FAMILY LAW

FAMILY LAW

Text, Cases, and Materials

SECOND EDITION

Sonia Harris-Short and Joanna Miles

OXFORD

UNIVERSITY PRESS

OXFORD
UNIVERSITY PRESS

Great Clarendon Street, Oxford OX2 6DP

Oxford University Press is a department of the University of Oxford.
It furthers the University's objective of excellence in research, scholarship,
and education by publishing worldwide in

Oxford New York

Auckland Cape Town Dar es Salaam Hong Kong Karachi
Kuala Lumpur Madrid Melbourne Mexico City Nairobi
New Delhi Shanghai Taipei Toronto

With offices in

Argentina Austria Brazil Chile Czech Republic France Greece
Guatemala Hungary Italy Japan Poland Portugal Singapore
South Korea Switzerland Thailand Turkey Ukraine Vietnam

Oxford is a registered trade mark of Oxford University Press
in the UK and in certain other countries

Published in the United States
by Oxford University Press Inc., New York

Contains public sector information licensed under the Open Government Licence v1.0
(http://www.nationalarchives.gov.uk/doc/open-government-licence
/open-government-licence.htm)

Crown copyright material is reproduced
with the permission of the Controller, HMSO
(under the terms of the Click Use Licence)

Database right Oxford University Press (maker)

First published 2007
This edition 2011

British Library Cataloguing-in-Publication Data

Data available

Library of Congress Cataloging in Publication Data

Data available

Typeset by Newgen Imaging Systems (P) Ltd., Chennai, India
Printed in Great Britain
on acid-free paper by
Ashford Colour Press, Gosport, Hampshire

ISBN 978-0-19-956382-1

3 5 7 9 10 8 6 4 2

PREFACE TO THE SECOND EDITION

The second edition of this book shares the same aims of the first edition: to provide readers with a thorough understanding of the law relating to the family and to do so in a way that stimulates critical reflection on that law: how and why has the law developed as it has, what policies is it seeking to pursue, does it achieve the right balance between the rights and interests of individual family members and wider public interests, how does it operate in practice? But we seek in this edition to provide readers with a slightly slimmer volume which is more fully integrated with the Online Resource Centre.

The Online Resource Centre provides a wealth of useful information, not least of which are our regular updates on changes to the law since the manuscript was completed. It also contains questions, suggestions for further reading, and supplementary materials. Some of these support topics covered in the book, while others provide information for interested readers on less central material not systematically addressed in the book. A guide to using this book and the online materials will be found on the Online Resource Centre.

We continue to be grateful to those whom we thanked in our last preface, some of whom have provided further assistance. We have been very well supported in preparing this new edition by the team at OUP, initially Alex Clabburn and latterly Anna Winstanley and colleagues. Sonia would once again like to give particular thanks to her husband Tim and her children Isaac and Olivia (the new arrival!) for their love, patience, and support. Bringing the second edition in on time was very much a 'family effort'.

Authorship of the various chapters remains as it was for the first edition. We have endeavoured to state the law as it was on 1 October 2010. The first set of updates on developments since then will be on the Online Resource Centre by October 2011.

This edition of the book is dedicated to Howard Miles (1943–2008).

New to this edition:

- coverage of the same-sex marriage case *Schalk and Kopf v Austria*
- full treatment of *Stack v Dowden* and subsequent case law, and its implications for ownership of the family home
- a fully updated chapter on child support, following the reforms implemented by the Child Maintenance and Other Payments Act 2008
- a revised account of the law of ancillary relief in light of the developing case law, including *Charman v Charman* and *B v B*
- a fully updated section on private ordering on divorce following the decision of the Supreme Court in *Radmacher v Granatino*
- a fully revised chapter on the allocation of legal parenthood following assisted reproduction in light of the reforms contained within the Human Fertilisation and Embryology Act 2008

- detailed coverage of the debate surrounding the importance attributed to genetic fatherhood in the wake of reforms to the birth registration system and changing judicial approaches to parental responsibility and shared residence
- full analysis of key Supreme Court and House of Lords decisions on the importance to be attributed to the fact of biological parenthood in residence disputes (*In Re B (A Child)*) and on the threshold conditions for state intervention into the family where the child is at risk of harm (*Re B (Children) (Care proceedings: standard of proof)* and *Re S-B (Children)*)
- a fully updated chapter on adoption in light of developing case law under the Adoption and Children Act 2002

SHS
JM

PREFACE TO THE FIRST EDITION

This book has two principal aims: to provide readers with a thorough understanding of the law relating to the family and to do so in a way that stimulates critical reflection on that law: how and why has the law developed as it has, what policies is it seeking to pursue, does it achieve the right balance between the rights and interests of individual family members and wider public interests, how does it operate in practice?

As part of the *Text, Cases, and Materials* series, alongside our own description of and commentary on the law, the book includes a large number of extracts from primary sources, both statute and case law, and from official data, academic commentaries, qualitative research findings, and policy and reform papers. Several of these extracts are edited for use in the book. Deletions are indicated by … and textual insertions and editorial amendments made by us are contained in square brackets. We have generally removed all original footnotes and references from the extracts; where an original footnote is retained, we have indicated this in the footnote. The occasional footnotes attached to extracts are otherwise our own.

Many valuable resources for family lawyers are now available on the internet. Wherever a source to which we have referred is online, we have indicated this by use of the Online Resource Centre logo in the bibliography. Only where a source is available exclusively online have we included the full website details in the bibliography. Readers wishing to access any of that material can visit the Online Resource Centre, where they will find links to all sources marked with the Online Resource Centre logo. The Online Resource Centre also provides links to a number of websites of general use and interest to the family lawyer.

Inevitably, it has not been possible to cover all of the issues relating to families in England and Wales today that we might have wished to include. In particular, we do not discuss public funding for family proceedings, criminal offences against children and reasonable chastisement, international child abduction, inter-country adoption, the law relating to the elderly and other vulnerable adults, the law of succession, immigration law, private international law, European law relating to the family, or housing law. We have been able to give only brief attention to the laws of taxation and social security, formalities for marriage and civil partnership, wardship, and disputes regarding the child's name and relocation. We have, however, included material on some of these topics in the Online Resource Centre.

There are a number of people to whom we are immensely grateful, for reading draft chapters, advising on specific issues, or both: Stuart Bridge, John Eekelaar, Jonathan Herring, Matthew Jolley, Mavis Maclean, Judith Masson, Jo McCaffrey, Clare McGlynn, Howard Miles, Cheryl Morris, Rebecca Probert, Daniel Robinson, Nick Wikeley, and the anonymous reviewers for Oxford University Press. We have also benefited greatly from the research assistance of Gemma Nicholls, Anna Shadboldt, Phil Harris, and Andrew Brown. Any errors and omissions are, of course, our own. We also thank all the students whom we have taught family law and the wider family law community: we have learnt a lot from them all, and still have more to learn. Thanks are also due to Angela Griffin, our original commissioning editor at OUP, and to Melanie Jackson and the rest of the team who have seen us through the project and accommodated our various needs. Finally, Sonia would like to thank her husband Tim for his love, understanding, and unwavering support throughout this project. She dedicates her chapters to him and their beautiful son, Isaac.

Sonia Harris-Short is responsible for chapters on the law relating to children: chapters 8–13. Joanna Miles is responsible for chapters covering issues relating to adults and financial and property disputes: chapters 2–7. We co-wrote chapter 1. We have endeavoured to state the law as it was at 1 October 2006. Twice yearly updates on developments in areas of law addressed in the book will be posted on the website.

SHS
JM

ACKNOWLEDGEMENTS

We are grateful to all authors and publishers of copyright material used in this book and in particular to the following for permission to reprint from the sources indicated:

Extracts from Law Commission Reports, Legal Services Commission Reports, DFES, DHSS, Cafcass, and ONS publications are Crown copyright material. Crown copyright material is reproduced with the permission of the Controller, HMSO (under the terms of the Click Use licence). Parliamentary material is reproduced with the permission of the Controller of HMSO on behalf of Parliament. This book contains public sector information licensed under the Open Government Licence v1.0 (http://www.nationalarchives.gov.uk/doc/open-government-licence/open-government-licence.htm).

American Bar Association and the author for extract from *Family Law Quarterly*: Mary Ann Glendon, 'Is There a Future for Separate Property?', (1974) 8 *Family Law Quarterly* 315.

Wiley-Blackwell for extract from *Modern Law Review*: G. Douglas, 'The Intention to be a Parent and the Making of Mothers', (1994) 57 *Modern Law Review* 636.

Susan Boyd for extracts from C. Smart and S Sevenhuijsen (eds), *Child Custody and the Politics of Gender*: S. Boyd, 'From gender specificity to gender neutrality? Ideologies in Canadian Child Custody Law', in C. Smart and S. Sevenhuijsen (eds), *Child Custody and the Politics of Gender* (London: Routledge, 1989).

Cambridge University Press for extracts from *Social Policy & Society*: Jan Pahl, 'Individualism in Couple Finances: Who pays for the children?', (2005) 4 *Social Policy & Society* 381.

Hart Publishing Ltd for extracts from A. Bainham, S. Day Sclater, and M. Richards (eds), *What is a Parent? A Socio-Legal Analysis* (Oxford: Hart Publishing, 1999).

The Incorporated Council of Law Reporting for extracts from *Appeal Cases* [AC], *Chancery Division* Law Reports [Ch], *Family Division* Law Reports [Fam], *Probate Division* Law Reports [P], and *Weekly Law Reports* [WLR].

Jordan Publishing Ltd for extracts from *Child and Family Law Quarterly* and *Family Law Reports* [FLR]: R. Deech, 'The unmarried father and human rights', (1992) 4 *Journal of Child Law* (continued as *Child and Family Law Quarterly*) 3; L. Smith, 'Clashing symbols? Reconciling support for fathers and fatherless families after the Human Fertilisation and Embryology Act 2008', (2010) 22 *Child and Family Law Quarterly* 46; P. Hayes, 'Giving due consideration to ethnicity in adoption placements—a principled approach', (2003) 15 *Child and Family Law Quarterly* 255; C. Smith and J. Logan, 'Adoptive parenthood as a "legal fiction"—Its consequences for direct post-adoption contact', (2002) 14 *Child and Family Law Quarterly* 281; *B v B (Minors) (Custody, Care and Control)* [1991] 1 FLR 402.

Robert Mnookin for extracts from *Law & Contemporary Problems*: R. H. Mnookin, 'Child Custody Adjudication: Judicial Functions in the Face of Indeterminacy', (1975) 39 *Law & Contemporary Problems* 226.

New Zealand Council of Law Reporting and **LexisNexis New Zealand** for extract from *New Zealand Law Reports* [NZLR]: *C v C* [1942] NZLR 356.

Oxford University Press for extracts from J. Dewar, 'Land, Law and the Family Home', in S. Bright and J. Dewar (eds), *Land Law: Themes and Perspectives* (Oxford: OUP, 1998); from *Current Legal Problems*: H. Reece, 'The Paramountcy Principle. Consensus or Construct?', (1996) 49 *Current Legal Problems* 267.

Oxford University Press Journals for extracts from *International Journal of Law and the Family*: T. Campbell, 'The Rights of the Minor: As Person, As Child, As Juvenile, As Future Adult', (1992) 6 *International Journal of Law and the Family* 1.

Polity Press for extract from C. Smart and B. Neale, *Family Fragments*? (Cambridge: Polity Press, 1999).

Reed Elsevier (UK) Ltd trading as LexisNexis Butterworths for extracts from *All England Law Reports* [All ER], and *Family Court Reports* [FCR].

Sweet & Maxwell Ltd for extract from *Law Quarterly Review* and *Journal of Social Welfare and Family Law*: J. Eekelaar, 'Do parents have a duty to consult?', (1998) 114 *Law Quarterly Review* 337; L. Fox Harding, 'The Children Act 1989 in Context: Four Perspectives in Child Care Law and Policy (I)', (1991) *Journal of Social Welfare and Family Law* 179.

Every effort has been made to trace and contact copyright holders but this has not been possible in every case. If notified, the publisher will undertake to rectify any errors or omissions at the earliest opportunity.

OUTLINE TABLE OF CONTENTS

TABLE OF CONTENTS

3   FAMILY PROPERTY AND FINANCES   117

4 | DOMESTIC VIOLENCE 203

5 | ENDING RELATIONSHIPS: DIVORCE AND SEPARATION 283

10   PARENTAL RESPONSIBILITY   653

13 ADOPTION 888

TABLE OF CASES

TABLE OF STATUTES

TABLE OF STATUTORY INSTRUMENTS

TABLE OF EUROPEAN MATERIALS

TABLE OF INTERNATIONAL
CONVENTIONS AND INSTRUMENTS

ABBREVIATIONS

AA 1976	Adoption Act 1976
ACA 2002	Adoption and Children Act 2002
ADR	alternative dispute resolution
AID	artificial insemination by donor
BCS	British Crime Survey
CA 1989	Children Act 1989
CA 2004	Children Act 2004
CAA 2006	Children and Adoption Act 2006
Cafcass	Children and Family Court Advisory and Support Service
CAO	child assessment order
CASC	Children Act Sub-Committee, Advisory Board on Family Law
CB	child benefit
CFR	Children and Family Reporter
C-MEC	Child Maintenance and Enforcement Commission
CMOP 2008	Child Maintenance and Other Payments Act 2008
CPA 2004	Civil Partnership Act 2004
CPAG	Child Poverty Action Group
CPC	child protection conference
CPS	Crown Prosecution Service
CSA	Child Support Agency
CSA 1991	Child Support Act 1991
CTC	child tax credit
DCA	Department for Constitutional Affairs
DCLG	Department of Communities and Local Government
DCSF	Department for Children, Schools and Families
DEO	deduction from earnings order
DfES	Department for Education and Skills
DH / DOH	Department of Health
DHSS	Department of Health and Social Security
DPMCA 1978	Domestic Proceedings and Magistrates' Courts Act 1978
DSS	Department of Social Security
DTI	Department of Trade and Industry
DVCVA 2004	Domestic Violence, Crime and Victims Act 2004
DWP	Department for Work and Pensions
ECHR	European Convention on Human Rights
EEA	European Economic Area
EHRC	Equality and Human Rights Commission
EPO	emergency protection order
FJC	Family Justice Council
FLA 1986	Family Law Act 1986

FLA 1996	Family Law Act 1996
FLRA 1969	Family Law Reform Act 1969
FLRA 1987	Family Law Reform Act 1987
FPR 2010	Family Procedure Rules 2010, SI 2010/2955
GAL	guardian ad litem
GRA 2004	Gender Recognition Act 2004
HFEA	Human Fertilisation and Embryology Authority
HFEA 1990	Human Fertilisation and Embryology Act 1990
HFEA 2008	Human Fertilisation and Embryology Act 2008
HMRC	Her Majesty's Revenue and Customs
HO	Home Office
HRA 1998	Human Rights Act 1998
ICCPR	International Covenant on Civil and Political Rights
IRO	independent reviewing officer
JSA	income-based jobseeker's allowance
Law Com	Law Commission
LCD	Lord Chancellor's Department
LPA 1925	Law of Property Act 1925
LRA 2002	Land Registration Act 2002
MA 1949	Marriage Act 1949
MCA 1973	Matrimonial Causes Act 1973
MOJ	Ministry of Justice
NRP	non-resident parent
OECD	Organisation for Economic Cooperation and Development
ONS	Office for National Statistics
PHA 1997	Protection from Harassment Act 1997
PRO	parental responsibility order
PWC	parent with care
SAA 1985	Surrogacy Arrangements Act 1985
Scot Law Com	Scottish Law Commission
SGO	special guardianship order
TOLATA 1996	Trusts of Land and Appointment of Trustees Act 1996
UNCRC	United Nations Convention on the Rights of the Child 1989
WTC	working tax credit

1

INTRODUCTION TO FAMILY LAW

The purpose of this chapter is to introduce you to:

- the idea of family law
- some key themes and debates which feature in several areas of family law and are dealt with in later chapters of the book
- this book and its companion Online Resource Centre

We hope that you will find it helpful.

1.1 FAMILIES AND FAMILY LAW IN ENGLAND AND WALES TODAY

1.1.1 WHAT IS 'FAMILY'?

This apparently simple question is actually a complex one to which people might offer different answers in different contexts. To many, 'family' implies a group linked by blood relationship and by marriage, and commonly by a shared home. The world of advertising would have us believe that we all live, or at least grew up, in nuclear families: households composed of two parents and their children. However, the reality of domestic life for many people diverges from that traditional image, as figures from the 2001 Census show.[1]

Marriage remains the preferred way of organizing family life, with just over half of all adults in 2001 living in a married couple. However, since the 1970s, the popularity of marriage has been declining and divorce is much more common. Increasing numbers of couples live together without getting married and 45 per cent of children are now born to parents who are not married.[2] Thirty per cent of households in England and Wales contain dependent children: 59 per cent are headed by a married couple, 11 per cent by a cohabiting

---

[1] ONS (2003). We provide more detailed statistical information on several of the issues identified here in later chapters.
[2] O'Leary et al (2010).

couple, and 22 per cent by a lone parent.[3] Some children are adopted, fostered, or otherwise 'parented' by people other than their biological parents. Same-sex couples are gaining social acceptance and legal recognition: they can register a civil partnership in order to acquire rights and responsibilities akin to those of spouses, adopt children together, or become parents using assisted reproduction. Some households, particularly in ethnic minority communities, comprise 'extended' families of more than two generations and/or adult siblings.[4] Many people, particularly in early and late adult life, share households with friends in platonic relationships. Increasing numbers of young people remain in their parents' homes into adulthood. Many individuals live alone, but are nevertheless members of families by virtue of blood and other ties; some couples physically live apart and yet still regard themselves as being 'together'. In one way or another, all of these groups may consider themselves 'family'.

Whether, to what extent, and how the law recognizes this growing diversity in family life is of central importance for family lawyers. The supportive and protective functions of 'family law' are reserved to those the law accepts as 'family'. For those whom the law rejects, denied formal recognition of their family status, solutions must be found elsewhere. For example, those who have not formalized their relationships by marriage or civil partnership cannot access the specialist financial remedies applicable on divorce to spouses and civil partners. The general law of contract, trust, and property must be relied upon to determine financial and property disputes between such individuals on relationship breakdown. A key issue for contemporary family law is therefore to decide which social 'families' to admit to 'family law', how to regulate their relationships, and whether to confer more extensive rights and duties on some categories of family than others, for example by privileging marriage.

1.1.2 WHAT IS FAMILY LAW?

If defining 'family' is hard, defining 'family law' is also surprisingly complicated. In jurisdictions with codified laws, we might expect to find a code containing the Family Law of that country.[5] Identifying a corpus of family law for England and Wales is less straightforward. Much of the law that regulates family life in this jurisdiction is specifically devised for families, but to some extent aspects of the general law are relevant too.

The shape and focus of family law has also changed substantially over the decades. As Rebecca Probert has highlighted, a family law textbook written in the 1950s would have looked very different from ours.[6] At that point in the social and legal history of the English family, marriage was almost universal, cohabitation almost unheard of, and divorce rare by comparison with today's standards. It was therefore more natural to focus on law governing the ongoing relationship between the spouses (and not much else). Much has changed since then. The law relating to children has dramatically expanded, such that the parent-child relationship now takes centre stage, regarded by some commentators as the central relationship of family law. And rather than the functioning family, it is the pathology of family breakdown that has come to preoccupy the discipline. Divorce and its financial consequences, domestic violence, disputes over the upbringing of children, and protection of children from abuse within the home now constitute the core of family law.

---

[3] ONS (2003).
[4] ONS (2005a), 21–2.
[5] Müller-Freienfels (2003).
[6] Probert (2004a), 903–5.

In recognition of the breadth of contemporary 'family' and 'family law', this book examines the law relating to a wide range of 'families', not just those based on marriage, and addresses issues relevant to the ongoing family, as well as those arising on relationship breakdown.

1.2 THEMES AND ISSUES IN CONTEMPORARY FAMILY LAW

You will find that studying family law involves quite a lot of 'black letter' law, particularly in areas which are regulated closely by statute. Our understanding and evaluation of the law is considerably enriched by thinking about various theoretical and policy implications of the social issues with which family law is concerned, and this is something that we try to do throughout the book. Indeed, an important feature of contemporary family law scholarship is the identification of broad trends in the way in which law has been used to regulate the family in many Western jurisdictions.[7] Throughout this book, you will encounter a number of inter-related themes, issues, and perspectives on family law. We introduce the most important of these in this section in order to set the scene for the specific debates that you will read about in the following chapters.

1.2.1 A RIGHTS-BASED APPROACH TO THE FAMILY?

Welfare versus rights

Family law has oscillated between rights-based and welfare-based approaches to the family. Should family law be based on the notion that individual family members have rights and duties that they exercise against each other and against the state? (And, if so, what rights should those be?) Or should family law, and family dispute resolution, be based on welfare-based criteria, which seek to achieve the 'best' outcome for the parties in their particular circumstances? The rights–welfare spectrum relates closely to a similar tension between law based on rules and law based on discretion, which we discuss next. A lawmaker who wishes to enforce rights and duties may naturally adopt a rule-based approach. But a lawmaker concerned to achieve the best outcome in all the circumstances of the individual case may prefer to rely on discretion, affording decision-makers flexibility to produce optimal outcomes.

As Stephen Parker has related,[8] historically, both rights-based and welfare-based approaches have been evident in legal regulation of the family. One or other predominates at particular points in time, but neither is ever completely absent. Put at its most basic, from an approach initially dominated by rights (principally those of the husband and the father), the twentieth century witnessed a clear shift towards a welfare-orientated approach (exemplified by the welfare principle and the redistribution of property and finance on divorce), and now a new rights-based model is doing battle with the welfare approach.

In general terms, a rights-based approach reflects the view that the state should not seek to bring about certain consequences, such as maximization of social welfare, but simply protect individuals' rights to pursue their own vision of the 'good life'. Pre-twentieth century

---

[7] See for example Dewar (2003).
[8] Parker (1992), 321–5 on which the following draws.

rights-based family law consisted of a fairly rigid system of rules prescribing fixed roles for each family member which were ostensibly applied without regard to the implications for the individuals concerned. A utility-based model, by contrast, involves identifying a social goal and balancing individual interests to attain it. Broad discretion is conferred on judges to conduct this interest-balancing exercise guided only by vaguely defined 'goals and standards'. However, as Parker explains, growing dissatisfaction with the broad discretionary nature of a welfare-orientated approach led to a renewed focus on a more rule-orientated, rights-based approach. Needless to say, the rights of contemporary family law are rather different in substance from those of the nineteenth century, not least in being gender-neutral. But the result has been an uneasy tension in many areas of family law as it tries to accommodate both welfare and rights. As Parker puts it, 'by the late 1980s…a kind of normative anarchy reigned within family law, with some measures tugging in the direction of rights and others in the direction of utility'.[9]

Contemporary rights in family law: the European Convention on Human Rights

The Human Rights Act 1998 (HRA 1998) has intensified this ideological 'struggle' between rights and utility in family law. The HRA 1998 gave effect to the European Convention on Human Rights (ECHR) in domestic law. Despite continuing opposition and scepticism, a more rights-based approach to the family is therefore unavoidable. The HRA 1998 has implications for statutory interpretation, the development of case law, and the exercise of judicial discretion. Consequently, sound knowledge of the HRA, the ECHR, and the Strasbourg jurisprudence is now essential for any family lawyer in this jurisdiction. In this section, we introduce the key ECHR Articles likely to be encountered by family lawyers.

ONLINE RESOURCE CENTRE

Readers requiring information on the operation of the HRA 1998 will find further guidance and materials on the Online Resource Centre.

Article 3

In some areas of family law—child protection and domestic violence—the most basic human rights may be at stake.

Article 3

No one shall be subjected to torture or to inhuman or degrading treatment or punishment.

Article 3 subjects the state to a negative obligation: it must not perpetrate abuse itself or through its agents. Like other Convention rights, Article 3 has also been held to impose positive obligations on the state, here requiring the state to take reasonable steps to protect both adults and children from abuse perpetrated by others.[10] In extreme cases, Article 2—the

---

9 Ibid, 325.
10 *Z and others v UK* (App No 29392/95, ECHR) (2001).

right to life—may also be implicated; it too imposes positive obligations on the state. The state's obligations towards children who are suffering or at risk of suffering harm are particularly far-reaching.

Article 6

Article 6—along with Article 8[11]—creates procedural rights for those involved in family law disputes, whether between the state and family members (for example, child protection and adoption) or between private individuals (for example, contact disputes).

Article 6(1)

In the determination of his civil rights and obligations or of any criminal charge against him, everyone is entitled to a fair and public hearing within a reasonable time by an independent and impartial tribunal established by law. Judgment shall be pronounced publicly but the press and public may be excluded from all or part of the trial in the interests of morals, public order or national security in a democratic society, where the interests of juveniles or the protection of the private life of the parties so require, or to the extent strictly necessary in the opinion of the court in special circumstances where publicity would prejudice the interests of justice....

Especially in the context of child protection, conferring procedural rights on parents (often via Article 8) is regarded as one way of balancing parents' rights against children's right to be protected from suspected abuse. Procedural rights are as important as substantive rights (i.e. the right to a particular outcome), bringing both instrumental and non-instrumental advantages. Conferring procedural rights on individuals likely to be affected by the outcome of a decision-making process may improve the accuracy and quality of that decision: those individuals may have unique knowledge to contribute to the process and so should be allowed to participate in it. But procedural rights also perform a dignity-protecting function: they acknowledge affected individuals' entitlement to participate in decisions affecting them, rather than simply subjecting them arbitrarily to the closed decision-making of a third party. Whether doing so makes any practical difference to the outcome does not matter for these purposes—what matters is that the affected individual is heard.

Ascertaining what 'fairness' requires under Article 6 involves weighing the applicant's demands against the exigencies of the particular procedure involved and the rights of other parties to those proceedings,[12] in a manner similar to the proportionality exercise conducted under Article 8 (below). Articles 6 and 8 have been found to apply both to court-based and out-of-court decision-making, and may support various rights, for example: to participate in decision-making affecting the applicant;[13] to be legally represented before decision-making forums;[14] to legal aid;[15] to adequate notice of proceedings (rather than 'ex parte' proceedings, conducted without notifying the respondent);[16] to be given access to key evidence;[17]

---

[11] *W v UK* (App No 9749/82, ECHR) (1988).

[12] *Ashingdane v UK* (App No 8225/78, ECHR) (1985).

[13] *Re M (Care: Challenging Decisions by Local Authority)* [2001] 2 FLR 1300.

[14] E.g. on children's rights to participate in legal proceedings: *Sahin v Germany* (App No 30943/96, ECHR) (2001).

[15] *Airey v Ireland (No 1)* (App No 6289/73, ECHR) (1979).

[16] In the context of child protection proceedings see pp 877–8.

[17] E.g. in relation to child protection: *TP and KM v UK* (App No 28945/95, ECHR) (2001); *Re G (Care: Challenge to Local Authority's Decision)* [2003] EWHC 551.

and to be given access to a court or other forum to enforce legal rights.[18] Articles 6 and 8 also offer protection regarding the effect of delay on the disposal of cases,[19] and the privacy or otherwise of legal proceedings and judgments in family cases.[20]

Article 8

Article 8 is a key provision for family lawyers, carrying potential significance for almost any sort of family law dispute. Any case under Article 8 will have three stages: demonstrating that the right applies; showing that the state has breached its duty; determining whether that breach can be justified by the state.

Article 8

> 1. Everyone has the right to respect for his private and family life, his home and his correspondence.
>
> 2. There shall be no interference by a public authority with the exercise of this right except such as is in accordance with the law and is necessary in a democratic society in the interests of national security, public safety or the economic well-being of the country, for the prevention of disorder or crime, for the protection of health or morals, or for the protection of the rights and freedoms of others.

To establish a case under Article 8, the applicant must first show that the complaint falls within the scope of Article 8(1). The right to respect for private life and the right to respect for family life arise most commonly in family law cases; the right to respect for the home may also be relevant, for example, in relation to rights to succeed to a tenancy or to occupy property.

The right to respect for private life has been particularly important for those who have traditionally struggled to establish 'family life' rights, such as same-sex couples and transgendered applicants, or where no family ties currently exist. The scope of private life protection while not unlimited[21] is potentially extremely broad, covering 'physical and psychological integrity', 'physical and social identity', 'gender identification, name and sexual orientation and sexual life', 'personal development', 'personal autonomy', and 'the right to establish and develop relationships with other human beings and the outside world'.[22] It has been invoked in various situations.

The right to respect for *family* life is the most frequently invoked provision of the Convention in domestic family law proceedings, in both private and public law cases. Establishing the existence of family life is not always straightforward. A well-established line of authority makes it clear that Article 8 only affords respect to *existing family relationships*: it does not safeguard the 'mere desire' to found a family or create new familial relationships.[23] Moreover, until recently the European Court of Human Rights has clearly favoured the traditional

---

[18] See 6.4.7 on parents' rights to enforce child support; and 12.8 on challenging implementation of care measures on behalf of young children.

[19] E.g., in relation to child-related disputes: *Glaser v UK* (App No 32346/96, ECHR) (2000); *Re D (Intractable Contact Dispute: Publicity)* [2004] EWHC 727; see chapter 11.

[20] In relation to child contact disputes: *B and P v UK* (App Nos 36337/97, 35974/97, ECHR) (2001); *Re B (A Child) (Disclosure)* [2004] EWHC 411; and in relation to disputes between adults: *Clibbery v Allan* [2002] EWCA Civ 45.

[21] *M v Secretary of State for Work and Pensions* [2006] UKHL 11; cf Scherpe (2006c).

[22] *Van Kück v Germany* (App No 35968/97, ECHR) (2003), [69].

[23] *Fretté v France* (App No 36515/97, ECHR) (2003), [32].

heterosexual married unit, where 'family life' between the various individuals, including children of the marriage, is established automatically by the simple fact of the marital tie.[24] Establishing family life where the adult parties are unmarried has been more difficult.[25] However, the Court has been increasingly willing to embrace de facto as well as de jure family life.[26] Importantly, this has included relationships between transgendered, gay, and lesbian parents and their children.[27] Most recently, as we discuss in chapter 2, the European Court has held that both opposite-sex and same-sex cohabiting couples living in a stable de facto partnership fall within the notion of 'family life', whether or not they have children.[28]

Once the applicant has established the existence of one of the relevant interests protected by Article 8 (whether private life or family life, etc) it must then be determined whether the state is, prima facie, in breach of any of its obligations. This raises the question of what the right 'to respect' for private and family life entails. Article 8 imposes a range of specific obligations on the state. Many of those are negative: for example, prohibiting the state from removing children from their parents. Others are positive, requiring the state to act in a particular way. As noted earlier, sometimes Article 8 imposes *procedural* obligations: for example, requiring that parents be given the opportunity to be consulted about decisions made by the state in relation to their children.[29] We shall come across many examples of Article 8 obligations throughout the book. By way of example, here are some types of situation in which Article 8 *might* plausibly be invoked—we shall see later whether successfully or not:

- to achieve the legal recognition of transgendered persons in their acquired gender;
- to protect the competing interests in cases of domestic violence: the victim's right to physical and psychological integrity, versus the alleged perpetrator's right to remain undisturbed in his own home;
- to recognize the parental status of unmarried fathers;
- to protect the competing interests of parties to disputes relating to the upbringing of a child following parental separation, particularly residence and contact arrangements;
- to protect the mutual family life interests of parents and children where it is proposed to take a child into state care, and to protect their ongoing relationship once a care order has been made;
- to protect parents' interests when adoption of their child is proposed.

Article 8 is a 'qualified' right, which means that even if the state is prima facie obliged to respect the right in a particular way it may be justifiable for it to do otherwise. As we can see from the examples just given, in many Article 8 cases private parties will be asserting competing rights, and some decision clearly has to be made between them. Protecting one person's rights will necessarily entail encroaching on the rights of the other; for example, protecting a non-resident parent's right to have contact with his child against the wishes of the resident parent will necessarily interfere with the resident parent's right to respect for family life.

Article 8(2) provides the framework within which we resolve these conflicts and ascertain the true extent of each party's right. Once it has been demonstrated that the applicant has a

---

[24] *Al Nashif v Bulgaria* (App No 50963/99, ECHR) (2003).
[25] *Marckx v Belgium* (A/31, ECHR) (1979).
[26] *Lebbink v Netherlands* (App No 45582/99, ECHR) (2004).
[27] *X, Y and Z v the United Kingdom* (App No 2180/93, ECHR) (1997); *Salgueiro De Silva Mouta v Portugal* (App No 33290/96, ECHR) (2001).
[28] *Schalk & Kopf v Austria* (App No 30141/04, ECHR) (2010), [90]–[95].
[29] *W v UK* (App No 9749/82, ECHR) (1988).

right under Article 8(1) which has been interfered with in some way by the state, the burden then shifts to the state to justify its action. Article 8(2), in common with the other qualified Convention rights, sets out three basic criteria that must be met in order for the interference to be justified: it must be (i) 'in accordance with the law'; (ii) pursue one of the legitimate aims specified in the list in Article 8(2); and (iii) be 'necessary in a democratic society'. In practice, the first two requirements of Article 8(2) are usually easily satisfied. Often, the state will have acted in accordance with domestic law to protect the rights and interests of a child, unquestionably a 'legitimate aim'.

The most difficult test to satisfy is showing that the interference with the applicant's rights was 'necessary in a democratic society'. This test comprises several requirements: the interference must correspond with a pressing social need, be based on relevant and sufficient reasons, and be proportionate to the aim being pursued. The key concept here is proportionality, the tool used to resolve conflicts between competing parties' rights, or between rights and other 'legitimate aims'. The concept of proportionality is also relevant to several other provisions, including Articles 6 and 14. The Strasbourg Court has also used criteria akin to those found in Article 8(2) when seeking to ascertain the scope of positive obligations under various Articles.[30] The proportionality test requires the decision-maker to carry out a balancing exercise, weighing the various rights and interests in order to determine whether the degree of interference with the applicant's rights is no more extensive than is required to meet the needs of the stated aim. But applying the proportionality test is not a mechanical, value-neutral exercise: it is impossible to determine the proper relationship between competing rights and interests without ascribing each of them relative weight—the question is a normative rather than factual one: 'which right *ought to* prevail?'; or 'how extensive *ought* the state's obligation to be?'.

Article 12

By contrast with the breadth of Article 8, Article 12 has a very specific focus.

Article 12

Men and women of marriageable age have the right to marry and to found a family, according to the national laws governing the exercise of this right.

The rights protected under Article 12 are expressed in unqualified terms and, although subject to 'national law', at least as regards the right to marry, it is impermissible to read into Article 12 the same limitations as set down in Article 8(2).[31] The position as regards the right to found a family is more uncertain.[32] Although the European Court has generally interpreted Article 12 cautiously and conservatively, evolving social conditions and trends may prompt change. As we shall see in chapter 2, recent developments concerning the right of transgendered persons to marry[33] signal a shift away from the traditional concept of marriage as a heterosexual, biological-sex-based relationship, to one based more broadly on gender and social function, opening the door to formal recognition of transgender, and perhaps

---

[30] *Rees v UK* (App No 9532/81, ECHR) (1986), [37]; *Osman v UK* (App No 23452/94, ECHR) (2000), [99], quotation of Commission decision, para 91.

[31] *R (Baiai) v Sec. of State for Home Department* [2008] UKHL 53, [15].

[32] Ibid. and see *R (Mellor) v Secretary of State for the Home Department* [2001] EWCA Civ 472, [28]–[29]. For further discussion see pp 621–2.

[33] *Goodwin v UK* (App No 28957/95, ECHR) (2002).

in time even same-sex, relationships.[34] Article 12 has also become potentially important in the field of reproduction as individuals seek to take advantage of new reproductive technologies. The controversial issue of whether Article 12 offers a legal basis for an individual right to become a parent, whether through natural intercourse, assisted reproduction or adoption, is discussed in chapters 9 and 13.

Article 14

Article 14 is the Convention's non-discrimination clause. As we shall see in chapter 2, it has been used with notable success in the English courts since the HRA came into force to advance the legal rights of same-sex couples.

Article 14

The enjoyment of the rights and freedoms set forth in this Convention shall be secured without discrimination on any ground such as sex, race, colour, language, religion, political or other opinion, national or social origin, association with a national minority, property, birth or other status.

The principle of non-discrimination has been described by Baroness Hale as 'essential to democracy'—guaranteeing that power is not exercised arbitrarily, everyone is valued equally, and where distinctions are drawn between different groups such distinctions have a rational basis.[35]

It is important to appreciate that Article 14 is not a freestanding anti-discrimination provision: it only guards against discrimination in the exercise of other Convention rights. Any claim under Article 14 must therefore begin by demonstrating that the factual circumstances of the case fall within the scope of one of the other rights. However, this does not require the applicant to demonstrate that that other right has itself been breached. Article 14 also demands that if the state chooses to grant rights beyond those required by the Convention, it must not do so in a discriminatory way: it must grant that right equally unless the difference in treatment can be justified.[36]

A resistance to rights?

The return to a rights-based approach to the family, prompted by the HRA 1998, gives previously excluded groups such as transgendered individuals and same-sex couples a more promising language in which to argue for change, providing them with rights that they can assert against the state in order to demand legal recognition. However, the rights-based discourse has not met with unanimous support from family lawyers. Some family lawyers, including members of the family bench, have shown deep-seated resistance to the (re)introduction and potential predominance of rights-based reasoning. The continuing ambivalence about the rights of individual family members has meant that the impact of the HRA 1998 on the balance between welfare and rights in family law has varied considerably depending on the nature of the dispute.

---

[34] But see *Schalk & Kopf v Austria* (App No 30141/04, ECHR) (2010), discussed at 2.3.2.
[35] *Ghaidan v Godin-Mendoza* [2004] UKHL 30, [131]–[132].
[36] Ibid., [135].

There are various reasons for the resistance to rights-based reasoning in family law.[37] For some conservative groups, the perceived alliance between strong liberal values and human rights discourse breeds concern that, by emphasizing individualism, equality, and non-discrimination, rights-based reasoning will undermine the traditional family unit and the values it protects.[38] More moderate commentators are concerned that the individualistic focus of rights-based reasoning is inappropriate when dealing with the interdependence of contemporary family life.[39] Scepticism about rights-based reasoning is particularly strong in cases relating to children, where there are concerns that focusing on rights will lead to children's interests being marginalized. Jane Fortin, for example, has warned that the 'Strasbourg jurisprudence may not always augur well for British children' and that rights-based discourse, including the discourse of children's rights, may well be hijacked by the parental rights lobby, particularly fathers, to further their own claims and interests at the expense of the child.[40] Those concerns are understandable. It is only fairly recently that the notion of parents holding autonomous 'proprietary' rights over their children has given way to a welfare-based discourse which strives to put children's interests at the heart of the decision-making process.[41] For many family lawyers, the principle that children's interests should be paramount in decisions concerning their future welfare and upbringing is sacrosanct; to revert to reasoning dominated by the individual rights of parents would be a retrograde step.

Despite these concerns, family law has not escaped the pressures of a domestic legal, political, and social culture increasingly wedded to the concept of rights. Rights-based arguments have found a natural home in family law disputes. A rights-based, more rule-oriented approach can lead to more principled, 'just' outcomes.[42] The discourse of rights demands that the individual needs and interests of all family members are identified and weighed. Clear articulation of the parties' individual needs and interests may bring predictability, transparency, and accountability in family law decision-making. It can also address concerns that welfare-based approaches allow legitimate rights and interests to be obscured by children's interests.

One of the most controversial issues in carrying out the balancing exercise demanded by Article 8(2) is the weight to be accorded to the child's interests, in particular whether they are to be the paramount consideration such that any interference with an adult's rights will automatically be deemed 'necessary in a democratic society' if undertaken with the aim of protecting a child's rights and interests. This is an important issue, not least because of its implications for the traditional welfare-orientated approach of English law, explored in depth in chapter 8. It exemplifies, more clearly than any other area of family law, the ideological struggle between welfare and rights in the post-HRA era.

1.2.2 RULES VERSUS DISCRETION

The legislature has adopted two principal modes of law-making in relation to the family: (i) the imposition of rules; and (ii) the creation of judicial (or executive) discretion. Some legislation creates prescriptive, exhaustive rules to govern particular disputes; child support law is the classic example of this approach. Here, the courts' function is confined to determining the meaning of statutory language and applying it to the facts of the case, though

---

[37] Harris-Short (2005), on which the following draws.
[38] E.g. Hafen and Hafen (1995–96).
[39] E.g. Herring (1999a), 232–5.
[40] Fortin (1999a), 251.
[41] Parker (1992), 321–5.
[42] Dewar (1998a), 473.

this is not a straightforward or value-neutral task. Other legislation confers wide discretion on the family courts: the statute may set down broad principles, or just indicate relevant factors for the courts to consider, giving no close indication of the 'right' outcome for any particular case. Many areas of family law, such as decisions about future arrangements for children's residence and contact and financial provision on divorce, are heavily discretionary. Here, the courts' role is very different: interpretation of the legislation is less difficult and less important to the determination of individual cases. Instead the emphasis is on the courts' assessment of the individual circumstances of each case, and their judgment of what will be a 'fair' outcome, or one which best promotes the welfare of particular family members, guided only rather loosely by general statutory principles.[43]

As noted earlier, this contrast between rules and discretion is associated with the contrast between rights-based and welfare-based approaches to family disputes. It is also connected with broader questions about the social function of family law: should family law endeavour to modify the behaviour of individuals within families, or should it simply offer an (apparently) morally neutral forum for decision-making?

There are various pros and cons to rules and discretion. Does discretion create inconsistency and so unfairness? Are rules equally capable of yielding unjust outcomes? Does discretion render the system unpredictable and so impede private negotiation? Are rules preferable insofar as they can be used by the state to try to affect our behaviour? A strong reason in favour of discretion in family law is that family life is so variable that it would be impossible to lay down sufficiently nuanced rules in advance. Discretion thus maximizes 'individualized justice': achieving the fairest outcome in each individual case.[44] However, rules also have advantages. As Carl Schneider has observed, rules have 'democratic legitimacy': they are publicly accessible and readily susceptible to public debate. They also further one of the most fundamental principles of justice: that like cases should be treated alike. It is suggested that where the rules to be applied to a particular dispute are clear and democratically sanctioned even losing parties should feel satisfied they have been treated fairly rather than abandoned to the vagaries of individual judges' personal prejudices and preferences.[45] Yet, as Schneider also points out, this confidence in the capacity of rules to guard against a sense of injustice in family disputes may be naïve. Rather than passively accept defeat, the losing party is very likely to contend that the rules are wrong or have been unfairly applied to the circumstances of their case. Falling back on the individualized justice afforded by discretion, our disaffected litigant is likely to call for a more careful examination of the individual circumstances of his or her case in order to ensure justice is done.

A particular concern of opponents of discretion is that it hampers negotiated settlements. It is often said that parties 'bargain in the shadow of the law',[46] that they negotiate in light of what they anticipate a court would order in their case. This can sometimes be difficult, given the highly discretionary—and so rather unpredictable—nature of family law. By contrast, rules would provide clear guidance about how a court is likely to resolve the dispute, helping parties to negotiate settlements out of court, but also performs the important normative function of telling disputants how society believes the dispute *ought* to be resolved.[47] As we shall see in various chapters, this normative function of family law has become particularly important and controversial in the context of divorce and post-divorce parenting, as the

[43] This has implications for the proper handling of case law in the family field, an issue discussed on the Online Resource Centre.

[44] Dewar (1997), 311–14.

[45] Schneider (1992), 74–7.

[46] Mnookin and Kornhauser (1979).

[47] Ibid.

state has sought through more subtle and diffuse methods to re-inject some sense of 'family values' and 'responsibility' in the wake of the removal of 'fault' from family law. We are not faced then simply with a choice between rules and discretion, but more fundamentally with a dilemma regarding the proper purposes of family law: to modify behaviour in line with some moral code (better effected by rules), or to resolve practical problems by reference to more (apparently) value-neutral principles? Dewar has observed that there has indeed been a shift in several jurisdictions (particularly in areas such as child support, spousal support, and post-divorce parenting) away from discretion (and welfare), partly as a result of attempts to reinvigorate the moral messages conveyed by the law with a view to delivering more 'just' and principled outcomes for men, women, and children.[48]

1.2.3 STATE INTERVENTION VERSUS PRIVATE ORDERING

The extent to which the law is able to exert moral force in contemporary family life is closely tied to its willingness to intervene in family decision-making. The more emphasis placed upon the privacy of the family unit, the more difficult it is for the state to enforce its normative standards and interests. The problem is particularly acute in the context of family breakdown. If the state is neutral about how such disputes should be resolved, families can be left to settle their own problems. By contrast, if the state is committed to promoting, for example, a particular model for the division of family assets on divorce, it may be expected to try to enforce its view of the 'right' or 'preferable' outcome through the law. However, state intervention in family life has always been controversial.

The privacy of the family unit is fiercely protected within liberal western thought. Intervention in this protected realm by outside agencies has typically been perceived as harmful and undesirable. However, as Andrew Bainham explains, the private realm is not 'naturally preconstituted'.[49] Its boundaries are constructed by the state to serve the state's interests. Whilst the concept of family privacy is an important constraint on state intervention, it is not an inherent good. Consequently, where the privacy accorded to the family unit serves the wider public interest the state will happily adhere to a 'hands-off' approach; but when the family fails to serve that wider public interest, the state will not hesitate to intervene. Bainham illustrates this point with the example of child-rearing. Child-rearing can be understood as a private matter subject to state intervention only when certain norms are breached. However, it may be more accurately understood as an inherently public matter which, whilst typically delegated to parents, remains subject to the state's overriding control and scrutiny.[50]

Whichever conceptualization is preferred, the public interest in regulating the family is such that state intervention into the private realm will sometimes be justified. This will most often be the case when the family is in crisis, for example, where children are being abused within the family home. The state may also have an interest in enforcing financial obligations between family members. The difficulty for the state lies in deciding where to draw the line between those cases in which the privacy of the family should be protected and those in which the public interest, whether social, economic, or moral in nature, is sufficiently strong to merit intervention.

---

[48] Dewar (1997), 313–16 and Dewar (1998a), 473–4.
[49] Bainham (1990), 206–7 on which the following draws.
[50] Ibid.

This is an important and difficult question for the state. Adopting a non-interventionist policy sends out a strong message about the value placed on the rights and interests at stake. For this reason, a non-interventionist policy towards the family has been subjected to convincing criticism, particularly by the feminist school, who point out that it reinforces the status quo and legitimizes 'structural inequalities between the sexes'.[51] It is argued, for example, that the state's formerly non-interventionist policy in areas such as domestic violence allowed abuse of vulnerable family members to go unchecked. Private ordering on family breakdown runs a similar risk. If parties' agreements on matters such as family property and finances are not subjected to outside scrutiny and control, power rather than principle may dictate the outcome of negotiations. Similar concerns exist about private ordering in the context of child-related disputes, where the supposedly paramount interests of children, who are particularly vulnerable on breakdown of the family unit, may be lost as parents pursue their own interests. If the normative and protective function of family law is to be taken seriously, there is a strong argument that greater legal intervention is needed in such cases. Throughout the book, we shall consider whether English law has found the correct balance between the protection of family privacy and the need to safeguard certain individual rights, principles, and standards through greater state intervention.

The problems associated with private ordering may also hamper the success of the latest mode of family governance. Instead of intervening by way of the traditional mechanisms of substantive legal rules and adjudication, the state is attempting to regulate family, and perhaps—more broadly—social, behaviour via the 'soft law' of guidance on standards of responsible behaviour by divorcing couples and separating parents. These new initiatives entail the state attempting to intervene in or influence the minutiae of people's private lives and interactions in a novel and more subtle way than the court order. It raises interesting questions about the public/private boundary, the proper role of the state, and the practical limits of governance.

1.2.4 GENDER ISSUES

The interests of some groups and individuals have at various times been neglected by family law. Commentators from various schools of thought and proponents of reform have sought to draw attention to these omissions. Feminism has long been the most dominant of these discourses, highlighting the historical oppression of women by the law in general and family law in particular. By contrast, the turn of the twenty-first century has witnessed a burgeoning fathers' rights movement and the growth of masculine studies which have sought to encourage equivalent examination of the position of men within the family.

Feminist perspectives

There is a wealth of literature bringing a variety of feminist perspectives to family law. Feminist scholars do not speak with one voice, various schools of thought taking very different approaches to a range of family law issues. For example, views differ sharply on whether women have legitimate claims to ongoing financial support following divorce; and on whether perceived judicial bias towards women in residence and contact disputes should be supported as recognizing and valuing women's care-giving role, or resisted as

---

[51] Ibid., 207.

further entrenching traditional stereotypes portraying women's natural and appropriate role as resting within the private realm of the family. However, despite the diversity, feminist writers share some core concerns which have an important bearing upon many areas of family law.

The 'difference' of gender

The first such concern is the issue of gender itself and whether gender does and/or should make a difference. For 'liberal feminists', gender is unproblematic: all that is required to secure true equality is the removal of legal and structural barriers to women's full participation in the public sphere.[52] For 'difference' or 'cultural feminists', however, gender is crucial: they focus on 'the perception that women and men have differing modes of reasoning and different socially-constructed roles which are explanatory of women's inferiority and exclusion from the gendered, male, world'.[53] The work of Carol Gilligan, an educational psychologist, is most closely associated with the 'difference' school of feminist thinking. Based on her research into the moral development of boys and girls, she suggests that men and women think differently and approach moral problems in different ways.[54] Although controversial, Gilligan's work has a potentially important application to many legal issues. She describes the 'ethic of care', which she identifies with feminine thinking, as an approach which sees moral problems within a web of complex relationships to be resolved through dialogue and communication. This supports a model of family justice based more firmly on negotiation, mediation, and other forms of alternative dispute resolution than the adversarial, rights-based approach of traditional adjudication. Gilligan's work on the importance of resolving disputes by situating them within the context of the realities of people's lives has also been advanced as the most appropriate model for resolving disputes over residence and contact, in preference to the abstract, rights-based reasoning which has come to dominate recent debates.[55]

Gender also matters for the radical feminist school. Gender is here understood as the manifestation of power disparities between men and women as created and sustained by the law. As Barnett explains, 'from this perception, woman's role is determined by her socially constructed gender, which ensures her inequality and subordination in relation to law and society which is characterised by male dominance'.[56] The insights of radical feminists have made an important contribution to our understanding of men's violence against women, particularly within the domestic sphere.

The public/private divide

A second core concern of feminist writers is the public/private divide and its role in securing what O'Donovan terms 'the universal oppression of women'.[57] It is argued that whereas men have been identified with the rational, economically productive world of work and politics, women have been identified with the emotionally driven world of the family where work is undertaken for love not money.[58] This has led to an economic and power imbalance between the sexes which, in turn, has secured men's dominance over women in all spheres of life.

---

[52] Barnett (1998), 17–18.
[53] Ibid.
[54] Graycar and Morgan (2002), 194–5.
[55] See, for example, Neale and Smart (1999).
[56] Barnett (1998), 18.
[57] O'Donovan (1985), 15.
[58] Ibid., 8–9.

Moreover, it is argued that the exclusion of women from the public sphere of government, politics, and work, and the reluctance of public bodies to intervene in what is regarded as the quintessentially private realm of family life, have rendered women invisible to the law and allowed dominance, inequality, violence, and abuse to continue unchecked. The law's historically muted response to the problem of domestic violence provides a strong example of legislators' reluctance to intervene in the 'private affairs' of family members. It is sobering to remember that it was only in 1991 that rape within marriage was criminalized. As Barnett argues, 'that which law does not explicitly proscribe infers implicit acceptance'. In the now seminal phrase 'the personal is political'.[59]

Women as mothers

The confinement of women within the private sphere of domestic life is closely related to feminism's third core concern: women's traditional mothering role and its implications for achieving women's equality. Whether the reproductive and maternal role of women should be a cause for celebration or concern, it has relevance to several areas of family law, from financial provision on divorce to residence disputes. The close association between the enduring inequalities faced by women and their child-bearing and child-rearing responsibilities has been the subject of much comment by both radical and liberal feminists.

For radical feminists, women's mothering role can be deeply problematic. Katherine O'Donovan argues that women's confinement in the private sphere as a result of their reproductive and child rearing role has secured their subordination to the dominance of men, who, she contends, are able to maintain this dominance and authority by distancing themselves from the domestic work of raising a family. She argues that women's continuing subordination is rooted in both biology and culture: law and society has constructed male and female roles on the basis of an interpretation of biology that dictates that 'biological differences should determine the social order'. Thus the answer for a radical feminist is to free women from mothering: 'to abolish current methods of biological reproduction through the substitution of artificial methods and the socialisation of child care'.[60]

Liberal feminists have similar concerns about how traditional assumptions about the 'natural', biologically determined role of women within the family have limited women's opportunities in the public world of work, although their solutions to this problem are less drastic. Clare McGlynn's analysis of the 'ideology of motherhood' underpinning judicial decision-making in family law within the European Union is instructive for domestic lawyers, particularly regarding residence and contact disputes and the perceived bias operating against fathers in such cases. According to McGlynn, the 'ideology of motherhood' reflects a deep-rooted belief that 'all women need to be mothers, that all mothers need their children and that all children need their mothers'.[61] This belief permeates the law such that motherhood is simply accepted as the natural, appropriate, and inevitable role for all women. From here, child-care is readily understood as the primary responsibility of women, underpinned by a welfare discourse that identifies the physical and emotional needs of all young children with their mothers. To protect this core relationship, the mother–child relationship is thus privileged by the law to the detriment of women's equality in the wider public sphere. However, as McGlynn points out, this privileging of motherhood is not just damaging for women but also for men, denying fathers an active caring role within the family. The answer

---

[59] Barnett (1998), 65–6.
[60] O'Donovan (1985), 15–16.
[61] McGlynn, citing Anne Oakley, (2001), 326.

for McGlynn is not to negate the importance of the mothering role, but to reject the privileging of motherhood over fatherhood. It is, she argues, 'parenting' not 'mothering' which should be valued, opening up an egalitarian vision of life in which both men and women are free to participate as equal partners in the private and the public spheres.[61a]

However, the world of gender neutrality to which liberal feminist scholars such as McGlynn would aspire is not a vision shared by all feminists. Indeed, in a world which remains deeply gendered, entrenching 'formal equality' within the law based on a gender-blind vision of life may be a cause of further oppression for many women. As noted above, for some feminists, gender does make a difference and the key to achieving equality is not to ignore and suppress those differences but to ensure the law attributes equal value and respect to female experiences. On family law issues bearing upon the mother–child relationship, cultural/difference feminists would thus be more receptive to approaches which sought to support and uphold the mothering work of women and the perhaps unique mother–child bond, seeing it not as a source of oppression but as a source of empowerment and strength.

Men and the family

Much less developed than feminist jurisprudence is a growing body of work focusing on men's engagement with the law. Many men are becoming increasingly disenchanted with what they perceive as the bias towards women in family law, particularly the law relating to children. This disenchantment has coincided with an important 'repositioning' of fatherhood in contemporary political, legal, and cultural thought. Recent years have seen the strong emergence of what Richard Collier terms the idea of the 'new democratic family'.[62] Central to this model of the family is a vision of fatherhood which is active, engaged, and emotionally involved. Thus we see a move away from the dominant normative construction of the father as detached economic provider, towards a more 'progressive' idea of father as 'hands-on' parent. This re-visioning of fatherhood was strongly promoted by the Labour Government who introduced a range of initiatives aimed at encouraging and supporting fathers, particularly economically and socially vulnerable men, to engage successfully in family life.[63]

However, as Collier explains, this emerging image of the 'new' 'hands-on father' is not unproblematic. The 'new father' is just one of several conflicting popular images of fatherhood in contemporary discourse.[64] There remains, for example, strong political and cultural allegiance to the concept of the father as the 'guarantor of social and familial order'. Firmly rooted in appeals to traditional notions of masculinity, the father is here perceived as strong and authoritarian, the disciplinarian within the family charged with ensuring correct behaviour. In this regard he is expected to provide a positive role-model for his children, particularly his sons, by fulfilling his primary role as economic provider. Yet, strongly contradicting these overwhelmingly positive images of fatherhood, is continuing suspicion and distrust about the role of men in family life. Thus the negative perception of at least some men as irresponsible and feckless, the 'deadbeat dad' who is superfluous to the family, remains entrenched in popular discourse. Still further away from any positive conception of the father is the legal, political, and cultural acceptance of the dangerous family man—a man who callously subjects his family to harmful violence and abuse.

61a Ibid., 326–30.
62 Collier (2003), 245.
63 Ibid., 245–7, 249–51. See also Gillies (2009), 52.
64 Collier (2003), 257–9 on which the following draws.

Moreover, there are serious concerns about the extent to which the rhetoric surrounding the emergence of the new 'hands-on' father is rooted in the actual practices of family life. Indeed, as Richard Collier argues, there would appear a serious disjuncture between the rhetoric and the reality of 'new fatherhood'.[65] Rather than a revolution in the traditional gendered division of labour in the UK, the empirical evidence strongly suggests that women continue to take on the bulk of the domestic labour whilst men remain principally committed to paid employment outside the home.[66] Despite various recent initiatives, parenting and employment practices thus remain deeply gendered, the evidence suggesting that rather than embracing the opportunity for change, men, and perhaps some women, remain resistant to political pressure to cede their traditional roles.

This debate signals some important dangers for family law. The recent focus on fatherhood and the rhetoric surrounding the 'new' 'hands-on' father has led to what Collier describes as a 'devaluing and systematic negation of the social importance of mothers and mothering'.[67] This devaluing of motherhood is particularly problematic given it appears to be occurring against a 'mythical' understanding of contemporary fatherhood. Family law decision-making based on unfounded assumptions about contemporary equality between the sexes risks betraying the investment made by women in their parenting role, and ultimately the welfare of the child. The extent to which the role of fathers has changed, and whether such changes demand a different approach by the law to parent–child relationships, will be an important question throughout the child law chapters.

1.2.5 SEXUAL ORIENTATION

Until recently entirely excluded, the lesbian, gay, and bisexual community have now clearly 'arrived' in family law, prompting questions about the proper regulation of same-sex—and opposite-sex—relationships, some of which draw on lessons learned from the feminist project. Sexual orientation only becomes problematic for law and society where it departs from the 'norm' of heterosexuality. For centuries, individuals with non-heterosexual orientation were outlaws. Anal intercourse, even if consensual, was a serious criminal offence, subject to the death penalty until 1861. The offence of gross indecency—introduced in 1885—was aimed explicitly at gay behaviour. Lesbianism, by contrast, inhabited the shadows: the suggestion in 1921 that lesbian acts be brought within the scope of the offence of 'gross indecency' was dismissed on the basis that criminalization would 'tell the whole world there is such an offence, . . . bring it to the notice of women who have never heard of it, never dreamed of it. I think this is a very great mischief'.[68] Needless to say, quasi-conjugal relationships between same-sex couples received no legal recognition. And many consider that that should continue to be the case.

However, over the last 60 years English law's approach towards gay and lesbian individuals, their sexual relationships, their place in civil society, and their relationships has been transformed. Kees Waaldijk has suggested that most countries follow a series of standard legislative steps towards recognition of same-sex relationships: first, homosexual acts are decriminalized and any distinctions between opposite-sex and same-sex sexual relations, such as the age of consent, are removed from criminal law; second, the civil law prohibits

---

[65] Ibid., 255–6.
[66] See data cited in chapter 3.
[67] Collier (2003), 266.
[68] Lord Birkenhead, quoted in Playdon (2004), 136.

any discrimination against homosexuals in employment and the provision of goods and services; third, family law is extended to embrace same-sex relationships in various ways, ending finally with acceptance of same-sex marriage.[69]

Just as feminism is not a single school of thought, nor are advocates for gay and lesbian rights a homogenous group, and some criticize the way in which the new liberalism has been achieved and the potential implications of reform. The principal motive for reform has been equality. As we noted above, Article 14 ECHR has been used successfully on several occasions in Strasbourg and domestically to further the cause of gay and lesbian law reform, even though sexual orientation is not expressly enumerated as one of the prohibited grounds of discrimination.[70] The concept of equality is not, however, straightforward. The argument that same-sex couples should be treated in the same way as opposite-sex couples is conceptually simple, carries political and legal weight, and is readily accepted by the general population. As Craig Lind argues,[71] it is somewhat inevitable in today's political climate that this version of equality appears to be taking us inexorably towards the 'full equality' symbolically enshrined in same-sex marriage. However, equality is more complex than this suggests. True equality does not require that all people be treated the same. Sometimes it demands that different people be treated differently. The crucial question for family lawyers is thus whether 'admission to marriage and other forms of heterosexual family regulation enhance the 'real' equality of lesbians and gay men?'[72]

The main concern here is the potentially 'normalizing' effects of formal equality arguments and their suppression of the diversity of gay and lesbian life.[73] As Cameron asks: 'on whose terms – and on what basis – is recognition to be gained? Are our relationships to be recognised only if they are in all respects, save for the gender of our partners, indistinguishable from traditional heterosexual marriages?'[74] The dilemma is a very real one for political activists. It is through emphasizing the 'sameness' of homosexuality that the greatest legal and political mileage is likely to be made. So, Cameron asks, is assimilation to the heterosexual norm and rejection of the rich diversity and difference of same-sex relationships to be the inevitable price of equality? And is this a price worth paying for the holy grail of marriage? These are crucial questions. We shall see in chapter 2, in particular, the extent to which English family law has made recognition of same-sex relationships dependent upon compliance with heterosexual norms.

1.2.6 CULTURAL DIVERSITY

The cultural and religious diversity of the population of England and Wales raises important issues for family law. The 2001 Census revealed that 4.6 million people or 7.9 per cent of the UK population are from an ethnic minority community. There is considerable diversity within the ethnic minority population, which includes those of Indian, Pakistani, Bangladeshi, Black Caribbean, Black African, Chinese, and mixed-race origin,[75] as well as a growing number of European migrants. Religious identity is also an increasingly important

---

[69] Waaldijk (2003).

[70] See *Salguiero da Silva Mouta v Portugal* (App No 33290/96, ECHR) (2001).

[71] Lind (2004), 115–19.

[72] Ibid., 119.

[73] See further Eskridge (2001); Halley (2001); Norrie (2000).

[74] Cameron (2001), v.

[75] ONS (2005b), 1.

consideration. While the majority religion within Great Britain remains Christianity with over 41 million people (70 per cent of the total population in 2001) identifying as Christian, the next largest religious groups are Pakistani Muslims (686,000); Indian Hindus (471,000); Indian Sikhs (307,000); Bangladeshi Muslims (261,000); and white Jews (259,000). There is also a significant Buddhist population drawn from a wide range of ethnic groups.[76]

Given this diversity, religious and cultural factors play an increasingly important role in family disputes. The family sits at the heart of most cultural and religious communities. It is through the family that cultural and religious practices and beliefs are transmitted and preserved for the next generation. Cultural and/or religious practices are therefore often particularly strongly entrenched within the protected, private realm of family life. Traditions surrounding core family practices such as marriage and child-rearing practices are particularly resistant to change and, within immigrant communities, are often strongly defended when felt to be under threat from the assimilating pressures of the majority population. As John Eekelaar observes: '[i]t is natural that adults should be deeply concerned about the cultural context in which their children grow up. They tend to see it as part of their own interests'.[77] Respect for cultural identity is also a key part of liberalism's respect for individual liberty and choice, respect that extends to both adults and children.

The difficult question facing multicultural societies is to what extent minority practices and beliefs, whether rooted in religion or culture, should be accommodated within the law when in conflict with the normative standards of the majority population. An overly prohibitive approach can lead to charges of cultural imperialism, even racism. An overly tolerant approach can constitute an affront to the mores of the majority population, who may then complain that their own traditions and values are being undermined and eroded. Perhaps more persuasively, the application of different principles and standards to different ethnic and religious groups generates concern that vulnerable individuals within those communities are being denied equal treatment and protection under the law. The suggestion (at least as reported in the media) by Dr Rowan Williams, the Archbishop of Canterbury, that some form of legal pluralism was 'unavoidable' in the UK and that Islamic courts should be able to apply Sharia Law to a range of family disputes caused a popular outcry.[78] It was condemned by David Cameron, then leader of the Opposition, as 'dangerous' and 'illiberal'.[79]

The potential for difficulty arises in several areas of family law, and the cultural norms and practices at stake are hugely significant to the communities in question.[80] Minority practices with respect to marriage have attracted considerable attention. The first wave of immigration following the Second World War raised the difficult question of whether polygamous marriages and child marriages entered into abroad should be recognized by English law.[81] Inter-generational conflict between first and second wave immigrants and their children generated disputes over arranged marriages, argued by the younger generation to be forced and so invalid.[82] In the context of divorce, women from various communities have looked to English law to help address difficulties in obtaining a divorce in accordance with their personal religious law.[83] Intra-cultural and religious disputes concerning marriage and divorce

[76] Ibid., 6.
[77] Eekelaar (2004), 178.
[78] See <http://news.bbc.co.uk/1/hi/uk/7239409.stm> accessed 6 December 2010.
[79] See <http://news.bbc.co.uk/1/hi/uk_politics/7264740.stm> accessed 6 December 2010.
[80] Murphy (2000), 650–1.
[81] See Shah (2003).
[82] Matrimonial Causes Act 1973 (MCA 1973), s 12: see 2.7.1.
[83] See 5.5.7.

require the English courts to navigate a difficult path between according appropriate respect to the cultural and religious mores of the community, whilst seeking to do justice between the parties in accordance with the norms of English law. This task is made particularly difficult when differing interpretations of the cultural/religious norms and practices at the heart of the dispute are advanced by the opposing parties. Clearly, Parliament and the courts must be responsive to the potential difficulties caused, especially for women, by traditional family practices. However, there are again no simple answers. Measures intended to protect vulnerable individuals within ethnic minority communities, such as refusing to recognize polygamous or child marriages on the basis of protecting basic human rights and promoting gender equality, can have the opposite effect, leaving the most vulnerable groups unprotected and driving prohibited practices, such as polygamy, underground.[84] Prakash Shah suggests that a more effective response is to afford official recognition to these diverse cultural and religious practices, bringing them within the protective scope of English law.[85]

Cultural and religious conflict can also arise in various contexts relating to children. In the private law arena, disputes between parents of different religious and/or ethnic backgrounds over the upbringing of their children are increasingly common.[86] The weight to be accorded to cultural and religious identity in the context of adoption has also been controversial, trans-racial adoption dividing many commentators and communities.[87] Less well-recognized, but equally important, is the potential impact of different child-rearing practices within ethnic minority communities on the outcome of residence and contact disputes. In contrast to the model of the nuclear family which predominates in the West, the extended family has a much more central role in many Asian and African cultures, as is reflected in the typical household size amongst ethnic minority communities in Great Britain.[88] Care must be taken that parents, particularly mothers, from these communities are not unfairly prejudiced in residence disputes because they fail to comply with the patterns of child-care predominating in western nuclear families.[89] Similarly, members of the extended family should not be overlooked as full-time carers for children because of the much less significant role played by equivalent relations within western families. Similar considerations apply in the public law context. On the one hand, social workers and the courts must be alert to the dangers of cultural imperialism in misinterpreting culturally rooted child-rearing practices as harmful or abusive.[90] On the other hand, social workers and the courts must be equally alert to the danger of the 'culture' argument being manipulated by parents with the result that vulnerable children are left in dangerous situations of abuse, one of the many contributing factors to the death of Victoria Climbié.[91]

There is no clear policy in English law determining how cases involving sensitive cultural or religious issues should be dealt with. However, the need for tolerance and restraint is vital. In the words of Munby J:

> We live, or strive to live, in a tolerant society increasingly alive to the need to guard against the tyranny which majority opinion may impose on those who, for whatever reason, comprise

---

[84] Shah (2003), 399.
[85] Ibid.
[86] See, for example, *Re J (child's religious upbringing and circumcision)* [2000] 1 FCR 307.
[87] Eekelaar (2004), 182.
[88] ONS (2004), 17.
[89] See *Re K (Residence order: securing contact)* [1999] 1 FLR 583.
[90] See *Re K* [2005] EWHC 2956.
[91] Eekelaar (2004), 190.

a weak or voiceless minority...[T]he starting point of the law is a tolerant indulgence to cultural and religious diversity and an essentially agnostic view of religious beliefs...The court recognises no religious distinctions and generally speaking passes no judgment on religious beliefs or on the tenets, doctrines or rules of any particular section of society. All are entitled to equal respect.[92]

1.2.7 SHOULD LAW AND LAWYERS KEEP OUT OF THE FAMILY?

The family courts remain the lynchpin of the family justice system. As the family court system has evolved, it has acquired a distinctive character. More flexible and informal than other parts of the legal system, the family court system prides itself on its conciliatory approach to family disputes. However, the family court system is currently under severe pressure. Alongside swathing cuts to family legal aid which threaten to deprive many vulnerable families of access to legal advice and support, the family courts have been subjected to increasingly strong criticism—particularly from fathers' rights groups.[93] A range of problems have been identified, most notably expense, unacceptable delays, lack of transparency, and inadequate attention to the views of children. Steps have been taken to address some of these concerns. For example, whilst most family cases are still heard in private with the parties protected by tight reporting restrictions,[94] accusations that the family courts are administering 'secret justice' behind closed doors have been met to some extent by allowing greater media access to the courts[95] and lifting some of the restrictions on the publication of information relating to the proceedings.[96]

However, the perceived problems with the family court system have lent strong impetus to the search for more 'effective' alternatives. This search has been underpinned by the increasing popularity of a communitarian ideology that emphasizes the importance of duties and responsibilities in family life, rather than the self-interest and individualistic focus said to permeate 'rights-based' adversarial litigation. Furthermore, the mindset which accompanies adversarial litigation is believed to exacerbate hostility, something considered particularly damaging in the context of family relationships. To lawyers' eyes, the question may seem at best counter-intuitive and at worst self-destructive, but is law and the legal system really suitable for dealing with family disputes at all?

Recent government initiatives indicate a clear desire to move private family law away from dispute resolution and adjudication in the courts towards 'private ordering' in informal settings, where direct negotiation and settlement are promoted. Private ordering can be achieved via various routes. A number of different forms of alternative dispute resolution (ADR) now operate outside the formal court structure, some involving lawyers, some not. As more disputes move outside the courts, the legal process is becoming increasingly marginalized within the family justice system. Indeed, rather than turning to the law for solutions, therapeutic, social work interventions, and mediation are now strongly promoted as more promising alternatives. It should be noted, however, that privately negotiated settlements

---

92 *Pawandeep Singh v Entry Clearance Officer, New Delhi* [2004] EWCA Civ 1075, [67].
93 See, for example, Geldof (2003).
94 Administration of Justice Act 1960, s 12; CA 1989, s 97(2). See generally, DCA (2006a), 14–16.
95 Family Procedure Rules, SI 2010/2955, r 27.10–27.11.
96 Children, Schools and Families Act 2010, Part II.

are not generally enforceable, both parties remaining free to seek a court order inconsistent with the agreement.[97]

Mediation

It has been said that '[t]he main 'story' of private family law over the past two decades has been the emergence of mediation'.[98] 'Mediation' often used to be referred to as 'conciliation', a term that may readily be confused with 'reconciliation':[99] counselling designed to salvage damaged relationships. While mediation might include a therapeutic element designed to enable the parties to adjust to the future, for example to help them to cooperate in joint parenting after separation, it does not aim to reunite couples. Family mediation involves an impartial third party, the mediator, assisting the separating couple to reach an agreement about the future arrangements for their property, finances, and children. The mediator plays a purely facilitative role. He or she has no power to impose a settlement on the parties. As Walker explains, 'it is seen as a more sensible way of settling family disputes and as a civilised and civilising procedure, a process which returns to, or keeps control in, the couple.'[100]

Interest in mediation as an alternative to lawyer-based dispute settlement on relationship breakdown peaked in the 1990s, when it became a key component of subsequently abandoned divorce reforms in the Family Law Act 1996. Previously restricted mostly to disputes over children and used by few parents, mediation was envisaged for the future as 'the norm rather than the exception', to be used for all aspects of a divorce, including finances and property.[101] Mediation has recently returned to the spotlight, as a central focus of the review of the family justice system announced in January 2010. The guiding principles for that review include that 'mediation should be used as far as possible to support individuals themselves to reach agreement about arrangements, rather than having an arrangement imposed by the courts.'[102] One of the proposals under consideration is that it should be compulsory for all parties to child-related disputes to attend at least one mediation session before being able to take their dispute to court.[103]

There are strongly opposing views about the merits or otherwise of mediation as a form of family dispute resolution. Although a major initial impetus for reform was the hope that mediation would lead to cost-savings (a hope disappointed by research),[104] mediation was perceived by the Conservative Government championing the divorce reforms of the 1990s to offer other benefits.[105] Whilst mediation was described as a forward-looking rather than backward-looking process, it was said that it enabled spouses to address what went wrong with the marriage, accept responsibility for the breakdown, face the questions of fault and blame, and begin to address the anger and hurt caused. So, it was said, it would reduce parties' emotional suffering, avoid the polarization of litigation, and more effectively identify marriages capable of being saved. As well as improving substantive outcomes, a number

---

[97] See 7.7.
[98] Davis (2000), para 1.1.
[99] Conciliation Project Unit (1989), para 20.18.
[100] Walker (2000), 401–2.
[101] LCD (1993), para 7.11.
[102] Family Justice Review, Terms of Reference. Available at: <www.justice.gov.uk/news/docs/family-justice-review-terms-reference.pdf>.
[103] See, <www.justice.gov.uk/news/newsrelease200110a.htm> .
[104] E.g. Davis (2000).
[105] Identified at LCD (1993), [7.4]–[7.20].

of claims were made about the benefits of the mediation *process*: that it was an empowering experience, improved communication, helped couples to reach their own agreements and cooperate in post-divorce parenting, and developed parties' negotiating skills for the future. In contrast, litigation and lawyers were presented in a wholly negative light: it was suggested that the law encouraged spouses to take up unreasonable and opposing stances, locked them into dispute, exacerbated the already high levels of pain and distress, and all at higher financial cost.[106]

Many commentators were concerned that the debates were based on polarized (and rather distorted) depictions of what mediation and the legal system were each supposed to offer.[107] Mediation was said to have been 'dangerously idealised'[108] as the harbinger of cheap conflict-free divorce, while law and lawyers were pilloried for fanning the flames of conflict and invariably viewed as inevitably and irrationally inducing contested litigation. Research has never supported either stereotype.[109] Recent research finds that the practice of very many divorce lawyers is forward-looking and focused on reaching early settlements with minimal conflict.[110] This push for settlement is overlooked by the Family Justice Review principle noted above, which wrongly assumes that the only alternative to mediation is litigation. Moreover, in the longer term, lawyer-negotiated agreements have been found to be just as enduring as mediated agreements.[111] Where parties can only communicate through their lawyers, research suggests that lawyer involvement helped to reduce rather than increase tension.[112] There is also little to support the argument that lawyers provoke their clients into adopting unreasonable, highly legalistic, and costly positions. Again, the opposite would appear to be the case, lawyers encouraging their clients to behave reasonably within the parameters prescribed by law. These findings thus undermine many of the negative assumptions commonly made about lawyers' activities. Furthermore, as Eekelaar, Maclean, and Beinart argue, it is important not to lose sight of the benefits from being able to rely on the partisan help and advice of a lawyer.[113] There is, for example, nothing inherently wrong in a party to a divorce seeking to uphold his or her rights to proper financial support. A 'bad' privately mediated agreement could leave that individual in an extremely vulnerable position (potentially at a cost to the state). Privately mediated agreements which represent nothing more than an expression of the existing power relations between the parties can be dangerously unfair. It is this last concern that really exemplifies why mediation is not the panacea some consider it to be.

Indeed, alongside research into family lawyers we must consider the body of research and associated literature on the advantages, disadvantages, uses, and outcomes of mediation, and on the public's willingness to use it. Sceptics have had wide-ranging concerns about mediation's ability to deliver on its supposed benefits. Does mediation offer party control, or merely replace one set of professionals (lawyers, judges) with another (mediators), who may be unable to maintain a neutral, orchestrating role and to avoid interposing their view of the 'right' outcome?[114] Does mediation thereby become a form of informal

---

106 Ibid., [7.3].

107 E.g. Eekelaar, Maclean, and Beinart (2000), ch 1; Walker (1996); Eekelaar (1995).

108 Brown and Day Sclater (1999), 158. On the tension between 'insiders' and 'outsiders' researching and evaluating mediation, and between lawyers and mediators, see Roberts (1992) and Dingwall and Greatbatch (1993); Walker (1996).

109 For a useful survey, see Eekelaar, Maclean, and Beinart (2000), ch 1.

110 Eekelaar, Maclean, and Beinart (2000), 183–7. Eekelaar (1995), 206–9.

111 Eekelaar (1995).

112 Eekelaar, Maclean, and Beinart (2000), 183–7.

113 See also Davis (2000), 20.1

114 Dingwall (1988); Piper (1996); Davis (2000), para 18.6.

adjudication without the safeguards of formal legal process?[115] If mediation does offer party control, does it thereby privatize and reinforce power imbalances between the parties that the legal process could have evened out? Is mediation inherently likely to be better suited to either men or women?[116] How, if at all, can mediation be used where one party has abused the other, and what safeguards can help identify such cases?[117] Since children may not participate directly or at all in the process, can mediation ensure that their interests are given adequate attention?[118] It has also been suggested that as mediation comes under pressure to professionalize and its 'success' is measured by reference to its ability to settle the parties' immediate dispute, therapeutic goals may now be receiving less attention, so that some of the distinctive benefits of mediation are being lost.[119]

For now, 'customer' ambivalence and lack of familiarity with the process[120] means that mediation remains a small part of the family justice system. One recent survey found that whilst 90 per cent of parents agree on contact outside the formal court process, only 5 per cent of those parents use mediation services.[121] Another study[122] into the cost and effectiveness of mediation found that the introduction of public funding for mediation and the requirement that clients attend a meeting to assess their suitability for mediation led only to a small increase in mediated settlements. Those who engaged in mediation found it a positive experience, women generally more so than men, particularly regarding child disputes; but these participants were essentially volunteers,[123] from whom a positive response might be expected. Given that fact, agreement rates (over half of child disputes and a third of financial disputes) were relatively disappointing. Moreover, responses received to the service of solicitors were more positive, especially in their handling of financial disputes.[124] If parties who are willing to try mediation struggle to settle their disputes this way, it is doubtful that cases currently being handled by lawyers would fare any better if pushed into mediation. It must also be remembered that evidence suggesting that mediated cases settle more quickly, cheaply, and less acrimoniously than litigated disputes may not be comparing like with like: it may not be mediation that makes those cases easier, but the characteristics of the parties involved in those disputes.

However, despite such findings and the abandonment of the divorce reforms which had originally prompted government enthusiasm for mediation, mediation remains central to family policy. Public funding is available for couples to mediate their disputes, with necessary lawyer support, rather than litigate.[125] The Labour Government strongly promoted alternative dispute resolution (ADR) in contact cases as a way of trying to effect a change in adult behaviour when settling disputes over children.[126] And, as noted above, the current

[115] Stylianou (1998).

[116] Bottomley (1984); Davis (1988), 5–6; Davis and Roberts (1989); Roberts (1996); Davis (2000), para 17.2.

[117] Raitt (1996); Piper and Kaganas (1997); Greatbatch and Dingwall (1999); Davis (2000); Humphreys and Harrison (2003), 239–40.

[118] Richards (1995), 224; Davis (2000), para 18.10; Diduck (2003), 118–19.

[119] Walker and McCarthy (2004). See also Davis (2000), paras 18.3, 29.9, 30.2.

[120] National Audit Office (2007).

[121] DCA, DfES, and DTI (2004), para 21.

[122] Davis (2000).

[123] 'Suitability' for mediation tended to be understood in terms of 'willingness' to undergo mediation: ibid., para 15.4.

[124] Ibid., paras 20.2–20.3. Newcastle Centre for Family Studies (2004), ch 6.

[125] See generally Black et al (2007), ch 2; and the Legal Services Commission's Funding Code and accompanying Guidance for Decision-Making.

[126] DCA, DfES, and DTI (2004), para 43.

review of the family justice system is considering giving a greater role to mediation, and recent proposals for reform of legal aid (discussed on the Online Resource Centre) would give mediation a very significantly increased role, and family lawyers a very radically reduced role in publicly funded cases. Mediation undoubtedly offers benefits to some clients, where both are committed to the process. But it seems that considerable cultural change is needed before the general public will embrace mediation with the enthusiasm that has marked the approach of successive governments.[127]

Changing the legal profession

Mediation is just one of several initiatives which it is hoped will encourage settlement and divert cases from the courts. The Labour Government promoted a number of such schemes in the context of its contact reforms.[128] These reforms did not reject a continuing role for the legal profession, but instead sought to move the focus of legal practice from advocacy and adjudication towards more 'neutral', conciliatory approaches. The family solicitor is no longer expected to act solely as legal adviser and advocate, but also arbitrator, negotiator, mediator, information-provider, and even counsellor. The new 'collaborative law' method, for example, involves the clients expressly opting for a path in which the solicitors conduct the case exclusively with the objective of promoting settlement; should settlement fail, the client has to instruct new solicitors to litigate instead. For those clients who do get as far as court, in-court conciliation services provided by Cafcass are intended to reduce the number of cases that proceed to a formal hearing. Naturally, each of these initiatives has funding implications, and depend for their success on adequate public or private resourcing.

1.3 CONCLUDING THOUGHTS

Family law is an intellectually stimulating and challenging subject. But it also matters beyond the lecture room. Family law affects real people and their lives on a daily basis. Family life can be full of love and happiness: a rich and rewarding experience. But it can also be a cause of great pain and sadness. Families often turn to the law for help. Getting the law right is therefore important. We hope you enjoy studying it as much as we do.

 ONLINE RESOURCE CENTRE

You will find materials supplementing the discussion in this chapter on the Online Resource Centre which we hope you will find useful. In addition to the topics addressed here, you will find sections on:

- *The Sources of Family Law*: Statute Law; Case Law; International and European Law; Non-Legal Sources.
- *The Family Justice System*: The Family Courts; Who's Who in the Family Courts; Transparency; Legal Aid and Mediation.

---

[127] Walker (2000), 412.
[128] DCA, DfES, and DTI (2005); see 11.5.4.

Also available on the Online Resource Centre are:

A Guide to using this textbook and the Online Resource Centre

Questions, suggestions for further reading, and supplementary materials for each chapter (including updates on developments in family law since this book was published).

The Online Resource Centre will be found at **www.oxfordtextbooks .co.uk/orc/harrisshort_tcm2e/.**

2

FAMILY RELATIONSHIPS
BETWEEN ADULTS

CENTRAL ISSUES

1. Formerly confined largely to traditional conceptions of marriage, family law has recently opened its doors to same-sex relationships and individuals with gender dysphoria. Once outlaws, same-sex couples can now register civil partnerships. Once in legal limbo, trans people can have their acquired gender formally acknowledged, and form legally recognized relationships in that gender.

2. Article 12 of the European Convention on Human Rights (ECHR) enshrines the right to marry, to some extent limiting states' ability to restrict access to marriage. But it has been held that the ECHR does not require the recognition of same-sex marriage.

3. A wide range of legal consequences flow automatically from two status-based relationships: marriage and civil partnership. The law of nullity—which sets out the grounds on which a marriage or civil partnership is void or voidable—identifies who has the right to acquire each status, and tells us something about the law's conception of each status.

4. For many faiths, marriage is the basis for family life. English marriage law currently gives a privileged position to Anglican rites in the formation of marriage, and only monogamous marriages can be created in England and Wales. But English law has also had to deal with questions raised by the marriage traditions of other faiths practised in this country.

5. English law increasingly recognizes relationships that have not been formalized in marriage or civil partnership, but tends still to focus on couples. Relationships between platonic companions, adult relatives who share a home, and individuals in different households receive less attention. Should law move 'beyond conjugality' and recognize the wider range of relationships that are important to people's domestic lives and identities?

2.1 INTRODUCTION

A man and a woman go through a civil marriage ceremony to give the woman the status necessary to acquire a British passport; after the ceremony, they go their separate ways.[1]

---

[1] *Vervaeke v Smith* [1983] 1 AC 145, see below p 80.

Another couple go through a Sikh marriage ceremony and live together as husband and wife for nearly 40 years.[2] A same-sex couple cohabit for over 20 years until the death of one partner, who had been nursed by the other for several years following an accident.[3] Two unmarried elderly sisters live together for their entire life, for the last 30 years in the house built by their brother on land inherited from their parents.[4] Which of these relationships is recognized in English law, on what basis, and with what consequences?

This chapter seeks to answer the first two of those questions in relation to these and other examples. There are many situations in which legal recognition of relationships between two or more adults is relevant, several (but by no means all) of which are addressed in this book: for example, determining rights to inherit on intestacy, calculating welfare benefits entitlements, accessing remedies against domestic violence and financial remedies on relationship breakdown, protection of the shared home in the event of insolvency, enjoyment of tax exemptions, and eligibility to apply to adopt a child together.

Identifying which relationships would be recognized for these sorts of legal purpose, and how, used to be relatively easy. Family law focused on marriage and the legal consequences that flow automatically from it. Little recognition was afforded to unmarried opposite-sex couples, none to same-sex couples, and blood relatives appeared only on the periphery. Transgendered people were not recognized in their acquired gender and so, if heterosexual, were unable to marry their chosen partner. Those excluded from law's concept of family sought admission to it, for the dignity, status, and legitimacy that flows from legal recognition, and for access to various rights and responsibilities accompanying it.

Status-based family law has recently expanded in response to these claims. Same-sex partners can formalize their relationships by registering a civil partnership, a status which confers almost all of the legal consequences that flow from marriage. 'Trans' people can obtain legal recognition of their acquired gender and formalize relationships with their partners, whether by marriage or civil partnership. Identifying these status-based relationships is largely straightforward: legal recognition flows from the fact of marriage or civil partnership, proved and, in the case of civil partnership, created by registration.

Increasing recognition has also been granted to relationships not formalized in marriage or civil partnership. Cohabitants, whether opposite-sex or same-sex, have gradually acquired more legal recognition, though far less extensive than that of spouses and civil partners. Identifying 'non-formalized' relationships is less straightforward than ascertaining whether parties are married. The law recognizes these relationships where they *function* like a family or, more specifically, like spouses. This 'functional' approach to identifying relationships involves a close factual inquiry into how the individuals interact in everyday life.

However, recognition of these relationships has prompted further questions. Commentators have asked whether marriage is an unnecessary legal concept.[5] They are not advocating the abolition of marriage, but asking why we attach certain legal rights and duties to some relationships, traditionally marriage, and not others. The fact that parties happen to be spouses or civil partners may not seem to be a necessary or even sufficient reason for particular legal consequences to arise from their relationship, either at all or from that type of relationship alone. The next candidates for legal recognition tend to be couples who cohabit in a relationship akin to marriage or civil partnership. But then, it is

---

[2] *Chief Adjudication Officer v Bath* [2000] 1 FLR 8, see below p 77.
[3] *Fitzpatrick v Sterling Housing Association Ltd* [2001] 1 AC 27, see below p 39.
[4] *Burden v United Kingdom* (App No 13378/05, ECHR), see below p 113.
[5] E.g. Clive (1980), Hoggett (1980).

asked, what about individuals who share a home, who may or may not be blood relations, and do not have an intimate (sexual) relationship? Why focus on couples or pairs, and not on wider networks?

The basic question is what characteristics of relationships *should* be relevant to determining the scope of legal recognition in each context? The answer depends on what we think is the purpose or function of each law and so which relationships ought to be included, given that purpose. But there may be other objectives at stake: should the law actively promote marriage by attaching certain privileges exclusively to it, and continue to impose special rules on entry into marriage, to preserve a particular understanding of what marriage itself entails? Or should a more neutral stance be taken on relationship-form, focusing instead on the practical situation of a family regardless of status? We consider some of the evidence relevant to debates on these questions in the last section of the chapter. First, we examine the demographic data about families in England and Wales today.

2.2 FAMILY RELATIONSHIPS IN ENGLAND AND WALES

The transformation of family law reflects substantial change in patterns of relationship formation in recent decades.

Marriage and civil partnership

The proportion of married couple households is still high. But the number of marriages contracted each year has declined markedly since the 1970s, a trend common across Europe.[6] In 2008, the marriage rate (i.e. the number marrying per thousand unmarried people in the population aged over 16) was at its lowest since these calculations began in 1862, and the number of marriages contracted in England and Wales was the lowest since 1895 (when, of course, the population was much smaller). The average age at marriage has also significantly increased, the mean age at first marriage for both sexes now being at or over 30 years.[7] However, these data regarding numbers and rates may be under-estimates because they do not include marriages contracted abroad. Government data suggest that as many as 10 per cent of marriages between UK residents may now be occurring abroad, and that this figure is rising annually with the growth in 'wedding package holidays'.[8]

While the marriage rate and overall number of marriages have dropped, the number of *remarriages* has stayed fairly constant since the 1970s, having risen after divorce law was liberalized in 1969. Remarriages (for one or both parties) therefore now constitute a large proportion of total marriages—around 37 per cent of all marriages contracted in England and Wales in 2008.[9]

Patterns of marriage vary between ethnic groups. Data regarding marriages in Great Britain in which at least one spouse is below pensionable age are revealing. The highest proportion of such marriages is found amongst Asian households, at just over half; they are also least likely to contain cohabiting couples. By contrast, just 37 per cent of white British households contain spouses, and less than one-fifth of black households.[10]

6 OECD (2008).
7 ONS (2010c).
8 Government Actuary's Department (2005).
9 ONS (2010b).
10 ONS (2005b), 22.

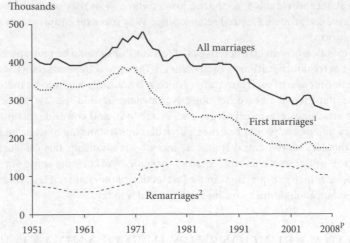

Figure 2.1 Marriages: United Kingdom, 1951–2008

Source: Reproduced from the Office for National Statistics, by Crown copyright © 2010; General Register Office for Scotland; Northern Ireland Statistics and Research Agency. ONS (2010b), provisional data.

Civil partnerships were first registrable in December 2005. By the end of 2009, 40,2327 partnerships had been registered in the United Kingdom, over 90 per cent of them in England and Wales.[11] There were twice as many registrations in 2006 than in subsequent years, doubtless including a large backlog of couples who had been waiting (some for decades) to have the opportunity to formalize their relationship. The total number of registrations to date far exceeds the lower end of the government's original projection that by 2050 there would be between 21,000 to 42,500 civil partnerships in Great Britain.[12]

Cohabitation

It is hard accurately to measure the incidence of cohabitation and characteristics of cohabitants since such relationships are not registered. But various surveys and the Census give insight into their prevalence. While marriage rates are falling, cohabitation is increasing, particularly amongst younger cohorts.[13] Over 2 million cohabiting couples were recorded in England and Wales by the 2001 Census. Government projections suggest that by 2033, there will be 3.8 million (opposite-sex) cohabiting couples and that many more older people will be cohabiting, not least as current cohorts of young cohabitants age without converting their relationships into marriage.[14]

Amongst opposite-sex couples, cohabitation is commonly used as a prelude to marriage, which is being postponed. It seems increasing numbers of couples may not marry at all, despite evidence of widespread intentions to do so.[15] However, many of these cohabiting

---

[11] ONS (2010f), table 1.
[12] DTI (2004), 33–6.
[13] See Law Com (2006), Part 2.
[14] ONS (2010d).
[15] See Coast (2009), de Waal (2008), discussed at p 109 below.

relationships 'terminate' on the parties' marriage, rather than by separation. Recent analysis of longitudinal Census data found that two-fifths of couples who had been cohabiting in the 1991 survey were married to each other by 2001, one-fifth were still cohabiting with each other, and the remainder had separated.[16] Older cohabitants are more likely to be divorced and perhaps to cohabit instead of marrying. Although the average length of cohabitation is shorter than the average marriage and levels of commitment vary, cohabiting relationships are not universally characterized by a lack of commitment.[17] Moreover, the average duration of cohabiting relationships is increasing. The Census data cited above suggest that quite a substantial proportion of cohabiting relationships endure in that form beyond 10 years. More recent data collected in 2006 by the British Social Attitudes survey found a mean duration of 4.6 years for past cohabitations; relationships ongoing at the date of the survey had lasted on average 6.9 years, 8.5 where the couple had children.[18]

The other very significant recent demographic change has been the boom in births outside marriage, whether to cohabitants or to parents who are not living together at birth. In 2008, 45 per cent of births occurred outside marriage, nearly 30 per cent registered to parents living at the same address.[19] Data from the Millennium Cohort Study show that, amongst parents of children born in 2000, cohabitants' relationships were less stable than those of spouses. Three years after the birth, while 95 per cent of mothers who were married at the child's birth were still living with the father, only 83 per cent of originally-cohabiting mothers were doing so, nearly a third having married the father by then. After five years, more cohabiting parents had separated.[20]

We discuss some of the policy questions raised by this growth in cohabitation and its apparent instability as a family form in the last part of the chapter in light of further empirical data about the characteristics of individuals who do and do not marry.

Other relationships within and between households

Not everyone lives in couple-based families. Three in ten households—7.5 million in total—contain an individual living alone or, less commonly, two or more unrelated adults.[21] Other households may contain more than one family, or be composed of several adult generations of the same family, elderly siblings or friends who live together for companionship, or adult children living with and caring for their elderly parents.[22] Demographers now collect data about those who 'live apart together': couples who share an intimate relationship, without living in the same household. There may be anything between 1 to 2 million such relationships.[23]

2.3 GENDER AND SEXUAL ORIENTATION

Historically, many 'family' relationships were not legally recognized because they failed to fit the law's family template: a married couple with children, or as Katherine O'Donovan

---

[16] Wilson and Stuchbury (2010).
[17] Lewis et al (1999); Smart and Stevens (2000).
[18] Barlow et al (2008).
[19] O'Leary et al (2010).
[20] Calderwood (2008).
[21] ONS (2010e), table 2.2.
[22] Law Com (2002), para 1.7.
[23] Haskey (2005); Haskey and Lewis (2006).

once called it, the advertisers' 'cornflakes family'.[24] However, human rights arguments have recently been used to extend the legal conception of family to non-traditional family forms. Here we examine two issues: gender identity and the treatment of 'trans' people in law; and intimate relationships between parties of the same gender.

2.3.1 DETERMINING GENDER: TRANSGENDER AND INTER-SEX PEOPLE

Gender is important to the law of marriage and civil partnership: marriage requires one male and one female; civil partnership requires parties of the same sex.[25] But how is gender determined for these purposes? While the answer is usually straightforward, there are two classes of people for whom life is less simple: transgender or transsexual and inter-sex persons. There are thought to be just a few thousand trans people in the UK,[26] and up to 1 per cent of people at birth cannot be decisively labelled male or female.[27] However, the problems that these people encounter under a law which seeks to place everyone into one of two boxes—male or female—raise interesting questions, not least, why does the law insist on dividing us up in that way? While trans people clearly identify as either male or female and so accept the law's 'binary' male/female taxonomy, inter-sex individuals may regard themselves as belonging to a 'third' gender or reject the concept of gender entirely.[28]

It is important to emphasize at the outset that we are dealing here with gender identity (whether one is regarded as male or female), not sexual orientation (i.e. whether one is sexually attracted to members of the opposite or same sex). In medical terms, sex or gender is determined by various factors, the first immutable, the others more or less susceptible to medical intervention: chromosomes (XY for male, XX for female); gonads and other internal sex organs, genitalia; secondary sexual characteristics generated by hormones, such as body hair and body shape; upbringing, lifestyle, and self-perception, which might possibly have a neurological as well as psychological aspect.[29] For most of us, all of these factors are congruent and our gender is obvious from birth. However, for inter-sex and trans people, matters are more complex.

The rare inter-sex condition arises where an individual's physiology is ambiguous, featuring both male and female characteristics. As noted above, the law's binary scheme of gender struggles to cope with this natural phenomenon, but a judgement is simply made about which gender to ascribe to the individual concerned.[30] As Lord Nicholls has put it, 'that is the best that can be done'.[31]

Transsexualism is rather different. Here, the chromosomes, gonads, and genitalia all unambiguously denote either male or female gender, yet the people concerned believe themselves to be of the other sex, and can experience extreme distress at their situation. This phenomenon is now recognized as a psychiatric condition known as 'gender dysphoria'. Following psychiatric assessment, medical treatment available to deal with this condition now involves hormonal treatment to alter secondary sexual characteristics; living in society as the other sex, with psychiatric therapy and support; and ultimately, and if clinically

---

24 O'Donovan (1993), 30.
25 Matrimonial Causes Act 1973 (MCA 1973), s 11(c); Civil Partnership Act 2004 (CPA 2004), s 3(1)(a).
26 DCA (date unknown).
27 Chau and Herring (2004), 204.
28 Ibid.
29 *Bellinger v Bellinger* [2003] UKHL 21, [5].
30 E.g. *W v W (Physical Inter-sex)* [2001] Fam 111.
31 *Bellinger v Bellinger* [2003] UKHL 21, [6].

appropriate, increasingly extensive surgery, which can remove unwanted gonads and genitalia, and construct genitalia and bodily features of the other sex.[32]

The common law and transgender people

Until recently, English law's treatment of trans people in relation to marriage was governed by *Corbett v Corbett*, which concerned the validity of a marriage contracted between a man and a transsexual woman (i.e. a biological male). At that time, scientific understanding of these cases was less well-developed and gender-reassignment surgery and other techniques less advanced than they are today. The common law which then governed this issue rendered marriage void if not between 'a man and woman'.[33] What is most striking about Ormrod J's decision in the case, a feature that we shall encounter in case law on other topics addressed in this chapter, is the exclusive, question-begging nature of the reasoning: he sets up the issue in such a way that his answer—that an individual born a man cannot be legally recognized as a woman for the purpose of marriage—is unavoidable. His view about the 'essential role of a woman in marriage' is also noteworthy:[34]

Corbett v Corbett (otherwise Ashley) [1971] P 83, 105–6 (Fam Div)

ORMROD J:

...[S]ex is clearly an essential determinant of the relationship called marriage because it is and always has been recognised as the union of man and woman. It is the institution on which the family is built, and in which the capacity for natural hetero-sexual intercourse is an essential element. It has, of course, many other characteristics, of which companionship and mutual support is an important one, but the characteristics which distinguish it from all other relationships can only be met by two persons of opposite sex....

Since marriage is essentially a relationship between man and woman, the validity of the marriage...depends, in my judgment, upon whether the respondent is or is not a woman....The question then becomes, what is meant by the word "woman" in the context of a marriage, for I am not concerned to determine the "legal sex" of the respondent at large. Having regard to the essentially hetero-sexual character of the relationship which is called marriage, the criteria must, in my judgment, be biological, for even the most extreme degree of transsexualism in a male or the most severe hormonal imbalance which can exist in a person with male chromosomes, male gonads and male genitalia cannot reproduce a person who is naturally capable of performing the essential role of a woman in marriage. In other words, the law should adopt in the first place...the chromosomal, gonadal and genital tests, and if all three are congruent, determine the sex for the purpose of marriage accordingly, and ignore any operative intervention.

Challenges under the European Convention on Human Rights

Steps were taken to reduce the embarrassment that trans people might otherwise encounter in their daily lives—notably, by reissuing driving licences, passports, and National Insurance cards in their new names—and gender reassignment procedures were available on the NHS.

---

[32] Ibid., [7]–[9].
[33] See now MCA 1973, s 11(c): 'male and female'.
[34] Diduck and Kaganas (2006), 47–50.

However, the *Corbett* line prevailed, denying trans people legal and so societal recognition. The law was repeatedly challenged before the European Court of Human Rights throughout the 1980s and 1990s with two principal complaints: first, the state's refusal to amend the record of gender on birth certificates and the associated difficulties to which this gave rise; second, the state's refusal to recognize acquired gender for the purposes of marriage. It was argued, for years unsuccessfully, that this violated Articles 8, 12, and 14.[35] However, English law's approach to trans people became increasingly isolated within Europe and beyond, and in 2002 the European Court found the UK position incompatible with the Convention. Two successful challenges were brought, one by Christine Goodwin, a male-to-female trans person who had had gender-reassignment surgery. She had had several discriminatory and humiliating experiences relating to employment, pension entitlements, loan, and other transactions because of her gender status and unalterable birth certificate; and she could not marry her male partner as the law still regarded her as male.[36]

The first issue was whether the UK was in breach of a positive obligation under Article 8, failing to respect Christine Goodwin's private life by not recognizing her acquired female gender:

Goodwin v UK (App No 28957/95, ECHR) (2002)

90. . . . [T]he very essence of the Convention is respect for human dignity and human freedom. Under Article 8 of the Convention in particular, where the notion of personal autonomy is an important principle underlying the interpretation of its guarantees, protection is given to the personal sphere of each individual, including the right to establish details of their identity as individual human beings . . . In the twenty first century the right of transsexuals to personal development and to physical and moral security in the full sense enjoyed by others in society cannot be regarded as a matter of controversy requiring the lapse of time to cast clearer light on the issues involved. In short, the unsatisfactory situation in which post-operative transsexuals live in an intermediate zone [as] not quite one gender or the other is no longer sustainable. . . .

93. . . . [T]he Court finds that the [UK] Government can no longer claim that the matter falls within their margin of appreciation, save as regards the appropriate means of achieving recognition of the right protected under the Convention. Since there are no significant factors of public interest to weigh against the interest of this individual applicant in obtaining legal recognition of her gender re-assignment, it reaches the conclusion that the fair balance that is inherent in the Convention now tilts decisively in favour of the applicant. There has, accordingly, been a failure to respect her right to private life in breach of Article 8 . . .

In reaching this conclusion, the Court had noted the administrative and other problems that would be encountered in providing a mechanism for the recognition of individuals in an acquired gender, but did not feel that these were insuperable:

91. . . . [T]he Court considers that society may reasonably be expected to tolerate a certain inconvenience to enable individuals to live in dignity and worth in accordance with the sexual identity chosen by them at great personal cost . . .

---

[35] *Rees v UK* (App No 9532/81, ECHR) (1986); *Cossey v UK* (App No 10843/84, ECHR) (1993); *Sheffield & Horsham v UK* (App Nos 22985/94, 23390/94, ECHR) (1998); on the issue of recognition for the purpose of acquiring paternity through artificial reproduction, see *X, Y, Z v UK* (App No 21830/93, ECHR) (1997): see 9.2.3. For discussion of these Articles, see the Online Resource Centre and, on Art 12 specifically, below.

[36] See also *I v UK* (App No 25680/94, ECHR) (2003).

The Court then turned to Article 12. In previous cases, the Court had found no breach in the UK's refusal to let trans people marry in their new gender. It had accepted that the right to marry protected the traditional concept of marriage between those of the opposite sex, as the basis of the family, and that states were free to adopt biological criteria for determining sex for this purpose. But the Convention is commonly described as a 'living instrument': its interpretation and application can change over time as circumstances change. This time, as with Article 8 above, it held that the UK could no longer shelter behind a wide margin of appreciation on this issue, and—importantly—detached the legal concept of marriage from procreation:

> 98. Reviewing the situation in 2002, the Court observes that Article 12 secures the fundamental right of a man and woman to marry and to found a family. The second aspect is not however a condition of the first and the inability of any couple to conceive or parent a child cannot be regarded as *per se* removing their right to enjoy the first limb of this provision.
>
> 99. The exercise of the right to marry gives rise to social, personal and legal consequences. It is subject to the national laws of the Contracting States but the limitations thereby introduced must not restrict or reduce the right in such a way or to such an extent that the very essence of the right is impaired...
>
> 100. It is true that the first sentence [of Article 12] refers in express terms to the right of a man and woman to marry. The Court is not persuaded that at the date of this case it can still be assumed that these terms must refer to a determination of gender by purely biological criteria [as held by Ormrod J in *Corbett v Corbett*...]. There have been major social changes in the institution of marriage since the adoption of the Convention as well as dramatic changes brought about by developments in medicine and science in the field of transsexuality. The Court has found above, under Article 8..., that a test of congruent biological factors can no longer be decisive in denying legal recognition to the change of gender of a post-operative transsexual. There are other important factors—the acceptance of the condition of gender identity disorder by the medical professions and health authorities within Contracting States, the provision of treatment including surgery to assimilate the individual as closely as possible to the gender in which they perceive that they properly belong and the assumption by the transsexual of the social role of the assigned gender. The Court would also note that Article 9 of the recently adopted Charter of Fundamental Rights of the European Union departs, no doubt deliberately, from the wording of Article 12...in removing the reference to men and women...
>
> 101. The right under Article 8 to respect for private life does not... subsume all the issues under Article 12, where conditions imposed by national laws are accorded a specific mention. The Court has therefore considered whether the allocation of sex in national law to that registered at birth is a limitation impairing the very essence of the right to marry in this case. In that regard, it finds that it is artificial to assert that post-operative transsexuals have not been deprived of the right to marry as, according to law, they remain able to marry a person of their former opposite sex. The applicant in this case lives as a woman, is in a relationship with a man and would only wish to marry a man. She has no possibility of doing so. In the Court's view, she may therefore claim that the very essence of her right to marry has been infringed....
>
> [The Court held that no separate issue arose under Article 14.]

Shortly after this decision, the House of Lords was called on to consider the issue in light of the Human Rights Act 1998 (HRA 1998) in *Bellinger v Bellinger*.[37] A post-operative

---

[37] [2003] UKIIL 21.

male-to-female trans person, supported by her male partner, sought a declaration that their marriage, contracted over 20 years earlier, was valid. The House of Lords held that the marriage was void under English law and that, while this was incompatible with the ECHR, reform must be left to Parliament.

The Gender Recognition Act 2004

The European Court held that it is for individual states to decide how to go about recognizing individuals in their new gender. The Gender Recognition Act 2004 (GRA 2004) accordingly creates a mechanism whereby transgendered adults can obtain full legal recognition of their 'acquired gender', defined in s 1(2)(a) as the gender in which the person is living, by applying for a gender recognition certificate from the Gender Recognition Panel, composed of legally and medically qualified individuals.[38] By April 2010, over 2,500 certificates had been issued.[39]

Gender Recognition Act 2004

2 Determination of applications

(1) ... [T]he Panel must grant the application if satisfied that the applicant–

  (a) has or has had gender dysphoria,

  (b) has lived in the acquired gender throughout the period of two years ending with the date on which the application is made,

  (c) intends to continue to live in the acquired gender until death, and

  (d) complies with the requirements imposed by and under section 3.

  ...

(3) The Panel must reject an application under section 1(1) if not required by subsection (1) ...to grant it...[40]

Applicants are not required to have had or to propose to have any gender reassignment surgery; it may not be clinically appropriate for certain individuals to do so. The application must be accompanied by two reports from appropriately qualified persons, one of whom (either a registered medical practitioner or chartered psychologist) must practise in the field of gender dysphoria. These reports must describe the applicant's diagnosis and any gender-reassignment treatment undertaken or planned. The applicant must also make a statutory declaration that the conditions in s 2(1)(b) and (c) are met, and a declaration regarding his or her marital or civil partnership status.[41]

Where the applicant is a spouse or civil partner, an interim gender recognition certificate is issued pending the annulment of that relationship.[42] Otherwise, a full gender recognition certificate is issued immediately.[43] We consider at 2.6.1 below the decision of the European

---

[38] GRA 2004, Sch 1.

[39] Gender Identity Research and Education Society (GIRES) website: <http://www.gires.org.uk/grp.php> accessed July 2010.

[40] Alternative criteria apply to applications for recognition of gender changed outside the UK.

[41] GRA 2004, s 3.

[42] Ibid., ss 4(3), 5, and 5A; see 2.7.4.

[43] Ibid., s 4(2).

Court in *Parry v UK*, in which a Christian married couple unsuccessfully challenged this procedure, objecting that they could not remain married and have the husband's change of gender recognized.

The general effects of a full certificate are set out in section 9:

Gender Recognition Act 2004

9 General

(1) Where a full gender recognition certificate is issued to a person, the person's gender becomes for all purposes the acquired gender (so that, if the acquired gender is the male gender, the person's sex becomes that of a man and, if it is the female gender, the person's sex becomes that of a woman).

(2) Subsection (1) does not affect things done, or events occurring, before the certificate is issued; but it does operate for the interpretation of enactments passed, and instruments and other documents made, before the certificate is issued (as well those passed or made afterwards)...

Other provisions deal with the implications of gender recognition in specific contexts, including amendment of birth certificates, parental status, and welfare benefit and pension entitlement.[44] Trans people may now marry a partner of the opposite sex from that of their acquired gender, or form a civil partnership with a same-sex partner. We examine some unusual issues associated with the gender rules for marriage and civil partnership when we address the law of nullity at 2.6.1 and 2.7.4 below.

2.3.2 SAME-SEX RELATIONSHIPS

It is easy to assume that by 'same-sex' we effectively mean gay, lesbian, or bisexual. But where the law is concerned about parties' respective genders, that is all that it is concerned about; the parties' sexual orientation is legally irrelevant. A marriage between a gay man and a lesbian woman would be valid simply because they are respectively male and female.[45] Nevertheless, the vast majority of same-sex pairs seeking legal recognition will be couples. Moreover, for a non-formalized relationship between parties of the same-sex to be recognized, it may be necessary to show that they have, or had, a sexual relationship.[46]

For most of family law's history, same-sex relationships have been legally and socially invisible. When homosexual activity was criminal, social invisibility was essential. But even once the criminal laws were relaxed, enduring social disapproval meant that same-sex relationships were not *positively* recognized in law. Such recognition has been afforded by English law only very recently. But it has developed rapidly to the point that same-sex and opposite-sex relationships are treated on an equal footing for most family law purposes.[47] We trace those recent developments here in order to clear the way for consideration of the present legal

---

[44] Ibid., Schs 3 and 5, s 12.
[45] MCA 1973, s 11(c); see 2.7.5–6 on the requirement of consummation.
[46] See 2.8.2.
[47] See Cretney (2006a).

treatment of formalized and non-formalized relationships. That later discussion will refer to the gender pattern of relationships only to the extent that it remains legally relevant.

Historical exclusion from 'family'

The starting point is *Harrogate Borough Council v Simpson*.[48] This case, like the two landmark cases that departed from it, arose in the context of succession to tenancies by family members living with the tenant on his or her death. Different legislation applies, depending on the type of tenancy involved, identifying specified classes of person who are entitled to inherit. The question was whether a same-sex partner fell within the scope of any of the specified relationships. Under the legislation applicable in this case, the claimant could succeed only by showing that she was a member of the tenant's family, as described by s 50(3) of the Housing Act 1980:

> A person is a member of another's family within the meaning of this chapter if he is his spouse, parent, grandparent, child, grandchild, brother, sister, uncle, aunt, nephew or niece... or if they live together as husband and wife.

Ms Simpson, the defendant, had lived with Mrs Rodrigo, the deceased, for a year and a half in a lesbian relationship. She argued that they could be regarded as having 'lived together as husband and wife', using functional arguments (considered in detail at 2.8.1 below): she argued that their relationship fulfilled many of the same functions as a marriage, notwithstanding both parties being female, and so should be regarded as being akin to marriage for these purposes: they shared a household in a permanent, monogamous, faithful, sexual, and loving relationship. But the Court of Appeal were utterly unpersuaded:

Harrogate Borough Council v Simpson (1985) 17 HLR 205, 209 (CA)

WATKINS LJ:

[Counsel for the plaintiffs] contends that, if Parliament had wished homosexual relationships to be brought into the realm of the lawfully recognised state of a living together of man and wife for the purpose of the relevant legislation, it would plainly have so stated in that legislation, and it has not done so. I am bound to say that I entirely agree with that. I am also firmly of the view that it would be surprising in the extreme to learn that public opinion is such today that it would recognise a homosexual union as being akin to a state of living as husband and wife. The ordinary man and woman...would in my opinion not think even remotely of there being a true resemblance between those two very different states of affairs. That is enough, I think, to dispose of this appeal, which...I would unhesitatingly dismiss.

Ms Simpson applied to the European Commission of Human Rights, arguing that the bar on her succeeding to the tenancy violated her rights under Articles 8 and 14. Her case was declared inadmissible. Her case under Article 8 failed because the ECHR did not then recognize the existence of 'family life' between same-sex partners; nor on the facts was her 'private life' implicated. But had she suffered discrimination in enjoyment of her right to respect for her home contrary to Article 14? She had clearly been treated differently from an opposite-sex partner, but that different treatment was held to be justifiable. Like *Corbett v Corbett* in the trans gender context, the exclusive reasoning here on the scope of family leaves no room for same-sex couples to be accommodated:

---

[48] [1986] 2 FLR 91.

Simpson v United Kingdom (App No 11716/85, ECommHR) (1986)

7....The Commission finds that the aim of the legislation in question was to protect the family, a goal similar to the protection of the right to respect for family life guaranteed by Article 8...The aim itself is clearly legitimate. The question remains, however, whether it was justified to protect families but not to give similar protection to other stable relationships. The Commission considers that the family (to which the relationship of heterosexual unmarried couples living together as husband and wife can be assimilated) merits special protection in society and it see no reason why a High Contracting Party should not afford particular assistance to families. The Commission therefore accepts that the difference in treatment between the applicant and somebody in the same position whose partner had been of the opposite sex can be objectively and reasonably justified....

Fitzpatrick—same-sex partners accepted as 'family'

The next challenge, under the Rent Act 1977, was more successful, and paved the way for same-sex relationships to be admitted to family law. The claimant's case could not have had stronger factual merits. The deceased, Mr Thompson, and the appellant, Mr Fitzpatrick, had lived together in a 'close, loving and faithful' relationship in Mr Thompson's rented flat for 10 years when the deceased was rendered tetraplegic after an accident. Mr Fitzpatrick personally provided the constant care which Mr Thompson needed until his death eight years later. Could Mr Fitzpatrick succeed to the tenancy? The Rent Act provision offered him two arguments: first, by showing, as Ms Simpson had failed to do, that he had been living with Mr Thompson 'as his or her wife or husband'; or second, by showing that he had been a 'member of [Mr Thompson's] family'.[49] Inclusion within the quasi-spousal category would provide greater security of tenure than the 'family' category. Crucially, unlike the equivalent Housing Act provision, the 'family' provision was not defined by an exhaustive list of relationships, so left room for judicial interpretation.

The House of Lords rejected the first argument, on the basis that the statutory wording could not accommodate a same-sex partnership. However, a majority was prepared to find that Mr Fitzpatrick had been a member of Mr Thompson's family.[50] The following passages exemplify the majority's attitude towards same-sex relationships in this context. Mr Fitzpatrick's case was based, like Ms Simpson's, on functional arguments. We explore that aspect of his argument and the House of Lords' response to it in greater detail at 2.8.1 below. The following extracts relate to the question of statutory interpretation: whether a same-sex partner is capable of being a member of the tenant's family for the purposes of the legislation:

Fitzpatrick v Sterling Housing Association Ltd [2001] 1 AC 27, 44, 51

LORD NICHOLLS:

I am in no doubt that this question should be answered affirmatively. A man and woman living together in a stable and permanent sexual relationship are capable of being members of a family for this purpose. Once this is accepted, there can be no rational or other basis on which the like conclusion can be withheld from a similarly stable and permanent sexual relationship between two men or between two women. Where a relationship of this character exists, it

---

[49] Rent Act 1977, Sch 1, paras 2(2) and 3(1).
[50] For commentary, see Sandland (2000), Diduck (2001).

cannot make sense to say that, although a heterosexual partnership can give rise to membership of a family for Rent Act purposes, a homosexual partnership cannot. Where sexual partners are involved, whether heterosexual or homosexual, there is scope for the intimate mutual love and affection and long-term commitment that typically characterise the relationship of husband and wife. This love and affection and commitment can exist in same-sex relationships as in heterosexual relationships. In sexual terms a homosexual relationship is different from a heterosexual relationship, but I am unable to see that the difference is material for present purposes. As already emphasised, the concept underlying membership of a family for present purposes is the sharing of lives together in a single family unit living in one house . . .

LORD CLYDE:

The concept of the family has undergone significant development during recent years, both in the United Kingdom and overseas. Whether that is a matter for concern or congratulation is of no relevance to the present case, but it is properly part of the judicial function to endeavour to reflect an understanding of such changes in the reality of social life.

Post-Human Rights Act: the assimilation of same-sex couples into family law

Lord Slynn observed that the exclusion of members of same-sex couples from the more beneficial quasi-spousal category might be regarded as incompatible with the ECHR once the HRA 1998 came into force.[51] The House of Lords reached that conclusion in *Ghaidan v Godin-Mendoza*.[52] It was successfully argued that the survivor's rights under Article 14 in conjunction with Article 8 (right to respect for the home) were violated by denying a same-sex partner the security of tenure enjoyed by an opposite-sex partner on death of the tenant. Before *Mendoza* reached the House of Lords, the European Court had resiled from its position in *Simpson*. The *Karner* case involved equivalent Austrian tenancy succession law. The Austrian government argued that different treatment of same-sex partners was justified in order to protect the traditional family:

Karner v Austria (App No 40016/98, ECHR) (2004)

37 The Court reiterates that, for the purposes of Art. 14, a difference in treatment is discriminatory if it has no objective and reasonable justification, that is, if it does not pursue a legitimate aim or if there is not a reasonable relationship of proportionality between the means employed and the aim sought to be realised... Furthermore, very weighty reasons have to be put forward before the Court could regard a difference in treatment based exclusively on the ground of sex as compatible with the Convention... Just like differences based on sex, differences based on sexual orientation require particularly serious reasons by way of justification....

40 The Court can accept that protection of the family in the traditional sense is, in principle, a weighty and legitimate reason which might justify a difference in treatment ...

---

[51] [2001] 1 AC 27, 34.
[52] [2004] UKHL 30.

41 The aim of protecting the family in the traditional sense is rather abstract and a broad variety of concrete measures may be used to implement it. In cases in which the margin of appreciation afforded to Member States is narrow, as is the position where there is a difference in treatment based on sex or sexual orientation, the principle of proportionality does not merely require that the measure chosen is in principle suited for realising the aim sought. It must also be shown that it was necessary to exclude persons living in a homosexual relationship from the scope of application of [the tenancy succession provision] in order to achieve that aim. The Court cannot see that the Government has advanced any arguments that would allow such a conclusion....

And so the Court found a violation of Article 14 in conjunction with Article 8. It was against this background that the House of Lords considered Mr Mendoza's claim. It was common ground: that the complaint fell within the ambit of Article 8's right to respect for the home; and that—in being excluded from the quasi-spousal category of Rent Act tenancy succession—Mr Mendoza had been treated differently from a survivor of an opposite-sex relationship because of his sexual orientation. But could the difference of treatment on that ground be justified? This long extract from Baroness Hale's judgment provides a powerful vindication of the rights of same-sex couples to be free from discrimination in this (and many other) spheres:

Ghaidan v Godin-Mendoza [2004] UKHL 30

BARONESS HALE:

138. We are not here concerned with a difference in treatment between married and unmarried couples. The European Court of Human Rights accepts that the protection of the 'traditional family' is in principle a legitimate aim: see *Karner v Austria*...para 40. The traditional family is constituted by marriage. The Convention itself, in article 12, singles out the married family for special protection by guaranteeing to everyone the right to marry and found a family. Had paragraph 2 of Schedule 1 to the Rent Act 1977 stopped at protecting the surviving spouse, it might have been easier to say that a homosexual couple were not in an analogous situation. But it did not. It extended the protection to survivors of a relationship which was not marriage but was sufficiently like marriage to qualify for the same protection. It has therefore to be asked whether opposite and same-sex survivors are in an analogous situation for this purpose.

139. There are several modern statutes which extend a particular benefit or a particular burden, granted to or imposed upon the parties to a marriage, to people who are or were living together 'as husband and wife'[53]... Working out whether a particular couple are or were in such a relationship is not always easy. It is a matter of judgement in which several factors are taken into account. Holding themselves out as married is one of these, and if a heterosexual couple do so, it is likely that they will be held to be living together as such. But it is not a prerequisite in the other private and public law contexts and I see no reason why it should be in this one. What matters most is the essential quality of the relationship, its marriage-like intimacy, stability, and social and financial inter-dependence. Homosexual relationships can have exactly the same qualities of intimacy, stability and inter-dependence that heterosexual relationships do.

[53] See 2.8.2 below.

140. It has not been suggested to us that the nature of the sexual intimacies each enjoys is a relevant difference. Nor can the possibility of holding oneself out as a legally married couple be a relevant difference here. Homosexuals cannot hold themselves out as legally married, but they can if they wish present themselves to the world as if they were married. Many now go through ceremonies of commitment which have the same social and emotional purpose as wedding ceremonies – to declare the strength and permanence of their commitment to one another, their families and friends. If the Civil Partnership Bill now before Parliament becomes law, an equivalent status will be available to them.

141. The relevant difference which has been urged upon us is that a heterosexual couple may have children together whereas a homosexual couple cannot. But this too cannot be a relevant difference in determining whether a relationship can be considered marriage-like for the purpose of the Rent Act. First, the capacity to bear or beget children has never been a prerequisite of a valid marriage in English law.... Even the capacity to consummate the marriage only matters if one of the parties thinks it matters: if they are both content the marriage is valid.[54] A marriage, let alone a relationship analogous to marriage, can exist without either the presence or the possibility of children from that relationship. Secondly, however, the presence of children is a relevant factor in deciding whether a relationship is marriage-like but if the couple are bringing up children together, it is unlikely to matter whether or not they are the biological children of both parties. Both married and unmarried couples, both homosexual and heterosexual, may bring up children together. One or both may have children from another relationship: this is not at all uncommon in lesbian relationships and the court may grant them a shared residence order so that they may share parental responsibility. A lesbian couple may have children by donor insemination who are brought up as the children of them both: it is not uncommon for each of them to bear a child in this way.[55] A gay or lesbian couple may foster other people's children. When the relevant sections of the Adoption and Children Act 2002 are brought into force, they will be able to adopt: this means that they will indeed have a child together in the eyes of the law. Thirdly, however, there is absolutely no reason to think that the protection given by the Rent Act to the surviving partner's home was given for the sake of the couple's children.... It is the longstanding social and economic interdependence, which may or may not be the product of having brought up children together, that qualifies for the protection of the Act....

142. Homosexual couples can have exactly the same sort of interdependent couple relationship as heterosexuals can. Sexual 'orientation' defines the sort of person with whom one wishes to have sexual relations. It requires another person to express itself. Some people, whether heterosexual or homosexual, may be satisfied with casual or transient relationships. But most human beings eventually want more than that. They want love. And with love they often want not only the warmth but also the sense of belonging to one another which is the essence of being a couple. And many couples also come to want the stability and permanence which go with sharing a home and a life together, with or without the children who for many people go to make a family. In this, people of homosexual orientation are no different from people of heterosexual orientation.

143. It follows that a homosexual couple whose relationship is marriage-like in the same ways that an unmarried heterosexual couple's relationship is marriage-like are indeed in an analogous situation. Any difference in treatment is based upon their sexual orientation. It requires an objective justification if it is to comply with article 14. Whatever the scope for a 'discretionary area of judgment' in these cases may be, there has to be a legitimate aim

---

[54] See 2.7.5 below.
[55] See now the Human Fertilisation And Embryology Act 2008, discussed in chapter 9.

before a difference in treatment can be justified. But what could be the legitimate aim of singling out heterosexual couples for more favourable treatment than homosexual couples? It cannot be the *protection* of the traditional family. The traditional family is not protected by granting it a benefit which is denied to people who cannot or will not become a traditional family. What is really meant by the 'protection' of the traditional family is the *encouragement* of people to form traditional families and the *discouragement* of people from forming others. There are many reasons why it might be legitimate to encourage people to marry and to discourage them from living together without marrying. These reasons might have justified the Act in stopping short at marriage. Once it went beyond marriage to unmarried relationships, the aim would have to be encouraging one sort of unmarried relationship and discouraging another.... But,... it is difficult to see how heterosexuals will be encouraged to form and maintain such marriage-like relationships by the knowledge that the equivalent benefit is being denied to homosexuals. The distinction between heterosexual and homosexual couples might be aimed at discouraging homosexual relationships generally. But that cannot now be regarded as a legitimate aim. It is inconsistent with the right to respect for private life accorded to 'everyone', including homosexuals, by art 8 since *Dudgeon v UK* (1981) 4 EHRR 149. If it is not legitimate to discourage homosexual relationships, it cannot be legitimate to discourage stable, committed, marriage-like homosexual relationships of the sort which qualify the survivor to succeed to the home. Society wants its intimate relationships, particularly but not only if there are children involved, to be stable, responsible and secure. It is the transient, irresponsible and insecure relationships which cause us so much concern.[56]

144. I have used the term 'marriage-like' to describe the sort of relationship which meets the statutory test of living together 'as husband and wife'. Once upon a time it might have been difficult to apply those words to a same-sex relationship because both in law and in reality the roles of the husband and wife were so different and those differences were defined by their genders. That is no longer the case. The law now differentiates between husband and wife in only a very few and unimportant respects. Husbands and wives decide for themselves who will go out to work and who will do the homework and child care. Mostly each does some of each. The roles are inter-changeable. There is thus no difficulty in applying the term 'marriage-like' to same-sex relationships. With the greatest respect to my noble and learned friend, Lord Millett, I also see no difficulty in applying the term 'as husband and wife' to persons of the same sex living together in such a relationship. As [counsel for the Secretary of State] said in argument, this is not even a marginal case. It is well within the bounds of what is possible under section 3(1) of the Human Rights Act 1998. If it is possible so to interpret the term in order to make it compliant with convention rights, it is our duty under section 3(1) so to do.[57]

Pre-empting further deployment of s 3 of the HRA 1998 to other legislation, Parliament amended several statutes expressly to include same-sex couples.[58] Surprisingly perhaps, all of this progress was made, and civil partnership (to which we turn next) introduced, despite the fact that the ECtHR had not yet held that same-sex couples enjoy 'family life' for the purposes of Article 8. That step finally came in 2010 in *Schalk and Kopf v Austria*,[59] largely in light of the growing legal recognition and social acceptance of same-sex partnerships across

[56] See also *Rodriguez v Ministry of Housing of the Governmenet of Gibraltar* [2009] UKPC 52.

[57] Their Lordships were unanimous regarding the Convention arguments, but Lord Millett dissented on the use of the HRA 1998, s 3.

[58] Notably, amendments made by Schedules to the CPA 2004.

[59] (App No 30141/04, ECHR) (2010) discussed below.

Europe. This development reinforces the steps that English law had already taken to include same-sex relationships firmly within the scope of English 'family' law.[60]

Civil partnership or 'gay marriage'?

Same-sex marriage is highly controversial wherever it is raised, opposed—for very different reasons—by conservative religious organizations, feminist and radical queer commentators.[61] Marriage is an icon—for some, to be preserved in its traditional, religious form; for others, an important prize to be won, even if civil partnership affords identical rights and duties; and for others still, a patriarchal monolith to be avoided in favour of more diverse, egalitarian ways of living, or simply an irrelevance in contemporary society.

The CPA 2004 enables same-sex partners to contract a relationship which, in its legal characteristics and consequences, is almost identical to marriage but is packaged under a different label. Recent amendments relating to non-formalized same-sex relationships accordingly adopt a new statutory formula: same-sex couples need not demonstrate that they live together 'as if they were husband and wife', rather that they live together 'as if they were civil partners'.[62] But although the institutions of marriage and civil partnership, and their non-formal analogues, are kept semantically distinct, they are intended to operate socially and legally in the same way[63] in order to achieve equality for same-sex couples.[64]

Is civil partnership 'gay marriage'?

The equality policy did not extend to same-sex couples being allowed to *marry*. The Government denied claims that civil partnership is 'gay marriage', but failed to convince some opponents:

Hansard, *Official Report*—Civil Partnership Bill debates
Hansard HL Deb, vol 660, cols 403–5, 22 April 2004: 2nd Reading

Baroness O'Cathain:

The Government have stated many times, even in recent months when they knew that the Bill was about to be introduced, that they do not intend to legalise same-sex marriage....[On] 11 February this year [Lord Filkin]...said: "The concept of same-sex marriage is a contradiction in terms, which is why our position is utterly clear: we are against it, and do not intend to promote it or allow it to take place"...

...The Government's consultation document on civil partnerships said: "It is a matter of public record that the Government has no plans to introduce same-sex marriage".

So apparently we are all agreed. Only gay rights groups want gay marriage. The rest of us are opposed to it.

---

[60] *M v Secretary of State for Work and Pensions* [2006] UKHL 11, [23].

[61] For discussion of the various viewpoints, see Crompton (2004), Eskridge (2001), Norrie (2000), Finnis (1993), Bamforth (2001), (2007b), Auchmuty (2008).

[62] See, for example, CPA 2004, Sch 8, para 13(3), amending Rent Act 1977, Sch 1, para 2(2).

[63] There are some exceptions in the conditions for creating valid marriage and civil partnership: see 2.5 below.

[64] Women and Equality Unit (2003a), paras 1.1–1.2.

There is just one problem: despite what has been said already in this debate, I firmly believe that this Bill creates gay marriage...

The Government may deny this, but I am sure that the man in the street will see this as being a gay marriage...The Guardian on 30 June called civil partnership: "legal marriage in all but name".

It is just wrong to create a parody of marriage for homosexual couples.

Hansard HC Deb, vol 426, col 776, 9 November 2004: Report Stage

Jacqui Smith [Deputy Minister for Women and Equality]:

We introduced [the Bill] with a specific purpose, which is to provide legal recognition for unrelated same-sex couples who do not currently have the option, which is available to opposite-sex couples, to marry. We seek to create a parallel but different legal relationship that mirrors as fully as possible the rights and responsibilities enjoyed by those who can marry, and that uses civil marriage as a template for the processes, rights and responsibilities that go with civil partnership. We are doing this for reasons of equality and social justice...We had some discussion about this in Committee, and our view was that, unless there was an objective justification for a difference in the approaches taken to civil marriage and civil partnership, no difference should exist. There are very few areas in which any difference does exist. The whole point, however, is that civil partnership is not civil marriage, for a variety of reasons, such as the traditions and history—religious and otherwise—that accompany marriage. It is not marriage, but it is, in many ways—dare I say it?—akin to marriage. We make no apology for that.

The media has persisted in referring to civil partnership as 'gay marriage', and government ministers have inevitably lapsed occasionally into that language. For example, in seeking to deflect arguments that siblings who have lived together long-term should enjoy similar inheritance tax exemptions to spouses and civil partners, it was said that, 'The civil partnership issue is rather a distraction in this context. We are talking about marriage, including marriages involving same-sex couples'.[65] But despite the social currency of 'gay marriage', while civil partners enjoy substantive equality with spouses, denying them the *legal* title deprives them of formal equality.[66] We explore the implications of that approach further below.

Same-sex marriage: international comparison and human rights obligations

Increasing numbers of jurisdictions have opened up marriage to same-sex couples: including the Netherlands, Belgium, Spain, Canada, South Africa, Sweden, Norway, Portugal, Iceland, Argentina, and a couple of American states. Others have done the opposite, specifically affirming marriage as an opposite-sex union.[67] The sensitivities surrounding marriage have prompted a proliferation of new family forms offering different ways of

---

[65] Kitty Ussher MP (Economic Secretary, HM Treasury), Hansard HC Deb, vol 478, col 830, 1 July 2008. We examine the *Burden* case from which this particular debate arose at 2.8.3.

[66] Auchmuty (2008).

[67] Marriage Amendment Act 2004 (Aus); Defense of Marriage Act 1996 (US), see Feldblum (2001).

accommodating same-sex relationships in law.[68] Many jurisdictions have created registered partnership schemes which, like UK civil partnership, confer all or most of the rights and duties of spouses on registered partners. Other schemes confer less extensive rights and duties and are easier to enter and exit than marriage.

So there is increasing international recognition of same-sex relationships, even same-sex marriage. But is it required by international human rights law? The right to marry is enshrined in various terms in several human rights instruments.[69]

European Convention on Human Rights, (1953) Article 12

Men and women of marriageable age have the right to marry and to found a family, according to the national laws governing the exercise of this right.

International Covenant on Civil and Political Rights, (1966) Article 23

1. The family is the natural and fundamental group unit of society and is entitled to protection by society and the State.
2. The right of men and women of marriageable age to marry and to found a family shall be recognized....

Charter of Fundamental Rights of the European Union, (2000) Article 9

The right to marry and the right to found a family shall be guaranteed in accordance with the national laws governing the exercise of these rights.

Of these, only the EU Charter was passed after registered partnership schemes and same-sex marriage had arrived on the legal map. Although Article 9 makes no reference to same-sex partnerships, it does not refer to 'men and women', thus making room for—though not requiring—same-sex marriage.[70] However, despite the fact that following the Lisbon Treaty the EU Charter is now legally binding on EU institutions and member states implementing EU instruments,[71] the European Court of Justice has so far declined to recognize registered partnerships as equivalent to marriage under EU law.[72] The UN Human Rights Committee has held that the exclusion of same-sex couples from marriage does not breach Article 23 of the International Covenant on Civil and Political Rights (ICCPR).[73]

Until recently, the European Court of Human Rights had only been called on to consider the nature of the relationship protected by Article 12 in relation to trans people. These cases did not challenge the opposite-sex model, but disputed how sex is determined for the

---

[68] See Curry-Sumner (2006).

[69] Article 12 ECHR is considered more generally at 2.4.3.

[70] See the Commentary to the Charter, cited by the European Court of Human Rights in *Schalk and Kopf v Austria* (App No 30141/04, ECHR) (2010).

[71] On the supposed UK opt-out from this aspect of the Treaty, see Barnard (2008).

[72] *D and Sweden v Council* (C-122/99P) [2001] ECR I-4319; Caraccioclo Di Torella and Reid (2002). Directive 2004/38 requires recognition of same-sex couples' partnerships if they move between member states, but only if the law of the receiving state recognizes the type of relationship.

[73] Views of 17 July 2002 (*Joslin et al v New Zealand*, CCPR/C/75/D/902/1999).

purposes of that model. Some commentators argue that Article 12, alone or in conjunction with Article 14, could be interpreted to require same-sex marriage.[74] The UK Government concluded that declining to allow same-sex couples to marry was compatible with Article 12, and the Joint Committee on Human Rights endorsed that view.[75] The President of the Family Division upheld that view in *Wilkinson v Kitzinger*.[76] The issue was finally tested at European level in 2010 in a case against Austria.

Austria has created its own registered partnership scheme for same-sex couples. That scheme is different from UK civil partnership, affording many but by no means all of the legal consequences of marriage, in particular excluding registered partners from the right to apply to adopt a child, including a step-child, or to undergo artificial insemination. Before that scheme was introduced, Messrs Schalk and Kopf asked the competent authorities to allow them to marry. They objected that their inability to marry violated their rights under Article 12 and Article 14 in conjunction with Article 8, arguing in particular that the growing trend across Europe to recognize same-sex partnerships in some way meant that the Convention should, as a living instrument, now be interpreted to protect their rights in this regard. They sought to rely by analogy on the developments in relation to trans people and on the wording of Article 9 of the EU Charter. It was also argued that the option now available to them to have a registered partnership was not an adequate substitute, in view of the less extensive rights enjoyed by registered partners.

The Court rejected the complaint, but made a number of important pronouncements along the way which mark a significant change in the Convention jurisprudence on same-sex relationships. The Court was unanimous in its decision on Article 12:

Schalk and Kopf v Austria (App No 30141/04, ECHR) (2010)

58. The Court is not persuaded by the applicants' [living instrument] argument. Although, as it noted in *Christine Goodwin*, the institution of marriage has undergone major social changes since the adoption of the Convention, the Court notes that there is no European consensus regarding same-sex marriage. At present, no more than six out of forty-seven Contracting States allow same-sex marriage.

59. . . . [T]he present case has to be distinguished from *Christine Goodwin*. In that case . . . the Court perceived a convergence of standards regarding marriage of transsexuals in their assigned gender. Moreover, *Christine Goodwin* is concerned with marriage of partners who are of different gender, if gender is defined not by purely biological criteria but by taking other factors including gender reassignment . . . into account.

60. Turning to the comparison between Article 12 of the Convention and Article 9 of the [EU Charter], . . . the latter has deliberately dropped the reference to men and women. . . . The commentary to the Charter . . . confirms that Article 9 is meant to be broader in scope than the corresponding articles in other human rights instruments . . . At the same time the reference to domestic law reflects the diversity of national regulations, which range from allowing same-sex marriage to explicitly forbidding it. By referring to national law, Article 9 of the Charter leaves the decision whether or not to allow same-sex marriage to the States. In the words of the commentary: " . . . it may be argued that there is no obstacle to recognize same-

---

[74] E.g. Murphy (2004), Morris and Nott (2005).

[75] Explanatory Note 53, para 700, accompanying the original Civil Partnership Bill; Joint Committee on Human Rights (2004), paras 15–16.

[76] [2006] EWHC 2022.

sex relationships in the context of marriage. There is, however, no explicit requirement that domestic laws should facilitate such marriages."

61. Regard being had to Article 9 of the Charter, therefore, the Court would no longer consider that the right to marry enshrined in Article 12 must in all circumstances be limited to marriage between two persons of the opposite sex. Consequently, it cannot be said that Article 12 is inapplicable to the applicants' complaint. However, as matters stand, the question whether or not to allow same-sex marriage is left to regulation by the national law of the Contracting State.

62. In that connection the Court observes that marriage has deep-rooted social and cultural connotations which may differ largely from one society to another. The Court reiterates that it must not rush to substitute its own judgment in place of that of the national authorities, who are best placed to assess and respond to the needs of society.

The Court was divided 4:3 on the arguments under Articles 14 and 8. The majority reached a number of important conclusions, first (with which the minority agreed) about the scope of Article 8:

93. The Court notes that since 2001, [when an earlier case rejecting the existence of 'family life' between same-sex partners was decided], a rapid evolution of social attitudes towards same-sex couples has taken place in many member States. Since then, a considerable number of member States have afforded legal recognition to same-sex couples...Certain provisions of EU law also reflect a growing tendency to include same-sex couples in the notion of "family"...

94. In view of this evolution, the Court considers it artificial to maintain the view that, in contrast to a different-sex couple, a same-sex couple cannot enjoy "family life" for the purposes of Article 8. Consequently, the relationship of the applicants, a cohabiting same-sex couple in a stable *de facto* [i.e. not formalized] partnership, falls within the notion of "family life", just as the relationship of a different-sex couple in the same situation would.

This conclusion opened the route to the Article 14 argument. The applicants' complaint fell within the scope of Article 8 and, the Court went on, the applicants were similarly situated to a different-sex couple (who of course could marry) in relation to their 'need for legal recognition and protection of their relationship'. However, the majority held that the applicants could not achieve via Articles 14 and 8 what they had failed to achieve directly via Article 12: there could be no right to marry. Since the applicants could now register their relationship under Austrian law, the Court expressly noted that it was not being asked to determine whether failure to provide *any* sort of legal recognition would violate Article 14 in conjunction with Article 8. Moreover, Austria could not be found to have violated the applicants' rights by not introducing registered partnership earlier than it did: since there is not yet a majority of states which recognize same-sex relationships, it remains a matter for individual states when they introduce such laws.[77] Where a state does legislate, the *extent* of the rights conferred on same-sex couples—and any difference between their rights and those of spouses—falls within the state's margin of appreciation. There was therefore

---

[77] It was at this point that the dissenters parted company with the majority, considering that the latter afforded too wide a margin of appreciation to the government given the paucity of reasoning offered to justify (even in broad terms) the different treatment of same-sex couples.

no violation of Articles 14 and 8 by virtue of the lesser legal consequences flowing from registered partnership.

Schalk and Kopf is an important landmark in the legal recognition of same-sex relationships. While the substantive claim failed, the Court's reasoning—particularly its recognition of 'family life' and acceptance that Article 12 is applicable to same-sex marriages (if not—yet?—so as to require that they be allowed) lays the foundations for success in a future case once more states have legislated in this area and the margin of appreciation is consequently narrowed. One important point for English law for the time being is that if a scheme such as that introduced in Austria which creates quite substantial differences between marriage and registered partnership passes muster under the Convention, there can be no question of UK civil partnership law being found to be deficient, since it closely tracks marriage law with only very minor exceptions other than the denial of the title of 'marriage'. *Schalk and Kopf* therefore offers no hope for the parties in *Wilkinson v Kitzinger*, a case concerning the recognition in English law of same-sex marriages contracted abroad. However, *Schalk and Kopf* does require some modification of the reasoning underpinning the decision in *Wilkinson*, to which we now turn.

The CPA 2004 provides that same-sex couples with registered relationships (including marriages) from other jurisdictions will be treated as having formed a civil partnership.[78] Susan Wilkinson and Celia Kitzinger, a lesbian couple dissatisfied by this, sought a declaration that their Canadian marriage was recognized as a marriage by English law, arguing that not to do so violated Articles 8, 12, and 14. They argued that to offer same-sex couples the 'consolation prize' of civil partnership rather than the 'gold standard' of marriage is offensive and demeaning, breaching basic principles of equality. They rejected the government's 'separate but equal' approach on the basis that marriage is still regarded as the superior institution.[79] Their arguments failed.

As we have already noted, the President concluded that Article 12 was not breached, though he did find that the applicants' complaint fell within the ambit of Article 12 for the purposes of a claim under Article 14.[80] This is supported by the approach taken to Article 12 in *Schalk and Kopf*. However, he also considered ('family life' not applying to same-sex couples at that date—see now *Schalk and Kopf*) that the parties' 'private life' was not even implicated, never mind breached, by the refusal to recognize the parties' relationship as a marriage.[81] That view requires modification: the Court in *Schalk and Kopf* clearly assumed that that complaint fell within the ambit of Article 8 for the purposes of setting up the Article 14 claim. More interesting and problematic for the future are the President's observations about the claimed violation of Article 14 in conjunction with Article 12, as they represent English law's reasoning within its margin of appreciation for declining to treat same-sex couples on a par with opposite-sex couples. The President rejected the argument that same-sex couples were not analogous to opposite-sex couples for these purposes: the opposite-sex requirement of marriage was itself the subject of the complaint. But he nevertheless concluded that the difference of treatment pursued a legitimate aim in an appropriate and proportionate manner. It may be doubted whether the dissenting judges in *Schalk and Kopf* would find it entirely persuasive.

---

[78] CPA 2004, ss 212–18, Sch 20.
[79] *Wilkinson v Kitzinger* [2006] EWHC 2022, [5]–[6].
[80] Ibid., [60]–[63], [108]–[110].
[81] Ibid., [85]–[88], [106]–[107].

Wilkinson v Kitzinger [2006] EWHC 2022 (Fam)

SIR MARK POTTER P:

116. In my view the aim is indeed legitimate and in principle is recognised as such [by the ECHR: the protection of the traditional family based on marriage bonds]. On the question of the proportionality of any discriminatory measure reflecting that aim, in this case the CPA, it is complained…that, in denying [the applicant] and the first respondent the name and formal status of marriage and "downgrading" her Canadian marriage to the status of civil partnership, the impact of the measure upon her is one of hurt, humiliation, frustration and outrage. I can understand her feelings in that respect. At the same time, it is certainly not clear that those feelings are shared by a substantial number of same-sex couples content with the status of same-sex partnership.

117. Regrettable as the adverse effects have been upon the petitioner and those in her situation who share her feelings, they do not persuade me that, as a matter of legislative choice and method, the provisions of the CPA represent an unjustifiable exercise in differentiation in the light of its aims.

118. It is apparent that the majority of people, or at least of governments, not only in England but Europe-wide, regard marriage as an age-old institution, valued and valuable, respectable and respected, as a means not only of encouraging monogamy but also the procreation of children and their development and nurture in a family unit (or "nuclear family") in which both maternal and paternal influences are available …

119. The belief that this form of relationship is the one which best encourages stability in a well regulated society is not a disreputable or outmoded notion based upon ideas of exclusivity, marginalisation, disapproval or discrimination against homosexuals or any other persons who by reason of their sexual orientation or for other reasons prefer to form a same-sex union.

120. If marriage…is[,] by longstanding definition and acceptance, a formal relationship between a man and a woman, primarily (though not exclusively) with the aim of producing and rearing children as I have described it, and if that is the institution contemplated and safeguarded by Article 12, then to accord a same-sex relationship the title and status of marriage would be to fly in the face of the Convention as well as to fail to recognise physical reality.

121. Abiding single sex relationships are in no way inferior, nor does English law suggest that they are by according them recognition under the name of civil partnership. By passage of the CPA, United Kingdom law has moved to recognise the rights of individuals who wish to make a same sex commitment to one another. Parliament has not called partnerships between persons of the same sex marriage, not because they are considered inferior to the institution of marriage but because, as a matter of objective fact and common understanding, as well as under the present definition of marriage in English law, and by recognition in European jurisprudence, they are indeed different.

122. The position is as follows. With a view (1) to according formal recognition to relationships between same sex couples which have all the features and characteristics of marriage, save for the ability to procreate children, and (2) preserving and supporting the concept and institution of marriage as a union between persons of opposite sex or gender, Parliament has taken steps by enacting the CPA to accord to same-sex relationships effectively all the rights, responsibilities, benefits and advantages of civil marriage save the name, and thereby to the remove the legal, social and economic disadvantages suffered by homosexuals who wish to join stable long-term relationships. To the extent that by reason of that distinction it discriminates against same-sex partners, such discrimination has a legitimate aim, is reasonable and proportionate, and falls within the margin of appreciation accorded to Convention states.

Several points in this passage are open to criticism. Empirical research supports the view that the attitudes of same-sex couples to the advent of civil partnership and its distinctiveness from marriage are indeed varied,[82] but Nick Bamforth has criticized the President's failure to engage more fully with what is a crucial piece of symbolism for couples such as these.[83] The President's approach to marriage is characterized by the same exclusive reasoning which bedevils *Corbett v Corbett* and *Simpson v UK*, discussed above, and has been criticized for its 'heteronormative' approach which presupposes traditional gender roles at odds with many contemporary opposite-sex relationships.[84] As one Canadian court has put it: 'Stating that marriage is heterosexual because it has always been heterosexual is merely an explanation for the opposite-sex requirement of marriage; it is not an objective that is capable of justifying [different treatment]'.[85] His reasoning also sits somewhat uncomfortably alongside the judgment of Baroness Hale in *Ghaidan v Godin-Mendoza*, extracted above. As Baroness Hale—and the European Court in *Goodwin v UK* and *Schalk and Kopf*—make clear, procreation is not (as a plain matter of English law) a necessary correlative of marriage. Nor is it obvious how the practice of marriage in its traditional form is promoted by the exclusion from its ambit of same-sex couples who wish to live a similar life. We address some of these issues further below when we examine the requirements for valid marriage and civil partnership imposed by the law of nullity. But for the foreseeable future, the pragmatic approach of the UK Parliament which confers the legal consequences of marriage on same-sex couples who wish to formalize their relationship without conferring the sensitive title of 'marriage' seems likely to withstand further judicial scrutiny.

The issue of normalization

Not all gay and lesbian rights commentators have welcomed the way in which same-sex couples have been admitted to the law's family. There are concerns about the law's 'normalizing' tendency: accepting same-sex relationships only insofar as they conform to heterosexual models of relationship. The adoption of a 'marriage model' for civil partnership, rather than the creation of a more distinctive model for same-sex partners, has also been questioned. Alison Diduck takes up this theme in relation to *Fitzpatrick*, observing that the House of Lords did not adopt a new definition of 'family', but simply enlarged the categories of people falling within it.[86] She regards this technique as problematic:

A. Diduck, 'A Family by any other Name ... or Starbucks™ comes to England', (2001) 28 *Journal of Law and Society* 290, 292–4

On the one hand, for example, by enlarging the number of different types of 'personal associations' to which the concept of family can be applied, the Lords arguably presented a clear challenge to law's heteronormative construction of the family. They may have legitimated heretofore 'pretended'[87] families, at least for the purpose of this housing law. But on the other, what is the family to which Mr Fitzpatrick is now legally entitled to belong? While all

---

[82] Mitchell, Dickens, and O'Connor (2009), ch 3.
[83] See generally Bamforth (2007a), from p 156.
[84] Harding (2007); Auchmuty (2008).
[85] *Halpern et al v Attorney General of Canada et al* (2003) 169 OAR 172.
[86] [2001] 1 AC 27, 34–40, per Lord Slynn, 43–6, per Lord Nicholls, 48–50, per Lord Clyde.
[87] Local Government Act 1988, s 28, repealed by Local Government Act 2003, s 122.

the judges spoke of the flexibility of the word family, of its lack of definitive characteristics, they did make some attempt to outline those characteristics ...

Query, from a critical perspective, what happened here. The 'hallmarks' of family were not questioned; its constitution, that is, being a couple, was not questioned and the functional nature of the relationship between its members was not questioned—a stable commitment, caring, sharing, support, and an exclusive sexual relationship are still required. In this light, the particular facts of the *Fitzpatrick* case are important, and may have provided a sufficiently compelling basis for the court to reward Mr Fitzpatrick's claim for justice. ... By his actions of devoted care and sexual fidelity Mr Fitzpatrick came to embody the 'good', that is the sacrificing and dedicated partner of family ideology....

Diduck is concerned that admission to the law's concept of family comes only on condition that one behaves in the 'expected' manner:

Boyd and other ... scholars have previously brought to our attention the deradicalizing potential of widening the net of traditional families, however, and I wish to argue that important lessons can be learned from their insights. Boyd, for example, says that each time a case to redefine spouse or family is brought forward, a challenge to heteronormativity is made, but often the way that legal arguments have to be formulated and, I would add, the way the decision is ultimately framed means that the potentially disruptive gay/lesbian subject is absorbed back into familiar roles and his or her disruptive potential is displaced. We can see evidence of this in the *Fitzpatrick* case. In arguing first for legal recognition as a spouse, and alternatively as family, Fitzpatrick was forced to submit that his relationship with Mr Thompson was 'akin to marriage', and the way the court framed its decision seems to suggest that it agreed.

Diduck finds traditional equality arguments problematic because applicants must demonstrate that they are treated differently from analogous individuals. The claim's success therefore hangs on gay and lesbian applicants showing that their relationships are the same as heterosexual ones: this 'retains the pitfall of instantiating in law characteristics, relationships, and subjectivities already dominant'.[88] Craig Lind argues that this creates new demarcations: homosexuality per se no longer bars admission to 'family', but those whose relationships fail to make the grade in other respects—for example, because not monogamous, or because not perceived as being sufficiently committed—remain excluded:[89]

C. Lind, 'Sexuality and Same-Sex Relationships in Law', in Brooks-Gordon et al (eds), *Sexuality Repositioned* (Oxford: Hart Publishing, 2004), 122–4, 126

[A]lternative ways of living domestic lives are being marginalised by the ... process of normalisation. People who are unsuited to these lifestyles remain outsiders in society. And the question we must ask ourselves is whether or not we have really progressed when we have managed to enlarge the group of the privileged and retain our prejudices in relation to others.

---

88 Diduck (2001), 304.
89 See further Eskridge (2001); Halley (2001); Norrie (2000).

But others take a different view, either regarding normalization as unproblematic or rejecting the view that the concept of family will remain fixed. The 'conservative approach', outlined by Lind in this extract, rejects the notion that marriage is institutionally unacceptable and embraces normalization:

For some ..., what distinguishes people with same-sex desire from those with different-sex desire is only their desire. In all other respects lesbians and gay men are 'normal'. Furthermore, their identity is perceived as immutable. And inequality arising out of an immutable, unchosen, characteristic, it is argued, is unjust. The argument goes on to assert that society could easily remedy that inequality by extending the privileges of the majority to the minority. Sexuality should be an irrelevant consideration in legal regulation; in the regulation of family relationships, for example, lesbians and gay men should be able to attract exactly the same legal regulation as different-sex couples. Society would, in effect, acknowlege the 'normality' of lesbians and gay men by adapting its significant institutions to provide for them. Even amongst those who acknowledge the constructed nature of sexuality there are those who take the view that a socially responsible sexuality is a constrained sexuality...Fitting same-sex desire into the normal patterns of life is an acceptable way of controlling it so that it becomes socially responsible rather than socially obnoxious. Normalisation of sexuality should occur...

By contrast, the 'liberal approach' maintains that extending legal recognition to same-sex relationships will not just result in those families being normalized to the standard family model. Rather, the arrival of same-sex relationships within 'family' has the potential to transform our understandings of what family is and how it should work, recognizing the diversity that exists between different family forms, and undermining the notion of one 'normal family structure':

This view is typically liberal in its idealisation of equal treatment, based on freedom of choice and a notion of individual agency. But its embrace of the creation of a diverse family ethic is also postmodern ...It claims to have, in other words, a radical underbelly. Giving same-sex couples access to ordinary family regulation will, it is argued, go some way (if not all the way) towards addressing the concerns of feminists and others about the patriarchal nature of family regulation. Recognising same-sex relationships will force an internal transformation in the basic tenets of all relationships...Although the desire to be married is regarded as a conservative phenomenon...the desire to compel the state to recognise same-sex marriage is radical. It brings into public discourse a different way of being married. Same-sex couples will be bound to behave differently from the norm of marriage...This is particularly true in relation to gendered roles and other unquestioned behavioural patterns in different sex family lives...For this reason same-sex relationships destabilise the ideal of marriage. Same-sex couples introduce a reflective element into expectations of behaviour in relationships. As a result of this characteristic they will, it is argued, reveal different ways of being married. In particular, they will undermine gendered power in relationships. A more equitable family ethic will emerge. Same-sex families will, in effect, live the feminist ambition for a family life characterised by real equality. In doing so they will, in effect, foster its achievement beyond their own families. Ideologically suspect relationships will benefit from the disruption to the norm that normalisation of abnormal relationships will cause.

The transformative potential is not limited to 'leadership by example', however. The fact that there is a debate surrounding same-sex marriages will create (indeed, has created) a discourse around the nature of marriage, adult relationships and state regulation. It has increased the scope and variety of relationships that are socially recognised and the mechanisms that the state is prepared to use to regulate them. It has, in effect, led to a tangible increase in the diversity of recognised family forms in society. This, it is argued, is a radical departure from the married/single binary which has been the dominant feature of modern family life. . . .

These hoped-for radicalizing effects of bringing same-sex relationships within family law are yet to be seen, and Diduck and Lind doubt that they will arrive.[90] Early empirical research into the impact of civil partnership and other developments extending rights and duties to same-sex couples reveals a diversity of opinion within the gay and lesbian community similar to that found amongst commentators:

M. Mitchell, S. Dickens, and W. O'Connor, *Same-Sex Couple and the Impact of Legislative Changes* (London: NatCen, 2009), executive summary and para 10.2

Where civil partnership was equated with marriage, this could affect [individuals'] decision-making process [about whether to enter a civil partnership] in different ways. For some the perceived similarity was an attraction, because they regarded civil partnership as an important step in moving towards equality with heterosexual couples. For others it was a deterrent because they associated marriage with undesirable heterosexist assumptions and loss of freedom to self-define relationships. Viewing civil partnership as different to marriage could also act as an incentive and deterrent. An incentive where it was believed that civil partnership in its current form was more attractive than marriage; a deterrent where its lack of equality with marriage was felt to be a reason for not having anything to do with it . . .

Decisions about civil partnership were also sometimes related to feelings about whether same-sex couples were the same as or different from heterosexual couples. Some participants saw little difference in the everyday patterns of their lives, so did not think that becoming more like heterosexual couples was a reason against civil partnership. In other cases there was a conscious desire to become part of the 'mainstream' or demonstrate through civil partnership that same-sex relationships were no different to heterosexual ones. Conversely, the view that same-sex couples were different sometimes acted as a deterrent to entering civil partnership; for example that [sexual exclusivity] or financial inter-dependency were undesirable . . .

10.2 . . . [D]epending on the perspective that participants took, views differed about whether civil partnership should be made equal to marriage, whether it should remain an institution specifically for same-sex couples, or whether indeed it should be opened up to heterosexual couples or even to other types of relationships (for example siblings and friends). Those most likely to desire equality with marriage in all respects were the people who expressed a desire to be recognised as part of the mainstream . . . Those who welcomed the idea of a separate institution argued that same-sex relationships were different (and, in some cases, better) and deserved their status. The solution that appeared to have the best fit with the diverse set of views expressed above was for both marriage and civil partnerships to be made open to same-sex and heterosexual couples. This was regarded as a means of increasing equality (and reducing exclusion) and choice amongst all types of couples about which institution best suited their relationship, if indeed any at all.

In light of this last suggestion it is worth noting that the legal complaints have not come from one direction. Just as some same-sex couples are aggrieved at their exclusion from marriage,

---

[90] See also Diduck (2005), Stychin (2006), Auchmuty (2008).

so some opposite-sex couples keen to avoid what they regard as the patriarchal baggage of traditional marriage (however irrational that opinion may seem in light of contemporary marriage law[91]) aspire to the fresh opportunity to create new, equal relationships through civil partnership. There are media reports in the UK[92] and Austria[93] of opposite-sex couples seeking to challenge their exclusion from civil/registered partnership, just as Ms Wilkinson and Kitzinger and Messrs Schalk and Kopf complained about their exclusion from marriage. It is probable the European Court of Human Rights would afford states an ample margin of appreciation on this question, but the cases nevertheless raise important questions about our approach to the legal regulation of adult relationships. Some jurisdictions have retained marriage in its traditional form but made its new institution open to all: for example the French *pacte civil de solidarité* and New Zealand's civil union. But the Netherlands has pursued full equality by both extending marriage to same-sex couples and its registered partnership scheme to opposite-sex pairs. It will be interesting to see in coming decades whether this approach—providing a smorgasbord of options from which all couples have a free choice—gains wider currency.

2.4 STATUS-BASED RELATIONSHIPS: MARRIAGE AND CIVIL PARTNERSHIP

English law recognizes two formalized relationships: marriage and civil partnership, status-based relationships whose recognition flows simply from the parties completing state-prescribed formalities. The legal existence or validity of a marriage or civil partnership does not generally depend upon the parties subsequently behaving in a particular way, so, for example, they need not cohabit.[94] We begin by examining the essential legal nature of such relationships and the right to form them, before turning to the conditions that must be satisfied in order to create them.

2.4.1 THE NATURE OF MARRIAGE AND CIVIL PARTNERSHIP

Marriage has long been regarded as multifaceted: at once a religious institution, a contract between the parties, and a legal status from which particular rights and responsibilities flow, both between the parties themselves, and vis-à-vis the spouses and third parties, including the state.[95] As such, marriage is difficult to categorize juristically:

K. O'Donovan, *Family Law Matters* (London: Pluto Press, 1993), 43–4

As a contract, so presented in legal discourse throughout the history of the common law, it cannot stand. Its terms are not negotiated by the parties, but prescribed by law. It is not a contract freely entered into by any adult but is open only to certain persons under specified

---

[91] Hale (2009), 194.
[92] The case of Freeman and Doyle, reported by *The Guardian*, 24 November 2009.
[93] The case of Ratzenboeck and Seydl, reported on the BBC website, 17 May 2010.
[94] *Draper v UK* (App No 8186/78, ECHR) (1980), [60].
[95] *Lindo v Belisari* (1795) 1 Hag Con 216, 230; *Niboyet v Niboyet* (1878) 4 PD 1, 11; *Bellinger v Bellinger* [2001] EWCA Civ 1140, [99] and [128].

conditions according to law. Termination of marriage can occur only as denoted by law, and not by the partners. Within the legal married state, the law's prescriptions allocate roles ascriptively, according to gender, and not according to the wishes of the parties. Legal marriage requires the sacrifice of personal autonomy but not on equal terms for the parties. An ascriptive quality, gender, is incorporated in the legal institution [notably, the marital rape exemption, see 4.2.3]. This differentiation of partners produces inequality.

Where the notion of marriage as free contract is rejected, writers tend to use the word 'institution' instead, and this may be an appropriate word. When one enters an institution one does so on terms set by that body, one is bound by rules to which one consents on entry. However, the membership may collectively agree a change of rules. It is not easy to apply this analysis to marriage. It is the law, not the partners, which lays down the rules, not only of entry, but also of membership. Collective agreement on the alteration of the rules by the partners is not possible. We are up against something not easily analysed in institutional terms. Marriage has contractual and institutional elements, but it is also *sui generis*, a law unto itself.

As for its religious aspect, much of current marriage law has origins in ecclesiastical law. But it is questionable whether the contours of contemporary, secular marriage law should continue to be shaped by Christian doctrine in a multi-cultural, multi-faith society in which it has been possible to contract a civil marriage since 1836.[96]

The nature of civil partnership attracted attention during parliamentary debates. Section 1 of the CPA 2004 describes civil partnership as a 'relationship'. Some thought it ought to be described as a 'contract'. The Government disagreed:

Hansard, *Official Report*—Civil Partnership Bill debates

Hansard HL Deb, vol 662, cols 1361–2, 24 June 2004: Report Stage

Baroness Scotland of Asthal:

The noble Lord wishes to describe civil partnership as a contract. However, civil partnership is not governed by the law of contract and there is no room for individual variation of the statutory rules governing eligibility, or governing formation or dissolution of a civil partnership, nor of those setting out its consequences.

The change of status from single person to civil partner affects a couple's relationship with each other. After the formation of their civil partnership they would have an entirely new legal relationship with each other. Forming a civil partnership also affects their status; in other words, their position as an individual in relation to everyone else. Each would now be a civil partner. This change of status is permanent in that on the ending of a civil partnership, civil partners do not revert to being single people. They will be marked by having been in a civil partnership in that they will be former civil partners or a surviving civil partner. Civil partnership is a new statutory relationship that provides same-sex couples with legal recognition of their life together as a couple.

While marriage and civil partnership combine contract and status, save for one recent change which we discuss below at 2.5.3, it is clear that civil partnership has no religious

---

[96] Marriage Act 1836.

aspect in law. Adopting the rules that apply to civil marriages, no religious service may be used while the registrar is officiating at the signing of the civil partnership document (the act which creates a civil partnership).[97] The decision to create the separate institution of civil partnership rather than simply permit same-sex marriage was undoubtedly influenced by the fact that many regard marriage as a religious sacrament incapable of accommodating same-sex unions.

One of the key debates relating to marriage and civil partnership today is the extent to which couples can in fact devise their own terms for the relationship by mutual consent. Since marriage arises from the mutual consent of the parties, should they be similarly free to divorce simply because both wish to do so? Should they be free to agree their property and financial arrangements on separation?[98] For the time being, the law formally continues to prescribe the grounds for divorce, to require application to court to terminate the legal status, and retains the power to intervene in parties' financial settlements: as O'Donovan observes, having joined the club, members cannot simply change the rules as it suits them.

2.4.2 THE SIGNIFICANCE OF STATUS

Historically, marriage had a profound and unequal effect on the legal status of the individuals who became husband and wife. Any account of the legal effects of marriage (specifically) must begin with this classic exposition:

W. Blackstone, *Commentaries on the Laws of England*, vol 1 (1765, Facsimile edn: Chicago: University of Chicago Press, 1979), 430

By marriage, the husband and wife are one person in law: that is, the very being or legal existence of the woman is suspended during the marriage, or at least is incorporated and consolidated into that of her husband: under whose wing, protection, and *cover*, she performs every thing . . . Under this principle, of an union of person in husband and wife, depend almost all the legal rights, duties, and disabilities, that either of them acquire by the marriage.

The common law doctrine of unity fused husband and wife's legal personalities into one person, and, as Lord Denning once pithily put it, that person was the husband.[99] This fiction generated some slightly surprising consequences. For example, spouses were unable to sue each other in tort.[100] Nor (still) can they be guilty of conspiring with each other.[101] That dubious benefit aside, lack of distinctive legal personality caused wives substantial disabilities, as we shall see in chapters 3 and 4 when we examine the laws of family property and domestic violence. As John Stuart Mill put it in his essay on *The Subjection of Women* (1869): 'If married life were all that it might be expected to be, looking to the laws alone, society would be a hell upon earth'. But over the course of the late nineteenth century and throughout the twentieth century, wives' legal disabilities and husbands' rights of control were gradually

---

[97] CPA 2004, ss 2(5) and 6.

[98] See 5.7.2 and 7.7.

[99] *Midland Bank v Green (no 3)* [1982] Ch 529, 538.

[100] Until the Law Reform (Husband and Wife) Act 1962.

[101] This exemption is now justified on the basis of marital sanctity and confidentiality, rather than marital unity: Criminal Law Act 1977, s 2(2)(a), *Midland Bank v Green (no 3)* [1979] Ch 496, 521. The Law Commission has recommended abolition of this immunity: Law Com (2009), para 5.16.

removed. Marriage has, at least in theory, developed from legally-condoned patriarchy to a 'partnership of equals':

Sheffield City Council v E and another [2004] EWHC 2808, [2005] Fam 326

MUNBY J:

111 ...[I]n *Durham v Durham* (1885) ... Sir James Hannen P described the contract of marriage in these terms:

"It is an engagement between a man and woman to live together, and love one another as husband and wife, to the exclusion of all others. This is expanded in the promises of the marriage ceremony by words having reference to the natural relations which spring from that engagement, such as protection on the part of the man, and submission on the part of the woman." ...

116 It seems to me that...these observations about the husband's duty to protect and maintain and the wife's duty of submission have now to be read with very considerable caution. Indeed, I doubt that they any longer have any place in our contemporaneous understanding of marriage,...as a civil institution whose duties and obligations are regulated by the secular courts of an increasingly secular society. For, although we live in a multicultural society of many faiths, it must not be forgotten that as a secular judge my concern...is with marriage as a civil contract, not as a religious vow...

131 Today both spouses are the joint, co-equal heads of the family. Each has an obligation to comfort and support the other. It is not for the husband alone to provide the matrimonial home or to decide where the family is to live. Husband and wife both contribute. And where they are to live is, like other domestic matters of common concern, something to be settled by agreement, not determined unilaterally by the husband. In so far as the concept of consortium—the sharing of a common home and a common domestic life, and the right to enjoy each other's society, comfort and assistance—still has any useful role to play, the rights of husband and wife must surely now be regarded as exactly reciprocal.

The notion that spouses owe each other legal duties to comfort, support, and cohabit is problematic. None of them is specifically enforceable,[102] but divorce may be obtained on the basis of desertion, separation, or behaviour such that the petitioner cannot reasonably be expected to live with the respondent.[103]

Civil partnership has nothing like the history and ideological baggage of marriage.[104] It is a creature of modern statute largely replicating existing matrimonial legislation, the exemption from criminal liability for conspiracy included. The common law doctrines of unity and consortium presumably have no application to civil partnership.[105] However, as Munby J observed in the *Sheffield* case, it is doubtful whether those doctrines have any modern significance for spouses: although never formally abolished, they have been encroached upon and compromised substantially by legislation.[106]

---

[102] The action for restitution of conjugal rights was abolished in 1970: Law Reform (Miscellaneous Provisions) Act: see Cretney (2003a), ch 4 and Gaffney-Rhys (2006).

[103] MCA 1973, s 1. See chapter 5.

[104] Though see the concerns of commentators such as Diduck (2005), discussed at 2.3.2.

[105] Harper et al (2005), 42.

[106] Bridge (2001), 15.

We shall examine particular rights and duties arising from marriage and civil partnership throughout the book.[107] It will be clear that, while their status is less distinctive than it was historically, spouses and civil partners still enjoy a special position in English law. In each chapter, we shall examine the contrast with the legal treatment of cohabitants, in particular, whose de facto relationships are created and ended informally and attract rather fewer and less intensive legal consequences.

2.4.3 A RIGHT TO MARRY, OR NOT TO MARRY?

Marriage and civil partnership are vehicles for the acquisition of distinctive rights and duties, many of which cannot be created by private contract. Whether one has the right to form a marriage or civil partnership is therefore a vital question. It has been said that English law has always recognized the right to marry,[108] but the right is now expressly enshrined in Article 12 ECHR and various other international conventions. The importance and universal recognition of this right was described by Baroness Hale in a case concerning procedural restrictions placed on marriages by non-EEA nationals in an effort to prevent sham marriages contracted purely for immigration purposes:

R (on the application of Baiai and others) v Secretary of State for the Home Department and others [2008] UKHL 53

BARONESS HALE:

44. . . . As Chief Justice Warren . . . said [in *Loving et ux. v Virginia* 388 US 1 (1967) a landmark US Supreme Court decision quashing bans on mixed-race marriages] "Marriage is one of the 'basic civil rights of man', fundamental to our very existence and survival". Even in South Africa, where marriage is not constitutionally protected because of fears that this might entrench a particular model of marriage within a multi-cultural society, "the provision of the constitutional text would clearly prohibit any arbitrary state interference with the right to marry or to establish and raise a family. The text enshrines the values of human dignity, equality and freedom" (see *Minister for Home Affairs v Fourie*, Case 60/04 Constitutional Court of South Africa, para 47, Sachs J). Denying to members of minority groups the right to establish formal, legal relationships with the partners of their choice is one way of setting them apart from society, denying that they are "free and equal in dignity and rights".

45. Even in these days, when many in British society believe that there is little social difference between marrying and living together, marriage still has deep significance for many people, quite apart from the legal recognition, status, rights and obligations which it brings. "Marriage law . . . goes well beyond its earlier purpose in the common law of legitimising sexual relations and securing succession of legitimate heirs to family property. And it is much more than a piece of paper." (Sachs J, para 70). It brings legal, social and psychological benefits to the couple when they marry, while they are married and when it ends.

---

[107] For exhaustive analysis of the effects of marriage, see Lowe and Douglas (2007), ch 3.
[108] *R (on the application of the Crown Prosecution Service) v Registrar General of Births, Deaths and Marriages* [2002] EWCA Civ 1661, [20].

We have seen already that not everyone enjoys this right—Article 12 is not breached where marriage remains confined to opposite-sex couples[109]—and Article 12 expressly preserves the right of states to govern the exercise of the right. But the state's freedom is not unlimited, as was explored in *Baiai*. In this extract, Lord Bingham responds to the suggestion that the right to marry in Article 12 is an absolute right:[110]

R (on the application of Baiai and others) v Secretary of State for the Home Department and others [2008] UKHL 53

LORD BINGHAM:

13. If by "absolute" is meant that anyone within the jurisdiction is free to marry any other person irrespective of age, gender, consanguinity, affinity or any existing marriage, then plainly the right protected by article 12 is not absolute. But equally plainly...it is a strong right....In contrast with articles 8, 9, 10 and 11 of the Convention, it contains no second paragraph permitting interferences with or limitations of the right in question which are prescribed by law and necessary in a democratic society for one or other of a number of specified purposes. The right is subject only to national laws governing its exercise.

14. The Strasbourg case law reveals a restrictive approach towards national laws. Thus it has been accepted that national laws may lay down rules of substance based on generally recognised considerations of public interest, of which rules concerning capacity, consent, prohibited degrees of consanguinity and prevention of bigamy are examples....But from early days the right to marry has been described as "fundamental", it has been made clear that the scope afforded to national law is not unlimited and it has been emphasised that national laws governing the exercise of the right to marry must never injure or impair the substance of the right and must not deprive a person or category of person of full legal capacity of the right to marry or substantially interfere with their exercise of the right....

16. The Strasbourg jurisprudence requires the right to marry to be treated as a strong right which may be regulated by national law both as to procedure and substance but may not be subjected to conditions which impair the essence of the right.

In *Baiai*, it was held that it was legitimate to seek to prevent sham marriages for immigration purposes by imposing restrictions on the right to marry, but that such restrictions must be proportionate and non-discriminatory in their operation; the scheme in question failed that test. Other notable cases involving the UK have involved marriage by prisoners; the adverse finding in *Draper v UK*[111] prompted amendments to the Marriage Act 1949 (MA 1949) to allow marriages in prisons. Such restrictions must also have a clear basis in law: a general statutory discretion not to issue a marriage licence to a remand prisoner could not be exercised on the basis that the marriage would frustrate his impending trial, his intended wife then no longer being compellable as a witness.[112]

These cases involved situations where the parties had the capacity to marry and were proposing to comply with the relevant formalities. As we have seen in relation to same-sex

---

[109] See *Schalk and Kopf v Austria* (App No 30141/04, ECHR) (2010), discussed above.

[110] Article 12 is inapplicable in this sense to civil partnership; however, analogous restrictions on access to civil partnership might breach Article 8.

[111] (App No 8186/78, ECHR) (1980).

[112] *R (on the application of the Crown Prosecution Service) v Registrar General of Births, Deaths and Marriages* [2002] EWCA Civ 1661; see also *Frasik v Poland* (App No 22933/02, ECHR) (2010).

couples and trans people, domestic rules regarding capacity to marry and the formalities required to create a marriage must also be compatible with Article 12. For example, Article 12 was invoked, without substantial analysis or adjudication in court, to permit the Prince of Wales to contract a civil marriage; it had previously been understood that members of the Royal Family were able to marry in England and Wales only in an Anglican ceremony.[113] But Article 12 is relevant to the wider populous too, and on examining the law of nullity we shall see how current English law fares under Article 12.

Recent cases in the English courts have also considered what is in effect the right *not* to marry, implicit in Article 12. A marriage to which one or both parties is not consenting is not valid, but the courts have developed their inherent jurisdiction to intervene and prevent a marriage where it is feared either that the marriage would be forced,[114] or that one party may lack the mental capacity to consent to marriage or be unable to make a fully informed, genuine choice to enter a particular marriage.[115] The marriage in the latter type of case might often be valid, since English law takes a narrow view of what must be understood and consented to for a marriage to be valid. But the 'serious emotional and psychological harm' that might nevertheless be suffered has been held to justify the grant of protective orders designed to 'ensure that any marriage really is what [the individual] wants'.[116]

2.5 CREATING A VALID MARRIAGE OR CIVIL PARTNERSHIP

The law does little to provide *positive* definitions of marriage and civil partnership. The most famous, if 'positively misleading',[117] definition of marriage comes from the nineteenth century: 'I conceive that marriage, as understood in Christendom, may...be defined as the voluntary union for life of one man and one woman to the exclusion of all others.'[118]

This statement was not accurate even when it was first made, not least because marriage can be terminated by divorce, so may not endure for the parties' joint lives. But, rightly or wrongly, it is nevertheless frequently cited as a starting point for discussion of marriage. We discover rather more about the law's conception of marriage and civil partnership from the *negative* law of nullity. That law performs a dual function. It sets out those characteristics or conditions that are so fundamental to the law's understanding of marriage and civil partnership that if one or more of them is absent or not satisfied, the relationship cannot or may not be regarded as valid. It also provides a mechanism whereby an apparent marriage or civil partnership which fails to satisfy any of those criteria can be unravelled.

2.5.1 THE LAW OF NULLITY: VOID, VOIDABLE, AND NON-MARRIAGES

It is important to appreciate the distinction between nullity and divorce (or, in the case of civil partnership, dissolution). Divorce entails the termination of what had been a valid

---

[113] The Registrar-General's determination is reported at (2005) FL 345; for comment, Probert (2005b).

[114] This has now been overtaken by statutory remedies created by the Forced Marriage Act 2007, which we address on the Online Resource Centre.

[115] The cases are surveyed in *Re SA (Vulnerable Adult with Capacity: Marriage)* [2005] EWHC 2942.

[116] Ibid., [126] per Munby J.

[117] Probert (2007a), 323.

[118] *Hyde v Hyde* (1866) LR 1 P&D 130, 133, per Lord Penzance.

marriage. Nullity is concerned with the validity of a purported marriage from its inception. However, the distinction is not clear cut, as the law of nullity distinguishes between void and voidable marriages and civil partnerships:

Law Commission, *Report on Nullity of Marriage*, Law Com 33
(London: HMSO, 1970)

3....[T]he present distinction between valid, void and voidable marriages correspond[s] to factual differences in the situations of the parties which call for different relief from the courts. The difference between the three types of marriage may be summarised thus:

(a) A valid marriage is one which is in no sense defective and is, therefore, binding on the parties (and on everyone else); it can only be terminated by death or by a decree of divorce, which decree acknowledges the existence of a valid marriage and then proceeds to put an end to it.

(b) A void marriage is not really a marriage at all, in that it never came into existence because of a fundamental defect; the marriage is said to be void *ab initio*; no decree of nullity is necessary to make it void and parties can take the risk of treating the marriage as void without obtaining a decree. But either of the spouses or any person having a sufficient interest in obtaining a decree of nullity may petition for a decree at any time, whether during the lifetime of the spouses or after their death. In effect, the decree is a declaration that there is not and never has been a marriage.

(c) A voidable marriage is a valid marriage unless and until it is annulled; it can be annulled only at the instance of one of the spouses during the lifetime of both, so that if no decree of nullity is pronounced during the lifetime of both spouses, the marriage becomes unimpeachable as soon as one of the spouses dies.

4. In many Civil Law countries marriages which we would regard as void are treated as voidable in the sense that a marriage once formally celebrated cannot be disregarded until it has been set aside. This seems to be based on the importance which those countries place on official records. The English view, however, is that registration of a marriage merely records the celebration of marriage and affords no guarantee of its validity. To require legal proceedings to be instituted before partes could regard themselves as free from a marriage which was palpably invalid because, for example, one party was already married to another or was under the age of 16, would, in our view, add needlessly to the expense to the parties and to the public.

Although no court proceedings are needed to 'end' a void marriage, they may still be desirable: to provide the certainty of a court order definitively stating the legal position; and to invoke the court's jurisdiction to order financial provision and property adjustment between the parties. It may seem surprising that a void marriage should attract any legal consequences. However, in some cases, one or both parties might have honestly believed the marriage was valid. For example, an innocent party to what is later discovered to have been a bigamous marriage may have compromised his or her position assuming the marriage to be valid to a point where his or her need for financial relief is as great as that of a party to a valid marriage.[119] Whether a remedy is awarded depends on the court's discretion; where the applicant is responsible for the relationship's invalidity, no remedy may be forthcoming.[120]

---

[119] The availability of this jurisdiction in void cases was confirmed in *S-T (formerly J) v J* [1998] Fam 103.
[120] See p 483.

The last, rather curious category is the 'non-marriage'. These are purported marriages which depart so far from what constitutes a marriage under English law, usually because no attempt has been made to comply with the required formalities, that they cannot be regarded even as a void marriage and so *no* legal consequences flow from them. This is a particularly grave conclusion when one or both parties honestly believed the marriage to be valid. As we shall see below, it seems that the courts have recently been stretching the boundaries of this category in forced marriage cases in order to achieve just outcomes, but on a questionable legal basis.

2.5.2 THE PRACTICAL IMPORTANCE OF THE LAW OF NULLITY

If the significance of the law of nullity were measured by reference to the number of nullity decrees granted, we would conclude that it was relatively unimportant. In 2009, just 290 petitions were filed for nullity, compared with 132,144 divorce petitions.[121] This in part reflects the limited scope of the grounds for nullity and the breadth of the bases on which divorce may be obtained. However, much more significant is the role of the law of nullity in delineating the scope of the right to marry or form a civil partnership, and the unknown numbers of individuals who might wish to marry or form a civil partnership, but are unable to do so because of the entry rules prescribed by the law. Restricting access to these institutions to certain types of relationships tells us something more about the law's view of the social function of marriage and civil partnership. The most interesting questions, then, are why have *these* entry requirements been imposed; and why are the grounds on which a marriage or civil partnership may be voidable not relegated to the law of divorce?

2.5.3 FORMAL REQUIREMENTS FOR CREATING MARRIAGE AND CIVIL PARTNERSHIP

Before we examine the grounds for nullity, we must outline the formal requirements for creating a marriage or civil partnership. Since marriage and civil partnership transform the parties' legal status, both between themselves and as against the world, it is unsurprising that public formalities must be performed. The rules are intended to ensure that the parties are free to marry and consent to do so, and to establish with complete certainty who enjoys the legal status of spouse or civil partner.[122] Requiring parties to jump through specific procedural hoops, rather than permitting them to create marriages by whatever method they privately choose, is compatible with Article 12.[123] Specifically, the European Court of Human Rights has held that a state does not violate Article 8, 12, or 14 in refusing to recognize religious marriages and requiring parties who wish to have a religious ceremony additionally to complete further formalities to create a civil law marriage.[124]

English law relating to formalities for marriage (specifically) suffers from 'bewildering' complexity, entirely the product of history.[125] There are several parallel rules. Which

---

[121] MOJ (2010), table 2.5.
[122] Law Com (1973a), Annex, para 4.
[123] *X v Federal Republic of Germany* (App No 6167/73, ECHR) (1974).
[124] *Şerife Yiğit v Turkey* (App No 3976/05, ECHR) (2009); *Muñoz Díaz v Spain* (App No 49151/07, ECHR) (2009).
[125] Law Com (1973a), Annex, para 6.

rules apply depends on the location and/or religious format, if any, of the intended ceremony. The Church of England enjoys a privileged position as the one religious body whose
own buildings, ceremony, and celebrants are qualified to create and register marriages
without any further state sanction, and which can use its own forms of preliminary procedure. Before 1836, marriage could generally *only* be solemnized in an Anglican church,
save that Jews and Quakers were permitted to use their own marriage practices. In 1836,
the option of civil marriage was created,[126] and civil marriages may now be celebrated in
approved premises (such as hotels and stately homes), as well as register offices.[127] Since
1992, civil ceremonies have outnumbered religious ceremonies, in 2008 accounting for
two-thirds of all marriages.[128] Adherents to other Christian denominations and other
deist faiths may now marry in their own religious premises, provided further requirements regarding the registration of the building and presence of an authorized celebrant
are satisfied.[129]

Until recently, civil partnership was a clearly non-religious institution: the original CPA
2004 entirely barred the use of religious premises as a venue for the creation of a civil
partnership and required that the registration be conducted by a registrar, not a religious
celebrant. This scheme, which followed that for civil marriage, frustrated faith groups such
as Liberal Jews and Quakers which support same-sex partnerships and would like to be
able to host registration ceremonies. Section 202 of the Equality Act 2010 has accordingly
removed the bar on use of religious premises, leaving the matter instead to the decision
of each faith group. The Act emphasizes that there is no obligation on religious organizations to host civil partnerships if they do not wish to do so.[130] However, it remains the case
that the registration process itself must be conducted by a registrar, not by the religious
celebrant. It is likely that couples in these faith groups will follow the registration with a
religious ceremony.

The formal requirements for marriage and civil partnership can broadly be divided into
three categories: (i) the preliminary procedures—giving public notice of intention to marry
or register a civil partnership, in order to allow interested parties to lodge objections (for
example, on the grounds that the parties do not have the capacity to marry); (ii) rules that
must be satisfied and procedures that must be completed to create the marriage or civil
partnership—regarding the time and location of the ceremony, the identity of the celebrant,
the presence of witnesses, and (for marriage) the exchange of particular words or (for civil
partnership) the signing of the civil partnership document; and (iii) bureaucratic registration requirements, recording and so proving the existence of the marriage or civil partnership—in the case of marriage, this is a separate stage; in the case of civil partnership, the act
of registration both creates and records the legal status. Different rules apply at stages (i) and
(ii) to different types of marriage: Anglican, Jewish, Quaker, of another faith, or civil. The
registration requirement is universal.

Failure to comply with the prescribed form does not necessarily render the marriage or
civil partnership void.[131] Some defects may result in nullity. Other breaches do not affect

---

[126] Marriage Act 1836.

[127] MA 1949, ss 46A–B.

[128] ONS (2010b).

[129] MCA 1973, ss 35, 41–4; Places of Worship Registration Act 1855.

[130] Not yet in force at January 2011. Cf the employment law obligations of civil registrars, regardless of
any personal objection that they might have on religious grounds: *Ladele v Islington LBC* [2009] EWCA
Civ 1357.

[131] See 2.6.2.

validity, though someone—usually the registrar or equivalent person—may be guilty of a criminal offence.[132] Conversely, if failure to comply with the formal requirements is sufficiently fundamental, the resulting union may be regarded as a non-marriage.

Rationalization and simplification of the law in this area is long overdue, and may in time be required in order to avoid a challenge under Article 14 ECHR in conjunction with Articles 12 and 9, barring discrimination in the exercise of the right to marry on grounds of religion. It is not obvious that the special status of the Church of England, and the relatively disadvantageous positions of other faiths and denominations, should be maintained. However, following recent European Court of Human Rights case law, it might be argued that the universal availability of civil marriage to members of all faiths or none means that there is no violation of Article 14 in conjunction with Article 12.[133] Reform proposals published in 2003, which have thus far failed to reach the statute book, would provide uniform rules for *all* marriages (and now civil partnership), and in other respects provide a marriage law far better suited to twenty-first century social conditions in this jurisdiction.[134]

ONLINE RESOURCE CENTRE

More detailed discussion of the formal requirements for the creation of marriage and civil partnership may be found on the Online Resource Centre.

2.6 GROUNDS ON WHICH A MARRIAGE OR CIVIL PARTNERSHIP IS VOID

The grounds on which marriage and civil partnership are void, summarized in the table below, are identified in the MCA 1973, s 11 and CPA 2004, s 49. They fall into two categories: (i) the first address the parties' 'capacity' to marry or 'eligibility' to form a civil partnership; (ii) the last concerns the failure to observe specified formalities. Since the law of civil partnership has been modelled on marriage, we shall treat marriage and civil partnership together, highlighting differences as we go.

2.6.1 CAPACITY TO MARRY OR FORM A CIVIL PARTNERSHIP

With the exception of minimum age, the rules relating to capacity do not wholly bar individuals from becoming a spouse or civil partner. The issue is whether the given *couple* have the capacity to marry *each other*.

---

[132] MA 1949, ss 75–7; CPA 2004, ss 31–3. Parties may be guilty of perjury if they make false declarations: Perjury Act 1911, s 3, CPA 2004, s 80.

[133] *Muñoz Díaz v Spain* (App No 49151/07, ECHR) (2009), though the complaint in that case was one of ethnic rather than religious discrimination, so the point may still be regarded as open: paras 79–81. Contrast *Şerife Yiğit v Turkey* (App No 3976/05, ECHR) (2009), where Turkish law, which recognizes no religious marriages at all, was upheld.

[134] General Register Office (2003); Probert (2002a) and (2004b); Barton (2002).

Marriage: MCA 1973, s 11	Civil Partnership: CPA 2004, s 49
Void if parties not male and female respectively	Void if parties not of the same sex
Void if within the prohibited degrees	Void if within the prohibited degrees
Void if both parties not over 16	Void if both parties not over 16
Void if either party already a spouse or civil partner	Void if either party already a spouse or civil partner
Void if rules regarding polygamy breached	[no equivalent ground]
Void if certain formal requirements disregarded	Void if certain formal requirements disregarded

Opposite-sex or same-sex

The principal distinction between marriage and civil partnership lies in the parties' genders (not their sexual orientation): spouses must be of the opposite sex, civil partners the same sex.[135] Gender for these purposes is determined by biological criteria or, in the case of trans people with a gender recognition certificate, by acquired gender; without such a certificate, biological criteria still apply.

The law's treatment of gender potentially generates some interesting phenomena. Gender identification is entirely separate from sexual orientation: a female-to-male trans person may want a female partner (and marriage) or a male partner (and civil partnership). Before the GRA 2004, ostensibly same-sex marriages were possible: a female-to-male trans person could marry a man, as the law would still regard him as female. Even now, that paradox is not consigned to legal history, since acquired gender is only recognized if the individual applies under the GRA 2004.[136] If gay or lesbian trans people wish to *marry* their partners, they can do so by declining to have their acquired gender recognized and so legally remaining in their biological sex.[137]

However, these procedures and paradoxes do create dilemmas for some, as *Parry v UK* demonstrates.[138] Since marrying and having three children, the husband had (with the wife's support) undergone gender reassignment. The husband wanted that gender recognized in law, but under the GRA scheme could not acquire a full gender recognition certificate without first annulling the marriage.[139] Once of the same sex in law, the parties could then become civil partners via a fast-track procedure. But, as committed Christians married for over 45 years, they wished to be *married*, despite the legal similarity of civil partnership. As the Court succinctly put it: 'the legislation clearly puts the applicants in a quandary – the first applicant must, invidiously, sacrifice her gender or their marriage'.

The applicants argued unsuccessfully that this violated their rights under Articles 8 and 12, the Court deploying a wide margin of appreciation in what it clearly regards as a culturally, socially, and morally sensitive area of law. The Court agreed that there was a 'direct and invasive effect on the applicants' enjoyment of their right to respect for their private

---

[135] MCA 1973, s 11(c); CPA 2004, ss 3(1)(a) and 49(a).
[136] Probert (2005a).
[137] McCafferty (2002) reports two instances of this, in the US and Aldershot.
[138] (App No 42971/05, ECHR) (2006).
[139] See above p 36.

and family life'. However, since they could acquire a legal status akin to marriage in civil partnership, it found no breach of the Convention. Maintaining the 'bright line' rule that marriage is for partners of the opposite sex and civil partnership for those of the same sex was held to strike a fair balance between the interests of the applicants and the wider community.

The number of couples directly affected by this decision is very small.[140] But, alongside *Bellinger v Bellinger*[141] and *Wilkinson v Kitzinger*,[142] the case has wider significance for its affirmation of marriage in English law as an opposite-sex institution and its rejection of arguments for extending marriage beyond its traditional reach in order to enable excluded couples to enjoy what they clearly view as the social, emotional, and other benefits attaching uniquely to marriage.

There is a further issue raised by the gender requirements for marriage and civil partnership. Same-sex couples (where neither is transgendered) who object to the creation of a parallel institution rather than the extension of marriage to same-sex couples might endeavour to marry. Opposite-sex couples with the converse complaint, perhaps having ideological objections to marriage, might try to create a civil partnership.[143] Should either situation arise (by the unlikely eventuality of the parties disguising the truth from or securing the cooperation of a registrar), how would the law respond?

The point was given some attention in transgender cases before the recent reforms, where it was suggested that 'a marriage void for the reason that the two parties are of the same sex is not merely void but a meretricious marriage which cannot give rise to anything remotely matrimonial in character', despite it being possible to obtain a nullity decree in such cases.[144] However, the cases where nullity decrees were granted involved transgender (rather than same-sex) parties, who were seeking to adopt the law's model of marriage, but disputing the criteria by which gender was judged.

By contrast, it is doubtful whether the courts would issue decrees in clearly same-sex cases.[145] Before the CPA 2004, treating a same-sex marriage as void would have had considerable practical significance, entitling parties to apply for discretionary remedies then reserved to opposite-sex couples (though the courts might have refused to grant relief). It was understood when the precursor to the MCA 1973, s 11(c) was enacted that no remedy would be available in such cases.[146] Post-CPA, recognizing a same sex 'marriage' as void would not give the 'spouses' any practical benefits that they cannot obtain through civil partnership. However, the traditional concept of marriage as a union of man and woman, and the nature of civil partnership as an institution for same-sex couples, are probably sufficiently fundamental that were a marriage to be contracted by parties of the same biological or legally recognized sex, or a civil partnership by opposite-sex partners, it would be treated

---

[140] Submissions made by the applicants in a similar case relating to Scottish law, *R and F v UK* (App No 35748/05, ECHR) (2006), report that there are only two to three dozen applications for gender recognition in the UK where the applicant is married and the spouses wish to remain so.

[141] [2003] UKHL 21, discussed above at p 35.

[142] [2006] EWHC 2066, discussed above at p 49; cf now *Schalk and Kopf v Austria* (App No 30141/04, ECHR) (2010).

[143] See above p 55.

[144] *S-T (formerly J) v J* [1998] Fam 103, 146.

[145] Cf *Talbot v Talbot* (1967) 111 Sol Jo 213. Contrast recent cases of forced marriage contracted abroad where the courts have refused to recognize the marriage at all rather than declare it to be voidable: e.g. *B v I* [2010] 1 FLR 1721, discussed below at p 82.

[146] Cretney, Masson, and Bailey-Harris (2002), 38, citing Hansard HC Deb, 2 April 1971, vol 814, col 1838 (Mr Leo Abse); Hansard HL Deb, 22 April 1971, vol 317, col 816 (Lord Chancellor Hailsham).

as a non-marriage/non-civil partnership. Since such couples know that their actions challenge the law of marriage and civil partnership, depriving them of access to 'void' status and its associated remedies may not be unjust.[147]

Prohibited degrees of relationship and associated formalities

The law of marriage has always barred unions between certain relatives. Over the centuries, the range of prohibited relationships has gradually narrowed[148] and the degree of prohibition on one remaining category (step-relations) relaxed. The most recent relaxation, removing all restrictions on marriages between parents- and children-in-law, was prompted by a decision of the European Court of Human Rights. B and L, both divorced, were father- and daughter-in-law. They had been cohabiting for some time, along with B's grandson (L's son), and wished to marry, but were barred from doing so under the law then in force until both B's first wife (the mother of B's son whom L had married) and B's son (L's first husband) had both died (a hypothetical and quite unpredictable eventuality), or unless they invoked a costly and cumbersome procedure, with 'no discernable rules or precedent', to obtain a personal Act of Parliament permitting their marriage. The majority of a group appointed by the Archbishop of Canterbury had earlier concluded that this bar could not be justified.[149] The restrictions were held to breach B and L's right to marry under Article 12.

B v United Kingdom (App No 36536/02, ECHR) (2006)

36 Article 12 expressly provides for regulation of marriage by national law and given the sensitive moral choices concerned and the importance to be attached to the protection of children and the fostering of secure family environments, this Court must not rush to substitute its own judgment in place of the authorities who are best placed to assess and respond to the needs of society....[A] large number of Contracting States...have a similar bar in their law, reflecting apparently similar concerns about allowing marriages of this degree of affinity.

37 The Court must however examine the facts of the case in the context pertaining in the United Kingdom. It observes that this bar on marriage is aimed at protecting the integrity of the family (preventing sexual rivalry between parents and children) and preventing harm to children who may be affected by the changing relationships of the adults around them. These are, without doubt, legitimate aims.

38 Nonetheless, the bar on marriage does not prevent the relationships occurring...There are no incest, or other criminal law, provisions to prevent extra-marital relationships between parents-in-law and children-in-law being established notwithstanding that children may live in these homes. It cannot, therefore, be said that in the present case the ban on the applicants' marriage prevents any alleged confusion or emotional insecurity to the second applicant's son...

The Court was also unimpressed that the private Act of Parliament route had enabled some parties in the applicants' position to marry. In response to the government's argument that

[147] See Law Com (1970), para 32.
[148] E.g. Marriage (Enabling Act) 1960; Marriage (Prohibited Degrees of Relationship) Act 1986. See Cretney (2003a), ch 2.
[149] Archbishop of Canterbury's Group (1984).

the bar should be retained because this procedure ensured that exceptions were made only in cases where no harm would arise, it commented:

> 40...that there is no indication of any detailed investigation into family circumstances in the Parliamentary procedure and that in any event a cumbersome and expensive vetting process of this kind would not appear to offer a practically accessible or effective mechanism for individuals to vindicate their rights. [The Court] would also view with reservation a system that would require a person of full age in possession of his or her mental faculties to submit to a potentially intrusive investigation to ascertain whether it is suitable for them to marry...

The in-law restrictions were subsequently repealed.[150]

The current law—identical in effect for marriage and civil partnership—is most clearly set out in the CPA 2004.[151] Different rules apply to (i) consanguineous and some adoptive[152] relationships, where marriage or civil partnership is absolutely barred; and (ii) step-relationships, where it is permitted in certain cases:

Civil Partnership Act 2004, Sch 1, Part 1: Prohibited Degrees of Relationship[153]

Absolute prohibitions

1 (1) Two people are within prohibited degrees of relationship if one falls within the list below in relation to the other.

Adoptive child
Adoptive parent
Child
Former adoptive child
Former adoptive parent
Grandparent
Grandchild
Parent
Parent's sibling
Sibling
Sibling's child

(2) In the list "sibling" means a brother, sister, half-brother or half-sister.

Qualified prohibitions

2 (1) Two people are within prohibited degrees of relationship if one of them falls within the list below in relation to the other, unless—

(a) both of them have reached 21 at the time when they register as civil partners of each other, and

---

150 Marriage Act 1949 (Remedial) Order 2006, SI 2007/348.

151 CPA 2004, s 3(1)(d), (2); MCA 1973, s 11(a)(i).

152 Adoption and Children Act 2002 (ACA 2002), s 74: adopted persons remain members of their birth family for the purposes of these rules; within their adopted family they are barred only from parent/child unions.

153 Following *B v UK* (App No 36536/02, ECHR) (2006), para 3 was not commenced and is due to be repealed. For marriage, see MA 1949, s 1 and Sch 1, as amended.

> (b) the younger has not at any time before reaching 18 been a child of the family in relation to the other.
>
> Child of former civil partner
> Child of former spouse
> Former civil partner of grandparent
> Former civil partner of parent
> Former spouse of grandparent
> Former spouse of parent
> Grandchild of former civil partner
> Grandchild of former spouse
>
> (2) "Child of the family", in relation to another person, means a person who—
>
> (a) has lived in the same household as that other person, and
>
> (b) has been treated by that other person as a child of his family.

Where parties falling within the qualified prohibitions wish to marry or become civil partners, additional formal preliminaries apply, though it seems that failure to comply does not invalidate the union.[154]

The rules prohibiting marriage between relations were based originally on biblical grounds.[155] Latterly, the prohibitions have been justified by reference to the genetic health of any offspring of such unions.[156] It is curious that identical restrictions apply to civil partnerships, since same-sex couples cannot (yet) procreate with the genetic material of both partners. Genetic problems can arise between unrelated persons and between cousins, who may marry in English law, and the prohibitions extend to adoptive and step-relations. So the rules are better rationalized on social grounds: the undesirability of relatives forming conjugal relationships disrupting other family relationships. The special limits imposed on marriages between step-relations reflect concerns about abuse of power by older family members. Barring such marriages may deter people from pursuing these relationships at all. It is significant that the criminalization of sexual activity between family members now largely corresponds with the remaining prohibited degrees.[157] One curious exception relates to adoptive relationships, where marriage between adoptive parent and child is absolutely barred, even though sexual activity between them, once both are adult, is apparently permitted.[158] However, the law fails to pursue the social rationale to its logical limit. For example, why are adopted relatives (aside from parent and child) excluded from the prohibitions?[159] Why can people marry former *cohabiting* partners of their parents without restriction? While step-grandparents and child are barred from marrying before both are 21 where the younger has at *any* time when under 18 been treated as a child of the step-grandparent's family in the same household, the criminal law seems not to ban sexual activity between them once the child is over 16 and they no longer share a household.[160] Given these inconsistencies, the prohibited degrees may yet be subject to further reform.[161]

---

[154] MA 1949, ss 16(1A)–(2B), 27B–C; Marriage (Registrar-General's Licence) Act 1970, s 3; CPA 2004, Sch 1, Part 2.

[155] Canon law has biblical origins: Leviticus ch 18 and 20; Deuteronomy 27; 1 Corinthians 5.

[156] Law Com (1970), paras 51–3; Archbishop of Canterbury's Group (1984); cf Human Fertilisation And Embryology Act 1990, s 31ZB.

[157] Sexual Offences Act 2003, ss 64–5, and where one party is under 18, ss 25–9.

[158] ACA 2002, s 74.

[159] Law Com (1970), para 50; sexual activity between adult adoptive relations is not criminal.

[160] Sexual Offences Act 2003, s 27(4).

[161] See Gaffney-Rhys (2005), 957; cf Cretney (2006b).

The age of the parties and associated formalities

Until 1929, the minimum age for marriage was 12 for a girl and 14 for a boy.[162] The basic rule now is that no person under the age of 16 may enter into marriage or civil partnership.[163] In the case of marriages between step-relations, the prohibited degrees rules raise the age limit to 21. However, the legal bars are rather low compared with the average age on first marriage, now around 30.[164] The Law Commission considered but rejected the argument that marriages of children should be merely voidable (valid unless annulled at the instance of one of the parties); or ratifiable (void unless affirmed by the parties after majority is attained).[165] Under-age marriages are therefore void, and so vulnerable to challenge by third parties, even many years after the child in question has reached majority and is happily married, and even if both parties were ignorant that either of them was under 16 at the time of marriage. The basic age rule corresponds with the criminal law of sexual offences against children[166] and child abduction.[167] It may be surmised that the bar is designed to protect children from undesirable sexual activity. The age limits also reflect the seriousness of marriage and civil partnership and the obligations inherent in them, and the need for a mature consent.[168]

Mature minors, aged 16 or 17, may validly marry or become civil partners. But special formal requirements apply, depending (in the case of marriage) on whether the marriage is preceded by civil or Anglican preliminary procedures. Save in the rare case of widowed children, some Anglican marriages, all marriages preceded by civil preliminary procedures, and civil partnerships involving 16 and 17-year-olds ordinarily require the consent of a parent with parental responsibility and/or of another statutorily defined 'appropriate person'.[169] Where those eligible to consent are absent, inaccessible, or under a disability, the court may consent instead, or the registrar may dispense with the consent requirement. If a person whose consent is required refuses to consent, court consent may be obtained.[170] Court consent is required where the child is a ward of court. However, failure to *obtain* appropriate consent will not of itself invalidate a marriage or civil partnership.[171] Only where an appropriate person positively registers *dissent* and no court consent is substituted is the marriage or civil partnership void.[172] In the case of Church of England marriages preceded by the publication of banns, parental consent is not required; but if the parent or other appropriate person has publicly and openly declared his or her dissent in church when the banns are published, any later marriage under those banns will be void.[173] In the case of civil partnership, it is clear that dissent renders the partnership void

---

[162] Age of Marriage Act 1929 raised age to current level of 16; see Cretney (2003a), 57–8.

[163] MCA 1973, s 11(a)(ii), MA 1949, ss 2 and 3; CPA 2004, ss 3(1)(c) and 4.

[164] ONS (2010c), table 5.

[165] Law Com (1970), paras 16–20.

[166] Sexual Offences Act 2003, principally ss 5–13; in the case of sexual offences involving mature minors, note the marriage/civil partnership exception in ss 23 and 28.

[167] Child Abduction Act 1984, s 2.

[168] For international human rights instruments in this field and comparative examples, see Gaffney-Rhys (2009).

[169] MA 1949, s 3; CPA 2004, Sch 2, Part 1. For analysis of these rules, see Probert (2009a).

[170] MA 1949, s 3(1); CPA 2004, Sch 2, Part 2.

[171] In the case of civil marriages, MA 1949, s 48(1)(b). The parties may be guilty of perjury: Perjury Act 1911, s 3(l); CPA 2004, s 80.

[172] MA 1949, ss 30 and 49(b); CPA 2004, s 49(c).

[173] MA 1949, ss 3(3) and 25(c); for marriages under common licence, ss 16(1)(c), (2) and 25(c).

even if the parties were unaware of the impediment; the position in relation to marriage is arguably less clear.[174]

The age limits selected by English law may not be compatible with the marriage practices of some minority religions observed in the UK. An application to Strasbourg challenging this as incompatible with Articles 9, 12, and 14 ECHR was declared inadmissible, the age limits falling with the state's freedom to regulate marriage.[175]

The requirement of parental consent for child spouses was originally designed to prevent imprudent marriages. However, as Munby J has observed, in contemporary society where the average age at marriage is now close to 30, the numbers of teenagers marrying at all is relatively small[176] and children whose parents withhold consent to marriage are simply likely to cohabit instead. The greater concern now is not to prevent unwise marriages by children, but forced ones: not to uphold parental rights to resist a child's proposed marriage, but to prevent an abuse of parental power by forcibly engineering a marriage.[177] Prior to the Forced Marriage Act 2007, which we discuss on the Online Resource Centre, the courts had developed their wardship and inherent jurisdiction to protect children (and vulnerable adults) in such cases;[178] and immigration rules now place an age bar of 21 on marriage visas.[179] The duress entailed in such cases renders the marriage voidable, and we will consider this issue further below in that context.

Monogamy

Under English law, marriage and civil partnership are monogamous states: one may only have one spouse or civil partner at any one time and one cannot simultaneously be a spouse and a civil partner.[180] A marriage or civil partnership contracted where either party is already a spouse or civil partner is automatically void, regardless of the parties' knowledge, and remains void even if the other spouse or civil partner subsequently dies or a divorce is obtained. Parties who knowingly give false information regarding their status in this regard for the purpose of procuring a marriage or civil partnership commit an offence.[181] However, the statutory offence of bigamy is confined to marriage.[182]

Cases may arise where one party's original spouse or partner has been missing for some time, and is honestly and reasonably presumed to be dead. A second union will nevertheless be void if it transpires that the 'deceased' was still alive at the time of the ceremony. However, it is possible to apply for an order presuming the death of the missing party and dissolving that marriage or civil partnership accordingly. The missing party is presumed dead if continuously absent for seven years and the applicant has no reason to believe that he or she has been alive during that time. If that presumption does not apply, the applicant bears a heavy burden of establishing reasonable grounds for believing the missing party to be

---

[174] The issue turns on the effect of ss 49(b) and 25(c) on the declaration of voidness made by ss 30 and 3(3) respectively.

[175] *Khan v UK* (App No 11579/85, ECHR) (1986).

[176] Compare the figures for 2008 with 1981, ONS (2010c), table 5.

[177] *A Local Authority v N, Y and K (by her children's guardian)* [2005] EWHC 2956, [78]–[84].

[178] Ibid.; see also Probert (2009a).

[179] Though note *Bibi v Secretary of State for the Home Department* [2010] EWCA 1482.

[180] MCA 1973, s 11(b); CPA 2004, ss 3(1)(b), 49(a).

[181] Perjury Act 1911, s 3; CPA 2004, s 80.

[182] Offences Against the Person Act 1861, s 57.

dead.[183] Once the order has been made, the 'survivor' may then validly form a new marriage or civil partnership.[184]

Polygamy

Rules about polygamous unions apply only to marriage. Since no jurisdiction permits polygamous civil partnership, the issue does not arise. Polygamy has required attention from English law as a result of migration from jurisdictions where polygamy is lawfully practised.[185] English law does not itself permit the creation of polygamous marriages, so any purportedly polygamous marriage created by a ceremony conducted in England and Wales will at best be void,[186] and may be treated as a non-marriage. To create a valid marriage through a ceremony conducted, for example, in a mosque that ceremony must comply with the formal requirements set out in the MA 1949 for non-Anglican religious marriages, and will create a monogamous marriage.[187]

But does English law recognize polygamous marriages contracted abroad by those domiciled in England and Wales?[188] There is a distinction between actually and potentially polygamous marriages. If a man takes more than one wife, those marriages are actually polygamous. A marriage is only *potentially* polygamous when a husband takes his first wife under a law permitting him to take another. In 1972, Parliament adopted a policy of cultural assimilation: any polygamous marriage, whether actually polygamous or potentially so, contracted by someone domiciled in England and Wales would be void. As Sebastian Poulter observed, 'the provision was framed so widely that it was liable to bar, for example, Muslims from the Indian subcontinent who had acquired a domicile of choice here, from returning to their countries of origin to enter into a first marriage through an Islamic wedding. This restricted them in their choice of ceremony since an Islamic form of marriage cannot validly be contracted in England.'[189] After unsatisfactory judicial attempts to mitigate the resulting harshness the Law Commission recommended reform.[190] If a *potentially* polygamous marriage is contracted abroad by someone domiciled in England and Wales, it is now valid.[191] If a second marriage is then celebrated abroad by either party, the first marriage will not be invalidated since validity is determined at the start of marriage. But if either party to that second marriage is domiciled in England and Wales, that second—actually polygamous—marriage will be void.[192]

2.6.2 DISREGARD OF FORMAL REQUIREMENTS

Void marriages

The rules about which formal defects invalidate particular types of marriage are as labyrinthine as the laws relating to the formalities themselves. Perplexingly, the Marriage Acts

---

[183] *Chard v Chard* [1956] P 259.

[184] MCA 1973, s 19; CPA 2004, s 55.

[185] See 1.2.6. On associated immigration rules, see Immigration Act 1988, s 2; Immigration Rules, r 278; *Bibi v United Kingdom* (App No 19628/92, ECtHR) (1992).

[186] *R v Bham* [1966] 1 QB 159.

[187] See p 64 above.

[188] English law's recognition of marriages contracted abroad by those domiciled abroad is an issue of private international law: see Collins (2000), ch 17.

[189] Poulter (1998), 50–1.

[190] Law Com (1985a).

[191] MCA 1973, s 11(d).

[192] Ibid.

are silent about the effects of failing to comply with some formalities, but it is generally accepted that in the absence of provision expressly rendering a marriage void, it will be valid despite the formal defect.[193] A broad picture can be identified, which largely corresponds with the rather clearer rules governing the formal validity of civil partnerships. We have already considered the effect of breach of the requirements regarding mature minors and step-relations.

Some formal requirements are mandatory—their non-observance will render the marriage or civil partnership void if the parties know (or, in the case of marriage, are guilty of 'knowing and wilful disregard' of the fact) that they are failing to comply with a mandatory requirement. It has not been decided whether the parties need know only that they have failed to comply with the relevant formality, or whether it must additionally be shown that they know that the effect is to invalidate the marriage; the CPA 2004, s 49(b) simply requires that both parties 'know' of the relevant defect. Broadly speaking, a marriage or civil partnership is void where the parties know that the ceremony or registration was conducted: without completion of the key preliminary requirements; in a place other than that specified in the original notice; after expiry of the period of time following completion of the preliminaries during which the marriage or partnership may be celebrated; or without a properly authorized celebrant or registrar being present.[194]

Other requirements are directory—their non-observance may involve a criminal offence by the registrar or other responsible person, but will not invalidate the union, even if the parties know that they have failed to comply with them. For example, breaches of the rules regarding the time of the ceremony, public access to it, the presence of witnesses, use of the prescribed words, and failure to register are not invalidating.[195]

Non-marriages

Some departures from the formal requirements are so substantial that the courts have held there to be no marriage at all. A recent illustration is provided by *Hudson v Leigh*. The parties wished to marry. The wife, a devout Christian, wanted to marry in a religious ceremony, but the husband, a wealthy 'atheist Jew', did not. They compromised. They would have a Christian ceremony (in South Africa) which would satisfy the wife that they were 'married in the eyes of God', but it was agreed by them and the celebrant that the service would not create a legal marriage. Specific passages from the normal wedding service were accordingly omitted, in particular, the question whether anyone present knows any lawful impediment to their marriage, and any reference to the parties as 'lawful' husband or wife, or to their being 'lawfully' married. The service proceeded as planned. The parties then returned to London where, it had been understood, they would get married in a civil ceremony. Unfortunately, their relationship broke down between fixtures, and the wife began divorce proceedings.

But could they divorce? Not if there were no valid marriage to begin with. And the wife would not be entitled to a decree of nullity and the right to apply for ancillary relief consequent upon that decree unless there was a void marriage. The wife argued that the South African ceremony had created a lawful marriage, or at least a void marriage, contending that cases suggesting the existence of a third category—the so-called 'non-marriage'—were

---

193 *Campbell v Corley* (1856) 4 WR 675.
194 MA 1949, ss 25, 30, and 49; CPA 2004, s 49(b)(c).
195 Law Com (1973a), Annex, para 120; see also MA 1949, ss 24 and 48.

wrongly decided. The husband argued that the ceremony amounted only to a non-marriage, and that the wife therefore had no right to apply for ancillary relief. The husband won. The South African ceremony was certainly defective as a result of South African marriage formalities law so at least void.[196] But the judge went further, holding there was no marriage at all:

Hudson v Leigh [2009] EWHC 1306

BODEY J:

69. I would find it unrealistic and illogical to conclude that there is no such concept as a ceremony or event which, whilst having marriage-like characteristics, fails in law to effect a marriage. Such is the ingenuity of human beings that we will always be able to come up with some sort of ritual or happening which one party claims created a marriage but which the other says fell short of doing so. Rare though this will be, the law has to be able to determine the issue without being constrained (except of course where statute so requires) to go down the nullity route.... Rebecca Probert [(2002a) suggests that] the 'marriage within a play' example (such as in Romeo and Juliet)...is a 'non-marriage'...because it in no way ever purports to be a real marriage, a feature which she suggests is linked to, but distinct from, the issue of the parties' intentions. The concept of 'non-marriage' should she argues: " ...also apply to alternative, self-devised rituals, should anyone wish to argue the legal validity of, for example hand-fasting or a broomstick wedding" (these being old rites here and on the continent, thought by some in days gone by to create married status).[197]

70. It is inherently difficult to come up with examples (of a questionable ceremony, ritual or event) which do not appear fanciful; but take a nervous and eccentric couple who wished to have a full dress-rehearsal of their wedding ceremony, so as to be sure that everything would go alright [sic.] on the day. Assume that the vicar was present and that he used the full wording of the marriage service. Assume wedding-outfits, bridesmaids, flowers, music, an Order of Ceremony and the presence of many of the intended guests, but with its being known that the occasion was not the real thing. What if that the relationship were then to break down prior to the actual wedding day?

71....[I]t was but a rehearsal and was neither arranged to, nor intended to, nor was it purporting to achieve any legal outcome at all (even though in principle the parties' underlying wish and purpose was to be married)....I distinguish the possible example of where the minister is intending to celebrate a marriage in the normal way, but where the parties are participating for a (perhaps) drunken bet, or dare: that is a very different matter and would call for quite different considerations should it arise...

Bodey J then set out key factors for determining the status of a purported marriage:

79....[I]t is not in my view either necessary or prudent to attempt in the abstract a definition or test of the circumstances in which a given event having marital characteristics should be held not to be a marriage. Questionable ceremonies should I think be addressed on a case by case basis, taking account of the various factors and features mentioned above including particularly, but not exhaustively: (a) whether the ceremony or event set out and purported to

---

[196] The formal validity of the marriage was governed by South African law, as the law of the place where the ceremony had occurred.

[197] See Probert (2009b) on the falsity of these beliefs.

be a lawful marriage; (b) whether it bore all or enough of the hallmarks of marriage; (c) whether the three key participants (most especially the officiating official) believed, intended and understood the ceremony as giving rise to the status of lawful marriage; and (d) the reasonable perceptions, understandings and beliefs of those in attendance [though these cannot be decisive in converting an occasion which all three participants fundamentally meant not to be effective into a marriage in law]. In most if not all reasonably foreseeable situations, a review of these and similar considerations should enable a decision to be satisfactorily reached.

He accordingly made a declaration that there never was a marriage.

It may be felt that no injustice was done to the wife in that case. The same might not always be said about some of the cases involving non-Anglican marriages where parties have married in accordance with their own religious rites without complying with the additional formal requirements imposed by secular English law. It has been said that 'a marriage which purports to be conducted under these Acts may nevertheless be void for want of formality... But unless a marriage purports to be of the kind contemplated by the Marriage Acts, it is not... a marriage for the purposes of s 11'.[198]

In *Gandhi v Patel*,[199] the parties had a lavish Hindu wedding conducted by a Brahmin priest in an Indian restaurant in London, but did not observe any formal requirements of English law; they could only have created a valid marriage by marrying 'again' in a register office or other approved or registered premises.[200] Unbeknownst to the wife, the husband was already married, so any marriage would in any event have been void for that reason. But would the restaurant marriage even count as a void marriage, given the informal circumstances of its creation? The issue arose when the husband died having made no financial provision for the wife in his will. She sought to apply to court under its powers to redistribute property from the deceased's estate amongst certain family members.[201] To be eligible to apply under that legislation, she had to prove at least a void marriage.[202] The beneficiaries of the husband's estate argued that the marriage was not even void and that she was therefore ineligible. The judge decided that the ceremony created only a non-marriage, relying on dicta in a case concerning the celebration of a wedding under Islamic rites in a private flat:

A-M v A-M (Divorce: Jurisdiction: Validity of Marriage) [2001] 2 FLR 6 (Fam Div)

HUGHES J:

[58]... No doubt it is possible to envisage cases where the question whether a particular ceremony or other event does or does not purport to be a marriage of the kind contemplated by the Marriage Acts is a fine one. *Gereis v Yagoub* [1997] 1 FLR 854 was one such, where [the judge] concluded that but for the absence of notice to the superintendent registrar and the lack of registration of the building the ceremony would have been one valid in English law; the decision may have been a merciful one. It is clear, however, that the present ceremony did not begin to purport to be a marriage according to the Marriage Acts, with or without fatal defects. It was not conducted under the rites for the Church of England, nor

---

198 *A-M v A-M (Divorce: Jurisdiction: Validity of Marriage)* [2001] 2 FLR 6.
199 [2002] 1 FLR 603.
200 Which could include a temple: MA 1949, ss 35, 41–4; Places of Worship Registration Act 1855.
201 Inheritance (Provision for Family and Dependants) Act 1975.
202 Ibid., ss 1(1)(a) and 25(4).

was there ever any question of an application for, still less a grant of, a superintendent registrar's certificate, and it was conducted in a flat which was clearly none of the places which were authorised for marriage. The ceremony was consciously an Islamic one rather than such as is contemplated by the Marriage Acts . . . [N]obody purported to conduct or take part in a Marriage Act 1949 ceremony, and the fact that no one applied their mind to how English law would view what they did does not alter that conclusion . . . [T]he . . . ceremony is neither a valid marriage in English law nor one in respect of which jurisdiction exists to grant a decree of nullity.

Rescuing a non-marriage: the presumption of marriage

Non-marriages often arise where a valid marriage would be created were the facts to occur in another jurisdiction. The conclusion that these ceremonies create nothing but a non-marriage may seem particularly harsh for recent migrants to England who marry in accordance with rites from their own faith or ethnic community and who, unlike actors in a stage play or couples rehearsing, may honestly believe that they are validly married. Although religious premises may be authorized as registered premises for civil marriages, it appears that not many have been.[203] It has been suggested that increasing numbers of couples may be 'marrying' via religious rites only, a state of affairs that raises particular concerns for women in these communities.[204]

In some cases the courts have been prepared to rescue individuals from this legal blackhole via the presumption of marriage. This presumption comes in two forms: it may be presumed that parties are married, despite the lack of positive evidence of a valid ceremony, where they have cohabited for such a period of time and in such circumstances that they are reputed to be married; alternatively, where there is evidence of a ceremony having taken place, and the parties have subsequently lived together as husband and wife, it will be presumed that the ceremony complied with the formal requirements of English law.[205]

In *Chief Adjudication Officer v Bath*,[206] the parties went through a Sikh wedding ceremony which did not fulfil English law's formal requirements; there was no marriage certificate. Nevertheless, the couple lived as man and wife for nearly 40 years, during which time the man paid his tax and national insurance contributions on the basis that he was married. The woman later applied for a widow's pension, but her application was refused because there was no evidence of a valid marriage. The Court of Appeal held the marriage to be valid: the facts required to demonstrate that the marriage was void owing to defective formalities could not be proved. However, Evans LJ also considered, alternatively, that the presumption of marriage saved the marriage. His conclusion, and the other non-marriage and presumption cases, have been cogently criticized by Rebecca Probert: it is one thing to presume that a valid marriage occurred when there is no evidence of any ceremony, or no evidence that the ceremony that did occur was formally valid, quite another to presume a marriage where the only known ceremony was plainly invalid and there is no evidence that a further ceremony might have occurred.[207]

---

[203] ONS (2006a), table 3.43; MA 1949, ss 35, 41–4; Places of Worship Registration Act 1855.
[204] Talwar (2010).
[205] *Chief Adjudication Officer v Bath* [2000] 1 FLR 8, [20].
[206] Ibid.
[207] Probert (2002a), 412–13.

By contrast, it was conceivable in *A-M v A-M (Divorce: Jurisdiction: Validity of Marriage)*[208] that the parties, domiciled abroad, might have contracted an Islamic marriage by proxy, the wife having granted power of attorney to her husband for this purpose. But Probert queries whether the English courts should presume that a marriage has been contracted in these circumstances. In that case, it was advantageous to the wife to presume a marriage, but in other circumstances the assertion of a marriage by proxy, a procedure readily open to abuse, might be undesirable as a matter of policy, not least since the UK is a signatory to the UN Convention on Consent to Marriage which requires that consent be given in person.[209] She concludes that the courts are using the presumption of marriage in an unprincipled manner in order to achieve fair outcomes for parties to non-Christian faiths who seem to be particularly susceptible to a finding of 'non-marriage' for want of proper formalities.[210] It would be preferable if proposed reforms of marriage formalities were enacted, making it easier for adherents to non-Anglican faiths to contract valid marriages in this jurisdiction within their own faith communities.[211]

2.7 GROUNDS ON WHICH A MARRIAGE OR CIVIL PARTNERSHIP IS VOIDABLE

Since a voidable marriage or civil partnership is valid unless and until annulled on the application of one of the parties during their joint lives, we might ask why these grounds should exist at all, rather than simply leaving dissatisfied parties to divorce. However, the concept of the voidable marriage is important for faith groups, since to annul a marriage because of some impediment present from the outset is doctrinally distinct from dissolving a valid marriage.[212] The category of voidable marriage has therefore been retained—and extended to civil partnership (notwithstanding the wholly secular nature of that institution). Annulment of voidable unions now takes effect prospectively: the existence of the marriage or civil partnership prior to the decree is unaffected.[213]

The voidable grounds for marriage and civil partnership are mostly shared, and it will be assumed in the following discussion that principles from the case law relating to marriage apply to civil partnership. However, some sex-related grounds—concerning failure to consummate and venereal disease—apply only to marriage. Why this should be is intriguing in two senses: why they should apply only to marriage, and why they should apply to marriage at all.

Nearly all of the grounds on which marriage and civil partnership may be voided may be regarded as in some way relating to a defect in the parties' consent,[214] either in the sense that no consent was given, or that the apparent consent was vitiated by the presence or absence of some crucial factor or condition with or without which the consent could not be fully effective.

---

[208] [2001] 2 FLR 6.

[209] Probert (2002a), 416.

[210] Cf the Coptic Orthodox Christians in *Gereis v Yagoub* [1997] 1 FLR 854.

[211] General Register Office (2003), though see Probert (2004b) for criticism.

[212] Law Com (1970), Part III.

[213] MCA 1973, s 16; CPA 2004, s 37(3).

[214] Law Com (1970), para 24(b).

Marriage: MCA 1973, s 12	*Civil Partnership: CPA 2004, s 50*
Voidable if lack of valid consent by either party	Voidable if lack of valid consent by either party
Voidable if either party suffering from mental disorder rendering 'unfit' for marriage	Voidable if either party suffering from mental disorder rendering 'unfit' for civil partnership
Voidable if respondent pregnant by a third party at time of marriage	Voidable if respondent pregnant by a third party at time of civil partnership
Voidable on grounds relating to gender recognition	Voidable on grounds relating to gender recognition
Voidable on grounds relating to non-consummation	[no equivalent ground]
Voidable if respondent had venereal disease at time of marriage	[no equivalent ground]

Statutory bars prevent decrees of nullity in some circumstances.[215] Several of the voidable grounds are subject to specific bars which we examine below. But a general, estoppel-type bar applies to all grounds:

Matrimonial Causes Act 1973, s 13(1)[216]

The court shall not...grant a decree of nullity on the ground that a marriage is voidable if the respondent satisfies the court—

(a) that the petitioner, with knowledge that it was open to him to have the marriage avoided, so conducted himself in relation to the respondent as to lead the respondent reasonably to believe that he would not seek to do so; and

(b) that it would be unjust to the respondent to grant the decree.

This provision, which replaced the old defence of approbation, was considered in *D v D (Nullity: Statutory Bar)*.[217] The court noted differences between the old defence and s 13: the matter need no longer be considered from the perspective of public policy, but simply in terms of what is required to do justice between the individual parties. The test's two-part nature may make it hard to invoke. Given the jurisdiction to provide financial relief and property adjustment on making nullity decrees, and the ready availability of divorce, the bar may rarely be imposed.

2.7.1 LACK OF VALID CONSENT

Consent lies at the heart of both marriage and civil partnership. The need for consent—and the right not to be married without it—is recognized by several international human rights

---

[215] MCA 1973, s 13; CPA 2004, s 51.
[216] CPA 2004, s 51(1).
[217] [1979] Fam 70.

Conventions.[218] The issue has arisen recently in relation to forced marriage and parties with limited mental capacity, often in cases concerned to prevent such marriages going ahead at all, rather than in subsequent nullity proceedings.

The MCA 1973 and the CPA 2004 provide that marriage or civil partnership will be voidable wherever one party did not 'validly consent' to it, enumerating situations in which that might be so: 'duress, mistake, unsoundness of mind, or otherwise'.[219] Lack of consent may be relied on by either party, not only the party whose consent it is claimed was lacking. Proceedings on this ground must ordinarily be initiated within three years of the marriage or civil partnership.[220]

Before examining the bases on which consent might be vitiated or absent, we must identify what it is that must be consented to. *Vervaeke v Smith* is instructive on this point and on English law's attitude towards the institution of marriage. The petitioner was a Belgian prostitute who married an Englishman in order to acquire British nationality and so avoid deportation.[221] The couple parted immediately after the ceremony, never intending to live as husband and wife and never doing so. The issue of the marriage's validity arose years later when the petitioner sought to inherit from her second 'husband'. She could only succeed if the first marriage was void[222] for want of consent. She failed in the English courts, but subsequently obtained a decree of nullity in Belgium which she then sought to have recognized in England. In the course of considering—and refusing—that application, the House of Lords approved remarks of Ormrod J:

Vervaeke (formerly Messina) v Smith and others [1983] 1 AC 145, 151–3

"Where a man and a woman consent to marry one another in a formal ceremony, conducted in accordance with the formalities required by law, knowing that it is a marriage ceremony, it is immaterial that they do not intend to live together as man and wife....[I]f the parties exchange consents to marry with due formality, intending to acquire the status of married persons, it is immaterial that they intend the marriage to take effect in some limited way or that one or both of them may have been mistaken about or unaware of some of the incidents of the status which they have created. To hold otherwise would impair the effect of the whole system of law regulating marriages in this country, and gravely diminish the value of the system of registration of marriages upon which so much depends in a modern community. Lord Merrivale in *Kelly (Orse. Hyams) v. Kelly*...said: 'In a country like ours, where the marriage status is of very great consequence and where the enforcement of the marriage laws is a matter of great public concern, it would be intolerable if the marriage of law could be played with by people who thought fit to go to a register office and subsequently, after some change of mind, to affirm that it was not a marriage because they did not so regard it.'..."

---

218 Including Universal Declaration of Human Rights, Art 16; UN Convention on the Elimination of All Forms of Discrimination Against Women, General Recommendation No 21; UNCRC, Arts 19 and 35; UN Convention on Consent to Marriage, Minimum Age for Marriage and Registration of Marriage, Art 1.

219 MCA 1973, s 12(c); CPA 2004, s 50(1)(a).

220 MCA 1973, s 13(2)(4)(5); CPA 2004, s 51(2)–(4). Cf *B v I* [2010] 1 FLR 1721, a decision under the inherent jurisdiction addressed below in relation to duress.

221 Cf the new rules designed to prevent such marriages considered in *R (on the application of Baiai and others) v Secretary of State for the Home Department* [2008] UKHL 53.

222 Until 1971, lack of consent rendered marriage void rather than merely voidable: would the English courts' reasoning apply equally under the present law? Cf Bradney (1984) on duress cases.

Interestingly, Lord Hailsham went on to contrast the approaches of English and Belgian law, the latter having granted a decree of nullity where the former would not. As the Belgian court had put it in this case:

> "According to section 146 Civil Law, there is no marriage when there is no consent. The consent being an essential condition and element of the marriage, the lack of consent has as consequence the absolute invalidity of that marriage. As the parties...delusively indulged in a marriage ceremony without in fact really consenting to a marriage, they behaved against public policy. The disturbance of public order, the protection of what belongs to the essence of a real marriage and of human dignity, exact that such a sham-marriage be declared invalid."

While English law reaches the opposite result, it is striking that its reasons for declaring the marriage valid are at root very similar to the reasons offered by Belgian law for reaching the opposite conclusion: upholding the seriousness of the institution of marriage as a matter of public policy.

Duress

The law on duress has received considerable attention in a series of cases involving forced marriages. It is important to appreciate the difference between forced and arranged marriages:

Re SK (Proposed Plaintiff) (An Adult by way of her Litigation Friend)
[2004] EWHC 3203

SINGER J:

> 7....[T]here is a spectrum of forced marriage from physical force or fear of injury or death in their most literal form, through to the undue imposition of emotional pressure which is at the other end of the forced marriage range, and that a grey area then separates unacceptable forced marriage from marriages arranged traditionally which are in no way to be condemned, but rather supported as a conventional concept in many societies. Social expectations can of themselves impose emotional pressure and the grey area...is where one may slip into the other: arranged may become forced but forced is always different from arranged.

Statutory remedies now exist to protect potential and actual victims of forced marriages. The courts have also developed the inherent jurisdiction to protect suspected victims[223] and generally to ensure that vulnerable individuals are able to give full and genuine consent to any marriage proposed for them, beyond what the law of nullity requires by way of consent for the marriage to be valid.[224] Prevention is better than cure.[225]

---

[223] *Re SK (Proposed Plaintiff) (An Adult by way of her Litigation Friend)* [2004] EWHC 3202 (Fam).
[224] *Re SA (Vulnerable Adult with Capacity: Marriage)* [2005] EWHC 2942.
[225] *NS v MI* [2006] EWHC 1646, [7] per Munby J.

ONLINE RESOURCE CENTRE
We examine the Forced Marriage Act 2007 on the Online Resource Centre.

Our principal concern here, however, is with the diagnosis and cure: to determine when a marriage or civil partnership may be annulled owing to duress. Forced marriages are voidable under the MCA 1973; arranged marriages, to which both parties consent, are not. One wrinkle in this scheme has been introduced by recent cases involving the recognition of forced marriages contracted abroad. The victims brought their proceedings too late in terms of the MCA 1973: as noted above, nullity petitions based on lack of consent must be brought within three years of the ceremony. That period cannot be extended, say, because the victim of a forced marriage was prevented by family circumstances (which may be tantamount to false imprisonment) from seeking assistance and bringing proceedings. The courts have sought to 'avoid' the time bar by granting declarations under the inherent jurisdiction that the ceremony created no marriage capable of recognition in English law—i.e. treating the case as one of non-marriage.[226] Whilst the outcome may appear just, releasing victims of forced marriages without incurring the stigma (in their community's eyes) of a divorce, it must be doubted whether these cases are rightly decided under the law as it stands.

That problem aside, the chief difficulty lies in navigating Singer J's 'grey area' between forced and arranged marriages. The courts have shown considerable sensitivity towards minority cultural practices.[227] It is clear that the duress may come from other party to the marriage or from third parties. However, the law is uncertain because there are competing lines of authority, one espousing a subjective test, the other a more restrictive, objective test. Since there are Court of Appeal decisions on both sides, that court and those below it remain free to apply either test until the House of Lords resolves the issue.[228] However, the subjective test is generally preferred, some judges and commentators considering that it already represents the law.[229] When assessing cases decided before 1971 espousing an objective test, it may be important to bear in mind that lack of consent then rendered a marriage void, rather than voidable, and so a stricter test may have been considered desirable.[230] But whichever test were applied to these facts the reported cases would arguably have been decided the same way.

The objective test

In *Buckland v Buckland*, the husband, a member of the armed forces serving in Malta, found himself in an awkward position. Falsely alleged to be the father of a young girl's child, he was told by his senior officers and lawyer that his only escape from prosecution

---

226 *B v I* [2010] 1 FLR 1721; *SH v NB* [2009] EWHC 3274; see also *KC and NNC v City of Westminster Social and Community Services Department and anor* [2008] EWCA Civ 198 and Probert (2008a).

227 Ibid., [37]; see also Scottish cases, e.g. *Mahmud v Mahmud* 1994 SLT 599; for criticism, see Bradney (1984), (1994); Lim (1996).

228 *Young v Bristol Aeroplane Co Ltd* [1944] KB 718; *Ashburn Anstalt v Arnold* [1989] Ch 1, 21.

229 *NS v MI* [2006] EWHC 1646 (Fam); Masson, Bailey-Harris, and Probert (2008), para 2-041.

230 Bradney (1984), 279. Note also, however, that when void, no time bar would have applied to forced marriages, a problem that has been avoided in recent cases by invoking the inherent jurisdiction: *B v I* [2010] 1 FLR 1721.

and imprisonment for under-age sex would be to marry the girl. The judge set out a three-stage test in declaring the marriage void:

Buckland v Buckland (orse Camilleri) [1968] P 296, 301 (Probate Div)

SCARMAN J:

[I]n a case where it is alleged that the petitioner's consent to marriage has been vitiated by fear, it must be shown, first, that fear of sufficient degree to vitiate consent was present; and, secondly, that the fear was reasonably entertained.... [A] third proposition may be stated to the effect that, even if the fear is reasonably entertained, it will not vitiate consent, unless it arises from some external circumstance for which the petitioner is not himself responsible.

The conclusion which I have reached, on the facts in the present case, is that the petitioner agreed to marry the girl because he was afraid, and that his fear was brought about by an unjust charge preferred against him... The fear which originated in this way was greatly strengthened by the advice given to the petitioner by his own solicitor and by his superior officer. I am satisfied that when he presented himself in the church for the marriage ceremony, he believed himself to be in an inescapable dilemma—marriage or prison: and, fearing prison, he chose marriage...

Accordingly, in my judgment, he is entitled to a declaration that the marriage ceremony was null and void.

The test was elaborated in *Szechter v Szechter*.[231] A Polish Jewish woman in very poor health married an academic at Warsaw University (who divorced his wife, with her full consent, to facilitate the plan) in order to enable the woman to escape totalitarian Poland, where she had been imprisoned for offences against the regime. She had served several months of imprisonment and lengthy interrogation before trial, during which time she faced various, very serious threats; the circumstances were causing her already fragile health to fail. The court considered *Buckland* on the way to annulling the marriage:[232]

Szechter v Szechter (orse Karsov) [1971] P 286, 297–8 (Probate Div)

SIR JOCELYN SIMON P:

[T]he instant case seems to me to be stronger than... *Buckland v. Buckland*. It is, in my view, insufficient to invalidate an otherwise good marriage that a party has entered into it in order to escape from a disagreeable situation, such as penury or social degradation. In order for the impediment of duress to violate an otherwise valid marriage, it must, in my judgment, be proved that the will of one of the parties thereto has been overborne by genuine and reasonably held fear caused by threat of immediate danger (for which the party is not himself responsible) to life, limb or liberty, so that the constraint destroys the reality of consent to ordinary wedlock.

Two Court of Appeal cases approved this line of authority. Both involved arranged marriages which were held to be valid; indeed, it is questionable whether either case would have

---

[231] [1971] P 286.
[232] Polish law was formally determinative, but the position under English law was also considered.

succeeded under the subjective test, considered below. In *Singh v Singh*,[233] a young woman married under parental pressure—not under a threat to life, limb, or liberty, but rather out of a sense of reluctant duty to her parents and religion. In *Singh v Kaur*,[234] it was the husband who gave in to family pressure. Aged 21 and having always lived at home, he was threatened that if he did not marry, he would lose his job in the family business, and have no income or transport:

Singh v Kaur (1981) 11 Fam Law 152 (CA)

ORMROD LJ:

[O]ne can see that, through our English eyes, he is in a sad position but, at the same time, he has to make up his mind, as an adult, whether to go through with the marriage or whether to withstand the pressure put upon him by his family. It is quite clear that this court cannot possibly...hold that this marriage is invalid by reason of duress unless it can be shown that there were threats to his life, limb and liberty. Quite clearly, the evidence falls far, far short of that. There was no threat of that kind and...it would be a very serious matter if this court were, even if it could in law, to water down Sir Jocelyn Simon's test...because there are many of these arranged marriages, not only in the Sikh community in this country but in other communities, and not only Asiatic communities. There are other European communities who adopt this custom, and it would be a most serious thing for this court to introduce any less rigorous burden of proof in these matters than that which the court decided was right in the case of *Singh v Singh*...

The subjective test

The alternative, subjective test does not require any particular type of threat, but simply focuses on the state of mind of the party in question, which is not measured against any objective standard of steadfastness. The test originates in *Scott v Sebright*: the young bride was blackmailed by a rogue who had borrowed her fortune to pay his debts, and threatened her with bankruptcy, scandal-mongering within the drawing rooms of polite London society, and (immediately before the ceremony) death, should she not marry him. That last threat would clearly have satisfied the objective test, but the court did not express itself so narrowly:

Scott (falsely called Sebright) v Sebright (1886) LR 12 PD 21, 23–4, 31 (Probate Div)

BUTT J:

The Courts of law have always refused to recognize as binding contracts to which the consent of either party has been obtained by fraud or duress, and the validity of a contract of marriage must be tested and determined in precisely the same manner as that of any other contract. True it is that in contracts of marriage there is an interest involved above and beyond

---

[233] [1971] P 226.
[234] (1981) 11 Fam Law 152.

that of the immediate parties. Public policy requires that marriages should not be lightly set aside, and there is in some cases the strongest temptation to the parties more immediately interested to act in collusion in obtaining a dissolution of the marriage tie. These reasons necessitate great care and circumspection on the part of the tribunal, but they in no wise alter the principle or the grounds on which this, like any other contract, may be avoided. It has sometimes been said that in order to avoid a contract entered into through fear, the fear must be such as would impel a person of ordinary courage and resolution to yield to it. I do not think that is an accurate statement of the law. Whenever from natural weakness of intellect or from fear—whether reasonably entertained or not—either party is actually in a state of mental incompetence to resist pressure improperly brought to bear, there is no more consent than in the case of a person of stronger intellect and more robust courage yielding to a more serious danger. The difficulty consists not in any uncertainty of the law on the subject, but in its application to the facts of each individual case....

Here, however, the facts clearly pointed to the conclusion that no true consent had been given.

Having received only passing reference in *Singh v Kaur*,[235] the subjective test found support from the Court of Appeal in *Hirani v Hirani*.[236] A young Hindu woman was threatened with eviction from the family home should she not submit to an arranged marriage, precipitated by her parents' abhorrence of her dating a Muslim. Ormrod LJ delivered the short judgment, curiously overlooking the previous Court of Appeal cases endorsing an objective test, to which he had been a party. He adopted a limited reading of *Szechter v Szechter*, at odds with his reading of the case in *Singh v Kaur*. Like the judge in *Scott*, he drew an analogy with contract:[237]

Hirani v Hirani (1983) 4 FLR 232, 234 (CA)

ORMROD LJ:

...[T]he matter can be dealt with quite shortly by referring to a recent case in the Privy Council dealing with duress and its effect on a contract. It is a case called *Pao On v Lau Yiu Long* [1980] AC 614. Lord Scarman, giving the opinion of the Privy Council and dealing with the duress question, at p. 635 said this:

'Duress, whatever form it takes, is a coercion of the will so as to vitiate consent.'

He then quoted a dictum of Kerr J in another case...:

'There must be present some factor "which could in law be regarded as a coercion of his will so as to vitiate his consent".'

The crucial question in these cases, particularly where a marriage is involved, is whether the threats, pressure, or whatever it is, is such as to destroy the reality of consent and overbears the will of the individual. It seems to me that this case, on the facts, is a classic case of a young girl, wholly dependent on her parents, being forced into a marriage with a man she has never seen and whom her parents have never seen in order to prevent her (reasonably, from her parents' point of view) continuing in an association with a Muslim which they would

---

[235] (1981) 11 Fam Law 152.
[236] (1983) 4 FLR 232.
[237] Note *Mahmood v Mahmood* 1993 SLT 589, 591.

regard with abhorrence. But it is as clear a case as one could want of the overbearing of the will of the petitioner and thus invalidating or vitiating her consent.

Hirani was applied in *P v R (Forced Marriage: Annulment: Procedure)*,[238] the facts of which would readily satisfy the objective test. A British Pakistani family took their daughter to Pakistan for a relative's funeral. During the visit, the parents arranged a marriage which the daughter was forced to go through with under threat of violence in circumstances where she was unable to escape owing to illness, close supervision, and lack of funds and knowledge of the local area. Her apparent assent during the ceremony was caused by her mother standing behind her and pushing her head to create the appearance of a nod. The marriage was patently voidable for want of consent.

Mistake

Mistakes only vitiate consent and render marriage (and presumably civil partnership) voidable where they relate either to the identity (not merely the attributes) of the other party, or to the nature of the ceremony. Such mistakes may be spontaneous or induced by the fraud of the other party or a third party. Other mistakes will not render marriage or civil partnership voidable, though the courts have a protective jurisdiction to prevent marriages involving vulnerable individuals going ahead under such misapprehensions.[239]

Mistake as to identity

C v C [1942] NZLR 356, 358–9 (Supreme Court, New Zealand)

CALLAN J:

The topic was carefully considered...in...*Moss v Moss*... : "But when in English law fraud is spoken of as a ground for avoiding a marriage, this does not include such fraud as induces a consent, but is limited to such fraud as procures the appearance without the reality of consent"..."Error about the family or fortune of the individual, though produced by disingenuous representations, does not at all affect the validity of the marriage"....Now my duty is to accept that statement of law and apply it to the facts of this case, and I have a clear opinion that this is a case of real consent although induced by fraud, and not a case of no consent or absence of consent. The petitioner truly consented to marry the human being to whom she was married by the Registrar. It is true that he was married under the name of Michael Miller, the Australian boxer, whereas in truth he is Samuel Henry Coley, a New Zealander, not a boxer at all, and a person of very different fortune of the person he represented himself to be, of no fortune at all really. But I am also satisfied that Michael Miller, as a human being, meant really nothing to this lady. What she was interested in was the man before her, the man who, after this very rapid courtship, proposed marriage to her, and she accepted that human being because she believed, on his fraudulent representations, that his position as to fortune and his prospects were ample for starting her in a good way in the married state...The point was

---

238 [2003] 1 FLR 661.
239 *Re SA (Vulnerable Adult with Capacity: Marriage)* [2005] EWHC 2942: concern that a marriage arranged for a deaf and dumb young Pakistani woman should only proceed with her full and genuine consent to the specific marriage proposed.

that she was willing to marry this man whom she believed to be able to support her, and the identity of Michael Miller in the matter was merely accidental. It is possible to conceive a case...where this principle can be applied successfully. Suppose A. proposes marriage to B. by correspondence, never having seen B. before, but really on what A. knows about B.'s family circumstances and so on, or perhaps A. has not seen B. for very many years, and that proposal is accepted, and then on the day of the marriage C. fraudulently impersonates B., and gets away with it, because A. does not know the present personal appearance of B. There would be, I should think, a case of no true consent. But that is not this case.

However, the line between mistakes as to identity and attributes may not be certain. In *Militante v Ogunwomoju*,[240] the court voided a marriage involving an illegal immigrant who had assumed the identity of someone living legally in the UK. *Moss v Moss* was cited, but the refined arguments of *C v C* were not considered in the very short judgment. One commentator notes that it is not known whether the petitioner 'thought she was marrying another man, or simply [as in *C v C*] that she thought the man had a different name'.[241]

Mistake as to the nature of the ceremony

In these cases, a language barrier often creates the confusion. For example, in *Valier v Valier (otherwise Davis)*,[242] the Conte Jerome Valier, an Italian resident of France who had fallen on hard times, was working in a garage and was 'not quick on the uptake' when spoken to in English. He went through a marriage ceremony with May Winifred Davis, aspiring actress, at St Giles', London register office. Not realizing that he had thus been married, he later married the Marchesa Balbi in Italy. His London marriage was annulled on the ground that he had no idea when he attended the register office and signed a document, which he never subsequently saw or read, that he was contracting a marriage. In Italy, engaged couples must sign a document at the town hall and wait three weeks before obtaining a licence to marry, the marriage then being solemnized at the town hall and thereafter in church. He mistakenly thought that he was merely performing this preliminary. The marriage was annulled.[243]

Unsoundness of mind

Ability to give valid consent to marriage or civil partnership requires mental capacity to do so. The appropriate test for determining capacity was analysed in a case concerning E, who had spina bifida and hydroencephalus, and was alleged to have a mental age of 13 and to be vulnerable to exploitation. She had formed a relationship with an older man, S, who had several convictions for serious sex offences. E's local authority, SCC, applied under the inherent jurisdiction for injunctive relief to prevent their planned marriage.[244] Munby J had to identify the appropriate test for capacity so that the expert witnesses charged with assessing E's capacity could be properly instructed. The starting point is that adults are presumed to have capacity and it is for those who assert that an individual lacks capacity to prove that. No one, including the court, can consent to marriage on behalf of an individual

---

[240] [1993] 2 FCR 355.
[241] Douglas (1994a).
[242] (1925) 133 LT 830.
[243] See also *Mehta v Mehta* [1945] 2 All ER 689.
[244] The jurisdiction to issue such injunctions was confirmed in *M v B, A and S (by the Official Solicitor)* [2005] EWHC 1681.

who lacks capacity to marry; and if the individual has capacity, the court cannot interfere with his or her decision just because it thinks the decision unwise.[245] Capacity is assessed on an issue by issue basis, the test being whether the individual understands the nature and quality of the relevant transaction. In the case of marriage, what does that involve?:

Sheffield City Council v E and another [2004] EWHC 2808, [2005] Fam 326

MUNBY J:

68. ... The law ... can be summed up in four propositions. (i) It is not enough that someone appreciates that he or she is taking part in a marriage ceremony or understands its words. (ii) He or she must understand the nature of the marriage contract. (iii) This means that he or she must be mentally capable of understanding the duties and responsibilities that normally attach to marriage. (iv) That said, the contract of marriage is in essence a simple one, which does not require a high degree of intelligence to comprehend. The contract of marriage can readily be understood by anyone of normal intelligence.

69. There are thus, in essence, two aspects to the inquiry. The first is whether the person understands the nature of the marriage contract. But this, as the authorities show, merely takes us to the central question: does he or she understand the duties and responsibilities that normally attach to marriage? This in turn leads on to two further questions. (1) What are the duties and responsibilities that normally attach to marriage? In other words, what are the essential attributes of the contract of marriage that the person has to be mentally capable of "understanding"? ... (2) What is meant for this purpose by "understanding"?

As to that, Munby J provided this summary:

132. ... Marriage, whether civil or religious, is a contract, formally entered into. It confers on the parties the status of husband and wife, the essence of the contract being an agreement between a man and a woman to live together, and to love one another as husband and wife, to the exclusion of all others. It creates a relationship of mutual and reciprocal obligations, typically involving the sharing of a common home and a common domestic life and the right to enjoy each other's society, comfort and assistance.[246]

Importantly—given the undesirability of E's intended spouse—Munby J held that the test is also a general one (did E have the capacity to marry generally, not to marry S, specifically), and a test of capacity to enter this type of transaction (marriage), not a test of the wisdom of the specific marriage contemplated:[247]

85. ... [T]he *nature of the contract of marriage* is necessarily something shared in common by all marriages. It is not something that differs as between different marriages or depending upon whether A marries B or C. The implications for A of choosing to marry B rather than C may be immense. B may be a loving pauper and C a wife-beating millionaire. But this has nothing to do with the nature of the contract of marriage into which A has chosen to enter.

---

[245] *Sheffield City Council v E* [2004] EWHC 2808, [18]–[23], [101].

[246] We considered the general validity of this statement at p 58 above.

[247] Cf the theoretical scope for a court considering the marriage of a minor to withhold consent on best interest grounds: see Probert (2009a), 249.

> Whether A marries B or marries C, the contract is the same, its nature is the same, and its legal consequences are the same. The emotional, social, financial and other implications for A may be very different but the nature of the contract is precisely the same in both cases.

Munby J found it unnecessary to address the argument under Article 12: that Sheffield County Council's approach, purporting to vet E's choice of spouse, plainly interfered with the right of both E and S to marry. But having outlined the various advantages, legal and non-legal, to be derived from marriage, he concluded:

> 144. There are many people in our society who may be of limited or borderline capacity but whose lives are immensely enriched by marriage. We must be careful not to set the test of capacity to marry too high, lest it operate as an unfair, unnecessary and indeed discriminatory bar against the mentally disabled.
>
> 145. Equally, we must be careful not to impose so stringent a test of capacity to marry that it becomes too easy to challenge the validity of what appear on the surface to be regular and seemingly valid marriages...

However, it is worth noting the particular cultural view about the function of marriage that underlies English law's approach to these issues. This is highlighted in a recent case concerning the Islamic marriage (in Bangladesh, via telephone call to England) of a severely mentally disabled young man, IC (who patently lacked capacity to marry as a matter of English law), which was not recognized by the English court:

KC and NNC v City of Westminster Social and Community Services Department
[2008] EWCA Civ 198

WALL LJ:

44. The appeal throws up a profound difference in culture and thinking between domestic English notions of welfare and those embraced by Islam. This is a clash which...this court cannot side-step or ignore. To the Bangladeshi mind,...the marriage of IC is perceived as a means of protecting him, and of ensuring that he is properly cared for within the family when his parents are no longer in a position to do so.

45. To the mind of the English lawyer, by contrast, such a marriage is perceived as exploitative and indeed abusive. Under English law, a person in the position of IC is precluded from marriage for the simple reason that he lacks the capacity to marry....Furthermore, as IC is incapable of giving his consent to any form of sexual activity, NK [the wife] would commit a criminal offence in English law by attempting...any form of sexual contact with him.

46. To the mind of the English lawyer, the marriage is also exploitative of NK, although the evidence is that she entered into it with a full knowledge of IC's disability. The English lawyer inevitably poses the theoretical question: what young woman of marriageable age, given a free choice, would ally herself for life in marriage to a man who she will have to care for as if for a child; with whom, on the evidence, she will be unable to hold a rational conversation, let alone any form of normal social intercourse; by whom she cannot have children, and indeed with whom any form of sexual contact will, under English law...constitute a criminal offence?[248]

---

[248] Probert (2008a), 403–4.

Commenting on the case, Rebecca Probert notes that the Law Commission in 1970 had deliberately categorized these marriages as voidable, not void (so rendering them less susceptible to outside challenge[249]), and suggesting that English courts may be becoming stricter in determining questions about consent because of concerns about forced marriage.

'Or otherwise'

One other situation which might vitiate an apparent consent involves intoxication. Probably only extreme intoxication temporarily depriving the individual of *capacity* to consent will suffice; mere loss of inhibition through drink, which causes the individual to provide a consent that he or she would not have given when sober, will not:

Sullivan v Sullivan, falsely called Oldacre (1818) 2 Hag Con 238, 246, 248 (Consistory Court)

SIR WILLIAM SCOTT:

Suppose three or four persons were to combine to [procure a marriage] by intoxicating another, and marrying him in that perverted state of mind, this Court would not hesitate to annul a marriage on clear proof of such a cause connected with such an effect. Not many other cases occur to me in which the co-operation of other persons to produce a marriage can be so considered, if the party was not in a state of disability, natural or artificial, which created a want of reason or volition amounting to an incapacity to consent... [But i]f he is capable of consent, and has consented, the law does not ask how the consent has been induced.

2.7.2 MENTAL DISORDER RENDERING PERSON 'UNFIT' FOR MARRIAGE OR CIVIL PARTNERSHIP

This ground[250] may be relied upon by either party, and must ordinarily be invoked within three years of the ceremony.[251] It must be distinguished from mental incapacity vitiating consent. Here, the individual is competent to consent, but the nature of his or her disorder is such that he or she is nevertheless 'unfit' for marriage or civil partnership at the time of the ceremony. This is more difficult territory than the consent ground, as it appears to require an evaluation of the individual's behaviour, and an understanding of what it is for which he or she must be 'fit'. In *Bennett v Bennett*, Ormrod J posed the question as follows: 'Is this person capable of living in a married state, and of carrying out the ordinary duties and obligations of marriage?'—but did not elaborate.[252] Munby J's contemporary view of marriage in *Sheffield City Council v E* may be helpful here, as are his observations about the value of marriage to people with mental health problems.[253] In *Bennett*, the wife was occasionally violent and periodically hospitalized with neurosis. The court remarked that she might be a person

---

[249] Subject to the possibility of nullity proceedings being commenced by the incapacitated party's litigation 'next friend': ibid., 405.

[250] MCA 1973, s 12(d); CPA 2004, s 50(1)(b).

[251] MCA 1973, s 13(2)(4)(5); CPA 2004, s 51(2)–(4).

[252] [1969] 1 WLR 430, 434.

[253] [2004] EWHC 2808, see extract above.

to whom it would be difficult to be married and would need an understanding husband. But her mental illness was not so extreme as to make her unfit. Indeed, Ormrod J's experience of the divorce courts suggested to him that there were many people of normal mental state who might be thought considerably less fit for marriage than this wife.[254] It remains to be seen what qualities will be judged necessary to render someone fit for civil partnership.

The existence of a marriage or civil partnership provides a statutory defence to some of the sexual offences involving persons with mental disorders, though not for those offences involving individuals with disorders impeding that person's choice regarding the sexual activity in question, or for those offences involving inducements, threats, or deception.[255]

2.7.3 THE RESPONDENT WAS PREGNANT BY ANOTHER AT THE TIME OF THE CEREMONY

This ground[256] may only be relied upon by the other party, must ordinarily be invoked within three years of the ceremony, and that party must have been ignorant that the respondent was pregnant by another at the time of the ceremony.[257] The ground was introduced in 1937, the courts having declined to regard such mistakes as sufficiently fundamental to vitiate husbands' consent to marriage—pregnancy is an 'attribute' only, and not an issue going to the wife's identity.[258] It has been suggested that the ground is justified on two bases: that the husband only married the wife because he believed the child to be his own; and/or that the husband believed the wife to be chaste.[259] The latter is rightly regarded as inappropriate to modern conditions. The lack of equivalent ground upon which it can be complained that a male partner is fathering children elsewhere suggests that the concern is not (male) sexual fidelity or chastity. It may be better to leave female infidelity resulting in pregnancy, in extreme cases, to the law relating to duress (as in *Buckland*) or to the divorce courts.

In the case of civil partnership, it is (currently) biologically impossible for one female to be pregnant *other than* by someone who is not her (female) civil partner. Where the parties have together embarked on a course of assisted reproduction, necessarily using donor sperm, the non-pregnant party ought not to be allowed to complain.[260] The requirement that she be ignorant of her partner's pregnancy at the time of the civil partnership registration goes some way to ensure justice, and the general, estoppel-type bar to nullity practically eliminates the possibility of annulment in such cases.

2.7.4 GROUNDS RELATING TO GENDER RECOGNITION

The importance of gender to both marriage and civil partnership is emphasized by two voidable grounds relating to trans people. If one party was unaware at the time of the ceremony

---

[254] [1969] 1 WLR 430, 434.

[255] Sexual Offences Act 2003, s 43; cf ss 30–7.

[256] MCA 1973, s 12(f); CPA 2004, s 50(1)(c).

[257] Ibid., s 13(2)–(5); s 51(2)–(4), (6).

[258] *Moss v Moss* [1897] P 263.

[259] Hayes and Williams (1999), 503–4. The authors question why this particular 'attribute' mistake should have been selected; why not the belated discovery that one's spouse is a convicted rapist?

[260] See 9.4.3 on the Human Fertilisation and Embryology Act 2008 and its 'agreed parenthood conditions' which may apply here.

that the other is a trans person whose present legal gender derives from a gender recognition certificate, the marriage or civil partnership will be voidable on the application of the first party.[261] The second ground caters for trans people who are spouses or civil partners when they apply for gender recognition. They must annul that relationship before they can obtain a full gender recognition certificate. In the meantime, they receive an interim certificate, which provides a ground for having the union voided.[262] Either party has six months from the issue of the interim gender recognition certificate in which to apply.[263] If the parties wish to continue to share a legal relationship following issue of the full certificate, special procedures allow them to reconstitute themselves as spouses or civil partners, whichever is now the appropriate form of relationship, without being subject to the usual waiting periods.[264] The compatibility of this process with the ECHR was confirmed in *Parry v UK*, discussed above at 2.6.1.

2.7.5 GROUNDS UNIQUE TO MARRIAGE: THE SEXUAL NATURE OF MARRIAGE

A marriage, but not a civil partnership, may be annulled on the ground that the respondent had communicable venereal disease at the time of the marriage, or on the ground that the marriage was not consummated either because of the respondent's wilful refusal to do so or because either party was incapable of doing so. Civil partners aggrieved in similar circumstances must seek dissolution instead. Why this should be can only be explained, if at all, by reference to the rationales underpinning these grounds and the particular meaning of consummation. It is notable that some other jurisdictions have removed these grounds for marriage. Both grounds imply that the parties have a sexual relationship. However, it is questionable whether the law should have anything to say regarding this aspect of the parties' relationship. Indeed, close examination of the definition of consummation causes many of our *assumptions* about what the ground might be about, and so why its retention might be justified, to fall away. This in turn raises interesting questions about the scope of marriage and civil partnership, and why we confer certain rights and responsibilities on some categories of relationship and not others.

The respondent had communicable venereal disease at time of marriage

It is not clear what 'venereal disease' covers,[265] and in particular whether only serious infections such as HIV are included, or all sexually transmitted diseases, including minor, relatively common, and readily treatable conditions such as chlamydia. It is significant that the ground was introduced in the pre-antibiotic age. This ground may be relied on ordinarily only within the first three years of marriage, and only if the petitioner was ignorant of the problem at the date of the marriage.[266] Given the reasons offered by

[261] See MCA 1973, ss 12(h) and 13(3); CPA 2004, ss 50(1)(e) and 51(6).
[262] MCA 1973, s 12(g); CPA 2004, s 50(1)(d).
[263] MCA 1973, s 13(2A); CPA 2004, s 51(5).
[264] MA 1949, s 39A; CPA 2004, s 96 and Sch 3.
[265] MCA 1973, s 12(e).
[266] Ibid., s 13(2)–(5).

government for not adopting this ground for civil partnership, its retention for marriage must be questioned:

Hansard, *Official Report*—Civil Partnership Bill Debates

HC Standing Committee D, col 162, 26 October 2004

Mrs McGuire [Parliamentary Under-Secretary of State]:

[T]he Government's intention in drafting the Bill was that civil partners would be treated in the same way as spouses except where there was justification for a difference in treatment. This was one matter on which we felt that there was justification for difference. It is a medical fact that men and women may carry certain sexually transmitted infections for many years without knowing it, and we do not believe that it is appropriate in present-day circumstances to include that as a ground for nullifying a civil partnership. The deliberate transmission of a sexually transmitted infection might well be considered as a basis for dissolution, as a factor proving unreasonable behaviour.

I suggest that were we starting now to create marriage law, it would be highly questionable whether we would include such a provision in that law. It is a provision from a bygone age when, perhaps, we were less informed about sexually transmitted diseases. The Government have clearly stated in their national strategy for sexual health and HIV that we need to de-stigmatise the whole issue of sexually transmitted infections if we are to tackle the increasing infection rate...Suggesting that sexually transmitted diseases should be treated differently from any other communicable diseases in that regard is counterproductive to that aim.

Failure to consummate

A marriage may be annulled where not consummated owing either to the wilful refusal of the respondent or to incapacity of either party.[267] Neither ground is subject to the three-year limitation period applying to most of the other voidable grounds, and so may be raised at any time until consummation occurs. Until the introduction of the special gender recognition ground, wilful refusal to consummate was the only ground clearly related to problems post-dating the marriage, rather than facts present at the time of the ceremony; it has been noted that the statute does not expressly confine incapacity to cases where the condition existed at the time of the ceremony, leaving open the possibility of a nullity decree on grounds of supervening incapacity.[268] Despite suggestions that this ground should be demoted to the law of divorce, it remains part of nullity law.[269] It is necessary to examine three issues: first, the meaning of 'consummation'; and then the two ways in which lack of consummation may give grounds for nullity: incapcity and wilful refusal to consummate.

---

[267] Ibid., s 12(a) and (b).
[268] Masson, Bailey-Harris, and Probert (2008), 2-027.
[269] Cf Morton Commission (1956), paras 88–9, 283; Law Com (1970), para 27.

Consummation

Both grounds rely on the concept of consummation:

D-E v A-G, falsely calling herself D-E (1845) 1 Rob Eccl 279, 298 (Consistory Court)

DR LUSHINGTON:

Sexual intercourse, in the proper meaning of the term, is ordinary and complete intercourse; it does not mean partial and imperfect intercourse: yet I cannot go the length of saying that every degree of imperfection would deprive it of its essential character. There must be degrees difficult to deal with; but if so imperfect as scarcely to be natural, I should not hesitate to say that, legally speaking, it is no intercourse at all. I can never think that the true interest of society would be advanced by retaining within the marriage bonds parties driven to such disgusting practices. Certainly it would not tend to the prevention of adulterous intercourse, one of the greatest evils to be avoided... If there be a reasonable probability that the lady can be made capable of vera copula—of the natural sort of coitus, *though without power of conception*—I cannot pronounce this marriage void. If, on the contrary, she is not and cannot be made capable of more than an incipient, imperfect, and unnatural coitus, I would pronounce the marriage void.[270] [emphasis added]

The cases have been preoccupied then, not with the question of fertility, but with what 'ordinary and complete intercourse' entails. No other form of sexual activity counts. The case law makes for extraordinary reading. Often, the issue is whether the wife has a sufficiently accommodating vaginal cavity which can be penetrated, and whether the husband is capable of sufficient penile penetration of it. The 'impervious cul-de-sac' of the wife in *D-E v A-G* was deemed insufficiently deep, at $2\frac{1}{2}$ inches, to permit consummation. As medical science advanced, so too did the courts' willingness to accept artificially created, or extended, vaginas as meeting the requirements, though only when created in a biological female.[271] As for the husband's contribution, ejaculation in the vagina, at least, is not required, but an erection of some endurance is: the efforts of the husband whose erection 'collapsed' immediately upon penetration could not 'without a violation of language be described as ordinary and complete intercourse'.[272] The courts have been divided on the acceptability of *coitus interruptus* for these purposes,[273] but no less authority than the House of Lords has condoned the use of condoms, further underlining the fact that procreation need not be intended or anticipated as a possible by-product of the exercise.[274] This point is driven home by *Clarke (otherwise Talbott) v Clarke*,[275] in which *despite* the wife's conceiving a child by a rogue, persistent sperm, the marriage was nevertheless unconsummated for want of actual intercourse. Whether any sexual satisfaction is obtained is irrelevant to the legal perfection

---

[270] Now only voidable.

[271] *S v S (otherwise C)* [1954] 3 All ER 736; *SY v SY (orse W)* [1963] P 37; cf *Corbett v Corbett* [1971] P 83. Unless the courts review their approach to consummation in such cases, the marriages of trans women remain vulnerable to voidability on this ground, though the estoppel bar to nullity may apply: MCA 1973, s 13.

[272] *W (orse K) v W* [1967] 1 WLR 1554.

[273] *Cackett (orse Trice) v Cackett* [1950] P 253; cf *Grimes (otherwise Edwards) v Grimes* [1948] P 323.

[274] *Baxter v Baxter* [1948] AC 274.

[275] [1943] 2 All ER 540.

of the intercourse,[276] and intercourse need only occur once for the marriage to be consummated. The parties' sexual compatibility is therefore not the issue; that is a matter for the divorce courts. Pre-marital intercourse between the parties does not preclude a finding of non-consummation if the act is not repeated after marriage.[277] We turn now to the two grounds based on the concept of consummation.

Incapacity

The incapacity to consummate may be physical. If it is curable by non-dangerous surgery, a refusal to undergo treatment might amount to wilful refusal.[278] Alternatively, the incapacity may be psychological. In *Clarke*,[279] the wife had an invincible repugnance to sexual intercourse, described in the language of 1940s psychology as 'frigidity'. Care must be taken to differentiate incapacity from wilful refusal, since while a spouse may plead his or her own incapacity, wilful refusal may only be relied on by the other party. In *Singh v Singh*, the claim of invincible repugnance was rejected on the evidence: mere lack of desire to consummate did not suffice, and might instead amount to wilful refusal.[280] However, psychological incapacity can be specific to one person, so the aversion need not relate to sexual relations per se.[281]

Wilful refusal

Not any refusal to have intercourse suffices. Since consummation need occur only once, refusal to repeat the exercise will not render the marriage voidable, though it might give grounds for divorce. 'Wilful refusal' was described in *Horton v Horton* as a 'settled and definite decision reached without just excuse', viewed in light of the whole history of the marriage.[282] Here, consummation had been delayed by the war, and an unsuccessful attempt subsequently made. The court acknowledged that in such 'false start' cases, one or both parties would frequently be reluctant and hesitant to try again, and in light of the wife's evident anxiety to resolve the problem, she could not be said to be wilfully refusing. Nor, according to *Potter v Potter*, is natural loss of ardour to be equated with wilful refusal.[283] The parties in *Ford v Ford* were frustrated by the husband's imprisonment in an institution with no facilities for conjugal visits, and rules specifically prohibited intercourse during prison visits. Whilst other prisoners and their spouses were apparently content to take their chances, the husband's disinclination to do so did not constitute wilful refusal.[284] The concept of wilful refusal has acquired a special meaning in the context of marriages between parties whose faith demands that a religious ceremony be performed, as well as a civil marriage ceremony, before intercourse is permitted. In *Kaur v Singh*, the husband's refusal to perform his obligation to arrange such a ceremony was itself interpreted as a wilful refusal to consummate.[285]

---

[276] *SY v SY (orse W)* [1963] P 37.
[277] *Dredge v Dredge (otherwise Harrison)* [1947] 1 All ER 29.
[278] *D v D (Nullity: Statutory Bar)* [1979] Fam 70.
[279] [1943] 2 All ER 540.
[280] [1971] P 226.
[281] *G v M* (1885) 10 App Cas 171.
[282] [1947] 2 All ER 871.
[283] (1975) 5 Fam Law 161.
[284] (1987) 17 Fam Law 232.
[285] [1972] 1 WLR 105.

2.7.6 THE CASE OF CONSUMMATION: A CRITIQUE OF MARRIAGE AND CIVIL PARTNERSHIP

Consummation has always been regarded as integral to marriage.[286] As Lord Denning once remarked, 'No one can call a marriage a real marriage when it has not been consummated'.[287] So important is consummation that express pre-marital agreements not to have sex have been struck down as being void on grounds of public policy, though the courts' views seem to depend upon the age of the parties. As the court observed in *Morgan v Morgan*,[288] while agreements between young couples never to cohabit and have sexual relations have been struck down on grounds of public policy,[289] an agreement between an elderly and/or infirm couple who wish to marry purely for companionship is a different matter. It would be unjust for one to be permitted subsequently to have the marriage annulled for incapacity to consummate when it had never been intended that it should be consummated. Further evidence of the seriousness of marriage, and the consummation requirement, is provided by the intervention of the Queen's Proctor in *Morgan*.[290] The Queen's Proctor is a Crown officer statutorily empowered to intervene in matrimonial and civil partnership proceedings to represent the public interest in the interpretation of the legislation, and to guard against fabrication of evidence by parties who wish to obtain an annulment or divorce. The court in *Morgan* observed that it 'must always treat nullity cases as of national importance irrespective of the wishes of the parties'.[291] However, the current location of non-consummation amongst the voidable grounds confers some degree of privacy, letting the parties decide whether they wish to enjoy a purely companionable marriage; the estoppel bar may prevent nullity actions from succeeding in such cases (see s 13(1), discussed above).

The requirement of consummation may seem particularly perplexing in view of its one-off nature. However, a historical view again throws useful light on the matter: until 1991, husbands were permitted to have sexual intercourse with their wives regardless of whether they were then actually consenting, the original act of consummation and the resultant marital status entitling the husband to sexual relations thereafter.[292] Consummation and the (now historical) marital rape exemption—and what they imply about the institution of marriage—has inevitably attracted academic comment, in particular from law and gender scholars:[293]

K. O'Donovan, *Family Law Matters* (London: Pluto Press, 1993), 46–8

The marriage contract establishes the possession of the wife's body by her husband, but she has no corresponding right. After consummation further heterosexual acts are assumed to take place in accordance with male desire. It is evident that the law approves heterosexuality in marriage but withholds its constitutive power from other relationships not legally approved.

---

286 We explore the widespread but erroneous belief that an agreement to marry followed by intercourse created a valid marriage prior to 1753 on the Online Resource Centre.
287 *Ramsay-Fairfax (orse Scott-Gibson) v Ramsay-Fairfax* [1956] P 115, 133.
288 [1959] P 92, 101.
289 *Brodie v Brodie* [1917] P 271.
290 MCA 1973, ss 8 and 15; CPA 2004, s 39.
291 [1959] P 92, 96.
292 See now *R v R* [1992] 1 AC 599.
293 E.g., Collier (1995), ch 4; O'Donovan (1993), 66–8.

> The requirement of consummation places primacy on penetrative sex, an act constitutive of masculinity....Reported cases reveal bizarre knowledge against which questions were asked about 'how long, and how wide, and how far, and whether, and what'. Determination of the standard, the norm, against which to measure the answers created a 'knowledge' of male sexuality and a discourse of normal masculinity. Law's insistence on consummation as the final performative act constituting marriage marginalises other sexual practices. The missionary position, in which the woman lies under the man and facing him in readiness for coition, has been privileged in this discourse...
>
> ...The story of marriage as an institution in which the sexes are united and opposed relates to the uncovering of the sexual contract. Not only is a particular form of marriage constituted, with a delineation of social roles and hierarchy, but marriage has much to say about the meaning of masculinity and femininity. Marriage establishes 'orderly access by men to women's bodies' according to Pateman. This law of male sex-right embodies women as sexual beings. Although personal autonomy over sexuality has largely been won by women today, elements of the history of marriage remain. The story helps to understand what it is to be masculine or feminine in modern civil society. No matter how much we try to avoid replicating patriarchal marital relations, these are reproduced in the institution of marriage...

Marriage also has a religious aspect, again evidenced by consummation:

> The sacred character of marriage as an institution calls on a past, understood and shared tradition, and on an eternal future, a perpetuity. Marriage is an emblem of continuity, of reproduction of the race...Not only are sexual needs to be met but marriage is the place for the veneration of motherhood, for deference to patriarchy, for the continuance of tradition, learned yet known anew by each generation and in each generative act.
>
> Through marriage the couple become one flesh, one body. In legal terms, this biblical notion takes form in the constitution of the couple as a unit headed by the husband....The 'consummation most devoutly to be wished for' is the final performative act of consecration of the marriage....

However, despite this patriarchal reading of marriage, O'Donovan observes that those excluded from marriage (trans persons, same-sex couples) wish to join the institution. These individuals are clearly seeking something from marriage, but not necessarily endorsing its traditional form. Those potential benefits of marriage are described in a dissenting opinion in *Cossey v UK*, one of the early, unsuccessful, transgender cases to appear before the European Court of Human Rights. Judge Martens examined the reasoning in *Corbett v Corbett*[294] regarding the importance of biological sex for the purposes of marriage and the inadequacy of the artificially constructed vagina for the purposes of consummation:

Cossey v UK (App No 10843/84, ECHR) (1993)

JUDGE MARTENS (dissenting):

4.5.1...[It] is arbitrary and unreasonable in this context to ignore successful gender reassignment surgery and to retain the criterion of biological sex.

---

[294] Extracted above at 2.3.1.

4.5.2 This is all the more so because Mr Justice Ormrod's arguments are clearly unacceptable. Marriage is far more than sexual union, and the capacity for sexual intercourse is, therefore, not "essential" for marriage. Persons who are not or are no longer capable of procreating or having sexual intercourse may also want to and do marry. That is because marriage is far more than a union which legitimates sexual intercourse and aims at procreating: it is a legal institution which creates a fixed legal relationship between both the partners and third parties...; it is a societal bond, in that married people (as one learned writer put it) "represent to the world that theirs is a relationship based on strong human emotions, exclusive commitment to each other and permanence"; it is, moreover, a species of togetherness in which intellectual, spiritual and emotional bonds are at least as essential as the physical one.

Although consummation is clearly not based on procreation,[295] procreation has extraordinary persistence in judicial accounts of marriage. As we noted earlier, it formed a key plank in the reasoning in *Wilkinson v Kitzinger*,[296] even though the European Court has now removed it from its conceptualization of the relationship protected by Article 12.[297] But the curious nature of consummation and the omission of any equivalent from civil partnership law invite questions about why the legal privileges of marriage, and now civil partnership, should only attach to relationships of a particular type. The government rather struggled to articulate during the passage of the Civil Partnership Bill why no sexual relationship should be required, and yet the prohibited degrees should still apply, barring civil partnership between blood relatives.[298] The Church of England's observations on civil partnership are thought-provoking, both about the (lack of) analogy with marriage, and what that implies about who should be eligible to acquire the legal status, and consequent rights and obligations, associated with marriage and civil partnership. This debate would be reopened by the Burden sisters,[299] whose case we consider later in this chapter:

Church of England, *Response to Civil Partnership consultation* (2003)

12....[T]here is an ambiguity at the heart of the Government's proposals about the nature of the proposed partnerships and about what precisely the couple are promising to be to each other. This is reflected in the shifting language in the document between 'gay, lesbian and bisexual' couples in some places and 'same sex partnerships' (potentially a wider category) in others. In a matter of this kind clarity is crucial.

13. The extremely close parallel between the new arrangements and the legal framework for marriage is likely to deter some people who might otherwise register—for example those who choose to share a home with others for a substantial period and may wish to benefit from the new partnership provisions in relation to successor tenancy rights but are not homosexual. Conversely, gay and lesbian couples will receive less protection than they might expect from a legal framework so akin to marriage—no apparent protection against sexual infidelity within a supposedly exclusive relationship, no equivalent to a nullity process should a sexual relationship be wilfully refused...

---

[295] *Baxter v Baxter* [1948] AC 274.

[296] [2006] EWHC 2022 (Fam); see also *Bellinger v Bellinger* [2003] UKHL 21, [46]–[47] and [64].

[297] *Goodwin v UK* (App No 28957/95, ECHR) (2002); *Schalk and Kopf v Austria* (App No 30141/04, ECHR) (2010).

[298] See, for example, the exchange between Baroness Scotland and Lord Tebbit, Hansard HL Deb, vol 666, col 1479, 17 November 2004.

[299] *Burden v UK* (App No 13378/05, ECHR) (2008).

14. We would urge the Government to be clearer and more consistent over what it is trying to achieve. Is the primary aim to remedy injustice and create some new legal rights and
safeguards for those who are not married but who may wish to share important parts of their
lives with each other, whether or not within a sexual relationship? If so, the logical approach
would be to remove the prohibited degrees of relationship, thereby enabling, say, two brothers or two sisters to access the new set of rights. Indeed, if this is the primary aim it could be
argued that they should not be confined to same-sex couples.

15. If, on the other hand, the Government's primary aim is to confer rights on gay and
lesbian people in long-term, committed relationships, the logic would be for the legal framework to acknowledge the sexual nature of the relationship. The hybrid nature of the present
proposals is a recipe for confusion.

Several attempts were made to amend the Civil Partnership Bill to allow non-conjugal relationships to be registered, including those involving parties who fall within the prohibited
degrees.[300] Although unsuccessful, the debates increased awareness that marriage itself is a
legal concept, as well as an important social, cultural, and religious institution. But why do
particular legal rights and duties attach to marriage and civil partnership at all, and only to
those institutions and not other relationships? If the legal consequences are justified simply
on the basis that the parties have elected to form a legal union, why cannot any two people
elect to do so? The fact that the law only permits certain pairings to become spouses and
civil partners suggests that there is more to it than party autonomy. But it is appropriate to
ask what the justification is for confining marriage and civil partnership to presumptively
sexual relationships between legal strangers. There is, in fact, nothing to prevent *unrelated*
platonic pairs from forming a marriage or civil partnership and so acquiring that distinctive legal status. But the cultural aura of romantic love surrounding both institutions, and
implied by the prohibited degrees, inevitably inhibits this. Should there be some mechanism whereby related or unrelated individuals could register their relationships in order
to acquire a general legal status, or to nominate particular individuals to benefit in specific
legal contexts? In the absence of any registration option, such relationships can only be recognized on a non-formal basis. It is to those relationships that we now turn.

2.8 NON-FORMALIZED RELATIONSHIPS: COHABITANTS AND OTHER 'FAMILY'

Increasing numbers of people have relationships which they may regard as 'familial' but which
are not formalized in marriage or civil partnership. In matters relating to children, the nature
of the parents' relationship is now largely irrelevant. But in those branches of law dealing with
the relationship between the adults, the specific recognition of relationships of cohabitants
and others remains patchy. Perhaps surprisingly, this is even the case for blood relatives, who
are undoubtedly 'family' but whose relationships nevertheless rarely feature as the subject of
specific legal rights or duties. In the absence of family law provision, parties are left to use the
general law of property, contract, and trusts to ascertain their legal position. As we shall see in
later chapters, that law is not often suited to the particular context of family disputes.

---

[300] See Glennon (2005), Stychin (2006); e.g. Hansard HL Deb, vol 660, cols 405 et seq, 22 April 2004,
Baroness O'Cathain.

Where they are recognized, there is no uniformly defined set of 'second-tier', non-formalized relationships. Various formulae are used in different areas of the law to describe other family relationships to which rights and duties attach. The principal non-formalized family type is the relationship of 'cohabitants': couples who live together in circumstances akin to marriage and civil partnership. Ironically, where parties to such relationships have potential access to legal remedies, they have to work rather 'harder' than spouses and civil partners to get it, even though the rewards are usually less generous. Spouses and civil partners are recognized simply because they have successfully acquired their legal status. Even parties to void marriages and civil partnerships achieve quite substantial recognition and potential protection. This recognition flows regardless of how the parties actually live their lives, as *Vervaeke v Smith*[301] illustrates: the parties' relationship in that case was non-existent in social and functional terms, yet they had the status of spouses, and so held the passport to a wide range of legal rights and duties. By contrast, those seeking recognition as cohabitants must demonstrate that their relationship actually functions in the way that we imagine many marriages in fact do (but legally need not do).

However, although spouses are not subjected to such scrutiny as a precondition of legal recognition, many legal remedies turn on the exercise of the courts' discretion, and they examine all the circumstances before making any order. If, as in *Vervaeke v Smith*, a marriage or civil partnership is in fact just an empty legal shell, a remedy is likely to be unnecessary or inappropriate, and none is likely to be granted. Moreover, although formalized and non-formalized relationships are treated differently in many respects, there has been some convergence between them. Many of the traditional rights and duties of husband and wife have been eroded, making status per se less significant as a source of automatic rights and duties. Divorce is easier to obtain. Non-formalized relationships are recognized in some areas. It might be argued that the logical conclusion of these developments is that marriage and civil partnership ought no longer to have any automatic legal implications: as Eric Clive put it, that marriage is unnecessary as a legal concept.[302] Instead, the law should adopt an entirely functionalist or 'de facto' model, providing rights, duties, and remedies for parties to those relationships which in fact need them for practical reasons, given their stability, duration, economic interdependence, and so on, not purely because of their legal ('de jure') form.[303]

England and Wales is currently a long way from adopting a thoroughgoing functional approach, and Lisa Glennon argues that the inception of civil partnership reinforced the emphasis on formal conceptions of family.[304] The marriage/civil partnership passport remains important to many areas of law. This may seem ironic at a time when marriage numbers and rates are at an historical low and cohabitation ascendant.[305] However, any move to reduce the legal significance of marriage would face stiff opposition; indeed, the Conservative Party is keen that the position of marriage should be enhanced, particularly in the tax system.[306] Increasing the legal consequences automatically attaching to non-formalized, cohabiting relationships would also be opposed by those who specifically wish to preserve personal autonomy outside marriage.[307] Nevertheless, recent years have seen growing recognition of non-formalized family relationships, and so we address them here.

---

[301] See above p 80.
[302] (1980).
[303] See also Bailey-Harris (1996); Probert and Barlow (2000); Dewar (2003).
[304] (2008).
[305] Auchmuty (2008); see 2.2 above for statistical data.
[306] Conservative Party (2010).
[307] See, for example, discussion in Law Com (2006), Part 5; Deech (2009b).

2.8.1 IDENTIFYING 'FAMILY'

A panoply of tests

The term 'family' itself appears infrequently in domestic legislation, mainly appearing in statutes governing tenancy succession, which we considered earlier.[308] Since the HRA 1998 came into force, the English courts have also had to address the scope of 'family life' for the purposes of Article 8. As we have seen, same-sex couples and opposite-sex cohabitants, with[309] or without children[310] are now regarded by the Strasbourg Court as having 'family life'. Some time before the European Court reached that position, both English case law interpreting 'family' under the tenancy succession legislation and recent domestic legislation had already accommodated a wide range of non-traditional family forms.[311] But there remain limits to what English courts will regard as constituting 'family' for these purposes, and little legislation extends beyond 'cohabitants' to confer rights on other forms of relationship.

The parliamentary draftsman has produced a panoply of descriptive terms, many of which are undefined and have yet to receive judicial attention. The concept of 'associated person' governs eligibility to access remedies regarding domestic violence, forced marriage, and occupation of the home.[312] This umbrella term covers a broad range of relationships, exhaustively listed by the legislation, including spouses, civil partners, cohabitants (opposite and same-sex), relatives, and platonic home-sharers. A recent addition to the repertoire of 'family' concepts—the 'intimate personal relationship...of significant duration'—does not require the parties to live together, or to have a blood or formalized relationship, but otherwise its scope is unclear.[313] It will be interesting to see whether 'intimate' is taken to connote a sexual relationship, or whether it might encompass other relationships, such as between carers and their dependants. 'Partners [living] in an enduring family relationship' are eligible to adopt[314] and to acquire parenthood via surrogacy.[315] Certain blood relations are specifically excluded from the scope of this expression, but the terms are otherwise left undefined. It remains to be seen how 'enduring' will be interpreted and proved, and whether 'partner' will receive the same interpretation as 'cohabitant' and similar terms, discussed below, though it has been held that there is no need for parties to such a relationship to cohabit.[316]

Sharing a household

Some statutes, either expressly or as a result of judicial interpretation, require that the parties share a 'household'. Merely living under the same roof does not mean that you share a household: the latter requires a degree of domestic interaction. But someone may be a member of a household despite periodical absence from it. *Kotke v Saffarini* concerned a compensation claim under the Fatal Accidents Act 1976. The applicant had to show that she had been living with the deceased in the same household as (if) husband and wife for two

---

308 See 2.3.2.
309 *Saucedo Gomez v Spain* (App No 37784/97, ECHR) (1999).
310 *Schalk and Kopf v Austria* (App No 30141/04, ECHR) (2010).
311 See 2.3.2, above; the 'home' aspect of Art 8, in conjunction with Art 14 ECHR was key to these cases.
312 Family Law Act 1996 (FLA 1996), s 62.
313 FLA 1996, 62(3)(ea).
314 ACA 2002, s 144(4)–(7).
315 Human Fertilisation and Embryology Act 2008, s 54.
316 *T and M v OCC and C* [2010] EWHC 964.

years immediately before his death. Two years before the death, the deceased had owned a house in Doncaster where he slept on several nights a week and kept most of his belongings, from which he commuted conveniently to work in London, and which he retained as his official address. The applicant lived in Sheffield. The deceased stayed with her there at weekends, when they shared shopping expenses. They were discussing buying a house together, but their plans were delayed by the deceased's negative equity problem. Were they sharing a household at this point? The applicant subsequently became pregnant, and was left with a young baby when the deceased died, having only recently moved in:

Kotke v Saffarini [2005] EWCA Civ 221

POTTER LJ:

28. . . . Use of [the word 'household'] embodies a concept somewhat elusive of definition, combining as it does both the physical connotation of a place i.e. a particular house or home and personal connotations of association i.e. the family or household resident within it. Both aspects are covered by the various dictionary definitions available. . . .

29. In the context of matrimonial law, and in particular the phraseology of s 2(5) of the Divorce Reform Act 1969 ("For the purposes of this Act a husband and wife shall be treated as living apart unless they are living with each other in the same household") it has been said:

"First, it does not use the word 'house', which relates to something physical, but 'household', which has an abstract meaning. Secondly, that the words 'living with each other in the same household' should be construed as a single phrase . . . On the contrary, use is again made of words with a well settled matrimonial meaning—'living together', a phrase which is simply the antithesis of living apart, and 'household', a word which essentially refers to people held together by a particular kind of tie, even if temporarily separated . . . " (per Sachs LJ in *Santos v Santos*).

30. In *Gully v Dix* [2004] EWCA Civ 139 . . . the Court of Appeal was concerned with the question whether the claimant fell within s 1(1A) of the Inheritance (Provision for Family and Dependants) Act 1975 as amended by the Law Reform (Succession Act) 1995 which applies to a person who—" . . . during the whole of the period of two years immediately before the date when the deceased died . . . was living— (a) in the same household as the deceased, and (b) as the husband or wife of the deceased . . . "

31. The issue in the case was whether Mrs Gully, who, without marrying the deceased, had co-habited with him for many years, but had left the deceased and lived apart from him for the last three months of his life, was yet able to demonstrate that she was living in the same household as the deceased during the whole of the period of two years immediately before the date of his death. The judgment of Ward LJ . . . referred . . . to the observations of Sachs LJ in *Santos v Santos* quoted above and stated:

"24. In my judgment, similar considerations must apply to the meaning to be given to the statute with which we are presently concerned. Thus the claimant may still have been living with the deceased in the same household as the deceased at the moment of his death even if they had been living separately at that moment in time. The relevant word is 'household' not 'house', and 'household' bears the meaning given to it by Sachs LJ. Thus they will be in the same household if they are tied by their relationship. The tie of that relationship may be made manifest by various elements, not simply their living under the same roof, but the public and private acknowledgment of their mutual society, and the mutual protection and support that binds them together. In former days one would possibly say one should look at the whole consortium vitae." . . .

41. . . . It is clear from the authorities that in principle a person may be a member of household A, albeit he has a second house or home elsewhere at B to which he departs temporarily from time to time. . . .

59. . . . We consider the judge was correct in drawing a distinction between wanting and intending to live in the same household, planning to do so, and actually doing so. It was the judge's decision that, on all the evidence before him, the relationship of these parties did not cross the statutory threshold into the final stage. The evidence showed that the deceased retained his home in Doncaster, leaving there his wardrobe and possessions, and living out of an overnight bag (as it were) at Sheffield until such time as he could dispose of his own house and purchase a new home with the claimant. That situation, coupled with the claimant's acknowledgment that it was only after the pregnancy that they really began to plan a life together, was sufficient to justify the judge's finding that the situation only changed after the pregnancy when . . . the deceased's centre of gravity began to move and they really began to make plans. The mere sharing of the shopping expenses when the claimant and the deceased were together [in Sheffield] was evidence of a sharing relationship, but one which fell short of the establishment of a joint household.

The functional approach in action

Most of the tests for identifying non-formalized relationships turn on 'functional' criteria. This approach developed in the context of the 'family' requirement in the tenancy succession legislation. There was a clear evolution in the case law, as courts' perception of the 'ordinary meaning' and the 'ordinary man's view' of family evolved. A decision in the 1950s refused to characterize an opposite-sex cohabiting couple as 'family': only a marital, parental, or quasi-parental relationship would suffice.[317] But by the 1970s, the courts accepted that an 'ordinary person' would regard such a relationship as familial, provided it was sufficiently permanent.[318] Even in the 1980s, as we have seen, a similar relationship between a same-sex couple was denied 'family' status.[319] Platonic home-sharing by unrelated individuals also failed the test, however close and longstanding their relationship.[320] The issue arose again in relation to a same-sex relationship in *Fitzpatrick* (the facts of which are described on p 39 above). Ward LJ in the Court of Appeal provided a nice account of the functional approach:

Fitzpatrick v Sterling Housing Association Ltd [1998] Ch 304, 336–9 (CA)

WARD LJ (dissenting):

Since the inception of the Rent Acts in or before 1920, the home of members of the tenant's family has been preserved for them. As the decided cases show, the meaning of family has been progressively extended. The movement has been away from the confines of relationships by blood and by marriage to the reality of family life, and from de jure to de facto relationships. . . . The trend in the cases, as I see them, is to shift the focus, or the emphasis, from structure and components to function and appearance—what a family does rather than what it is, or, putting it another way, a family is what a family does. I see this as a functionalist approach to construction as opposed to a formalist approach. Thus whether the *Joram*

---

[317] *Gammans v Ekins* [1950] 2 KB 328; see Probert (2004c); cf *Sheffield City Council v Wall* [2010] EWCA Civ 922.
[318] *Dyson Holdings Ltd v Fox* [1976] QB 503; cf *Helby v Rafferty* [1979] 1 WLR 13.
[319] *Harrogate BC v Simpson* (1985) 17 HLR 205.
[320] *Ross v Collins* [1964] 1 WLR 425; *Sefton Holdings Ltd v Cairns* (1988) 20 HLR 124..

Developments Ltd. v. Sharratt [1979] 1 WLR 928 test is satisfied, i.e. whether there is "at least a broadly recognisable de facto familial nexus," or a conjugal nexus, depends on how closely the alternative family or couple resemble the traditional family or husband and wife in function if not in precise form...

A family unit is a social organisation which functions through linking its members closely together. The functions may be procreative, sexual, sociable, economic, emotional. The list is not exhaustive. Not all families function in the same way.

...Whilst there clearly is no right of self-determination it cannot be immaterial to have regard to the view the parties have of their own relationship. If the officious commuter on the Clapham omnibus had paid a visit to the deceased's household, asked all the relevant questions about their relationship and asked the deceased finally, "What is Mr. Fitzpatrick to you? Is he one of the family?," it seems to me to be inconceivable that the deceased would not have testily suppressed him by replying, "Of course he is." I doubt whether the ordinary man would be surprised by the answer...I am quite certain that he would not treat the answer as an abuse of the English language. Indeed I am satisfied that the ordinary man is liberated enough to accept in 1997..., looking broadly at the plaintiff's life and comparing it with the other rich patterns of family life he knows, that the bond between the plaintiff and the deceased was de facto familial.

Ward LJ was dissenting in the Court of Appeal. When the case reached the House of Lords, a majority were persuaded that Mr Fitzpatrick's relationship to the deceased tenant had been familial. Lord Slynn's judgment reflects the functional character of the majority's reasoning, focused on the purpose of the housing legislation:

Fitzpatrick v Sterling Housing Association Ltd [2001] 1 AC 27, 34–40, 48–9, 51

LORD SLYNN:

[I have found this question] difficult largely because of preconceptions of a family as being a married couple and, if they have children, their children; difficult also because of the result in some of the earlier cases when applying the law to the facts. It is, however, obvious that the word "family" is used in a number of different senses, some wider, some narrower. "Do you have any family?" usually means "Do you have children?". "We're having a family gathering" may include often distant relatives and even very close friends. "The family of nations", "the Christian family" are very wide. This is no new phenomenon. Roman law, as I understand it, included in the familia all members of the social unit though other rights might be limited to spouses or heirs...

If "family" could only mean a legal relationship (of blood or by legal ceremony of marriage or by legal adoption) then the plaintiff must obviously fail. Over the years, however, the courts have held that this is not so...

Given...that the word ["family"] is to be applied flexibly, and does not cover only legally binding relationships, it is necessary to ask what are its characteristics in this legislation and to answer that question to ask further what was Parliament's purpose. It seems to me that the intention in 1920 was that not just the legal wife but also the other members of the family unit occupying the property on the death of the tenant with him should qualify for the succession...

The hall marks of the relationship were essentially that there should be a degree of mutual interdependence, of the sharing of lives, of caring and love, of commitment and support. In respect of legal relationships these are presumed, though evidently are not always present as the family law and criminal courts know only too well. In de facto relationships these are capable, if proved, of creating membership of the tenant's family. If, as I consider, this was the purpose of the legislation, the question is then who ... today ... are capable in law of being members of the tenant's family. It is not who would have been so considered in 1920. . . .

In particular if the [amendment which introduced a specific provision for cohabitants] had not been made I would have had no hesitation in holding today when, it appears, one-third of younger people live together unmarried, that where there is a stable, loving and caring relationship which is not intended to be merely temporary and where the couple live together broadly as they would if they were married, that each can be a member of the other's family for the purpose of the 1977 Act.

If, as I think, in the light of all the authorities this is the proper interpretation of the Act of 1920 I hold that as a matter of law a same-sex partner of a deceased tenant can establish the necessary familial link. They are capable of being in Russell LJ's words in *Ross v Collins* ... : "A broadly recognisable de facto familial nexus." It is then a question of fact as to whether he or she does establish the necessary link . . .

It seems to be suggested that the result which I have so far indicated would be cataclysmic. In relation to this Act it is plainly not so. The onus on one person claiming that he or she was a member of the same-sex original tenant's family will involve that person establishing rather than merely asserting the necessary indicia of the relationship. A transient superficial relationship will not do even if it is intimate. Mere cohabitation by friends as a matter of convenience will not do ... Far from being cataclysmic it is ... in accordance with contemporary notions of social justice. In other statutes, in other contexts, the same meaning may or not be the right one. If a narrower meaning is required, so be it. It seems also to be suggested that such a result in this statute undermines the traditional (whether religious or social) concept of marriage and the family. It does nothing of the sort. It merely recognises that, for the purposes of this Act, two people of the same sex can be regarded as having established membership of a family, one of the most significant of human relationships which both gives benefits and imposes obligations.

The functional approach, as applied by the judges, has been criticized by some commentators for its tendency to make legal recognition contingent upon compliance with one particular model of 'family' relations to the exclusion of others.[321] Conversely, Probert has argued that we should be wary of too quickly assuming the functional equivalence of certain relationships: it may be the case that some family forms do function more effectively and that there may consequently be a case for privileging them in law; we need to examine the evidence.[322]

In the following extract, Australian scholar Jenni Millbank describes the feminist roots of the functional approach, comparing it with normative alternatives:

J. Millbank, 'The role of "functional family" in same-sex family recognition trends', (2008) 20 *Child and Family Law Quarterly* 155, 156

Functional family approaches accord with a core objective of feminist legal scholarship and law reform projects – to centre 'lived lives' rather than legal doctrine or formal legal categories. Not coincidentally, therefore, many of the proponents of functional family approaches in relationship law are feminist and progressive scholars who embrace the idea of dynamic change in law to reflect changing social practices. By positing law's role as reflecting and assisting actual families' experiences and needs, rather than as encouraging or mandating a particular

---

[321] See Diduck (2001) above p 52.
[322] Probert (2009c), 322.

family form, functional family approaches run directly counter to normative approaches to law such as the so-called 'channelling' purpose of famliy law. The 'channelling function' has been expressed as one which 'supports social institutions which are thought to serve desirable ends', such as marriage, by 'channelling' people towards them. In this competing view, law's role is to tell people, both individually and collectively, how they should form families (and, to a greater or less extent, to provide inducements for those who listen to these messages, and impose punitive consequences on those who do not). Not coincidentally, proponents of the normative or channelling approach to family law are often conservative scholars and religious organisations, who wish to maintain established legal traditions and use them to (attempt to) stem or reverse changing social practices.

2.8.2 COHABITANTS

The functional family most frequently recognized in law is cohabitation, which now encompasses same-sex as well as opposite-sex relationships.[323] The law has not always been as accommodating of unmarried couples as it is today.[324] But since the 1970s, both courts and Parliament have become increasingly aware of the needs of the growing number of cohabitants.

The legal definitions

Many statutory provisions refer to couples who 'live together as if they were husband and wife', or 'as if they were civil partners', expressly drawing an analogy between them and marriage/civil partnership in a way some commentators find restrictive. In some contexts (like *Kotke v Saffarini*, above), parties must have lived together in this manner for a minimum period before they become entitled to the relevant legal protection; this may require investigation, since cohabiting relationships do not always have a firm start and end date, unlike marriage and civil partnership. Cohabitation is not defined uniformly throughout the law. Given the range of formulae now used to describe non-formalized relationships, it may not be immediately obvious to any one couple what all their legal rights and duties are.

As we shall see in later chapters, the courts' willingness to accept a given relationship as cohabitation may be conditioned by the context and the remedy sought. Here, we outline the test commonly used throughout family law to ascertain whether a couple are 'living together as husband and wife'. The test is borrowed from social security law, which treats cohabitants in the same way as spouses for certain purposes.[325] Like *Fitzpatrick*'s approach to defining 'family', it focuses on the way in which the couple functions as a unit.

Crake v Supplementary Benefits Commission [1982] 1 All ER 498, 502–3, 505

WOOLF J:

...[For the purposes of the social security rule] it is not sufficient, to establish that a man and woman are living together as husband and wife, to show that they are living in the same household. If...they are living together in the same household, that may raise the question

---

[323] See 2.3.2.
[324] Though see Probert (2004c) for a discussion of the varied history of cohabitants in law.
[325] See 3.8.2.

whether they are living together as man and wife, and, indeed, in many circumstances may be strong evidence to show that they are living together as man and wife; but in each case it is necessary to go on and ascertain, in so far as this is possible, the manner in which and why they are living together in the same household; and if there is an explanation which indicates that they are not there because they are living together as man and wife, then…they are not two persons living together as husband and wife.

It is impossible to categorise all the explanations which would result in [the rule] being inapplicable but it seems to me that if the reason for someone living in the same household as another person is to look after that person because they are ill or incapable for some other reason of managing their affairs, then that in ordinary parlance is not what one would describe as living together as husband and wife.…

Quite clearly if that were not the position, housekeepers performing no other functions, other than those of housekeepers, could be regarded as falling within this paragraph. A couple who live together because of some blood relationship could be treated as falling within this paragraph. In my view it was not the intention of Parliament that they should. What Parliament had in mind was…that where a couple live together as husband and wife, they shall not be in any different position whether they are married or not…

Woolf J then adopted the 'six signposts' which have become a standard set of criteria for identifying a cohabiting relationship:

[They] are admirable signposts to help a tribunal…to come to a decision whether in fact the parties should be regarded as being within the words 'living together as husband and wife'. They are: whether they are members of the same household; then there is a reference to stability; then there is a question of financial support; then there is the question of sexual relationship; the question of children; and public acknowledgment…

It has been said that it is most important to evaluate the parties' 'general relationship', in light of six signposts, rather than just ticking off those boxes, but that had the parties never had a sexual relationship, it might be difficult to classify them as cohabitants.[326] It is unclear whether same-sex cohabitants, who must live 'as if civil partners' to be recognized, will ordinarily be expected to share a sexual relationship, in view of the fact that the CPA 2004 carefully avoids basing civil partnership on a sexual relationship.[327] It would not be surprising if the courts nevertheless placed some weight on the presence of a sexual relationship, not least as most civil partnerships may be expected to be sexually intimate relationships.

The diversity of couple-relationships has been recognized, whilst still invoking the judgement of the ordinary person:

Re Watson (decd) [1999] 3 FCR 595, 601 (Ch Div)

NEUBERGER J:

[O]ne must beware of indulging in too much over-analysis. Anyone who reads newspapers or law reports does not need to be told that marriages, like, perhaps even more than, other human relationships, can vary from each other in multifarious ways. However, in my

---

326 *Re J (Income Support: Cohabitation)* [1995] 1 FLR 660, 665–6.
327 Cretney (2006a), 33–4. But see, for example, the Child Support Act 1991, Sch 1, para 10C(6).

judgment, when considering whether two people are living together as husband and wife, it would be wrong to conclude that they do so simply because their relationship is one which a husband and wife could have. If the test were as wide as that, then, bearing in mind the enormous variety of relationships that can exist between husband and wife, virtually every relationship between a man and a woman living in the same household would fall within s 1(1A). It seems to me that, when considering the question, the court should ask itself whether, in the opinion of a reasonable person with normal perceptions, it could be said that the two people in question were living together as husband and wife; but, when considering that question, one should not ignore the multifarious nature of marital relationships.

The Court of Appeal has approved the suggestion that the parties must have made a 'lifetime commitment to permanence', and the relationship must be 'openly and unequivocally displayed to the outside world' for the parties to be regarded as 'living together as husband and wife' in the context of tenancy succession.[328] But the fact that one party remains formally married to someone else may not automatically prevent cohabitants from being found to constitute a family.[329]

Couples who 'live apart together', perhaps *unable* to reside permanently together in one location owing to the constraints of their respective employments and so who maintain separate homes (as in *Kotke v Saffarini*[330]), will not be regarded as cohabiting. They may be economically interdependent to some extent, and be as intimate and committed as many cohabitants, yet lack of a shared household precludes their legal recognition in many contexts.

Some policy questions

The legal regulation of cohabitants—couples who (given the ready availabilty of divorce) are generally free to marry or form civil partnerships—is a hotly contested area of family policy. These debates have recently focused on whether cohabitants should have access to financial remedies on relationship breakdown, a topic we address in chapter 7. The basic dispute concerns whether form of relationship is more important than function.

As we noted at 2.2 above, the cohabiting population is heterogenous: people cohabit at different life stages for different reasons. Cohabitation is increasingly used as a prelude or alternative to marriage, and is lasting longer. Social attitudes towards relationships are becoming more liberal, especially amongst younger cohorts of the population.[331] Two-thirds of people consider that there is little social difference between marriage and cohabitation, and only one in four think spouses make better parents than cohabitants.[332] But the important *legal* differences between marriage and cohabitation are not fully appreciated. While some deliberately do not formalize their relationship in order to avoid the legal consequences of doing so, the British Social Attitudes Survey in 2000[333] made startling revelations about the so-called 'common law marriage myth'—the erroneous belief that couples who live together have the same legal status as spouses:[334]

---

[328] *Nutting v Southern Housing Group Ltd* [2004] EWHC 2982; *Helby v Rafferty* [1979] 1 WLR 13.
[329] *Watson v Lucas* [1980] 1 WLR 1493: applying the 'member of the tenant's family' Rent Act test.
[330] *Kotke v Saffarini* [2005] EWCA Civ 221, see extract above.
[331] Haskey (2001a), 5–7.
[332] Duncan and Phillips (2008).
[333] Barlow et al (2001).
[334] Rebecca Probert's research has convincingly demonstrated that there is no historical foundation for this belief: cohabitation was not formerly recognized as a form of marriage. We discuss this research on the Online Resource Centre.

A. Barlow, 'Regulation of Cohabitation, Changing Family Policies and Social Attitudes: A Discussion of Britain within Europe', (2004) 26 *Law and Policy* 57, 72–3

That people see cohabitation or marriage as personal lifestyle choices was underlined by their surprising lack of awareness about the different legal consequences of these relationships. Fifty-six percent of the BSA national survey believed that cohabiting for a period of time gave rise to a common-law marriage giving them the same legal rights as married couples. Among cohabitants, this false belief rose to 59 percent and the in-depth sample found that the source of this was most often family and friends although the media and official social security application forms had also informed a significant number of views. None of the interviewees had sought legal advice specifically in relation to their position as cohabitants...When you add to this the finding by another research team, that 41 percent of their sample of 173 engaged couples (73 percent of whom were cohabiting) thought that marriage would not change the legal nature of their relationship (Hibbs, Barton and Beswick 2001), a disturbing picture of legal misperceptions emerges. What is more worrying still to policymakers, is that consciously at least, in most cases people's perceptions of the legal consequences had no impact on their decision to cohabit or marry.

Such misconceptions about the law are concerning if they mean that individuals are organizing their lives oblivious of the legal implications of their arrangements. Moreover, public ignorance of the law will impair attempts by government to engineer behaviour by providing certain rights to marriage and withholding them from other relationships.[335]

How should the law respond? Many—particularly those keen to promote marriage—consider that rather than make the law match people's beliefs we should better educate the public about the law. A government-funded campaign has sought to dispel the 'common law marriage myth'. The British Social Attitudes survey of 2006 suggests that this had some, albeit relatively limited, impact on people's understanding of the law.[336] The majority still believing that cohabitants enjoy the same status as spouses was smaller than in 2000: 51 per cent of the whole sample, 53 per cent of cohabitants. Only 37 per cent (39 per cent of cohabitants) knew that to be untrue. But there was increased uncertainty: more people (10 per cent, from 6 per cent) stated that they were unsure about cohabitants' legal position. However, many more people believed marriage offers greater financial security than cohabitation: 61 per cent, from 37 per cent in 2000.

However, while attitudes may be increasingly liberal, that does not mean marriage is regarded as irrelevant: only a small minority—9 per cent of all respondents, and 19 per cent of cohabitants—think that marriage is 'just a piece of paper'.[337] Recent surveys find a large majority of young people aspire to marry.[338] This will please those commentators and policy-makers who wish actively to encourage marriage, on the basis that formalizing a relationship in marriage ensures a more stable, committed relationship than cohabitation.[339] However, the empirical basis for these views is doubtful. It is true that cohabiting relationships are more susceptible to breakdown than marriages. But it is important to compare like with like: for example, many cohabiting relationships are between young couples, and youth is known to be a predictor of

---

[335] Barlow and Duncan (2000).
[336] Barlow et al (2008).
[337] Ibid.
[338] De Waal (2008): survey of 20–35-year-olds; Coast (2009): survey of under 35s who are currently cohabiting.
[339] E.g. Centre for Social Justice (2009).

relationship instability, whether married or not; meanwhile, many long-term cohabitations are indistinguishable from marriages. While spouses may generally report higher levels of commitment, it is hard to disentangle cause and effect, as the following extract—which focuses on the impact of relationship form for children—explains. While the process of making the promises entailed in marriage may have some stabilizing effect,[340] overall, marriage may be the product of pre-existing commitment, rather than a creator of commitment:[341]

British Academy Working Group, *Social Science and Family Policies* (London: British Academy, 2009), 48–50

But is marriage the cause or consequence of that commitment? There are no studies to date that adequately deal with that issue...

[Another] consideration involves the major factors involved in 'selection effects', meaning the fact that those who marry before they have children are likely to be rather different sorts of people from those who have children while cohabiting. The factors predisposing childbirth outside marriage include being economically worse off, lower educational attainments, less religious commitment, the experience of sex before 16, having a widowed mother, black ethnicity, having been a teenage parent, and having a low income.... Accordingly, it is quite possible that the disadvantages experienced by children born to those who are unmarried but living together have more to do with the characteristics of the people concerned than with whether or not they are legally married...[342]

Bearing in mind these findings, a thought experiment can be carried out. If legal steps were taken to ensure that more people in the high risk group married, what would happen to marriage stability? The evidence suggests that probably it would lessen and that the differences between the married and the cohabiting would diminish.... [I]t cannot be claimed that we have adequate evidence on the pros and cons of marriage versus non-marital cohabitation.... Also, the scientific findings make it very clear that any conclusions on the benefits of marriage must be based on considerations that include differences between people who do, and who do not, choose to marry. In other words, people choose whether or not to marry, and the differences in child outcomes between groups of married and cohabiting couples with children may reflect the sorts of people who choose to marry, rather than the effects of the marital situation as such. That is not to say that marriage does not engender commitment. But we cannot ascribe all the differences between the married and non-married to the degree of commitment between partners (either as a cause or consequence of marriage).

Human rights issues

ECHR case law currently offers limited support for arguments in favour of the equal treatment of cohabitants with spouses and civil partners. Importantly, recent decisions of the European Court in relation to the UK under Article 14 (discrimination in the exercise of Convention rights on grounds of marital status) have supported the maintenance of bright-line rules based on support for the traditional family based on marriage or, in the civil partnership era, on the parties having undertaken public, legally binding commitments towards

---

[340] Probert (2009c), 325.
[341] De Waal (2008).
[342] See also Goodman and Greaves (2010).

each other.[343] The issue has generally arisen in the context of welfare benefits or taxation[344] in relation to which the Court has consistently held that the distinctive legal status of spouses means that spouses and cohabitants are not analogous, so the different treatment does not require justification. Case law involving other states has considered access to financial remedies on separation and death. It has been held that while a cohabiting couple with children have 'family life' under Article 8, the state has no positive duty under that Article to provide access to such remedies.[345] In *Saucedo Gomez v Spain*, the Commission considered whether failure to provide remedies violated Article 14 in conjunction with Article 8. But while it seemed prepared to accept that cohabitants and spouses might be regarded as analogous in that context, it held that states were justified in distinguishing between marriage and cohabitation to promote the traditional concept of family.[346]

English courts and the Privy Council have also usually declined to find any discrimination in these cases, at least where the couple in question could have formalized their relationship in law.[347] However, the House of Lords held in *Re P*[348] that Northern Irish adoption law was incompatible with Article 14 in conjunction with Article 8 by refusing to permit unmarried couples to be considered as potential adopters. In this context, where the child's best interests are paramount, the law could not rationally exclude an entire class of potential adopters simply because of their marital status. However, the House acknowledged that in other contexts maintaining a bright-line rule distinguishing married from unmarried couples could be lawful, certainly where the parties were free to marry.[349] The question must be considered in relation to specific issues rather than as a blanket rule. Whether different treatment can be justified depends considerably on the context.

2.8.3 THE PLATONIC, NON-CONJUGAL FAMILY

Another set of families which have attracted recent attention, particularly during the Civil Partnership Bill debates,[350] are platonic relationships, often between legal strangers (i.e. those not already related by blood or formalized relationship). Few laws expressly apply, or have been interpreted as applying, to platonic home sharers and friends, or even blood relationships. Relationships with a sexual aspect are readily classified as quasi-conjugal and so fall within the scope of laws applying to cohabitants. But (subject to the possibility that living together 'as if civil partners' may be interpreted platonically), the absence of sexual intimacy probably excludes platonic relationships from laws applicable to 'cohabitants'. Just as marriage (in particular) is based on sex, so too, it seems, must its analogues. Even where the parties are of the same sex, if they are related within the prohibited degrees or if there are more than two of them they will presumably not be regarded as being akin to civil partners. Platonic home-sharers who are not blood or adoptive relatives have also been even

---

[343] E.g. *Courten v UK* (App No 4479/06, ECHR) (2008); *MW v UK* (App No 11313/02, ECHR) (2009); *Burden v UK* (App No 13378/05, ECHR) (2008), *Shackell v UK* (App No 45851/99, ECHR) (2000). The one exception related to the taxation of unmarried fathers' child maintenance payments: *PM v UK* (App No 6638/03, ECHR) (2006).

[344] See 3.8.2.

[345] *Johnson v Ireland* (1987) ECHR A-112.

[346] (App No 37784/97, ECHR) (1999).

[347] E.g. *Ratcliffe v Secretary of State for Defence* [2009] EWCA Civ 39; cf *Rodriguez v Minister of Housing of the Government of Gibraltar* [2009] UKPC 52.

[348] [2008] UKHL 38,

[349] Ibid., at [13]–[16] and [108]–[110].

[350] Glennon (2005).

excluded from judicial interpretations of the ambit of 'family' in the tenancy succession stat-utes, however longstanding and close the relationship.[351] But they do fall within some of the more broadly framed concepts used by family law statutes. For example, the mere sharing of a household in a non-commercial context makes parties 'associated persons' for the pur-poses of domestic violence legislation.[352] By contrast with English law, some jurisdictions have brought non-sexual, caring domestic relationships within the scope of family law more generally,[353] in the case of Tasmania, including where the parties are related by family.[354]

One reason for English law's reluctance to extend beyond conjugal and quasi-conjugal couples, certainly to parties not related by blood, might be the perceived difficulties of defin-ing family beyond those examples and so of drawing a clear line (assuming that such rela-tionships cannot be formalized in law). However, some would say that the line drawn by the *present* law is unsustainable:

Fitzpatrick v Sterling Housing Association Ltd [2001] 1 AC 27, 64 and 67

LORD HUTTON (dissenting):

A further difficulty which confronts the argument on behalf of [Mr Fitzpatrick] is that if it is correct and if the underlying purpose of the legislation is to provide a secure home for a person who shares his or her life with the tenant in a relationship of mutual affection, commit-ment and support, it is difficult to see why two elderly spinsters who live together for mutual support and companionship in old age without any sexual element in their relationship and who give each other devoted care should not qualify as members of the same family. I do not consider that the absence of a sexual relationship distinguishes such a case from the present one. The sexual relationship between a couple is a very important and enriching part of their life together, but I am unable to accept that there is such a distinction between an elderly homosexual couple who once had an active sexual relationship and two elderly spinsters who never had a sexual relationship that the homosexual couple should be regarded as mem-bers of each other's family and the spinsters should not. If the courts depart from the require-ment of . . . [a broadly recognisable familial nexus, which the dissenting judges in *Fitzpatrick* take to require a heterosexual, (and so) marriage-like relationship] it is difficult to discern what criterion would include one person residing with the tenant and exclude another.

English law's exclusion of such relationships from various legal rights and duties raises dif-ficult and interesting questions. It can be argued that if the law's purpose is to assist those in practical need, the presence or absence of a sexual or blood relationship should be irrelevant to legal recognition. For example, in the context of financial and property rights and rem-edies, the existence of economic interdependence, or dependence, might be felt the more obvious criterion for identifying relationships eligible for legal recognition.[355] The restric-tions on access to marriage and civil partnership, particularly the rules regarding prohibited degrees, combined with the absence of legal protection for non-formalized relationships, leave some deserving parties with no mechanism for acquiring the legal protection they

---

[351] *Ross v Collins* [1964] 1 WLR 425, 432; *Sefton Holdings Ltd v Cairns* (1987) 20 HLR 124.

[352] FLA 1996: see chapter 4.

[353] See Australian states' experience, for example Property (Relationships) Act 1984 (NSW), as amended; Domestic Relationships Act 1994 (ACT).

[354] Relationships Act 2003 (Tas), s 5.

[355] Bailey-Harris (1998), 85.

might be thought to need or deserve. While parties can protect themselves to some extent through contract, declarations of trust, and wills, that will not solve all of their problems, particularly where the complaint involves an issue of public law such as taxation.

The Burden sisters' case

These issues hit the headlines when the Burden sisters unsuccessfully challenged English tax law before the European Court of Human Rights.[356] The unmarried Burden sisters have lived together all their lives, for the last 30 years in a jointly-owned house currently worth £875,000, built by their brother on land inherited from their parents. When one dies, the survivor will have to pay inheritance tax on the deceased sister's share of the house.[357] Spouses or civil partners in the same position would be exempt from inheritance tax. And that was the basis of the sisters' complaint: why should they not be able to enjoy a similar exemption, having lived interdependently for decades? Being related within the prohibited degrees, they cannot arrange their affairs to avoid the liability by forming a civil partnership. The case has provoked debate on why only spouses and civil partners should be able to enjoy the exemption—and why marriage and civil partnership are open only to pairs unrelated by family.

The sisters formulated their complaint as a breach of Article 14 taken in conjunction with Article 1 to Protocol 1 of the ECHR (the right to peaceful enjoyment of possessions), marshalling an impressive range of arguments. They argued that their position is analogous to spouses or civil partners, having 'chosen to live together in a loving, committed and stable relationship for several decades, sharing their only home, to the exclusion of other partners'.[358] The fact that their relationship is not sexual could not be relevant, as civil partnership law has no sexual aspect. They argued that they should not be prejudiced by the fact that their relationship arose initially by accident of birth and that it entails no legally enforceable financial obligations expressly elected by them by formalizing their relationships: being unable in law to form a civil partnership, their decision to live together should itself be regarded as an equivalent exercise of self-determination to assume responsibility for each other.[359] If the purposes of the tax exemption, as described by the Government, is to promote stable and committed relationships, that purpose applies equally to adult siblings who live together in such circumstances, so denying them the same exemption serves no legitimate aim.[360] They argued that English law should reach beyond conjugality by introducing a statutory scheme conferring certain fiscal benefits on pairs of siblings or other close relations who had lived together for a minimum period and not married or formed civil partnerships with third parties. In response to the suggestion that extending such a tax exemption would deprive the public purse of revenue, they argued that this would potentially be offset by gains in other areas: for example, people would be encouraged to care for disabled and elderly relations and so avoid the need for state-funded care.[361]

Their case failed both at first instance and on appeal to the Grand Chamber. The court of first instance reached no decision on whether the sisters' position was analogous to that of

---

[356] *Burden and Burden v United Kingdom* (App No 13378/05, ECHR) (2008).
[357] Despite suggestions that this would mean selling the house, this appears unlikely to be necessary: see Auchmuty (2009).
[358] Judgment of first instance ECtHR, [50].
[359] Cf the Government's argument, [46] and [48].
[360] Ibid., [51]. Cf the Government's argument, [47].
[361] Ibid., [52].

spouses and civil partners, who are exempt from inheritance tax. Instead, it found that the difference in treatment could in any event be justified within the state's margin of appreciation. Two dissenting judges noted that while the state might have been able to justify its position by reference to Article 12 had the tax exemption been confined to spouses, the position changed once it was extended to civil partners: 'once the legislature decides that a permanent union of two persons could or should enjoy tax privileges, it must be able to justify why such a possibility has been offered to some unions while continuing to be denied to others'.[362] This meant that it was important to examine the point left undecided by the majority. While earlier case law had compared the treatment of spouses with cohabitants— i.e. people who were free to acquire the privileged legal status but had not done so[363]—the sisters' position was quite different, being barred by their blood relationship from formalizing their relationship and so acquiring the tax exemption.[364]

By contrast, the majority of the Grand Chamber considered that the sisters fell at the first hurdle: their position is not analogous to that of spouses and civil partners. The majority's reasoning here is generally regarded as somewhat weak. They took what may be called a formalistic (and somewhat circular) approach, failing to engage with arguments about the functional similarity between the sisters and spouses in relation to the issue of inheritance tax and possible loss of a shared home:

Burden and Burden v UK (App No 13378/05, ECHR) (2008)

62....[T]he relationship between siblings is qualitatively of a different nature to that between married couples and homosexual civil partners...The very essence of the connection between siblings is consanguinity, whereas one of the defining characteristics of a marriage or [civil partnership] is that it is forbidden to close family members...The fact that the applicants have chosen to live together all their adult lives, as do many married and Civil Partnership Act couples, does not alter this essential difference between the two types of relationship.

63. Moreover, the Grand Chamber notes that it has already held that marriage confers a special status on those who enter into it. The exercise of the right to marry is protected by Article 12 of the Convention and gives rise to social, personal and legal consequences...

65. As with marriage, the Grand Chamber considers that the legal consequences of civil partnership..., which couples expressly and deliberately decide to incur, set these types of relationship apart from other forms of co-habitation. Rather than the length or the supportive nature of the relationship, what is determinative is the existence of a public undertaking, carrying with it a body of rights and obligations of a contractual nature. Just as there can be no analogy between married and Civil Partnership Act couples, on the one hand, and heterosexual or homosexual couples who choose to live together but not to become husband and wife or civil partners, on the other hand (see *Shackell v UK*), the absence of such a legally binding agreement between the applicants renders their relationship of co-habitation, despite its long duration, fundamentally different to that of a married or civil partnership couple.

The weaknesses of the majority reasoning were recognized by two other judges who, while also dismissing the appeal for reasons similar to those of the first instance court, were

---

362 Dissenting judgment of Judges Bonello and Garlicki, [2].
363 E.g. *Shackell v UK* (App No 45851/99, ECHR) (2000).
364 Judges Bonello and Garlicki, [3].

expressly critical of the majority's approach to whether the sisters are in an analogous position to spouses and civil partners:

JUDGE BJÖRGVINSSON:

The reasoning of the majority . . . is in my view flawed by the fact that it is based on comparison of factors of a different nature and which are not comparable from a logical point of view. It is to a large extent based on reference to the specific legal framework which is applicable to married couples and civil partnership couples but which does not, under the present legislation, apply to the applicants as cohabiting sisters. However, although in the strict sense the complaint only relates to a difference in treatment as concerns inheritance tax, in the wider context it relates, in essence, to the facts that different rules apply and that consanguinity between the applicants prevents them from entering into a legally binding agreement similar to marriage or civil partnership, which would make the legal framework applicable to them, including the relevant provisions of the law on inheritance tax.

I believe that in these circumstances any comparison of the relationship between the applicants, on the one hand, and the relationship between married couples and civil partnership couples, on the other, should be made without specific reference to the different legal framework applicable, and should focus only on the substantive or material differences in the nature of the relationship as such. Despite important differences, mainly as concerns the sexual nature of the relationship between married couples and civil partner couples, when it comes to the decision to live together, closeness of the personal attachment and for most practical purposes of daily life and financial matters, the relationship between the applicants in this case has, in general and for the alleged purposes of the relevant inheritance tax exemptions in particular, more in common with the relationship between married or civil partnership couples, than there are differences between them. Despite this fact, the law prohibits them from entering into an agreement similar to marriage or civil partnership and thus take advantage of the applicable rules, including the inheritance tax rules. That being so, I am not convinced that the relationship between the applicants as cohabiting sisters cannot be compared with married or civil partner couples for the purposes of Article 14 of the Convention. On the contrary there is in this case a difference in treatment of persons in situations which are, as a matter of fact, to a large extent similar and analogous.

Taking functionalism to its logical conclusion

In the following extract, Alison Diduck, writing from a Canadian perspective, outlines how a purely functional approach can be taken to determining the proper reach of legal regulation. It is worth considering how this approach might be applied to a situation such as the Burdens':

A. Diduck, 'Shifting Familiarity', (2005) 58 *Current Legal Problems* 235, 249

In 2001, the Law Commission of Canada . . . observed the growing diversity in family life and it concluded that recognising and supporting the great variety of caring personal adult relationships is 'an important state objective'. It identified certain basic principles and values that the state must attend to when it devises a principled and comprehensive approach to the needs of all in relationships. It concluded that the state must value equality and autonomy, personal security, privacy, freedom of conscience and religion and coherence and efficiency. It further concluded that the distinction between conjugal and non-conjugal is inconsistent with the value of equality, since conjugality 'is not an accurate marker of the qualitative attributes of personal adult relationships that are relevant to practical legislative [and policy] objectives'. It said that 'the state's role should be neutral regarding the roles that people assume in their personal relationships'.

Instead, then, of simply arguing that some relationships currently excluded should be included in legal recognition, it proposed that we start from scratch and 'look at the way governments have relied upon relational status in allocating rights and responsibilities', and try to design a legislative regime that accomplishes its goals by relying less on whether people are living in certain kinds of relationships. Sometimes some characteristics of the relationship will be important, other times they would not be, but conjugality would never be important.

On the one hand this approach runs the risk of even broader familialisation,[365] yet on the other, it eschews the word family completely in these contexts, and focuses on the variety of personal and caring relationships in which people live. Instead of being concerned about families, then, it is concerned about the individual rights and responsibilities that accrue from different relationships and about how the law can help distribute them among people more equitably. For me the change in language is important. It allows us to think outside the 'family' box.

2.9 CONCLUSION

Whether individuals have the legal status of spouse or civil partner—and whether they are legally permitted to acquire that status—still makes a considerable difference to their treatment in many areas of the law. Other family relationships between adults are acknowledged in some areas, but not others. Extending legal rights and duties beyond marriage is often politically controversial, many fearing that such developments undermine the institution of marriage. We shall consider in later chapters what practical impact continued difference of treatment has on the individuals involved, and whether it can be justified.

ONLINE RESOURCE CENTRE

Questions, suggestions for further reading, and supplementary materials for this chapter (including updates on developments in this area of family law since this book was published) may be found on the Online Resource Centre at **www.oxfordtextbooks.co.uk/orc/harrisshort_tcm2e/**.

---

[365] Diduck is concerned that apparently liberal designation of a relationship as 'family' is a way to enforce particular *obligations*.

3

FAMILY PROPERTY AND FINANCES

CENTRAL ISSUES

1. The ownership, occupation, and use of the family home, other property, and resources within families are principally governed by the general law of property. That law has been criticized for failing adequately to deal with the particular needs of the family context. Recent judicial development of specific principles for 'domestic' cases has not been uncontroversial, and has not addressed all of the problems in this area of the law.

2. By contrast with many European jurisdictions, English family property law is based on the notion of 'separate property'. No property is deemed to be jointly owned or held in 'community' simply by virtue of marital or other family status. Each individual's property rights must therefore be addressed separately. Various reform recommendations made in the 1970s and 1980s proposing automatic co-ownership of matrimonial property were not implemented.

3. Most of the few statutory provisions providing specific 'family' rules apply only to spouses and civil partners, and deal with occupation of the family home rather than its ownership. Family members with no right of ownership have only limited power to influence the owner's decisions regarding sale or mortgage of the home.

4. The law imposes a mutual duty of support between spouses and civil partners, enforceable in private law. The public law of welfare benefits and tax credits assumes that cohabitants also support each other, but cohabitants have no means of securing support from their partner.

5. The law relating to welfare benefits, tax credits, and taxation of the family sheds interesting light on law's concept of family, adopting different definitions of family according to the particular policy goals at stake.

3.1 INTRODUCTION

Much of family law deals with family 'pathology': the consequences of family breakdown. By contrast, the law addressed in this chapter applies as much to happy families as it does to those in trouble. However, much of this law is not 'family' law, in the sense of law devised specifically for the family. Indeed, it has been said that 'there is really no such thing in English law as "family property"', despite the social importance of family.[1]

But why does ownership of resources within an intact family matter? If the family is together, does it matter who technically owns what, who has a legal right to occupy the home, or who earns the money used to support the family? Determining who has what rights, in particular regarding the family home, can be crucial. For example, if the home and mortgage used to purchase it are in the name of one spouse, who defaults on the repayments, what rights do the other spouse and any other occupants have to resist the mortgagee which wishes to realize its security by repossessing the family home? What if one family member is bankrupt—can the home and other property be preserved for the rest of the family? If one party dies, what property is his and so to be inherited by others?

While there is no coherent family property law, there is a limited corpus of legislation touching on various aspects of family property and finances. However, those 'family law' provisions are based on a narrow view of what counts as 'family'. Most statutory provisions deal exclusively with spouses and civil partners. The position of other family members— including children, blood relatives, cohabitants, and other home sharers—remains governed almost entirely by the general law. But as increasing numbers of families in England and Wales are not based on marriage or civil partnership, family law is called upon to extend its reach. Some aspects of the 'public law' of family finances—those relating to welfare benefits and tax credits—already apply to cohabitants. However, even the special provisions relating to spouses and civil partners while they are together have a fairly limited ambit. So to determine the property and financial rights of family members, we must examine the general law. By contrast, as we shall see in chapters 6 and 7, there are substantial 'family law' provisions dealing with economic consequences of family breakdown. Those laws focus principally on support of minors, and financial provision and property adjustment between separating spouses and civil partners. Save in relation to children (and on death), little family law currently deals with the end of cohabiting and other 'family' relationships. Much of the general law discussed in this chapter therefore determines the outcomes of financial disputes when such relationships end.

It has been said that 'so far as possible the law should be kept out of the intimate life of the family'.[2] That perhaps explains why there is so little specific family law in this area. However, 'family privacy' may be counterproductive for economically weaker family members. It is important to examine the implications of the law for *individuals*, some of whom it may serve better than others. An unequal division of assets and income may create or sustain dependency and poverty within the family, particularly for women.[3] Those with no rights to occupy the home and to contribute to decisions about transactions such as sale or mortgage may be powerless to influence one of the most fundamental aspects of family life—the place in which it is carried on.

---

[1] Law Com (1971), para 0.1.
[2] Royal Commission on Marriage and Divorce (1956), para 647.
[3] See generally O'Donovan (1985), various chapters in Miles and Probert (eds) (2009).

The law regarding family property and finances also reveals something about the law's understandings of different types of relationships and the roles of individuals within them, as Kevin Gray has suggested:

K. Gray, *Reallocation of Property on Divorce* (Abingdon: Professional Books, 1977), 1

Family law uniquely represents a conjunction of law, sociology, ethics, religion and economics. This statement is particularly true of that part of family law which touches upon the property relations of husband and wife. There is a sense in which the law of matrimonial property is concerned, not with property at all, but with human relations and ideologies in respect of property. Just as the general law of property provides "the basis for a broad range of social and economic assessments that are intrinsic to the way in which the community defines its culture," the law of matrimonial property "comprises a substantial portion of the secular definition of marriage." The law regulating the spouses' property relations is fundamentally an index of social relations between the sexes, and, for this reason, affords a peculiar wealth of commentary on such matters as the prevailing ideology of marriage, the cultural definition of marital roles, the social status of married women, and the role of the state *vis-à-vis* the family.

This last sentence prompted the following response from Carol Smart:

C. Smart, *The Ties that Bind* (London: Routledge, 1984), 101–2

This statement written by an academic lawyer, rather than a sociologist, reveals the extent to which law has been increasingly conceptualised as a social construct which is profoundly imbued with ideological content. However, there still appears to be a tendency to identify the law as both passive (i.e. as an index) and homogenous. The law relating to family structure is neither of these; it actively regulates the behaviour of family members and through a variety of methods encourages marriage and reproduces the 'social relations between the sexes'. It is not homogenous because different fields of law advocate different principles even where the family is concerned, and family law itself 'speaks' with a variety of different voices . . . None the less Gray is correct when he argues that an analysis of law and its implementation is a valuable site of analysis of—or peculiar wealth of commentary on—the social organisation of households and the sexual division of labour.

3.2 THE SOCIAL CONTEXT

In order to evaluate the suitability and fairness of the law relating to family property and finances, we need some awareness of the current housing and economic standing of different families and family members.[4]

3.2.1 THE FAMILY HOME

Key questions considered in this chapter concern the family home: who owns it, and what rights, if any, other family members have in it. Data for 2008–9 reveal that 68 per cent of the

---

[4] We consider lone parents at the start of chapter 6.

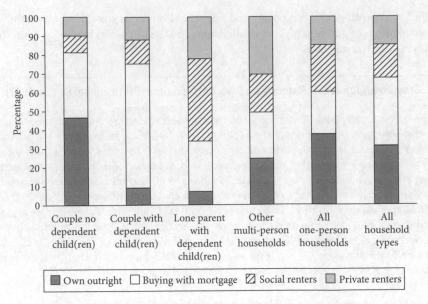

Chart 3.1 Household type by tenure, from DCLG (2010), fig 2

Source: Reproduced from English Housing Survey Headline Report 2008–9, by Crown copyright © 2010.

English live in owner-occupied homes, 18 per cent in social housing (rented) and 14 per cent in privately rented accommodation.[5] Housing tenure varies both by marital status and by whether the family includes dependent children. In 2007–8, while 83 per cent of spouses lived in owner-occupied property, only 62 per cent of cohabitants, 56 per cent of single people, and 54 per cent of divorced and separated people did so. Conversely, 29 per cent of divorced and separated individuals lived in social housing, 21 per cent of single people, 16 per cent of cohabitants, and 9 per cent of spouses.[6]

3.2.2 THE FAMILY ECONOMY

The law attaches great significance to property ownership, which usually derives from purchasing that property or contributing financially to its acquisition. Each family member's economic power is therefore important. Women's employment patterns, particularly following motherhood, have changed markedly over the last 30 years, as increasing numbers of women, including mothers, have entered the workforce. However, as can be seen from Chart 3.2, the vast majority of part-time employees are women, and a large proportion of working women, mostly mothers, work only part-time. More female than male employees have opted for flexible working patterns to accommodate child-care.[7]

A considerable proportion of working-age women are economically inactive, most commonly because they are looking after family or home (44 per cent of all economically inactive women aged 16–59, and 71 per cent of the 25–34 age group);[8] in 2005, only 6 per cent of all economically inactive men cited that reason, the most common reasons for male economic

---

[5] DCLG (2010), table 1.

[6] DCLG (2009), table 1.7; for equivalent Welsh data, see Welsh Assembly Government (2009), ch 12.

[7] ONS (2010e), table 4.11.

[8] Ibid., ch 4

United Kingdom
Thousands

Chart 3.2 Economic activity and inactivity status: by sex and age, 2009, from ONS (2010e), fig 4.2

Source: Reproduced from the Labour Force Survey by the Office for National Statistics, by Crown copyright © 2010.

¹ The Labour Force Survey asks people to classify themselves as full time or part time based on their own perceptions.

Note: Data are at Q2 and are not seasonally adjusted. See Appendix, Part 4: Labour Force Survey.

inactivity being long-term sickness or disability, and studying.[9] Indeed, while being a mother of dependent children makes a woman less likely to be employed, the opposite is true for men: a higher proportion of fathers of dependent children are in paid employment than other men.[10] And the younger the child, the less likely the mother is to work.[11]

Many parents positively choose a traditional division of roles. However, for mothers who want to improve their economic position by playing a greater role in the workforce, labour law rights are crucial. Recent years have seen both an increase in family-friendly employment legislation and a considerable growth in registered child-care places.[12] However, parents' views about the accessibility and affordability of child-care services vary.[13] Moreover, it has been argued that emphasis on bringing women to work, for example through improved maternity leave, means that not enough has been done in law, policy, and workplace culture to encourage and enable *men* to shoulder more caring tasks by taking up existing (and new) leave entitlements and adopting more flexible working patterns.[14] Until that is done, the burden of juggling work and family responsibilities is likely to rest predominantly with women.

So although far more women are working now than in the 1960s, men's and women's engagement with the labour market remain very different. Women's employment patterns over their lifetime are substantially affected by child-care, home-making, and other unpaid

[9] ONS (2006b), table 4.26.
[10] Ibid., ch 4.
[11] ONS (2009a), table 4.3.
[12] HM Treasury et al (2004), B.17.
[13] Lyon, Barnes, and Sweiry (2006), ch 16.
[14] EHRC (2009), Scott and Dex (2009), Lewis (2009), James (2009).

caring responsibilities (for example, for older relatives).[15] This places many women in an inferior economic position in their relationships, having less money at their disposal for personal spending and saving,[16] pension building,[17] contribution to household expenses, and to acquisition of the family home. As we will see below and in chapter 7, this potentially disadvantages them significantly in property law and, if the parties are not spouses or civil partners, on relationship breakdown.

3.3 FAMILY PROPERTY SYSTEMS: SEPARATE PROPERTY

English law operates a system of 'separate property': there is no such thing as 'family property' which is jointly owned and controlled by family members by virtue of their relationship. Instead, each individual has whatever rights of ownership he or she enjoys under the general law of property and trusts.

Historically, this was not so for spouses. The law of husband and wife imposed special rules on the capacity of each spouse to hold property. It is helpful to consider those rules before we examine the current law (which applies in almost[18] exactly the same way to spouses, civil partners, cohabitants, and any other person seeking to assert an interest in property), in order to see how and why English law has reached its current position.

3.3.1 THE OLD LAW OF HUSBAND AND WIFE

As we noted in chapter 2, at common law, the doctrine of unity prescribed that husband and wife were one person in law, represented by the husband.[19] This had profound implications for wives' property:[20] in principle, wives were disabled from owning property so all personal property of the wife owned prior to marriage or acquired during it, including any earnings, were the husband's. The position regarding the wife's real property (land) was more complicated: the husband took control of that property during the marriage; if a child was born, the husband would have a life interest in the property; but if he predeceased the wife, she would be able to recover any land that he had disposed of without her consent.[21] As a result of these laws, and wives' disabilities in contract and tort law, Cretney concludes that 'it is not a great exaggeration to say that the common law robbed the married woman of full human personality'.[22] Equity, however, took a different view, and so wealthy parents would ensure that their daughters' property was protected by trust before they married. But that avenue was not practically available to the poorer classes and—of particular importance to working class wives—could not protect a wife's earnings. As John Stuart Mill put it in his powerful essay of 1869, *The Subjection of Women*: 'The two are called "one person in law", for the purpose of inferring that whatever is hers is his, but the parallel inference is never drawn that whatever is his is hers; the maxim is not applied against the man, except to make him responsible to third parties for her acts, as a master is for the acts of his slaves or of his cattle.'[23]

---

[15] On patterns of unpaid work in the home and its impact on earnings, see ONS (2007), ch 2; Bryan and Sanz (2008); Scott and Dex (2009).

[16] Vogler et al (2008).

[17] Price (2009).

[18] A few statutory rules apply to spouses and civil partners.

[19] See 2.4.2.

[20] This summary is taken from Cretney (2003a), 90–3.

[21] See Doggett (1992), 36–59; Kahn-Freund (1955); O'Donovan (1985), ch 2.

[22] Cretney (2003a), 91.

[23] Mill (1869), 463.

There were limited compensations for the wife's disabilities: for example, she had a right at common law to be maintained by her husband, would be presumed to be acting as his agent in the purchase of 'necessaries', and so could pledge his credit with tradesmen;[24] he would be liable for any tort she committed.[25] But her essential disability remained, while her unmarried sister enjoyed the same property-holding status as men.

Katherine O'Donovan has argued that the common law was largely based on ideological and economic rationales.[26] The ideological basis was the doctrine of unity and the wife's consequent subjection to the husband's control. But the common law also served an economic function: by denying them economic power and rendering them dependent on their husbands, wives were pushed into motherhood and unpaid domestic service in the home, while husbands went out into the market to earn a 'family wage'. The law therefore sustained the traditional division of labour between spouses and the separation of the public world inhabited by men from the private world of women.[27]

3.3.2 REFORM: SEPARATE PROPERTY AND SEPARATE LIABILITY FOR SPOUSES

The Married Women's Property Acts of 1870 and 1882 brought key reform. This legislation followed sustained campaigns by the early women's movement, with the support of sympathetic (male) parliamentarians, moved by the injustice experienced in particular by working class wives.[28] The current law is found in early twentieth century legislation:

Law of Property Act 1925, s 37

A husband and wife shall, for all purposes of acquisition of any interest in property…be treated as two persons.

Law Reform (Married Women and Tortfeasors) Act 1935

1 Capacity of married women

Subject to the provisions of this Act, a married woman shall—

(a) be capable of acquiring, holding, and disposing of, any property; and

(b) be capable of rendering herself, and being rendered, liable in respect of any tort, contract, debt, or obligation; and

(c) be capable of suing and being sued, either in tort or in contract or otherwise;

(d) be subject to the law relating to bankruptcy and to the enforcement of judgments and orders,

[24] Since she could own no property, a wife could not make a contract herself, having no means of fulfilling it.

[25] These were necessary results of wives' incapacity regarding property: Kahn-Freund (1955), 271–2.

[26] O'Donovan (1985), 30–5.

[27] Women (married or not) had no vote until the early twentieth century and were excluded from professional occupations, public office, and reading for university degrees: Representation of the People Acts 1918 and 1928 and Sex Disqualification (Removal) Act 1919.

[28] Holcombe (1983).

in all respects as if she were a feme sole [single woman].

2 Property of married women

(1) Subject to the provision of this Part of this Act all property which—

    (a) immediately before the passing of this Act was the separate property of a married woman or held for her separate use in equity; or

    (b) belongs at the time of her marriage to a woman married after the passing of this Act; or

    (c) after the passing of this Act is acquired by or devolves upon a married woman,

shall belong to her in all respects as if she were a feme sole and may be disposed of accordingly.

3 Abolition of husband's liability for wife's torts and ante-nuptial contracts, debts and obligations

Subject to the provisions of this Part of this Act, the husband of a married woman shall not, by reason only of his being her husband, be liable—

    (a) in respect of any tort committed by her whether before or after the marriage, or in respect of any contract entered into, or debt or obligation incurred, by her before the marriage; or

    (b) be sued, or made a party to any legal proceeding brought, in respect of any such tort, contract, debt, or obligation.

4 Savings...

(2) For the avoidance of doubt it is hereby declared that nothing in this Part of this Act—...

    (c) prevents a husband and wife from acquiring, holding, and disposing of, any property jointly or as tenants in common, or from rendering themselves, or being rendered, jointly liable in respect of any tort, contract, debt or obligation, and of suing and being sued either in tort or in contract or otherwise, in like manner as if they were not married; ...

In the middle of the last century, a series of decisions involving Lord Denning MR sought to establish a doctrine of 'family assets' under which spouses would readily be found to co-own their home and other property central to family life. Lord Denning's initiative was quashed by the House of Lords in *Pettitt v Pettitt*, which firmly established that the general law of property applies between husband and wife, 'while making full allowances in view of that relationship'.[29]

So the general law applies to determine all family members' property rights. Under that law, the question for the judge is 'whose is this?' and not, as on divorce, 'to whom shall this be given?'.[30] But despite the suggestion that 'allowances' would be made for the parties' relationship, the general law is generally thought to be unsuited to the circumstances of family life, and the position of women in particular. 'Separate property' is perhaps not all that its proponents might have hoped as a measure for wives' economic emancipation. The nineteenth century reformers, motivated by a political philosophy of individualism, sought

---

29 [1970] AC 777, 813.
30 *Pettitt v Pettitt* [1970] AC 777, 798.

formal equality: married women should have the same rights as any other person to own property. The basic appeal of that claim seems irresistible. However, while wives now had the legal *power* to own property, many were in *practice* unable to acquire any property owing to their confinement to the domestic sphere and the basis on which the general law allows interests in property to be acquired.[31] As Katherine O'Donovan put it, 'So long as equality remains a formal notion, like the Ritz hotel which is open to all, structural obstacles will prevent those for whom opportunities are opened from taking advantage of them.'[32] Despite the increasing numbers of wives and mothers who engage in paid employment, these problems remain.

It is important, however, to remember the statutory remedies available between spouses and civil partners on relationship breakdown; for the benefit of children who live apart from one or both parents; and for a wide range of family members in the event of death, under the laws of intestacy and family provision.[33] Given the scope for property sharing entailed in these schemes, it is rather misleading to describe English family property law as a separate property regime.[34]

3.4 THE CURRENT LAW: ASCERTAINING OWNERSHIP OF LAND

Different rules apply to determine the ownership of land and other assets. The law ordinarily insists on compliance with certain formal requirements for the creation and transfer of interests in land, whereas interests in other forms of property can be created and transferred orally. However, even in the case of land, interests may arise informally under the laws of implied trust, in particular the 'common intention' constructive trust, and proprietary estoppel. Those areas of law have received particular attention from commentators and law reformers, and we give them most attention.

It is impossible here to provide a full account of this complex area of law; readers are advised to refer to a specialist textbook on land law.[35] The following discussion assumes basic understanding of English law's concepts of land, estates, and interests in land; the distinction between legal and equitable ('beneficial') ownership; the concepts of joint tenancy and tenancy in common; the system of land registration; and the concept of overreaching.

3.4.1 TRANSFERS AND EXPRESS TRUSTS: FORMAL REQUIREMENTS

Interests in land can be expressly created and transferred only by signed writing. A declaration of trust in relation to land must ordinarily be manifested and proved by some signed writing of the settlor(s).[36] All transfers of land and interests in land are void unless made by

---

[31] See Smart (1984), 29–30, 47–9.
[32] O'Donovan (1985), 167.
[33] See chapters 6 and 7. A brief outline of the law applying on death of a family member may be found on the Online Resource Centre for chapter 7.
[34] Kahn-Freund (1955) 284–6; Simon (1964), 18.
[35] Gray and Gray (2009).
[36] Law of Property Act 1925 (LPA 1925), s 53(1)(a) and (b).

deed.[37] If the property is transferred into the name of one person, prima facie that individual becomes both legal and beneficial owner. If property is owned by two or more people, it is held on trust. Usually, the property is transferred into the parties' joint names so that they are both legal owners (once registered as proprietors).[38] The legal owners should, ideally, also declare (in writing) the basis on which they, and any others, hold the beneficial interest in the property: do they all have beneficial shares; if so, as joint tenants or tenants in common; and if as tenants in common, what size share does each party have?[39] Any such express declaration of trust determines the shares in which the beneficial interest is held.[40] Express joint ownership of homes is now very common amongst spouses, but rather less so amongst cohabiting couples.[41]

The law permits some important exceptions to these formal requirements, allowing beneficial interests to arise by implied (resulting and constructive) trusts and proprietary estoppel.[42] These allow someone (who may or may not be on the legal title) to acquire a beneficial share in property, even if there is no valid express declaration of trust in his or her favour. However, implied trust and estoppel law is notoriously complicated and uncertain, so it is preferable that parties think specifically about how the beneficial title of property is to be held and declare an express trust. The courts' exasperation with those who fail to do so is exemplified in *Carlton v Goodman*.[43] Mr Goodman and Ms Carlton had bought a house in joint names and with a joint mortgage, to be occupied only by Mr Goodman, he alone paying the mortgage instalments. They had not expressly declared how the beneficial title was to be held, so the case was decided by reference to the law of resulting trust (an exercise which is less than easy in the context of mortgage-financed purchase):

Carlton v Goodman [2002] EWCA Civ 545

WARD LJ:

44. I would add only this. The conveyancer who acted for these parties thought at one time that she had discussed with Mr Goodman whether or not he wished to declare their beneficial interest in the conveyance and record that they held as joint tenants, the rules of survivorship having been explained to him [i.e. that where property is held on a joint tenancy, in the event of the death of one of two joint tenants, the survivor is immediately sole owner of the whole property]. When she gave evidence she eventually concluded that she did not have any such discussion with Mr Goodman and the judge had no hesitation in concluding that no such discussion had taken place. It was common ground that Anita [Carlton] was not involved in any such discussion. I ask in despair how often this court has to remind conveyancers that they would save their clients a great deal of later difficulty if only they would sit

---

[37] Ibid., s 52.

[38] Land Registration Act 2002 (LRA 2002), s 27. The legal title may be held by up to four people: Trustee Act 1925, s 34(2), LPA 1925, s 34(2).

[39] A clause providing that the survivor of the trustees can give a valid receipt for the proceeds of sale or other disposition of the property does not constitute an express declaration of a beneficial joint tenancy: *Stack v Dowden* [2007] UKHL 17.

[40] *Goodman v Gallant* [1986] Fam 106; subject, for example, to vitiating grounds such as fraud; the possibility of a subsequent express variation of their interests: *Singla v Browne* [2007] EWHC 405; or a supervening constructive trust arising: *Qayyum v Hameed* [2009] EWCA Civ 352.

[41] Haskey (2001b), table 2.

[42] LPA 1925, s 53(2).

[43] See also the 'cautionary tale' of *Kernott v Jones* [2010] EWCA Civ 578, [61].

> the purchasers down, explain the difference between a joint tenancy and a tenancy in common, ascertain what they want and then expressly declare in the conveyance or transfer how the beneficial interest is to be held because that will be conclusive and save all argument. When are conveyancers going to do this as a matter of invariable standard practice? This court has urged that time after time. Perhaps conveyancers do not read law reports. I will try one more time: ALWAYS TRY TO AGREE ON AND THEN RECORD HOW THE BENEFICIAL INTEREST IS TO BE HELD. It is not very difficult to do.

Land Registry rules now make it more likely that parties will address their minds to beneficial ownership, as the land registration process asks purchasers to complete a form on which they should state how the beneficial interest is to be held.[44] However, there is some ambiguity regarding this form. It was widely assumed that it was compulsory for purchasers to set out their beneficial interests on the form, a view supported by the text of the form itself.[45] However, comments by Baroness Hale in *Stack v Dowden* cast doubt on this, suggesting that completion of that part of the form is optional.[46] It is certainly the case that Land Registry will register transfers even if that part of the form has not been completed and executed; as a default measure, pursuant to LRA 2002, s 44 it enters a restriction on the register, a step which (whilst not being conclusive of the matter) tends to be interpreted by others as meaning that the parties wish to be beneficial tenants in common, rather than joint tenants—we explain the significance of that distinction in the next paragraph. Land Registry has recently conducted an in-depth review of this issue.[47]

This is a difficult area. The penalty for those who do not complete the form is that they are left to thrash out their respective rights under the law of implied trusts. However, recent research suggests that many purchasers who currently do complete and execute the form (thereby making a binding express declaration of trust) may not fully appreciate the significance of their choice and so may get an unpleasant surprise should their relationship break down. In particular, it seems that many couples select a beneficial joint tenancy on the basis that this will mean, in the event of their relationship ending by death, that the survivor will automatically acquire title to the whole property under the doctrine of survivorship.[48] However, what is less well-appreciated is that if a cohabiting relationship instead ends by separation, on severance of the beneficial joint tenancy the equity in the property (the capital value remaining after the mortgage loan has been repaid) will be divided 50:50, regardless of the parties' respective financial contributions to the property's acquisition.[49] With a tenancy in common, by contrast, the parties must draft wills to ensure inheritance by the survivor, but can specify whatever life-time shares in the property they like on whatever basis, financial contribution or otherwise.[50]

[44] LRA 2002, s 44(1), and Land Registration Rules 2003, r 95(2)(a); Form FR1 in the case of first registration, and Form TR1 in the case of a transfer of registered land.

[45] See Dixon (2007a).

[46] [2007] UKHL 17, [52].

[47] Land Registry (2008), 62.

[48] See findings of Douglas, Pearce, and Woodward (2007a, 2007b).

[49] See further, and for the contrast with spouses and civil partners, chapter 7.

[50] Though compare the construction placed on the declaration of trust in *Chopra v Bindra* [2009] EWCA Civ 203, which purported to create survivorship in what was otherwise a tenancy in common: the court construed the survivorship clause as conferring a contingent remainder interest on the survivor in the other party's share. The parties thus achieved separate, unequal interests during their joint lives, but with survivorship (in effect) on death. For comment, see (2009) FL 584.

At the very least, purchasers need to be alerted to the significance of their choices, by information (on the Land Registry form or on accompanying documents) and legal advice provided at the point of conveyancing, particularly where potentially conflicting interests mean that parties should receive independent advice.[51] Private ordering—parties deciding at the outset how they wish to deal with their property—has many advantages, not least the avoidance of protracted subsequent litigation under the law of implied trusts. But it can only be as good as the knowledge with which the parties act. Moreover, the Land Registry form and associated advice is only likely to draw people's attention to the question of beneficial ownership if they purchase land together. It does not help where the property is bought in the name of one party only, or where one party moves into property already acquired by the other. There therefore remain many cases where resort must be had to the law of implied trusts and estoppel.

3.4.2 IMPLIED TRUSTS OF LAND AND PROPRIETARY ESTOPPEL: INTRODUCTION

Whether the legal title is held solely or jointly, if there is no express declaration of trust, a trust may be implied by law. The law of implied trusts identifies the extent of the beneficial interests, if any, held by joint legal owners who failed to declare an express trust, and enables individuals who are not on the legal title to acquire a beneficial interest. The law of proprietary estoppel may also generate an interest in property for a claimant. Before embarking on an examination of this area, comments from a Court of Appeal judge—prompted by the morass of complex and often apparently contradictory case law—deserve repetition:

Stack v Dowden [2005] EWCA Civ 857

CARNWATH LJ:

75. To the detached observer, the result [of this case law] may seem like a witch's brew, into which various esoteric ingredients have been stirred over the years, and in which different ideas bubble to the surface at different times. They include implied trust, constructive trust, resulting trust, presumption of advancement, proprietary estoppel, unjust enrichment, and so on. These ideas are likely to mean nothing to laymen, and often little more to the lawyers who use them.

3.4.3 IMPLIED TRUSTS OF LAND: THE PRESUMPTIONS OF RESULTING TRUST AND ADVANCEMENT

In order to appreciate the current law, we need first to examine two presumptions, one of which (resulting trust) is less relevant in family cases than formerly, the other of which (advancement) was recently abolished (though not retrospectively) by statute. Both presumptions are (or were) based on what the courts assume—in the absence of evidence—to be the 'common sense' view of what parties would intend in such circumstances.

---

[51] See findings of Douglas, Pearce, and Woodward (2007a, 2007b).

The presumption of resulting trust

Generally, if property is transferred into the name of A, but B funded the purchase, the law will presume that the parties intended that A would hold the land on a resulting trust for B to the extent of B's contribution. So if A and B buy property, whether in A's name or in A and B's joint names, and they contribute 40 per cent and 60 per cent of the purchase price respectively, A (or, if in joint names, A and B) hold the property on trust for A and B in shares of 40:60. Such a resulting trust only arises where B makes direct financial contributions to the acquisition of the property, for example, payments of deposits, the assumption of personal liability under a mortgage,[52] entitlement to a discount on the purchase price under 'right to buy' legislation,[53] and—depending on the circumstances and type of mortgage—payment of mortgage instalments.[54] Indirect financial contributions (such as paying other household bills or contributing to a common pool from which household expenses are met) and non-financial contributions to the parties' relationship (such as home-making and child-rearing) are irrelevant.[55] Since a resulting trust is only presumed, where there is evidence that B's contribution was intended as a gift or a loan to A, B acquires no share.[56]

This exclusive focus on financial contributions makes it difficult for some family members to acquire a share in land under this presumption. However, although the presumption of resulting trust remains part of the law, it is now less likely to determine the outcome of family property cases, owing to important developments relating the common intention constructive trust.[57]

The presumption of advancement

The presumption of advancement, abolished prospectively by s 199 of the Equality Act 2010,[58] was an interesting relic of the law's historical treatment of certain family relationships.[59] It remains good law for cases arising from events occurring or obligations arising before the Act comes into force. Where a husband or father made a transfer to his wife or child—but not where a wife or mother did so[60]—the law initially presumed not a resulting trust, but a gift.[61] This presumption was not replicated in the civil partnership legislation (unsurprisingly, given its gendered nature), nor did it apply between cohabitants.[62]

The presumption was based on an increasingly dubious assumption that a husband or father would intend to make a gift, given his natural and moral obligation to his wife or child[63] and their economic dependence on him.[64] By contrast, a wife or mother would not be

---

[52] Cf *Stack v Dowden* [2007] UKHL 17, [120] per Lord Neuberger.

[53] *Springette v Defoe* [1992] 2 FLR 388.

[54] *Huntingford v Hobbs* [1993] 1 FLR 736; *Carlton v Goodman* [2002] EWCA Civ 545; *Curley v Parkes* [2004] EWCA Civ 1515; *McKenzie v McKenzie* [2003] 2 P & CR DG6.

[55] *Gissing v Gissing* [1971] AC 886.

[56] *Re Sharpe (a bankrupt)* [1980] 1 WLR 219.

[57] Cf *Curley v Parkes* [2004] EWCA Civ 1515, where constructive trust was, curiously, not argued.

[58] Not in force as at October 2010; see Glister (2010) for incisive analysis.

[59] See generally Gray and Gray (2009), from 7.2.33.

[60] Gender inequality in the parental context was questioned in *Gross v French* (1976) 238 EG 39; note also developments in some Commonwealth jurisdictions: Gray and Gray (2009), 7.2.37.

[61] *Dyer v Dyer* (1788) 2 Cox Eq Cas 92; it was extended by statute to fiancés: Law Reform (Miscellaneous Provisions) Act 1970, s 2(1), *Mossop v Mossop* [1989] Fam 77; cf *Mercier v Mercier* [1903] 2 Ch 98.

[62] *Soar v Foster* (1858) 4 K & J 152, 162.

[63] *Bennet v Bennet* (1879) 10 Ch D 474, 477.

[64] *Pettitt v Pettitt* [1970] AC 777, 793.

taken to intend to make a gift in such cases, but rather to retain an interest under resulting trust. As early as 1970, the House of Lords in *Pettitt* considered that the force of the presumption was much weakened in contemporary conditions.[65] In any event, there was almost always evidence, however slight, from which the parties' actual intentions could be deduced, readily rebutting the presumption.[66]

The presumption of advancement was widely thought to be incompatible with human rights law.[67] Its retention prevented the UK's ratification of a Protocol to the ECHR:

Article 5 of the Seventh Protocol of the European Convention on Human Rights

Equality between spouses

Spouses shall enjoy equality of rights and responsibilities of a private law character between them, and in their relations with their children, as to marriage, during marriage and in the event of its dissolution.

Following the passage of the Equality Act 2010, ratification should now be possible.

3.4.4 IMPLIED TRUSTS: 'COMMON INTENTION' CONSTRUCTIVE TRUSTS

Following the House of Lords decision in *Stack v Dowden*,[68] the common intention constructive trust is the principal form of implied trust in the 'domestic' context[69] where parties acquire a home together in joint or sole names, or where one moves into the other's home and claims a beneficial interest.[70] The voluminous but inconsistent case law in this area gives property and trust lawyers considerable doctrinal difficulty. *Stack* itself was a controversial decision that generated a large academic literature and a powerful, many would say more orthodox, minority speech from Lord Neuberger. The decision left many points of uncertainty which subsequent case law has, giving various answers, begun to explore.

There are three inter-related stages to be proved in establishing a common intention constructive trust: (i) a common or shared intention between the parties that the claimant should have a beneficial share in the property; on which (ii) the claimant has detrimentally relied, such that it would be unconscionable for the owner to deny the claimant's interest; and finally (iii) quantification of that interest. The following discussion of these elements is organized around the categories of case identified in *Stack* in which those three ingredients are differently interpreted and applied: cases in which the legal title is held jointly (joint-names cases), and those in which it is held by one party (sole-name cases).

---

[65] For criticism, see Auchmuty (2007), 180–3.
[66] *Pettitt v Pettitt* [1970] AC 777, at 793, 811, 814, and 824.
[67] See Andrews (2007); cf Glister (2010).
[68] [2007] UKHL 17.
[69] Contrast 'commercial' cases: *Stack v Dowden*, ibid., [57]–[58]. We explore this distinction below at p 144.
[70] There are various other contexts in which a constructive trust might arise: see Gray and Gray (2009), from 7.3.11; e.g. *Staden v Jones* [2008] EWCA Civ 936; *De Bruyne v De Bruyne* [2010] EWCA Civ 519.

A trust based on the parties' intentions, not fairness?

Following *Stack*, the court's task is to identify what the parties intended, not to impose the solution which it considers fair:

Stack v Dowden [2007] UKHL 17

BARONESS HALE:

60. . . . The search is to ascertain the parties' shared intentions, actual, inferred or imputed, with respect to the property in the light of their whole course of conduct in relation to it.

She then turned to the issue of quantification, considering two competing tests, first from *Oxley v Hiscock*:

'each is entitled to that share which the court considers fair having regard to the whole course of dealing between them in relation to the property'[71]

the other formulated by the Law Commission:

'If the question really is one of the parties' "common intention", we believe that there is much to be said for adopting what has been called a "holistic approach" to quantification, undertaking a survey of the whole course of dealing between the parties and taking account of all conduct which throws light on the question what shares were intended.'[72]

She preferred the Law Commission test:

61. . . . That may be the preferable way of expressing what is essentially the same thought, for two reasons. First, it emphasises that the search is still for the result which reflects what the parties must, in the light of their conduct, be taken to have intended. Second, therefore, it does not enable the court to abandon that search in favour of the result which the court itself considers fair. For the court to impose its own view of what is fair upon the situation in which the parties find themselves would be to return to the days before *Pettitt v Pettitt* [earlier HL decision] . . .

62. Furthermore, although the parties' intentions may change over the course of time, producing . . . an "ambulatory" constructive trust, at any one time their interests must be the same for all purposes. They cannot at one and the same time intend, for example, a joint tenancy with survivorship should one of them die while they are still together, a tenancy in common in equal shares should they separate on amicable terms after the children have grown up, and a tenancy in common in unequal shares should they separate on acrimonious terms while the children are still with them.

---

[71] [2004] EWCA Civ 546, [69].
[72] Law Com (2002), para 4.27.

Subsequent cases have largely adhered to this approach, emphasizing (sometimes very pointedly) that decisions must be based on intention, however 'unfair' the outcome.[73] However, one difficult issue that blurs this otherwise sharp distinction is the notion of an 'imputed' intention. In *Midland Bank v Cooke*, Waite LJ had suggested that a constructive trust could be found, at least on the basis of financial contributions, even where the parties 'had been honest enough to admit that they never gave ownership a thought or reached any agreement about it', thinking it 'unrealistic' to expect them to have had such conversations.[74] True as his view of the world may be, the orthodox view of the law—previously established by the House of Lords in *Pettit v Pettitt* and *Gissing v Gissing*—distinguishes sharply between inferred and imputed intentions, rejecting reliance on the latter:

Stack v Dowden [2007] UKHL 17

LORD NEUBERGER:

126. An inferred intention is one which is objectively deduced to be the subjective actual intention of the parties, in the light of their actions and statements. An imputed intention is one which is attributed to the parties, even though no such actual intention can be deduced from their actions and statements, and even though they had no such intention. Imputation involves concluding what the parties would have intended, whereas inference involves concluding what they did intend.

127. To impute an intention would not only be wrong in principle and a departure from [*Pettitt v Pettitt* [1970] AC 777 and *Gissing v Gissing* [1971] AC 886] in this very area, but it would also involve a judge in an exercise which was difficult, subjective and uncertain.... It would be difficult because the judge would be constructing an intention where none existed at the time, and where the parties may well not have been able to agree. It would be subjective for obvious reasons. It would be uncertain because it is unclear whether one considers a hypothetical negotiation between the actual parties, or what reasonable parties would have agreed. The former is more logical, but would redound to the advantage of an unreasonable party.

Given this orthodoxy, it was surprising in *Stack v Dowden* that Lord Walker and Baroness Hale both appeared, without any substantial discussion of the point or clear definition of the concept, to endorse reliance on imputed intention, certainly in relation to the quantification of shares, but perhaps also (their speeches are not clear on this point) in determining whether a trust arises at all.[75] As Lord Neuberger observed, to allow the court to impute to the parties an intention they never had comes very close to imposing the court's view of what is fair, the very approach rejected by the majority.[76] This development has generated considerable discussion amongst property lawyers[77] and some consternation in the lower courts. In *Kernott v Jones*, a joint-names case in which one party alone had paid the mortgage for 12 years following the parties' separation, rather different views were expressed on the matter by the first instance judge and on appeal:

[73] E.g. *James v Thomas* [2007] EWCA Civ 1212, [38].
[74] [1995] 4 All ER 562, 575.
[75] [2007] UKHL 17, [33] and [60]; see also dicta in *Abbott v Abbott* [2007] UKPC 53.
[76] Ibid., [127]; see also *Kernott v Jones* [2010] EWCA Civ 578, [77] per Rimer LJ.
[77] E.g. Piska (2008, 2009), Swadling (2007), Lee (2008), Gardner (2008).

Jones v Kernott [2009] EWHC 1713

JUDGE NICHOLAS STRAUSS QC

30. I think that...what Baroness Hale said [at para 61] was intended to qualify [the test in *Oxley v Hiscock*, above], not to contradict it. In my view, what the majority in *Stack* held was only that the court should not *override* the intention of the parties, in so far as that appears from what they have said or from their conduct, in favour of what the court itself considers to be fair. The key words used by Baroness Hale are that the court must not *impose* its view. [emphasis in original]

31. To the extent that the intention of the parties cannot be inferred, the court is free, as the key passage [para 61 of *Stack*] makes clear – to impute a common intention to the parties. Imputing an intention involves, as Lord Neuberger points out, attributing to the parties an intention which they did not have, or at least did [not] express to each other. The intention is one which the parties 'must be taken' [*Stack,* para 61] to have had. It is difficult to see how this process can work, without the court supplying, to the extent that the intention of the parties cannot be deduced from their words or conduct, what the court considers to be fair...

The case then went to the Court of Appeal, where the majority—in particular Rimer LJ— took a very different view:

Kernott v Jones [2010] EWCA Civ 578

RIMER LJ:

77. As for Baroness Hale's statement in [60] that the court must or can also look for the parties' *imputed* intentions, I do not, with the greatest respect, understand what she meant. It is possible that she was using it as a synonym for *inferred*,... in which case it adds nothing. If not, it is possible that she was suggesting that the facts in any case might enable the court to ascribe to the parties an intention that they neither expressed nor inferentially had: in other words, that the court can invent an intention for them. That, however, appears unlikely, since it is inconsistent with Baroness Hale's repeated reference to the fact that the goal is to find the parties' intentions, which must mean their real intentions. Further, the court could and would presumably only consider so imputing an intention to them if it had drawn a blank in its search for an express or an inferred intention but wanted to impose upon the parties its own assessment of what would be a fair resolution of their differences. But Baroness Hale's rejection of that as an option at paragraph [61] must logically exclude that explanation....

The Supreme Court is likely to have to revisit this (and other) questions relating to the interpretation and application of *Stack v Dowden*, as *Kernott v Jones* is due to be heard there on a further appeal in May 2011.

In the meantime, courts hearing other cases have mostly declined even to mention the possibility of imputing intention, focusing instead on the (restrictive) basis on which an intention might be inferred. As we shall see below, the courts have set claimants in sole-name cases a very high hurdle to establish the existence of a common intention that the claimant should have an interest at all. But we turn first to joint-name cases.

Cases where the legal title is in joint names

This was the situation in *Stack v Dowden* itself. Mr Stack and Ms Dowden, parents of four children, were legal co-owners of a home purchased 10 years into their 20-year cohabiting relationship. The purchase was funded by a deposit, other capital from Ms Dowden, and a joint mortgage. Throughout the relationship, she was the higher earner. They had separate bank and savings accounts. He paid off the mortgage interest; she paid all other household bills; both helped pay off the capital sum due under the mortgage. Overall, her financial contribution to the acquisition of this property and their previous home had been the greater. There was, of course, no express declaration of the parties' beneficial shares in the property.

The House of Lords held that in 'domestic' cases where the property is held in the parties' joint names (which means that there must be *a* trust) but no beneficial interests have been expressly created, the fact of putting title in joint names will 'at least in the vast majority of cases' demonstrate that the parties intended that both would have a beneficial share.[78] The majority appear to assume detrimental reliance on this presumed intention by whichever party most benefits from it.[79] As to the size and nature of those shares, it is *strongly* presumed in such cases that 'equity follows the law', creating a beneficial joint tenancy.[80] This would entail the parties having equal shares in the event of the property being sold following separation (at which point the joint tenancy would in practice be severed), and the survivor taking all should the other owner(s) die. As Lord Neuberger observed, this effectively creates a gender- and relationship status- neutral presumption of advancement in favour of whichever party made the lesser (or even no) financial contribution to the purchase.[81] As such, it is a very valuable presumption.

The onus lies with whichever party wishes to claim a larger share—here, Ms Dowden—to rebut the presumption of beneficial joint tenancy. One might have thought it could be rebutted where parties had made different levels of financial contribution to the acquisition of the property, effectively invoking instead the presumption of resulting trust.[82] However, the majority rejected this approach, arguing that in contemporary circumstances 'the importance to be attached to who paid for what in a domestic context may be very different from its importance in other contexts or long ago'. But Baroness Hale, for the majority, emphasized that only rarely would the presumption be rebutted by a finding, discerned from the parties' 'whole course of conduct in relation to the property', that other beneficial shares were intended:[83]

Stack v Dowden [2007] UKHL 17

BARONESS HALE:

68. The burden will...be on the person seeking to show that the parties did intend their beneficial interests to be different from their legal interests, and in what way. This is not a task to be lightly embarked upon. In family disputes, strong feelings are aroused when couples split up. These often lead the parties, honestly but mistakenly, to reinterpret the past in self-exculpatory

---

[78] *Stack v Dowden* [2007] UKHL 17, [55], [63].

[79] Gray and Gray (2009), 7.3.37, 7.3.66; Gardner (2008) and Etherton (2009) may go too far in suggesting that detrimental reliance is no longer required at all, particularly in sole-name cases: the House of Lords certainly did not expressly remove that element from the test.

[80] [2007] UKHL 17, [53]–[56].

[81] Ibid., [112].

[82] Lord Neuberger would take this approach where the only additional evidence is different levels of financial contribution: [2007] UKHL 17, [110]–[122].

[83] Ibid., [60].

or vengeful terms. They also lead people to spend far more on the legal battle than is warranted by the sums actually at stake. A full examination of the facts is likely to involve disproportionate costs. In joint names cases it is also unlikely to lead to a different result unless the facts are very unusual...It cannot be the case that all the hundreds and thousands, if not millions, of transfers into joint names using the old forms[84] are vulnerable to challenge in the courts simply because it is likely that the owners contributed unequally to their purchase.

How is the court to ascertain what the parties intended? Having indicated that the presumption would rarely be rebutted, Baroness Hale's subsequent observations appear to provide considerable room for parties to attempt to do just that:

69. In law, "context is everything" and the domestic context is very different from the commercial world. Each case will turn on its own facts. Many more factors than financial contributions may be relevant to divining the parties' true intentions. These include: any advice or discussions at the time of the transfer which cast light upon their intentions then;[85] the reasons why the home was acquired in their joint names; the reasons why (if it be the case) the survivor was authorised to give a receipt for the capital monies; the purpose for which the home was acquired; the nature of the parties' relationship; whether they had children for whom they both had responsibility to provide a home; how the purchase was financed, both initially and subsequently; how the parties arranged their finances, whether separately or together or a bit of both; how they discharged the outgoings on the property and their other household expenses. When a couple are joint owners of the home and jointly liable for the mortgage, the inferences to be drawn from who pays for what may be very different from the inferences to be drawn when only one is owner of the home. The arithmetical calculation of how much was paid by each is also likely to be less important. It will be easier to draw the inference that they intended that each should contribute as much to the household as they reasonably could and that they would share the eventual benefit or burden equally. The parties' individual characters and personalities may also be a factor in deciding where their true intentions lay. In the cohabitation context, mercenary considerations may be more to the fore than they would be in marriage, but it should not be assumed that they will always take pride of place over natural love and affection. At the end of day, having taken all this into account, cases in which the joint legal owners are taken to have intended that their beneficial interests should be different from their legal interests will be very unusual.

70. This is not, of course, an exhaustive list. There may also be reasons to conclude that, whatever the parties' intentions at the outset, these have now changed. An example might be where one party has financed (or constructed himself) an extension or substantial improvement to the property, so that what they have now is significantly different from what they had then.

Far from discouraging arguments attempting to rebut the presumption of beneficial joint tenancy, the majority's approach quickly attracted criticism from practitioners who suggested that it may be worthwhile regularly attempting rebuttal.[86] Indeed, practitioners may feel fortified by the fact that *Stack* was one of those 'very unusual' cases, from which Stack and

---

[84] I.e. forms containing the 'valid receipt' clause, discussed at n 39 above, which was held in *Stack* not to constitute an express declaration of trust, hence the resort to implied trust law.

[85] E.g. the draft declaration of trust considered in *Williamson v Sheikh* [2008] EWCA Civ 990; the claimant was a minor at the date of purchase, so could not appear on the legal title.

[86] See, for example, Barnes (2007).

Dowden emerged with 35:65 shares, essentially reflecting the financial contributions that each had made to the purchase. The factors which lead Baroness Hale to conclude that Stack and Dowden intended to hold 35:65 rather than as beneficial joint tenants were: that they had contributed unequally the purchase price;[87] that they had kept their money in separate accounts, not pooled it; and that they had divided responsibility for household outgoings rigidly: he paid the mortgage interest and endowment policy instalments, she all other household bills. This financial separation, and Mr Stack's apparent failure to commit at least 'to do what he could' towards family expenditure,[88] persuaded Baroness Hale that this relationship was not a 'partnership' in which a beneficial joint tenancy was intended. This despite the parties' having chosen to put *this* asset in joint names, the length of their relationship, their raising four children together, and the fact that they contributed equal proportions of their earnings to the purchase.[89] We examine below empirical evidence about cohabitants' money management practices which suggests that such cases are less unusual than Baroness Hale supposes.[90]

The outcome suggests that the presumption of resulting trust, formally abandoned, remains close by:[91] the presumption of beneficial joint tenancy seems rather quick to yield to unequal financial contributions. As Lord Neuberger has observed extra-judicially, 'If the presumption of equality is to be rebutted because the contributions are significantly different, it is a pretty useless presumption: the only time you need it, it isn't there'.[92] Indeed, it is telling that Lord Neuberger reached the same conclusion of 35:65 shares, but by starting with the presumption of resulting trust and then considering whether that presumption could be rebutted by evidence of a common intention that Mr Stack should have more.[93] He concluded that there was no such intention, and so concurred with the 65:35 split.

However, later cases paint a different, arguably contradictory picture. In *Fowler v Barron*,[94] the parties had cohabited for 23 years and had two children. Mr Barron, a retired fireman on a pension, looked after the children while Ms Fowler worked. Without any legal advice or express discussion, they put their house in joint names (with no declaration of trust) and took out a joint mortgage, despite having no intention that Ms Fowler would help pay the debt. Mr Barron contributed the deposit and paid the mortgage, and all of the utility, council tax, and other general household bills. Ms Fowler made no financial contribution to the house or general household costs. Her wages were used to buy her clothes and to meet the children's various expenses. The Court of Appeal set out its general approach to the presumption of beneficial joint tenancy as follows:

Fowler v Barron [2008] EWCA Civ 377

ARDEN LJ:

35. In determining whether the presumption is rebutted, the court must in particular consider whether the facts as found are *inconsistent* with the inference of a common intention

---

[87] This appeared to be a sufficient ground for Lord Hope, [11], which indicates, despite his approval of Baroness Hale's reasoning, sympathy for Lord Neuberger's minority approach.

[88] [2007] UKHL 17, [91].

[89] George (2008).

[90] See also *Kernott v Jones* [2010] EWCA Civ 578, [75].

[91] See in particular Lord Hope: [2007] UKHL 17, [11].

[92] Neuberger (2008), para 15.

[93] See in particular, [2007] UKHL 17, [131]–[137].

[94] [2008] EWCA Civ 377.

to share the property in equal shares to an extent sufficient to discharge the civil standard of proof on the person seeking to displace the presumption arising from a transfer into joint names. [emphasis added]

This elaboration of how the presumption works is important. Evidence which is *consistent* with a beneficial joint tenancy does *not necessarily* mean that parties *intended* a beneficial joint tenancy—the facts may be equally consistent with a tenancy in common (quite possibly in shares other than 50:50) or sole beneficial ownership. But that will not displace the presumption. The party seeking to rebut the presumption, here Mr Barron, must establish facts positively *inconsistent* with a beneficial joint tenancy. Viewed in this way, the task facing Mr Barron looks daunting (and *Stack*'s outcome perhaps too favourable to Ms Dowden).

In *Fowler*, there was only circumstantial evidence of the parties' common intention regarding ownership of the property. The trial judge found that Mr Barron had intended that Ms Fowler should become sole owner of the property on his death: this is consistent with joint tenancy's doctrine of survivorship. But that he had not intended that she should get an equal share should they separate: this is evidently inconsistent with a beneficial joint tenancy. However, this 'secret' intention had not been communicated to Ms Fowler, so could not form the basis of a *common* intention.[95] The parties had executed mutual wills, leaving each other their interests in the property: this implied that both thought each had *a* share (at least) during their lifetime.[96] Ms Fowler's position may appear to be weaker than Mr Stack's. Despite being party to the mortgage, Ms Fowler, unlike Mr Stack, had made no personal financial contribution to the mortgage or other regular household expenditure. Like Stack and Dowden, the parties had never had a joint bank account. *Perhaps* like Mr Stack (we know little about these aspects of *Stack v Dowden*), Ms Fowler had not been primary carer for the children since she was working. Nevertheless, the Court of Appeal felt able to uphold the presumption of beneficial joint tenancy, thus giving shares of 50:50.

Fowler v Barron [2008] EWCA Civ 377

ARDEN LJ:

41. ...Mr Barron paid some items properly described as household expenses, such as the council tax and utilities bills, whereas she paid for other such items. The division was perfectly logical if...she did most of the shopping for the children. The further inference that...it is appropriate to draw is that the parties intended that it should make no difference to their interests in the property which party paid for what expense. Those payments also throw light on their intentions in this respect. The inference from this, especially when taken with the evidence as to mutual wills...was that the parties simply did not care about the respective size of each other's contributions....

45. In a case where the parties have made unequal contributions to the cost of acquiring their home, it is obvious that in some cases there may be a thin dividing line between the case where the parties' shared intention is properly inferred to be ownership of the home in equal shares, and the case where the parties' shared intention is properly inferred to be that the party who has contributed less should have a smaller interest than the other. The resolution of such cases must however all depend on the facts. In my judgment it is important to

---

[95] Ibid., [36]–[37].
[96] Ibid., [6], [42].

return to the ratio in *Stack*. The essential reasoning of the House was (1) that, where parties put their home in joint names, the burden is on the one asserting that they own the property other than in equal shares to rebut the presumption of beneficial joint ownership that arises from their legal co-ownership, and (2) that the court must have regard to all the circumstances which would throw light on their shared intentions and not just their financial contributions to the cost of acquiring the property. It is necessary to consider the resolution of the facts in *Stack* with these principles in mind. In other words, it was not the fact that the parties made unequal contributions to the cost of acquiring their property . . . that mattered so much as the inferences as to their shared intentions to be gleaned from the evidence overall.

Arden LJ sought to justify upholding the presumption of beneficial joint tenancy on the basis of factual differences from *Stack* that, with respect, do not obviously *favour* Ms Fowler: for example, the mutual wills; the lack of other substantial assets; the fact that she had made no financial contribution (why should that give her more rather than less than Mr Stack?); that, without a share, she might become reliant on state support, which—in Arden LJ's view— the parties could not reasonably be inferred to have intended; and their treatment of their money as a common pool (despite the lack of joint account).[97]

The outcome is perhaps more convincing without attempting to distinguish it in detail from *Stack*:

TOULSON LJ:

53. In *Stack v Dowden* the House of Lords regarded the facts as very unusual. In the present case there was nothing at all unusual about the circumstances in which the property was acquired. It was bought and conveyed into the parties' joint names . . . at a time when they had a 9 month old baby . . . They had been in a relationship for 4 years. They had not been cohabiting, but Miss Fowler said . . . that the birth . . . "was the spur for us to become a proper family unit". The judge found that the property was bought in order to provide a home for themselves and their son. . . . They were joint borrowers and jointly liable [on the mortgage]. The judge found that whatever either of them thought about the question of ownership of the property at the time of the transfer, nothing was ever said. Looking at the matter at the time of acquisition, there was in my judgment nothing to rebut the ordinary presumption in such circumstances that the parties were intended to be joint beneficial owners in equal shares. . . .

56. . . . [He summarizes the factors listed in [69] of Baroness Hale's judgment in *Stack*, and goes on:] The judge in his analysis of the facts looked only at financial matters. That is too narrow an approach when addressing issues of inferred common intention. In this case the property served as a family home for the parties and their children from the time of its acquisition until the time of the breakdown of the relationship. During those 17 years Miss Fowler contributed to the life and wellbeing of the family in financial and other ways . . . In that family context I would reject any argument that a common silent intention should be inferred from the parties' conduct that their property interests were to be varied so as to reduce Miss Fowler's original share.

If anything, therefore, the difficulty lies not in Ms Fowler having a 50 per cent share, but in Mr Stack not doing so. It may transpire that the analysis in *Fowler v Barron* will prove to be more typical, and *Stack extremely* unusual.[98] In *Kernott v Jones*, the presumption of

[97] Ibid., [46].
[98] See *Kernott v Jones* [2010] EWCA Civ 578, [72] and [75].

beneficial joint tenancy was upheld notwithstanding the parties' 12-year separation, during which time the woman alone had funded the mortgage without any child support payments from the man, who had acquired his own home.[99]

Cases where the legal title is in the sole name of one party

Stack v Dowden was not concerned with property purchased in one party's name, but dicta in the decision nevertheless apply in this sphere. In particular, the intention- rather than fairness-based approach has been followed in the sole-name cases. The starting point, as in joint names cases, is that equity follows the law. Here, that means that equity presumes sole beneficial ownership from sole legal ownership. The onus is therefore on the party not on the legal title to prove a beneficial interest.[100] It is in these cases that the three analytical stages— intention, detrimental reliance, quantification—are more clearly evident.

Finding a 'common intention' to share beneficial ownership

The first stage is to establish a common intention that the claimant should have a beneficial share at all. Earlier House of Lords authority indicates that 'common intention' can arise in two ways, express or inferred:

Lloyds Bank v Rosset [1991] 1 AC 107, 132–3, 131

LORD BRIDGE:

The first and fundamental question which must always be resolved is whether, independently of any inference to be drawn from the conduct of the parties in the course of sharing the house as their home and managing their affairs, there has at any time prior to acquisition, or exceptionally at some later date, been any agreement, arrangement or understanding reached between them that the property is to be shared beneficially. The finding of an agreement or arrangement to share in this sense can only, I think, be based on evidence of express discussions between the partners, however imperfectly remembered and however imprecise their terms may have been. Once a finding to this effect is made it will only be necessary for the partner asserting the claim to a beneficial interest against the partner entitled to the legal estate to show that he or she has acted to his or her detriment or significantly altered his or her position in reliance on the agreement in order to give rise to a constructive trust or a proprietary estoppel.

The judges have sometimes been generous here, being prepared to find an express common intention where the owner has given some excuse for not putting the claimant on the legal title. Whilst those owners clearly had no intention that their partners should have any share, the reasonable understanding by the claimants of what was said supported the objective finding of a common intention to share.[101] Gardner considers that finding a common intention to share the beneficial ownership here may recognize the owner's moral obligation, but is nonetheless problematic: as he puts it, someone who gives a bogus excuse for declining an invitation to a boring party does not thereby indicate an intention to attend.[102]

---

[99] [2010] EWCA Civ 578. Cf the sole name case, *Holman v Howes* [2007] EWCA Civ 877.
[100] *Stack v Dowden* [2007] UKHL 17, [56].
[101] E.g. *Eves v Eves* [1975] 1 WLR 1338; *Grant v Edwards* [1986] Ch 638.
[102] Gardner (1993), 265.

Lord Bridge's exposition of the law continued with the 'inferred' category of intention:

> In sharp contrast with this situation is the very different one where there is no evidence to support a finding of an agreement or arrangement to share, however reasonable it might have been for the parties to reach such an arrangement if they had applied their minds to the question, and where the court must rely entirely on the conduct of the parties both as the basis from which to infer a common intention to share the property beneficially and as the conduct relied on to give rise to a constructive trust. In this situation direct contributions to the purchase price by the partner who is not the legal owner, whether initially or by payment of mortgage instalments, will readily justify the inference necessary to the creation of a constructive trust. But, as I read the authorities, it is at least extremely doubtful whether anything less will do.

This was bad news for Mrs Rosset. She had been married to Mr Rosset for 12 years and had two children. The newly acquired home was in his sole name, there was no evidence of an express common intention to share, and she had made no direct financial contribution to the acquisition or renovation of the property. What she had done was to supervise the renovations, carried out decorating work herself daily, and obtained building materials while her husband was working abroad:

> [T]he judge based his inference of a common intention that Mrs Rosset should have a beneficial interest ... essentially on the basis of what Mrs Rosset did in and about assisting the renovation of the property ... Yet by itself this activity ... could not possibly justify any such inference. It was common ground that Mrs Rosset was extremely anxious that the new matrimonial home should be ready for occupation before Christmas if possible. In these circumstances it would seem the most natural thing in the world for any wife, in the absence of her husband abroad, to spend all the time she could spare and to employ any skills she might have, such as the ability to decorate a room, in doing all she could to accelerate progress of the work quite irrespective of any expectation she might have on enjoying a beneficial interest in the property. The judge's view that some of this work was work "upon which she could not reasonably have been expected to embark unless she was to have an interest in the house" seems to me, with respect, quite untenable.

It is clear that a common intention to share cannot be inferred from non-financial contributions[103] or from the unilateral conduct of one party.[104] However, the case law remains ambiguous about the relevance of *indirect* financial contributions to the purchase.[105] There is a strong argument that they should, at least where payment of other household bills enables the other party to pay the mortgage:

Le Foe v Le Foe and another [2001] 2 FLR 970, 973

JUDGE NICHOLAS MOSTYN QC

> I have no doubt that the family economy depended for its function on [the wife's] earnings. It was an arbitrary allocation of responsibility that [the husband] paid the mortgage, service charge and outgoings, whereas [the wife] paid for day-to-day domestic expenditure.

---

103 *Burns v Burns* [1984] Ch 317.
104 *Holman v Howes* [2007] EWCA Civ 877, [31].
105 Contrast *Gissing v Gissing* [1971] AC 886; *Le Foe v Le Foe and Woolwich Building Society plc* [2001] 2 FLR 970; *Buggs v Buggs* [2003] EWHC 1538 (Ch); *Mollo v Mollo* [2000] WTLR 227.

In *Stack v Dowden*, Lord Walker opined that, whether or not Lord Bridge's doubts about their adequacy in *Rosset* were rightly held at that time, 'the law has moved on'.[106] Baroness Hale acknowledged that it could be argued that Lord Bridge had set the hurdle 'rather too high'.[107] Some commentators have argued that *Stack*'s 'holistic analysis' of party intention applies at this stage too, displacing the *Rosset* test entirely.[108] However, early Court of Appeal decisions following *Stack v Dowden* took a restrictive approach in sole-owner cases,[109] declining to adopt the suggested relaxation in the categories of contribution from which intention to share might be inferred.[110] Indeed, they are as strict as *Fowler v Barron*—here to the *disadvantage* of the party who made little or no financial contribution—in identifying evidence that rebuts the relevant presumption. This is particularly notable where claimants have sought to acquire an interest in property acquired by the defendant before the parties' relationship began.[111]

For example, in *James v Thomas*,[112] the parties had cohabited for 15 years in a property previously acquired in his sole name by Mr Thomas with mortgage finance. Miss James worked unpaid in his business throughout the relationship (that work including heavy labour[113]), only latterly becoming a formal business partner. The parties were reliant on the business for their livelihood; the mortgage and all outgoings on the property were paid from the business profits. When their relationship ended, the claimant claimed a beneficial share of the home.[114] First, the court found no evidence of an express common intention to share the beneficial title: Mr Thomas' remarks (regarding improvement to the property) that 'this will benefit us both' were construed as statements regarding shared use and enjoyment of the property, not shared beneficial ownership.[115] The court also declined to infer an intention, despite Miss James' substantial non-financial contribution to the business (and so, it might be argued, indirectly to the mortgage repayments) and to the property's renovation. This despite the fact that the court had accepted in principle, following *Stack*, that it was entitled to examine the whole course of dealing between the parties in relation to the property in search of a common intention to share beneficial ownership:[116]

James v Thomas [2007] EWCA Civ 1212

SIR JOHN CHADWICK:

27. Although it is possible to envisage circumstances in which the fact that one party began to make contributions to capital repayments due under a mortgage might evidence an agreement that that party was to have a share in the property, the circumstances of this

---

[106] [2007] UKHL 17, [26].

[107] Ibid., [63]; see also dicta in *Abbott v Abbott* [2007] UKPC 53.

[108] See Megarry and Wade, *The Law of Real Property*, relied on in *Hapeshi v Allnatt* [2010] EWHC 392, though the facts there would have satisfied the *Rosset* test.

[109] Failed claims include *Negus v Bahouse* [2007] EWHC 2628 (Ch); *Tackaberry v Hollis* [2007] EWHC 2633 (Ch); *James v Thomas* [2007] EWCA Civ 1212; *Morris v Morris* [2008] EWCA Civ 257.

[110] Though note *Webster v Webster* [2008] EWHC 31, [33] where a common intention to share was inferred from indirect contributions to the family budget (payment for furnishings, utilities, clothing, and food for the children). This finding, which is not closely analysed in the judgment, was superseded by a larger award under the Inheritance (Provision for Family and Dependants) Act 1975.

[111] Piska (2009), 229.

[112] [2007] EWCA Civ 1212. See also *Morris v Morris* [2008] EWCA Civ 257.

[113] Cf *Eves v Eves* [1975] 1 WLR 1338.

[114] She was in any event entitled to her share of the business assets on dissolution of the partnership.

[115] [2007] EWCA Civ 1212, [33].

[116] Ibid., [19].

case are not of that nature. On the facts found by the judge, the only source of funds to meet Mr Thomas' commitments under the mortgage, as well as all other household and personal expenses, was the receipts of the business. While the parties were living together they were dependent on the success of the business to meet their outgoings. It was not at all surprising that, in the early days of their relationship, Miss James should do what she could to ensure that the business prospered. That is not to undervalue her contribution, which, as Mr Thomas recognised, was substantial. But it is to recognise that what she was doing gives rise to no inference that the parties had agreed (or had reached a common understanding) that she was to have a share in the property: *what she was doing was wholly explicable on other grounds.* [emphasis added]

Similarly, in *Morris v Morris*[117] a wife unsuccessfully claimed a beneficial interest in the family farm, owned at law by the husband's mother.[118] Here too the Court of Appeal emphasized the need for 'exceptional circumstances'[119] before any common intention to share beneficial ownership could be inferred from conduct, particularly conduct after the property had already been acquired. Sir Peter Gibson talked in terms of conduct which 'can only be explained on the footing that [the claimant] believes that she was acquiring an interest in the land'.[120] The wife's apparently full (and unpaid) involvement in a joint business venture on the farm was insufficient.

The courts have shown reluctance to infer a common intention to share beneficial ownership even where the parties were cohabiting when the property was purchased. In *Thomson v Humphrey*,[121] the court emphasized that previous properties had also been held in the sole name of the defendant, and attached significant weight to a cohabitation agreement confirming that the claimant had no interest but which she had refused to sign. Her lack of signature did not indicate a common intention to share ownership: on the contrary, the unsigned agreement simply made it harder for her to show that her partner, the legal owner, intended that she should have a share.

Remarkably, during the trial in *James v Thomas*, Mr Thomas conceded that Miss James should in fairness have a share given her contributions. Sir John Chadwick agreed that they could properly have settled the case on that basis. But perceptions of fairness could not affect the outcome in court:

James v Thomas [2007] EWCA Civ 1212

SIR JOHN CHADWICK:

38.... Her interest in the property (if any) must be determined by applying the principles of law and equity which (however inadequate to meet the circumstances in which parties live together in the twenty-first century) must now be taken as well-established. Unless she can bring herself within those principles, her claim... must fail. As Baroness Hale... observed in

---

117 [2008] EWCA Civ 257.
118 The wife's case was made more difficult to sustain by the various business and property-holding structures, the mother and husband's farming business letting the farm from the mother, and the wife's equestrian business, run on the farm, borrowing money from the husband's company and contributing to the costs of building a manège.
119 At [23].
120 [2008] EWCA Civ 257, [25]; see also *Walsh v Singh* [2009] EWHC 3219.
121 [2009] EWHC 3576.

> *Stack v Dowden*...it is not for the court to abandon the search for the result which reflects what the parties must, in the light of their conduct, be taken to have intended in favour of the result which the court itself considers fair.

Detrimental reliance

If a common intention to share beneficial ownership can be found, the claimant's detrimental reliance on that intention must next be shown. Where common intention is inferred from direct financial contributions, those contributions also readily constitute detrimental reliance. In express common intention cases, the claimant must show detrimental reliance separately. While financial contribution, direct or indirect, to the purchase is not required at this stage, the courts have generally required that the conduct relied on be 'referable' to the acquisition of an interest in the property, and not something which the claimant would have done anyway. This approach effectively excludes 'normal' domestic contributions to family life from consideration. However, it has been observed that a wider range of conduct has sometimes been admitted at this stage in express intention cases than is permitted as a basis for finding the intention to share in inferred intention cases.[122]

Here again, however, recent cases have taken a hard line, insisting that the conduct relied upon be clearly referable to the acquisition of a beneficial interest, excluding even quite extensive domestic and business conduct on the basis that it was explicable for other reasons. In *James v Thomas*,[123] the judge considered that, assuming sufficient evidence of a relevant common intention, the claimant's conduct could not constitute detrimental reliance:

James v Thomas [2007] EWCA Civ 1212

> 36. It would unreal to think that Miss James did what she did in reliance on such a promise. The true position...is that she worked in the business, and contributed her labour to the improvements to the property, because she and Mr Thomas were making their life together as man and wife. The Cottage was their home: the business was their livelihood. *It is a mistake to think that the motives which lead parties in such a relationship to act as they do are necessarily attributable to pecuniary self-interest.* [emphasis added]

Compared with some pre-*Stack* cases, recent cases fall at the stricter end of the spectrum, privileging the mercenary-minded over those who simply get on with life.[124]

Quantification

If intention and detrimental reliance are proved, the court must quantify the parties' beneficial shares. At this point, the general approach in *Stack v Dowden* applies.[125] Having regard to all the factors identified by Baroness Hale in paragraph 69 of *Stack*, extracted above, the court must discern the shares which the parties intended (expressly or otherwise), not simply achieve an outcome which it thinks fair. Baroness Hale also suggested that in sole-owner

---

[122] E.g. *Grant v Edwards* [1986] Ch 638, 657A–B, per Browne-Wilkinson V-C; cf the stricter approach of Nourse LJ, at 648G–H; *Hammond v Mitchell* [1991] 1 WLR 1127; *Eves v Eves* [1975] 1 WLR 1338; *Cox v Jones* [2004] EWHC 1486.

[123] [2007] EWCA Civ 1212.

[124] Compare Gray and Gray's analysis of the case law prior to these cases: (2009), 7.3.46.

[125] *Holman v Howes* [2007] EWCA Civ 877.

cases, the question of who paid for what may have greater relevance than it does in joint names cases.[126]

The first reported application of *Stack v Dowden* in a sole-owner case was a Privy Council decision, *Abbott v Abbott*,[127] in which Baroness Hale again gave the lead judgment. The husband (the owner) had conceded that the wife had an interest in the property and that she had contributed financially to its acquisition, applying her income towards the mortgage instalments. The only issue, therefore, was the size of her share. The case and its outcome were not dissimilar from *Midland Bank v Cooke*.[128] The parties had been married for nearly 20 years and had children. All their income went into a joint account from which they paid the mortgage, for which they were jointly liable; their home had been built on land given to them both by the husband's mother. Examining the whole course of the parties' conduct, the Privy Council upheld the trial judge's conclusion that the wife was intended to have a half-share. As in *Cooke*, the fact that the parties were married might also have reinforced the case for equal shares. It should not be expected that equal shares will generally be found in sole-name cases: it will all depend on what view of the parties' intentions the court derives from the facts.

What is a 'domestic' case?

The *Stack v Dowden* approach to common intention constructive trusts is predicated on a distinction between the 'domestic' or 'consumer' and 'commercial' contexts. Early in her speech, Baroness Hale noted:

Stack v Dowden [2007] UKHL 17

42....the recognition in the courts that, to put it at its lowest, the interpretation to be put on the behaviour of people living together in an intimate relationship may be different from the interpretation to be put upon similar behaviour between commercial men. To put it at its highest, an outcome which might seem just in a purely commercial transaction may appear highly unjust in a transaction between husband and wife or cohabitant and cohabitant.

Lord Hope agreed:

3....Where the parties have dealt with each other at arms length it makes sense to start from the position that there is a resulting trust according to how much each party contributed....But cohabiting couples are in a different kind of relationship. The place where they live together is their home. Living together is an exercise in give and take, mutual co-operation and compromise. Who pays for what in regard to the home has to be seen in the wider context of their overall relationship. A more practical, down-to-earth, fact-based approach is called for in their case. The framework which the law provides should be simple, and it should be accessible.

---

[126] Ibid., [69].

[127] [2007] UKPC 53. The case concerned the law of Antigua and Barbuda, where there is no equivalent of the Matrimonial Causes Act 1973 (MCA 1973); property law therefore determines spouses' entitlements on divorce.

[128] [1995] 4 All ER 562.

Baroness Hale, for the majority, built on this analysis in identifying the appropriate starting point:

> 54. ... It should only be expected that joint transferees would have spelt out their beneficial interests when they intended them to be different from their legal interests. Otherwise, it should be assumed that equity follows the law and that the beneficial interests reflect the legal interests in the property. I do not think that this proposition is controversial ... It has even more force ... in the consumer context.[129]

From this flowed the very strong presumption in *domestic* joint name cases of beneficial joint tenancy, and the holistic search for the parties' intentions regarding beneficial co-ownership. *Stack* thus exemplifies what Dewar has called the 'familialization' of trusts law: developing trust law doctrine in a way that better accommodates the family context.[130] Lord Neuberger, by contrast, strongly contested the wisdom and propriety of judges developing specific principles for 'domestic' cases:

> 101. The determination of the ownership [of] the beneficial interest in a property held in joint names primarily engages the law of contract, land and equity. The relevant principles in those areas have been established and applied over hundreds of years, and have had to be applied in all sorts of circumstances. While both the nature and the characteristics of the particular relationship must be taken into account when applying those principles, the court should be very careful before altering those principles when it comes to a particular type of relationship ...
>
> 102. ... A change in the law, however sensible and just it seems, always carries a real risk of new and unforeseen uncertainties and unfairnesses. That is a particular danger when the change is effected by the court rather than the legislature, as the change is influenced by, indeed normally based on, the facts of a particular case, there is little room for public consultation, and there is no input from the democratically elected legislature.
>
> 107. ... [W]hile the domestic context can give rise to very different factual considerations from the commercial context, I am unconvinced that this justifies a different approach in principle to the issue of the ownership of the beneficial interest in property held in joint names ...

But what is the scope of the majority's 'familial' trusts law?[131] *Stack* involved a long-term cohabiting couple with four children and their shared home. Consider these examples: the purchase of a holiday home, or of a pied-à-terre occupied by only one party during the working week; blood relatives who live together; the joint purchase by an adult child and his or her parent of a home to be occupied for the foreseeable future by the parent alone;[132] or a purchase by friends. What if cohabitants or spouses are also business partners—is the case nevertheless 'domestic'?[133] If 'mercenary considerations' may be 'more to the fore' between

---

[129] Contrast various business contexts where, especially, the parties would presumably not wish the doctrine of survivorship to apply: [2007] UKHL 17, [57].

[130] Dewar (1998b).

[131] Cf Law Com (2002).

[132] Cf *Abbey National Bank v Stringer* [2006] EWCA Civ 338; *Ledger-Beadell v Peach and Ledger-Beadell* [2006] EWHC 2940.

[133] Lord Walker suggested that the doctrine of resulting trust might remain relevant here: [2007] UKHL 17, [32].

cohabiting couples than between spouses,[134] what prominence might we to expect such considerations to have in other cases?

Case law is exploring these issues. In *Adekunle v Ritchie*,[135] the presumption of beneficial joint tenancy was applied to a mother and son who had in joint names purchased a property which both occupied for some years until the mother's death. The judge held that the circumstances were sufficiently unusual to depart from the presumption, suggesting that outside the context of cohabiting couples, it may be easier to conclude that the parties did not intend a beneficial joint tenancy.[136] The primary purpose of this purchase had been to acquire a home for the mother, who could not use the 'right to buy' option over her council house without the son's assistance in obtaining a mortgage; the parties had kept their finances separate; the mother had nine other children with whom she had good relations, and so it was inconceivable that she would have intended to have a beneficial joint tenancy with the son, with the effect that he would take the house (her only sizeable asset) on her death under the doctrine of survivorship.[137] However, the son was clearly intended to have some interest, since the property had been put in joint names with a joint mortgage; he had lived in the house when it was bought; he had made some financial contribution to the mortgage payments. The judge found that the parties' financial contributions justified at most a 25 per cent share for the son, but (for reasons that were not closely articulated) increased his share to a third pursuant to the 'holistic' examination required by *Stack*. Judge Behrens was clearly less than comfortable in conducting that exercise, acknowledging the 'subjectivity and uncertainty' of the task highlighted by Lord Neuberger in his minority opinion in *Stack*.[138]

By contrast, in *Laskar v Laskar*,[139] the Court of Appeal held that the presumption of beneficial joint tenancy did not apply at all where mother and daughter purchased the mother's former council house in joint names with a joint mortgage as an investment: the property was let (the rent covering the mortgage) and the mother moved to live with another daughter. A family relationship does not of itself attract the presumption:

Laskar v Laskar [2008] EWCA Civ 347

LORD NEUBERGER:

15. . . . It is by no means clear to me that the approach laid down by Baroness Hale . . . in [*Stack*] was intended to apply in a case such as this. In this case, although the parties were mother and daughter and not in that sense in an arm's length commercial relationship, they had independent lives, and . . . the purchase of the property was not really for the purpose of providing a home for them. . . .

17. It was argued that this case was a midway between the cohabitation cases of co-ownership where property is bought for living in, such as *Stack*, and arm's length

---

[134] *Stack v Dowden* [2007] UKHL 17, [69].

[135] [2007] EW Misc 5 (EWCC).

[136] Ibid. at [65]. Dixon suggests that rather than being unusual this may simply feel 'unfair': (2007b), 459–60.

[137] At [66]–[67].

[138] At [68].

[139] [2008] EWCA Civ 347.

commercial cases of co-ownership, where property is bought for development or letting. In the latter sort of case, the reasoning in *Stack v Dowden* would not be appropriate and the resulting trust presumption still appears to apply. In this case, the primary purpose of the purchase of the property was as an investment, not as a home. In other words this was a purchase which, at least primarily, was not in "the domestic consumer context" but in a commercial context. To my mind it would not be right to apply the reasoning in *Stack v Dowden* to a case such as this, where the parties primarily purchased the property as an investment for rental income and capital appreciation, even where their relationship is a familial one.

He further held that even if the presumption *did* apply, it would readily be rebutted for various reasons, several similar to those relied on in *Adekunle*.[140] The case was therefore decided, in the absence of any agreement between the parties, on the basis of the parties' financial contributions to the property, resulting in a one-third share for the daughter. Such a strictly mathematical approach to the parties' shares (by contrast, perhaps, with the wider range of factors considered in *Adekunle*) was said to be not unreasonable, since the purchase was an investment.[141]

These two cases show that even if the presumption of beneficial joint tenancy is prima facie applicable, it may readily be rebutted in non-conjugal cases, and the case will then be decided as if the presumption had not applied at all. More generally, we can conclude from these decisions that it is *use of property as a home by the parties together* that attracts both the presumption of beneficial joint tenancy in joint-names cases and the holistic analysis of the parties' intentions in quantifying the beneficial interests.

Before exploring some of the criticisms that have been made of the common intention constructive trust, we complete the picture of land ownership by examining two other claims that may be available in these cases.

3.4.5 PROPRIETARY ESTOPPEL

The ingredients of a proprietary estoppel claim are superficially similar to common intention constructive trusts, and the courts often elide the two,[142] but there are key differences. Indeed, it has been remarked that proprietary estoppel is generally the lesser remedy, in terms of the likely outcome for the claimant.[143] It must be shown first that the legal owner has made some representation or assurance to the claimant that the latter has or will have an interest in property. The claimant must have relied on that to his or her detriment, in circumstances making it unconscionable for the legal owner to deny the claimant an interest. In deciding whether the necessary unconscionability exists, the court should take a broad approach, looking at the matter 'in the round'.[144] It then determines what remedy is 'necessary to satisfy the equity' that has arisen.

---

140 Ibid., [19].
141 Ibid., [33].
142 Lord Walker in *Stack v Dowden* [2007] UKHL 17 retracted from that position: [37].
143 Ibid.; *Q v Q* [2008] EWHC 1874, [113].
144 *Gillett v Holt* [2001] Ch 210; *Jennings v Rice* [2002] EWCA Civ 159.

As in the constructive trust context, the House of Lords has recently distinguished between 'domestic' and 'commercial' proprietary estoppel cases:[145]

Yeoman's Row Management Ltd v Cobbe [2008] UKHL 55

LORD WALKER:

68. ...In the commercial context, the claimant is typically a business person with access to legal advice and what he or she is expecting to get is a *contract*. In the domestic or family context, the typical claimant is not a business person and is not receiving legal advice. What he or she wants and expects to get is an *interest* in immovable property, often for long-term occupation as a home. The focus is not on intangible legal rights but on the tangible property which he or she expects to get. The typical domestic claimant does not stop to reflect (until disappointed expectations lead to litigation) whether some further legal transaction (such as a grant by deed, or the making of a will or codicil) is necessary to complete the promised title.[146]

The nature of domestic cases is such that it is more likely to be reasonable for parties to rely on informal assurances where a business man should insist on legal formality. Writing extra-judicially, Lord Neuberger has noted that emotional or social factors in domestic relationships in which such assurances are made may impede parties from insisting that those assurances be formalized, and that it would be 'unreal' to expect that they should. There is therefore more room for proprietary estoppel to operate in domestic cases than in the commercial context, where parties can be expected formally to protect their legal position rather than rely on informal assurances.[147]

While there are some unorthodox suggestions in constructive trust cases—including *Stack v Dowden* itself—that a common intention never held by the parties can nevertheless be imputed to them,[148] the assurance or representation underpinning a proprietary estoppel claim must actually exist. However, in domestic cases the courts may more readily find that an assurance was intended to be taken seriously and that the claimant's reliance on it was therefore reasonable. As Lord Walker recently remarked in *Thorner v Major*, whether an assurance has sufficient clarity is 'hugely dependent on context': it need only be 'clear enough'.[149] In *Thorner*, the claimant had worked unpaid for decades on his taciturn cousin's farm, the cousin having given several somewhat oblique, allusive indications that he would leave the farm to the claimant. He died without a will, leaving the claimant with nothing. In the context of the parties' relationship and the deceased's character, his remarks and conduct were regarded as sufficiently clear to underpin a claim to the farm in proprietary estoppel, a finding that would never be made in a commercial case. Proprietary estoppel, like the common intention constructive trust, is therefore responsive to the familial context. Nevertheless, even in a domestic case the assurance must relate to a particular asset or ascertainable pool of assets.[150] A general promise that the respondent will support the claimant or that the claimant will be 'financially' secure in the future is not enough.[151]

The detrimental reliance requirement raises problems similar to those experienced in constructive trust cases for claimants who have made only domestic contributions to family

---

[145] For criticism, see Mee (2009), 374.

[146] See also Lord Neuberger at [96]–[97].

[147] Neuberger (2009), 542, contrasting the decisions in *Yeoman's Row Property Ltd v Cobbe* [2008] UKHL 55 and *Thorner v Major* [2009] UKHL 18.

[148] We discuss this below at 3.4.7.

[149] [2009] UKHL 18, [56].

[150] *Jennings v Rice* [2002] EWCA Civ 159; *Thorner v Major* [2009] UKHL 18.

[151] *Lissimore v Downing* [2003] 2 FLR 308; *Layton v Martin* [1986] 2 FLR 227.

life. While domestic contributions are not ruled out entirely,[152] it may be difficult to show such actions were not explicable as a normal aspect of family life, as such not constitute detrimental reliance on the assurance.[153]

But proprietary estoppel again diverges from constructive trust on deciding what remedy is necessary to satisfy the equity. The basis of the remedy is uncertain: should the court be seeking to meet the claimant's expectation in full, or simply to compensate losses incurred in reliance on it, or something in between? Recent cases emphasize that the remedy must be proportionate to the detriment sustained and the claimant's expectation.[154] The court has considerable remedial flexibility It is not confined to awarding a beneficial share in the relevant property. It can instead award monetary compensation[155] or some other sort of interest in the property,[156] or even conclude that no remedy is required because benefits enjoyed by the claimant during the relationship counter-balance any disadvantage sustained.[157] The claimant's expectation may therefore not be met, distinguishing proprietary estoppel from the intention-based outcome of the constructive trust.

3.4.6 IMPROVEMENT TO PROPERTY BY SPOUSE OR CIVIL PARTNER

Statute provides another basis on which (specifically) a spouse, civil partner, or fiancé may acquire a beneficial interest in property belonging to the other.[158] Where one party makes a substantial contribution in 'money or money's worth' to the improvement of land or other property beneficially owned by one or both parties, the contributor will (absent contrary agreement) be found to have acquired a share, or an enlarged share, in that property. The size of that share is as agreed by the parties or, absent any agreement, as seems just in all the circumstances. Unlike the common intention constructive trust or proprietary estoppel, this provision enables certain domestic contributions (contributions of 'money's worth') to generate a beneficial interest without having to prove any intention or assurance that the contributor will thereby acquire a share.[159] The status of the parties' relationship is effectively substituted for that requirement. But it applies only where the contributions 'improve' the property; day-to-day housekeeping and maintenance, acquisition of furnishings and domestic appliances for the home do not suffice.[160]

3.4.7 CRITICISMS OF THE CURRENT LAW RELATING TO OWNERSHIP OF LAND

Many commentators have criticized the law as unfair and uncertain.[161] Property ownership is now theoretically equally open to all, but the preconditions required for property owner-

---

[152] *Greasley v Cooke* [1980] 1 WLR 1306; *Campbell v Griffin* [2001] EWCA Civ 990.

[153] *Lissimore v Downing* [2003] 2 FLR 308; *Coombes v Smith* [1986] 1 WLR 808; cf *Grant v Edwards* [1986] Ch 638, 656; *Wayling v Jones* [1995] 2 FLR 1029; *Henry v Henry* [2010] UKPC 3.

[154] *Jennings v Rice* [2002] EWCA Civ 159; *Gillett v Holt* [2001] Ch 210.

[155] *Dodsworth v Dodsworth* (1973) 228 EG 1115; *Jennings v Rice* [2002] EWCA Civ 159.

[156] E.g. the entire freehold: *Pascoe v Turner* [1979] 1 WLR 431; a life interest: *Greasley v Cooke* [1980] 1 WLR 1306.

[157] *Sledmore v Dalby* (1996) 72 P & CR 196.

[158] Matrimonial Proceedings and Property Act 1970, s 37; Civil Partnership Act 2004 (CPA 2004), s 65; Law Reform (Miscellaneous Provisions) Act 1970, s 2; CPA 2004, s 74(2); *Dibble v Pfluger* [2010] EWCA Civ 1005. The provision originates in Law Com (1969), paras 56–8.

[159] Cf *Stack v Dowden* [2007] UKHL 17, [70].

[160] See *In re Nicholson (Deceased)* [1974] 1 WLR 476.

[161] For a useful survey pre-*Stack v Dowden*, see Law Com (2006), Pt 4.

ship to arise where there is no express declaration of trust often—particularly in sole-name cases—prevent family members not engaged in paid employment from acquiring ownership of assets on which family life is based. Particular problems arise with common intention constructive trusts from the need to base the trust on the parties' intentions regarding property ownership, and the courts' general reluctance (in sole-name cases) to infer such intentions from anything other financial contributions to the acquisition of the property. As more couples cohabit outside marriage, the law discussed here is becoming increasingly significant in practice because cohabitants who separate depend principally on the general law to divide their property. Criticism of the law therefore merits close examination. We address five problem areas relating particularly to constructive trusts: (i) the empirical basis for the approach developed in *Stack v Dowden*; (ii) the problems surrounding 'intention'; (iii) the understanding of detrimental reliance; (iv) the situation of the homemaker; and (v) the uncertainty of the law.

The empirical basis for *Stack v Dowden*

Legal presumptions fill the gaps where there is no actual evidence of what parties intended, on the basis that, given circumstance y, individuals can (the courts think) generally be expected to intend x. The presumption of beneficial joint tenancy that accordingly arises from parties taking joint legal title is in turn rebutted (in the absence of express evidence on this point) if the case is found to be (factually) 'very unusual', such that the parties must have intended something else. In the course of their judgments, both Baroness Hale and Lord Neuberger sought to describe what people may, or may not, be taken to intend in particular circumstances. But, crucially, they offered rather differing assessments of the same facts.[162]

The majority's presumption of beneficial joint tenancy was based on the strong assumption that putting the house in joint names is a meaningful decision:

Stack v Dowden [2007] UKHL 17

BARONESS HALE:

66. . . . [I]t will almost always have been a conscious decision to put the house into joint names. Even if the parties have not executed the transfer, they will usually, if not invariably, have executed the transfer which precedes it. Committing oneself to spending large sums of money on a place to live is not normally done by accident or without giving it a moment's thought.

But as Baroness Hale acknowledged, parties' actions regarding house purchase are not necessarily as deliberate or even voluntary as we might assume:

67. This is not to say that the parties invariably have a full understanding of the legal effects of their choice: there is recent empirical evidence from a small scale qualitative study to confirm that they do not [(Douglas, Pearce, and Woodward (2007b)]. But that is so whether or not there is an express declaration of trust and no-one thinks that such a declaration can be overturned, except in cases of fraud or mistake . . . Nor do they always have a completely free choice in the matter. Mortgagees used to insist upon the home being put in the name of the

---

162 Contrast [2007] UKHL 17, [66]–[67], Baroness Hale with [113]–[116], Lord Neuberger.

person whom they assumed would be the main breadwinner. Nowadays, they tend to think that it is in their best interests that the home be jointly owned and both parties assume joint and several liability for the mortgage. (It is, of course, a matter of indifference to the mortgagee where the beneficial interests lie.) Here again, this factor does not invalidate the parties' choice if there is an express declaration of trust, nor should it automatically count against it where there is none.

However, it is one thing not to ignore the fact of purchase in joint names, quite another to erect a strong presumption that the parties thereby intended a beneficial joint tenancy. If parties who *expressly* declared a beneficial joint tenancy fail to appreciate its significance, it is difficult to presume that parties who bought a home together without making such a declaration nevertheless intended to create a beneficial joint tenancy, particularly (perhaps) where they contributed different amounts to the purchase.[163] In practice, evidence of clear, *common* intention about property ownership seems scarce:

G. Douglas, J. Pearce, and H. Woodward, 'Money, Property, Cohabitation and Separation: patterns and intentions', in J. Miles and R. Probert (eds), *Sharing Lives, Dividing Assets* (Oxford: Hart Publishing, 2009)

In our study, we found that the type of ownership of property – joint or sole, joint tenancy or (rarely) tenancy in common – established at the point of purchase was selected for a variety of reasons or no conscious reason at all. Whilst one would expect that cohabitants might have poor recollections of conversations and advice which had taken place several years before they were interviewed, our discussions with practitioners confirmed that, even at the time, most couples are not interested in such matters. Moreover, as some cohabitant respondents explained, a joint meeting with a conveyancer may not be the right time or setting in which to consider coolly how to protect one's individual interests. At the same time, other, more wily (or more astute) cohabitants may be able to mislead partners so that they fail to assert their own interests or may not have any to protect. The complexity of the law and the opacity of the legal jargon may contribute to the parties' lack of understanding of their positions, and explanations written by lawyers for whom such language is commonplace may not be sufficiently clear to overcome the difficulties.

Baroness Hale and Lord Neuberger also attached different significance to parties' money management practices as a reflection of their intentions regarding beneficial ownership of the home.[164] Empirical research into couples' money management shows that more spouses than cohabitants pool their resources, but that cohabiting *parents* act more like spouses in their money management than childless cohabitants.[165] That Stack and Dowden, long-term cohabiting parents, did *not* pool their resources may thus seem 'unusual'. However, researchers caution against making assumptions about the nature and commitment of couples' relationships, never mind their intentions regarding ownership of their *home*, from simplistic analysis of their general money management.[166] There

---

[163] Lord Neuberger: [2007] UKHL 17, [113].
[164] Compare [2007] UKHL 17, [86]–[92] and [131]–[137], [143].
[165] Vogler (2009).
[166] Barlow, Burgoyne, and Smithson (2007), 62–3.

are many pragmatic reasons for keeping money separate (e.g. access to extra credit and tax-free allowances, management of personal debts, even sheer inertia) which do not necessarily indicate that parties regard themselves as separate financial entities; as in *Fowler v Barron*, separate bank accounts may conceal a de facto pooling arrangement.[167] Lord Neuberger remarked that 'there is a substantial difference, in law, in commercial terms, in practice, and almost always in terms of value and importance, between ownership of a home and the ownership of a bank account or, indeed, furniture, furnishings and other chattels'.[168] For him, parties' treatment of their household finances, whether pooled or separate, does not necessarily cast light on their intentions regarding home ownership where the parties have made different financial contributions to its purchase. Conversely, if they generally keep their finances separate but put the *home* into joint names (as Stack and Dowden did), that might suggest they had different intentions regarding the home. But even there, he would be cautious about drawing any inference about joint ownership.[169]

Empirical research can improve our understanding of how people behave in relation to their property and finances, and what they think about them, in order to inform courts and policy-makers. Real life is more complicated than neat legal presumptions can accommodate. Gillian Douglas and colleagues drew the following conclusions from their study of cohabitants' property disputes, having analysed their data in light of Baroness Hale's 'paragraph 69' factors:

G. Douglas, J. Pearce, and H. Woodward, 'Money, Property, Cohabitation and Separation: patterns and intentions', in J. Miles and R. Probert (eds), *Sharing Lives, Dividing Assets* (Oxford: Hart Publishing, 2009), 159

Couples' relationships vary infinitely, in terms of why they cohabit initially and why they remain cohabiting, their economic and domestic positions, their personalities, the dynamics of their relationship, the changes they undergo as life proceeds, and how far they can or do make financial contributions to keeping the relationship going and acquiring property during it. The way they hold property, and the way they organise their finances, as our study and others' demonstrate, may in turn reflect this myriad of circumstances and does not always conform to what one might logically or rationally predict or assume. It is arguable whether, on the breakdown of their relationship, a couple should be held to arrangements which have arisen during their relationship in response to circumstances as if they were by common intention.

Baroness Hale's list of factors was intended to capture and encapsulate this variety and to indicate which elements might be relevant to establishing the parties' 'true intentions', but our study gives little encouragement to the belief that it will provide a clear pointer towards those cases which are 'unusual' enough to warrant departure from the legal title. On the basis of our findings, we are more inclined to agree with the view of Lord Neuberger:

'To say that factors such as a long relationship, children, a joint bank account, and sharing daily outgoings of themselves are enough, or even of central importance, appears to me not merely wrong in principle, but a recipe for uncertainty, subjectivity, and a long and expensive examination of the facts.'

---

[167] Burgoyne and Sonnenberg (2009).
[168] [2007] UKHL 17, [133].
[169] Ibid., [134].

The problem of intention

As Douglas et al's research suggests, ascertaining parties' intentions regarding beneficial ownership is difficult. It is hard enough to discern what each individually might have
intended, harder to divine commonly held intentions, assuming that they ever existed.[170] As
we noted above, whether we can effectively abandon that search by imputing to the parties
an intention that they never actually had is a controversial issue to which the Supreme Court
is likely to have to return in *Kernott v Jones*.[171]

Finding express evidence of common intention

Happy families rarely think about what each individuals' entitlements in relation to the
home may or may not be, and are even less likely to discuss them expressly:

Lloyds Bank v Rosset [1991] 1 AC 107, 127–8

LORD BRIDGE

Spouses living in amity will not normally think it necessary to formulate or define their
respective interests in property in any precise way. The expectation of parties to every happy
marriage is that they will share the practical benefits of occupying the matrimonial home
whoever owns it. But this is something quite distinct from sharing the beneficial interest in
the property asset which the matrimonial home represents. These considerations give rise
to special difficulties for judges who are called on to resolve a dispute between spouses who
have parted and are at arm's length as to what their common intention or understanding with
respect to interests in property was at a time when they were still living as a united family and
acquiring a matrimonial home in the expectation of living in it together indefinitely.

One judge has described as 'grotesque' the idea of 'a normal married couple spending the
long winter evenings hammering out agreements about their possessions'.[172] But failure to
devote at least one or two evenings to that exercise may cause uncertainty and insecurity in
the longer term. These cases can devolve into a 'painfully detailed retrospect':

Hammond v Mitchell [1991] 1 WLR 1127, 1139 (Fam Div)

WAITE J:

The primary emphasis accorded by the law in cases of this kind to express discussions
between the parties ("however imperfectly remembered and however imprecise their
terms") means that the tenderest exchanges of a common law courtship may assume an
unforeseen significance many years later when they are brought under equity's microscope
and subjected to an analysis under which many thousands of pounds of value may be liable
to turn on fine questions as to whether the relevant words were spoken in earnest or in dalli-
ance and with or without representational intent. This requires that the express discussions
to which the court's initial inquiries will be addressed should be pleaded in the greatest detail,
both as to language and as to circumstance.

---

[170] Probert (2008b), 345.
[171] [2010] EWCA Civ 578.
[172] *Pettitt v Pettitt* [1970] AC 777, 810.

This undertaking is now bypassed in joint-names cases to the extent that a common intention to hold a beneficial joint tenancy will be presumed. But it remains key to sole-name cases, unless intention can instead be inferred or—possibly—imputed.

The subjective and gendered nature of intention

As Lord Neuberger noted, imputing intention is a subjective exercise, but so too is inferring an actual common intention. Several items on Baroness Hale's paragraph 69 list are inherently subjective: for example, the 'nature of the parties' relationship'; the parties' 'individual characters and personalities'. In neither case is it clear what specific issue she has in mind and what, if anything, each might suggest about the parties' intentions about the ownership of their home.[173] All depends on the judge's analysis of the facts and his or her decision regarding inferences about the parties' intentions which may properly be drawn from them, rendering outcomes unpredictable.

Moreover, Anne Bottomley has argued that 'intentions' are often construed differently by men and women. She bases her argument on an analysis of reported cases:[174]

A. Bottomley, 'Self and Subjectivities: Languages of Claim in Property Law',
(1993) 20 *Journal of Law and Society* 56, 61–3

Evidence given in [*Lloyds Bank v Rosset*] is not, in my opinion, unusual and illustrates this point:

As soon as we heard he was likely to get the money, we looked round, looked for a suitable home for us and children. I always understood we were going to share whatever we had, big or little. We always discussed it as being ours. The only discussion was in very general terms. We needed a house; we would go out and look for one we could own as a couple for a family. When we found [the house], he said he was glad he would be able to provide a proper home, a place where we could be secure. I understood it would be jointly ours. He'd always indicated it would be a joint venture. Everything we did in the past had been jointly done. If you live with someone, you don't 'dissect'. It was the accepted thing.

This was enough for the trial judge and Court of Appeal, but the more 'orthodox' Lord Bridge was not so easily satisfied:

He wanted explicit evidence that there was an agreement about ownership.

I pause to observe that neither a common intention by spouses that a house is to be renovated as a 'joint venture' nor a common intention that the house is to be shared by parents and children as the family home throws any light on their intentions with respect to beneficial ownership of the property.

[She also quotes the extract from pp 127–8 of Lord Bridge's judgment, set out above.]
   ... It seems to me that this is not only a requirement of a certain jurisprudential approach but also a mode of reasoning and language use which is more conducive to men than women. This may in part be due to material factors and differences in socio-economic strengths and roles, but evidence drawn from psychoanalytical material would suggest that this division

---

173 See Lord Neuberger's analysis: [2007] UKHL 17, [131]–[139]; and Douglas et al (2009).
174 Probert (2001) argues that it may not be safe to draw generalizations from this source.

derives from the construction of gender identity. In other words, it is far more deeply embedded than a simple analysis of economic difference and consequent relative power relations would reveal.

... There is some evidence from the case material to suggest that women too often read silence as positive assent and lack of specificity as covering a number of issues with equal firmness rather than evading the particular issue.

There is also evidence of the great difficulty some women experience in raising issues about property as well as their difficulty in persuading their partners to confront the issue through discussions.

The high hurdle for claimants in sole-name cases

As we have seen, the courts continue to be especially conservative in finding a common intention that the claimant should have a share in sole-name cases. Yet as Simon Gardner has observed,[175] what is odd is not so much the refusal to infer a common intention to share from non-financial contributions in those cases, but rather that the courts should be so quick to assume the existence of such an intention where there is a direct financial contribution to property acquisition. Such contributions might equally be motivated by other intentions, yet there the law assumes 'pecuniary self-interest'.[176] This approach deprives many claimants of a share where either the intention to share might well have existed (albeit unexpressed and not evidenced by the required sort of conduct) or where no intention was held at all, because people in intimate relationships seldom consider ownership of their home. It may be that we cannot expect property law to provide 'fair' outcomes, but these cases fuel further the calls for statutory reform, not least to provide financial relief at the end of non-marital relationships.[177]

Abandoning intention?

While Bottomley would nevertheless retain a concept of intention in this context, other commentators have argued that intention provides the wrong starting point in the family sphere. The focus should instead be on the parties' relationship:

S. Gardner, 'Rethinking Family Property', (1993) 109 *Law Quarterly Review* 263, 282–3

A doctrine centred on the parties' own thinking ostensibly takes its stand on the recognisable individualist platform that the law should not impose obligations on persons other than by their consent. However, it has long been a commonplace that palpable thinking on the subject of property rights is unlikely to be forthcoming on the part of those who are emotionally committed to one another. So if the true facts are adhered to, it is natural that individualist doctrines will give a remedy only infrequently in such cases.

A doctrine centred on the fact of the relationship would allow the law to bypass such specific reference to the parties' thinking, and so give remedies more freely—as indeed seems to be the courts' instinct. The challenge now is to point to some defensible analysis which proceeds on the strength of the parties' relationship rather than of their thinking....[One]

---

[175] Gardner (1993), 264–5.
[176] *James v Thomas* [2007] EWCA Civ 1212.
[177] See chapter 7.

possible analysis ... argues that in at least some cases, the intrinsic logic of trust and collaboration is that the parties should be seen not as keeping separate accounts, ... but as pooling their efforts and their rewards: each operating on joint behalf of both. Being thus in effect mutual fiduciaries, they would hold the relevant property on a trust whose obligations follow from the ideas of trust and collaboration: either, simply, to share the property equally, or to provide for the adequate future support of each.

More recently, in response to *Stack v Dowden*, Gardner has refined this approach to argue that the court's task is to 'effectuate the implications of the parties' relationship'. Thus, where the relationship is found to be 'materially communal', as it was in *Fowler v Barron*,[178] the parties pooling their financial and other resources in a common endeavour in life, the outcome should be equal sharing of the beneficial interest; in other circumstances, as in *Stack v Dowden*, a resulting trust analysis should determine the parties' shares.[179] Attractive as this approach may seem, it suffers from similar empirical and evidential problems as the intention-based test in relying on judicial characterization of the parties' relationship.

The problem of detrimental reliance

The law regarding detrimental reliance in relation to both constructive trust and proprietary estoppel has been accused of gender bias, to the potential disadvantage of both female and male claimants, in generally requiring 'conduct on which the [claimant] could not reasonably have been expected to embark, unless she was to have an interest in the house'.[180] So how do the courts construe parties' conduct?

L. Flynn and A. Lawson, 'Gender, sexuality and the doctrine of detrimental reliance', (1995) 3 *Feminist Legal Studies* 105, 116–18

In their construction of normality, the decisions of the courts display the tenacious hold of the 'separate spheres' ideology [i.e. that woman's place is in the home, and man's place out in the labour market]. All the behaviour which is placed in the realm of the domestic, no matter how arduous, will not amount to detriment because it can be expected of any woman in an intimate relationship with a man. Behaviour which takes the [female] claimant outside the domestic realm is categorised as abnormal, and, in order to explain it, must be placed in the context of a market-like transaction giving rise to a property interest [rather than the product of love or desire to live in a comfortable home]. According to the authorities one cannot expect women, out of the love they have for their partners or of the desire to live in a comfortable place, to pay towards mortgage instalments.[181] Nor is it reasonable to expect to them to spend small sums on improvements, at least when those small sums represent a quarter of all their worldly wealth and their partner is a comparatively rich man.[182] A woman cannot be reasonably expected to wield 14-lb. sledge-hammers[183] or work cement mixers[184] out of

---

178 [2008] EWCA Civ 377.
179 Gardner (2008); see also Harding (2009) on the communitarian aspects of *Stack v Dowden*.
180 *Grant v Edwards* [1986] Ch 638, 648G–H per Nourse LJ; cf the more generous test at 657A–B, per Browne-Wilkinson LJ.
181 *Grant v Edwards* [1986] Ch 638.
182 *Pascoe v Turner* [1979] 1 WLR 431.
183 *Eves v Eves* [1975] 1 WLR 1338.
184 *Cooke v Head* [1972] 1 WLR 518.

love or the desire for more pleasant surroundings. Prompted by such motives, however, it is reasonable to expect women to leave their husbands, move in with their lovers, bear their babies, refrain from seeking employment,[185] wallpaper, paint and generally decorate and design their lovers' houses, and to organize builders working on those same houses, even when this includes the purchase and delivery of building materials.[186] In order to succeed, female claimants must show that they "did much more than most women would do",[187] or rather that they did more than the judges would expect most women to do. If the claimant's conduct is of a type regarded by judges as "the most natural thing in the world for a wife"[188] to have done, she will not succeed. The use of the stereotype as a norm, from which deviation has to be established, is an almost inevitable consequence of adopting Nourse LJ's test. [footnotes from the original]

Similarly, as Lawson observes,[189] men may not be regarded as incurring detriment by undertaking stereotypically 'male' tasks, such as gardening, DIY, and house-decoration.[190] How the courts would react to the male partner in an opposite-sex relationship who undertook child-care and looked after the house while his partner went out to work remains to be seen.[191] More problematic and revealing for this test are same-sex relationships. *Wayling v Jones*,[192] a proprietary estoppel case, involved a 20-year long gay partnership, in which the younger man (Wayling) acted as the other's companion and gave him substantial professional assistance (as a trained chef) in running his hotel and restaurant businesses.

L. Flynn and A. Lawson, 'Gender, sexuality and the doctrine of detrimental reliance', (1995) 3 *Feminist Legal Studies* 105, 118–19

Homosexuality is a troubling presence in such a scheme. One of the problems with same-sex sexual relations is that they call into question the inevitability of basic social norms which underlie patriarchy. While this is not to suggest that homosexuality cannot be appropriated by patriarchal modes of representation, homosexuality is always, to some extent, a challenge. At a basic level it upsets the images of the 'real man' or the 'authentically feminine', disrupting strongly held codes of masculinity and femininity. For the most part, the anxiety which this provokes results in hostility to lesbians and gay men. But when the normalcy-dependent test of detriment is applied to male-male relationships the unnatural qualities of these relations between men can operate in favour of the cohabiting claimant. In the separate spheres ideology which resurfaces in this field, it is not normal for a man to undertake caring, domestic duties. As a result, it is necessary for Balcombe LJ to explain (and to elevate) Wayling's domestic behaviour in the description of him acting as companion and chauffeur in exchange for monetary support. Wayling's activities have a visibility here which no woman's would possess. However, the Court of Appeal does not dwell on this aspect of the case because it can turn to a more conventional pattern of behaviour. Wayling has also engaged in non-domestic activity with Jones, and his work in the various hotels and restaurants which they

---

185 *Coombes v Smith* [1986] 1 WLR 808.
186 *Lloyds Bank v Rosset* [1991] 1 AC 107.
187 *Cooke v Head* [1972] 1 WLR 518, 519.
188 *Lloyds Bank v Rosset* [1991] 1 AC 107, 131.
189 Lawson (1996).
190 *Pettitt v Pettitt* [1970] AC 777.
191 Though note the facts and outcome in *Fowler v Barron* [2008] EWCA Civ 377.
192 [1995] 2 FLR 1029.

ran is deemed to constitute detrimental behaviour. Wayling, a man who lives with another gay man, who works inside and outside the domestic sphere, is visible in a way in which a woman living with Jones would not have been. All of his private behaviour is unnatural and so could amount to detriment in the eyes of a court. All of his public behaviour in the market is conventional and familiar; he does the type of things which men do which are the foundations of contracts and property transactions.

The position of the homemaker

Where legal title to the home is in joint names, family members who have devoted themselves to raising children and looking after the home now benefit from the strong presumption of beneficial joint tenancy that arises following *Stack v Dowden*. It is unclear how the homemaker would fare should the other party seek to rebut that presumption, given the apparent magnetism that financial contributions had in *Stack* itself and the lack of attention to the issue of responsibility for child-care in that case.[193] But later cases augur more favourably for the homemaker.[194] More problematic is the position of the homemaker whose partner is the sole legal owner and presumptive sole beneficial owner too. In the absence of express common intention to share, she will struggle to establish any share in the property for want of both evidence of common intention and proof of detrimental reliance.

The case most commonly used to illustrate the law's perceived unfairness is *Burns v Burns*,[195] which would be decided identically today. Mrs Burns and her partner, who were unmarried although she had taken his name, lived together for nearly 20 years in a house purchased in his name. Mrs Burns raised their children and looked after the home. When the children were older, she took up employment, but was not earning significant income until 15 years into their relationship. From her earnings, she paid some household bills and bought items for the house, including a washing machine, tumble dryer, and furniture. Her partner paid the mortgage instalments. When they separated, she was able to keep the washing machine and other goods that she had bought, but was held to have no share in the home. There was no express common intention that they share the beneficial interest, and in the absence of any financial contribution to the acquisition of the house, no such intention could be inferred. She had little to show for nearly 20 years' contribution to her family, despite her having 'worked just as hard as the man' in her domestic sphere.[196] But Fox LJ concluded that 'the unfairness of that is not a matter which the courts can control. It is a matter for Parliament'.[197]

As Rebecca Probert has observed, the world has changed both legally and socially since Mrs Burns' case. Many family homes are now expressly jointly owned, legally and beneficially, so most couples do not need to rely on the law of implied trusts and estoppel. *Stack v Dowden*, of course, has much to offer homemakers in joint-names cases. Sex equality legislation, more family-friendly employment law, and increased child-care provision have opened up the labour market to many more women, who are therefore more likely to make financial

---

[193] Probert (2008b), 349 is concerned that this augurs badly for homemakers.
[194] Cf the unusual division of responsibilities in *Fowler v Barron* [2007] EWCA Civ 377; *Abbott v Abbott* [2007] UKPC 53, a sole-name case.
[195] [1984] Ch 317.
[196] Ibid., 345, per May LJ.
[197] Ibid., 332.

contributions of a sort that will generate an interest in sole-name cases.[198] But, as the data at 3.2.2 above indicate, full economic equality between the genders has not yet been achieved.

John Eekelaar has strongly criticized the law:

J. Eekelaar, 'A Woman's Place—A Conflict Between Law and Social Values', (1987) 51 *Conveyancer and Property Lawyer* 93, 94

What is significant is that the fact that a woman bears a man a child, that she and the child move into a house with him in the clear expectation that this will constitute the environment in which the child will be nurtured and protected and that she devotes her time fully to the child and the house, cannot together be counted as evidence of an intention that the woman should have an interest in the house, with the relative security of occupation it can bring and the expectation of a share in its capital value should the relationship terminate. Only a person's "financial behaviour" can be considered in deciding what the original intentions might have been.

…Mrs. Burns (as she called herself) was held to have acquired no beneficial interest whatever in the home. No intention that she should do so could be spelt out of her activities after the house was bought. In looking for evidence of such intention, the court confined itself entirely to her income-generating pursuits. Her domestic duties were thought incapable of showing such an intention. "The mere fact that the parties live together and do the ordinary domestic tasks is, in my view, no indication at all that they intended to alter the existing property rights of either of them." The "mere" fact that the bearing and upbringing of a child is the decisive event which for most women permanently reduces their earning capacity, throwing them into dependency on men for their security in both the short and long term is to count as nothing when considering whether the parties may have intended that some form of such security may have been provided. The very activity which deprives a woman of her independent means of acquiring security and saving capital is excluded when deciding whether an alternative form of security was intended. A woman's place is often still in the home, but if she stays there, she will acquire no interest in it.

The uncertainty of the law in practice

Both constructive trust and proprietary estoppel cases are fraught with uncertainty, not least at the stage of quantifying the claimant's interest or deciding how to satisfy the equity. Moreover, as we have seen, uncertainty infects earlier stages of both types of claim, so it is often unclear whether and on what basis any interest will be found. In the case of the common intention constructive trust, there is ample scope for argument, not least about whether the case is a 'domestic' one to which the *Stack v Dowden* approach applies at all, and then in undertaking the wide-ranging factual survey necessary to identify the parties' intentions. It has been observed, in relation to joint-names cases, that it may be impossible to know whether the case in front of you is a 'very unusual' one, in which the presumption of beneficial joint tenancy may be rebutted, unless and until you have examined the 'paragraph 69 factors'.[199] Contrary to Baroness Hale's hopes, this simply promotes costly

---

[198] Probert (2001).
[199] Probert (2008b), 345.

litigation. John Mee has been similarly critical of the flexibility that exists in proprietary estoppel. The thrust of his remarks may also be applied to constructive cases:

J. Mee, 'The Limits of Proprietary Estoppel: *Thorner v Major'*, (2009) 21 *Child and Family Law Quarterly* 367, 383

The existence of an open-ended discretionary estoppel jurisdiction may lead to family quarrels becoming exponentially more bitter through a descent into litigation. A family member who feels ill-used upon a relative's death may be inclined to swallow his disappointment and get on with his life until he learns of the possibility that, if the court sees things his way, he may obtain a remedy against the other people in the family....[A] great deal depends on the court's response to highly subjective issues. Moreover, the uncertainty surrounding the conceptual basis of a claim in proprietary estoppel, including the failure of the courts to date to deal adequately with the issue of remedies, makes it very difficult for the parties to avoid the expense and trauma of a court hearing by reaching an amicable settlement.

3.5 THE CURRENT LAW: ASCERTAINING OWNERSHIP OF OTHER PROPERTY

Title to most forms of property other than land can be acquired without completing onerous formalities. The discussion in the following extract, concerned particularly with whether and how *co*-ownership of property other than land might arise, applies as much to non-spouses as to husband and wife.

Law Commission, *Family Law: Matrimonial Property*, Law Com No 175 (London: HMSO, 1988b)

2.1 In deciding who owns property acquired by the spouses during the marriage the law at present places great weight on who paid for the property. Superficially this may seem reasonable but two examples may serve to show how the results may not reflect the spouses' wishes.

(i) Husband and wife decide to buy a washing machine; one Saturday they look together at various makes and decide to discuss it over the weekend. They decide upon the make they want and on Monday, the husband, who happens to pass on his way to work a shop which has the particular machine in stock, goes and buys the machine. On sale, ownership of the machine passes to the husband.

(ii) A husband is paid in cash, and his wife receives a monthly salary cheque. Because of this, they use his money for rent, food and other day to day necessities, and her money for bills and larger purchases. Consequently all the furniture in the house belongs to her.

Further, the emphasis on who pays creates great disadvantage for a non-earning spouse, who, whatever other contributions he or she may be making to the couple's life together, is likely to end up owning very little of the property which both of them may well regard as "joint".

2.2 It might be thought that the couple could avoid these results by choosing co-ownership. However, co-ownership cannot arise simply because the parties intend to own property in this way. Intention alone is insufficient; there must be some act which is effective to create the co-ownership....

There are various ways—in the vast majority of cases, determined by the general law—in which ownership or co-ownership of property other than land can arise within a family.[200] First, simply paying for an item generates beneficial ownership under the doctrine of resulting trust, which applies equally to property other than land.[201] The common intention constructive trust and proprietary estoppel can also be used outside the land context to create beneficial ownership of chattels and other property.[202] More specifically, property purchased using funds pooled, either in cash or in a bank account held jointly both legally and beneficially,[203] will belong to both parties. Otherwise, one party purchasing an item for joint use does not of itself generate joint ownership.[204] Second, ownership of chattels can be transferred either by using a deed or by the property being delivered to the new (co)owner with an intention to transfer ownership. It can be difficult to prove delivery between spouses,[205] especially in such a way as to create co-ownership. Third, an owner of property can in theory orally[206] declare himself to hold the asset on trust for another, provided it is made clear that he intends to become a trustee and does not just indicate a wish that the other party should have an interest. Fourth, special statutory rules determine the ownership of property bought with savings made from a housekeeping allowance.[207]

The Law Commission's view of the current law is that creating co-ownership (specifically) can be difficult:

> 2.4...[E]ven when a married couple have thought about it and wish their property to be co-owned, creating co-ownership may present difficulties. In what we suspect is the more usual case, where the couple have not thought about it at all, but if asked would say that they *assumed* much of their property was co-owned, they would be wrong.

In the next two sections, we focus on two specific issues: express trusts and bank accounts.

Express trusts of other property

As noted above, express trusts of property other than land can be created orally, provided that the speaker manifests a clear intention to create or transfer the relevant interest. As with express common intention constructive trusts of land, this creates scope for litigation over conversations held long ago. In one case, a yacht (bought with the man's funds and in which the parties intended to sail the world following his divorce) was found to be owned by the parties in half-shares, owing to conversations in which he had repeatedly referred to the boat as 'ours':

Rowe v Prance [1999] 2 FLR 787, 792–5 (Ch Div)

NICHOLAS WARREN QC (sitting as a deputy judge of the High Court):

In his witness statement, [Mr Prance] says that he meant this in the sense that people might refer to the hotel or restaurants they visit together as 'our' hotel or restaurant; and that he

---

[200] The following discussion is taken largely from Law Com (1988b), para 2.2.
[201] As does the presumption of advancement, recently abolished: see 3.4.3.
[202] E.g. *Parrott v Parkin* [2007] EWHC 210, in relation to a boat.
[203] See further below.
[204] Law Com (1988b), para 2.3 considers how the law of agency might apply.
[205] *Re Cole* [1964] Ch 175.
[206] Cf the writing requirement for land: 3.4.1 above.
[207] See 3.8.1 below: Married Women's Property Act 1964, now the Matrimonial Property Act 1964.

would refer to the previous boats he had owned as 'our' boat to the crew he had on board. In oral evidence, he gave a rather different explanation. He said he did not like to boast, and preferred to refer to the boat as 'our' boat so as to remove the spotlight—my word not his—as it were from him....I found all that very unconvincing. I consider that Mr Prance's use of the word 'our' on many occasions was a reflection of how he wanted Mrs Rowe to think things were. It was the only expression of his intention and it is the effect of those words with which I am concerned....

...There was...a conversation in which Mrs Rowe raised the issue of her security [She had given up her rented accommodation and put her furniture in storage to live on the boat....[The] response from Mr Prance...was that her security was his ability to sail the boat *and her interest in it.*

Unlike many assets, ownership of boats has to be registered. In this case, the boat was registered in Mr Prance's sole name. What bearing did that have?

[Ms Rowe] asserts that she was told by Mr Prance that the boat could not be registered in their joint names because she did not hold an Ocean Master's certificate....Of course, no such certificate is necessary for yacht ownership at all. But if Mr Prance *did* say something to that effect, it is strong evidence of ownership on the part of Mrs Rowe: otherwise Mr Prance would not have made such a statement but would have said—if there was an occasion for him to need to say anything at all—that the boat was entirely his....

I am satisfied that Mr Prance effectively constituted himself an express trustee of the boat....

The judge then turned to the size of the parties' shares:

Nothing express was said to that effect, but the regular use of the word 'our' indicates to me an intention that there was no distinction to be drawn by Mr Prance between himself and Mrs Rowe so far as concerned ownership of the boat. Moreover, the discussion about security indicates that Mrs Rowe was intended to have a substantial interest. If I am reading too much into the first of these factors (the use of 'our') in deciding that it points to equality, and given also that the second factor (the reference to security) does not necessarily require equality, I consider that I should apply the maxim that equality is equity and hold that the shares are equal.

Since the property at stake was not land, Mrs Rowe did not need to prove any detrimental reliance on Mr Prance's oral statements about ownership of the boat in order to make them binding. Those who live in houseboats and caravans[208] may therefore acquire a stake in their homes more readily than those who live between bricks and mortar.

Bank accounts

Like land held in the name of one party, a sole-name bank account may be subject to a trust giving rise to a beneficial interest in favour of another person. Since a bank account is personal property, an express trust over it may arise orally. In *Paul v Constance*, the repeated statement that 'the money is as much yours as mine', in relation to funds in a bank account

---

[208] Unless the caravan constitutes a fixture, and so land: see Gray and Gray (2009), 1.2.46 et seq.

held in the name of the man but on which his partner had the right to draw, was held to confer on her a half interest in those funds.[209] Conversely, the fact that an account is held in joint names does not necessarily mean that both parties are beneficially entitled to the fund, either at all or to the same degree. This depends on the parties' intentions:

Law Commission, *Cohabitation: The Financial Consequences of Relationship Breakdown*, Law Com CP 179 (London: TSO, 2006)

Ownership of funds in bank accounts

3.38... If the account is fed from the resources of one party, A, but is held in joint names with B merely for convenience—for example, to give B access to funds—B has no beneficial interest in the money in the account until he or she actually exercises the right to draw funds from it. While it remains in the account, the money will belong, under resulting trust principles, to A as the party who fed the account. If B has made no contribution to the account, A will be entitled to terminate B's access to the funds at any time.[210]

3.39 Where both parties contribute to the account, pooling their resources, they will at least be found to own the funds on a resulting trust basis in accordance with their contributions. However, both in pooling cases and in cases where A has provided all the funds, the presumption of resulting trust might be displaced, for example, where there is an express declaration of trust or common intention to the effect that the parties should share the account in some other proportions. Indeed, the court might find that the parties intended to be joint tenants of the beneficial interest, each equally entitled to the whole of the fund.

3.40 Property purchased with funds from a joint account will ordinarily belong to whoever acquires title to that property, even if that person had no or only a part-share in the funds when they were in the account.[211] If, unusually, there is evidence that the assets acquired were intended to be held in the same way as the funds in the account, then that property will be held accordingly.[212] [some footnotes retained from original]

In this context, as with land, the courts may be quicker with spouses and civil partners than with others to imply an intention to pool both funds in the account and property acquired from those funds.[213]

3.6 FAMILY PROPERTY SYSTEMS: OPTIONS FOR REFORM

The law currently picks its way through the parties' intentions and contributions in order to establish whether a given asset is 'his', 'hers', or 'theirs', and if the last, in what shares. But there has long been wide public support for the proposition that the matrimonial

---

209 [1977] 1 WLR 527.
210 *Stoeckert v Geddes (No 2)* [2004] UKPC 54.
211 Ibid.
212 *Jones v Maynard* [1951] Ch 572.
213 E.g. *Jones v Maynard* [1951] Ch 572.

home should be jointly owned.[214] Ought the law prescribe that particular assets are, by law, automatically 'theirs' in equal shares?[215]

3.6.1 BASIC QUESTIONS FOR REFORM OF FAMILY PROPERTY LAW

Any 'family property' regime must address three basic questions: (1) to whom should the scheme apply? (2) to what property should it apply? (3) on what basis should property be shared, and what rights should each party have in relation to it? Major reform is properly a matter for the legislature, rather than judicial development,[216] so that the scheme can be confined to clearly identified situations for which it would be appropriate, and tailored accordingly. What we are principally contemplating here are options for a family property law, created by statute specifically for the family context, not a mere evolution of general property law.

The various answers which can be given to these three questions reflect differing views about the purpose of the law, ideological views about the family relationships involved, and the implications they should have for the property relations between the parties. Reform could be driven by various goals, alone or in combination, for example: to provide more certain determination of property rights; to recognize the economic value of domestic contributions; to protect the position of economically weaker family members; to align the law with public beliefs about what the law is or should be, and so better reflect parties' likely intentions; to promote a particular ideological view about marriage or other family relationships.

None of the three questions can be answered independently from each other. Lorna Fox has developed a useful pair of spectrums on which to evaluate family property regimes.[217] First, does the scheme apply 'broadly' or 'narrowly': to various relationships, or only to a limited class, such as spouses and civil partners? Secondly, is the level of protection 'deep' or 'shallow': do the rights take effect against third parties, or merely bind other family members? Viewed in these terms, a 'deeper' answer to question (3) might merit a 'narrower' answer to question (1): if a scheme confers substantial entitlements (such as automatic co-ownership of a pool of assets), it is likely to be appropriate for a more limited range of relationships.

It is impossible wholly to detach discussion of the position during relationships from the position when they end. For all except spouses and civil partners, the law currently applicable during the relationship largely dictates the division of assets on separation. Moreover, some of the options that have been mooted in this area for spouses (and now civil partners) would apply both during and following marriage. For example, the law could provide that certain property is co-owned in equal shares during marriage and that spouses retain those shares when it ceases; there might be separate rules governing the question of maintenance (income provision) following divorce, but the basic property rights could be fixed. A possible fourth question to add to our list, therefore, is 'at what point in the relationship should

---

[214] Law Com (1973b), paras 4 and 22; public support for joint ownership may not be based on legally relevant reasons: Cooke, Barlow, and Callus (2006), 25.

[215] Kahn-Freund (1952), 135.

[216] *Pettitt v Pettitt* [1970] AC 777, 794–5; *Burns v Burns* [1984] Ch 317, 332 per Fox LJ, and 345 per May LJ; *Stack v Dowden* [2007] UKHL 17, contrast Baroness Hale at [47]–[48], and Lord Neuberger at [101]–[107].

[217] Fox (2003).

family property rights conferred by the scheme arise: only during the relationship; only when it ends; or all the way through?'.

We shall see later in this chapter that various rights, short of full ownership, can be and to some extent have been conferred by legislation on some family members, in particular in relation to the home. Some argue that, given these rights, and the statutory remedies available on divorce and death, there is no need to amend the law of property ownership during relationships. However, it has been said that 'it is a poor and incomplete kind of marital justice which is excluded from continuing marriage relationships and allowed to operate only when those relationships end'.[218] Various proposals have therefore been made to confer property rights on family members during relationships. The Law Commission during the 1970s and 1980s sought to devise co-ownership schemes that could operate during marriage, but none has ever been implemented.[219] More recently, its *Sharing Homes* project considered ownership of the shared home in a wider range of domestic situations, not just on marriage.[220] Renewed interest in joint ownership has arisen following comparative studies of laws applying elsewhere in Europe.[221] Some reform options, modelled on the matrimonial property laws of some European and other jurisdictions, involve 'community' or sharing of wider pools of property and debts. Some propose joint ownership of the home and essential household goods. Others, like the *Sharing Homes* project, simply seek to make the law of trusts better suited to the social and economic realities of family life.

3.6.2 COMMUNITY OF PROPERTY REGIMES

Many jurisdictions have systems of community property for spouses. The range of property covered varies. For example, the Netherlands operates a 'full' or 'universal' community of property; France operates a 'community of acquests', defined in the extract below.[222] Community systems operate on an 'opt-out' basis, allowing couples to choose either separation of property or a form of community different from the default regime. One important characteristic of these systems is that they create an 'immediate' community from the point of marriage. By contrast, systems of 'deferred' community, such as those in Sweden and New Zealand, only arise when the relationship ends; separate property applies during the relationship. The basic precepts of 'immediate' community schemes have been evaluated by the Scottish Law Commission:

Scottish Law Commission, *Matrimonial Property*, Scot Law Com No 86
(Edinburgh: HMSO, 1984)

A "full community property" system

3.2 In a "full community property" system practically all the property of a married couple, including property owned by one of them before the marriage or inherited during it, would be automatically subject to a special form of joint ownership. It would not belong to one spouse or the other but would become "community property". Special rules would be necessary to

---

[218] Law Com (1978), para 0.11.
[219] Law Com (1971), (1973), (1978), (1982a), (1988b).
[220] Law Com (2002).
[221] Cooke, Barlow, and Callus (2006), 2.
[222] Ibid., ch 1.

regulate the management of the community property [by the couple jointly] ... Among the usual consequences of a full community system are these:

(a) The community property is liable for the debts of both spouses. So one spouse may lose all the property he or she brings into the marriage if the other is a spendthrift or becomes bankrupt.

(b) The community property is divided equally on divorce. So one spouse may lose half of the property he or she brings into the marriage, even after a very short marriage.

(c) The community property is divided equally on the death of *either* spouse. So if one spouse dies after, say, a year of marriage, the surviving spouse may have to pay half of the property he or she brought into the marriage to the heirs of the other...

A law introducing a full community system would be extremely complex. In countries with such systems many couples contract out of them. In our view the effect of introducing such a system...would be that many couples would be put to the expense and inconvenience of opting out of it by marriage contract....

A "community of acquests" system

3.3 Under most "community of acquests" systems the only property which becomes community property is that which is acquired by the spouses during the marriage otherwise than by gift or inheritance. There will usually be an equal division of such property on the dissolution of the marriage by death or divorce and joint liability for at least some debts. The advantage of such systems is that they give expression to the idea of marriage as an equal partnership. The disadvantages are complexity and r[i]gidity.

3.4...[T]he important question is whether a community of acquests system would have significant advantages in practice, on the dissolution of a marriage or during its subsistence, over a rule of separate property during marriage with rules for a division of property on dissolution of the marriage by death or divorce...So far as the position on death or divorce is concerned, there is no reason why a rule of separate property during marriage should not co-exist with satisfactory rules for the division of property on death or divorce...So far as the position during marriage is concerned, we do not believe that a community of acquests system would bring about significant benefits for many people. We know from the family property survey that there is already a great deal of voluntary sharing of property by married couples under our system. A community of acquests system would not make very much, if any, practical difference in cases where there already is considerable voluntary sharing and it would be unlikely to make very much practical difference, during the marriage, in those cases where there is little or no sharing. The crucial problem here is the day to day management of the community funds...To require the consent of *both* spouses to any dealing with community assets would be unwieldy. That leaves two solutions—to allow either spouse to deal with any part of the community property, or to allow each spouse to deal with the property he or she brought into the community. The first solution leaves both spouses at risk, while neither protects the non-earning spouse. Of course, the general rules on the management of the spouses' property could be qualified by special rules for the protection of the non-earning spouse, but that is also the case in separate property systems. The aspect of a community of acquests system which appealed to the minority of commentators supporting this type of system was the governing principle itself. In our view, any advantage of adopting this governing principle would, during the marriage, be more symbolic than real and would be outweighed by the disadvantages of introducing a community of acquests system.

The Scottish Law Commission felt that the principal disadvantage of community property was the 'excessive legal complexity' it might entail. Some spouses would fall within the scheme, others would opt out; third parties would need to know who was in and who was out, and that might require a register. For those within the scheme, detailed rules would have to pre-scribe what assets fell within the community: how should gifts, inheritances, compensation for injury, and so on be categorized? Even within the scheme, unless universal community were adopted, each marriage would have three pots of property—his, hers, and theirs—and further rules would have to deal with the relationship between these three pots. For example, if the wife sold an asset acquired before marriage and used the proceeds to buy something during the marriage, should that new asset be hers or theirs? What if the wife spent money restoring a painting belonging to the husband: should his fund have to compensate hers? On balance, the Commission felt that it would be easier and cheaper simply to let those who wished to share par-ticular assets do so under the general law, rather than to erect a complex scheme of community property from which the process of opting-out might be rather more elaborate and costly.[223]

In researching some European systems, Cooke, Barlow, and Callus[224] found lawyers and notaries were broadly satisfied with the law, though the degree of public awareness and understanding of the law was questioned. The simplicity of the 'universal' Dutch commu-nity system was appreciated: all property is included. Nevertheless, the researchers did not advocate the adoption of any form of immediate community of property in England and Wales. They considered that the original rationale of such schemes—to protect the interests of wives who looked after home and family rather than undertaking paid employment—sits uneasily with contemporary women's independence, and noted that the trend within Europe is to move away from full and immediate community in favour of more limited and deferred systems. Moreover, the results of their English attitudinal survey suggested that the key *debt*-sharing feature of community systems would be unacceptable, even given the option to opt out.[225] The traditional marriage vow—'for better, for worse, for richer, for poorer'—may not translate comfortably into law.

3.6.3 JOINT OWNERSHIP OF HOME, CONTENTS, AND OTHER ASSETS

Automatic co-ownership

The Law Commission has focused on joint ownership of key family assets, particularly the home, rather than community property schemes. The following remarks still have some force, despite *Stack v Dowden*.

Law Commission, *Third Report on Family Property: The Matrimonial Home (Co-ownership and Occupation Rights) and Household Goods*, Law Com No 86 (London: HMSO, 1978)

0.9 ... The present law about the ownership of the matrimonial home during marriage is not only highly technical and sometimes uncertain in application, but inappropriate in

---

[223] Scots Law Com (1984), paras 3.5–3.6.
[224] Cooke, Barlow, and Callus (2006), ch 3.
[225] See also Law Com (1988b), paras 4.17–4.18 on debt-sharing.

substance. The rules now applied to determine the ownership of the home are essentially the same as those which determine the ownership of a commercial or investment property: they ignore the fact that the home is the residence of a family as well as being, in many cases, its major capital asset. Husband and wife each contribute to the home in their different ways—the wife's contributions are no less real because they may not be financial—and the home is essential to the well-being of the family as a whole. In our view these factors make the matrimonial home a unique item of property, and one to which a unique law of co-ownership should apply ...

The Commission accordingly developed a scheme whereby spouses would enjoy statutory co-ownership of the matrimonial home as joint tenants. The scheme would not apply where they were express co-owners under the general law or in other prescribed circumstances. The courts would retain their powers on divorce and death to adjust spouses' property rights under the scheme. The Matrimonial Homes (Co-ownership) Bill 1980 was put before Parliament but withdrawn before being fully debated.[226] The Commission later took the view that, since joint ownership of the matrimonial home had become standard practice, there was no pressing need for its controversial scheme.[227] Instead, it advocated statutory joint ownership of certain other property (not acquired for business purposes), including household goods and cars:[228]

Law Commission, *Family Property: Matrimonial Property*, Law Com No 175 (London: HMSO, 1988b)

2.8 The present law [of ownership of property other than land] is unsatisfactory because its application may not result in co-ownership of property even when a married couple desire this. Actual ownership may be held to depend on factors which neither party considered significant at the time of acquisition. In its treatment of money allowances and gifts of property the law discriminates between husband and wife.[229]

...

4.1 Money may be spent by spouses for many different purposes. However we believe that it is possible to distinguish two main purposes; first the use or benefit of the spouses jointly and, secondly, other uses or benefits. There is evidence to suggest that spouses regard much of their property as jointly owned even when in law it is probably not. Dissatisfaction with the present law arguably stems from the fact that ownership of the money used and property acquired with it is quite unconnected with the purposes for which it is to be used. The policy of our reform is to create a direct connection between the purposes for which money is spent and its ownership. Accordingly our proposal has two main limbs:

(i) where money is spent to buy property, or property or money is transferred by one spouse to the other, for their joint use or benefit the property acquired or money transferred should be jointly owned.

(ii) where money or property is transferred by one spouse to the other for any other purpose, it should be owned by that other.

---

226 See Fox (2001) and Cretney (2003a), 136–41 on the parliamentary history of the Bill and its collision with *Williams & Glyn's Bank v Boland* [1981] AC 487; Law Com (1982a).
227 Law Com (1988b), para 4.3.
228 On the importance of these assets, see Kahn-Freund (1971), 503.
229 See now the Equality Act 2010, ss 198–200; not in force at October 2010.

In both cases, the general rule should give way to a contrary intention on the part of the paying or transferring spouse, provided that the contrary intention is known to the other spouse....

4.11... Since the proposals apply to purchases by a spouse or transfers by a spouse, anything owned before the marriage will necessarily be excluded. Likewise gifts or inheritances received by one spouse during the marriage are excluded, although the spouse who has received them may still make a transfer to the other spouse or to both of them jointly, in which case the new rules will apply. Most importantly, our proposals are designed for the property bought or transferred for the purposes of the couple's domestic life together ...

Various forms of joint ownership have occasionally resurfaced in reform proposals.[230] But joint ownership schemes have been subject to criticism:

Scottish Law Commission, *Matrimonial Property*, Scot Law Com No 86 (Edinburgh: HMSO, 1984)

3.10 There appear to be four arguments for a scheme of statutory co-ownership of the matrimonial home:

(i) It would give expression to the idea of marriage as an equal partnership.

(ii) It would reward the contributions in unpaid work by a non-earning spouse, particularly a housewife.

(iii) It would bring the law more into line with the views of most married people.

(iv) It would give effect to the view that the matrimonial home should be owned in common because it is used in common.

These arguments can, however, be met by the following arguments:

(i) Statutory co-ownership of the matrimonial home would not be a good way of giving expression to the idea of marriage as an equal partnership. In some cases it would go too far, particularly if it applied to a home owned before marriage, or acquired by gift or inheritance during the marriage. These are not the results of the spouses' joint efforts. In other cases it would not go far enough and could produce results which were unfair as between one spouse and another. If the wife, say, owned the home and the husband owned other property, he could acquire a half share in the home without having to share any of his property. A spouse with investments worth thousands of pounds could allow the other to buy a home and then claim half of it without contributing a penny. The scheme would also work very unevenly as between different couples. If Mr A had invested all his money in the matrimonial home while his next-door neighbour Mr B had mortgaged his home to its full value in order to finance his business, the law would operate very unevenly for the benefit of Mrs A and Mrs B [though the scheme could require both spouses' consent to mortgaging]. It would, in short, be a hit or miss way of giving effect to the partnership ideal.

(ii) Statutory co-ownership of the matrimonial home would not be a good way of recognising contributions in unpaid work by a non-earning spouse. It would benefit the

---

[230] Law Reform Advisory Committee for Northern Ireland (2000); Barlow and Lind (1999); Lord Lester's Civil Partnership Bill (HL), s 9; Cooke, Barlow, and Callus (2006).

undeserving as well as the deserving. Extreme cases can be imagined. A man might marry a wealthy widow, encourage her to buy an expensive house, claim half her house and leave her. Even in less extreme cases statutory co-ownership would be a poor way of rewarding unpaid work. [Some] housewives would get nothing from the new law because its effects would be confined to owner-occupiers [as opposed to tenants[231]] ... Even where the new law did apply, its effects would be totally arbitrary. Not only would the net value of the home vary enormously from case to case, and from time to time, but so too would the respective values of the spouses' contributions.

(iii) Statutory co-ownership would not necessarily bring the law into line with the views of most married people. [The English Law Commission public survey asked whether the home should be legally jointly owned, but did not ask whether that outcome should be achieved by way of a default statutory rule to that effect—Law Com (1973), para 22.]

(iv) It is not self-evident that property which is used in common should be owned in common. Even if this proposition were accepted, it would lead further than co-ownership between spouses. It would lead to co-ownership between the members of a household, including for example, children and parents.

And there were further objections. As with community property, the scheme would be formidably complex, potentially requiring detailed legal advice to protect each spouse's interests, in turn potentially fomenting dispute between otherwise happy spouses, and not necessarily yielding fairer outcomes in return:

(v) A scheme for statutory co-ownership of the matrimonial home would be very complex ... Should, for example, co-ownership come about automatically by operation of law (in which case how would third parties, such as people who have bought the house in good faith, be protected) or should it come about, say, on registration of a notice [on the land register] by the non-owner spouse (in which case would non-owner spouses bother to register before it was too late)? Should co-ownership apply to a house owned by one spouse before the marriage? Should it apply to a home which is part of a commercial or agricultural property? Should it apply to a home bought by one spouse after the couple have separated? If not, should it make any difference if the spouses resume cohabitation for a short period? Should the spouses become jointly liable for any debts secured on the home? When should it be possible for one spouse, or both, to opt out of co-ownership and how should this be done? Should a spouse be able to claim half of the sale proceeds of one home, refuse to contribute to the purchase price of a new home, and then claim half of that one too? If not, how can this be remedied without forcing a spouse to invest in a home he or she does not want to invest in? These are just some of the less technical questions that would have to be answered. .... [A]lthough statutory co-ownership of the matrimonial home seems attractively simple in general terms, it turns out to be surprisingly complicated ...

It was also doubted, given the predominance of joint ownership by spouses under the general law, whether many would want to take advantage of a new scheme. Moreover, since death or divorce would trigger the specific rights and remedies available following those events, superseding the parties' interests under the joint ownership regime, it was felt that little practical benefit would arise from the scheme at all.

---

[231] Law Com (1982a) recommended co-ownership of most leases too.

Automatic co-ownership would at least avoid the need that certainly still arises in some cases in England and Wales[232] to grapple with the law of implied trusts in order to establish parties' beneficial interests in the absence of an express declaration of trust. But because it would have to take effect as joint *equitable* ownership only, Cooke, Barlow, and Callus have argued[233] that very little would be gained in practice. The interest would presumably be overreachable (though overreaching would only occur if there were two trustees). Third parties dealing with the property would in any event seek waivers from all adult occupiers to prevent an overriding interest being asserted. Conferring a share in the property would therefore give no extra power or protection to the non-owner. At the same time, they argued, the increased possibility of an unknown occupier 'coming out of the woodwork' with an overriding interest would cause lending institutions and other third parties to oppose such reform. The only way to guard against this—to bar statutory co-ownership interests from being overriding and to require registration, as the Law Commission recommended[234]— would seriously weaken the theoretical protection for the non-owning spouse: experience from the use of statutory home rights, addressed below, suggests registration would be very unlikely.

Presumption of joint ownership

An alternative might be to presume joint ownership of certain assets, rather than impose it automatically, in an effort to circumvent the complexity and uncertainty involved in seeking to establish ownership of property under the general law. This approach is taken in Scotland in relation to some types of money and property for both spouses and civil partners[235] and (with rather weaker presumptions, applying in some respects to a narrower range of property) cohabitants.[236] The Law Commission rejected this technique for English law. As a rule of evidence, presumptions only assist where there is no evidence supporting a finding of legal ownership, or the evidence is finely balanced, and do not supply the certainty of a rule.[237] Of course, *Stack v Dowden* created precisely this presumption—in strong form— where land is bought in joint names. Readers should refer back to the discussion and criticism of that decision and subsequent case law earlier in this chapter to decide whether the Law Commission's scepticism was well-founded.

3.6.4 BUT IS COMMUNITY OR JOINT OWNERSHIP APPROPRIATE?

Technical problems aside, there is considerable disagreement about whether it is socially and ideologically appropriate to translate the equal partnership of marriage (and now civil partnership) into equal sharing of family property where that is not expressly chosen by the parties.[238]

[232] The Scottish Law Commission's views must be assessed in light of the different general law of property that applies there, in particular, the lack of implied trusts law.

[233] Cooke, Barlow, and Callus (2006), pp 25–6.

[234] Law Com (1982a).

[235] Family Law (Scotland) Act 1985, ss 25–6. Scot Law Com (1984), paras 4.2–4.8.

[236] Family Law (Scotland) Act 2006, ss 26–7. Scot Law Com (1992), paras 16.7–16.13.

[237] Law Com (1988b), para 3.2; compare Scot Law Com (1992), para 16.9 on the practical effect of the spouses' presumption.

[238] E.g. Zuckerman (1978), 51–7; Deech (1980a).

Calls for joint ownership of key family assets by spouses emerged powerfully from the 1950s, when spouses were expected to perform distinct roles in marriage and there was no capital redistribution following divorce. Automatic joint co-ownership would ensure that wives' contributions were valued and their economic position protected. Female labour market participation has increased substantially since the 1950s. But many women are still not employed, and many others work only part-time. If joint ownership is viewed as a means of providing greater economic equality between spouses, there may remain a case for automatic joint ownership.

Alternatively or additionally, automatic sharing or community of property (and of liabilities) could be regarded as a contemporary manifestation of the 'community' that marriage or civil partnership should be understood to create. This could be thought to flow from the parties' express commitment to the legal status of spouse or civil partner, without implying that either party is economically dependent.[239] The parties' chosen legal status could be treated at least as presumptive evidence that they intend to share certain assets. The idea of equal partnership has become a powerful factor shaping property settlements on divorce,[240] and it may be desirable that it should also shape property entitlements during marriage. Indeed, if most spouses use their property as if it were jointly owned, regardless of the technical position, why not reflect that in law? Or should property ownership be left for the parties to arrange as they wish, from a starting point of separation? The following discussion by Mary Ann Glendon was written in the mid-1970s, but much of her analysis remains relevant:

M. Glendon, 'Is there a future for separate property?', (1974) 8 *Family Law Quarterly* 315, 323–7

There is an eternal tension in matrimonial law, in social attitudes, and in every marriage between the community of life that marriage involves and the separate, autonomous existence of the individuals who are associated in this community of life. Emphasis on one or other aspect varies from time to time in the law, in societies and in the lives of couples. John Stuart Mill's idea that marriage ought to be likened to a partnership, and its expression in [marital property regimes that involve sharing] emphasizes the community aspect of marriage.

But there is another idea that has regained great currency in contemporary society and which is in conflict with the ideology of community. This is the notion that marriage exists primarily for the personal fulfillment of the individual spouses and that it should last only so long as it performs this function to the satisfaction of each. [Hence the introduction in many jurisdictions of no-fault, unilateral divorce and clean break divorce settlements.[241]] . . .

. . . [However,] [t]he increased labor force participation of married women includes so much intermittent and part-time work that it cannot be seen as a move towards imminent economic [in]dependence of most married women. Thus, from one point of view, the stage is set for the introduction of more mechanisms to enable each spouse to share in the other's acquests. However, three additional questions must be asked at this point.

In the first place, the factual economic dependence of great numbers of married women must be distinguished from their potential for being economically independent. . . . Therefore, we must ask whether their potential, rather than their actual, status should be emphasized in framing laws affecting the economic relations of spouses.

[239] E.g. Kahn-Freund (1955), 267–8; (1959), 248–9.
[240] *Miller v Miller; McFarlane v McFarlane* [2006] UKHL 24.
[241] See chapters 5 and 7.

Secondly, how much weight should be given to the fact that laws emphasizing and responding to the factual dependence of married women may tend to perpetuate dependence and to discourage the acquisition of skills and seniority needed to make married women economically independent and equal in the labour market?

Finally, ... [c]onceding the compatability of sharing mechanisms with current economic behavior of spouses, how can we assess their compatability with current marriage behavior and ideologies? Is ideology at cross-purposes, in the short run at least, with economic reality? A leading French writer, Dean Savatier, advises married women that their choice is between "la finance" and "la gloire", and counsels them to take the bucks. Others think it is not just a question of choosing between financial security here and now and an illusion of glory later. They feel that opting for devices which shore up the economic role of housewife will, in the long run, work to the economic detriment of women. Certainly a factor to be considered here is the question of whether the role of housewife should be discouraged before a solution to the problem of child care can be seen.

These questions are thorny but cannot be overlooked by law reformers. Many different conceptions of marriage coexist in society at the present time. It is impossible to say which predominates. But when the widespread expectation that marriage will last only so long as it performs its function of providing personal fulfillment is put together with the reality of unilateral divorce, a diminished sense of economic responsibility after divorce, the increasing economic independence of married women, and the expansion of social welfare, the resulting state of affairs does not lead inevitably to the sharing of worldly goods ...

Seen in this light, the system of separation of assets with the possibility it has always offered for purely voluntary co-ownership may come to have the most appeal for the greatest number of people.

Whatever the rationale for joint ownership might be, ought such a scheme extend to cohabitants? The Scottish Law Commission thought not:[242]

Scottish Law Commission, *Matrimonial Property*, Scot Law Com No 86 (Edinburgh: HMSO, 1984)

4.23 We expressed the provisional view ... that a scheme of statutory co-ownership of the matrimonial home could not apply to unmarried couples cohabiting as man and wife. Such a scheme would involve fixed property rights and this would be inappropriate for a relationship as varied as cohabitation. It would presumably be unacceptable to allow a half share in a person's house to be acquired by a person of the opposite sex after, say, one week of cohabitation as man and wife. A minimum duration of two or three years would probably have to be required. Even then, however, there would be practical difficulties in deciding whether a couple came within the definition, and in applying any provisions allowing "opting out" before marriage. Third parties dealing with one of the parties would be placed in an impossible position. Similar objections applied, in our view, to extending a scheme for statutory co-ownership of household goods to unmarried cohabiting couples. They would apply *a fortiori* to any more general community property scheme.

---

242 See also Law Com (1982a), para 111; cf Law Com (1988b), para 4.21.

By contrast, the Law Reform Advisory Committee for Northern Ireland, while recognizing the diversity of cohabiting relationships, recommended that automatic co-ownership of the home,[243] housekeeping money, and household goods should apply to those cohabiting either for two years or who have a child:[244]

Law Reform Advisory Committee for Northern Ireland, *Matrimonial Property, Report No 10* (Belfast: TSO, 2000)

4.9 The argument against extending [property rights] to cohabitants is that by applying these protections and drawing these inferences, society would or might be perceived as equating the cohabitation relationship with marriage, thereby further undermining the married state and contributing to an increase in cohabitational relationships and thereby further weakening the stable family unit which draws its full strength only from the married state. Society, it would be argued, would be placing cohabitation on the same moral and functional plane as marriage.

4.10 However, where parties are living in a committed and stable relationships to the extent of sharing their lives and pooling their financial, emotional and physical resources in the common venture of living together as a unit, it is difficult to justify treating their property rights and interests differently from spouses. Their intentions are likely to be the same and the organisation of their financial affairs will be unlikely to differ to any material degree. If the existing law produces potentially unfair and unreal results so far as married couples and particularly wives are concerned, then the results so far as such cohabitants are concerned are likely to be equally unfair and unreal. ...

4.13 ... [O]ur recommendations would represent an enhancement of the position of women in relationships. It would be hard to justify the strengthening of the position of women in marriage relationships and leave untouched the position of women in unmarried relationships who are already in a weaker and more vulnerable position than wives, in view of the absence of the presumption of advancement and ... the lack of availability of any appropriate adjustment powers which the court may exercise in a divorce context.

However, the Committee's perception about the way cohabitants as a group arrange their financial affairs and how they view their property may not be empirically supported: while some do pool, that is not the case for all, especially where there are no children.[245] Moreover, the mere fact of cohabitation may not warrant conferring substantial property rights on the non-owner, particularly if that party has made no particular contribution to or economic sacrifice for the relationship.[246]

3.6.5 MODIFIED TRUSTS LAW FOR THE 'SHARED HOME'

Instead of creating automatic co-ownership, attempts might be made to adapt the law of trusts to deal more predictably and fairly with family situations. Many commentators have pointed to how other Commonwealth courts (notably in Australia, Canada, and New Zealand) have developed more flexible laws of remedial constructive trust, which are not

---

[243] See also Barlow and Lind (1999).
[244] For criticism see Fox (2001).
[245] Vogler (2009).
[246] Cf Scot Law Com (1984), para 3.10(ii), extracted above.

dependent on finding (or creating) a common intention by the parties that ownership be shared.[247]

The Law Commission's *Sharing Homes* project sought to develop a new statutory trust of the 'shared home', to displace the general law of implied trusts and estoppel. The ownership of 'shared homes' would be determined by reference to the parties' various financial and non-financial contributions to their shared life. To use Lorna Fox's terminology, while the scheme was confined narrowly to just one asset (the home), the project was otherwise both wide and deep.[248] It covered all domestic home-sharers, including relatives and platonic friends living together, and conferred full property rights, rather than lesser rights (e.g. to occupy the home). This breadth and depth was its downfall. The Commission felt unable to devise a scheme that would: (i) release cases from the strictures of the current law (particularly the need to find a common intention regarding ownership and the narrow range of relevant contributions); whilst also (ii) producing appropriate outcomes for the full range of relationships. For example, an outcome which would be fair between a married or cohabiting couple may not be fair between an adult child and the parents to whose home he has returned. Parties in those situations are likely to have differing (if often unarticulated) views about whether and when certain contributions should give rise to shared ownership of the property.[249]

The Commission concluded that the law of implied trusts should instead be refined judicially: (i) by inferring the required common intention for a constructive trust in cases where one party has made indirect financial contributions to the acquisition of the property; and (ii) by adopting a holistic approach to the quantification of interests under such trusts.[250] That brings us again to *Stack v Dowden*, in which Baroness Hale consciously took up that invitation. But, as we noted above, subsequent cases suggest that the 'familialization' of trusts law effected by *Stack* has so far had little impact in sole-name cases.

In another sense, however, the *Sharing Homes* project could be regarded as having been too *narrow*. Rebecca Probert has argued that if the justification for reform is to ensure that domestic and other non-financial contributions to inter-personal relationships are properly valued, another raft of candidates for a new scheme emerge:

R. Probert, 'Trusts and the modern woman—establishing an interest in the family home', (2001) 13 *Child and Family Law Quarterly* 275, 285

A ... justification for reform might be that, on principle, domestic contributions should be treated in the same way as financial contributions. This would require reform to embrace both married and cohabiting couples. However, it should also be noted that those who share a home are not the only ones who make contributions to each other's welfare. Recent statistics on the extent to which informal care is being provided found that while 4% of adults were caring for someone who lived with them, 7% were providing equally significant levels of care for someone who lived in another household.[251] The only justification for excluding the latter from consideration would be the assumption that their services are provided out of 'love and affection', which would merely perpetuate one of the major deficiencies of the current law.[252]

---

[247] See Gray and Gray (2009), 7.3.77 et seq; Rotherham (2004); Mee (1999); Gardner (1993).
[248] Fox (2003).
[249] Law Com (2002), paras 3.55–3.74. See Miles (2003); Fox (2003); Mee (2004).
[250] Law Com (2002), 86. For criticism, see Mee (2004), Probert (2002b).
[251] See now data from ONS (2010e), pp 113 et seq.
[252] See extract from Flynn and Lawson (1995), p 156 above.

3.6.6 SHOULD WE FOCUS ON 'OWNERSHIP' DURING RELATIONSHIPS AT ALL?

Many proposals relating to intact families have focused on ownership. But ownership may not be the most helpful 'conceptual starting point':[253]

J. Dewar, 'Land, Law and the Family Home', in S. Bright and J. Dewar (eds), *Land Law: Themes and Perspectives* (Oxford: OUP, 1998b), 353–4

I want to suggest that, in devising a legislative strategy in this context, we need not think exclusively in terms of ownership; and that ownership thinking may have become something of a strait-jacket. Instead, I want to suggest that, in line with the English tradition of pragmatism in this area, we should think functionally. Thinking functionally about the family home means asking what rights family members need in relation to it. If we can identify what those are or might be, we can set about conferring them directly, without necessarily invoking the language of ownership. This means avoiding the Law Commission's strategy [in pre-*Sharing Homes* projects] of creating equal ownership in order to confer rights incidental to that ownership. The focus would be on status as the mechanism for conferring the necessary rights, not on property. Of course, this begs the question of what we mean by familial 'status' for these purposes, who would qualifying for it, and how the different interests of family members and third parties would be weighed against each other: but at least the strategy would be clear.

In order to get discussion going on these lines, I suggest that there are four broad rights that family members need in relation to the family home: a right of *control over dealings* (such as mortgages or sales); a right of *occupation or enjoyment*; a right of *capital entitlement on sale*, and a right, on the termination of the relationship, to have *basic needs met out of the family resources represented by the family home*.

. . . [T]he incidents of property ownership have been developed judicially in such a way that co-owners of a family home already have many of these rights secured to them—through what I have called the 'familialization' of property law. An equitable interest in land, for example, can form the basis of securing the first two rights of consent to dealings and enjoyment through occupation; and ownership remains pre-eminent in determining the third right, at least where there are no statutory alternatives available for doing so. But, in a family context, or more specifically a context of gender inequality, it needs to be asked whether ownership is a sufficient or necessary basis for securing these rights.

I would suggest that it is neither. It is not necessary, because there are existing instances in which some of these rights are secured to family members *as such*, regardless of their rights of ownership (for example, occupation orders under the Family Law Act 1996, or property distribution orders under the Matrimonial Causes Act 1973); and there is no reason why a status-based logic, which bypasses ownership, could not be extended to securing the other rights mentioned.

Nor is it sufficient, given the weight of evidence suggesting that, despite judicial development, the rules of ownership acquisition operate unfavourably in a family context, especially against women, by according pre-eminence to money contributions to acquisition; and in the light of the fact that ownership is a very crude device for securing all four of the rights mentioned above, especially the fourth. For example, an a priori assumption of equal ownership would translate into a principle of equal division on separation, yet that is a rule that legislatures

[253] See also Deech (1984); Miles (2003).

have generally avoided, on the basis that equal division can lead to serious post-separation inequalities. Instead, distribution of property has to be seen in the light of the parties' post-relationship needs and of other powers concerning maintenance for spouses and children. Vindication of the fourth right therefore requires more than a simple rule about ownership.

... [T]here is a sense in which all four of the rights mentioned are already secured, to some degree, by means of existing legislation ... To that extent, we might say that ownership is in any case fast becoming obsolete as a significant conceptual category in this area; and that, in its pragmatic way, English statute law is groping towards a satisfactory regime for the family home, despite its continuing theoretical attachment to the doctrine of separation. But ... that statutory regime has arisen piecemeal, and varies significantly in its application according to status or the procedural context in ways that are not obviously justified.

If, instead, we were to view the current maze of the law relating to the family home through the grid of the four rights mentioned above, and at the same time reduce our attachment to ownership as the sole vehicle for attaining these rights, we might get some greater clarity about the proper policy in this important area of social and economic life.

Some commentators advocate family ownership schemes, in preference to reliance on the exercise of judicial discretion in favour of economically vulnerable individuals.[254] They emphasize the 'symbolic' value of property ownership,[255] and the psychological security it can provide. However, addressing more specific issues—such as the right to occupy the home, and financial remedies on relationship breakdown—rather than, or alongside, ownership helps us to focus clearly on our objectives. While property ownership itself may seem too substantial an entitlement for some categories of family members, any or all of the 'sub-rights' identified by John Dewar might be appropriate. Unpacking the question in this way may offer a more productive strategy for dealing with today's diverse family relationships.

John Mee observed that the *Sharing Homes* project could be said to have tried to 'treat the symptom of disputes over the ownership of houses rather than address the underlying problem of the fall-out from the breakdown of informal relationships'.[256] Indeed, in concluding its project, the Law Commission diagnosed:

...a wider need for the law to recognise and to respond to the increasing diversity of living arrangements in this country. We believe that further consideration should be given to the adoption, necessarily by legislation, of new legal approaches to personal relationships outside marriage, following the lead given by other jurisdictions...[257]

A flexible scheme of remedies on relationship breakdown may indeed be preferable to a system of fixed property rights. The reform agenda has accordingly shifted from property ownership during relationships to providing fairer outcomes via court-based remedies at the *end* of non-marital relationships, tailored specifically to the type of relationship involved. In the following sections of this chapter, we examine the first two 'rights' suggested by Dewar—occupation rights and control over dispositions of the home—which have to some extent been conferred by legislation independently of ownership. We address the financial and property remedies provided by English law on relationship breakdown in chapters 6 and 7.

---

[254] See Bottomley (1998); Law Com (1971), para 22.
[255] O'Donovan (1985), 112.
[256] Mee (2004), 417.
[257] Law Com (2002), 86; see now Law Com (2006) and (2007).

3.7 RIGHTS IN RELATION TO THE FAMILY HOME AND ITS CONTENTS

Although English law confers no automatic joint or community ownership on any family members, there are some basic 'mitigations'[258] to the separate property regime, conferring limited rights and protections short of ownership on some family members. The current law in this area is limited in its scope and application. To adopt Fox's typology again, English law can be regarded as both narrower and shallower than that of many other jurisdictions.[259] The rights are largely confined to spouses and civil partners, and even they enjoy relatively limited protection. Our focus in this chapter is on the basic rights of members in the intact family. We reserve detailed discussion of disputes between family members regarding occupation of the home to chapters 4, 6, and 7.[260]

3.7.1 RIGHTS TO OCCUPY THE FAMILY HOME

The general law

The right to occupy property is ordinarily governed by the law of property or contract. Whether the right is proprietary or merely contractual is important if it becomes necessary to assert the right against someone other than the individual who granted it.

Where property is co-owned and so subject to a trust, the beneficial owners have a statutory right to occupy the trust property if a purpose of the trust is to make the property available for their occupation and the property is in fact available and suitable for their occupation.[261] Since the right to occupy flows from ownership of an estate in the land, anyone claiming that right must be able to demonstrate that he or she is a beneficial freehold owner or tenant under a lease. A proprietary estoppel claim may also generate a right to occupy.[262] As a proprietary right, the beneficial owner's or estoppel claimant's right can bind third parties.

A right to occupy property may also be conferred by written or oral, express or (more problematically) implied contract.[263] If the contract does not grant a lease, it takes effect simply as a personal right and so does not ordinarily bind third parties. There are statutory constraints on terminating contractual licences, but these do not apply to licences to share property with the resident owner or a member of the owner's family.[264] While a contractual licence cannot lawfully be terminated other than in accordance with the agreement,[265] the court will not enforce by injunction a licence of a shared home;[266] the wrongfully ejected licensee will be left to a remedy in damages.

A licence to occupy may be granted, expressly or impliedly, on a gratuitous basis (without the intention to create legal relations and valuable consideration necessary to create a

---

[258] Kahn-Freund (1959), 247.

[259] Fox (2003).

[260] Under Children Act 1989 (CA 1989), Sch 1, Family Law Act 1996 (FLA 1996), and Trusts of Land and Appointment of Trustees Act 1996 (TOLATA 1996).

[261] TOLATA 1996, s 12; Gray and Gray (2009), 7.5.44 et seq.

[262] E.g. *Greasley v Cooke* [1980] 1 WLR 1306.

[263] E.g. *Tanner v Tanner* [1975] 1 WLR 1346; cf *Horrocks v Foray* [1976] 1 WLR 230. *Coombes v Smith* [1986] 1 WLR 808. On the various categories of licensee, see Gray and Gray (2009), 10.2–10.5; 10.3.12 et seq on the difficulties with contractual licences in family cases.

[264] Protection from Eviction Act 1977, s 3A(2)–(3).

[265] The court may have to imply terms regarding termination, e.g. reasonable notice: *Chandler v Kerley* [1978] 1 WLR 693.

[266] *Thompson v Park* [1944] KB 408.

contract). This is the most tenuous basis for occupation, easily terminated by the licensor withdrawing the permission. It has been said that the right to respect for the home under Article 8 ECHR requires that reasonable notice be given to terminate a licence to occupy property as a home,[267] but the owner's right to terminate a bare licence is otherwise unqualified; no reason need be given.

Since many spouses now elect to own or lease their homes jointly, most spouses enjoy rights to occupy as a matter of property law. Spouses and other family members who do not have a beneficial interest in the shared home may at best—in terms of the general law—occupy by virtue of a bare licence. However, some family members enjoy special occupation rights by virtue of their family status.

Spouses and civil partners: statutory 'home rights'

The rights of the wife at common law

At common law, a wife with no right to occupy the matrimonial home under the general law enjoys a personal right to occupy it[268] simply by virtue of being a wife. This is an aspect of the wife's common law right to be maintained by the husband.[269] The nature and scope of this right has been explored by the House of Lords:

National Provincial Bank Ltd v Ainsworth [1965] AC 1175, 1229–30, 1232–3

LORD UPJOHN:

[T]he law has never adjudicated between the parties where or how they are to live. It is for the spouses to decide where and in what state they and the family are to live, be it in the Ritz or a caravan. The choice from time to time of the matrimonial home is entirely a matter for decision within the domestic forum; though, no doubt ... where there is a difference of opinion between the spouses as to the place of the matrimonial home someone must have the casting vote. A wife on entering a matrimonial home, the property of her husband, has no rights, even inchoate, in that home which the law will recognise or protect ... But, on the other hand, having regard to the duty of the spouses to live together the court does not, during the subsistence of the marriage, merely give effect to the strict legal and equitable rights of a spouse qua owner of the property as though the spouses were strangers. Recognising the obligations of the spouses to live together[270] the court will only make orders with regard to the occupation of the matrimonial home subject to those obligations ...

[A] wife does not remain lawfully in the matrimonial home by leave or licence of her husband as the owner of the property. She remains there because as a result of the status of marriage it is her right and duty so to do and if her husband fails in his duty to remain there that cannot affect her right to do so. She is not a trespasser, she is not a licensee of her husband, she is lawfully there as a wife, the situation is one sui generis ...

---

[267] *Parker v Parker* [2003] EWHC 1846, para 276. 'Home' rights under Art 8 can be asserted even by those with no legal right to occupy the property: *Prokopovich v Russia* (App No 58255/00, ECHR) (2006).

[268] The right only applies to property which is or has been the matrimonial home: *Hall v King* [1988] 1 FLR 376; in relation to other property, the wife may have only a bare licence. It is unenforceable if the home is owned by or with third parties: *Chaudhry v Chaudhry* [1987] 1 FLR 347

[269] Query whether it may therefore be abolished by the Equality Act 2010: see 3.8.1.

[270] See the concept of consortium, at p 58 above; the action for restitution of conjugal rights was abolished in 1970: see Cretney (2003a), ch 4

But apart from authority, what is the extent and ambit of her right to continue in occupation? I have already pointed out that…she has no special rights in the particular house where the spouses are living…[If the husband deserts the wife, her] rights as a wife continue as before, they are not increased by breach of duty on the part of the husband, but being in breach himself he may find it difficult to turn her out of the house where she is lawfully living awaiting his return and the court may prevent the husband by injunction from dealing with his property to the prejudice of the wife without safeguarding her position … But then many things may happen: he may offer alternative accommodation to the wife: he may offer her substantial maintenance to go and live elsewhere … [P]rovided the wife's marital rights are adequately safeguarded in some such way the court would not normally refuse to evict a wife if the husband wants to deal with his property. Or he may return and resume cohabitation [at which point] the domestic forum resumes exclusive jurisdiction. Or the wife may change her position. She may commit a matrimonial offence which may lead the court to refuse her the right to continue under her husband's roof;[271] she may obtain (as in this case) a decree of judicial separation which at all events brings the husband's desertion to an end … Such a decree must necessarily be an important though not conclusive factor if the husband is seeking to turn his wife out of occupation. Finally, any right on the part of the deserted wife to remain in occupation terminates when the marriage terminates.

It is unclear whether a husband enjoys equivalent rights against a property-owning wife.[272] Civil partnership, a creature of statute, confers no such common law entitlements. However, the significance of any common law right to occupy is superseded by statutory 'home rights' which are enjoyed equally by husbands, wives, and civil partners.

Statutory 'home rights'

In order to appreciate the significance of home rights (formerly called 'matrimonial home rights'), it is necessary to review the background to their creation. One of Lord Denning's initiatives to protect wives' interests in the family home was the 'deserted wife's equity': could the wife's common law right to occupy the matrimonial home (as wife rather than co-owner) be enforced both against the husband who had deserted her and against a third party to whom the deserting husband had sold or mortgaged the property? Several Court of Appeal decisions held that it could. However, while a wife may still be able to assert her common law right to occupy as against a landlord in leasehold cases,[273] the House of Lords in *Ainsworth* held that no such right was enforceable against third parties in the context of freehold land where the husband had deserted the wife:

National Provincial Bank Ltd v Ainsworth [1965] AC 1175, 1233–4, 1242

LORD UPJOHN:

The right of the wife to remain in occupation even as against her deserting husband is incapable of precise definition, it depends so much on all the circumstances of the case, on the exercise of purely discretionary remedies, and the right to remain may change overnight by

---

[271] Cf the regulation of statutory home rights under FLA 1996, s 33; see 4.5.3.
[272] *Seel v Watts and Butterworth* [1954] CLY 2861 concluded not; but compare *Harman v Glencross* [1985] Fam 49, 58.
[273] E.g. *Metropolitan Properties Co Ltd v Cronan* (1982) 44 P&CR 1. The position is now covered by FLA 1996, s 30(4).

the act or behaviour of either spouse. So as a matter of broad principle I am of opinion that the rights of husband and wife must be regarded as purely personal inter se and that these rights as a matter of law do not affect third parties [even if they have full notice of the desertion].

In this case your Lordships are dealing with essentially conveyancing matters. It has been the policy of the law for over a hundred years to simplify and facilitate transactions in real property. It is of great importance that persons should be able freely and easily to raise money on the security of their property. Of course an intending purchaser is affected with notice of all matters which would have come to his notice if such inquiries and inspections had been made by him as ought reasonably to have been made (section 199 of the [LPA] 1925[274]). But surely any inquiry, if it is to be made reasonably, must be capable of receiving a positive answer as to the rights of the occupier and lead to a reasonably clear conclusion as to what those rights are? The answer "I am a deserted wife" (if given) only gives notice of a right so imprecise, so incapable of definition, so impossible of measurement in legal phraseology or terms of money that if he is to be safe the mortgagee will refuse to do business and much unnecessary harm will be done … It does not seem to me that an inquiry as to the marital status of a woman in occupation of property is one which the law can reasonably require to be made; it is not reasonable for a third party to be compelled by law to make inquiries into the delicate and possibly uncertain and fluctuating state of affairs between a couple whose marriage is going wrong. Still less can it be reasonable to make an inquiry if the answer to be expected will probably lead to no conclusion which can inform the inquirer with any certainty as to the rights of the occupant. These considerations give strong support to the opinion I have already expressed that the rights of the wife must be regarded as purely personal between herself and her husband.

LORD WILBERFORCE:

The ultimate question must be whether such persons can be given the protection which social considerations of humanity evidently indicate without injustice to third parties and a radical departure from sound principles of real property law.

The House of Lords held they could not. However, Parliament promptly filled the gap with 'matrimonial home rights', originally in 1967: the relevant provisions are now consolidated in the FLA 1996. That legislation, unlike the common law, is gender neutral, and applies to civil partners. These rights are enforceable against the other spouse or partner, provide eligibility to apply for an occupation order against the other spouse or partner, and (if registered on the appropriate land register) are enforceable against third parties as a charge:

Family Law Act 1996

30 Rights concerning home where one spouse or civil partner has no estate etc.

(1) This section applies if—
  (a) one spouse or civil partner ("A") is entitled to occupy a dwelling-house by virtue of—
    (i) a beneficial estate or interest or contract; or
    (ii) any enactment giving A the right to remain in occupation; and
  (b) the other spouse or civil partner ("B") is not so entitled.

---

[274] Cf registered land: LRA 2002.

(2) Subject to the provisions of this Part, B has the following rights ("home rights")—

(a) if in occupation, a right not to be evicted or excluded from the dwelling-house or any part of it by A except with the leave of the court given by an order under section 33;

(b) if not in occupation, a right with the leave of the court so given to enter into and occupy the dwelling house.

(3) If B is entitled under this section to occupy a dwelling-house or any part of a dwelling-house, any payment or tender made or other thing done by B in or towards satisfaction of any liability of A in respect of rent, mortgage payments or other outgoings affecting the dwelling-house is … as good as if made or done by A.

(4) [Provisions regarding security of leasehold tenure—see n 273 above]

(5) If B—

(a) is entitled under this section to occupy a dwelling-house or any part of a dwelling-house, and

(b) makes any payment in or towards satisfaction of any liability of A in respect of mortgage payments affecting the dwelling-house,

the person to whom the payment is made may treat it as having been made by A, but the fact that that person has treated any such payment as having been so made does not affect any claim of B against A to an interest in the dwelling-house by virtue of the payment.

(6) [Provision regarding the operation of (3)-(5) where A is a beneficiary of trust property—rights bind trustees as they bind A]

(7) This section does not apply to a dwelling-house which—

(a) in the case of spouses, has at no time been, and was at no time intended by them to be, a matrimonial home of theirs; and

(b) in the case of civil partners, has at no time been, and was at no time intended by them to be, a civil partnership home of theirs.

(8) B's home rights continue—

(a) only so long as the marriage or civil partnership subsists, except to the extent that an order under section 33(5) otherwise provides; and

(b) only so long as A is entitled as mentioned in subsection (1) to occupy the dwelling-house, except where provision is made by section 31 for those rights to be a charge on an estate or interest in the dwelling-house.

(9) It is hereby declared that a person—

(a) who has an equitable interest in a dwelling-house or in its proceeds of sale, but

(b) is not a person in whom there is vested (whether solely or as joint tenant) a legal estate in fee simple or a legal term of years absolute in the dwelling-house,

is to be treated, only for the purposes of determining whether he has home rights, as not being entitled to occupy the dwelling-house by virtue of that interest.

31 Effect of home rights as a charge on dwelling-house

(1) Subsections (2) and (3) apply if, at any time during a marriage or civil partnership, A is entitled to occupy a dwelling-house by virtue of a beneficial estate or interest.

(2) B's home rights are a charge on the estate or interest.

(3) The charge created by subsection (2) has the same priority as if it were an equitable interest created at whichever is the latest of the following dates—

    (a) the date on which A acquires the estate or interest;

    (b) the date of the marriage or the formation of the civil partnership; and

    (c) 1st January 1968 (the commencement date of the Matrimonial Homes Act 1967).

[(4)–(7) Provisions regarding trusts—where only A and B are or could be beneficiaries, B's interest is a charge binding on the trustees]

(8) Even though B's home rights are a charge on an estate or interest in the dwelling-house, those rights are brought to an end by—

    (a) the death of A, or

    (b) the termination (otherwise than by death) of the marriage or civil partnership,

    unless the court directs otherwise by an order made under section 33(5)....

(10) If the title to the legal estate by virtue of which A is entitled to occupy a dwelling-house (including any legal estate held by trustees for A) is registered under the Land Registration Act 2002 or any enactment replaced by that Act—

    (a) registration of a land charge affecting the dwelling-house by virtue of this Part is to be effected by registering a notice under that Act; and

    (b) B's home rights are not to be capable of [operating as an overriding interest by virtue of B's actual occupation of the property under] ... paragraph 2 of Schedule 1 or 3 to that Act.

    ...

[(12)–(13) Provision regarding the priority of home rights in unregistered land: home rights are registrable as a Class F land charge under the Land Charges Act 1972, s 2]

63 Interpretation...

(5) It is hereby declared that this Part applies as between the parties to a marriage even though either of them is, or has at any time during the marriage been, married to more than one person.[275]

Statutory home rights are 'purely personal': they do not entitle that spouse to give any other person a right to occupy the property, and cannot be assigned or disposed of.[276] However, home rights are more concrete than wives' old common law right: they do not depend for their continued existence on the parties' conduct (for example, there is no need for the owning spouse to have deserted the other), but they may be terminated by court order.[277] The rights may be asserted against the other spouse over more than one property, but can only be registered and so bind third parties in relation to one.[278] In order to bind a third party, they must be appropriately registered.

---

[275] Presumably meaning 'validly married': cf *Ramsamy v Babar* [2003] EWCA Civ 1253.
[276] *Wroth v Tyler* [1974] Ch 30.
[277] See FLA 1996, s 33; conduct is a relevant factor: s 33(6); see 4.5.3.
[278] FLA 1996, Sch 4, para 2.

Children

With the exception of those who have a right to occupy by virtue of a beneficial interest in the property,[279] the status of children is unclear. Statutory home rights confer no right to occupy on any children (or anyone else) who lives with the spouse.[280] Case law, perhaps surprisingly, suggests that even minor children occupy their parents' home under only a bare licence.[281] Parents could in theory therefore withdraw permission for their own children to live with them. While that may be appropriate in the case of adult children, it would sit somewhat incongruously alongside parents' ordinary responsibilities to children under 18; a parent who evicts his or her minor child may be guilty of child neglect and attract child protection proceedings.[282] It has accordingly been argued that these obligations, together with Article 8 ECHR and Article 16 of the United Nations Convention on the Rights of the Child (UNCRC) (no child 'shall be subjected to arbitrary or unlawful interference with his or her...home'), demand that children attract a protected occupation status in their home, at least vis-à-vis their parents or de facto carers, if not against third parties.[283]

Other family members with no right to occupy under the general law

All other family members—cohabitants, adult children, parents, relatives, and non-commercial[284] home-sharers—who cannot establish a proprietary or contractual right to occupy the property under the general law have only limited rights. Most are bare licensees, who need only be afforded 'reasonable' notice if required by the owner to leave,[285] and who have no right that will bind a third party. The only extra family law protection is for cohabitants (and former spouses and civil partners with no home rights), who may be able to obtain relatively short-term occupation orders under the FLA 1996.[286] The Law Society's recommendation that cohabitants with children or whose relationships have lasted two years should also have home rights has not been adopted.[287]

3.7.2 DECISION-MAKING ABOUT SALE AND OTHER TRANSACTIONS RELATING TO THE FAMILY HOME

The general law

Under the general law, decisions about sale, mortgage, and other dispositions of property are for the legal owner(s). Where all occupiers of the property are legal owners, all must

---

[279] Such interest must be registered to bind third parties, since a minor cannot be in 'actual occupation' for the purposes of establishing an overriding interest under LRA 2002, Sch 3, para 2: *Hypo-Mortgage Services Ltd v Robinson* [1997] 2 FLR 71; Gray and Gray (2009), 8.2.92. A minor cannot hold a legal estate in land: LPA 1925, s 1(6): Gray and Gray (2009) 1.7.27, 4.2.3, 7.5.14. In the leasehold context, see *Kingston upon Thames BC v Prince* [1999] 1 FLR 593.

[280] *Wroth v Tyler* [1974] Ch 30, though the interests of certain children are relevant to decisions of the court regulating home rights under FLA 1996, s 33; see 4.5.3.

[281] E.g. *Metropolitian Properties Co Ltd v Cronan* (1982) 44 P&CR 1.

[282] E.g. Children and Young Persons Act 1933, s 1; on child protection, see chapter 12.

[283] Gray and Gray (2009), 10.2.16.

[284] Lodgers, tenants, and employees of the owner are subject to relevant housing and employment law.

[285] E.g. *Hannaford v Selby* (1976) 239 EG 811.

[286] See 4.5.3.

[287] Law Society (2002).

consent to any disposition, so each has a right of veto. For most spouses, who jointly own their homes, the general law therefore ensures both have equal say.

Adults who are not on the legal title but who have beneficial shares in the property have no right of veto, unless the trust specifically requires that their consent be obtained.[288] A beneficiary of property held by a sole trustee can at least delay a disposition by registering a restriction which, in effect, will prevent the disposition from going ahead without a second trustee being appointed.[289] But if the owner can find someone else willing to become a trustee, the disposition may proceed, overreaching the beneficiary's interest.[290] In the case of trusts created after 1996, beneficiaries have a right to be consulted, so far as is practicable. Trustees must give effect to the majority view, so far as that is consistent with the general interest of the trust.[291] Failure to comply with the statutory duty to consult will not, of itself, affect any purchaser of the property.[292] In case of dispute regarding transactions over the property, one or other party can refer the case to the court under TOLATA 1996, which we discuss at 7.8.3.[293]

Family law protection?

No right as family member to be consulted about or veto transactions

English law does not straightforwardly provide any family member with a right to be consulted about transactions regarding the family home, in that capacity, rather than as a co-owner of the property. Lord Wilberforce in *National Provincial Bank Ltd v Ainsworth* considered that such a requirement would 'create impossible difficulties for those dealing with the property of a married man', requiring, as it would, the wife's consent to all dealings affecting the home.[294] Nor does English law prevent or limit use of the family home as security for business loans, preferring instead to maximize the marketability of that asset.[295] Such loans may be essential for the livelihood of a family dependent on that business. But that may not of itself justify depriving family members of a say in whether their home should be used for that purpose, given the risks involved.[296]

The FLA 1996 provisions regarding home rights give spouses and civil partners some leverage over such decisions if they have registered their rights.[297] But it has been asked whether the owner-spouse should be obliged to give the other advance notice of any proposed transaction which would affect the latter's right of occupation, alerting the other to the need to take steps to protect his or her home rights. The law could even require that the latter's active

---

[288] TOLATA 1996, s 10, likely only to be the case with express trusts. In registered land, such a right will operate only as a personal right against the trustees unless reflected in a restriction on the register: LRA 2002, s 40.

[289] LRA 2002, s 40.

[290] See Hopkins (2009), 320–1: overreaching conceptualizes the home as an investment.

[291] TOLATA 1996, s 11. The 'majority' is calculated by the size of the parties' interests.

[292] Unless an appropriate restriction has been entered to prevent the registration of a disposition unless consultation has taken place: LRA 2002, s 40. In relation to unregistered land: TOLATA 1996, s 16(1).

[293] See 7.8.3.

[294] [1965] AC 1175, 1248.

[295] See *Barclays Bank v O'Brien* [1994] 1 AC 180, 188. Compare the 'homestead' legislation of some Canadian provinces and US states, and New Zealand's Joint Family Homes Act 1964, which to a greater or lesser extent puts the home 'off limits' to creditors: Fox (2005).

[296] Even if those family members would not think twice about consenting: Fehlberg (1997).

[297] See discussion on the Online Resource Centre.

consent to any such transaction be obtained, so that any purported sale or mortgaging of the family home would be void without it.

The Law Commission's proposals for statutory co-ownership of the matrimonial home would have provided the 'incidental advantage' of giving the otherwise non-owning spouse control over dispositions of the property: a disposition without the spouse's consent (or without having dispensed with it by court order) would have no legal effect. However, consistent with the approach to statutory home rights, the right would in most cases have been enforceable against third parties only if the co-ownership interest had been registered.[298] But the Commission rejected the view that a spouse should be entitled to prevent any disposition of the matrimonial home, regardless of whether he or she co-owned it: such a right 'would represent a drastic inroad into accepted concepts of property'.[299]

By contrast, many other jurisdictions give spouses statutory rights of consultation and veto which are enforceable without prior registration. Some of those countries operate full community of property during marriage, but, as Dewar suggests, there is no reason why the right to control dispositions of key assets cannot be enjoyed independently of ownership.[300] Since the right attaches only to spouses (and, if adopted in England, to civil partners), third parties can easily check the legal status of the person with whom they wish to transact (marital status being a matter of public record) and so ascertain whether there is a spouse whose consent must be obtained. Commonly, non-compliance with such requirements renders the relevant transaction voidable for a given period,[301] or even void (unless the third party is a purchaser for value in good faith, who is unaware that the vendor or mortgagor is married).[302] In practice most purchasers and mortgagees check whether there are any other adults occupying the property in order to get them to waive whatever rights they may have (whether as co-owners, home rights holders, or otherwise). But English law would arguably benefit from a more formalized mechanism for obtaining consent, at least from spouses and civil partners, if not also from cohabitants and other family members.

Can the court prevent a disposition?

If a non-owning spouse or other family member cannot prevent the disposition privately, can he or she do so via court order?[303] The law here is not entirely clear. The fact that someone has statutory home rights (even if registered) or the benefit of an occupation order under the FLA 1996 does not prevent the owner from selling or mortgaging the property[304] or, probably, terminating a tenancy of it.[305] However, it may be possible to obtain an injunction prohibiting dispositions of the property. Where divorce proceedings are in progress, the courts have specific powers to prevent certain types of transaction.[306] It has also been held that s 17 of the Married Women's Property Act 1882 empowers the court to grant an injunction barring sale unless the husband provides alternative accommodation for the wife, as an aspect

---

298 Law Com (1978), paras 0.12 and 1.417(79)–(116); Law Com (1982a), paras 90–105.

299 Law Com (1982a), para 110(iii). See also Law Com (1978), paras 2.87–2.89.

300 Dewar (1998b); e.g. in Sweden, where there is no community of property during marriage.

301 E.g. Swedish Marriage Code, ch 7, s 5: see generally Cooke, Barlow, and Callus (2006), ch 5.

302 Irish Family Home Protection Act 1976, s 3.

303 Royal Commission on Marriage and Divorce (1956) thought he or she should be able to: para 670.

304 Law Com (1992), para 4.19; *Davis v Johnson* [1979] AC 264, 343 and 349. Even though the owner might be required by order to continue to pay the mortgage or rent: FLA 1996, s 40.

305 *Harrow LBC v Johnstone* [1997] 1 WLR 459; Lowe and Douglas (2007), 255 query whether an order under the FLA 1996 might prohibit the respondent from giving notice to quit.

306 MCA 1973, s 37; CPA 2004, Sch 5, Part 14: see p 482.

of the common law duty to provide a home for the wife; the courts might now regard wives as being subject to this duty as well as husbands. This power seems to survive the creation of statutory home rights.[307] Even outside the context of marriage, it might also be possible to use s 37 of the Supreme Court Act 1981 to restrain a disposition which would prejudice rights enjoyed under an occupation order or home rights.[308] Such an injunction could not bar dispositions of the property for any period longer than the underlying occupation order or home rights endured. Otherwise, however, the owner is free to do as he or she wishes with the property.

3.7.3 PROTECTING OCCUPATION AGAINST THIRD PARTIES

Suppose that the legal owner mortgages the home and defaults on the payments, or sells the property. Can a family member with beneficial ownership or a statutory home right defend an action for possession of the home by third party? To answer this question, we must first ask whether the third party is bound by the family member's interest under the general law or pursuant to the statutory home rights regime. Even if the third party *is* bound by a family member's proprietary interest, it may still be able to secure the family's eviction from the home by forcing a sale to realize its interest; different legal provisions apply depending on whether the third party is a purchaser, secured creditor, or trustee in bankruptcy. In the case of binding home rights, the third party can apply for an occupation order under the FLA 1996 scheme. The law in this area and its application in practice have been criticized for giving too much weight to the commercial interests of the third parties and insufficient weight to the use value of the property as a family home.

ONLINE RESOURCE CENTRE
Readers wishing to learn more about this area of the law should visit the Online Resource Centre for chapter 3, where the law and critical commentaries are explained in detail.

3.7.4 RIGHTS REGARDING THE CONTENTS OF THE FAMILY HOME

Ownership of the contents of the family home—furniture, furnishings, kitchen equipment, crockery and cutlery, household linen, and so on—is entirely a matter for the general law. Ordinarily, the use and possession of that property flows from ownership. In the course of normal family life, of course, the technical owner of the spoons, towels, and sofa, whoever he or she may be (the parties may have no idea), will give implicit permission to all other family members to use that property.

The only family law specifically addressing use of such property is an adjunct to the occupation order regime discussed in chapter 4. When making an occupation order under the FLA 1996, the court can include additional provisions granting either party possession or use of

---

[307] *Lee v Lee* [1952] 2 AC 489; *Halden v Halden* [1966] 1 WLR 1481; *Gurasz v Gurasz* [1970] P 11.
[308] Cf *Moore v Moore* [2004] EWCA Civ 1243.

furniture or other contents.[309] The 'width' of this protection is governed by the width of the FLA 1996 regime—only those eligible to apply for and who have obtained an occupation order benefit from it. So, save for those family members who have a beneficial interest in the home, only current and former spouses, civil partners, and cohabitants can access this provision.

No other property, such as the family car,[310] attracts similar protection, and there is no protection where occupation of the home is not in issue. The Law Commission's recommendation that the courts have power to make orders between spouses regarding the use and possession of 'household goods' (including cars), and independently of disputes over occupation, has not been enacted.[311]

3.8 FAMILY FINANCES

An examination of family finances involves both private law and two aspects of public law, welfare benefit and tax law. The state's role in regulating and supporting families through these avenues is significant not only for its practical impact. The scope of these laws also reflects interestingly on the law's conception of 'family', in terms both of the breadth of family and the presumed roles of individuals within it.

Research about couples' money management practices is important for evaluating the law. Times have changed significantly from the days of the man's 'family wage', which supported a male breadwinner/female homemaker model of marriage. But economic inequalities remain.

J. Pahl, 'Individualisation in Couple Finances: Who Pays for the Children?',
(2005) 4 *Social Policy and Society* 381, 381–4

Patterns of money management within the household have changed dramatically over the past half century. Fifty years ago in the UK there were widespread and commonly shared notions about the allocation of money within the family, about the form which 'proper' families should take and about the ways in which the welfare state should cater for the needs of individuals within families. The Beveridge Report [(1942), on which the modern welfare state, introduced by the National Assistance Act 1948, was based] argued that,

All women by marriage acquire a new economic and social status with risks and rights different to those of the unmarried. On marriage a woman gains a legal right to maintenance by her husband as a first line defence against risks which fall directly on the solitary woman; she undertakes at the same time to perform vital but unpaid service and becomes exposed to new risks, including the risk that her married life may be ended prematurely by widowhood or separation. . . .Beveridge, 1942: 49

This statement encapsulates the idea that the married couple should be a financial unit, within which the man would be the breadwinner and a woman would accept financial dependence in exchange for financial security. This idea was translated into social security legislation which gave married women a right to a pension on the basis of their husbands' contributions and a widow's pension if he died before she did. It reflected a situation in which less than half of women aged 16 to 59 were in paid work in 1961, compared with 68 per cent in 2000. . .

---

[309] FLA 1996, s 40; see generally 4.5.3.
[310] Occupation orders can be made over caravans or houseboats used as the family home: ibid., s 63.
[311] Law Com (1978), Book Three.

Studies carried out at the time showed that the ways in which couples organised their finances reflected the idea of the male breadwinner. Zweig's study [in 1961] of 337 men in south and central England showed that 70 per cent gave their wives a housekeeping allowance, while 16 per cent handed over the whole wage packet, either keeping back a sum for themselves or receiving a sum back from the wife for their pocket money. Only 16 per cent of couples pooled their income, and Zweig commented that this system was particularly common among younger couples and when both partners were earning. He also noted 'a very peculiar arrangement' which was described by one respondent as 'What she makes is hers, what I make is mine' ...

By the 1980s the situation had changed. From being a minority way of managing money, pooling had become the most common system. My first study, which reported on interviews with 102 couples and used data collected in 1982–84, found that 56 per cent of couples pooled their money, typically in a joint bank account; in 22 per cent of couples the husband gave his wife a housekeeping allowance; 14 per cent used a whole wage system; and 9 per cent were classified as maintaining independence in financial matters ...

Changing patterns of money management reflected changing ideologies about marriage. The Beveridge acceptance of economic inequality within marriage was being challenged, not least by feminists, and there was a new reluctance, among some couples at least, to seeing one partner as the breadwinner and the other as financially dependent ... The classic statement by couples who pool their money is, 'It's not my money; it's not his/her money; it's our money'. This would seem to perpetuate the idea that the couple is a financial unit, but it also implies an ideal of equality between the two individuals making up the couple. Many of those interviewed in the 1980s expressed anxiety about the differences in earning power between men and women and saw the pooling of money as a way to diminish its impact....

... [T]he fastest growing [money management] system ... is 'partial pooling'. This depends on each partner having their own personal income, so that each can keep some money under their own personal control, while contributing some to a common pool; the system also relies on the couple agreeing a distinction between joint and personal spending.... [Both partial pooling and independent management] express an essential individualism. If couples do not pool their money or maintain a common kitty, this is often because one or both want to maintain a degree of autonomy or privacy in their money management practices.... [Research from the late 1990s showed that] independent management of money was particularly characteristic of younger couples, of those without children and of those where the woman was in full time paid work.

Recent research has found that the system adopted varies by relationship status. While spouses are more likely to operate as a single economic unit, cohabitants are more likely to operate independently. However, cohabiting *parents* are much more likely to pool: they appear to behave more like spouses in their financial practices.[312] While this similarity between spouses and some cohabitants is reflected to an extent in welfare benefit and tax credit law, private law treats the two types of relationship very differently.

3.8.1 PRIVATE LAW

The law in this area is important owing to the continued imbalance in earning power between many parents, married or not, described at 3.2.2 above. Where one parent (usually the mother) gives up or reduces paid employment to take on the role of primary carer, that

---

[312] Vogler (2009).

person is rendered to some extent dependent on the wage-earner. However, private law relating to income and savings from earnings is similar to that governing ownership and use of property. Ownership of such funds is largely determined by the general law: the earner is exclusively entitled to his or her income, and is under no general obligation to share it with any family member. Nor does any family member have a right to know what others' income is.[313] The general position is mitigated by basic 'maintenance' obligations. But, save in relation to minors, they arise only where the relationship between the parties is formalized in marriage or civil partnership.[314] English law does not impose wider family duties of support. Even between spouses, the practical significance of the obligation is limited.

The common law duty of husbands to support wives

Having disabled wives from owning property, including any wages that they might earn through paid employment, the common law obliged husbands to maintain their wives. But the obligation was not directly enforceable:

R (Kehoe) v Secretary of State for Work and Pensions [2005] UKHL 48

BARONESS HALE:

53. The common law courts would not intrude into the matrimonial relationship, or trespass upon the jurisdiction of the ecclesiastical courts over that relationship, by ordering the husband to make payments to his wife. But a wife who was living with her husband did have the apparent authority to contract as his agent for the expenses of the household. And if they were living apart, the common law recognised her agency of necessity, the right to pledge her husband's credit for necessaries according to her station in life. Unlike the housekeeping authority, this could not be countermanded by the husband. But the agency of necessity subsisted only if the wife was justified in living apart from her husband. Hence she would lose it for ever if she was guilty of adultery, no matter how badly her husband had behaved; . . . it would be suspended while she was in desertion . . .; but if they were obliged to live apart through no fault of hers, for example because of illness, the obligation continued.

The wife's agency of necessity was abolished in 1970, when the court's modern-day powers to order financial provision on divorce, judicial separation, and nullity were created.[315] The common law duty to maintain was superseded in practice by gender neutral legislation empowering the courts to make enforceable maintenance orders between spouses and civil partners. It was finally abolished by the Equality Act 2010.[316]

Statutory maintenance obligations

The courts can order payment of maintenance *during* marriage and civil partnership under various statutes.[317] In practice, the power is exercised, if at all, only where the relationship

---

[313] Cf the old law which required married couples to complete a single tax return, completed by the husband, which would ensure that he knew her income, but not vice versa.

[314] See chapters 6 and 7; contrast the public law of welfare benefits, 3.8.2.

[315] Matrimonial Proceedings and Property Act 1970, s 41.

[316] S 198; not in force as at October 2010.

[317] Domestic Proceedings and Magistrates' Courts Act 1978 (DPMCA 1978), CPA 2004, Sch 6; MCA 1973, s 27, CPA 2004, Sch 5, Pt 9: Cretney (2003a), ch 11.

has broken down (but is not subject to dissolution, separation, or nullity proceedings[318]). The law is reluctant to intervene in the intact family in order to preserve 'family privacy'.[319] Although orders may now be made and enforced while the parties are living together, orders for maintenance made in the magistrates' court automatically expire after six months' continuous cohabitation by the parties.[320] The basis on which these orders may be made and enforced is very similar to that governing equivalent powers on dissolution, judicial separation, and nullity, so we shall not examine them in detail here.[321] Where there are minors, child support is payable in the event of parental separation (whether married or not); that is far more significant than maintenance for the benefit of the spouse, which is rare.[322]

The courts can also make financial orders to secure payments relating to property subject to an occupation order under the FLA 1996,[323] but these powers are 'not intended as a disguised form of maintenance for those who are not entitled to it'.[324] Although the power is exercisable in favour of a cohabitant, it therefore cannot be used as a means of requiring the respondent to support that individual, to whom no duty to maintain is owed.

One special rule of ownership: savings from housekeeping money

One statutory provision creates co-ownership of a specific pool of money, originally only within marriage. Like the presumption of advancement, the statutory rule about ownership of savings made from housekeeping money, in its original form, was something of an historical curio and raised human rights problems. It cast interesting light on historical understandings of the family and family members' roles. As originally enacted, it read as follows:

Married Women's Property Act 1964, s 1

If any question arises as to the right of a husband or wife to money derived from any allowance made by the husband for the expenses of the matrimonial home or for similar purposes, or to any property acquired out of such money, the money or property shall, in the absence of any agreement between them to the contrary, be treated as belonging to the husband and wife in equal shares.

This explicitly gendered provision—husbands earn wages from which an 'allowance' for housekeeping is made to housewives (who receive no personal income or wages)—was introduced to protect the interests of the thrifty housewife who made savings from the housekeeping money.[325] It followed a case which held that, in the absence of any other agreement, the husband solely owned that money or any property acquired with it, in that case, a winning football pools coupon.[326] Although applauded for treating marriage as a partnership which should give rise

---

[318] As to that, see chapter 7.
[319] Boden and Childs (1996), 114; O'Donovan (1985), 112, 182.
[320] DPMCA 1978, s 25; CPA 2004, Sch 6, para 29.
[321] But note the particular 'grounds' on which maintenance orders may be made in this context: DPMCA 1978, s 1; MCA 1973, s 27(1); CPA 2004, Sch 6, para 1; Sch 5, para 39. For case law examples see *Barnes v Barnes* [1972] 1 WLR 1381; *Blower v Blower* [1986] 1 FLR 292; *Robinson v Robinson* [1983] Fam 42; *Vasey v Vasey* [1985] FLR 596.
[322] Though no official data on use of this jurisdiction are available: see Cretney (2003a), 472–3.
[323] FLA 1996, s 40.
[324] Law Com (1992), para 4.41.
[325] Cf the gender-neutral Scottish presumptions: Family Law (Scotland) Act 1985, ss 25–6, and Family Law (Scotland) Act 2006, ss 26–7.
[326] *Hoddinott v Hoddinott* [1949] 2 KB 406.

to joint ownership of property, the provision was criticized as far too narrow. Why, for example, should joint ownership only arise from housekeeping money, and not from savings made directly by the husband from his wage for expenditure on items for the family's use?[327]

Like the presumption of advancement, this provision appeared to be incompatible with Article 5 of the Seventh Protocol. The Equality Act 2010 accordingly amends the provision prospectively (relabelling it 'Matrimonial Property Act 1964') to make it gender neutral—so it applies equally to savings made by a husband to whom an allowance is made by the wife—and to extend it to civil partners.[328] Whether many, if any, couples will ever rely on it is doubtful, given the substantial decline of the housekeeping allowance money management system, particularly among young couples.[329]

Leaving it to the parties

In the absence of any effective legal regulation of family finances during the currency of relationships, the matter is left to the parties.[330] This raises concerns that by keeping out of the family, the law simply protects the more economically powerful, who can decide to what extent to share their money with the rest of the family. Research on money management in opposite-sex relationships suggests that where couples do not pool their resources and give each party equal decision-making power over and access to the funds, there can be marked imbalances between the parties, prejudicing the lower earning party (often the woman). The resulting strain on the relationship may even precipitate separation.[331]

It has been argued that the failure to give an entitlement to share in the family finances (and the family home) to those undertaking unpaid work in the home encourages the perception that that work is of no value.[332] One campaigning organization seeks 'wages for housework' from the state. Women spend more time on domestic work than men (even when both are in paid employment), while men spend more time in paid employment than women.[333] Gross unpaid household production in 2000 (including the provision of housing) was worth £877 billion to the national economy.[334] A state-paid wage for housework seems unlikely. But the value of this work—and the economic sacrifices made by those who devote themselves to home and family, in terms of lost opportunity to develop and maximize earning capacity—do need to be recognized. We shall see in chapter 7 that they are acknowledged on divorce. The question here is whether they ought to receive firmer recognition *during* relationships by the conferment of further private law entitlements.

3.8.2 FAMILIES IN THE TAX AND BENEFIT SYSTEMS

We turn finally to the law relating to welfare benefits and tax.[335] This area of law is important for what it reveals about the relative responsibilities of family and state to support

---

327 Kahn-Freund (1959), 250–1.
328 Ss 200–1: not in force as at October 2010.
329 On the practices of under-35s, see Vogler (2009).
330 We deal with the law relating to formal maintenance agreements in 7.7.2.
331 Vogler (2005).
332 Taub and Schneider (1998), 334.
333 Scott and Dex (2009).
334 ONS (2006b), table 5.27.
335 For detailed discussion of particular benefits, tax credits, and taxes, see CPAG (2010), an authoritative, user-friendly guide to welfare benefit and tax credit law; Douglas (2000a), Wikeley (2007c); on tax law, Lee (2010), Salter (2007).

economically weaker individuals. Rather than examine the law in detail, we briefly address three broad issues: family members' liability to support each other; 'aggregation' provisions, which assume the existence of economic support within families; and use of welfare benefits and tax credits to alleviate the relative poverty of individuals *within* the family unit. We also consider how this law can be used to incentivize particular behaviour, for example by providing tax advantages for spouses. We shall see that broader and narrower concepts of family are used in different areas: as Nick Wikeley has observed, welfare benefit law has 'always treated "the family" as a protean term, depending on the respective policy goals of the benefits schemes in question'.[336]

Public law liability of family members to support each other

Historically, the scope of family responsibility, enforceable by the state, was wider than it is today:

R (Kehoe) v Secretary of State for Work and Pensions [2005] UKHL 48

BARONESS HALE:

56. Statutory recognition of the parental duty to maintain dates back to the Elizabethan poor laws, culminating in the Poor Relief Act of 1601 ..., s 7 of which provided that

"...the father and grandfather, and the mother and grandmother, and the children of every poor ... person ... being of a sufficient ability, shall, at their own charges, relieve and maintain every such poor person in that manner, and according to that rate, as by the justices of peace of that county where such sufficient persons dwell, or the greater number of them, at their general quarter sessions shall be assessed; upon pain that every one of them shall forfeit 20s for every month which they shall fail therein."

The practice was to order, not only payment for the future, but also repayment of money already spent by the overseers of the poor.... Thus the principle of family responsibility or solidarity was laid down....

60. There is [now] ... a system, descended from the Poor Law, for recovering the costs of public assistance from 'liable relatives'. We have already seen the extent of the family obligations between parents, grandparents and children ... Obligations towards wives, and then husbands, came later [in 1834] ...

61. The Poor Law was abolished by the National Assistance Act 1948. In the post war welfare state, it was expected that most areas of need would be covered by national insurance benefits [paid for via contributions made from employees' earnings] and that means-tested benefits would be a safety net for the few who were not covered by the national insurance scheme. The 1948 Act retained the possibility of recovery from a 'liable relative' but reduced those liable: under section 42, a man was liable to maintain his wife and children ... and a woman was liable to maintain her husband and children. Neither was liable to maintain a *former* spouse.

Wikeley argues that the law here had a 'preventative' rather than 'restorative' function, seeking to encourage intra-family responsibility and so avoid the need to enforce it.[337] But the law's view of family responsibility for these purposes is now narrow and based on formalized,

---

336 Wikeley (2007c).
337 Ibid.

conjugal relationships rather than, as formerly, kin-based relationships, and no longer enforces liability up the generations (adult children to their parents) as well as down.[338] The liable relative procedure, now chiefly confined to spouses and civil partners,[339] in practice applies only where they are living apart; where they share a household, any means-tested benefit payments are reduced by aggregating the parties' income and capital for means-testing (discussed below). Where one spouse or civil partner living apart from the other makes a claim for a relevant means-tested benefit, the Department for Work and Pensions (DWP) may seek a voluntary contribution from the other, or apply to the magistrates' court to recover sums paid out; the magistrates have a discretion about how much, if anything, to require liable persons to pay, on pain of criminal prosecution.[340]

Assumptions about economic roles and support within families

Historically, at least, the gendered model of breadwinner/homemaker family has been dominant in welfare benefit law. Contribution-based benefits were originally set up following the Beveridge Report in 1942 such that a wife's entitlement to contribution-based benefits depended upon her husband's contributions, rather than her own.[341] Spouses and civil partners are now largely treated individually for the purposes of contribution-based benefits (such as contribution-based jobseeker's allowance).[342] But, though the law is now gender neutral, they can still base claims for bereavement benefits and one type of state retirement pension on their spouse or partner's contribution record. It has been held that exclusion of cohabitants from these benefits does not violate the ECHR.[343] It is significant also that jobseeker's allowance rules require claims by one partner in a couple without children (including cohabitants) to be made by both parties, and both must therefore be available for and actively seek employment. Wikeley argues that the prime motivation for this development was not equality within relationships (reducing the dependence of one partner on the other), but a desire to tackle welfare dependency generally.[344]

While the family is intact, some welfare benefit laws adopt a rather wider view of 'family' than the liable relative procedure. In some instances, this advantages claimants: where the rules recognize de facto support provided within families by those under no legally enforceable obligation to do so. For example, if a claimant of means-tested benefits is supporting an elderly relative by allowing that individual to occupy a dwelling owned (and previously occupied) by the claimant, the value of that property can be excluded from means-testing.[345] But in other contexts, the rules operate to *reduce* benefits payable, making *assumptions* about economic roles and support within intact families. In relation to spouses and civil partners, this is relatively uncontroversial since they have private law obligations to support each other. However, public law goes further, assuming support where there is no corresponding private law remedy to enable the individual affected to secure it. The main example of this is cohabitants.[346] The key means-tested benefits are currently income support and income-based

---

338 See generally Maclean and Eekelaar (1997) ch 3, and 42–3; Oldham (2001).

339 And sponsors of migrants to the UK: CPAG (2010), 776; see generally Wikeley (2008).

340 Social Security Administration Act 1992, ss 105–8; CPAG (2010), 771.

341 Douglas (2000a), 261; CPAG (2010), 746.

342 See generally CPAG (2010), ch 31.

343 *Shackell v UK* (App No 45851/99, ECHR) (2000).

344 Wikeley (2007c).

345 Ibid.; CPAG (2010), 953, 973.

346 For other examples, e.g. treatment of adult children at home under the age of 25 and other close 'non-dependent' relatives in relation to housing benefit, see Wikeley (2007c); CPAG (2010), 838.

jobseeker's allowance (JSA). Income support is designed for those not in or available for full-time paid work owing to their own sickness or disability, or because of child-care or other caring responsibilities;[347] JSA is for those seeking paid employment.[348] Both are payable in respect of all members of the 'family', but is paid to and in the name of only one of them.[349] 'Family' for these purposes is defined narrowly as 'couples': not only spouses and civil partners living in the same household (separated spouses and civil partners are assessed individually), but also cohabitants, whatever the duration of the relationship. Under the aggregation or 'cohabitation' rule, couples are therefore treated as an economic unit.[350] They can make only one claim, in the name of only one of them. Someone whose partner is in full-time work cannot claim income support, and the income and capital of both parties is aggregated for means-testing.[351]

Much of the case law exploring the meaning of 'cohabitation' and 'living together as husband and wife' (and now 'as civil partners'[352]) has arisen in this context.[353] The cohabitation rule has been controversial, not least because the DWP may have to inquire about the couple's intimate life and sleeping arrangements in order to establish whether they are 'cohabiting' rather than, for example, living together because one party is ill or disabled and the other is caring for him or her.[354] It has been suggested that investigating parties' sexual relationships may raise issues under Article 8 ECHR.[355]

Is the rule as it applies to cohabitants justifiable?

N. Harris, 'Unmarried cohabiting couples and Social Security in Great Britain', (1996) 18 *Journal of Social Welfare and Family Law* 123, 127–8

The basic argument used to justify the rule has been that it would be unfair if an unmarried partner was entitled to receive benefit that would be denied to a married person whose partner was in employment … This equity principle led the Finer Committee [DHSS (1974)] … to conclude that the rule should continue. It is also argued that if the law places unmarried partners in a more advantageous position than married couples in this way, it might serve to discourage marriage … (However, it has always been argued that the cohabitation rule discourages stable relationships between unmarried partners.) The Supplementary Benefits Commission (SBC) also argued that discouraging marriage in this way might 'present an obstacle to the legitimation of children' … The rule was, it was claimed, in tune with contemporary social attitudes—most people, the SBC argued, considered such a rule to be fair and equitable.

The rule's retention also reflects the lack of feasible alternative:

One possibility that has been discussed, in relation to income-related benefits, is assessment of each partner's actual contribution to the household, and especially that of the

---

[347] CPAG (2010), ch 13.

[348] Ibid., ch 15.

[349] A joint claim for JSA must be made where neither party is responsible for children, but even in those cases, the benefit is paid to only one partner: ibid., 394, 406.

[350] Social Security Contributions and Benefits Act 1992, s 137.

[351] Ibid., ss 124(1)(c), 134(2), 136(1).

[352] Jones (2007).

[353] See *Crake v Supplementary Benefits Commission* [1982] 1 All ER 498; *Re J (Income Support: Cohabitation)* [1995] 1 FLR 660; CPAG (2010), ch 30; DWP (2010b), vol 3, ch 11.

[354] Harris (1996); *Butterworth v Supplementary Benefits Commission* [1982] 1 All ER 498.

[355] Harris (1996), 137.

working partner. The SBC ... considered that the administrative difficulties and expense in assessing entitlement on this basis made it unworkable. Lister, ... however, argued that rather than complete aggregation of each partner's resources there might be 'possible reduction of benefit according to the resources actually at the woman's disposal in relation to her needs as defined by the statutes'. This would have been consonant with an argument used to justify differential treatment of married and cohabiting couples under the law generally, namely that a decision not to marry may imply an intention, by the parties, to have a relationship which is truly different in character (e.g. looser) than marriage ... It would also weaken the broad dependency assumption, under which women have traditionally been faced with a loss of independent income as a result of being forced to rely on a joint payment made to the man ..., although since 1983 either party can be the claimant ... It has also been argued that the rule 'assumes ... a support obligation which the law does not recognise' ... (unmarried partners owe no legal obligation to support each other under English law) and 'ignores the unequal distribution of income within the family which disadvantages women' ...

The question of how the practical difficulties and high administrative costs ... can be overcome remains unanswered. Nevertheless, there continues to be discussion about 'individualisation', which involves assessing each partner's benefit entitlement, and paying them, independently. Because members of married and unmarried couples would be treated the same way, the principle behind the cohabitation rule would continue to apply, but the disadvantages to women in particular would be reduced ...

Research[356] examining how couples manage money received by one of them as income support or JSA has found that, although benefits are less commonly regarded as 'belonging' to one party than earnings, there remains evidence of a 'breadwinner' stereotype:

A. Morris, 'Couples and benefits claims: a comment on *Relying on the State, Relying on Each Other*', (2000) 7 *Journal of Social Security Law* 228, 233–5, 239–40

For example, [most] JSA claimants were men, and only the man's name appeared on the cheque. This was taken to reflect "state recognition and validation of the role of males as head of the household". Bearing in mind that JSA requires the claimant to be actively seeking work, this can be explained (in the light of societal expectations) by the fact that in-work patterns are replicated in benefit management and perception. In other words, unemployment alone does not disrupt the idea that the man is responsible for fulfilling the role of the provider ...

Traditional gender roles are also apparent in the way in which one particular benefit is generally perceived and treated. Child benefit is seen as "belonging" to the mother rather than the father. This raises interesting questions as to the role played by the benefits system in reinforcing stereotypical gendered views. Child benefit is not only payable by default to the mother [an example of a benefit directed "at the purse not the wallet"] it also appears to be regarded as particularly appropriate that women should claim it because it is their role to "look after" the children ...

However, while benefit claims might be made in the name of the man, the man would not necessarily manage the money once it arrived, though money management patterns and their practical and psychological implications can be complex:

[356] Snape and Molloy (1999).

[E]arlier research...has already established that the lower the income, the more likely it is that there will be a system of female management.... [T]he fact that one partner set the budget and allocated expenditure did not necessarily mean that they had *physical* control of the money. The issue of control is especially problematic—even where financial management is handed over to a woman, her partner may still question her allocation or request additional personal money ...

However, it is a central finding that there was nothing in the data "to indicate that women were financially deprived in couples using the less equitable systems [of money management]. Indeed, ... there was generally a shared sense that household income had to be pooled in order to survive on the amount received ..." ... Nevertheless, there was an identifiable feeling of psychological dependency where men were named claimants. Women could then feel that they were invisible within the system. There was a view that dependency was reinforced by the fact that only one name appeared on the benefit cheque ... The idea of benefit-splitting (each receiving half the benefit in their own name) was not favourably received by couples who felt it would run counter to the idea of sharing which is the basis of the way benefits are allocated to couples. The result of splitting would be to give each individual a sum which would probably be insufficient and necessitate pooling in any event. Women also felt that their role as manager of the household budget could be undermined by splitting.... One reform which is suggested is that naming both partners as entitled to access [the money by being entitled to cash the benefit cheque] might be sufficient to counter feelings of psychological dependency and anonymity.

Benefits can now be paid directly into bank accounts—but that then makes access to funds dependent on access to that account.

Alleviating child poverty and poverty within families

Alleviating child poverty is an important governmental objective. Children's needs are currently dealt with separately from their carers' via universal (for the time being) child benefit (CB) and means-tested tax credits.[357] Child tax credit (CTC) and working tax credit (WTC) are tax-free payments administered by Her Majesty's Revenue and Customs (HMRC).[358] For the time being, they are available more widely than means-tested welfare benefits as the means-ceiling (defined by reference only to income, and not capital) is higher, covering more than just the poorest, and they can be claimed by those in full-time work. The credits are intended to supplement earned income (and/or benefits), encouraging claimants to enter or stay in the labour market and not depend on benefits. They pursue two key policies: supporting families and tackling child poverty, and 'making work pay'.[359] WTC may be claimed by couples without children and by single people, as well as by parents.

Both tax credits and child benefit are payable to those with 'responsibility' for a child, whether or not that person is the child's parent or in a couple. The law here takes a functional approach, recognizing de facto responsibility for raising children, regardless of legal or relationship status.[360] A 'child' is someone under 16, or 20 if criteria regarding educational and

---

[357] CPAG (2010), ch 4 and Part 6.

[358] The whole area of welfare benefits is (as at October 2010) being re-examined by the Coalition Government, so the various benefits and tax credits discussed here may undergo radical reform in the near future.

[359] HM Treasury and Inland Revenue (2002), 2.2.

[360] Wikeley (2007c).

employment status as a 'qualifying young person' are met.[361] Only one CTC and CB payment is available per child. A person is responsible for a child if he or she 'normally lives with' that person, or that person has the main responsibility for the child.[362] A claim by someone living in a couple must be made jointly, and the aggregation rule applies for means-testing. Income from CTC is excluded from means-testing for WTC, so both credits are often payable. The amount of credit payable depends on family circumstances (including number and age of children, whether lone parent or a couple) and income (not capital). WTC also covers a set proportion of child-care costs, to help parents who wish to engage in paid employment to do so. But it is only available for 'relevant' child-care, essentially registered/approved childminders and child-care facilities, and cannot meet the costs incurred by relatives and others caring for the child informally. Ann Mumford has argued that this, together with tax credits' drive to get more mothers working, devalues care provided by families for their own members.[363] Moreover, as we noted at 3.2.2, many parents still find affordable child-care hard to find.

A key feature of CB, CTC, and the child-care component of WTC is that they are paid directly to the child's 'main carer', a payment to 'purse rather than wallet'. Where the parents are living together, the mother will receive CB. In the case of a joint claim by a couple for tax credit, the 'main carer' will be either the person nominated by them or, if they cannot agree, identified by HMRC.[364] The rest of WTC is paid to the worker (if only one partner is employed), to whichever partner is nominated by the couple, or, if they cannot agree, to whomever HMRC decides. This feature of CB and tax credits is intended to ensure that some money reaches women, who may otherwise receive no funds directly, and who, research suggests, are more likely to spend it for the benefit of the children.[365] However, since means-testing is based on aggregated income, a woman with a wealthy partner may not be eligible for any tax credit, and so receive only the more limited CB.[366] Where parents are separated, the main carer is generally the mother. There is no facility for payments to be split pro rata where care is shared, and it has been held that no Article 14 discrimination on grounds of gender arises against fathers with whom the child spends a substantial part (but not most) of the week who accordingly receive no payment.[367]

Tax law and the family

Key questions for tax law are whether the family is to be treated as a unit for tax purposes, and if so, how that unit should be defined, or whether family members should be taxed individually.[368] As David Salter has observed, answers to these questions depend on political judgment and may be culturally specific.[369] We briefly outline two key themes: historical treatment of wives by income tax law; and the treatment of different family forms for tax purposes.[370] In the next section, we consider the use of tax and benefit law to promote particular family forms.

361 CPAG (2010), 57 and 1243.
362 Ibid., 63 and 1244.
363 Mumford (2007), 206.
364 CPAG (2010), 1289.
365 Lundberg, Pollak, and Wales (1997).
366 See Douglas (2000a); Pahl (2005), 9.
367 *Humphreys v Revenue and Customs Commissioners* [2010] EWCA Civ 56.
368 Salter (2007).
369 Ibid.
370 See more generally Mumford (2007), Young (2009).

Tax law took over one hundred years to catch up with the implications of wives' separate property and income.[371] Until relatively recently, married couples[372] were treated as a unit for income tax purposes: the husband completed the tax return on which any income of the wife would be deemed to be the husband's, and he was liable pay the resulting tax. This rule reflected wives' subordination to their husbands,[373] and allowed wives whose income was not taxed at source no financial privacy within their marriages. But the rule also prejudiced poorer husbands whose income-rich wives declined to contribute towards payment of the resulting tax bill.[374] The rules were gradually relaxed, until entirely separate income taxation for spouses was introduced in the late 1980s. For income tax purposes, spouses are therefore treated largely like any other individuals.[375] But it has been observed that there is some incongruity in spouses and others being treated individually for tax purposes while their incomes are aggregated for the purposes of welfare benefit and tax credit law, compromising the financial privacy that independent taxation was intended to provide for wives.[376]

Historically, husbands also received a special tax allowance, worth one and a half times the ordinary personal allowance, a rate which assumed that the wife was not in paid employment and was being supported by the husband. As Claire Young has argued, this sort of allowance reinforced spouses' traditional roles, encouraging and privatizing wives' dependency within the family, and failing to reward them personally for the economic value of their work.[377] If the wife was working, and was well-paid, spouses risked being taxed more highly than an unmarried couple, each of whom enjoyed a full personal allowance.[378] Independent taxation of wives ensured that spouses were no longer *penalized* by the taxation system. Not long after, the married person's tax allowance was withdrawn in order to help fund the new tax credit system, which is targeted more widely at families with children, including cohabiting and lone parent families. However, spouses and civil partners[379] still receive some special tax treatment. The most high profile example is their exclusive enjoyment of exemption from inheritance tax, which has been held not to violate the Convention rights of cohabiting couples.[380] As we discussed at 2.8.3, the Burden sisters unsuccessfully sought to assert a wider concept of 'family' for this purpose.[381]

Some current questions

Fiscal policy is controversial. Concerns have recently been expressed about two features of current tax and benefit laws: (i) the so-called 'couple penalty' that can arise from the

---

[371] Deech (1984), 256.

[372] *Rignell v Andrews* [1991] 1 FLR 332: not cohabitants.

[373] Cf the view of the Royal Commission on Income Tax (1920), cited in *Lindsay v UK* (App No 11089/84, ECHR) (1986).

[374] Williams (1947), 29.

[375] Cf the litigation in *Jones v Garrett*, discussed by Salter (2007).

[376] Salter (2007), Wikeley (2007c).

[377] Young (2009).

[378] Complaint that Art 1 of Protocol 1 and Art 8, in conjunction with Art 14, ECHR were violated where spouses attracted higher tax than cohabitants was held inadmissible: *Lindsay v UK* (App No 11089/84, ECHR) (1986).

[379] Inland Revenue (2004).

[380] *Holland v IRC* [2003] STC (SCD) 43.

[381] *Burden v UK* (App No 13378/05, ECHR) (2008).

aggregation rule that applies to couples claiming welfare benefits and tax credits; and (ii) the limited specific recognition of marriage (and, we would add, civil partnership) in the tax system.

The 'couple penalty' argument focus on the fact that, given certain characteristics (notably income-level and whether both parties are working), some couples would be better off in terms of their benefits and tax credit entitlement were they to live separately.[382] The aggregation rule, it is said, may discourage some couples from living together in order to maximize benefits entitlements, destabilizing family life.[383] Conversely, however, failure to *disclose* the fact of cohabitation is a common benefit fraud.[384] Of course, one function of the aggregation rule is to recognize the economies of scale that couples can achieve, reducing the per capita spend, compared with a single person. Nevertheless, there has been political pressure to remove the 'couple penalty' in order to encourage the formation and maintenance of co-residential relationships, not least for the benefit of children. However, a recent review of international research in this area concluded that there is only mixed evidence of the couple penalty having this effect in practice, noting in particular the impact of factors other than financial incentives and disincentives, which theories that have regard purely to financial matters fail to take into account; where there is an impact, it tends to be small and vary considerably between different groups of the population.[385] Given the evidence of the penalty having only marginal impact within a complex picture, researchers have cautioned against attempts to 'fix' the system, not least on grounds of likely cost to the state (simply removing the penalty by assessing everyone individually would cost around £34 billion on current figures) and the potential of new rules to create new, unwanted impacts on individuals' behaviour.[386]

So, if penalties are not the problem (or cannot readily be fixed), what about the lack of premium for spouses? The withdrawal of the married person's allowance and introduction of marriage-neutral tax credits has been criticized by those who consider the tax and benefit system should be used to encourage marriage, and child-rearing within marriage, instead of cohabitation or lone parenthood.[387] In any event, as John Eekelaar argues, tax incentives must be carefully designed if they are to be effective, particularly as society changes—even assuming that fiscal policy has the power to affect social behaviour at all:[388]

J. Eekelaar, 'Uncovering Social Obligations: Family Law and the Responsible Citizen', in M. Maclean (ed.), *Making Law for Families* (Oxford: Hart Publishing, 2000), 22–3

It is not difficult to see how fiscal policy may affect family life. Financial measures may be a clear expression of a wish to reward or deter certain behaviour patterns. These also operate against a backdrop of legal and social norms. Where there is a social norm that cohabiting adults "ought to" be married, for example, a tax allowance for married couples

382 E.g. Centre for Social Justice (2009), 6.3.
383 Smart and Stevens (2000), 36.
384 DWP (2010a), table 4.1.
385 Stafford and Roberts (2009).
386 Adam and Brewer (2010).
387 O'Neill (2005); Centre for Social Justice (2009), 6.3.
388 See Henshaw (2006), para 31–5 on incentive effects of child support rules.

will support that norm. But failure to keep track of evolving norms can be self-defeating. For example, the "old" system whereby a husband and wife's incomes were aggregated for taxation purposes, the "married allowance" deducted and the tax levied on the husband, assumed that ordinarily the husband will have far greater income than the wife: that is, that the domestic role will be assumed by her. Indeed, it could be seen as a measure in support of a norm that she *should* assume that role because, if she had high earned or unearned income, depending on the size of any allowance permitted for the wife's earned income, the total tax liability would be greater than it would be if the couple were taxed separately (at lower rates). However, changes in the social norm that women should adopt the domestic role were too rapid and the application of that taxation regime began (at least theoretically) to threaten another social norm: that adults who cohabit should be married. For, if the woman's income was above a certain level, it would be financially better for the couple to live together without marrying and be taxed separately. That was the position in the UK until separate taxation was allowed for earned income in 1972, and for unearned income in 1990. However, there is no evidence that these factors affected the marriage rate, which declined steadily throughout that period, and although there is now a modest tax benefit to be obtained from marrying (soon to be removed [the married person's allowance]), this seems to have done little (if anything) to arrest the decline in the marriage rate. Perhaps the experience of taxation and family life shows the relatively weak influence even fiscal measures can have when confronted by deep-seated changes in social norms.

Taxation rules can also be used for symbolic reasons: to signify relationships, behaviours, or transactions that are valued by the state. In 2010, the Conservative Party proposed an allowance for basic rate taxpaying spouses that would net up to £150 per year. Considerably less valuable than the old married person's tax allowance, it would still be costly for the state. It must be doubted whether such a low-value benefit would send the strong message that its proponents intend. It would surely not encourage many couples to marry—or to stay together.[389]

3.9 CONCLUSION

English law of family property and finances is complex, drawn from a variety of general law and statutory sources. It has been widely accepted that the general law gives inadequate attention to the needs of the family context and that unfair outcomes arise as a result. *Stack v Dowden* has not removed that problem, and has created problems of its own. By contrast, welfare benefit laws specifically recognize a wide range of family relationships; but here the law is perhaps at its most complicated, different relationships being recognized in different contexts in order to advance particular policy goals. Thorough-going review of private law in this area seems unlikely in the foreseeable future. Attention is instead currently focused on the situation on family breakdown. The next four chapters examine the specialist statutory rights and remedies that govern such cases.

---

[389] IFS (2010). On the wider policy issue of promoting marriage over cohabitation, see generally 2.8.2 above.

ONLINE RESOURCE CENTRE

Questions, suggestions for further reading, and supplementary materials for this chapter (including updates on developments in this area of family law since this book was published) may be found on the Online Resource Centre at www.oxfordtextbooks.co.uk/orc/harrisshort_tcm2e/.

4

DOMESTIC VIOLENCE

CENTRAL ISSUES

1. Domestic violence is a widespread problem, experienced particularly by women in opposite-sex couples.

2. Historically, domestic violence has been regarded as a 'private' problem, and the state has failed to protect victims. Government policy is now clearly aimed at reducing domestic violence and supporting victims. States' duties to protect victims of domestic violence under human rights law are increasingly well understood.

3. A key issue for current policy is how to provide an integrated response to domestic violence, involving criminal, civil, and family law, providing material and emotional support to victims, and giving appropriate weight to victims' wishes and interests.

4. The civil law provides remedies principally under the Family Law Act 1996 (FLA 1996). The family courts can make non-molestation orders and occupation orders between parties to a wide range of domestic relationships.

5. The family courts have strong powers to enforce orders made under the FLA 1996. Breach of a non-molestation order is now also a criminal offence, a controversial development.

6. Specific legislation deals with the problem of forced marriage.

4.1 INTRODUCTION

Domestic violence destroys many relationships, impairs the emotional, social, and psychological development of children who witness it, and can have devastating, long-term effects on the immediate victims. It has been estimated that domestic violence costs public services and the wider economy over £5.7 billion a year. The pain and suffering of victims is calculated to cost £17 billion a year.[1]

Domestic violence impacts on many areas of family law. Should a court make an order for contact between parent and child if that parent has abused the other? Does domestic violence warrant intervention by the state to protect children who are not the primary victims?

---

[1] Walby (2004).

Should domestic violence affect financial provision on divorce? Can mediation safely be used where there is a history of domestic violence? We address these specific questions elsewhere. This chapter focuses on what the law can do directly to punish and rehabilitate perpetrators and to protect victims.

A central theme in any discussion of domestic violence is the dichotomy between the public and private spheres. Domestic violence used to be regarded as private problem, ignored by the state and society. Since the 1970s, the state has increasingly recognized its responsibility to tackle domestic violence. The state's role may initially appear obvious: domestic violence is criminal conduct. We might therefore expect offences committed in the domestic context to be treated just like any other crime. Recent initiatives do seek to improve the criminal justice system's response to domestic violence, both in dealing with perpetrators and supporting victims. However, the dynamics of domestic violence raise complicated issues, particularly in relation to the extent to which victims can, or should be able to, control the course of any criminal proceedings. While domestic violence has rightly emerged from the privacy of the family home, victims may still have legitimate private interests that may affect how the state deals with perpetrators.

Important as the criminal law increasingly is as a response to domestic violence, this chapter focuses mainly on the family courts' powers. 'Non-molestation orders' can be used to prohibit a wide range of abusive conduct. 'Occupation orders' can secure the victim's right to occupy a home that was shared by the parties, and exclude the abuser. We discuss occupation orders principally here in the context of domestic violence, but they have wider significance: see chapter 3, regarding family members' rights to occupy the home; and chapter 7, regarding the financial and property implications of separation, particularly for family members other than spouses and civil partners. We shall see that the line between public and private has also come under scrutiny in the family court context: the recent criminalization of breach of non-molestation orders has blurred the boundaries between the civil and criminal justice systems, again with implications for victims' ability to control their family's fate. Determining the proper legal response to domestic violence is far from straightforward.

ONLINE RESOURCE CENTRE

We discuss the specific issues surrounding forced marriage and the Forced Marriage (Civil Protection) Act 2007 on the Online Resource Centre.

4.2 BACKGROUND ISSUES: DOMESTIC VIOLENCE AND KEY POLICY QUESTIONS

4.2.1 WHAT IS 'DOMESTIC VIOLENCE'?

The expression 'domestic violence' has no general legal definition,[2] but this definition is now used by all government agencies dealing with the problem:

> any incident of threatening behaviour, violence or abuse (psychological, physical, sexual, financial or emotional) between adults who are or have been intimate partners or family members, regardless of gender or sexuality.

---

[2] Cf Housing Act 1996, s 177, recently considered by the Supreme Court: *Yemshaw v Hounslow LBC* [2011] UKSC 3.

An adult is any person aged 18 or over; 'family members' covers mother, father, son, daughter, brother, sister, and grandparents, whether directly related, in-laws, or step-family.[3] The inclusion of family members as perpetrators brings activities such as elder abuse,[4] forced marriages, 'honour crimes', and female genital mutilation within domestic violence policy.[5]

As we discuss below, domestic violence is widely regarded as a gender-based problem:[6] most victims, and most serious victims, are women in opposite-sex relationships. 'Domestic violence' may therefore be misleadingly gender neutral. The expression 'violence against women' is sometimes preferred, though it may inhibit other victims—in same-sex relationships or heterosexual men—from coming forward.[7] However, family law's remedies for domestic violence—and the government's definition—apply to a broader range of more or less loosely 'familial' relationships, characterized by physical, emotional, and often financial closeness. We shall see that the parties' proximity poses potential difficulties as it can make victims reluctant or unable to pursue legal remedies that objectively appear best suited to ending the violence.

The use of the word 'domestic' is controversial, associated with historical trivialization of the problem. Police were particularly criticized, their expression 'it's just a domestic' betraying a failure to take violence in the home as seriously as violence committed in public.[8] Some commentators also object to 'victim', preferring 'survivor'. Hoff described the women she met when researching domestic violence as 'knowledgeable, capable people who developed strategies for coping within the violent relationship, as well as for eventually leaving it. Their ability to cope with life-threatening crises in spite of self-blame and intimidations from others that they were somehow responsible for their plight, reveals them more as survivors than as helpless victims.'[9] Throughout this chapter, we use various terms, including 'victim', the word used throughout the criminal justice system. In discussing civil remedies, we use 'applicant' and 'respondent'.

4.2.2 EVIDENCE ABOUT DOMESTIC VIOLENCE

The prevalence of domestic violence

It is difficult accurately to measure the prevalence of domestic violence, not least because agencies have used differing definitions for data collection.[10] There are particular gaps in our knowledge about violence against groups who are inhibited for various reasons from coming forward: men, members of black and ethnic minority communities, and those in same-sex relationships.[11] But it is clear that domestic violence is under-reported and under-recorded. Its contribution to official crime and civil court figures is therefore misleadingly small.[12] Many victims do not regard themselves as victims of a criminal offence. Researchers are quite frequently the first people—and the police the last—to whom the abuse has been disclosed, if it is disclosed at all.[13] The British Crime Survey (BCS) is an important data source on what it now

---

[3] HO (2005), para 10.
[4] See O'Keeffe et al (2007).
[5] HO (2005), para 10; and (2006a), paras 8, 12–14.
[6] HO (2006a), foreword.
[7] Donovan et al (2006).
[8] Mullender and Morley (1994), 11.
[9] Hoff (1990), 229.
[10] HM CPS Inspectorate and HMIC (2004), 8.
[11] HO (2006a), 45.
[12] Smith (1989).
[13] Roe (2010), tables 3.17 and 3.18.

calls 'intimate violence', since it collects information about offences which never reach the legal system and offers the additional privacy of a self-completion questionnaire, which has yielded five times as many reports of abuse than face-to-face interviews.[14] Since the BCS is based on private households, those living in refuges, who might have experienced the worst abuse, are unrepresented. But even with these and other limitations,[15] the figures gathered are high.

In evaluating the data, particularly when analysing the prevalence of abuse directed at women and men respectively, we need to distinguish between the different categories of domestic abuse, or 'intimate violence', covered by the survey. It now counts not just the use and threat of physical violence,[16] but also financial and emotional abuse: preventing the victim from having a fair share of the household money; stopping the victim from seeing friends and relatives; repeatedly belittling the victim so that he or she felt worthless. Sexual violence and stalking by current and former partners and other family members are also counted. Abuse by a current or former partner and other 'family' abuse are distinguished. The headline findings from the most recent survey on the extent of 'intimate violence' of all types were as follows:[17]

S. Roe, 'Intimate violence: 2008/09 BCS', in K. Smith et al (eds), *Homicides, Firearm Offences and Intimate Violence 2008/09* (2010), 60–1 and fig 3.1

Women were more likely than men to have experienced intimate violence across all the different types of abuse. In contrast, men, particularly young adults, are at greater risk of experiencing any violent crime.

Figure 4.1 Prevalence of intimate violence since age 16, by sex, 2008/09 BCS

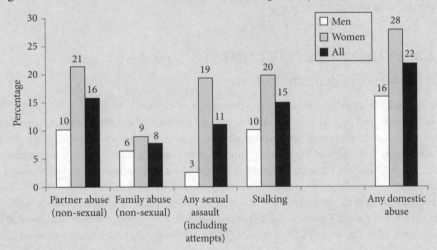

Source: Reproduced from Kevin Smith et al (eds), *Homicides, Firearm Offences and Intimate Violence 2008/09*, The Home Office, by Crown copyright © 2010.

- Overall, more than one in four women (28%) and around one in six men (16%) had experienced any domestic abuse since the age of 16. These figures are equivalent to an estimated 4.5 million female victims of domestic abuse and 2.6 million male victims.

---

[14] Walby and Allen (2004), 112.

[15] Various restrictions and methodological problems are described in Mirlees-Black (1999), Walby and Allen (2004).

[16] Cf the earlier survey reported by Mirlees-Black (1999).

[17] The most comprehensive report of survey findings is Walby and Allen (2004).

- Since the age of 16, partner abuse (non-sexual) was the most commonly experienced of the separate types of intimate violence among both men and women. About one in five (21%) and one in ten (10%) men reported having experienced such abuse since the age of 16.

- Six per cent of women and four per cent of men reported having experienced any domestic abuse in the past year, equivalent to an estimated one million female victims of domestic abuse and 600,000 male victims.

- In the last year partner abuse (non-sexual) and stalking were the most common of the separate types of intimate violence, with around four per cent of women and three per cent of men reporting having experienced each.

Although reports of domestic violence in the Survey appear to have decreased substantially since the mid-1990s,[18] with a further general decline over the five years to 2008/09, domestic violence remains a 'volume crime', constituting about 14 per cent of all violent crime reported in the face-to-face BCS interviews.[19] It is the highest offence for repeat victimization: in 2009/10, 76 per cent of all domestic violence was a repeat incident and over 30 per cent of victims had experienced at least three incidents.[20] It has been estimated that nearly one million children in the UK could be living with domestic violence.[21]

Gender asymmetry

The orthodox view is that there is considerable 'gender asymmetry' in the experience of domestic violence. However, it is difficult accurately to identify the pattern and frequency of abuse by reference to the parties' gender, and researchers using different methodologies have reached apparently contradictory conclusions about the incidence of violence by women against men. Gathering reliable evidence of male victimization through official records is especially problematic: 41 per cent of male victims of partner abuse (in the broad sense) reporting abuse in the last year for the 2008/9 BCS had not told anyone about it.[22] Since domestic violence is regarded principally as violence against women, BCS findings regarding frequency of male victimization appear surprisingly high. However, closer inspection of crime survey and other data reveals a more subtle picture, reinforcing the orthodox view.[23]

The tables accompanying Roe's BCS 2008/9 report reveal detailed differences between men and women's experience of domestic abuse. In particular, nearly twice as many women as men reported any partner abuse at some time in their life, women had typically experienced abuse for longer periods, and were more likely to have been injured or experienced emotional effects as a result of the abuse. Notably, women reported higher rates of both non-physical abuse and threats/force than men and had experienced more incidents of abuse in the last year, with men more likely to have experienced non-physical abuse[24] than

---

[18] Cf suggestions that the drop might be partly attributable to methodological differences between surveys: Walby and Allen (2004), 114.

[19] Flatley et al (eds) (2010), table 3.01.

[20] Ibid., 24.

[21] UNICEF (2006).

[22] Roe (2010), table 3.18. For discussion of reasons for this under-reporting, see Walby and Allen (2004).

[23] Mirlees-Black (1999), Walby and Allen (2004), Dobash and Dobash (2004); discussed by Kaganas (2007), 144–6.

[24] The 'emotional abuse' aspect of the definition may have been used to support the claim that men denied contact with their children suffer 'domestic violence' to a similar extent as women: see Kaganas (2007).

threats/force.[25] When viewed in context, it is clear that much of women's use of force is isolated and defensive or reactive, rather than sustained and controlling.[26] Recent research by Marianne Hester examining incidents of domestic violence reported to the Northumbrian police similarly found that the vast majority of incidents were perpetrated by men against women, and that violence used by men against women was far more severe than that used by women.[27] Domestic violence can also have fatal consequences, and here gender difference is very clear. The principal suspect in relation to 53 per cent of female homicide victims and 7 per cent of male victims in 2008/9 was a partner or ex-partner; the principal suspect in relation to 15 per cent of female victims and 8 per cent of male victims was another family member.[28]

Causes and risk factors

If gathering reliable statistical evidence about the prevalence and experience of domestic violence is difficult, reliably identifying its causes is harder. There are several theories, each of them controversial in their way, suggesting different strategies for dealing with domestic violence.[29] Some theories focus on the psychology of the particular individuals involved, both perpetrator and victim: the former having an unusually aggressive or jealous personality, the latter being unusually insecure or even masochistic. Some cases may be explained inter-generationally, parties repeating behaviour witnessed by them as children in their own families.[30] Some theories focus on social and economic deprivation; others on alcohol and other substance abuse. Feminist theories, explored in more detail in the next section, view domestic violence as a manifestation of patriarchy, of male power being systematically exercised over women.

In reality, no one theory can explain any one incident of domestic violence. Theories which in some way blame the victim are highly controversial and inconsistent with researchers' findings about the determination of 'survivors' to escape.[31] Rather than seeking to identify the cause, it is easier to identify correlations or risk factors that heighten the probability of abuse.[32] The following factors have been identified as increasing the likelihood of being a victim: being female; of young age (16–24); being separated, divorced, or single; pregnancy; living as a lone parent; low household income and living in rental accommodation.[33] Perpetrators, by contrast, tend to be characterized by: being male, having a history of criminal and delinquent behaviour, unemployment, frequent substance abuse; low income and education; inadequate social networks; stress and other negative consequences of low income and poor accommodation; and various psychological traits such as a tendency to deny personal responsibility for their circumstances, jealousy and heightened dependence, lack of empathy.[34]

However, whilst certain characteristics increase the risk, abuse is not confined to any social or economic class or ethnic group, age, or gender pattern. The perception that

---

[25] Roe (2010), various tables.
[26] Dobash and Dobash (2004).
[27] Hester (2009).
[28] Coleman and Osborne (2010), 14–15.
[29] Law Com (1992), from para 2.6.
[30] Morley and Mullender (1994), 6–7.
[31] Edwards (1989), 164–72; Hoff (1990); Dobash and Dobash (1992), ch 7.
[32] Walby and Myhill (2001).
[33] HO (2006a), 56–8; Roe (2009), 62–5.
[34] HO (2006a), 56–8.

domestic violence is particularly prevalent in lower socio-economic classes may reflect the greater visibility of disadvantaged groups, who are more likely to come to public agencies' attention. Victims in more affluent households may have better private support networks that enable them to keep abuse private,[35] and be less likely to report abuse to police and medical agencies.[36] Other studies have revealed no differences in the incidence of violence by reference to socio-economic status[37] or ethnicity, though poverty and social exclusion may be *consequences* of abuse.[38]

R. Morley and A. Mullender, *Preventing Domestic Violence to Women* (London: Home Office, 1994)

Attempting to isolate particular groups of people prone to domestic violence may be defended as a way of furthering an understanding of the causes and hence cures of the problem. However, the message from research is clear. While class, ethnicity, drinking, childhood experiences and indeed other psychological/social factors may in some cases contribute to the establishment of violent relationships and/or their continuation, domestic violence to women is far too common throughout society to isolate specific groups as constituting *the* problem.

Ending the relationship

Ending the relationship does not always stop the violence; indeed, separation sometimes precipitates abuse.[39] Many victims suffer some form of abuse in the context of contact arrangements between children of the family and the now ex-partner.[40] Separation puts some victims at higher risk of homicide, as abusers' behaviour becomes increasingly serious and obsessive.[41] Fear of abuse commencing or worsening, together with family responsibilities and cultural, physical, or economic barriers may therefore inhibit victims, particularly women, from leaving their relationship or even reporting the abuse:

C. Humphreys and R. Thiara, 'Neither justice nor protection: women's experiences of post-separation violence', (2003) 25 *Journal of Social Welfare and Family Law* 195, 196

'Why doesn't she leave?' is probably one of the most frequently asked questions for those who witness a woman suffering domestic violence. Implicit in this question is frustration and mystification that women are failing to 'look after themselves', and often their children, by remaining caught in a web of violence and abuse. This individualizing discourse places the responsibility on the woman for leaving herself open to continued violence and abuse. It

---

[35] Law Com (1992), para 2.2; Select Committee (1975), para 7.
[36] Walby and Allen (2004), 98.
[37] Finney (2006).
[38] Walby and Allen (2004), 90.
[39] Ibid., 62–9.
[40] See 11.5.2.
[41] See work discussed by Paradine and Wilkinson (2004), 14.

further implies that there is a clear line separating her life in the abusive relationship and the safety and security which awaits her once she separates.

Post-separation violence is a fear and frequently a reality for women and children who attempt to escape from abusive and violent relationships. However, it is often over-looked as a danger and remains an area where the failure of effective intervention leaves women and children vulnerable and unprotected. The effect of this failure is not neutral, but compounds the abuser's control and the woman's sense of entrapment.

The justice gap

Even taking more modest estimates of the prevalence of domestic violence, there is a vast 'justice gap' between the number of cases in the legal system and the estimated 1.6 million victims each year (see extract above) many of whom will be repeat victims and so between them experience many more individual *incidents* of abuse.[42] Police are thought to be aware of only 23 per cent of the worst cases of domestic violence, of which only a quarter result in an arrest.[43] And only about 25,000 applications for civil orders relating to domestic violence are made each year.

4.2.3 FEMINIST CRITIQUES OF DOMESTIC VIOLENCE LAW, POLICY, AND PRACTICE

We have seen from the statistical evidence cited above that domestic violence may be principally viewed as a problem of violence against women. Feminist scholars have accordingly been at the forefront of critiques of the law and domestic violence. While feminist theories classically offer an explanation of the abuse of women by men, they can be applied more widely to abuse of power by the dominant party in any unequal relationship, such as the abuse of vulnerable older people by family members or 'carers'.[44] Michelle Madden Dempsey has argued that in order properly to understand the phenomenon and so tailor appropriate responses to it, it is important to distinguish instances of domestic violence in its 'strong sense'—where it carries this aspect of control and abuse of power in an unequal relationship—from other instances of violence between family members.[45]

Central to feminist analysis of domestic violence is the dichotomy between the public and private spheres. The law and its agents have been accused of regarding domestic violence as a private matter, not a concern for the state. The state and wider society have thus enabled abuse to continue free from outside interference, and so condoned it. Historically, those charges are unanswerable. Until relatively recently, the law paid no special attention to domestic violence, instead placing wives in an inferior position. The common law permitted husbands to use 'reasonable' chastisement on their wives and to confine them in order to control their behaviour and to enforce the right to consortium.[46] These rights flowed from the law's understanding of the marital relationship:

---

[42] Roe (2010), 64.
[43] Walby and Allen (2004).
[44] Freeman (1989), 743–5.
[45] Madden Dempsey (2006).
[46] See Cretney (2003a), ch 4.

W. Blackstone, Commentaries on the Laws of England, vol 1 (1765. Facsimile edn: Chicago: University of Chicago Press, 1979), 430, 432–3

By marriage, the husband and wife are one person in law: that is, the very being or legal existence of the woman is suspended during the marriage, or at least is incorporated and consolidated into that of the husband: under whose wing, protection, and *cover*, she performs every thing…Under this principle, of an union of person in husband and wife, depend almost all the legal rights, duties, and disabilities, that either of them acquire by marriage….

The husband also (by the old law) might give his wife moderate correction. For, as he is to answer for her misbehaviour, the law thought it reasonable to intrust him with this power of restraining her, by domestic chastisement, in the same moderation that a man is allowed to correct his servants or children; for whom the master or parent is also liable in some cases to answer. But this power of correction was confined within reasonable bounds…But…this power of correction began to be doubted: and a wife may now have security of the peace against her husband; or, in return, a husband against his wife. Yet the lower rank of people, who were always fond of the old common law, still claim and exert their antient privilege: and the courts of law will still permit a husband to restrain a wife of her liberty, in case of any gross misbehaviour….[47]

The law also granted husbands immunity from liability for rape:

M. Hale, *The history of the pleas of the Crown* (1736, London: Professional Books, 1971), 629

…the husband cannot be guilty of a rape committed by himself upon his lawful wife, for by their mutual matrimonial consent and contract the wife hath given up herself in this kind unto her husband, which she cannot retract.

These rights were eroded over time, but it was not until 1891 and 1991 that the courts definitively declared each right no longer to exist.

The Queen v Jackson [1891] 1 QB 671, 678–9, 680

LORD HALSBURY LC:

I confess that some of the propositions which have been referred to during the argument are such as I should be reluctant to suppose ever to have been the law of England. More than a century ago it was boldly contended that slavery existed in England; but, if any one were to set up such a contention now, it would be regarded as ridiculous. In the same way, such quaint and absurd dicta as are to be found in the books as to the right of a husband over his wife in respect of personal chastisement are not, I think, now capable of being cited as authorities in a court of justice in this or any civilized country … The [case] seems to me to be based on the broad proposition that it is the right of the husband, where his wife has wilfully absented herself from him, to seize the person of his wife by force and detain her in his

---

[47] Doggett (1992), ch 2, argues that husbands' right to control wives was the very *essence*, not the mere consequence, of the doctrine of coverture.

house until she shall be willing to restore to him his conjugal rights. I am not prepared to assent to such a proposition.

Regina v R [1992] 1 AC 599, 616

LORD KEITH OF KINKEL:

The common law is ... capable of evolving in the light of changing social, economic and cultural developments. Hale's proposition reflected the state of affairs in these respects at the time it was enunciated. Since then the status of women, and particularly of married women, has changed out of all recognition in various ways...Apart from property matters and the availability of matrimonial remedies, one of the most important changes is that marriage is in modern times regarded as a partnership of equals, and no longer one in which the wife must be the subservient chattel of the husband. Hale's proposition involves that by marriage a wife gives her irrevocable consent to sexual intercourse with her husband under all circumstances and irrespective of the state of her health or how she happens to be feeling at the time. In modern times any reasonable person must regard that conception as quite unacceptable.

However, even once all adults *theoretically* enjoyed equal protection from the general criminal and civil laws, commentators continued to highlight the legal system's failure to treat domestic violence as seriously as other offences. This failure to intervene was attributed to a perception prevalent in various public agencies and wider society that domestic violence is a 'private' matter:[48]

J. Pahl, *Private Violence and Public Policy: the needs of battered women and the response of public services* (London: Routledge and Kegan Paul, 1985), 13–15

In a culture which, both explicitly and implicitly, assumes fundamental linkages between such concepts as 'woman', 'wife', 'family', 'home' and 'private', it is no accident that violence against a woman, perpetuated by her husband within their family home, is somehow seen as a different sort of crime from violence against a stranger in a public place. We can see these linkages exemplified in many different statements which have been made on the subject, most especially in the justifications for non-intervention given both by violent husbands, and also by people who might well have intervened had the violence occurred between strangers in a public place.

Pahl drew on two examples from evidence given to the 1975 Parliamentary Select Committee on Domestic Violence. The first was from the Association of Chief Police Officers:

It is important to keep 'wife battering' in its correct perspective and realise that this loose term is applied to incidents ranging from a very minor domestic fracas where no Police action is really justified, to the more serious incidents of assaults occasioning grievous bodily harm and unlawful woundings. Whilst such problems take up considerable Police time during say, 12 months, in the majority of cases the role of the Police is a negative one. We are, after all, dealing with persons 'bound in marriage', and it is important for a host of reasons, to maintain the unity of the spouses. (Select Committee Report, 1975, 366).

---

[48] Pizzey (1974); Pahl (1985); Edwards (1989); Hoff (1990); Dobash and Dobash (1992).

The second example given by Pahl was from the Home Office, addressing the scope of criminal injuries compensation:

> It can perhaps be argued that the Government (or the police) cannot have the same day to day responsibility for the day to day behaviour of members of a household within their own walls. Some disagreement may be inevitable within a family. Even a degree of minor violence may be normal in some homes. It can perhaps be argued that the point at which the State should intervene in family violence should be higher than that which is expected in the case of violence between strangers. Or even that the State has no particular responsibility for compensating those who suffer violence in circumstances which are largely (in the case of adult members of a family) under their own control. (Select Committee Report, 1975, 418)

According to Pahl:

> Both these statements suggest that the intervention of the state is less appropriate when the individuals concerned are linked by family ties as opposed to being strangers, and when the incident takes place in a private rather than a public place. To question this is not to advocate that there should be a policeman in every bedroom nor is it to argue for the abolition of privacy or domestic life. However, for our topic it is important to consider more carefully the ways in which the public-private boundary is defined; more specifically, it is important to consider *whose* privacy is being respected or violated in particular circumstances.... [T]he notion of privacy is not an absolute value, ... some people's privacy appears to be more inviolate than other people's privacy, and ... by looking at how 'the private' is defined and maintained we can understand a great deal about the power relations in a particular society.

E. Schneider, 'The Violence of Privacy', in M. Fineman and R. Mykitiuk (eds), *The Public Nature of Private Violence* (New York: Routledge, 1994), 44

> Although social failure to respond to problems of battered women has been justified on grounds of privacy, this failure to respond is an affirmative political decision that has serious public consequences. The rationale of privacy masks the political nature of the decision. Privacy thus plays a particularly subtle and pernicious ideological role in supporting, encouraging, and legitimating violence against women. The state plays an affirmative role in permitting violence against battered women by protecting the privileges and prerogatives of battering men and failing to protect battered women, and by prosecuting battered women for homicide when they protect themselves.

Domestic violence and the concept of privacy which has allowed it to flourish are viewed as the product of deep-seated, patriarchal ideology, present throughout the law and society:

M. Freeman, 'Legal ideologies, patriarchal precedents, and domestic violence', in M. Freeman (ed), *State, Law, and the Family: critical perspectives* (London: Tavistock, 1984), 72

> [G]iven the position of women in society the behaviour of violent husbands is rational, if extreme. It is not necessary for husbands to have formal rights such as to chastise their

wives. That they once had this right and exercised it is sufficient. It helped to form and then to reinforce an ideology of subordination and control of women. The ideology remains imbricated in the legal system even if one of its grosser manifestations has virtually disappeared. Wife battering remains one of its legacies and if this too is to go the ideology must be dismantled. The legal system has been committed to a patriarchal ideology. It is this that must be challenged if violence against women is to diminish and ultimately to cease.

L. Hoff, *Battered Women as Survivors* (London: Routledge, 1990), 234, 241

Terms such as the 'battered wife syndrome' and 'domestic violence' reveal an interpretation of wife battering as only a 'family' or medical problem and tend to mask the political and broader social ramifications of the more explicit term 'violence against women' ...

[W]oman abuse is more than a personal crisis. It is a public health problem which arises from traditional values that regard women as appropriate objects of violence and male control; from the chronic problem of women's continued economic disparity in a wealthy industrialized society; and from the gender-based division of labour regarding child-care.

On this view, improving the law's response to individual perpetrators may alleviate a symptom, but it will not destroy the underlying infection. Domestic violence will not be rooted out until the structural inequality of women in society is removed, for example through fundamental reform of employment law and child-care practices, yielding a more equal division of responsibilities within the home, to give men and women more equal economic power; and through initiatives designed to educate children and the public generally about healthy relationships and appropriate inter-personal behaviour, and to raise awareness of domestic violence.[49]

4.2.4 THE HUMAN RIGHTS DIMENSION

One relatively new arrival in legal discourse about domestic violence in this jurisdiction is human rights law.[50] Until recently, human rights arguments in this sphere have tended to focus on proportionate and fair treatment of perpetrators (especially under Articles 6 and 8 of the European Convention on Human Rights (ECHR)), rather than protecting victims or children affected by the violence. However, the European Court of Human Rights was finally called upon to consider domestic violence as a human rights violation in a number of recent cases, notably *Opuz v Turkey*.[51] In this section, we outline the law set out in *Opuz* and other human rights arguments that may be made for the protection of victims of domestic violence. We shall pick up on particular issues in the English context in the course of the chapter.

The applicant's husband in *Opuz* had over several years perpetrated serious attacks on the applicant and her mother, threatening to kill them. Despite arresting the husband, the police released him from custody, the women withdrew their complaints (under threat from the husband), and the prosecutor dropped the charges. He was later convicted for a multiple stabbing of the applicant, but sentenced only to pay a fine. Despite the women's appeals for further action, nothing was done. Shortly afterwards, the husband killed the mother,

---

[49] E.g. Hoff (1990); Law Com (1992), para 2.8; HM Government (2009).
[50] See generally Choudhry and Herring (2006a), (2006b), (2010), ch 9.
[51] (App No 33401/02, ECHR) (2009); *Kontrova v Slovakia* (App No 7510/04, ECHR) (2007).

claiming that he had to do so to protect his 'honour'. Extraordinarily, he was again released pending an appeal, going on to threaten again to kill the applicant and her new partner. The police responded simply by circulating his picture and fingerprints to facilitate an arrest should he appear again near the applicant's home.

The applicant successfully claimed violations of Articles 2, 3, and 14 ECHR, arguing that the Turkish state had breached its positive obligations to protect her and her mother, and that its lacklustre policing, prosecution, and sentencing of domestic violence constituted discrimination against women, the principal victims of that official inactivity. The Court took a robust approach, drawing on its own case law concerning the state's obligations (in particular) regarding child protection, and referring extensively to other international conventions and policies regarding the prevention of violence and discrimination generally against women. In short, Turkish law and practice were found wanting. It should have been possible to prosecute the husband despite the victims' withdrawal given the seriousness of his offences and continuing threat to the women. The response of police and prosecutors was found 'manifestly inadequate', having no impact on the husband's behaviour; the few judicial interventions were chastised for exhibiting 'a certain degree of tolerance' of his conduct.[52]

Article 2

The following passage sets out the Court's approach to Article 2, the right to life, which was breached in this case:

Opuz v Turkey (App No 33401/02, ECHR) (2009)

128. ... Article 2§1 enjoins the State ... to take appropriate steps to safeguard the lives of those within its jurisdiction ... This involves a primary duty on the State to secure the right to life by putting in place effective criminal law provisions to deter the commission of offences against the person backed up by law enforcement machinery for the prevention, suppression and punishment of breaches of such provisions. It also extends in appropriate circumstances to a positive obligation on the authorities to take preventive operational measures to protect an individual whose life is at risk form the criminal acts of another individual ...

129. Bearing in mind the difficulties in policing modern societies, the unpredictability of human conduct and the operational choices which must be made in terms of priorities and resources, the scope of the positive obligation must be interpreted in a way which does not impose an impossible or disproportionate burden on the authorities. Not every claimed risk to life, therefore, can entail for the authorities a Convention requirement to take operational measures to prevent that risk from materialising. For a positive obligation to arise, it must be established that the authorities knew or ought to have known at the time of the existence of a real and immediate risk to the life of an identified individual from the criminal acts of a third party and that they failed to take measures within the scope of their powers which, judged reasonably, *might have been expected to avoid* that risk. Another relevant consideration is the need to ensure that the police exercise their powers to control and prevent crime in a manner which fully respects the due process and other guarantees which legitimately place restraints on the scope of their action to investigate crime and bring offenders to justice, including the guarantees contained in Articles 5 and 8. [emphasis added]

---

[52] Ibid., [170].

The italicized words are significant: the applicant is not required to prove causation, that prompt action by the state *would have prevented* the death. It is enough that it *might* have done. However, in other respects the test set out in *Opuz* may be difficult to satisfy. Considerable operational discretion was afforded to the police by the House of Lords in *Van Colle* (a case brought under the Human Rights Act 1998 (HRA 1998)) and the joined appeal in *Smith* (brought in negligence) in relation to police inaction in the face of threats which culminated in fatal and near-fatal assaults.[53] Mandy Burton has expressed concern that following these decisions the question of what police 'ought to have known' for the purposes of Article 2 may be assessed on the basis of information already available to them, and not on the basis of further information they might have discovered had they investigated more actively.[54] If correct, this puts the onus on victims to ensure that they put as much information as possible before the police about the history of their case in requesting action.[55]

Article 3

Here too the state has positive obligations, as under Article 2. The Court in *Opuz* recognized that sufficiently serious domestic violence can constitute 'ill-treatment' within the scope of Article 3, whether it entails physical injury or psychological pressure, and so potentially trigger the state's positive duty under that Article to protect 'vulnerable individuals'.[56] The applicant here was vulnerable, not least because of the history of violence and fear of further violence from the husband.[57] States have some discretion in deciding how to act given local conditions, but must operate within the ambit of common international values and understandings of states' duties 'relating to the eradication of gender-based violence'.[58] This the Turkish state had lamentably failed to do.

Article 14

The Court turned finally to the charge of discrimination on grounds of gender under Article 14 in conjunction with Articles 2 and 3. The Court here particularly drew on growing international legal and political measures to combat violence against women:

Opuz v Turkey (App No 33401/02, ECHR) (2009)

186.... The [UN Convention on the Elimination of All Forms of Discrimination Against Women (CEDAW)] defines discrimination against women under Article 1 as '...any distinction, exclusion or restriction made on the basis of sex which has the effect or purpose of impairing or nullifying the recognition, enjoyment or exercise by women, irrespective of their marital status, on a basis of equality of men and women, of human rights and fundamental freedoms in the political, economic, social, cultural, civil or any other field.'

---

[53] *Chief Constable of the Hertfordshire Police v Van Colle* and *Smith v Chief Constable of Sussex Police* [2008] UKHL 50, applying *Osman v UK* (App No 23452/94, ECHR) (1998).

[54] Ibid., [86].

[55] Burton (2010, 2009a); Choudhry and Herring (2010), 356–62.

[56] *Opuz v Turkey* (App No 33401/02, ECHR) (2009), [158]–[161].

[57] The Court also referred to the inferior position of women generally in the particular region of Turkey: ibid., [160].

[58] Ibid., [164]–[165].

187. The CEDAW Committee has reiterated that violence against women, including domestic violence, is a form of discrimination against women...

188. The UN Commission on Human Rights expressly recognised the nexus between gender-based violence and discrimination by stressing in resolution 2003/45 that 'all forms of violence against women occur within the context of *de jure* and *de facto* discrimination against women and the lower status accorded to women in society and are exacerbated by the obstacles women often face in seeking remedies from the State.'...

191....[T]he State's failure to protect women against domestic violence breaches their right to equal protection of the law and...this failure does not need to be intentional.

The Court went on to find that while the legislative framework in Turkey was not itself discriminatory, discrimination nevertheless arose from

192....the general attitude of the local authorities, such as the manner in which the women were treated at police stations when they reported domestic violence and judicial passivity in providing effective protection to victims.

It concluded that:

198....the applicant has been able to show, supported by unchallenged statistical information, the existence of a prima facie indication that the domestic violence affected mainly women and that the general and discriminatory judicial passivity in Turkey created a climate that was conducive to domestic violence.

Article 8

Balancing rights

Owing to the seriousness of the abuse involved in that case, *Opuz* did not address the state's obligation to protect victims under Article 8. However, less serious abuse may fall within the scope of victims' right to respect for private and family life, and state inactivity may accordingly violate Article 8.[59] The key difference between Article 8 and Articles 2 and 3, however, is that Article 8 is a qualified right. Respondents might seek to assert their rights under Article 8 to resist, for example, removal from the parties' home or civil injunctions or bail conditions which inhibit their relationship with the parties' children. We shall explore the potential impact of Article 8 in the English context when we examine occupation orders at 4.5.4 below. However, two points raised by Choudhry and Herring should be noted here.[60] First, they have argued that Article 17 may preclude respondents from asserting their Convention rights in these cases:

Article 17

Nothing in this Convention may be interpreted as implying for any State, group or person any right to engage in any activity or perform any act aimed at the destruction of any of the rights and freedoms set forth herein or at their limitation to a greater extent than is provided for in the Convention.

---

[59] *Bevacqua v Bulgaria* (App No 71127/01, ECHR) (2008).
[60] Choudhry and Herring (2006a).

On this basis, they argue, perpetrators of domestic violence should forfeit their right to respect for private life and home where necessary to protect victims and their Article 8 rights from the threat posed by the abuse. Some support for this approach may be drawn from the remark in *Opuz* (made without reference to Article 17) that 'in domestic violence cases perpetrators' rights cannot supersede victims' human rights to life and to physical and mental integrity',[61] the latter rights falling within the scope of Article 8. Secondly, where children are affected by the violence, their rights will often be determinative or at least highly influential in an Article 8 balancing exercise.

Balancing rights and victim withdrawal

One other aspect of Article 8 was explored in *Opuz*. The Turkish state argued that its relative inactivity following the withdrawal of the victims' complaints was intended to respect the parties' family life under Article 8. If individuals do not want the state to intervene in their lives, can the state ignore those wishes? The problem of victim withdrawal divides commentators,[62] particularly once—as in England and Wales—the state has deliberately adopted a more rigorous approach to tackling domestic violence. Should the criminal or civil law be used, or both? Should legal proceedings be taken even where the victim opposes such intervention? Is a *legal* response necessarily the most constructive one? Some writers are concerned that improvements to the *civil* justice response to domestic violence may reinforce the idea of domestic violence as a *private* problem, when perpetrators should instead be subject to the public condemnation of criminal justice.[63] On the other hand, victims may wish to retain the control that the civil justice system (on the face of it) allows them. Many victims seem reluctant to bring or co-operate with any legal proceedings, often for negative reasons: they may not perceive themselves as victims of criminal or even wrongful behaviour;[64] they may blame themselves for their predicament;[65] they may fear reprisals from the perpetrator; indeed—as in *Opuz*—they may have been directly threatened by him. While it is important to help victims overcome these barriers to taking remedial action, the state cannot simply ignore their aversion to using the law. Some victims view legal intervention, particularly criminal justice, as detrimental to the interests of themselves and their families. It is said that the state should aim to empower victims to make informed choices about whether and how to engage with the legal system, thus preserving their autonomy.[66] Otherwise, victims escape the patriarchal control of their abusers only to be subjected to control by the state.[67] However, others caution against placing inappropriate weight on 'victim autonomy', given the difficulties some victims have in exercising truly free choice. The independent interests of children affected by the violence, and of wider society, may also mean that victims' wishes cannot invariably be prioritized.[68]

In *Opuz*, the Turkish authorities were found to have breached both Articles 2 and 3 through their approach to victim withdrawal: they had failed to explore why the victims withdrew their complaints, had not weighed up countervailing factors which favoured continuing the prosecution without them, and had instead 'given exclusive weight to the need

---

61 *Opuz v Turkey* (App No 33401/02, ECHR) (2009), [147].
62 Morris and Gelsthorpe (2000), 412.
63 E.g Edwards (1989).
64 Roe (2010).
65 Hoff (1990).
66 Hoyle and Sanders (2000).
67 Schneider (1994).
68 Choudhry and Herring (2006a); see generally Miles (2001), Dobash and Dobash (1992), ch 4.

to refrain from interfering in what they perceived to be a "family matter".[69] The Court specifically endorsed the approach of the English prosecuting authority, the CPS, to victim withdrawal. This involves weighing up a number of factors (such as the seriousness of the offence, the nature of any injuries, whether the attack was planned and armed, its effect on any children in the household, the risk of recurrence, the history and current state of the parties' relationship and the likely impact on it of any prosecution, and so on) in deciding whether it is in the public interest to prosecute. A key factor for the CPS is the safety of the victim and any children.[70] The Court supported this approach on the basis that

> 144....in some instances, the national authorities' interference with the private or family life of the individuals might be necessary in order to protect the health and rights of others or to prevent commission of criminal acts.

Indeed, the victim's Article 2 rights might take precedence over her *own* Article 8 right to respect for private and family life.[71]

4.3 THE CRIMINAL LAW AND DOMESTIC VIOLENCE

While its response to domestic violence is far from unimpeachable, the UK is considerably further along the road mapped by the European Court in *Opuz* than Turkey. For example, the CPS policy endorsed by the European Court explicitly identifies domestic violence not just as a crime of violence but of coercive control, reflecting a feminist-inspired, 'strong sense' of domestic violence of the sort described by Madden Dempsey.[72] In this section, we outline the principal features of English criminal law and justice applicable to domestic violence. At 4.7.2 we examine the increasing interaction between criminal and civil law in this field, and the problems that raises.

4.3.1 THE CRIMINAL LAW

The criminal law now protects all adults, regardless of marital status. Despite the lack of any specific offence of 'domestic violence',[73] the law is fairly well-equipped to deal with the various physical, sexual, psychological, and financial manifestations of domestic violence. Relevant charges include assault, wounding, grievous bodily harm, homicide offences, sexual offences, false imprisonment, kidnap, blackmail, criminal damage, witness intimidation, breach of the peace, and other public order offences.[74] Less severe forms of abuse, such as stalking and other forms of harassment fall under the Protection from Harassment Act 1997[75] (PHA 1997) and offences relating to misuse of computers and telecommunications. Cases of domestic harassment constitute the largest category of prosecutions under the PHA

---

[69] *Opuz v Turkey* (App No 33401/02, ECHR) (2009), [143].
[70] See CPS (2009), para 6.3.
[71] *Opuz v Turkey*, [140].
[72] CPS (2009), para 2.1; Madden Dempsey (2006).
[73] Cf Tadros (2005); HO (2003); and the FLA 1996, s 42A, discussed at 4.7.2.
[74] See CPS (2009), Annex A; Ormerod (2008).
[75] PHA 1997, ss 2 and 4. Recent statistics on use of the PHA 1997: HO (2003), 63.

1997.[76] The PHA 1997 empowers the criminal courts to issue restraining orders.[77] These closely resemble civil law injunctions, designed to protect victims by prohibiting offenders from behaving in a specified manner; they may now be made following conviction for any offence (not just harassment) or even on acquittal.[78] Breach of a restraining order is itself an offence. Breach of a non-molestation order granted by a *civil* court under the FLA 1996, discussed below, is also now a criminal offence.

Some victims of domestic violence find themselves on the wrong side of the criminal law, notably women who have killed abusive partners. The law's response to these cases has long been questioned, and the law of homicide, particularly the defences available to murder, has recently been reformed, though whether to the benefit of these women is not yet clear.[79]

4.3.2 THE CRIMINAL JUSTICE SYSTEM

Despite the criminal law's potential in this field, the criminal justice system has been accused of dismissing domestic violence as a trivial, private matter. Police were reluctant to intervene, particularly if victims did not demonstrate a clear commitment to pursue the case; arrest and charge rates were low; even where charges were brought, incidents were often 'down-crimed', i.e. the abuser merely cautioned or charged with a less serious offence than that actually committed; courts were criticized for lenient sentencing.[80] Women reported feeling 'more endangered than protected by the prosecution process'.[81] Their experience of using the system has been described as 'double victimization'.[82] Even quite recently it has been suggested that domestic violence has been 'decriminalized' in some areas.[83]

However, in recent years, there has been a renewed drive from government to tackle domestic violence on all fronts, underpinned by research identifying more effective ways of tackling domestic violence.[84] The new strategy has three core components: (i) prevention of violence, (ii) provision of support to victims through a coordinated multi-agency response; and (iii) protection and justice through the legal system, with criminal justice at the forefront.[85] Progress and targets (for arrest and conviction rates, etc) have been regularly monitored.[86]

New initiatives aim to ensure a robust, effective, and consistent criminal justice response, designed to protect victims from repeat abuse during and after legal proceedings, and to call perpetrators to account. Domestic violence is emphatically regarded as criminal; if anything, the domestic context may be an aggravating factor.[87] Police and CPS policies are pro-arrest and pro-prosecution, with or (if necessary and in the public interest) without victims' agreement.[88] Police powers have been significantly enlarged: an arrest may now be made for

---

[76] Harris (2000).

[77] PHA 1997, s 5.

[78] Ibid., ss 5–5A.

[79] Coroners and Justice Act 2009, ss 54–6; Norrie (2010), 285; Quaid and Itzin (2000); McColgan (1993).

[80] See generally Pahl (1985); Edwards (1989); Grace (1995); Dobash and Dobash (1992); Rumney (1999) on rape; Harris (2000) on the PHA 1997.

[81] Humphreys and Thiara (2003), 203.

[82] Edwards (1989), 153.

[83] Humphreys and Thiara (2003), 211, referring to research in Surrey in 2001.

[84] Hester and Westmarland (2005).

[85] HM Government (2009).

[86] E.g. HO (2009).

[87] CPS (2009), para 1.2.

[88] See generally: HO (2000); ACPO (2008); CPS (2009); Ellison (2003).

any offence,[89] including now breach of family courts' non-molestation orders under the FLA 1996 and breach of civil injunctions and restraining orders made under the PHA 1997. Since the victim will often be the only witness, police are encouraged to gather as much other evidence as possible to reduce the extent to which prosecution depends on victim testimony.[90] Decisions about charges are for the CPS, not the police, or the victim. Where victims wish to retract their evidence, pursuant to the policy endorsed by the European Court in *Opuz v Turkey*,[91] prosecution will nevertheless proceed if there is enough evidence and it is in the public interest. Decisions to retract should also be closely investigated to ensure they are not the product of pressure or threats. Where defendants are bailed pending trial, appropriate bail conditions should be used to protect victims. Specific sentencing guidelines seek to ensure that domestic offences are properly penalized. Their starting point is that domestic violence is no less serious than other crime; several aggravating features are identified as meriting stiffer penalties.[92] Sentencing under community rehabilitation orders may now include referral to 'perpetrator programmes', designed to reform offenders' attitudes and behaviour through counselling and group work, whilst also providing support for victims to help manage any continuing risk.

If victims are to be encouraged, or even required,[93] to participate in criminal justice, they need support and protection. Where victims attend court, that ordeal can be alleviated to some extent through protections for 'vulnerable and intimidated' witnesses.[94] All crime victims now have rights to information about the progress of their case and within court proceedings.[95] Specialist Domestic Violence Courts have become central to the new strategy, and their experiences have informed policy development across the system. Hearings in these courts are conducted with specially trained police, prosecutors, and magistrates, and can offer a fast-track procedure, minimizing delays. They also provide independent advocates for high-risk victims and the hub of a multi-agency response to domestic violence.[96] The 'advocates' are not lawyers, but individuals who support victims through the criminal justice process; liaise between police, prosecutors, courts, other agencies, and victims; and help victims access material and emotional resources to start a new life free from abuse.[97]

However, ensuring effective implementation of official policy by agents on the ground is always more difficult,[98] given entrenched working practices, attitudes, and cultures within the police and CPS. The risk of ECHR violation in an individual case therefore remains.[99] Under-funding of certain initiatives has also been a problem. Success or failure of the new strategies can be measured, not without difficulty, by reference to 'attrition' from the emergency phone call through to conviction. An analysis of attrition in 2004 made disappointing findings in this respect:

[89] Serious Organised Crime and Police Act 2005, amending the Police and Criminal Evidence Act 1984, s 24.

[90] *Re C* [2007] EWCA Civ 3463.

[91] Discussed above at 4.2.4.

[92] Sentencing Guidelines Council (2006a), (2006b); Burton (2008a), 63–6; *R v McNaughten* [2003] EWCA Crim 3479; *R v Liddle* [2000] 1 Cr App R (S) 131.

[93] Victims can be compelled to give evidence: but victim retraction has commonly marked discontinuation of the case: Cretney and Davis (1997); cf CPS (2009), Part 5.

[94] Youth Justice and Criminal Evidence Act 1999, Part II, Chapter I; CPS (2009), Part 11.

[95] DVCVA 2004; HO (2006b).

[96] Cook et al (2004); Vallely et al (2005); Burton (2008a), ch 7.

[97] Kelly (1999); Hester and Westmarland (2005); HO (2006a), Section 2; ACPO (2008) 6.2.5.

[98] Grace (1995); Kelly (1999).

[99] Choudhry and Herring (2006a), 107; Burton (2010), 136–7. For a survey of recent research, see Burton (2008a), ch 6

HM CPS Inspectorate and HM Inspectorate of Constabulary, *Violence at Home: A Joint Thematic Inspection of the Investigation and Prosecution of Cases Involving Domestic Violence* (2004), 9

The key stages identified are incidents to which police are called, potential crime reports, crime reports, arrests, charges, convictions. Between every stage there is roughly a 50% reduction. Inspectors concluded that of the 463 incidents to which police were called, there should have been approximately 260 crime reports with potential offenders. In the event, 118 crimes were actually recorded and charges were made in relation to 21%. The CPS file sample showed that typically 50% of those charged would be convicted (guilty plea or conviction after contested hearing); that is to say 11% of those matters recorded as crime led to a conviction. Whilst in some respects alarming, it should be recognised that positive police action at the early stages may have stopped or prevented violence to the satisfaction of the victim, who in many instances did not want the matter to go further.

Attrition in relation to domestic violence offences within the judicial process is higher than for offences generally. However, the picture appears to be an improving one. In the past many prosecutors had an inbuilt expectation that a bind-over would suffice, or in any event the victim would later withdraw. The fact that over half the cases received by the CPS resulted in convictions, provides a much more positive picture.

Better quality investigation and provision of information by police; higher standards of review by CPS specialists and more robust application of the revised policy; and in some areas the development of domestic violence cluster courts, are having a positive impact on the delivery of successful outcomes.

More recent figures show further progress. Several Specialist Domestic Violence Courts reach convictions in over 70 per cent of prosecuted cases.[100] More important perhaps is the percentage of cases in which *arrest* leads to conviction: in areas with specialist courts, arrest rates are over 80 per cent,[101] and general figures show that arrest-to-conviction rate improved from 13.5 per cent in 2004/5 to 19 per cent in 2007/8.[102] But that leaves 20 per cent of cases reported to police in which, for some reason, there is no arrest.[103] Some research has found a conviction rate from *report* to conviction as low as 4 per cent.[104]

There remains considerable room for improvement. There is a vast gulf between the total number of incidents, estimated by the British Crime Survey, and calls to the police. In 2008/9, 80 per cent of incidents of partner abuse (in the broad sense) against female victims and 90 per cent against male victims went unreported.[105] In 2008/9, only 36 per cent of victims of intimate violence (many of whom had had no contact with the system) regarded the criminal justice system as a whole to be effective, and 51 per cent to be fair, smaller proportions in both instances than victims of other types of crime and non-victims.[106] While popular with many victims, perpetrator programmes are controversial and badly under-funded; their effectiveness in reducing recidivism is under review.[107] Nearly a third of victims still

---

[100] HMCS, HO, and CPS (2008).
[101] Ibid.
[102] HO (2008), 23.
[103] See Roe (2010), figure 3.5 for police action in cases brought to their attention.
[104] Hester (2005).
[105] Roe (2010), table 3.18.
[106] Roe (2010), table 3.20.
[107] Home Affairs Select Committee (2008), ch 9; HO (2008), 32–3; Hester et al (2006); Burton (2006); Williamson and Hester (2009); Respect (2010).

retract their statements, though the proportion of such cases which nevertheless continue, and result in conviction or a guilty plea, has risen.[108]

However, 'improvement' of the criminal justice response may not be best, or solely, measured by reference to arrest and conviction rates. Nor is victim retraction necessarily a failure, provided the victim was properly supported. Not all victims may not measure success in these terms.[109] The goal must be for victims to become 'domestic violence free', something which arrest, victim retraction, and conviction rates cannot reliably measure.[110] Some victims may not view prosecution and conviction as a constructive step towards that goal, particularly if they want the relationship to continue in some form. But whether and when the system should respect victims' opposition to arrest or prosecute is controversial. Pro-arrest and pro-prosecution policies bring into sharp relief the difficult question of what weight to give to victims' wishes and the associated human rights issues. The importance of victim choice is recognized in the current policy framework,[111] but ultimately, the public interest and affected children's interests may be determinative.[112]

On any view, however, the criminal justice system is only one, and perhaps not always the best, option, alongside housing, welfare, counselling, and other social tools—and the civil law, to which we now turn.[113]

4.4 THE CIVIL LAW AND DOMESTIC VIOLENCE: INTRODUCTION

By contrast with criminal justice, the principal purpose of civil law is protection of the victim rather than punishment of the abuser.[114] Civil law remedies are dispensed on a lower standard of proof[115] in private hearings. The general civil law is available to victims of domestic violence. However, the laws of tort and property in practice have only limited ability to protect victims from abuse and provide them with a safe and secure home.[116]

The common law variously prohibits intentional interferences with the person: assault and battery; false imprisonment; the rule in *Wilkinson v Downton*,[117] applied in *Khorasandjian v Bush*[118] to harassing behaviour likely to cause psychiatric injury.[119] These can be remedied by damages and with injunctions. However, behaviour such as persistent phone-calling or stalking may not be actionable at common law if no physical or psychiatric injury is caused or likely, or if the claimant has no property right on which to base a claim.[120] Invasions of privacy may generate a claim, at least regarding disclosure of confidential information; but there is no general privacy tort, and the circumstances in which privacy-related claims may be made are

---

[108] CPS (2006).
[109] Kelly (1999), Hoyle (1998); cf Hester (2005).
[110] Women's Aid (2005); Robinson and Cook (2006).
[111] HO (2005), para 21.
[112] CPS (2009).
[113] Hoyle and Sanders (2000); Robinson and Cook (2006); cf Lewis, R. (2004).
[114] Law Com (1992), para 2.11.
[115] Cf Edwards and Halpern (1991), 98–9.
[116] Law Com (1992), paras 3.13–3.17.
[117] [1897] 2 QB 57.
[118] [1993] QB 727.
[119] See Lunney and Oliphant (2010), ch 2.
[120] Claimants must have proprietary rights in the affected property to sue for nuisance: ibid., ch 12.3.

unclear.[121] Injunctions can only be granted against tortious behaviour, though they can also prohibit non-tortious conduct to the extent necessary to protect claimants' interests.[122] The laws of property and trespass only assist claimants with relevant proprietary rights to secure their homes, however long they have occupied the property.[123] Victims exclusively entitled to occupy the home can enforce that right and, if their abusers are not so entitled, can evict them as trespassers. But eviction is not possible where the parties are co-owners, or where the victim has no rights at all. The civil courts' enforcement powers are also limited, and civil procedures different from those of the family courts.[124] Courts issuing injunctions at common law cannot attach powers of arrest to apprehend defendants in the event of breach.

These limitations of the general law contributed to calls for reform to deal directly and appropriately with domestic violence as a specific social problem. The Women's Aid Movement in the 1970s brought the subject of domestic violence to public attention,[125] prompting a Parliamentary Select Committee to examine the matter.[126] Two important statutes designed to improve the protection of victims of domestic violence were enacted: the Domestic Violence and Matrimonial Proceedings Act 1976 and the Domestic Proceedings and Magistrates' Courts Act 1978.[127] These Acts created special statutory remedies for spouses and cohabitants: non-molestation orders and 'ouster' orders regulating occupation of the matrimonial and quasi-matrimonial home. Ousters built on orders already available between spouses under the Matrimonial Homes Act 1967.[128] The new Acts also empowered family courts to attach powers of arrest to their orders.

However, the implementation of these Acts was heavily criticized. The schemes were complex, incoherent, and of limited scope. Different levels of court had powers to make different types of order between different categories of party under different criteria.[129] Judges were reluctant to make ouster orders and to attach the new powers of arrest.[130] Solicitors, the gatekeepers of the civil justice system, discouraged many victims from taking action.[131] The Law Commission re-examined the civil law remedies,[132] and, after one abortive effort in 1995,[133] Parliament passed the FLA 1996, amended by the Domestic Violence, Crime and Victims Act 2004 (DVCVA 2004). This legislation forms the main focus of this chapter. We also briefly consider the Protection from Harassment Act 1997.

4.5 THE FAMILY LAW ACT 1996, PART IV

The FLA 1996 is the principal source of family law remedies for domestic violence. It provides two types of order: non-molestation orders and occupation orders. These respectively protect victims from physical and other forms of abuse, and offer victims security in the

---

[121] *Wainwright v Home Office* [2003] UKHL 53; *Campbell v MGN Ltd* [2004] UKHL 22.

[122] *Burris v Azadani* [1995] 1 WLR 1372.

[123] See 3.7.1 and 7.8.3.

[124] Law Com (1992), para 3.15.

[125] Pizzey (1974).

[126] Select Committee (1975).

[127] Note also the Homeless Persons Act 1977: housing law and domestic violence are discussed in a supplement to this chapter on the Online Resource Centre.

[128] See 3.7.1–3.7.2 on the history of that Act.

[129] Law Com (1992), paras 1.2, 2.21–2.30.

[130] McCann (1985); Edwards (1989).

[131] See Burton (2008a), ch 3.

[132] Law Com (1992).

[133] See Cretney (1998), 2.

home. The Act's procedures and enforcement provisions are designed for the domestic violence context.

4.5.1 THE RANGE OF RELATIONSHIPS COVERED: 'ASSOCIATED PERSONS'

Unlike the 1970s legislation, which applied only to spouses and cohabitants, the FLA 1996 protects a wide range of 'associated persons'. However, the Act does not offer the same level of protection to all categories of associated person. Non-molestation orders are equally available across the board. But the nature of the parties' relationship affects whether occupation orders are available at all, and, if so, the basis on which they are made. This makes the identification of the type of 'associated person' relationship between the parties, in particular whether or not they are 'cohabiting', crucial.

Family Law Act 1996

62 Meaning of ... 'associated persons'

(3) For the purposes of this Part, a person is associated with another person if—

    (a)   they are or have been married to each other;

    (aa) they are or have been civil partners of each other;

    (b)   they are cohabitants or former cohabitants;

    (c)   they live or have lived in the same household, otherwise than merely by reason of one of them being the other's employee, tenant, lodger or boarder;

    (d)   they are relatives;

    (e)   they have agreed to marry one another (whether or not that agreement has been terminated);[134]

    (eza) they have entered into a civil partnership agreement (as defined by section 73 of the Civil Partnership Act 2004) (whether or not that agreement has been terminated);[135]

    (ea) they have or have had an intimate personal relationship with each other which is or was of significant duration;

    (f)   in relation to any child, they are both persons falling within subsection (4); or

    (g)   they are parties to the same family proceedings (other than proceedings under this Part).

(4) A person falls within this subsection in relation to a child if—

    (a)   he is a parent of the child; or

    (b)   he has or has had parental responsibility for the child.

One other individual whom the courts must consider, and in favour of whom a non-molestation order may be made,[136] is the 'relevant child'. A child is any person under the age of 18;[137] a 'relevant child' is defined in s 62(2) as:

[134] See FLA 1996, ss 44, 42(4), 33(2).
[135] Ibid., s 44, ss 42(4ZA), 33(2A).
[136] 4.5.2.
[137] FLA 1996, s 63.

> (a) any child who is living with or might reasonably be expected to live with either party to the proceedings;
>
> (b) any child in relation to whom an order under the … Adoption and Children Act 2002 or the Children Act 1989 is in question in the proceedings; and
>
> (c) any other child whose interests the court considers relevant.

Some of the terms used in s 62(3) to define 'associated person' themselves require definition. 'Relatives' is broadly defined:

> ### 63 Interpretation of Part IV
>
> (1) In this Part— …
>   'relative', in relation to a person, means—
>
> (a) the father, mother, stepfather, stepmother, son, daughter, stepson, stepdaughter, grandmother, grandfather, grandson, granddaughter of that person or of that person's spouse, former spouse, civil partner or former civil partner, or
>
> (b) the brother, sister, uncle, aunt, niece, nephew or first cousin (whether of the full blood or of the half blood or by marriage or civil partnership) of that person or of that person's spouse, former spouse, civil partner or former civil partner,
>
> and includes, in relation to a person who is cohabiting or has cohabited with another person, any person who would fall within paragraph (a) or (b) if the parties were married to each other or were civil partners of each other.

The definition of 'cohabitant' was amended to include same-sex couples, following *Ghaidan v Godin-Mendoza*:[138]

> ### 62 Meaning of 'cohabitants' …
>
> (1) For the purposes of this Part—
>
> (a) 'cohabitants' are two persons who are neither married to each other nor civil partners of each other but are living together as husband and wife or as if they were civil partners; and
>
> (b) 'cohabit' and 'former cohabitants' are to be read accordingly, but the latter expression does not include cohabitants who have subsequently married each other or become civil partners of each other.

But what exactly does it mean to be 'living together as husband and wife or as if civil partners'? We considered this and similar concepts in chapter 2, but we must examine the courts' approach in the context of the FLA 1996.

The leading case is *G v F (Non-molestation Order: Jurisdiction)*,[139] the facts of which demonstrate the difficulties of categorizing relationships which have not been formalized in marriage or civil partnership, and are not based on blood relationship. The parties were sexual partners.

[138] [2004] UKHL 40; see 2.3.2.
[139] [2000] Fam 186.

When their relationship began, they had separate homes but spent most nights together. Two years later, they discussed marriage. When the man had to sell his home, he deposited the proceeds in the parties' joint account and most of that money was spent on improvements to the woman's house, the anticipated matrimonial home. Initially they continued to maintain separate homes, the man renting a flat, but he subsequently moved in with her. Only weeks later, he moved out, withdrawing his funds from the joint account from which he also removed his name. Shortly afterwards, the relationship ended, having lasted just over three years. The woman sought a non-molestation order, arguing that the parties were 'associated persons' by virtue of being 'cohabitants'. The magistrates concluded that the parties were not 'cohabitants', applying the 'six signposts' from social security law.[140] Their decision was overturned:

G v F (Non-molestation Order: Jurisdiction) [2000] Fam 186, 196

WALL J:

In my judgment, the evidence is sufficient to support the proposition that the applicant and the respondent were cohabitants within the meaning of section 62(3)(b) of the Act. Of the "admirable signposts" set out in *Crake v Supplementary Benefits Commission*..., three are present. There was plainly a sexual relationship; there is evidence that they lived in the same household, and there was substantial evidence ... that the applicant and the respondent operated a joint account into which the proceeds of sale of the respondent's previous property were paid. The respondent asserts also that money was spent on the applicant's property. In my judgment ... the respondent's evidence taken as a whole is sufficient to demonstrate that he and the applicant were, indeed, cohabitants. It is true that the relationship was not stable, although in one way or another it appears to have lasted [for three years] ...

[T]he message of this case ... is that where domestic violence is concerned, [courts] should give the statute a purposive construction and not decline jurisdiction, unless the facts of the case ... are plainly incapable of being brought within the statute. Part IV of the Family Law Act 1996 is designed to provide swift and accessible protective remedies to persons of both sexes who are the victims of domestic violence, provided they fall within the criteria laid down by section 62. It would, I think, be most unfortunate if section 62(3) were narrowly construed so as to exclude borderline cases where swift and effective protection for the victims of domestic violence is required. This case is, after all, about jurisdiction; it is not about the merits. If on a full inquiry the applicant is not entitled on the merits to the relief she seeks, she will not get it.

This case signals a generous approach to the interpretation and application of the 'associated person' categories. But the relationship must still fall within one of those categories. When the case was decided, had the parties not been regarded as 'cohabitants' or as having 'lived in the same household' (s 62(3)(c)), and if the court had found no evidence of an agreement to marry, that would have been the end of it; the applicant would have been left to the general law and the PHA 1997, discussed below. However, s 62(3)(ea) now brings non-cohabiting but intimate relationships within the Act. It is not clear how 'intimate personal relationship of significant duration' will be interpreted. The Explanatory Notes to the amending Act state that:

---

[140] *Crake v Supplementary Benefits Commission* [1982] 1 All ER 498; see 2.8.2.

> It will be for the court to decide on whether the relationship meets these criteria. This covers a long-standing relationship which may, or may not, be a sexual relationship, but which is an intimate and personal one. It does not include long-term platonic friends or "one-night stands".[141]

It might be interpreted to include relationships between vulnerable adults and non-residential carers.

The concept of 'associated person' is the widest concept of 'family' in law. Some of the relationships necessarily involve the parties living together: paras (b) and (c). Many others do not: paras (a), (aa), and (d)–(g). Some involve blood or other legal relationship: paras (a), (aa), (d), (e), (eza), and (f). Some categories turn on factual rather than legal factors: paras (b), (c), and (ea). The definition of 'relative' is particularly wide, not least given the inclusion of 'in-law' relationships based on cohabitation rather than marriage or civil partnership. Despite its breadth, there are arguable omissions. For example, the Act does not protect new partners of those whose former partners resent the new relationship and direct their frustration at the new partner. Although undoubtedly 'associated' with the person on the third side of this love triangle, the new and ex-partners have no associated person relationship with each other so no order can be made between them.

The rationale for the initial coverage of the Act was described by the Law Commission, on whose recommendations the Act is largely based:

Law Commission, *Family Law: Domestic Violence and Occupation of the Family Home,* Law Com No 207 (London: HMSO, 1992)

> 3.17 The need to extend the scope of injunctions in family proceedings beyond the scope of the law of tort has been explained by reference to the special nature of family relationships. When problems arise in close family relationships, the strength of emotions involved can cause unique reactions which may at times be irrational or obsessive. Whilst these reactions may most commonly arise between spouses and cohabitants, they can also occur in many other close relationships which give rise to similar stresses and strains and in which the people concerned will often continue to be involved with one another …
>
> 3.19 … As we see it, there are three possible choices:
>
> (i) [to extend the law to include *former* spouses and cohabitants, and possibly people with parental responsibility for the same child];
>
> (ii) to remove all restrictions on applicants and throw the jurisdiction open to all as has been done in some Australian states; or
>
> (iii) to choose a middle path and widen the range of applicants to include anyone who is associated with the respondent by virtue of a family relationship or something closely akin to such a relationship.
>
> On reflection, we have concluded that the third is the best alternative. The first might exclude people who have a genuine need for protection in circumstances which most people would regard as a family relationship in the broader sense … [e.g.] people who lived together on a long term basis whether as close friends or in a homosexual relationship. We think that the second alternative goes too far. We do not think it is appropriate that this jurisdiction should be available to resolve issues such as disputes between neighbours, harassment of tenants

---

141 Explanatory Notes to the Domestic Violence, Crime and Victims Act 2004, para 24.

by landlords or cases of sexual harassment in the workplace. Here there is no domestic or family relationship to justify special remedies or procedures and resort should properly be had to the remedies provided under property or employment law. Family relationships can, however, be appropriately distinguished from other forms of association. In practice, many of the same considerations apply to them as to married or cohabiting couples. Thus the proximity of the parties often gives unique opportunities for molestation and abuse to continue; the heightened emotions of all concerned give rise to a particular need for sensitivity and flexibility in the law; there is frequently a possibility that the relationship will carry on for the foreseeable future; and there is in most cases the likelihood that they will share a common budget, making financial remedies inappropriate.

On the face of it, the breadth of 'associated person' exemplifies 'functional' approaches to family, extending family law beyond its traditional confines. But the Law Commission's rationale and the breadth of 'associated person' have been criticized for diluting the concept of domestic violence as a phenomenon particularly experienced by women in marital and cohabiting relationships:

H. Reece, 'The End of Domestic Violence', (2006) 69 *Modern Law Review* 770, 782, 790–1

Contrary to the Law Commission's rendition, the four features of proximity, heightened emotions, the possibility of a continuing relationship and the likelihood of a common budget had little to do with special protection against domestic violence for wives and female heterosexual cohabitants. Such protection was primarily associated with proximity only when coupled with isolation, controlled rather than heightened emotions in the context of unequal power, barriers to leaving the relationship rather than the mere possibility that the relationship would continue and financial dependence as opposed to a common budget ...

In many contexts, there are progressive aspects to expanding our understanding of the concept of family. But if the boundaries of the family are also treated as the boundaries for enhanced protection against domestic violence then in this context expanding the boundaries of the family is regressive, because expansion endangers the specificity of the category of domestic violence. Domestic violence used to be treated as a problem specific to the traditional marital or quasi-marital union, caused partly by women's inferior position within the home and family, 'but now the violence between those in close emotional relationships is seen as a wider problem, being restricted not just to wives nor even to domestic situations'. Intimacy is replacing inequality as the touchstone of domestic violence law ...

Feminist commentators have commonly interpreted the state's *apparent* concern to protect women from domestic violence as motivated by a *real* concern to preserve the status of the traditional nuclear family. They have suggested that the state achieves this objective by minimising domestic violence in various connected ways. The claim that domestic violence occurs in every type of relationship seems to be the reverse of minimising domestic violence, but in fact it is another method, because if domestic violence occurs everywhere then domestic violence occurs nowhere ...

However, as Mandy Burton has noted, structural inequalities can be found outside spousal and quasi-spousal relationships.[142]

---

[142] Burton (2008), 19.

4.5.2 NON-MOLESTATION ORDERS

Family Law Act 1996

42 Non-molestation orders

(1) In this Part a "non-molestation order" means an order containing either or both of the following provisions—

(a) provision prohibiting a person ("the respondent") from molesting another person who is associated with the respondent;

(b) provision prohibiting the respondent from molesting a relevant child.

. . .

(5) In deciding whether to exercise its powers under this section and, if so, in what manner, the court shall have regard to all the circumstances including the need to secure the health, safety and well-being—

(a) of the applicant . . . ; and

(b) of any relevant child.

(6) A non-molestation order may be expressed so as to refer to molestation in general, to particular acts of molestation, or to both.

(7) A non-molestation order may be made for a specified period or until further order. . . .

63 Interpretation of Part IV . . .

'health' includes physical or mental health

Non-molestation orders are available on the same basis between all categories of associated person. They can be obtained by an applicant for the protection of a relevant child without also protecting the applicant himself.[143] In this section we examine the concept of molestation and the court's discretion to make an order. We address issues relating to applications for and enforcement of non-molestation orders later in this chapter.

Molestation

'Molestation' is undefined, as the Law Commission recommended.[144] It is implicit from s 42(5) that molestation is something that may prejudice the health, safety, and well-being of victims. Case law provides some further guidance, cases decided under the 1970s legislation remaining instructive. Neither actual nor threatened violence is required.[145] Molestation, or its close cousin harassment, 'includes within it an element of intent, intent to cause distress or harm'.[146]

In *Vaughan v Vaughan*,[147] after the wife had successfully petitioned for divorce on grounds of cruelty,[148] the husband followed her between home and workplace, despite constant requests not to and his knowing that she was frightened of him owing to his past violence;

---

[143] *Re A (Non-molestation proceedings by a child)* [2009] NI Fam 22.

[144] Law Com (1992), para 3.1.

[145] *Horner v Horner* [1982] Fam 90, 93.

[146] *Johnson v Walton* [1990] 1 FLR 350, 352.

[147] [1973] 1 WLR 1159.

[148] This was one of the grounds for divorce before 1969: 5.4.

her health consequently suffered. The husband claimed that he simply wanted to ask her to see and speak to him. The court resorted to the dictionary:

Vaughan v Vaughan [1973] 1 WLR 1159, 1162–3, 1165 (CA)

DAVIES LJ:

There are two different definitions …: "meddle hostilely or injuriously" … "to cause trouble to; to vex, annoy, put to inconvenience". It seems to me that, in the circumstances of this case, taking into consideration this lady's health, of which the husband was to some degree aware, and taking into consideration the fact that he knew she was frightened of him, molestation has plainly been made out in the present case.

STEPHENSON LJ:

"Molest" is a wide, plain word which I should be reluctant to define or paraphrase. If I had to find one synonym for it, I should select "pester". Whether communication amounts to molestation is a question of fact and degree. I have no doubt that what this man did … to this woman, with the knowledge of his past conduct which both of them had, was to molest her.

Molestation was also found in *Horner v Horner*, where the husband accosted the wife in public, repeatedly telephoned the school where she worked and made demeaning comments about her to the school secretary, and displayed abusive posters about her on the school railings in sight of her pupils' parents.[149] The aggrieved ex-partner in *Johnson v Walton* was alleged to have instigated articles about the parties' relationship in the press illustrated by semi-nude photographs of the applicant. The court held that, if done with intent to distress the applicant, this was clearly molestation.[150]

Molestation was not found in *C v C (Non-molestation Order: Jurisdiction)*. The respondent instigated articles in the press critical of the applicant's behaviour during the marriage and previous relationships. The applicant was concerned that these articles would damage his reputation, and that of the charity for which he worked, with adverse financial consequences.

C v C (Non-molestation Order: Jurisdiction) [1998] Fam 70, 73

STEPHEN BROWN P:

[Counsel for the husband] submits that although in this case there is no direct threat to, or "molestation" of [the husband] in the physical sense by his former wife, nor is there any direct interference by telephoning or by sending letters or communications directly to [him], nevertheless, on the basis of the fact that she has given information to newspaper reporters resulting in the publication of … articles [offensive to him] in the newspapers, that amounts to conduct which would justify the application of section 42 …

… [T]here is no legal definition of "molestation". … It is a matter that has to be considered in relation to the particular facts of particular cases. It implies some quite deliberate conduct that is aimed at a high degree of harassment of the other party, so as to justify the intervention of the court. There is no direct communication … between the former wife and the former husband in this case …

---

[149] [1982] Fam 90.
[150] [1990] 1 FLR 350.

> Endeavours have been made … to widen the concept of molestation. It does not include enforcing an invasion of privacy per se. There has to be some conduct which clearly harasses and affects the applicant to such a degree that the intervention of the court is called for.
>
> It is further significant that in section 42(5) the [FLA 1996] provides … [The judge then sets out s 42(5)]
>
> It is significant … that section 42 is to be found in Part IV of the Family Law Act 1996, which is concerned with the general topic of domestic violence. In this particular case the marriage between these parties has been finally ended; they are quite separate individuals, and the material complained of is some alleged revelations by the former wife of what she regarded as her former husband's misconduct. In my judgment it comes nowhere near molestation as envisaged by section 42 … I believe this is a misconceived endeavour to seek to impose what might be called a gagging order … It is not "molestation" as much as damage to his reputation with which [the husband] is concerned.

Stephen Brown P did not refer to *Johnson v Walton*, which had been cited in argument. It seems hard to distinguish these cases, unless the wife in *C v C (Non-molestation Order: Jurisdiction)* did not intend to cause distress. The suggestion that the FLA 1996 is unsuited to cases between ex-partners overlooks the reality that much abuse arises on relationship breakdown; 'associated person' is defined specifically to include former relationships. However, it is important to police the limits of molestation. 'Molestation' should be broadly defined in order to attract remedies where the general law cannot. But in some situations there are good reasons why the general law—of harassment, defamation, privacy, breach of confidence, and so forth—denies a remedy, for example to protect freedom of expression where there is no sufficiently strong countervailing interest to be protected.[151] The mere fact that the parties have a relationship falling within the scope of the FLA 1996 does not invariably warrant overriding limitations of the general law.

The suggestion that 'molestation' includes a mental element—an 'intent to cause distress or harm'; 'deliberate' conduct 'aimed' to harass—raises interesting questions where the behaviour derives from mental health problems over which the respondent has no control. The wife's mental illness in *Banks v Banks*[152] caused her verbally and physically to abuse her husband. A non-molestation order was refused. It is not clear whether that was because the wife's behaviour could not be regarded as molestation, or because the judge simply exercised his discretion to refuse an order.[153]

Research suggests that it is harder to get non-molestation orders in cases where the abuse is not physical.[154] The recent criminalization of breach of non-molestation orders, discussed below, may further raise the bar, if courts are reluctant to expose respondents to the risk of criminal sanction.[155]

The court's discretion

Even if molestation is found, the court has a discretion whether to make an order and if so, in what terms and for what duration. Section 42(5), set out above, lists some factors

---

151 Article 10 ECHR; cf *R v Debnath* [2005] EWCA Crim 3472; *Hipgrave v Jones* [2004] EWHC 2901, [21].
152 [1999] 1 FLR 726.
153 Cf the less serious mental condition of the respondent in *Gull v Gull* [2007] EWCA Civ 900.
154 Burton et al (2002), discussed by Burton (2008a) from 39.
155 Cf *Majrowski v Guy's and St Thomas's NHS Trust* [2005] EWCA Civ 251, [83]; Noon (2008).

to which the court must have regard, but, as usual, it is directed to have regard to 'all the circumstances'.

Banks v Banks arguably supplies an example of the judge simply declining to make an order. *Chechi v Bashir*[156] provides another, rather unusual example. A family feud over land led to cross-allegations of violence to person and property, some attracting criminal charges. One brother sought a non-molestation order against other relatives. The trial judge refused an order on various grounds, two of which were upheld. But the Court of Appeal rejected his first objection: that the existence of the family relationship was incidental to the dispute. Butler-Sloss LJ noted the Law Commission's rationale for extending the law to a wide range of relationships, remarking that:

> Although the dispute between the parties is in origin about land, it is patently overlaid and magnified by the family relationship … The depth of the dissension and the violent reaction on both sides must owe a great deal to family ill-feeling.[157]

Where molestation is found, the court will usually grant an order. The order may prohibit 'molestation' generally, the use or threat of violence, intimidation, pestering, and harassment, or the encouragement or instruction of anyone else to do so. It may include specific prohibitions: e.g. from coming within a defined area around the applicant's home or workplace; from telephoning, writing to, or otherwise communicating with the applicant, except for defined purposes or through defined routes, for example through the applicant's solicitor. The potentially criminal consequences of breach may now encourage courts to draft orders more tightly, to try to avoid any ambiguity about the conduct prohibited. It is better to prohibit specific behaviour rather than 'molestation' generally.[158] Where the parties are parents, the order may need to be carefully drafted to facilitate contact between the respondent and child, without jeopardizing the applicant's safety and well-being.[159] Whilst the principal objective is to protect victims whose rights under Articles 3 and 8 (or even Article 2) are at stake, the court must be careful not to impose any greater restriction on respondents' freedom than is necessary and proportionate to the objective of protecting applicants' and any relevant children's rights and interests. Otherwise it risks violating respondents' Convention rights, particularly Articles 8 and 10.[160]

Orders may last for a specified time or indefinitely. In *Re B-J (Power of Arrest)*, a non-molestation order was made indefinitely in the context of ongoing disputes regarding contact between the respondent father and the parties' 10-year old child, C, who no longer wanted contact with her father and his new family:

In re B-J (A Child) (Non-molestation Order: Power of Arrest) [2001] Fam 415 (CA)

HALE LJ

26 [Counsel for the father] argues that an indefinite order was wrong. [He relied on *M v W (Non-molestation Order: Duration)* [2000] 1 FLR 107, in which Cazalet J said]:

---

[156] [1999] 2 FLR 489.
[157] Ibid. at 493.
[158] See Platt et al (2009) 6.69.
[159] See 11.5.
[160] Cf *R v Secretary of State for the Home Department, ex parte Craven* [2001] EWHC Admin 850.

" ... the object of non-molestation orders is designed to give a breathing space for the parties and, unless there are exceptional or unusual circumstances, it should be for a specified period of time. If this latter course is not taken then many years may go by and a party may find himself or herself suddenly arrested under an order made many years previously when much has since changed and the original order has lost the substance of its main purpose."

29 In my judgment, that passage both underestimates the range of purposes for which non-molestation orders were designed and contains a serious fallacy. A non-molestation order is indeed sometimes, even often, designed to give a breathing space after which the tensions between the parties may settle down so that it is no longer needed. But in other cases it may be appropriate for a much longer period, and it is not helpful to oblige the courts to consider whether such cases are "exceptional" or "unusual". [The judge then set out s 42(5) and (7) and went on:] ...

31 These provisions implemented the recommendations of the Law Commission [(1992) para 3.28]:

" ... protection should be available when and for as long as it is needed. Fixed time limits are inevitably arbitrary and can restrict the courts' ability to react flexibly to problems arising within the family. In particular, it is important that non-molestation orders should ... be capable of enduring beyond the end of a relationship, although in some cases, short term relief will be all that is necessary or desirable."

Earlier, the Commission had rejected the idea of a two-tier system of short- and long-term remedies, with different criteria, at para 2.43:

"The distinction between short and long term remedies certainly arises in practice ... But this distinction does not always correspond to the requirements of particular categories of applicant and is not therefore a justification for requiring the courts to distinguish between short and long term orders in each case. Sometimes the need for a long term order may be apparent from the outset. Often, having solved the immediate problem the parties do not need to return. ... In principle the criteria upon which a decision is based should be appropriate to the nature of the remedy sought: the duration of the remedy is simply a matter of judgment according to the circumstances of the particular case."

...

33 A non-molestation order rarely prohibits a person from doing something which would otherwise be completely unobjectionable. It is not usually appropriate to use or threaten violence, or to harass, pester or molest another person. There are obviously cases, of which this is one, in which the continuing feelings between parties who separated long ago are such that a long-term or indefinite order is justified. The order in this case was made for the benefit of C as much as for her mother: it is to C's benefit that her mother is not threatened or pestered.

Since a non-molestation order 'rarely prohibits ... something ... completely unobjectionable', it is unlikely that long-term orders, simply by reason of their duration, violate respondents' rights under the ECHR. But indefinite orders are less likely to be made if they could be breached by respondents in the course of everyday activity.[161]

4.5.3 OCCUPATION ORDERS

Occupation orders can be made in relation to a dwelling-house in which the parties have lived or do live together as their home or, in some cases, in which they intended to live

[161] James (2007).

together.[162] They can perform two basic functions: (i) confer a personal right to occupy on someone otherwise not entitled to (under contract or property law), or enforce a pre-existing right to occupy; and (ii) exclude from the property another party, or otherwise regulate that party's occupation of the home, even if that party is the sole owner. They can support non-molestation orders, physically separating the parties and so reducing opportunities for abuse.

The rules governing occupation orders are more complex than those for non-molestation orders, since the FLA 1996, departing to some extent from the Law Commission's proposals, differentiates sharply between different categories of applicants for occupation orders, depending on their marital status and entitlement to occupy the property. In consequence, five sections deal with five types of case:

- s 33: associated persons (of any category), where the applicant is 'entitled to occupy' the property or has 'home rights' under s 30;[163]

- s 35: former spouses or former civil partners, where the applicant is not entitled to occupy the property, but the respondent is entitled;

- s 36: cohabitants or former cohabitants, where the applicant is not entitled to occupy the property, but the respondent is entitled;

- s 37: current and former spouses and civil partners, where neither party is entitled to occupy the property;

- s 38: cohabitants or former cohabitants, where neither party is entitled to occupy the property.

Entitlement to occupy for these purposes flows from 'a beneficial estate or interest or contract or ... any enactment giving ... the right to remain in occupation'.[164] We discussed the relevant law for these purposes in chapter 3. Beneficial owners or co-owners of property, contractual licensees, and statutory tenants all have relevant rights to occupy and so fall within s 33. So too do spouses and civil partners (and sometimes ex-spouses/civil partners) with home rights under s 30 of the Act. Those occupying merely under a bare licence are not entitled for these purposes, so may only apply under one of ss 35-8.

Figures 4.2 and 4.3 provide an overview of the five categories. Features on these diagrams such as the 'balance of harm' test are explained in the text below.

It is important to select the appropriate section, as each:

- has different qualifying criteria;

- confers different powers regarding the types of order that can be made and the terms that can be included;

- allows for different maximum duration of orders;

- requires the court to consider different factors in exercising its discretion to make an order, to define the order's terms, and to determine its duration;

- in some cases constrains the court's discretion by *requiring* it to make an order in certain circumstances, under the 'balance of harm test'.

---

[162] FLA 1996, ss 33, 35-6; contrast ss 37-8. Law Com (1992), para 4.4.
[163] See 3.7.1.
[164] E.g. s 33(1)(a)(i).

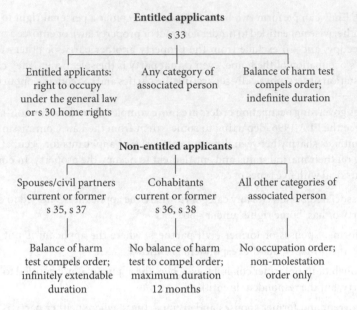

Figure 4.2 Features of different categories of occupation order

A hierarchy of property-owning and family forms emerges from the occupation order scheme. The best protection is enjoyed by applicants who are entitled to occupy the property, whatever sort of 'associated person' relationship they have with the respondent, and to spouses/civil partners with home rights under s 30. Applicants who are not entitled to occupy the property are ranked according to the type of relationship they have with the respondent: spouses and civil partners (current and former) secure the better treatment under ss 35 and 37; cohabitants (current and former) have a lesser measure of protection under ss 36 and 38. Other non-entitled individuals—such as adult children living at home with their parents, other 'home-sharers', even if they are related—cannot apply for an occupation order at all. They are left to remedies under the general law discussed in chapter 7 and non-molestation orders.

We shall examine the components of each section closely, in each case addressing: qualifying criteria; terms that the order may contain and its potential duration; and factors bearing on the court's discretion. Having set out the framework for each section, we examine a key feature of the FLA 1996 scheme: the balance of harm test.

Section 33: entitled applicants—associated persons

The qualifying criteria

Section 33 is in one sense the widest category, covering any type of 'associated person' relationship. However, that generosity is limited since this section is available only to applicants who are entitled to occupy the property or who have s 30 home rights in relation to it. The order must relate to a dwelling that has been or is or has at any time been intended by both parties to be their home together.[165]

---

[165] FLA 1996, s 33(1).

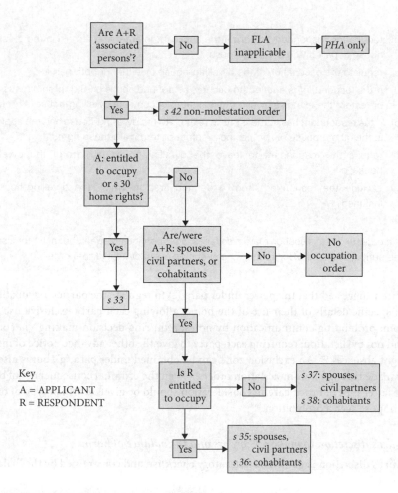

Figure 4.3 FLA 1996: choosing the right section

The order's terms and duration

Because the applicant already has the right to occupy the property, there is no need for the order to confer such a right, though the court might be asked to declare that the right exists.[166] The applicant may have been ejected from the property by the respondent or otherwise wish to enforce his or her right to occupy. The applicant may also want the respondent's occupation to be regulated, even terminated.

Family Law Act 1996, s 33

. . .

(3) An order under this section may—

    (a) enforce the applicant's entitlement to remain in occupation as against the [respondent];

---

[166] Ibid., s 33(4).

(b) require the respondent to permit the applicant to enter and remain in the dwelling-house or part of the dwelling-house;

(c) regulate the occupation of the dwelling-house by either or both parties;

(d) if the respondent is entitled [to occupy, as defined above p 287], prohibit, suspend or restrict the exercise by him of his right to occupy the dwelling-house;

(e) if the respondent has home rights in relation to the dwelling-house and the applicant is the other spouse or civil partner, restrict or terminate those rights;

(f) require the respondent to leave the dwelling-house or part of the dwelling-house; or

(g) exclude the respondent from a defined area in which the dwelling-house is included.

...

(10) An order under this section may, in so far as it has continuing effect, be made for a specified period, or until the occurrence of a specified event or until further order.

It has been suggested that the power under para (c) to regulate the parties' occupation can govern specific details of their use of the home: allowing each party exclusive use of one bedroom; prohibiting communication by notes; requiring decision-making via consultation and not by dictation; requiring each party to give the other advance notice of intended overnight absences.[167] An exclusion zone can be obtained under para (g), but is also commonly made through non-molestation orders. Given the criminal consequences of breaching the latter type of order, careful consideration should be given to which type of order to use to impose such a prohibition.[168]

The court's discretion to make s 33 orders and the balance of harm

The court's discretion is guided by a statutory checklist, and constrained by the 'balance of harm' test.

Family Law Act 1996, s 33

...

(6) In deciding whether to exercise its powers under subsection (3) and (if so) in what manner, the court shall have regard to all the circumstances including—

(a) the housing needs and housing resources of each of the parties and of any relevant child;

(b) the financial resources of each of the parties;

(c) the likely effect of any order, or of any decision by the court not to exercise its powers under subsection (3)... on the health, safety or well-being of the parties and of any relevant child; and

(d) the conduct of the parties in relation to each other and otherwise.

---

[167] *G v G (occupation order)* [2000] 3 FCR 53, 59.
[168] Soni (2007).

> (7) If it appears to the court that the applicant or any relevant child is likely to suffer significant harm attributable to conduct of the respondent if an order under this section containing one or more of the provisions mentioned in subsection (3) is not made, the court *shall make* the order *unless* it appears to it that—
>
> (a) the respondent or any relevant child is likely to suffer significant harm if the order is made; and
>
> (b) the harm likely to be suffered by the respondent or child in that event is as great as, or greater than, the harm attributable to conduct of the respondent which is likely to be suffered by the applicant or child if the order is not made. [emphasis added]...

The effect of the balance of harm test in subsection (7) is that where the applicant 'wins' that test, the court has *no* discretion as to *whether* to make an order, but retains discretion regarding the order's precise terms and duration. In *Chalmers v Johns*, it was said that the court should first check whether the test in subsection (7) was met, before addressing the subsection (6) factors. If the test in (7) is satisfied, the court knows it must make an order. If not, it has a broad discretion under (6).[169] This suggests that subsection (6) has no function unless and until that balance of harm test has been applied. If the applicant wins the test, subsection (6) simply guides the court's decision as to the terms and duration of the order; if the applicant loses, subsection (6) helps the court to decide whether nevertheless to make an order (and, if so, in what terms and for how long). However, the balance of harm test cannot be conducted in a vacuum. Assessing likely harm may require an examination of the subsection (6) factors, such as the parties' housing resources. It is also clear that an application may be made where there is no question of the balance of harm test being satisfied in favour of the applicant, but an occupation order is nevertheless desirable.[170]

Section 35: non-entitled former spouse or civil partner; entitled respondent

The qualifying criteria

Section 35 applies to former spouses and civil partners where the respondent is entitled to occupy but the applicant need not be.[171] It applies only to *former* spouses and civil partners because *current* spouses or civil partners of respondents who are entitled to occupy the property enjoy home rights under s 30, and so fall within s 33. Since home rights ordinarily terminate on dissolution of marriage and civil partnership, such individuals may require an alternative basis on which to seek occupation orders: hence s 35. The order must relate to a dwelling that has been or is or has at any time been intended by both parties to be their home together.[172]

The order's terms and duration

Section 35 cases involve non-entitled applicants and entitled respondents. Unlike applicants under s 33, these applicants have no right to be in the property themselves, never mind a

---

[169] [1999] 2 FCR 110, 114.
[170] *Grubb v Grubb* [2009] EWCA Civ 976.
[171] Note s 35(11)–(12) and equivalent provisions in s 36 allow applicants to use these sections without prejudicing any future claim they might wish to make regarding their entitlement to occupy and a consequent s 33 application.
[172] FLA 1996, s 35(1).

right to exclude the entitled party. So, if any order is made at all, it must first confer on the applicant a right to occupy. Different subsections apply according to the applicant's situation at the date of the hearing:

Family Law Act 1996, s 35

...

(3) If the applicant is in occupation, an order under this section must contain provision—

    (a) giving the applicant the right not to be evicted or excluded from the dwelling-house or any part of it by the respondent for the period specified in the order; and

    (b) prohibiting the respondent from evicting or excluding the applicant during that period.

(4) If the applicant is not in occupation, an order under this section must contain provision—

    (a) giving the applicant the right to enter into and occupy the dwelling-house for the period specified in the order; and

    (b) requiring the respondent to permit the exercise of that right....

If the court decides to make an order in those terms, it additionally has the power under s 35(5) to regulate the respondent's occupation of the property. Its powers here match those under paras (c), (d), (f), and (g) of s 33(3), set out above. The duration of any order made under s 35 is limited to six months, but it may be extended on one or more unlimited occasions for further specified periods not exceeding six months each.[173]

The court's discretion to make s 35 orders and the balance of harm

There are potentially two stages to any case under s 35: first, the court must consider whether to make an order giving the applicant a personal right to occupy the property for the order's duration; if it does that, the court must then consider whether to attach a provision regulating the respondent's occupation. Different considerations apply at each stage. Subsection (6) sets out the criteria for the first stage, determining whether it is appropriate to give a right to occupy to the non-entitled former spouse or civil partner:

Family Law Act 1996, s 35

...

(6) In deciding whether to make an order under this section containing provision of the kind mentioned in subsection (3) or (4) and (if so) in what manner, the court shall have regard to all the circumstances including—

    (a) the housing needs and housing resources of each of the parties and of any relevant child;

    (b) the financial resources of each of the parties;

    (c) the likely effect of any order, or of any decision by the court not to exercise its powers under subsection (3) or (4), on the health, safety or well-being of the parties and of any relevant child;

---

[173] Ibid., s 35(10).

(d) the conduct of the parties in relation to each other and otherwise;

(e) the length of time that has elapsed since the parties ceased to live together;

(f) the length of time that has elapsed since the marriage or civil partnership was dissolved or annulled; and

(g) the existence of any pending proceedings between the parties—

    (i) for an order under section 23 ... or 24 of the Matrimonial Causes Act 1973 (property adjustment orders in connection with divorce proceedings, etc.);

    (ia) for a property adjustment order under Part 2 of Schedule 5 to the Civil Partnership Act 2004;[174]

    (ii) for an order under paragraph 1(2)(d) or (e) of Schedule 1 to the Children Act 1989 (orders for financial relief against parents);[175] or

    (iii) relating to the legal or beneficial ownership of the dwelling-house.[176] ...

If the parties separated and divorced years ago, the case for giving the ex-spouse the right to occupy a dwelling that had been intended to be, but in the event never was, the matrimonial home is not obviously strong. However, orders will sometimes be appropriate, in particular where the children's needs require it. *S v F (occupation order)*[177] provides an interesting example outside the context of domestic violence. The parties had divorced and both remarried. Their teenage children lived with the mother in the former matrimonial home. She decided to move to Somerset, without consulting the children or the father, then living in Malaysia. The son insisted on staying in London to complete his education. The mother (it might be said) effectively abandoned him, and he went to live with an aunt. The father applied for an occupation order to provide a home for his son in the former matrimonial home. He also sought financial provision from the mother under the Matrimonial Causes Act 1973; those proceedings were pending at the time of the occupation order application:

S v F (occupation order) [2000] 3 FCR 365, 372 (Fam Div)

JUDGE CRYAN:

I must have regard to the length of separation, seven years, and the time since [the divorce], five years, and take those factors into account.... They are long periods and are together factors which have caused me to pause. But it seems to me that I have to see the timescale in the context of a continuing common parental responsibility and the use to which this property is put. It was still the children's home until they went to [Malaysia this summer].

I must also have regard to the present applications for ancillary relief.

Balancing all these [and other] factors I take the view that I should make an order permitting the father to return to the property forthwith for a period of six months, or until the ancillary relief proceedings between the parties have been resolved, whichever is the shorter.

Turning to the second stage, the court may then be invited to regulate the respondent's occupation by making provision under s 35(5). From this point, the case proceeds as under

---

[174] See 7.3.2.

[175] See 6.5.1.

[176] See 3.4 and 7.8.3.

[177] [2000] 3 FCR 365.

s 33: the court must first apply the balance of harm test in s 35(8). As in s 33, if the applicant wins that test, provision regulating the respondent's occupation *must* be included, leaving the court with discretion only as to the order's particular terms and duration. Again, as in s 33, should the applicant *not* win the test, the court retains a discretion to make provision regulating the respondent's occupation. Wherever the court has a discretion, it must have particular regard to paras (a)–(e) of s 35(6).[178]

Section 36: non-entitled current or former cohabitant; entitled respondent

The qualifying criteria

Like s 35, this section is available between applicants who are not entitled to occupy the property and respondents who are.[179] It too is limited to a particular class of 'associated person': current and former cohabitants. The order must relate to a dwelling that has been or is or has at any time been intended by both parties to be their home together.[180]

The order's terms and duration

Cases under s 36, like those under s 35, have two potential stages: first, securing the applicant's occupation; and secondly, regulating the respondent's occupation. The types of order that may be made here are the same as under s 35. However, the duration of s 36 orders differs: in the first instance it may be made for a period not exceeding six months, but only *one* extension (again of up to six months) is permitted.[181]

The court's discretion to make s 36 orders and the balance of harm

The two-stage pattern for orders under s 36 means that again there are different sets of criteria for the two stages. The subsection (6) criteria for the first stage—giving the applicant the right to occupy—are different in some respects from those applying under s 35:

Family Law Act 1996, s 36

. . .

(6) In deciding whether to make an order under this section containing provision of the kind mentioned in subsection (3) or (4) and (if so) in what manner, the court shall have regard to all the circumstances including—

(a) the housing needs and housing resources of each of the parties and of any relevant child;

(b) the financial resources of each of the parties;

(c) the likely effect of any order, or of any decision by the court not to exercise its powers under subsection (3) or (4), on the health, safety or well-being of the parties and of any relevant child;

(d) the conduct of the parties in relation to each other and otherwise;

---

[178] FLA 1996, s 35(7).
[179] See n 171.
[180] FLA 1996, s 36(1).
[181] Ibid., s 36(10).

(e) the nature of the parties' relationship and in particular the level of commitment involved in it;

(f) the length of time during which they have cohabited;

(g) whether there are or have been any children who are children of both parties or for whom both parties have or have had parental responsibility;

(h) the length of time that has elapsed since the parties ceased to live together; and

(i) the existence of any pending proceedings between the parties—

   (i) for an order under paragraph 1(2)(d) or (e) of Schedule 1 of the Children Act 1989 (orders for financial relief against parents);[182] or

   (ii) relating to the legal or beneficial ownership of the dwelling-house.[183] ...

At the second stage—regulating the respondent's occupation—there is another major difference between this section and ss 33 and 35. In those sections, the balance of harm can *require* the court to include provision regulating the respondent's occupation. By contrast, under s 36(7) and (8), the court is directed only to 'have regard to' the balance of harm 'questions', along with the first four factors in subsection (6). So, the court must consider whether the applicant or any relevant child is likely to suffer significant harm attributable to the respondent's conduct if such provision is not made; and whether the respondent or any relevant child is likely to suffer significant harm if such provision is made; and it must ascertain which side of the balance weighs more heavily. But even if the applicant's likely harm is clearly greater than the respondent's, the court is not obliged to regulate the respondent's occupation; it retains full discretion.

Sections 37 and 38: current and former spouses, civil partners, and cohabitants, where neither party is entitled to occupy

The qualifying criteria

Both sections deal with cases where *neither* party is entitled to occupy the property in relation to which the order is sought. They may, for example, be living by personal licence in a third party's property, or even be squatting. The sections are limited to current and former spouses and civil partners (s 37), and current and former cohabitants (s 38). The property must be or have been the matrimonial or civil partnership home (s 37) or one in which the parties cohabit or have cohabited (s 38); no order can be made in relation to property merely intended to be a joint home.[184]

The order's terms and duration

Since neither party is entitled to occupy the property, that limits the type of order available:

Family Law Act 1996, ss 37(3) and 38(3)

...

(3) An order under this section may—

---

[182] See 6.5.1.
[183] See 3.4 and 7.8.3.
[184] FLA 1996, ss 37(1) and 38(1).

(a) require the respondent to permit the applicant to enter and remain in the dwelling-house or part of the dwelling-house;

(b) regulate the occupation of the dwelling-house by either or both of the parties;

(c) require the respondent to leave the dwelling-house or part of the dwelling-house; or

(d) exclude the respondent from a defined area in which the dwelling-house is included....

The duration of orders under each section differs as it does in ss 35 and 36: under s 37 (spouses and civil partners), an unlimited number of six-month orders may be made; under s 38 (cohabitants), only two six-month orders are available.[185]

The court's discretion in ss 37 and 38 and the balance of harm

Here too, the position largely corresponds with that under ss 35 and 36 respectively. Under s 37 (spouses and civil partners), the court is bound by the balance of harm test, and its remaining discretion is guided by the factors set out in s 33(6). Under s 38 (cohabitants), the court must merely have regard to the balance of harm 'questions' and a checklist matching that in s 33(6).[186]

Ancillary orders under section 40

Section 40 empowers the court to attach additional provisions dealing with incidental matters on making an occupation order under ss 33, 35, and 36 (only):

Family Law Act 1996, s 40

(1) The court may on, or at any time after, making an occupation order under section 33, 35, or 36—

(a) impose on either party obligations as to—

(i) the repair and maintenance of the dwelling-house; or

(ii) the discharge of rent, mortgage payments or other outgoings affecting the dwelling-house;

(b) order a party occupying the dwelling-house or any part of it (including a party who is entitled to do so [as defined above, p 235] to make periodical payments to the other party in respect of the accommodation, if the other party would (but for the order) be entitled to occupy the dwelling-house [as defined above];

(c) grant either party possession or use of furniture or other contents of the dwelling-house;

(d) order either party to take reasonable care of any furniture or other contents of the dwelling-house;

(e) order either party to take reasonable steps to keep the dwelling-house and any furniture or other contents secure.

---

[185] Ibid., ss 37(5) and 38(6).
[186] Ibid., s 38(4).

(2) In deciding whether and, if so, how to exercise its powers under this section, the court shall have regard to all the circumstances of the case including—

(a) the financial needs and financial resources of the parties; and

(b) the financial obligations which they have, or are likely to have in the foreseeable future, including financial obligations to each other and to any relevant child.

(3) An order under this section ceases to have effect when the occupation order to which it relates ceases to have effect.

To think that this appears to be rather petty detail would be to misunderstand the nature of domestic abuse:

H. Conway, 'Money and Domestic Violence—escaping the *Nwogbe* trap', (2002) 32 *Family Law* 61

The predominant feature of domestic violence is less physical assault than the exercise and maintenance of power held by one party over the other.... Often ill-treatment is manifested in a financial way, with the income and monetary arrangements for the family being in the sole domain of one of the parties, thus leading to unacceptable levels of control over the life of the other partner.

It is a further feature of domestic violence that in many cases an abuser will be imaginative and vindictive in seeking ways around the law to continue his abuse. Unless orders are drafted carefully, using the ability to specify particular forms of behaviour as molestation, a level of abuse may continue, although it might not legally form the basis for a power of arrest being activated or a committal application being founded.

[Hence s 40, which was] partly intended to prevent the undermining of occupation orders by such actions that would make continued occupation of the home under an order either impossible (for example, because of repossession) or intolerable (for example, because the property is stripped of all the furniture).

We shall see at 4.7.1 that insofar as it involves ordering payment of outgoings to third parties (such as landlords, local authorities, etc), the effectiveness of s 40 is seriously limited by problems surrounding its enforcement.

The balance of harm test and questions

Under the 1970s legislation, judges appeared reluctant to take what they regarded as the 'Draconian step' of excluding respondents from their own homes. Lower courts initially held that occupation orders could not be made at all in favour of non-entitled cohabitants against their property-owning partners. The House of Lords in *Davis v Johnson*, by majority, overturned those decisions.[187] Lord Scarman's powerful speech emphasized the importance of ensuring that property rights should not be allowed to undermine the protection offered to victims whose fundamental rights to integrity and safety of the person were at stake, whether as a result of the property owner's violence or the risk of homelessness should an order not be made.[188] However, many courts continued to emphasize the 'Draconian' nature

[187] [1979] AC 264.
[188] Ibid., 348.

of occupation orders and the need for strong justification for ejecting property owners.[189] Even the House of Lords regarded occupation orders as a 'first aid' measure rather than a long-term solution.[190]

The balance of harm test and the corresponding 'questions' that apply to ss 36 and 38 were intended to ensure that applicants in need of protection receive it. Research suggests that occupation orders are now made more frequently than under the old legislation.[191]

Breaking the test into separate steps helps us to see more clearly what it involves and how it is 'won' or 'lost' in sections 33, 35, and 37.

- Is the applicant or any relevant child **likely** to **suffer significant harm** attributable to the respondent's conduct if the relevant type of order is *not* made? If not, the test has not been satisfied, so the court is not *required* to make the order but may *choose* to do so.

- If such harm is likely, is the respondent or any relevant child likely to suffer significant harm if the order *is* made? If not, the applicant wins by default and so the court must, under ss 33, 35, and 37, make an order.

- If such harm is likely, the court must weigh the respective harm on each side of the balance.

- If the harm on the applicant's side of the balance is *greater than* the harm on the respondent's side, then an order *must be made*.

- If the harm on the respondent's side is greater, *or if the scales are evenly balanced*, then the court is not obliged to make an order, but may choose to do so.

In ss 36 and 38 (applications by non-entitled cohabitants), the court simply asks these questions, but is never obliged to make an order, retaining full discretion. We next examine three key components of the test, indicated above in bold.

'Significant harm'

The core concept, 'harm', is more serious than mere 'hardship':

Family Law Act 1996, s 63(1)

... "harm"—

(a) in relation to a person who has reached the age of eighteen years, means ill-treatment or the impairment of health; and

(b) in relation to a child, means ill-treatment or the impairment of health or development; ...

"development" means physical, intellectual, emotional, social or behavioural development; "health" includes physical or mental health...

---

[189] Cases treating children's interests as the first consideration were overruled in *Richards v Richards* [1984] 1 AC 174; Burton (2008a), 35.

[190] *Davis v Johnson* [1979] AC 264, 343, and 349.

[191] Edwards (2001).

The harm must be 'significant', which is taken here, as in the context of child protection law, to mean 'considerable, noteworthy or substantial'.[192]

Likely

The significant harm must be 'likely'. By analogy with child protection law, this does not mean that the harm must be 'more likely than not' to occur—a greater than 50 per cent chance. It is sufficient that there is a 'real possibility' of that harm occurring. But that prognosis must be based on facts that have themselves been proved on the balance of probabilities, and not on mere suspicions.[193] By contrast with child protection law, the test is concerned only with the likelihood of harm in the future. The fact that harm may have occurred in the past or present is irrelevant if it is unlikely to endure.

It has been argued that this focus on the future and the courts' particular interpretation of the likelihood test in the FLA 1996 may deny remedies to worthy applicants. In *B v B (occupation order)*,[194] the respondent's serious violence caused the applicant to flee the parties' home with their baby. At the time of the application, they were safely (though unsatisfactorily) housed elsewhere. In asking whether the applicant and child were likely to suffer significant harm in the future, the court focused on their housing situation, not on the respondent's violence. Felicity Kaganas has criticized the court's approach: Parliament can hardly have intended that victims should be deprived of the protection of an occupation order by fleeing their home.[195]

At what point should the likelihood of harm be assessed: the time of the hearing or some earlier point? Kaganas advocates an approach similar to that used for the threshold test in child protection cases,[196] whereby the court would ask whether significant harm was likely when the applicant took steps to protect herself, by calling the police, leaving the home, etc. Alternatively, she suggests that the courts should consider whether harm is likely should the applicant return home. Applicants otherwise face an invidious choice: on the one hand, they could remain in a violent home in order to satisfy the balance of harm test; or, on the other hand, they could escape to safety, but thereby fail the test and so perhaps fail to secure an occupation order.

'Attributable to the conduct of the respondent'

A further limitation is that it must be shown that the likely harm on the applicant's side of the scales is 'attributable to the conduct of the respondent'. This makes the test harder for the applicant to win, and it did not form part of the Law Commission's recommendations, which focused on need rather than conduct.[197] What sort of link between the conduct and the harm is required?

The first question is whether it must be shown that the respondent *intends* to harm the applicant or relevant child. In *G v G (occupation order)*,[198] the parties were divorcing but still living in the same household with their children. The wife sought an occupation order.

---

[192] *Chalmers v Johns* [1999] 2 FCR 110, 117, adopting *Humberside County Council v B* [1993] 1 FLR 257. See 12.5.3.
[193] *Re H and others (minors) (sexual abuse: standard of proof)* [1996] AC 563.
[194] [1999] 2 FCR 251.
[195] Kaganas (1999a), 201.
[196] Ibid.; Children Act 1989 (CA 1989), s 31(2); see 12.5.3.
[197] Law Com (1992), para 4.34.
[198] [2000] 3 FCR 53.

The strain between the parents was found by the judge to be causing significant harm to the wife and children, but was it attributable to the husband's conduct? The first instance judge thought not. His remarks could describe the ending of many relationships:

G v G (occupation order: conduct) [2000] 3 FCR 53, 57 (CA)

Quoting the first instance judge:

... [T]o a great extent the conduct of the father is ... unintentional. I do not believe ... that this is a father who sets out to be unpleasant ... [M]uch of the present strain and worry is the result of the meeting of two apparently incompatible personalities, and that the great differences between them are aggravated by this awful no-man's land in which they have now been living for a year....

... [I]n all the circumstances of this thoroughly difficult case, bearing in mind the length of the marriage [15 years] and that much of the difficulties are to do with character and temperament and other factors unavoidable on an adult relationship breakdown, I am not persuaded that it would be appropriate ... to make an occupation order.

On appeal, the wife successfully argued that unintended conduct and resulting harm should be considered:

THORPE LJ:

13. ... Plainly, the word attributable on its proper construction could not dissociate the tension that the judge found evident in the complaint from the conduct by the husband that he had found proved. Plainly, the court's concentration must be upon the effect of conduct rather than on the intention of the doer. Whether misconduct is intentional or unintentional is not the question. An applicant under s 33 is entitled to protection from unjustifiable conduct that causes harm to her or the children of the family. The effect is what the judge must assess. Tiny wounds may be inflicted with great malice: great blows may be struck unintentionally. Of course, lack of intent might support a plea of accidental injury. But where something is not done accidentally it is not to be dismissed on the grounds that it was not done deliberately.

Secondly, 'attributable' implies some causal relationship between conduct and harm. But how far can the 'chain of causation' stretch before harm can no longer be attributed to the respondent's conduct?

F. Kaganas, 'B v B (Occupation Order) and Chalmers v Johns: Occupation orders under the Family Law Act 1996', (1999) 11 Child and Family Law Quarterly 193, 198

Section 33(7) does not prevent the courts, in assessing the harm to a respondent or relevant child, from taking cognisance of factors such as their housing needs and resources; the provision does not limit the types of harm that are relevant here and it appears that any harm that would be likely to stem from the making of an order can be taken into account. Indeed, in explaining the operation of the balance of harm test, the Law Commission, while suggesting that this would not normally constitute significant harm, specifically cited as an example of potential hardship to a respondent difficulty of finding alternative accommodation. But doubts have been expressed as to whether considerations of this nature can be taken into account when determining whether there is a risk of significant harm to the applicant or child. In relation to the applicant or child, subsection 7 provides that it is only the likelihood of harm attributable to the conduct of the respondent that can be considered. It has accordingly been suggested that the harm suffered by an applicant or child as a result of having to flee to overcrowded or unsuitable accommodation because of the respondent's violence may be attributable to the inadequate provision of refuges and housing rather than to the conduct of the respondent. Against this, however, it could be argued that such harm can be attributed to both factors; although it is not the respondent's conduct that renders the available accommodation unsatisfactory, it is his conduct that forces the applicant and the child to occupy it. On this reasoning, the harm suffered by the applicant and child as a result of the move whether caused by inhabiting a dangerous environment or, say, by the disruption for a child of having to change schools, would fall within the purview of subsection 7.

This was the approach taken in *B v B (occupation order).*[199] Having fled the family home owing to the husband's violence, the wife and baby were housed by the local authority in temporary, extremely poor, bed and breakfast accommodation: mother and child occupied one room with a shower and shared a bed; 12 other people lived in the house, with only one kitchen, one toilet, and two bathrooms; there was no garden, but a park 10 minutes away. The judge found that, particularly in winter when poor weather would confine them to their room, this accommodation was likely significantly to impair the baby's health and development. The appeal court agreed that this was attributable to the father's conduct.

Application of the balance of harm test and the residual statutory discretion

One difficulty with the test is its hypothetical nature: the court must consider what is likely to happen should it make, or not make, an order. At that stage, the court does not know what precise terms any order that it might make would contain. For the test to make practical sense, the court should consider the harm in the light of specific possibilities. For example: what harm is the applicant likely to suffer if we do not regulate the respondent's occupation or, alternatively, suspend the respondent's right to occupy; and what harm is the respondent likely to suffer if we do make either sort of provision? In almost all cases, a non-molestation order will also be sought and made. The court will then have to predict how effective that order will be. If a non-molestation order has been made, will that stop the violence and remove any real possibility of further harm?

The appellate courts continue to be cautious. They are reluctant to make interim orders excluding one party, particularly where there are ongoing family proceedings with implications for the home's future occupation. In *Chalmers v Johns*, the parties had had a long relationship, were joint tenants of their home, and had a child aged seven. Each party had assaulted the other over the years, causing no more than minor injury. The mother, in particular, had problems with alcohol. The father had called out the police on three previous occasions in the last year, but although the mother had been arrested each time, she had not been charged.

---

[199] [1999] 2 FCR 251.

Chalmers v Johns [1999] 2 FCR 110, 112, 115–16 (CA)

THORPE LJ:

The final call out came on 5 May. On this occasion it was the mother who called the police. On this occasion she was observed to have minor injury. On this occasion the police seemed to have taken a more robust line, for they arrested the father and charged him with common assault. Apparently he was bailed on condition that he vacated the family home pending trial. That trial took place on 5 June. The justices acquitted the father and so he was free to return to the family home.

The mother's emotional reaction is not established but can be imagined. She exercised her right to leave, taking the youngest child with her and sadly that has to date constituted a final separation. I say that because it does seem very sad that this couple after 25 years of shared family life and obvious attachment each to the other should have determined, at least on one side, that a continuing relationship is impossible.

There have been a welter of applications to the court following the mother's departure. On 11 June she applied for a non-molestation and an occupation order. On 19 June the father applied for a residence order and an occupation order. On 13 July she applied for a transfer of tenancy and for a residence order. Those applications have been before the court either for directions, or for conciliation or for interlocutory application.... [At one hearing an order for contact was made, allowing regular staying contact between the youngest child and the father in the family home.]

When with her mother [that child, A] is in unsatisfactory temporary council accommodation, which is said to be a mile and a half from school. The family home is about ten minutes' walk from the school ...

The residence order, determining whether A would live with her father or mother, had not yet been made. The instant appeal had been brought by the father against an interim occupation order excluding him from the family home and allowing the mother to return, with the daughter. Thorpe LJ overturned the judge's finding that the balance of harm test was satisfied, and turned to the exercise of the discretion. He remarked that this was 'a very slight' case as domestic violence cases go, such that it did not fall within the scope of the balance of harm test at all. That left the question whether to make an order to the court's discretion. The fact that the residence order hearing was just a month away was considered highly relevant:

On that occasion the court will have before it all the issues and principally which of these two parents, if they have to remain separate, should have the primary responsibility for A's care; which of the two, if they must be separate, should have the sole tenancy of the family home; and whether there should be orders of a more permanent character under the Family Law Act 1996.... As a matter of generality, ... a court should be cautious to make a definitive order at an interlocutory stage with a final hearing only six or seven weeks distant. The gravity of an order requiring a respondent to vacate the family home, an order overriding proprietary rights, was recognised in cases under the [1970s legislation] and a string of authorities in this court emphasise the draconian nature of such an order, and that it should be restricted to exceptional cases.... [T]he wider statutory provisions contained in the Family Law Act [do not] obliterate that authority. The order remains draconian, particularly in the perception of the respondent. It remains an order that overrides proprietary rights and it seems to me that it is an order that is only justified in exceptional circumstances. Of course there will be cases where the character of the violence or the risk of violence and the harm to the victim or the risk of harm to the victim is such that the draconian order must be made, must be made immediately, and must be made at the earliest interlocutory stage. But I simply do not see this case on its facts approaching anywhere near that category. Conventionally the court has given careful consideration to the control of domestic disharmony by the imposition of [non-molestation] orders before resorting to the draconian order. It is to be noted that in the history of this case, there is clear evidence of such judicial management having proved highly effective ...

It may have been difficult to satisfy the balance of harm test on these facts, and the violence was being controlled by non-molestation orders. But there is something to be said for enabling the parties to live apart pending the final hearing and so removing the tension that would otherwise exist (even if non-molestation orders are made). An order would also have enabled the mother and daughter to return to the family home and so closer to the child's school. Kaganas considers that Thorpe LJ's focus on violence (specifically) and property rights undermines Parliament's intention to emphasise the broader interests of victims and children and to give the courts power to achieve 'sensible' solutions to the problems associated with relationship breakdown.[200]

G v G (occupation order)[201] is open to similar criticism. There had been no violence, but the husband's conduct and the tense atmosphere over the divorce were making the home miserable, particularly for the children. Again the court refused an interim order pending the final hearing of the residence and financial applications: those proceedings had been accelerated, the husband would be away on business much of the time, and the judge had prescribed detailed rules regarding the parties' occupation of the property and their behaviour towards each other until the hearing. The judge considered that 'the friction between the parties was only the product of their incompatible personalities and the heightened tensions that any family has to live with whilst the process of divorce and separation is current'.[202]

The reluctance to use occupation orders as a matter of course on relationship breakdown was also shown in another case:

Re Y (children) (occupation order) [2000] 2 FCR 470, 478 and 480 (CA)

SEDLEY LJ:

The purpose of an occupation order, however large its grounds may be, is not to break matrimonial deadlocks by evicting one of the parties ... To use the occupation order as a weapon in domestic warfare is wholly inappropriate. Parliament has made provision for it as a last resort in an intolerable situation, not as a move in a game of matrimonial chess.[203]

B v B (occupation order),[204] aspects of which we have already considered, was an unusual case in which an order was withheld despite serious violence, and illustrates the importance of housing law to occupation order cases. The wife and baby had fled to temporary bed and

---

[200] Kaganas (1999a), 197.
[201] [2000] 3 FCR 53.
[202] Ibid., 58.
[203] [2000] 2 FCR 470, 478, and 480.
[204] [1999] 2 FCR 251.

breakfast accommodation following serious violence by the husband against the wife. He remained in the home with his six-year-old son from a previous marriage. Having fled the home because of domestic violence, the wife was entitled to permanent rehousing by the local authority, as someone having a 'priority need' for accommodation and not 'intentionally homeless'.[205] The husband would also have priority need by virtue of having his son with him, but, if ejected from the home by an occupation order because of his violence, he would be regarded as intentionally homeless. As such, he and his son would be given only temporary accommodation and advice and assistance in seeking a home.[206] Since the husband was caring full-time for his son, he could not afford to rent private sector accommodation:

B v B (occupation order) [1999] 2 FCR 251, 258–61 (CA)

BUTLER-SLOSS LJ:

The respective housing needs of the parties are, in one sense, equal. Each needs two-bedroom accommodation provided by the local authority; but the 'housing resources', using that term to include the duty owed to each by the local authority, were quite different. Unsatisfactory as [the wife's] current temporary accommodation is, there is every prospect that in the reasonably foreseeable future she and [the baby] will be rehoused by the local authority in suitable two-bedroomed accommodation. There is no such prospect for [the husband and his son, MB] if the occupation order stands.

As we discussed above, the judge had found, and the Court of Appeal agreed, that the baby was likely to suffer significant harm in the poor accommodation and that this could be attributed to the respondent's conduct. However, the Court of Appeal also found that were the husband and his son evicted from the home to allow the wife and baby to return, the son would suffer significant harm: he had already suffered from his parents' separation and would have to change schools for the fifth time in 18 months, further impairing his social, educational, and emotional development.

In our judgment, and whilst in no sense under-estimating the difficulties and frustrations of living with and caring for a toddler in bed and breakfast accommodation, the essential security for a child of [the baby's] age is being where her mother is. Furthermore, ... on the evidence, Mrs B's residence in bed and breakfast accommodation is likely to be temporary.

For MB the position is much more complex. His security depends not just on being in the care of his father, but on his other day-to-day support systems, of which his home and his school are plainly the most important ...

In our judgment, if, on the facts of this case, the respective likelihoods of harm are weighed so far as the two children are concerned, the balance comes down clearly in favour of MB suffering the greater harm if an occupation order is made.

However, Butler-Sloss LJ was at pains to emphasize that this was an unusual case, and that the husband should not think that the court condoned his behaviour:

... This case turns on its own very special facts. We have no sympathy for Mr B. He has behaved towards his wife in a manner which the judge found to be disgraceful. He treated her

---

[205] Housing Act 1996, s 193.
[206] Ibid., s 190.

with serious domestic violence. Such conduct is unacceptable, and plainly falls to be considered within s 33(6)(d). Thus, were it not for the fact that he is caring for MB, and that MB has particular needs which at present outweigh those of [the baby], an occupation order would undoubtedly have been made.

The message of this case is emphatically *not* that fathers who treat their partners with domestic violence and cause them to leave home can expect to remain in occupation of the previously shared accommodation. Equally, such fathers should not think that an application for a residence order in relation to a child or children of the relationship will prevent occupation orders being made against them.

Part IV of the 1996 Act is designed to protect cohabitants from domestic violence and to secure their safe occupation of previously shared property. Nothing in this judgment should be read as weakening that objective.

Each case will, of course, turn on its facts. The critical, and highly unusual facts of this case are (1) that MB is not a child of the parties; (2) that there is no question of MB being cared for by Mrs B or anyone other than Mr B; (3) that Mr B is thus the full-time care of a child who is likely to suffer greater harm that the harm which will be suffered by Mrs B and [the baby] if an occupation order is made. It is the position of MB alone which … makes it inappropriate for an occupation order to be made on the facts of this case.

The courts are alert to what they regard as undue reliance on public housing entitlements. In *Re Y (children) (occupation order)*,[207] it had been suggested that the local authority would find it easier to rehouse the wife than the husband, who had special accommodation needs associated with his disability. But the authority might find the wife intentionally homeless if she were evicted by an occupation order and might regard the husband as having a greater need. In any event, the Court of Appeal held that an occupation order was not merited: the home was large enough to share, and mutual undertakings made by the parties seemed to have brought their behaviour under control. The local authority's ability to reduce tension by housing one party was not regarded as a reason either to require that party to leave, or to refuse to make an order in favour of that party. If a home can safely be shared, or if the applicant for an occupation order can make a good case under the FLA 1996 for an order evicting the other party, the court considered that it should not engineer an outcome that throws the party with stronger housing entitlements on the local authority. As Sedley LJ pithily put it, 'the purpose of an occupation order… [is not] to use publicly-funded emergency housing as a solution for domestic strife'.[208]

Difficult issues may arise where the parties' home is shared with the extended family, a situation not uncommon in certain minority ethnic communities. Prior to the FLA 1996, in *Chaudhry v Chaudhry* a judge declined to make an occupation order in favour of a blameless wife where the matrimonial home was owned by the husband together with his father, and occupied by several members of his family who had been alleged to have attacked the wife. The judge found that requiring the husband to permit the wife to occupy the property would create a 'miserable situation which would lead to violence and … an impossible situation'. Divorce proceedings were in any event pending, and these would resolve the issue of the wife's accommodation in the longer term.[209] Under the FLA 1996, the court could now make non-molestation orders against the husband's family, and, provided that the applicant had

---

[207] [2000] 2 FCR 481.
[208] Ibid., [30].
[209] [1987] 1 FLR 347.

home rights or was otherwise entitled to occupy the property, could also make an occupation order against them under s 33. Were the balance of harm test satisfied, an occupation order would now have to be made. But where the applicant cannot invoke s 33, no occupation order interfering with the wider family's occupation of the home would be possible: ss 35–8 only permit orders to be made against the applicant's spouse, civil partner, or cohabitant, not other 'associated persons'.

Mary Hayes has advocated a more expansive use of occupation orders:

M. Hayes, 'The Law Commission and the Family Home', (1990) 53 *Modern Law Review* 222, 223–4

… [I]t is a dangerous social policy which regulates the right to occupy the matrimonial home … only where there is proof of violence…. Such a rigid approach could provoke a wife, desperate to live apart from her husband, but needing to stay in the family home (perhaps because of the children) either falsely to accuse him of violence or, in an extreme case, to precipitate an act of violence against herself …

[I]s it reasonable to expect spouses to remain together under the same roof, where one of them has decided that the marriage has broken down to such a degree that he or she wants the other spouse to leave the home and is prepared to apply to a court to achieve this purpose? … [W]here one spouse is in an economically weak position, and especially where housing must be provided for the children, that spouse … may not be able to separate from her husband without recourse to, and the assistance of, the courts.

The decisions in *G v G* and *Re Y* have also been criticized for under-estimating the impact on children of living in a high-tension household.[210]

Grubb v Grubb[211] now provides an example of an occupation order being made in favour of a wife in a non-violent case pending the resolution of the parties' financial issues following their stressful, defended divorce. It demonstrates the potential for occupation orders to alleviate pressures experienced by families on relationship breakdown. Crucially, the husband had adequate alternative accommodation and the wife was prepared to vacate the family home as soon as he provided somewhere else for her to live.

4.5.4 A HUMAN RIGHTS AUDIT OF THE OCCUPATION ORDER SCHEME

Unlawful discrimination contrary to Article 14?

One of the occupation order scheme's most striking features is its differential treatment of different types of applicant. What is the justification for this? Does it amount to discrimination in violation of Article 14 ECHR, in conjunction with Articles 2, 3, and 8? The Law Commission's original proposals had distinguished between applicants by reference to their property entitlement, but not in terms of marital status.[212] This was unacceptable to parliamentarians who feared that marriage would be undermined (apparently oblivi-

---

210 Choudhry and Herring (2010), 370.
211 [2009] EWCA Civ 976.
212 Law Com (1992), Part IV; spouses and cohabitants were treated identically, but the Law Commission did not extend occupation orders to 'other' non-entitled associated persons.

ous that cohabitants had been included in the legislation since the 1970s), and who forced the insertion of the distinctions between spouses (and now civil partners) and cohabitants. There are four key differences: (i) the applicability of the balance of harm test; (ii) the checklists; (iii) the duration of orders; and (iv) the fact that non-entitled individuals in other forms of 'associated person' relationship cannot apply at all.

The differences regarding the balance of harm and duration of orders in ss 35 and 36 seem hard to explain. The parties in s 35 made a formal legal commitment (now dissolved) to each other, which the s 36 cohabitants never have. That lack of legal commitment does not inhibit cohabitants applying under s 33, though there they are entitled to occupy the property, which s 36 applicants are not. Property entitlement is clearly important. That may explain the difference between ss 35 and 36: since the respondent is entitled to occupy and the applicant not, the applicant needs particular justification for invading the respondent's right, and the s 35 parties' (former) marital status arguably provides that. But protection of property rights cannot explain the difference between ss 37 and 38. Here both parties are non-entitled, so it is not obivous why spousal applicants should be in a better position than cohabitants. Section 36 requires the courts to examine the degree of commitment in the cohabitants' relationship when deciding whether to give the applicant a right to occupy.[213] But even marriage-like relationships of 20 years that easily clear that hurdle are still denied the balance of harm test available to the divorced applicant, even after a short marriage. Can it plausibly be argued that protection of the traditional family based on marriage provides sufficient justification for the different treatment of otherwise similarly situated victims of domestic violence? While bright-line rules distinguishing spouses/civil partners from others may be tenable in the welfare, fiscal and financial context, it is not clear that such distinctions should be made where fundamental rights to personal security are at stake.[214]

The importance given to property rights—and even to sex—is evident in the exclusion of non-entitled individuals in 'other' associated person relationships from the occupation order scheme. It is not clear (from a functional perspective) why the existence of a relationship formalized by marriage or civil partnership or one that functions similarly (in sexual terms[215]) should be a prerequisite for non-entitled applicants to seek an occupation order, particularly where a principal aim is to secure protection from violence in the domestic sphere.[216] The standard requirement that the property be one that is, or was, or was intended to be lived in by the parties together might be thought adequate justification. As Wall J emphasized in *G v F (Non-molestation Order: Jurisdiction)*,[217] the courts can always refuse to make orders where the merits of individual cases are weak.

These features of the occupation order scheme may not withstand close scrutiny under Article 14. But, at least for those falling within the scope of the scheme, the *theoretical* difference of legal treatment may not yield very different outcomes, which may cure any discrimination on the face of the legislation. The balance of harm issue does not become relevant in applications between cohabitants unless and until the court has made an order giving the applicant the right to occupy. In making that order under s 36, the court has determined that the parties' relationship is sufficiently serious that it should attract remedies of this nature. That being so, and if the balance of harm 'questions' are answered in the applicant's favour, it is hard to imagine a court then refusing to make such an order. The court could do

---

213 FLA 1996, s 36(6)(e).
214 See 2.8.2 on relevant human rights case law, none of it dealing with domestic violence.
215 Cf 2.7.6 on the curious nature of civil partnership in this regard.
216 Though see Reece (2006).
217 [2000] Fam 186, extracted above.

nothing to overcome the different rules concerning the duration of orders for cohabitants, but it could at least ensure that an order was made.

The implications of Articles 2, 3, and 8 ECHR

Indeed, applicants' rights under Articles 2, 3, and 8 ECHR may limit the courts' discretion under the FLA scheme.[218] The conflict between victims' rights of personal protection and respondents' property rights has always been prominent in debates about the legal response to domestic violence. The ECHR provides a new framework within which the balance between the rights of victim and perpetrator must be struck, presaged by Lord Scarman's remarks in *Davis v Johnson*, described above.[219] As we noted at 4.2.4, where Article 2 or 3 applies, there is no balancing to be done: these rights are absolute—victim protection is paramount, and the state is under a duty to take reasonable steps to protect victims' rights. No case has yet addressed the implications of parties' Convention rights for occupation orders, but we can formulate the likely arguments.

Under the HRA 1998, s 6, the courts must act compatibly with parties' Convention rights. Choudhry and Herring argue that 'significant harm' in the balance of harm test should be found wherever the abuse or its impact on children in the household reaches the Article 3 threshold.[220] This would ensure that orders are made wherever, as in s 33, satisfaction of the balance of harm test mandates an order. However, it can further be argued that Articles 2 and 3 effectively require a court to exercise its discretion in cohabitants' cases to make an order where not doing so might expose the applicant to a risk of death or ill-treatment bad enough to fall within Article 3.[221]

In less serious cases, Article 8 requires the courts to balance parties' competing rights: victims' rights to respect for family, private life, and home, in the form of their personal integrity and residential security (even in a home in which they have no property right, provided they have sufficient and continuing links with the property[222]); respondents' rights to respect for their home and to family life with their children; and children's competing rights to safety and a relationship with both parents. As in *B v B (occupation order)*, the rights of another child may also need to be considered.[223] In cases under s 36, the respondent's rights could be asserted as a legitimate reason for the court to decline to make an order or to limit its duration. However, wherever the applicant or any relevant child stand to suffer the greater harm, that should—as Lord Scarman argued as a matter of purely domestic law—arguably determine the balancing exercise under Article 8. As discussed above at 4.2.4, this argument may be reinforced by reference to Article 17, discounting the respondents' rights.

If these arguments are accepted, non-entitled cohabitants under ss 36 and 38 may find that the differences on the face of the statute rarely result in different treatment in practice, save in relation to the duration of orders.[224] Any incompatibility with the Convention may therefore largely be avoided. In light of these arguments, in suggesting that an occupation

---

[218] See also Choudhry and Herring (2006a).

[219] [1979] AC 264.

[220] (2006b).

[221] Such a 'reading down' of the legislation would be possible under HRA 1998, s 3: *R (Friends Provident Life and Pensions Ltd) v Secretary of State for Transport, Local Government and the Regions* [2001] EWHC (Admin) 820. Cf Choudhry and Herring (2006b), 779–80, 783.

[222] *Harrow LBC v Qazi* [2003] UKHL 43.

[223] [1999] 2 FCR 251.

[224] A court cannot 'interpret' the duration provisions under the HRA 1998, s 3 to remove any limitation that was held incompatible with Article 2, 3, 8, or 14. A declaration of incompatibility would be required.

order will only be justified in 'exceptional' circumstances,[225] Thorpe LJ may be said to take an inappropriately reserved starting point.

4.5.5 APPLICATIONS, ORDERS, AND UNDERTAKINGS

The FLA 1996 simplified the law by giving the same powers to all levels of court: family proceedings court, County Court, and High Court. In practice, the County Court deals with most cases: in 2001 (the last year in which this data was collected), 99 per cent of all non-molestation orders and occupation orders made were made there.[226]

Orders on application by one party or of the court's own motion

Usually, the order is made on the application of a qualifying 'associated person'. Leave is required for applications by children under 16 years old, and may only be granted if the court 'is satisfied that the child has sufficient understanding to make the proposed application'.[227] The more usual course, wherever possible, would be for an adult associated person to apply on the child's behalf.[228] However, the court can make a non-molestation order in someone's favour even though no application has been made, so more orders than applications are made.[229]

Family Law Act 1996, s 42

...(2) The court may make a non-molestation order— ...

(b) if in any family proceedings to which the respondent is a party the court considers that the order should be made for the benefit of any other party to the proceedings or any relevant child even though no such application has been made....

(4A) A court considering whether to make an occupation order shall also consider whether to exercise the power conferred by subsection (2)(b) ...

'Family proceedings' encompasses proceedings under the inherent jurisdiction and under various statutes,[230] including the FLA 1996; proceedings for financial relief during and on the dissolution of marriage or civil partnership;[231] private and public law proceedings in relation to children,[232] including (in this context) cases in which the court has made an emergency protection order in relation to a child with an exclusion requirement;[233] adoption cases;[234] and applications for parental orders in surrogacy cases.[235] Civil proceedings under the PHA 1997 are not 'family proceedings'.

---

[225] *Chalmers v Johns* [1999] 2 FCR 110, extracted above, p 250.
[226] Dibdin, Sealy, and Aktar (2001), 60.
[227] FLA 1996, s 43(2): see 8.5.5.
[228] *Re A (Non-molestation proceedings by a child)* [2009] NI Fam 22.
[229] MOJ (2009), tables 5.8 and 5.9.
[230] FLA 1996, s 63.
[231] Matrimonial Causes Act 1973 (MCA 1973), Civil Partnership Act 2004 (CPA 2004), Schs 5–7, Domestic Proceedings and Magistrates' Court Act 1978 (DPMCA 1978).
[232] CA 1989, Pts I, II, and IV.
[233] Ibid., s 44A; FLA 1996, s 42(3).
[234] Adoption and Children Act 2002.
[235] Human Fertilisation and Embryology Act 2008, s 54.

Third party applications?

The Act also potentially allows both non-molestation orders and occupation orders to be made on the application of a third party. Section 60 permits rules of court to allow specified persons to act on behalf of others, which may prescribe:

> (a) conditions to be satisfied before a representative may make an application to the court on behalf of another; and
>
> (b) considerations to be taken into account by the court in determining whether, and if so how, to exercise any of its powers under [Part IV of the Act] when a representative is acting on behalf of another.[236]

Policy attention having shifted to criminal justice, there are no plans to make any such rules, so third party applications are not currently possible. However, third parties can apply for orders relating to forced marriage (discussed on the Online Resource Centre), and the Crime and Security Act 2010 would introduce new powers for the police to issue 'domestic violence protection notices' and then to apply for corresponding orders. It is currently uncertain whether the 2010 provisions will be brought into force, and so this remains a live issue. Should third party applications should be allowed and, if so, in what form? For example, should victims' consent to the application have to be obtained? What types of third party should be empowered to act? Agencies or private individuals (e.g. relatives)? And if agencies, which—police, CPS, housing and social services departments, refuge workers? Mandy Burton conducted a survey amongst professionals working in the domestic violence field. Two-thirds of respondents to the survey supported implementation of s 60, with police and refuge workers being preferred as potential applicants. The principal advantage of third party applications would be that victims would no longer have to act to protect themselves:

M. Burton, 'Third party applications for protection orders in England and Wales: service provider's views on implementing Section 60 of the Family Law Act 1996', (2003) 25 *Journal of Social Welfare and Family Law* **137, 139–41, 146**

> First, respondents felt that the confidence of some survivors may be so eroded by their experience of domestic violence that they would be unable to recognise that their situation called for a remedy, let alone undertake the daunting task of pursuing an order from a position of such low self-esteem. It was thought that the support of the third party could be beneficial in rebuilding the confidence of the survivor. Second, the survivor would know that she was believed by the third party, a boost to confidence in addition to that accruing from the order itself. Third, respondents also argued that third party applications would remove any blame attributed to the survivor for invoking the protection offered by the legal system against the perpetrator. It was felt that the survivor would be able to simply tell the perpetrator that the application had nothing to do with her; she could 'hide behind' the third party. Thus third party applications could deflect the blame coming from the perpetrator and also, in some situations, the extended family and wider community. This latter factor was considered to be particularly important for survivors in ethnic minority communities, where pursuing redress for domestic violence can lead to being ostracized by the whole community … An important consideration for women, in deciding whether to pursue a civil remedy, is weighing up the

---

236 FLA 1996, s 60(3).

prospect of the remedy being effective against the chances that pursuing it may result in further violence. Many respondents in this study commented that women were put off pursuing civil protection by fear of reprisals. Respondents who favoured implementation of Section 60 saw third party applications as beneficial in reducing a survivor's fear of reprisals. It was thought that women would be less likely to be subjected to pressure by the respondent if a third party application was being made, because there would be no point in the respondent intimidating his partner with a view to getting her to withdraw the case.

However, that is not to say that the matter was regarded as entirely straightforward, particularly if the victim's consent were required and if it were necessary to rely on her evidence to obtain the order. Either potentially puts victims in danger:

Respondents who opposed implementation, about a quarter (16/60) of those interviewed, pointed out that third party applications might not reduce the survivor's fear of reprisals. The perpetrator would still believe the woman to have played some part in the application being made, even if the extent of her involvement was merely alerting an outside agency to the existence of violence. Thus, the woman would still be blamed for the application. However, their main objection ... was that third party applications would reinforce a survivor's low self-esteem and confidence. It would reaffirm a survivor's belief that they are unable to obtain remedies themselves and deprive them of the benefits that may be gained by actively and fully engaging in the process of successfully pursuing a remedy. On the other hand, this objection to implementation does not address the argument that women may need third party applications not because they lack confidence to pursue remedies but because they lack financial resources ...

... About a third of respondents felt that public funding had become more difficult to obtain [owing to changes in the rules] ... It was noted that survivors who failed the means test for public funding might be unable to find the several thousand pounds that could be required to obtain an order and then perhaps return to court two or three times for its enforcement. Implementation of Section 60 will of course have resource implications for the third party, but it would at least remove the financial burden of seeking and enforcing a remedy from the survivor.

Over half of Burton's respondents opposed allowing s 60 applications to proceed without the victim's consent. This would:

reinforce the lack of power and control that the survivor had already experienced due to the domestic violence. A comparison was ... made with mandatory prosecutions .... Even amongst respondents who supported mandatory prosecution, there were some who felt that there was a difference between pursuing a prosecution without the victim's consent and obtaining a protective order without her consent and cooperation.

Consent was considered important principally for pragmatic reasons—without victims' co-operation, obtaining evidence and enforcing orders would be hard. But there are also important human rights considerations. Pursuing a case against victims' wishes, certainly without even consulting them, would arguably breach their rights under Article 8 ECHR. However, where children or other vulnerable individuals are affected by the violence, state intervention might still be justified.[237] As we discussed at 4.2.4, it may even be argued that

---

[237] Cf the exclusion requirements that can be attached to emergency protection and interim care orders, CA 1989, ss 38A and 44A: 12.6.2 and 12.7.

victims' own need for protection justifies intervention against their wishes.[238] Insisting on victim consent might deprive s 60 of its chief advantage: ensuring action to protect victims who are too petrified to protect themselves.

A quarter of Burton's respondents also identified a potential symbolic virtue of s 60 applications:

> [I]t would affirm the responsibility of the state, through public bodies, to provide protection for survivors of domestic violence.... [A] clear message would be sent out by third party applications that domestic violence is a public matter not a private matter; it is a legitimate sphere of state intervention in the interests of society as a whole.

However, giving police access to this power might further 'decriminalize' domestic violence if they used this route rather than prosecute.[239]

Ex parte orders

Ordinarily, respondents must have at least two days' notice of proceedings. But cases involving domestic violence are often urgent. The court should be able to provide immediate protection. Orders can therefore be obtained without giving notice:

Family Law Act 1996, s 45

Ex parte orders

(1) The court may, in any case where it considers that it is just and convenient to do so, make an occupation order or a non-molestation order even though the respondent has not been given such notice of the proceedings as would otherwise be required by rules of court.

(2) In determining whether to exercise its powers under subsection (1), the court shall have regard to all the circumstances including—

    (a) any risk of significant harm to the applicant or a relevant child, attributable to conduct of the respondent, if the order is not made immediately

    (b) whether it is likely that the applicant will be deterred or prevented from pursuing the application if an order is not made immediately; and

    (c) whether there is reason to believe that the respondent is aware of the proceedings but is deliberately evading service and that the applicant or a relevant child will be seriously prejudiced by the delay involved [in commencing the proceedings].

(3) If the court makes an order by virtue of subsection (1) it must afford the respondent an opportunity to make representations relating to the order as soon as just and convenient at a full hearing [i.e. a hearing of which notice has been given to all parties in accordance with the rules of court]....

---

[238] Choudhry and Herring (2006a).
[239] Humphreys and Kaye (1997), 410–12; Burton (2003a), 142–3.

Many applications are made on an ex parte basis, but research suggests that *occupation* orders are particularly difficult to obtain ex parte.[240] These applications do have drawbacks:

Law Commission, *Family Law: Domestic Violence and Occupation of the Family Home,* Law Com No 207 (London: HMSO, 1992)

5.6 The danger of a misconceived or malicious application being granted or the risk of some other injustice being done to the respondent is inevitably greater where the court has only heard the applicant's side of the story and the respondent has had no opportunity to reply. Also, on ex parte applications, the judge has no opportunity to try to resolve the parties' differences by agreed undertakings or otherwise to reduce the tension of the dispute. Equally, there is no opportunity to bring home the seriousness of the situation to the respondent and to underline the importance of complying with the order ...

In many cases involving violence, 'reducing tension' is an inadequate response and an ex parte order will be appropriate.[241] But it is important that the procedure *as a whole* is fair to the respondent and complies with Article 6 ECHR. Compliance should be ensured by the fact that the legislation entitles the respondent to an inter partes hearing and to have an ex parte order set aside.[242]

Undertakings

Instead of making an order, courts can accept undertakings from one or both parties: a voluntary promise to the court, commonly to do what an order would otherwise have required. Before the FLA 1996, undertakings were popular amongst some applicants and professionals—and still are[243]—but their use was not uncontroversial:

A. Kewley, 'Pragmatism before principle: the limitations of civil law remedies for the victims of domestic violence', (1996) 18 *Journal of Social Welfare and Family Law* 1, 3–6

[An applicant] who accepts ... an undertaking in lieu of a court injunction, will not have to testify in court, an experience which the evidence suggests many women would prefer to avoid if an alternative option is available to them.

Undertakings appear to be popular with judges and lawyers ... because the practice of accepting them means that an expensive, protracted and difficult hearing of the case is avoided and that the practical effect—[with the exception of the power of arrest: see below]—is much the same as if an ... order is granted in that breach of the undertaking may theoretically be punishable [as] contempt of court. Some practitioners consider that in some ways such undertakings are likely to be more effective than orders ... because they are given freely and voluntarily by the respondent to the judge rather than to an estranged ex-partner and that, having been given to the court, are the more likely to be honoured, because

---

[240] Barron (2002); Burton et al (2002).
[241] Kaganas (1999a), 196–7.
[242] Cf *Re J (Abduction: Wrongful Removal)* [2000] 1 FLR 78.
[243] Burton (2008a), 40.

the judge has the authority to punish any future non-compliance. It is apparent that domestic violence victims may sometimes be subject to considerable pressure from their lawyers to accept an undertaking instead of a court order because lawyers' training and practical experience are characterized by the need to avoid lengthy and expensive disputes if at all possible by a process of negotiation and compromise between the parties. Moreover, there is evidence that a complainant may be subject to pressure to accept an undertaking from the respondent even where there has been a breach of a previous undertaking or court order ... and where the woman has understandable doubts about the probable effectiveness of accepting the undertaking offered to her....

It is one thing to accept an undertaking from the respondent instead of getting the vindication and the protection of an order. But in some cases, the victim might even be required to give a 'cross undertaking' in return:

[I]t is viewed by some courts as a 'sensible' or 'fair' way of keeping the domestic peace in that blame is not being attached to either party's conduct but that each of the parties undertakes to behave reasonably in the future.... A victim of violence may feel understandably aggrieved in such a case where she infers that she is being held partly to blame for the abuse that she has had to endure.

Finally, the acceptance of an undertaking denies the victim of violence a chance for the court formally to find fault and to condemn, through the granting of the injunction, the violence that has taken place.... By giving an undertaking on a purely voluntary basis, the respondent has not been required to accept any responsibility for his or her actions nor has he or she been required to acknowledge having been culpable of any wrongdoing. In such circumstances, failure to obtain the required court order ... may also leave the [victim] understandably disillusioned with the whole legal process and reluctant to seek to obtain legal redress if, as experience has shown, it is likely that the violence or harassment will be repeated in the future.

While an undertaking can be enforced as if it were a court order, it is not possible to attach a power of arrest to an undertaking. This has implications for their use, as we shall see below when we consider enforcement of orders.

4.6 CIVIL REMEDIES UNDER THE PROTECTION FROM HARASSMENT ACT 1997

Protection from Harassment Act 1997

1 Prohibition of harassment

(1) A person must not pursue a course of conduct—

    (a) which amounts to harassment of another, and

    (b) which he knows or ought to know amounts to harassment of the other.

(2) For the purposes of this section, the person whose conduct is in question ought to know that it amounts to harassment of another if a reasonable person in possession of the

4 DOMESTIC VIOLENCE | 263

same information would think the course of conduct amounted to harassment of the other.

(3) Subsection (1) does not apply to a course of conduct if the person who pursued it shows—...

    (c) that in the particular circumstances the pursuit of the course of conduct was reasonable.

    ...

3 Civil remedy

(1) An actual or apprehended breach of section 1 may be the subject of a claim in civil proceedings by the person who is or may be the victim of the course of conduct in question.

(2) On such a claim, damages may be awarded for (among other things) any anxiety caused by the harassment and any financial loss resulting from the harassment....

7 Interpretation of this group of sections ...

    (2) References to harassing a person include alarming the person or causing the person distress.

    (3) A "course of conduct" must involve conduct on at least two occasions. ...

    (4) "Conduct" includes speech.

'Harassment' has no statutory definition. As with 'molestation' under the FLA 1996, the law leaves room for flexible interpretation:

Hipgrave v Jones [2004] EWHC 2901

TUGENDHAT J:

20. Harassment can cover a very wide range of conduct. It may involve actions alone, or words alone ... or both. The actions may be so grave as to amount to criminal offences against public order, or against the person, which cause serious alarm, or they may be little more than boorishness or insensitive behaviour, so long as it is sufficient to cause distress. The words may be, at one extreme, incitements to, or threats of, violence that cause alarm, or at the other extreme, unwelcome text messages sent, for example, to a woman wrongly perceived to be a girlfriend ...

21. The PHA is one of the many different common law and statutory provisions which provide remedies to protect privacy ...It is relevant to have regard to Art 8 of the [ECHR] in interpreting it, to the extent that it implements the state's positive obligation to protect individuals from interference with their private lives. But it is also necessary to have regard to the fact that an order under the Act [often an injunction prohibiting the harassing behaviour] may interfere with the private lives of defendants and their freedom of expression ...[244]

---

[244] Cf *R v Debnath* [2005] EWCA Crim 3472 on the scope of a restraining order.

One important limitation is that 'harassment' arises from a 'course of conduct':[245] an iso-lated event or several unconnected instances of harassing behaviour will not suffice. This may sometimes prove problematic.[246] Whether a course of conduct constitutes harassment is judged objectively.[247]

This legislation was introduced primarily to deal with stalking by strangers, but it has substantial application to family cases, where stalking and other forms of harassment are common, particularly following relationship breakdown. Nevertheless, use of the PHA 1997 between partners has been regarded as inappropriate in some circumstances. The following observation was made in a *criminal* case, where the defendant had hit his partner and pulled her hair on several occasions:

R v Hills [2001] 1 FCR 569

OTTON LJ:

31. It is to be borne in mind that the state of affairs which was relied upon by the prosecu-tion was miles away from the 'stalking' type of offence for which the Act was intended. That is not to say that it is never appropriate so to charge a person who is making a nuisance of himself to his partner or wife when they have become estranged. However, in a situation such as this, when they were frequently coming back together and intercourse was taking place (apparently a video was taken of them having intercourse) it is unrealistic to think that this fell within the stalking category which either postulates a stranger or an estranged spouse. That was not the situation when the course of conduct relied upon was committed.

Given the frequent difficulty of pinpointing the end point of a relationship,[248] attempting to draw the line in the way Otton LJ suggests may artificially limit the potential of the PHA 1997 to offer valuable remedies, whether or not victims are seeking to end the relationship. A County Court judge has declined the suggestion that he should be slow to apply the PHA 1997 in a domestic context—in that case, a campaign of harassment directed at a young wife by her mother-in-law—stating that 'a judge should be very slow to refuse on policy grounds to grant a statutory remedy if the provisions of the statute apply to the facts of the case'.[249]

One major advantage of the PHA 1997 is its universal application: unlike the FLA 1996, it does not require any particular type of relationship between the parties. It also offers a mon-etary remedy, though where the parties share a household that may not be advantageous: any award might come out of already shared resources.[250] But the Act only deals with har-assment and provides no remedies regarding the occupation of a shared home. If abuser and victim share a home, obtaining an injunction with the threat of arrest may not prevent the abuse recurring. Even if the behaviour does not recur, victims may feel vulnerable sharing a home with the respondent and so will have to invoke the occupation order scheme of the FLA 1996, if eligible to do so.

---

245 PHA 1997, ss 1(1), 7(3); *R v Curtis* [2010] EWCA Crim 123.
246 *R v Hills* [2001] 1 FCR 569: a criminal case, but the point is identical for civil law.
247 *R v Colohan* [2001] EWCA Civ 1251.
248 Humphreys and Thiara (2003).
249 *Singh v Bhakar* [2006] 1 FLR 880, [162]–[163].
250 Cf the award made in *Singh v Bhakar*, ibid.; see generally Noon (2008).

4.7 ENFORCEMENT OF ORDERS UNDER THE FLA 1996 AND THE PHA 1997

Research has suggested that the family justice system has still been failing some victims when it comes to enforcing orders.[251] The enforcement of non-molestation orders has recently, and controversially, been reformed to bring the weight of the criminal justice system behind the family court. The resulting parallel jurisdiction of the family, civil, and criminal courts complicates the law relating to enforcement.

4.7.1 OCCUPATION ORDERS

Breach of an occupation order is a contempt of court, and exclusively a matter for the family court. There are two routes to arrest: either the applicant may return to court for a warrant; or the family court can attach a power of arrest to the original order. The latter power permits the police to arrest the respondent without returning to court for a warrant where the officer has reasonable cause to suspect a breach.[252] Where a warrant is sought, the court must be satisfied on evidence given under oath that there are reasonable grounds for believing that a breach has occurred.[253] Whether arrested under an original power of arrest or pursuant to a warrant, respondents must be brought to court within 24 hours of arrest; either the matter is dealt with then or the respondent is remanded or released on bail until a later hearing.[254]

It has been argued that since the court lacks any substantial power to penalize minors for contempt, it should have no power to attach a power of arrest to orders made against minors. This argument has been rejected in view of the mandatory language of s 47 and the functions of powers of arrest:

Re H (Respondent under 10: Power of arrest) [2001] 1 FCR 370 (CA)

HALE LJ:

16. ..., [I]t is not the sole purpose of a power of arrest to provide a convenient short route to the court's power to commit for contempt of court. That is one of its purposes and a very helpful one, but it also has the purpose of taking the person concerned away from the scene. In a case such as this, the immediate object was to ensure that the young man did indeed leave the family home and that objective can readily be secured by a power of arrest.

Under the 1970s legislation, powers of arrest were rarely attached to orders.[255] The FLA 1996 now requires their use in certain situations:

---

[251] Barron (2002); Burton et al (2002); Humphreys and Thiara (2003).
[252] FLA 1996, s 47(6).
[253] Ibid., s 47(9).
[254] Ibid., s 47(7).
[255] Law Com (1992), para 5.11.

Family Law Act 1996

47 Arrest for breach of order

. . .

(2) If—

    (a) the court makes an occupation order; and

    (b) it appears to the court that the respondent has used or threatened violence against the applicant or relevant child,

it shall attach a power of arrest to one or more provisions of the order unless satisfied that in all the circumstances of the case the applicant or child will be adequately protected without such a power of arrest.

(3) Subsection (2) does not apply [to ex parte orders], but in such a case the court may attach a power of arrest to one or more provisions of the order if it appears to it—

    (a) that the respondent has used or threatened violence against the applicant or a relevant child; and

    (b) that there is a risk of significant harm to the applicant or child, attributable to conduct of the respondent, if the power of arrest is not attached to those provisions immediately. . . .

Powers of arrest and undertakings

Since undertakings are voluntary, no power of arrest can be attached to them.[256] In order to ensure that a power of arrest is available wherever one would be appropriate, the court cannot accept an undertaking instead of making an occupation order if, were it to make an order, it would be obliged to attach a power of arrest.[257] Wherever courts consider accepting undertakings, they must therefore ensure that a power of arrest is unnecessary. Official data last reported for 2005 suggests that undertakings are accepted in only a minority of cases.[258] But the reliability of these figures is dependent on the courts' record keeping: often no formal record was made of undertakings prior to the FLA 1996.[259] The use of orders and undertakings still varies regionally.[260]

Lawyers and courts must ensure that those in need of the full protection of a court order are not left in a vulnerable position. It has often been observed that the effectiveness of legislation can be, and has been, undermined by the attitudes of those responsible for implementing it.[261] Nevertheless, some of the concerns expressed by Kewley[262] may be alleviated by the FLA 1996. For example, it is questionable whether a proper hearing can now be avoided, for without testing the evidence the court cannot decide—as it is required to—whether a power of arrest (and so an order) is necessary and so whether an undertaking may be lawfully accepted. Where a power of arrest is required, victims ought now to obtain the justice and affirmation of a court order.

---

[256] FLA 1996, s 46(2).
[257] Ibid., s 46(3).
[258] DCA (2006c), table 5.9.
[259] Kewley (1996), 3.
[260] Edwards (2001); Burton et al (2002).
[261] Smart (1989), 164; Kewley (1996), 7.
[262] Ibid., and extracted above, p 261.

Duration of powers of arrest

Where a power of arrest is attached to an occupation order, the court must decide how long that power should last. The Act specifically provides that the power of arrest attached to an ex parte order may last a shorter period than the order itself[263] but says nothing about orders made at an inter partes hearing. Before the introduction of s 42A (discussed below), powers of arrest would very often be attached to non-molestation orders of indefinite duration. Is it necessary or might it be inappropriate for the power of arrest to be similarly unlimited in time? The Court of Appeal decided that powers of arrest can operate for a shorter period than the inter partes order to which they are attached, mindful of respondents' rights:

In re B-J (A Child) (Non-molestation Order: Power of Arrest) [2001] Fam 415 (CA)

HALE LJ:

43 There is nothing inherently incompatible between the mandatory duty contained in section 47(2) and [the flexibility of allowing powers of arrest shorter than the order to which they are attached]. The court would have to be satisfied that the victim would be adequately protected with only a shorter power of arrest. The cases in which the court could be satisfied of this might be difficult but are not impossible to imagine.... The great variety of circumstances in which Part IV orders, especially perhaps occupation orders, may be required make this by no means impossible, although it may not be common. One thing, however, is clear from section 47(2): the criterion is whether or not the applicant or child will be adequately protected without the power of arrest, not whether its continued existence will be inconvenient for others.

44 Given the inherent difficulties of predicting the future, and in particular when people will be safe, however, it would usually be preferable to attach the power for the same time as the order. Once it can be shown that the victim will be adequately protected without it, or without a different power, the obvious course is to vary the order [under s 49] so as to remove the power of arrest or reduce its scope....

47 ... If there is a case in which an order is appropriate but the court is indeed satisfied that the victim will be adequately protected by a time-limited power of arrest, an order which gives a larger power of arrest without warrant might ... be incompatible with Convention rights. The court would then have to read section 47(2) [under s 3 of the HRA 1998] so as to permit this.

49 ... In the context of the liberty of the subject, statutes are normally to be construed in such a way as to limit rather than enlarge the powers of the state. Powers of arrest for breach of the orders of a civil court are themselves unusual, although amply justified by the need effectively to secure the performance of the obligations contained in the order.... [T]o require the court to attach a power of arrest for a longer period than the court is satisfied is required for the protection of victims is manifestly unjust to the respondent; it may also indirectly lead to injustice to the victims if the court is thereby deterred, either from making an order for the appropriate period, or from attaching a power of arrest....

Similar arguments may be made when deciding the *parts* of the order to which a power of arrest should be attached; if the power is necessary only for some types of breach it should not be applied to the whole order.

[263] FLA 1996, s 47(4).

Use of powers of arrest

Under earlier legislation, a power of arrest was attached to only one-third of all orders. The FLA 1996 has ensured that powers of arrest are more frequently attached. Edwards reported a considerable increase in the attachment of a power of arrest in 2001: they were made in 75 per cent of occupation order cases and, when the courts had the power to do so (see below), in 80 per cent of non-molestation order cases.[264] More recent data show a declining number of occupation orders, though a greater proportion of those orders that are made have powers of arrest attached.[265]

Provisions ancillary to occupation orders under s 40

An important limitation on the courts' powers was exposed in *Nwogbe v Nwogbe*.[266] The court had made an occupation order with s 40 provisions requiring the respondent to pay the rent and other outgoings on the property from which he had been excluded. He failed to pay. The wife brought contempt proceedings. The Court of Appeal reluctantly found itself powerless. The maze of relevant statutes offer no way of enforcing payment of money to a third party in this context, whether by imprisonment or less serious measures, such as attachment of earnings. Without some other basis on which the respondent can be ordered to pay money directly to the applicant, who can then pass it on to the third party, this form of s 40 provision is useless. Where the parties are spouses or civil partners, the problem might be avoided by relying on the various matrimonial financial orders.[267] But cohabitants and other associated persons may have no such alternative. Parliament has yet to remedy this deficiency, despite strong criticism from the Court.

4.7.2 NON-MOLESTATION ORDERS AND INJUNCTIONS UNDER THE PHA 1997

Breach of these orders and injunctions is not exclusively a matter for the family or civil court which made them. The PHA 1997 introduced a novel combination of civil and criminal law, replicated in recent reform of the FLA 1996. These developments raise controversial questions of policy and practice, in particular about the treatment of domestic violence as a public or private issue.

The Protection from Harassment Act 1997

Claimants under the PHA 1997 may seek damages or an injunction from the High Court or County Court. But where an injunction has been made 'for the purpose of restraining the defendant from pursuing any conduct which amounts to harassment' and 'without reasonable excuse the defendant does anything which he is prohibited from doing by the injunction', the defendant is guilty of a criminal offence under s 3 for which an arrest may be made without obtaining a warrant.[268] The s 3 offence relating to breach of civil injunctions carries up to five years' imprisonment, a heavier penalty than that available for the basic criminal

---

[264] Edwards (2001).
[265] MOJ (2009), table 5.9.
[266] [2000] 2 FLR 744.
[267] See 7.3.
[268] Police and Criminal Evidence Act 1984, s 24, as amended.

offence of harassment under s 2, which is triable only by magistrates and so punishable by up to six months' imprisonment. This heavier maximum penalty recognizes the seriousness of conduct which is not only generally criminalized but which has also been specifically prohibited in the individual case by a civil court. Alternatively, the claimant can seek an arrest warrant from the civil court for the matter to be dealt with as contempt of court. The Act guards against double punishment: if the breach has been punished as a civil contempt, criminal proceedings are barred, and vice versa.[269]

Non-molestation orders under the Family Law Act 1996

The FLA 1996 was amended by the DVCVA 2004 to enhance, and dramatically alter, the enforcement of non-molestation orders on the same model. Non-molestation orders were originally enforced like occupation orders. Now, although breach of a non-molestation order is still a contempt of the family court which made it, that court cannot attach a power of arrest to its order, though a warrant can later be issued. Like breach of a PHA injunction, breach of a non-molestation order is now also a criminal offence:

Family Law Act 1996

42A Offence of breaching non-molestation order

(1) A person who without reasonable excuse[270] does anything that he is prohibited from doing by a non-molestation order is guilty of an offence.

(2) In the case of an [ex parte order], a person can be guilty of an offence under this section only in respect of conduct engaged in at a time when he was aware of the existence of the order.

(3) Where a person is convicted of an offence under this section in respect of any conduct, that conduct is not punishable as contempt of court.

(4) A person cannot be convicted of an offence under this section in respect of any conduct which has been punished as a contempt of court.

(5) A person guilty of an offence under this section is liable—

(a) on conviction on indictment, to imprisonment for a term not exceeding five years, or a fine, or both; and

(b) on summary conviction, to imprisonment for a term not exceeding twelve months, or a fine ..., or both....

46 Undertakings ...

(3A) The court shall not accept an undertaking ... instead of making a non-molestation order in any case where it appears to the court that—

(a) the respondent has used or threatened violence against the applicant or a relevant child; and

(b) for the protection of the applicant or child it is necessary to make a non-molestation order so that any breach may be punishable under section 42A.

---

[269] PHA 1997, s 3(7)–(8).

[270] The burden lies with the prosecution to prove there was no such excuse: *R v Richards* [2010] EWCA Crim 835; cf *R v Nicholson* [2006] EWCA Crim 1518 on the contents of the defence.

The Explanatory Notes accompanying the 2004 Act explained that the purpose of the reform was to permit police to arrest for breach of an order without needing a power of arrest to have been attached to the order or a warrant subsequently issued.[271] Victims therefore no longer need to rely on family courts deciding to attach a power of arrest to the order in order to secure the respondent's immediate arrest. The power to arrest a respondent endures for the lifetime of the order.

The CPS policy guidance states that the new offence 'aims to place complainants at the heart of the criminal justice system' and accordingly 'gives complainants a choice' about whether breach of non-molestation order will be dealt with criminally or as a contempt of the family court.[272] It suggests that where the conduct which breached the non-molestation order was not (otherwise) criminal in nature, the public interest may be better served by leaving the matter to be dealt with by application from the victim to the family court, rather than by criminal prosecution. But the possibility of parallel criminal and civil proceedings is also contemplated. Breach of an order may be prosecuted either for that specific offence only, for a substantive criminal offence (such as assault), or both. Whatever offence is charged, the fact that a court order has been breached should be regarded as an aggravating feature.[273] Where both breach of the order and a substantive offence are charged, consecutive sentences should be considered to reflect the seriousness of the conduct.[274] Sentencing guidelines also emphasize that since the purpose of the non-molestation order was to protect the victim from harm, the primary aim of sentencing should be achieving compliance with the order and protecting the victim.[275]

Evidently, the criminal justice system is only useful as an enforcement mechanism for civil and family orders if the police know about those orders' existence and their terms, particularly where the behaviour they proscribe would not otherwise constitute an offence. Since harassment is an offence under the PHA 1997, there may be few cases in which breaches of *non-molestation* orders will not, independently of the order, involve an offence. However, 'harassment' and 'molestation' are amorphous concepts: matters would be far clearer for the police if they knew what specific behaviour had been prohibited. Where a non-molestation order has been made, where the applicant is acting in person and requests it, the court is responsible for delivering the relevant documentation to the police; otherwise, the duty formally rests with the applicant,[276] though internal guidance instructs court staff to send to the police copies of orders in relation to which an arrest may be made in the event of breach.

Reform was strongly promoted by the Government, which argued that it brought several advantages:

Hansard, *Official Report*—Domestic Violence, Crime and Victims Bill debates
Hansard HL Deb, cols GC237–8, 240, 19 January 2004

Baroness Scotland of Asthal, Minister of State:

There are a number of reasons why contempt of court is not a sufficient or effective sanction. Contempt of court is of course a very serious matter and has always been so. However, many

---

[271] Para 15.
[272] CPS (2008).
[273] Sentencing Guidelines Council (2006b), para 2.2.
[274] Ibid., para 2.1.
[275] Ibid., paras 3.3–3.4.
[276] Family Proceedings Rules 2010 (FPR 2010), SI 2010/2955, r 10.10.

victims with whom we have spoken have stressed to us the disdain in which the offender holds the non-molestation order—even where a power of arrest is attached to that order. We are concerned that the sanction for breach of a non-molestation order must bring home to the respondent the seriousness of that breach. That is why we wish to make breach a criminal offence....

Making breach a criminal offence would also extend the range of sanctions available to the courts to punish the offender. Contempt of court limits the sanctions to imprisonment or fine. Where a breach is a criminal offence, the courts would also be able to impose the usual range of community sentences. Sections 189 and 190 of [the Criminal Justice Act 2003] provide that, on conviction, conditions can [in certain cases] be imposed to do with curfew, mental health, drug treatment, voluntary activities, residence and supervision. If the person does not comply with those conditions, a suspended sentence can take effect....

That gives the court an opportunity to deal with the offending behaviour. Many partners who find themselves involved in domestic violence are in need of anger management, drug treatment and a whole series of other interventions that will inure to the benefit not only of that partner, but of partners who may come afterwards.... [In] the analysis of partners who kill, it is very unusual indeed if those persons have not had a series of partners whom they have abused on the way to the murder that they eventually commit. It is not simply the complainant on the day whom we have to protect, but all the other partners who may come afterwards. That should exercise our attention, because of the nature of domestic violence....

... Some women do not wish to criminalise their husbands but wish to have the abuse stopped. It will be possible to continue to do that through the civil route. But we should also take on board that the very abusive nature of domestic violence often erodes the will of the woman, who may need the greater support offered by the criminal court as well as that of the civil court, and that an intervention of that nature may prove necessary.

Many have said that they have benefited from having a police officer come to the door to arrest and remove the assailant. The courts can apply those provisions with flexibility and speed. We do not accept that they will be longer drawn-out as a result of the procedures. We will be assisted greatly by the way in which case management is currently dealt with and the fact that the CPS is working very closely with the police and the courts to get together protocols so that we have a holistic approach to domestic violence.

Hansard HC Deb, Proceedings of Standing Committee E, col 45, 22 June 2004

The Parliamentary Under-Secretary of State for the Home Department, Paul Goggins MP:

[Introducing s 42A would involve] a rebalancing between civil and criminal in the system. That is entirely in keeping with the spirit of this legislation, which is to empower and protect the victim on the one hand while also sending out a very clear message that Parliament—and the country—regards with increasing seriousness crimes associated with domestic violence and intends the penalties to be heavy and the protection to be stronger. There may be some rebalancing, and that would be entirely right.

The meaning of 'rebalancing' here is somewhat unclear and its wisdom debatable. The reforms tend to push domestic violence towards the public realm of the criminal justice system, whilst 'further blur[ring] already muddied waters regarding the objectives of sanctions for breach of civil orders and criminal sanctions'.[277] The policy objectives need to be

[277] Burton (2003b), 305–8.

clarified. The choice between criminal and civil/family proceedings has many implications: for the sanctions available; for the degree of victim involvement in and control over the proceedings; for evidential rules; and for the public and police perception of these cases. Is the objective to protect the victim for the future, or to punish the abuser? Criminal law has traditionally focused on the latter, family and civil law on the former.

Criminalization of breach relieves victims of the financial and psychological burden of bringing enforcement proceedings themselves, just as third party applications for civil orders might do. Moreover, increased use of the criminal law sends out strong messages about society's disapproval of domestic abuse. However, criminalizing breach of civil orders as such may—ironically—undermine this aim. Charging the new offence under s 42A of the FLA 1996, instead of an ordinary criminal offence applicable to the facts, may downgrade domestic violence by giving the impression that it is not 'real crime'. Indeed, police and prosecutors might feel encouraged to require victims to pursue civil remedies before the criminal law steps in at all. Much will depend upon prosecutors' practice.

Opponents also raised questions about victim control.[278]

M. Burton, 'Criminalising Breaches of Civil Orders for Protection from Domestic Violence', (2003) *Criminal Law Review* 301, 305–6

Domestic violence is not just an individual matter but an offence against the state. The onus should not be on the victim to seek enforcement of the order, rather through criminal proceedings the state should mark society's disapproval of the defendant's conduct in breaching the order. The difficulty with this model is that the victim's interests may become supplanted by a wider public interest and the victim's views may become marginalised in relation to any decisions that may be taken by the prosecuting authorities about whether to prosecute for breach of a non-molestation order. If the conduct is grave enough to warrant criminalisation then it has been argued that it is right that the victim should lose control over the prosecution process, albeit that they should be kept informed of its progress. However, it can be questioned whether breach of a non-molestation order should result in the victim's wishes being subordinated to a wider public interest. It may be in practice that the police and CPS would not prosecute for breaches of a non-molestation order where the victim did not want them to, however, the possibility remains.... Perhaps prosecutors would feel that the victim should have more influence in relation to cases which came to them by the indirect route of breach of a civil order rather than the direct route of the police charging the defendant for assault or other general offences related to domestic violence. However, as far as victim decision-making in legal interventions is concerned, the victim has a more prominent role in civil interventions. There may be value in preserving that role and not, even theoretically, subordinating it to a wider public interest.

Victims preferring to take civil proceedings cannot elect from the outset to have a power of arrest attached to the order, so they have to return to the family court to obtain a warrant if they wish to enforce the order through that route. If victims call the police when a breach occurs, the case is likely to be taken through the criminal justice system. Unless the victim manages to bring enforcement proceedings in the family courts before the criminal process

---

[278] See in particular Hansard HL Deb, vol 656, cols GC 229–30, 19 January 2004, Lord Thomas of Gresford.

has concluded, civil enforcement will be barred by the rules against double punishment.[279] Victims have no party status in criminal proceedings, so are not directly represented by their own lawyer. Victims might be deterred from seeking non-molestation orders at all if they know that their partners might gain a criminal record as a result of any breach and that decisions regarding charge and prosecution, in the public criminal courts, will be beyond their control.

Concerns were also expressed that the courts might start applying a more stringent standard of proof when making a non-molestation order, by analogy with anti-social behaviour orders. Although the wider rules of civil evidence apply to ASBOs, it has been held that the potential criminal consequences of breach mean that the *criminal* standard of proof applies not only to adjudication on alleged breaches, but also to the *making* of these orders.[280] These fears may be alleviated by *Hipgrave v Jones*, which held that the civil standard of proof applies to injunctions under the PHA 1997.[281] It seems highly likely that the same approach will be taken to non-molestation orders. However, the fact that breach constitutes an offence might sometimes make the courts reluctant to make the order at all. The prospect of a power of arrest instigating *contempt* proceedings being invoked dissuaded the court from making a non-molestation order in *Chechi v Bashir*, the case involving brothers feuding over a land dispute.[282] It was felt that this would put too much power into the hands of the applicant. The prospect of *criminal* proceedings may weigh even more heavily against making an order, though it may be hoped that in paradigm domestic violence cases these sorts of considerations would not influence courts' decisions.

However, criminal punishment—if not very carefully managed—may be counter-productive, prejudicing victims' safety rather than protecting them. Short prison sentences may simply aggravate the situation. Fines may also be problematic where victim and abuser live in the same household; it has even been known for victims to pay fines themselves.[283] An alternative approach to improve protection of victims would be to enhance the family courts' enforcement and sentencing powers. Family courts already hold many attractions with their more accommodating rules of evidence, the opportunity for proceedings to be held in private, and their speed of action. The currently limited menu of civil and family law sanctions may not best serve victims' interests. Notably, family courts cannot order participation in a perpetrator programme or other community sentences. Opponents of the reform preferred this route.

Early evidence of the impact of change

Early anecotal and more robust survey-based evidence suggested that concerns about criminalization deterring victims (or even courts) from making orders might have been well-founded.[284] It has been suggested that police are not treating these breaches seriously, not arresting or not charging, and issuing cautions inappropriately.[285] Breach of a non-molestation order could be dealt with by family courts in a matter of hours: the police were obliged to bring respondents to court within 24 hours of arrest. By contrast, the criminal

---

279 FLA 1996, s 42A(3), (4); PHA 1997, s 3.
280 *R (McCann) v Manchester Crown Court; Clingham v Kensington and Chelsea RLBC* [2002] UKHL 39.
281 [2004] EWHC 2901.
282 [1999] 2 FLR 489.
283 Pizzey (1974).
284 See generally Burton (2009b).
285 Home Affairs Select Committee (2008).

justice system can take weeks to act, and at rather greater cost; and the CPS has a discretion whether to charge the defendant at all. Delay increases the chances of victim withdrawal.[286] Information-transfer to the criminal justice agencies has also proved problematic.[287]

Judges reported that fewer victims seemed to be applying for non-molestation orders in the first place,[288] concerns corroborated by two early surveys based on court data.[289] One of those surveys, by Judge Platt, found an average drop of 25 per cent in applications for non-molestation orders comparing the two six-month periods before and after the new law, suggesting that some applicants may be applying for occupation orders to achieve the effects of a non-molestation order without the threat of criminalization. He suggested three other possible explanations, operating alone or together. The first, highly unlikely, is that the risk of criminalization has suddenly reduced the occurrence of domestic violence. Secondly, some victims might be by-passing family proceedings and going straight for criminal proceedings, an explanation supported by the increase in prosecutions in that year. Finally, victims may be deterred from using the family courts now that the threat of criminal sanctions hangs over respondents. Platt strongly suspects this to be a factor, though Burton has suggested that the problem may be the opposite: that victims' groups had welcomed criminalization of breach, but had since been disappointed by police inaction.[290] A number of other practical factors are hampering victims' access to the family courts (notably reduced availability of legal aid[291]) and impeding the successful implementation of the new provisions. However, as Burton points out:

M. Burton, 'Civil law remedies for domestic violence: why are applications for non-molestation orders declining?', (2009) 31 *Journal of Social Welfare and Family Law* 109

Victims' help-seeking behaviour is influenced by a range of factors, not all of which are related to their perceptions about the relevance or potential usefulness of the legal process and civil remedies. Many victims do not even consider the legal system, so the idea that they would be 'encouraged' or 'put off' by changes to legal criteria, the attitudes of legal personnel or the availability of [legal aid] funding seems unlikely. Nevertheless, for those who do wish to use civil remedies, or could be encouraged to do so, some improvements could be made. These include a greater level of specialisation in the civil justice system to ensure that those using the FLA are well informed about the legal framework, the funding criteria and, most importantly, the dynamics of domestic abuse and how to respond sympathetically and appropriately to victims.

Hester et al caution that research over a longer period than they were able to undertake (only July–Nov 2007) is needed to discern whether the drop in applications is a product of the new Act rather than a consolidation of longer term trends pre-dating the change.[292] Indeed,

---

286 Minute of evidence given by District Judge Mornington to the Home Affairs Select Committee (2008), Q 55, 22 January 2008.
287 Hester et al (2008) report several further practical problems with implementation of the new law.
288 Gibb (2008); Millward (2008).
289 Platt (2008); Hester et al (2008). See also Burton's review for the Legal Services Commission (2008b).
290 Burton (2009b), 117.
291 Cf HO (2008), 27. Legal aid criteria require victims to cooperate with criminal prosecution before they can obtain legal aid for civil remedies.
292 Hester et al (2008), 27

the latest court statistics do show the number of orders returning to well above 20,000 in 2009.[293] This issue will have to be revisited as more data becomes available.

Restraining orders under the PHA 1997

An analogous blurring of criminal and civil jurisdictions, though one operating in the opposite direction, is created by the introduction of powers enabling criminal courts to issue civil-style restraining orders against defendants who have been acquitted of any offence for which they were prosecuted, if the court 'considers it necessary to do so to protect a person from harassment by the defendant'.[294] Evidence that was inadmissible in the unsuccessful criminal proceedings but which would be admissible in proceedings under s 3 of the 1997 Act may be introduced by either prosecution or defence.[295] Effectively, this involves mini-civil proceedings following the criminal trial. This new power has attracted criticism, for example, for staining the character of defendants who have been acquitted.[296] But the Joint Committee on Human Rights nevertheless judged the provision to be compatible with Articles 8 and 6 ECHR.[297] Less controversially, the Act permits restraining orders to be made on *conviction* for any offence. Whilst the availability of this remedy may be felt to compromise the clarity of an acquittal, these provisions illustrate how victim protection can be achieved by integration of criminal and civil-style proceedings within one court. But it is questionable whether criminal judges, and CPS lawyers, are best placed to determine what the circumstances of the individual case require. Crucially, victims are not a party to the criminal proceedings, but may have essential information necessary for the court to decide what form of restraining order to make. However, there is considerable support amongst professionals involved in domestic violence cases for these new powers, anticipating that these orders could potentially have a large and positive impact on the disposal of such cases.[298]

4.7.3 SANCTIONS FOR BREACH IN THE FAMILY AND CIVIL COURTS

If the criminal route is not used,[299] the respondent in breach of an order will be brought to the family or civil court under a power of arrest or warrant. Contempt proceedings in the family court are 'criminal proceedings' for the purposes of Article 6 ECHR, carrying the rights to legal representation and against self incrimination.[300] If the respondent is found guilty of contempt (on a criminal standard of proof), the court must decide what sanction to impose. Family courts had been criticized for imposing nominal sanctions. The suggestion in *Ansah v Ansah*[301] that in most cases 'stern warnings' will suffice was said to downgrade

---

[293] MOJ (2010), table 2.9.

[294] PHA 1997, s 5A.

[295] Ibid., s 5A(2).

[296] Liberty (2003).

[297] Joint Committee on Human Rights (2003a).

[298] Hester et al (2008), 30.

[299] For early sentencing decisions in the criminal courts for breach of non-molestation orders, see *R v Briscoe* [2010] EWCA Crim 373; *R v Franks* [2010] EWCA Crim 1030.

[300] *Hammerton v Hammerton* [2007] EWCA Civ 248.

[301] [1977] Fam 138, 144, per Ormrod J.

the seriousness of domestic violence.[302] Recent decisions have emphasized the importance of proper penalties. When assessing these cases, it is important to remember that the maximum penalty available to the civil and family courts sentencing for contempt is only two years' imprisonment.[303] In *A-A v B-A*,[304] the husband's rape was punished by 12 months' imprisonment. In a case where the respondent seriously assaulted the applicant at midday outside her solicitors' offices, the trial judge's 'wholly inadequate' sentence of 14 days was increased on appeal to three months:[305]

Wilson v Webster [1998] 2 FCR 575, 578–9 (CA)

THORPE LJ:

There is an element in this matter of public confidence. Domestic violence is a serious matter. It would appear that Parliament has taken particular note of the incidence of domestic violence and the courts who have to deal with incidents of domestic violence must take it very seriously indeed. This was, in my judgment, an exceptional case. This was a quite deliberate attack on this lady in breach of the undertaking at midday in the centre of a city when she had just left her solicitor's offices. He punched her, he punched her to the ground and continued punching her and desisted, it would seem, when he was finally pulled away from her. This is not a matter which could receive a mere caution, it was certainly a matter which required serious punishment...

Each case will be dealt with on its own merits but I hope that county court judges will take seriously the views of this court that matters of this kind are to be dealt with seriously.

Recent Court of Appeal cases have sought to provide guidance on sentencing for contempt under the FLA 1996, seeking to work out what the parallel jurisdictions of the criminal courts and the civil courts under the PHA 1997 mean for family courts' sentencing. The basic guidance for family contempt sentencing derives from *Hale v Tanner*:

Hale v Tanner [2000] 1 WLR 2377 (CA)

HALE LJ:

Family cases, it has long been recognised, raise different considerations from those elsewhere in the civil law. The two most obvious are the heightened emotional tensions that arise between family members and often the need for those family members to continue to be in contact with one another because they have children together or the like. Those two factors make the task of the court, in dealing with these issues, quite different from the task when dealing with commercial disputes or other types of case in which ... sanctions have to be imposed for contempt of court. Having said that:

(1) These cases have to come before the court on an application to commit. That is the only procedure which is available. Not surprisingly, therefore, the court is directing its mind to

---

[302] McCann (1985), 83–4.

[303] Contempt of Court Act 1981, s 14. Minors cannot be imprisoned for contempt: see *Re H (Respondent under 18: power of arrest)* [2001] 1 FCR 370.

[304] [2001] 2 FLR 1.

[305] Cf *Gull v Gull* [2007] EWCA Civ 900; *Nicholls v Nicholls* [2008] EWCA Civ 121 where longer sentences were passed for non-violence but serial breaches.

whether or not committal to prison is the appropriate order. But it does not follow from that that imprisonment is to be regarded as the automatic consequence of the breach of an order. Clearly it is not. There is, however, no principle that imprisonment is not to be imposed at the first occasion … Nevertheless, it is a common practice, and usually appropriate in view of the sensitivity of the circumstances of these cases, to take some other course on the first occasion.

(2) There is the difficulty … that the alternatives are limited. The full range of sentencing options is not available for contempt of court. Nevertheless, there is a range of things that the court can consider. It may do nothing—make no order. It may adjourn, and in a case where the alleged contemnor has not attended court, that may be an appropriate course to take, although I would not say so in every case; it depends on the reasons that may be thought to lie behind the non-attendance. There is a power to fine. There is a power of sequestration of assets and there are mental health orders. All of those may, in an appropriate case, need consideration, particularly in a case where the court has not found any actual violence proved.

(3) If imprisonment is appropriate, the length of the committal should be decided without reference to whether or not it is to be suspended. A longer period of committal is not justified because its sting is removed by virtue of its suspension.

(4) The length of the committal has to depend upon the court's objectives. There are two objectives always in contempt of court proceedings. One is to mark the court's disapproval of the disobedience to its order. The other is to secure compliance with that order in the future. Thus, the seriousness of what has taken place is to be viewed in that light as well as for its own intrinsic gravity.

(5) The length of the committal has to bear some reasonable relationship to the maximum of two years which is available.

(6) Suspension is possible in a much wider range of circumstances than it is in criminal cases. It does not have to be the exceptional case. Indeed, it is usually the first way of attempting to secure compliance with the court's order.

(7) The length of the suspension requires separate consideration, although it is often appropriate for it to be linked to continued compliance with the order underlying the committal.

(8) Of course, the court has to bear in mind the context. This may be aggravating or mitigating. The context is often the break-up of an intimate relationship in which emotions run high and people behave in silly ways. The context of having children together, if that be the case, cannot be ignored. Sometimes that means that there is an aggravation of what has taken place, because of the greater fear that is engendered from the circumstances. Sometimes it may be mitigating, because there is reason to suppose that once the immediate emotions have calmed down, the molestation and threats will not continue.

(9) In many cases the court will have to bear in mind that there are concurrent proceedings in another court based on either the same facts or some of the same facts which are before the court on the contempt proceedings. The court cannot ignore those parallel proceedings. It may have to take into account their outcome in considering what the practical effect is upon the contempt proceedings. They do have different purposes and often the overlap is not exact, but nevertheless the court will not want, in effect, the contemnor to suffer punishment twice for the same events.

(10) It will usually be desirable for the court to explain very briefly why it has made the choices that it has made in the particular case before it…. [I]t would be appropriate in most cases for the contemnor to know why he or she was being sentenced to a period of imprisonment; why it was the length that it was; if it was suspended, why the suspension was as it was, but only very briefly.

An important part of the exercise is that the contemnor should understand the importance of keeping court orders, of not breaking them and the likely consequences if they are so broken.

In *H v O*, it was said that the fact that breaches occurred in the context of a contact dispute should be regarded as an aggravating rather than mitigating factor.[306] But what should the court do where there are parallel or prior proceedings in another court concerning related conduct?

Lomas v Parle [2003] EWCA Civ 1804, [2004] 1 WLR 1642

THORPE LJ:

47 ...[A] perpetrator may face sentence for the same act which amounts to both a breach of an injunction made in family proceedings and also a crime under the Protection from Harassment Act 1997. Of course, the sentencing courts do not share the same objective and operate in different ranges. The judge in the family proceedings has to fit a custodial sentence within a range of 0–24 months. An important objective for him is to uphold the authority of the court by demonstrating that its orders cannot be flouted with impunity. Nevertheless there will be a shared deterrent objective in the punishment of domestic violence by imprisonment .

48 ... [T]he first court to sentence must not anticipate or allow for a likely future sentence. It is for the second court to sentence to reflect *the prior sentence* in its judgment in order to ensure that the defendant is not twice punished for the same act. It is essential that the second court should be fully informed of the factors and circumstances reflected in the first sentence. The defendant is often publicly funded to defend the proceedings in each court and may well have different solicitors and counsel in each justice system. There is, therefore, an obligation on the first court to ensure that the basis of its sentence is fully expressed, and that a transcript of its judgment is made available to the second court ...

50 Within the constraints of the two-year limit on sentences for harassment in breach of [non-molestation orders] and the different scale which this necessarily involves, judges should as far as possible ensure that sentences passed under section 42 [FLA 1996] are not manifestly discrepant with sentences for harassment charged under sections 3, 4 or 5 of the Protection from Harassment Act 1997. The experience of counsel before us is that the level of sentencing under the [PHA 1997] is very significantly higher than the present level of sentencing for comparable incidents leading to committal for breach of [non-moleslation orders under FLA 1996]. Of course, domestic violence may also be the subject of other criminal charges varying from common assault to murder. The more serious the offences, the less scope there will be, in view of the two-year limit, to maintain any relationship between family and criminal court sentences—if indeed such cases are brought before the family court at all. [emphasis added]

The recommendation that family courts endeavour to issue sentences corresponding with those that might be issued by a criminal court under the PHA 1997 is problematic. Since the PHA 1997, and now the FLA 1996, s 42A, permit a maximum of five rather than just two years' imprisonment in criminal cases, and many other criminal offences carry higher penalties than the family courts can impose, it will often be impossible for the family court to 'keep up'. One answer may be to bring proceedings under the PHA 1997 or to prosecute breach of the non-molestation order instead of using contempt proceedings.[307]

---

[306] [2004] EWCA Civ 1691, [38].

[307] *Robinson v Murray* [2005] EWCA Civ 935, [13]. Since PHA 1997 proceedings are not 'family proceedings', a court faced with an application under that Act or under the FLA 1996 cannot simply elect to make an order under the other Act instead.

In a case where the respondent has already been sentenced in criminal proceedings for overlapping and other related incidents, the second court must tread carefully to avoid punishing the respondent twice for the same conduct.[308] How should such parallel proceedings be managed? Wilson LJ has accordingly refined Thorpe LJ's remarks in *Lomas v Parle*:

Slade v Slade [2009] EWCA Civ 748

WILSON LJ:

[He referred to s 3(7)(8) of the PHA 1997, which bars double jeopardy under that Act and went on...]

21. [T]he terminology of subsections (7) and (8) reflects true principle, namely that it is the *conduct* which is not twice punishable. Thus in my view we should not be misled by the words in [48] of *Lomas v Parle* [italicized above]: the second court should not so much reflect "the prior sentence" in its judgment as to decline to sentence for such of the conduct as has already been the subject of punishment in the criminal court. It follows that, even if a civil judge were to regard the punishment given by the criminal court for certain conduct as too lenient, it would be improper for him to use his power of committal in respect of that self-same conduct in order to top up the punishment to what he regards as a proper level. What he must do is to sentence only for such conduct as was not the subject of the criminal proceedings...

He went on to consider how the family court should sentence as contempt conduct which, in breach of the family court's order or an undertaking made to the court, had already been punished in criminal proceedings:

23....No doubt the seriousness or otherwise of the breach of the obligation to the civil court...will in part be informed by what one might call its *context*, namely (for example) whether it was the first breach or the last in a series of breaches, by the existence or otherwise of warnings of the consequences of a breach or further breaches and by the propinquity in time between the creation of the obligation and the breach. But how much further can the judge go into the circumstances or the *content* of the breach without sentencing for the conduct for which sentence has already been passed? In the most general terms, the judge must surely be entitled to assess the conduct's gravity: for the graver the conduct, the more serious the contempt of the civil court. But...any more profound assessment risks trespass upon the area for which sentence has already been passed. And, even when the breach is serious, the civil court must rigorously remind itself that, however problematical, its function is to sentence only for the fact of a serious contempt and not for the content of the serious contempt.

4.8 THE FUTURE: INTEGRATING CRIMINAL, CIVIL, AND FAMILY PROCEEDINGS?

The FLA 1996 was designed to streamline non-criminal remedies for domestic violence. The introduction of the PHA 1997, and the various reforms blurring the criminal, civil, and

---

[308] FLA 1996, s 42A(3), (4); PHA 1997, s 3. *Chechi v Bashir* [1999] 2 FLR 489: parallel civil proceedings for damages for assault, trespass to land, and damage to property contributed to the refusal to make a non-molestation order.

family jurisdictions—not least the criminalization of breach of non-molestation orders and the use of restraining orders on acquittals, and the possibility of police applications should the Crime and Security Act 2010 be implemented—have introduced fresh complexity and fragmentation.[309] The overlap between the criminal, civil, and family courts potentially causes wasteful duplication of effort and penalties from different courts dealing with the same basic facts, and a muddle of orders pursuing different objectives in relation to different aspects of the parties' lives. But it is usual for just one legal strategy to be pursued, not least because of the lack of integration between the civil/family and criminal justice systems.[310]

Victims are not represented directly before the court at all in criminal proceedings, and family solicitors retained to deal with connected family proceedings may lack the expertise, or the funding, to advise on related criminal proceedings. But proceedings dealing directly with domestic violence are often only part of the picture. Many cases involve child-related proceedings, for example in relation to contact between children of the family and the respondent. A criminal court may be ignorant of these proceedings, their outcome, and their implications for the matter before it: it might issue a restraining order in terms which precluded contact ordered by a family court; or, a restraining order having been made by a criminal court, a family court might subsequently wish to order contact to proceed in a manner barred by the indefinite restraining order; or the parties themselves might wish to agree such contact. As matters stand, the parties would have to return to the criminal court to seek variation of its restraining order before contact could proceed as ordered or desired. Important issues might get lost in the process.[311]

The answer may be to combine the family, civil, and criminal jurisdictions within one integrated domestic violence court, ideally on a 'one family, one judge' model enabling the same judge, as far as possible, to deal with all aspects of the family's legal problems. This option was highlighted in *Lomas v Parle*,[312] in light of US experience:

M. Burton, 'Domestic Violence—From Consultation to Bill: Closer integration of the civil and criminal justice systems', (2004) 34 *Family Law* 128, 131–2

The coordination of the civil and criminal functions in the new court has been evaluated as the single most important aspect of the process. The researchers note that, prior to the formation of the new court, victims of domestic violence were shuttled between various courts seeking different relief. In the integrated court, victim safety had increased because victims could obtain all forms of relief from the one court. And the situation in the past, where conflicting orders were sometimes made in criminal and civil proceedings, has been resolved....

It appears ... that an integrated specialist domestic violence court has the potential to resolve not only any information-sharing problems that exist in the traditional judicial system but also 'evidence-sharing' problems. Specially trained judges in integrated domestic violence courts have no difficulties applying the different evidential burdens and tailoring relief to the whole case before them. Rather than compromising neutrality, specialisation, it seems, creates judicial expertise and promotes continuity and consistency in decision-making.

---

[309] Burton (2004a).
[310] Humphreys and Thiara (2003), 202.
[311] See Hansard HC Proceedings of Standing Committee E on the Domestic Violence, Crimes and Victims Bill, 29 June 2004: discussion of amendments to cl 10.
[312] [2003] EWCA Civ 1804, [52].

It should not be thought that the integration of civil and criminal matters in a single special-ist court is completely without detriment to victims. Kellitz observes that integrated systems that include family proceedings, or systems where there is a high level of information sharing, may deter some women from accessing the system for fear of losing their children … Epstein has also commented that integration may maximise women's access to services but also 'can reduce their ability to decline such services if they wish to do so' … Women who want help with the civil justice route may be pushed into pursuing the criminal justice route as well. Implementation of a specialist domestic violence court has to remain responsive to the indi-vidual victim's needs and wishes. Judicial burnout has been identified as a further potential problem … Nevertheless, the benefits of specialisation on the fully integrated model, seem to outweigh the problems to the extent that it has become the preferred model for new courts in the US.

The increasing overlap between the family, civil, and criminal jurisdictions, and the impli-cations of domestic violence for other aspects of family life before the courts, demand a holistic approach of the sort that integrated courts could provide. Very disappointingly, however, a recent pilot project of an integrated court in Croydon ended in failure, with very few cases being put through the system, and the government has dropped the idea for the time being.[313]

4.9 CONCLUSION

A poor response from the legal system to domestic violence can be worse than the victim not turning to the law at all.

C. Humphreys and R. Thiara, 'Neither justice nor protection: women's experiences of post-separation violence', (2003) 25 *Journal of Social Welfare and Family Law* 195, 210

[In their research sample there was] a smaller group of chronic and serious offenders [who] were unresponsive to normative frameworks. 'Brushes' with the law which result in being charged with minor offences, cautions, binding over or short custodial sentences had no effect and in fact served to reinforce the abuser's belief that there are no effective constraints or sanctions on his behaviour. They can increase the dangers to women, who will be seen to have 'transgressed' having called the police or given evidence against the abuser. Moreover, poor and ineffective action from law enforcement and prosecution services may serve to confirm a woman's belief that she is outside help and, therefore, has no option other than to seek to appease the abuser.

The legal system must provide effective and timely protection and assistance for victims. However, important as it is, the law's ability to deal with domestic violence is limited. The vast majority of victims never reach a courtroom. The activities of other government and voluntary sector agencies are vital to victims' safety. Current policy aims to achieve

---

[313] Hester, Pearce, and Westmarland (2008); HO (2009), 24.

an integrated, multi-agency approach, to secure prevention and support, justice and protection.[314] Education, particularly among young people, is important to root out attitudes which tolerate or even support domestic abuse, and to encourage victims and others to speak out. Proper resourcing and training for all agencies and individuals involved with families experiencing domestic violence are essential. Social exclusion and other risk factors associated with domestic violence must be tackled. Only these non-legal measures will secure a significant reduction in the prevalence of domestic violence.

ONLINE RESOURCE CENTRE

Questions, suggestions for further reading, and supplementary materials for this chapter (including updates on developments in this area of family law since this book was published) may be found on the Online Resource Centre at **www.oxfordtextbooks.co.uk/orc/harrisshort_tcm2e/**.

---

[314] HO (2009).

5

ENDING RELATIONSHIPS: DIVORCE AND SEPARATION

CENTRAL ISSUES

1. The law of divorce has always been controversial owing to its implications for the institution of marriage and the family. Attempts to reform the law trigger heated political debate.

2. Divorce used to be fault-based, available only on proof that the respondent had committed a 'matrimonial offence'. Since 1969, divorce has been available on the basis that the marriage has irretrievably broken down. But that ground can be satisfied only by proving one of five 'facts', three of which (adultery, behaviour, and desertion) are generally fault-related, two of which (based on separation) do not require proof of fault.

3. The law of civil partnership dissolution is largely identical to the law of divorce, with the notable exception that there is no 'fact' based on 'adultery'. Like the omission of sex-related grounds from the law of nullity, this has interesting implications for the nature of civil partnership.

4. In practice, the procedure for uncontested cases severely limits the extent of any real adjudication on questions of fault on divorce.

5. Attempts to introduce no-fault divorce in the Family Law Act 1996 (FLA 1996) foundered owing to Government concerns that new provisions designed to save saveable marriages and to encourage use of mediation would be ineffective. Those provisions have never been brought into force. The Matrimonial Causes Act 1973 (MCA 1973) (in which the 1969 reforms were consolidated) remains the law in force today.

6. Current family policy is concerned with finding ways to encourage couples, whether married or cohabiting, to deal responsibly with the consequences of relationship breakdown, particularly for their children.

5.1 INTRODUCTION

Thousands of families are touched by divorce every year. That sad fact attracts a range of responses. Some see divorce as the death of family, symptomatic of moral decay, of 'broken

Britain',[1] a cause of social dislocation, economic cost to society, and damage to children. Divorce and separation must therefore be curtailed and marriage promoted as the functional and ideological 'gold standard'. Others are more sanguine, seeing divorce as a common stage in contemporary family life beyond which family continues, albeit reconfigured across two households. On this view, the issue is how law can enable families to adjust and maintain good relationships after relationship breakdown, particularly where the couple have children.[2] These concerns apply equally to couples who cohabit and become parents without marrying. Issues surrounding parenting and property arrangements on separation are as pressing for them as they are for divorcing spouses. But while separating spouses and cohabitants share many practical problems, spouses and civil partners may wish (and need) to end their relationship not only in fact but also in law. Simply separating does not extinguish the legal status of marriage or civil partnership. The legal rights and duties attaching to the status continue, and, while they may cohabit with another, the parties are unable to marry or form a civil partnership with anyone else. Releasing the parties from their legal status is the job of the law of divorce, the principal focus of this chapter.

There is a human right to marry, but the European Convention on Human Rights (ECHR) does not recognize a right to divorce.[3] Nevertheless, all European states (except Malta) now permit divorce and Article 12 ECHR entitles divorcees to remarry without unreasonable restrictions.[4] However, each state is free to determine the basis on which divorce is granted and there is considerable variety across Europe.[5] Divorce in England and Wales is governed by the MCA 1973 and equivalent provisions of the Civil Partnership Act 2004 (CPA 2004). Civil partnerships are terminated by 'dissolution', but the procedures and substantive law (with the notable omission of the law relating to adultery) are the same as divorce. Unless clear from the context, references here to 'divorce' and associated terminology include civil partnership dissolution. The MCA 1973 provides a 'mixed economy' divorce system, combining fault-based and 'no-fault' elements. It had been expected that the MCA 1973 would be replaced by the FLA 1996, which would have placed divorce on an entirely no-fault basis and transformed the procedure for obtaining divorce. For reasons that we shall explore later, the relevant Parts of that Act will never be brought into force, but the FLA 1996 remains central to discussion of divorce reform.

Like its law of nullity,[6] a society's divorce law (or its absence) reveals something about that society's understanding of the nature and significance of marriage, and about the boundaries between public and private, between community interest and individual interest. It involves basic questions about the role of the state and the law in regulating adults' private lives and the nature that that regulation should take. If the law makes no provision for divorce, then marriage is a lifelong status. If divorce is permitted, on what basis? Is marriage a status terminable only if one party commits some 'offence' regarded by the state as sufficiently grave to excuse the innocent party from continued participation in the marriage? Is it a contract dissoluble by mutual consent, its terms (to that extent) implicitly agreed by the

---

[1] This concept was invoked by the Conservative Party in the 2010 election campaign.

[2] Hasson (2006). Lewis (2001a), 162 observes that it is difficult to prove the cause and effect relationship between divorce and outcomes for children, since it is hard to disentangle the impact of divorce (specifically) on children's outcomes from other factors affecting families before, during, or after separation.

[3] *Johnson v Ireland* (App No 9697/82, ECHR) (1986).

[4] *F v Switzerland* (App No 11329/85, ECHR) (1987), [32]: three-year ban on remarriage by a serial divorcee and adulterer was unreasonable.

[5] Boele-Woelki et al (2004).

[6] 2.6, 2.7.

parties, rather than the state? Or can marriage last only for so long as both parties assᵣ
its continuation, allowing one party to end it unilaterally? Even if divorce is freely availᵣ
in this sense, might the law seek in other ways to influence parties' behaviour regarding
divorce, for example by imposing waiting periods?

5.2 THE RISE IN DIVORCE

Most marriages end by death, but the number and proportion of marriages ending by divorce
increased dramatically during the last century. This overall trend is matched across much of
Europe, although differences in laws, social, cultural, and religious factors are reflected in
countries' divorce rates.[7] In one sense at least, changes in the substantive and procedural law
governing divorce contributed to this increase: it is now legally possible for many of those
who wish to divorce to do so when previously they could not. But this does not itself mean
that more marriages now fail: before the law permitted divorce, many couples in unhappy
marriages physically separated.[8] Some formed new relationships which, without a divorce
from the earlier marriage, could not be formalized by marriage. A restrictive divorce law
may therefore not have kept unhappy couples together, but simply prevented them from
terminating their legal relationship.[9]

Another major contributing factor to increasing divorce was the huge social changes of the
twentieth century, especially regarding women's position in the home and their increased
participation in the labour market, birth control, sexual morality, declining levels of religious
adherence, and the transformation of home and family from a unit of production to a haven
from the outside world. These changes have affected people's expectations of marriage, now
principally regarded as a source of companionship through life.[10] Moreover, greater long-
evity has exposed more marriages to the test of time: in 1820, the same proportion of marriages ended by death within 15 years of marriage as ended by divorce in 1980.[11] However,
the relationship between social behaviour and law reform is complex. Commentators and
researchers disagree about whether and to what extent reforms liberalizing divorce either
responded to social demand or increased the divorce rate amongst couples who would otherwise have been prepared to stay together.[12]

5.2.1 DIVORCES IN ENGLAND AND WALES

In the early 1900s, around 500 divorces were granted each year. Thereafter, the numbers rose
after each reform enlarging the grounds on which divorce could be obtained.[13] After 1923,
there were about 2,500 divorces annually, from 1937, around 7–8,000. Social upheaval during and following the Second World War unsurprisingly generated an exceptional 60,300
divorces in 1947, but otherwise around 25–30,000 divorces were granted per year post-war

[7] OECD (2008).

[8] See recent data for Ireland, noted by Ellman (1997), 219.

[9] Law Com (1988a) paras 2.15–2.16.

[10] Rheinstein (1972), 273–6; Phillips (1991), ch 9.

[11] Walker (1991).

[12] Cf Law Com (1988a), paras 2.14–2.22; Deech (1990), 242; Gibson (1994), 223; Richards (1996); Mansfield,
Reynolds, and Arai (1999); Rowthorn (1999); Binner and Dnes (2001); Smith (2002); González and Viitanen
(2006); Allen and Gallagher (2007) provide a useful review of the research data.

[13] See 5.4.

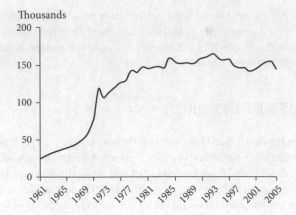

Figure 5.1 Divorces, England and Wales (including annulments): ONS website

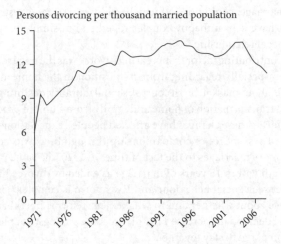

Figure 5.2 Persons divorcing per thousand married population (England and Wales): ONS website

Source: Reproduced from the Office for National Statistics, by Crown copyright © 2010.

until the 1960s.[14] This increase was partly attributable to the availability of legal aid (from 1948 until the mid-1970s) which made divorce available to those who had previously been unable to afford it. During the 1960s, the number of divorces doubled independently of any major substantive legal change.[15] Following reform in 1969—which introduced the law in force today—the number of divorces each year spiked, quickly exceeding 100,000 per year and peaking at 180,523 across the UK in 1993. But, after a small post-millennium rise, since 2004, numbers have fallen markedly. In 2008, 136,026 divorces were granted across the UK, 121,779 in England and Wales.[16] It is anticipated that the *numbers* of divorces will drop over

[14] Stone (1990), table 13.1.
[15] The Matrimonial Causes Act 1963 amended the laws of condonation and collusion: Cretney (2003a), 349–51; there was also some liberalization in the case law during the 1960s: ibid., 352–3.
[16] ONS (2010a).

the coming decades as fewer people marry. Those who do marry increasingly do so later in life, reducing the number of youthful marriages which are more prone to divorce.[17]

Another useful measure is the divorce *rate*: how many people each year divorce per 1,000 members of the married population. This statistic is unaffected by changes in the overall population or the number of marriages and so more accurately indicates the frequency of divorce. In England and Wales, the divorce rate in 1961, before the 1969 reforms, was 2.1 per 1,000 of the married population.[18] By 1971, it was 6.0; it peaked at 14.1 in 2004, but since then has dropped away and in 2008 was 11.2, a rate last seen in 1979.[19] This drop suggests that the current married population are more likely to stay married. Indeed, while the divorce rate and numbers of divorces have declined, so too has the marriage rate: far fewer people are now marrying, and those who do marry are doing so later in life.[20] Many of those who do marry are therefore probably more likely to stay together, and vice versa. Recent projections suggest that if current divorce rates continue, around 45 per cent of marriages will end in divorce, almost half of those divorces will occur before the tenth wedding anniversary, and that only 10 per cent of spouses who married in 2005 will reach their 60th wedding anniversary.[21]

What divorce statistics cannot tell us about is the breakdown of cohabitation. Owing to the informal nature of these relationships, gathering data about them is challenging, but survey evidence indicates that their breakdown rate is significantly higher than that of spouses.[22]

5.2.2 WHO DIVORCES?

Twice as many divorces are granted to wives as to husbands,[23] which presumably indicates that twice as many divorce petitions are presented by wives. However, the petitioner's identity does not necessarily indicate which spouse instigated the separation.[24] Just as mean age at first marriage is rising,[25] so is mean age at divorce. In 2008, the mean age of divorcees was 43.9 for men and 41.4 for women. The median duration of marriage at divorce in 2008 was 11.5 years;[26] many couples will have separated some time before divorce is obtained, so the duration of their 'live' relationships will have been shorter than that. Just over half of couples divorcing today have at least one child aged under 16. In 2007, over 117,193 dependent children experienced parental divorce.[27] Just as an increasing proportion of marriages are remarriages, so an increasing proportion of those divorcing are doing so for the second time: since 1981, the proportion has doubled to one in five.[28] The divorce rate is considerably higher for younger couples (around 26 per 1,000 for couples aged 25–29) than for older ones (below 10 per 1000 for those aged 55–59, and considerably lower for those over 60).[29] The ris-

---

[17] ONS (2010d), tables of projected numbers of marriages and divorces.
[18] Law Com (1988a), Appendix A.
[19] ONS (2010a).
[20] See 2.2.
[21] Wilson and Smallwood (2008).
[22] See discussion at 2.8.2.
[23] ONS (2010a).
[24] Davis and Murch (1988), 64–6.
[25] See 2.2.
[26] ONS (2010a).
[27] ONS (2008), table 4.
[28] ONS (2010a).
[29] ONS (2008), table 3.

ing age at first marriage is therefore contributing to the fall in divorce rates noted in the last section, as fewer young marriages are contracted.

Various factors are associated with an increased likelihood of divorce, including: early (especially teenage) marriage; premarital cohabitation, whether with the spouse or another; prior relationship breakdown; premarital births; parental divorce; poor economic circumstances (also associated with young marriage); poor psychological and physical well-being.[30] Similar characteristics are associated with separation by unmarried couples.

5.3 THE NATURE, FUNCTION, AND LIMITS OF DIVORCE LAW

Before examining current divorce law and reform options, we sketch some inter-related themes which have been debated since judicial divorce was introduced in 1857. It is striking how timeless many of the political concerns about marriage and divorce seem to be, despite massive social and legal change over time. A law of divorce can assume various shapes, depending on the chosen degree, nature, and purpose of state intervention and the state's view of marriage. How can and should the law be used in relation to divorce?

5.3.1 REGULATION OR REGULARIZATION?

Divorce law can have more or less substantial roles, described by John Eekelaar as 'regulation' and 'regularization'. Regularization:

> accepts, fatalistically, that separation and divorce will occur whatever the legal process does. It wishes to ensure that that process does not add to its harms, and leaves it largely to the people involved to settle the consequences. The legal process is therefore largely confined to ensuring that cases are processed efficiently and formalities attended to properly.[31]

Marriage and civil partnership can be created by a relatively straightforward, low-cost administrative process. The law could adopt a similarly hands-off stance at the end, effecting divorce by an administrative, rather than judicial, process instigated by both parties, or even (unlike marriage) by one of them. Divorce would thus be the product of private decision. There may be disputes about *consequences* of divorce, for example regarding children or finances in which the state might assert an interest to protect vulnerable family members or the public purse. But judicial determination of these ancillary issues would not detract from the essentially private, administrative nature of the underlying divorce.

By contrast, 'regulation' implies some more substantial role for the law, imposing restrictions on divorce which reflect the seriousness of that step and, by implication, the importance of marriage to the welfare of the parties, any children of the marriage, and society at large. The precise *nature* of that role and those restrictions would depend upon the state's view of marriage and its interest in it. But it would be more paternalistic, interventionist, and directive than mere 'regularization'.

---

[30] Clarke and Berrington (1999); Kiernan and Mueller (1998); Coleman and Glenn (2010).
[31] Eekelaar (1991b), 142.

5.3.2 FAULT OR 'NO-FAULT'?

The legal system characteristically dispenses justice, adjudicating on right and wrong. Divorce law could do the same, providing 'justice' for a wronged party and enforcing responsibility for wrongdoing. A fault-based divorce law identifies various 'matrimonial offences', commission of which render the 'guilty' spouse vulnerable to the penalty of being divorced on the other's application. This to some extent reflects a contractual view of marriage,[32] the guilty party's breach excusing the other from continued performance of the contract and entitling that party to some form of compensation. But, undermining the contract analogy, the couple do not decide what constitutes a breach: that is determined for them by the law of divorce (though it is for the innocent party, once a breach has occurred, to decide whether to instigate divorce). A fault-based law also performs an exhortatory function, establishing a moral code for marriage. However, there are various problems with administering fault-based divorce, and most—though not all—options for reform remove fault, leaving parties a greater or lesser degree of freedom to divorce simply because one or both of them consider that the marriage has broken down.[33]

5.3.3 'EASIER' OR 'HARDER' DIVORCE AND SUPPORTING THE INSTITUTION OF MARRIAGE

A perennial theme is whether the law makes divorce too easy or too hard, and whether any reform would make divorce easier or harder. This is also linked to the degree of support which the law appears to offer the institution of marriage: easy divorce is said to undermine it, hard divorce to support it. These political debates continue despite Otto Kahn-Freund's observation over 40 years ago that 'it is a hopeless quest to promote the stability of marriage by making divorce "difficult" and...the problem is far more complex and more profound than the crude question whether divorce should be a little more or a little less "easy".'[34] Davis and Murch expand on this theme:

G. Davis and M. Murch, *Grounds for Divorce* (Oxford: Clarendon Press, 1998), 148

It is tempting to view this debate in light of a liberal/conservative battleground, with the liberals seeking 'easier' divorce through shorter time periods or the abandonment of fault, whilst the conservatives struggle to maintain some disincentive to ill-considered termination of marriage through longer time periods or the maintenance of fault. But 'fault' and time constraints, whilst they may each be thought to make divorce more difficult, make it more difficult *in different ways*—and for different people. In other words, there are arguments for and against delay; there are also arguments for and against fault; but they are not the *same* arguments and they should not be lumped together under the heading of 'easier' or 'more difficult' divorce.

For example, a law which allows a spouse to obtain a divorce in under six months because of the other's adultery would be rendered considerably 'harder' if fault were replaced by a

---

[32] See discussion at 2.4.1.
[33] See 5.7, and compare Rowthorn (1999) and Ellman (1997).
[34] Kahn-Freund (1967), 181.

uniform one-year separation requirement. On the other hand, such a reform would make divorce 'easier' for a spouse who currently has to be separated for *two* years before divorce is permitted. But that same reform would be 'harder' for those individuals if it required them to use the one-year period to resolve all issues regarding their children and finances. All of this overlooks the emotional pain of divorce, even for those who ostensibly desire it, which the law can do little to alleviate.[35] Divorce in that sense is never 'easy'.

It is often said that the law of divorce should seek to support the institution of marriage, but again what this implies for the ease or difficulty of divorce is ambiguous. A restrictive divorce law, for example requiring proof of grave fault by the respondent, could be said to support marriage by emphasizing the seriousness of matrimonial obligations and requiring people to remain married, however dissatisfied they may be, unless one partner commits a relevant offence. The same law could be said to undermine marriage by insisting that marriages of poor quality be upheld, even if the parties had long since separated. By contrast, an 'easy' divorce law which released those who were dissatisfied with their marriages could be said to support the institution by reserving marriage and its legal consequences for 'good quality' relationships.[36] Might such a law encourage people to adopt a 'throw-away' approach to marriage and give up too soon? But is the law the, or even a, principal determinant of people's behaviour in this regard? And, if it is, how might it best seek to influence them?

5.3.4 CAN DIVORCE LAW AFFECT MARITAL AND DIVORCING BEHAVIOUR?

Commentators disagree on whether divorce law should simply provide a mechanism for individuals to terminate their marriage, or whether it can or should go further, seeking to influence relationship behaviour. We have noted the arguments about whether liberal divorce causes more marriages to fail. But other questions arise. Can and should divorce law be based on fault to deter whatever behaviour gives grounds for divorce? Does divorce law affect parties' willingness to invest in their marriages, easier divorce reducing parties' reliance on marriage?[37] If divorce is hard, might some be dissuaded from marrying at all? If so, would that be a good or bad thing? Can the law rescue couples from divorce by helping them to save saveable marriages? It has been said that the notion that divorce law can save individual marriages (as opposed to the institution more generally) is one that 'conventional wisdom has long firmly rejected'.[38] Nevertheless, the idea that something should be done to 'save saveable marriages' has persistent political appeal.[39] The law might also encourage parties to divorce in a particular manner. Recent government publications have emphasized 'responsibility' on divorce.[40] The concern here is not with responsibility to respect the lifelong commitment of marriage or a guilty party's duty to accept responsibility (blame) for its breakdown. Rather, the new concept of responsibility requires *both* parties to 'divorce responsibly';[41] 'responsible' couples resolve their differences by way of mediation rather than via lawyers and the courts. However, whether law can steer parties' behaviour in this

---

[35] See Law Com (1990), paras 3.46–3.47; LCD (1993), 6.51–6.53.

[36] Cf *Reiterbund v Reiterbund* [1974] 1 WLR 788, extract below p 317; *Vervaeke v Smith* [1983] 1 AC 145, extract above p 80; Smart (2000), 371.

[37] See 5.7.1.

[38] Cretney (1996a), 45.

[39] E.g. LCD (1993), (1995). See Hasson (2006).

[40] LCD (1993), (1995); HO (1998).

[41] Reece (2003).

manner is questionable. Evidence that such attempts would fail caused major reforms to be abandoned.[42]

5.3.5 A LEGAL OR NON-LEGAL APPROACH?

While terminating spousal status is inevitably a legal process, the legal system need not have a monopoly over resolving the practical issues that arise on divorce (regarding children and financial settlements) or over determining whether the spouses' relationship has ended. Non-legal disciplines may have roles here: education and information provision, therapeutic intervention such as marriage counselling and social work, and mediation[43] may be able to perform some of those functions that the state is keen to pursue but which the *legal system* cannot fulfil. In particular, the legal system may be unable to save marriages or to enable parties to cope psychologically with divorce. But the law could provide a framework for the delivery and funding of such services when divorce is sought or earlier. Whether the legal system can help couples to co-operate in resolving the practical consequences is hotly contested by lawyers and mediators.[44] Non-legal approaches to relationship support and breakdown have become increasingly prominent. However, the current law of divorce, experienced by most couples as a fault-based process, sits somewhat uneasily alongside the outlook of non-legal disciplines.

5.4 A BRIEF HISTORY OF DIVORCE LAW TO 1969

Until 1857, divorce by way of court order terminating marriage did not exist.[45] The ecclesiastical courts issued decrees of nullity and various remedies short of divorce. A valid marriage could only be ended by Private Act of Parliament, a route open only to the wealthy. Following a Royal Commission, the ecclesiastical courts' jurisdiction was replaced by a new civil court with the power to dissolve marriages. Under the Matrimonial Causes Act 1857, divorce could be obtained by the husband on the ground of his wife's adultery, and by the wife on the ground that her husband had been guilty of incestuous adultery, bigamy with adultery, rape (of someone other than the wife[46]), sodomy, bestiality, or adultery coupled either with desertion for two years or with cruelty. The lack of gender equality persisted until 1923, when wives were permitted to petition on grounds of adultery alone.[47] Adultery was effectively the sole ground for divorce until 1937:

Law Commission, *Facing the Future: A Discussion Paper on the Ground for Divorce*, Law Com No 170 (London: HMSO, 1988a)

2.1 Before the Divorce Reform Act 1969, a divorce could only be obtained [under the Matrimonial Causes Act 1937] by proving that the respondent had committed a matrimonial offence (the only material offences were adultery, cruelty and desertion for three years). A petitioner who was himself guilty of such an offence, or had somehow contributed to

---

[42] See 5.8.
[43] Mediation is not to be confused with counselling and reconciliation: see 1.2.7.
[44] Ibid.
[45] For the long history, see Stone (1990) and Cretney (2003a), Part II.
[46] At that time, husbands could not be guilty of raping their wives: see 4.2.3.
[47] Probert (1999).

the offence of the other, or had condoned it, might be refused relief.[48] No divorce could be granted within three years of marriage, unless special leave was given on the ground that the petitioner would suffer exceptional hardship or that the respondent was guilty of exceptional depravity.

2.2 Since the 1950s there had been increasing disillusionment with the operation of the fault-based law.[49] It was clear that there was no real barrier to consensual divorce where both parties wanted it and one was prepared to commit, or perhaps appear to commit, a matrimonial offence to supply the necessary ground [though technically collusion was an absolute bar to divorce until 1963]. On the other hand, where parties were not prepared to resort to such expedients, there was often no remedy, even though the marriage had irretrievably broken down. It was argued by the proponents of reform that the court was in no position to allocate blame; that in many cases both parties were at fault, and that matrimonial offences were often merely symptomatic of the breakdown of the marriage rather than the cause. However, the majority of the Royal Commission on Marriage and Divorce (the Morton Commission of 1956) affirmed the matrimonial offence as the sole basis of divorce because they saw this as the only means to ensure the stability of the institution of marriage. Three attempts, in Private Members' Bills, to introduce a provision allowing for divorce after long periods of separation were unsuccessful. Finally, the publication in 1966 of the report of the Archbishop of Canterbury's Group [Mortimer Commission], entitled *Putting Asunder—A Divorce Law for Contemporary Society*, paved the way for reform. The report found the existing law concentrated exclusively on making findings of past delinquencies, whilst ignoring the current viability of the marriage. It therefore recommended that the matrimonial offence be abolished and be replaced by the principle of breakdown as the sole ground for divorce. It was envisaged that the court would determine whether the marriage had broken down after considering all the evidence.

2.3 The Lord Chancellor referred *Putting Asunder* to the Law Commission, whose response was published later in the same year, entitled Reform of the Grounds of Divorce—the Field of Choice. The Commission agreed with the Archbishop's Group's criticisms of the existing law. In particular, it found that the need to prove a matrimonial offence caused unnecessary bitterness and distress to the parties and their children. The law did not accord with social reality, in that many spouses who could not obtain a divorce simply left the "empty shells" of their marriages and set up "stable illicit unions" with new partners.[50] The Commission also agreed that where both parties wanted to end the marriage, divorce was easily available if they were prepared to commit or appear to commit a matrimonial offence. The Commission considered the objectives for a good divorce law to be:

(i) To buttress, rather than to undermine, the stability of marriage; and

(ii) When, regrettably, a marriage has irretrievably broken down, to enable the empty legal shell to be destroyed with the maximum fairness, and the minimum bitterness, distress and humiliation. . . .

2.4 Thus, both bodies agreed that the fault principle was unsatisfactory and that the law should be reformed to allow marriages which had irretrievably broken down to be dissolved in a humane fashion. The difficulty, of course, was how to identify those marriages which had irretrievably broken down. The Law Commission did not favour the solution advocated by the

---

[48] The law barred divorce (absolutely or on a discretionary basis) where the petitioner had colluded with the respondent in drafting the petition, condoned or connived in the respondent's offence, or had also committed a matrimonial offence: see Cretney (2003a), 176–7.

[49] See Law Com (1966), paras 19 et seq.

[50] Ibid., paras 33 et seq.

Archbishop's Group. First, it considered the proposed inquest impracticable partly because breakdown was not a justiciable issue. Secondly, it was concerned that such an inquest into the conduct of the parties in order to determine breakdown would cause unnecessary bitterness and humiliation and prevent the marital ties being dissolved with decency and dignity. After consultations between the various interested bodies, a compromise solution was reached whereby breakdown would become the sole ground for divorce, but would be inferred from the existence of one of a number of facts rather than by judicial inquest. This solution was enacted in the Divorce Reform Act 1969.

5.5 THE PRESENT LAW OF DIVORCE AND JUDICIAL SEPARATION

The present law of divorce, found in the Matrimonial Causes Act 1973, is largely as enacted in 1969. The corresponding law of 'dissolution' applying to civil partnerships is modelled on divorce law, with some difference of terminology, e.g. 'dissolution' rather than 'divorce', and 'applicant' rather than 'petitioner'. We use the traditional terminology of divorce here, but note that new Family Procedure Rules (which came into force in April 2011) bring much of the language of divorce into line with the terminology adopted for civil partnership.[51] The only difference of *substance* between divorce and dissolution law is that civil partnership may not be dissolved on the basis of 'adultery', though sexual infidelity by a civil partner would probably satisfy the 'behaviour' fact.[52] We focus largely on the substantive law under which divorce must be obtained. But it is essential also to understand divorce procedure, since it casts a rather different light on contemporary divorce practice.

5.5.1 THE GROUND FOR DIVORCE AND DISSOLUTION: IRRETRIEVABLE BREAKDOWN OF MARRIAGE OR CIVIL PARTNERSHIP

There is now only one ground for divorce or dissolution and it is not fault-based: that the marriage or civil partnership has irretrievably broken down. This fact must be established at the date of the hearing, not at the date of filing the petition.[53] But one or both parties cannot simply assert that fact, however clear it may be. For example, in *Buffery v Buffery*, the parties had grown apart and could not longer communicate, but would have to wait to obtain their divorce on a separation fact.[54]

Matrimonial Causes Act 1973, s 1[55]

(1)...[A] petition for divorce may be presented to the court by either party to a marriage on the ground that the marriage has broken down irretrievably.

---

[51] FPR 2010.
[52] Cf 2.7.5 and 2.7.6 on the omission of consummation from the nullity grounds in the CPA 2004.
[53] *Pheasant v Pheasant* [1972] Fam 202.
[54] [1988] 2 FLR 365.
[55] CPA 2004, s 44.

> (2) The court hearing a petition for divorce shall not hold the marriage to have broken down irretrievably unless the petitioner satisfies the court of one or more of the following facts…

Three of those facts—adultery, desertion, and behaviour by the respondent—appear principally fault-based, though the behaviour fact can apply in situations that involve no fault, as such, by the respondent. Petitioners need not have 'clean hands'.[56] The other two—based on separation, for two years if the respondent consents to the divorce, for five years without that consent—are no-fault facts. English law therefore operates a 'mixed system' of divorce, comprising both fault-based and no-fault elements.

The requirement that the petitioner must prove a 'fact' means parties cannot divorce immediately by mutual consent, a right which might have been thought implicit in the irretrievable breakdown test. Something more substantial must also be proved. Divorce is in that sense a public, not a private matter. Conversely, even if it is accepted on all sides that the marriage has broken down irretrievably, the party with grounds to petition is entitled *not* to instigate proceedings.[57]

The fact-based approach to breakdown seeks to overcome the problem that, 'except in the clearest of cases, [whether a marriage has broken down irretrievably] is not a justiciable issue'.[58] What courts can adjudicate upon are more specific allegations of the sort comprised in the 'facts'. Curiously, however, there is no need to prove that the 'fact' *caused* the breakdown.[59] Once the 'fact' is proved, the court must grant a decree of divorce, *unless* it is satisfied on all the evidence that—notwithstanding proof of the 'fact' and the petitioner's wish to be divorced—the relationship has *not* irretrievably broken down.[60] This effectively requires petitioners to prove their 'fact', and leaves respondents with the uphill task of trying to persuade the court that the relationship remains viable.[61]

5.5.2 THE FACTS: ADULTERY BY THE RESPONDENT

Matrimonial Causes Act 1973, s 1(2)(a)

> …the respondent has committed adultery and the petitioner finds it intolerable to live with the respondent.

The proscribed behaviour

This fact applies only to marriages, and so is not available in civil partnership cases. Adultery entails voluntary intercourse by one spouse with a third party of the opposite sex.[62] Sexual

---

[56] Contrast the old discretionary bars to divorce: Cretney (2003a), 188–95.

[57] E.g. they might delay for tactical reasons, such as to preserve matrimonial home rights (3.7.1): *Stevens v Stevens* [1979] 1 WLR 885.

[58] *Pheasant v Pheasant* [1972] Fam 202, 206.

[59] *Buffery v Buffery* [1988] 2 FLR 365, 366.

[60] Notwithstanding *Cotterell v Cotterell* [1998] 3 FCR 199, the court must examine the fact before assessing whether the marriage has broken down irretrievably.

[61] MCA 1973, s 1(4); CPA 2004, s 44(4). Cretney (2003a), 367 records that in no reported case has a respondent succeeded, though many apparently try, at least initially: Davis and Murch (1988), 102.

[62] Presumably including someone with a full gender recognition certificate and appropriate constructive surgery (Gender Recognition Act 2004); cf case law regarding consummation in such cases: see 2.7.5.

activity between one spouse and someone of the same sex does not constitute adultery, though it may satisfy the behaviour fact. No reported case has considered whether artificial insemination by another man without the husband's consent constitutes adultery.[63] The old case law still offers guidance. The wife's lover in *Dennis v Dennis*, Mr Spillett, was found to be 'unable to effect his purpose', owing to nerves:

Dennis v Dennis (Spillett cited) [1955] P 153, 160

SINGLETON LJ:

I do not think that it can be said that adultery is proved unless there be some penetration. It is not necessary that the complete act of sexual intercourse should take place. If there is penetration by the man of the woman, adultery may be found, but if there is no more than an attempt, I do not think that a finding of adultery would be right.

Attempts at intercourse and the actual commission of lesser sexual acts, even those that might result in conception, were therefore held to be insufficient. Intercourse is not regarded as voluntary where the respondent is raped.[64] The effect of intoxicants on the respondent may not be so serious as to render intercourse involuntary. If voluntarily consumed alcohol disinhibits the respondent, causing him or her to have sex when he or she would not have done so sober, and even to have no memory of the event, the intercourse may still be adulterous. Contrast the case where intoxication deprives the respondent of the power to give any valid consent to intercourse.[65] Special issues arise where the respondent has validly contracted a polygamous marriage in another jurisdiction.[66]

The intolerability requirement

It is not enough to prove adultery. Petitioners must also prove that they find it intolerable to live with the respondent. But must the adultery and intolerability be connected—must the latter arise in consequence of the former? It was held in *Roper v Roper* that it must, otherwise a wife could take the chance occurrence of her husband's adultery to get the divorce that she had always wanted because of the irritating way in which he blew his nose. Nor could the petitioner simply to *say* that she found it intolerable to live with the respondent: she might actually want a divorce because she was sexually attracted to another man.[67] However, when the Court of Appeal considered the question two years later, it took another view, which now represents the law:

Cleary v Cleary and Hutton [1974] 1 WLR 73, 76 and 78 (CA)

DENNING LJ:

As a matter of interpretation. I think the two facts in section [1(2)(*a*)] are independent and should be so treated. Take this very case. The husband proves that the wife committed

---

[63] Cretney (2003a), 254, n 28.

[64] *Redpath v Redpath* [1950] 1 All ER 600: unclear whether the burden of proving lack of consent falls on the respondent.

[65] *Goshawk v Goshawk* (1965) 109 SJ 290.

[66] Collins (2000), 18-021; Law Com (1985a), para 4.16; *Onobrauche v Onobrauche* (1978) 8 FL 107; *Quoraishi v Quoraishi* [1985] FLR 780.

[67] [1972] 1 WLR 1314, 1317.

adultery and that he forgave her and took her back. That is one fact. He then proves that, after she comes back, she behaves in a way that makes it quite intolerable to live with her. She corresponds with the other man and goes out at night and finally leaves her husband, taking the children with her. That is another fact. It is in consequence of that second fact that he finds it intolerable—not in consequence of the previous adultery. On that evidence, it is quite plain that the marriage has broken down irretrievably. He complies with section [1(2)(a)] by proving (a) her adultery which was forgiven; and (b) her subsequent conduct (not adultery), which makes it intolerable to live with her.

I would say one word more. In *Rayden on Divorce*…it is suggested…: "It may even be his own adultery which leads him to find it intolerable to live with the respondent." I cannot accept that suggestion. Suppose a wife committed adultery five years ago. The husband forgives her and takes her back. He then falls in love with another woman and commits adultery with her. He may say that he finds it intolerable to live with his wife, but that is palpably untrue. It was quite tolerable for five years: and it is not rendered intolerable by his love for another woman. That illustration shows that a judge in such cases as these should not accept the man's bare assertion that he finds it intolerable. He should inquire what conduct on the part of the wife has made it intolerable. It may be her previous adultery. It may be something else. But whatever it is, the judge must be satisfied that the husband finds it intolerable to live with her.

Scarman LJ agreed, noting s 1(3) of the MCA which requires the court 'so far as it reasonably can' to 'inquire…into the facts alleged' by each party. The judge must therefore be satisfied on the balance of probabilities that the petitioner is telling the truth in claiming that he or she finds it intolerable to live with the respondent. Yet he appreciated that in undefended cases there may be rather little evidence on which the judge could base his finding other than the petitioner's own statements. We shall see later that this problem has been aggravated by the procedure now adopted in undefended cases.[68]

The relevance of continued cohabitation

A final issue is the relevance of continued cohabitation by the parties after the petitioner discovered the adultery:

Matrimonial Causes Act 1973, s 2(1)

One party to a marriage shall not be entitled to rely for the purposes of section 1(2)(a) above on adultery committed by the other if, after it became known to him that the other had committed that adultery, the parties have lived with each other for a period exceeding, or periods together exceeding, six months.

We explore the meaning of 'lived with each other' for these purposes when we examine the two separation facts. Essentially, it has been interpreted to mean sharing a household as husband and wife. Living under the same roof, even sharing a household, may therefore not prevent reliance on adultery, provided that the parties are not living 'as husband and wife'. The clock starts running from discovery of the last incident; so where there are multiple

---

[68] 5.5.7.

adulterous liaisons, petitioners who have continued to live with their spouse for over six months from the last known incident will not be prevented subsequently from relying on *later* adultery once it is discovered.[69] Cohabitation of less than six months is disregarded.[70]

The proof of adultery

Respondents usually concede guilt in the relevant court forms. Otherwise, proof must be found elsewhere. It has been said that 'being a secret matter, as a rule [adultery] has to be inferred from evidence of inclination and opportunity, and if evidence is given of a guilty intention and of acts of gross indecency, adultery itself may readily be inferred'.[71] Evidence that a third party is the father of a child conceived by the wife after marriage may evidence adultery. So too would conviction of the husband for rape. The standard of proof has never been formally settled, and in practice now the issue seldom arises, since the vast majority of divorces are undefended. Prior to the 1969 Act, the House of Lords in *Blyth v Blyth* expressed divergent views.[72] Some of their Lordships considered that the judge had to be 'satisfied' of the facts beyond reasonable doubt. Others adopted the normal civil standard—the balance of probabilities—assessed in light of the seriousness of the allegation.

5.5.3 THE FACTS: BEHAVIOUR OF THE RESPONDENT

Matrimonial Causes Act 1973, s 1(2)(b); Civil Partnership Act 2004, s 44(5)(a)

...the respondent has behaved in such a way that the [petitioner/applicant] cannot reasonably be expected to live with the respondent.

This fact is frequently—but erroneously—referred to as 'unreasonable behaviour'. It is not the behaviour that must be unreasonable (though it may often be so) but the expectation that the petitioner should live with the respondent.[73] It has been said that this is an 'increasingly low' bar.[74]

The behaviour

The case law has considered a wide range of behaviour. The most serious cases involve violence and sexual assault. Others involve emotional abuse (for example, a campaign of attrition by the husband designed to secure the wife's departure from the shared home);[75] financial irresponsibility causing problems for the family;[76] over-ambitious home improvement projects (inter alia, lifting all the floorboards and not replacing them for a two-year

---

[69] *Carr v Carr* [1974] 1 WLR 1534.

[70] MCA 1973, 2(2).

[71] *Dennis v Dennis (Spillett cited)* [1955] P 153, 161.

[72] [1966] AC 643.

[73] *Bannister v Bannister* (1980) 10 FL 240.

[74] *Miller Smith v Miller Smith* [2009] EWCA Civ 1297 [15].

[75] *Stevens v Stevens* [1979] 1 WLR 885; see also the boorish behaviour in *Livingstone-Stallard* [1974] Fam 47; *Birch v Birch* [1992] 1 FLR 564.

[76] *Carter-Fea* (1987) 17 FL 131.

period, depositing 30 tons of rubble from beneath the floorboards in the garden, and leaving the lavatory without any door for eight months, all of which prevented the petitioner and children from conducting any sort of social life from the house);[77] questioning the children's paternity;[78] and various complaints regarding the couple's lack (usually) of sexual and intimate life.[79] Behaviour extraneous to the marriage—such as the commission of criminal offences by the respondent—might also suffice. 'Behaviour' preceding desertion and desertion itself cannot provide a basis for this fact; petitioners could otherwise avoid the two-year requirement of the desertion fact.[80]

Difficult questions arise regarding respondents with mental health problems or other disabilities who are not responsible for their actions, or who may be entirely inactive owing to their problems. Two questions arise: (i) whether 'negative' behaviour suffices; and (ii) whether any behaviour, positive or negative, arising from mental or other illness does so. No appellate decision has considered these questions, but they were fully explored in *Thurlow v Thurlow*. The wife for many years suffered from epilepsy and a severe, worsening, neurological disorder which ultimately required full-time institutional care. The husband, who knew about the wife's condition before the marriage and that it might deteriorate, had done his best to care for her at home; their relationship had become 'more like a nurse and a patient'. Rees J concluded that negative behaviour could suffice; so too could 'involuntary' behaviour caused by physical or mental illness:

Thurlow v Thurlow [1976] Fam 32, 40–6 (Fam Div)

REES J:

The husband's case therefore consists of allegations of both negative and of positive behaviour on the part of the wife. The negative behaviour alleged and proved is that [over three years] . . . she gradually became a bedridden invalid unable to perform the role of a wife in any respect whatsoever until she reached a state in which she became unfitted even to reside in an ordinary household at all and required to be removed to a hospital and there reside for the rest of her life. The positive behaviour alleged and proved is that during the same period she displayed bad temper and threw objects at her mother-in-law and caused damage by burning various household items such as towels, cushions and blankets. From time to time she escaped from the home and wandered about the streets causing alarm and stress to those trying to care for her.

I am satisfied that by July 1972 the marriage had irretrievably broken down and since the wife, tragically, is to spend the rest of her life as a patient in a hospital the husband cannot be expected to live with her. But the question remains as to whether the wife's behaviour has been such as to justify a finding by the court that it is unreasonable to expect him to do so. . . . [I]t is not sufficient to identify a state of affairs wherein there is a dead marriage coupled with an impossibility of cohabitation. It must be shown that it is the behaviour of the respondent which justifies a conclusion by the court that the petitioner cannot reasonably be expected to endure cohabitation. A state of affairs in which there is merely a dead marriage and inevitable separation of the parties can be dealt with under section 1(2)(e) [MCA 1973] by obtaining a decree after five years. . . . It is worth observing that in cases in which a

---

[77] *O'Neill v O'Neill* [1975] 1 WLR 1118.
[78] Ibid.
[79] *Dowden v Dowden* (1978) 8 FL 106; *Mason v Mason* (1980) 11 FL 143; *Pheasant v Pheasant* [1972] Fam 202.
[80] *Morgan v Morgan* (1973) 117 SJ 223; *Stringfellow v Stringfellow* [1976] 1 WLR 645.

respondent is mentally ill it will rarely, if ever, be possible to make use of section 1(2)(d) [two year separation with respondent's consent to divorce] because of doubt as to the capacity to give a valid consent....

Questions of interpretation of the words in section 1(2)(b)...which arise from the facts in the instant case include the following: Does behaviour which is wholly or mainly negative in character fall within the ambit of the statute? Is behaviour which stems from mental illness and which may be involuntary, capable of constituting relevant behaviour?

I consider these questions separately. As to the distinction which has been made between "positive" and "negative" behaviour I can find nothing in the statute to suggest that either form is excluded. The sole test prescribed as to the nature of the behaviour is that it must be such as to justify a finding that the petitioner cannot reasonably be expected to live with the respondent. It may well be that in practice such a finding will more readily be made in cases where the behaviour relied upon is positive than those wherein it is negative. Spouses may often, but not always, be expected to tolerate more in the way of prolonged silences and total inactivity than of violent language or violent activity...

But there remains for consideration the kind of case in which the conduct or behaviour relied upon is total passivity (sometimes described as a "cabbage" existence). I do not pause, at this stage, to consider whether the behaviour stems from mental illness or from a sudden accidental physical injury or from a malicious campaign of withdrawal from all aspects of matrimonial life with an intention of injuring the other spouse....

He concluded that it could sometimes be proper to find that a petitioner could not reasonably be expected to live with such behaviour:

I have found support for this view in a recent succinct statement of the law by Sir George Baker P. in *Katz v. Katz* [1972] 1 W.L.R. 955 ...:

"Section 2 (1) (b) of the Divorce Reform Act 1969, under which this petition is brought, requires first that the husband 'has behaved.' Behaviour is something more than a mere state of affairs or a state of mind, such as for example, a repugnance to sexual intercourse, or a feeling that the wife is not reciprocating his love, or not being as demonstrative as he thinks she should be. Behaviour in this context is action or conduct by the one which affects the other. Such conduct may either take the form of acts or omissions or may be a course of conduct and, in my view, it must have some reference to the marriage."

Accordingly upon principle and authority I conclude without hesitation that "negative" as well as "positive" behaviour is capable of forming the basis of a decree of divorce under section 1(2)(b)...

I now turn to the question as to whether behaviour which stems from mental illness and which may be involuntary is capable of falling within the statute.

Having reviewed various authorities, the judge concluded that it could, depending on its impact on the petitioner:

Accordingly the facts of each case must be considered and a decision made, having regard to all the circumstances, as to whether the particular petitioner can or cannot reasonably be expected to live with the particular respondent.... The granting of the decree to the petitioner does not necessarily involve any blameworthiness on the part of the respondent, and, no doubt, in cases of misfortune the judge will make this clear in his judgment.

Rees J then outlined submissions made by the wife regarding a respondent who had become a 'human vegetable' following an accident. For such a person to be divorced on the basis of their 'behaviour' would, it was argued, be contrary to Parliament's intention and unjustly impute wrongdoing where none could be found. It was argued that divorce in such cases should instead be available only following five years' separation.[81] That would in turn ensure that safeguards specifically available in separation cases (under ss 5 and 10[82]) were available. Rees J focused on the need to protect the other spouse:

> There is no completely satisfactory answer to these submissions but what may properly be said is that the law as laid down in *Williams v. Williams* [1964] A.C. 698 does provide a remedy by divorce for a spouse who is the victim of the violence of an insane respondent spouse not responsible in law or fact for his or her actions and in no respect blameworthy. The basis for that decision is the need to afford protection to the petitioner against injury. So also in the insanity cases where the behaviour alleged is wholly negative and no violence in deed or word is involved but where continuing cohabitation has caused, or is likely to cause injury to health, it should be open to the court to provide a remedy by divorce. Before deciding to grant a divorce in such cases the court would require to be satisfied that the petitioner could not reasonably be expected to live with the respondent and would not be likely to do so in the cases referred to by [counsel for the wife] unless driven to it by grave considerations which would include actual or apprehended injury to the health of the petitioner or of the family as a whole.... The safeguard provided for the interests of respondents is that it is the judge and not the petitioner who must decide whether the petitioner can reasonably be expected to live with the respondent; and that decision is subject to review upon appeal.
>
> I do not propose to state any concluded view upon the case postulated in which a spouse is reduced to a human vegetable as the result of a road traffic accident and is removed at once to hospital to remain there for life. When that case does arise for decision I apprehend that the petitioner may face very considerable difficulties in establishing that there was any, or any sufficient, behaviour towards him or her or alternatively that such behaviour as there was justified a conclusion that the petitioner could not reasonably be expected to live with him or her.

Whether, given that behaviour, the petitioner can reasonably be expected to live with the respondent

Like the adultery fact, the behaviour fact has two parts, but here they are linked: the behaviour and an evaluation of its impact on the petitioner. Moreover, while the intolerability test in adultery cases is simply a question of subjective fact, the 'reasonableness' test is more complex. It has been said that reference to the Book of Common Prayer and its 'for better, for worse' test is misplaced.[83] But the courts are—rightly or wrongly—required to identify the acceptable limitations and burdens of married life.

One question is how far the apparently objective concept of reasonableness is conditioned by the parties' particular characteristics. In *Pheasant v Pheasant*, Ormrod J noted the ambiguity of the word 'expected'. One interpretation, focusing on the petitioner's 'expected' future conduct—is there any prospect of the petitioner staying with the respondent?—would, he suggested, make the other facts 'superfluous':

---

[81] MCA 1973, s 1(2)(e); see 5.5.5 below.
[82] See 5.5.6 below.
[83] *O'Neill v O'Neill* [1975] 1 WLR 1118, 1121.

Pheasant v Pheasant [1972] Fam 202, 207–9 (Fam Div)

ORMROD J:

[Counsel for the petitioner] has not contended for this construction and concedes that the word "expected" is used in its other sense, which approximates to "required". He submits that the matter should be approached very largely, if not entirely, from the point of view of the petitioner, and that the court should consider … whether it is reasonable to require this petitioner to go on living with this respondent, having regard to her behaviour, giving that word its widest meaning and including both acts and omissions. This is sometimes called the subjective, in contrast to the objective approach, but so stated the antithesis is, in my opinion, misleading. In matrimonial cases there are two subjects to be considered … whose personalities are constantly interacting with one another throughout their relationship.

In my judgment, this construction is untenable for several reasons. It places the primary emphasis upon the petitioner and his personal idiosyncrasies, whereas the paragraph clearly places the primary emphasis on the behaviour of the respondent. A respondent whose behaviour is beyond reproach by any standards other than the petitioner's would be liable to be divorced without any possibility of resistance except to rely on section [1(4)] and try to show that the marriage has not finally broken down. [Counsel for the petitioner] faces this and says that under the modern law the court is concerned only to crush empty shells. Had this been the intention of the statute, paragraph (b) need only have provided that a decree could be granted if the court is satisfied that the petitioner finds life with the respondent unbearable. Once again the other four paragraphs would be surplusage and the court would be faced with an untriable issue. The experience of this particular trial which proceeded on [counsel for the petitioner's] assumption, should have convinced any doubters of the utter impracticality of such an inquiry. In the end it became reduced to a series of almost hysterical assertions by the petitioner and calm rebuttals by the respondent. So far from saving "bitterness, distress and humiliation" it produced a degree of humiliation of the petitioner which is unique in my experience …

[My preferred approach is to] consider whether it is reasonable to expect this petitioner to put up with the behaviour of this respondent, bearing in mind the characters and the difficulties of each of them, trying to be fair to both of them, and expecting neither heroic virtue nor selfless abnegation from either. It would be consistent with the spirit of the new legislation if this problem were now to be approached more from the point of view of breach of obligation than in terms of the now out-moded idea of the matrimonial offence. It must also be borne in mind that the petitioner is still free to make his own decision whether to live with his wife or otherwise. The court is only concerned with the next stage, i.e. whether he is entitled to have his marriage dissolved.

Whilst the matrimonial offence doctrine certainly has no place in the modern law, the concept of breach of obligation may be problematic, particularly in cases of mental health problems.[84]

The courts have considered the reasonableness test several times.[85] In assessing what is reasonable, regard will be had to the particular individuals involved, despite the fact that the wording of s 1(2)(b) appears to create an objective test:

---

[84] See *Katz v Katz* [1972] 1 WLR 955, 961.

[85] For recent Court of Appeal decision, see *Birch v Birch* [1992] 1 FLR 564, which endorsed the extracts set out above.

Ash v Ash [1972] Fam 135, 140 (Fam Div)

BAGNALL J:

In order, therefore, to answer the question whether the petitioner can or cannot reasonably be expected to live with the respondent, in my judgment, I have to consider not only the behaviour of the respondent as alleged and established in evidence, but the character, personality, disposition and behaviour of the petitioner. The general question may be expanded thus: can this petitioner, with his or her character and personality, with his or her faults and other attributes, good and bad, and having regard to his or her behaviour during the marriage, reasonably be expected to live with this respondent? It follows that if a respondent is seeking to resist a petition on the first ground upon which Mr Ash relies, he must in his answer plead and his evidence establish the characteristics, faults, attributes, personality and behaviour on the part of the petitioner upon which he relies....

[I]t seems to me that a violent petitioner can reasonably be expected to live with a violent respondent; a petitioner who is addicted to drink can reasonably be expected to live with a respondent who is similarly addicted; a taciturn and morose spouse can reasonably be expected to live with a taciturn and morose partner; a flirtatious husband can reasonably be expected to live with a wife who is equally susceptible to the attractions of the other sex; and if each is equally bad, at any rate in similar respects, each can reasonably be expected to live with the other.

The Court of Appeal has twice endorsed the following test:[86]

Livingstone-Stallard v Livingstone-Stallard [1974] Fam 47, 54

DUNN J:

Coming back to my analogy of a direction to a jury, I ask myself the question: Would any right-thinking person come to the conclusion that this husband has behaved in such a way that this wife cannot reasonably be expected to live with him, taking into account the whole of the circumstances and the characters and personalities of the parties?

In *Birch v Birch*, the Court of Appeal added that in judging the behaviour by reference to the petitioner's capacity to tolerate it, 'the court would consider to what extent the respondent knew or ought reasonably to have known of that capacity'.[87] However, the dicta in *Ash v Ash*[88] perhaps go too far in suggesting that violence is acceptable, even if reciprocated. Bagnall J sought to support his view by reference to the Law Commission's aim 'to buttress, rather than undermine, the stability of marriage'. But it is questionable whether the institution of marriage is much supported by divorce law apparently condoning domestic violence.

In *Thurlow*, the court found the fact to be satisfied on the following test:

---

86 See *O'Neill v O'Neill* [1975] 1 WLR 1118; *Birch v Birch* [1992] 1 FLR 564.
87 Ibid., 568.
88 [1972] Fam 135, 140.

Thurlow v Thurlow [1976] Fam 32, 44, 46 (Fam Div)

REES J:

... If the behaviour stems from misfortune such as the onset of mental illness or from disease of the body, or from accidental physical injury, the court will take full account of all the obligations of the married state. These will include the normal duty to accept and to share the burdens imposed upon the family as a result of the mental or physical ill-health of one member. It will also consider the capacity of the petitioner to withstand the stresses imposed by the behaviour, the steps taken to cope with it, the length of time during which the petitioner has been called upon to bear it and the actual or potential effect upon his or her health. The court will then be required to make a judgment as to whether the petitioner can fairly be required to live with the respondent....

... It will be for the judge to decide subject to review on appeal whether the behaviour is sufficiently grave to make it unreasonable to expect the petitioner to endure it. In reaching the decision the judge will have regard to all the circumstances including the disabilities and temperaments of both parties, the causes of the behaviour and whether the causes were or were not known to the petitioner, the presence or absence of intention, the impact of it upon the petitioner and the family unit, its duration, and the prospects of cure or improvement in the future.

Since no causal connection between the fact relied on and the breakdown of the marriage is required, in some cases the behaviour post-dates the breakdown, itself caused by the *petitioner's* earlier behaviour. Such circumstances are taken into account in applying the reasonableness test. We might expect both parties in such cases to be keen to divorce, so, save where the respondent seeks some tactical advantage from keeping the marriage formally alive, this point will rarely arise.[89]

The relevance of continued cohabitation

As in the case of adultery, the Act instructs the court what relevance to attach to cohabitation following the last behaviour complained of. The relevance of cohabitation here is different from the adultery cases. Under s 2(3)[90] continued cohabitation of under six months since the last event relied on as behaviour is disregarded in deciding whether the petitioner can reasonably be expected to live with the respondent. Unlike adultery, there is no bar on use of the behaviour fact where the cohabitation lasts beyond six months; but nor is that irrelevant to the reasonableness test. In extreme cases the petitioner may have had no choice but to remain in the home, even the same bed, as the respondent:

Bradley v Bradley [1973] 1 WLR 1291, 1295 (CA)

SCARMAN LJ:

There are many, many reasons why a woman will go on living with a beast of a husband. Sometimes she may live with him because she fears the consequences of leaving. Sometimes

---

[89] *Stevens v Stevens* [1979] 1 WLR 885.
[90] CPA 2004, s 45(1), (2).

it may be physical duress, but very often a woman will willingly make the sacrifice of living with a beast of a husband because she believes it to be in the true interest of her children. Is such a woman to be denied the opportunity...of calling evidence to show that, although she is living with him, yet the family situation is such and his behaviour is such that she cannot reasonably be expected to do so? It seems to me...that there is no logical difficulty in the way of the wife; and the Act plainly envisages that she should have the opportunity of placing her case before the court.

The behaviour fact and civil partnership 'adultery'

Since the adultery fact is unavailable in civil partnership cases, civil partners wishing to complain of sexual infidelity must rely instead on the behaviour fact. This was the government's intention.[91] Indeed, given the narrowness of the adultery test, many forms of sexual infidelity practised by spouses also have to proceed under this fact. It may be that the outcome will not be different, though use of the behaviour fact involves the ostensibly more stringent 'reasonableness' test, instead of the subjective 'intolerability' test. Conversely, applicants using this fact enjoy the more generous approach to continued cohabitation.

However, all of this depends upon judicial evaluation of whether sexual infidelity is something that makes it unreasonable to expect the applicant to live with the respondent. This requires an examination of what civil partnership is for. As we saw in chapter 2, the law of nullity studiously avoids referring expressly to any sexual relationship between civil partners, even though many civil partners do have sexual relationships. In dealing with dissolution cases based on this fact, the judges will have to decide whether that cultural expectation of sexual intimacy and the applicant's expectation of exclusivity is enough to justify dissolution on this basis.[92]

5.5.4 THE FACTS: DESERTION FOR TWO YEARS BY THE RESPONDENT

Matrimonial Causes Act 1973, s 1(2)(c); Civil Partnership Act 2004, s 44(5)(d)

... the respondent has deserted the [petitioner/applicant] for a continuous period of at least two years immediately preceding the [presentation of the petition/making of the application]

Desertion and the separation facts compared

Desertion is the last of the facts originating in the old law of divorce. Some of its basic ingredients are similar to the no-fault separation facts introduced in 1969. The features which distinguish it from separation are: (i) the deserter must have no justification for leaving; and (ii) the party not in desertion must not consent to the other's absence, although now wishing to divorce the deserter. Where, as is likely, the deserter also wants to divorce, the parties may proceed under the next fact: two years' separation with the respondent's consent to divorce.

---

[91] Women and Equality Unit (2003b), 35.
[92] Cretney (2006a), 32–8.

Desertion is therefore likely to be used only where two-year separation (or some other fact[93]) is unavailable because the deserter refuses to consent to divorce, or where the petitioner perceives that some tactical advantage is to be gained by relying on desertion. The deserter may only petition for divorce without the other's consent if the desertion last five years, on the basis of five years' separation.

The basic elements of desertion

The essence of desertion lies in destroying the 'consortium vitae' of marriage without justification or consent. It consists of two elements, one physical—de facto separation—and the other mental—the 'animus deserendi', i.e. the intention to bring the matrimonial union to an end.[94] Both must be present throughout a two-year period without consent or other justification. If the original separation is unaccompanied by the requisite intention, it is enough that that intention arises later, provided both separation and intention are present together for two years.[95] The two-year clock may be stopped for up to six months in total during attempted reconciliations.[96]

Physical separation

The physical separation required for desertion is not as complete as the word might suggest. A mere refusal of sexual intercourse will not suffice.[97] However, one spouse may desert the other even though they remain living under the same roof. At various points in history, notably in the aftermath of the Second World War and during housing market slumps, this has been important for those unable to find alternative accommodation. The key here is the concept of the shared 'household':

Hopes v Hopes [1949] P 227, 235–6 (CA)

DENNING LJ:

One of the essential elements of desertion is the fact of separation. Can that exist whilst the parties are living under the same roof? My answer is: "Yes". The husband who shuts himself up in one or two rooms of his house, and ceases to have anything to do with his wife, is living separately and apart from her as effectively as if they were separated by the outer door of a flat. They may meet on the stairs or in the passageway, but so they might if they each had separate flats in one building. If that separation is brought about by his fault, why is that not desertion? He has forsaken and abandoned his wife as effectively as if he had gone into lodgings. The converse is equally true. If the wife ceases to have anything to do with, or for, the husband and he is left to look after himself in his own rooms, why is not that desertion? She has forsaken and abandoned him as effectively as if she had gone to live with her relatives....I find myself in agreement with all the decisions of the Divorce Division except perhaps *Wanbon v. Wanbon*...where the parties were said to be still in one household. If

---

[93] Desertion will often be accompanied by adultery, but not necessarily by behaviour: *Stringfellow v Stringfellow* [1976] 1 WLR 645.

[94] *Lang v Lang* [1955] 1 AC 402, 417.

[95] *Hopes v Hopes* [1949] P 227, 231.

[96] MCA 1973, s 2(5); CPA 2004, s 45(6).

[97] *Weatherley v Weatherley* [1947] AC 628.

> that means that, although living at arms length, they were still sharing the same living room, eating at the same table and sitting by the same fire, then I cannot agree with the finding of desertion....[Desertion exists] where the parties are living separately and apart. In cases where they are living under the same roof, that point is reached when they cease to be one household and become two households; or, in other words, when they are no longer residing with one another or cohabiting with one another.

Parties may sometimes be prevented from physically cohabiting, for example, because one spouse has been hospitalized. Desertion can occur here even though the parties had no common home which could be left: 'desertion is not the withdrawal from a place, but from a state of things...The law does not deal with the mere matter of place. What it seeks to enforce is the recognition and discharge of the common obligations of the married state'.[98] So a husband could be in desertion by leaving the district and setting up home with another woman while his wife was in hospital, despite continuing to support the wife financially.[99]

Intention, communication, and consent

It is not necessary that the deserting spouse should communicate his or her intention to desert to the other. However, it must be shown that the innocent spouse does not consent to the deserter's absence, and that requires knowledge of the intention to desert. This may be difficult. Suppose that, at the outset, the innocent spouse consents to the other's physical absence on the understanding that it is for some temporary purpose, but the other—without the remaining spouse's knowledge—subsequently forms an intention to desert. It has been held that unless and until the remaining spouse withdraws consent to the other's absence, desertion cannot be found. Surprisingly, that spouse's lack of knowledge of the other's intention to desert seems not automatically to vitiate consent to the other's continued absence.[100]

Respondents experiencing mental health problems may leave without intending to desert. Capacity to form, and actual formation of, intention must be proved, and the respondent will be judged on the facts as he or she honestly believes them to be.[101] Where the respondent has fluctuating capacity and had the required intention at some point, the court may treat desertion as continuing during periods of incapacity if it would (without the incapacity) have inferred from the evidence that the desertion continued at that time.[102]

Justification and constructive desertion

A party is only in desertion where there is no justification for his or her departure. That justification may be actual, reasonably believed,[103] or, in case of delusion at least, honestly believed.[104] For such justification to be found, the cause must be 'grave and weighty'.[105] In such cases, the tables may be turned and the party who left may be entitled to petition for

---

98 *Pulford v Pulford* [1923] P 18, 21–2.
99 *Yeatman v Yeatman* (1868) 1 P&D 489.
100 *Nutley v Nutley* [1970] 1 WLR 217; cf *Santos v Santos* [1972] Fam 247, below at 5.5.5.
101 *Perry v Perry* [1964] 1 WLR 91.
102 MCA 1973, s 2(4); CPA 2004, s 45(5).
103 *Everitt v Everitt* [1949] P 374.
104 *Perry v Perry* [1964] 1 WLR 91.
105 *Yeatman v Yeatman* (1868) 1 P&D 489, 494.

divorce on the basis of 'constructive desertion': where one spouse's conduct drives the other party away and the latter is justified in leaving.

Lang v Lang [1955] AC 402, 417–8 (PC)

LORD PORTER:

[T]he party truly guilty of disrupting the home is not necessarily or in all cases the party who first leaves it. The party who stays behind (their Lordships will assume this to be the husband) may be by reason of conduct on his part making it unbearable for a wife with reasonable self-respect, or powers of endurance, to stay with him, so that he is the party really responsible for the breakdown of the marriage. He has deserted her by expelling her: by driving her out. In such a case the factum is the course of conduct pursued by the husband— something which may be far more complicated than the mere act of leaving the matrimonial home. It is not every course of conduct by the husband causing the wife to leave which is a sufficient factum. A husband's irritating habits may so get on the wife's nerves that she leaves as a direct consequence of them, but she would not be justified in doing so. Such irritating idiosyncrasies are part of the lottery in which every spouse engages on marrying, and taking the partner of the marriage "for better, for worse." The course of conduct—the "factum"—must be grave and convincing.

This involves determining what behaviour the departing spouse is expected to tolerate before his or her departure will be justified and constructive desertion by the remaining spouse found. Like the behaviour fact, this requires the courts to make value judgments about married life, and the nature of civil partnership, which are likely to change as social conditions and understandings of the nature of those relationships alter.[106] Most of the case law predates introduction of the behaviour fact, but at a time when its forerunner— 'cruelty'—afforded grounds for divorce. Cruelty was a stricter concept than 'behaviour', and conduct not amounting to cruelty could justify departure and so create constructive desertion.[107] It is hard now to imagine conduct justifying desertion which would not itself satisfy the 'behaviour' fact. But if one party simply orders the other to leave, it will still be dealt with as desertion.[108]

Intention to desert in cases of constructive desertion will be inferred where the other spouse's departure is the natural and probable consequence of the respondent's behaviour, but that inference can be rebutted where the evidence shows that the respondent did not intend the petitioner to leave. As in the criminal law, it is necessary to distinguish between intention and desire: the respondent may not want the petitioner to go, but nevertheless know that that will be the effect of his or her conduct and so intend it.[109]

Refusal to accept the deserter's return

Desertion ends if the parties are reunited. If the petitioner unreasonably refuses to let the respondent back, the 'petitioner' will now be in desertion. However, petitioners are sometimes

---

[106] *Hall v Hall* [1962] 1 WLR 1246.
[107] *Timmins v Timmins* [1953] 1 WLR 757.
[108] *Morgan v Morgan* (1973) 117 SJ 223.
[109] *Lang v Lang* [1955] AC 402.

justified in refusing respondents' offers to return and the original desertion is deemed to continue. This was the outcome in *Everitt*, where the wife's reasonable (though, as it turned out, erroneous) belief that the husband had committed adultery during his desertion justified her refusing his offer to return, even though she knew that such adultery could not now be continuing.[110] If the respondent had committed domestic violence against the petitioner prior to desertion (actual or constructive), that too would justify a refusal to resume cohabitation.

5.5.5 THE SEPARATION FACTS

Matrimonial Causes Act 1973, s 1(2)(d)(e); Civil Partnership Act 2004, s 44(5)(b)(c)

... the parties...have lived apart for a continuous period of at least two years immediately preceding the presentation of the petition (... "two years' separation") and the respondent consents to a decree being granted.
    ... the parties...have lived apart for a continuous period of at least five years immediately preceding the presentation of the petition (... "five years' separation").[111]

These two facts were introduced in 1969, providing the first no-fault bases for divorce in English law. The five-year separation fact is the sole fact available to a 'guilty' party whose spouse does not want to divorce.[112] The introduction of these facts contributed to the sudden rise in divorces shortly after the legislation came into force, as the 'backlog' of long-dead marriages in which neither party had committed—or wished to plead—any fault could finally be dissolved.[113]

Separation shares some ground with the basic concepts underpinning desertion, but there is no need here to prove that one party had left without the other's consent or that the departure was unjustified. As in the case of desertion, the clock can stop running for a period or periods of time adding up to no more than six months of resumed cohabitation.[114] The Court of Appeal considered the essential ingredients of separation in *Santos v Santos*. A key question was whether the concept of 'living apart', which is central to the separation facts, was a purely physical state or included some sort of mental element, bearing in mind that the meaning of the term must be the same for both separation facts, but distinctive from desertion. Sachs LJ took the view that 'living apart' required something more than physical separation:

Santos v Santos [1972] Fam 247, 259–63 (CA)

SACHS LJ:

"Living apart": prima facie meaning

[T]he phrase "living apart" when used in a statute concerned with matrimonial affairs normally imports something more than mere physical separation [namely a recognition by one or

---

110 [1949] P 374.
111 The CPA provisions reflect the different procedural terminology.
112 See Law Com (1966), paras 85 et seq.
113 Richards (1996), 152. Cretney describes witnessing such divorces being granted: (1996a), 41.
114 MCA 1973, s 2(5); CPA 2004, s 45(6).

both spouses that the marriage is no longer subsisting]. . . . It follows that its normal meaning must be attributed to it in the 1969 Act, unless one is led to a different conclusion either by the general scheme of the statute coupled with difficulties which would result from such an interpretation or alternatively by some specific provision in that statute.

The 1969 Act: general scheme: questions for consideration

[The lack of express provisions for dealing with the hospitalization of mentally ill spouses, long-term imprisonment etc.] tend to highlight some linked problems bearing on the meaning of "living apart" which have caused us concern.

He then posed himself three questions:

If these words import an element additional to physical separation, can that element depend on a unilateral decision or attitude of mind; if so, must its existence be communicated to the other spouse; and, in any event, how can it be identified so that it is in practice capable of judicial determination?

Obviously this element is not one which necessarily involves mutual consent, for otherwise the new Act would not afford relief under head (e) in that area where it was most plainly intended to be available—where the "innocent" party adheres to the marriage, refusing to recognise that in truth it has ended, often despite the fact that the "guilty" one has been living with someone else for very many years. So it must be an element capable of being unilateral: and it must in our judgment involve at least a recognition that the marriage is in truth at an end—and has become a shell, to adopt a much-used metaphor.

If the element can be unilateral in the sense of depending on the attitude of mind of one spouse, must it be communicated to the other spouse before it becomes in law operative? That is a question that gave particular concern in the course of the argument. There is something unattractive in the idea that in effect time under head (e) can begin to run against a spouse without his or her knowledge. Examples discussed included men in prison, in hospital, or away on service, whose wives, so far as they knew, were standing by them: they might, perhaps, thus be led to fail to take some step which they would later feel could just have saved the marriage. On the other hand, communication might well be impossible in cases where the physical separation was due to a breakdown in mental health on the part of the other spouse, or a prolonged coma such as can occasionally occur. Moreover, need for communication would tend to equate heads (d) and (e) with desertion . . . something unlikely to be intended by the legislature.[115] Moreover, bowing to the inevitable is not the same thing as intending it to happen.

In the end we have firmly concluded that communication by word or conduct is not a necessary ingredient of the additional element.

On the basis that an uncommunicated unilateral ending of recognition that a marriage is subsisting can mark the moment when "living apart" commences, "the principal problem becomes one of proof of the time when the breakdown occurred" . . . . How, for instance, does a judge in practice discharge the unenviable task of determining at what time the wife of a man immured long term in hospital or one serving a 15 year sentence changes from a wife who is standing by her husband (in the sense of genuinely keeping the marriage alive until he recovers or comes out) to one who realises the end has come but visits him merely from a sense of duty arising from the past? Sometimes there will be evidence such as a letter, reduction or cessation of visits, or starting to live with another man. But cases may well arise

---

[115] Cf *Nutley v Nutley*, n 100 above and associated text.

where there is only the oral evidence of the wife on this point. . . . In some cases, where it appears that the petitioning wife's conduct is consistent with a continuing recognition of the subsistence of the marriage, automatic acceptance of her uncorroborated evidence inconsistent with such conduct would not be desirable. On the other hand, there can be cases where a moment arrives as from which resumption of any form of married life becomes so plainly impossible, e.g. on some grave disability becoming known to be incurable, that only slight evidence is needed—for the nature of the breakdown is so patent.

The difficulties arising from some of these problems at one stage led to hesitation as to whether after all "living apart" in this particular Act might not refer merely to physical separation. . . . [But] injustices and absurdities . . . could result from holding that "living apart" refers merely to physical separation; these . . . outweigh any hard cases or difficulties that can arise from the standard interpretations.

One category under head (e) is exemplified by the case of a long-sentence prisoner whose wife has, with his encouragement, stood by him for five years—only for her to find that when he comes out he files a petition for divorce relying on ground (e). But the more usual categories relate to men who could unjustly find time running against them through absences on public service or on business in areas where, out of regard for the welfare of the wife or the children of the family, the former remains in this country: particularly hardly could this bear on men whose home leave did not for some years total the six months referred to in [s 2(5) MCA 1973].

Turning from hardships under head (e) to absurdities under head (d), read in conjunction with [s 2(5) MCA 1973], it is plain that in cases arising under the latter head the spouses can spend up to 20 per cent. of their time together without interrupting the continuity of the separation (i.e. six months in two years and six months). Thus if living apart means mere physical separation, a man who got home on leave for less than 20% of the two to two-and-a-half years immediately preceding the filing of the petition would be in a position to satisfy the court under head (d), even though he and his wife had been on excellent terms until they had a row on the last day of his last leave. As petitions under head (d) are normally undefended, there would be no evidence to rebut this presumption that the breakdown of the marriage was irretrievable and the decree would be granted. Unless—contrary to our view—the Act intended to permit divorce by consent simpliciter such a result would be absurd. On the contrary the tenor of [s 1(2) MCA 1973] is to ensure that under heads (c), (d) and (e) a breakdown is not to be held irretrievable unless and until a sufficiently long passage of time has shown this to be the case . . .

[S 2(6) MCA 1973] . . . makes it clear beyond further debate that when two spouses are living in the same house, then, as regards living apart, a line is to be drawn, in accordance with the views of Denning LJ [in *Hopes v Hopes*, see above], and they are to be held to be living apart if not living in the same household.

And so he concluded that *in the vast majority of cases*, it would be necessary to prove more than mere physical separation: it cannot be said that the parties are living apart 'where both parties recognise the marriage as subsisting'. Where a separation started on a 'voluntary' basis, the judge would have to determine at what point either or both parties no longer regarded the marriage as subsisting, but rather a 'mere shell'. However:

We have deliberately refrained from speaking unequivocally of "all cases" (as opposed to "the vast generality of cases") arising under heads (d) and (e) for the same reason that we have not sought to attempt any definition either of "consortium" or of "absence of consortium";

similarly we have gone no further than to specify the attitude of mind that precludes its being said that the parties are living apart. This is because there may arise wholly exceptional cases: to take an extreme and one hopes a particularly unlikely example, there may one day fall to be dealt with a case were some misfortune has caused both spouses to be of unsound mind for more than five years. Such cases can only be dealt with when they arise—and it can then be decided whether resort can be had to inferences to be drawn from the hopelessness of the situation in which the parties find themselves.

Sachs LJ was concerned that judges should carefully investigate the facts, and not simply rubber-stamp applications on the basis of written evidence. However, we shall see that the special procedure now used for undefended divorces effectively leaves the judge in no position to do much more than rubber-stamping.[116]

The issue addressed by Denning LJ in *Hopes* had received some attention in relation to separation prior to *Santos*. The 'living apart' requirement can be difficult for couples who continue living in the same house for laudable reasons. In *Mouncer v Mouncer*, the parties stayed under the same roof and tried to carry on a semblance of normal domestic life for the benefit of their two children. They slept in separate rooms, but usually ate all together (the wife having cooked) and, bedrooms aside, shared use of the other rooms; they both worked part-time, each doing chores while the other was at work; the wife no longer did the husband's laundry. Could they be said to be 'living apart'? The judge found such a conclusion impossible where they were—as here—still living 'in the same household':

Mouncer v Mouncer [1972] 1 WLR 321, 322–3 (Fam Div)

WRANGHAM J:

There have, of course, been many cases in which it has been held under the former law that husband and wife were living apart even though they lived under the same roof...It is, however, to my mind plain that if this case were being considered under the old law it would be held that this husband and wife were living together ...: see *Hopes v Hopes*. It is contended on the part of both the husband and the wife that the test under the new legislation is wholly different. [The first part of section 2(6) MCA 1973] provides that for the purposes of the Act, a husband and wife shall be treated as living apart unless they are living *with each other* in the same household. It is argued that the effect of this subsection is that spouses are to be treated as living apart unless they fulfil two separate requirements. First they must be living with each other; second, they must be living in the same household. On the facts of this case it is said the parties may be said to be living in the same household but they were not in any real sense living with each other. The wife had done all she could to reject her husband as a husband and to break the matrimonial relation between them by refusing to share his bedroom. It is hard to see how husband and wife who share a household could ever be said not to be living with each other unless rejection of a normal physical relationship coupled with the absence of normal affection is sufficient for this purpose. But if the effect of [s 2(6)] is that spouses are to be treated as living apart whenever one spouse has refused the right of intercourse, and they are (as of course they naturally would be in such circumstances) on bad terms, that would mean that the law...has been altered, and I think that if Parliament had intended to do that, it would have done so specifically.

116 5.5.7.

The truth, in my opinion, is that [the first part of s 2(6)] does not lay down two separate requirements at all. A clue to the true meaning of the subsection can be discovered from comparison with [the second part of s 2(6)] which provides: "References in this section to the parties...living with each other shall be construed as references to their living with each other in the same household." It is plain that in that subsection the words "in the same household" are words of limitation. Not all living with each other is sufficient for the purposes of [that part of s 2(6)], only living with each other in the same household. And in my view the same applies to [the first part of s 2(6)]. What it means is that the husband and wife can be treated as living apart, even if they are living with each other, unless that living with each other is in the same household. It follows that in my judgment the draftsman...was not providing for a case where parties live in the same household but do not live with each other. Indeed I do not think that there is such a case....For these reasons I have come to the conclusion that it is not proved that these spouses were living apart. [emphasis added]

However, contrary to Wrangham J's opinion, it may be possible for spouses to live in the same household without living 'with each other'. It could have been argued in *Mouncer* that they were living in the same household not 'with each other' as spouses, but in some other capacity, there as co-parents. *Fuller v Fuller* provides a rather different illustration of such a case:

Fuller v Fuller [1973] 1 WLR 730, 732 (CA)

LORD DENNING MR:

From 1964 to 1968 the parties were undoubtedly living apart. The wife was living with [Mr Penfold as his] wife in that household, and the husband was separate in his household. From 1968 to 1972 [after having suffered a coronary thrombosis and being advised that he ought not to live alone] the husband came back to live in the same house but not as a husband. He was to all intents and purposes a lodger in the house. [Section 2(6)] says they are to be treated as living apart "unless they are living with each other in the same household". I think the words "with each other" mean "living with each other as husband and wife". In this case the parties were not living with each other in that sense. The wife was living with Mr Penfold as his wife. The husband was living in the house as a lodger. It is impossible to say that husband and wife were or are living with each other in the same household. It is very different from *Mouncer v Mouncer*...where the husband and wife were living with the children in the same household—as husband and wife normally do—but were not having sexual intercourse together. That is not sufficient to constitute "living apart". I do not doubt the correctness of that decision. But the present case is very different....I would allow the appeal and pronounce the decree nisi of divorce.

Although Lord Denning attempts to distinguish *Mouncer*, the contrary argument can be made. If the Fullers were not living 'with each other' by virtue of their new status as landlady and lodger, it is not clear why the Mouncers could similarly be regarded as not living with each other now that they did so as co-parents. Indeed, parties who behave like the Mouncers—sharing the task of parenting following relationship breakdown—act compatibly with contemporary notions of good parenting post-divorce. It would be unfortunate for such responsible behaviour to disqualify couples from divorcing on this no-fault basis.

Two-year separation and the consent requirement

The separation facts are differentiated by the requirement in the two-year cases that the respondent consent to the divorce. That consent must exist at the time of the decree,[117] must be made positively, rather than simply inferred from lack of protest,[118] and is ordinarily supplied by the respondent completing the relevant court form. Consent must be full and informed: the respondent must have had the information necessary to understand the consequences of consenting to the decree.[119]

5.5.6 BARS AND OTHER RESTRICTIONS ON DIVORCE AND DISSOLUTION

There are several bars and restrictions on divorce, some of which apply to all facts, others to just one or both of the separation facts. In practice, the principal function of most of these bars is to provide bargaining power to one party: to hold up the divorce (and so the opportunity to remarry) pending a desirable settlement of ancillary matters, particularly financial issues. Divorce is rarely delayed substantially, let alone barred outright, by a bar or restriction being invoked.

Time bar on divorce

It is not possible to petition for divorce or apply for dissolution of a civil partnership during the first year of the union.[120] However, it is possible to rely on events during that first year to prove the fact relied on. For example, parties could separate immediately after the wedding and petition for divorce on the basis of two-years' separation on their second wedding anniversary. The remedy of judicial separation provides relief, including access to financial remedies, where necessary during that first year.[121] Nullity proceedings can also be brought immediately where grounds to do so apply.[122] Occupation and non-molestation orders under the FLA 1996 can provide protection from domestic violence.[123]

This bar delays divorce and so delays remarriage. To that extent, it might be argued that it breaches the right to marry under Article 12 ECHR. In *F v Switzerland*,[124] it was briefly asserted that this sort of rule does not violate the Convention. Although the Court offered no reasoning, it may be inferred that since the rule operates during a marriage, and as a condition of divorce, it can be distinguished from the bar on remarriage arising *after* divorce which was successfully challenged in that case. Since the Convention does not confer a right to divorce, it cannot restrict the terms on which divorce may be granted, so a time bar of this sort is legitimate. But once a divorce has been granted—as in *F*—the state must not disproportionately restrict the right to remarry.

---

[117] *Beales v Beales* [1972] Fam 210.

[118] *McGill v Robson* [1972] 1 WLR 237.

[119] MCA 1973, s 2(7); CPA 2004, s 45(3)–(4). The court can rescind a decree nisi (before the decree absolute has been granted—see p 324 below) if the petitioner is found to have misled the respondent, intentionally or not, about any matter which the respondent took into account in deciding to consent: MCA 1973, s 10(1); CPA 2004, s 48(1).

[120] MCA 1973, s 3; CPA 2004, s 41.

[121] MCA 1973, ss 17–18; CPA 2004, ss 56–7; see 5.5.9 below.

[122] See 2.5–2.7.

[123] See chapter 4.

[124] (App No 11329/85, ECHR) (1987).

Arrangements for children of the family

The court is required during divorce, nullity, and judicial separation proceedings to consider whether it ought to exercise any of its powers under the Children Act 1989 in relation to any relevant children of the family.[125] The court can delay the decree absolute where it considers that it may need to make an order under that Act, further consideration of the case is required before it can make its decision, and exceptional circumstances make it desirable in the interests of the children to delay the divorce. Although this specific *restriction* on divorce is rarely applied, orders for contact between children and the non-resident parent following divorce are increasingly common.[126]

Financial protection for respondents in separation cases

Respondents in separation cases against whom no 'fact' has been found are entitled to apply under s 10 to have their financial position post-divorce considered by the court before the divorce is finalized.[127] In cases involving middle-aged clients, the respondent's solicitor (unless instructed otherwise) may be negligent if he or she does not file a s 10 application to enable a proper investigation of the financial circumstances, particularly regarding pension rights, to be made prior to grant of the decree absolute.[128] If loss of potential pension rights associated with ongoing marital status—principally a widow's pension—could put the respondent in financial difficulty, the divorce should be delayed until compensatory provision has been explored.[129]

Where such an application has been made, the court may not ordinarily grant the decree absolute unless satisfied in all the circumstances either that: (i) no financial provision ought to be made by the petitioner, or (ii) the financial provision that has been made[130] is reasonable and fair or the best that can be made in the circumstances. The low standard of 'the best [financial provision] that can be made in the circumstances' recognizes that where resources are limited financial hardship may be unavoidable, yet divorce should still permitted. This test must be compared with the hardship bar, below. Even if *not* satisfied that the best possible provision has been made (or that no provision should be made), the court may still finalize the divorce if: (i) it is desirable to do so in the circumstances without delay, and (ii) the petitioner has made satisfactory undertakings to make provision approved—in fairly firm and achievable outline[131]—by the court. Courts are wary of allowing cases to proceed with mere undertakings if, having obtained the desired divorce, the petitioner might fail to cooperate further in ancillary relief proceedings.[132]

---

[125] MCA 1973, s 41; CPA 2004, s 63.

[126] See 11.5.

[127] MCA 1973, s 10(2)–(4); CPA 2004, s 48(2)–(5). It may be used to seek compensation for arrears accrued under past financial obligations: *Garcia v Garcia* [1992] Fam 83.

[128] *Griffiths v Dawson & Co* [1993] 2 FLR 315.

[129] See 7.3.3.

[130] Not merely proposed: *Wilson v Wilson* [1973] 1 WLR 555.

[131] *Grigson v Grigson* [1974] 1 WLR 228.

[132] Cf *Wickler v Wickler* [1998] 2 FLR 326, regarding the court's power to permit a respondent to apply for decree absolute under s 9(2).

The hardship bar in five-year separation cases

The introduction of the five-year separation fact was highly controversial. For the first time, blameless spouses could be divorced against their wishes, even on the petition of a spouse guilty of adultery, desertion, and worse. This was a seismic shift: the old law of matrimonial offences was clearly being supplanted by no-fault divorce. There was particular concern about the plight of older wives abandoned by mid-life-crisis husbands seeking younger models, leaving the wives in financial difficulty. In order to prevent the new law becoming a 'Casanova's charter', under s 5 the grant of the decree nisi can be barred in some five-year separation cases. In the event, the five-year separation fact has been used as much by women as men,[133] and the facts and judgments required to invoke the bar are so demanding that it rarely prevents divorce. But it might be deployed successfully as a delaying tactic to help secure good financial settlements:[134]

Matrimonial Causes Act 1973, s 5[135]

(1) The respondent to a petition for divorce in which the petitioner alleges five years' separation may oppose the grant of a decree on the ground that the dissolution of the marriage will result in grave financial or other hardship to him and that it would in all the circumstances be wrong to dissolve the marriage.

(2) Where the grant of a decree is opposed by virtue of this section, then—

 (a) if the court finds that the petitioner is entitled to rely in support of his petition on the fact of five years' separation and makes no such finding as to any other fact [under s 1(2)], and

 (b) if apart from this section the court would grant a decree on the petition,

 the court shall consider all the circumstances, including the conduct of the parties to the marriage and the interests of those parties and of any children or other persons concerned, and if of opinion that the dissolution of the marriage will result in grave financial or other hardship to the respondent and that it would in all the circumstances be wrong to dissolve the marriage it shall dismiss the petition.

(3) For the purposes of this section hardship shall include the loss of the chance of acquiring any benefit which the respondent might acquire if the marriage were not dissolved.

Grave financial or other hardship arising from dissolution of the union

It must be proved that hardship 'will' arise; a mere risk of hardship is not sufficient. Moreover, the hardship—financial or otherwise[136]—must be 'grave'. This may be contrasted with 'substantial' and 'significant', generally interpreted to mean 'more than trivial'. 'Grave' is a much higher threshold: 'important', or 'very serious'.[137]

The hardship must result specifically from the change of legal status effected by the divorce.[138] Much of the hardship arising on divorce is attributable to the physical, rather

---

[133] Gibson (1994), 173; for most recent data, ONS (2008), figure 2.
[134] Law Com (1988a), para 3.29.
[135] CPA 2004, s 47.
[136] *Rukat v Rukat* [1975] Fam 63.
[137] *Reiterbund v Reiterbund* [1975] Fam 99, 107; *Archer v Archer* [1999] 1 FLR 327.
[138] Contrast s 10: *Garcia v Garcia* [1992] Fam 83, 89.

than legal, separation of the parties, in particular the need to maintain two households, rather than one, from the same pool of resources. That sort of hardship is irrelevant to s 5. Most of the reported cases instead concern loss of pension rights, in particular widows' pensions, where it is clearly loss of spousal status that would cause the hardship: if not married to the deceased at his death, the respondent will not be his widow and so not qualify for the pension. However, 'grave' financial hardship of that sort now arises less frequently because the courts have substantial powers to adjust the parties' property and pension rights and to order periodical payments from income.[139] The courts' powers regarding pensions are much greater than they were when many of the reported cases considering s 5 were decided. Many cases can therefore now proceed under s 10 (see above) for proper pension or alternative compensatory provision to be made, rather than be barred absolutely under s 5.[140] Only where the rules of the particular pension scheme preclude sharing and there are insufficient other assets available to compensate the spouse is grave financial hardship likely to be proved. If the hardship can be alleviated only by steps which the courts have no power to order, the petitioner will have to implement satisfactory proposals to mitigate it.[141] Welfare benefits might also alleviate potential hardship.[142]

Cases of financial hardship are perhaps relatively easy to decide as the hardship claimed is objectively measurable. Cases of 'other' grave hardship have generally involved claims regarding social stigmatization following divorce as a result of religious or cultural mores in the respondent's home country or community.[143] These claims are more intangible. None of the reported cases has succeeded. The wife in *Rukat v Rukat* was of Roman Catholic Sicilian extraction, for whom divorce was on moral and religious grounds an anathema. She felt that if she were divorced she and her child would not be able to return to Sicily because of community attitudes. However, there was no evidence that anyone would know she had been divorced, or (if they did) that her fears of social ostracism would be realized once it were understood that the divorce involved no fault on her part, not least since it was known that she and her husband had been living apart for over 25 years. The Court of Appeal found that no grave hardship had been proved. Lawton LJ considered the nature of the test to be applied:

Rukat v Rukat [1975] Fam 64, 73–4, 75–6 (CA)

LAWTON LJ:

The [MCA 1973]...has now been in operation a few years. As far as counsel knows, and as far as I know, no one has yet succeeded in a defence under that part of section [5] under which this wife comes to this court for help; and I have asked myself the question whether the courts may not have whittled away the defence provided by Parliament by setting far too high a standard of proof.

---

[139] 7.3.

[140] Cf *Le Marchant v Le Marchant* [1977] 1 WLR 559, 562; though 'the best that can be done' under s 10 may not be enough to alleviate the hardship: *Parker v Parker* [1972] Fam 116, 118.

[141] *Le Marchant v Le Marchant* [1977] 1 WLR 559; *K v K (Financial Relief: Widow's Pension)* [1997] 1 FLR 35.

[142] *Reiterbund v Reiterbund* [1975] Fam 99; *Jackson v Jackson* [1993] 2 FLR 848.

[143] Several cases involve Hinduism: *Banik v Banik* [1973] 1 WLR 860; *Parghi v Parghi* (1973) 117 SJ 582; *Balraj v Balraj* (1981) 11 FL 110.

One has to start, I think, by looking at the context in which the phrase "grave financial or other hardship" occurs. The word "hardship" is not a word of art. It follows that it must be construed by the courts in a common-sense way, and the meaning which is put upon the word "hardship" should be such as would meet with the approval of ordinary sensible people. In my judgment, the ordinary sensible man would take the view that there are two aspects of "hardship"—that which the sufferer from the hardship thinks he is suffering and that which a reasonable bystander with knowledge of all the facts would think he was suffering. That can be illustrated by a homely example. The rich gourmet who because of financial stringency has to drink vin ordinaire with his grouse may well think that he is suffering a hardship; but sensible people would say he was not.

If that approach is applied to this case, one gets this situation. The wife undoubtedly feels that she has suffered a hardship; and the judge...found that she was feeling at the time of the judgment that she could not go back to Sicily. That, if it was genuine and deeply felt, would undoubtedly be a "hardship" in one sense of that word. But one has to ask oneself the question whether sensible people, knowing all the facts, would think it was a hardship. On the evidence, I have come to the conclusion that they would not.

Ormrod LJ agreed, remarking that:

Making all allowances for the sacramental views of some people, to keep in existence a marriage which has been dead for 25 years requires, in my judgment, a considerable amount of justification.

And it would be wrong in all the circumstances to dissolve the union

These last words of Ormrod LJ bring us to the second limb of the test: even if the court finds that grave hardship will arise, it may nevertheless grant the divorce because the bar can only succeed if it would be 'wrong' to dissolve the marriage or civil partnership.

Reiterbund v Reiterbund [1974] 1 WLR 788, 797–8 (Fam Div)[144]

FINER J:

It seems to me that the word "wrong" must there be construed to mean "unjust." However, in determining whether in all the circumstances it would be wrong, or unjust, to dissolve the marriage, it seems to me that the court must be careful to avoid subverting the policy which led to the inclusion of section 1(2)(e)...as one of the facts establishing irretrievable breakdown by, so to speak, treating the paragraph (e) "fact" as of a lower order than the other four. Irretrievable breakdown is now the sole ground for divorce, and it may be established through any one of the matters set out in section 1(2), all of which carry equal weight in expressing the object of the legislation. It seems to me, therefore, that in considering the section 5 defence, the court has to exclude from its consideration that a petition based on five years' separation is brought by a "guilty" husband (in the phraseology of the old law) against a non-consenting wife, for this would be tantamount to striking section 1(2)(e) out of the Act altogether....The parties in this case are not young, but even if there were no prospect at all of the husband marrying again (and there is at least a hint that he may) I do not consider that it would be

---

[144] Affd. [1975] Fam 99.

> wrong to dissolve this marriage. On the contrary, I think it is a case which is well within the
> policy embodied in the new law which aims, in all other than exceptional circumstances, to
> crush the empty shells of dead marriage.

Where the parties are young, it will be extremely difficult to satisfy this test:

Mathias v Mathias [1972] Fam 287, 300, 301 (CA)

DAVIES LJ:

On the second part of the subsection, I would say, . . . that, so far from its being wrong to dissolve this marriage, I am absolutely satisfied that it would be wrong not to do so. The ages
of the parties are about 35 and 32 respectively. We do not know the age of [the husband's
fiancée], but no doubt she is a young woman. All three of the parties, the husband, the wife
and [the husband's fiancée], would, in the ordinary course of events, have many years to live;
and in my view, unless there were strong reasons to the contrary, it would be ridiculous to
keep alive this shell of a marriage and prevent perhaps all three of the parties settling down
to a happier life in happier circumstances. The cohabitation lasted for some two and three-
quarter years. They have been living apart now for some seven and three-quarter years. I
should have thought that the sooner that latter situation is put an end to the better.

The relevance of conduct

Section 5 requires the court to consider the parties' conduct in deciding whether to apply the
bar. Although divorce law and financial settlements on divorce are no longer fault-based, it
has been held that conduct, good or bad, must be taken into account here.[145]

Special protection for parties to some religious marriages

Some marriages cannot be wholly dissolved by civil divorce. Although the state recognizes
the divorce for all purposes, the religious law under which a marriage was contracted may
not recognize civil divorce, and further procedures may have to be completed before the parties will be free to remarry in accordance with their religious rites.[146] Conversely, religious
divorces obtained in the UK will not dissolve marriage for civil law purposes; there must be
a civil divorce.[147] This perhaps contrasts oddly with the recognition of certain religious marriage ceremonies as being competent to create a marriage for civil law purposes.[148]

Difficulty arises where only one spouse wishes to remarry under religious law but cannot
do so without the other's cooperation. For example, under Jewish law, the parties are only
divorced if the husband gives and the wife accepts a formal document issued under the auspices of a rabbinic court called a 'Get'. If the husband is content to remarry outside the faith, he
has no incentive to fulfil this procedure, and that leaves the wife effectively unable to remarry
within her faith, and any children she might have will be illegitimate under Jewish law.

---

[145] *Brickell v Brickell* [1974] Fam 31.
[146] See Morris (2005); Schuz (1996), writing before the reform discussed in the text.
[147] Family Law Act 1986, s 44; *Sulaiman v Juffali* [2002] 1 FLR 479.
[148] Schuz (1996); see 2.5.3, particularly in relation to Jewish and Quaker marriages, which proceed
entirely under their own rites without any additional civil requirements save registration.

Following a series of cases[149] highlighting the problem faced by some Jewish wives, a new provision designed expressly to deal with the problem—s 10A—was introduced in 2002.[150] This empowers the court, if it is just and reasonable to do so, to withhold the decree absolute until both parties have taken any steps required to dissolve the marriage under their religious law. In many cases (assuming that the intransigent party wants a civil divorce), the threat of invoking s 10A may produce the desired result. Evidently, no equivalent issue arises for civil partners.

5.5.7 THE PROCEDURE FOR DIVORCE AND DISSOLUTION

The nature of the judge's task under the MCA 1973 has been described thus:

Ash v Ash [1972] Fam 135, 141 (Fam Div)

BAGNALL J:

The only circumstances in which the court will have to decide...whether the marriage has broken down irretrievably must be when one of the spouses is asserting the affirmative of that proposition and the other is asserting the negative. Simple assertion either way, it seems to me, cannot suffice. What I have to do is to examine the whole of the evidence placed before me, including and giving not inconsiderable weight to the assertions of the parties, and make up my mind, quite generally, whether it can be said that in spite of the behaviour of the husband, and the reaction to that behaviour of the wife, the marriage has not broken down irretrievably. In my opinion, in performing that general exercise on a survey of the evidence, only a general answer is appropriate and no useful purpose would be served by seeking to place quantitative weight on one consideration or another. Performing the best survey that I can of the evidence, and having regard to the personalities of the parties as displayed in the witness box, I have concluded that I cannot be satisfied on all the evidence that the marriage has not broken down irretrievably and accordingly I must pronounce a decree nisi.

However, the judge's job is rather different in undefended divorces, which are now decided under the 'special procedure'. The reality of modern divorce law cannot be appreciated without reference to this procedure. That reality is far from what we might expect from the face of the substantive law that we have just discussed, and raises fundamental questions about the relevance of that law.

The judicial duty to inquire and the special procedure

Since 1857, statute has required divorce judges to perform an inquisitorial function.[151] When reform was being considered during the 1960s, the Archbishop's Group desired a thorough judicial investigation into the end of couples' relationships. For practical reasons, that approach was rejected.[152] However, although not required to conduct a wide-ranging

---

[149] See, for example, *N v N (divorce: ante-nuptial agreement)* [1999] 2 FCR 583; *O v O (Jurisdiction: Jewish Divorce)* [2000] 2 FLR 147, in which s 9(2) was used to delay granting a decree absolute to the respondent husband.

[150] Divorce (Religious Marriages) Act 2002: it currently applies only to Jewish marriages.

[151] See generally Booth Committee (1985), paras 2.13 et seq. and Eekelaar (1994).

[152] Law Com (1966), paras 60 et seq.

inquiry into the various causes of the claimed irretrievable breakdown, the judges still have a limited inquisitorial role:

Matrimonial Causes Act 1973, s 1[153]

(3) On a petition for divorce it shall be the duty of the court to inquire, so far as it reasonably can, into the facts[154] alleged by the petitioner and into any facts alleged by the respondent.

(4) If the court is satisfied on the evidence of any [of the five facts set out in s 1(2)], then, unless it is satisfied on all the evidence that the marriage has not broken down irretrievably, it shall, subject to section 5 [the hardship bar, see above p 315], grant a decree of divorce.

The reality of divorce trials, which were heard in the High Court, had long since failed to live up to the image projected by the substantive law, even pre-1969 when the concept of the matrimonial offence still prevailed.

C. Gibson, *Dissolving Wedlock* (London: Routledge, 1994), 175–80

It is not known whether the guardianship of High Court divorce judges made couples more decorous within their marital relationships. But it is clear that the vast majority of divorces were undefended petitions which were speedily processed by Special Divorce Commissioners masquerading as High Court judges.[155] Undefended cases, as Mr Harvey QC explained in a caustic exposition of the post-war divorce procedure, 'works almost on the slot machine principle'....Sir Hartley Shawcross, the Attorney-General, recalled to the House of Commons in 1951: 'One used to handle these undefended cases at the rate of about one in two minutes...it did not impress me at the time that there was any real principle operating in practice in the administration of our divorce laws'.

When the 1969 legislation came into force, that inquiry ostensibly remained the function of the senior judiciary, and appellate decisions emphasized the importance of judges making factual findings even in undefended cases, rather than merely rubber-stamping the petition.[156] The distance between substance and procedure would soon become greater with the introduction of the so-called 'special procedure'.[157]

[By] 1977 the divorce process had been changed into a private arrangement validated within an administrative setting. This most radical transformation in the approach to, and meaning of, divorce took place without serious Parliamentary debate. The new process was essentially the outcome of a cost-saving exercise rather than a purposeful Parliamentary rethinking of what the legislative, administrative and social needs of a modern divorce policy should be.

---

[153] CPA 2004, s 44(2).

[154] *Darnton v Darnton* [2006] EWCA Civ 1081, [8]–[9].

[155] County Court judges had been designated as High Court judges for the purposes of granting divorces locally to help process the otherwise unmanageable numbers of cases.

[156] See, for example, *Santos v Santos* [1972] Fam 247, 263–4.

[157] See Black et al (2007), ch 9; *Pounds v Pounds* [1994] 1 FLR 775, 778; FPR 2010, r 7.20(2).

When introduced in 1973 the new arrangements were properly termed 'special procedure', for availability was restricted to petitioners without dependent children who sought divorce on the fact of two years'...separation. Two further extensions have meant that since April 1977 all undefended divorces are dealt with by special procedure. And this, in fact, is the general everyday procedure used by 99.9 per cent of all petitioners. The parties are not required to appear before a judge unless there are dependent children or... there are ancillary matters to be resolved. The district judge examines the papers in his office for both conformity to administrative requirements and assurance that the petition and its supporting affidavit evidence meets the substantive requirements for divorce. When satisfied on these two counts the district judge certifies his approval. This is the crucial decision, for with this certificate to hand the divorce judge must pronounce the decree nisi.

As Gibson goes on to explain, the extension of what had been a 'special' procedure to all undefended cases, regardless of the fact relied on, effected a 'fundamental change...to the administration and regulation of divorce':

The Bishop of Durham could write to *The Times* (4 April 1977):

I am disturbed at the implications of divorce by post, and even more disturbed by the apparently casual manner in which such a fundamental change has been made...To avoid public action tilts the concept of marriage breakdown dangerously in the direction of divorce by consent, and in doing so widens the gulf between Christian and purely contractual understandings of marriage. I believe it would be an immeasurable loss if those who, from both sides, wish to widen this gulf were given encouragement to do so by a piece of administrative convenience.

But executive endorsement of special procedure was not governed by a radical belief that divorce should now be seen as an essentially administrative process that no longer required a court hearing. Rather, at a time of economic crisis, causing the Treasury to insist on major cuts in public spending and the government to announce that there was to be little or no increase in expenditure on legal aid for the next five years, the Lord Chancellor concluded that there was only one area within civil legal aid where sizeable savings could justifiably be made. This was the field of divorce...

When Lord Chancellor Elwyn-Jones announced in 1976 the extension of the special procedure to all undefended divorces he also declared that legal aid would no longer be available in such proceedings. The rationale behind this change was that as determination of the undefended petition would not now require a court hearing there was no longer need for a lawyer's attendance at court. However, legal aid would still be available where the need for a hearing arose for which legal representation was necessary. This covered contested petitions and such matters as disputes over ancillary questions involving maintenance, property or arrangements for children. Ancillary proceedings were, in the words of the Lord Chancellor, 'the areas of real contest between the parties to divorce proceedings today, not the question whether the petitioner should get a decree'...

The divorce process has been radically transformed from a public judicial inquest titularly undertaken by High Court judges to a private administrative ratification of the spouses' decision to divorce.

Given the near-universal application of the procedure, the label 'special' is a 'complete misnomer'.[158] It has been said that its objectives are 'simplicity, speed and economy', so that,

---

[158] *Day v Day* [1980] Fam 29, 32, per Ormrod LJ.

whilst the essentials of the petition must be satisfactory and its contents proved, 'there should be no room for over-meticulousness and over-technicality in approach'; substance should be preferred over form.[159] It has also been said that 'the judge's duty pursuant to s 1(3)...to enquire, so far as he reasonably can, into the facts alleged by the petitioner is...emasculated almost into invisibility'.[160] However, one study concluded that even within the narrow boundaries of the special procedure, there remained some room for strict judicial control, if only over form and procedure, if the judge wished to exert it.[161]

Stephen Cretney has suggested that 'in relation to divorce, procedural change has over the years often had more impact than changes in the substantive law', and certainly affected public perceptions of the law.[162] The special procedure necessarily deeply affected the courts' ability to make any effective inquiry in undefended divorces and so reduced the influence of the substantive law.[163]

This must be borne in mind when considering the case law on the 'facts'. Many of those cases were decided before the special procedure arrived, or were defended. The judges were therefore able to conduct a far deeper inquiry than the special procedure permits. Some of the instructions given to the judge by that case law are effectively impossible to implement under the special procedure. The substantive law clearly impacts on special procedure cases, as the evidence submitted must fulfil the substantive requirements. However, it is only in defended cases that the judge has room to operate in the way envisaged by the case law. Divorce is therefore more easily obtained than the face of the legislation and case law may suggest.

Davis and Murch conclude that 'we have...moved to a position where the *state*'s interests in the breakdown of marriage has receded almost to vanishing point...in favour of an increased emphasis on private agreement'.[164] Ruth Deech has observed that 'conceptually and procedurally, it is far more difficult to terminate those other pillars of a stable life, employment and a tenancy, than marriage'.[165] Whatever the MCA 1973 and CPA 2004 may imply on their face about the public interest in marriage and civil partnership and the consequent restrictions on obtaining a divorce, the reality is very different. The grant of divorce may rest with a judge, but that judge is essentially discharging an administrative responsibility rather than adjudicating in any substantial sense.

Defended cases

Defended divorces are now extremely rare. Even by 1966—before the current law came into force—93 per cent of divorces were undefended.[166] Statistics on defended divorces have not been collected centrally since 1991. In that year, 153 defended divorces were listed for trial in the High Court, of which 82 went to trial; in none was a decree granted. Figures for defended divorces in the county courts were last reported for 1989, when 511 cases were listed for

---

159 *R v Nottingham County Court, ex parte Byers* [1985] 1 WLR 403, 406, per Latey J.

160 *Bhaji v Chauhan* [2003] 2 FLR 485, 487, per Wilson J.

161 Ingleby (1989), 240.

162 Cretney (2003a), 165. The different procedures under the Divorce (Scotland) Act 1976 are probably a cause of most Scottish divorces' reliance on separation rather than fault-based facts: Law Com (1990), para 3.17; Harvie-Clark (2005).

163 Booth Committee (1985), para 2.8.

164 Davis and Murch (1988), 13.

165 Deech (2009a).

166 Law Com (1966), para 20.

trial and 259 resulted in divorce decrees.[167] To put these figures in perspective, in 1991 over 153,000 divorce decrees were granted.[168]

However, the relatively tiny number of defended cases does not indicate that all cases passing via the special procedure are factually undisputed. Davis and Murch describe defended divorce as a 'seriously underestimated problem'.[169] Many respondents may wish to defend the petition, particularly where it is based on the behaviour fact and the detailed allegations are disputed. The respondent may agree that the marriage has irretrievably broken down, but vehemently deny the allegation that his or her behaviour is the problem. However, legal aid is now rarely available to defend a divorce. Public funding is currently only available if the respondent can satisfy the legal aid authorities that there is a 'substantial defence with sufficient prospects of success and there are substantial practical benefits to be gained from avoiding the decree'.[170] Public funding is unlikely to be provided where, although the detail of some allegations can be disputed, there is nevertheless sufficient basis on which to grant the divorce. For example, if a behaviour petition drags on beyond two years of the parties' being separated, a divorce will be available on the basis, legal aid will probably be terminated, and the defendant's financial situation is likely to dictate that he concede to a divorce on that basis.[171] Only the most persistent respondents with private means or the confidence to act as a litigant in person are therefore likely to defend. The vast majority of respondents who might have wished to defend reluctantly concede defeat rather than see the case go to trial.[172] It might be wondered whether this practical lack of legal aid violates unwilling respondents' rights under Article 6 ECHR.[173] However, in the absence of a blanket ban on public funding for such cases,[174] such a challenge seems unlikely to succeed.[175] It has been held to be unarguable that lack of legal representation or advice in divorce proceedings, whether that be the result of the litigant's choice or not, breaches Article 6 ECHR.[176]

Where a defence does proceed, the respondent is entitled to a proper hearing. The petition must provide adequate detail regarding the facts alleged; specific findings of fact should be made; and a circuit judge, not a recorder, should hear the case. That did not occur in *Butterworth*, where the litigant in person respondent was faced with 'hopelessly general' allegations:

Butterworth v Butterworth [1997] 2 FLR 336, 339 (CA)

BUTLER-SLOSS LJ:

At the end of the day, looking at this case, although I am sure that the recorder did his best to hear the evidence and to try to come to a decision between the parties, the impression given, even if incorrect, is that it is unreasonable for husbands to object to divorces and that the evidence in support of the petition is somewhat of a formality. That is far from the truth.

[167] LCD (1990), table 5.6.
[168] LCD (1992), table 5.3.
[169] Davis and Murch (1988), 100.
[170] Black et al (2007), 11.06. Cf proposals in 2011 substantially to cut legal aid for all private family cases.
[171] Ibid., 11.10.
[172] Davis and Murch (1988), chs 7–10.
[173] Kay (2004).
[174] Cf *Airey v Ireland (No. 1)* (App No 6289/73, ECHR) (1979); *Steel and Morris v UK* (App No 68416/01, ECHR) (2005).
[175] Cf *Santambrogio v Italy* (App No 61945/00, ECHR) (2005).
[176] *Darnton v Darnton* [2006] EWCA Civ 1081, [16].

All courts hope that spouses whose marriages fail will bury them decently and will not litigate the divorce in public with the consequential adverse effect upon each of the parties and
upon their children. But the present state of the English law of divorce gives the respondent
to a divorce petition the right to oppose it and to have the allegations made in the petition
against him properly proved to the satisfaction of the court to the civil standard of the balance
of probabilities.

These are potentially serious allegations [of violence, alcoholism etc]. They are allegations
that this respondent does not wish to have made against him. The fact that most other
respondents do not bother too much does not prevent him having the right to say: 'I do not
agree with them. Prove them', and I have to say that the allegations made in this petition
were not proved.

The two-stage process

Whether conducted via the special procedure or defended, divorce proceeds in two stages.
Once the papers have been examined, or the defended trial heard, and the judge is satisfied
that the ground for divorce is made out, he or she initially issues a decree nisi.[177] After six
weeks, the petitioner may apply for the decree absolute.[178] If the petitioner has not done this
within three months of the six-week point, the respondent may apply for the decree absolute to be made, or for the decree nisi to be rescinded.[179] If the application is made over 12
months from the first possible date, the court may require evidence to account for the delay
before deciding whether to grant the decree absolute, not least to ascertain whether recent
events cast doubt on the findings made to support the decree nisi. If dissatisfied, the court
can rescind the decree nisi.[180] The eventual grant of the decree absolute has been described
as an administrative rather than judicial procedure.[181] But only at that point are the parties
divorced and so free once more to marry or form a civil partnership.

Fraud unravels everything, so a decree absolute may be rescinded if it is discovered that
the divorce was obtained on false evidence.[182] Procedural errors, whether committed by
the parties or the court itself, may also render a decree absolute void. This may have adverse
implications for a party who has, on the faith of the decree absolute, since remarried. In
Dennis v Dennis, the petitioner wife was not sent notice of the husband's application for the
decree absolute, which was in any event made earlier than it ought to have been, and the
court then failed to send the wife a copy of the decree. When the errors came to light, the
court of its own motion reopened the case to declare the decree void, a result which neither
party wanted, but in relation to which there was no discretion. This rendered void the husband's remarriage. The husband argued that this breached his rights under Articles 8 and 12
ECHR, but the court found no prima facie violation of either Article.

---

177 MCA 1973, s 1(5); in civil partnership law: 'conditional order', CPA 2004, s 37(2).

178 MCA 1973, s 1(5); 'final order': CPA 2004, s 38(1); Matrimonial Causes (Decree Absolute) General
Order 1972.

179 MCA 1973, s 9(2); CPA 2004, s 40(2). The court has a discretion whether to make the final order on
the respondent's application, and may decline to do so if it might prejudice the petitioner, in particular in
relation to ongoing ancillary relief proceedings: *Wickler v Wickler* [1998] 2 FLR 326. *Darnton v Darnton*
[2006] EWCA Civ 1081.

180 *Court v Court* [1982] Fam 105; FPR 2010, r 7.32(3).

181 *Dennis v Dennis* [2000] Fam 163, 183.

182 *Moynihan v Moynihan* [1997] 1 FLR 59.

Dennis v Dennis [2000] Fam 163, 180–1 (Fam Div)

WALL J:

Regulation of marriage and divorce is clearly a function of the state. Freedom to marry, in a society which practi[s]es monogamy, depends upon capacity to marry. There is nothing, in my judgment, in Part I of the Matrimonial Causes Act 1973 which is ambiguous, or which cannot be said to be Human Rights Act compliant... The statute sets out a scheme to enable spouses to divorce each other by means of clear and well-recognised procedures... [T]he provision... of a two-stage process leading to the final decree of divorce is not only unexceptionable, but is designed to protect the status and rights of both parties. Divorce affects not only personal status and capacity to remarry, but also inheritance and pension rights. A woman in the petitioner's position is plainly entitled at all times to know what her marital status is; and, if that status is to be changed, she is entitled to have notice of and to be heard on the question. These, in my judgment, are as much rights under articles 8 and 12 as the respondent's rights under the same articles. As it happens, on the facts of this case, the petitioner's inheritance and pension rights in the context of her marital status would not have been affected if I had been able to hold that the decree absolute was voidable rather than void; however, the position might well have been different if, for example, the respondent had died in the intervening period.

The role of the Queen's Proctor

The delay between decrees nisi and absolute also provides an opportunity for intervention by the Queen's Proctor, the Crown officer charged with representing the public interest in the law and practice of divorce against manipulation by private individuals who wish to evade the substantive law and effectively divorce on their own terms.[183] The Queen's Proctor may be called upon to act as amicus curiae in cases raising difficult points of law, where it may be in neither party's interests to oppose the divorce. When divorce was based on the concept of matrimonial offence, divorce was prohibited where the parties had colluded to create the grounds for divorce or the petitioner had connived at or condoned the respondent's offence (notably where the husband undertook to commit adultery—or to give the impression of having done so—with another woman in a hotel). The Queen's Proctor would investigate where it was suspected that such activities were afoot.[184] His evidence could deprive spouses who both wished to be divorced of the decree they sought. These bars and the role of the Queen's Proctor emphasized the public interest in the sacrosanct nature of the marriage bond.[185]

Nowadays, opportunities for proctorial intervention are more limited, the old bars of collusion, connivance, and condonation having gone. However, there may still be cases— particularly where a quick divorce is wanted—where parties falsely assert the facts required to obtain the desired outcome. Under the special procedure where no oral testimony is required and the paperwork appears satisfactory, suspicion of perjury may rarely arise. But once suspicions are aroused, an oral hearing of the undefended petition may follow, the Queen's Proctor intervening to oppose the divorce. In *Bhaji v Chauhan*, five almost identically worded petitions crossed the same judge's desk. In each case, one party was a

---

[183] The Queen's Proctor may also intervene in nullity and judicial separation cases.
[184] The lengths to which these inquiries might go are vividly portrayed in A.P. Herbert's *Holy Deadlock*.
[185] Cretney (2003a), 176–7.

UK national, the other an Indian national who was given leave to enter the UK because of the marriage. In each case, the marriage was alleged to have broken down shortly after indefinite leave to remain in the UK had been obtained. The papers were sent to the Queen's Proctor who then intervened to prove that the petitions were a sham:

Bhaji v Chauhan, Queen's Proctor Intervening (Divorce: Marriages Used for Immigration Purposes) [2003] 2 FLR 485 (Fam Div)

WILSON J:

[20] This hearing may serve to bring to public attention the opportunity which exists for serious abuse both of our immigration rules and of our divorce laws; and inevitably one wonders whether the abuse is more widespread than is reflected in this handful of five petitions presented in the county court in Bolton.... The opportunity for abuse of our divorce laws is the opportunity to procure an immediate divorce by the inclusion of false allegations of unreasonable behaviour in a petition presented once the marriage has been successfully used in securing indefinite leave. I am well aware that, after 2 years of separation, one spouse can, with the other's consent, lawfully obtain a divorce. Indeed it was submitted to me that there is no point in my dismissing the petitions because the parties to all the marriages will within the next year have become separated for 2 years and will thus be entitled to a divorce by consent. With respect, that argument entirely misses the point. In England and Wales divorce is not yet available simply upon joint demand following separation. This unusual hearing has exposed a concerted attempt to bypass the requirements of the present law and, by use of bogus allegations of behaviour, to secure the immediate dissolution of marriages which have outlived their perceived usefulness.

Encouraging reconciliation

Several statutory provisions seek to encourage reconciliation before the parties reach the point of no return. Whether any of these provisions do—or ever could—save saveable marriages is doubtful; indeed, they were not introduced with any great hopes that they would.[186]

The bar on initiating divorce proceedings in the first year of marriage may be viewed as an attempt to encourage spouses to make a go a new union.[187] If at any point during the divorce proceedings, the court considers that reconciliation might be reasonably possible, it can adjourn proceedings to allow efforts to be made in that direction.[188] But, given the special procedure, it is difficult to see how the court can make that judgment. If the petitioner has sought legal advice in connection with the divorce, the solicitor must certify *whether* he or she has discussed the possibility of reconciliation with the petitioner and supplied details of appropriate couple counselling services.[189] But since many petitioners act in person rather than with legal advice there may be no solicitor on hand to perform even this limited duty.[190]

---

[186] See Law Com (1966), paras 29–32.
[187] See 5.6.6 above.
[188] MCA 1973, s 6(2); CPA 2004, s 42(3).
[189] MCA 1973, s 6(1); CPA 2004, s 42(2).
[190] Law Com (1988a), para 3.9; Booth Committee (1985), para 4.42.

The substantive law also seeks to facilitate reconciliation by allowing the clock running in desertion and separation cases to stop for up to six months in total should the parties cohabit again, and by permitting some degree of continued cohabitation in adultery and behaviour cases.[191] The policy of promoting reconciliation has also shaped interpretation of the substantive law. It has been held that it is necessary only to prove irretrievable breakdown at the date of the hearing, not on the date of filing the petition. Were it otherwise, the court's power to adjourn pending a possible reconciliation would be of no value, and 'petitioners would be discouraged by their legal advisers from making or accepting any overtures for reconciliation while the proceedings were pending', a result which 'would clearly be contrary to the policy of the Act'.[192]

5.5.8 THE FACTS IN PRACTICE

The five facts are used to differing extents by the divorcing population as a whole and by husband and wife petitioners respectively. The most relied upon fact (both overall and amongst wives) is behaviour, accounting for nearly half of divorces today. The separation facts, in particular the two-year fact, have been more popular than adultery. But the hope that the separation facts would be the most popular has proved unfounded.[193] Desertion cases are extremely rare.

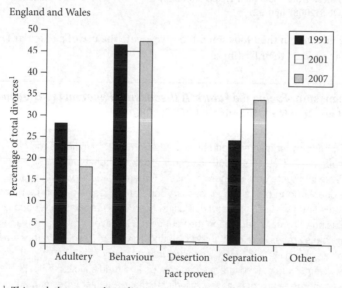

[1] This excludes cases where divorces were granted to both parties and annulments.

Figure 5.3 Facts proven at divorce as percentage of total divorces, 1991, 2001, and 2007

Source: Reproduced from *Population Trends* No 133 by the Office for National Statistics, by Crown copyright © 2008 (ONS (2008), figure 1).

[191] MCA 1973, s 2; CPA 2004, s 45.
[192] *Pheasant v Pheasant* [1972] Fam 202, 205–6.
[193] Law Com (1966), paras 92–3. Compare the position in Scotland: n 162 above.

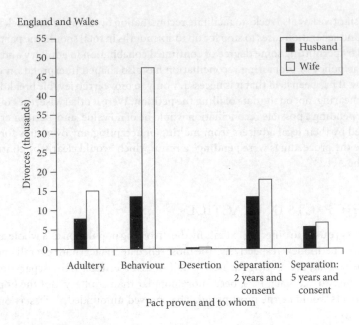

Figure 5.4 Facts proven at divorce and to whom granted, 2007

Source: Reproduced from *Population Trends* No 133 by the Office for National Statistics, by Crown copyright © 2008 (ONS (2008), figure 2).

Studies conducted in the 1980s sought to investigate the use of particular facts. The Law Commission reported their findings:

Law Commission, *Facing the Future: A Discussion Paper on the Ground for Divorce,* Law Com No 170 (London: HMSO, 1988)

2.11 Perhaps the most marked trend discernible from the statistics is the increased use of the behaviour fact...Haskey's study has shown that the behaviour fact is more likely to be used by those in lower socio-economic classes whereas adultery and separation are more frequently used among the middle classes. A correlation has also been found between the age at divorce and fact used. Thus, those using five years' separation tend to be the oldest and those using two years' separation the youngest. However, amongst those with dependent children behaviour is dominant among "young" divorces. Generally, those with dependent children are more likely to use the behaviour and adultery facts.

2.12 [Davis and Murch, who interviewed parties and read solicitors' files] have concluded that these phenomena do not necessarily indicate that particular types of marital misconduct are more prevalent among particular groups. Rather, the evidence suggests that behaviour and adultery are frequently used because of the need to obtain a quick divorce. In particular, it is noteworthy that the separation grounds are least used by those petitioners who are least able to effect separation—women, in lower social classes, and particularly those with dependent children. Davis and Murch found that 28 per cent of those petitioning on the basis of behaviour and 7 per cent of those petitioning on the basis of adultery were still living together when the petition was filed. These same groups are also more likely to need to have ancillary issues relating to [child residence], maintenance and housing determined quickly. This is most likely to occur once the petition has been filed.

2.13 The choice between adultery and behaviour seems to depend on social mores and on the state of the relations between the parties, as much as upon their marital history. Thus, adultery would seem to carry less stigma particularly among the middle classes and is more likely to be employed than behaviour where the parting was consensual or at least amicable. Behaviour petitions seem much less likely to have been discussed between the parties or their solicitors in advance and sometimes take respondents completely by surprise.

5.5.9 JUDICIAL SEPARATION

One or both parties, perhaps for religious reasons, may not wish to divorce but nevertheless wish to separate without risking an adverse finding of desertion.[194] Other individuals may require early protection where they find themselves in an impossible, even violent relationship before they can petition for divorce. A decree of judicial separation ('separation order', in the case of civil partnership) cannot require either party to leave the matrimonial home (an occupation order would be required for that[195]), but on making the decree the court can order financial relief, as it can on divorce and annulment.[196] This releases spouses from the duty to cohabit without effecting any change of status, save in relation to inheritance on intestacy.[197]

In order to obtain a decree, it is necessary to prove that one of the five (or, in the case of civil partnership, four) facts applies. But the court is not required to find that the union has irretrievably broken down. Should the parties wish subsequently to divorce, the same fact can be relied on, but judicial separation cannot simply be converted into a divorce; it is necessary to petition and produce evidence again.[198] Comparatively small numbers of judicial separation orders are now made each year—in 2008, there were just 421 petitions and 214 decrees of judicial separation.[199]

5.6 EVALUATION OF THE CURRENT LAW

The original objectives of the current law were first set out in 1966:

Law Commission, *Reform of the Grounds of Divorce: The Field of Choice*, Law Com No 6 (London: HMSO, 1966)

15. ... [A] good divorce law should seek to achieve the following objectives:

(i) To buttress, rather than to undermine, the stability of marriage; and

(ii) When, regrettably, a marriage has irretrievably broken down, to enable the empty legal shell to be destroyed with the maximum fairness, and the minimum bitterness, distress and humiliation.

...

---

[194] Cf MCA 1973, s 18(1); there is no equivalent provision in the CPA, but absence pursuant to an order for separation clearly provides justification under the law of desertion.

[195] See 4.5.3.

[196] See 7.3.4.

[197] MCA 1973, ss 17–18; CPA 2004, ss 56–7; Law Com (1990), paras 4.2–4.11; Cretney (2003a), 149 ff.

[198] MCA 1973, s 4; CPA 2004, s 46.

[199] MOJ (2009), table 5.5.

18. In addition to these two main objectives, another important requirement is that the divorce law should be understandable and respected. It is pre-eminently a branch of law that is liable to affect everyone, if not directly at any rate indirectly. Unless its principles are such as can be understood and respected, it cannot achieve its main objectives. If it is thought to be hypocritical or otherwise unworthy of respect, it will not only fail to achieve those objectives but may bring the whole of the administration of justice into disrespect.

The defects of the current law, assessed against those criteria and others, have been catalogued many times: by the Law Commission,[200] the Government,[201] and academic researchers.[202]

Law Commission, *The Ground for Divorce*, Law Com No 192 (London: HMSO, 1990)

Criticisms of the present law and practice

2.7 The criticisms of the present law...add up to a formidable case for reform.

(i) It is confusing and misleading

2.8 There is a considerable gap between theory and practice, which can only lead to confusion and lack of respect for the law. Indeed, some would call it downright dishonest. There are several aspects to this. First, the law tells couples that the only ground for divorce is irretrievable breakdown, which apparently does not involve fault. But next it provides that this can only be shown by one of five "facts", three of which apparently do involve fault. There are several recent examples of divorces being refused despite the fact that it was clear to all concerned that the marriage had indeed irretrievably broken down. The hardship and pain involved for both parties can be very great.

2.9 Secondly, the fact which is alleged in order to prove the breakdown need not have any connection with the real reason why the marriage broke down. The parties may, for example, have separated because they have both formed different associations, but agree to present a petition based on the behaviour of one of them, because neither wishes their partner to be publicly named [see MCA 1973, s 49]. The sex, class and other difference in the use of the facts make it quite clear that these are chosen for a variety of reasons which need have nothing to do with the reality of the case. This is a major source of confusion, especially for respondents who do not agree with the fact alleged. As has long been said, "whatever the client's reason for wanting divorce, the lawyer's function is to discover grounds".

2.10 The behaviour fact is particularly confusing. It is often referred to as "unreasonable behaviour", which suggests blameworthiness or outright cruelty on the part of the respondent; but this has been called a "linguistic trap", because the behaviour itself need be neither unreasonable nor blameworthy: rather, its effect on the petitioner must be such that it is unreasonable to expect him or her to go on living with the respondent, a significantly different and more flexible concept which is obviously capable of varying from case to case and court to court....

2.11 Finally, and above all, the present law pretends that the court is conducting an inquiry into the facts of the matter, when in the vast majority of cases it can do no such thing [owing to the special procedure]. This is not the fault of the court, nor is it probably any more of a

---

[200] Most fully, Law Com (1988a), Part III.
[201] LCD (1993), (1995).
[202] E.g. Davis and Murch (1988), Eekelaar (1991b), Gibson (1994).

problem under the present law and procedure than it was under the old. It may be more difficult to evaluate the effect of the respondent's behaviour from the papers than from the petitioner's account in the witness box, but it has always been difficult to get at the truth in an undefended case. Moreover, the system still allows, even encourages, the parties to lie, or at least to exaggerate, in order to get what they want. The bogus adultery cases of the past may have all but disappeared, but their modern equivalents are the "flimsy" behaviour petition or the pretence that the parties have been living apart for a full two years. In that "wider field which includes considerations of truth, the sacredness of oaths, and the integrity of professional practice", the present law is just as objectionable as the old.

(ii) It is discriminatory and unjust

2.12 83% of respondents to our public opinion survey thought it a good feature of the present law that couples who do not want to put the blame on either of them do not have to do so, but these couples have to have lived apart for at least two years. This can be extremely difficult to achieve without either substantial resources of one's own, or the co-operation of the other spouse at the outset, or an ouster order from the court.[203] . . . The law does recognise that it is possible to live apart by conducting two separate households under the same roof. In practice, this is impossible in most ordinary houses or flats, especially where there are children: it inevitably requires the couple to co-operate in a most unnatural and artificial lifestyle. It is unjust and discriminatory of the law to provide for a civilised "no-fault" ground for divorce which, in practice, is denied to a large section of the population. A young mother with children living in a council house is obliged to rely upon fault whether or not she wants to do so and irrespective of the damage it may do.

2.13 The fault-based facts can also be intrinsically unjust. "Justice" in this context has traditionally been taken to mean the accurate allocation of blameworthiness for the breakdown of the marriage. Desertion is the only fact which stills attempts to do this . . . Desertion, however, is hardly ever used, because its place has been taken by the two separation facts. A finding of adultery or behaviour certainly need not mean that the respondent is any more to blame than the petitioner for the breakdown of the marriage. . . .

2.14 This inherent potential for injustice is compounded by the practical problems of defending or bringing a cross-petition of one's own. It is extremely difficult to resist or counter allegations of behaviour. Defending them requires time, money and emotional energy far beyond the resources of most respondents. Even if the parties are prepared to go through with this, what would be the point? If the marriage is capable of being saved, a long-fought defended divorce, in which every incident or characteristic that might amount to behaviour is dragged up and examined in detail, is not going to do this. It can only serve to make matters worse and to consume resources which are often desperately needed elsewhere, particularly if there are children. . . . Small wonder, then, that lawyers advise their clients not to defend and that their clients feel unjustly treated.

(iii) It distorts the parties' bargaining positions

2.15 Not only can the law be unjust in itself, it can also lead to unfair distortions in the relative bargaining power of the parties. When a marriage breaks down there are a great many practical questions to be decided: with whom are the children to live, how much are they going to see the other parent, who is to have the house, and what are they all going to live on? Respondents to Facing the Future [the Law Commission's earlier discussion paper] told us that the battles which used to be fought through the grounds for divorce are now more likely to be

---

203 See 4.5.3 on occupation orders under the FLA 1996.

fought through the so-called ancillary issues which in practice matter so much more to many people. The policy of the law is to encourage the parties to try and resolve these by agreement if they can, whether through negotiation between solicitors or with the help of a mediation or conciliation service. Questions of the future care of children, distribution of family assets, and financial provision are all governed by their own legal criteria. It is not unjust for negotiations to be affected by the relative merits of the parties' cases on these matters. Yet negotiations may also be distorted by whichever of the parties is in a stronger position in relation to the divorce itself. The strength of that position will depend upon a combination of how anxious or reluctant that party is to be divorced and how easy or difficult he or she will find it to prove or disprove one of the five facts. That might not matter if these represented a coherent set of principles, reflecting the real reasons why the marriage broke down; but as we have already seen, they do not. The potentially arbitrary results can put one party at an unfair disadvantage.

(iv) It provokes unnecessary hostility and bitterness

2.16 A law which is arbitrary or unjust can exacerbate the feelings of bitterness, distress and humiliation so often experienced at the time of separation and divorce. Even if the couple have agreed that their marriage cannot be saved, it must make matters between them worse if the system encourages one to make allegations against the other. The incidents relied on have to be set out in the petition. Sometimes they are exaggerated, one-sided or even untrue. Allegations of behaviour or adultery can provoke resentment or hostility in a respondent who is unable to put his own side of the story on the record. We are not so naive as to believe that bitterness and hostility could ever be banished from the divorce process. It is not concerned with cold commercial bargains but with the most intimate of human relations. The more we expect of marriage the greater the anger and grief when marriage ends. But there is every reason to believe that the present law adds needlessly to the human misery involved....

(v) It does nothing to save the marriage

2.17 None of this is any help with the law's other objective, of supporting those marriages which have a chance of survival. The law cannot prevent people from separating or forming new relationships, although it may make it difficult for people to get a divorce. The law can also make it difficult for estranged couples to become reconciled. The present law does make it difficult for some couples—in practice a very small proportion—to be divorced, but it does so in an arbitrary way depending upon which facts may be proved. It also makes it extremely difficult for couples to become reconciled. A spouse who wishes to be divorced is obliged either to make allegations against the other or to live apart for a lengthy period. If the petitioner brings proceedings based on behaviour, possibly without prior warning, and sometimes while they are still living together, the antagonism caused may destroy any lingering chance of saving the marriage. The alternative of two or five years' separation may encourage them to part in order to be able to obtain a divorce, when their difficulties might have been resolved if they had stayed together. From the very beginning, attention has to be focussed on how to prove the ground for divorce. The reality of what it will be like to live apart, to break up the common home, to finance two households where before there was only one, and to have or to lose that day-to-day responsibility for the children which was previously shared, at least to some extent: none of this has to be contemplated in any detail until the decree nisi is obtained. If it had, there might be some petitioners who would think again.

2.18 It is a mistake to think that, because so few divorces are defended, the rest are largely consensual. There are many, especially behaviour cases, in which the respondent indicates an intention to defend, but does not file a formal answer, or files an answer which is later withdrawn. Some of these are a reaction to the unfairness of the allegations made against them, but some reveal a genuine desire to preserve the marriage. A defended suit is not going to do this, and if a case is, or becomes, undefended, there is little opportunity to explore the possibility of saving the marriage. An undefended divorce can be obtained in a matter of weeks. If both parties are contemplating divorce, the system gives them every incentive to obtain a "quickie" decree based on behaviour or separation [sic. presumably adultery was meant, rather than separation], and to think out the practical consequences later.

(vi) It can make things worse for the children

2.19 The present system can also make things worse for the children. The children themselves would usually prefer their parents to stay together. But the law cannot force parents to live amicably or prevent them from separating. It is not known whether children suffer more from their parents' separation or from living in a household in conflict where they may be blamed for the couple's inability to part. It is probably impossible to generalise, as there are so many variables which may affect the outcome, including the age and personality of the particular child. But it is known that the children who suffer least from their parents' break-up are usually those who are able to retain a good relationship with them both. Children who suffer most are those whose parents remain in conflict.

2.20 These issues have to be faced by the parents themselves, as they agonise over what to do for the best. However regrettably, there is nothing the law can do to ensure that they stay together, even supposing that this would indeed be better for their children. On the other hand, the present law can, for all the reasons given earlier, make the conflict worse. . . . It is often said that couples undergoing marital breakdown are too wrapped up in their own problems to understand their children's needs. There are also couples who, while recognising that their own relationship is at an end, are anxious to do their best for their children. The present system does little to help them to do so.

Conclusion

2.21 These defects alone would amount to a formidable case for reform. The response to Facing the Future very largely endorsed its conclusion that "Above all, the present law fails to recognise that divorce is not a final product but part of a massive transition for the parties and their children."

And so the Law Commission concluded that the most suitable role for the law on divorce lay in adjudicating not on the breakdown of the marriage itself, but instead on the practical issues—residence and contact with children, financial and property matters—that inevitably flow from divorce where agreement cannot be reached. While the law may not itself be the source of the bitterness and hostility so often seen on divorce, the current law does nothing to help the parties come to terms with the life-changes associated with divorce.

Divorcing couples, lawyers, and government have also expressed the concern that for many people, divorce is too quick and 'easy' and so might encourage precipitate divorce where a marriage could be saved.[204] The median duration of divorce proceedings under the two principal fault-based facts is under six months; some couples get from petition to decree absolute in as little as three months.[205] In one sense, this appears to undermine suggestions

---

204 Davis and Murch (1988), 66–70.
205 LCD (1995), para 2.7.

that divorce is made 'harder' by requiring that it be based on fault. Given the ease with which fault may be alleged and the briskness of the special procedure, the 'quickie' divorce may seem rather attractive to prospective divorcees. But the fact that divorce may be readily available does not necessarily encourage irresponsible behaviour; divorce is rarely entered into lightly.[206] Indeed, it has been said that where it is clear that a marriage has irretrievably broken down, spouses who are forced to rely on the five-year separation fact are made to wait too long for their divorce and so for access to the full powers of the court to provide financial relief.[207] Nor does the law systematically protect the economically weaker party. The Law Commission found it anomalous that the special protection of ss 5 and 10 should be available only to respondents in separation cases. Reliance on a separation fact does not necessarily mean that the respondent is blameless; nor, given the difficulty of clearly ascribing blame for marital breakdown, does the selection of a fault-based fact necessarily indicate that the respondent is undeserving of the court's protection.[208]

But the case for reform is not universally accepted:

R. Deech, 'Divorce Law and Empirical Studies', (1990) 106 *Law Quarterly Review* 229, 242–3

As far as the divorce grounds go, there is certainly no public or professional clamour for reform. And if the rate of divorce is really levelling off, then also there is no need for reform because it is evident that we have exhausted the possibilities of *de jure* ending all *de facto* breakdowns. If all those people whose marriages have broken down can obtain divorces under existing law, there is no need to liberalise it...[Deech then argues that further liberalization of divorce law would only further increase divorce rates.]

[Insofar as research suggests that the long-term harm caused to children occurs at the point of separation,] any alteration to divorce law is irrelevant to children's post-divorce suffering and...we should not delude ourselves that the nature of the divorce petition can make a real improvement...

Even the widely held perception of the grounds of adultery, behaviour and desertion as acrimonious and unfair may be overstated. It is not usually the spouses who choose the grounds relied on but their solicitors, and there may well be more long drawn out legal difficulties [e.g. occupation orders, interim maintenance, disputes regarding child residence and contact] in the lapse of separation periods than where the quick grounds are relied on. It is also probably not the case...that immediate consensual divorces are available. There is always a waiting period, currently of seven or eight months on average between service of petition and decree absolute. So it is the *grounds* that are immediate, not the decree, and some studies report that petitioners do not take sudden decisions to divorce.

5.7 OPTIONS FOR REFORM OF DIVORCE LAW AND THE PROCESS OF DIVORCE

Given the many criticisms of current law and procedures for divorce, now replicated for dissolution of civil partnership,[209] anxiety about the rising divorce rate, the apparent 'ease'

---

[206] Walker (1991).
[207] Law Com (1988a), para 3.12.
[208] Ibid., paras 3.19 and 3.31.
[209] See Hasson (2006), 285–90.

of divorce, and the claimed effects of divorce on children and society, ought the law to be reformed, and if so how?[210] There are a number of perspectives from which reform might be approached, between them suggesting different models for divorce law which may in turn suggest different understandings about the nature of marriage.[211] The first focuses on the role of fault. The others are all forms of no-fault divorce. The options are not mutually exclusive, and many reform proposals—like current English law—offer several alternative routes to divorce.[212]

5.7.1 REAFFIRMING THE CENTRALITY OF FAULT?

The Morton Commission of 1956 considered that the role of divorce law was to give relief where wrong had been done.[213] There is still popular support for fault: 84% of respondents to a public opinion survey for the Law Commission conducted in the late 1980s supported divorce for fault, though not as the sole basis for divorce.[214] But jurisdictions worldwide have been retreating from fault. It has been said that the legal concept of marriage which requires spouses to be subservient to a particular view of moral duty has been replaced by a concern for the quality of individual relationships and the psychological well-being of the individuals involved.[215]

Some commentators and legislators seek to resist this trend, considering that fault should remain a central feature of divorce law and family justice more generally. Ruth Deech has recently made the case for fault in these terms:

R. Deech, 'Divorce law – a disaster?', (2009a) Gresham lectures 2009–10

It seem[s] to me to be clear that [the lack of morality in public life] is because over the last forty years or so we have abandoned, in terms of approbation/disapprobation, law and categorisation, any pressure to conform to basic, long unchallenged tenets of private morality. At the time I applauded the liberalising laws of the 1960s and still think that on balance they did more good than harm – the legalisation of abortion and homosexuality, the ending of the criminalisation of suicide, [ending] the stigmatising of illegitimacy, and the liberalising of contraception and divorce. Yet the effect, when taken all together a few decades on, is to live in a society where there are no constraints on private morality, no judgmentalism, no finger wagging or name calling, only acceptance of anything that anyone does, short of the criminal law, in the name of the pursuit, if not of individual happiness, then at least individual choice....So individual happiness is pitted against, and prevails over the good of one's family and others.

Contemporary debate about fault was first stimulated by the divorce reforms in Part II of the Family Law Act 1996, which (we shall see below) was never brought into force. It would have removed fault entirely from English divorce law. Members of the House of Lords had expressed concerns during the passage of the Act about what they saw as the removal of individual responsibility from marriage. As Lord Stallard put it, 'No fault, to me, means no

---

[210] See generally Harvie-Clark (2005); Boele-Woelki et al (2004); Law Com (1988a) and (1990).
[211] See the themes considered earlier: 5.3.
[212] Including those of the Commission for European Family Law: Boele-Woelki et al (2004).
[213] Royal Commission on Marriage and Divorce (1956), para 69(xii).
[214] Law Com (1990), 183.
[215] Ellman (2000), 344; this is not to say that people no longer feel a sense of obligation and commitment within their intimate relationships: see Lewis (2001b).

responsibility, no commitment and no security'.[216] Meanwhile, economist Robert Rowthorn offered the following analysis:

R. Rowthorn, 'Marriage and trust: some lessons from economics', (1999) 23
Cambridge Journal of Economics 661, 662–3

[M]arriage should be seen as an institution for creating trust between individuals in the sphere of family life, and…legal and social policy should be fashioned so as to allow this function to be effectively performed. Many of the legal and social reforms which have been implemented in modern times have undermined the ability of marriage to perform its basic role as a trust-creating institution. To get married is no longer such a major commitment and no longer offers the degree of security which it once did, since divorce is now relatively easy and the responsibilities and rights of the married and the unmarried are increasingly similar. These developments are often presented as an advance in human freedom since they allow individuals to exit unilaterally from unhappy relationships at minimum cost to themselves and with minimum delay. However, this is a one-sided view, since it ignores the benefits and freedoms associated with trust and security. The fact that individuals can now exit easily, and unilaterally, from a relationship makes it difficult for couples to make credible commitments to each other. They can promise anything they want, but many of these promises are no longer legally enforceable, and many are undermined by social policies which reward those who break their promises. By eroding the ability of couples to make credible commitments to each other, modern reforms have deprived them of an important facility which, for all its defects, the old system provided.

… The marriage contract has been diluted to the point that it is now much less binding than the average business deal. While employment law has increased job security and protection for workers, legal security in the family has been weakened and in many Western countries the marriage contract can now be terminated at will virtually without penalty. Marriage is now one of the few contracts where the law and government policy frequently protect the defaulting party at the expense of his or her partner.

Arguments surrounding fault in this area are hotly contested. Fault-based divorce is viewed by some as a tool for influencing behaviour: to deter divorce and to deter bad behaviour during marriage (i.e. whatever behaviour would give the other spouse grounds for divorce).[217] It is also argued that the knowledge that divorce may only occur if each party misbehaves (or consents to divorce, where divorce is also available on the basis of mutual consent) would encourage spouses to 'invest' in the marriage for their mutual benefit (for example, by one spouse reducing paid employment in order to raise the children), safe in the knowledge that their investments are protected for so long as the other party has no grounds for divorce.[218] But others question whether deterrence of bad behaviour is properly or realistically the role of divorce law, rather than criminal or tort law. If conduct is not sufficiently grave to warrant the intervention of criminal or tort law, or cannot be defined sufficiently clearly for those purposes, that may suggest that it is not something that should or can be adjudicated on by the divorce courts.[219] The threat of the 'sanction' of divorce may only be as strong as the guilty party's desire not to be divorced and that party's unwillingness to satisfy the terms

---

216 Hansard HL Deb, vol 569, col 1651, 29 February 1996.
217 E.g. Royal Commission on Marriage and Divorce (1956), para 69 (xxxvii).
218 E.g. Rowthorn (1999).
219 E.g. Ellman (1997), 226.

that the innocent party may demand as a condition for agreeing to divorce.[220] Alternatively, it is suggested that a guilty party who *wants* divorce can be punished under fault-based law by the innocent party withholding divorce. But critics have argued that this course of action may rarely be in the interests of the innocent party, who may be rather better protected by the courts' ancillary powers triggered by divorce.[221] Many also question whether law is a sufficiently sophisticated mechanism for influencing conduct within marriage and encouraging commitment; social norms may be more potent.[222] Moreover, the practical reasons rehearsed by the Law Commission for rejecting fault remain,[223] though proponents of fault contest their validity.[224] Ascribing guilt and innocence in intimate relationships is often far from straightforward, and the legal system is said to be ill-equipped to identify correctly the causes of a marriage's demise. The process of adjudicating fault can only be damaging to the parties' future relations as joint parents of their children and, if done properly (assuming even that it could be), would be extremely costly for the parties and the family justice system.

The debate about fault and no-fault divorce has been particularly strong in the US, where no-fault divorce was introduced during the 1970s, many states permitting divorce on unilateral demand after six months' separation, often alongside traditional fault-based grounds.[225] The guilty party can therefore obtain a divorce fairly easily. But rather than advocate a wholesale return to fault-based divorce, some commentators have sought to promote 'covenant marriage', a special class of marriage which couples can select at the outset. Covenant marriage has more restrictive grounds for divorce and spouses must participate in pre-divorce counselling. The concern is principally to secure the position of the spouse who is unwilling to divorce, reflecting a private contract view of marriage, rather than the old public interest that sought to uphold marriage by keeping parties together in the absence of fault, even where both wish to part. So while an innocent party can instigate divorce immediately on fault-based grounds, divorce is not available only on proof of fault. Louisiana's covenant marriage law permits unilateral divorce following a more onerous two years' of separation. So even under this scheme, divorce is not drastically restricted. Three states have enacted covenant marriage laws, but the take-up has been very low.[226] The principal architect of the Louisiana covenant marriage statute makes the case for this new form of marriage:

E. Spaht, 'Louisiana's covenant marriage law: recapturing the meaning of marriage for the sake of the children', in A. Dnes and R. Rowthorn (eds), *The Law and Economics of Marriage and Divorce* (Cambridge: CUP, 2002), 110–11

Restoration of "moral discourse" to divorce law . . . troubles most critics of the covenant marriage law more than any other aspect of the legislation. The "moral discourse" consists of society's collective condemnation of certain conduct within the marital relationship. Returning

---

[220] Ibid.

[221] Eekelaar (2006b), 105–11. One response to this would be to open up wider remedies outside the divorce context.

[222] Contrast Deech (1990); Schuz (1993); Eekelaar (2000).

[223] See extract above pp 330–1 and Law Com (1990), paras 3.6–3.9, 3.40; O'Donovan (1993), 110–15; Scott (2002), 50–1.

[224] Rowthorn (1999), 684–5.

[225] See Ellman (2000).

[226] Louisiana (La Rev Stat Ann Sect 9:272–275, 307–9), Arizona (Ariz Rev Stat Ann Sect 25-901–906), Arkanas (Covenant Marriage Act of 2001); Bills have been introduced in several other states, but not yet been passed.

to objective moral judgments about a spouse's conduct threatens the notion that morality cannot be legislated. Congress and legislatures do it every day. Only when the morals to be legislated have the potential of impeding the affected person's "liberty" to leave his or her family when he or she so chooses and be considered legally "a single person" do we hear objections. In matters of breach of contract, no one has objected to assigning *blame* for failure to perform a contract, requiring that contracts be performed in good faith, and assessing damages based upon whether the party breached the contract in good faith or bad faith. If principles of contract law involve moral judgments in the context of a relationship between strangers,[227] why should the law hesitate to make a moral judgment about spouses who have been married for thirty years and have three children?

Another argument against the restoration of fault to divorce law is the assertion that fault cannot be proven, thus, those who desire divorce will be relegated to perjury, allegedly a widespread practice prior to no-fault divorce. Fault in the nature of adultery or physical abuse sufficient for an immediate divorce [under covenant marriage law] may be proven by mere preponderance of the evidence (more likely than not), and that evidence need only be circumstantial, not direct. Surely, it is no more difficult to prove adultery by a spouse than to prove which driver's fault, and the degree of that fault expressed in a percentage, caused a car accident. As a response to the expressed concern about widespread perjury, the answer is that the judiciary and attorneys bear responsibility. Even though perjury should surely be condemned, the fraud upon the court did at least require *cooperation of both spouses* and precluded the current practice [under no-fault divorce] of legalized desertion by one spouse.

Spaht goes on to argue that, logically, the revival of fault should extend to the determination of ancillary issues such as child custody and financial relief. If fault-based divorce law is to achieve its aims, it may indeed be logical to ensure that a finding of fault is reflected in decisions about the future residence of any children and the distribution of the parties' assets: the children would live with the 'innocent' party, who could claim financial recompense from the 'guilty' party for lost expectations on divorce.[228] Adopting fault as the key criterion for these decisions would entail a major reversal in policy, prioritizing 'justice' between the spouses over the welfare and rights of individual children. This proposal has therefore been criticized by Carol Smart for returning children to the status of 'trophies in the adversarial system'.[229] Moreover, John Eekelaar and others have argued that financial settlements on divorce can promote 'responsibility' on divorce and protect parties' investments in marriage via mechanisms other than fault.[230]

Other commentators, with a very different set of concerns, have cautioned against attempts to 'sanitize' divorce by removing any opportunity for parties to express their sense of grievance. From a psychological perspective, the emotional conflict accompanying divorce is neither trivial nor pathological, but a normal part of the process of bereavement experienced on divorce.[231] It may be desirable for the divorce process to contain that conflict, rather than simply try to deny or reduce it,[232] and to recognize that current norms associated with 'good'

---

[227] By contrast with many other legal systems, English contract law has no general good faith doctrine.

[228] Rowthorn (1999), 671; Dnes (1998), 345 argues instead that, rather than find fault in a tradition sense, a party who unilaterally seeks divorce without good cause should be regarded as being 'in breach', and so treated as the guilty party. Determining whether 'good cause' exists might, however, reintroduce traditional fault arguments.

[229] Smart (2000), 380.

[230] Eekelaar (2006b), 105–11; Ellman (1997); see 7.5.6 on the marginal relevance of fault in English law of financial and property adjustment on divorce.

[231] Day Sclater (1999), 180.

[232] Brown and Day Sclater (1999), 158; Walker (1991), 236.

divorce, such as the importance of joint parenting following separation, may actually fuel conflict.[233] The question is whether the *legal* forum, whether via the grounds for divorce or otherwise, provides the environment or context in which the emotional consequences of divorce can be most satisfactorily addressed.

5.7.2 DIVORCE BY MUTUAL CONSENT?

The Law Commission found substantial support for divorce on the basis of mutual consent: 90 per cent of survey respondents thought that divorce should be available on this basis.[234] Long gone are the days when the public interest demanded that parties be prevented from reaching agreements regarding divorce. It is probably no exaggeration to say that most of today's divorces are now effectively obtained on this 'ground', albeit that the petition will be framed in terms of one of the fault-based facts (in order to secure a quick divorce) or two-years' separation. If so, adopting mutual consent as an immediate ground for divorce could be viewed simply as 'a technical fix aimed at improving the functioning of the judicial system rather than…a fundamental change in family policy'.[235] Whether it would be perceived that way is another matter: like any no-fault option, this purely *private* view of marriage which removes the state from any adjudicative role over its dissolution might attract opposition. But it would certainly be readily comprehensible.[236]

Current English law expressly contemplates divorce by mutual consent only where the parties have been separated for two years. There are significantly fewer cases of divorce on this basis than on the fault-based facts. If it were thought desirable that more cases should proceed on a no-fault basis, but that a separation requirement remained appropriate (rather than allowing immediate divorce by consent), the law could try to encourage reliance on the 'separation with consent' fact by reducing the period of separation required. The time periods for the separation facts in Scotland are now one and two years respectively.[237]

If mutual consent were to become a ground for divorce, increased procedural safeguards would be needed to ensure that consent had been given in a free and informed way.[238] Mutual consent could not, however, serve as the sole ground for divorce. There are situations in which one party should be free to instigate divorce without consent (especially where the respondent is guilty of some grave fault), and an exclusive mutual consent ground could replicate the 'distortions' of bargaining position for which the current law is criticized.[239] The question is whether the law should identify specific circumstances in which one party should be able to instigate divorce (whether based on specific categories of fault or on a period of separation), or whether divorce on unilateral demand should be adopted.

5.7.3 DIVORCE ON UNILATERAL DEMAND?

If divorce should be available where a marriage has irretrievably broken down, the corollary may be to accept that divorce should be available not only where the parties agree on

---

[233] Collier (1999), 262.
[234] Law Com (1990), 183.
[235] Ellman (2000), 341. This was true as early as 1966: Law Com (1966), para 79.
[236] Cretney (1992), 474.
[237] Family Law (Scotland) Act 2006, s 10; also abolishes desertion fact and the hardship bar, ss 11–12.
[238] Law Com (1988a), para 5.18.
[239] See Law Com (1990), para 2.15, above.

that course, but wherever *one* party desires it. On this view, consent of both ought not to be a necessary precondition: the marriage contract needs the consent of both parties for it to *continue*. Moreover, it might be safe to assume that those best placed to determine whether a marriage has irretrievably broken down are the parties themselves—if one party wishes to divorce, that is surely the best evidence available that divorce is appropriate. Many believe that the legal system cannot undertake that evaluation—the issue is not justiciable.[240] The desire that the dissolution of marriage ought to be 'subject to an authority that is independent of the will of the parties…a real exercise of judgment by the Court, acting on the community's behalf' in order to make the notion of lifelong obligation meaningful,[241] may be unrealizable. Given the difficulty of defending divorce petitions and the lack of serious scrutiny under the special procedure, many divorces are already effectively granted on this basis, and not only in cases based on the only no-fault unilateral fact, five-year separation.[242]

However, the public may be less willing to accept this reasoning: only a third of respondents to the Law Commission survey in the late 1980s thought divorce on unilateral demand would be acceptable. Like any other no-fault option, divorce on unilateral demand entails a very different conception of marriage and the nature and extent of the public interest in divorce from a fault-based law. The state is entirely removed from adjudication on the end of the marriage, and can only protect the unwilling party via decisions relating to ancillary issues relating to any children and the allocation of the parties' assets.[243] Unlike divorce by mutual consent, no-fault unilateral divorce is criticized for undermining each spouse's ability to rely upon the marriage contract, and so damaging the quality of their partnership.[244]

However, even if divorce on unilateral demand were acceptable, we would still need to consider whether divorce should be available immediately on that basis, or whether the parties should be required to separate (currently under English law for five years, under Louisiana's covenant law for two years, or for its standard marriage contract just six months), or simply to wait for a period of time before divorce proceedings could be initiated, and if so, why and for how long. This brings us to consideration of divorce as a process over time.

5.7.4 DIVORCE AS A PROCESS OVER TIME: THE FLA 1996

In these days of mass divorce, it has been suggested that the focus has shifted from delivering substantive justice to aggrieved parties to considerations related to 'consumer choice, efficiency and pragmatism'.[245] The values and interests at stake may now be reduced to 'easy and public access to divorce, the promotion of consensual divorce above unilateral divorce, the autonomy of the spouses and the protection of the weakest spouse'.[246] But the state may not be prepared to give up all attempts to regulate divorcing behaviour. The 'consumers' of divorce may not be left entirely free to divorce as and when they wish to. If the law can no longer be used to restrict the *substantive* grounds on which a divorce may be obtained, could the law be used to slow down and influence the decision-making *process*, either to

---

240 Law Com (1988a), paras 4.6–4.7.

241 Mortimer Commission (1966), para 48.

242 Law Com (1988a), para 5.20.

243 Ibid., para 4.14. Even if the divorce itself were not granted on the basis of fault, ancillary decisions still could be: see Ellman (1997), 218; Dnes (1998).

244 Rowthorn (1999); see also Scott (2002).

245 O'Donovan (1993), 112.

246 Boele-Woelki et al (2004), 48–9, discussing scrutiny of agreements on the consequences of divorce.

guard against precipitate divorces, or to encourage those determined to divorce to do so in a particular way? At the very least, 'Would it not be ironic if a consumer were allowed to "back out" of an agreement to purchase life assurance or a timeshare after a "cooling-off" period, but would be bound with immediate effect to an agreement to divorce?'[247]

A period of separation

The law currently enforces a cooling-off on those who wish to divorce without proof of fault by requiring that they separate for two or five years. Separation affords the sole ground for divorce in Australia (one year) and New Zealand (two years).[248] The separation facts are criticized for discriminating against those who may find it difficult to satisfy the legal test for separation.[249] But that could be avoided by reform enabling the court, as in Australia and New Zealand, to order financial relief to facilitate separation by would-be petitioners.[250] Indeed, it is because they seek immediate access to the courts' adjustive powers over the parties' assets that so many people rely on the immediate, fault-based facts instead.[251] But some commentators still doubt whether a separation ground would in practice operate satisfactorily and reduce conflict.[252]

A 'period of reflection and consideration': the FLA 1996

Another option is exemplified by Part II of the FLA 1996. This legislation was based on recommendations made by the Law Commission, subsequently revised by the Government and further amended during its passage through Parliament.[253] The scheme received considerable support when originally proposed and would have revolutionized English divorce law. Irretrievable breakdown would have remained the sole ground for divorce, but there the similarity to the current law would have ended. The 'facts' would have been abolished, non-adversarial terminology adopted, and joint applications for divorce made possible. Separation prior to divorce would not have been required. Instead, the ground for divorce would have been established by a statement, made by the applicant(s) following the mandatory 'period of reflection and consideration', that the marriage had irretrievably broken down. During that period, parties would have been expected to consider whether their marriage could be saved and, if not, to resolve issues relating to the future care of their children and their property. The clock would only have started to run three months after the applicant(s) had attended a mandatory information meeting. Mediation came to be seen as a key way for parties to negotiate these issues on divorce.

Under the new law, divorce would have taken much longer for parties who currently rely on the quick fault-based facts.[254] The only remaining significant element of *substantive* law

---

[247] Schuz (1993), 581.

[248] Family Law Act 1975 (Aus); Family Proceedings Act 1980 (NZ).

[249] See extract above p 331.

[250] Law Com (1990), para 3.25. See also Commission for European Family Law's proposals: Boele-Woelki et al (2004).

[251] Davis and Murch (1988), 141.

[252] Ibid., 142–5; cf Davies (1993) reporting the success of the separation ground in other jurisdictions; but that success may be partly attributable to greater availability of housing in those countries: Davis and Murch (1988), ibid.

[253] Law Com (1988a), (1990); LCD (1993), (1995).

[254] LCD (1995), para 2.7.

requiring adjudication would have been provided by the hardship bar,[255] which was lowered during the passage of the Bill from 'grave' to 'substantial' hardship, and which (since divorces could no longer be categorized by reference to the fact relied on) would have been available in all cases. The bar on divorce in the first year of marriage would still have applied, and the court would have retained its power to delay divorce in the interests of the children.

The 'period of reflection and consideration' and associated aspects of the reform were not intended to operate neutrally in the way that a period of separation does. Instead, a new role for the state on divorce and new obligations for divorcing spouses were envisaged.[256] As Carol Smart has described, the radical nature of the proposed change generated fierce debate between two groups: those who advocated the retention of fault to provide clear, public 'rules of conduct' for marriage, the cornerstone of family and society, viewing divorce as punishment for those who broke those rules; and those who viewed family in more fluid, private terms, where moral questions were negotiable and private. The Family Law Act 1996, a victory for the second group, marked a significant change in the state's role with regard to marriage and divorce:

C. Smart, 'Divorce in England 1950–2000: A Moral Tale?', in S. Katz, J. Eekelaar, and M. Maclean (eds), *Cross Currents: Family Law and Policy in the US and England* (Oxford: OUP, 2000), 376–7

As with the debates some decades earlier, the main point of contention in the 1990s was over the best method(s) for the state to deploy in order to facilitate/ensure supportive, stable, and responsible family relationships... The core elements of the Bill, namely the information meetings, the period of reflection, and the preference for mediation over litigation, all constituted a prime example of the practice of governance as opposed to government. The theme of the legislation was based on the idea that people need knowledge about divorce and the financial problems it brings, the difficulties it creates for children, and the need to plan such things as resuming work and pension provision. The period of reflection was proposed as a form of 'time out' in which emotions could settle down in order to allow the divorcing couple to become more rational and more competent citizens, equipped either to manage the transition to divorce, or to change their minds and stay married. Mediation was intended as a way of helping to plan and to resolve any outstanding differences and problems mutually. The modern citizen envisaged by the Family Law Bill was the fact-gathering, rational, caring parent who would make decisions on the basis of knowledge. This citizen could be compared (unfavourably) with the divorced spouse of the former fault-based system who was encouraged to look backwards and cherish resentments and blame, who seized upon children as weapons in the battle, and who—in their emotional haze—failed to make proper provision either for themselves or for their former partners and children. The aim of governance would be to produce the former citizen. The aim of government in the latter scenario would be to adjudicate on who should be rewarded and who punished, while admonishing the most guilty for their failure.

Even amongst those who favour no-fault divorce, the new law was not universally supported. It was criticized for being unrealistic in its aspiration that couples 'will be required

---

[255] See 5.5.6.
[256] See generally Reece (2003).

to spend time reflecting on whether their marriage can be saved, and, if not to face up to the consequences of their actions and make arrangements to meet their responsibilities'.[257]

S. Cretney, 'Divorce Reform: Humbug and Hypocrisy or a Smooth Transition?', in M. Freeman (ed), *Divorce: Where Next* (Aldershot: Dartmouth, 1996a), 52–3

This is a very laudable aspiration. But how is this 'requirement' to be enforced? May not some of those concerned prefer to spend their time in the far more pleasurable activity of conceiving—necessarily illegitimate—babies? May not some spend the time seeking means of exploiting their emotional or financial advantage, or brooding on grievances and perhaps using the available legal procedures as a way of seeking satisfaction for the wrongs they have suffered? The way in which the Law Commission's proposals were presented seemed almost reminiscent of those earnest Victorian reformers who invented the so-called 'separate system'—prisoners deprived of all corrupting influences would be driven to reflect in their solitude on the evil of their ways and thereby be well prepared to receive the sympathy, advice and religious consolation provided for those truly humbled by their experience. It was, of course, all very well-intentioned; and yet succeeded in inflicting scarcely imaginable cruelty on hundreds of helpless human beings. We would all hope that the parties will indeed give anxious consideration to whether the marriage has broken down irretrievably and to the consequential arrangements. We must all hope that mediation and counselling will be successful in this respect. But the evidence for believing that these expectations will be fulfilled is not overwhelmingly convincing.

Cretney also accused the new law of hypocrisy: that the emphasis on reflection and consideration concealed what in fact amounted to divorce on unilateral demand:

It is true that the government's proposals will end the sometimes damaging ritual of filing a petition alleging—perhaps unjustly—that the other spouse has committed adultery or been guilty of behaviour such as to make it unreasonable for the spouses to go on living together. But a man who has behaved cruelly and unreasonably will still be able to insist on divorce against the wishes of his wife; and the wife's anger, grief and bitterness may reasonably not be assuaged by assurances that the new law promotes consideration and reflection—and that since her case is a simple one she is not to receive any public help to pay a lawyer who will defend her interests. There seems to be a serious risk that countless people will find themselves uncomprehendingly ensnared in a monstrous and costly legal/social work/counselling nightmare. The Law Commission...identifies the 'incoherence' of the law and the confusion thereby caused to people caught up in the divorce process as one of the law's most significant weaknesses; and the Commission rightly attributes these defects to the compromise nature of the 1969 divorce reforms. But there is a serious risk that the incoherence and confusion will be perpetuated and even increased. We shall still have to pretend that the ground for divorce is the breakdown of the marriage; whereas the reality is that it is the wish of one party to divorce the other. The information and mediation sessions merely conceal that simple truth and, in so doing, they make matters worse.

The scheme could also be criticized for being patronizing and unduly restricting access to divorce for at least some couples. The decision to divorce is rarely taken lightly or

---

[257] LCD (1995), para 4.16.

quickly.[258] Many couples (especially, perhaps, those without children) may have separated and resolved all arrangements for the future long before initiating divorce proceedings. How might such couples feel if required to reflect and consider for a further year? Might such a system encourage people to set that clock ticking early—perhaps enticing them into a divorcing mindset too early—to ensure that the option of immediate divorce would be there once the decision was reached?

It has also been asked whether such a scheme should be accompanied by an alternative track for immediate divorce by mutual consent—or even unilaterally—where the parties have been separated for a defined period and/or where they have no minor children.[259] Immediate divorce is available in Sweden if both parties want it and they have no minor children. If only one party wishes to divorce or if the parties have children, they must ordinarily wait for a six-month period of reflection (during which they need not separate). But if they have been separated for two years, a divorce may be granted immediately.[260] John Eekelaar has observed that were childless marriages to be left effectively unregulated at divorce, there would be little to distinguish them from childless cohabitation; 'marriage will [to that extent] have become, in Clive's (1980) phrase, an "unnecessary legal concept"'.[261]

On the other hand, many couples are reported bitterly to regret having got divorced (though that may not mean that they would not still *want* a divorce, in the circumstances). The law might therefore be justified in imposing some waiting period on all cases. To deny immediate divorce to those who genuinely wish to have it may be a small price to pay for a system which does not risk propelling those undergoing emotional stress towards a divorce which they may later regret.

Recent reform proposals have been variations on the theme of the FLA 1996. Resolution, the specialist family law solicitors' group, are keen proponents of a more straightforward no-fault divorce law. Under their scheme,[262] parties intending to divorce would attend information meetings regarding local legal and non-legal services (including counselling, mediation, help with parenting) that might assist them. One or both parties could then lodge a statement of marital breakdown that would start a six-month waiting period, which could be shortened in exceptional circumstances or by reference to the length of any separation immediately preceding the lodging of the statement (thus potentially reducing the waiting period, apparently, to nothing). Parties who had not already separated would not have to do so during that period. On the conclusion of the waiting period, either party could apply for divorce by filing a declaration that the marriage had broken down. The s 5 hardship bar would be abolished, but the s 10(2) power to delay divorce retained.

The more modest proposals of the Centre for Social Justice, a body advising the Conservative Party, would simply introduce a waiting period to the current MCA scheme.[263] Parties would have to give notice of intention to divorce and then wait three months before being entitled to apply for divorce. After three months (and within six months) of that notice, either or both parties together would be allowed to petition for divorce in the ordinary way. To ensure that the waiting period afforded parties space to reflect, no application for financial relief could be made during that time. The waiting period would be intended

---

[258] See Davis and Murch (1988).
[259] For criticism of allowing children to affect the duration of any period, see LCD (1995), paras 4.17–4.18.
[260] Swedish Marriage Code, Chapter 5.
[261] Eekelaar (1991b), 171.
[262] See Shepherd (2009).
[263] Centre for Social Justice (2009). See also Deech (2009a).

to help save saveable marriages and allow for time to attend information meetings, attempt reconciliation, or commence mediation or other alternative dispute resolution.

5.8 WHERE NEXT FOR ENGLISH DIVORCE LAW?

5.8.1 THE DEMISE OF THE FLA 1996

Part II of the FLA 1996 was never brought into force. The decision to abandon the scheme was taken following the results of pilot projects designed to explore the best format for the initial information meetings which were a key part of the scheme. The pilots were devised simply to test the format for information delivery (and were necessarily conducted in the context of the current law), but the Government evaluated the results by reference to the likelihood, following receipt of the information, of parties electing to use mediation rather than seeking legal advice in relation to their divorce.[264]

This reflected the way in which the Law Commission's original scheme had changed in emphasis as it developed in the hands of successive Governments and in Parliament.[265] The Law Commission had conceived of the period for reflection and consideration principally as a way of proving irretrievable marital breakdown. It was envisaged that parties could use mediation and other non-legal services during that period; but use of mediation was not central to the Law Commission's scheme. However, when the Conservative Government took over the project, divorce reform become inextricably linked with concerns to save marriages and the promotion of mediation in preference to legal services, and it was because of this that the information meetings were introduced. It became clear under the subsequent Labour Government that these meetings would not be neutral conduits for the delivery of factual information. 'Information' for these purposes had a persuasive function, aimed at steering parties towards attempts to save their marriage or, if that were impossible, towards behaving 'responsibly' in relation to their divorce. 'Responsibility' for these purposes was synonymous with use of mediation.[266]

Given these ambitions for marriage-saving and mediation, the Labour Government was unsurprisingly 'disappointed'[267] by the results of the pilot projects. Only a small minority of couples were diverted to marriage counselling; counselling had limited success in preventing divorce, but did perform the valuable function of helping individuals cope with the transition through divorce and improve the quality of their post-divorce relationship, particularly important where they had children. The failure of the meetings to save more marriages was perhaps unsurprising: only one member of the couple had to attend the information meeting and that person was often too far down the psychological road to divorce for the meeting to affect the decision to end the marriage. Nor were the meetings particularly successful in diverting couples into mediation: only 10 per cent of individuals attending the meetings went to mediation with their spouses within two years of the meeting, while 73 per cent went to lawyers in that time.[268] Interim results had found 39 per cent reporting that having attended the information meeting they were now *more likely* to seek legal advice.[269] This

---

[264] Newcastle Centre for Family Studies (2001b), 21.
[265] See Eekelaar, Maclean, and Beinart (2000), ch 1.
[266] See Reece (2003), Eekelaar (1999).
[267] LCD (1999).
[268] Newcastle Centre for Family Studies (2001a).
[269] LCD (1999).

was not the ringing public endorsement of mediation for which the Government had hoped, particularly bearing in mind that all of those who participated in the pilot projects were volunteers, who might therefore have been expected to be more amenable to new options.

The pilot projects reported many positive findings—an overwhelming majority (90 per cent) of those who had attended meetings were glad to have done so. The information meetings succeeded in 'increasing knowledge and empowering citizens to take informed decisions'.[270] Yet despite these good outcomes, Part II of the FLA 1996 was abandoned.[271] The Government's disappointment that parties still wished to use lawyers rather than mediators and so failed to match the image of 'responsible' divorce attracted strong criticism from John Eekelaar, worried by the implications of the Government's position for the rule of law:

J. Eekelaar, 'Family Law: keeping us "on message" ', (1999) 11 *Child and Family Law Quarterly* **387, 395–6**

I do not wish to argue against the importance of people being under duties and having responsibilities. Indeed, to the extent that any individual has rights, others (individually or collectively) will have responsibilities to respect those rights. It is also the case that an individual's rights and duties are not exhausted by their statement in the law. This is obvious in the case of moral rights and duties. It is also true in relation to an individual's socially constructed rights and duties: so, while, for example, the law may not require an able, adult, child to give any assistance to his or her indigent parent, there may well be a socially accepted obligation to provide it. But in the examples discussed here, we have an apparent tension between what the state proclaims in its law and how it wants people actually to behave. The legal framework of marriage and divorce has, under the influence of liberal individualism, become a neutral edifice within which parties have worked out their lives according to a wide variety of beliefs and customs. Now the state is actively intervening, through institutions of its creation or to which individuals will be strongly steered, in an attempt to bring about certain forms of behaviour which are not legally required, and may not even be consistent with widely accepted social norms.

Eekelaar went on to note that the FLA 1996 allowed grants to be made for research into marital breakdown, its causes, and prevention methods, and funding for marriage counselling. He raised no objection to this expenditure, accepting that it might be thought right, even a matter of duty, for the state to seek through various means to promote 'good' behaviour. But are there limits to the appropriateness of such state intervention?

Perhaps we would not feel uncomfortable if the state were to do this to modify behaviour to make people more racially tolerant, for example, or to discourage domestic violence. One might not even feel too uncomfortable with a scheme which attempts to motivate people to earn their income rather than rely on welfare benefits. Is it different when we are dealing with marriage and divorcing behaviour? It may be. The legal provisions themselves [i.e. the FLA 1996, and the substantive law governing children and property division on divorce] have largely moved away from a prescriptive role to a position of neutrality, although they do provide a range of options which are available to protect the vital interests of those who are harmed in their personal lives. This has emerged from gradual acceptance that the way

---

270 Walker (2000), 410.
271 LCD (2001).

people organise their personal lives evolves in response to changing moral, social and economic factors which are not easily controlled by governments. There can, I think, be no objection to the government playing a part, although by no means the sole part, in influencing those factors. We may, however, become uncomfortable when the government intervenes at key points in the institutional processes of marriage and divorce and attempts to impose its own vision of how people should be behaving at those times. At best, it risks being made to appear foolish and ineffectual. Worse, it can appear heavy handed, domineering and insensitive in an area of behaviour to which all citizens have a strong claim to privacy, provided that they do not threaten the clear interests of other individuals. But my main objection is *where it utilises the institutions of law itself to obstruct individuals from access to the rights conferred on them by law.* This could be deeply corrupting of the law itself. We should not forget that both marriage and divorce are *rights* and that post-divorce settlements *do* reflect legal entitlements (however imperfectly expressed in the discretionary system). Disenchantment with some of the excesses of the legal process should never obscure these facts. The role of the legal profession has perhaps never been more important in helping people to negotiate their way through some of the hazards which changing behaviour patterns and an increasingly complex material world visit on them.

5.8.2 CURRENT POLICY INITIATIVES SURROUNDING RELATIONSHIP BREAKDOWN

Despite recent proposals from non-governmental bodies, no reform of divorce law is in prospect and we are left with the MCA 1973, replicated in the CPA 2004, and its many shortcomings. However perfunctory the special procedure may be, couples have no choice but to use the courts to get a divorce (the change of legal status). But the *consequences* of relationship breakdown (divorce or not)—the future upbringing of any children and division of the parties' assets—need not be determined (exclusively) via lawyers or litigation. Despite the demise of Part II of the 1996 Act, non-mandatory information provision, marriage-saving, mediation, and relationship support following divorce therefore remain firmly on the policy agenda. Initiatives focusing on these services are being developed within the existing legislative and procedural framework.

One answer to the information meeting problem is to move it to a much earlier stage: before the wedding.[272] Not least given evidence that many couples about to marry are oblivious of the legal significance of the step that they are taking,[273] there is a strong case for giving engaged couples at least basic *legal* information about their planned change of status when they give notice of their intention to marry or form a civil partnership.[274]

Reconciliation is only paid 'lip service' in the MCA scheme.[275] It was never expected that intervention at such a late stage could save many marriages. But work is being undertaken to develop and publicize the availability of pre-marriage support and marriage counselling, to encourage couples to use counselling as a way of preparing for married life, equipping them to deal with problems in their relationships, and to seek help early when their relationships falter.[276] The aim is to prevent divorce from becoming the place of first resort and counselling

---

[272] Schuz (1993), 631; Davis and Murch (1988), 70; HO (1998), ch 4.
[273] Hibbs, Barton, and Beswick (2001).
[274] HO (1998).
[275] Eekelaar (1991b), 26.
[276] HO (1998) and LCD (2002).

being considered too late for it to be effective in saving marriages. However, even if 'too late' for marriage-saving, it is recognized that counselling can have an important function in helping couples to rebuild a post-divorce relationship as joint parents: moving from 'linked lives to linked futures'. Marriage-saving, or civil partnership-saving, should not therefore be the only measure of success for information provision and relationship support services.[277]

The debate stimulated by the Family Law Act saga about the relative merits of mediation and lawyers as the principal agents for helping couples to reach arrangements regarding their children and property on divorce continues. Although the Government decided not proceed with the main body of the divorce reforms, public funding for mediation was introduced, and various initiatives seek to encourage use of mediation.[278] As we noted at 1.2.7, it has had a prominent place in the 2010 Family Justice Review and in the 2011 consultation on the future of legal aid for private law family cases. However, since mediation depends for its suitability and success on the willingness of both parties to participate, couples cannot be forced in this direction. As Janet Walker observes, 'voluntariness is the central tenet of mediation, and no amount of government or professional "desire" will render it possible, necessary or desirable for large numbers of couples to mediate. Access to justice in its traditional sense must remain.'[279]

It is also important to note that insofar as the concern is to protect the interests of those experiencing relationship instability and breakdown, including children, there is a case for considering how the law—or the provision of services by the state or other agencies—might assist *all* families in that position, not just those whose situation falls within the realms of divorce law. Recent initiatives regarding the provision of information, relationship support, and mediation are therefore directed at cohabitants as well as spouses and civil partners.[280]

 ONLINE RESOURCE CENTRE
For more information on mediation visit the Online Resource Centre.

5.9 CONCLUSION

The British Social Attitudes Survey shows that a large majority think it better to divorce than to continue in an unhappy marriage.[281] However, they would likely be less satisfied with the way in which English law currently handles divorce. As we have seen, English divorce law retains a large fault-based component which is relied upon by most divorcing spouses, at least in part because that secures them a quick divorce. Shortly after the FLA 1996's tenth anniversary, Sir Nicholas Wall—now the President of the Family Division—called for fault-based divorce to be removed. He founded his arguments for no-fault divorce on support for the institution of marriage:

I do believe strongly in the institution of marriage as the best way to bring up children and that's one of the reasons why I would like to end the quick and easy divorces based on the fault system. I think that it actually undermines marriage.[282]

---

277 Newcastle Centre for Family Studies (2004), ch 5.
278 Walsh (2004).
279 Walker (2000), 407.
280 See HO (1998); LCD (2002).
281 Ross and Sacker (2010), table 6.3.
282 Verkaik (2006).

While some want fault to be reinstated in divorce law and beyond, for commentators such as Sir Nicholas Wall, fault simply promotes conflict in a way that is inimical to maintaining good relations post-divorce, and the current system does little to encourage parties to contemplate the consequences of divorce. Whether the FLA 1996 would have been any more successful in encouraging consideration and reflection before divorce is a moot point. It may be some years before the subject of divorce reform is broached again in Parliament. Until then, spouses and now civil partners must continue to use the curious combination[283] of the MCA 1973 (experienced by most couples as fault-based) and its rather less than 'special' procedure, whilst being encouraged (despite their mutual recriminations) to approach divorce constructively to pave the way for a co-operative life after divorce.

ONLINE RESOURCE CENTRE

Questions, suggestions for further reading, and supplementary materials for this chapter (including updates on developments in this area of family law since this book was published) may be found on the Online Resource Centre at **www.oxfordtextbooks.co.uk/orc/harrisshort_tcm2e/.**

---

[283] Cf LCD (1993), para 7.8.

6

FINANCIAL AND PROPERTY PROVISION FOR CHILDREN

CENTRAL ISSUES

1. The principal responsibility for maintaining minor children lies with their legal parents, whether or not the parents were ever married or civil partners.

2. Financial and property provision for children who live apart from one or both parents is dealt with by the Child Maintenance and Enforcement Commission (C-MEC) and the courts.

3. Under the Child Support Act 1991 (CSA 1991), most recently amended by the Child Maintenance and Other Payments Act 2008 (CMOP 2008), C-MEC has principal jurisdiction to secure from non-resident parents payment of regular child maintenance—child support—calculated by reference to a statutory formula.

4. The CSA 1991 originally applied automatically wherever the parent with care of the child was claiming means-tested benefits, diverting much of the maintenance received to reduce the state's welfare bill rather than benefiting the

child. Recent reforms have removed this requirement. Any child maintenance received now goes directly to the parent with care, with no reduction in benefits.

5. The courts have residual jurisdiction to order periodical payments for the benefit of children in certain circumstances. The courts also have exclusive jurisdiction to make capital and property adjustment orders for the benefit of children. They make their decisions pursuant to a wide statutory discretion.

6. Following the 2008 reforms, the focus on private ordering for child maintenance has attracted widespread criticism, not least that the reforms have been driven by concern for operational efficiency rather than any conceptual analysis of children's rights to financial support.

7. Non-resident parents continue to complain that child support and contact decisions are not more closely linked.

6.1 INTRODUCTION

This chapter is concerned with financial support for children who live apart from one or both parents, whether in a lone-parent family, step-family, or with other carers.[1] The development of the law has been driven by the rapid rise in lone-parent families, and the implications for their financial support. In 1971, families headed by lone-parents accounted for only 7 per cent of families with dependent children. Now they make up over a quarter of such households,[2] and feature disproportionately amongst the poorest households.[3] Lone mothers have lower employment rates than other mothers,[4] and are more likely than other parents to claim benefits or tax credits.[5] Since the vast majority of lone parents are *mothers*, the poverty of these families has been regarded as a matter of gender equity.[6] But the issue has recently been conceptualized in terms of child poverty. The Labour Government set itself an ambitious target to eliminate child poverty by 2020, a target adopted by the subsequent Coalition Government.[7]

There are three ways in which child poverty might be alleviated:

- by the state providing direct financial support to children's households, such as benefits and tax credits, and support in kind, such as subsidized child-care facilities to enable parents to work;

- by parents (especially lone mothers) boosting household income via paid employment; and

- where children do not live with both parents, by the parent with whom the child does not mostly live ('non-resident parents', usually men) transferring income and capital to the child's household.

All three routes may be adopted at any one time to varying degrees: determining the proper balance between them is controversial and depends on current political preferences.[8] The basic initial question is whether principal responsibility for children's maintenance, in lone-parents families and otherwise, lies with the state or private individuals. State obligation aside, the key question within the private sphere is how responsibility for supporting children should be allocated between parents who are separated. We shall see that the balance between state and private support has recently altered radically in English law, placing a heavier burden on the state.

The state has an interest in ensuring that parents maintain their children, not only to help reduce child poverty and improve those children's quality of life, but also because if parents fail to maintain their children (whether financially or in terms of practical care), the state may have to do so instead.[9] However, international human rights instruments do not require the state to assume the whole burden. The United Nations Convention on the Rights of the Child 1989 (UNCRC) places primary responsibility for supporting children on parents,

---

[1] We do not address the position of children looked after by the state.

[2] ONS (2010e), 17.

[3] DWP (2009), ch 4.

[4] ONS (2006b), 53–4, ONS (2010e), table 4.3.

[5] Maplethorpe et al (2010), ch 7.

[6] Barnes, Day, and Cronin (1998), 71; see also Flaherty et al (2004), ch 6 on women and poverty; see 3.2.2 above on the economics of intact families.

[7] HM Government (2010), para 14. See also Child Poverty Act 2010; Fortin (2009b), from 337.

[8] See Lewis (1998) and (2000), 94–6 for analysis of recent child support history in these terms. On possible roles for the state, see Eekelaar and Maclean (1986), 107–12.

[9] See 3.8.2 and chapter 12.

and envisages only a 'safety net' function for the state,[10] requiring it to 'take all appropriate measures to secure the recovery of maintenance for the child from the parents or other persons having financial responsibility for the child'.[11]

The Labour Government improved state support for children, increasing child benefit, introducing child tax credit, and extending child-care facilities. But it also sought to reinforce private responsibility to support children by getting more lone parents (including parents of pre-school children) into paid employment. Most recently, the Welfare Reform Act 2009 moved lone parents from income support to jobseeker's allowance, with its rules regarding participation in work-seeking activities. But while employment rates amongst lone parents have increased, most of the jobs obtained have been low-skilled or elementary and therefore low paid: lone parents' earnings may not be enough to lift these families out of poverty.[12] Many parents, especially lone parents, also complain about the continuing lack of affordable, flexible, good quality child-care.[13] The recession that began in 2008 further hampered efforts to improve children's prospects via this route. However, these policies are controversial for denying the social and economic value conferred on society by individuals caring for their own children, and the moral value of choosing to care rather than work.[14] Moreover, the evidence about ensuring good outcomes for children would suggest caution in choosing between full-time parental care and long hours in nursery or some other non-parental child-care.[15]

But whether lone parents are in work or claiming benefits, to what extent can 'non-resident parents' or other private individuals also be expected to contribute to a child's financial support? On whom should private obligations to maintain children be imposed: should the duty arise from legal or social parenthood? What if the legal parent[16] has had no social relationship with the child or no legal relationship with the other parent?[17] We shall see in this chapter that English law imposes principal private financial responsibility for children on their legal parents. That liability is enforced in various ways, and with increasing vehemence, almost regardless of the parents' marital status. But the law provides remedies only for separated families, most commonly where the parents are not living together. Unlike Scottish law, English law generally does not permit children themselves to obtain support from their parents when they are together—and, even when they are apart, strictly limits the right of children themselves to apply for support.

All aspects of financial and property provision for children used to be dealt with by the courts. But the law relating to financial support of children was split in two by the Child Support Act 1991, which largely moved the issue of child maintenance from the courts to an administrative body, formerly the Child Support Agency (CSA), now the C-MEC. Under the latest reforms, where the parents cannot agree on maintenance, C-MEC calculates the regular 'child support' due from the 'non-resident parent' by reference to a rule-based statutory formula and enforces payment. However, the courts retain exclusive jurisdiction, exercising a statutory discretion, to award capital provision and property adjustment for children, and

---

10 See in particular Articles 18, 26, and 27 UNCRC; see Fortin (2009b), 334–5.

11 Article 27(4) UNCRC, referred to in *Smith v Secretary of State for Work and Pensions* [2006] UKHL 35, [77]–[78], per Baroness Hale: she doubted whether Article 8 ECHR entailed the right to receive regular, reasonable maintenance; see also [65], per Lord Walker.

12 Flaherty et al (2004), 168.

13 Gingerbread (2008).

14 Fineman (2004), Family and Parenting Institute (2009).

15 See Fortin (2009b), 340–2.

16 See chapter 9.

17 See 6.7.3. On theories underlying parents' obligations, see Altman (2003); Eekelaar (1991a); Wikeley (2006a), ch 1.

a residual jurisdiction to make periodical payments orders in certain circumstances. The contrasting jurisdictions of C-MEC and courts illustrate the contrast between rules and discretion in family law.[18]

Child support paid under the CSA 1991 is potentially just one part of the jigsaw of financial and property provision for children. But that in turn is often just part of a larger puzzle of financial remedies between separated parents. The importance of financial remedies for the children differs markedly depending on the nature of the parents' relationship. Where the parents were spouses or civil partners, provision for children is part of the package of financial remedies available on divorce/dissolution. We shall see in chapter 7 that the courts have substantial powers to order financial provision and property adjustment between those parents. Where there are dependent children, orders made under that legislation, particularly regarding the family home, are fashioned giving first consideration to those children's welfare. Capital or property orders specifically for the benefit of the child are therefore less necessary (and may not be feasible financially). However, child support is payable as calculated by C-MEC or agreed by the parties and, if there are surplus resources, additional provision for the children—such as payment of school fees—might also be made. By contrast, where the parents were not spouses or civil partners, remedies between the adults are considerably more limited, leaving the primary carers of the children to shoulder alone the potential long-term economic effects of their role, such as reduced earning capacity or pension-savings owing to time taken out of the labour market.[19] Remedies for the benefit of children assume considerable significance in this context, as substantial indirect benefit can accrue to primary carers from financial remedies for the child. However, that indirect benefit ceases once the child becomes independent: child support then ceases to be payable and any court orders benefiting the child terminate, potentially leaving these parents in a precarious economic position.

This area of the law has been in flux for some time, and so we begin this chapter with a brief history, before examining the law as it emerged following the latest statutory reform of child support. That new law places considerable weight on private ordering, and so we consider separately parties' options for making their own arrangements for the financial support of children, together with some other significant themes which emerge from the technical legal material set out earlier in the chapter. The latest reforms effected by the CMOP 2008, which created C-MEC, have not (as of winter 2010) all been implemented, but for the most part we describe the law as it will be once that is done. Some materials included in this chapter which pre-date CMOP 2008 refer to the Child Support Agency, the precursor to C-MEC, but we have edited them to refer to C-MEC. The terms 'child support' and 'child maintenance' are used inter-changeably. Changes to the constitutional position of C-MEC were announced in October 2010 as part of the Coalition Government's review of 'quangos'. The details of those changes, at the time of writing, are unknown. Any substantial changes which affect the discussion in this chapter will be noted in due course on the Online Resource Centre.

 ONLINE RESOURCE CENTRE
Readers wishing to access material on the law pre-CMOP 2008, in particular the treatment of so-called 'public law cases', should visit the Online Resource Centre.

---

[18] See 6.7.5 and 1.2.2.
[19] Maclean and Eekelaar (1993), 215.

6.2 A BRIEF HISTORY OF FINANCIAL PROVISION FOR CHILDREN

6.2.1 PUBLIC AND PRIVATE LAW OBLIGATIONS TO MAINTAIN CHILDREN PRIOR TO 1993

The legal history of child maintenance obligations is complex, related in the following account by Baroness Hale. Nick Wikeley has doubted whether she is correct in asserting a right for the *child* to be maintained, rather than a right for the parent with care to receive maintenance for the child's support.[20] But her survey is nevertheless valuable.

She began her survey with Blackstone, who considered that parents had an obligation to maintain their children as a matter of natural law;[21] but the common law offered no direct means of enforcing it:

R (Kehoe) v Secretary of State for Work and Pensions [2005] UKHL 48

BARONESS HALE:

51. Our law has always recognised the right of a child who is too young to fend for herself to be provided for by her parents. The problem has always been to find an effective method of enforcement. The child was too young to do so and the married mother had no separate right to sue her husband. Hence the machinery of enforcement was laid down in the Poor Laws...[22]

52. But the fact that the father's obligations were measured by the Poor Laws did not mean that the courts of law and equity would ignore them. The principles underlying the later statutory concept of 'wilful neglect to maintain' a wife or child, even the later liability to reimburse the public purse for benefits expended, were those developed by the common law. Hence, just as the husband's common law duty to maintain his wife would normally be discharged by providing the home which they shared, the father's duty to maintain his children would be discharged by providing them with a home...

53. The common law courts would not intrude into the matrimonial relationship, or trespass upon the jurisdiction of the ecclesiastical courts over that relationship, by ordering the husband to make payments to his wife. But a wife who was living with the husband did have the apparent authority to contract as his agent for the expenses of the household. And if they were living apart, the common law recognised her agency of necessity...

54. ...[O]nce it became possible for the wife to obtain custody of a child even against the father's will, the law recognised that her agency of necessity extended to necessaries for a child in her custody as well as for herself.

55. A further recognition by the common law of a duty to maintain was the opinion of the judges that it was an indictable misdemeanour at common law for a person under a duty to provide for an infant of tender years to neglect to do so and thereby injure his health...[See now s 1 of the Children and Young Persons Act 1933.] A parent or person 'legally liable to maintain' a child is deemed to have neglected him for this purpose if he has failed to provide adequate food, clothing, medical aid or lodging, even if he is not living with the child...

---

[20] See Wikeley (2006b), extracted at p 388 below.
[21] Blackstone (1765), book 1, ch XVI.
[22] See extracts in 3.8.2.

Baroness Hale then traced the history of the nineteenth century statutes which first recognized the right in private law of one parent to obtain an order for periodical payments from the other for the child's benefit, both legitimate and illegitimate. These latter statutes were the forerunners of today's private law: the matrimonial and civil partnership legislation in which provision for children is considered alongside that for the adults, and Sch 1 to the Children Act 1989, which also provides for children of unmarried parents. Meanwhile, the successors of the Poor Laws retained the public law 'liable relative' procedure, enabling the state to recoup welfare benefits from relevant family members, here the non-resident parent of the child, whether or not the parents were married.[23] The operation of these laws in the 1970s and 1980s generated the political case for the child support legislation of 1991.

62. It was...intended that the receipt of national assistance, later to become supplementary benefit, and later still income support, should not carry a stigma. As Dr Stephen Cretney relates...in keeping with this new entitlement-based approach the benefit authorities changed their policy about seeking recovery from liable relatives. Instead of routinely seeking this, they would try to reach an agreement with the husband or father, and accept any offer which they considered reasonable. Rather than take proceedings themselves, they would encourage the mother to do so. The disadvantage for the mother was that she would then not know from week to week how much benefit she would get, because it all depended how much maintenance the husband or father had paid that week. The sensible solution eventually found was that she would assign or 'divert' any payment made into the magistrates' court to the benefit authorities. They could then issue her with an order book which she could safely cash each week. Although the benefit authorities retained their power to seek recovery from the liable relative, in practice this was rarely done even in cases where the mother had, for whatever reason, chosen not to bring proceedings.

63. It was scarcely surprising that the courts would have this changed climate in mind when deciding what orders for financial provision should be made. They were not supposed to take means-tested benefits into account as a resource available to the wife and mother, but neither were they supposed to order a sum which would reduce the husband and father's income below that which he would receive for himself and his new family were he also on benefit: see *Barnes v Barnes* [1972] 1 WLR 1381....

64. It became common for divorcing parties to agree a 'clean break', in which the wife and children would retain the family home, where the mortgage interest would be met by the benefit authorities, while the husband was relieved of any further maintenance liabilities...The fact that there were still both private and public law liabilities to maintain the children receded into the background, especially as the risk that the benefit authorities would proceed against the absent parent were so slim...

6.2.2 THE BIRTH, DEVELOPMENT, AND DEMISE OF THE CHILD SUPPORT AGENCY, 1993–2008

The creation of the Child Support Agency and the maintenance regime for which it was responsible by the CSA 1991 was motivated by various economic and moral concerns. The first was that those formally liable to support children were not doing so, leaving the

---

[23] See extracts in 3.8.2.

state to foot the resulting welfare benefits bill for the burgeoning population of lone-parent families.[24] The evidence suggested that non-resident parents were not significantly contributing to children's support either via private law maintenance orders or through the liable relative procedure for recouping welfare benefits. As Bradshaw and Millar recorded, there were good reasons for the decline in use of the liable relative procedure, not least the 1980s recession and the growth in births out of wedlock, which made it harder to identify the fathers; enforcement action was therefore unlikely to prove cost-effective. Mothers claiming benefits were not penalized for failing to cooperate in any endeavours made by the state to obtain maintenance from the father.[25] But nor did mothers have any incentive to assist the benefit authorities or bring private law proceedings: where maintenance orders *were* made, they rarely exceeded mothers' benefits entitlements, so simply reduced their benefits, leaving them and their children no better off than they would have been without maintenance from the father.[26]

This fuelled political arguments about 'welfare dependency' and its cost to the state, underpinned by concerns—exploded by research, but tenacious nevertheless—that the situation was incentivizing lone-motherhood. It was time, it was thought, for lone mothers' welfare benefits to be reduced by pursuing non-resident parents more vigorously for maintenance. Economic concerns coincided with moral concerns, also generated by the rises in divorce and lone-parenthood,[27] as this extract from a speech given by Margaret Thatcher reveals:

Prime Minister Margaret Thatcher, National Children's Homes George Thomas Society lecture, January 1990[28]

[W]hen one of the parents not only walks away from marriage but neither maintains nor shows any interest in the child, an enormous unfair burden is placed on the other. Nearly four out of five lone mothers claiming income support received no maintenance from the fathers. No father should be able to escape from his responsibility and that is why the Government is looking at ways of strengthening the system for tracing an absent father and making the arrangements for recovering maintenance more effective.

'Parenthood is for life' was the new soundbite; 'feckless fathers' were the new scapegoats.[29]

The response was the CSA 1991, quickly enacted with cross-party support. Despite the benefit authorities' apparent tolerance of lone parents' past reliance on benefits, it was decided that a new administrative body—the Child Support Agency—should become responsible for extracting regular child maintenance from non-resident parents, instead of the courts.[30] The maintenance payable by 'absent parents' to 'parents with care' for their children would be calculated with a statutory formula, rather than on a discretionary, case-by-case basis. This would 'produce consistent and predictable results', with prompt collection, enforcement,

---

[24] Bradshaw and Millar (1991), 64.
[25] Ibid., 78–9.
[26] Law Com (1982b), para 3.24.
[27] Maclean and Eekelaar (1993), 210–11.
[28] Extracted in Cretney (2003a), 474.
[29] Contrast the contemporaneous discussion of unmarried fathers and parental responsibility: 10.3.3.
[30] For a detailed history, see Wikeley (2006a), ch 5.

and payment of maintenance to parents with care, organized by a single authority.[31] The courts would largely be confined to making capital orders.

A central part of the system was that the Agency took jurisdiction over cases in which lone parents were claiming benefits, effectively replacing the liable relative procedure. This was intended to ensure that welfare payments made to parents with care were reimbursed by the liable non-resident parents. Benefits cases constituted the vast bulk of the Agency's caseload, clearly suggesting that the priority lay in cutting welfare benefit expenditure.[32]

The Agency was hampered from the outset by chronic administrative problems[33] and the vociferous opposition[34] of 'absent parents' and, to a lesser extent, parents with care.[35] 'Absent parents' had many complaints, not least the label 'absent' which implied that they played no role in their children's lives; the terminology was later changed to 'non-resident parent'. Many non-resident parents had second families or had made 'clean break' settlements on divorce,[36] and those who had previously been paying little or no maintenance claimed to be suffering hardship owing to the higher levels of maintenance now required.[37] The original Act's complex formula required large amounts of information and staff time to administer, was difficult to understand, and produced assessments which were frequently wrong and even more frequently challenged, or simply not paid. Legal aid not being available for legal representation in dealing with the Agency and appeal tribunals, many parents had to cope without a lawyer.[38] Many non-resident parents responded by simply resisting payment, which was unfortunate given that the investment of staff time on assessment left few resources for enforcement. The formula was simplified considerably and some limited discretion introduced—though not for cases already in the system. Having to operate different assessment systems for different cases depending on when they entered the system compounded the Agency's woes, as did a diabolical IT system.[39]

Described as 'one of the greatest public administration disasters of recent times',[40] the Agency never met its creators' expectations. The system continued to be dogged by severe administrative difficulties,[41] high running costs, and low rates of maintenance recovery. Reform was announced in 2006, following a review by Sir David Henshaw.[42]

6.2.3 THE BIRTH OF C-MEC

C-MEC, accompanied by a radically reformed child support system—again with cross-party support—emerged following the Henshaw recommendations.

---

[31] DSS (1990), paras 5.1–5.2.
[32] Cf Wikeley (2006a), 129–30.
[33] Ibid., 126–33.
[34] See generally Diduck (2003), ch 7; Fortin (2009b), 346–7; and Davis et al (1998).
[35] See Glendinning et al (1994).
[36] See 7.6.2 and 6.6.2.
[37] Wallbank (1997), Collier (1994).
[38] Davis et al (1998), 126.
[39] On the operational problems, see Henshaw (2006), paras 18–20.
[40] Family Law Week (2007).
[41] Wikeley (2006a), 140–3.
[42] Henshaw (2006); DWP (2006b).

D. Henshaw, *Recovering child support: routes to responsibility* (London: TSO, 2006)

12. Improving enforcement of social norms and responsibilities was a key objective in the creation of the CSA. This was in response to the low levels of lone parents receiving maintenance. However, 16 years later the figures have barely improved. Although many non-resident parents do take financial responsibility for their children and pay regular maintenance, there is a widespread belief amongst others that it is possible and, in some cases, acceptable to avoid paying. This contributes to the fact that only around 30 per cent of parents with care are receiving any maintenance at all. Compliance with arrangements made through the CSA is lower than for arrangements made through other routes.

13. Cost-efficiency for the taxpayer has consistently been poor. In 2004/05, the CSA recovered £120 million in Income Support expenditure against costs of £425 million. In the region of £80 million was saved through other routes. Therefore, the system runs at a net cost to the taxpayer of around £200 million. There is also outstanding debt, in the form of unpaid maintenance, of over £3 billion.... One of the reasons for poor cost-efficiency is that...only a very small proportion of the Agency's caseload has the potential to recover funds for the state (that is a case with a positive liability where the parent with care is on benefits).

The Henshaw Report identified several policy and operational problems. The recommendations were radical.

D. Henshaw, *Recovering child support: routes to responsibility* (London: TSO, 2006), 4–5

- At the moment, all parents with care claiming benefits are forced to use the Child Support Agency to agree maintenance. Around 70 per cent of new applicants are required to use the Agency. This requirement prevents parents from making private arrangements between themselves. As a result, it creates a large group of clients who do not wish to use the service.

- Reducing benefit entitlement pound for pound against maintenance collected means that neither parent has an incentive to co-operate with the Child Support Agency. Parents with care can see little or no increase in income and non-resident parents see money paid going to the state, not to their children.

- The complex nature of the cases makes it difficult for the system to keep up. Many of the clients have difficult situations with volatile income, regular movements in and out of work and complicated personal relationships....

Key recommendations

- The state should only get involved when parents cannot come to agreement themselves, or when one party tries to evade their responsibilities. Removing the barriers that currently prevent some parents from making their own arrangements would allow the state to focus on the more difficult cases and where effective enforcement is needed.

- Parents who are able to should be encouraged and supported to make their own arrangements. Such arrangements tend to result in higher satisfaction and compliance and allow individual circumstances to be reflected. We should end the policy of forcing all parents with care claiming certain benefits to use the Child Support Agency.

- Those who want a private arrangement to be legally enforceable would be able to obtain a consent order. This operation should be available to all parents. Those unable to use other routes would have access to the government back-up service.

- Allowing most parents with care to keep the maintenance paid would encourage both parents to co-operate, increasing the maintenance going to children.

- Safeguards can be introduced to prevent those parents with care in receipt of significant amounts of maintenance from also having full access to state benefits.

The Government immediately accepted many of these recommendations. Of the radical change in the treatment of parents with care on benefits and the raising of the maintenance disregard, a 'virtual abandonment' of the original CSA policy,[43] it said:

Hansard, *Official Report*—Ministerial Statement on Child Support Redesign

Hansard HC Deb, vol 449, cols 597–9, 24 July 2006

The Secretary of State for Work and Pensions (Mr. John Hutton):

Both those changes will help more families to receive more maintenance and reduce the risk of child poverty. They reflect both the rights of children to be properly maintained by their parents and the right of society to ensure that parental responsibilities are properly discharged. We also agree that the delivery of child support requires a fresh start. We will therefore create a new organisation to replace the CSA and we will strengthen enforcement powers.

The White Paper preceding the Bill that was to become CMOP 2008 set out 'four new principles' for a reformed child maintenance system. Compare these principles with the Secretary of State's remarks in the extract above: any reference to a right of the *child* is gone:

DWP, *A new system of child maintenance*, Cm 6979 (London: TSO, 2006b), paras 15–16

- **help tackle child poverty** by ensuring that more parents take responsibility for paying for their children and that more children benefit from this;

- **promote parental responsibility** by encouraging and empowering parents to make their own maintenance arrangements wherever possible, but taking firm action – through a **tough and effective enforcement regime** – to enforce payment where necessary;

- **provide a cost-effective and professional service** that gets money flowing between parents in the most efficient way for the taxpayer; and

- **be simple and transparent,** providing an accessible, reliable and responsive service that is understood and accepted by parents and their advisers and is capable of being administered by staff.

[43] Fehlberg and Maclean (2009).

These four principles refocus the child maintenance system on meeting the needs of children. They make tackling child poverty the first and most critical test for reform, and they establish and enforce clear rights and responsibilities – the right of a person to make a claim and the resulting responsibility of the non-resident parent to pay.

And so was born C-MEC in the CMOP 2008, in turn amended in some important respects shortly afterwards by the Welfare Reform Act 2009. It is the law as stated following those statutes—much of it contained in a heavily amended CSA 1991—that we discuss in the next parts of this chapter.

6.3 OVERVIEW OF THE CURRENT LAW

The law governing financial and property provision for children is contained in several statutes whose inter-relationship is complex. In order to get an overview, it is helpful to divide the topic along two lines: (i) the identity of the children involved and their relationship with the potential payer; (ii) the type of remedy sought: see fig 6.1.

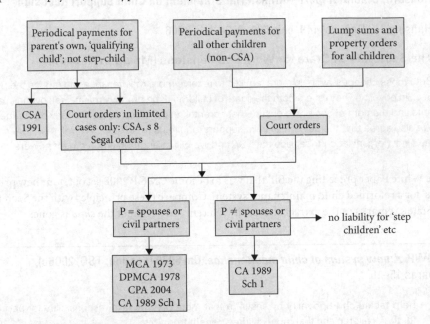

Figure 6.1 Financial and property provision for children

6.3.1 THE PARTIES' RELATIONSHIPS

Like most areas of contemporary child law, financial and property provision is almost blind to parents' marital status. What matters is the legal parent–child relationship. Parents' liability for their own children must be distinguished from the liability of step- and other social parents in relation to other 'children of the family'. Only spouses and civil partners may be liable to provide for children other than their own. Step-parental liability does not arise in cohabiting relationships,[44] or following a joint enterprise in creating a child by

---

[44] Children Act 1989 (CA 1989), s 105; Matrimonial Causes Act 1973 (MCA 1973), s 52; Civil Partnership Act 2004 (CPA 2004), s 72.

artificial insemination from which legal parenthood did not arise,[45] even if the non-parent has parental responsibility for the child via a residence order.

6.3.2 C-MEC OR COURT?

The law treats periodical payments and other forms of relief, such as lump sum and property adjustment orders, very differently. The courts have exclusive jurisdiction over the latter. C-MEC has principal jurisdiction over periodical payments for parents' *own* children under the CSA 1991. The court may only order periodical payments in limited circumstances: where C-MEC lacks jurisdiction in parent-child cases, in relation to step-children and others who are not the respondent's child, and where the CSA 1991 explicitly permits it. We examine the child support legislation in 6.4 and the courts' jurisdiction in 6.5.

6.4 CHILD SUPPORT: THE CURRENT LAW

The law relating to child support is highly technical.[46] The situation is complicated by the fact that there are several categories of case within the child support system, all subject to different rules: cases pre-dating 1993, cases which arose between 1993 and 2003, cases dating from March 2003, and—in due course—cases that will be decided under the new formula introduced by CMOP 2008, due to come into force from 2011 and to which existing cases may be migrated. We examine that most recent law, in anticipation of its full implementation; some aspects of CMOP 2008, which apply to all cases whenever they arose, are already in force.

The primary legislation is often framed in general terms, conferring a power for regulations to be made or rather opaquely referring to 'prescribed' matters. We therefore have to examine secondary legislation that fleshes out the Act and defines many of the terms used; where those regulations refer to 'the Secretary of State' performing various functions which have now been transferred to C-MEC,[47] we have edited the extracts accordingly.

6.4.1 THE RELEVANT PARTIES

We begin by identifying the parties relevant to child support claims: the 'qualifying child'; the 'non-resident parent'; the 'person with care'; and 'relevant other children'. The Act ordinarily applies only where each of the first three is habitually resident in the United Kingdom.[48]

The 'qualifying child'

First, the Act only applies if the child for whom support is sought meets the definition of 'child' in s 55. If the child fails to meet these criteria, the courts may instead have jurisdiction over child maintenance. In broad outline, a 'child' for these purposes is anyone under the age of 16; and anyone under the age of 20[49] who is either in full-time non-advanced education (i.e. below degree level), or is registered for (but has not commenced) work or

[45] *T v B* [2010] EWHC 1444; cf the new agreed parenthood provisions in the Human Fertilisation and Embryology Act 2008, discussed at 9.4.3.

[46] For detailed treatment see Bird and Burrows (2009) and CPAG's Child Support Handbook for the current year.

[47] CMOP 2008, s 13(3) and Schs 2–3.

[48] CSA 1991, s 44.

[49] As at October 2010, the ceiling is 19, rather than 20, CMOP 2008, s 42 (which amends CSA 1991, s 55) not yet being in force

work-based learning.[50] If the individual is or has been a spouse or civil partner (including in a void union), he or she is not a 'child' in this context.[51] In order to be a 'qualifying' child, s 3 provides that it must be shown that either one or both of his parents is in relation to him a 'non-resident parent'. Child support is therefore not payable within intact families: the child must be separated from at least one parent.

The 'non-resident parent'

The child's qualifying status turns on having at least one non-resident parent. 'Parent' is defined by s 54 as 'any person who is in law the mother or father of the child'.[52] The CSA 1991 does not cover step-parents, from whom maintenance can only be obtained through the courts. The other key point is that no significance is attached to the relationship, if any, between the parents; they need never have married, cohabited, or had any substantial relationship. The bare fact of legal parentage suffices.

A parent is a 'non-resident' parent under s 3(2) if:

(a) that parent is not living in the same household with the child; and

(b) the child has his home with a person who is, in relation to him, a person with care.

'Not living in the same household' may include parents who live under the same roof as the child but maintain a separate household from the child and person with care.[53]

The 'person with care'

3(3) A person is a "person with care", in relation to any child, if he is a person—

(a) with whom the child has his home;

(b) who usually provides day to day care for the child (whether exclusively or in conjunction with any other person); and

(c) who does not fall within a prescribed category of person.

(4) The Secretary of State shall not, under subsection (3)(c), prescribe as a category—

(a) parents;

(b) guardians;

(c) persons in whose favour residence orders under section 8 of the Children Act 1989 are in force . . .

(5) For the purposes of this Act there may be more than one person with care in relation to the same qualifying child. . . .

The regulations made under s 3(3)(c) exclude local authorities and their foster parents from the scope of 'person with care'.[54]

---

[50] Child Support (Maintenance Calculation Procedure) Regulations 2000, SI 2001/157, Sch 1, as amended for the current age limit of 19. For detailed rules, see CPAG (current year), ch 2.3

[51] CSA 1991, s 55(2), (3).

[52] See chapter 9.

[53] See 5.5.5 for interpretation of the equivalent expression in divorce law.

[54] Child Support (Maintenance Calculation Procedure) Regulations 2000, SI 2001/157, reg 21. SI 2001/155 reg 9 deals with the payment of maintenance where care is shared between a person with care and the local authority.

The terminology of 'non-resident parent' and 'person/parent with care' is unsatisfactory. It has been a source of grievance for fathers where separated parents have a shared residence arrangement for the child. Both parents might claim to be 'persons with care', even if any residence order is in the name of one parent only. The following rule applies where two or more people who do not live in the same household each provide day to day care for the child:[55]

Child Support (Maintenance Calculations and Special Cases) Regulations 2000, SI 2001/155, reg 8

(2) . . a parent who provides day to day care for a child of his is to be treated as a non-resident parent for the purposes of the Act in the following circumstances—

(a) a parent who provides such care to a lesser extent than the other parent, person or persons who provide such care for the child in question; or

(b) where [those caring for the child] include both parents and the circumstances are such that care is provided to the same extent by both but each provides care to an extent greater than or equal to any other person who provides such care for that child—

(i) the parent who is not in receipt of child benefit[56] for the child in question; or

(ii) if neither parent is in receipt of child benefit for that child, the parent who, in the opinion of [C-MEC], will not be the principal provider of day to day care for that child. . . .

'Day to day care' is defined, broadly speaking, to mean care of not fewer than 104 nights in a 12-month period.[57]

The 'relevant other child'

The existence of a 'relevant other child' may impact on the amount of child support payable in respect of qualifying children. A child is 'relevant' if the non-resident parent or his partner with whom he shares a household (whether as spouses, civil partners, or cohabitants of the opposite or same sex) receive child benefit in relation to that child.[58]

6.4.2 GENERAL PRINCIPLES

Child Support Act 1991, s 1

The duty to maintain

(1) For the purposes of this Act, each parent of a qualifying child is responsible for maintaining him.

(2) For the purposes of this Act, a non-resident parent shall be taken to have met his responsibility to maintain any qualifying child of his by making periodical payments of maintenance

---

[55] *C v Secretary of State for Work and Pensions and B* [2002] EWCA Civ 1854.
[56] See Social Security Contributions and Benefits Act 1992, Sch 10, para 5 and Child Benefit (General) Regulations, SI 2006/223, Part 3: rules regarding payment of child benefit.
[57] Child Support (Maintenance Calculations and Special Cases) Regulations 2000, SI 2001/155, reg 1.
[58] Sch 1, para 10C.

> with respect to the child of such amount, and at such intervals, as may be determined in accordance with the provisions of this Act.
>
> (3) Where a maintenance calculation made under this Act requires the making of periodical payments, it shall be the duty of the non-resident parent with respect to whom the calculation is made to make those payments.

While the Act closely defines non-resident parents' duties, it says nothing about how parents with care discharge their maintenance responsibility. But it is implicit in the Act—and in the formula for calculating non-resident parents' liability—that parents with care fulfil their duty by virtue of caring for the child.

Unlike the rest of child law, there is no general welfare principle in the CSA 1991. Given the rule-based rather than discretionary nature of the Act, that is perhaps unsurprising. Where C-MEC does have discretion, for example with regard to variations from the formula or in taking enforcement action, a welfare principle applies. The principle is relatively weak, requiring only that 'regard' be had to the child's welfare, not paramount or even first consideration. But it is wide ranging: the welfare of *any* child likely to be affected must be considered, not just that of the qualifying child and 'relevant other children'.[59]

6.4.3 ROUTES TO RECEIVING CHILD MAINTENANCE

Until recently, there were two categories of application for child support: 'public law' or 'benefits' cases concerning parents with care who were claiming relevant means-tested benefits, and 'private law' cases under CSA 1991, s 4. Maintenance was calculated on the same basis in both, but the cases reached the Agency (as it then was) via different routes and the means of payment to persons with care might differ. All change with CMOP 2008 and the arrival of C-MEC. The public/private distinction has been removed (this reform is already in effect), and private arrangements are encouraged.

Reform of benefits cases

Prior to the radical reforms effected by CMOP 2008, parents with care receiving certain means-tested welfare benefits were compelled to cooperate with the Agency in securing maintenance from the non-resident parent. Those who refused to cooperate risked a substantial cut in their benefits unless they could show 'good cause' for doing so; this was a particular issue for victims of domestic violence.[60] The small consolation offered to parents with care who cooperated was that they would be permitted to retain the first £10 per week of total maintenance recovered from the non-resident parent, regardless of the number of children; the balance (up to the value of their benefits) went to the state.

ONLINE RESOURCE CENTRE

Readers who require further information on the pre-CMOP 2008 treatment of these cases are directed to the materials on the Online Resource Centre.

---

[59] CSA 1991, s 2.
[60] See CSA 1991, ss 6 and 46.

The most radical reforms effected by CMOP 2008 were the removal of all compulsion on parents with care and the introduction of a *total* maintenance disregard. For completeness, the liable relative rule was also abolished as it applied to the support of children.[61] This profoundly alters the roles of non-resident parents and state in supporting children: the state now provides a basic level of support (via income support/jobseeker's allowance and/or tax credits) wherever parents with care claim benefits, and the contribution (if any) of non-resident parents, rather than relieving the state of this burden, entirely supplements the parent with care's income. As Henshaw observed, this policy could make an immediate and significant contribution to the target to eliminate child poverty.[62] But that will depend on how many non-resident parents pay maintenance, and that will depend on the wisdom of moving principally to a system of private ordering.

A new emphasis on private ordering

The other key plank of the Henshaw recommendations was that all parents with care should enjoy the freedom to reach a private agreement with non-resident parents for child support. That freedom was always enjoyed in private cases—CMOP 2008 simply extends it across the board. Since parties negotiating privately will often wish to bargain 'in the shadow of the law', we first examine the law that would apply were they not to reach agreement. We shall then address the detailed legal framework for private ordering in this area and its practical implications at 6.6 and 6.7.2 below.

Application to C-MEC where agreement fails

No one is now *obliged* to apply to C-MEC. If the parties cannot reach agreement or become dissatisfied with an agreement reached earlier, either can apply to C-MEC for a maintenance calculation under the CSA 1991, s 4. The one person who cannot apply for a maintenance calculation (other than in Scotland[63]) is the qualifying child.

Duties to supply information

Section 4(4) of the CSA 1991 requires applicants to C-MEC to provide information necessary to trace the non-resident parent and facilitate the calculation and recovery of child support. Sections 14 to 15 of the CSA 1991 and associated regulations[64] oblige a wide range of individuals and agencies to provide particular categories of information, regarding non-resident parents' whereabouts, income, and circumstances. C-MEC's inspectors have statutory powers to enter certain premises (other than dwellings) and make inquiries in order to obtain required information. Failure to comply is an offence punishable by fine.

Disputes about parentage

Child support applications sometimes trigger disputes regarding parentage, usually paternity.

---

[61] For criticism, see Wikeley (2008).
[62] Henshaw (2006), para 24.
[63] CSA 1991, s 7.
[64] Child Support Information Regulations 2008, SI 2008/2551.

Child Support Act 1991, s 26

Disputes about parentage

(1) Where a person who is alleged to be a parent of the child with respect to whom an application for a maintenance calculation has been made or treated as made ("the alleged parent") denies that he is one of the child's parents, the Commission shall not make a maintenance calculation on the assumption that the alleged parent is one of the child's parents unless the case falls within one of those set out in subsection (2).

The cases set out in subsection (2) correspond with categories of parentage, and means of establishing it, recognized throughout child law:[65]

- the presumption that the husband of the mother from conception to birth is the father;
- the presumption that the man registered as the father on the child's birth certificate is the father;
- positive results from, or inferences derived from refusals to participate in, scientific testing to determine parentage;
- adoptive parenthood;
- parenthood derived in the context of assisted reproduction under the Human Fertilisation and Embryology Act 1990 (HFEA 1990) or 2008; and
- declarations of parentage made under the Family Law Act 1986 (FLA 1986), and findings of paternity made in the course, principally, of CA 1989 proceedings.

If none of those cases applies, the person with care or C-MEC may apply to the court under the FLA 1986 for a declaration of parentage. The court is likely to direct scientific tests, whose outcome may bring the case within the third category above.[66] In practice, applicants are expected to resolve paternity disputes before applying to C-MEC.[67]

6.4.4 THE MAINTENANCE CALCULATION

One of the chief operational changes recommended by Henshaw and adopted in CMOP 2008 related to the formula whereby child support is calculated. It is not expected that the new formula will come into effect until 2011 at the earliest, but we describe the law as it will be under that new system.

ONLINE RESOURCE CENTRE

Readers who require information based on the formula in operation for so-called 'new' cases (arising post-2003) pending implementation of the CMOP formula are directed to the discussion on the Online Resource Centre.

---

[65] See chapter 9.
[66] *F v Child Support Agency* [1999] 2 FLR 244.
[67] Boden and Childs (1996), 152.

Different rates apply depending on the non-resident parent's income and status. Where C-MEC has insufficient information to make the proper calculation immediately, it may make a default calculation, which requires payment at a set rate based on average income: £30 per week for one child, £40 for two, £50 for three or more.[68] Non-resident parents may make voluntary payments exceeding these amounts where they anticipate that the eventual calculation will be higher and wish to prevent the accumulation of arrears.[69]

Basing the calculation on gross historic income

Under the pre-CMOP system, child support is normally calculated as a fixed percentage (depending on the number of qualifying children) of the non-resident parent's current net income. Henshaw recommended a formula which would yield largely the same figures, but based—for (hoped for) administrative ease[70]—on the non-resident parent's *gross* income for the *last* year. Under CMOP, the calculation will therefore be based on historic gross weekly earned[71] income (based on the non-resident parent's tax return for the previous year). In theory, income in a past tax year is a known, fixed amount, provided via the tax authorities, which should speed up assessment considerably. The calculation will provide an amount payable for the current year, and not require regular revision as circumstances change.[72] However, non-resident parents' income for the last tax year may be very different—higher or lower—than their current income. Non-resident parents who experience a substantial drop in income may struggle to pay a bill calculated on this basis. It is therefore proposed that where the difference in income is 25 per cent or greater, current income data will be used instead.[73] C-MEC's administrative burden may be eased by such a high threshold having to be passed before calculations have to be revised. But it may pose significant trouble for non-resident parents caught by the legacy of past riches falling just below that threshold, who may find their payments unaffordable.[74]

The basic rate[75]

The basic rate applies to non-resident parents with gross weekly incomes over £200. The formula is a fraction of that income, depending on the number of qualifying children. For the first £800 of gross income, non-resident parents must pay 12 per cent of income for one qualifying child, 16 per cent for two qualifying children, and 19 per cent for three or more.[76] Additional income between £800 and £3,000 is subject to a basic rate of 9 per cent for one, 12 per cent for two, and 15 per cent for three or more qualifying children. Income

---

[68] Child Support (Maintenance Calculation Procedure) Regulations 2000, SI 2001/157, reg 7. This also applies pending revisions and supersessions: see 6.4.8.

[69] CSA 1991, s 28J; Child Support (Voluntary Payments) Regulations 2000, SI 2000/3177; child support is generally payable from the date on which the non-resident parent is (or would have been, but for his or her intentional avoidance) notified of the application to C-MEC.

[70] DWP (2006b), ch 4; cf the cautionary notes sounded by Wikeley (2007a), paras 19–21.

[71] Self-employed non-resident parents who can divert income from earned into unearned sources pose significant challenges: *Smith v Secretary of State for Work and Pensions* [2006] UKHL 35; Wikeley (2007a), paras 19–21.

[72] DWP (2007b), para 16.3.

[73] DWP (2006b), para 25.

[74] See Work and Pensions Select Committee (2007), paras 125–34; DWP (2007b), para 16.

[75] CSA 1991, Sch 1, para 2.

[76] CMOP 2008, Sch 4. Cf CSA 1991, Sch 1.

over £3,000 per week is ignored, as is the income of the parent with care and any partner of either parent. As we shall see below, income above the £3,000 threshold can be the subject of court-ordered periodical payments.[77]

The CMOP formula and its staged nature across different income levels were required to keep maintenance bills largely the same following the shift to gross income. But it is rather less arithmetically neat than the pre-CMOP formula based on all net income up to £2,000, under which non-resident parents paid 15 per cent of net income for one qualifying child, 20 per cent for two, and 25 per cent for three or more. The new figures are rather less easy to remember and apply, which will make private ordering to that extent more burdensome.

Cases where the non-resident parent has 'relevant other children'

If the non-resident parent has one or more 'relevant other children', the gross income is reduced (by 12, 16, or 19 per cent, according to the number of such children) before the basic rate percentage is applied to the remainder. This formula was adopted instead of a proposal that the basic rate be applied to all qualifying and relevant children of the non-resident parent, and for the maintenance to be apportioned equally between them.[78]

The reduced rate[79]

The reduced rate applies to non-resident parents on gross incomes of between £100 and £200 per week, and to whom neither the flat nor the nil rate applies. Regulations set the rate: they pay £7 for the first £100, and then a set percentage (different from the basic rate percentages) over the remaining amount, depending on the number of any relevant other children.

The flat rate[80]

A flat rate of £7 per week is payable by non-residents parents who earn less than £100 per week or who (or whose partners) are on one of several prescribed benefits, pensions, or allowances. Where the non-resident parent's partner[81] is also a non-resident parent in respect of whom a maintenance calculation is in force and who receives one of the prescribed benefits, each is required to pay just half the flat rate. Even those living on benefits are required to accept some financial responsibility for their children.[82]

The nil rate[83]

The nil rate applies to non-resident parents with gross weekly incomes of £7 or less, and those who fall into one of several categories prescribed in regulations, including students,

---

[77] 6.5.2 on 'top-up' orders.

[78] DSS (1999), paras 2.9–2.15.

[79] CSA 1991, Sch 1, para 3 and Child Support (Maintenance Calculations and Special Cases) Regulations 2000, SI 2001/155, reg 3.

[80] Ibid., Sch 1, para 4 and SI 2001/155, reg 4.

[81] As defined in Sch 1, para 10(C)(4) and (5).

[82] Barnes et al (1998), 66 view this as an expensive public relations exercise, since the costs of collecting this sum generally outweigh the income received.

[83] CSA 1991, Sch 1, para 5 and Child Support (Maintenance Calculations and Special Cases) Regulations 2000, SI 2001/155, reg 5.

children,[84] prisoners, and those aged 16–17 who receive certain means-tested benefits or whose partner does so.[85]

Apportionment

What happens where non-resident parents have qualifying children by two or more partners, and each child lives with his or her other parent?

Child Support Act 1991, Sch 1, para 6

(1) If the non-resident parent has more than one qualifying child and in relation to them there is more than one person with care, the amount of child support maintenance payable is (subject to [rules regarding shared care]) to be determined by apportioning the rate between the persons with care.

(2) The rate of maintenance liability is to be divided by the number of qualifying children, and shared among the persons with care according to the number of qualifying children in relation to whom each is a person with care.

Shared care

It may sometimes be difficult, or seem erroneous, to identify one parent as 'non-resident' where the child spends time with both, perhaps under a shared residence order or order for staying contact.[86] This is reflected in basic and reduced rate cases by a pro rata deduction in the notionally non-resident parent's liability. The amount of reduction depends on the number of nights the child spends with the non-resident parent:

Child Support Act 1991, Sch 1, para 7[87]

(1) This paragraph applies only if the rate of child support maintenance payable is the basic rate or reduced rate [or is determined under special rules applicable to certain maintenance agreements, under para 5A].

(2) If the care of the qualifying child is, or is to be, shared between the non-resident parent and the person with care, so that the non-resident parent from time to time has care of the child overnight, the amount of child support maintenance which he would otherwise have been liable to pay the person with care [as calculated above] is to be decreased in accordance with this paragraph.

(3) First, there is to be a decrease according to the number of such nights which the Commission determines there to have been, or expects there to be, or both during a prescribed twelve-month period.

---

[84] As defined in s 55(1), above.
[85] See SI 2001/155, reg 5 for complete list, and reg 1 for definition of terms.
[86] See 11.4.5 and 11.5.
[87] Supplemented by SI 2001/155, reg 7.

(4) The amount of that decrease for one child is set out in the following Table—

Number of nights	Fraction to subtract
52 to 103	One-seventh
104 to 155	Two-sevenths
156 to 174	Three-sevenths
175 or more	One-half

(5) If the person with care is caring for more than one qualifying child of the non-resident parent, the applicable decrease is the sum of the appropriate fractions in the Table divided by the number of such qualifying children.

(6) If the applicable fraction is one-half in relation to any qualifying child in the care of the person with care, the total amount payable to the person with care is then to be further decreased by £7 for each such child.[88]

(7) If the application of the preceding provisions of this paragraph would decrease the weekly amount of child support maintenance (or the aggregate of all such amounts) payable by the non-resident parent to the person with care (or all of them) to less than £7, he is instead liable to pay child maintenance at the rate of £7 per week, apportioned (if appropriate) in accordance with paragraph 6.

In flat rate cases, the fact of shared care for at least 52 nights over 12 months reduces the £7 assessment to nil.[89]

The issue of shared care was considered by Henshaw and the following consultation process. Consultees to the White Paper had mixed views. One group in particular, Families Need Fathers, have argued that the shared care rules should be abolished in order better to recognize and promote shared parenting and the costs incurred by the 'non-resident' parent.[90] Henshaw and the Work and Pensions Select Committee advocated no liability in cases where care is shared 50:50.[91] But in the event, the rules were tweaked only slightly to allow maintenance to be determined on the basis of the *expected* level of shared care.

The facts of *R (Plumb) v Secretary of State for Work and Pensions*[92] demonstrate the unfairness of the old rules[93] (under which 104 nights per annum attracted a deduction) and the potential unfairness of the current rules. The non-resident father, who was unemployed and receiving jobseeker's allowance, provided substantial amounts of care for the child under contact arrangements involving frequent staying contact (but fewer than 104 nights per annum) and considerable after-school and weekend day-care and meals. The re-partnered mother was earning £15,000 in her full-time job, which provided tied accommodation. The father's liability could not be reduced to reflect this arrangement. Under the current law, there would be a deduction for shared care (and since this would now be a flat rate case, Mr Plumb would receive a nil assessment). But that deduction would only apply in relation

---

[88] See DSS (1999), para 7.17: this effectively shares the child benefit paid to the person with care.

[89] CSA 1991, Sch 1, para 8.

[90] Families Need Fathers (2007). Note also that child benefit and child tax credit cannot be shared. See also Gilmore (2007).

[91] Henshaw (2006), Work and Pensions Select Committee (2007).

[92] [2002] EWHC 1125.

[93] Though no breach of the ECHR was found.

to overnight stays: no account could be taken of the actual level of care or expenditure on the child made by each parent. Mr Plumb made substantial provision for his child—an estimated 1,600 hours and 260 meals per annum. Yet non-resident parents who provided no day-care or evening meals for the child would receive an identical deduction, simply on the basis of overnight stays. The pro rata deduction is also insensitive to such matters as which parent pays for items such as clothing.

It is questionable whether this rough and ready mechanism produces just results for either parent. A daytime-hours rule was rejected by government on the basis that hours could not be reliably counted.[94] It may not be possible to count nights much more reliably, particularly on the boundaries between bands, where one night more or fewer makes a big difference. There is a clear incentive for parents to argue about contact because of its impact on child support liability. We explore this further at 6.7.3 below.

Set-off

Following CMOP 2008, C-MEC now has the power to treat child support liability as having been satisfied by setting off counter-liabilities (in cases where the two parents are at once parents with care and non-resident parents in relation to two children) or other payments to which the person with care agreed. These latter payments include payments made in respect of certain mortgages, rent, utility bills, council tax, and the cost of essential repairs to the child's home.[95]

6.4.5 VARIATIONS

The basic formula and ancillary rules regarding shared care and apportionment operate strictly mathematically.[96] However, C-MEC has discretion to vary the amount payable in cases falling in one of the categories specified in the Act and accompanying regulations.[97] Variations—up or down—are designed to relieve specific injustices that might arise under the formula. Either party may apply for a variation at the outset or once a maintenance calculation is in force.[98] Once it has been decided to allow the variation, detailed regulations govern how the variation affects the maintenance calculation.[99] It must first be shown that one of the 'cases' for a variation applies.

The first case—special expenses

The first case concerns 'special expenses' of the non-resident parent which, it is argued, should reduce the maintenance payable.[100] Regulations deal exhaustively with the nature

---

[94] DSS (1999), para 7.20.

[95] CSA 1991, s 41C and Child Support (Management of Payments and Arrears) Regulations 2009, SI 2009/3151, paras 5–7.

[96] *R v Secretary of State for Social Security, ex parte Biggin* [1995] 1 FLR 851.

[97] See DSS (1995); CSA 1991, ss 28A–G, Schs 4A and 4B; Child Support (Variations) Regulations 2000, SI 2001/156.

[98] CSA 1991, ss 28A and 28G. The latter variations take effect by way of a revision under s 16 or a superseding decision under s 17: see 6.4.8.

[99] SI 2001/156, regs 22–30.

[100] CSA 1991, Sch 4B, para 2.

and level of expenses that may be claimed to justify the variation.[101] Broadly speaking, they fall under the following headings:

- average weekly travel and accommodation costs incurred regularly by the non-resident parent in maintaining contact with the qualifying child;

- the maintenance element of boarding school fees, up to 50 per cent of the non-resident parent's income;

- repayment of certain debts, including mortgages, incurred for the benefit of certain members of the family (and not exclusively for the benefit of the non-resident parent) before the non-resident parent acquired that status, and when the non-resident parent and the person with care were a couple;[102]

- repayment of limited categories of mortgage, loan, and endowment insurance policies. Here, any mortgage must, inter alia, have been taken out to facilitate the purchase of, or repairs or improvements to, a property by someone *other than* the non-resident parent, though that property must have been the home of both parents as a couple, and is now the home of the person with care and qualifying child. A variation on this basis is expressly excluded if the non-resident parent has any legal or equitable interest in, or charge over, the property,[103] which excludes any variation on this basis where one of the property arrangements common on divorce—*Mesher* and *Martin* orders—has been adopted;[104]

- costs necessarily incurred in relation to the long-term illness or disability of a relevant other child (less amounts received by way of disability living allowance[105] or other financial assistance received in respect of the illness or disability).

In relation to the first four categories, weekly expenses (in aggregate) below £15 per week (for those with a weekly income of £200 or more) or £10 (for those with a lower income) are not taken into account. If C-MEC considers any expenses to be unreasonably high or to have been unreasonably incurred, it may substitute such lower amount as it considers reasonable, which may be nil or below the £15/£10 threshold. More importantly, perhaps, there is evidence that some non-resident parents are not aware of the possibility of variation for these contact-related expenses.[106]

The second case—pre-1993 property and capital transfers

The second category of variation also gives grounds for a reduction in maintenance payable where a clean break settlement had been reached on divorce.[107] It is now only of historical interest, as the last such cases close.[108]

---

101 Child Support (Variations) Regulations 2000, SI 2001/156, regs 10–15.

102 Ibid., reg 12. Although payment of mortgages over the home of the person with care and qualifying child are included, it seems that variations are not intended to be available where the non-resident parent retains any interest in that property: see next bullet in text.

103 Ibid., reg 14.

104 See 7.3.2.

105 See CPAG (2010), ch 7.

106 Atkinson and McKay (2005), 113.

107 CSA 1991, Sch 4B, para 3.

108 See 6.6.2 below.

The third case—assets, income, and lifestyle incompatible with calculation

The final case[109] aims to prevent non-resident parents paying less than they should, in view of the fact that the formula only takes into account their earned income, rather than view their financial circumstances in the round.[110] The following, in broad terms, may therefore give grounds for a variation:[111]

- beneficial ownership or control of certain assets with an equity exceeding £65,000; there are various exclusions, in particular the home of the non-resident parent or any child of his or hers;

- the non-resident parent automatically falling within the nil or flat rate category, but nevertheless having an income exceeding £100 per week;

- the non-resident parent having the ability to control the amount of his income and C-MEC believing that he has unreasonably reduced his income in order to reduce his child support liability, for example by paying an unreasonably high salary to his spouse for working in his business;

- the non-resident parent having a lifestyle inconsistent with his declared income.

The discretion

Even if one of the 'cases' applies, C-MEC has a discretion whether to allow a variation, structured by the CSA 1991 and regulations. In addition to the general welfare principle in s 2, specific factors are set out. These factors are instructive about the policies underpinning child support:

Child Support Act 1991

28E Matters to be taken into account

(1) In determining whether to agree to a variation, the Commission shall have regard . . . to the general principles set out in subsection (2) . . .

(2) The general principles are that—

(a) parents should be responsible for maintaining their children whenever they can afford to do so;

(b) where a parent has more than one child, his obligation to maintain any one of them should be no less than his obligation to maintain any other of them.

(3) In determining whether to agree to a variation, the Commission shall take into account any representation made to it—

(a) by the person with care or non-resident parent concerned; . . .

(4) In determining whether to agree to a variation, no account shall be taken of the fact that—

(a) any part of the income of the person with care concerned is, or would be if the Commission agreed to a variation, derived from any benefit; or

---

109 CSA 1991, Sch 4B, para 4.
110 E.g. *Phillips v Peace* [1996] 2 FCR 237.
111 See SI 2001/156, regs 18–20.

(b) some or all of any child support maintenance might be taken into account in some manner in relation to any entitlement to benefit. . . .

28F Agreement to a variation

(1) The Commission may agree to a variation if—

(a) it is satisfied that the case is one which falls within one or more of the cases set out in Part 1 of Schedule 4B or in regulations made under that Part [described above]; and

(b) it is its opinion that, in all the circumstances of the case, it would be just and equitable to agree to a variation.

(2) In considering whether it would be just and equitable in any case to agree to a variation, the Commission—

(a) must have regard, in particular, to the welfare of any child likely to be affected if it did agree to a variation; and

(b) [to factors specified in regulations] . . .

Child Support (Variations) Regulations 2000, SI 2001/156

21 Factors to be taken into account and not to be taken into account

(1) The factors to be taken into account in determining whether it would be just and equitable to agree to a variation in any case shall include—

(a) where the application is made on any ground—

(i) whether in the opinion of [C-MEC], agreeing to a variation would be likely to result in a relevant person ceasing paid employment;

(ii) if the applicant is the non-resident parent, the extent, if any, of his liability to pay child maintenance under a court order or agreement in the period prior to the effective date of the maintenance calculation; and

(b) where an application is made on the ground [of special expenses], whether, in the opinion of [C-MEC]—

(i) the financial arrangements made by the non-resident parent could have been such as to enable the expenses to be paid without a variation being agreed; or

(ii) the non-resident parent has at his disposal financial resources which are currently utilised for the payment of expenses other than those arising from essential everyday requirements and which could be used to pay the expenses.

(2) The following factors are not to be taken into account in determining whether it would be just and equitable to agree to a variation in any case—

(a) the fact that the conception of the qualifying child was not planned by one or both of the parents;

(b) whether the non-resident parent or the person with care of the qualifying child was responsible for the breakdown of the relationship between them;

(c) the fact that the non-resident parent or the person with care of the qualifying child has formed a new relationship with a person who is not a parent of that child;

(d) the existence of particular arrangements for contact with the qualifying child, including whether any arrangements are being adhered to;

(e) the income or assets of any person other than the non-resident parent, other than the income or assets of a partner of a non-resident parent taken into account [in 'lifestyle' cases];

(f) the failure by a non-resident parent to make payments of child support maintenance, or to make payments under a maintenance order or a written maintenance agreement; or

(g) representations made by persons other than the relevant persons.

6.4.6 TERMINATION OF THE CALCULATION

The maintenance calculation ceases to have effect on: (i) the death of the non-resident parent or person with care; (ii) there no longer being any qualifying child; or (iii) the non-resident parent ceasing to be a parent of the qualifying child (e.g. following adoption).[112]

6.4.7 COLLECTION AND ENFORCEMENT OF C-MEC MAINTENANCE CALCULATIONS[113]

For an Act otherwise rather thin on detail and reliant on secondary legislation, CMOP 2008, amending the CSA 1991, is extremely comprehensive on enforcement. Even here, however, much is left to regulations, to the dismay of the parliamentary Joint Committee on Human Rights which, whilst content that the changes were not incompatible with parties' rights under the European Convention on Human Rights (ECHR), were concerned that important details necessary to secure that position should be enshrined in primary legislation.[114] While critics argue that the effectiveness of the CSA's existing armoury of enforcement powers had not been properly tested, the Government was keen to send a strong signal about the importance of non-resident parents meeting their responsibility to pay child maintenance. So much so that in summer 2007, it briefly instituted a 'naming and shaming' policy of defaulting non-resident parents who had been convicted of offences related to child maintenance.[115]

Many of these new powers are not in force at the time of writing, but we discuss the law as it will be once CMOP 2008 is fully implemented.

'Enforcement' via reliance on tax records

Whilst not an issue of enforcement as such, the calculation of maintenance based on historical gross income data obtained via the tax authorities will itself act as an early-stage 'enforcement' power. To some extent, non-resident parents' ability to frustrate maintenance calculations by withholding information about their financial position (particularly when self-employed) may be hampered by this new procedure. However, the information

[112] CSA 1991, Sch 1, para 16(1).

[113] CSA 1991, ss 29–41B.

[114] Joint Committee on Human Rights (2007), paras 1.9–1.12, and generally on human rights issues arising from C-MEC's powers.

[115] For criticism see Joint Committee on Human Rights (2007), 1.38.

available to C-MEC will only be as good as that available to the tax authorities, who have not tended to investigate the affairs of low-earning taxpayers.[116] Concerns have been raised about non-resident parents' rights under Article 8 ECHR which arise from this form of information-sharing, given the poor track record of various government departments with data security.[117]

Collection and receipt of child support

Where a C-MEC maintenance calculation is in place, either party can request that C-MEC collect payments of child support and transmit them to the person with care.[118] Parties may alternatively arrange direct payment to the person with care once C-MEC has determined the amount due.[119]

Payment may be made by various means including standing order, direct debit, cheque, cash, or debit card.[120] Collection of child maintenance should, however, now become more efficient by C-MEC regularly issuing deduction from earnings orders[121] (DEOs) addressed to the non-resident parent's employer, as a standard means of collection. (DEOs are not available for self-employed non-resident parents, the most problematic group.) No court involvement or default by the non-resident parent is required before DEOs can be made. Other payment methods will be permitted only where there is good reason (relating to potential adverse employment or family consequences arising from the disclosure of the non-resident parent's status as parent)[122] why DEOs or direct debit (the other form of payment with high compliance rates) *cannot* be used.[123] A portion of non-resident parents' income is protected for these purposes, so DEOs cannot reduce their circumstances unreasonably. Non-resident parents may appeal to the magistrates' court against a DEO, but only on very limited grounds.[124] The DEO will not operate until the deadline for appealing has passed. Parkinson has argued that in order to respect non-resident parents' dignity, C-MEC should ensure that they are given the option of direct debit instead of DEO wherever possible.[125]

Enforcement by C-MEC

Two separate issues arise at each stage: (i) the enforcement tools available; and (ii) whether court sanction is required for their use. All of these tools are available only to C-MEC: the person with care has no direct means of enforcing maintenance, as we discuss below.

The enhanced arsenal at C-MEC's disposal

Pre-CMOP, the enforcement arsenal lay beyond the gateway of the 'liability order', which could only be obtained from the court. However, the courts' discretion *not* to make that

116 Wikeley (2007a), para 20.
117 Joint Committee on Human Rights (2007), 1.26.
118 CSA 1991, s 4(2)(a).
119 See Bell, Kazimirski, and La Valle (2006).
120 Child Support (Collection and Enforcement) Regulations 1992, SI 1992/1989, Part II.
121 CSA 1991, ss 29 and 31; SI 1992/1989, reg 3 and Part III.
122 SI 1992/1989, reg 3.
123 Hansard HC WS col 137WS, Parliamentary Under-Secretary of State for Work and Pensions, 15 September 2008.
124 CSA 1991, s 32(5)(6); SI 1992/1989, reg 22; *Secretary of State for Social Security v Shotton* [1996] 2 FLR 241.
125 Parkinson (2007).

order was limited. Indeed, they were, and where still involved in enforcement, are precluded from examining the correctness of the underlying maintenance calculation: that is a matter for the Act's statutory appeal system.[126] CMOP 2008 has moved the deployment of most weapons from the courts to C-MEC itself. In many instances it is now for the aggrieved non-resident parent to engage the court (or, in the case of liability orders, tribunal) in the enforcement process by bringing an appeal against C-MEC's proposed action. C-MEC is free to implement its enforcement action before the deadline for appealing expires, provided that it thinks the liability in question would not be affected by a successful appeal or—more surprisingly—it nevertheless considers that it would be fair to proceed in all the circumstances.[127] In taking any enforcement action, C-MEC is subject to its general duty under s 2 of the CSA 1991 to have regard to the welfare of any child likely to be affected by its decision.[128]

It seems likely that most features of the new enforcement regime are compatible with the ECHR. However, the Government accepted that they engaged several rights of non-resident parents, in particular their right to respect for private life (Article 8), their right to a fair trial in the determination of civil rights and obligations (Article 6), and their right to peaceful enjoyment of possessions (Article 1 of Protocol 1).[129] Whether these rights are respected will often depend in practice on how C-MEC operates its discretion in relation to enforcement action, having regard to its obligations as a public authority under s 6 of the Human Rights Act 1998 (HRA 1998) to act compatibly with Convention rights.

Given the limited scrutinizing role that the courts had in pre-CMOP enforcement action, depriving them of the power to authorize enforcement action, whilst symbolically significant and intended to save C-MEC precious time by avoiding court delays[130] may be thought to have little impact on practical outcomes. However, serious concerns have been expressed about the implications of this move for citizens' right of access to court, which we explore below.

Unlike any other financial liabilities (including court-ordered periodical payments), there is no limitation period during the child's minority on collection of child support arrears.[131] C-MEC can now even chase defaulters beyond the grave.[132] C-MEC may impose penalty payments of up to 25 per cent of the sums due, which go to the state; the person with care gains no compensation or interest for late payment.[133]

Deduction orders

Where the non-resident parent is in default, C-MEC can make regular or lump sum deduction orders (addressed to the institution holding the account) from various bank accounts in relation to both arrears and future payments.[134] This tool should be particularly useful against recalcitrant self-employed non-resident parents to whom DEOs cannot be applied.

---

126 See 6.4.8; *Farley v Child Support Agency and another* [2006] UKHL 31.

127 E.g. CSA 1991, s 32A(3).

128 *Brookes v Secretary of State for Work and Pensions and C-MEC* [2010] EWCA Civ 420.

129 Cf *R (ota Denson) v Child Support Agency* [2002] EWHC 154: court-based liability order scheme held not to engage Article 8 or Article 1 of Protocol 1, but if engaged, readily justifiable; *Brookes v Secretary of State for Work and Pensions and C-MEC* [2010] EWCA Civ 420, [39]: doubted obiter whether, short of imprisonment, Article 8 engaged by enforcement action—but cf disqualification and curfew orders, discussed below.

130 Though delays may commonly have been the fault of the Child Support Agency not the courts.

131 Cf Burrows (2010).

132 CSA 1991, s 43A.

133 CSA 1991, s 41A; SI 1992/1989, Part IIA.

134 CSA 1991, ss 32A–K, SI 1992/1989, Part IIIA.

These powers are backed up by the facility for C-MEC to apply to court for an anti-avoidance order, modelled on powers exercisable by the matrimonial courts. These orders are available on the ground that the non-resident parent has failed to pay and—intending to avoid payment—is about to make or has made a reviewable disposition, i.e. a disposition other than one made for valuable consideration to a third party acting in good faith and with no notice of the intention to avoid paying maintenance.[135]

Liability orders and associated remedies

Beyond that, C-MEC itself can make liability orders,[136] a power that formerly lay with the courts.[137] C-MEC can then supply details of the child maintenance debt to credit reference agencies;[138] concerns were expressed by the Joint Committee on Human Rights that this had implications for non-resident parents' rights under Article 8 ECHR.[139] C-MEC can also enforce the liability order without court sanction by various means.

First, it can take control of certain of the non-resident parent's goods and sell them in order to pay the outstanding debt.[140] Under the law currently in force,[141] certain items of property are immune from this remedy:

Child Support Act 1991, s 35

(3) The Commission may, in exercising his powers...against the liable person's goods, seize—

  (a) any of the liable person's goods except—

    (i) such tools, books, vehicles and other items of equipment as are necessary to him for use personally by him in his employment, business or vocation;

    (ii) such clothing, bedding, furniture, household equipment and provisions as are necessary for satisfying his basic domestic needs; and

  (b) any money, banknotes [and other valuable securities, etc] belonging to the liable person.

(4) For the purposes of subsection (3), the liable person's domestic needs shall be taken to include those of any member of his family with whom he resides....

Regulations provide for an appeal to the magistrates by 'any person aggrieved' by such action, but only in relation to procedural defects; the court cannot question the underlying maintenance calculation.[142]

Second, armed with its own liability order, C-MEC can go on to make (without application to court) a third party debt order, requiring third parties holding the liable person's funds to pay them to C-MEC as directed in the order. Finally, C-MEC can make a charging

---

[135] CSA 1991, s 32L, modelled on MCA 1973, s 37.

[136] CSA 1991, ss 32M–N.

[137] This change was not in force as at October 2010.

[138] CSA 1991, s 49D(3).

[139] (2007), 1.28; cf *R (ota Denson) v Child Support Agency* [2002] EWHC 154, [47].

[140] CSA 1991, s 35(1).

[141] These provisions are due to be replaced by the Tribunals, Courts and Enforcement Act 2007, Part 3 and associated regulations, which will presumably include similar exemptions.

[142] SI 1992/1989, reg 31.

order, giving it a security interest in any property subject to the order, so that in the event of sale (which may be expressly ordered for this purpose), a specified sum from the proceeds goes to C-MEC.[143]

'Wilful refusal or culpable neglect'

The next tranche of enforcement powers arise only when the remedies considered so far have failed to yield all or part of the debt, and where C-MEC or (in some instances) the court finds that the non-resident parent has been guilty of 'wilful refusal or culpable neglect' to pay. These terms were explained in a different—but for our purposes similar—context as follows:

R (Sullivan) v Luton Magistrates' Court [1992] 2 FLR 196

Those are words which set the degree of blameworthiness necessary to attract an imprisonment order at a very high level. It is not just a matter of improvidence or dilatoriness. Something in the nature of a deliberate defiance or reckless disregard of the court's order is required.

Burrows and Bird note that outside the context of imprisonment—e.g. curfew orders, driving disqualification—the threshold might be set a little less high, although the interference with liberty entailed in all of these measures, the threshold cannot be lowered too far.[144]

Disqualification from holding driving licence or travel authorization

The most controversial new powers exercisable by C-MEC concern disqualification from driving and confiscation of passports, to be trialled for a two-year period.[145] Pre-CMOP, magistrates had the power to disqualify from driving for up to two years in cases of wilful refusal to pay or culpable neglect. The Government was keen to move this power—and with it a new power to confiscate passports—to C-MEC. Its attempts to do so in CMOP 2008 failed following objections that it was unconstitutional for an administrative body to be empowered to remove passports. Unbowed, the Government secured the passage of similar provisions in 2009, amending relevant sections of the CSA 1991.[146]

Under ss 39B–F of the CSA 1991, C-MEC will be able to make a 'disqualification order' in relation to non-resident parents' driving licence, travel authorization (usually passport), or both for up to one year. The grounds for such action will be the same as previously applied by magistrates: that attempts to recover the debt by other means had failed entirely or partly, and that there has been wilful refusal or culpable neglect to pay. The Act requires C-MEC, before exercising this power, to consider 'whether the person needs the relevant document in order to earn a living'.[147] But while it will also be bound by s 2 to have regard to the welfare of any child likely to be affected by its decision and by s 6 of the HRA 1998 to act compatibly with Convention rights, there is no specific duty to consider whether the parent needs to drive

---

[143] CSA 1991, s 36.
[144] (2009), 9.34.
[145] Welfare Reform Act 2009, ss 52–3.
[146] Not in force as at October 2010.
[147] CSA 1991, s 39B(4).

or travel on a passport to have contact with the child. To ensure that it acts compatibly with Article 8 ECHR where contact might be hampered, C-MEC will have to be able to justify its action as necessary and proportionate under Article 8(2).[148] In this regard, the Government would doubtless say that these orders are intended not as punishment but encouragement, and that it lies within the non-resident parent's power to ensure contact can proceed uninhibited: he need only pay the bill.[149] But then, opponents counter, one might as well empower C-MEC to impose curfews or imprison people without court sanction (cf below).[150]

The controversy lies in these serious interferences with non-resident parents' private and family life being made administratively rather than judicially. The court can be required to reconsider the matter afresh only if the non-resident parent lodges an appeal—though doing so will risk the court *extending* the order to take effect for up to two years.[151] Pursuing an appeal may not be entirely straightforward, one reason why the Joint Committee on Human Rights recommended that these provisions be dropped:

Joint Committee on Human Rights, *Legislative Scrutiny: Welfare Reform Bill*
Fourteenth Report of Session 2008–09, HL Paper 78, HC 414 (2009)

1.65 Resolution and Families Need Fathers have raised some concerns about the change now proposed in the current Bill:

Fundamentally, they conflict with the citizen's direct access to the courts when the state could be seen to be acting in a way clearly against the person's interests and their right to a fair trial.

If the Commission makes these Orders administratively, there are no safeguards to have the matter properly considered. If the Orders are made administratively, they are effectively being made by Civil Servants, who may be quite junior in position and, again, there are no 'checks and balances'. The Bill attempts to deal with this by providing that the seizure will only take place by an administrative decision if the individual decides not to appeal to the court. But that is well short of direct and full access to the court. Many of the individuals concerned may be poorly equipped to take sound advice from the legal profession or elsewhere when confronted with the threat to confiscate any of these documents.

1.66 The common law right to a fair hearing may require that an individual is invited to make representations before an order is made and that they are given adequate notice of the intention of C-MEC to make a disqualification order. The Bill only provides for the non-resident parent to be given notice of the order when it is made. In addition, in light of the importance of the right to appeal, we consider that this notice should specifically inform individuals of their right to appeal and that the order will not come into force until the appeal is exhausted.

1.67 Resolution and Families Need Fathers told us that administrative failures could undermine the fairness of any process operated by C-MEC:

[T]he provisions depend crucially on C-MEC's ability to communicate effectively with the persons whose licence or documents they are confiscating…We understand an individual will have the opportunity to submit an appeal, but this is effectively reversing the burden of proof to the paying party to demonstrate why the Order should not remain in place.

---

[148] *R (Plumb) v Secretary of State for Work and Pensions* [2002] EWHC 1125, [19]; for unsuccessful argument in this vein in other contexts: *Logan v UK* (App No 24875/94, ECHR) (1996); *Burrows v UK* (App No 27558/95, ECHR) (1996).

[149] Cf Hansard HL Deb, col GC142, 2 July 2009, Lord McKenzie of Luton.

[150] Ibid., Lord Pannick.

[151] CSA 1991, s 39CB(7).

Even if these points were met, however, the Joint Committee retained serious reservations about the procedure, given Article 6's requirements of a fair hearing in the determination of civil rights and obligations. One concern related to costs: for the non-resident parent to secure the full, independent, and impartial hearing to which Article 6 entitles him, he would have to bear the initial costs of launching an appeal, a burden which might be too much for some.[152] The CSA 1991 provides no guarantee that the appellant's costs will be met by C-MEC should the appeal succeed. Contrary to the concerns of Resolution and Families Need Fathers that the procedure effectively reversed the onus of proof, the Joint Committee considered that Article 6 might demand otherwise—with the net result that empowering C-MEC to issue these orders could simply end up duplicating effort, as many parents inevitably sought an appeal:

> 1.80 While the penalties imposed are not as restrictive as committal or curfew, they may have a significant impact on individuals, in particular where a licence or passport is necessary for the non-resident parent's work or business. In respect of travel, the right to leave and enter one's country of nationality is recognised in a number of international human rights instruments, including the Universal Declaration of Human Rights and Article 2 of the Fourth Protocol of the ECHR (to which the UK is not a party). Against this background, it is likely that a high standard of scrutiny must be applied to any Order issued by C-MEC in order to comply with the right to a fair hearing. In reconsidering whether the non-resident parent has 'wilfully refused to pay' or is 'culpably negligent', Article 6 may require that any doubt should lie with the non-resident parent. On appeal the court may be required to treat the hearing as if it were an application by C-MEC, requiring evidence that the Order has been properly made. Against this background, we can see little value in the proposed changes to outweigh the potential for injustice in cases where sanctions are imposed administratively and non-resident parents are deterred from pursuing an appeal in light of the costs involved.

Noting that, pre-CMOP 2008, where courts have heard direct applications for driving disqualifications and committals, no order was made in a quarter of cases and the vast majority of orders that were made were suspended (to take effect only if the non-resident parent still refused to pay), the Committee concluded:

> 1.81 ...While we recognise the legitimate policy aim of securing appropriate support for children by non-resident parents, it would be inappropriate to introduce new administrative sanctions with the principal goal of deterring individuals from pursuing a fair hearing to which they are lawfully entitled.
> 1.82 ...We consider that in practice these hearings will vary little from...an application by C-MEC for an order. The proposal to introduce an administrative stage only reduces the likelihood that non-resident parents will, in practice, have disqualification or suspension tested by an independent and impartial tribunal. We recommend that these proposals should be removed from this Bill.

We shall see once the provisions have been in force for two years whether these predictions were well-made.

---

[152] Joint Committee on Human Rights (2009), 1.73.

Court-based sanctions: curfew orders and committal to prison

If those options fail, the last resort remedies may only be obtained from the magistrates' courts, again following a finding that the non-resident parent is guilty of wilful refusal to pay or culpable neglect to do so: curfew orders or committal to prison for up to six weeks.[153] The courts are slow to exercise what is now an anomalous power to imprison debtors; the vast majority of sentences issued to date have been suspended. Concerns have been raised about the compatibility with Article 6 of the procedure for committal hearings in relation to child support debts.[154] Curfew orders—orders of up to six months' duration requiring the person to remain at specified places for specified periods of time of between two and 12 hours a day[155]—are an innovation of CMOP 2008. The court is directed to ensure that any curfew avoids any conflict with the non-resident parent's religious beliefs, employment, or education—but conflict with contact arrangements is again not mentioned. As with C-MEC's disqualification orders, courts considering curfews will need to address this issue in order to act compatibly with Article 8 ECHR. Breach of a curfew risks imprisonment for a specified period—or until the debt is paid, if earlier.[156] For completeness, non-resident parents subjected to a curfew or committed to prison are now searched for cash on the spot—no opportunity to recover arrears, it seems, is to be missed.[157]

No enforcement of C-MEC calculations by persons with care

Enforcement proceedings lie exclusively in the hands of C-MEC, which has full discretion as to whether and how to pursue cases; it can also accept part payment or write off arrears in certain circumstances.[158] Persons with care cannot take enforcement proceedings, nor do they have party status in proceedings brought by C-MEC. They may only empower C-MEC to act for them and then only where a C-MEC calculation has been made.[159] We examine the position of those who opted for private ordering below at 6.6.

The exclusion of parents with care from the enforcement process was unsuccessfully challenged in *R (Kehoe) v Secretary of State for Work and Pensions*. The case raises fundamental questions about the nature of the child support obligation. The Kehoes had been married with four children. Following the divorce, Mrs Kehoe applied to the Agency (as it then was). For 10 years, with some success, it extracted maintenance from Mr Kehoe, but the process was painful and substantial arrears accumulated. Mrs Kehoe felt that she could have done rather better at enforcing her child support assessment than the Agency was apparently able to do. She argued that the system violated Article 6 ECHR by preventing her, as a person with care, from judicially enforcing her civil right to receive child maintenance from the non-resident parent. The House of Lords, Baroness Hale dissenting, held that persons with care have no such civil right and that Article 6 was therefore not engaged. The majority view was based on its interpretation of the CSA 1991, in particular parts of s 4:

---

153 CSA 1991, ss 39H–P and 40.
154 Burrows (2009a).
155 CSA 1991, s 39I(1), (3).
156 Ibid., s 39N(4).
157 Ibid., ss 39L and 40(10)–(10C). These powers, and curfew orders, were not in force at August 2010.
158 Ibid., ss 41D–E.
159 Ibid., s 4(2)(b). Nor may they apply for a court order: ibid., s 8—see p 392 below.

Child Support Act 1991, s 4

Child support maintenance

(1) A person who is, in relation to any qualifying child..., either the person with care or the non-resident parent may apply to the Commission for a maintenance calculation to be made under this Act with respect to that child...

(2) Where a maintenance calculation has been made in response to an application under this section the Commission may, if the person with care or non-resident parent with respect to whom the calculation was made applies to it under this section, arrange for—

(a) the collection of the child support maintenance payable in accordance with the calculation;

(b) the enforcement of the obligation to pay child support maintenance in accordance with the calculation.

(3) Where an application under subsection (2) for the enforcement of the obligation mentioned in subsection (2)(b) authorises the Commission to take steps to enforce that obligation whenever it considers it necessary to do so, the Commission may act accordingly....

R (Kehoe) v Secretary of State for Work and Pensions [2005] UKHL 48

LORD BINGHAM:

3. It is necessary first to examine whether Mrs Kehoe has a right to recover financial support for the maintenance of the children... from Mr Kehoe under the domestic law of England and Wales. Under the law as it stood before 1991 it was clear that she had such a right under the [MCA 1973, the DPMCA 1978...and the CA 1989]. But these procedures were judged by the government of the day to be unsatisfactory...

Lord Bingham then examined the history and provisions of the CSA 1991 as it stood pre-CMOP 2008 (including its treatment of benefits cases—see 6.4.3 above), and continued:

5....In Huxley v Child Support Officer [2000] 1 FLR 898, 908, Hale I J...helpfully characterised the regime established by the 1991 Act:

"The child support system has elements of private and public law but fundamentally it is a nationalised system for assessing and enforcing an obligation which each parent owes primarily to the child. It replaces the powers of the courts, which can no longer make orders for periodical payments for children save in very limited circumstances. Unless she can secure a voluntary agreement at least as high as that which the CSA would assess, the PWC [parent with care] is expected to look to the Agency to assess her child support according to the formula, whether or not she is on benefit. The fact that it does her no direct good if she is on means-tested benefits, and that much CSA activity so far has been in relation to parents on benefit, does not alter the fundamental characteristics of the scheme."

6. That a caring parent in the position of Mrs Kehoe was given no right of recovering or enforcing a claim to child maintenance against a...non-resident parent was not a lacuna or inadvertent omission in the 1991 Act: it was the essence of the new scheme, a deliberate

legislative departure from the regime which had previously obtained. The merits of that scheme are not for the House in its judicial capacity to evaluate. But plainly the scheme did not lack a coherent rationale. The state has an interest, most directly in cases where public funds are disbursed, but also more generally that children should be adequately supported. It might well be thought that a single professional agency, with the resources of the state behind it and an array of powers at its commend, would be more consistent in assessing and more effective and economical in enforcing payment than individual parents acting in a random and uncoordinated way. It might also be thought that the interposition of an independent, neutral, official body would reduce the acrimony which had all too frequently characterised applications for child maintenance by caring against absent or non-resident parents in the past which, however understandable in the aftermath of a fractured relationship, rarely enured to the benefit of the children. For better or worse, the process was deliberately changed.

That seriously undermined Mrs Kehoe's argument under Article 6, which guarantees access to an impartial tribunal for the determination of substantive civil rights and obligations, but does not itself decide *what* substantive rights and obligations individuals should enjoy. Article 6, therefore, could not supply Mrs Kehoe with a right to recover child maintenance to which she had no right in English law.

10. Sympathetic though one must be with Mrs Kehoe, who appears to have suffered extreme frustration and a measure of loss, one cannot in my opinion ignore the wider principle raised by this case. This is that the deliberate decisions of representative assemblies should be respected and given effect so long as they do not infringe rights guaranteed by the Convention...Whether the scheme established by the 1991 Act is on balance beneficial to those whom it is intended to benefit may well be open to question, but it is a question for Parliament to resolve and not for the courts, since I do not consider that any article 6 right of Mrs Kehoe is engaged.

The narrow approach of the majority to the interpretation of the CSA 1991 is exemplified by this extract, edited for the post-CMOP context:

LORD HOPE:

33....[N]owhere in the Act is it said that the [non-resident] parent owes a duty, or is under an obligation, to pay [the child support due] to the person with care. Nor is it said anywhere that the person with care has a right which she can enforce against the absent parent.

34....Where an assessment is made, [the person with care and the non-resident parent] are...given the right by section 4(2) to apply to [C-MEC] to arrange for its collection and enforcement. But enforcement is not something which they can demand. Section 4(2) makes it clear that enforcement of the obligation to pay child support maintenance is at the discretion of [C-MEC], not at the discretion of the person who applies for its enforcement.

35. I would conclude that the 1991 Act has deliberately avoided conferring a right on the person with care to enforce a child maintenance assessment against the [non-resident] parent. Enforcement is exclusively a matter for [C-MEC]. It follows that the person with care has no right to apply to a court for the enforcement of the assessment...It is a matter of substantive law, not of procedure.

And so Lord Hope concluded that her claim fell outside Article 6. But rights which, from Lord Hope's perspective, had not been expressly *stated* by the Act, for Baroness Hale had not been expressly *removed* and so survived the CSA scheme. While she agreed that the scheme deprived parents of the right to *enforce* maintenance, she concluded that the underlying right (in her view, of the child) to *receive* maintenance was intact, raising an issue under Article 6. Her approach to the issues, as so often, was distinctive:

BARONESS HALE: [dissenting]

49. This is another case which has been presented to us largely as a case about adults' rights when in reality it is about children's rights. It concerns the obligation to maintain one's children and the corresponding right of those children to obtain the benefit of that obligation. The issue is whether the restrictions placed on direct access to the courts to enforce that obligation by section 8(1) and (3) of the [CSA 1991—see p 392 below] are compatible with article 6 of the [ECHR]. Article 6 is concerned only with the fair and impartial adjudication and enforcement of the rights recognised in domestic law. It does not guarantee any particular content to those rights. Put another way, the issue is whether the 1991 Act has defined the extent of the obligation and that right or whether it has merely altered the machinery for assessing and enforcing them. If it is the latter, then the underlying right still exists and the Act's provisions may be regarded as procedural only. If it is the former, then all that survive are the rights set out in the Act itself. In my view, it is not possible to answer that question by looking only at the rights contained in the 1991 Act itself. They have to be set in the context of the scope of the parents' obligations and the children's rights as a whole. The 1991 Act is only one of a number of ways in which the law recognises these.

She then set out the history of the public and private law in this area, extracted earlier in this chapter and in chapter 3, and the current position, noting public law's liable relative procedure (since abolished by CMOP 2008 in relation to children), the common law duty of fathers to maintain their children, and the various court-based financial remedies for children considered at 6.5 below.

70. It is obvious, therefore, that the obligation of a parent to maintain his children, and the right of those children to have the benefit of that obligation, is not wholly contained in the 1991 Act. Far from it. The Act left all the previous law intact, merely precluding the courts from using their powers in cases where the Agency was supposed to do it for them...The 1991 Act contemplates that, as a minimum, children should have the benefit of the maintenance obligation as defined under the formula; but it does not contemplate that children should be limited to their rights under that Act; in appropriate circumstances, they may be supplemented or replaced in all the ways recounted earlier.

71. That being the case, it is clear to me that children have a civil right to be maintained by their parents which is such as to engage article 6...Their rights are not limited to the rights given to the parent with care under the [CSA 1991]. The provisions of that Act are simply a means of quantifying and enforcing part of their rights. I appreciate that the line between a procedural and a substantive bar is not always easy to draw...The formula is a substantive definition of the extent of the basic right. But in my view the continued existence of the wider rights, together with the wider objective of the 1991 Act to improve the provision made for children by their non-resident parents, places the collection and enforcement provisions of

the Act on the procedural rather than substantive side of the line. A civil right to be maintained exists and *prima facie* children are entitled to the benefit of the article 6 rights in the determination and enforcement of that right.

72. The problem is that this is exactly what the system is trying to do. It is trying to enforce the children's rights. It is sometimes, as this case shows, lamentably inefficient in so doing. It is safe to assume that there are cases, of which this may be one, where the children's carer would be much more efficient in enforcing the children's rights. The children's carer has a direct and personal interest in enforcement which the Agency, however good its intentions, does not. Even [under the pre-CMOP scheme] in benefit cases, where the state does have a direct interest in enforcement, it is not the sort of interest which stems from needing enough money to feed, clothe and house the children on a day-to-day basis. Only a parent who is worrying about where the money is to be found for the school dinners, the school trips, the school uniform, sports gear or musical instruments, or to visit the "absent" parent, not only this week but the next and the next for many years to come, has that sort of interest. A promise that the Agency is doing its best is not enough. Nor is the threat or reality of judicial review. Most people simply do not have access to the Administrative Court in the way that they used to have access to their local magistrates' court. Judicial review may produce some action from the Agency, but what is needed is money from the absent parent. Action from the Agency will not replace the money which has been irretrievably lost as a result of its failure to act in time.

Having found that Article 6 was engaged, and that the Act's attempt to improve enforcement of the child's right to maintain was a legitimate aim, she then moved on to consider whether depriving the parent with care of the right to enforce maintenance assessed under the Act was proportionate:

74. . . . I do not find that an easy question to answer . . . While the child support scheme was under review in the late 1990s, there was considerable debate about whether the courts should regain their power to make the basic award on the application of the parent with care. The formula would remain the same in all cases, but parents who were not receiving means-tested benefits would be able to apply to the courts rather than the Agency to award it. This was, however, rejected after careful consideration by the Government ([see DSS (1999), ch 8]). One can see why. The Government did not want to create 'one law for the rich and one for the poor'. It would be difficult to apply to the common case where the parent with care is sometimes in receipt of relevant benefits and sometimes is not . . .

75. This is just the sort of policy choice in a socio-economic field which the courts are usually prepared to leave to the judgment of Parliament. . . . It would be difficult to hold that the scheme as a whole is incompatible with the children's rights to a speedy determination and enforcement of their claims.

76. But if I am right that the children's civil rights to be properly maintained by their parents are engaged, it follows that the public authority which is charged by Parliament with securing the determination and enforcement of their rights is under a duty to act compatibly with their article 6 right to the speedy determination and effective enforcement of those rights. Indeed [counsel for the Secretary of State] did not seek to argue that they were not. He accepted, for the sake of the issue before the House, that if article 6 was engaged in this case, the claim under section 7 of the [HRA 1998] for failing to act in compliance with those rights should proceed. It stands to reason that if the state is going to take over the enforcement of a person's civil rights it has a duty to act compatibly with article 6 in doing so. . . .

The majority decision that there is no 'civil right' for the purposes of Article 6 to receive maintenance for one's children under the CSA 1991 has been branded 'disturbing'.[160] Nick Wikeley described the majority's reasoning as 'profoundly disappointing in their adoption of an unduly literalist and positivist approach to the question of statutory construction in *Kehoe*'. And there were further criticisms:

N. Wikeley, 'A duty but not a right: child support after R *(Kehoe) v Secretary of State for Work and Pensions',* (2006) 18 *Child and Family Law Quarterly* 287, 293–5

First, the two members of the majority who delivered short concurring speeches both relied in part on Mrs Kehoe's right to bring judicial review proceedings against the Secretary of State (in the guise of the Agency) as an indication that she was not without redress… [T]he proposition that judicial review is an adequate remedy will be greeted with at best some bemusement, and at worst hollow laughter, by those practitioners who have acted for parents with care in similar cases before the Administrative Court.

Secondly,…the majority placed considerable weight on the argument that the 1991 Act (which excluded the parent with care from the enforcement process) was an entirely new scheme which had 'replaced' the previous unsatisfactory private law remedies. This reading allowed the 1991 Act to be construed in isolation, so reinforcing the narrow perspective on the rights in issue.

Wikeley argued that the case law relating to those aspects of the CSA 1991 relied upon for this argument does not determine the point, and that other case law—not cited—is inconsistent with the majority's conclusion that the Act altered the parties' substantive rights. He was also doubtful that the decision would pass muster before the European Court of Human Rights, given the possibility that they would regard a CSA maintenance calculation, certainly one endorsed by an appeal tribunal, as a judicial determination of a civil right:.

Thus, the government's position in *Kehoe* may be difficult to sustain, not least as the outcome of the decision might well seem peculiar to a continental judiciary which will be more familiar with concepts of family solidarity. The Strasbourg bench will doubtless be even more puzzled once it is explained to them that, if the separating parents successfully negotiate a financial settlement and the parent with care is not on benefit, then a civil court may make a consent order embodying the terms of that agreement. It has never seriously been questioned that the parent with care enjoys a civil right to child maintenance in such circumstances.…[The significance of this point] was simply ignored by the House of Lords. Moreover, if the Strasbourg court turns over this particular stone, they will find that the unfortunate paradoxes generated by the decision in *Kehoe* simply multiply…

Wikeley identifies four examples of this incoherence. First, a parent with care clearly has a right to *apply* for a maintenance assessment: if that assessment is delayed, Article 6 is engaged; but according to *Kehoe*, delays in *enforcing* an assessment once made fall outside Article 6. Secondly, a parent with care who has obtained a top-up order from the courts from a wealthy non-resident parent in addition to a C-MEC assessment (see 6.5.2 below) will have a civil right to enforce the former, but not the latter: 'it would seem that English law accords

---

[160] Douglas (2004b), discussing the same decision of the majority in the Court of Appeal.

rather greater protection to the child's right to luxury rather than to mere subsistence'. Thirdly, whether the parent with care has a civil right for the purposes of Article 6 depends on whether the non-resident parent co-operates in obtaining a consent order for maintenance (see 6.5.2 below), which will engage Article 6. If not, the parent with care must proceed via the CSA, which will not: 'It hardly seems right that the whim of one party...should determine the legal rights of the other party in this way'. Finally, *non-resident* parents' Article 6 rights are clearly engaged by the process, allowing them to make arguments which, if successful, may prejudice the parent with care.[161]

While it may reach the better result, Baroness Hale's judgment was not unproblematic in suggesting that English law recognizes maintenance as a right of the *child*, rather than of the parent with care:

N. Wikeley, 'A duty but not a right: child support after *R (Kehoe) v Secretary of State for Work and Pensions',* (2006) 18 *Child and Family Law Quarterly* 287, 297–9, 301

If this is right, it requires a fundamental rethinking on the part of family law scholars. The traditional understanding was set out by J.C. Hall, writing in 1966: 'There was no civil obligation to maintain one's child at common law or in equity, but statute has imposed a duty'.

The common law cases provide scant support for the proposition that the common law clearly established a right of the child to maintenance, particularly where illegitimate.

What then of the legislative intervention prior to the 1991 Act? Baroness Hale...carefully explored the development of the various statutory codes for maintenance, both in public and private law. The public law mechanisms, dating back to the Poor Relief Act 1601, were always primarily concerned with indemnifying the public purse and discouraging immorality, and provide little support for the notion that children enjoy maintenance rights. Admittedly, the private law legislative measures have historically made a sharp distinction between spousal maintenance and child maintenance. However,...these statutes...all proceed on the assumption that it is the parent with care who will institute proceedings to enforce the maintenance obligation. In effect, the default position in English law is that children have no personal right to sue for maintenance. This might simply be seen as indicative of a mere lack of legal capacity, but the weight of authority [including that relating to tax and social security] would suggest that it points to the absence of any underlying legal right. We are thus some way from the position in the USA, where it seems to be accepted that 'the right to support lies exclusively with the child, and that a parent holds the child support payments in trust for the child's benefit'....

Wikeley will have been disappointed by the outcome of Mrs Kehoe's appeal to Strasbourg. The Court did not decide whether Article 6 was engaged (i.e. whether, contrary to the majority of the House of Lords, she had a civil right under domestic law to which Article 6 could attach). But even assuming that it was engaged, the Court found that Article 6 was not infringed. Mrs Kehoe had access to the remedy of judicial review. The Court considered (somewhat naïvely, given Wikeley's condemnation of this 'remedy') that it would not be

---

[161] Wikeley (2006b), 294–5.

unduly onerous to require her to use judicial review repeatedly, anymore than she would probably have had to take enforcement action directly against Mr Kehoe repeatedly had she been entitled to do so. In conclusion, the Court made the following observations:

Kehoe v United Kingdom (App No 2010/06, ECHR) (2008)

49....The provision of a state enforcement scheme for maintenance payments *inter alia* benefits the many parents with care of children who do not have the time, energy, resources or inclination to be embroiled in ongoing litigation with the absent parent [sic.] and allows the State to pursue those absent parents who default on their obligations leaving their families on the charge of the social security system and the taxpayer. The mere fact that it is possible to envisage a different scheme which might also allow individual enforcement action by parents in the particular situation of the applicant is not sufficient to disclose a failure by the State in its obligations under Article 6.

Despite suggestions by Henshaw that the issue be reviewed, *Kehoe* survived CMOP 2008 unscathed. Enforcement therefore remains a matter exclusively for C-MEC. This may be thought surprising since the state's interest in the payment of child support is attenuated now that parents with care claiming benefits are no longer required to apply for child support and any maintenance they receive is disregarded entirely in assessing their benefits claims. Allowing parents to enforce maintenance would also, as Henshaw observed, be consistent with the new policy of encouraging parents to take responsibility for child support through private arrangements, relieving the state of the burden to act.[162] As Gillian Douglas has observed, the removal of compulsion in public law cases could be said to reinstate the parent's right to seek child support by once more providing *all* parents with a choice of mechanisms for obtaining payment from the non-resident parent, and so clearly to engage Article 6.[163] But the reasoning of the European Court in *Kehoe* makes it doubtful whether this would affect its view of the compatibility of the English scheme with Article 6. It is unlikely that a domestic court would find that *Kehoe* had been implicitly overruled, given the government's clear intention that *Kehoe* not be affected by the changes made to the child support scheme by CMOP 2008 (apparently anxious that parents with care with difficult cases should not be burdened with the cost of enforcement),[164] and the style of statutory interpretation deployed by the House of Lords.[165]

6.4.8 CHALLENGING C-MEC DECISIONS

Absent any mechanism for enforcing a C-MEC maintenance calculation against the non-resident parents *directly*, persons with care (and non-resident parents wishing to challenge C-MEC decisions) are left to the various (quite limited) indirect remedies exercisable against *C-MEC* where it fails to recover the maintenance due.

---

[162] Henshaw (2006), para 67.
[163] Douglas (2009).
[164] DWP (2007b), para 28.
[165] Cf Burrows (2009b).

Revisions and supersessions[166]

Under the CSA 1991, s 16, any C-MEC decision, for example a maintenance calculation or variation decision, may be revised by C-MEC on its own initiative or on application from either party. The grounds on which revisions may be made are set out in regulations. Applications must ordinarily be made within one month of the decision.[167]

If there has been a change of circumstances or the original decision was made in ignorance of, or under a mistake as to, some material fact, an application under s 17 superseding the original decision should be made. Supersession is not allowed where it would make less than 5 per cent difference in the non-resident parent's income figure on which the calculation is to be based.[168]

Statutory appeals[169]

Thereafter, remedies lie outside C-MEC. Appeals against various categories of C-MEC decision—including original maintenance calculations, revision and supersession decisions, and enforcement action—may be brought not before a court, but instead within the new tribunal system,[170] and thereafter (on points of law) to the Court of Appeal. No public funding for legal representation is available for litigants before tribunal proceedings. Appeals against disqualification orders go to court.

Judicial review

The only other way of challenging C-MEC decisions before an external body is by judicial review,[171] which does not re-examine the merits of the case.[172] The judicial review court may, however, consider arguments that C-MEC has acted incompatibly with the ECHR.[173] The adequacy of judicial review as a remedy for those aggrieved by Child Support Agency (and now C-MEC) decisions, actions, and inaction has been doubted.[174]

Suing C-MEC?

Disappointed parents with care and children cannot sue C-MEC, either in negligence or under the HRA 1998 where it fails to enforce a maintenance calculation effectively. The decision in *Rowley v Secretary of State for Work and Pensions*[175] that no duty of care is owed was reinforced in part by the *Kehoe* decision: the House of Lords' failure to allude to any possibility of an

---

[166] Social Security and Child Support (Decisions and Appeals) Regulations 1999, SI 1999/991, Part II.

[167] Ibid., reg 3A.

[168] Ibid., reg 6B.

[169] CSA 1991, ss 20–24; SI 1999/991, Part IV; Tribunal Procedure (First Tier Tribunal) (Social Entitlement Chamber) Rules 2008, SI 2008/2685; Tribunal Procedure (Upper Tribunal) Rules 2008, SI 2008/2698. See Bird and Burrows (2009), ch 8; CPAG (current year), ch 18.

[170] Tribunals, Courts and Enforcement Act 2007.

[171] The Independent Case Examiner investigates claims of maladministration, but does not produce legally binding decisions, though the DWP may offer ex gratia financial redress where loss has been incurred.

[172] See Craig (2008).

[173] HRA 1998, ss 3–4, 6–8.

[174] *Farley v Child Support Agency* [2006] UKHL 31, [20]; *R (Kehoe) v Secretary of State for Work and Pensions* [2005] UKHL 48, [72].

[175] [2007] EWCA Civ 598.

action in negligence was regarded as significant. The statutory scheme for challenging C-MEC decisions, together with judicial review, were held to be inconsistent with any common law duty of care also being owed.[176] Similar reasoning undermined the claimants in *Treharne v Secretary of State for Work and Pensions*.[177] The children (some now adult) in respect of whom maintenance arrears had not been enforced sued the CSA under the HRA 1998, claiming a breach of the state's positive obligations towards them under Article 8, resulting in their having had a somewhat deprived upbringing. The judge held that since the CSA 1991 scheme is itself compliant with Article 8, there was no scope for HRA claims to be brought in individual cases: instead the remedies provided by the CSA 1991 scheme, and judicial review, should be pursued.[178]

It was also held in *Treharne* that Article 8 did not create an economic right to receive regular, reasonable maintenance.[179] The right to respect for family life is concerned, it was said, to guard against impairment of the 'love, trust, confidence, mutual dependence and unrestrained social intercourse which are the essence of family life',[180] and the right to respect for private life to protect 'the sphere of personal and sexual autonomy'. While family and private life may be tougher as a result of the state's failure to recover unpaid maintenance, that 'cannot be said to affect the core values attached to those concepts'.[181]

6.5 COURT-BASED PROVISION: THE CURRENT LAW

Where the courts have jurisdiction, they operate under various (broadly similar) statutes depending on the nature of the proceedings and the parties' relationship. We must consider first whether the courts have jurisdiction at all. It is necessary to discuss periodical payments separately from other forms of order.

6.5.1 LUMP SUM AND PROPERTY-RELATED ORDERS

The courts have exclusive jurisdiction, unaffected by the CSA 1991, to make lump sum orders and orders in relation to property: property adjustment orders, property settlements, and orders for sale. The jurisdiction of County Courts and High Court is unlimited by reference to the value of the claim or type of order sought;[182] magistrates' courts may only make lump sum orders of up to £1,000.[183] Where C-MEC lacks jurisdiction to make a maintenance calculation, capital orders can be used to meet income requirements.[184]

6.5.2 PERIODICAL PAYMENTS

More complicated is the courts' jurisdiction to order periodical payments to or for the benefit of children. It is necessary to distinguish between cases where C-MEC has jurisdiction to make a maintenance calculation and those where it does not.

---

[176] Ibid., [66]–[77].
[177] [2008] EWHC 3222 (QB).
[178] Ibid., [15]–[18], [28].
[179] Ibid., [19]–[20], [29], [30].
[180] Ibid., [24], quoting from *M v SSWP* [2006] UKHL 11, [5] per Lord Bingham.
[181] Ibid., [31].
[182] MCA 1973, Part II; CPA 2004, Sch 5; CA 1989, Sch 1.
[183] Domestic Proceedings and Magistrates' Courts Act 1978 (DPMCA 1978), s 2(3); CPA 2004, Sch 6, para 2(2); CA 1989, Sch 1, para 5(2).
[184] *V v V (Child Maintenance)* [2001] 2 FLR 799.

Where C-MEC has jurisdiction

First, the general rule is that the courts have *no* power to order maintenance where C-MEC has potential or actual jurisdiction—that is, where there is a qualifying child in respect of whom a maintenance calculation could be or has been made.[185] The courts must not use capital orders (such as lump sums or property adjustment) as a means of evading this general rule; capital orders should be confined to meeting the child's capital rather than day-to-day income needs—such as home and furnishings, or a car for the primary carer's use.[186] A lump sum order will not be regarded as a maintenance order for these purposes unless specified to be for the purpose of maintenance.[187]

However, there are some exceptions to the general rule, set out in CSA 1991, s 8, and the courts have identified another situation in which they may order periodical payments.

Consent orders

The most significant exception is that the courts can make periodical payment orders for the benefit of children with the consent of both parties.[188] Parties can thereby confer jurisdiction on the courts, and so avoid engaging with C-MEC. A standard practice has emerged to exploit this exception fully:

V v V (Child Maintenance) [2001] 2 FLR 799 (Fam Div)

WILSON J:

[18] My experience...has been that, even when parties require the court to determine other claims for ancillary relief [on divorce], they have often reached agreement upon the level of periodical payments for the benefit of the children; and that they are keen for the court to make an order in that respect with a view...to excluding the possibility of [a maintenance calculation under the CSA] and to securing the facility for the court to resolve any future issue about the level of such payments in the exercise of its variation jurisdiction. In that event the court proceeds without difficulty to make the order under s 8(5).

[19] Even, however, when parties remain at odds as to the level of periodical payments for the children, they often wish the court to determine that issue as well as the other issues, thereby perhaps obviating the need for a return to court for a topping-up order[189] following [a maintenance calculation] and in any event securing the court's ongoing jurisdiction in the event of future such dispute. In my experience the court invariably wants to accommodate the parties in that regard. But, in the light of the general prohibition, how can it do so? Over the last 8 years the following mechanism, which I believe to be entirely legitimate, has evolved, namely that at the outset of the hearing the court makes an order by consent for periodical payments for the benefit of the children in the sum of five pence each and that at the end of the hearing it varies that order to the level of payments which it thinks fit.

[20] It may be argued that, technically, such a mechanism requires the preparation of three documents:

---

[185] See CSA 1991, s 8.

[186] *Phillips v Peace* [1996] 2 FCR 237; *N v D* [2008] 1 FLR 1629.

[187] *AMS v Child Support Officer* [1998] 1 FLR 955.

[188] CSA 1991, s 8(5); Child Maintenance (Written Agreements) Order 1993, SI 1993/620. On consent orders generally, see 7.7.1.

[189] Ibid., s 8(6).

(a) a written agreement between the parties for the husband to pay five pence for the benefit of each of the children;[190]

(b) a nominal order, duly perfected, which reflects that agreement;[191] and

(c) a notice of application, duly issued, to vary that order.[192]

[21] My experience is that the written agreement at (a) and the notice of application at (c) rarely come into existence. I have no problem with that. My view is that, if the words 'by consent' appear above the nominal order, they satisfy the requirement of a written agreement and that any requirement for the issue of a notice of application can and should be waived.

However, we shall see below that consent orders cannot be relied on long term.

Top-up orders

The next exception to the general rule against the court ordering periodical payments concerns wealthy non-resident parents. C-MEC's maintenance calculation only covers gross income of up to £3,000 per week. The CSA 1991, s 8(6) preserves a power for the courts, where a maintenance calculation is in force in relation to the first £3,000,[193] to make top-up periodical payments orders in relation to the remaining income. This does not automatically give the courts jurisdiction in 'big money' cases; parents with care must obtain a maintenance calculation before they can apply for this 'top-up' order.

Expenses connected with education and disability

The courts have jurisdiction to make orders designed to meet costs incurred in the child's education or training for a trade, profession, or vocation,[194] and to cover expenses attributable to the child's disability.[195] This power does not extend to nursery and child-minding fees.[196] Unlike 'top-up' orders, these orders may be made even if there is no maintenance calculation in force.

C v F (disabled child: maintenance orders) [1999] 1 FCR 39, 46 (CA)

BUTLER-SLOSS LJ:

In general a court considering this difficult assessment should take into account in the broadest sense the expenses attributable to the child's disability. The additional help needed, the cost of feeding…additional help, a larger or better-appointed house, heating, clothing, car expenses, respite care are only some of the expenses which immediately spring to mind. The expenses attributable to the disability, broadly assessed, the income and allowances coming into the family housing the child under a disability have to be weighed in the balance against the income, assets, liabilities and outgoings of the person asked to meet some or all of those expenses.

---

[190] Ibid., s 8(5) and Child Maintenance (Written Agreements) Order 1993, SI 1993/620 require a written agreement which is then reflected in the court order.

[191] Thus complying with s 8(5) and SI 1993/620.

[192] CSA 1991, s 8(3A) allows the courts to vary validly made maintenance orders.

[193] Note obiter suggestion in *CF v KM* [2010] EWHC 1754, [4]–[6] that the court can determine that the non-resident parent's income exceeds that threshold, even if any current C-MEC calculation assumes a lower income.

[194] CSA 1991, s 8(7).

[195] Ibid., s 8(8); 'disability' for these purposes is defined in s 8(9).

[196] *Re L M (a minor)* (CA), 9 July 1997, unreported.

'Segal' orders

In addition to the situations specified in CSA 1991, s 8, the courts have carved out one further exception where it is making orders following the parents' divorce:[197]

Dorney-Kingdom v Dorney-Kingdom [2000] 3 FCR 20, 24–5 (CA)

THORPE LJ:

...A practice has grown up, finding its origins before District Judge Segal in the Principal Registry, to make an order for spousal maintenance under s 23(1)(a) of the Matrimonial Causes Act 1973 that incorporates some of the costs of supporting the children as part of a global order. When a Segal order is made an important ingredient is that the overall sum will reduce pro tanto from the date upon which [C-MEC] brings in a [maintenance calculation]. The utility of the Segal order is obvious, since in many cases the determination of the ancillary relief claims will come at a time when [C-MEC] has yet to complete its assessment of liability. It is therefore very convenient for a district judge to have a form of order which will carry the parent with primary care over that interim pending [C-MEC's] determination.

The proscription on the court making orders for child periodical payments other than by agreement, expressed in s 8(3) of the statute, could be said to be challenged, if not breached, by the mechanism of the Segal order. However, it seems to me to be just within the bounds of legitimacy, since it is no sort of ouster of or challenge to the jurisdiction of [C-MEC], but merely a holding until such time as [C-MEC] can carry out its proper function. But it seems to me absolutely crucial that if legitimacy is to be preserved, there must be a substantial ingredient of spousal support in the Segal order. If in any case there is a determination that the primary carer has no entitlement to periodical payments on her own account, any form of order that is not an agreed order plainly circumvents the statutory prohibition.

Variation of a court order duly made

The final exception is an adjunct of the foregoing four: the courts may vary maintenance orders that they have made, provided no maintenance calculation has subsequently been made by C-MEC.[198] While *V v V (Child Maintenance)* demonstrates how this facility can be used to maximize the consent order exception,[199] commentators are divided on whether any variation of a consent order must itself be made by consent.[200]

Where C-MEC does not have jurisdiction

Where C-MEC lacks jurisdiction to make a maintenance calculation, the courts have exclusive jurisdiction to order periodical payments for the benefit of a child, constrained only by the limits of the legislation under which they are acting. These situations are:

- Where maintenance is sought from a step-parent or other person who is not a 'parent', and so in relation to whom the child in question is not a 'qualifying child' for the purposes of the CSA 1991.

---

[197] Cf C-MEC default calculations and voluntary payments: 6.4.4.
[198] CSA 1991, s 8(3A).
[199] [2001] 2 FLR 799.
[200] See Wikeley (2006a), 209–10.

- Where the child is not a 'qualifying child' in relation to anyone—for example, if the child is older than the various age limits prescribed for the CSA 1991, or if there is no non-resident parent.
- Where maintenance is sought from a person with care.[201]
- Where any one or more of the person with care, non-resident parent, and qualifying child is not habitually resident in the United Kingdom.[202]
- Where C-MEC's jurisdiction is ousted by binding private ordering: see 6.6.[203]

It is important to distinguish between cases where C-MEC does not have jurisdiction, and those where C-MEC *does* have jurisdiction, but has concluded or would conclude that no maintenance calculation should be made, for example because the non-resident parent's situation warrants a nil calculation. The result produced by the CSA 1991 in such cases cannot be circumvented by resorting to the courts.[204]

6.5.3 THE STATUTORY SCHEMES

When the courts have jurisdiction to make orders, one of four statutes generally applies: the MCA 1973, DPMCA 1978, CPA 2004, or CA 1989, Sch 1 (see fig 6.1 above, p 360). The courts' powers under these Acts can be broadly divided into three categories, the first two applying only between spouses and civil partners:

- Cases of failure to maintain a child during marriage or civil partnership: DPMCA 1978/ CPA 2004, Sch 6 (magistrates' court); MCA 1973, s 27/CPA 2004, Sch 5, Pt 9 (County Court and High Court).
- Financial provision on or following divorce/dissolution, nullity, or judicial separation: MCA 1973, Pt II and CPA 2004, Sch 5.
- A more widely available jurisdiction to order financial provision for the benefit of a child under CA 1989, Sch 1, regardless of the nature of the relationship between the parents (available at all three levels of court).

For ease of exposition, we refer to each jurisdiction as proceedings or provisions relating to 'failure to maintain', 'divorce', and 'under the CA 1989', respectively. We refer collectively to the Acts other than the CA 1989 as 'matrimonial legislation'.

The extent of the courts' powers under each Act is slightly different.[205] The appropriate choice of statute turns on various factors. The parents' marital or civil partnership status and the level of court in which the application is to be made are obviously significant. There is no need to show that one parent is 'non-resident' for the court to exercise its powers. But there are certain restrictions on the making and duration of orders under some of the statutes where the parents are living together. The type of order sought and the identity of the applicant and respondent are also relevant. In order to gain an overall impression of the nature

---

[201] CSA 1991, s 8(10); see Wikeley (2006a), 198.
[202] CSA 1991, s 44.
[203] Ibid., s 4(10).
[204] Ibid., s 8(2).
[205] We do not address issues regarding the parties' domicile, habitual residence etc.

and extent of the courts' powers, we shall approach the law thematically, rather than Act by Act, highlighting differences as they arise.

The orders available

On application between spouses and civil partners for failure to maintain, only periodical payment (secured and unsecured) and lump sum orders may be made. In all other cases, including under the CA 1989, several remedies are available: periodical payments; lump sums;[206] property settlements; and property transfers.[207] In proceedings on divorce, periodical payment and lump sum orders can require payment to a third party, for example direct payment of school fees.[208] Periodical payments need not be payable from the respondent's income; maintenance can be paid from accumulated or borrowed capital.[209] Those courts can also vary ante- and post-nuptial settlements for the benefit of the child, and order sale of property as an adjunct to secured periodical payment, lump sum and property adjustment orders.[210] None of these additional powers arises under the CA 1989, Sch 1. We examine what each type of order entails in chapter 7.[211]

Who can be made liable for whom?

Each Act permits orders to be made not only against parents for the benefit of their own children, but also against certain adults for the benefit of 'children of the family'. Where the parties are spouses or civil partners:

> 'child of the family', . . . means—
>
>   (a) a child of both of those parties; and
>
>   (b) any other child, not being a child who is placed with those parties as foster parents by a local authority or voluntary organisation, who has been treated by both of those parties as a child of their family.[212]

It is not material, when determining whether a child is a 'child of the family', that a husband had so treated a child mistakenly believing that he was the father;[213] the court can consider those circumstances in deciding what, if any, order to make. But the definition of 'child of the family' depends on the relevant adults having formalized their relationship: cohabitants have no liability for each other's children.

---

[206] Magistrates can only order unsecured periodical payments and lump sums of up to £1,000: CA 1989, Sch 1, paras 1(1)(b) and 5(2); DPMCA 1978, s 2; CPA 2004, Sch 6, para 2(2).

[207] MCA 1973, ss 23 and 24; CPA 2004, Sch 5, Parts 1 and 2; CA 1989, Sch 1, para 1: see *Phillips v Peace* [2004] EWHC 3180; cf *B v B* [2007] EWHC 789.

[208] MCA 1973, s 23(1)(d)–(f); CPA 2004, Sch 5, para 2(d)–(f); the same applies in proceedings for failure to maintain, though not in the magistrates' court.

[209] *SW v RC* [2008] EWHC 73.

[210] 'Property adjustment' here includes transfers, settlements, and variation of settlements: MCA 1973, s 24A, CPA 2004, Sch 5, Part 3.

[211] A series of cases have considered the question of making Sch 1 orders to cover the applicant's legal costs: see most recently *CF v KM* [2010] EWHC 1754.

[212] E.g. MCA 1973, s 52; CPA 2004, Sch 5, para 80(2); CA 1989, Sch 1, para 16(2): cognate definition of 'parent'.

[213] *W(RJ) v W(SJ)* [1972] Fam 152.

Who can apply?

In proceedings for failure to maintain and on divorce, a current or former spouse or civil partner may apply against the other for an order in relation to a child of the family. Though they may not make an original application in proceedings for failure to maintain, children over 16 may apply for *variation* of existing orders.[214] If granted leave, children of the family may intervene in divorce proceedings to apply for financial relief. The child's guardian,[215] and a person who has or is entitled to apply for a residence order[216] in relation to the child may also apply.[217]

A far broader range of persons may apply under CA 1989, Sch 1, not least because the Act applies whatever the nature of the relationship between the parents. Since 45 per cent of children are now born to unmarried parents,[218] this Act potentially has substantial practical importance.[219] It covers disputes arising between spouses, civil partners, cohabitants, or those connected only by shared parenthood; and between parents and other individuals who enjoy certain other legal relationships with the child. A parent, guardian,[220] special guardian,[221] or person in whose favour a residence order has been made[222] may apply for relief from a parent or, where the applicant is not a parent, from both parents. 'Parent' here includes those in relation to whom a child is a 'child of the family', making spouse or civil partner step-parents potential applicants and respondents.[223]

As we have seen, the CSA 1991 gives children no standing to apply for a maintenance calculation for themselves.[224] The opportunities for children to apply under the CA 1989 are limited, and reserved for older teenagers. Children over 18 may in certain circumstances apply for lump sum or periodical payments orders against their parents, but not against step-parents or others. No such application can be made where a periodical payments order was in force when the child attained 16. Children over 16 may, however, apply for variation of existing orders.[225] No children can apply for orders if their parents are living with each other in the same household.[226] They cannot apply for property adjustment orders against anyone.

The child's age and the duration of orders

Ordinarily, no order for financial provision or for the transfer or settlement of property may be made in favour of children aged 18 or above. The courts have held that while there is no rule against property orders extending into adulthood, they should do so only exceptionally. Whilst it is commonplace for orders to last until the end of an undergraduate degree, including a gap year, they will not be made to last beyond that stage, notwithstanding the

---

214 DPMCA 1978, s 20(12); MCA 1973, s 27(6A); CPA 2004, Sch 5, para 55, and Sch 6, para 39.
215 CA 1989, s 5.
216 Ibid., ss 8 and 10(4).
217 Family Procedure Rules 2010 (FPR 2010), SI 2010/2955, r 9.10.
218 ONS (2009c).
219 *Re P (child: financial provision)* [2003] EWCA Civ 837.
220 CA 1989, s 5.
221 Ibid., s 14A.
222 Ibid., s 8.
223 Ibid., Sch 1, para 16(2).
224 Cf the position in Scotland: CSA 1991, s 7.
225 CA 1989, Sch 1, para 6(4).
226 Ibid., Sch 1, para 2.

increasing trend for children to remain at home post-university.[227] Statutory rules govern periodical payment orders. They generally last until age 17, or 18, if the court thinks it appropriate. However, orders may be made to endure beyond 18 (and so beyond the age limit of the CSA 1991[228]) or be made in the first instance after the child has reached that age, if: (a) the child is receiving instruction at an educational establishment or is training for a trade, profession, or vocation; or (b) there are special circumstances that justify the order.[229] *Downing v Downing* illustrates orders being made to support the adult child through higher education.[230] *C v F (disabled child: maintenance orders)* considered the 'special circumstances' exception in relation to disability, Butler-Sloss LJ observing that:

> It is part of the philosophy of the Children Act that a young person in [the child's] position with a total dependence upon others for the rest of his life should look for continuing financial support from his parents for whatever period may be necessary.[231]

Butler-Sloss and Thorpe LJJ concluded, *obiter*, that once the child ceased to be a 'qualifying child' for the purposes of the CSA 1991, the restriction on the courts' powers imposed by s 8(8) of that Act—that its periodical payments order could only cover expenses connected with the disability, and not with any other needs—would also cease, freeing the court to make orders for any purpose.

Periodical payments orders terminate on the payer's death.[232] Payments may cease to be payable, or may not be ordered at all, if the parents are living together. Under the magistrates' court 'failure to maintain' jurisdiction and the CA 1989, Sch 1, an order may be made for the child's benefit while the parents are living together. But such an order will terminate after the parties' have lived together, or resumed cohabitation, for over six months.[233]

6.5.4 THE GROUNDS FOR ORDERS AND THE COURTS' DISCRETION

The 'failure to maintain' provisions specify the ground on which orders under those Acts may be made for the child's benefit: that the respondent has failed to provide, or make a proper contribution towards, reasonable maintenance for the child in question.[234] The other legislation does not specify any ground for the exercise of the courts' powers. Nevertheless, the courts tend to confine themselves to providing for the child's 'maintenance', however broadly that term is construed.[235] Each statute sets out a checklist of factors for the courts to consider in exercising their discretion very similar to those applying to financial provi-

---

227 *Re N (A child)* [2009] EWHC 11.
228 See discussion in *C v F (disabled child: maintenance orders)* [1999] 1 FCR 39.
229 DPMCA 1978, s 5; CPA 2004, Sch 6, para 27; MCA 1973, ss 27(6) and 29; CPA 2004, Sch 5, para 49; CA 1989, Sch 1, para 3.
230 [1976] Fam 288.
231 [1998] 2 FLR 1, 3.
232 DPMCA 1978, s 5(4); CPA 2004, Sch 6, para 27(6); CA 1989, Sch 1, para 3(3); MCA 1973, s 29(4); and CPA 2004, Sch 5, para 49: save for arrears due.
233 DPMCA 1978, s 25(1); CPA 2004, Sch 6, para 29; CA 1989, Sch 1, para 3(4).
234 DPMCA 1978, s 1(b); CPA 2004, Sch 6, para 1; MCA 1973, s 27(1); CPA 2004, Sch 5, para 39(1).
235 *A v A (Financial Provision for Child)* [1995] 1 FCR 309. CA 1989, Sch 1, para 5 expressly permits lump sums to cover expenses incurred in connection with the child's birth.

sion between spouses and civil partners on divorce/dissolution. The checklists are broadly identical, but we highlight differences.[236]

Only in proceedings on divorce is it expressly stated that 'first consideration' must be given to the welfare while a minor of any child of the family.[237] The welfare principle in the CA 1989 does not apply to decisions about children's maintenance,[238] but it has nevertheless been held that the child's welfare is at least a relevant consideration.[239]

Re P (a child: financial provision) [2003] EWCA Civ 837

THORPE LJ:

44....I would only wish to amplify [that] by saying that welfare must be not just 'one of the relevant circumstances' but, in the generality of cases, a constant influence on the discretionary outcome. I say that because the purpose of the statutory exercise is to ensure for the child of parents who have never married and who have become alienated and combative, support and also protection against adult irresponsibility and selfishness, at least insofar as money and property can achieve those ends.

In deciding whether and, if so, how to exercise their powers under the Acts, the courts must consider all the circumstances, particularly:[240]

- the child's financial needs;
- the child's income, earning capacity (if any), property, and other financial resources;
- in matrimonial proceedings: the current or former spouses/civil partners' income, earning capacity (including that earning capacity which it would be reasonable to expect each party to take steps to acquire), property and other financial resources; their financial needs, obligations, and responsibilities, both now and likely in the foreseeable future;
- under the CA 1989, Sch 1: to those same aspects of the parents' financial situation; and, where the applicant is not a parent of the child, to the financial situation of that person. Under the CA 1989, the court is not directed to consider any earning capacity that it would be reasonable to expect a party to take steps to acquire;
- any physical or mental disability of the child (and in matrimonial proceedings other than in the magistrates' court, of either spouse/civil partner);
- the standard of living enjoyed by the family before: (i) the failure to make reasonable provision for the child (failure to maintain cases); (ii) the breakdown of the marriage/civil partnership (divorce cases). This factor is not listed in the CA 1989, Sch 1, where the parents may never have lived together or with the child;[241]
- the manner in which the child was being, or was expected to be, educated or trained.

---

[236] DPMCA 1978, s 3; CPA 2004, Sch 6, para 6; MCA 1973, ss 25(1), (3)–(4), and 27(3A); CPA 2004, Sch 5, paras 20 and 22; CA 1989, Sch 1, para 4.
[237] MCA 1973, s 25(1).
[238] See ss 1 and 105, definition of 'upbringing'.
[239] J v C (child: financial provision) [1998] 3 FCR 79.
[240] See n 236.
[241] But see N v D [2008] 1 FLR 1629.

Where orders are sought for the benefit of a 'child of the family' who is not in law the respondent's child, the court must also consider:

- whether the respondent has assumed any responsibility for the child's maintenance; and, if he did, the extent to and the basis on which he assumed that responsibility; and the length of time during which he discharged that responsibility;
- whether in assuming and discharging that responsibility the respondent did so knowing that the child was not his own;
- the liability of any other person to maintain the child: for example, the child's legal parent, who may be liable to make child support payments.

6.5.5 PRINCIPLES FROM THE CASE LAW

Most reported cases involve extremely wealthy respondents and parents who did not marry. In 'ordinary wealth' divorce cases, child support liability generally consumes respondents' free income, and the parties cannot afford to litigate, so very few reported cases address their situation. Capital and property orders, particularly regarding the former matrimonial home, are more likely to be made for the benefit of primary carers than for children, but the children obtain substantial indirect benefit from such orders. By contrast, where the respondent is wealthy and/or the parties were not spouses or civil partners so there is no jurisdiction to adjust capital or make income orders between the adults, orders for the child may be financially feasible and important for the welfare of the child's household.[242]

Unwanted births and births to unmarried parents

Applications for financial provision sometimes prompt respondents to claim that the conception was accidental, the birth unwanted, and the relationship between the parents, and between respondent parent and child, insubstantial.

J v C (child: financial provision) [1998] 3 FCR 79, 81–3 (Fam Div)

HALE J:

...[A]lthough para 4(1) of Sch 1 to the 1989 Act tells me to consider all the circumstances, I do not consider that any great weight should be attached either to the circumstances of T's birth or to the length or quality of her [parents'] relationship. There is nothing in the private law provisions to distinguish between different children on such grounds. The policy of the Child Support Act 1991 was that people who had children should support them, whether or not those were wanted children. As a general proposition children should not suffer because their parents are irresponsible or uncaring towards them. I note that there is an example of an order being made against a father who had wanted the mother to have a termination in the case of *Phillips v Peace* [1996] 2 FCR 237....

...The underlying principle [is] that children should not suffer just because their parents had, for whatever reason, not been married to one another.

Equally of course they should not get more...[243]

---

[242] Cf Law Com (2006), paras 4.34–4.46 on the under-use of the CA 1989, Sch 1.

[243] See also the remarks of Thorpe LJ in *Re P (a child: financial provision)* [2003] EWCA Civ 837 regarding welfare, extracted above.

The basic objective: meeting the child's needs

The courts view their objective as being simply to cater for the child's needs, however wealthy the respondent parent. By contrast with spouses and civil partners, who can generally claim a form of entitlement to share family assets on divorce,[244] children are merely dependants to be maintained until adulthood.[245] However, in assessing the extent of the child's needs, the courts have regard to the resources and standard of living of the respondent parent (and, where applicable, the standard of living enjoyed by the family during the parents' relationship[246]), taking the view that the child's situation should bear some reasonable resemblance to that of the parent.[247] Determining the extent of the child's 'needs' is an uncertain art.[248] Whilst orders must be 'for the benefit of the child', it is enough for a 'welfare' benefit, rather than a financial benefit, to accrue to the child. So orders may be made transferring property from one parent to the other in order to make it available for the child's occupation with that parent.[249]

Orders made under this legislation are ordinarily intended only to benefit the child during minority or until completion of education, not for life.[250] It would therefore be improper to order an outright transfer of property (e.g. a home), rather than a settlement of that property during the child's dependence. It would similarly be inappropriate to order periodical payments that would not be exhausted in meeting the child's needs during the term of the order.[251]

Indirect benefit for others

These orders may be made 'for the benefit of the child' only. Applicants who were not the respondent's spouse or civil partner cannot obtain adjustive orders for their own benefit. However, orders made for the benefit of the child can provide such individuals (and any other children living with them for whom the respondent is not liable[252]) with substantial indirect benefit. The courts have generally been happy to contemplate such indirect benefit, considering it to be in children's best interests that those living with them enjoy standards of living similar to their own.[253] In particular, the child's need for a carer requires that that carer's needs, particularly regarding accommodation, be considered.[254] However, the courts are alert to claims that are, in substance, for the benefit of the carer or her other children rather than the respondent's child.[255] In *Morgan v Hill*, the Court of Appeal emphasized that whilst

---

[244] See 7.5.4.

[245] *A v A (Financial Provision for Child)* [1995] 1 FCR 309; *Kiely v Kiely* [1988] 1 FLR 248.

[246] *N v D* [2008] 1 FLR 1629, [23].

[247] *J v C (child: financial provision)* [1998] 3 FCR 79, 87.

[248] Gilmore (2004b), 112; compare the 'reasonable requirements' concept used on divorce: see 7.5.2, 7.5.4.

[249] *K v K (Minors: Property Transfer)* [1992] 1 WLR 530.

[250] *A v A (Financial Provision for child)* [1995] 1 FCR 309. Cf *Tavoulareas v Tavoulareas* [1998] 2 FLR 418; criticized by Gilmore (2004b).

[251] *Re P (a child: financial provision)* [2003] EWCA Civ 837, [49], in relation to the carer's allowance.

[252] *Morgan v Hill* [2006] EWCA Civ 1602; cf the child born later in *Phillips v Peace* [2004] EWHC 3180, [11].

[253] *A v A (Financial Provision for Child)* [1995] 1 FCR 309; *J v C (child: financial provision)* [1998] 3 FCR 79.

[254] *Haroutunian v Jennings* (1980) 1 FCR 62.

[255] *J v C (child: financial provision)* [1998] 3 FCR 79; *Re S (Unmarried Parents: Financial Provision)* [2006] EWCA Civ 479.

it was difficult to disentangle the indirect costs (e.g. of housing, running a car, and so on) pertaining to each individual in the household (contrast the identifiable direct costs of food and clothing for each person), it was important in principle not to lose sight of the extent of the respondent's liability. It suggested that where the primary carer has children with different parents, it might be fairest to bring consolidated actions against both respondents and apportion the liability for the children between them.[256] We explore this issue insofar as it relates to the 'carer element' of periodical payments below.

Property orders

The following extract exemplifies the courts' approach to capital orders, here regarding a child's housing under the CA 1989, Sch 1. As is typical of the reported cases, the respondent was wealthy. Ward J considers the factors in para 4:

A v A (Financial Provision for Child) [1995] 1 FCR 309, 315–16 (Fam Div)

WARD J:

The father is so rich he could transfer this property and not even be aware that he had done so. His obligations and responsibilities are to provide for the maintenance and education of his child until she has completed that education, including her tertiary education, and reached independence. There is no special circumstance which imposes on him any moral duty to advance capital or income to her once he has fulfilled that duty. Her financial needs are to be considered, and it is noticeable that they are the "financial needs of the child", which again suggests that adult needs are not ordinarily relevant. The child has no income. She has no physical or mental disability. I must have regard to the manner in which she was being or was expected to be educated or trained, and the implication in those words is once more that the obligation to maintain ceases when that educational training ceases....There is no special circumstance I can find which would require this father to do more than maintain his daughter until she is independent. I therefore reject her claim for the transfer of the property to her absolutely.

The judge refused simply to accept an undertaking from the father that he would allow the child to occupy the property: the child needed the security of a beneficial interest in the home, and so made a property settlement order for the child:[257]

The terms of the trust...should be that the property be conveyed to trustees...to hold the same for A for a term which shall terminate six months after A has attained the age of 18, or six months after she has completed her full-time education, which will include her tertiary education, whichever is latest. I give her that period of six months to find her feet and arrange her affairs. The trustees shall permit her to enjoy a reasonable gap between completing her school education and embarking upon her further education.

I have regard to para. 4(1)(b) which requires me to consider the financial needs, obligations and responsibilities of each parent and also subpara. (c) which requires me to have regard to the financial needs of the child. The mother's obligation is to look after A, and A's financial

---

[256] [2006] EWCA Civ 1602, [38]–[39].
[257] See also *Re P (a child: financial provision)* [2003] EWCA Civ 837, [45].

need is to provide a roof over the head of her caretaker. It is, indeed, [the] father's obligation to provide the accommodation for the living-in help which A needs. Consequently, it must be a term of the settlement that while A is under the control of her mother and thereafter for so long as A does not object, the mother shall have the right to occupy the property to the exclusion of the father and without paying rent therefor, and for the purpose of providing a home and care and support for A.

Periodical payments: the carer's allowance

Where the courts have jurisdiction in relation to periodical payments, for example in 'top-up' cases under the CSA 1991, s 8(6), and where the available funds are extensive, they include an allowance to cover the needs of the child's carer. This practice was affirmed in the Court of Appeal's first decision under the CA 1989, Sch 1. This extract describes the approach that should be taken in 'big money' cases and addresses capital provision, before turning to the question of maintenance and the carer's allowance. The parents had not married, so the non-resident parent had no responsibility to support the parent with care in her own right. Thorpe LJ first determined what housing and associated lump sum orders were required for furnishings, a car, and so on:

Re P (a child: financial provision) [2003] EWCA Civ 837

THORPE LJ:

47. Those issues settled the judge can proceed to determine what budget the mother reasonably requires to fund her expenditure in maintaining the home and its contents and in meeting her other expenditure external to the home, such as school fees, holidays, routine travel expenses, entertainments, presents, etc. In approaching this last decision, the judge is likely to be assailed by rival budgets...Invariably the applicant's budget hovers somewhere between the generous and the extravagant. Invariably the respondent's budget expresses parsimony....But it is worth emphasising the trite point that...an order for periodical payments is always variable and will generally have to be revisited to reflect both relevant changes of circumstance and also the factor of inflation. Therefore...the court should discourage undue bickering over budgets. What is required is a broad commonsense assessment. What the court first ordains may have a comparatively brief life before a review is claimed by one or other party.

48. In making this broad assessment how should the judge approach the mother's allowance, perhaps the most emotive element in the periodical payments assessment? The respondent will often accept with equanimity elements within the claim that are incapable of benefiting the applicant (for instance school fees or children's clothing) but payments which the respondent may see as more for the benefit of the applicant than the child are likely to be bitterly resisted. Thus there is an inevitable tension between the two propositions, both correct in law, first that the applicant has no personal entitlement, second that she is entitled to an allowance as the child's primary carer. Balancing this tension may be difficult in individual cases. In my judgment, the mother's entitlement to an allowance as the primary carer (an expression which I stress) may be checked but not diminished by the absence of any direct claim in law.

49. Thus...the court must recognise the responsibility, and often the sacrifice, of the unmarried parent (generally the mother) who is to be the primary carer for the child, perhaps

the exclusive carer if the absent parent disassociates from the child. In order to discharge this responsibility the carer must have control of a budget that reflects her position and the position of the father, both social and financial. On the one hand she should not be burdened with unnecessary financial anxiety or have to resort to parsimony when the other parent chooses to live lavishly. On the other hand whatever is provided is there to be spent at the expiration of the year for which it is provided. There can be no slack to enable the recipient to fund a pension or an endowment policy or otherwise to put money away for a rainy day. In some cases it may be appropriate for the court to expect the mother to keep relatively detailed accounts of her outgoings and expenditure in the first and then in succeeding years of receipt. Such evidence would obviously be highly relevant to the determination of any application for either upward or downward variation.

Whilst keeping accounts may be sensible, these observations have been questioned: requiring that accounts be regularly reported to the respondent may be unhelpful, intrusive, a cause of friction, and so counter-productive.[258] As to the question of making savings, it was noted in *Re C (Financial Provision)* that the primary carer should be allowed to save up for recurrent expenditure which arises less frequently than annually: it is *personal* saving which is barred.[259]

Thorpe LJ made the following observations in quantifying the carer element (note that the father had 'unlimited means' and the court had approved budgets of £1m to acquire central London accommodation for the child and mother and £100,000 for its furnishing):

42.... [In] *A v A* [above, decided in 1995], in explaining his quantification of an allowance for the mother's care Ward J said:

"I bear in mind a broad range of imprecise information from the extortionate demands (but excellent service) of Norland nannies, to au pair girls and mother's helps, from calculations in personal injury and fatal accident claims and from the notice-boards in the employment agencies I pass daily. I allow £8,000 under this head. It is almost certainly much less than the father would have to pay were he to be employing staff, but to allow more would be—or would be seen to be—paying maintenance to the former mistress who has no claim in her own right to be maintained."

43. I cannot agree with that reservation. I believe that a more generous approach to the calculation of the mother's allowance is not only permissible but also realistic. Nor would I have regard to calculations in either personal injury or fatal accident claims. It seems to me that such cross-references only risk to complicate what is an essentially broad-brush assessment to be taken by family judges with much expertise and experience in the specialist field of ancillary relief....

54. In making an independent assessment [of the periodical payments order] in the exercise of my own discretion, I have regard to the likely cost of running the home that the trustees will buy for the mother and L [the child]. I have regard to the fact that the mother is to be L's primary carer. I would not relate that to the cost of a Norland nanny. That would be to demean the mother's role. Mothers provide 24-hour care for children. That level of care would be difficult to buy in, even for a father as rich and resourceful as this. In the real world nannies are entitled to days off, weekends off and holidays.... I would take a broad-brush figure of £70,000 per annum from which the father is entitled to deduct the amount of state

[258] *Re P* [2003] EWCA Civ 837, [75] per May LJ; *Re C (Financial Provision)* [2007] 2 FLR 13; cf accounting for the expenditure of a lump sum paid for a specific purpose: *Re N (a child)* [2009] EWHC 11, [32]–[33].
[259] [2007] 2 FLR 13.

benefits that the mother receives for L. Of course it is easy to say that that represents a liability of approximately £1,500 a week for a two-year-old child. But that is a distortion of the reality that £70,000 is a budget to enable the mother to run the home for [the child] and to provide her additional needs....

As May LJ noted in *Re P*, cases like are atypical and so should not be used as a benchmark for future cases.[260]

In *F v G (Child: Financial Provision)*, a full carer's allowance was made even though the mother was working full-time. The court considered that she should be able to choose whether to spend that allowance on hiring child-care and continue to work, securing her own financial future, or alternatively to work part-time and care for the child herself.[261] This was not considered to offend *Re P*'s prohibition on any 'slack' being made available to the parent with care: any savings would derive from her own earnings, should she choose to work.

A carer's allowance can also be justified in relation to teenage children, even when at university: they still need someone to provide a home for them, and can be as demanding in terms of a carer's time and attention, albeit in very differently, as younger children.[262]

GW v RW (Financial Provision: Departure from Equality) exemplifies a different approach to fixing periodical payments.[263] This was a big money case where the court had full jurisdiction over child maintenance because the parent with care and children were not habitually resident in the UK. The parents were divorcing, so their financial and property disputes had been dealt with under the MCA 1973; the wife, broadly speaking, was awarded 40 per cent of the substantial assets. We examine the CSA 1991, s 4(10), referred to in this extract, below. Judge Mostyn identified two main principles:

GW v RW [2003] EWHC 611

NICHOLAS MOSTYN QC (sitting as a deputy High Court judge):

74....First, I am of the view that the appropriate starting point for a child maintenance award should almost invariably be the figure thrown up by the...child support rules. The Government's express policy in making awards of child maintenance susceptible to abrogation and replacement by a maintenance calculation by the CSA (see 4(10)(aa) Child Support Act 1991) was that child maintenance orders should be negotiated:

'...in the shadow of the CSA. All parties will know that either parent can turn to the CSA in future, and that it will therefore be sensible to determine child maintenance broadly in line with CSA assessment rates.' [See DSS (1999), ch 8]

If a child maintenance order, whether made by consent or after a contest, is markedly at variance with the calculation under the [child support] regime then there will be a high temptation for one or other party after the order has been in force for a year, and after giving two months' notice, to approach the CSA [as it then was] for a calculation. Quite apart from the obvious acrimony that this would engender, a calculation in a different amount to the figure originally negotiated or

---

[260] See also *Re S* [2006] EWCA Civ 479.
[261] [2004] EWHC 1848, [44]–[54].
[262] *N v D* [2008] 1 FLR 1629, [24]–[25]; *H v C* [2009] EWHC 1527.
[263] See also *E v C (Calculation of Child Maintenance)* [1996] 1 FLR 472; *A v M* [2005] EWHC 1721.

awarded may cast doubt on the fairness of the original ancillary relief settlement between the parties, leading to further litigation. These spectres should be avoided at all costs.

75. The second principle is that notwithstanding that the income of the parent with care is disregarded in the calculation of child support…it is reasonable to expect the parent with care who has received a substantial share of the parties' assets to contribute to the support of the children.…It should be noted that the Government justified the omission of the parent with care's income in the new formula on the ground that she would from her own resources be making a substantial contribution to the support of the children.…

77. Having regard to these principles my decision is as follows:

77.1. I am satisfied that there should be some increase on the starting point of the maximum CSA calculation that would be applicable here. The husband has an income well in excess of the capped amount of [£2,000 per week—the then ceiling for the CSA]. I am also of the view that where a proportionate division of the main assets has been effected [60% to H, 40% to W] then that proportion should inform the division of the child maintenance costs.…I therefore award general maintenance of [60% of those costs] per child per annum payable quarterly in advance…to continue until each respective child attains 18 years of age or completes full time tertiary education if later.…Once a child enters tertiary education the payments will be made, as H has suggested, as to two-thirds to the child direct and one-third to W.

77.2. In addition H will pay all the educational costs of the children, to include reasonable extras until the conclusion of full-time tertiary education.

77.3. H will also pay all the costs of travel for contact, to include the cost of an accompanying nanny until the younger child's seventh birthday.

The child support formula can legitimately and sensibly provide a *starting point* for determining the level of court-ordered periodical payments, not least as a guide to determining the extent of the child's needs, as measured by reference to the non-resident parent's living standard (insofar as that is roughly reflected in his income level). However, the courts are required to have regard to a wider range of circumstances than that, and so must be free to depart from the formula where fairness requires it.

6.5.6 ENFORCEMENT OF COURT ORDERS

The courts have broad powers to enforce their own orders, corresponding with those available in matrimonial and civil partnership cases.[264] The enforcement powers of the CSA 1991 were originally modelled on the powers to enforce court orders, but post-CMOP 2008 C-MEC enjoys a wider range of options to enforce its calculations (including disqualification orders and curfews) than the courts have for their orders.

6.6 'VOLUNTARY ARRANGEMENTS' AND OTHER PRIVATE ORDERING

A key recommendation of Henshaw was that all parents should be free and encouraged to make their own arrangements for child support, without the intervention of a public authority. The statutory objectives and duties of C-MEC are important here:

264 See 7.3.6.

Child Maintenance and Other Payments Act 2008

2 Objectives of the Commission

(1) The Commission's main objective is to maximise the number of children who live apart from one or both of their parents for whom effective maintenance arrangements are in place.

(2) The Commission's main objective is supported by the following subsidiary objectives –

(a) to encourage and support the making and keeping by parents of appropriate voluntary maintenance arrangements for their children;

(b) to support the making of applications for child support maintenance under the Child Support Act 1991 and to secure compliance when appropriate with parental obligations under that Act...

4 Promotion of child maintenance

The Commission must take such steps as it thinks appropriate for the purpose of raising awareness among parents of the importance of –

(a) taking responsibility for the maintenance of their children, and

(b) making appropriate arrangements for the maintenance of children of theirs who live apart from them

5 Provision of information and guidance

(1) The Commission must provide to parents such information and guidance as it thinks appropriate for the purpose of helping to secure the existence of effective maintenance arrangements for children who live apart from one or both of their parents...

In this section, we consider to the legal framework within which such private arrangements can be made. We consider the policy implications the new emphasis on private ordering at 6.7.2.

6.6.1 MAINTENANCE AND OTHER FINANCIAL AGREEMENTS AND CONSENT ORDERS FOR THE BENEFIT OF CHILDREN

Private ordering of maintenance

The statutory provisions governing the legal effect of private ordering undertaken in relation to child maintenance (i.e. matters falling within the jurisdiction of C-MEC) are quite difficult to follow, but their overall effect—which we explain below—is clear:

Child Support Act 1991

4 ...

(10) No application [to C-MEC] may be made at any time under this section with respect to a qualifying child or any qualifying children if—

(a) there is in force a written maintenance agreement made before 5th April 1993, or a maintenance order made before [6th April 2002], in respect of that child or those children and the person who is, at that time, the non-resident parent; or (aa) a maintenance order made on or after [6th April 2002] is in force in respect of them, but has been so for less than the period of one year beginning with the date on which it was made;...

8 ...

(11) In this Act "maintenance order", in relation to any child, means an order which requires the making or securing of periodical payments to or for the benefit of the child and which is made under—

(a) Part II of the Matrimonial Causes Act 1973;

(b) the Domestic Proceedings and Magistrates' Courts Act 1978;...

(e) Schedule 1 to the Children Act 1989;

(ea) Schedule 5, 6 or 7 to the Civil Partnership Act 2004; or

(f) any other prescribed enactment,[265] and includes any order varying or reviving such an order.

9 Agreements about maintenance

(1) In this section "maintenance agreement" means any agreement for the making, or for securing the making, of periodical payments by way of maintenance...to or for the benefit of any child.

(2) Nothing in this Act shall be taken to prevent any person from entering into a maintenance agreement.

(3) Subject to section 4(10)(a)..., the existence of a maintenance agreement shall not prevent any party to the agreement, or any other person, from applying for a maintenance calculation with respect to any child to or for whose benefit periodical payments are to be made or secured under the agreement.

(4) Where any agreement contains a provision which purports to restrict the right of any person to apply for a maintenance calculation, that provision shall be void...[266]

First, 'voluntary' (as C-MEC calls them) maintenance agreements: parties are free to make such agreements, which are theoretically enforceable as contracts.[267] However, like separation agreements made between spouses on divorce[268] (with the exception of agreements made pre-1993) the existence of such an agreement cannot prevent either party at any time applying to C-MEC for a maintenance calculation which will then replace the agreement, which will no longer be enforceable.[269]

Parties who wish to attain greater certainty from private ordering should enshrine their agreement in a consent order. Such orders made before 6 April 2002 are fully binding for their duration; neither party can undermine the order by applying to C-MEC. However, the position relating to consent orders made since that date is more complicated. Whilst

---

[265] Child Support (Maintenance Arrangements and Jurisdiction) Regulations 1992, SI 1992/2645, as amended, reg 2.

[266] Further subsections relate to courts' powers to vary certain maintenance agreements.

[267] *Darke v Strout* [2003] EWCA Civ 176.

[268] See 7.7.

[269] CSA 1991, s 10(2); SI 1992/2645, reg 4.

theoretically capable of variation and enforcement for their duration, once the order has been in place for one year, either party is free to apply to C-MEC for a maintenance calculation which will, again, supplant what the parties agreed, and deprive the court of jurisdiction.[270] So, for their first year of operation, consent orders offer more security than mere agreements; but after that year, they are as vulnerable as agreements to C-MEC's intervention. The bar in s 4(10)(aa) on applying for child support during the first year of a consent order for maintenance does not apply to orders made for either educational fees or special expenses associated with the child's disability: such orders are designed to deal with matters other than the child's basic maintenance.[271]

It follows that parties' ability to avoid using C-MEC through private ordering requires ongoing, mutual consent. As was observed in *GW v RW (Financial Provision: Departure from Equality)*,[272] it makes sense for parties seeking to avoid C-MEC's involvement to consider what the CSA 1991 formula would provide were it applied to their case. Then neither party will have any incentive to apply to C-MEC. In fashioning orders in contested cases, courts consider the potential maintenance calculation that would be made. A court invited to enshrine in a consent order a maintenance agreement which departed substantially from the calculation that C-MEC might be expected to make is likely to ask careful questions before making the order.

One key Henshaw recommendation that was rejected by Government was that the 12-month rule rendering consent orders vulnerable to attack via C-MEC should be dropped, leaving such cases entirely within the court system. Others argued for a return to an entirely court-based system, in which child maintenance would be addressed alongside all the other financial and other issues over which the courts have jurisdiction on relationship breakdown.[273] But others were concerned that the emphasis on court-based private ordering may be detrimental to children and primary carers where there was an imbalance of power, and costly to those who cannot readily access the courts.[274] The Government firmly opposed both ideas:

DWP, *Report on the child maintenance White Paper: Reply by the Government*, Cm 7062 (London: TSO, 2007b)

7.1...The Government wants to give parents the choice of resolving child maintenance either by private agreement, or by recourse to a straightforward and transparent administrative process. It is the Government's view that providing a further parallel State child maintenance system operating on very different principles and with the ability to set very different levels of child maintenance would add a further level of complexity that would not, for the vast majority of clients, lead to a better service.

8.1....The 12-month rule ensures that Consent Orders contain fair and consistent levels of child maintenance and provides parents with a route back into the assessment, collection and enforcement services of C-MEC if their order breaks down. Removal of the 12-month rule would keep parents locked into the court system and would enable the courts to make awards that were not consistent with the formula.

---

270 Ibid., s 10(1) and reg 3.
271 Child Support Act 1995, s 18(6).
272 [2003] EWHC 611 (Fam), [74].
273 Pirrie (2006).
274 CPAG (2006).

> 8.2 We want parents to agree fair and sustainable child maintenance arrangements, and to
> ensure that, if agreements do break down or circumstances change, children can continue
> to receive maintenance because their parents will still have the opportunity to access the
> services provided by C-MEC.
>
> One of the faults of the past was that courts authorised clean-break settlements leaving
> children stranded in poverty without any ongoing child maintenance. The Government does
> not want to return to this past scenario and the 12-month rule appears to be effectively dis-
> couraging this type of settlement.

The Government promised to explore with stakeholders ways of improving the interface
between family court and C-MEC to help families resolve all issues smoothly.

Private ordering of other financial issues for children

Parents are free to reach private agreements regarding financial and property provision falling outside C-MEC's jurisdiction for the benefit of children: for example, an agreement to
hold a house on trust for child and primary carer to occupy, or regarding school fees. Again,
parents may simply conclude an agreement or—for greater certainty—obtain a consent
order. The latter option is fully binding—and variable—like any other order.[275] An agreement not so formalized will be binding as a contract, save that, just as C-MEC's jurisdiction
over maintenance cannot be ousted by agreement, nor can the courts' powers over the matters for which it has jurisdiction. Either party may therefore apply to court for provision
different from that agreed, or ask the court to vary the agreement either because of a change
of circumstances or because the agreement 'does not contain proper financial arrangements
with respect to the child'.[276] The Court of Appeal held in *Morgan v Hill* that the same principles apply whichever route is taken.[277] The applicant need only show lack of proper financial arrangements; no higher threshold of inadequacy need be crossed. But any variation
or departure via a court order from what had been agreed must be just having regard to
all the circumstances, and the existence and terms of the agreement are a 'very important
circumstance'.[278] This approach, similar to that taken between spouses on divorce, discourages applications made merely because parties become dissatisfied with their bargain.

6.6.2 DISCOURAGING THE 'CLEAN BREAK'

Parties not only have reason to fix periodical payments at levels prescribed by the CSA 1991.
They are also strongly encouraged to view periodical payment, so calculated, as the only, or
at least the primary, means of discharging the child support obligation. Some parents might
prefer to do so by some means other than regular income payments in order to achieve a
clean break: i.e. make capital transfers now in lieu of maintenance and so terminate the
parties' financial relationship.[279] This was a common settlement prior to the CSA 1991.[280]
But because private ordering over maintenance cannot be guaranteed to stick, non-resident

---

[275] See 7.7.1.

[276] CA 1989, Sch 1, para 10; MCA 1973, s 35.

[277] [2006] EWCA Civ 1602, [34].

[278] Ibid., [28]; cf *Edgar v Edgar* [1980] 1 WLR 1410, discussed at 7.7.2.

[279] See 7.6.

[280] *R (Kehoe) v Secretary of State for Work and Pensions* [2005] UKHL 48, [64] extracted above, p 354.
For the problems encountered when the CSA 1991 was implemented, see *Crozier v Crozier* [1994] Fam 114;

parents may be unwilling to make such settlements. Parents therefore need to take account of potential periodical child support obligations when negotiating other aspects of their financial settlement on divorce.

6.7 POLICY QUESTIONS RELATING TO FINANCIAL SUPPORT OF CHILDREN

The law relating to financial and property provision for children raises several important policy questions. In this section we explore six issues: child support as a matter of child's right or parent's responsibility; public intervention, family privacy, and private ordering; the relevance of legal and social parenthood to child support liability; the contrast between rules and discretion; and the choice between judicial and administrative fora for determining the extent of financial responsibility for children.

6.7.1 CHILDREN'S RIGHT OR PARENTS' RESPONSIBILITY?

Key government papers on child support have had child-centred titles: 'Children Come First'—'Children First: a new approach to child support'—'Children's Rights and Parents' Responsibilities'. The Henshaw report asserted that 'children have a right to appropriate support', though also used the language of 'welfare'.[281] Various questions arise when attempting to formulate a rights-based approach to financial provision for children, not least: what is the content of the right and against whom is it exercisable? Readers may wish to refer to the extracts at 8.5.2 from the theoretical work of MacCormick and Eekelaar on whom Nick Wikeley relies in developing his rights-based approach:

N. Wikeley, *Child Support: Law and Policy* (Oxford: Hart Publishing, 2006a), 8–10

[C]hildren's basic interests mean that children have a right that their essential needs for food, shelter and clothing are satisfied. This right may be conceptualised in two parallel and complementary ways. First, it might be characterised as a fundamental human right, which is vested in children by virtue of their membership of the wider community and irrespective of their own parents' particular circumstances. In the United Kingdom, the availability of child benefit as a universal social security benefit may be seen as a tangible manifestation of this principle, in that it reflects a (modest) contribution by society at large to assist all parents (for the most part) in meeting the costs of raising their children. The resource implications for the state of the child's fundamental human right to support may be more extensive in some circumstances: [e.g. orphans]. Secondly, the child's right to support might be construed as a correlative claim-right, in the sense that failure to satisfy those needs would amount to a breach of duty by an individual subject to corresponding obligations. The decision to impose such a duty on a particular individual – for example, the child's parent(s) – will be the outcome of a process of weighing up a range of considerations drawn from the realms of moral insight and social policy. These factors will also influence the priority which is accorded

---

Smith v McInerney [1994] 2 FLR 1077, and the introduction of the special variation ground for such cases in 1995.

[281] Henshaw (2006), 2; see also Hutton (2006).

within society to the child's correlative right to (private) child support, as against the contribution made by (public) child support.

One undoubted benefit of such a twin-track approach to understanding the child's right to support is that it would appear to command widespread popular support. A further advantage of this framework is its universality in that it is not predicated on family breakdown; in principle it applies just as much to children who live in intact families as to those whose parents have separated (or indeed whose parents have never lived together at all). Yet in practice...the state is inhibited from seeking to regulate the distribution of resources within the private domain of the intact family. For this reason, the problems of identifying and quantifying a child's basic needs remain largely hidden from view. It is the public fact of separation that throws these questions into sharp relief: even if we assume that child support is first and foremost a call on parental income, how do we define a child's basic needs?

The options range from securing a minimum, uniform subsistence level of support for all children, or relating maintenance to the standard of living of the particular family, an approach which gets further from the needs-based paradigm and so from a fundamental human right:

[I]t may be possible to resolve this dilemma by returning to Eekelaar's analysis of children's rights in terms of basic, developmental and autonomy interests. Applying this taxonomy, we might argue that children enjoy a fundamental human right to child support in terms of having their basic living needs met, and that these are to be satisfied by a combination of public and private resource (the precise balance between those two sources to be determined by both value judgments and social policy considerations). On top of this, we might also contend that children have at the very least a legitimate expectation that they will benefit from the standard of living enjoyed by both their parents, irrespective of with which parent they actually happen to reside. This is, admittedly, a question of values and political choices rather than fundamental human rights. Obviously, the state itself cannot fund such expectations...One may, however, suggest that it is not unreasonable for the state to create the legal structures within which such expectations may be realised. The nomenclature of legitimate expectations, rather than rights, is deliberate, in that it implies that such expectations may be subject to compromise where there are other compelling interests to take into account. Its importance, however, lies in the message that child support is not simply a question of ensuring that food is put on the table and clothes on the child's back. Rather, child support is about improving the child's overall life chances – a matter in which society at large has a considerable interest and investment.

Current English law cannot readily be explained in rights-based terms, notwithstanding Baroness Hale's speech in the *Kehoe* case[282] and the radical change in the state's interest in recovery of child support post-CMOP 2008. Pre-CMOP, when the state was the principal beneficiary of child support in public law cases, the notion that this was a child's rights measure was very problematic.[283] But even now that child support fully supplements children's household income, the matter remains doubtful. There is no reference in governmental

---

[282] *R (Kehoe) v Secretary of State for Work and Pensions* [2005] UKHL 48: see Wikeley (2006b), p 387 above.

[283] Parker (1991).

policy documents to the UNCRC's guarantees.[284] The legislation does not conceptualize financial provision as a children's rights issue: attempts to affirm the child's right to maintenance on the face of CMOP 2008 failed.[285] As we have seen, children have no right to apply to C-MEC and limited opportunities to apply to court for financial provision. The new focus on private ordering leaves children dependent on parents' actions: whether maintenance is paid at all, in what form and amount, depends on adults' agreement or on the person with care applying to C-MEC or court. CMOP 2008's reinstatement of family privacy in this sphere, discussed below, detracts from any notion that the child has an independent right to be maintained. As Stephen Parker has observed, if anyone has a right here it is the person with care[286]—but even that right is doubtful after *Kehoe*. Moreover, it is perhaps an odd fundamental human right which applies only to the children of parents who are living apart:

S. Parker, 'Child Support in Australia: Children's Rights or Public Interest?', (1991) 5 *International Journal of Law and the Family* 24, 55

What particular class of children is intended as the class of right-holder? It cannot be children in one-parent families because, for example, a child whose father has died or disappeared is not covered by the Scheme. The obvious counter to this is that the putative right is to share in *parental* income and that the establishment of a guaranteed maintenance scheme for *all* children (which would belong to the more contestable class of welfare rights) was never intended. Whilst this might be true, it is difficult to see what exactly the child gains in insisting that the *parent* provides the money,[287] when set alongside the advantage of simply having the benefit of that amount of money from somewhere. A Scheme more obviously in line with this theory of children's rights would guarantee to all children the same sort of income as in the normal case [of children living with two parents] but quite separately institute a reimbursement mechanism for those absent parents who can be tracked down.[288]

It may be more appropriate to focus on the second part of the title of the Government's 1999 paper: 'Parents' Responsibilities'. Rebecca Bailey-Harris's comments on the Australian system are again apposite to the UK context:

R. Bailey-Harris, 'Child Support: is the Right the Wrong One?', (1992) 6 *International Journal of Law and the Family* 169, 171

[A]rguably *any* rights analysis is inappropriate: the scheme is more properly viewed as being based on obligation ie the enforcement of parental *obligations* to support their children. The language employed in the [Australian legislation—compare CSA 1991, s 1] is of symbolic significance: it is framed entirely in terms of parental duty. It is not suggested that an obligations analysis is necessarily less capable of promoting the child's interests than a rights analysis;[289] nevertheless the two approaches must be recognized as conceptually distinct.

---

[284] Henricson and Bainham (2005), 44.
[285] E.g. Hansard HL Deb, vol 698, cols GC275–80, 29 January 2008.
[286] Parker (1991), 53–5.
[287] Cf Altman (2003), Eekelaar (1991a).
[288] Compare the Finer Committee proposals (DHSS (1974)) for a guaranteed maintenance allowance for all lone-parent families: Lewis (1998) and Douglas (2000a).
[289] See O'Neill (1992).

If the Child Support Scheme is to be analyzed in obligation terms, the nature of the parental obligation it creates merits analysis. It arises from procreation and not from nurturing; it is not necessary for a liable parent to have lived with the custodian. It is an obligation which may exist without any correlative benefit..., the legislation having set its face squarely against any necessary link between access [i.e. contact between non-resident parent and child] and financial support.

We explore the emphasis on legal parenthood, regardless of the degree of social relationship between non-resident parent and child at 6.7.3 below.

'Parental responsibility' has been in the foreground of child support debates, but its meaning has changed over time. While Margaret Thatcher was concerned about the irresponsibility of feckless fathers who paid nothing towards their children's upbringing, the latest reforms adopt a rather different approach. It is important to appreciate that the meaning of 'parental responsibility' here does not correspond with the term as used in s 3 of the CA 1989, discussed in chapter 10, not least because child support is payable by 'parents' whether or not they have 'parental responsibility' (as defined by s 3) for the child. The concept is being deployed here in a wider sense,[290] reflected in CMOP 2008, s 4 and CSA 1991, s 1.[291] In its exhortation of 'effective' private arrangements which ensure that an 'appropriate' level of child support is paid, CMOP 2008 contains echoes of the sort of 'responsibility' which features in divorce law and policy debates.[292] Just as Government wishes spouses to 'divorce responsibly', so it is desirous that parents make 'responsible' arrangements for child maintenance and act 'responsibly' by endeavouring to make private agreements rather than by relying on the state to do it for them.[293]

However, just as it is questionable whether divorcing couples would use a 'period of reflection and consideration' in the responsible manner intended by divorce policy-makers, so it is doubtful to what extent parents will (be able to) reach private arrangements for child maintenance that provide a proper level of financial support— and so contribute to child poverty targets—in the absence of a more assertive role for the state. As Wikeley has observed, the policy is not helped by CMOP 2008's expression 'voluntary maintenance arrangements' which scarcely emphasizes any *duty* of the non-resident parent to provide support.[294] The rhetoric of 'parental responsibility' may be rather empty. But if the CSA 1991/CMOP 2008 regime is as weak on parental responsibility as it is on children's rights, then what is it about? Some might argue that it is driven by pragmatic, operational efficiency concerns of the state, and not by rights, interests, or concerns of the individuals involved, least of all the child.[295]

6.7.2 PUBLIC AND PRIVATE

The dichotomy between public and private spheres, and the justification for state (public) intervention in family (private) life, is a prevalent theme in family law.[296] Several issues pertaining to that theme arise in relation to financial provision for children: the state's roles in

---

[290] Cf discussion of parental responsibility by Fox Harding (1991a, 1991b), and Eekelaar (1991c).

[291] Set out above at pp 407 and 363.

[292] See chapter 5.

[293] Cf discussion of this theme at 5.8.1.

[294] (2007b), 442.

[295] Fortin (2009b), 354; Wikeley (2007b).

[296] See 1.2.3.

intact and separated families; the nature of the privacy afforded to families; and the impact of family privacy and private ordering on vulnerable family members.

Protecting the private sphere

Financial or property provision cannot be sought for or by children living with both parents. Only where one or both parents are non-resident or are severing their legal relationship does the law offer any remedy. The private realm of the nuclear family is immune from state interference. But we must beware of viewing family law in purely negative terms: in *defining* what is 'dysfunctional' and therefore warrants legal intervention, the law implicitly promotes 'accepted', and so private, family forms and behaviours.[297] The non-intervention of law in intact families has implications for the status and rights of children.

A. Diduck, *Law's Families* (London: Butterworths, 2003), 166

When children and parents live in the same household, the law says very little about how they carry out their financial obligations to each other. It is clear, however, that children have no right to share in the overall family wealth, but simply the right to be supported during their dependence....Law thus does not assume democracy or children's economic 'citizenship' within the family, but rather relies upon an idea of children's status to endorse their (economic) dependency.

This can produce strange inequalities. For example, the restrictions on children's right to make applications against their own parents may place the children of separated parents in a stronger position than those who still live with both parents. While children of divorced parents may apply for support during university, children from intact families may not, even if their parents are not supporting them adequately, and even though their eligibility for student loans and grants is generally determined by reference to parental resources.[298]

Pre-CMOP 2008, the public/private line was drawn very differently where the parent with care was on benefits. The state actively intervened in family life to recoup welfare benefits paid out from child support received, requiring parents with care to cooperate in this exercise despite the very limited personal benefit (up to £10 per week) that would accrue to them in consequence. Meanwhile, the privacy of 'middle class' families not reliant on state support was preserved, not required to engage with the CSA regime unless one party wished to do so. The radical reforms effected by CMOP 2008, not only removing compulsion in benefit cases and creating a full maintenance disregard, but also abolishing the liable relative rule as it applied to children, considerably reinforce the privacy of all families.

A limited form of privacy

However, the privacy available is somewhat limited. We saw in 6.6 that there are strong incentives for parents to agree financial provision along C-MEC lines. 'Private ordering'

---

[297] O'Donovan (1985).
[298] Education (Student Support) Regulations 2009, SI 2009/1555, Sch 4; Maclean and Eekelaar (1997), 43.

so understood seems to have procedural rather than substantive content: the parties' free-dom is to behave amicably within the substantive framework set down by the law, not to agree their own terms. Where they do apply to C-MEC, they cede even procedural privacy: enforcement falls entirely into the hands of the state.[299] Once the state in the form of C-MEC has been engaged, the family moves itself into the public sphere and so loses control. By contrast, C-MEC has no power to enforce privately negotiated maintenance arrangements. Parents who have managed to reach agreement must therefore use the courts' more limited enforcement powers, and remain vulnerable to the possibility of the other party unilaterally removing the case from the private judicial system into the public administrative sphere by simply applying to C-MEC for a maintenance calculation.[300] The lack of simple enforcement mechanism for voluntary agreements may discourage many parents with care from trying the voluntary route instead of applying initially to C-MEC.[301] The Government justified its policy on the basis that parents whose private arrangement fails should have easy access to C-MEC, which, it is said, will provide 'swift intervention'. In echoes of past child sup-port debates, the new administrative body was repeatedly portrayed in the parliamentary debates as hyper-efficient, by contrast (at least implicitly) with the courts to which parties might otherwise have to turn (and get 'stuck') if the 12-month rule relating to enforcement of consent orders were abolished.[302] It remains to be seen whether C-MEC will perform any better than its ill-fated predecessors: much will depend on the size and nature of its caseload and effectiveness of its IT systems.

So, child support is privatized insofar as liability rests with private individuals, but 'pub-licized' insofar as the state controls nearly all aspects of that liability. This undermines what one commentator describes as the 'important principle of autonomy for parents in whom the state has no direct financial interest (other than the raising of taxes)'.[303]

The dangers of private ordering

Private ordering does not come without dangers. Most fundamentally, it has been argued that privatizing child support—by making child maintenance the primary responsibility of private individuals rather than the state—ensures women's dependence on men.[304] The dysfunctional, fatherless family is forced by the state (certainly pre-CMOP 2008 in benefits cases) to 'reconnect' via the enforcement of financial obligations.[305] However, the greater danger may arise post-CMOP 2008 now that private ordering is the preferred route and application to C-MEC depends entirely on private action.

Several commentators, including the Work and Pensions Select Committee,[306] expressed concerns about this policy, particularly where there is an imbalance of power or information[307] between the parents, and about the consequent 'moral hazard' of non-resident parents avoid-ing their responsibilities. The Government was confident that offering full information and

---

[299] R (Kehoe) v Secretary of State for Work and Pensions [2005] UKHL 48.

[300] See 6.6.

[301] Wikeley (2007b), 446–7.

[302] E.g. Hansard HL Deb, GC525, 5 February 2008; HC Public Bill Committee, cols 246–7, 9 October 2007.

[303] Mostyn (1999), 97.

[304] Lewis (1998), 275.

[305] Diduck (1995), 539.

[306] Work and Pensions Select Committee (2007), para 179; see also Hansard, Public Bill Committee, col 49 (Nick Wikeley) and cols 70, 72 (Janet Allbeson) 17 July 2007; Hansard HL Deb, GC 382–3.

[307] Parents negotiating privately do not have the benefit of courts' powers to require disclosure.

support to parents with care would empower them to seek the child maintenance to which they are entitled, if not by agreement then via C-MEC. But there is an important distinction between simply providing information and support, and providing *independent advice* tailored to the circumstances of each family, and there are many obstacles to fair agreements being reached.

Headline findings from research conducted prior to CMOP 2008 into the experiences and views of different categories of separated parents (PWCs: parents with care; NRPs: non-resident parents; benefit and non-benefit cases; Agency clients and others) are instructive about the potential of the new approach:[308]

N. Wikeley et al, *Relationship separation and child support study,* DWP RR 503, summary (2008)

The demographic profile of separated families...

- **CSA benefit PWCs**, obliged to use the CSA. Relationship with ex-partner may or may not have been acrimonious. Most economically disadvantaged of all the groups.

- **CSA non-benefit PWCs** have used the CSA voluntarily. Most acrimonious relationship with ex-partner, of all the groups, indicating that they may have chosen to go to the CSA due to difficulties setting up private maintenance arrangements.

- **Non-CSA 'happy' PWCs**. Less acrimony between co-parents, more likely to have higher incomes. Non-use of the CSA may be due to a lack of need.

- **Non-CSA 'unhappy' PWCs**. Never in a relationship and/or no current contact with co-parent, more likely to have lower incomes. Non-use of the CSA may be due to a lack of information about the CSA and/or the co-parent.

Financial arrangements...

- Around six in ten non-CSA PWCs had no maintenance arrangement at all; about three in ten had a private arrangement; and one in ten were subject to a court order or consent order.

- On average, non-CSA PWCs reported receiving almost twice as much in maintenance as CSA PWCs.

- CSA PWCs were less likely than other parents to regard the amount of child maintenance being paid as fair.

- Only a minority of parents discussed financial matters with their ex-partners. CSA NRPs were more comfortable about doing this than PWCs (especially those who were clients of the CSA).

- Three-quarters of CSA NRPs claimed to be providing informal support (i.e. payments or purchases for their children or the PWC), whilst fewer than half the CSA PWCs acknowledged receipt of such assistance....

Parents' views on the new emphasis on private arrangements...

- Whilst around half of non-CSA PWCs and CSA NRPs thought parents should ideally make maintenance arrangements privately between themselves, only a fifth of CSA PWCs shared this view.

---

[308] See also Coleman et al (2007).

- The main advantages associated with private arrangements were: being quicker and easier; helping to reduce conflict; and being more private. The main disadvantages were: the NRP might not be willing/able to pay; they may cause conflict; and that they require parents to have a good relationship.

- CSA PWCs took a much more negative view of private maintenance arrangements than other parents and had greater concerns about monitoring and support in the case of problems.

- Around half non-CSA PWCs and CSA NRPs felt confident about being able to make a private arrangement using new information and guidance servces, compared to about a quarter of CSA PWCs.

- Around four in ten CSA NRPs felt confident about being able to make a private arrangment with support from a trained, impartial advsier, compared to about two in ten PWCs...

Conclusion

The study's findings indicate considerable support among parents for the principle that parents should make private child maintenance [arrangements] where possible and suggest that effective (and relatively intensive) information and guidance services could play a key role in facilitating this. However, it has also shown that more than two-thirds of the CSA's existing clientele saw themselves as likely to use C-MEC, with CSA PWCs expressing especially negative views in regard to the possibility of making private arrangements.

A number of factors have emerged as potential threats to the feasibility of private arrangements. The strong connection in parents' minds between contact and maintenance shown by past research is supported by this study, with NRPs displaying a particularly strong commitment to this link. Therefore, where there are disputes over contact, it is likely to be particularly difficult for parents to agree maintenance arrangements between themselves.

In addition, a number of issues have been identified about which PWCs and NRPs appear to have differing opinions, particularly in regard to the proper effects of additional factors on the maintenance obligation. NRPs feel that shared care, informal support, a new child and (it is implied) an increase in the PWC's income ought rightly to reduce their obligation; PWCs by and large disagree. Where so many causes of potential disharmony are present, it is clear that encouraging more parents to make private arrangements will not be an easy task. The fact that only a minority of separated parents ever discusses financial issues with their ex-partners also highlights the radical nature of the [reform].

Studies examining negotiation of other financial claims suggest that women often sacrifice legal entitlements in order to attain other 'relationship' objectives, even if they have full legal *advice*, never mind if they have only received 'information and support' from a statutory body such as C-MEC.[309] And the bargaining position of parents with care will only be as strong as C-MEC turns out to be: if it is as inefficient as its predecessor, it will present a somewhat empty threat.

In sum, parents with care on benefit may be unable or unwilling, for all sorts of reasons, to secure child maintenance from the other parent.[310] A quarter of CSA PWCs in Wikeley et al's study indicated that they would probably not make any arrangement for maintenance

---

[309] See Wikeley (2007b), 446.

[310] Suggestions that third parties should be enabled to apply to C-MEC in certain cases have not been taken forward: Hansard HC, Public Bill Committee, col 251, 9 October 2007.

once free to decide for themselves. Where no (or no satisfactory) agreement is reached and, for whatever reason, no application to C-MEC is made, the child's household will not benefit from the maintenance disregard, and the child will be maintained by any earnings of the parent with care and by the state via benefits payments and tax credits without any contribution from the non-resident parent.

6.7.3 LEGAL AND SOCIAL PARENTHOOD

As we have seen, parents have differing views about the link between child support payments and the social relationship between the liable party and the child. Should child support liability inexorably flow from legal, rather than social parenthood? And what links should exist between financial support and contact?

Who should pay for whom?

Much opposition to the CSA 1991 has arisen from differing perceptions about who should be liable for whom, and which children should have priority call on adults' income. This issue is particularly pressing given the growing number of step-families. Establishing such new family bonds has long been recognized as an optimum way for mothers and children to improve their economic lot after breakdown of the parents' relationship.[311] Because the law places primary responsibility for children's maintenance on legal parents, some families are in a chain of households along which money is passed: the father in one household pays child support to children from his first relationship, while new step-fathers of his children in turn send money to another household for children from their earlier relationships, and so on.[312] There are inevitably breaks in the chain, leaving some non-resident parent/step-parents supporting two sets of children.[313] As Jane Millar astutely observes, 'people's lives are far messier in reality than [the Child Support Act] policy can easily allow for'.[314] Few can afford to sustain two households.[315]

In the early days of the CSA 1991, commentators considered the likely impact of its reinforcement of obligations deriving from legal parenthood:

M. Maclean and J. Eekelaar, 'Child Support: The British Solution', (1993) 7
International Journal of Law and the Family 205, 226

The creation of children is now more likely to have lasting effect on the lives of men, as it always has for women. We are less certain, however, about the extent to which the scheme subordinates the social family to the biological principle. Whether this will enhance individual responsibility as is hoped is unpredictable and, in a society where so many family relationships cross households, it may not make good economic sense to shift resources across families to such an extent and with such cost.

---

[311] Marsh and Vegeris (2004).
[312] Barton (1999), 705 advises non-resident parents to join such households in order to reduce their own liability whilst their new household also enjoys that income from the other non-resident parent.
[313] Davis et al (1998), 229.
[314] Millar (1996), 189.
[315] Gibson (1991), 343

R. Boden and M. Childs, 'Paying for Procreation: Child Support Arrangements in the UK', (1996) 4 *Feminist Legal Studies* 131, 156

This biological determinism as the basis for financial obligations indicates how heavily involved the state is in defining the private realm of the family and family obligations. In their real lives people may have assumed kinship responsibilities with regard to step-children and new partners. Yet here the state is retrospectively redetermining obligations based on biological parentage, refusing to recognise the private realm social relationships which may exist. One type of kinship, that based on biology, is privileged over that based on social or cultural foundations. The state is not reasserting the rightful role of the private realm of the family, it is imposing its own definition of that role in an attempt to relieve itself of a public expenditure commitment [pre-CMOP 2008]. One result may be an adverse effect on women whose partners are deemed to have more important financial commitments to previous children.

Research confirmed that this emphasis on biological (legal) parenthood clashes with some social perceptions. Like attitudes towards private ordering, here too there was a difference of opinion between parents with care and non-resident parents:

M. Maclean and J. Eekelaar, *The Parental Obligation: a study of parenthood across households* (Oxford: Hart Publishing, 1997), 149–50

[T]he "social" dimension of parenthood plays a far more important part in the performance of the parental role (and therefore probably in the perception of parental obligations) than the policy underscoring the Child Support Act allowed. This is seen in the following major findings: *first*, a strong association between the maintenance of contact with and support by the "outside" parent and the age of the child at separation; *secondly*, the strong negative effect which the presence or subsequent acquisition of a partner by either parent had on the maintenance of contact with and support by the "outside" parent of children with whom they had not lived, or with whom they had lived only for a relatively short time; and *thirdly*, the strong association between payment of support and the exercise of contact.

However, the attitudinal survey showed that there was a strong gender factor lying behind people's perceptions of their cross-household support obligations. The fathers [non-resident parents] related their obligations much more closely to the exercise of social parenthood both by themselves and by another man who may have joined the mother's household than the mothers would have allowed. In view of such a division, we should perhaps not speak of *a* social rule, but of *two conflicting* social rules. The empirical data strongly showed the fathers acting consistently with the viewpoints they expressed in the attitudinal survey. They can be said to assume a social rule which can be formulated in three stages: (i) a prior social parenthood developed in a household can be extended beyond that household after parental separation; (ii) social parenthood so extended can create a social obligation to provide support; and (iii) such social obligations can co-exist with the social obligations associated with subsequently acquired social parenthood. Since each stage is dependent on the preceding stage for its existence, *if an initial social parenthood had not existed, or, if it had existed, if it was not extended after separation*, the men will be reluctant to view any support obligation based solely on their natural fatherhood as co-existing with subsequent social parenthood and will be inclined to assume that the obligation attaches to a man who later takes on social parenthood with respect to their child.

The researchers concluded that the implications of their findings for the scope of child support obligations were complicated:

> It could not be right to conclude that fathers...should have no support obligations towards the children they have procreated simply because they have not lived with them. It also seems dangerous to say that only those fathers who have looked after their children should have continuing obligations towards them, for this seems to punish virtue. Furthermore, the mothers saw that natural fatherhood, at least when initiated in marriage, created in itself a strong support obligation and were less likely than fathers to see this as lapsing if the child acquired a stepfather. It is not surprising that mothers should place more weight on natural parenthood and fathers more weight on social parenthood because, for almost all mothers, but by no means all fathers, natural parenthood and social parenthood coincide.
>
> ...A support obligation which accompanies or arises from social parenthood is embedded in that social parenthood; thus the payment of support can be seen as part of the relationship maintained by continued contact. But an obligation based on natural parenthood rests on the policy of instilling a sense of responsibility for individual action and equity between fathers who do and fathers who do not exercise social parenthood.

This re-emphasis of the obligations of legal parenthood reversed the courts' previous 'pragmatic policy' of allowing men to move on, economically, to new families. It accordingly attracted huge opposition.[316] Some fathers claimed (unsuccessfully on the facts) that their Article 8 ECHR rights were being interfered with insofar as child support obligations contributed to the break-up of second families.[317] The CSA 1991 does now make some allowance for the costs of children in the non-resident parent's new family, both in the basic formula and as grounds for variation where a relevant other child has a long-term illness or disability. However, the formula chosen for accommodating other children in the basic calculation makes clear that a parent's first responsibility remains with the first family, regardless of the income of that family's household, the resources of the parent with care and any new partner of hers not being taken into account.

Contact and child support

A large-scale survey of CSA clients made the following findings:

N. Wikeley et al, *National Survey of Child Support Agency Clients,* DWP Research Report No 152 (Leeds: Corporate Document Service, 2001), 153

> A question which underpins much of the discussion concerning the expectation that NRPs [non-resident parents] pay significant sums in child support concerns the appropriateness of requiring such payments in circumstances where the father (as it usually is) has little, if any, contact with his children and so does not derive any benefit from his 'investment'....[It] is important to acknowledge that a survey methodology cannot possibly do justice to the complexities of this issue.

---

316 Diduck (2003), 181.
317 *Burrows v UK* (App No 27558/95, ECHR) (1996).

As one might have expected, NRPs were more likely to assert as an absolute principle that payment of 'full' maintenance should entitle the NRP to have regular contact with his children. Only 16 per cent dissented. A majority of PWCs likewise seemed willing to sign up to this as an absolute principle, although 25 per cent equivocated, suggesting (wisely) that the answer to this question would depend on the particular circumstances of the case.

We gave this theme a somewhat sharper edge by asking whether, in circumstances where the NRP is denied contact with his children, he should pay less maintenance. (This, needless to say, is to oversimplify the 'contact' issue, certainly as it would be perceived by many parents with care.) The question nonetheless exposed sharp differences between the attitudes of NRPs and PWCs...NRPs were much more likely to assert that a denial of contact should lead to a reduced maintenance obligation. Over 50 per cent supported this proposition without any qualification. Less than 20 per cent of PWCs took the same view.

Researchers have found correlations between frequency of contact and both payment rates and parents' perception of the child support system as fair.[318] Maclean and Eekelaar concluded that fathers do not exercise contact *because* they are paying support, but, if the child support system were to encourage more non-resident parents to maintain contact with their children, that might be beneficial to both those parents and to the children.[319]

Child support has also been strongly linked in the public mind with contact and understandings of parental responsibility, in the wide sense. Fathers objected to the terminology of the original Act: the expression 'absent parent' (replaced in 2000 by 'non-resident parent') implied irresponsibility and total absence from their children's lives after separation from the parent with care. Some fathers are increasingly motivated to seek equal parenting post-separation, objecting to the implication that fatherhood essentially entails no more than providing money.[320] But as Collier notes:

...such an association of 'being' a father with an established economic link with children is implicit in the arguments of those campaigning against the CSA who have made a clear correlation between levels of payments and [contact]. The more that is paid, it is argued, the greater [contact] rights there should be...[321]

Despite the popular view, in key respects, contact—or no contact—is irrelevant to the C-MEC maintenance calculation and court-based finacial liability. For example, whether the non-resident parent has contact with the child is specified as a factor *not* to be taken into account when C-MEC decides whether to permit a variation. There is no deduction for parents who never see the children for whom they are paying. However, some contact issues are now recognized, not least the variation ground designed to alleviate non-resident fathers' difficulty in affording the costs of maintaining contact with the children whom they were supporting;[322] and the rules regarding shared care arrangements.

---

318 Wikeley at al (2001); Davis and Wikeley (2002).

319 (1997), 128; cf Bradshaw et al (1999) and Wilson (2006) on the complex social inter-relationship of contact and maintenance.

320 Wallbank (1997); and see chapter 11.

321 Collier (1994), 386.

322 The argument in *Logan v UK* (App No 24875/94, ECHR) (1996) that this violated Article 8 failed the facts.

J. Wallbank, 'The Campaign for Change of the Child Support Act 1991: Reconstituting the "Absent" Father', (1997) 6 *Social and Legal Studies* 191, 197

This change can be interpreted in a number of ways: it might be viewed as consolidating the government's commitment to ensuring that parental contact with children is maintained; alternatively the change might be considered as part of a package of changes which attempted to appease the mass of middle-class fathers who voiced their grievances about the Act in a vociferous manner; less cynically perhaps it could have been a very real attempt to respond to the problems caused by the inflexibility of the formula. Whatever the motivation...the change has the effect of highlighting the desirability of maintaining links between a father and his child(ren)....

So contact and child support *have* become linked to some extent. One feared disadvantage of allowing reductions in child support to reflect staying contact is an increase in the number of disputed contact and shared residence cases under the CA 1989, s 8. Non-resident parents have clear financial (as well as emotional) incentives to maximize contact; parents with care conversely have financial incentives to try to minimize contact arrangements which will attract the shared care rule. Contact in such troubled circumstances may benefit no one.

Henshaw's recommendation that child support liability be removed entirely where parents provide equal amounts of care was not taken up.[323] This may simply stoke further resentment since, as Wikeley has explained, there is a mismatch between the policy objectives of the shared care rules and the perspectives of non-resident parents. The rules are designed to support contact with non-resident parents, viewed as important for child welfare, and to improve payment of child support, following known correlations between regular contact and maintenance payment. But non-resident parents tend to view shared care rules as a way of reflecting their direct expenditure on the child while in their care, discounting their maintenance liability.[324] Contact arrangements may well impact on private arrangements made in the post-CMOP world, in both directions: no payment where no contact, reduced payment where substantially shared contact. Research will doubtless examine this issue in due course.

The courts have also been called upon to consider the relationship between child support and practical parenting. It has been held that a father's *failure* to pay maintenance ought not to be given substantial weight in courts' decisions to grant parental responsibility (in the strict sense), at least where the father has otherwise demonstrated devotion to the child; parental responsibility should not be withheld to extort maintenance.[325] However, it was held in *Re B (Contact: Child Support)*[326] that it would be inappropriate when making orders for *contact* to have regard to the impact that different contact arrangements might have on non-resident parents' child support liability, in particular under the shared care rules:[327] that would be to introduce a factor unrelated to the child's welfare into the CA 1989 decision-making process. This decision has been strongly criticized by Stephen Gilmore, who argues that—reflecting a wider trend[328]—the decision neglects parents' rights to contact with their

---

[323] Henshaw (2006), para 117; see Gilmore (2007), 372.
[324] Wikeley (2006a), 313–14.
[325] *Re H (Parental responsibility: maintenance)* [1996] 1 FLR 867.
[326] [2006] EWCA Civ 1574.
[327] 6.4.4.
[328] See 8.4.4.

children under Article 8 ECHR which, while they may frequently be outweighed by the child's interests, cannot be simply ignored. If a decision about contact so increases the non-resident parents' child support liability that exercising that contact becomes problematic, an Article 8 issue arises and cannot be sidelined as 'irrelevant'.[329]

6.7.4 THE FORMULA: COST-SHARING OR RESOURCE-SHARING?

One of the most complex but important issues in child support is the formula whereby liability is calculated and its underlying objective. The choice of formula partly depends on whether the aim is to achieve 'collective justice' between the parents (and child) or 'distributive justice' between parents and state, the former compensating the latter for monies paid out for the child.[330] Commentators have suggested two principal types of formula:[331]

- Cost-sharing: the cost of raising the child (measured objectively and so regardless of parental wealth) should be shared equally, or equitably, between the parents. This approach risks ignoring the lost economies of scale in lone-parent families, and so risks miscalculating the 'true' costs of child-rearing in that context. There are also difficulties in selecting an appropriate objective measure of need.

- Resource-sharing: the child should share a given proportion of the non-resident parent's resources, perhaps to ensure similar standards of living for non-resident parent and child. Unlike cost-sharing, this entails different children receiving different maximum levels of support according to parental wealth, 'need' being interpreted by reference to the parent's standard of living.

These map on to what Nick Wikeley identifies in the extracts at 6.7.1 as the fundamental right to relief of 'basic need', and the further legitimate expectation that extends beyond that, given the parents' means. As he goes on to argue, whether the underlying rationale is one of cost-sharing or resource-sharing should enable one to answer in a principled way whether issues such as the parent with care's income, shared care, new partners, or children from new relationships should be brought into the formula.[332]

The original Child Support Act adopted a mixed approach. The calculation began on a cost-sharing basis: income support scales were used to identify the basic cost of raising a child and that figure was then split according to parental resources. But the scheme included potential for resource-sharing: where the non-resident parent was wealthy, that parent would pay a greater proportion (up to 100 per cent) of the amount required to meet the child's objectively calculated needs; and the child could, subject to a ceiling, receive more than the basic cost-scale required. Initially focused on achieving distributive justice between state and non-resident parent by cutting the welfare state budget, the basic formula neglected to accommodate factors which might be thought relevant in achieving justice between the private individuals involved: for example, capital settlements already made for benefit of children, contact costs, obligations to new families, and resources of the parent with care's

---

[329] Gilmore (2007).
[330] Maclean and Eekelaar (1997), 42.
[331] Eekelaar and Maclean (1986), ch 7; Parker (1991); Wikeley (2006a), ch 1.
[332] (2006a), 25–7.

new partner.[333] These are all factors which the courts can take into account.[334] Non-resident parents' hostility to the exclusion of such factors led to the incorporation of some of these private law elements in the child support scheme.[335]

Since the 2000 reforms of the CSA 1991, which introduced the 'fraction of net income per child' formula, the basic model has become one of resource-sharing. The percentages adopted were based on evidence that intact families on average spend 30 per cent of their income on a child; the scheme divides that in half for the separated family, so each parent notionally contributes 15 per cent of their income for one child.[336] However, the suitability of the percentages and the manner of their deployment are questionable. The new percentages based on gross income in CMOP 2008 seek to produce the same net effect in the parent with care's hands, so these criticisms still apply:

J. Fortin, *Children's Rights and the Developing Law* (3rd edn, Cambridge: CUP, 2009), 347–8

The new formula seemed to have little philosophical basis. The government simply maintained that the proposed base rate of 15% of the payer's net income was 'roughly half the average that an intact two-parent family spends on a child', the assumption being that this is what a non-resident parent *should* also pay. As Parkinson pointed out, the government cited only one piece of research to substantiate such a claim. The new formula not only ignored the fact that expenditure is greater for older children but also that when two-parent families spend 30% of their income on their children, fathers contribute far more of this total than mothers. In the UK, the norm is the 'one-and-a-half-earner household', with a high proportion of women working short part-time hours on low rates of pay. To argue that non-resident fathers should only contribute half what two parents spend on their children was nonsensical, given that mothers' incomes, if they existed at all, were far lower than that of fathers. There was certainly no attempt to argue that it would produce levels of maintenance matching actual child-care costs.

Conversely, unlike the courts' discretion and the original child support rules, the new formula for child support takes no account of the income of the parent with care or any new partner of that parent, who may be fulfilling a social obligation to support the qualifying children in that family. The non-resident parent must pay regardless of the economic circumstances of each household, so parents with care receive child support regardless of whether it is actually 'needed'.[337] Such cases may be few: in 2000, 96 per cent of earning non-resident parents' former partners were on weekly incomes below £100.[338] Moreover, disregarding the income of parents with care may act as a work incentive, so increasing the income of the child's household.[339] But many non-resident parents may regard this as unfair.[340] There are alternative models:

---

[333] Maclean and Eekelaar (1997), 39 and 42; Davis et al (1998), 217.
[334] See *Re P (a child: financial provision)* [2003] EWCA Civ 837; Mostyn (1999), 101; and the effect of the statutory checklists. For discussion of pre-CSA 1991 case law, see Eekelaar and Maclean (1986), 113–5.
[335] Wallbank (1997).
[336] DSS (1999), para 2.5; Middleton et al (1997), para 16.
[337] Douglas (2004a), 206.
[338] Wikeley (2000), 822.
[339] As Davis et al (1998), 229–30 suggest, many parents with care would need a drastic increase in income to make this viable, given other barriers to employment; though note now that tax credits can assist with child-care costs.
[340] Gillespie (2002).

N. Mostyn, 'The Green Paper on Child Support—Children First: a new approach to child support', (1999) 29 *Family Law* **95, 100**

...[I]t is a fact of life that the parent with care will spend a part of her income on the child. But that obvious truism cannot lead to the conclusion that the paying parent should therefore pay the same whatever the income of his former partner might be. Every child requires a finite amount of support. That obligation should be shared rateably between the parents in the ratios of their respective incomes. Only thus will the system reflect the legal obligation on each parent to support the child in question...A percentage system does not fit easily with these precepts, while for all its faults the [previous] system clearly [did]. The Australians have addressed the problem by reducing the paying parent's assessable income by [that part of the caring parent's income which exceeds average weekly income plus social security allowances received for the child]. This seems a fair way of dealing with the problem. If...[something like this is not adopted here] there will be massive discontent with the new system...

6.7.5   RULES OR DISCRETION?

Child support law invites a comparison of rule-based and discretion-based regimes.[341] Discretion claims some advantages over rule-based systems, as demonstrated by the original CSA 1991, before the introduction of variations:

Phillips v Peace [1996] 2 FCR 237, 239 (Fam Div)

JOHNSON J:

It is of the essence of the policy underlying the Child Support Act 1991 that child support is to be assessed according to a mathematical formula which is to be applied rigorously, seemingly without any significant element of discretion to cater for the needs of a child in the circumstances of the child with whom I am concerned....This is quite contrary to the practice of the court which for generations, in seeking to assess entitlements to financial support for former spouses or children, has sought to achieve a result which is fair, just and reasonable, based on the realities and the practicalities.

But court-based discretion carries disadvantages too:

G. Davis, S. Cretney, and J. Collins, *Simple Quarrels* **(Oxford: OUP, 1994), 256**

...along with discretion goes *uncertainty: the elevation of professional judgment* (because only lawyers, who deal with these matters all the time, have the necessary knowledge and skill to weigh up the competing factors); *an almost limitless need for information about family finances* (because discretion, if it is to be justified at all, has to be based on a minute examination of differing circumstances); and *the demand for large amount of professional time* (because the discretion, if it is not to be exercised arbitrarily, takes time). In practice, of course, there is a limit to the amount of lawyer-time which divorcing couples can purchase, and also a limit to the amount which the State is prepared to support. Court-time is likewise expensive and has, somehow, to be rationed.

[341] 1.2.2.

As we shall see in chapter 7, these question also arise in relation to financial provision between spouses on divorce, where child support is one part of the package:

E. Jackson et al, 'Financial Support on Divorce: the Right Mixture of Rules and Discretion?', (1993) 7 *International Journal of Law and the Family* 230, 231–2

In any child support system which depends on discretion, there will tend to be public dissatisfaction if one father finds out that he pays twice as much as his neighbour, or one mother discovers that she receives half as much as hers. In a situation where dissatisfied payers can and do just cease payments without much fear of recourse, it is important to minimize public mistrust. In addition to the problems of inconsistency, a system of discretion will make it very difficult for lawyers to predict the outcome of an adjudication. This may mean that more couples will fight full adversarial battles, and have to bear increasing legal costs and the strain of protracted litigation. Alternatively they may accept unsatisfactory settlements in preference to the high-cost, high-risk strategy of litigation....

International dissatisfaction with discretionary approaches meant that several jurisdictions moved towards rule-based systems for child support, in part to remove the apparent arbitrariness of different discretionary awards, in part in pursuit of administrative efficiency:

It might be thought that, in making the 'ancillary' matters part of an administrative process, divorce can cease to be a time for conflict and instead simply be the civilized ordering of a couple's affairs. Nonetheless, the rush to simplicity and certainty may underestimate the complexity of the issues to be resolved and fail to do justice to them. The divorce represents a substantial upheaval for the spouses and their children, and it takes a great deal of time to work out how their domestic arrangements should be restructured. Indeed, there are so many complex issues that it is difficult to envisage a formula that could encompass them all. Most couples just want to sort out a workable solution and not become embroiled in protracted legal battles. If thoroughness is sacrificed in the interests of administrative efficiency, simplicity and cost-cutting, problems may not be addressed adequately at the time of the divorce and may re-emerge later with extra complications.

...As family law continues to move towards interlocking systems, rules, and formulae, it might be timely to question if there should be limits to these trends. What, if anything, is worth retaining from a discretion-based system? Can the trend towards rules go too far? To what extent does discretion...allow divorcing people to be flexible, responsive to need, and open to compromise? Will formula-based approaches to maintenance gain in predictability, generosity, and consistency but at a cost of greater rigidity and an inability to make adjustments to the overall financial package?

Even though discretion may not facilitate the resolution of disputes without the need for legal representation and may lead to inconsistencies, it might nevertheless be fairer for the decision-maker to examine each case individually before deciding how much this father should pay.

As these authors suggest, rule-based systems are not a panacea. But nor is it a straight choice between rule and discretion. The history of the Child Support Act is instructive about the advantages and pitfalls of different rule-based systems. Rule-based systems can follow one of two basic patterns. Like the original, incrementally developed Child Support Act scheme, they can be razor-sharp but highly complex, seeking to accommodate every conceivable variable and so demanding considerable information. At the other end of the spectrum, exemplified by the current scheme, they can be rather blunter: easy to understand, but potentially unfair in occasional cases whose idiosyncrasies do not quite fit the rationale underpinning the basic rule. Horton evaluates these two approaches, writing at a time when the Government was simply proposing to sharpen the original, razor-sharp formula:

M. Horton, 'Improving child support—a missed opportunity', (1995) 7 *Child and Family Law Quarterly* 26, 27–8

This first [highly detailed] approach has a number of drawbacks. Collecting lots of information takes time, increases the scope for errors in calculation, and renders checking by the parents themselves almost impossible. Further, debate on the fairness of the formula will hinge largely on whether a particular item is classed as essential and thus taken into account in the calculation. If enough parents consider a particular item to be essential, this may create pressure for the formula to be altered to take account of that item.... In addition, the prescriptive and detailed nature of the regulations means that the rules are often in a form inaccessible and unintelligible to the general public and, indeed, to the parents affected....

A second approach is taken by the Australian child support scheme [and now by the CSA 1991]. It is radically different and has few of the above pitfalls. It recognises that, as in most areas of family law, there is no right answer, and trying to do too much by means of a formula itself can be troublesome. Instead, this approach keeps the formula very simple, and thus easily understood by those affected. Where the simple formula leads to injustice in the particular case, there can be a discretionary modification to or departure from the simple formula.... [The] nearest similarity is with the taxation system, with simple percentages used to work out child support liability, the percentage used depending on the number of children involved.... At its simplest, the Australian approach requires just two pieces of information, the number of children and the parent's income. The small number of variables means quicker and less error-prone decision-making. This approach does not aim at perfect individualised justice, but at consistent, predictable, and simple adjudication, and aims to prevent injustice through the departure system, as opposed to attempting perfect justice in every case.

In line with Horton's second approach, the current English system seeks to deal with at least some of the potential unfairness that blunt rules can entail by allowing discretion to soften the impact of the rules in specified cases: the variation grounds. But in keeping with a desire to avoid a return to the unbridled discretion of the courts and so to ensure that non-resident parents pay 'proper' levels of support, that discretion is very limited and carefully defined, and exercised by C-MEC, not by the courts. Some of those whose circumstances fall beyond the reach of that discretion may feel hard done by. It seems that we are inevitably faced with a choice between imperfect systems.

6.7.6 ADMINISTRATIVE OR JUDICIAL FORUM?

Outside the context of voluntary arrangements, the separation of child support from other issues arising on breakdown of the parental relationship—child contact and residence, financial and property provision between the parents, capital provision for the child—means that no one forum can take a holistic view.[342] This sits rather uneasily alongside the longstanding

---

[342] See *V v V (Child Maintenance)* [2001] 2 FLR 799, [11].

policy to facilitate the resolution of all issues in one forum. Nor can a flexible view of 'child support' be taken. Provision of accommodation for the child cannot be a substitute for regular maintenance, even if that might in all the circumstances be more beneficial to the individual child on welfare grounds, and more fair or practical between the adult parties.

Instead, courts and parents must cope with what James Pirrie calls the 'pinball effect': the court making its adjudication on issues within its jurisdiction on the assumption that C-MEC will require a certain level of child support; C-MEC then bringing in a different calculation, forcing the parties to return to court to vary the orders made earlier.[343] Although the *basic* formula is relatively straightforward and predictable (though potentially problematic because of its use of historical data), the final child support calculation becomes less predictable if parents invoke variation grounds.

Resolution have long proposed that where courts are already dealing with a case, they (not C-MEC) should have jurisdiction to handle child support. This would be particularly useful for financially complex cases, which burdened the Agency considerably and may continue to trouble C-MEC. Under this proposal, it was envisaged that the courts would use the Child Support Act formula and variations unless justice demanded departure from them:

J. Pirrie, 'Report of the Child Support Agency, March 2002', (2003) 33 *Family Law* **105, 109**

When we presented this proposal to Government, we argued it from a client perspective, primarily pointing out that:

(1) Clients were ill-served by having to go through two processes where they only needed one. (If the court knows what the financial data is, why can it not get on and fix the level for child maintenance at the same time?)

(2) Individuals are ill-served by a state that appears to be operating two different state organs, analysing income data and coming up with radically different answers.

(3) The processes do not fit together well. Parties may not separate until after the court has made its adjudication and it may be months before the CSA is able to fix the level of child maintenance, an important part of the overall package. What does the parent with care do while she waits for the situation to be resolved?

Attempts to introduce amendments to give effect to this policy through CMOP 2008 failed.

6.8 CONCLUSION

Child support has long been a controversial issue, illustrating a number of key debates in contemporary family law. The nature of family obligations—should responsibility attach to legal status, or to the actual performance of social family roles? The relationship between family and state—should financial obligations be a matter for families to agree amongst themselves wherever possible, or should the state intervene in all or any cases? Family law

---

[343] Pirrie (2003), 109. This effect was worse when non-resident parents' housing costs were a crucial ingredient for the original CSA formula, but could not be known until the parents' property settlement had been reached: Maclean and Eekelaar (1993), 221; see also the carer's allowance element of the old formula: Gibson (1991), 337.

techniques—are family disputes better dealt with by way of wide discretion or more certain rules, and by courts or administrative agencies? Ironically, the figure who often fades into the background is the child. Ultimately, perhaps the question should be: what system of private law obligations and state-based provision would best cater for children's needs, and what *rights* of children in this sphere should we recognize?

ONLINE RESOURCE CENTRE

Questions, suggestions for further reading, and supplementary materials for this chapter (including updates on developments in this area of family law since this book was published) may be found on the Online Resource Centre at **www.oxfordtextbooks.co.uk/orc/harrisshort_tcm2e/.**

7

PROPERTY AND FINANCES WHEN RELATIONSHIPS END

CENTRAL ISSUES

1. English law has no special regime of property ownership *during* marriage and civil partnership. However, on relationship breakdown, it treats different types of family distinctly.

2. On divorce/dissolution, the courts have wide discretionary powers under the Matrimonial Causes Act 1973 (MCA 1973) and Civil Partnership Act 2004 (CPA 2004) to make orders for 'ancillary relief': adjusting the parties' property rights and requiring ongoing financial provision between them in order to achieve a 'fair' result in all the circumstances.

3. The House of Lords in *Miller; McFarlane* [2006] UKHL 24 identified three elements of a 'fair' outcome: meeting need; compensating for 'relationship-generated disadvantage'; and equal sharing. The statute requires that first consideration be given to the welfare of minor children of the family. It is usually only possible to meet the parties' needs, insofar as limited resources allow.

4. The 'clean break' principle encourages the courts where appropriate to terminate ongoing financial ties between the parties, for example, by ordering one-off capital transfers rather than periodical payments.

5. The law is ambivalent about private ordering in this sphere. Parties can make agreements binding on divorce only by converting them into an order by consent and cannot deprive each other of the right to apply to court by agreement. But a court invited to grant relief inconsistent with an agreement will have regard to its terms and in some circumstances determine that fairness requires that its order should reflect what the agreement provides.

6. On the breakdown of other family relationships, laws considered in previous chapters determine the outcome of property disputes: those governing parties' property ownership; occupation of the shared home; and financial and property provision for the benefit of children. These parties can regulate their affairs by contract.

7.1 INTRODUCTION

If we relied on newspapers for information about financial settlements on divorce, we would obtain a seriously distorted impression. The media relate stories about the wives of premiership footballers, entrepreneurs, and rock stars seeking multi-million pound 'pay-outs'. The reality for thousands of families affected by divorce each year is 'just about keeping heads above water'. Family solicitors and courts must conjure as beneficial (or as least detrimental) an outcome as possible for all parties from limited assets. We discussed chapter 6 the various financial remedies for children whose parents live apart, whatever the legal status of the parents' relationship. Our focus here is on remedies for the benefit of the adults. In that context, the law distinguishes sharply between marriage/civil partnership[1] and other relationships.

Spouses and civil partners have access to powerful statutory remedies on divorce/dissolution, enabling the courts to adjust property rights and order ongoing financial provision, regardless of the parties' property rights.[2] These orders are misleadingly referred to as 'ancillary relief',[3] reflecting a time when the main issue would be whether the marriage should be dissolved at all, and the grant of financial provision was a subsidiary consequence.[4] The main dispute is now more likely to concern the financial settlement, the vast majority of divorces themselves being undefended. But the expression remains a useful shorthand for the courts' powers in these cases. One key issue is the basis on which those powers are exercised. The rationales on which the transfer of resources on divorce is justified reveal something about the nature of the economic relationship created by marriage and civil partnership.

The picture is very different on breakdown of other family relationships. The general law provides almost the only basis for resolving property disputes. There is little scope for adjusting property rights, and no periodical financial support. As we saw in chapter 3, the outcomes produced by the property and trust law have been heavily criticized, fuelling calls for reform.

7.2 THE SOCIAL CONTEXT

Economic problems on relationship breakdown, marital or not, are most acutely felt where the parties are parents.[5] Many couples adopt specialized roles within the family economy, at least for some periods of their relationship, one party concentrating on breadwinning and paying the mortgage, while the other gives up or limits paid employment to look after home and family.[6] While they are together, all will usually at least appear to be well: they have a home, an income, and may be accumulating savings and a pension for later life which will support both spouses. The fact that technically each party owns his or her 'separate property' and has no claim over the other's assets may not seem to matter. But relationship breakdown exposes the vulnerabilities created by role-specialization in a separate property system, particularly for an individual who worked unpaid in the home. Without the wealth-transfer

---

[1] Identical legislation applies to spouses and civil partners; for ease of exposition, we shall generally refer to 'divorce' and 'spouses'; but see 7.4.

[2] Cf *Tee v Hillman* [1999] 2 FLR 613; *Miller Smith v Miller Smith* [2009] EWCA 1297.

[3] The Family Procedure Rules 2010 (FPR 2010) replace this terminology with the concept of 'financial orders': r 2.3.

[4] Cretney (2003a), 396, 402.

[5] E.g. Eekelaar and Maclean (1986), Eekelaar (1998a), Hale (2004).

[6] Diduck (2003), 149–52.

informally enjoyed during the relationship, such individuals are economically vulnerable on separation.[7] With reduced earning-capacity, reduced occupational or private pension and other personal savings,[8] and often with continuing child-care obligations that limit opportunities to maximize any earning capacity, many primary carers (and the children living with them) experience substantial drops in their standard of living.[9] Financial settlements on divorce therefore relate to a wider discussion of gender and social policy on issues such as child-care and employment rights.[10] Even with the benefit of special statutory remedies, the negative economic impact of divorce is often great, particularly during a time of recession and especially for primary carers. At least one party may often have to rely on state support to some extent, whether welfare benefits or social housing.[11] Questions arise about the respective responsibility of private individuals and the state to support the family after divorce.[12]

Feminist scholars disagree about the appropriate response:

J. Carbone, 'Feminism, Gender and the Consequences of Divorce', in M. Freeman (ed), *Divorce: Where Next?* (Ashgate: Dartmouth, 1996), 181–2

As a descriptive undertaking, there is near unanimity, both within feminist circles and without, as to the role of gender in accounting for the economic consequences of divorce. Women generally, for reasons attributable to gender, earn less than men. Marriage increases the gap as married women, who bear the overwhelming responsibility for child-rearing, earn less than single women, while married men increase their earnings over single men. At divorce, mothers overwhelmingly retain physical custody of their children, and the pressures of single parenthood interfere with labour force participation...Accordingly, divorce almost inevitably lowers the standard of living of the custodial family and, for systemic reasons related to gender, leaves the vast majority of divorced women in a financially more precarious position than their former husbands.

Despite the near unanimous embrace of this picture of divorce, there is considerable disagreement, both within feminist circles and without, as to the implications. The disagreement starts with the central feature of the gendered division of family responsibilities: what Mary Becker describes as mothers' greater, and qualitatively different, attachment to their children...

Nonetheless, feminists have been slow to call attention to this central difference in men and women's approach to family. When feminist scholarship does acknowledge it, it is without agreement on cause and effect. And although the source of women's greater attachment to children may well be irrelevant to the determination of public policy, feminists are no closer to agreement on possible solutions. 'Liberal' feminists believe that it is the gendered division of labour itself that ensures women's subordination to men and that, unless there is genuinely shared responsibility for childbearing, equality is impossible. 'Cultural feminists' or 'feminists of difference' believe that the principal problem is not that women disproportionately care for children, but that society so undervalues child-rearing. In between are many feminists who believe that equality requires both greater sharing of the responsibility for child-rearing *and* greater support for the child-rearing role.

[7] Rake (2000), ch 4.

[8] Ibid., ch 6; Price (2009).

[9] Eekelaar and Maclean (1997), esp. tables 7.8–7.10; Fisher and Low (2009).

[10] See Herring (2005a).

[11] 34 per cent entrants to the social rented sector in 2007/8 who had previously been owners cited divorce or separation as their reason for moving: DCLG (2009), 108, table 4.5.

[12] Ferguson (2008), Miles (2011).

Meanwhile, the other spouse's desire to move on after divorce, an aspiration apparently legitimized by no-fault divorce,[13] may make it increasingly difficult for (usually) him to support the first family. While his income is less likely to have been damaged by separation,[14] if he is required to support the first family, his financial *obligations* may increase and he may take some time to find accommodation.[15] The family economy that supported one household struggles to support two, and the interests of women and children in second families conflict with those in the first. This has long been a cause of protest against child support policy, and has also influenced the development of ancillary relief law.

7.3 REMEDIES ON DIVORCE: THE ORDERS AVAILABLE

The courts' powers on divorce expanded over twentieth century,[16] and now provide a flexible toolkit for transferring resources. The choice of tools and the amounts transferred in each case depend on the *basis* for exercising the powers—in what circumstances and for what purpose should orders be made? We address that in the next section. Here, we ask the mechanical question—what can the court do?

The aim is produce a financial 'package' achieving the optimum outcome for the parties and their children, using whatever powers are available.[17] Child maintenance is often an important component. If the parties have not agreed to confer jurisdiction on the court to order child maintenance via a consent order, the court must tailor its orders around C-MEC's anticipated child support assessment. Given the extensive powers to make orders for the benefit of the primary carer on divorce, capital orders for the children may seldom be required.[18]

The first step in any ancillary relief case is to identify and value the assets available for distribution.[19] The courts' powers are exercisable only in relation to resources belonging to one or both spouses. They cannot make orders over third parties' property: for example, a beneficial share in the matrimonial home belonging to relatives cannot be distributed between the spouses.[20] Nor will the courts assume that family members or a new partner will deploy their resources to satisfy an order that the respondent cannot meet.[21] Some cases may involve parallel insolvency or other debt-related proceedings.[22]

7.3.1 FINANCIAL PROVISION

Periodical payments

Periodical payments are often referred to as 'maintenance', but they may be used for any purpose.[23] Commonly paid from income to help meet the recipient's day-to-day needs, they

---

13 Symes (1985), 52–3.

14 Eekelaar and Maclean (1997), table 7.11; Fisher and Low (2009).

15 Perry et al (2000).

16 See Cretney (2003a), ch 10.

17 Jackson et al (1993), 244–5.

18 Cf cases involving unmarried parents, discussed at 7.8.2.

19 *Charman v Charman* [2007] EWCA Civ 503, [67].

20 *TL v ML and others (ancillary relief: claim against assets of extended family)* [2005] EWHC 2860. See also cases relating to family trusts, e.g. *Charman v Charman* [2007] EWCA Civ 503.

21 Ibid.; cf if the third party has a fiduciary obligation to provide funds to the spouse, or the spouse controls the third party (e.g. family company cases).

22 See Burrows, Conway, and Eames (2006), ch 22; Schofield (2010). On legal aid, esp. the statutory charge: see Black et al (2007), ch 2H–L.

23 *Miller; McFarlane* [2006] UKHL 24, [31]–[34].

are simply a mechanism for transferring resources, weekly, monthly, or on some other time-table, between the parties. The order may last indefinitely ('for joint lives'), for a defined period, or until a specified event.[24] If the recipient marries or forms a civil partnership, the order automatically terminates. Otherwise, the order expires as provided for by its own terms, on the death of either party, or pursuant to a further order.[25] Periodical payments can be index-linked, so payments due increase automatically with rising costs of living. The order may require that payments be 'secured':[26] a capital sum is set aside from which payments can continue should the payer default or die, avoiding the need for enforcement proceedings or to seek continued support from the deceased's estate.[27] Periodical payments orders are now less common than they once were;[28] respondents' free income is more likely to be paid in formal or informal child support, rather than spousal support.

Lump sums

The court can order one party to pay the other a capital sum, in full or by instalments.[29] A large lump sum can generate income from interest or dividend payments.[30] While the amount payable and duration of liability under a periodical payments order can be varied, a lump sum order by instalments ordinarily provides certainty regarding total quantum,[31] but the timetable for payment can be varied. Lump sum orders are unaffected by subsequent marriage or civil partnership of the recipient.

7.3.2 PROPERTY ADJUSTMENT AND ORDERS FOR SALE

The courts have various powers to adjust the parties' rights over capital assets: transfer of property from one to the other; settlement of property for the benefit of one or both parties; varying or extinguishing the parties' interests under existing settlements.[32] These one-off orders cannot be varied, though there is limited scope for them to be set aside and appealed against outside the normal time limits.[33] The courts can order the sale of property to facilitate the performance of property adjustment orders, orders for lump sums, and secured periodical payments.[34]

Orders relating to the owner-occupied home

The family home is commonly the most valuable asset at stake, subject to any mortgage debt. The courts have devised various ways to retain the home for occupation by one party and any children, whilst preserving shares in its capital value for both adults. Pending a final determination of this issue, it may be appropriate to make occupation orders under the Family Law Act 1996 (FLA 1996).[35]

---

[24] MCA 1973, s 23(1)(a), (b); CPA 2004, Sch 5, para 2(1)(a), (b).

[25] MCA 1973, s 28; CPA 2004, Sch 5, para 47.

[26] MCA 1973, s 23(1)(b); CPA 2004, Sch 5, para 2(1)(b).

[27] Inheritance (Provision for Family and Dependants) Act 1975.

[28] MOJ (2010), tables 2.6–2.7; Barton and Bissett-Johnson (2000).

[29] MCA 1973, s 23(1)(c); CPA 2004, Sch 5, para 3.

[30] *Duxbury v Duxbury* [1990] 2 All ER 77.

[31] Cf *Westbury v Sampson* [2001] EWCA Civ 407.

[32] MCA 1973, s 24; CPA 2004, Sch 5, Part 2.

[33] See 7.6.3.

[34] MCA 1973, s 24A; CPA 2004, Sch 5, Part 3.

[35] *S v F (occupation order)* [2000] 3 FCR 365.

The house could be sold immediately and the proceeds (after any mortgage debt has been paid) divided in defined shares, providing each party with resources to fund new accommodation. However, in many cases involving dependent children there are insufficient resources remaining once the mortgage has been repaid (and given each party's ability to raise fresh mortgage finance) to enable both to rehouse.[36] If so, the house could instead be transferred outright to one spouse, perhaps in return for a lump sum payment or for that spouse forgoing other claims. Alternatively, the house might be made the subject of a settlement to allow one spouse and the children to occupy it until a specified date or event following which it will be sold and the proceeds split. Or it might be transferred absolutely to one party, but subject to a charge in favour of the other party to be realized on sale. Various events could be used as the trigger for sale: the principal examples are '*Mesher*' and '*Martin*' orders.

A *Mesher* order[37] settles the property on the parties in defined shares, to be realized on sale following the youngest child reaching a particular age, or finishing tertiary education, or (earlier) on further order, pending which time the property is occupied by the children with their primary carer. This may be feasible only if: (i) the other parent can obtain alternative accommodation without immediate access to his or her share of the capital; (ii) the primary carer will be able to procure new accommodation following the sale; and (iii) the parties can maintain mortgage or other outgoings on the former matrimonial home whilst also funding new accommodation for the other party. A *Mesher* order may be an unattractive option, simply 'postpon[ing] the evil day' for the party left in occupation.[38]

A *Martin* order[39] triggers sale on the occurrence of some event in the life of the spouse who will occupy the property, such as remarriage, cohabitation, death, or that spouse electing to leave the property. This potentially further delays the other party's access to his or her capital share, but provides greater protection for the occupying spouse, who may otherwise struggle to find alternative accommodation other than at public expense. However, it has been said that that 'protection' may seriously restrict the occupying party's freedom. That spouse may wish to move, for example to take up a new job or to be near family. But since the proceeds of sale must be shared, the occupying spouse's share may be insufficient to acquire a home in the new location.[40]

The court's powers are not unlimited. For example, it cannot order one party to pay sums to a third party (e.g. a mortgage lender) or to adjust the parties' respective liabilities under the mortgage. Any mortgagee must be given notice of the proceedings and an opportunity to be heard.[41] The mortgage terms may require the mortgagee's consent to any transfer, and, even if the property is transferred, the original mortgagor(s) remain liable to repay the loan unless the mortgagee consents to transfer the liability.[42] There are various ways of coping with these restrictions. Cases are commonly settled by one party 'undertaking' to do something, or to use best endeavours to achieve something, which the court cannot order.[43] Undertakings can be enforced as if they are court orders, though the court cannot

[36] Davis et al (2000), 54.
[37] [1980] 1 All ER 126.
[38] *Harvey v Harvey* [1982] Fam 83, 89.
[39] [1978] Fam 12.
[40] Deech (1982), 633.
[41] FPR 2010, r 9.13.
[42] *Livesey v Jenkins* [1985] AC 424, 444.
[43] See Black et al (2007), ch 18O.

order specific performance.[44] Since the orders made are likely to have depended on the undertakings, the orders could be set aside or varied if the undertakings were breached. The mortgagor can undertake to use best endeavours to secure the mortgagee's agreement to transfer the mortgage. An undertaking by one spouse to pay the mortgage can be supported by a nominal order for periodical payments; in the event of failure to pay, that order could be varied upwards to give the recipient funds with which to pay instead. Alternatively, the party who is not mortgagor could be required to indemnify the other for mortgage payments, or (if occupying) to pay an occupation rent.[45]

Orders relating to rented homes

The courts can transfer various types of tenancy to one party, whether the parties were joint tenants of the property or it was rented by one.[46] These powers arise principally under the FLA 1996, which sets out a checklist of factors which the court must consider in exercising its discretion.[47] The landlord is entitled to be heard before an order is made.[48] Where the landlord is a housing authority, it may in any event allocate new housing to one or both parties without a court order, at least where they are in agreement.[49] Access to social housing is a matter for the local authority, whose hands cannot be tied by court orders, for example, relating to joint residence.[50]

7.3.3 ORDERS RELATING TO PENSIONS

Pensions are increasingly important forms of saving and sources of future financial security. The courts have two direct powers over pension funds: pension attachment and pension sharing. Pension attachment is a type of financial provision order,[51] directed not at the pension-holder but at that spouse's pension trustees. When the pension or relevant death-in-service benefit falls due, some defined portion of the pension or benefit is paid to the other spouse. Neither the court nor the other spouse can control whether and when the pension will fall due, or how valuable it will be. Partly for that reason, pension attachment is little used.[52] The preferred option is pension sharing, available in relation to all except the basic state pension.[53] The court orders that part of one party's pension fund be debited from his or her fund and immediately transferred to the other spouse. Both parties thereafter have independent pension funds, avoiding the difficulties associated with pension attachment and achieving a clean break. Alternatively, especially if the pension is small, the value of the pension might be 'off-set' against other aspects of the settlement, for example giving a greater share in the value of the house to one spouse in return for no share of the pension.[54]

---

[44] See *N v N (divorce: ante-nuptial agreement)* [1999] 2 FCR 583, 596; *Livesey v Jenkins* [1985] AC 424, 444; *L v L* [2006] EWHC 956, [61]; cf Law Society (2003), para 293, casting doubt on the enforceability of undertakings.

[45] *Harvey v Harvey* [1982] Fam 83.

[46] FLA 1996, Sch 7; a property adjustment order can sometimes be used: Burrows, Conway, and Eames (2006), para 17[3].

[47] Ibid., para 5.

[48] Ibid., para 14(1).

[49] Law Com (2006), para 3.58.

[50] *Holmes-Moorhouse v Richmond LBC* [2009] UKHL 7: see p 752.

[51] MCA 1973, ss 25B–D; CPA 2004, Sch 5, Part 6.

[52] Black et al (2007), 17.47.

[53] MCA 1973, ss 21A, 24B–D; CPA 2004, Sch 5, Part 4.

[54] See Hitchings (2010), 107–8; Hess and Hay (2007); *Martin-Dye v Martin-Dye* [2006] EWCA Civ 681, [85].

7.3.4 WHEN MAY ORDERS BE MADE?

All orders are available on divorce and nullity, all bar pension sharing on judicial separation. Orders may be made at any time following the grant of decree nisi, but will not take effect until after decree absolute.[55] The intervening period can be covered by orders for 'maintenance pending suit'.[56] Orders may also be made after decree absolute; there is no formal limitation period, so orders can in theory be made long after the divorce, though such applications are difficult to sustain in practice.[57] A party who has remarried or formed a new civil partnership cannot apply at *any* time, except where the application was in the original petition for divorce/dissolution.[58]

7.3.5 VARIATION OF ORDERS

Once made, an order can be appealed within 14 days. We consider later the grounds on which final, non-variable orders may be set aside or appealed against out of time.[59] Additionally, certain types of order can be varied in light of changed circumstances: maintenance pending suit, periodical payments, lump sums by instalment (in relation to the timetable but not, ordinarily, the total payable), deferred lump sums payable by pension attachment, property settlements made on judicial separation (only), orders for sale and pension sharing orders (before decree absolute has been granted and the order taken effect).[60] A fresh lump sum or property adjustment order cannot be made on a variation application.[61] But the court may substitute a lump sum, property adjustment, or pension sharing order[62] to secure a clean break if periodical payments are to be discharged or time-limited. Once discharged, a periodical payment order cannot be revived. Where the court wishes to 'leave the door ajar' should circumstances change, it can reduce the order to a purely nominal amount.

7.3.6 ENFORCEMENT OF ORDERS

The courts have wide ranging powers to enforce orders made in ancillary relief proceedings.[63] They depend on the type of order and level of court which made it; orders of superior courts can be registered with the magistrates' court so that their collection and enforcement procedures can be used.[64] Key powers include attachment of earnings,[65] warrant of control: the seizure and sale of goods to pay the debt;[66] third party orders, requiring a third party (such as

---

[55] See p 324 above.

[56] MCA 1973, s 22; CPA 2004, Sch 5, para 38.

[57] Black et al (2007), 17.68; cf *Hill v Hill* [1998] 1 FLR 198.

[58] MCA 1973, s 28(3); CPA 2004, Sch 5, para 48; *Whitehouse-Piper v Stokes* [2008] EWCA Civ 1049.

[59] 7.6.3.

[60] MCA 1973, s 31(1)–(4C); CPA 2004, Sch 5, Part 11, para 50. On lump sums, see *Westbury v Sampson* [2001] EWCA Civ 407.

[61] *Pearce v Pearce* [2003] EWCA Civ 1054.

[62] MCA 1973, s 31(5), (7A)–(7G); CPA 2004, Sch 5, Part 11, para 53.

[63] Black et al (2007), ch 22.

[64] Maintenance Orders Act 1958.

[65] Attachment of Earnings Act 1971; Maintenance Enforcement Act 1991, s 1; Magistrates' Courts Act 1980, s 59.

[66] Court Services Act 2003, Sch 7; County Courts Act 1984, s 85; Magistrates' Courts Act 1980, s 76; see generally Tribunal, Courts and Enforcement Act 2007, Part 3, due to be implemented in 2012.

a bank) holding funds belonging to the liable party to pay them to the applicant;[67] charging orders, giving the applicant a security interest in property belonging to the payer realizable on sale;[68] and committal to prison for up to six weeks: the last resort to be used where the defaulting payer can pay but is wilfully refusing or culpably neglecting to do so.[69] Failure to execute relevant documentation for property adjustment or to give up vacant possession prior to sale can be rectified by the court executing the documents or making an order for possession.[70]

7.4 THE PRINCIPLES GOVERNING THE GRANT OF RELIEF: AN INTRODUCTION

Having identified the tools, we now examine the basis on which they may be used. English ancillary relief law allocates resources not in accordance with statutory rules but on the basis of a wide judicial discretion.

There are no cases yet exploring the application of this law to civil partnership. It seems probable (and probably legally necessary[71]) that the principles emerging from contemporary case law between spouses will be applied to civil partners. The following discussion assumes that that will be the case. However, the different features of many same-sex relationships (for example, the lesser likelihood that one partner will have given up paid work to care for children; the greater likelihood of explicit financial arrangements, possibly pre-dating their civil partnership) is likely to mean that the application of those principles will generate different outcomes in practice from many 'ordinary' divorces. As on divorce, however, all will depend on the features of individual cases: like cases should be treated alike, regardless of whether they are civil partnerships or marriages. As Wilson observes,[72] application of the principles in the civil partnership context may provide a valuable, more gender-neutral and ahistorical, context in which to re-evaluate the principles as they apply in the ideologically loaded, gendered context of marriage.[73]

7.4.1 A BRIEF HISTORY

The history of ancillary relief on divorce is closely related to that of divorce law itself. Fault-based divorce law pre-1969 was accompanied by fault-based financial provision:

Law Commission, *The Financial Consequences of Divorce: The Basic Policy*, Law Com No 103 (London: HMSO, 1980)

13. Prior to 1971 ... the main features of the law governing the financial consequences of divorce were based on the assumption that (subject perhaps to the exception that a wife who

---

[67] Rules of the Supreme Court 1965, SI 1965/1776, Ord 49; County Court Rules 1981, SI 1981/1687, Ord 30.
[68] Charging Orders Act 1979, s 1.
[69] Debtors Act 1869; Administration of Justice Act 1970, s 11; Magistrates' Courts Act 1980, ss 76, 93, 96.
[70] Supreme Court Act 1981, s 39; County Courts Act 1984, s 38.
[71] Given the arguments and reasoning in *Wilkinson v Kitzinger* [2006] EWHC 2022: Wilson (2007), 36.
[72] See also Lind (2004), extracted at 2.3.2 above.
[73] Wilson (2007), 37.

was technically "guilty" might nevertheless expect some financial provision) the function of divorce was to give relief where a wrong had been done. The right and duty of maintenance was related to the performance of reciprocal maintenance obligations; a husband who was at fault should continue to support his wife, but conversely it would be unjust to require a husband who had "performed substantially all his matrimonial obligations to continue to provide maintenance for a wife who had substantially repudiated hers." The concept of a life-long right to and duty of support was thus inextricably linked with the concept of divorce as a relief for wrongdoing.

The Divorce Reform Act 1969 radically replaced the concept of matrimonial offence with irretrievable breakdown of marriage, now the sole ground of divorce. This might have been expected to affect the basis on which ancillary relief should be granted. However, the Law Commission report on which the ancillary relief legislation of 1970 was based did not examine basic principles.[74] The abandonment of the contractual, fault-based model left something of a 'normative vacuum'.[75] The legislation required courts to consider a checklist of factors, of which the parties' conduct was just one factor. Orders could now be made in favour of *either* party, regardless of who had petitioned for the divorce. Following pre-1969 case law, the court was ultimately directed

> ...so to exercise [its] powers as to place the parties, so far as it is practicable and, having regard to their conduct, just to do so, in the financial position in which they would have been if the marriage had not broken down and each had properly discharged his or her financial obligations and responsibilities towards the other.[76]

The practical problems with this 'minimal loss' principle quickly became apparent.[77] The objective was usually unattainable as resources were insufficient to meet the parties' basic needs: the principle was more aptly described as 'equal misery' than 'minimal loss'.[78] There were concerns that the continuing obligations were causing financial hardship on husbands and their new families, but equally that wives were not receiving adequate provision and having to rely on welfare benefits.[79] Fundamentally, the minimal loss objective seemed incompatible with no-fault divorce.

Law Commission, *The Financial Consequences of Divorce: the Basic Policy*, Law Com No 103 (London: HMSO, 1980)

> 30. We think that the arguments against the retention of a principle of life-long support at the standard enjoyed during the marriage can most easily be analysed and considered under four heads:
>
> (i) A duty of life-long support is now out of date because it is rooted in the concept of marriage as a life-time union. If marriage were indeed still a life-long institution, it might

---

[74] Law Com (1969).
[75] Dewar (2003), 426.
[76] Matrimonial Proceedings and Property Act 1970, s 5(1).
[77] See Cretney (2003a), 427–8.
[78] *Miller; McFarlane* [2006] UKHL 24, [126] per Baroness Hale.
[79] Law Com (1980), paras 25–8.

perhaps be reasonable that the parties should expect that the benefits and burdens incident to the status of marriage would not be affected by divorce; but (it is said) in modern conditions it is unrealistic for married couples not to accept that there is a very real possibility that their marriage will break down. It is thus correspondingly unrealistic for them to suppose that if this should happen their financial position would remain unaffected.

(ii)   The change in the juristic basis of divorce from matrimonial offence to irretrievable breakdown has fundamentally altered the validity of the law's approach to support obligations. On this argument the obligation to provide life-long support is based on the analogy between marriage and contract, under which compensation would be available for its breach. Consequently, it is argued that now that divorce is available whenever the marriage has broken down, irrespective of whether one or other of the parties is in breach of his or her matrimonial obligations, it is inappropriate for the law to continue to found the parties' respective financial obligations after divorce on the now largely irrelevant notion of breach of duty; and it is unjust to do so since the present law may require a man to maintain his wife when she has herself been entirely responsible for the breakdown.

(iii) The objective of life-long support is almost invariably impossible to attain because in most cases one man's resources are insufficient to support two households.

(iv)   The concept of a life-long support obligation is based on wholly out of date views of the division of function between husband and wife as well as of the economic status of women.

The first and fourth of these arguments could be over-stated. While divorce was no longer rare, many of those marrying might still expect or intend a lifelong union.[80] While wives were more economically active, large differences in the employment patterns of spouses, particularly following the birth of children, meant that men and women were far from on an equal economic footing and many wives could not be self-sufficient on divorce.[81] The second argument had more weight, the courts having decided that detailed investigation of conduct, other than in extreme cases, would subvert the aims of no-fault divorce.[82] As the Law Commission asked, 'If...the essence of the obligation of life-long support on divorce is that it represents compensation for a wrong done to the financially weaker party, yet the courts no longer investigate the question of blame, how (it is asked) can the obligation to support still be justified?'[83] The policy represented by the minimal loss principle no longer commanded support.[84] The MCA 1973, Part II was accordingly amended in 1984,[85] giving us the law in force today.

7.4.2   THE CURRENT LAW: THE STATUTORY DISCRETION

Any examination of the current law must begin with the statute. In the following extract, we have italicized some of the key wording added in 1984. The clean break principle, s 25A,

---

[80] Ibid., paras 31–4.
[81] Ibid., paras 45–57.
[82] *Wachtel v Wachtel* [1973] Fam 72; see 7.5.6 below.
[83] Law Com (1980), para 41.
[84] Law Com (1981), para 17.
[85] Matrimonial and Family Proceedings Act 1984.

was introduced at the same time; we include the basic provision here for completeness, but discuss it later in the chapter.[86]

Matrimonial Causes Act 1973[87]

25 Matters to which the court is to have regard in deciding how to exercise its powers [to order financial provision, property adjustment, sale, and pension sharing]

(1) It shall be the duty of the court in deciding whether to exercise its powers [to order financial provision, property adjustment, sale, or pension sharing] and, if so, in what manner, to have regard to all the circumstances of the case, *first consideration being given to the welfare while a minor of any child of the family who has not attained the age of eighteen.*

(2) As regards the exercise of the powers of the court [to make such orders] in relation to a party to the marriage, the court shall in particular have regard to the following matters—

   (a) the income, earning capacity, property and other financial resources which each of the parties to the marriage has or is likely to have in the foreseeable future, *including in the case of earning capacity any increase in that capacity which it would in the opinion of the court be reasonable to expect a party to the marriage to take steps to acquire*;

   (b) the financial needs, obligations and responsibilities which each of the parties to the marriage has or is likely to have in the foreseeable future;

   (c) the standard of living enjoyed by the family before the breakdown of the marriage;

   (d) the age of each party to the marriage and the duration of the marriage;

   (e) any physical and mental disability of either of the parties to the marriage;

   (f) the contributions which each of the parties has made or is likely in the foreseeable future to make to the welfare of the family, including any contribution by looking after the home or caring for the family;

   (g) the conduct of each of the parties, *if that conduct is such that it would in the opinion of the court be inequitable to disregard it*;

   (h) in the case of proceedings for divorce or nullity of marriage, the value to each of the parties to the marriage of any benefit which, by reason of the dissolution or annulment of the marriage, that party will lose the chance of acquiring.[88] . . .

25A Exercise of the court's powers in favour of party to marriage on decree of divorce or nullity of marriage

(1) Where on or after the grant of a decree of divorce or nullity of marriage the court decides to exercise its powers [to make such orders] in favour of a party to the marriage, it shall

---

[86] 7.6.1.

[87] CPA 2004, Sch 5, Part 5 and para 80.

[88] This refers principally to pension benefits that would be enjoyed if the party remained married, e.g. a widow's pension.

be the duty of the court to consider whether it would be appropriate so to exercise those powers that the financial obligations of each party towards the other will be terminated as soon after the grant of the decree as the court considers just and reasonable. . . .

52 Interpretation

(1) In this Act—

"child" in relation to one or both of the parties to a marriage, includes an illegitimate child of that party or, as the case may be, of both parties;
"child of the family", in relation to the parties to a marriage, means—

(a) a child of both of those parties; and

(b) any other child, not being a child who is placed with those parties as foster parents by a local authority or voluntary organisation, who has been treated by both of those parties as a child of their family.

On applications to vary orders, the court must give first consideration to the welfare of minor children of the family, and have regard to all the circumstances, including any relevant change of circumstance. The clean break principle also applies.[89]

The most striking feature of these provisions is that no ultimate objective is identified. The 1984 legislation removed the minimal loss principle, but the 'replacements'—first consideration being given to the welfare of minor children, and the clean break principle—do not perform the same function.[90] If anything, they clash: the individualism implicit in the clean break principle jars with the idea of continuing obligations and constraints where there are dependent children.[91] The factors in the statutory checklist point in different directions, some suggesting forward-looking, needs-based awards, others encouraging a retrospective evaluation of parties' contributions. Since English law operates a separate property system, there must be some rationale for redistributing resources between the parties on divorce.[92] Without explicit legislative guidance, the courts have been left to give shape to their wide discretion. Their approach has evolved over the years, in turn generating a vast academic literature which seeks both to explain what the law is (which is less than straightforward) and to debate the principles which *should* govern ancillary relief awards.[93] As one practitioner recently put it:

There is something in the work of archaeologists that reflects the current difficulties faced by family lawyers. The excavation requires a large group of people to pick through the rubble to find a few nuggets, which are delivered to a learned few, who develop a theory to unlock the mysteries of the investigation.[94]

---

[89] MCA 1973, s 31(7); CPA 2004, Sch 5, Part 11.

[90] Cf Scottish law: Family Law (Scotland) Act 1985; Scot Law Com (1981); see Deech (1982).

[91] Diduck (2003), 142.

[92] *Miller; McFarlane* [2006] UKHL 24, [137], per Baroness Hale, citing a lecture by Ward LJ (2004).

[93] E.g. Eekelaar (1991a), ch 4; Diduck and Orton (1994); Eekelaar and Maclean (1997); Eekelaar (1998a); Diduck (2003), ch 6; Bailey-Harris (2005); Miles (2005), (2008); Cooke (2007).

[94] Pirrie (2007).

7.5 EXERCISING THE STATUTORY DISCRETION: PRINCIPLES FROM THE CASE LAW

The basic principle identified by the House of Lords is 'fairness'. But as Lord Nicholls famously remarked in *White v White*, 'fairness, like beauty, likes in the eye of the beholder'.[95] He developed this theme in *Miller; McFarlane*:

Miller v Miller; McFarlane v McFarlane [2006] UKHL 24

LORD NICHOLLS:

4. Fairness is an elusive concept. It is an instinctive response to a given set of facts. Ultimately it is grounded in social and moral values. These values, or attitudes, can be stated. But they cannot be justified, or refuted, by any objective process of logical reasoning. Moreover, they change from one generation to the next. It is not surprising therefore that in the present context there can be different views on the requirements of fairness in any particular case...

6. ... Implicitly the courts must exercise their powers so as to achieve an outcome which is fair between the parties. But an important aspect of fairness is that like cases should be treated alike. So, perforce, if there is to be an acceptable degree of consistency of decision from one case to the next, the courts must themselves articulate, if only in the broadest fashion, what are the applicable if unspoken principles guiding the court's approach...

9. The starting point is surely not controversial. In the search for a fair outcome it is pertinent to have in mind that fairness generates obligations as well as rights. The financial provision made on divorce by one party for the other, still typically the wife, is not in the nature of largesse. It is not a case of 'taking away' from one party and 'giving' to the other property which 'belongs' to the former. The claimant is not a suppliant. Each party to a marriage is *entitled* to a *fair* share of the available property. The search is always for what are the *requirements* of fairness in the particular case.

The speeches in *Miller; McFarlane* identified three broad principles, rationales, or 'strands' underpinning the 'fair' result: need, compensation, and (equal) sharing. The outcomes generated by these principles in individual cases vary substantially, depending on factors such as the scale of the parties' resources, whether they have children, the degree of financial interdependence, and the length of the marriage.

Miller and *McFarlane* were both 'big money' cases, but otherwise were very different. The Millers had been married for less than three years and had no children; the McFarlanes were married for over 16 years, with three children. Mrs Miller had been working in public relations until the first year of the marriage; Mrs McFarlane had given up a successful professional career in order to raise the family and support her husband, whose career prospered. The McFarlanes had started out in life together; Mr Miller had amassed a fortune before the marriage. What did 'fairness' demand in these very different cases? Moreover, since the vast majority of reported cases concern 'big money' couples, how do the principles apply in more 'everyday' cases?[96] The reality of everyday cases is very different from what the big money case law might imply.

---

[95] [2001] 1 AC 596, 599.
[96] Hitchings (2010).

Our discussion is principally organized around the three principles identified by the House of Lords. However, the courts regularly reiterate that the exercise remains a discretionary one, guided by the s 25 factors and focused on obtaining a result which is 'fair'. The courts resist attempts to treat the three rationales as 'separate heads of claim' in favour of a more holistic, 'intuitive' pursuit of fairness,[97] informed but not constrained by the three principles, or whichever of the principles is deemed relevant to the case.[98] But 'fairness' cannot be used as a sole criterion. To secure consistency in decision-making (itself an aspect of fairness), 'fairness' (even if supplemented with 'non-discrimination'[99]) cannot be left to the judgement of individual courts, but needs principled shape and content. So we need to analyse each rationale, explore their inter-relationship,[100] and consider when one might assume 'magnetic importance'.[101] Only then can we gain a sense of where the courts' intuition takes them and so try to develop a coherent view of the case law. However, the statutory provisions and the width of the court's discretion must be kept in mind: 'It is prudent to remember that [the House of Lords' speeches] are explanations of and expansions upon the statute, not the statute itself'.[102] That being so, we begin with the factor which must, by statute, be given first consideration.

7.5.1 FIRST CONSIDERATION: THE WELFARE OF THE CHILDREN

Although children's maintenance requirements are dealt with primarily via child support, children's interests may influence provision between the adults in various ways:

Miller v Miller; McFarlane v McFarlane [2006] UKHL 24

BARONESS HALE:

128. . . . [S]ection 25(1) . . . is a clear recognition of the reality that, although the couple may seek to go their separate ways, they are still jointly responsible for the welfare of their children. The invariable practice in English law is to try to maintain a stable home for the children after their parents' divorce. Research indicates that it is more successful in doing this than in securing a comparable income for them in future (see, eg [Arthur et al (2002)]). Giving priority to the children's welfare should also involve ensuring that their primary carer is properly provided for, because it is well known that the security and stability of children depends in large part upon the security and stability of their primary carers (see eg [Lewis (2001a)] p 178).

---

[97] E.g. *RP v RP* [2006] EWHC 3409, [58]; *P v P* [2007] EWHC 2877, [108]–[109]; *CR v CR* [2007] EWHC 3334, [83]; *B v B* [2008] EWCA Civ 543; *VB v JP* [2008] EWHC 112, [45], [52]; *McFarlane v McFarlane (no 2)* [2009] EWHC 891, [112], [118].

[98] See Wall LJ in *B v B* [2008] EWCA Civ 543, [50]–[51] asserting that only two principles have universal application: fairness and non-discrimination.

[99] Ibid.

[100] See 7.5.5.

[101] E.g. *McCartney v Mills McCartney* [2008] EWHC 401, [301].

[102] *Charman v Charman* [2006] EWHC 1879, [114] per Coleridge J.

Children's welfare in this context is only the first, not paramount, consideration.[103] It is only during the children's minority that their statutory priority applies. However, the courts acknowledge that children remain financially dependent and live at home long after reaching 18.[104] The interests of other children (such as children or step-children from a previous or subsequent relationship) may be relevant insofar as they affect parties' needs and obligations.[105] The interests of children frequently affect decisions about housing, and may also impact on whether and when it is reasonable to expect the primary carer to undertake paid employment.[106]

7.5.2 MEETING THE PARTIES' MATERIAL NEEDS

The first of the House of Lords' three principles derives from the second factor in the s 25 checklist: financial needs.

Miller v Miller; McFarlane v McFarlane [2006] UKHL 24

LORD NICHOLLS:

11. This element of fairness reflects the fact that to a greater or lesser extent every relationship of marriage gives rise to a relationship of interdependence. The parties share the roles of money-earner, home-maker and child-carer. Mutual dependence begets mutual obligations of support. When the marriage ends fairness requires that the assets of the parties should be divided primarily so as to make provision for the parties' housing and financial needs, taking into account a wide range of matters such as the parties' ages, their future earning capacity, the family's standard of living, and any disability of either party. Most of these needs will have been generated by the marriage, but not all of them. Needs arising from age or disability are instances of the latter.

As is most lavishly exemplified by *McCartney v Mills McCartney*,[107] the courts interpret 'need' by reference to the standard of living enjoyed by the parties;[108] the 'needs' or 'reasonable requirements' of the rich are therefore more substantial than the needs of the rest; they might even extend to a 'need' to keep horses.[109] Case law has explored various needs-related issues: provision of housing; the source of available resources to meet the parties' needs; the source of those needs; the needs and resources of second families. It is important to emphasize that in 'everyday' cases where resources are limited, needs (and associated pragmatic issues) will be the only really consideration (to the exclusion of compensation and equal sharing).[110] Need may also assume 'magnetic importance' in other contexts, for example after short marriages to which one party brought all the wealth, even if they have produced children.[111]

[103] *Suter v Suter* [1987] Fam 111, 123–4.
[104] *Richardson v Richardson (No 2)* [1994] 2 FLR 1051.
[105] *Roberts v Roberts* [1970] P 1.
[106] Eekelaar and Maclean (1986), 105.
[107] [2008] EWHC 401.
[108] *Miller; McFarlane* [2006] UKHL 24, [138] per Baroness Hale.
[109] *S v S* [2008] EWHC 519.
[110] Hitchings (2010).
[111] *McCartney v Mills McCartney* [2008] EWHC 401.

Housing first

Wherever there are minor children, the court's priority is securing accommodation for them, their primary carer, and (if possible)[112] the other parent:

M v B (ancillary proceedings: lump sum) [1998] 1 FCR 213, 220 (CA)

THORPE LJ:

In all these cases it is one of the paramount considerations, in applying the s 25 criteria, to endeavour to stretch what is available to cover the need of each for a home, particularly where there are young children involved. Obviously the primary carer needs whatever is available to make the main home for the children, but it is of importance, albeit it is of lesser importance, that the other parent should have a home of his own where the children can enjoy their contact time with him. Of course, there are cases where there is not enough to provide a home for either. Of course, there are cases where there is only enough to provide one. But in any case where there is, by stretch and a degree of risk-taking, the possibility of a division to enable both to rehouse themselves, that is an exceptionally important consideration and one which will almost invariably have a decisive impact on outcome.

Here the judge had the opportunity to make a division which would just about enable each to rehouse. True, if the wife was to go for [the house she preferred] it would require some sacrifice on the part of her family and some burden of future mortgage. True, on the husband's side it would entail taking advantage of his ability to defer the Law Society's charge in respect of his costs.[113] But those are the sort of methods to which the court regularly has to have recourse in cases where the money is only just enough . . .[114]

Even if the home is retained for occupation by the children and primary carer during the children's minority, it may be appropriate for the other spouse to retain a share in its capital value under a *Mesher* order.[115] But the parties' respective needs and resources may indicate that the primary carer should retain the property either on a *Martin* basis or outright.[116] One study indicates that some primary carers place such weight on securing immediate housing that they forgo periodical payments and the long-term security offered by a share of the other spouse's pension fund in order to secure the home.[117]

The source of available resources

The court must have regard to all available financial resources of the parties. We shall see that the source of assets is potentially important under the equal sharing principle. But all assets are in principle available for meeting the parties' needs, including wealth accumulated prior to the marriage; acquired by gift or inheritance during it;[118] or even years after separation.[119]

---

[112] E.g. *B v B (Financial Provision: Welfare of Child and Conduct)* [2002] 1 FLR 555.

[113] This is a reference to the statutory charge enabling the legal aid authority to recover its costs: Black et al (2007), ch 2.

[114] See also *Fisher-Aziz v Aziz* [2010] EWCA Civ 673.

[115] *Elliott v Elliott* [2001] 1 FCR 477; see p 436 above.

[116] *B v B (Mesher Order)* [2002] EWHC 3106.

[117] Perry et al (2000).

[118] *White v White* [2001] 1 AC 596, at 610.

[119] *Schuller v Schuller* [1990] 2 FLR 193; *Vaughan v Vaughan* [2010] EWCA Civ 349, [42].

The parties' ability to raise capital through secured loans is also relevant, whether to release the value of an otherwise illiquid asset or to acquire new property. Sometimes, the nature of the property may be such that it is fair to *limit* an award to the applicant's needs (with no sharing of the surplus), for example, where the main asset is a farm which has been in the respondent's family for generations.[120]

The relevance of welfare benefits entitlements to meet needs is a difficult area. Periodical payments simply decrease the recipient's entitlement to key benefits pound for pound.[121] From the recipient's perspective, an order may seem pointless unless and to the extent that its value exceeds the benefits. Nevertheless, it is generally considered undesirable that the state should support individuals whom other private persons could reasonably be expected to support.[122] So although a former spouse is not a 'liable relative' from whom benefits payments may be recouped by the state, respondents may ordinarily be expected to contribute to applicants' needs to the extent that they can afford to do so. Inevitably, however, financial settlements for low income families depend to some extent on welfare benefits, tax credits, and public housing.[123]

The mere fact that one party has needs following divorce and so is likely to become reliant on state support may not itself justify a needs-based award, particularly if the marriage was short or childless.[124] The law must determine when, on what basis, and for how long a former spouse, rather than the state, should have to support such individuals. This issue is closely related to the clean break principle.[125]

The source of the parties' needs

A key question is the type and source of needs for which awards may be made.[126]

North v North [2007] EWCA Civ 760

THORPE LJ:

32. ...There are of course two faces to fairness. The order must be fair both to the applicant in need and to the respondent who must pay. In any application under Section 31 [for variation of a periodical payment order] the applicant's needs are likely to be the dominant or magnetic factor. But it does not follow that the respondent is inevitably responsible financially for any established needs. He is not an insurer against all hazards nor, when fairness is the measure, is he necessarily liable for needs created by the applicant's financial mismanagement, extravagance or irresponsibility. The prodigal former wife cannot hope to turn to a former husband in pursuit of a legal remedy, whatever may be her hope that he might out of charity come to her rescue.

An ex-spouse is clearly potentially liable for needs generated by the relationship itself: for example, where one spouse gave up paid employment to raise the children and so is not

---

120 *P v P (Inherited Property)* [2004] EWHC 1364, [44]–[45].
121 Contrast the full maintenance disregard in relation to child support payments: see p 365 above.
122 *Peacock v Peacock* [1984] 1 All ER 1069; cf *Delaney v Delaney* [1991] FCR 161.
123 Burrows, Conway, and Eames (2006).
124 *SRJ v DWJ (financial provision)* [1999] 3 FCR 153, 160 per Hale J.
125 7.6.1.
126 See Eekelaar and Maclean (1986), 39–41.

self-sufficient; or where domestic violence caused some disability impairing the victim's earning capacity.[127] It is less clear whether and when responsibility may extend to needs which have not been produced by the marriage: for example, arising from long-term unemployment, illness, disability, or old age, particularly where those problems arise following separation.[128] Although not necessary for their decision, both Lord Nicholls and Baroness Hale considered this issue. While Lord Nicholls referred generally to needs arising from disability,[129] Baroness Hale's view was qualified:

Miller v Miller; McFarlane v McFarlane [2006] UKHL 24

BARONESS HALE:

137....The cardinal feature is that each [of the three principles: need, sharing, and compensation] is looking at factors which are linked to the parties' relationship, either causally or temporally, and not to extrinsic, unrelated factors, such as a disability arising after the marriage has ended.

138....The most common rationale is that *the relationship has generated needs* which it is right that the other party should meet...This is a perfectly sound rationale where the needs are the consequence of the parties' relationship, as they usually are. The most common source of need is the presence of children, whose welfare is always the first consideration, or of other dependent relatives, such as elderly parents. But another source of need is having had to look after children or other family members in the past. Many parents have seriously compromised their ability to attain self-sufficiency as a result of past family responsibilities. Even if they do their best to re-enter the employment market, it will often be at a lesser level than before, and they will hardly ever be able to make up what they have lost in pension entitlements. A further source of need may be the way in which the parties chose to run their life together. Even dual career families are difficult to manage with completely equal opportunity for both. Compromises often have to be made by one so that the other can get ahead. All couples throughout their lives together have to make choices about who will do what, sometimes forced upon them by circumstances such as redundancy or low pay, sometimes freely made in the interests of them both. The needs generated by such choices are a perfectly sound rationale for adjusting the parties' respective resources in compensation.

The Scottish Law Commission examined this area when recommending that awards should be possible on the grounds of 'grave financial hardship', one of five principles on which relief can be based under the Family Law (Scotland) Act 1985. But they felt that the principle should have limited operation:[130]

Scottish Law Commission, *Report on Aliment and Financial Provision*, Scot Law Com No 67 (Edinburgh: HMSO, 1981)

3.110...We do not think, for example, that a man who suffers hardship on being made redundant at the age of 52 should have a claim for financial provision against a former wife

---

[127] *Jones v Jones* [1976] Fam 8.
[128] E.g. *Ashley v Blackman* [1988] Fam 85; *Re G (Financial Provision: Liberty to Restore Application for Lump Sum)* [2004] EWHC 88.
[129] See [11], in extract above.
[130] See also Law Com (1980), para 72.

whom he divorced thirty years before. We think that the general principle should be that after the divorce each party bears the risk of *supervening* hardship without recourse against the other. It should therefore be made clear in the legislation that it is only where the likelihood of grave financial hardship is established at the time of the divorce that a claim will arise [on that basis]. We recognise that if the principle is framed in this way there will be cases falling narrowly on the "wrong" side of the line. The man or woman paralysed as a result of a road accident six months before the divorce would have a claim for financial provision. The man or woman who suffered a similar injury six months after the divorce would not. We consider, however, that a line has to be drawn somewhere and that the right place to draw the line is the date when the legal relationship between the parties comes to an end. After that each should be free to make a new life without liability for future misfortunes which may befall the other.

On this view, a former spouse cannot be expected to meet all needs, howsoever arising, however short the marriage, and however long ago the divorce.

By contrast, with the clarity of the Scottish position, the English cases do not clearly delineate the extent of responsibility for need. In *Seaton v Seaton*,[131] the wife was relieved of ongoing liability to support a husband who, having become dependent on her during the marriage after being sacked and failing to hold down a job because of drink, suffered a debilitating stroke shortly before the divorce which left him wholly dependent with no prospect of recovery. The precise reason for the decision was unclear: the husband's long-term dependency or his prior delinquency? By contrast, in *Fisher v Fisher*, the ex-husband was required to continue paying periodical payments to his former wife when she was unable to support herself through employment owing to the birth of a child fathered by a third party (though she was also looking after the child of the marriage).[132] Liability in relation to subsequent redundancy, illness, or disability might sometimes properly arise long after divorce. This is so at least where the former spouse's inability to support him- or herself, owing to lack of capital resources or pension fund, derives from having given up paid employment in order to care for the family during (and following) the marriage.[133] But in *North v North*, the prospering ex-husband was required to make modest annual payments to his ex-wife of 14 years, some 20 years after the divorce, when, having been financially secure in England, the wife's position became precarious following her emigration to Australia and unwise investment decisions. Importantly, the Court of Appeal rejected the husband's argument that an applicant in the wife's position should be required, as a matter of principle, to prove that 'despite her best efforts, her attempts at self-help had failed' before being able to proceed with an application to vary a periodical payments order. The circumstances relating to her present need were to be examined in the exercise of the court's broad discretion, in pursuit of the overarching objective to attain a fair result. On the facts, and given Thorpe LJ's statement of principle extracted above, the award of any periodical payment in this case is rather surprising.

The needs and resources of second families

The court must also consider the needs and obligations of the respondent and any new dependants, whether the respondent is legally or, as in the case of step-children or a

---

[131] [1986] 2 FLR 398.
[132] [1989] 1 FLR 432.
[133] E.g. *Whiting v Whiting* [1988] 1 WLR 565, 580.

cohabiting partner, only morally obliged to maintain them.[134] In *Vaughan v Vaughan (no 2)*, it was said that 'although [the court] should not go so far as to give priority to the claims of the first wife, it should certainly not give priority to the claims of the second wife'.[135] In *Delaney v Delaney*, the wife was renting the former matrimonial home with the two children; the husband had bought a new three-bed property with his girlfriend on a shared equity basis, wishing to start a family. Any obligation to the first family would leave the husband's household with an amount 'barely adequate to sustain any reasonable way of life'. The case arose pre-Child Support Act: the husband was relieved from an obligation to pay regular child maintenance, an outcome that could not be secured by a court today.[136] The Court of Appeal balanced support for the primary carer, who may have benefits entitlements, against the husband's new family.

Delaney v Delaney [1991] FCR 161, 165–6 (CA)

WARD J:

[T]he approach of this court in this case must be, first, to have regard to the need of the wife and the children for proper support. Having assessed that need, the court should then consider the ability of the husband to meet it. Whilst this court deprecates any notion that a former husband and extant father may slough off the tight skin of familial responsibility and may slither into and lose himself in the greener grass on the other side, nonetheless this court has proclaimed and will proclaim that it looks to the realities of the real world in which we live, and that among the realities of life is that there is a life after divorce. The ... husband is entitled to order his life in such a way as will hold in reasonable balance the responsibilities to his existing family which he carries into his new life, as well as his proper aspirations for that new future. In all life, for those who are divorced as well as for those who are not divorced, indulging one's whims or even one's reasonable desires must be held in check by the constraints imposed by limited resources and compelling obligations. But this husband's resources, even when one adds to them the contribution made by his girl friend, are very limited indeed.

The judge found that it was reasonable, since the first consideration was the interests of the children, that the husband should have accommodation suitable for them to have overnight stays; the chosen property was not extravagant. And in this case, it was appropriate only to make nominal orders in favour of the wife and children:

[I]f, having regard to the reasonable financial commitments undertaken by the husband with due regard to the contribution properly made by the lady with whom he lives, there is insufficient left properly and fully to maintain the former wife and children, then the court may have regard to the fact that in proper cases social security benefits are available to the wife and children of the marriage; that having such regard, the court is enabled to avoid making orders which will be financially crippling to the husband.... In my judgment, it is far better that the spirit of effecting a clean break and starting with a fresh slate be implemented in this case, not by dismissing the claims of the wife and the children, but by acknowledging that

---

[134] *Roberts v Roberts* [1970] P 1.
[135] [2010] EWCA Civ 349.
[136] See 6.6.2.

now and, it is likely, in the foreseeable future he will not be able to honour the obligations he has recognized towards his children.

Can the resources of a respondent's new partner can be considered in deciding what, if any, order to make against the respondent? If working, the partner can be expected to contribute to the respondent's household costs. But the court will not ordinarily make orders against respondents which can only be satisfied by using the resources of their new partner, or other third party, or by making orders that leave respondents dependent on a third party.[137]

Elsewhere, the question is whether and how a new partner of the (would-be) *recipient* of periodical payments is relevant.[138] Either the recipient has a new partner when the court is first invited to make the order, or a new partner arrives later, prompting an application to vary an order. Where the recipient marries or forms a civil partnership before any order has been made, any application is now barred by statute and any existing order for periodical payments automatically terminates.[139]

Cohabitation does not have the same effect. Commonly, orders state that periodical payments will cease if the recipient cohabits with a third party for six months. If no such term was included, the payer wishing to cease or reduce payment must seek a variation. A cohabitant who can afford to contribute to the recipient's household should do so to the extent that he or she has capacity to pay;[140] orders have been reduced, discharged, or rendered nominal accordingly.[141] But there is disagreement about the weight which should, in principle, be attached to the recipient's cohabitation. In *Atkinson v Atkinson*,[142] the Court of Appeal held that cohabitation was not to be equated with marriage, and that position was affirmed over 20 years later in *Grey v Grey*,[143] despite the 'heretical' reservations of Coleridge J in *K v K*.[144] Coleridge J had argued that given the rise in cohabitation and births outside marriage, and the functional and social equivalence of lengthy, settled cohabitation to marriage, it was too easy for an ex-spouse to avoid periodical payments being automatically terminated by cynically not marrying the new partner, thus putting the onus on the payer to seek a variation of the order. But the Court of Appeal is clear that the matter must be left to Parliament to determine. In the meantime, cohabitation is just another factor to weigh in the balance of fairness, albeit one that can attract considerable weight. This is a difficult issue. While many cohabiting relationships exhibit the characteristics of many marriages, others are less stable. Moreover, as the wife in *K v K* argued, cohabitants—unlike spouses—currently owe each other no legal obligations of support, whether during their relationship[145] or following separation. The 'legal paperwork' which accompanies marriage and civil partnership is therefore not insignificant. This clash between law and social practice is difficult to reconcile.

---

137 *Macey v Macey* (1982) 3 FLR 7; and n 21 above.

138 See also *Chadwick v Chadwick* [1985] FLR 606: whether *Martin* order more appropriate than outright transfer.

139 MCA 1973, s 28(1)(a), (3); CPA 2004, Sch 5, paras 47–8.

140 *Grey v Grey* [2009] EWCA Civ 1424, [28].

141 E.g. *Suter v Suter* [1987] Fam 111.

142 [1988] Fam 93.

143 [2009] EWCA Civ 1424.

144 [2005] EWHC 2886.

145 See 3.8.1.

7.5.3 COMPENSATION: RELATIONSHIP-GENERATED ECONOMIC DISADVANTAGE

Miller v Miller; McFarlane v McFarlane [2006] UKHL 24

LORD NICHOLLS:

13. Another strand, recognised more explicitly now than formerly, is compensation. This is aimed at redressing any significant prospective economic disparity between the parties arising from the way they conducted their marriage. For instance, the parties may have arranged their affairs in a way which has greatly advantaged the husband in terms of his earning capacity but left the wife severely handicapped so far as her own earning capacity is concerned. Then the wife suffers a double loss: a diminution in her earning capacity and the loss of a share in her husband's enhanced income. This is often the case. Although less marked than in the past, women may still suffer a disproportionate financial loss on the breakdown of a marriage because of their traditional role as home-maker and child-carer...

15. Compensation and financial needs often overlap in practice, so double-counting has to be avoided. But they are distinct concepts, and they are far from co-terminous. A claimant wife may be able to earn her own living but she may still be entitled to a measure of compensation.

Of the three principles identified by the House of Lords in _Miller; McFarlane_, the compensation strand is the one of which practitioners and courts have been most wary, perceived (rightly or wrongly) to be wholly novel and not to be found on the face of the legislation.[146] It has also attracted critical comment in principle.[147]

McFarlane was regarded as a 'paradigm case for compensation'.[148] Both spouses had highly successful professional careers, but they decided the wife should give up her career to look after the home and family. By the time of the divorce, the husband was earning over £750,000 net per annum, a sum which far exceeded the family's needs. The House of Lords held that annual periodical payments of £250,000 should be paid to the wife both to meet her needs and to compensate her for forgone earning capacity. However, it was not explained how the figure of £250,000 was reached, or to what extent it was intended to compensate rather than meet needs. This remains one of the most difficult outstanding questions from _McFarlane_. Lord Nicholls' and Baroness Hale's speeches suggest that there are potentially two, quite distinct, concerns: (i) loss of earning capacity sustained by a spouse who reduced or gave up paid employment in order to care for the family; (ii) enhancement of the other spouse's income and earning capacity which is partly attributable to the support provided by the homemaking spouse.

Compensating for loss of earning capacity

The idea of compensation for loss of earning capacity pre-dates _Miller; McFarlane_. Here, Hale LJ (as she then was) explains why a clean break would be inappropriate in this case:

---

[146] This is not entirely accurate: see _Charman v Charman_ [2007] EWCA Civ 503, [71]; Miles (2005).

[147] Deech (2009c).

[148] Ibid., and [93] per Lord Nicholls.

SRJ v DWJ *(financial provision)* [1999] 3 FCR 153, 160 (CA)

HALE LJ:

This was a long marriage. The couple had 27 years together. There were four children. It was a classic example of the sort of case where the wife could have continued to work as a teacher; indeed, she did for some of the time. But she gave up her place in the world of work to concentrate upon her husband, her home and her family. That must have been a mutual decision from which they both benefited. It means that the marriage has deprived her of what otherwise she might have had. Over the many years of that marriage she must have built up an entitlement to some compensation for that. It is not only in her interests but in the community's interests that parents, whether mothers or fathers, and spouses, whether wives or husbands, should have a real choice between concentrating on breadwinning and concentrating on home-making and child rearing, and do not feel forced, for fear of what might happen should their marriage break down much later in life, to abandon looking after the home and the family to other people for the sake of maintaining a career.

It is not only after long marriages that awards based on compensatory principles may be justified. In *B v B (Mesher Order)*, the parties had been married for only one year, but had a child, W. A lump sum was to allow the wife to buy a house for herself and W. Should this be done on a *Mesher* basis, reserving a portion of the capital for the husband on W's independence, or transferred outright to the wife? Munby J did not express himself in terms of compensation, and any 'compensation' may have corresponded with needs arising from the wife's child-care responsibilities. But the case has a strong compensatory flavour. Munby J agreed with the 'common sense view of the future realities', depicted by counsel for the wife, that:

B v B *(Mesher Order)* [2002] EWHC 3106, [2003] 2 FLR 285

MUNBY J:

... the wife's major contribution to this marriage ... is the fact that, for the next 16 years or so (and I put it that way because W is now approximately 2 years old), she will have the very considerable burden of looking after him and bringing him up ...

Furthermore ... in the nature of things the performance by the wife of her obligations ... will inevitably impact adversely upon her earning capacity. Not merely her capacity to earn an income during that part of her life, during W's early years when she will not be able to work at all; not merely during that part of W's later childhood during which she will be able to work part-time perhaps on an increasing scale. But even after W is off her hands, her continuing earning capacity, even when she is free to work full-time, will be significantly reduced, he says, by the fact that for a number of years she will have been out of the job market. She will therefore find herself, when W is 18, in her mid-forties, even if free to work full-time, not able to get the kind of job which will generate the kind of income which by then she could realistically have hoped to obtain had she not had the interruption of looking after W.

Moreover ... that impacts not merely upon her earning ability in the sense of her income, it impacts seriously (and he suggests decisively) upon her ability ... ever to generate capital, whether by way of acquiring a property on a mortgage, or more particularly by way of building up a pension fund.

Meanwhile, the husband would readily make back the capital and had substantial pension funds which were untouched by the order. The outright transfer of the house to the wife was therefore upheld.

By contrast with these cases where one spouse sacrifices earning capacity in order to look after home and family, it seems that a spouse who simply chooses—in pursuit of his own lifestyle preference—to reduce his earning capacity by changing from a financially lucrative career to a more personally satisfying but less well-paid job does not thereby generate a claim for compensation.[149]

Cases since *Miller; McFarlane* have taken a tentative approach to these arguments. It has sometimes been assumed that the wife has sustained economic disadvantage from devoting herself to raising the family, even if no professional career had been sacrificed,[150] on the basis that the length of absence from the labour market will have disadvantaged her.[151] In other cases, perhaps because the wife already stood to receive a substantial sum from the sharing principle, the courts have declined to find any disadvantage.[152] Where it has been found that the compensation principle applies, the courts have declined to analyse closely how it affects the quantum of the overall award, preferring to subsume the matter into their 'in the round' assessment of the fairness of their orders[153] or within a 'generous assessment of needs'.[154] Coleridge J has cautioned against (i) subjecting the compensation principle to the forensic techniques of negligence actions (such as use of expert evidence about wives' earning capacity); (ii) separating out needs, compensation, and sharing as if they are 'heads of damage' in a tort claim; and (iii) conducting speculative 'what if...?' explorations of the lost career.[155] There are related concerns about the compensation principle's potential to ride roughshod over respondents:[156]

Compensation usually considers only the position of the person who has suffered some detriment, regardless of the ability of the other person to pay. That is the antithesis of the exercise in ancillary relief, which involves striking a fair balance in the context of a finite kitty.[157]

The answer lies in the idea of achieving overall equality of outcome for the parties.[158] Failing to recognize career sacrifice would often leave an imbalance between the parties. But, clearly, the court's order should not simply create a new imbalance operating in the other direction. There are only limited assets available for division and these are not tort claims: the respondent is not paying the applicant damages for injury sustained owing to his blameworthy conduct, regardless of his own needs and legitimate claims. The sacrifice

---

[149] *Radmacher v Granatino* [2010] UKSC 42, [121], cf [186].

[150] Singer J accepted that that is not a requirement in *S v S* [2006] EWHC 2339, [116], but declined to uphold a compensation claim on the facts; *H v H* [2007] EWHC 459, [77].

[151] E.g. *Lauder v Lauder* [2007] EWHC 1227, [65]–[67], [69].

[152] *NA v MA* [2006] EWHC 2900 (Fam), [177]; *S v S* [2006] EWHC 2793, [59]; *S v S* [2006] EWHC 2339, [116]; *B v B* [2010] EWHC 193.

[153] *Lauder v Lauder* [2007] EWHC 1227; *RP v RP* [2006] EWHC 3409: husband's greater earning capacity was a factor (with the children's needs and the clean-break nature of the orders) justifying a 60:40 split in favour of the wife. This is a common ratio in the district courts: Hodson (2007).

[154] *Lauder v Lauder* [2007] EWHC 1227; *VB v JP* [2008] EWHC 112, [82].

[155] *RP v RP* [2006] EWHC 3409, [59]–[64]; approved in *VB v JP* [2008] EWHC 112, [52]. See also *McFarlane v McFarlane (no 2)* [2009] EWHC 891.

[156] Cf need: needs of both parties are relevant; equal sharing gives each party the same.

[157] *CR v CR* [2007] EWHC 3334, [79].

[158] *Vaughan v Vaughan* [2007] EWCA Civ 1085, [50]; *CR v CR* [2007] EWHC 3334, [95].

of curtailing paid employment should ordinarily be viewed as the product of a joint decision made as part of spouses' lifestyle choices for their relationship. The economic consequences should be fairly shared, given the finite resources that their partnership has generated and both parties' interests.[159] That must at least imply that the applicant cannot assert a claim regarding career sacrifice that would give her a stronger economic position and better standard of living than the respondent: there should at least be some form of 'economic equality' ceiling to compensation.[160]

Compensation received its most authoritative consideration to date in *VB v JP*:

VB v JP [2008] EWHC 112

POTTER P:

59. In my view there emerge from the post-*Miller* and *McFarlane* authorities . . . the following propositions in elaboration of, but consistent with, the House of Lords decision. First, it is at the exit of the marriage and in relation to the division / redistribution of the family assets that the consideration of the element of compensation immediately arises, but as a feature of the concept of fairness rather than as a head of claim in its own right. Second, on the exit from the marriage, the partnership ends and in ordinary circumstances the wife has no right or expectation of continuing economic parity ("sharing") unless and to the extent that consideration of her needs, or compensation for relationship-generated disadvantage so require. A clean break is to be encouraged wherever possible. Third, in big money cases, where the matrimonial assets are sufficient for a clean break to be achieved, a wife with ordinary career prospects is likely to have been compensated by an equal division of the assets and consideration of how the wife's career might have progressed is unnecessary and should be avoided.[161] Where, however, that is not the case and the parties accept or the court decides that fairness can only be achieved by an award of continuing periodical payments in respect of a wife's maintenance, then the matter of compensation in respect of relationship-generated disadvantage requires consideration, again as a strand or element of fairness. Fourth, in cases other than big money cases, where a continuing award of periodic payments is necessary and the wife has plainly sacrificed her own earning capacity, compensation will rarely be amenable to consideration as a separate element in the sense of a premium susceptible of calculation with any precision. Where it is necessary to provide ongoing periodical payments for the wife after the division of capital assets insufficient to cover her future maintenance needs, any element of compensation is best dealt with by a generous assessment of her continuing needs unrestricted by purely budgetary considerations, in the light of the contribution of the wife to the marriage and the broad effect of the sacrifice of her own earning capacity upon her ability to provide for her own needs following the end of the matrimonial partnership. These considerations are of course inherent in s. 25(a)(b)(d) and (f) of the 1973 Act.

The President regarded *McFarlane* as a case where the scale of the wife's disadvantage 'went well beyond the compensation afforded by a generous interpretation of her needs'. By implication, in such cases a closer examination of the quantum of appropriate compensation will

---

159 See *McFarlane v McFarlane (no 2)* [2009] EWHC 891, [44]–[45], [113]–[114].
160 See further Miles (2008).
161 See further below, 7.5.5.

be required.[162] It may also be necessary where a clean break is to be effected, in which case 'there is a particular necessity to concentrate on the adequacy of the sum ordered because it will finally settle the position between the parties'.[163] The extent of any losses depends on the applicant's qualifications and experience: contrast high-flying professionals such as Mrs McFarlane with someone who left school with no qualifications for low-paid, unskilled employment. It has been suggested that it would be 'discriminatory' if Mrs McFarlane received a larger award than a former shop assistant.[164] But the different outcomes here may be no more 'discriminatory' than the difference between the value of *any* awards in 'big money' and 'small money' cases: private law remedies mirror the features of individual cases.

When *McFarlane* returned to court on a variation application,[165] Charles J considered that, given the parties' long marriage and its character as a joint enterprise, fairness required that the wife should be able to maintain her current standard of living for the rest of her life (with no drop on retirement, as might otherwise have been expected). It could at least be said that, had she not given up her career, she would have been able to do that herself. Instead, the parties so conducted themselves that they would depend on the husband's income as the source of wealth. Rather than try to estimate the wife's earnings losses, the court's order focused on a fair distribution of the husband's wealth given the choices and plans that they had made. The resulting order was effectively a *very* generous assessment of need, an outcome which may disappoint the President given his remarks in *VB v JP*. However, it seems clear that following shorter marriages, and certainly childless marriages, rather less generosity should be expected.

Mitigation of loss

A related issue is how far applicants can reasonably be expected to 'mitigate' the projected loss by returning to paid employment once child-care obligations permit. The court must have regard to 'any increase in [the parties' earning] capacity which it would in the opinion of the court be reasonable to expect a party to the marriage to take steps to acquire'.[166] In making that assessment, courts will consider spouses' ages and the duration of their absence from the labour market.[167] But, as *SRJ v DWJ* indicates,[168] there are important social questions about what can reasonably be expected of parents of dependent children: some parents are happy to work, or feel they must do so, relying on child-care services; others prefer personally to undertake as much child-care as possible and limit work commitments accordingly. Where the child has special needs, opportunities for employment may be further restricted.[169] Hale LJ assumed that the parties' decisions in *SRJ v DWJ* about employment and child-care were mutual—but what if one party contends otherwise? Moreover, respondents may equally wish to make lifestyle choices after divorce that reduce their income and so limit their ability to make periodical payments.[170]

---

[162] [2008] EWHC 112, [60].

[163] Ibid., [61], [66].

[164] Brasse (2006).

[165] [2009] EWHC 891.

[166] MCA 1973, s 25(2)(a); CPA 2004, Sch 5, para 21(2)(a).

[167] *Leadbeater v Leadbeater* [1985] FLR 789.

[168] [1999] 2 FLR 176, 182.

[169] E.g. *P v P (Inherited Property)* [2004] EWHC 1364.

[170] Moor and Le Grice (2006).

New relationships

There is a potential clash between the fact that periodical payments can be made for any purpose and the fact that the recipient's remarriage automatically terminates the order.[171] A new spouse assumes a duty to maintain (i.e. to meet needs). While that properly supersedes the ex-spouse's duty to meet need, it does not obviously detract from a compensatory award. Nevertheless, the President in *VB v JP* remarked that a compensatory element of a periodical payments order can only last as long as the duty to maintain.[172] This being so, where it is felt that fairness demands compensation despite any future relationship, a capital award (such as lump sums payable by instalments) should be used instead.[173]

Little compensation in practice?

The courts are unlikely to address compensation frequently. The available resources often do not even cover the parties' needs: the need principle will predominate. There is also considerable overlap between the needs for which respondents should be liable and 'relationship-generated disadvantages'[174] meriting compensation: applicants who have been and following divorce will be looking after children of the marriage may have economic needs precisely because child-care responsibilities have impaired their earning capacity. Conversely, if an applicant is not self-sufficient simply, for example, because of idleness, imprudence, or other self-imposed difficulty, the respondent may have no responsibility, whether in terms of need or compensation.

Compensation for contribution to an enhanced earning capacity?

The House of Lords in *McFarlane* only touched briefly on arguments related to applicants' contribution to respondents' future earnings, for example by sacrificing her own employment so that they could focus on the respondent's career. Periodical payments exceeding needs were awarded in some earlier big money cases, ostensibly as part of a 'bridging period' prior to a clean break.[175] Although the courts were reticent about the basis of the awards, some could be recognizing the applicant's contribution to the respondent's earning capacity.[176] Notably, in *Parlour v Parlour*,[177] the wife had contributed to the acquisition and retention of the husband's earning capacity, having rescued the Arsenal footballer from a 'laddish' culture, enabling him to flourish under the subsequent management of Arsène Wenger.

Case law since *Miller; McFarlane* has explored this issue both as an aspect of compensation—for the applicant's inability now to share in those future earnings—and of equal sharing. Whichever way it is argued, many of the underlying concerns are similar. This highlights the importance of taking a holistic approach, not treating each principle as separate 'claims' to be totted up. For ease of exposition, we address this issue at 7.5.4 with the sharing principle.

---

171 See 7.3.1.
172 [2008] EWHC 112, [91].
173 *McFarlane (no 2)* [2009] EWHC 891, [103].
174 *Miller; McFarlane* [2006] UKHL 24, [140] per Baroness Hale.
175 E.g. *Q v Q (Ancillary Relief: Periodical Payments)* [2005] EWHC 402.
176 Cf *M v M* [2004] EWHC 688: award based on the wife's future contributions to caring for their special needs child.
177 [2004] EWCA Civ 872, [39]–[40], [46].

Compensating for the unequal exposure to risk on matrimonial breakdown?

John Eekelaar argues that both formulations of the compensation claim were misguided and directed at the wrong object:[178]

J. Eekelaar, 'Property and Financial Settlements on Divorce—Sharing and Compensating', (2006a) 36 *Family Law* 754, 756

Baroness Hale described the compensation as being for 'relationship-generated disadvantage'...Does this mean that *any* loss, or opportunity foregone, as a result of entering the relationship should be (fully?) compensated? Lord Hope remarked that it would be unfair if 'a woman who has chosen motherhood over her career in the interests of her family' were to be 'denied a fair share of the wealth that her husband has been able to build up...out of the earnings that he is able to generate when she cannot be compensated for this out of capital'...Yet there are strong arguments against approaching the compensation issue in this way. Some are practical. In many cases the financial benefits of an 'alternative life' are too speculative to provide an appropriate measure. But also, there must be a high possibility that, had the applicant not had the relationship with the respondent, he or she will have had one with another person. The 'alternative life' may never have happened anyway. As the [American Law Institute] put it:

'[The wife] has not lost a career, for that is not what she had sought. She instead lost the opportunity to have her children with someone with whom she would enjoy an enduring relationship. The most direct measure of her financial loss would compare her situation at divorce to the hypothetical situation had she married a different man'....

The compensation is, therefore, for the consequences of the differential risk between the parties of the consequences of the separation. As Lord Nicholls said, the compensation element would be 'aimed at redressing any significant prospective economic disparity between the parties arising from the way they conducted their marriage' (at para [13]). This must refer to the disparity after the separation, not before it. Suppose the respondent earns less than the applicant after separation, but the applicant would nevertheless have earned more were it not for the relationship. Surely there should be no claim against the respondent. If there is no disparity, so the risk has turned out even, there again seems no case for compensation...

Following this approach, Eekelaar recommends a presumptive formulaic approach to compensatory awards, based on duration of the marriage and presence or not of children. While the courts decry formulae, the outcome in *McFarlane (no 2)* to some extent reflects Eekelaar's approach, declining to value the wife's loss and instead focusing on a fair division of the fruits of the partnership represented by his income, given the length of their marriage.

7.5.4 ENTITLEMENT: EQUAL SHARING

The equal sharing principle originates in *White v White*. The Whites had been married for over 30 years and had three children, all adult by the time of the divorce. They had built up

---

[178] See also Ellman (2007).

a successful farming business together, the wife working as an active business partner and raising the family. The assets exceeded the parties' financial needs:

White v White [2001] 1 AC 596, 605–6, 608

LORD NICHOLLS:

In seeking to achieve a fair outcome, there is no place for discrimination between husband and wife and their respective roles. Typically, a husband and wife share the activities of earning money, running their home and caring for their children. Traditionally, the husband earned the money, and the wife looked after the home and the children. This traditional division of function is no longer the order of the day. Frequently both parents work. Sometimes it is the wife who is the money-earner, and the husband runs the home and cares for the children during the day. But whatever the division of labour chosen by the husband and wife, or forced upon them by circumstances, fairness requires that this should not prejudice or advantage either party when considering paragraph (f), relating to the parties' contributions. This is implicit in the very language of paragraph (f): "... the contribution which *each* ... has made or is likely ... to make to the *welfare of the family*, including any contribution by looking after the home or caring for the family". (Emphasis added.) If, in their different spheres, each contributed equally to the family, then in principle it matters not which of them earned the money and built up the assets. There should be no bias in favour of the money-earner and against the home-maker and the child-carer ...

A practical consideration follows from this. Sometimes, having carried out the statutory exercise, the judge's conclusion involves a more or less equal division of the available assets. More often, this is not so. More often, having looked at all the circumstances, the judge's decision means that one party will receive a bigger share than the other. Before reaching a firm conclusion and making an order along these lines, a judge would always be well advised to check his tentative views against the yardstick of equality of division. As a general guide, equality should be departed from only if, and to the extent that, there is good reason for doing so. The need to consider and articulate reasons for departing from equality would help the parties and the court to focus on the need to ensure the absence of discrimination.

Lord Nicholls addressed the established case law which confined wives in big money cases to awards satisfying their 'reasonable requirements', leaving the surplus to the husband, who had accumulated the wealth. He held that this approach had no support from the MCA 1973 or the objective of fairness, and went on:

If a husband and wife by their joint efforts over many years, his directly in his business and hers indirectly at home, have built up a valuable business from scratch, why should the claimant wife be confined to the court's assessment of her reasonable requirements, and the husband left with a much larger share? Or, to put the question differently, in such a case, where the assets exceed the financial needs of both parties, why should the surplus belong solely to the husband? On the facts of a particular case there may be a good reason why the wife should be confined to her needs and the husband left with the much larger balance. But the mere absence of financial need cannot, by itself, be a sufficient reason. If it were, discrimination would be creeping in by the back door. In these cases, it should be remembered, the claimant is usually the wife. Hence the importance of the check against the yardstick of equal division.

The facts of *White* fell squarely within the premise of Lord Nicholls' equality yardstick. But there was held to be good reason to depart from equality in recognition of financial help given by Mr White's father.

White had particular significance for older spouses. The needs associated with old age may be substantial but are time-limited. Pre-*White*, an elderly wife who needed only a small capital sum to generate income for the rest of her life might receive less following a decades-long marriage than a younger applicant after a shorter marriage. Where the assets exceed the parties' needs, *White* offered such applicants a substantial award reflecting their contributions over a long marriage, quite possibly an equal share of matrimonial property.[179]

However, *White* left many questions unanswered. Did the 'yardstick' of equal division apply only where assets exceeded the parties' needs?[180] Did it apply only to long marriages?[181] What if one party had arrived in the marriage with substantial wealth already?[182] What if one party inherited a large sum of money during the marriage?[183] Could either argue that the parties had therefore not 'contributed equally' to the family's welfare, so that the party who had made a 'stellar contribution' could take a larger share? And how, for these purposes, should the ostensibly incommensurable contributions of homemaker and breadwinner be measured and compared?[184]

Miller v Miller returned the question to the House of Lords on facts very different from *White*'s: a short, childless marriage to which the husband brought considerable wealth. How, if at all, should the equality yardstick be applied on facts such as these? And to what property should it apply? Their Lordships parted company on the latter point, albeit reaching the same outcome on the facts: £5 million to Mrs Miller (the matrimonial home and capital to generate nearly £100,000 per annum), under a third of the value of the wealth acquired during the marriage, less than one-sixth of Mr Miller's total estimated wealth, recognizing that the gains during marriage derived largely from pre-marital business endeavours. The main speeches were delivered by Lord Nicholls and Baroness Hale. Lord Hoffmann agreed with Baroness Hale; Lord Hope agreed with both on all points relevant to the disposal of the case; Lord Mance did likewise, but preferred Baroness Hale's analysis on some points. Regrettably, *Miller; McFarlane* also left several questions unanswered, and posed new problems, which subsequent Court of Appeal authority goes some way (unfortunately, not unambiguously) to address.

We begin with the basic principle, which is equally applicable to both long and short marriages:

Miller v Miller; McFarlane v McFarlane [2006] UKHL 24

LORD NICHOLLS

16. A third strand [after need and compensation] is sharing. This 'equal sharing' principle derives from the basic concept of equality permeating a marriage as understood today.

---

[179] See *White v White* [2001] 1 AC 596, 609, per Lord Nicholls, criticizing the '*Duxbury* paradox'.
[180] *Cordle v Cordle* [2001] EWCA Civ 1751.
[181] Cf *Foster v Foster* [2003] EWCA Civ 565; *GW v RW (Financial provision: departure from equality)* [2003] EWHC 611.
[182] *GW v RW* [2003] EWHC 611.
[183] *P v P (Inherited Property)* [2004] EWHC 1364.
[184] *Cowan v Cowan* [2001] Fam 97; *Lambert v Lambert* [2002] EWCA Civ 679; *Parlour v Parlour* [2004] EWCA Civ 872; *Sorrell v Sorrell* [2005] EWHC 1717.

Marriage, it is often said, is a partnership of equals. In 1992 Lord Keith of Kinkel approved [the] observation that 'husband and wife are now for all practical purposes equal partners in marriage': *R v R* [1992] 1 AC 599 [the marital rape exemption case]. This is now recognised widely, if not universally The parties commit themselves to sharing their lives. They live and work together. When their partnership ends each is entitled to an equal share of the assets of the partnership, unless there is a good reason to the contrary. Fairness requires no less. But I emphasise the qualifying phrase: 'unless there is good reason to the contrary'. The yardstick of equality is to be applied as an aid, not a rule.

17. This principle is applicable as much to short marriages as to long marriages: see *Foster v Foster* [2003] EWCA Civ 565 ... A short marriage is no less a partnership of equals than a long marriage. The difference is that a short marriage has been less enduring. In the nature of things this will affect the quantum of the financial fruits of the partnership.

18. A different approach was suggested in *GW v RW (Financial Provision: Departure from Equality)* [2003] 2 FLR 108 ... There the court accepted the proposition that entitlement to an equal division must reflect not only the parties' respective contributions 'but also an accrual over time' ... It would be 'fundamentally unfair' that a party who has made domestic contributions during a marriage of 12 years should be awarded the same proportion of the assets as a party who has made the domestic contributions for more than 20 years. ...

19. I am unable to agree with this approach. This approach would mean that on the breakdown of a short marriage the money-earner would have a head start over the home-maker and child-carer. To confine the *White* approach to the 'fruits of a long marital partnership' would be to re-introduce precisely the sort of discrimination the *White* case ... was intended to negate.

BARONESS HALE:

141. A third rationale [after needs and compensation] is *the sharing of the fruits of the matrimonial partnership*. One reason given by the Law Commission for not adopting any one single model was that the flexibility of section 25 allowed practice to develop in response to changing perceptions of what might be fair. There is now a widespread perception that marriage is a partnership of equals. The Scottish Law Commission found that this translated into widespread support for a norm of equal sharing of the partnership assets when the marriage ended, whatever the source or legal ownership of those assets ... A decade earlier, the English Law Commission had found widespread support for the automatic joint ownership of the matrimonial home, even during marriage ... [T]he authors of *Settling Up* [Arthur et al (2002)] p 56, found that "there appeared to be a relatively widespread assumption that an 'equal' or 50/50 division was the normal or appropriate thing to do", alongside a recognition of needs and entitlements (but their respondents' views on entitlements might not be quite the same as the lawyers', a point to which I shall return) ...

143. ... [T]here are many cases in which the approach of roughly equal sharing of partnership assets with no continuing claims one against the other is nowadays entirely feasible and fair. One example is *Foster v Foster* [2003] EWCA Civ 565..., a comparatively short childless marriage, where each could earn their own living after divorce, but where capital assets had been built up by their joint efforts during the marriage. Although one party had earned more and thus contributed more in purely financial terms to the acquisition of those assets, both contributed what they could, and the fair result was to divide the product of their joint endeavours equally. Another example is *Burgess v Burgess* [1996] 2 FLR 34, a long marriage between a solicitor and a doctor, which had produced three children. Each party could earn their own living after divorce, but the home, contents and collections which they had accumulated during the marriage could be equally shared. Although one party might have better

prospects than the other in future, once the marriage was at an end there was no reason for one to make further claims upon the other.

It was clear that equal sharing is in principle available whatever the duration of the marriage. But beyond that the scope and application of the principle is unclear. In the following sections, we ask:

- What is the status of the principle? In particular, is it a proper starting point or presumption?
- To what property does equal sharing apply?
- What constitutes 'good reason' to divide the assets other than in equal shares?

What is the status of the equal sharing principle?

Lord Nicholls in *White* had been adamant that it was improper for judges to curtail the wide discretion conferred by the MCA 1973 by treating equal sharing as a presumption or starting point, and so deployed it as a final 'check' having provisionally decided what outcome would be fair having regard to the s 25 checklist. However, in *Charman v Charman,* the Court of Appeal interpreted *Miller; McFarlane* as treating equal sharing as an appropriate—though not mandatory—starting point. In their view, the equal sharing principle means that 'property should be shared in equal proportions unless there is good reason to depart from such proportions'; 'departure is not *from* the principle but takes place *within* the principle'.[185] Unfortunately, the subsequent Court of Appeal decision *B v B* cast doubt on this approach, Hughes LJ treating equal sharing as a retrospective yardstick and Wall LJ emphasizing the width of the discretion to reach a 'fair' outcome.[186] This difference of view is regrettable, though it is worth noting that *B v B* was not a 'big money' case and that the wife had brought all the assets to the marriage: two reasons why one would in any case quickly depart from a starting point of equal sharing to make some other award. But the fact that unequal shares are likely to be the conclusion does not mean that there is no point taking equal shares as a starting point: it may be desirable at a normative level for applicants to be able to assert a prima facie entitlement under the equal sharing principle. We consider the interaction of equal sharing and need further at 7.5.5.

To what property does equal sharing apply?

We have seen that all assets are potentially available to satisfy needs- and compensation-based claims. But what property falls within the equal sharing pool? This is the key point on which Lord Nicholls and Baroness Hale disagreed:

Miller v Miller, McFarlane v McFarlane [2006] UKHL 24

LORD NICHOLLS:

20. . . . The rationale underlying the sharing principle is as much applicable to 'business and investment' assets as to 'family' assets . . .

---

[185] [2007] EWCA Civ 503, [65].
[186] [2008] EWCA Civ 543, [24], [50]–[60].

Matrimonial property and non-matrimonial property

22. ... The statute requires the court to have regard to all the circumstances of the case. One of the circumstances is that there is a real difference, a difference of source, between (1) property acquired during the marriage otherwise than by inheritance or gift, sometimes called the marital acquest but more usually the matrimonial property, and (2) other property. The former is the financial product of the parties' common endeavour, the latter is not. The parties' matrimonial home, even if this was brought into the marriage at the outset by one of the parties, usually has a central place in any marriage. So it should normally be treated as matrimonial property for this purpose. As already noted, in principle the entitlement of each party to a share of the matrimonial property is the same however long or short the marriage may have been.

23. The matter stands differently regarding property ('non-matrimonial property') the parties bring with them into the marriage or acquire by inheritance or gift during the marriage. Then the duration of the marriage will be highly relevant. The position regarding non-matrimonial property was summarised in the *White* case [2001] 1 AC 596, 610:

'Plainly, when present, this factor is one of the circumstances of the case. It represents a contribution made to the welfare of the family by one of the parties to the marriage. The judge should take it into account. He should decide how important it is in the particular case. The nature and value of the property, and the time when and circumstances in which the property was acquired, are among the relevant matters to be considered. However, in the ordinary course, this factor can be expected to carry little weight, if any, in a case where the claimant's financial needs cannot be met without recourse to this property.' ...

Flexibility

26. This difference in treatment of matrimonial property and non-matrimonial property might suggest that in every case a clear and precise boundary should be drawn between these two categories of property. This is not so. Fairness has a broad horizon. Sometimes, in the case of a business, it can be artificial to attempt to draw a sharp dividing line as at the parties' wedding day. Similarly the "equal sharing" principle might suggest that each of the party's assets should be separately and exactly valued. But ... [the] costs involved can quickly become disproportionate ...

27. Accordingly, where it becomes necessary to distinguish matrimonial property from non-matrimonial property the court may do so with the degree of particularity or generality appropriate in the case. The judge will then give to the contribution made by one party's non-matrimonial property the weight he considers just. He will do so with such generality or particularity as he considers appropriate in the circumstances of the case.

BARONESS HALE:

149. The question ... is whether *in the very big money cases* [emphasis added], it is fair to take some account of the source and nature of the assets, in the same way that some account is taken of the source of those assets in inherited or family wealth. Is the 'matrimonial property' to consist of everything acquired during the marriage (which should probably include periods of pre-marital cohabitation and engagement) or might a distinction be drawn between "family" and other assets? Family assets were described by Lord Denning MR in the landmark case of *Wachtel v Wachtel* [1973] Fam 72, at 90:

"It refers to those things which are acquired by one or other or both of the parties, with the intention that there should be continuing provision for them and their children during their joint lives, and used for the benefit of the family as a whole".

Prime examples of family assets of a capital nature were the family home and its contents, while the parties' earning capacities were assets of a revenue nature. But also included are other assets which were obviously acquired for the use and benefit of the whole family, such as holiday homes, caravans, furniture, insurance policies and other family savings. To this list should clearly be added family businesses or joint ventures in which they both work. It is easy to see such assets as the fruits of the marital partnership. It is also easy to see each party's efforts as making a real contribution to the acquisition of such assets. Hence it is not at all surprising that Mr and Mrs McFarlane agreed upon the division of their capital assets, which were mostly of this nature, without prejudice to how Mrs McFarlane's future income provision would be quantified.

150. More difficult are business or investment assets which have been generated solely or mainly by the efforts of one party. The other party has often made some contribution to the business, at least in its early days, and has continued with her agreed contribution to the welfare of the family (as did Mrs Cowan [*Cowan v Cowan* [2001] EWCA Civ 679]). But in these non-business-partnership, non-family asset cases, the bulk of the property has been generated by one party. Does this provide a reason for departing from the yardstick of equality? On the one hand is the view, already expressed, that commercial and domestic contributions are intrinsically incommensurable. It is easy to count the money or property which one has acquired. It is impossible to count the value which the other has added to their lives together. One is counted in money or money's worth. The other is counted in domestic comfort and happiness. If the law is to avoid discrimination between the gender roles, it should regard all the assets generated in either way during the marriage as family assets to be divided equally between them unless some other good reason is shown to do otherwise.

151. On the other hand is the view that this is unrealistic. We do not yet have a system of community of property, whether full or deferred. Even modest legislative steps towards this have been strenuously resisted. Ownership and contributions still feature in divorcing couples' own perceptions of a fair result, some drawing a distinction between the home and joint savings accounts, on the one hand, and pensions, individual savings and debts, on the other (*Settling Up*, [Arthur et al (2002)] chapter 5). Some of these are not family assets in the way that the home, its contents and the family savings are family assets. Their value may well be speculative or their possession risky. It is not suggested that the domestic partner should share in the risks or potential liabilities, a problem which bedevils many community of property regimes and can give domestic contributions a negative value. It simply cannot be demonstrated that the domestic contribution, important though it has been to the welfare and happiness of the family as a whole, has contributed to their acquisition. If the money maker had not had a wife to look after him, no doubt he would have found others to do it for him. Further, great wealth can be generated in a very short time, as the *Miller* case shows; but domestic contributions by their very nature take time to mature into contributions to the welfare of the family.

It fell to the Court of Appeal in *Charman* to discern a clear path through the thicket of House of Lords' speeches. The Court acknowledged that it could be argued that equal sharing should apply only to property generated during marriage other than by gift or inheritance: that would fit with the idea that sharing of the 'fruits of the partnership' grew from the parties' contributions during the marriage. However, the Court preferred the view that, subject to narrow exceptions, the principle applies to all of the parties' property, whether designated 'matrimonial' or not. It felt that any alternative would risk being discriminatory and undermine the sharing principle. But this does not make it unnecessary to identify different categories of property: the fact that certain property can be described as 'non-matrimonial', for example because acquired by one party before the marriage or post-separation, is likely to provide a 'good reason' for unequal sharing.[187]

Possible exceptions to equal sharing?

The Court in *Charman* was prepared to note—without deciding the point—that there may be two situations in which equal sharing of one category of assest would never be appropriate: so-called 'unilateral' or 'non-business-partnership, non-family assets', i.e. the fruits of a business in which only one spouse had worked, which were not used for the family's benefit.[188] The two cases in which such assets might never be shared are (i) short marriages, such as *Miller*, and (ii) dual-career marriages where the parties kept part of their assets separate.[189] The latter case, which the Court of Appeal would restrict narrowly, arose from dicta of Baroness Hale, endorsed by Lord Mance:

Miller v Miller; McFarlane v McFarlane [2006] UKHL 24

BARONESS HALE:

153....[I]n a matrimonial property regime which still starts with the premise of separate property, there is still some scope for one party to acquire and retain separate property which is not automatically to be shared equally between them. The nature and the source of the property and the way the couple have run their lives may be taken into account in deciding how it should be shared. There may be other examples. Take, for example, a genuine dual career family where each party has worked throughout the marriage and certain assets have been pooled for the benefit of the family but others have not. There may be no relationship-generated needs or other disadvantages for which compensation is warranted. We can assume that the family assets, in the sense discussed earlier, should be divided equally. But it might well be fair to leave undisturbed whatever additional surplus each has accumulated during his or her working life. However, one should be careful not to take this approach too far. What seems fair and sensible at the outset of a relationship may seem much less fair and sensible when it ends. And there could well be a sense of injustice if a dual career spouse who had worked outside as well as inside the home throughout the marriage ended up less well off than one who had only or mainly worked inside the home.

LORD MANCE:

170....[T]here can be marriages, long as well as short, where both partners are and remain financially active, and independently so. They may contribute to a house and joint expenses, but it does not necessarily follow that they are or regard themselves in other respects as engaged in a joint financial enterprise for all purposes. Intrusive inquiries into the other's financial affairs might, during the marriage, be viewed as inconsistent with a proper respect for the other's personal autonomy and development, and even more so if the other were to claim a share of any profit made from them. In such a case the wife might still have the particular additional burden of combining the bearing of and caring for children with work outside the home. If one partner (and it might, with increasing likelihood I hope, be the wife) were more successful financially than the other, and questions of needs and compensation

---

187 [2007] EWCA Civ 503, [66].

188 *S v S* [2006] EWHC 2793, [30].

189 [2007] EWCA Civ 503, [82]–[86].

had been addressed, one might ask why a court should impose at the end of their marriage a sharing of all assets acquired during matrimony which the parties had never envisaged during matrimony. Once needs and compensation had been addressed, the misfortune of divorce would not of itself, as it seems to me, be justification for the court to disturb principles by which the parties had chosen to live their lives while married.

If parties kept their assets separate during marriage, equal sharing on divorce seems discordant with those spouses' view of the marriage partnership. Moreover, Lord Mance's last remarks presage the Supreme Court decision in *Radmacher v Granatino* regarding the impact on the sharing principle of pre-nuptial and other agreements, discussed at 7.7 below.[190] Following parties' express agreements seems preferable to judicial inquiry into the character of their marriage, attempting to infer parties' intentions from conduct.[191]

When will there be good reason to divide the assets other than equally?

There are two categories of reason for departing from equal sharing:

- reasons relating to the rationale of the equal sharing principle itself, which give rise to departures 'within' the principle: we focus on these reasons here;
- reasons arising from competing principles—need, compensation, conduct, and the desirability of a clean break: we address these in following sections.

As Elizabeth Cooke has argued, the departures 'within' the principle betray the ambiguity in the rationale for equal sharing: is it based on the idea of marriage as a partnership which of itself justifies equal sharing of property; or is it based more or less precisely on the notion that the parties have actually made contributions of equal value and that it is these contributions which justify the equal share? If the 'partnership' approach is taken, it is harder to argue against equal sharing than under the 'valuation' approach, which invites dispute about what each party contributed (financially or otherwise) to the asset-pool and over what period.[192] In the following sections, we consider the treatment of non-matrimonial property and the relevance here of the duration of the marriage; resources acquired post-separation; 'stellar' contributions; and the approach to risky or illiquid assets. We then return to the issue of partnership *versus* valuation approach. The impact of parties' agreements about the division of property on divorce is addressed below at 7.7.

Duration of the marriage and treatment of 'non-matrimonial' property

Under s 25(2)(d), the court must consider 'the duration of the marriage'.[193] While the equal sharing principle in theory applies however long or short the marriage, the courts are more inclined to depart from equal sharing after short marriages in recognition that some of the property can be classed as 'non-matrimonial',[194] for example, having been accumulated

---

[190] Cf *Parra v Parra* [2002] EWCA Civ 1886, where parties had deliberately arranged to share assets equally.

[191] Cf the problems with intention in the trusts context, discussed at 3.4.7.

[192] Cooke (2007); see also Miles (2008).

[193] And CPA 2004, Sch 5, para 21(2)(d).

[194] On the issues of passive growth and conversion of pre-matrimonial to matrimonial property, see *Rossi v Rossi* [2006] EWHC 1482, [10]; *S v S* [2006] EWHC 2793, [31]–[35].

by one spouse before the marriage,[195] inherited by one of them,[196] or generated post-separation.[197] After long marriages, by contrast, the case for crediting the owner of non-matrimonial property will wane, especially if the property has been used to the family's benefit, such as to buy the family home.[198]

In contemporary social conditions, the courts take a functional approach to measuring duration for these purposes:

GW v RW [2003] EWHC 611

NICHOLAS MOSTYN QC (sitting as a deputy judge of the High Court):

33. ...[W]here a relationship moves seamlessly from cohabitation to marriage without any major alteration in the way the couple live, it is unreal and artificial to treat the periods differently. On the other hand, if it is found that the pre-marital cohabitation was on the basis of a trial period to see if there was any basis for later marriage then I would be of the view that it would not be right to include it as part of the "duration of the marriage" ...

34. By the same token I am of the view that it is equally unreal to characterise the 18 month period of estrangement, conducted under the umbrella of a divorce petition which alleged the irretrievable breakdown of the marriage, as counting as part of "the duration of the marriage" ...

This inclusion[199] of pre-marital cohabitation and engagement[200] is controversial.[201] To allow pre-marital cohabitation to be brought into account may detract from the unique significance of marriage as a status from which distinctive rights and duties flow.[202] But law may clash with the public attitudes and practices of many couples if a rigid line is drawn.[203] Post-divorce cohabitation following reconciliation might also contribute to the duration of their relationship for the purposes of an award based on the equal sharing principle made when the parties eventually separate again.[204]

The duration of the relationship, so measured, then has a bearing on the treatment of 'non-matrimonial' property: the shorter the marriage, the greater the reason to exclude it from equal sharing; the longer the marriage, the more likely the court will consider it fair to share it:

Miller v Miller; McFarlane v McFarlane [2006] UKHL 24

LORD NICHOLLS:

24. In the case of a short marriage fairness may well require that the claimant should not be entitled to a share of the other's non-matrimonial property. The source of the asset may be a

---

195 E.g. *McCartney v Mills McCartney* [2008] EWHC 401.
196 E.g. *B v B* [2008] EWCA Civ 543; *L v L* [2008] EWHC 3328; *K v L* [2010] EWHC 1234.
197 See below.
198 *L v L* [2008] EWHC 3328.
199 *Miller; McFarlane* [2006] UKHL 24, [149].
200 *H v H* [2004] EWHC 1066; *J v J* [2004] EWHC 53.
201 See Gilmore (2004a).
202 *Campbell v Campbell* [1976] Fam 347, 352.
203 Cf public beliefs and attitudes: Barlow et al (2001).
204 Assuming that the court still has jurisdiction to make the award: *Hill v Hill* [1998] 2 FLR 198.

good reason for departing from equality. This reflects the instinctive feeling that parties will generally have less call upon each other on the breakdown of a short marriage.

25. With longer marriages the position is not so straightforward. Non-matrimonial property represents a contribution made to the marriage by one of the parties. Sometimes, as the years pass, the weight fairly to be attributed to this contribution will diminish, sometimes it will not. After many years of marriage the continuing weight to be attributed to modest savings introduced by one party at the outset of the marriage may well be different from the weight attributable to a valuable heirloom intended to be retained in specie. Some of the matters to be taken into account in this regard were mentioned in the ... citation from the *White* case [see para 23, extracted at p 464 above]. To this non-exhaustive list should be added, as a relevant matter, the way the parties organised their financial affairs.

BARONESS HALE:

147. [Debates about stellar contributions: see p 471 below] are evidence of unease at the fairness of dividing equally great wealth which has either been brought into the marriage or generated by the business efforts and acumen of one party. It is principally in this context that there is also a perception that the size of the non-business partner's share should be linked to the length of the marriage: see, eg, Eekelaar "Asset Distribution on Divorce the Durational Element" (2001) 117 LQR 552; and "Asset Distribution on Divorce—Time and Property" [2003] Fam Law 828; and *GW v RW (Financial Provision: Departure from Equality)* [2003] 2 FLR 108.... [She then sets out her views on the distinction between matrimonial and non-matrimonial property, extracted above from p 464.]

152. My Lords, while I do not think that these arguments can be ignored, I think that they are irrelevant in the great majority of cases. In the very small number of cases where they might make a difference, of which *Miller* may be one, the answer is the same as that given in *White v White* ... in connection with pre-marital property, inheritance and gifts. The source of the assets may be taken into account but its importance will diminish over time. Put the other way round, the court is expressly required to take into account the duration of the marriage: section 25(2)(d). If the assets are not 'family assets', or not generated by the joint efforts of the parties, then the duration of the marriage may justify a departure from the yardstick of equality of division. As we are talking here of a departure from that yardstick, I would prefer to put this in terms of a reduction to reflect the period of time over which the domestic contribution has or will continue (see Bailey-Harris "Comment on *GW v RW (Financial Provision: Departure from Equality)*" [2003] Fam Law 386, at p 388) rather than in terms of accrual over time (see Eekelaar "Asset Distribution on Divorce-Time and Property" [2003] Fam Law 828). This avoids the complexities of devising a formula for such accruals.

Where the marriage is long, the courts have tended to take a broad brush approach to the treatment of non-matrimonial property in their awards.[205]

Resources acquired post-separation

Particular attention has been given to resources acquired post-separation, particularly City bonuses, which form part of the respondents' income stream. Arguments about these have been made both in terms of equal sharing and compensation for the lost opportunity to share in the respondent's future wealth. The basic argument is that the respondent would not

---

[205] E.g. *C v C* [2007] EWHC 2033; *H v H* [2008] EWHC 935.

have been able to acquire that earning capacity without the applicant's contributions and so it would be unfair for him to retain that surplus alone, leaving a large disparity between the parties' living standards, post-divorce.

In *H v H*, the wife had agreed to relocate to Japan with the children for the sake of the husband's career.[206] Charles J took a restrictive approach to the wife's claim related to the husband's post-separation bonuses, feeling it necessary to ensure that the 'pendulum does not swing too far' in favour of wives.[207] To succeed, she would have to satisfy a 'but for' test demonstrating the continuing influence of her input to the family's welfare as a factor contributing to an *enhancement* in the husband's future earnings, i.e. over and above what he could have earned alone. That would show that the future earnings were a fruit of the marital partnership, albeit now ended. That will be very difficult to prove, especially from purely domestic contributions:

H v H [2007] EWHC 459

CHARLES J:

82. ...[T]he wife's role and contribution to the marital partnership [which] was of great assistance to the husband in furthering his career is a consequence of the choices made by the parties to the marriage. Such a contribution as a supporter of the husband's career, as a home maker and as a caretaker of the children by a wife is substantial. In general, depending on, and subject to, factors such as the position at the start of the marital partnership and its length, on a non-discriminatory, equal and fair approach it founds the conclusion that pursuant to the yardstick there should be an equal division of the product of the husband's income earned *during* the marital partnership.

83. In my view the position changes when the marital partnership ends. This is because the joint venture and participation of the parties as equal partners in that marital partnership...ends. After that termination the focus is no longer on the effects of the contributions of the parties as equal partners in assessing the product of their partnership but with the *effects* of their separate contributions as the source of the husband's income in the future.

84. In considering the position after the termination of the marital partnership...it is the role and contribution of a wife during the marital partnership that forms the basis of the element of the husband's earning capacity and future income (i.e. his *enhanced* income or earning capacity) that can be said to be a fruit of that partnership. As Lord Nicholls points out...in *Miller & McFarlane* the spadework for rewards received towards the end, and after the end, of the marital partnership has been done during it. The wife's role and contributions have enabled the husband to create a working environment which has produced greater (enhanced) rewards of which she should have a fair share.

85. However, in my view the balance of his future income and earning capacity is the product of the husband's talents, energy and good fortune, notwithstanding that he has been supported by the wife, and they have been applied, expended and enjoyed during the marital partnership.

86. [A] wife who continues to act as the primary caretaker of the children of a marriage in a separate household continues to make a contribution to the welfare of the <u>family</u> (my emphasis), or the marriage, after the end of the marriage...In my view so does the husband

---

[206] [2007] EWHC 459.
[207] Ibid., [96].

who continues to meet their financial needs. But as this is looking at the position after the marriage is over these contributions whether described as being to the family or the marriage are not, in my view, contributions to the marital partnership because that is over.

87. I do not accept that such contributions by a wife to the family after the end of the marital partnership can generally be said to warrant a conclusion that a proportion of the husband's future income continues to be attributable to the wife's domestic contribution and thus a fruit of the marital partnership. [emphasis added]

Despite these conclusions, Charles J held that given the marriage's length, the wife's contributions, and the expected increase in the husband's income to which she could be said to have made some small (if incalculable) contribution, her award should include a 'run-off' component to help smooth the transition towards independent living.[208]

This reasoning may be compared with *CR v CR*,[209] where Bodey J appeared to be more sympathetic to a wife's claim relating to her husband's future earnings where there was a 'financial continuum'—i.e. he continued to work as he had during the marriage when the seeds of his post-separation success were sown—rather than 'any new source of risk, endeavour, or luck'. Bodey J considered that assets acquired by the husband following separation (indeed, for the rest of his life[210]) were a product of the wife's support of his career during the marriage. He accommodated that factor in what he regarded as 'the most straightforward and least controversial way': a generous assessment of the wife's needs.[211]

The Court of Appeal has yet to deal with bonuses, or the issue of husbands' future earning capacity. It remarked in *Charman* that this is 'an area of complexity and potential confusion' which that case did not involve.[212] Some judges, re-emphasizing the discretionary nature of the exercise, have felt no need to determine whether earning capacity is 'matrimonial property', instead simply taking into account the husband's earning capacity, and the fact (where relevant) that it has yielded substantial wealth post-separation, in the exercise of their discretion.[213] There is certainly an awareness of the 'imbalance', or inequality of outcome, that may remain even after substantial capital assets have been divided equally where the parties have widely different earning capacities.[214] Some commentators doubt the fairness of awards related to future earnings, certainly if they involve sharing future income (now generated by the respondent's hard work), rather than reimbursing expenditure on something like course fees.[215] These cases are likely to be treated as fact-specific, and such awards are unlikely to made as a matter of course.

Stellar contributions

A 'stellar' or 'special' contribution warranting departure from equal sharing will arise only exceptionally.

---

[208] Ibid., [90].
[209] [2007] EWHC 3334, [40]–[41].
[210] Ibid., [104].
[211] Ibid., [95]–[96].
[212] [2007] EWCA Civ 503, [67].
[213] E.g. *P v P* [2007] EWHC 2877, [121].
[214] E.g. *CR v CR* [2007] EWHC 3334, [95]; *Vaughan v Vaughan* [2007] EWCA Civ 1085, [50].
[215] E.g. Ellman (2005), 274–5.

Miller v Miller; McFarlane v McFarlane [2006] UKHL 24

BARONESS HALE:

146.... Following *White v White* ..., the search was on for some reason to stop short of equal sharing, especially in 'big money' cases where the capital had largely been generated by the breadwinner's efforts and enterprise. There were references to exceptional or 'stellar' contributions... These, in the words of Coleridge J in *G v G (financial provision: equal division)* [2002] EWHC 1339 (Fam) ..., opened a 'forensic Pandora's box'. As he pointed out ...:

"[W]hat is 'contribution' but a species of conduct? ... Both concepts are compendious descriptions of the way in which one party conducted him/herself towards the other and/or the family during the marriage. And both carry with them precisely the same undesirable consequences. First, they call for a detailed retrospective at the end of a broken marriage just at a time when parties should be looking forward, not back ... But then, the facts having been established, they each call for a value judgment of the worth of each side's behaviour and translation of that worth into actual money. But by what measure and using what criteria? ... Is there such a concept as an exceptional/special domestic contribution or can only the wealth creator earn the bonus? ... It is much the same as comparing apples with pears and the debate is about as sterile or useful."

A domestic goddess self-evidently makes a 'stellar' contribution, but that was not what these debates were about. Coleridge J's words were rightly influential in the later retreat from the concept of special contribution in *Lambert v Lambert* [2002] EWCA Civ 1685 ... It had already been made clear in *White v White* ... that domestic and financial contributions should be treated equally. Section 25(2)(f) of the 1973 Act does *not* refer to the contributions which each has made to the parties' *accumulated wealth*, but to the contributions they have made (and will continue to make) to the *welfare of the family*. Each should be seen as doing their best in their own sphere. Only if there is such a disparity in their respective contributions to the *welfare of the family* that it would be inequitable to disregard it should this be taken into account in determining their shares.

Or as Lord Nicholls put it:

68.... The wholly exceptional nature of the earnings must be, to borrow a phrase more familiar in a different context [conduct—see 7.5.6], obvious and gross.

Shortly after *Miller; McFarlane*, Mrs Charman received £48 million, a 37 per cent share of the fortune accumulated from scratch by the husband's business activities over the parties' nearly 30-year marriage. However, that award was reduced from what it might have been in recognition of his stellar contribution. The first instance judge considered how to recognize a successful stellar contribution argument in the award:

Charman v Charman [2006] EWHC 1879

COLERIDGE J:

125. If adjustment is appropriate, especially in these huge money cases, I think, it should be meaningful and significant and not a token one. It either means something and the court should so mark it or it does not ... The sharp carving knife rather than the salami slicer is the appropriate tool. Having said that any adjustment should not be so great as to actually impact

on the wife's standard of living where, as here, no conduct of the wife's is relevant other than it being conceded that she was a fully attentive wife and mother. But reduction in living standard is highly unlikely in this class of case, given that what is being divided up is the surplus fat in the case, way over and above any amount required to meet the payee spouse's needs

On appeal, the Court of Appeal provided admittedly arbitrary guidance on the thickness of slice which the knife should carve: somewhere between 55:45 and two-thirds:one-third in favour of the contributor.[216]

Accumulation of wealth does not of itself make a financial contribution 'stellar'; what is required is some spark of genius.[217] But nor is there some specific monetary threshold which must be exceeded before wealth-creation becomes 'special': that would encourage a presumption that a special contribution had been made wherever the threshold was exceeded.[218] When a court is considering financial remedies, contributions which have directly led to the acquisition of the assets being divided are perhaps easier to recognize and respond to in financial terms than more intangible domestic contributions; and the argument tends only to arise where there is considerable wealth available with which to acknowledge it.

Indeed, it is hard to envisage a stellar 'domestic' contribution, even (as is common) where one spouse is both engaging in paid employment and doing the larger share of the housework;[219] Thorpe LJ in *Lambert v Lambert* regarded as 'distasteful' the example of a mother caring for a handicapped child.[220] It is not obvious that these contributions are sufficiently rewarded by their equal share: the spouse who makes efforts way beyond the call of 'wifely' duty receives the same as one who made considerably less effort, whether because slapdash with the housework, or because blessed by healthy children or the assistance of domestic staff. However, arguing 'stellar' domestic contributions may tend to denigrate the other spouse's efforts at home, so may be ruled out as an attempt to impugn the respondent's 'conduct'.[221]

Risky and illiquid assets

Even if they fall within the equal sharing pool, the nature of particular assets may nevertheless justify unequal sharing. Where assets are 'illiquid', for example, because tied up in a family farm or private company, the courts do not insist on an equal division immediately, if at all: such assets cannot be divided like cash. To facilitate an 'orderly redistribution of wealth',[222] courts may effect equal sharing over time via periodical payments pending the release of the capital.[223] A fair distribution of 'copper-bottomed' and 'risk-laden' assets is generally also necessary.[224] The former, such as land and cash, have a reliable value, are readily saleable, but may yield a more modest income. The latter, such as shares, may yield a higher income but be less readily saleable, more susceptible to loss of capital value or income

---

[216] [2007] EWCA Civ 503, [90]–[91].
[217] Ibid., [80].
[218] Ibid., [87]–[88].
[219] See Scully (2003).
[220] [2002] EWCA Civ 1685, [45].
[221] *Sorrell v Sorrell* [2005] EWHC 1717; see 7.5.6.
[222] *N v N (Financial Provision: Sale of Company)* [2001] 2 FLR 69, 71.
[223] *F v F (Clean Break: Balance of Fairness)* [2003] 1 FLR 847.
[224] *Wells v Wells* [2002] EWCA Civ 476; cf *Myerson v Myerson* [2009] EWCA Civ 282, discussed below at p 488.

potential, or be difficult to value as capital at all and better treated as a source of income.[225] If one party is to have a larger share of the risk-laden assets (for example, a shareholding in a private company), it may be appropriate, given the extra risk thereby taken on, for that party to retain what may appear to be a larger share of the overall assets.[226]

The indeterminacy of the equal sharing principle

Having reviewed some of the key questions arising under the equal sharing principle, it is worth reverting to Cooke's question about its underlying rationale:[227] do we have a partnership approach or a valuation approach? In fact, somewhat incoherently, it seems we have both:

J. Miles, 'Charman v Charman (no 4): making sense of need, compensation and equal sharing after Miller/McFarlane', (2008) 20 Child and Family Law Quarterly 378, 385–6

For example, a starting point of equal sharing in relation to (almost) the entire asset pool implies a deep, universal partnership. Yet the grounds on which equal sharing might be denied 'within' that principle suggest alternative rationales. Either a rough valuation approach, which responds to the claim that one party has made an 'unmatched' contribution, whether a stellar contribution or some form of non-matrimonial wealth. Or a more sophisticated form of partnership, whereby the increasing duration of the marriage reduces scope for arguing that the partnership should take a shallower form....

Again, the partnership view is supported by the possible exceptions to equal sharing in relation to 'unilateral' assets: the short duration (how short?) or the spouses' financial independence makes universal partnership too intense. (Though...the shallower partnership entailed in the sharing of core 'matrimonial' assets is countenanced even in those cases). Equally, however, these cases could be presented as illustrations of the need for non-owner spouses to make some plausible claim that they have indirectly contributed to the acquisition of those assets: a valuation approach.

Other cases seem firmly to adopt valuation, for example, where applicants seek to share in post-separation earning capacity. Here the question has been framed in terms of whether the applicant can demonstrate the continuing influence of her contribution to the welfare of the family as a factor contributing to an enhancement in the respondent's earnings post-separation. At the very least, the termination of the marital partnership on separation excludes a partnership model, and requires that a valuation approach be taken to claims in relation to property acquired after that point. The court's remarks in Charman about the rare cases where one would permit a stellar contribution argument also lie with the 'valuation of contributions' rather than 'partnership' rationale:

'the statutory requirement in every case to consider the contributions which each party has made to the welfare of the family...would be inconsistent with a blanket rule that their past contributions to its welfare must be afforded equal weight.'

Unsurprisingly, it is in cases perceived to lie further from the paradigm of marital partnership – for example, short marriages or where property is acquired post-separation – that we apparently no longer feel comfortable with the implications of a partnership-based sharing

---

[225] *A v A* [2004] EWHC 2818.
[226] *N v N (Financial Provision: Sale of Company)* [2001] 2 FLR 69.
[227] Cooke (2007).

principle, and so fall back on a valuation approach, insisting on concrete demonstration of actual contribution to rebut the unmatched contribution argument.

In which case, perhaps we should simply adopt Baroness Hale's narrower approach to the scope of marital partnership.

7.5.5 THE INTERACTION OF NEED, COMPENSATION, AND EQUAL SHARING[228]

Needs dominate in the 'normal' case

As we emphasized earlier, in 'normal' cases, where the assets do not exceed the parties' needs (remembering that this concept is construed liberally by reference to the parties' standard of living), the equal sharing and compensation principles will be largely irrelevant. Particularly where the home is rented, there may be no significant capital to divide; the principal focus (tenancy transfer aside) will be on periodical payments, sharing any pension, and whether a clean break can be achieved.[229] If there is significant capital, the applicant, typically a wife who reduced her paid employment to raise the children, may receive rather *more* than half of the assets in order to protect the children's welfare and to cater for her needs as their primary carer. The court's principal aim is still to house any children, their primary carer, and, if possible, the other parent. If the objective is to give the parties an 'equal start on the road to independent living', unequal division may be necessary:[230]

Miller v Miller; McFarlane v McFarlane [2006] UKHL 24

BARONESS HALE:

136.... Giving half the present assets to the breadwinner achieves a very different outcome from giving half the assets to the homemaker with children...

142.... [A]n equal partnership does not necessarily dictate an equal sharing of the assets. In particular, it may have to give way to the needs of one party or the children. Too strict an adherence to equal sharing and the clean break can lead to a rapid decrease in the primary carer's standard of living and a rapid increase in the breadwinner's. The breadwinner's unimpaired and unimpeded earning capacity is a powerful resource which can frequently repair any loss of capital after an unequal distribution ... Recognising this is one reason why English law has been so successful in retaining a home for the children.

Cases where assets exceed needs

Where the assets do exceed the parties' needs, the interaction between the three principles becomes important.

The relationship between equal sharing and need is straightforwardly explained in *Charman*:

• Equal sharing may be departed from where need in fairness requires it.

---

[228] See Miles (2008).
[229] See 7.6.1 below.
[230] *Miller; McFarlane* [2006] UKHL 24, [144].

- But an applicant is not to be denied an equal share on the basis that it exceeds his or her needs.[231]

- Equal sharing is not to be applied only to any surplus remaining after the parties' needs have been met: that approach would encourage each party to inflate their budgets in order to secure a larger overall share. But the equal sharing principle may subsume any claim based on need where the share awarded is sufficient to cover those needs.[232]

The place of compensation is more difficult, generating concerns about the risk of double-counting:[233] i.e. the danger of 'compensating' the applicant several times over for the same disadvantage under more than one of the principles. The Court of Appeal in *Charman* left this point for future decision.[234] But we can work out some parameters. Just as equal sharing may subsume 'need', as Lord Nicholls noted in *Miller; McFarlane*,[235] so need will very often subsume compensation: the applicant's inability to support herself will often be symptomatic of the relationship-generated disadvantage she has sustained, so an award should only include a distinct compensatory element *to the extent that* that disadvantage can be identified as being greater than the applicant's needs (generously assessed[236]). Such cases will probably be rare. The relationship between equal sharing and compensation is harder. Some cases have adopted the suggestion (derived from Baroness Hale in *Miller; McFarlane*[237]) that compensation may sometimes be subsumed within equal sharing. In *CR v CR*, it was said that:

> a wife with...'ordinary' career prospects which are forfeited following her marriage to a husband who is or becomes a financial high-flyer, is highly likely to have been adequately 'compensated' for that forfeiture by the very fact of an equal division of the family's resources.[238]

This dictum contemplates: (i) an 'ordinary' wife, not one who, having sacrificed a lucrative career, may require a distinctive compensatory element in her award;[239] *and* (ii) a 'high-flying' husband and so a high marital living standard and extensive assets to be shared. The implication is that in such cases equal capital shares on a clean break basis will enable the wife to sustain a very comfortable standard of living; any larger award would have no practical impact on her situation. Contrast the case where the capital is insufficient to produce that outcome. Fairness then requires either that the wife receive a larger capital share to achieve a clean break, or that she receive periodical payments. In *CR v CR*, although the wife had only 'ordinary' career prospects, her 'very considerable wifely contributions' during the husband's prolonged absences on business merited recognition (as discussed above at p 471). His income for the foreseeable future was substantial, and so she received a larger capital share on a clean break. We discussed above at p 455 the need to ensure that any compensatory award is kept within proper bounds, in particular, by being subject to an economic equality ceiling.

---

231 [2007] EWCA Civ 503, [73].
232 Ibid., [73], [77(c)].
233 *RP v RP* [2006] EWHC 3409 (Fam), [64].
234 [2007] EWCA Civ 503, [73].
235 [2006] UKHL 24, [15].
236 *VB v JP* [2008] EWHC 112, [82].
237 [2006] UKHL 24, [154]; *Charman v Charman* [2007] EWCA Civ 503, [76(b)].
238 [2007] EWHC 3334, [92], endorsed in *VB v JP* [2008] EWHC 112, [59]; *B v B* [2010] EWHC 193.
239 *VB v JP* [2008] EWHC 112, at [60]; cf *McFarlane (no 2)* [2009] EWHC 891.

Whichever principle predominates in any individual case, all three have something important to tell us about the law's understanding of the economic relationship created by marriage (and, presumably, civil partnership). Even in those cases where assets do not exceed needs, there may be something vital to be gained from acknowledging that the applicant is *entitled* to at least half of the assets, and not merely a 'needy supplicant'. This may be particularly important where parties are negotiating privately, where the concept of entitlement may help reduce any imbalance in power that may be inherent in cases where the assets are all owned by the respondent.[240]

A move to guidelines, rules, or formulae?

Reform of ancillary relief was under active consideration before *White* and *Miller; MacFarlane* but not pursued[241] *Miller; McFarlane* itself prompted renewed calls for legislative reform because of various concerns, not least the lack of predictability in the law and the size of awards now being generated in 'big money' case[242] The Law Commission has thus far declined to undertake a project on ancillary relief as a whole.[243] Aside from debates about what the basis of ancillary relief should be, a more basic question being asked is whether a system based on judicial discretion too unpredictable and uncertain, discouraging settlement.[244] Should statute set out clear objectives, principles, and guidelines for the courts, or even prescribe rules determining how resources should be divided on divorce?[245] In particular, should English law adopt a version of deferred community of property?[246] The challenges are significant:

E. Jackson et al, 'Financial Support on Divorce: the right mixture of rules and discretion?', (1993) 7 *International Journal of Law and the Family* 230, 252–3

Ultimately it is the outcome of negotiations regarding financial arrangements on divorce which is important for the parties. Nonetheless, concentration on the final settlement disguises the importance of the reasoning process. The theoretical framework on which the issues are pinned is of great significance. If the legal regulation of economic distribution is underpinned by a belief in the importance of the satisfaction of rights-based claims, then clear rules are essential so that those rights may be prospectively evaluated. If, on the other hand, the law attempts to fulfil needs and expectations, discretion must be used to assess their relative importance in the light of competing claims and available resources.

One approach is not necessarily better than the other. The issues raised by the economics of divorce are many and diverse....[T]he most complex decision which must be made involves the family home. Here a settlement must deal with the settling-up of property rights in a substantial capital sum, while being sensitive to the importance of the continuing use-value of the home. The matter is further complicated by the fact that a decision concerning

---

240 Diduck (1999).
241 Ancillary Relief Advisory Group (1998): see (1998) FL 380; HO (1998), (1999).
242 E.g. *Charman v Charman* [2007] EWCA Civ 503, [106]–[126].
243 Law Com (2008), from para 5.4.
244 Cf findings of Hitchings (2009a).
245 E.g. Eekelaar (2006a), (2010); Law Society (2003); Douglas and Perry (2001). There are several international examples on which to draw: e.g. Rogerson (2002), Department of Justice (2008), Ellman (2005), (2007).
246 Cooke (2009), Cretney (2003b); Cooke, Barlow, and Callus (2006).

> the property rights of two adults must also take account of the needs of the children for a stable and satisfactory home environment. If rights are best served by clear rules and needs best served by the sensitive exercise of discretion, we appear to have reached an impasse. Perhaps it is best to acknowledge that the process is not susceptible to a clear and elegant exegesis. We should gain reassurance from the obvious care taken by solicitors in trying, as nearly as possible, to resolve the irresolvable.

Any attempt to reduce the principles from the existing case law to statutory guidelines or more prescriptive formulae would be controversial. The MCA's discretion is regarded as one of the great strengths of English family law.[247] Any reform, whether a codification of the case law, move to a community system, or attempt to devise a set of guidelines or formulae (even ones that were not prescriptive), would stimulate debate about what the substantive basis for ancillary relief awards should be—needs (which?), compensation (for what?), equal sharing (of what?)—and so about the nature of the economic relationship created by marriage and civil partnership. Such debate should be held in Parliament, not left to judicial development.[248]

ONLINE RESOURCE CENTRE

Further materials on this issue may be found on the Online Resource Centre.

7.5.6 THE PARTIES' CONDUCT

Conduct merits separate consideration as a distinctive reason for departing from equal sharing, or for curtailing or increasing[249] awards based on need or compensation. Conduct was central to ancillary relief under fault-based divorce, but under no-fault divorce is now rarely relevant.

Wachtel v Wachtel [1973] Fam 72, 89–90 (CA)

LORD DENNING MR:

Parliament has decreed: "If the marriage has broken down irretrievably, let there be a divorce." It carries no stigma, but only sympathy. It is a misfortune which befalls both. No longer is one guilty and the other innocent. No longer are there long contested divorce suits. Nearly every case goes uncontested. The parties come to an agreement, if they can, on the things that matter so much to them. They divide up the furniture. They arrange the custody of the children, the financial provision for the wife, and the future of the matrimonial home. If they cannot agree, the matters are referred to a judge in chambers.

When the judge comes to decide these questions, what place has conduct in it? Parliament still says that the court has to have "regard to their conduct" ... Does this mean that the

---

[247] Ancillary Relief Advisory Group (1998), para 5.2; Wilson (1999).
[248] Scot Law Com (1981), para 3.37.
[249] *Jones v Jones* [1976] Fam 8, 15.

judge in chambers is to hear their mutual recriminations and to go into their petty squabbles for days on end, as he used to do in the old days? Does it mean that, after a marriage has been dissolved, there is to be a post mortem to find out what killed it? We do not think so. In most cases both parties are to blame—or, as we would prefer to say—both parties have contributed to the breakdown.

It has been suggested that there should be a "discount" or "reduction" in what the wife is to receive because of her supposed misconduct, guilt or blame (whatever word is used). We cannot accept this argument. In the vast majority of cases it is repugnant to the principles underlying the new legislation, and in particular the [Divorce Reform] Act of 1969. There will be many cases in which a wife (though once considered guilty or blameworthy) will have cared for the home and looked after the family for very many years. Is she to be deprived of the benefit otherwise to be accorded to her by section [25(2)(f)] because she may share responsibility for the breakdown with her husband? There will no doubt be a residue of cases where the conduct of one of the parties is in the judge's words ... "both obvious and gross," so much so that to order one party to support another whose conduct falls into this category is repugnant to anyone's sense of justice. In such a case the court remains free to decline to afford financial support or to reduce the support which it would otherwise have ordered. But, short of cases falling into this category, the court should not reduce its order for financial provision merely because of what was formerly regarded as guilt or blame. To do so would be to impose a fine for supposed misbehaviour in the course of an unhappy married life. [Counsel for the husband] disputed this and claimed that it was but justice that a wife should suffer for her supposed misbehaviour. [The parties had been found equally responsible for the marital breakdown]. We do not agree. Criminal justice often requires the imposition of financial and indeed custodial penalties. But in the financial adjustments consequent upon the dissolution of a marriage which has irretrievably broken down, the imposition of financial penalties ought seldom to find a place.

The House of Lords affirmed this restrictive approach in *Miller; McFarlane*. Mrs Miller argued that the shortness of the marriage should not reduce her award because its shortness was caused by Mr Miller's affair. Her argument found favour with the lower courts, but was unanimously dismissed by the House of Lords.[250] They also dismissed the associated argument that a spouse should have his or her 'expectation' loss remedied on divorce, as if it were an action for breach of contract:[251]

Miller v Miller; McFarlane v McFarlane [2006] UKHL 24

LORD NICHOLLS:

'Legitimate expectation'

56. ... The judge [in *Miller*] said the key feature was that the husband gave the wife a legitimate expectation that in future she would be living on a higher economic plane.

57. By this statement I doubt whether the judge was doing more than emphasise the importance ... of the standard of living enjoyed by Mr and Mrs Miller before the breakdown of their short marriage. This is one of the matters included on the statutory check list. The

---

[250] [2006] UKHL 24, [59]–[63], [145], [164].
[251] Cf the history of fault-based divorce and the minimum loss principle: Law Com (1980), paras 10–12.

standard of living enjoyed by the Millers during their marriage was much higher than the wife's accustomed standard and much higher than the standard she herself could afford.

58. If the judge meant to go further than this I consider he went too far. No doubt both parties had high hopes for their future when they married. But hopes and expectations, as such, are not an appropriate basis on which to assess financial needs. Claims for expectation losses do not fit altogether comfortably with the notion that each party is free to end the marriage. Indeed, to make an award by reference to the parties' future expectations would come close to restoring the 'tailpiece' which was originally part of section 25. By that tailpiece the court was required to place the parties, so far as practical and, having regard to their conduct, just to do so, in the same financial position as they would have been had the marriage not broken down. It would be a mistake indirectly to re-introduce the effect of that discredited provision.

While surveys of the legal profession find strong support for the exclusion of conduct arguments in this context,[252] it is not popular with the divorcing public[253] and some parliamentarians.[254] Even some judges have expressed disquiet about the amorality implied by the exclusion of fault.[255] Recognizing fault, or responsibility for deciding to end marriage without good cause, is regarded by some commentators as a basic aspect of justice on divorce.[256] Nevertheless, fault seems destined to play only a peripheral role.

Where it is taken into account, like the parties' contributions, 'conduct' poses a challenge—how is the financial significance of conduct to be measured? In one recent case, the husband was convicted and imprisoned for attempted murder of the wife in front of the children. This was at the top end of the scale of conduct that should be taken into account:[257]

H v H (Financial Relief: Attempted Murder as Conduct) [2005] EWHC 2911

COLERIDGE J:

44 How is the court to have regard to his conduct in a meaningful way? I agree with [counsel for the husband] that the court should not be punitive or confiscatory for its own sake. I therefore consider that the proper way to have regard to the conduct is as a potentially magnifying factor when considering the wife's position under the other subsections and criteria. It is the glass through which the other factors are considered. It places her needs, as I judge them, as a much higher priority to those of the husband because the situation the wife now finds herself in is, in a very real way, his fault. It is not just that she is in a precarious position, which she might be for a variety of medical reasons, but that he has created this position by his reprehensible conduct. So she must, in my judgment and in fairness, be given a greater priority in the share-out.

---

[252] Solicitors Journal (2006).
[253] Law Com (1981), para 36; media reaction to *Miller*.
[254] An amendment to the FLA 1996 designed to give conduct greater prominence was never brought into force.
[255] Davis and Murch (1988), 16–17.
[256] E.g. economists such as Rowthorn (1999); Dnes (1998); cf Eekelaar (2006b) and Ellman (1997): see 5.7.1.
[257] See also *K v L* [2010] EWCA Civ 125.

The offence had impacted directly on the wife's mental health and destroyed her police career and earning capacity; she had had to move away from the area and would obviously receive no financial or other support from the husband in raising the children.

> 46 Those are the ways, in my judgment, in which this conduct has impacted directly on the wife's life and it is against that that I turn now to consider the needs of the parties, and first the needs of the wife and the children. It seems to me that so far as practical she should be free from financial worry or pressure. So far as housing is concerned, by far the most important aspect of her security is a decent and secure home for herself and the children. If she feels she is in a nice, new home of her choosing that will be beneficial therapeutically to her....
>
> 48 The husband too would like a home when he is released from prison. He would like a home, he says, similar to that of the wife's.... If it is possible to achieve that, then of course it is reasonable as well. But as I have indicated, because of his conduct, he has to come very much second place in the queue.
>
> 49 So far as incomes are concerned, again the wife should, in my judgment, be as secure as possible and not be under pressure to have to work more than she can really cope with. She wants no recourse to the husband so this will be on a clean break basis....

The judge awarded the wife three times as much of the assets as the husband.

It is not necessary to show that the 'victim' was entirely blameless before it will be equitable to take account of the other spouse's conduct.[258] Conduct after marital breakdown is relevant, even if several years after the divorce.[259] Relevant conduct is 'the elephant in the room; incapable of definition but easy to recognise'.[260] It induces not a 'gulp' but a 'gasp'.[261] 'Ordinary' instances of 'behaviour' and adultery on which many divorce petitions are based are insufficient.[262] Cases in which conduct has been taken into account have been extreme. They include inciting third parties to murder the other spouse,[263] assisting the other spouse's attempted suicide for personal gain,[264] other serious domestic violence,[265] and abduction of the parties' child.[266] In *K v K (Conduct)*, the court took into account the husband's serious drinking problem, his unreasonable failure to seek employment following redundancy, and his neglect of the house which forced its sale; meanwhile, the wife supported the household and endeavoured to pay the mortgage from her earnings. Since the separation, the wife had made considerable efforts to improve her financial situation, and the husband's application for ancillary relief was largely rejected.[267] In *Clark v Clark*, a younger woman heavily in debt married a millionaire approaching his 80s; exercised undue influence over him to persuade him to pay her debts, spend vast sums of money, and transfer substantial assets to her; refused to consummate the marriage or cohabit; and confined him at times to a caravan in the grounds or an annexe in the property, while she

---

[258] *Kyte v Kyte* [1988] Fam 145, 155.

[259] *Evans v Evans* [1989] 1 FLR 351.

[260] *Charman v Charman* [2006] EWHC 1879, [115] per Coleridge J.

[261] *S v S* [2006] EWHC 2793, [57].

[262] MCA 1973, s 1.

[263] *Evans v Evans* [1989] 1 FLR 351.

[264] *Kyte v Kyte* [1988] Fam 145.

[265] *H v H (Financial Provision: Conduct)* [1994] 2 FLR 801; cf *S v S* [2006] EWHC 2793, criticized by Choudhry and Herring (2010), 410.

[266] *B v B (Financial Provision: Welfare of child and conduct)* [2002] 1 FLR 555.

[267] [1990] 2 FLR 225.

resided in the main house with her boyfriend. Six years on, the old man, by then reduced to a 'pitiful' state, was rescued by relatives. The wife was perhaps lucky to receive the £175,000 that she did.[268]

Financial misconduct and anti-avoidance powers

The courts also take into account financial misconduct which has dissipated the assets available for division, for example by gambling the family assets and diverting funds from payment of the mortgage on the matrimonial home to a mistress;[269] fraudulently remortgaging the family home;[270] or simply unreasonably dissipating assets.[271] Unlike other forms of misconduct, this behaviour is more readily measurable in financial terms.

Special rules deal with conduct where a purpose[272] of the respondent was to 'defeat' the other party's claim, whether by preventing it from being made, reducing its amount, or frustrating or impeding its enforcement.[273] The court has statutory 'anti-avoidance' powers to recover assets which have been disposed of by the respondent,[274] restrain such transactions before they go ahead, and prevent the transfer of assets out of the jurisdiction.[275] It is not possible to challenge a completed disposition if it was made for valuable consideration (other than marriage or civil partnership[276]) to a person acting in good faith and without actual or constructive notice[277] of any intention on the part of the transferor to defeat his or her spouse's claim for ancillary relief. But any other past or proposed disposition[278] by a spouse is 'reviewable'. If made with the intention to defeat a claim, a reviewable disposition may be set aside. If made less than three years before the claim for ancillary relief, and it would defeat the claim, it will be presumed (and so for the respondent to prove otherwise) that the disposition was made with that intention.[279] Where a 'transfer' (for example, movement of funds between bank accounts) leaves a third party holding the asset on bare trust for the spouse, the asset will still be regarded as belonging to the spouse in any event.[280]

Where these powers cannot be relied upon to recover property and so return it to the pool of assets awaiting distribution (for example, because the third party to whom the assets were transferred was acting in good faith and without notice), the court can instead take the relevant conduct into account when deciding how to divide the assets. The spouse who disposed of the assets is likely to be penalized to some extent in the size of share received by him or her.[281]

---

[268] [1999] 2 FLR 498, 509.

[269] Suspected in *M v M (Third party subpoena: Financial Conduct)* [2006] 2 FCR 555.

[270] *Le Foe v Le Foe and Woolwich plc* [2001] 2 FLR 970.

[271] As in *Clark v Clark* [1999] 2 FLR 498: W dissipated £1 million of H's assets.

[272] It need not be the sole or main intention: *Kemmis v Kemmis* [1988] 1 WLR 1307.

[273] Special problems apply to the preservation of joint periodic tenancies in anticipation of tenancy transfer: *Newlon Housing Trust v Al-Sulaimen* [1999] 1 AC 313; Conway (2001), Bridge (1998).

[274] Cf *Ansari v Ansari* [2008] EWCA Civ 1456.

[275] MCA 1973, s 37; CPA 2004, Sch 5, Part 14.

[276] Curiously, the MCA and CPA refer respectively to 'marriage' and 'civil partnership', and neither to both; it might have been expected that each statute would encompass both possibilities, which are of equivalent significance.

[277] *Kemmis v Kemmis* [1988] 1 WLR 1307.

[278] Except provision in a will or codicil: MCA 1973, s 37(6); CPA 2004, Sch 5, para 75(2).

[279] Equivalent tests apply to planned dispositions.

[280] *Purba v Purba* [2000] 1 FLR 444.

[281] *Le Foe v Le Foe and Woolwich plc* [2001] 2 FLR 970.

Litigation misconduct

One spouse's conduct of the ancillary relief litigation may require the other party to incur unnecessary legal costs, for example, by failing to make full and prompt disclosure, concealing or disposing of assets, making groundless allegations or exaggerated claims, pursuing clearly futile legal points, or failing to accept a reasonable offer. Litigation misconduct can be taken into account either by reducing the offending party's share of the assets,[282] or more usually by making a costs order.[283] The costs rules seek indirectly to encourage parties to conduct their litigation in a reasonable and proportionate manner.[284] But a costs order may not always be the better option. In *Clark v Clark*, since the husband had effectively been funding both sides' legal costs, a costs order would not have imposed any real penalty on the wife, and so her misconduct of the litigation was properly reflected in the quantification of her award.[285]

Nullity cases: criminal offences relating to the marriage or civil partnership

Special issues arising in relation to marriages or civil partnerships which are void in circumstances involving commission of a criminal offence by one or both parties,[286] whether bigamy[287] or perjury on some issue material to the validity of the union. There is clearly no obstacle to the innocent spouse claiming ancillary relief on the nullity application. But should the 'guilty' spouse effectively be able to profit from his or her crime by making a claim?

In *Whiston v Whiston*, it was held that a bigamist could be barred as a matter of public policy from seeking ancillary relief from the innocent spouse.[288] But it has since been held in relation both to bigamy[289] and perjury (regarding the spouse's gender)[290] that such criminal behaviour does not necessarily bar an application by the guilty party. Instead, it should be one factor for the court to consider in exercising its wide discretion, albeit one that may yield a nil award in appropriate circumstances. In cases such as *Whiston* and *S-T (formerly J) v J*, the respondent is entirely innocent and so should not be required to satisfy any claims by the bigamist/perjurer. But where, as in *Rampal*, the respondent knew of the impediment to the marriage, and engineered the marriage despite it, orders against him or her are less obviously unjust. While acknowledging that *Whiston* would permit a claim by bigamists as culpable as the applicant in *Whiston* to be struck out, the court in *Rampal v Rampal (no 2)* preferred the discretionary route, which allows all the circumstances to be considered.[291]

'Positive' conduct

Relevant conduct may also be positive: for example, an argument that one party has made exceptional contributions to the family. We have addressed this issue in relation to equal

---

282 *F v F* (2008) FL 183.
283 *Young v Young* [1998] 2 FLR 1131, 1140.
284 FPR 2010, Part 28.
285 [1999] 2 FLR 498.
286 Cf where the marriage was merely void: *Mendal v Mendal* [2007] EWCA Civ 437.
287 There is no offence of bigamy in the case of civil partnership, though the 'bigamist' may be guilty of perjury.
288 [1995] Fam 198.
289 *Rampal v Rampal* [2001] EWCA Civ 989, [2002] Fam 85.
290 *S-T (formerly J) v J* [1998] Fam 103.
291 [2001] EWCA Civ 989; applied in *Hashem v Shayif* [2008] EWHC 2380.

sharing, where contributions and conduct are regarded as two sides of the same coin.[292] The relevance of parties' agreements is considered below in relation to private ordering.[293]

7.6 THE CLEAN BREAK PRINCIPLE

In this section we explore two issues related to finality on divorce: the clean break principle; and the grounds on which a non-variable order, designed to provide a once-and-for-all settlement of the parties' claims, may nevertheless be set aside.

7.6.1 TERMINATING ONGOING FINANCIAL RELATIONS BETWEEN THE PARTIES

The clean break principle was introduced on repeal of the minimum loss principle following heated debate about what financial obligations, if any, should survive divorce by way of maintenance payments. Some complained that ex-wives were becoming 'alimony drones', allowed by the law to live a life of 'parasitic'[294] idleness at the expense of their former husbands and their second families.[295] Women's groups and others strongly opposed the introduction of the clean break.[296] Subsequent research demonstrated that the concept of the alimony drone was unreal: most ex-wives received such low maintenance that, unless they were employed, it would simply be diverted to the state to recoup welfare benefit payments; ex-wives therefore had a clear incentive to work in order for maintenance payments to augment their income.[297]

The clean break principle is manifested by several statutory provisions. The court is required by s 25(2)(a) to have regard not only to current resources but also resources available to each party in the foreseeable future, including any increase in earning capacity which it would be reasonable to expect them to acquire. Section 25A requires the court to consider whether it would be appropriate to exercise its powers to grant ancillary relief in such a way as to terminate the parties' financial obligations to each other as soon as is just and reasonable after the divorce. Essentially, the court should ask itself whether it can produce a package of orders which achieves fairness without periodical payments or other ongoing ties. If it decides to effect an immediate clean break, it can simply dismiss any periodical payment application under s 25A(3); if it wants to leave the door open without requiring substantial payment now, it can make a nominal order, which could be varied upwards (or extinguished) later if circumstances change. Section 25A(2) focuses on the duration of periodical payment orders, which may be made for 'joint lives' or some shorter period. If the court makes such an order to alleviate need, it must consider whether it would be appropriate to make it only for a term long enough for the recipient 'to adjust without undue hardship to the termination of his or her financial dependence on the other party'.[298] This is reinforced by ss 28(1) and (1A) which empower the court to make a periodical payment order for a specific duration

---

[292] *Miller; McFarlane* [2006] UKHL 24, [164] per Lord Mance.
[293] 7.7.
[294] Deech (1977), 232; cf O'Donovan (1982).
[295] For accounts of the Campaign for Justice on Divorce, see Eekelaar (1991b), 34–6.
[296] Including the Law Society: Symes (1985), n 10.
[297] Eekelaar and Maclean (1986).
[298] Cf if made for compensatory purposes, as in the McFarlanes' case: *Miller; McFarlane* [2006] UKHL 24, [38]–[39], [97]: order made for joint lives.

and to bar any extension of that period. If no bar is imposed, the recipient can seek an extension, but on that application the court is required by s 31(7) to revisit its original decision under s 25A(2) in light of the current circumstances. So even if the available resources available on divorce did not permit a clean break at that stage, it can be effected later if possible, with the support of fresh capital orders.[299] The clean break can even be extended beyond the grave by barring any application by the ex-spouse under the Inheritance (Provision for Family and Dependants) Act 1975, s 15.[300]

The legal relevance and weight of the clean principle has been controversial. The Court of Appeal had begun to interpret the Act as imposing a duty to achieve a clean break wherever possible.[301] The House of Lords rejected this approach in *Miller; McFarlane*: the 'principle' is not a prima facie universal requirement,[302] but a practical consideration to be borne in mind when structuring the settlement which fairness—identified by reference to the three strands and s 25 checklist—demands in the individual case.

Miller v Miller; McFarlane v McFarlane [2006] UKHL 24

BARONESS HALE:

133. Section 25A is a powerful encouragement towards securing the court's objective by way of lump sum and capital adjustment (which now includes pension sharing) rather than by continuing periodical payments. This is good practical sense. Periodical payments are a continuing source of stress for both parties. They are also insecure. With the best will in the world, the paying party may fall on hard times and be unable to keep them up. Nor is the best will in the world always evident between formerly married people. It is also the logical consequence of the retreat from the principle of the life-long obligation. Independent finances and self-sufficiency are the aims. Nevertheless, section 25A does not tell us what the outcome of the exercise required by section 25 should be. It is mainly directed at how that outcome should be put into effect.

134. Hence, these…pointers [including the requirement that first consideration be given to the welfare of the children] do make it clear that a clean break is not to be achieved at the expense of a fair result…

While a clean break must always be considered, the courts have been cautious about imposing it, notably where there are dependent children whose needs continue to inhibit the primary carer's ability to undertake paid employment, or might do so in future.[303] Where children of the marriage have special needs demanding long-term care well into adulthood, lifelong payments may be appropriate.[304] A clean break may also be inappropriate where the children are independent but one spouse's earning capacity has been impaired by past child-care responsibilities.[305] In deciding whether and when a clean break can be achieved, some

---

[299] MCA 1973, s 31(7B); *Miller; McFarlane* [2006] UKHL 24, [131].

[300] For civil partners, see CPA 2004, Sch 5, paras 21(2)(a), 23, 47(1)–(4), 53 and Inheritance (Provision for Family and Dependants) Act 1975.

[301] *Fleming v Fleming* [2003] EWCA Civ 1841; *McFarlane; Parlour* [2004] EWCA Civ 872.

[302] Their Lordships appear to accept *Fleming v Fleming* [2003] EWCA Civ 1841 (despite its incompatibility with *Flavell v Flavell* [1997] 1 FLR 353) on the clean break principle as it applies to applications to extend fixed-term periodical payments orders: *Miller; McFarlane* [2006] UKHL 24, [97], [155].

[303] E.g. *B v B (Mesher Order)* [2002] EWHC 3106.

[304] *V v C* [2004] EWHC 1739.

[305] *Flavell v Flavell* [1997] 1 FLR 353.

view must be reached about applicants' prospects for improving their earning capacity, at least (where any award would be based on need) to the point of becoming self-sufficient. But the courts have warned against unduly optimistic forecasts, particularly where the applicant is middle-aged and would have to retrain: orders should not be made 'more in hope than in serious expectation'.[306] Even if periodical payments are not required immediately, the court may make a nominal order so that it retains jurisdiction to increase the amount payable should circumstances change.[307]

Equally, however, applicants have a duty to take reasonable steps to become self-sufficient and, it seems fair to suppose, to mitigate any loss of earning capacity that forms the basis of a compensation claim.[308] Ex-wives cannot 'freeload' on former husbands. But nor can respondents offload their responsibility on the state, by arguing that the applicant has ample welfare benefit entitlements.

7.6.2 THE CLEAN BREAK IN PRACTICE

Where there is enough capital to satisfy all the parties' claims, a clean break is readily achievable. The difficulties arise in normal cases, where the available capital is insufficient to cover the parties' needs. In practice, orders for periodical payments for the spouse are relatively uncommon, even between couples with dependent children,[309] and the number of capital orders being made has increased. This suggests that clean breaks have become more common,[310] though one small-scale study suggests that *Miller; McFarlane* may have prompted a revival of periodical payments as a vehicle for sharing wealth.[311] However, a clean break can only be effected between the spouses themselves: where there are dependent children, the requirement to pay child support precludes a full clean break. But paying child support is likely to consume respondents' free income, leaving no surplus to be used as periodical payments for the primary carer.

The advent of child support may have made it more difficult in other respects to negotiate a clean break. Before the Child Support Act 1991 (CSA 1991), divorcing parents often reached clean break settlements. Primary carers would forgo periodical payments entirely in return for an outright transfer of the home, some then resorting to welfare benefits for income.[312] The CSA 1991 (in theory at least) barred this option, requiring non-resident parents to pay child support whatever capital settlement had been reached on divorce.[313] This incentive for non-resident parents to abandon a claim to the capital has therefore gone.[314] However, whatever the law may appear to require or encourage, one study suggests that many parents continue to reach informal agreements outside the child support system which achieve a clean break, the parent with care forgoing claims against assets, including pension funds, and for maintenance in order to secure the home.[315] The promotion of voluntary agreements

---

306 Ibid., 358 per Ward LJ.

307 E.g. *Whiting v Whiting* [1988] 1 WLR 565.

308 See Eekelaar (1991b), 86–7.

309 MOJ (2010), tables 2.6–2.7; Perry et al (2000); Davis et al (2000).

310 Barton and Bissett-Johnson (2000).

311 Hitchings (2010), 102.

312 Barton (1998).

313 See 6.6.2.

314 Deech (1996), 95.

315 Perry et al (2000), even in some cases (pre-Child Maintenance and Other Payments Act 2008) where the parent with care was on benefits.

between all parents by the most recent child support reforms may lead to an increase in this pattern of settlement, despite the continued presence of C-MEC in the background.[316]

7.6.3 APPLICATIONS TO SET ASIDE AND FOR LEAVE TO APPEAL FINAL ORDERS

Clean break settlements seek to dispose of the parties' affairs once and for all using property settlement orders, property transfers, and pension sharing. Unlike periodical payments, these orders cannot be varied and the court's jurisdiction ordinarily ceases once an order is made and executed.[317] Such orders may only be altered later if there are grounds either (i) for the order to be 'set aside' because it is tainted by the outset by some underlying flaw; or (ii) for one party to be granted leave to appeal outside the usual time limit in the light of changed circumstances (akin to frustration).[318]

Orders can be set aside on limited grounds, including fraud, mistake, and non-disclosure or misrepresentation of facts which, had they been known or accurately represented, would have made a substantial difference to the order made.[319] These decisions reflect the 'duty of full and frank' disclosure which parties owe each other and the court.[320] Examples include the concealment of an impending remarriage[321] or lucrative new job,[322] and of the existence, value, and marketability of key assets.[323] Where the order is based on the parties' agreement, issues may arise regarding the circumstances surrounding that agreement. But it has been held that undue influence will not provide grounds for setting aside a consent order.[324] Nor will bad legal advice.[325]

Appealing out of time in light of new events is only exceptionally permitted, as the clean break achieved by capital orders would be undermined if parties were free to seek some alteration given changes in their fortunes. The leading authority involved the most dramatic change of circumstance conceivable: shortly after the court had ordered a clean break settlement, transferring the matrimonial home to the wife for her to occupy with the children, she killed the children and committed suicide. On what grounds could leave be granted to appeal against the order?

Barder v Calouri [1988] AC 20, 41, 43

LORD BRANDON:

My Lords, the question whether leave to appeal out of time should be given on the ground that assumptions or estimates made at the time of the hearing of a cause or matter have been invalidated or falsified by subsequent events is a difficult one. The reason why the question is difficult is that it involves a conflict between two important legal principles and a

---

[316] See also new off-setting powers: p 371.
[317] Cf *Thwaite v Thwaite* (1981) 2 FLR 280; *L v L* [2006] EWHC 956, [63]–[67].
[318] *Cornick v Cornick* [1994] 2 FLR 530; for full review of these mechanisms, see *L v L* [2006] EWHC 956.
[319] *Livesey v Jenkins* [1985] AC 424.
[320] Ibid. Cf *Imerman v Imerman* [2010] EWCA Civ 908.
[321] Ibid.
[322] *Bokor-Ingram v Bokor-Ingram* [2009] EWCA Civ 412.
[323] *Vicary v Vicary* [1992] 2 FLR 271.
[324] *Tommey v Tommey* [1983] Fam 15, doubted in *Livesey v Jenkins* [1985] AC 424, 440.
[325] *L v L* [2006] EWHC 956, [47]–[53].

decision as to which of them is to prevail over the other. The first principle is that it is in the public interest that there should be finality in litigation. The second principle is that justice requires cases to be decided, so far as practicable, on the true facts relating to them, and not on assumptions or estimates with regard to those facts which are conclusively shown by later events to have been erroneous...

A court may properly exercise its discretion to grant leave to appeal out of time from an order for financial provision or property transfer made after a divorce on the ground of new events, provided that certain conditions are satisfied. The first condition is that new events have occurred since the making of the order which invalidate the basis, or fundamental assumption, upon which the order was made, so that, if leave to appeal out of time were to be given, the appeal would be certain, or very likely, to succeed.[326] The second condition is that the new events should have occurred within a relatively short time of the order having been made. While the length of time cannot be laid down precisely, I should regard it as extremely unlikely that it could be as much as a year, and that in most cases it will be no more than a few months. The third condition is that the application for leave to appeal out of time should be made reasonably promptly in the circumstances of the case. To these three conditions... I would add a fourth, which it does not appear has needed to be considered so far, but which it may be necessary to consider in future cases. That fourth condition is that the grant of leave to appeal out of time should not prejudice third parties who have acquired, in good faith and for valuable consideration, interests in property which is the subject matter of the relevant order.

It was clear that a fundamental assumption of the order, shared by the parties and the court,[327] was that the wife and children would indefinitely require a suitable home. That was invalidated by their sudden deaths, and the order was set aside.

Subsequent cases to which these criteria have been applied include: the death[328] or remarriage of one party, at least insofar as it affects that spouse's need for housing;[329] misvaluation of key assets; significant changes in value generated by subsequent events (not mere market conditions or natural price fluctuations, however unforeseeable);[330] changes in the law of ancillary relief.[331] That the parties reconcile after the divorce and cohabit long-term seems not to constitute a *Barder* event.[332] Nor, at a time when few jobs are wholly secure, does redundancy.[333] The uncertain times of the credit crunch generated several attempts to appeal out of time by respondents who had elected to take the risky assets and lost out,[334] and by applicants who regretted having deliberately forgone a stake in speculative assets which then grew in value.[335] The courts rejected these applications on *Barder* principles: if

[326] On the basis that had the event been foreseen *at the time of the original order*, a different order would have been made: *Williams v Lindley* [2005] EWCA Civ 103, [2005] 2 FLR 710.

[327] *Dixon v Marchant* [2008] EWCA Civ 11, [25].

[328] E.g. *Smith v Smith (Smith and other intervening)* [1992] Fam 69.

[329] *Dixon v Marchant* [2008] EWCA Civ 11; cf *B v B (Financial Provision: Leave to Appeal)* [1994] 1 FLR 219; *Chaudhuri v Chaudhuri* [1992] 2 FLR 73. Cohabitation would probably also be relevant: cf *Cook v Cook* [1988] 1 FLR 521.

[330] See *Cornick v Cornick* [1994] 2 FLR 530, and cases reviewed therein; *Middleton v Middleton* [1998] 2 FLR 821.

[331] *S v S (Ancillary Relief: Consent Order)* [2002] EWHC 223. *White v White* [2001] 1 AC 596 not a *Barder* event because it was foreseeable at the relevant time.

[332] *Hill v Hill* [1997] 1 FLR 730 (FD), rvsd on different grounds in [1998] 1 FLR 198 (CA).

[333] *Maskell v Maskell* [2001] EWCA Civ 858, [4].

[334] *Myerson v Myerson* [2009] EWCA Civ 282.

[335] *Walkden v Walkden* [2009] EWCA Civ 627.

you deliberately choose risk over certainty, or certainty over risk, you cannot later complain that you struck the wrong deal. If leave is granted, the case is reconsidered in light of all the circumstances at the time of the appeal.[336]

7.7 PRIVATE ORDERING

Rarely are financial and property disputes on divorce resolved by contested litigation. Agreement is the norm, whether reached by lawyer-led negotiation, mediation, or privately.[337] The procedure for ancillary relief claims provides incentives and opportunities for settlement: the requirement of full and frank disclosure;[338] pre-trial 'first appointments' to define the issues in dispute;[339] settlement-oriented 'financial dispute resolution' appointments;[340] other in-court conciliation schemes; mediation facilities;[341] costs rules;[342] and various codes of conduct and protocols.[343] The proportion of divorces in which contested ancillary relief orders are made has declined.[344]

However, two basic questions arise. (1) Are agreements made on separation regarding parties' finances and property legally enforceable? (2) Can parties reach a binding agreement in advance, whether before or during marriage, about how their assets and income will be shared (or not shared) in the event of any future divorce? At present, no form of purely private ordering is straightforwardly enforceable.

The key underlying principle, untouched by the recent decision of the Supreme Court in *Radmacher v Granatino*,[345] comes from *Hyman v Hyman*:[346] parties cannot oust the jurisdiction of the matrimonial courts by agreement. So no agreement can prevent the court from considering what provision between the parties would be fair; and the court is not bound to determine that the parties' agreement produces a fair outcome—it can impose its own, different order. With that principle in mind, we shall work backwards from the point of divorce, starting with the only really secure form of private ordering—consent orders—and ending with the most controversial—pre-nuptial agreements.

7.7.1 CONSENT ORDERS

Given the 'settlement culture' of family justice, most parties agree how to divide their property and finances. However, to achieve certainty and finality they should enshrine that agreement in a court order: a 'consent order'.[347] Most orders for ancillary relief are

---

[336] *Smith v Smith (Smith and Others Intervening)* [1992] Fam 69.
[337] But settlement is not necessarily good: Diduck (2003), 153–8; and 1.2.3 and 5.8.
[338] *Livesey v Jenkins* [1985] AC 424.
[339] FPR 2010, r 9.15.
[340] Ibid., r 2.61D–E; *Rose v Rose* [2002] EWCA Civ 208; see generally Black et al (2007), ch 18.
[341] Settlements reached by legally aided clients through mediation are exempt from the statutory charge, a strong incentive to mediate, at least for that party.
[342] See n 284.
[343] Law Society (2006); Resolution (2000); President's Pre-Application Protocol [2000] 1 WLR 1480.
[344] Barton and Bissett-Johnson (2000).
[345] [2010] UKSC 42, [7], [52].
[346] [1929] AC 601.
[347] See *Xydhias v Xydhias* on whether agreement has been reached: [1999] 1 FLR 683; *Radmacher v Granatino* [2010] UKSC 42, [148]–[149] per Baroness Hale.

made by consent, rather than contested.[348] To obtain the order, parties present prescribed information to the court, essentially 'headline' data relevant to s 25, in light of which it will determine whether an order in those terms should be made, or whether further inquiry is necessary.[349] Once the agreement is transposed into an order, the parties' rights and obligations flow from that; the underlying agreement falls away.[350] As an order of the court, it cannot include provisions that the court could not have ordered in contested litigation, except as undertakings.[351] A consent order is as binding as one made following contested litigation, so can only be varied, appealed against, or set aside on the grounds discussed above.[352] Indeed, some decisions indicate that because a consent order is based on agreement, the court considering an application for variation or appeal out of time should be particularly slow to intervene.[353]

The court's role in making a consent order in ancillary relief cases is distinctive, lying somewhere between 'rudimentary rubber stamp' and 'forensic ferret', 'a watchdog, but not a bloodhound', 'entitled but not obliged to play the detective':[354]

Pounds v Pounds [1994] 1 WLR 1535, 1537–41 (CA)

WAITE LJ:

In most areas of our law, parties to litigation who are sui juris and independently advised can settle their differences on terms which are included by agreement in an order or rule of court . . . with the authority of a judge who may not be aware of the terms of the deal at all . . . , still less be concerned with any question as to their suitability or fairness. That is not so in financial proceedings between husband and wife, where the court does not act, it has been said, as a rubber-stamp: the judge will be concerned, whether the order be made by consent or imposed after argument, to be satisfied that the criteria of sections 25 and 25A of the Matrimonial Causes Act 1973 have been duly applied . . .

When the House of Lords ruled in *Livesey (formerly Jenkins) v Jenkins* [1985] A.C. 424 . . . that the duty of disclosure of assets was owed by spouses not only to each other but to the court, it did so upon the basis that it was the function of the court in every case, whether it was proceeding by consent of the parties or after a contested hearing, to be satisfied that the provision made by the order fulfilled the criteria laid down by section 25 . . . It is clear, however, that this was intended to be an assertion of general principle only, and not to impose on the court the need to scrutinise in detail the financial affairs of the parties who came to it for approval of an independently negotiated bargain. It could not be otherwise, for earlier that year Parliament had specifically enacted a more cursory regime for the scrutiny of consent orders [in MCA 1973, s 33A] of which subsection (1) reads as follows:

"Notwithstanding anything in the preceding provisions of this Part of this Act, on an application for a consent order for financial relief the court may, unless it has reason to think that there are other circumstances into which it ought to inquire, make an order in the terms agreed on the basis only of the prescribed information furnished with the application."

---

[348] MOJ (2010), table 2.6; Davis et al (2000) found only 4.6% cases went to a contested final hearing.

[349] MCA 1973, s 33A; CPA 2004, Sch 5, Part 13; FPR 2010, r 9.26: see *Pounds* extract, in text below.

[350] *De Lasala v De Lasala* [1980] AC 546, 560.

[351] *Livesey v Jenkins* [1985] AC 424, 444.

[352] See 7.3.5 and 7.6.3.

[353] *Richardson v Richardson (No 2)* [1996] 2 FLR 617.

[354] *B-T v B-T (Divorce: Procedure)* [1990] 2 FLR 1, 17; *L v L* [2006] EWHC 956, [73].

The "prescribed information" is that required by [FPR 2010, r 9.26—set out below as amended since *Pounds*] which provides:

... in relation to an application for a consent order—(a) the applicant must file two copies of a draft of the order in the terms sought, one of which must be endorsed with a statement signed by the respondent to the application signifying agreement, and (b) each party must file with the court and serve on the other party, a statement of information in the form referred to in Practice Direction 5A [PD 5A not published at time of writing: previous rules required information regarding:]—(a) the duration of the marriage [or civil partnership, as the case may be], the age of each party and of any minor or dependent child of the family; (b) an estimate in summary form of the approximate amount or value of the capital resources and net income of each party and of any minor child of the family; (c) what arrangements are intended for the accommodation of each of the parties and any minor child of the family; (d) whether either party has [subsequently married or formed a civil partnership or has any present intention to do so or to cohabit with another person;] ... (f) any other especially significant matters."

Forms for use in supplying those particulars were prescribed by practice direction ... They run to no more than two pages, and the space allowed in the boxes for financial information is very restrictive indeed [see currently Form D81[355]].

The effect of section 33A and the Rules and Directions made under it is thus to confine the paternal function of the court when approving financial consent orders to a broad appraisal of the parties' financial circumstances as disclosed to it in summary form, without descent into the valley of detail. It is only if that survey puts the court on inquiry as to whether there are other circumstances into which it ought to probe more deeply that any further investigation is required of the judge before approving the bargain that the spouses have made for themselves.

But it has been doubted whether the paternalism underpinning the rule in *Hyman v Hyman*, requiring parties to submit to the authority of the court in order to secure a binding settlement, is exercised in practice:

S. Cretney, 'From Status to Contract?', in F. Rose (ed), *Consensus ad Idem* (London: Sweet & Maxwell, 1996b), 277

[T]he question of whether a court can sensibly discharge [the function described by Waite LJ] ... is self-evidently difficult; and it may well be that different judges approach their tasks in different ways ... In reality, the sanction of the court is today obtained in almost all cases and agreements intended to make any but short-term financial arrangements without reference to the court are rare indeed. But it is difficult to be confident that the investigation which the court is able to carry out is sufficient to ensure that the terms embodied in its order do not take advantage of the vulnerability of one of the parties. ... [Given the limited information available to it,] it seems questionable how far the court is really in a position to make any informed judgment about the fairness of the agreement to which it is asked to give effect.[356]

However, significant investigation by the court may be undesirable: 'Officious inquiry may uncover an injustice, but it is more likely to disturb a delicate negotiation and produce the very costly litigation and the recrimination which conciliation is designed to avoid'.[357]

---

[355] <www.hmcourtsservice.gov.uk/courtfinder/forms/d81_e1205.pdf>.
[356] See also Davis et al (2000), 48 and 63–4.
[357] *Harris v Manahan* [1997] 1 FLR 205, 213.

Given the court's limited ability to review the underlying agreement, it has been said that the parties' lawyers have a corresponding responsibility to secure fair outcomes and to minimize scope for subsequent challenge.[358] Nevertheless, the interests of securing finality in emotionally fraught ancillary relief litigation dictate that orders cannot be set aside because of bad legal advice.[359]

7.7.2 SEPARATION AND MAINTENANCE AGREEMENTS

What then of agreements made at the point of divorce which have not been enshrined in a consent order? Separation agreements do not offer certainty and finality as it remains open to either party to apply to court for ancillary relief: that can only be avoided if the agreement is enshrined in a consent order. However, even if the parties intend to obtain a consent order, there is often a delay between agreement and order.[360] Moreover, since the court cannot make any orders[361] until the decree nisi is granted, agreements governing the parties' finances and property may need to be relied upon for some time in divorces proceeding on either of the 'separation' facts.[362]

Insofar as separation agreements deal with an actually impending separation or divorce, they are contractually valid.[363] Moreover, 'maintenance agreements', usually reached on divorce, have statutory recognition and *some* binding legal force:[364]

Matrimonial Causes Act 1973, s 34[365]

Validity of maintenance agreements

(1) If a maintenance agreement includes a provision purporting to restrict any right to apply to a court for an order containing financial arrangements, then —

(a) that provision shall be void; but

(b) any other financial arrangements contained in the agreement shall not thereby be rendered void or unenforceable and shall, unless they are void or unenforceable for any other reason (and subject to sections 35 and 36 below), be binding on the parties to the agreement.

(2) In this section and in section 35 below—

"maintenance agreement" means any agreement in writing *made ... between the parties to a marriage*, being—

(a) an agreement containing financial arrangements, whether made during the continuance or after the dissolution or annulment of the marriage; or

---

[358] *Dinch v Dinch* [1987] 1 WLR 252, 255.

[359] *L v L* [2006] EWHC 956. Contrast the position applying to separation agreements, nn 371–2 below. The lawyers might be liable in negligence: *Arthur JS Hall and Co (a firm) v Simons et al* [2002] 1 AC 615.

[360] Cf the circumstances in *Rose v Rose* [2002] EWCA Civ 208.

[361] Save maintenance pending suit: s 22; and financial provision: s 27, MCA 1973; CPA 2004, Sch 5, para 38 and Part 9.

[362] Cretney (1996b), 278.

[363] *Hyman v Hyman* [1929] AC 601; compare pre-nuptial agreements, below.

[364] See Cretney and Masson (1990), ch 21.

[365] And CPA 2004, Sch 5, paras 67–8.

> (b) a separation agreement which contains no financial arrangements in a case where no other agreement in writing between the same parties contains such arrangements;
>
> "financial arrangements" means provisions governing the rights and liabilities towards one another when living separately of the parties to a marriage (including a marriage which has been dissolved or annulled) in respect of the making or securing of payments or the disposition or use of any property, including such rights and liabilities with respect to the maintenance or education of any child, whether or not a child of the family. [emphasis added]

Section 34 ensures that, provided the agreement is in writing and valid under the general law of contract, an applicant seeking payment in accordance with its terms can sue on it.[366] While it is necessary to prove an intention to create legal relations, which may be problematic if the parties are apparently in domestic harmony,[367] that will not be difficult where the agreement is in writing and made with legal advice, particularly where a divorce is pending.[368]

However, although binding to that extent in contract, maintenance agreements and other separation agreements may be challenged via two routes: (i) an application under section 35 for variation of the agreement; (ii) the *Hyman* assurance that each party retains an unfettered right to apply for ancillary relief in the ordinary way, despite the agreement.

Section 35 empowers the court to alter maintenance agreements where:

> by reason of a change in the circumstances in the light of which any financial arrangements contained in the agreement were made or, as the case may be, financial arrangements were omitted from it (including a change foreseen by the parties when making the agreement), the agreement should be altered so as to make different, or, as the case may be, so as to contain, financial arrangements.[369]

The court has the discretion, to be exercised as appears 'just having regard to all the circumstances', to vary existing terms or insert wholly new terms into the agreement (for example, by making provision for the making of periodical payments where none had originally been agreed).

The MCA also preserves the *Hyman* principle that the maintenance agreement cannot prevent an application to court for alternative provision.[370] Parties seeking greater provision—or those no longer wishing to pay what they agreed—can therefore apply for ancillary relief in the ordinary way. However, the agreement is not ignored in those proceedings. Its existence[371] and circumstances surrounding it will be considered by the court when deciding under s 25 what order would be 'fair'.[372]

---

[366] It may be necessary to use a deed, in the absence of consideration from the payee; cf *Bennett v Bennett* [1952] 1 KB 249, which prompted enactment of the precursor of s 34. Cf *Xydhias v Xydhias* [1999] 1 FLR 683 on the compromise of an ancillary relief claim not concluded in a deed: *MacLeod v MacLeod* [2008] UKPC 64, [26].

[367] *Balfour v Balfour* [1919] 2 KB 571.

[368] *Merritt v Merritt* [1970] 1 WLR 1211.

[369] MCA 1973, s 35(2)(a); CPA 2004, Sch 5, para 69. Following death of one party, see MCA 1973, s 36. The court may also alter agreements insofar as they '[do] not contain proper financial arrangements with respect to any child of the family': s 35(2)(b): see 6.6.

[370] MCA 1973, s 35(1), (6); CPA 2004, Sch 5, para 72.

[371] Decided not by reference to contractual principles, but in the exercise of the court's discretion: *Xydhias v Xydhias* [1999] 1 FLR 683; see Cretney (1999).

[372] *Hyman v Hyman* [1929] AC 601, 609, and 629.

Separation agreements are generally made and acted upon in quick succession and in light of known circumstances. Difficulties may arise if one party thinks on reflection that he or she could have done better. They may also be tainted by the emotional turmoil of marital breakdown. The weight given to them may often depend upon whether each party had independent legal advice and the presence or absence of unacceptable pressure to agree terms which, in retrospect, may seem to be less generous than what a court might have awarded. The leading case on the approach to ancillary relief applications where there is a separation agreement is *Edgar v Edgar*. Contrary to her lawyers' advice that she was entitled to substantially more, the wife had agreed by deed to a capital sum and periodical payments and covenanted not to apply for further capital provision. She nevertheless applied to the court, claiming that she had made the agreement because she was desperate to leave the husband, by whose wealth and position she felt overpowered:

Edgar v Edgar [1980] 1 WLR 1410, 1417–18 (CA)

ORMROD LJ:

To decide what weight should be given, in order to reach a just result, to a prior agreement not to claim a lump sum, regard must be had to the conduct of both parties, leading up to the prior agreement, and to their subsequent conduct, in consequence of it. It is not necessary in this connection to think in formal legal terms, such as misrepresentation or estoppel; *all* the circumstances as they affect each of two human beings must be considered in the complex relationship of marriage. So, the circumstances surrounding the making of the agreement are relevant. Und[ue] pressure by one side, exploitation of a dominant position to secure an unreasonable advantage, inadequate knowledge, possibly bad legal advice,[373] an important change of circumstances, unforeseen or overlooked at the time of making the agreement, are all relevant to the question of justice between the parties. Important too is the general proposition that formal agreements, properly and fairly arrived at with competent legal advice, should not be displaced unless there are good and substantial grounds for concluding that an injustice will be done by holding the parties to the terms of their agreement. There may well be other considerations which affect the justice of this case; the above list is not intended to be an exclusive catalogue . . .

Eastham J. in the present case, approached the problem on these lines. He summarised the law in five propositions:

"(1) . . . (and this is not contested) notwithstanding the deed . . . , the wife is entitled to pursue a claim under section 23 of the Act. (2) If she does pursue such a claim, the court not only has jurisdiction to entertain it but is bound to take into account all the considerations listed in section 25 of the Act. (3) The existence of an agreement is a very relevant circumstance under section 25 and in the case of an arm's length agreement, based on legal advice between parties of equal bargaining power, is a most important piece of conduct to be considered under section 25. (4) Providing that there is equality above, the mere fact that the wife would have done better by going to the court, would not generally be a ground, for giving her more as, in addition to its duty under section 25, the court had a duty also to uphold agreements which do not offend public policy. (5) If the court, on the evidence, takes the view that having regard to the disparity of bargaining power, it would be unjust not to exercise its powers under section 23 (having regard to the considerations under section 25), it should exercise such powers even if no fraud, misrepresentation or duress is established which, at common law, would entitle a wife to avoid the deed."

---

[373] *Camm v Camm* (1983) 4 FLR 577: 'bad' does not connote 'negligent', 580, per Sir Roger Ormrod.

I agree with these propositions, subject to two reservations. First, as to proposition (4), I am not sure that it is helpful to speak of the court having "a duty" to uphold agreements, although I understand the sense in which the word was used. Secondly, the reference to "disparity of bargaining power" in proposition (5) is incomplete. ... [What is required is a situation] where one spouse takes an unfair advantage of the other in the throes of marital breakdown, a time when emotional pressures are high, and judgment apt to be clouded. ... There can be no doubt in that in this case, as in so many, there is a disparity of bargaining power. The crucial question, however, for present purposes, is not whether the husband had a superior bargaining power, but whether he exploited it in a way which was unfair to the wife, so as to induce her to act to her disadvantage.

The court found that it was fair to hold her to the agreement: the husband had not abused his position and the wife was driven by her desire to achieve independence.[374]

Cases vary in their description of the approach to be taken to separation agreements and the *Edgar* criteria, though differences of emphasis may simply reflect the facts of the individual cases. Sometimes, the approach seems to be that, unless the party seeking to depart from the agreement can show that the case satisfies one of the *Edgar* criteria, the court will give effect to the agreement.[375] At other times, the courts have emphasized that agreements are just one factor in the global s 25 analysis.[376] Amendments to the 1973 Act since *Edgar* requiring first consideration to be given to the welfare of minor children of the family deprive agreements of primary status in such cases.[377] Clearly, more weight will generally be given to agreements concluded with independent, good quality legal advice, and full disclosure.[378] But as *Radmacher v Granatino* (discussed below) shows, neither is a necessary precondition for a court to attach decisive weight to an agreement.

The Privy Council held in *MacLeod v MacLeod* that the same approach should be taken to variation applications and applications for ancillary relief in these cases, whichever route of challenge is adopted.[379] So the court hearing the ancillary relief application may decide in the exercise of its s 25 discretion to depart from the agreement given a change of circumstance. Baroness Hale suggested that what was needed was 'the sort of change which would make those arrangements manifestly unjust', though in *Radmacher* she retracted the word 'manifestly' as imposing too strict a test.[380] But, now going beyond what s 35 allows, the court under *Edgar* principles may also depart from the agreement because of the circumstances in which the agreement was made, though the mere fact that a court would have made different provision will not of itself justify departure from the parties' agreement.[381] Baroness Hale also invoked the general point of public policy that, regardless of any change of circumstance, an obligation that ought to be met by a family member should not be cast onto the public purse.[382]

The 'limbo' status of separation agreements—neither straightforwardly binding nor irrelevant—has attracted judicial criticism:

---

[374] Cf *Camm v Camm*, ibid., in which the wife was also found to have received bad legal advice.

[375] *Smith v McInerney* [1994] 2 FLR 1077; *X v X (Y and Z intervening)* [2002] 1 FLR 508.

[376] *Smith v Smith* [2000] 3 FCR 374: Black J held that *Smith* did not indicate a different approach: *A v B (Financial Relief: Agreements)* [2005] EWHC 314.

[377] E.g. *Richardson v Richardson (No 2)* [1994] 2 FLR 1051.

[378] See generally *X v X (Y and Z intervening)* [2002] 1 FLR 508, esp [103].

[379] [2008] UKPC 64, [41]; cf *Simister (no 1)* [1987] 1 FLR 194.

[380] [2010] UKSC 42, [168].

[381] Ibid., at [42].

[382] Ibid., at [41].

Pounds v Pounds [1994] 1 WLR 1535, 1550–1 (CA)

HOFFMANN LJ:

[I]t does seem to me that the law is in an unsatisfactory state. There are in theory various possible answers to the problem. One might be that an agreement between the parties, at least where each has independent legal advice, is binding upon them subject only to the normal contractual remedies based on fraud, misrepresentation, undue influence, etc. At present, the policy of the law as expressed in *Hyman v Hyman* ... is against such a solution. The court retains its supervisory role and only its order gives finality. Another answer might be that when parties are negotiating with a view to an agreement which will be embodied in a consent order, everything should be treated as without prejudice negotiation until the order is actually made. In the latter case, the parties would know that until the court had given its imprimatur, nothing which they had negotiated was legally binding or even admissible. If one of them changed his or her mind, they would have either to go back to the negotiating table or litigate the matter de novo. This may be tiresome, as in the case of a house purchase where one party changes his or her mind before contracts are exchanged. But the parties would at least know where they stood. The result of the decision of this court in *Edgar v Edgar* ... and the cases which have followed is that we have, as it seems to me, the worst of both worlds. The agreement may be held to be binding, but whether it will be can be determined only after litigation and may involve ... examining the quality of the advice which was given to the party who wishes to resile. It is then understandably a matter for surprise and resentment on the part of the other party that one should be able to repudiate an agreement on account of the inadequacy of one's own legal advisers, over whom the other party had no control and of whose advice he had no knowledge. The husband's counsel, who has considerable experience of these matters, told us that he reckoned that in Northampton an agreement has an 80 per cent chance of being upheld but that attitudes varied from district judge to district judge. In our attempt to achieve finely ground justice by attributing weight but not too much weight to the agreement of the parties, we have created uncertainty and ... added to the cost and pain of litigation.

7.7.3 POST-NUPTIAL AGREEMENTS

We turn now to agreements not made at the point of divorce, but earlier in the marriage—possibly during a 'rocky' patch[383] and/or varying an earlier pre-nuptial agreement[384]—setting out what would happen in the (hypothetical) eventuality of a future divorce.

Until the Privy Council decision in *MacLeod v MacLeod*, there were question marks over the validity of such 'post-nuptial' agreements: were they void on grounds of public policy for improperly contemplating and so potentially encouraging divorce? The Privy Council held that any such public policy objection no longer applies, and went on to conclude from the wording of s 34(2) italicized in the extract above (at p 492) that post-nuptial agreements fall within s 34's regulation of 'maintenance agreements'. On that view, provided they were made in writing with intention to create legal relations and consideration (or by a deed), such agreements would be valid and binding by statute.[385] It would further follow from this that post-nuptial agreements could be challenged in the same way as separation agreements: via s 35 or an application for ancillary relief subject to *Edgar* principles.

[383] E.g. *NA v MA* [2006] EWHC 2900.
[384] E.g. *MacLeod v MacLeod* [2008] UKPC 64.
[385] Ibid., [35]–[39].

However, the majority of the Supreme Court in *Radmacher* took the view (only obiter, as that case concerned a *pre*-nuptial agreement) that this interpretation of s 34 is erroneous: that Parliament in 1973 cannot have intended to include within s 34 agreements understood at that time still to be void on grounds of public policy.[386] Rather than align post-nuptial agreements with separation agreements, the majority of the Supreme Court preferred to align them with pre-nuptial agreements. We discuss the Court's approach to those agreements in the next section: in short, neither type of agreement is now void on grounds of public policy, the *Hyman* principle entitles the matrimonial court to order provision different from that agreed, but that court will give the agreement decisive weight where freely entered into with full appreciation of its implications unless it would not be fair to hold the parties to it.[387]

Given the law as it emerges from *Radmacher*, little may turn on the particular type of agreement involved: all are subject to the *Hyman* principle and all are treated in a fact-sensitive way in pursuit of a fair outcome. But it is clear that a substantial change of circumstances of the sort that will in fairness demand provision different from that agreed is more likely to occur between the conclusion of a post-nuptial agreement and subsequent divorce than following a separation agreement.[388] Like a pre-nuptial agreement, a post-nuptial agreement concluded early in the marriage will often try to cater for what will happen 'in an uncertain and unhoped for future'.[389] By contrast, a separation agreement generally deals with known circumstances prevailing at the time of the impending divorce.

7.7.4 PRE-NUPTIAL AGREEMENTS

We come finally to pre-nuptial agreements, referred to in some recent judicial decisions as 'ante-nuptial' agreements, which until recently have had the most tenuous status of all types of marital agreement. As just noted, they and post-nuptial agreements are regarded by the Supreme Court as appropriately subject to the same legal principles.

The public policy objection removed

Like any other marital agreement, pre-nuptial agreements are subject to the *Hyman* principle, but until recently their status (and that of post-nuptial agreements) was further weakened by the fact that they were regarded as entirely *void* as a matter of contract law on grounds of public policy.[390] This public policy objection had been stated in various ways over the years, but essentially it was regarded as objectionable that couples should reach agreements which potentially encouraged one or other party to instigate divorce. Baroness Hale described the argument in the following terms:

Radmacher v Granatino [2010] UKSC 42

143. . . . This rule was developed in the context of agreements or settlements which made some or better financial provision for the wife if she were to live separately from her husband. Such an agreement could be seen as encouraging them to live apart – for example, by

---

[386] [2010] UKSC 42, [54]–[55].
[387] Ibid., [75].
[388] Ibid., [65].
[389] Ibid., [59].
[390] *MacLeod v MacLeod* [2008] UKPC 64, [31]–[33].

encouraging her to leave him, if it was sufficiently generous or more than she would get if she stayed with him, or encouraging him to leave her, or to agree to her going, if it were not so generous. Such encouragement was seen as inconsistent with the fundamental, life-long and enforceable obligation of husband and wife to live with one another.

As a result, such agreements were simply unenforceable as contracts. However, somewhat confusingly,[391] despite being contractually void pre-nuptial agreements were not ignored and, in recent years in certain circumstances, were given substantial—even decisive—weight.[392]

The current law was definitively stated by the Supreme Court in *Radmacher v Granatino*. The Court, by majority (Baroness Hale dissenting in certain key respects), held first—and obiter—that the public policy objections to pre-nuptial agreements are now obsolete and so no longer apply.[393] The Privy Council in *MacLeod*, led by Baroness Hale, had reached the same conclusion (again arguably obiter) in relation to *post*-nuptial agreements but declined (clearly obiter) to extend its reasoning to *pre*-nuptial agreements. This purported distinction between pre- and post-nuptial agreements was heavily criticized by commentators and its coherence respectfully doubted by the Court of Appeal in *Radmacher*.[394] Since the duty of spouses to cohabit is no longer legally enforceable[395] (save insofar as desertion provides grounds for divorce), the basis for the public policy argument against both types of agreement has disintegrated.

The Privy Council had also suggested in *MacLeod* that parties to pre-nuptial agreements need protection from pressures to which parties to 'post-nups' are not subject: the agreement might be 'the price which one party may extract for his or her willingness to marry' at all.[396] But parties to post-nuptial agreements might be susceptible to equally powerful if different pressure, as *NA v MA* illustrates, the agreement being the price for the continuation of the marriage. Here the wife, who was entirely dependent on the husband and his family, was bullied into signing the agreement following the discovery of her adultery. The agreement was a non-negotiable condition of the marriage continuing (and of her returning home). He knew that she felt overwhelmingly guilty about the adultery and was desperate to save the marriage for the sake of the children. Baron J had no difficult in departing from this agreement on *Edgar* grounds given the wife's evident subjection to undue influence.[397]

In view of these similarities between the pre- and post-nuptial context, the Supreme Court in *Radmacher* therefore rejected a sharp distinction between pre- and post-nuptial agreements, preferring to treat them on the same footing.

The *Hyman* principle: the treatment of agreements in the matrimonial court

However, whilst all forms of nuptial agreements are now understood to be contractually valid, a majority of the Supreme Court regarded their contractual enforceability to be a 'red

---

[391] *Radmacher v Granatino* [2009] EWCA Civ 649, [64] per Rix LJ.

[392] Ibid.; *Crossley v Crossley* [2007] EWCA Civ 1491; *K v K* [2003] 1 FLR 120; *M v M (Pre-nuptial agreement)* [2002] 1 FLR 654.

[393] [2010] UKSC 42, [52].

[394] See Miles (2009).

[395] Since, in particular, the abolition of decree for restitution of conjugal rights: Matrimonial Proceedings and Property Act 1970, s 20.

[396] *MacLeod v MacLeod* [2008] UKPC 64, [36].

[397] [2006] EWHC 2900.

herring': because they are all subject to the *Hyman* principle, and so all susceptible to being departed from in the exercise of the matrimonial court's discretion under the MCA 1973 following divorce.[398] The key question therefore is what approach that court will take when faced with an application for ancillary relief in a case where the parties had reached a pre- or post-nuptial agreement. From this point, Baroness Hale largely agreed with the substance of the majority's position, though she adopted a different emphasis (regarded by Lord Mance is unlikely to make any difference in practice). The majority described their approach in the following terms, essentially providing a new starting point for cases where there is an agreement:

Radmacher v Granatino [2010] UKSC 42

75. *White v White* and *Miller v Miller* establish that the overriding criterion to be applied to ancillary relief proceedings is that of fairness and identify the three strands of need, compensation and sharing that are relevant to the question of what is fair. If an ante-nuptial agreement deals with those matters in a way that the court might adopt absent such an agreement, there is no problem about giving effect to the agreement. The problem arises where the agreement makes provisions that conflict with what the court would other-wise consider to be the requirements of fairness. The fact of the agreement is capable of altering what is fair. It is an important factor to be weighed in the balance. We would advance the following proposition, to be applied in the case of both ante- and post-nuptial agreements . . . :

"The court should give effect to a nuptial agreement that is freely entered into by each party with a full appreciation of its implications unless in the circumstances prevailing it *would not* be *fair* to hold the parties to their agreement." [italics added]

Baroness Hale preferred to formulate the test the other way around, asking 'Did each party freely enter into an agreement, intending it to have legal effect and with full appreciation of its implications. If so, in the circumstances as they now are, *would it be fair* to hold them to their agreement?'.[399] But whether expressed negatively or positively, what does 'fairness' consist of in this context? The majority went on:

76. That leaves outstanding the difficult question of the circumstances in which it will not be fair to hold the parties to their agreement. This will necessarily depend upon the facts of the particular case, and it would not be desirable to lay down rules that would fetter the flexibility that the court requires to reach a fair result. There is, however, some guidance that we believe that it is safe to give directed to the situation where there are no tainting circum-stances attending the conclusion of the agreement.

There are therefore two stages to the inquiry, though the court may in practice examine their combined effect in its pursuit of fairness.[400] First, are there any 'tainting circumstances' present at the outset, factors which detract from the weight to be accorded to the agreement? Even if not, would it nevertheless now be unfair to hold the parties to the agreement?

---

[398] *Radmacher* [2010] UKSC 42, [62]–[63]; cf Lord Mance [128] and Baroness Hale [159].
[399] Ibid., [169]. Cf Lord Mance [129].
[400] Ibid., [73].

Factors tainting the agreement from the outset

The Court identified several issues that might undermine an agreement from the outset, going beyond what contract law would in any event identify as a vitiating factor (such as fraud, duress, and so on).[401] Both parties must have entered into the agreement 'of their own free will, without undue influence and pressure, and informed of its implications'. But the absence of independent legal advice or full disclosure of each party's assets will not necessarily undermine the agreement: while both advice and disclosure might be 'obviously desirable', what matters is that 'each party should have all the information that is *material* to his or her decision, and that each party should intend that the agreement should govern the financial consequences of the marriage coming to an end',[402] an intention that the Court considers will be more readily found for agreements concluded after the decision in *Radmacher*.[403] The same will be true of parties who made their agreement under a foreign law which allows for binding nuptial agreements, whenever they concluded their agreement.[404] In considering whether the parties were under undue pressure, the court will have regard to their 'emotional state' and their circumstances at the time of the agreement, such as their 'age and maturity' and their relationship history; we might also add to the list whether the woman is pregnant:

> 72....[For couples where either or both have been married or in long-term relationships before] their experience of previous relationships may explain the terms of the agreement, and may also show what they foresaw when they entered into the agreement. What may not be easily foreseeable for less mature couples may well be in contemplation of more mature couples. Another important factor may be whether the marriage would have gone ahead without an agreement, or without the terms which had been agreed. This may cut either way.

The 'fairness' of upholding the agreement at the point of divorce

The next step will be to examine the 'fairness' of giving effect to the agreement at the point of divorce. In addition to the remarks made at paras 75 and 76 (extracted above) the Court identified several factors that would have a bearing on the fairness of the agreement. The agreement cannot 'prejudice the reasonable requirements of any children of the family', whose welfare are by statute the 'first consideration' on granting ancillary relief.[405] Beyond that, however, the court should respect the parties' autonomy and their choice about how to regulate their financial affairs: 'It would be paternalistic and patronising to override their agreement simply on the basis that the court knows best'. This will especially be the case where the agreement dealt with known circumstances. Agreements that simply preserve a particular item of 'non-matrimonial property', such as an inheritance, may also attract more weight.[406] Contrast an agreement dealing with 'the contingencies of an uncertain future',[407] where the passage of decades and the changed circumstances they brought may have rendered the agreement unfair.[408] Baroness Hale was particularly eloquent in her treatment of the last point:

---

401 Ibid., [71]–[72].
402 Ibid., [68]–[69].
403 Ibid., [70].
404 Ibid., [74].
405 Ibid., [77].
406 Ibid., [78]–[79].
407 Ibid., [78].
408 Ibid., [80].

Radmacher v Granatino [2010] UKSC 42

BARONESS HALE

175. The focus both of my test and that of the majority is upon whether it is now fair to give effect to the agreement. The longer it is since the agreement was made, the more likely it is that later events will have overtaken it. Marriage is not only different from a commercial relationship in law, it is also different in fact. It is capable of influencing and changing every aspect of a couple's lives: where they live, how they live, who goes to work outside the home and what work they do, who works inside the home and how, their social lives and leisure pursuits, and how they manage their property and finances. A couple may think that their futures are all mapped out ahead of them when they get married but many things may happen to push them off course – misfortunes such as redundancy, bankruptcy, illness, disability, obligations to other family members and especially to children, but also unexpected opportunities and unexplored avenues. The couple are bound together in more than a business relationship, so of course they modify their plans and often compromise their individual best interests to accommodate these new events. They may have no choice if their marriage is to survive. There may be people who enter marriage in the belief that it will not endure, but for most people the hope and the belief is that it will. There is also a public interest in the stability of marriage. Marriage and relationship breakdown can have many damaging effects for the parties, their children and other members of their families, and also for society as a whole. So there is also a public interest in encouraging the parties to make adjustments to their roles and life-styles for the sake of their relationship and the welfare of their families.

176. All of this means that it is difficult, if not impossible, to predict at the outset what the circumstances will be when the marriage ends. It is even more difficult to predict what the fair outcome of the couple's financial relationship will be...

Protecting need and compensation over equal sharing

Perhaps the most significant part of the Court's decision, following on from these concerns, is that if one party is left in a 'predicament of real need,' while the other enjoys a sufficiency or more' at the end of the marriage, a court may readily find an agreement making no provision for that party to be unfair; likewise where one spouse's devotion to the domestic sphere freed the other to accumulate wealth: there too allowing the breadwinner to keep all is likely to be viewed as unfair. In those circumstances, provision based on need and/or compensation is likely to be ordered, notwithstanding any agreement. But it is less likely that provision based on equal sharing will be ordered. Indeed, where neither party is in need on divorce (so that needs-based provision would not be warranted in any event), it may well be fair to make no provision at all.[409] In short: while a nuptial agreement may readily displace the equal sharing principle, provision for needs (and compensation) on divorce appears to constitute an irreducible core obligation of marriage, such that parties would be well-advised to make provision for each other's needs in order for their agreement to be regarded as fair. This conclusion therefore places significant weight on an issue which, as we discussed at 7.5.2 above, English law has yet satisfactorily to address: when does a former spouse come under an obligation to meet the other's needs, and how extensive (in terms of quantum and duration) is that obligation?

---

[409] Ibid., [81]–[82], and [178].

The Supreme Court's principles applied in practice

What did all this mean for Radmacher and Granatino? The German wife, Ms Radmacher, and French husband, Mr Granatino, were married for eight years and had two children, who were to split their time between the parents following divorce. She was fabulously wealthy with family money. The parties had a pre-nuptial agreement—concluded in Germany and subject to German law—which barred the husband from bringing any claim for financial provision on divorce and made no alternative provision for him. This agreement would have been enforced by both German and French courts. He had been a merchant banker on their marriage, but later gave up that career to pursue a rather more low-paid academic career as a scientist.

Was the agreement tainted from the outset? No. The parties had clearly intended that the agreement would be legally binding. True, they had used the services of a single notary and the husband had not taken the opportunity available to him to obtain independent advice; nor had he received full disclosure of his wife's wealth, or even a full translation of the agreement he was signing. However, it was quite clear that he clearly understood the essence of the agreement: the absence of legal advice and so on did not affect his decision to enter into the agreement.[410]

Given the circumstances at the time of divorce, would it nevertheless be unfair to hold the parties to the agreement? In the view of the majority: it was fair to hold them to the agreement to the extent that no provision was to be made for the husband in his own right once the children had reached independence. The wife had discharged the husband's substantial debts and the Court of Appeal had ordered ample provision for the benefit of the children from which the husband would indirectly benefit (e.g. through the provision of accommodation and substantial maintenance including a carer allowance) for the duration of the children's minority. But the husband had an earning capacity as a scientist; there was no evidence that he would at any point struggle to meet his own needs; nor was there any basis, in the majority's view, for provision based on compensation where his decision to take a cut in earnings by moving out of banking and into scientific research was 'not motivated by the demands of his family, but reflected his own preference'.[411] As for sharing, in recognition of the agreement and the fact that the wife's wealth was 'non-matrimonial property' (having been acquired prior to the marriage and/or from family sources), the husband had from the outset formulated his claim in terms of needs only. And the Court was content that it would be fair to hold him to his agreement to have no share in his wife's property—indeed, it would be unfair to depart from that agreement.[412]

Applying the *Radmacher* approach to earlier pre-nuptial agreement cases, it can be concluded that the case does not mark a radical departure from what has long been a developing practice of giving substantial—even decisive—weight to pre-nuptial agreements in appropriate circumstances.[413] Thus, in *Crossley v Crossley*, where the parties were independently wealthy, middle-aged divorcees who were married only for a very short period and were economically unaffected by the marriage, the Supreme Court's approach readily justifies the view that the parties should be held to their agreement that in the event of divorce each would simply go their separate ways without any claim against each other, and that it was therefore appropriate to curtail the evidence-gathering procedures that would be otherwise

---

410 Ibid., [114]–[117], upholding the Court of Appeal decision: see Miles (2009).
411 Ibid., [118]–[121]. Cf Baroness Hale, dissenting, [192]–[195].
412 Ibid., [123].
413 See also the similar outcome achieved in the post-nuptial context in *MacLeod* [2008] UKPC 64.

be required on ancillary relief cases.[414] By contrast, in *M v M (Prenuptial agreement)*[415] and *K v K (Ancillary Relief: Prenuptial Agreement)*[416] we see examples of the courts ordering essentially needs-only provision in the face of a less generous pre-nuptial agreement (which in *M v M* was tainted by improper pressure on the wife to sign the agreement) following a short marriage which had produced a child where the mother's economic position would be impaired by child-care responsibilities for some time.

7.7.5 REFORM?

Despite the decision of the Supreme Court in *Radmacher v Granatino*, it seems likely that calls for statutory reform will remain, and were made loudly by Baroness Hale in *Radmacher* itself.[417] Since some key aspects of the Supreme Court's decision may be regarded as obiter, particularly in relation to the status and treatment of post-nuptial agreements, it would be desirable to have a comprehensive, definitive statutory regime for all categories of agreement between spouses and civil partners. Some may wish to take the law a step further in favour of party autonomy and certainty: to free parties from the full width of the MCA 1973 discretion by replacing the *Hyman/Radmacher* framework with a statutory scheme under which agreements are prima facie binding and must formally be set aside before the court can exercise its wide s 25 discretion. In any event, Baroness Hale argues, it would be desirable for the law to be the subject of public consultation and parliamentary debate. Early in 2011, the Law Commission published a consultation paper on 'marital property agreements', covering pre-nuptial, post-nuptial, and separation agreements.

ONLINE RESOURCE CENTRE

Materials relating to the Commission's consultation paper will be found on the Online Resource Centre.

What might reform entail?

Any statutory scheme for enforceable marital property agreements may be expected to consist of at least two central features designed to deal, in particular, with concerns about unequal bargaining power in the private sphere[418] and changes of circumstance: (i) formality requirements necessary to give the agreement prima facie binding force which precludes any resort to the MCA 1973 regime, thus displacing the paternalistic *Hyman* rule that the courts must retain unfettered jurisdiction to grant ancillary relief;[419] (ii) a jurisdiction to set such agreements aside in certain circumstances so as then to permit the courts to grant ancillary relief in the normal way. The key questions then are what formalities should be prescribed and how high or low the hurdle for setting agreements aside should be set.

---

414 [2007] EWCA Civ 1491.
415 [2002] 1 FLR 654.
416 [2003] 1 FLR 120. Both cases are discussed in the first edition, pp 553–4.
417 [2010] UKSC 42, [133]–[135].
418 McLellan (1996).
419 See p 489.

The majority in *Radmacher* observed that if you are to have a scheme under which agreements are prima facie binding, it will be necessary to have 'black and white rules' regarding formalities in order to provide some prima facie certainty about an agreement's status.[420] What sort of formalities might be required? At the very least, the law should require that agreements be in writing, signed, and perhaps witnessed. But should both parties be required (at some cost) to obtain full disclosure from the other party and independent legal advice? Or should it be enough that each had reasonable opportunity to obtain either or both of these?[421] Should agreements have to have been made outside a defined period before the wedding (say, at least one month earlier) to try to minimize the pressure arising from the impending wedding? Such requirements are intended to protect the parties' interests and to reduce potential for vitiating circumstances such as undue influence to arise.

As to setting agreements aside, the jurisdictional bar should not be set so low as to render the freedom to make a binding agreement illusory. It can also be argued that the tougher the formalities for entering into such agreements, the higher should be the hurdle for setting them aside: parties who have gone to that much trouble (and expense) to make a binding agreement should not be left too vulnerable to having the agreement subsequently overridden. The general law would obviously apply, allowing agreements to be set aside where vitiated from the outset by a flaw such as fraud, duress, mistake, or undue influence—but should the statute identify any other initial vitiating factors beyond contract law? And then what about subsequent change of circumstance? As we have seen, this is a particular concern with pre-nuptial agreements and early post-nuptial agreements where a substantial amount of time—and life events—may have occurred between the date of the agreement and the date on which one party seeks to enforce it. Should any change of circumstance have to have been unforeseeable at the time agreement was reached before it can give grounds to set the agreement aside? Government proposals in 1999[422] were widely criticized for suggesting that agreements should be set aside wherever a child had been born since the agreement, even if that eventuality had been contemplated and catered for by the agreement.[423] Should it additionally have to be shown that 'significant' or 'manifest injustice' (or 'unfairness') would arise were the agreement to be enforced, 'injustice' for these purposes not arising merely because the judge would have ordered provision different from that agreed?[424] Is Lord Mance right to suggest that it makes no difference whether we ask 'would it be fair to uphold the agreement' or 'would it be unfair to uphold the agreement', or is the difference of emphasis significant and, if so, which formula is to be preferred? The more expansive the grounds for setting aside, the better the economic protection of arguably weaker parties, but the worse the promotion of certainty and party autonomy, and the less fair for the party who had in good faith relied on the enforceability of the agreement.

Finally, reform will have to consider the desirability of the Supreme Court's privileging of need- and compensation-based relief: is it right that the obligation (whatever its scope may be) to relieve one spouse from a 'predicament of real need' (just how needy is that?) should essentially be incapable of compromise by private agreement where the other party is able to

---

420 [2010] UKSC 42, [69].

421 Cf the functional approach to formalities taken in *Radmacher v Granatino*, discussed by Miles (2009). See also Hitchings' findings on practice pre-*Radmacher* (2009b).

422 HO (1999).

423 Cf *M v M (pre-nuptial agreement)* [2002] 1 FLR 654; *K v K (Ancillary Relief: Prenuptial Agreement)* [2003] 1 FLR 120.

424 Cf [2010] UKSC 42, [75]. For criticism, see George, Harris, and Herring (2009), 934–5. For examples of reform recommendations see Resolution (2010); Law Com (2007), Part 5 (in relation to cohabitants, but similar issues arise); HO (1999), adopted in *Radmacher v Granatino* at first instance: [2008] EWHC 1532.

meet the need in question and would, absent the agreement, be regarded as liable to meet it? Or should spouses and civil partners be entirely free to agree their own terms, whatever the impact on the parties (if not on their children) might be?

Arguments for and against greater enforceability

Giving marital property agreements greater legal force could be one way of increasing certainty for couples, and possibly reducing costs on divorce.[425] Following *Miller; McFarlane*'s endorsement of equal sharing, wealthy individuals are said to have become more anxious to protect existing and future assets via pre-nuptial agreements. It is even suggested that, if they cannot rely on a pre-nuptial agreement, some individuals might not marry at all.[426] Pre-nuptial agreements may also be popular amongst those who have experienced divorce and are willing to remarry only if their assets are protected, perhaps for the benefit of children from the earlier relationship. The experience of a previous hostile divorce may also make parties keen to minimize potential conflict by reaching prior agreement.[427] Enforcing private agreements may also recognize and promote diversity within marriage and civil partnership, permitting couples to make whatever arrangements suit them and their vision of marital life.[428] As the facts of *Radmacher* show, it may also better accommodate the challenges raised by globalization and the growing numbers of foreign couples living and then divorcing in England and Wales who had concluded an agreement which would be binding in their home jurisdiction.[429]

Most fundamentally, prior to *Radmacher*, it was argued that English law concerning marital agreements was unduly paternalistic and anachronistic, leaving English law out of line internationally.[430] Insofar as all agreements are still subject to the *Hyman* rule, this argument might still be made. When *Hyman v Hyman* was decided in 1929,[431] wives were still six years away from acquiring full legal capacity, so still in a legally inferior position.[432] The liberal principles which underpinned wives' legal emancipation should arguably lead us to accept that spouses and now civl partners, like other competent adults, should be free to agree economic arrangements. The Court of Appeal in *Radmacher*, endorsed by the Supreme Court, strongly emphasized autonomy, expressing concern about the 'very basis' of the law regarding pre-nuptial agreements:[433]

Radmacher v Granatino [2009] EWCA Civ 649

WILSON LJ:

127....Its usually unspoken premise seems to be an assumption that, prior to marriage, one of the parties, in particular the woman, is, by reason of heightened emotion and an

---

[425] Cf George, Harris, and Herring (2009).
[426] Cf HO (1998), para 4.22. Baroness Hale suggested that systematic research is needed on this issue; *MacLeod v MacLeod* [2008] UKPC 64, [33]; but anecdotal evidence is strong. See also Probert (2009c), 330.
[427] Cf the range of clients reported in Hitching's study (2009b).
[428] Shultz (1982).
[429] *Charman v Charman* [2007] EWCA Civ 503, [124]; e.g. *Radmacher v Granatino* [2009] EWCA Civ 649; see Miles (2009).
[430] E.g. Australia, Canada, New Zealand, Scotland, the US, and many European jurisdictions: Scherpe (2007a) and Scherpe (2011).
[431] [1929] AC 601.
[432] Cretney (1999), 359, pending the Law Reform (Married Women and Tortfeasors) Act 1935: see 3.3.
[433] See Thorpe LJ at [27] and Rix LJ at [83].

intensity of desire to marry, likely to be so blindly trusting of the other as to be unduly susceptible to the other's demands even if unreasonable. No doubt in its application to each case
the law must guard against the possible infection of a contract by one party's exploitation of
the susceptibility of the other. But, as a general assumption, the premise is patronising, in
particular to woman; and I would prefer the starting-point to be for both parties to be required
to accept the consequences of whatever they have freely and knowingly agreed.

English law's ambivalence about private agreements might be a remnant of the old laws
of divorce, when 'the fact that the parties had come to an agreement between themselves
was ... regarded not as a matter for satisfaction but rather as something which should
arouse the court's vigilance',[434] if not suspicion that the divorce might be collusive.[435] But
this sits awkwardly alongside contemporary encouragement to divorcing parties to settle
their affairs amicably, the promotion of voluntary (albeit non-binding) agreements for child
support,[436] and the possibility of divorce by consent after two years' separation. Concerns
that agreements might inappropriately transfer the burden of maintaining an ex-spouse on
the state could be dealt with by appropriate social security laws or, as *Radmacher* appears to
do, by limiting the force of agreements in cases of real need.[437] Again, as *Radmacher* shows,
children's interests can be protected in part by ensuring that their interests cannot be compromised by the parents' agreement.

But the arguments are not all one way, as it evident from the disagreement between
Baroness Hale, the only family judge on the Supreme Court panel in *Radmacher*, and her
family law colleagues in the Court of Appeal. Baroness Hale summarized some of the different views that might be taken, in a way that perhaps makes her own view evident:

Radmacher v Granatino [2010] UKSC 42

BARONESS HALE:

135. ...Some may regard freedom of contract as the prevailing principle in all circumstances; others may regard that as a 19th century concept which has since been severely
modified, particularly in the case of continuing relationships typically (though not invariably)
characterised by imbalance of bargaining power (such as landlord and tenant, employer and
employee). Some may regard people who are about to marry as in all respects fully autonomous beings; others may wonder whether people who are typically (although not invariably)
in love can be expected to make rational choices in the same way that businessmen can.
Some may regard the recognition of these factual differences as patronising or paternalistic;
others may regard them as sensible or realistic. Some may think that to accord a greater
legal status to these agreements will produce greater certainty and lesser costs should the
couple divorce; others may question whether this will in fact be achieved, save at the price of
inflexibility and injustice. Some may believe that giving greater force to marital agreements
will encourage more people to marry; others may wonder whether they will encourage more
people to divorce. Perhaps above all, some may think it permissible to contract out of the
guiding principles of equality and non-discrimination within marriage; others may think this a
retrograde step likely only to benefit the strong at the expense of the weak.

---

[434] Cretney and Masson (1990), 445.
[435] Cretney (2003a), 187–8.
[436] See chapter 6.
[437] Cretney (1999), 358; *MacLeod v MacLeod* [2008] UKPC 64, [41].

As she goes on to observe, that weaker party will very often be the woman.

The views of the family law profession as a whole were last measured before *White v White* was decided.[438] Judicial opinions, reported by Wilson J (as he then was) were mixed:

N. Wilson, 'Response of the Judges of the Family Division to Government Proposals...', (1999) 29 *Family Law* 159, 162–3

We have reservations about whether the law should strive to encourage pre-nuptial agreements. We all still believe strongly in the institution of marriage as a source of personal and social stability and wonder whether the pre-nuptial agreement conditions the couple to the failure of their marriage and so helps to precipitate it. This deserves research. Some of us also feel that the institution of marriage is devalued if, while entering it, a couple can elect to sever some of its most important, if contingent, legal effects.[439] Others of us consider, hesitantly, that marriage is for mankind, not vice versa, and that, subject to obvious limits, adults should be allowed to cast their relationships in their own way. We are at one that this is profoundly difficult terrain....

While the majority favoured only the minor development of adding agreements to the s 25(2) checklist, the minority were more bold:

Despite our unanimous lack of enthusiasm for the pre-nuptial agreement, the provisional view of the minority is that where there is an agreement, whether pre- or post-nuptial, which satisfies the elementary requirements, the shape of the law should be that it be enforced "unless...". The minority feels that the current law of ancillary relief has inherited a paternalistic strain, rather too hostile to contract (formerly collusion) and in this respect rather too jealous of its own discretion, for the protection, in effect, of the downtrodden wife, and that, while she still exists, she may no longer be apt as a governing stereotype; that even in *Edgar*, ... progressive though it was, the dicta too readily deprived agreements of weight, for example in their reference to bad legal advice; and that the overall balance needs gentle redress but, by means of the "unless" clause, making enforcement subject to the interests of the child and to a residual discretion to depart in the plain case.

Wilson LJ now firmly associates himself with the view that all classes of agreement should be 'presumptively dispositive'.[440]

Some proponents of agreements consider that negotiating one's own marriage contract could, at best, 'foster the norms of commitment, reciprocity and openness in personal relationships, norms which are integral to egalitarian and democratic relationships'.[441] But the experience could, at first sight at least, be less beneficial:

B. Fehlberg and B. Smyth, 'Binding Pre-Nuptial Agreements in Australia: the First Year', (2002) 16 *International Journal of Law, Policy and the Family* 127, 135

According to family lawyers, one of the major factors inhibiting entry into agreement is difficulty experienced at a personal level between couples during the process of negotiating

---

438 See Bridge (2001), 31–2.
439 See also [2010] UKSC 42, [132].
440 *Radmacher v Granatino* [2009] EWCA Civ 649, [128].
441 Kingdom (2000), 24. See also Rix LJ, *Radmacher* [2009] EWCA Civ 649, [73].

agreements. Relationship tension reportedly increased when the parties and their legal representatives began formal negotiations regarding the terms of the agreement. Family lawyers, mindful of the agreement's central purpose of offering certainty for the future, were evidently keen to sort out the fine details and to 'reality test' agreements (by asking 'what if?' questions). Yet this process was often confronting for clients as they sat with their beloved and their respective legal representatives around the negotiating table. One practitioner, for example, said that the three clients who had contacted her regarding entry into a pre-nuptial agreement had not gone ahead and entered an agreement due to 'difficulties in negotiation leading to abandonment of the agreement, and sometimes of the relationship'.

But might parties driven to separate by that experience in fact have had short-lived marriages in any event, owing to fundamental disagreements about financial issues? Would greater enforceability provide increased certainty and so reduce litigation? Perhaps not. Experience of other jurisdictions suggests that making pre-nuptial agreements binding simply shifts, rather than eliminates, disputes on divorce. Rather than argue about what the settlement should be, parties instead argue (first) about whether the pre-nuptial agreement is enforceable and about its interpretation.[442] Indeed, since English courts already give considerable weight to pre-nuptial agreements in certain circumstances which look not dissimilar from the sort of situations in which they would be enforced under a statutory scheme, it must be asked whether reform would make much difference in practice.[443]

As Baroness Hale highlighted in *Radmacher*, there are also concerns about gender imbalance: would agreements be used principally by men, pushing disadvantageous deals on economically vulnerable women? While women are more often in the more vulnerable economic position on divorce, it has been suggested that (at least some) women stand to benefit from pre-nuptial agreements, in particular older women with assets to protect, and those for whom formally agreed entitlements would give a sense of security.[444] Of course, as cases such as *Radmacher v Granatino* show, some women are the economically dominant party. The issue is therefore perhaps better understood in simple terms of economic vulnerability and power imbalance rather than gender.

What is certain is that there is plenty for the Law Commission to grapple with as it works on its current project.

7.8 REMEDIES ON OTHER TYPES OF FAMILY RELATIONSHIP BREAKDOWN

While spouses and civil partners have access to special statutory financial remedies on divorce, where other family relationships break down—for example, between cohabitants, blood relatives, platonic home sharers—the parties must use a patchwork of common law and statutory rights and remedies. These do not provide a coherent substantive or procedural response to the financial and property-related problems associated with family breakdown.[445]

---

[442] See sources cited by Fehlberg and Smyth (2002), 128–9; George, Harris, and Herring (2009).
[443] Scherpe (2007a).
[444] But possibly not: Fehlberg and Smyth (2002), 134; Miller (2003), 131.
[445] For detailed examination and criticisms of the law in the context of cohabitation, see Law Com (2006), Parts 3 and 4.

7.8.1 THE GENERAL LAW APPLIES

The starting point is that the general law determines ownership and other rights in relation to property: the parties' shared home, its contents, other chattels, bank accounts. The courts have no powers to adjust the parties' property rights, and neither party can be ordered to make periodical payments to the other.[446] Each party will leave with what the general law says he or she owns, and nothing more. It is in the context of relationship breakdown that the criticisms made of that law have most urgency.[447] Readers should refer to the discussion and criticism of *Stack v Dowden*, *Fowler v Barron*, *James v Thomas*, and *Kernott v Jones* in chapter 3.

7.8.2 REMEDIES FOR THE BENEFIT OF CHILDREN

The most substantial statutory remedies exist for the benefit of any children of the parties under the CSA 1991 and the Children Act 1989 (CA 1989), Sch 1.[448] These remedies potentially offer the primary carer of the children indirect benefit: that party's household income may be increased by receipt of child support; the provision of accommodation for the benefit of such children clearly benefits the primary carers. However, orders under the CA 1989 are relatively unusual outside the big money context, and various limitations on the court's powers, not least its inability to adjust the capital entitlements of the adult parties or order sale, may inhibit their usefulness. Moreover, since these remedies offer protection ordinarily only during the children's minority, any indirect benefit obtained by the primary carer ceases with the order. The CA 1989 does not apply where the children have left home, leaving the former primary carer, who may have been out of paid employment for years, with no remedy (direct or indirect) to address any ongoing economic vulnerability.[449]

7.8.3 DISPUTES REGARDING THE FORMER FAMILY HOME

Where the parties have shared a home, the most important issue on relationship breakdown is future occupation or sale of that property. The solution to this problem depends on: who owns or rents the property and whether it is solely or co-owned; the nature of the parties' relationship; and whether there are any children in whose favour an order might be made under the CA 1989, Sch 1. We address three categories of case:

(1) disputes between co-owners under the general law of trusts: Trusts of Land and Appointment of Trustees Act 1996 (TOLATA 1996);

(2) disputes between an owner and non-entitled applicant under the FLA 1996; and

(3) disputes between an owner and mere licensee under the general law.

We shall consider the interaction between the TOLATA 1996 and applications under the CA 1989, Sch 1 in relation to (1). However, both (2) and (3) must also be read subject to the important qualification that wherever the applicant has a dependent child of the respondent

---

[446] *Windeler v Whitehall* [1990] 2 FLR 505. But note the remedy of equitable accounting discussed on the Online Resource Centre.

[447] See 3.4.7.

[448] See chapter 6.

[449] See Law Com (2006), paras 4.34–4.46.

living with him or her, Sch 1 to the CA 1989 may apply, providing greater indirect protection (if only for the duration of that child's minority) than the FLA 1996 or general law would allow. We also consider tenancy transfers.

Disputes between co-owners

Suppose two or more family members who co-own the home are in dispute about its continued occupation. One wishes to remain in the property while the other wishes to sell it and release his or her capital share.[450] Whether the parties are co-trustees at loggerheads, or sole-trustee and beneficial co-owner, an application to court may be required. There may be up to three applications.

Disputes in relation to the occupation and sale of land held on trust may be heard under the TOLATA 1996, s 14. The court is required by s 15(1) to have regard to the following factors in determining a dispute regarding sale under s 14:

(a) the intentions of the person or persons (if any) who created the trust,

(b) the purposes for which the property subject to the trust is held,

(c) the welfare of any minor who occupies or might reasonably be expected to occupy any land subject to the trust as his home, and

(d) the interests of any secured creditor of any beneficiary.

In considering who, if anyone, should be allowed to continue to occupy the property, the court is also directed by s 15(2) to have regard to the circumstances and wishes of each of the beneficiaries who is in principle entitled to occupy.[451]

The law of trusts aside, if the parties' relationship falls within the scope of the wide 'associated person' category,[452] disputes regarding occupation (though not sale) could be dealt with by an occupation order under the FLA 1996, s 33. Finally, if the parties have dependent children, an application may be made under CA 1989, Sch 1 for orders relating to the future occupation of the parties' home and transfer or settlement of other assets for the benefit of the children.[453] We have examined these already in chapter 4 (FLA 1996), and chapter 6 (CA 1989).

While competing claims under these Acts should be heard together,[454] their combination is not straightforward, either procedurally (the first is a civil matter, the other two family proceedings) or substantively (each conferring different powers to be exercised on different criteria). As such, they compare unfavourably with the 'one-stop-shop' of the MCA 1973/CPA 2004. The CA 1989 gives particular prominence to the needs of the children, and should be considered first in any combined TOLATA/CA case. Applications regarding the future residence of any children should ideally be determined by the same judge.[455] Where there are no children, the FLA 1996, tailored specifically for the family context, may be regarded as more appropriate than the TOLATA 1996 for dealing with what are essentially family

---

450 See generally Hopkins (2009).
451 See also s 15(3)–(4).
452 FLA 1996, s 62(3): see 4.5.1.
453 The courts only have limited jurisdiction to make periodical payments orders: see 6.5.2.
454 *W v W (Joinder of Trusts of Land Act and Children Act Applications)* [2003] EWCA Civ 924, [5].
455 Ibid., [15] and [17].

disputes, not simply disputes between two individuals who happen to co-own property. However, the TOLATA 1996 must be used to obtain a ruling on the timing of any sale.[456]

Despite the procedural maze, this legislation can provide outcomes regarding the family home not dissimilar to those achievable under the MCA 1973. In many cases, the main purpose of the trust[457] will have been to provide a family home with children. Even after the adults have separated, the trust's purpose may still be fulfilled by providing a home for the children. However, trusts law may produce outcomes unsuited to the realities of family life.[458] Arden LJ's recent approach to the TOLATA 1996, s 15 in a family case has been criticized for making unrealistic expectations about whether and how parties will articulate their intentions about co-owned family homes.[459] In *W v W*, an unmarried couple had purchased a home in joint names. They started a family and so extended the house to provide an extra bedroom. The relationship broke down. The father, with whom the two children were to live, wished to retain the home. The mother wanted an immediate sale.

W v W (Joinder of Trusts of Land Act and Children Act Applications)
[2003] EWCA Civ 924

ARDEN LJ:

22. . . . The [father] submits that the judge was entitled to have regard to the intention of the parents formed after the trusts of land was created. [Arden LJ set out TOLATA 1996, s 15(1), and decided that the intention referred to in para (a) must be held in common by all parties creating the trust.]

23. The question then remains whether the intention could include intention subsequently come to . . . I do not myself consider that this is the correct construction. Parliament has used the word "intention" which speaks naturally to the intentions of persons prior to the creation of the trust. If that were not its meaning, then it is not clear whether the court should be looking at the parties' intentions at the date of the hearing or at some other antecedent point in time and, if so, what date. If Parliament meant the present intention, it would have used some such word as "wishes" rather than the word "intention" which implies some statement or opinion as to the future. In all the circumstances, I consider that the [father's] submissions on the point of law on this point are not correct.

24. I turn now to the . . . point . . . that the judge had failed to deal with a submission by the father that there was an additional purpose come to after the property was purchased and the parties had been living there . . . namely to provide a home for the children. I would accept that, for the purposes of section 15(1)(b), purposes could have been formulated informally, but they must be the purposes subject to which the property is held. The purpose established at the outset of the trust which, on the judge's finding, did not include the provision of a home for children, could only change if both parties agreed. There was no evidence from which the judge could find that the mother agreed to the additional purpose spoken to by the father . . .

Such a narrow reading of the mother's probable intentions following the birth of her two children, and the suggestion that it may not be possible to form intentions after the initial

---

[456] *Chan v Leung* [2002] EWCA Civ 1075, [16]–[48].
[457] TOLATA 1996, s 15(1)(b).
[458] See 3.4.7 for similar criticism of implied trusts and proprietary estoppel.
[459] Gray and Gray (2009), at 7.5.98, n 1; Probert (2007a).

creation of the trust, poses difficulties for applications to postpone sale for the sake of children of the family under the TOLATA 1996, and appears to neglect the independent status afforded to children's interests by s 15(1)(c). In the event, the property was sold as the father could afford alternative accommodation with his share of the proceeds.

Section 15(1)(c) aside, the children's needs may self-evidently support a claim under the CA 1989, Sch 1. In *Re Evers' Trust*, the court applauded the fact that it could make orders under the trusts legislation, and now under the CA 1989, Sch 1, very similar in effect to matrimonial *Mesher* and *Martin* orders.[460] Sale can therefore be postponed and one party permitted to occupy to the exclusion of the other, for example, until the children leave home or reach a prescribed age,[461] or until the occupying party marries or cohabits with a third party, dies, or no longer requires the property.[462] The court can require the occupant to pay 'rent' to the excluded party.[463] But where the property is to be occupied by one party with the children, the parties' obligations to those children may make it inappropriate to make such an order.[464] The key *difference* between these cases and the matrimonial/civil partnership context is that here the court cannot adjust the parties' shares in the property. Those are fixed by the law of trusts. Any capital award made under CA 1989, Sch 1 will revert to the payer once the children are independent.[465]

Occupation orders under the FLA 1996

What if the party wishing to remain in occupation has no beneficial interest in the property or other relevant entitlement under the general law? Even an individual with no such right (a 'non-entitled' person) may be able to obtain an occupation order under the FLA 1996[466] (and if there are dependent children, under the CA 1989, Sch 1). However, 'non-entitled' applications can only be brought by current and former spouses, civil partners, and cohabitants. Other family members, such as relatives and unrelated home-sharers, are left to the general law governing licences. Moreover, the protection offered by the FLA 1996 to non-entitled cohabitants and former cohabitants is limited, in terms both of the basis on which the court makes its decision and the duration of any potential order.[467] It can at best provide a short-term solution to the accommodation needs of non-entitled applicants. Moreover, while the court can make ancillary orders for the payment of various outgoings in relation to property subject to an occupation order, it cannot use that power to provide maintenance for either party.[468]

Disputes between sole owner and licensee under the general law

A licensee only has a right to occupy insofar as the terms of the licence permit: the owner can terminate the licence on giving reasonable notice. The situation of bare licensees is illustrated by *Hannaford v Selby*. The Selbys were the parents of Mrs Hannaford. The Hannafords and

---

460 [1980] 1 WLR 1327, 1333.

461 *Parkes v Legal Aid Board* [1997] 1 WLR 1547.

462 Cf *Holman v Howes* [2007] EWCA Civ 877 where an estoppel had arisen in the occupant's favour.

463 TOLATA 1996, s 13, subject to s 15 factors.

464 *Stack v Dowden* [2005] EWCA Civ 857, [61]–[63]; cf [2007] UKHL 17, [94] and [155].

465 See p 402 above; *Norris v Hudson* [2005] EWHC 2934.

466 Note also FLA 1996, ss 35(11)–(12), 36(11)–(12): can apply as a non-entitled applicant without prejudice to subsequently claiming a beneficial interest.

467 FLA 1996, ss 36 and 38.

468 Ibid., s 40; Law Com (1992), para 4.41.

the Selbys had agreed to share the Hannafords' new home, together with the Hannafords' children. The Hannafords bought the property with the proceeds of sale of their own house and mortgage finance. The Selbys, who had given up their secure council house, made no contribution to the purchase price, but did contribute to household expenses and Mr Selby kept the family in vegetables from the garden. Unfortunately, the arrangement was unsuccessful. In response to the Hannafords' possession proceedings, brought in anticipation of their selling the house, the Selbys unsuccessfully attempted to assert a beneficial interest in the property. They would now be 'associated persons' for the purposes of the FLA 1996.[469] But since they were not entitled to occupy the property, and self-evidently not, vis à vis the Hannafords, current or former spouses, civil partners, or cohabitants, they would not be able to apply for an occupation order under the FLA 1996. However, it was held that as licensees they were entitled to 'reasonable notice':

Hannaford v Selby (1976) 239 EG 811, 813 (Ch Div)

GOULDING J:

[Counsel for the Hannafords] submitted that three factors should be mainly taken into account in determining a reasonable notice in the circumstances. First was the time required by the defendants to find new accommodation. As to that it was clear from the evidence that efforts had been made by the defendants...to find new accommodation without success...It was clear that in Ipswich it was not easy to find premises, particularly unfurnished premises, to rent. It was not unlikely that the defendants, in view of their age, would find it difficult or impossible to get a substantial mortgage. That aspect pointed to a generous allowance of time. The second matter...pointed the other way—the family atmosphere in the home. There was evidence that the health both of Mrs Selby and of the Hannaford children was put under some strain by the unsatisfactory position in the house. Therefore it would be in the interests of all parties, including the defendants themselves, to make the difficult period in which they remained as brief as possible. [The] third submission was that the court should remember the fact that the plaintiffs had contracted to sell the house and the completion date was the next day, April 30 [judgment was given on April 29]. Once that date was passed, the plaintiffs would be in peril if unable to perform their own contract of sale, and would also be in a position in which they would be unable to complete the purchase they had undertaken. It might be that others would suffer inconvenience and loss.

These last considerations did not weigh with [the judge] to any appreciable extent. The plaintiffs decided to sell the house as a means of putting pressure on the defendants and before the defendants had taken advice or their position had been fully clarified. The plaintiffs must take the matter as they found it. The most important consideration was a reasonable chance for the defendants to find alternative accommodation...[The judge] was of opinion that as at February 1 1976 [the date on which they knew they were required to leave] a reasonable time would have been six months. He would accordingly give the defendants until July 31 to leave.

In some cases (especially involving domestic violence), the owner may be able to secure the more immediate eviction of a licensee with an occupation order under the FLA 1996, s 33.

---

[469] Ibid., s 62(3); 4.5.1.

Rented homes

There is one exception to the basic proposition that the courts have no adjustive powers outside the MCA 1973 and the CPA 2004. Where cohabitants rented their home, the courts have the same powers under the FLA 1996 to order a transfer of that tenancy as they do between spouses and civil partners.[470] The power applies only between former cohabitants and not between other home-sharers. Jurisdiction arises when the parties 'cease to cohabit'.[471] The criteria to which the court must have regard in exercising its discretion are set out in the Act.[472] The party to whom the transfer is made may be required to compensate the other.[473] The landlord of the property has a right to be heard before any such order is made.[474] Since many private sector tenancies now offer limited security of tenure in any event, the practical benefit offered by Sch 7 may be limited.[475]

The occupation order regime of the FLA 1996 applies to rented property as it does to owner-occupied property,[476] so a sole or joint tenant may apply for an occupation order under s 33 and a non-entitled cohabitant under s 36. The general law of licences also applies.

7.8.4 PRIVATE ORDERING

Parties can create their own solution, whether by agreement in advance or on separation, and so avoid the problems that may otherwise be encountered in trying to use the general law to determine disputes following separation. Any two or more people can regulate the ownership of property via express declarations of trust; they can likewise be found to have a common intention to share the beneficial ownership for the purpose of a constructive trust.[477] However, question marks have dogged the legal enforceability of *contracts* making financial arrangements between cohabitants. The courts may hesitate to find an intention to create legal relations between parties to an on-going relationship, as contrasted with parties clearly dealing at arm's length following relationship breakdown.[478] Just as domestic contributions struggle to count as detrimental reliance for the purpose of the laws of implied trusts and estoppel, it may be hard to establish consideration by promising to undertake such tasks.[479] However, these problems can be overcome with an appropriately drafted deed.

But another factor has bedevilled contracts between cohabitants: a contract for which the performance of extra-marital sexual relations appears to form part of the consideration is void on public policy grounds. While that is not a problem for contracts made following separation (where it is clear that the provision being agreed is a consequence of the relationship, rather than a condition of it), it is potentially problematic for contracts made earlier.[480] However, it is widely accepted that a contract made between cohabitants governing their property and financial entitlements, whether during the relationship or following its future

---

470 Ibid., Sch 7.
471 Cf *Gully v Dix* [2004] EWCA Civ 139.
472 FLA 1996, Sch 7, para 5.
473 Ibid., para 10.
474 Ibid., para 14(1).
475 Note also problems regarding notice to quit joint periodic tenancies: Law Com (2006), para 3.61.
476 E.g. *Chalmers v Johns* [1999] 2 FCR 110.
477 See 3.4.1.
478 E.g. *Jones v Padavattan* [1969] 1 WLR 328, 332.
479 *Horrocks v Foray* [1976] 1 WLR 230, 239.
480 Probert (2004d), 459 and generally, for analysis of the old cases.

demise, will be upheld.[481] This view was reinforced from the unlikely source of a case involving a 'Swedish sex slave'. A negligence action was brought against solicitors in connection with the drafting of an agreement for a 'master/slave' relationship between two men which provided, inter alia, that the property of the 'slave' would be transferred absolutely to the 'master'. In the course of striking out the claim on the merits, the judge considered the agreement's validity. Was it void because 'meretricious'? This agreement was, but others—simply governing cohabitants' property rights—could be valid. In considering the 'unlawfulness' of cohabitants' sexual relationship, the judge referred to Tony Honoré's book, *Sex Law*:

Sutton v Mischon de Reya and another [2003] EWHC 3166, [2004] 3 FCR 142

HART J:

[22]...'Whatever the reason, and however stable the relation, sexual intercourse between an unmarried couple is "unlawful" though it is not in general a crime...A contract for which the whole or part of the consideration is sexual intercourse (or any other sexual relation) outside marriage is void, as is a contract which tends to promote unlawful sexual intercourse. So, if Jack agrees to support Jill to whom he is not married on condition that she keeps house for him and that they have sexual intercourse, the whole agreement is void even if they mean it to be a legally binding one. It makes no difference that the agreement to have sex is understood rather than expressed.'

But, as [Honoré] went on to point out, that analysis does not prevent the cohabitors from entering into perfectly valid legal relations concerning their mutual property rights, or even (he suggests) as to other ancillary matters such as how they will divide up the work. Such a contract will not be a contract of cohabitation but a contract between cohabitors. He suggested that there was no reason why such a contract should not be upheld even though its tendency in fact might be to encourage the continuation of the "unlawful" sexual relationship.

[23] If that is the right distinction to draw (ie a distinction between a contract *for* sexual relations outside marriage and a contract *between* persons who are cohabiting in a relationship which involves such sexual relations), it is not, in my judgment, difficult even for a moron in a hurry...to see on which side of the line the cohabitation deed in this case falls. It was not a property contract between two people whose sexual relationship involved them in cohabitation. It was itself an attempt to express the sexual relationship in the property relations contained in the contract (or, as [counsel for the claimant] himself put it, the property relation "sprang from" the desire to give the sexual role-play verisimilitude). It was an attempt to reify an unlawful ideal.

While the remarks of Hart J are welcome, there is still no contemporary decision upholding a contract between cohabitants.[482] The Law Commission recommended that clarifying legislation would be welcome, for the avoidance of doubt.[483] Since these contracts do not displace any special statutory remedies akin to the MCA 1973, no *Hyman* point arises.[484]

However, it is questionable how many couples do or, if the law were clarified, would regulate their affairs by contract:

---

481 E.g. Masson, Bailey-Harris, and Probert (2008), 5-007; Wood, Lush, and Bishop (2005).
482 Though note contractual licence cases such as *Tanner v Tanner* [1975] 1 WLR 1346, *Chandler v Kerley* [1978] 1 WLR 693 involving 'mistresses' set up in a home by their partners.
483 Law Com (2007), para 8.25.
484 Cf 7.7 above.

R. Probert, 'Sutton v Mishcon de Reya and Gawor & Co—Cohabitation contracts and Swedish sex slaves', (2004d) 16 *Child and Family Law Quarterly* 453, 461–2

In a study by Lewis [(1999)], only one-quarter of respondents agreed with the statement that 'people who are going to live together or get married should write down beforehand how they will divide their finances in case they split up'. In the accompanying qualitative study, 20 of the 73 respondents were in favour of contracts: those opposed suggested that contracts were 'too cold', 'defeatist', and inappropriate in view of the way that relationships change over time and demand flexibility. Barlow and James [(2004)] have suggested that their more recent research suggests greater enthusiasm for a contractual solution. Certainly, their respondents were positive about the idea of a partnership register . . . but such a scheme confers status as well as regulating the rights of the parties, and may be more attractive for that reason. In any case, their enthusiasm was not matched by formal arrangements. The number who actually enter into a contract is likely to be considerably smaller than those who are willing to contemplate one in theory: first, both parties must agree in theory that a contract is a good idea, secondly, they must agree on what the terms of the contract are to be, and thirdly, they must actually get round to entering into such a contract. The failure of couples thus to regulate their lives is well documented.

7.8.5 NEW STATUTORY REMEDIES FOR COHABITANTS?

If a cohabiting relationship ends on the death of one of the parties, the survivor can seek financial provision under the Inheritance (Provision for Family and Dependants) Act 1975. There is no equivalent statutory scheme of financial relief on separation. Several other jurisdictions, including Scotland[485] and Ireland,[486] now have such remedies.[487] The Law Commission undertook a project in this area from 2005–7, initiated owing to concerns that the current law produces what many regard as unfair results, particularly at the end of long-term relationships and those in which the couple had a child.[488]

Reform of the law relating to cohabitation provokes strong responses.[489] The first question is whether the law should be reformed at all, and if so, in which cases. This is a large question of social policy, ultimately to be answered by Parliament. But if the answer is 'yes', then the same questions that surround debates of ancillary relief arise. On what basis should remedies be provided? Should the law of ancillary relief simply be extended to cohabitants, or should some other basis be found, and, if so, what basis? Should the remedies be rule-based, discretionary, or structured by statutory principles? Should binding private ordering be permitted?

For many, the idea that cohabitants should have access to statutory remedies on relationship breakdown is unacceptable. Rather than giving cohabitants the remedies that many mistakenly believe they already have,[490] the state should endeavour to educate the public about the substantial legal differences between marriage and civil partnership on the one hand, and cohabitation on the other.[491] Then, it is argued, those who continue to cohabit

---

485 Family Law (Scotland) Act 2006.
486 Civil Partnership and Certain Rights and Obligations of Cohabitants Act 2010.
487 See Law Com (2006), Appendix C.
488 See Arthur et al (2002).
489 Cf the history of the Family Violence and Domestic Homes Bill 1995, which preceded the FLA 1996: Hale (2004), 419 and see 2.8.2.
490 See the common law marriage myth: 2.8.2.
491 See the Living Together Campaign.

can confidently be said to have rejected marriage, and it would be unjustifiable to impose on them rights and duties that they have consciously rejected.[492] Those who wish to do so, it is said, can make their own arrangements via contract. Other opponents of reform fear that any legal recognition of cohabitation would undermine the institution of marriage, arguing that provision of legal recognition outside marriage will remove an incentive to marry.[493]

At the opposite end of the debate are those who argue that cohabitants should be brought within the MCA 1973. The economic vulnerability to which many cohabitants and their children are exposed on separation is no different from that encountered by divorcing spouses. These commentators regard the flexible MCA regime as the best tool to deal with these practical problems, enabling the courts to differentiate those short-term, childless relationships at the end of which no remedy is called for, from longer-term, more economically interdependent partnerships which merit relief. It is argued that this would bring the law into line with people's expectations and social practices.[494]

The Law Commission recommended a middle path, seeking to respect the autonomy of those couples who wish to keep the law out of their relationships, whilst providing protection to those left economically vulnerable on separation as a result of their contributions to the relationship.[495] The key aspects of the recommendations for remedies on separation[496] were as follows:

- A new statutory scheme should provide financial relief between 'eligible' cohabitants, without requiring the parties to have 'opted in' by prior registration or agreement.

- Cohabitants would be 'eligible' to apply for financial relief under a new scheme if they had:

  - been living as a couple in a joint household; and had either

  - had a child together (born during, before, or following their cohabitation) or

  - had lived together for a minimum duration, which should be set by statute somewhere within a range between two and five years.[497]

- Couples should be able to 'opt out' of the scheme and make their own binding arrangements at any time.

  - Such agreements would be enforceable provided they were in writing, signed by the parties, and made clear the parties' intention to disapply the statute. Independent legal advice would not be a precondition to the enforceability of an opt-out agreement.

  - The court should be entitled to set aside an otherwise binding opt-out agreement if its enforcement would cause manifest unfairness given circumstances at the time the agreement was made or a change of circumstances by the time it came to be enforced which had not been foreseen when the agreement was made.

- Where a couple were 'eligible' and there was no binding opt-out agreement, the courts should have a discretion to grant the same types of orders as under the MCA 1973, save

---

[492] E.g. Deech (1980b).
[493] E.g. generally, Morgan (2000). For evaluation of these arguments, see Law Com (2006), Part 5.
[494] E.g. Barlow et al (2005), Bailey-Harris (1996).
[495] Law Com (2007).
[496] The project also considered remedies on death: ibid., Part 6.
[497] Separate recommendations were made regarding eligibility where a couple have a child living with them who is not in law the child of both of them.

that periodical payments orders should only be available in respect of future child-care costs.

- Those orders should be granted to provide relief on a basis different from that applying between spouses on divorce.[498] The exercise of the court's discretion should be focused on addressing the economic impact of contributions arising from the parties' cohabiting relationship and made by the applicant to the parties' shared lives or to the welfare of members of their families.

- Specifically, an applicant would have to prove that following separation:

  - the respondent had a retained benefit (in the form of capital, income, or earning capacity acquired, retained, or enhanced) or that

  - the applicant had an economic disadvantage (in the form of lost future earnings; a diminution in current savings (including pension) as a result of expenditure or as a result of earnings lost during the relationship; or the future cost of paid child-care.

- Key examples of 'retained benefit' claims include those based on financial contributions to the acquisition of property held in the other's name or increasing the value of the other's property by physical labour such as building and decoration works. Economic disadvantage claims would be principally be brought by applicants whose earning capacity had been impaired as a result of giving up paid employment during the relationship in order to care for children of the family or other dependant relatives.[499]

The Law Commission's recommendations were met with various criticisms. Some opponents disagreed with the basic policy, whether wanting cohabitants to be subject to the same law as spouses; opposing *any* reform; or promoting alternative schemes. Other commentators criticized various aspects of the recommended scheme, expressing concern in particular about complexity and problems that might be encountered attempting to prove and quantify claims under it.[500] The Labour Government announced that it would defer any final decision pending research into the costs and efficacy of recent reform in Scotland introducing similar remedies between cohabitants in the Family Law (Scotland) Act 2006. This announcement was met with disappointment amongst the many organizations, such as Resolution, which have been campaigning for years for fairer outcomes between cohabitants on separation. Lord Lester and Mary Creagh MP, in conjunction with Resolution, promoted Bills to introduce new remedies (on a rather different basis from the Law Commission's recommendations), but both ran out of parliamentary time.[501] Research into the first three years' operation of the Scottish provisions has now been published.[502] Meanwhile, public attitudes appear strongly to support financial remedies between cohabitants in certain circumstances.[503]

Several commentators have argued that debates about remedies for cohabitants have been distorted by a focus on the formal status rather than functions of relationships, and so on the perceived need to give cohabitant-applicants 'less' than an equivalent divorce-applicant. This, combined with the equal sharing principle's emphasis of the marriage partnership (to a

---

[498] Appendix C to the Report explains the Commission's reasons for rejecting alternative schemes, including the MCA 1973.

[499] Appendix B to the Report illustrates the operation of the recommended scheme with examples.

[500] Probert (2007b), (2009d); Douglas, Pearce, and Woodward (2008).

[501] Cohabitation Bill [HL] (2008–9); for criticism, see Probert (2009d).

[502] Wasoff, Miles, and Mordaunt (2010).

[503] Barlow et al (2008).

large extent regardless of the parties' actual contributions), leaves individuals in function-ally similar circumstances being treated very differently:[504]

L. Glennon, 'The limitations of equality discourses on the contours of intimate obligations', in J. Wallbank, S.Choudhry, and J. Herring (eds), *Rights, Gender and Family Law* (Abingdon: Routledge, 2010), 197–8

The result is that familial caregiving is not considered as a valued activity in its own right, but is conceptualised through the lens of the relationship form in which it takes place. As such, it can be said that these mutually informing equality discourses [about the recognition of non-traditional family forms and about non-discrimination between breadwinner and home-maker], whilst having transformative potential, have failed to generate a root and branch approach to family law development which would strip back the assumptions upon which current norms are based and encourage a deeper connection between the functions which a family (family members) perform(s) and the obligations to which it (they) are subjected.

By contrast, a preferable approach to the construction of legal obligations between adults would de-emphasise relationship form and encourage a more direct consideration of rela-tionship functions. In this way, the focus on actual interdependencies, such as those arising through shared parenthood, would encourage a more direct and positive value to be placed on familial caregiving. It would also allow more accurate demarcations to replace the current bright line distinctions drawn between the married and unmarried which prevents a proper evaluation of the mutual dependencies which can arise in couple-based relationships of vary-ing forms. Such an approach . . . would help to bring legal ideology into line with the emerging social view, revealed in the recent British Social Attitudes Report, that 'most people seem to place the emphasis on successfully 'doing' family in practice, whatever situation people find themselves in, rather than on the supposed functionality of different family forms'.

Indeed, viewed in these terms, cohabitants are not the only candidates for remedies on rela-tionship breakdown. Australian states have extended financial relief in this area to other 'domestic' or 'personal' relationships, in some instances even without requiring that the parties ever shared a household.[505] English law recognizes some such relationships in the event of death, insofar as 'dependants' of the deceased—those who were being maintained, wholly or partially, by the deceased immediately before his or her death—may apply for pro-vision under the Inheritance (Provision for Family and Dependants) Act 1975. But for the time being, should their relationship founder during the parties' joint lives, these families, like cohabitants, remain reliant for their protection on the general law and limited statutory remedies.

 ONLINE RESOURCE CENTRE

Readers will find an outline of succession law on the Online Resource Centre.

---

[504] See also Wong (2009), Bottomley and Wong (2006). But compare Probert's reservations (2009c) about such arguments, noted at pp 109–10 above.

[505] Property (Relationships) Act 1984 (NSW); Domestic Relationships Act 1994 (ACT); Relationships Act 2003 (Tas); see Mee (2004), 427–9.

7.9 CONCLUSION

The law relating to family finances and property on relationship breakdown is highly technical in practice and conceptually sophisticated. However, beneath that complexity lie fundamental questions about the nature of marriage, civil partnership, and other family relationships. Are they relationships of dependency and support, joint ventures between equal partners, or associations between economically independent individuals? And what is the role of the state in all this: to intervene to protect the economically vulnerable or to stand back and allow parties freedom to make their own arrangements?

ONLINE RESOURCE CENTRE

Questions, suggestions for further reading, and supplementary materials for this chapter (including updates on developments in this area of family law since this book was published) may be found on the Online Resource Centre at **www.oxfordtextbooks.co.uk/orc/harrisshort_tcm2e/.**

FUNDAMENTAL PRINCIPLES IN THE LAW RELATING TO CHILDREN

CENTRAL ISSUES

1. The welfare of the child is the paramount consideration in most child-related disputes. This means the rights and interests of others are only relevant insofar as they bear upon the child's interests. This raises serious questions as to the compatibility of the paramountcy principle with Article 8 of the European Convention on Human Rights (ECHR).

2. Controversially, the paramountcy principle only applies where the 'upbringing' of a child is *directly* in issue before a *court*.

3. The welfare principle is criticized for its indeterminacy and lack of transparency. Measures to curtail judicial discretion, such as statutory checklists and scientific evidence, only partially address these problems.

4. Alternatives to the welfare principle remain closely wedded to its basic premises: that children should be afforded special consideration in the decision-making process.

5. Children's rights play an increasingly important role in English family law. Although difficult to uphold when children seek to act in ways considered inimical to their welfare, the rights of children are now widely recognized and respected.

6. The Children Act 1989 (CA 1989) enshrines a policy of non-intervention in private family life. Whether this can be successfully reconciled with the paramoutcy principle is debatable.

8.1 INTRODUCTION

Charlie is the father of a 10-year-old boy, Billy. Billy is very close to his mother, Mary, with whom he has lived since she separated from Charlie three years ago. Charlie sees Billy every weekend and was perfectly happy with this arrangement until Mary began to cohabit with Fred, who has one previous conviction for domestic violence. The conviction is now 10 years old and, having served three months in prison, Fred has never been charged again. Charlie is however convinced that Fred poses a risk to Billy and is therefore insisting that Billy come to live with him. In response, Mary has stopped all contact between Charlie and Billy claiming that Charlie is poisoning Billy's mind against Fred.

How should this dispute be resolved? Should the parents be left to decide where Billy should live? Or, whether or not Charlie and Mary can agree on what is best for Billy, should the state intervene to ensure that Billy's welfare, as the state perceives it, is protected? If Charlie and Mary cannot agree and decide to involve the court, what principles should the court apply in trying to resolve the dispute? Should Billy's welfare be the determining factor or should other considerations be taken into account?

When determining a dispute relating to a child there are several approaches the law could adopt. The first, most commonly termed the welfare approach, would seek to resolve all questions relating to a child's upbringing in accordance with his or her best interests. Paternalistic in outlook, at the heart of this approach is a desire to protect and nurture children through to adulthood, ensuring that all decisions are made with a view to maximizing the child's welfare. At its most extreme, proponents of this child-centred approach would argue that the *only* relevant consideration when making decisions which bear upon the child's future should be the child's best interests: in our scenario, the court should simply do what it thinks would be best for Billy. The second approach moves away from seeing the child as the exclusive concern to embrace the rights and interests of other family members, particularly the child's parents. This approach emphasizes that the independent rights and interests of the adults should be afforded due respect: in our scenario, the potentially competing rights and interests of Charlie, Mary, and possibly Fred, should be carefully identified and weighed in the decision-making process. The third approach—a 'children's rights approach'—is again orientated more towards the child but, at a conceptual level, is fundamentally different from the welfare approach. Many proponents of children's rights would agree with the key principle underlying the welfare approach: that the child should stand at the heart of the decision-making process. However, rather than seeing the child exclusively, or at least primarily, as a vulnerable object of concern, children's rights advocates emphasize children's capacity for autonomous decision-making and action. In other words, children are perceived as self-determining subjects of the law, particularly as they enter their teenage years. Following this approach, in our scenario, the court should ascertain from Billy whom he would prefer to live with and respect his wishes in the matter. The final approach, characterized by a 'non-interventionist' philosophy, focuses on the rights of the child's parents. Closely allied to the belief that parents know what is best for their children, it seeks to protect the privacy of the family unit and the fundamental right of a child's parents to raise their child in accordance with their own beliefs and values, free from state scrutiny and control. Applying this to Billy's case, unless Billy is believed to be at risk of significant harm from Fred, the state should, if possible, avoid intervening in this 'private' dispute, leaving Mary and Charlie to reach agreement over Billy's future and actively encouraging them to do so even if they initiate court proceedings.

Which of the above approaches is preferred will often depend on one's views on more fundamental questions such as how to create a fair and just relationship between children, their families, and the wider community. Those who advocate an exclusively child-centred approach typically believe that children deserve special protection and care. From this perspective, the particular vulnerability of children to abuse and their dependence on the adults around them justifies prioritizing the interests of the child. For some, this conviction is grounded in a broad societal concern with protecting the future generation. For others, the privileging of the child is rooted more narrowly in the belief that when parents decide to bring a child into the world they thereby willingly surrender their own rights and interests to those of the child. Opponents question whether it is appropriate to give children such privileged status within the network of family relationships on which they depend.[1] Returning to our dispute over Billy, is it fair that the wishes of Billy should prevail over the wishes of Charlie or Mary such that the views of the latter are rendered irrelevant? Treating the interests of children in isolation from the interests of their parents and siblings is perhaps not only naive given the realities of family life, but positively harmful in the message it sends to children regarding what constitutes fair and just relations between themselves and others. Is the child entitled to demand unreasonable sacrifices of its care givers? As Herring puts it: 'We do children no favours by regarding their interests as the only relevant ones. We must treat children with respect by bringing them up as members of families, of communities and of a society which values and upholds the rights and obligations of everyone, with the interests of children held in the highest esteem.'[2]

The purpose of this chapter is to examine these alternative approaches to child-related disputes and to explore the extent to which they have influenced the development of English law. We begin by exploring the welfare principle and its central role in child law today. The problems and limitations of the principle are addressed, before the chapter considers the alternatives to a welfare-orientated approach. Contemporary challenges to the welfare principle are explored, particularly the growing pressure from advocates of parental rights who now find vital support for their approach in the Human Rights Act 1998 (HRA 1998). We then consider children's rights as an alternative to a welfare-orientated approach. The different theoretical perspectives on the concept of children's rights are explored, before looking at the extent to which this approach has gained acceptance within domestic family law. Finally, the chapter considers the importance of the 'non-intervention' principle and the possible tension between a commitment to maximizing children's welfare whilst supporting only a minimalist role for the state, including promoting family dispute resolution in the private realm.

8.2 THE WELFARE PRINCIPLE

8.2.1 THE PARAMOUNTCY OF THE CHILD'S WELFARE

The welfare principle is central to the resolution of child-related disputes under English law. It is enshrined in s 1 of the CA 1989:

Children Act 1989, s 1

(1) When a court determines any question with respect to—

    (a) the upbringing of a child; or

    (b) the administration of a child's property or the application of any income arising from it,
      the child's welfare shall be the court's paramount consideration.

The same principle is enshrined in s 1 of the Adoption and Children Act 2002 (ACA 2002):

---

[1] See, in particular, Herring (1999a) and (1999b).
[2] Herring (1999a), 235.

Adoption and Children Act 2002, s 1

(1) This section applies whenever a court or adoption agency is coming to a decision relating to the adoption of a child.

(2) The paramount consideration of the court or adoption agency must be the child's welfare, throughout his life.

This means that whenever a court determines any question relating to the upbringing of a child, whether concerning adoption, residence, contact, medical treatment, or taking a child into state care, the child's welfare must be the paramount consideration.

The meaning of 'paramount'

In *J v C* [1970] the House of Lords had to interpret the word 'paramount' as then found in s 1 of the Guardianship of Infants Act 1925. Lord MacDermott gave the clearest judgment as to the meaning to be attributed to the term:

J v C [1970] AC 668, 710–11

LORD MacDERMOTT:

The second question of construction is as to the scope and meaning of the words "shall regard the welfare of the infant as the first and paramount consideration." Reading these words in their ordinary significance...it seems to me that they must mean more than that the child's welfare is to be treated as the top item in a list of items relevant to the matter in question. I think they connote a process whereby, when all the relevant facts, relationships, claims and wishes of parents, risks, choices and other circumstances are taken into account and weighed, the course to be followed will be that which is most in the interests of the child's welfare as that term has now to be understood. That is the first consideration because it is of first importance and the paramount consideration because it rules upon or determines the course to be followed.

It is widely accepted that 'paramount' means that the child's welfare is the *only* relevant consideration for the court when determining any aspect of the child's upbringing. The child's welfare is thus determinative, with other potentially relevant factors, such as the wishes and feelings of the child's parents, only taken into account insofar as they have a direct bearing upon the best interests of the child. As Herring explains: 'the present law's understanding of the welfare principle is individualistic. By this is meant that the child and his or her welfare are viewed without regard for the welfare of the rest of his or her family, friends and community. The claims of the other members of the family and of the community are only relevant to the extent they directly affect the child's welfare.'[3]

The meaning of 'welfare'

The child's 'welfare' or 'best interests' has been broadly defined in the case law to encompass: 'every kind of consideration capable of impacting on the decision. These include,

---

[3] Herring (1999a), 225.

non-exhaustively, medical, emotional, sensory (pleasure, pain and suffering) and instinctive (the human instinct to survive) considerations.[4] In order to give some substantive content to the welfare principle, both the CA 1989 and the ACA 2002 contain a 'checklist' of factors that the judge should take into account when trying to determine the welfare of any particular child. The checklists provide valuable guidance as to the most important matters to be considered. The checklist applied in child-related disputes falling under the CA 1989 is contained in s 1(3):

Children Act 1989, s 1

(3) In the circumstances mentioned in subsection (4), a court shall have regard in particular to—

   (a) the ascertainable wishes and feelings of the child concerned (considered in the light of his age and understanding);

   (b) his physical, emotional and educational needs;

   (c) the likely effect on him of any change in his circumstances;

   (d) his age, sex, background and any characteristics of his which the court considers relevant;

   (e) any harm which he has suffered or is at risk of suffering;

   (f) how capable each of his parents, and any other person in relation to whom the court considers the question to be relevant, is of meeting his needs;

   (g) the range of powers available to the court under this Act in the proceedings in question.

The application of the welfare checklist is only mandatory in the circumstances specified in s 1(4):

- a *contested* application to make, vary or discharge a s 8 order (i.e. a residence, contact, specific issue, or prohibited steps order);

- an application to make, vary, or discharge a special guardianship order or an order under Part IV of the Act (i.e. care and supervision orders), whether contested or not.

A similar checklist to be applied in the context of adoption is set down in s 1(4) of the ACA 2002.[5]

When will the welfare principle apply?

Although the welfare principle is of central importance in most legal disputes concerning children, there are some important limitations on when it applies.

'When "a court" determines any question'

The mandate in s 1 of the CA 1989 is only directed at the *courts*. It does not apply to any other decision-making body, public or private, exercising power and responsibility over

---

[4] *NHS Trust v MB* [2006] EWHC 507.
[5] See pp 901–2.

children. Parents' liberty to prioritize other needs and interests, including their own or those of siblings, when making decisions in the ordinary course of family life is unaffected. Similarly, local authorities taking decisions with respect to 'looked after' children do not have to prioritize the best interests of any individual child: they can take into account wider considerations, such as their own, usually limited, financial resources. This makes the welfare principle of much narrower application than is envisaged by Article 3(1) of the UN Convention on the Rights of the Child (UNCRC):

United Nations Convention on the Rights of the Child, Article 3

(1) In all actions concerning children, whether undertaken by public or private social welfare institutions, courts of law, administrative authorities or legislative bodies, the best interests of the child shall be a primary consideration.

However, the UNCRC's 'trade-off' for such broad application of the welfare principle, extending even to private institutions, is that the obligation imposed on state authorities is significantly weakened: the welfare of the child is only *a primary* as opposed to *the paramount* consideration. Making the child's welfare 'a primary consideration' allows considerable scope for the decision-maker to take into account a wide range of factors other than the particular interests of the child.

'Upbringing of the child'

One of the most significant limitations on the application of the welfare principle under the CA 1989 is that it only applies to questions where the 'upbringing of the child' is *directly* in issue. This is important because several questions which clearly affect a child's interests have been held to be only *indirectly* concerned with upbringing, including:

- Applications for an occupation or non-molestation order under Part IV of the Family Law Act 1996.[6]

- Applications for the use of scientific tests to determine the parentage of a child under s 20 of the Family Law Reform Act 1969.[7]

- Applications for leave to apply for a s 8 order (e.g. contact and residence orders) under s 10 of the CA 1989.[8]

- Disputes concerning publication of potentially damaging details about a child's background where the publicity does not relate directly to some aspect of the child's upbringing.[9]

Best interests of more than one child relevant

A third important limitation on the application of the welfare principle is where the upbringing of two or more children is in question in court proceedings in which: (i) they

---

6 See chapter 4.

7 *In re H (A Minor) (Blood Tests: Parental Rights)* [1997] Fam 89, 104. See pp 603–8.

8 *Re A and others (minors: residence order)* [1992] Fam 182. See pp 717–18.

9 *Re Z (a minor) (freedom of publication)* [1997] Fam 1. For the correct approach to such disputes post-implementation of the HRA 1998, see *In re S (FC) (a child) (Appellant)* [2004] UKHL 47.

both form the subject matter of the proposed orders before the court; and (ii) the best interests of each child, when taken individually, point to a different and irreconcilable outcome. In this situation, it is impossible for the court to fulfil its duty to give effect to the best interests of each child. Whichever approach the court adopts, the paramountcy principle will be compromised.

It is important to note that the problem only arises where *both children* are to be the subject of the proposed orders and all the proposed orders are to be determined in accordance with the paramountcy principle. Even though two or more minors are involved, if only one child will be made the subject of an order the issue will not arise.[10] The correct approach where two children are the subject of proposed orders was confirmed by the Court of Appeal in *Re A (Children) (Conjoined Twins: Surgical Separation)*.[11] The Court held that should a conflict develop between the paramount interests of two children, a balancing exercise weighing up the potential benefits and detriments of the possible outcomes to each of the two children must be undertaken and whichever course of action believed to cause the least overall harm adopted.[12] The case concerned an application for a declaration that it would be lawful for doctors to undertake surgical separation of conjoined twins, Jodie and Mary, against the wishes of the twins' parents and with the inevitable consequence that Mary, the weaker twin, would die. Without the separation both twins would die within a few months.

Re A (Children) (Conjoined Twins: Surgical Separation) [2001] Fam 147, 181–97 (CA)

WARD LJ:

[T]he operation will be in Jodie's interests [it would give her the chance of a normal life] but not in Mary's [the operation would hasten her certain death]. Can that conflict be resolved and if so how?

...[T]he question arises directly in this case and because it is the right to life of each child that is in issue, the conflict between the children could not be more acute. If the duty of the court is to make a decision which puts Jodie's interests paramount and that decision would be contrary to the paramount interests of Mary, then, for my part, I do not see how the court can reconcile the impossibility of properly fulfilling each duty by simply declining to decide the very matter before it. That would be a total abdication of the duty which is imposed upon us. Given the conflict of duty, I can see no other way of dealing with it than by choosing the lesser of the two evils and so finding the least detrimental alternative. A balance has to be struck somehow and I cannot flinch from undertaking that evaluation, horrendously difficult though it is...

Having conducted the required balancing exercise, Ward LJ concluded that the scales came down heavily in favour of giving Jodie the chance of a normal life. Permission was thus granted for the operation to be carried out.[13]

---

[10] *Birmingham City Council v H (a minor)* [1994] 2 AC 212, 218–23.

[11] [2001] Fam 147.

[12] Ibid., 181–97. This approach was suggested, obiter, by Wall J in *Re T and E (Proceedings: Conflicting Interests)* [1995] 1 FLR 581, 582–9. *Re A* is discussed in further detail below at pp 696–7.

[13] Brooke LJ agreed with Ward LJ on the issue of the children's best interests and how the conflict between them should be resolved. Robert Walker LJ, disagreed, finding that the operation would be in Mary's best

8.2.2 CRITICISMS OF THE WELFARE PRINCIPLE

Indeterminacy

The concept of the child's welfare is notoriously vague, leaving considerable discretion in the hands of individual judges as to what they consider to be in a child's best interests. This indeterminacy has been the subject of considerable criticism. In particular, it is argued that the nebulous nature of the principle allows cases to be determined in accordance with nothing more principled than the personal prejudices and untested assumptions of individual judges.

R. Mnookin, 'Child-Custody Adjudication: Judicial Functions in the Face of Indeterminacy', (1975) 39 *Law and Contemporary Problems* 226, 229–61

[T]he determination of what is "best" or "least detrimental" for a particular child is usually indeterminate and speculative. For most custody cases [roughly equivalent to a residence dispute], existing psychological theories simply do not yield confident predictions of the effects of alternative custody dispositions. Moreover, even if accurate predictions were possible in more cases, our society today lacks any clear-cut consensus about the values to be used in determining what is "best" or "least detrimental."

B. The Indeterminacy of Present-Day Standards

... When a judge must resolve a custody dispute, he is committed to making a choice among alternatives. The very words of the best-interests-of-the-child principle suggest that the judge should decide by choosing the alternative that "maximizes" what is best for a particular child. Conceived this way, the judge's decision can be framed in a manner consistent with an intellectual tradition that views the decision process as a problem of rational choice. In analyzing the custody decision from this perspective, my purpose is not to describe how judges in fact decide custody disputes nor to propose a method of how they should. Instead, it is to expose the inherent indeterminacy of the best interests standard.

1. Rational Choice

Decision theorists have laid out the logic of rational choice with clarity and mathematical rigor for prototype decision problems. The decision-maker specifies alternative outcomes associated with different courses of action and then chooses that alternative that "maximizes" his values, subject to whatever constraints the decision-maker faces. This involves two critical assumptions: first, that the decision-maker can specify alternative outcomes for each course of action; the second, that the decision-maker can assign to each outcome a "utility" measure that integrates his values and allows comparisons among alternative outcomes. Choice does not require certainty about the single outcome that will in fact flow from a particular action. Treating uncertainty as a statistical problem, models have been developed that allow decisions to be made on the basis of "expected" utility...

2. A Custody Determination under the Best-Interests-of-the-Child Principle

Assume that a judge must decide whether a child should live with his mother or his father when the parents are in the process of obtaining a divorce. From the perspective of rational

interests as well as Jodie's, because it would give them both back their bodily integrity. On his analysis no conflict therefore arose between the best interests of the two children.

choice, the judge would wish to compare the expected utility for the child of living with his mother with that of living with his father. The judge would need considerable information and predictive ability to do this. The judge would also need some source for the values to measure utility for the child. All three are problematic.

a. The Need for Information: Specifying Possible Outcomes

In the example chosen, the judge would require information about how each parent had behaved in the past, how this behavior had affected the child and the child's present condition. Then the judge would need to predict the future behavior and circumstances of each parent if the child were to remain with that parent and to gauge the effects of this behavior and these circumstances on the child. He would also have to consider the behavior of each parent if the child were to live with the other parent and how this might affect the child...

One can question how often, if ever, any judge will have the necessary information. In many instances, a judge lacks adequate information about even the most rudimentary aspects of a child's life with his parents and has still less information available about what either parent plans in the future...

b. Predictions Assessing the Probability of Alternative Outcomes

Obviously, more than one outcome is possible for each course of judicial action, so the judge must assess the probability of various outcomes and evaluate the seriousness of possible benefits and harms associated with each. But even where a judge has substantial information about the child's past home life and the present alternatives, present-day knowledge about human behavior provides no basis for the kind of individualized predictions required by the best-interests standard. There are numerous competing theories of human behavior, based on radically different conceptions of the nature of man, and no consensus exists that any one is correct. No theory at all is considered widely capable of generating reliable predictions about the psychological and behavioral consequences of alternative dispositions for a particular child...

c. Values to Inform Choice: Assigning Utilities to Various Outcomes

Even if the various outcomes could be specified and their probability estimated, a fundamental problem would remain unsolved. What set of values should a judge use to determine what is in a child's best interests? If a decision-maker must assign some measure of utility to each possible outcome, how is utility to be determined?

For many decisions in an individualistic society, one asks the person affected what he wants. Applying this notion to custody cases, the child could be asked to specify those values or even to choose. In some cases, especially those involving divorce, the child's preference is sought and given weight. But to make the child responsible for the choice may jeopardize his future relationship with the other parent. And we often lack confidence that the child has the capacity and the maturity appropriately to determine his own utility.

Moreover, whether or not the judge looks to the child for some guidance, there remains the question whether best interests should be viewed from a long-term or short-term perspective. The conditions that make a person happy at age seven to ten may have adverse consequences at age thirty. Should the judge ask himself what decision will make the child happiest in the next year? Or at thirty? Or at seventy? Should the judge decide by thinking about what decision the child as an adult looking back would have wanted made? In this case, the preference problem is formidable, for how is the judge to compare "happiness" at one age with "happiness" at another age?

Deciding what is best for a child poses a question no less ultimate than the purposes and values of life itself. Should the judge be primarily concerned with the child's happiness? Or with the child's spiritual and religious training? Should the judge be concerned with the economic "productivity" of the child when he grows up? Are the primary values of life in warm, interpersonal relationships, or in discipline and self-sacrifice? Is stability and security for a child more desirable than intellectual stimulation? These questions could be elaborated endlessly. And yet, where is the judge to look for the set of values that should inform the choice of what is best for the child? Normally, the custody statutes do not themselves give content or relative weights to the pertinent values. And if the judge looks to society at large, he finds neither a clear consensus as to the best child rearing strategies nor an appropriate hierarchy of ultimate values.

Lack of transparency and irrelevant considerations

Helen Reece has made a similarly strong attack on the welfare principle. Her concern focuses not on indeterminacy, but the way in which untested policies and principles which have little or nothing to do with the best interests of the child (some based on little more than ignorance or prejudice), are able to find their way into child-related disputes through the medium of the welfare principle.

H. Reece, 'The Paramountcy Principle: Consensus or Construct?', (1996) 49 *Current Legal Problems* 267, 273, and 293–8

The indeterminacy and value-laden nature of custody decisions lead critics to characterise the ultimate results as subjective, individualistic, and idiosyncratic, arbitrary, and capricious. A more extreme version of this criticism is that adjudication under the paramountcy principle yields something close to a random pattern of outcomes. Slightly more radical variants of this argument suggest that judges' decisions may be informed by their middle and upper-class backgrounds, by their patriarchal values, or simply by their personal prejudices...

[These criticisms of the welfare principle] miss the mark. It is true that the paramountcy principle itself is indeterminate, but this indeterminacy has enabled a determinate policy to take over; where one parent does not fit into the traditional mould, the results of residence disputes can be predicted with as much accuracy as can legal cases generally. It is true that these decisions are value-dependent, but they depend on a value rather than on values. It follows that the claim that results in children's cases are subjective and depend on the views of the individual judge is false...

It emerges that the indeterminacy of children's welfare has allowed other principles and policies to exert an influence from behind the smokescreen of the paramountcy principle. I am referring here to principles and policies which are extraneous to children's welfare... [such as the principle that a child should live with the parent who is best able to create a 'normal' family environment].

[O]nce we have recognised that children's welfare does not really determine the course to be followed, the paramoutcy principle becomes even less sacred: not only is the principle impossible to justify when taken at face value, the reality is that it is not even applied. We are now in a position to challenge the argument that the paramountcy principle is a harmless statement of intent. Montgomery's approach is to accept that decisions about children's welfare are shaped by judicial ideologies, but to argue that acceptance of this is neutral until the ideologies themselves can be exposed. Inability to expose judicial ideology is the very reason that the paramountcy principle is not harmless. Its danger lies in impeding open debate, open debate about which principles and which policies other than children's welfare should be given what weight in children's cases...

Indeed, this smothering of debate may not be so much the danger of, but rather the very purpose of, the paramountcy principle. King has argued that the paramountcy principle has an important symbolic function in legitimating the resolution of disputes. Whatever the contestants' view of the eventual decision, they unite with the judge in accepting the principle that the child's interests are paramount. The strength of the paramountcy principle lies in its apparent neutrality; it is a principle to which everyone can pay lip service but which can at the same time be used to justify any decision. It is not only the judiciary who rely on the neutrality of the paramountcy principle: politicians are likewise able to present policy decisions about children as neutral and objective, rather than political, ideological, or moral.

Not everyone agrees that the discretionary nature of the welfare principle with its attendant uncertainty and unpredictability is a problem. In fact, Herring perceives it as a positive strength.[14] However, there are various ways in which the law could try and address the concerns raised by Mnookin and Reece. One option would be to take a more 'scientific' approach to determining what will maximize the child's welfare, relying on 'objective', scientific evidence, drawn from a range of disciplines such as paediatrics, psychology, and sociology. The ready justification expert scientific evidence can provide for difficult and often controversial decisions has obvious attractions for the courts. Greater reliance on scientific evidence is not, however, without its problems. Mnookin doubts the value of this type of evidence in trying to predict future outcomes for an individual child.

R. Mnookin, 'Child-Custody Adjudication: Judicial Functions in the Face of Indeterminacy', (1975) 39 *Law and Contemporary Problems* 226, 258–60 and 287

While psychiatrists and psychoanalysts have at times been enthusiastic in claiming for themselves the largest possible role in custody proceedings, many have conceded that their theories provide no reliable guide for predictions about what is likely to happen to a particular child. Anna Freud, who has devoted her life to the study of the child and who plainly believes that theory can be a useful guide to treatment has warned: "In spite of...advances there remain factors which make clinical foresight, i.e. prediction, difficult and hazardous," not the least of which is that "environmental happenings in a child's life will always remain unpredictable since they are not governed by any known laws..."

Various studies have attempted to trace personality development to specific antecedent variables to show that these variables have the same effects on different children. This connection is now widely questioned by experimental psychologists...who think that infants experience external events in individual ways. The implication of this for prediction is described very well by Skolnick: "[I]f the child selectively interprets situations and events, we cannot confidently predict behaviour from knowledge of the situation alone"...

Having custody disputes determined by embracing more and more of the niceties of psychological and psychiatric theories requires careful analysis of the limits of these theories, their empirical bases, and the capacity of our legal system to absorb this new doctrine. In cases where, from the child's perspective, each claimant has a psychological relationship with the child, I doubt whether there would often be widespread consensus among experts about which parent would prove psychologically better (or less detrimental) to the child. Often each parent will have a different sort of relationship with the child, with the child attached to

---

[14] Herring (2005b), 161.

each. One may be warm, easy-going, but incapable of discipline. The other may be fair, able to set limits, but unable to express affection. By what criteria is an expert to decide which is less detrimental? Moreover, even the proponents of psychological standards have acknowledged how problematic it is to evaluate relationships from a psychological perspective unless a highly trained person spends a considerable amount of time observing the parent and child interact or talking to the child. Superficial examinations by those without substantial training may be worse than nothing. And yet, that is surely a high risk.

Even with the best trained experts, the choice would be based on predictions that are beyond the demonstrated capacity of any existing theory. While the psychologists and psychiatrists have made substantial therapeutic contributions, they are not soothsayers capable of predicting with any degree of confidence how a child is likely to benefit from alternative placements. When the expert does express a preference, it too often is based on an unexpressed value preference. What is psychologically least detrimental will usually be no more determinate for expert and nonexpert alike than what is in a child's best interests; and to reframe the question in a way that invites predictions based on the use of labels and terminology developed for treatment is both demeaning to the expert and corrupting for the judicial process.

The current limitations of scientific disciplines in trying to predict future outcomes is not the only concern. Commentators writing from a feminist perspective have noted how the legal process makes selective use of scientific evidence, often to provide apparently unqualified support for a particular ideological position or policy. Writing about contact, Felicity Kaganas is highly critical of the use of 'child welfare science' to reinforce an ideology on post-divorce parenting which prioritizes the importance of contact with non-resident fathers at the expense of the legitimate concerns and interests of mothers. As she points out, the scientific research on this issue is not straightforward.

F. Kaganas, 'Contact, Conflict and Risk', in S. Day Sclater and C. Piper (eds), *Undercurrents of Divorce* (Aldershot: Ashgate, 1999b), 99, 105–10

[The] elevation [of contact] into a priority for law, along with the goal of reducing conflict, has been coterminous with the growth of child welfare knowledge focusing on these matters and courts have turned to this body of knowledge in justifying their decisions. Even in 1973, Latey J in *M v M* invoked not only 'common sense' and 'human experience', but also referred to 'medical and other expert discovery' favouring contact...

The version of the research studies that has shaped the dominant discourse about divorce and contact is clearly a simplified one. In this version, divorce damages children and, in order to limit that damage it is essential to ensure that conflict is reduced or eliminated and that contact is maintained. The more nuanced and complex features of the research are absent...A recent review of research in the field confirms that it is characterised by greater complexity and greater uncertainty than the law allows. Rodgers and Pryor observe that, 'there is no simple or direct relationship between parental separation and children's adjustment, and poor outcomes are far from inevitable.' Nor can it be assumed, they say, that the disadvantages to children identified by researchers are attributable to the separation. And although they ultimately favour contact, they note that the loss or absence of a parent does not appear to have a very significant effect on children and that it is the quality and not the frequency of contact that matters. Furthermore, they identify factors such as the ability of parents to recover from the psychological distress as being important for children's ability to adjust.

> Moreover, there is conflicting research in this field. Yet little credence is attached to studies that contradict what Maclean and Eekelaar term the 'new orthodoxy'...

Whilst Kaganas recognizes that to some extent the law needs to simplify and reduce the complexity of the research evidence for its own purposes, she criticizes the way the child welfare science has been 'interpreted' to serve certain pre-defined ends:

> King and Piper argue that reductionism and the simplification of child welfare knowledge is an inevitable consequence of law's autopoetic nature. Law cannot incorporate external discourses, they say, without reconstructing them in a way that 'makes sense' within law, enabling it to codify events as lawful or unlawful. These legal reconstructions of the complex discourse of child welfare are 'necessarily simplistic because law by its very nature needs clear normative principles'.
>
> The process of reconstruction is unavoidable; the law cannot ignore child welfare science and still purport to be applying principles and making decisions that serve the best interests of children. Law as a system of communication has nothing to say about what is good or bad for children. In contemporary society this is the preserve of experts within child welfare science, whose expertise confers on their work a claim to truth. Child welfare science alone can claim authoritatively to tell us what will best serve children's interests and which events or choices will lead to which outcomes for children.
>
> Yet the need for clear normative principles legitimated by science does not of itself explain the way in which the law has reconstructed child welfare science in the context of contact. It has had to make choices from a range of available principles. It could, for example, have chosen to adopt the principle that contact should not be ordered against the wishes of the resident parent but chose, instead, the opposite. The reason for this must be that a decision to give the resident parent a veto would run counter to a dominant discourse surrounding contact which has been informed by political as well as child welfare imperatives. Currently, government and professional groupings, as well as popular culture reflected in the media, all espouse a particular understanding of the consequences of separation and divorce for children. This understanding has been accorded the status of taken-for-granted truth and cannot fail to impact on the legal system if it is to retain credibility. And the law, in making pronouncements consistent with the dominant discourse, confirms its 'rightness'.

Thus, whilst the scientific disciplines have an important contribution to make in improving understanding about how best to maximize children's welfare, the use of scientific evidence in the judicial process is not without significant difficulties.[15]

An alternative way in which the judge's discretion could be curtailed is to move towards a more transparent, rule-based system in which the guiding principles and values to be applied in determining a child's interests are more clearly articulated. However, to develop such rules or principles is a value-laden exercise fraught with just the same difficulties as more individualized decision-making. Whilst recognizing the problem of indeterminacy, Mnookin doubts whether a rule-based system would prove any more successful than the current discretionary model.

[15] See also Barnett (2000), 137–40.

R. Mnookin, 'Child-Custody Adjudication: Judicial Functions in the Face of Indeterminacy', (1975) 39 *Law and Contemporary Problems* 226, 262–4

[A]djudication by a more determinate rule would confront the fundamental problems posed by an indeterminate principle. But the choice between indeterminate standards and more precise rules poses a profound dilemma. The absence of rules removes the special burdens of justification and formulation of standards characteristic of adjudication. Unfairness and adverse consequences can result. And yet, rules that relate past events or conduct to legal consequences may themselves create substantial difficulties in the custody area. Our inadequate knowledge about human behavior and our inability to generalise confidently about the relationship between past events or conduct and future behavior make the formulation of rules especially problematic. Moreover, the very lack of consensus about values that make the best-interests standard indeterminate may also make the formulation of rules inappropriate: a legal rule must, after all, reflect some social value or values. An overly ambitious and indeterminate principle may result in fewer decisions that reflect what is known to be desirable. But rules may result in some conspicuously bad decisions that could be avoided by a more discretionary standard...

As we have seen, qualified steps towards the adoption of a more rule-based system are evident in the CA 1989 and the ACA 2002 in the form of the welfare checklists. However, whilst these checklists provide some substantive content to the welfare principle, they do not provide a complete answer to concerns about its vagueness and indeterminacy. No particular weight or order of priority is attributed to the various factors and there is no guidance as to whether, in certain situations, one or more of them will have particular importance. The judge is thus still afforded considerable discretion as to the weight to be attributed to each factor in any particular case. In some cases, the judge may simply disregard certain factors as irrelevant.

Why should the child's welfare be paramount?

As Reece remarks, 'the paramountcy principle rests on an astonishingly solid consensus, both inside and outside the discipline of Family Law'.[16] It may be thought that given the strong support for the welfare principle, the justification for prioritizing the interests of one child over all other interests would be self-evident. However, articulating a convincing reason why children should always take priority is not necessarily straightforward. Reece outlines the most common arguments, none of which she finds convincing.

H. Reece, 'The Paramountcy Principle: Consensus or Construct?', (1996) 49 *Current Legal Problems* 267, 276–81

Children are more vulnerable

This is the most common justification for the paramountcy principle. For example, Cretney writes that the 'welfare principle is widely supported because . . . children who are necessarily vulnerable and dependent must be protected from harm'. A variation of this argument is that children's welfare should be paramount as a way of 'bending the stick', that in a world run

---

16 Reece (1996), 268.

by adults, there would otherwise be a danger that children's interests would be completely overlooked.

This argument holds the key to the consensus behind the paramountcy principle. Resting as it does on vulnerability, it has great resonance in the current political climate, in which vulnerability generally attracts priority... Even on its own terms this argument is flawed: in a case under the Children Act, the child will not necessarily be the most vulnerable individual...

Since the argument explains the consensus behind the paramountcy principle, it could not be more crucial to recognise the fallacy contained at the heart of the argument. The fallacy lies in the equation of priority with protection. It is self-evident that, as a general rule, children need more protection than adults. From this statement it does not follow that children should be prioritized over adults...

Children must be given the opportunity to become successful adults

'[T]he care of our children must be a prime priority. Within each child is the person he will one day become. Inside each of us is the child we once were' [Baroness Strange]. According to this argument, childhood is important because of its psychological significance; unless we do what is best for children, they will not be able to flourish into adults. The argument is self-defeating because it makes the importance of childhood contingent on, and subordinate to, the importance of adulthood: if decisions are made which sacrifice adults' interests to children's interests, there is little point becoming a successful adult.

More broadly, this argument is self-defeating because it promotes the future at the expense of the present, and indeed Leach argues explicitly that children are important because they are our future. The resonance of this yearning for the future reflects a social malaise. Although a preoccupation with the future is often favourably contrasted with a preoccupation with the past, the reality is that both represent an attempt to escape the present. A society which puts its hope in simply reproducing itself is a society which has lost its sense of purpose. It reduces the destiny of humans to ensuring that others take their place.

Adults create children

'Grown-ups... make free decisions, pooled their genes, created a baby and have to take the consequences... Children come first. We invited them to life's party' [Libby Purves]. It is not self-evident that the creation is more important than the creator; the opposite argument is equally plausible and indeed forms the basis of most religions. Moreover, the argument only achieves coherence in relation to parents; when the paramountcy principle ignores the interests of anyone other than a natural parent, it ignores the interests of someone who had no control over whether the child was born.

Argument from Solomon

This argument, which again could only conceivably justify the paramountcy principle in its application to parents, is that the desire to sacrifice one's own interests to those of one's child is the very mark of being a parent. If the argument is that this is how things are, then it stands defeated by legal disputes between parents and children. If the argument is that this is what it means to be a good parent, first, this is not self-evident, and secondly... there are more important values than being a good parent.

Utilitarian arguments

... All the previous arguments have justified the importance attached to children's welfare as a primary good. Two final arguments return to the utilitarian premises which initiated the discussion, but cast the net more broadly to include effect on society. More specifically, Barton and Douglas argue that children are important for the continuity of order in society and Parker suggests that giving greater weight to children's welfare maximises the welfare of society. However, ... when we raise the discussion to the social level, as indeed we should, the reasons to reject the paramountcy principle are far stronger than any reasons to retain it.

Reece argues that prioritizing the interests of children over all other relevant parties simply cannot be justified. Why, she asks, is only one participant to the dispute, the child, valued?[17]

8.3   ALTERNATIVES TO THE WELFARE PRINCIPLE

Given the strong criticism of the welfare principle, the question inevitably arises as to whether there is a better approach to decision-making about children. There are several alternatives, reflecting Reece's view that decision-making in family law needs to be more transparent and disciplined and that automatically prioritizing the child's interests, regardless of the harm caused to others, is wrong. The alternatives thus seek to find a way to identify the legitimate rights and interests of all affected parties and to bring those interests fairly into the decision-making process.

8.3.1   RE-CONCEPTUALIZING THE WELFARE PRINCIPLE

Reece's concerns regarding the 'unduly individualistic' nature of the welfare principle are shared by Herring.[18] In light of these concerns, he has developed an alternative theory which he terms 'relationship-based welfare'.[19] This approach is based on the principle that a child should not be seen as an isolated individual but as an integral part of a wider family network. In his view, the inter-dependence of the child on this wider family network should constitute a core consideration in the decision-making process: not least because teaching the child the importance of respecting the needs and interests of others is core to the child's welfare.[20]

J. Herring, 'The Welfare Principle and the Rights of Parents', in A. Bainham, S. Day Sclater, and M. Richards (eds), *What is a Parent? A Socio-Legal Analysis* (Oxford: Hart Publishing, 1999b), 89, 101–3

The conception of the welfare principle adopted by the courts is often too narrowly individualist and focuses on a self-centred approach to welfare. A broader version of the welfare principle could allow consideration of the parent's interests. There are two elements to the

---

[17] Ibid., 275.
[18] Herring (1999a), 233.
[19] Herring (1999a) and (1999b).
[20] See also Herring and Taylor (2006), 533.

argument for pursuing a wider understanding of the welfare principle. The first is that it is part of growing up for a child to learn to sacrifice as well as claim benefits. Families, and society in general, are based on mutual co-operation and support. So it is important to encourage a child to adopt, to a limited extent, the virtue of altruism and an awareness of social obligation. It needs to be stressed that it is a very limited altruism that is being sought. Children should only be expected to be altruistic to the extent of not demanding from parents excessive sacrifices in return for minor benefits.

The second element of this approach is that the child's welfare involves ensuring that the child's relationships with the other family members are fair and just. A relationship based on unacceptable demands on a parent is not furthering a child's welfare...

It is in the child's welfare to be brought up in a family whose members respect each other and so, on occasion, sacrifices may be required from the child...

The effect of this approach is to move away from conceiving the problem as a clash between children and parents and in terms of weighing two conflicting interests, and towards seeing it rather as deciding what is a proper parent-child relationship. The child's welfare is promoted when he or she lives in a fair and just relationship with each parent. Understood in this way, the welfare principle can protect children while properly taking into account parent's rights.

The argument can also operate where a child's welfare may require a sacrifice for the obtaining of some greater social good...

Herring identifies a number of advantages to this approach:

First, it is more in accord with practice in many families...[M]ost family dynamics involve "give and take" and do not consider exclusively the child's interests. Secondly, it is in accord with what most of us would have wished when we were being brought up. I suspect that most adults would not have wanted their parents to have been obliged to make extraordinary sacrifices to pursue a minor increase in their welfare, but would have expected a fair level of sacrifice by the parents. Thirdly, this approach enables a court to consider explicitly the interests of all family members while still adhering to the welfare principle. This is what is done already, but covertly. Fourthly, this approach enables the interests of adolescents to be better understood. As a child becomes older the relationship with his or her parents changes, but in complex ways. It no longer becomes necessary for the parents to determine the child's own interests—the child can determine this for him or herself. Similarly, the demands that a child can make on a parent can lessen. Andrew Bainham refers to the "democratic model of decision making", which usefully captures the sense of co-operation within families focused upon by this approach to welfare. Fifthly, by focusing on a child's relationships this may encourage the law to develop ways in which a child's voice may be heard more effectively in proceedings.

As Herring notes, one advantage of his approach is that it does not entail abandoning the centrality of the paramountcy principle. Herring has the more limited objective of 're-conceptualizing' what we mean by welfare. In his view, we need to broaden our understanding of welfare from an individualistic to a relationship-based concept, securing a place for the rights and interests of others in the decision-making process by recognizing their importance to the child's welfare. However, it could be argued that this is not a marked departure, if a departure at all, from the approach under *J v C* whereby the rights and interests of others can be taken into account insofar as they bear upon the child's interests. The problem from the parents' perspective is that their rights and interests must still be mediated through the framework of the child's welfare—they are not given *independent* weight and recognition in the decision-making process. Herring's approach may also prove problematic from the child's perspective, in that once it is conceded that the rights and interests of the parents are relevant to the child's welfare, the child's welfare may be subsumed within the parents' interests. Eekelaar is critical of Herring's approach for this reason, pointing out that it was not so long ago that the view was taken that 'recognition of the pre-eminence of the father was in the child's interests'.[21] Arguably this problem continues today, but with the child's interests now being more commonly identified with the interests of the mother.[22]

Eekelaar proposes a more radical alternative which, in seeking to ensure that proper regard is paid to the interests of others, abandons the paramountcy principle.

J. Eekelaar, 'Beyond the Welfare Principle', (2002a) 14 *Child and Family Law Quarterly* 237, 242–5

It might appear that many dilemmas in family law involve resolving issues at which the future well-being . . . of various people are at stake. How are these issues best resolved? A crude utilitarian attempt at maximising the well-being of the greatest number could not be accepted, since this would pay insufficient regard to extreme adverse affects of certain outcomes on the well-being of particular individuals. The best solution is surely to adopt the course that avoids inflicting the most damage on the well-being of any interested individual. The methodology can be illustrated in this way. Suppose one could assign a value to the degree of benefit and detriment to the well-being of all interested parties under various possible solutions. The following would be a simple case. C is the child. X and Y are adult participants. Minus values indicate an outcome that has more detriment than benefit for the party:

- Solution 1: C (+15); X (+10); Y (−30).
- Solution 2: C (+10); X (+10); Y (−20).
- Solution 3: C (+5); X (−5); Y (−10).

Solution 1 would be chosen under the best interests test. Solution 2 would be chosen under general utilitarianism (since the overall benefit/detriment scores are: −5 (solution 1); 0 (solution 2); and −10 (solution 3)). Under the suggested methodology, solution 3 should be chosen, for although it reduces the benefit to C (and to X), the detriment to Y is far less . . .

It seems very difficult to advocate a solution that is, on these assumptions, the least beneficial to the child of all three solutions. But on closer examination, some merits appear. It *considerably* reduces the detriment for Y. It may be that the disadvantage to the child is a price worth paying . . . Of course, the evaluation of the benefits and detriments on various parties is a matter of judgment in each case, but this is true in all matters of adjudication, including, of course, the welfare test. It is a delusion to believe that such matters can be evaluated with scientific objectivity. Nevertheless, it is safe to say that special care must be taken in evaluating the impact or potential impact, of a solution on the well-being of children, for it is always necessary to remember children's vulnerability and the potential longer term effects on them, than on adults, of many decisions . . .

Although Eekelaar rejects the paramountcy principle, he still affords the child a privileged position within the decision-making process:

---

[21] Eekelaar (2002), 238.
[22] See, e.g., the recent relocation case of *Re C (Permission to Remove from the Jurisdiction)* [2003] EWHC 596.

Qualifications—privileges and appropriateness

Unfortunately, this does not conclude the matter. It might be difficult (but not impossible) to envisage solutions that hold *nothing but* detriment to the child. It is easier to imagine this for an adult. Yet it is possible to imagine an outcome for a child where detriments *exceed* benefits. How, then, would a decision be made between the following two solutions?

- Solution 1: C (+10); X (+10); Y (−30).
- Solution 2: C (−10); X (−15); Y (−15).

Here the price paid in solution 2 for reducing Y's detriment is to spread the hardship around relatively equally. It certainly would not satisfy general utilitarianism. Should it satisfy anyone? I think the answer must be to hold that no solution should be adopted where the detriments outweigh the benefits for the child unless that would be the result of *any* available solution, so that it is unavoidable. There should be no negative quantity for C. In this way, the interests of children would be *privileged* in the calculus, but not given priority. This could be justified on the basis that, whatever we might say about future generations, they at least have no control whatsoever over our actions. It behoves us, therefore, when considering the consequences of our actions, to treat our successors as always innocent and to allow them to start their lives, as far as possible, without deficits from what we have done. For the same reason, the privilege should allow resolution in favour of children where the value of benefits and detriments between them and other parties is minimal or very speculative.

Eekelaar's approach has the advantage that by separating out the individual rights and interests of all affected parties, it brings much greater transparency to the decision-making process. This is preferable to concealing those interests behind the obscurity of the welfare principle. Eekelaar also provides some comfort for strong adherents to a welfare-centred approach by continuing to privilege the children's interests in the form of a long-stop guarantee that no solution will ever be adopted which results in a net detriment to the child. The child's basic interests are thus safeguarded, whilst creating a better balance between the rights and interests of all parties. However, as Eekelaar acknowledges, the downside of his approach is its complexity, making it difficult to apply in practice.[23] This is perhaps inevitable. Family life is complex and disputes about a child are rarely easy to resolve. It is perhaps better to face this complexity than to hide behind the apparent safety of the welfare principle.

Whether one finds these alternatives to the welfare principle convincing, the question is no longer merely a matter for academic speculation. Following the implementation of the HRA 1998, there is a very real question whether the welfare-orientated approach of the CA 1989 and the ACA 2002 can be sustained in the face of the rights-based approach of the ECHR.

8.4 A RIGHTS-BASED APPROACH TO CHILD-RELATED DISPUTES: TAKING PARENTS' RIGHTS SERIOUSLY

Before considering whether the paramountcy principle can be reconciled to the rights-based approach of the ECHR, the potential relevance of the Convention to disputes concerning children must first be explored. Anyone seeking to take advantage of the ECHR and its

---

[23] Eekelaar (2002), 248.

right-based approach in a family dispute must first establish that they fall within the scope of the ECHR's protection. The most important provision of the ECHR here is the right to respect for family life, guaranteed under Article 8.

8.4.1 ESTABLISHING A 'RIGHT' UNDER ARTICLE 8(1)

In order to fall within the scope of Article 8(1), the applicant must first establish the existence of 'family life'. A well-established line of authority makes it clear that Article 8 only affords respect to existing family relationships: it does not safeguard the 'mere desire' to found a family or create new familial relationships.[24] Establishing the existence of family life is not always straightforward. The European Court has clearly favoured the traditional, heterosexual, married unit where the existence of family life between both the parents and the child is established automatically by virtue of the marital tie.[25] Establishing family life between parent and child where the parents are not married is more difficult. The relationship between unmarried mothers and their children was dealt with in the seminal case of *Marckx v Belguim*.[26] At the time of the application, illegitimate children suffered a number of disadvantages under Belgian law when compared with legitimate children, including the fact that no legal bond was automatically created between illegitimate children and their mothers by the mere fact of birth. The European Court held that Article 8 protects the family life of both the 'legitimate' and the 'illegitimate' family, thereby bringing the position of an 'illegitmate' child into line with that of a 'legitimate' child as regards the mother-child relationship.

The European Court has not, however, taken the same step with respect to the relationship between an unmarried father and his children. Although *Marckx* states unequivocally that Article 8 'makes no distinction between the "legitimate" and the "illegitimate" family', the European Court has not been prepared to assume the existence of family life between an unmarried father and his children on the basis of a mere biological bond. The father is therefore required to demonstrate the existence in practice of 'close personal ties' between himself and the child, or at least between himself and the child's mother, before he can claim the protection of Article 8. The Court has held that factors relevant to determining whether de facto family life has been established include cohabitation (usual but not essential), the nature of the relationship between the parents, and the father's demonstrable commitment to the child both before and after the birth.[27]

Although the European Court has treated the traditional married unit more favourably than the unmarried family, its willingness to embrace de facto as well as de jure family life has enabled unconventional family relationships to benefit from the protection of the ECHR. Importantly, this has included the relationship between transsexual parents and their children, and gay and lesbian parents and their children.[28]

Outside the immediate family unit of parents and child, the Court has suggested that the protection of 'family life' under Article 8 extends to include near relatives such as

---

[24] See, e.g., *Fretté v France* (App No 36515/97, ECHR) (2003), [32].

[25] *Al Nashif v Bulgaria* (App No 50963/99, ECHR) (2003); see also, *Kosmopoulou v Greece* (App No 60457/00, ECHR) (2004), [42].

[26] (A/31, ECHR) (1979–80), [31].

[27] *Lebbink v the Netherlands* (App No 45582/99, ECHR) (2004).

[28] *X, Y and Z v the United Kindgom* (App No 21830/93, ECHR) (1997); *Salgueiro Da Silva Mouta v Portugal* (App No 33290/96, ECHR) (2001).

grandparents, siblings, aunts, uncles, and cousins.[29] Rather oddly, the Strasbourg jurisprudence suggests that it may be easier for grandparents to establish 'family life' for the purposes of Article 8 than the child's father.[30]

8.4.2 ESTABLISHING A BREACH OF ARTICLE 8(1)

Once the existence of family life has been established, the enquiry moves on to consider whether the state is, prima facie, in breach of any of its obligations under Article 8. The specific obligations imposed on the state by Article 8 are many and varied. We give just a flavour here.

Perhaps the most fundamental obligation imposed on the state under Article 8 is to respect the 'mutual enjoyment by parent and child of each other's company', what the European Court describes as a 'fundamental element of family life'.[31] Any state action in the public or private sphere which prevents or hinders the parent and child from exercising this right, such as refusing a contact order or taking a child into state care, constitutes a prima facie violation of Article 8(1).[32]

The primary object of Article 8 is thus to protect individuals against arbitrary intervention by public authorities. However, as held in *Marckx v Belguim*, Article 8 also imposes positive obligations on the state, one of the most important of which is to ensure the integration of a child into his or her family.[33] A second positive obligation imposed on the state is to take all reasonable measures to reconcile parent and child where family life, for whatever reason, has broken down. This is now well established in both the public and private law context.[34]

Finally, Article 8 offers procedural as well as substantive protection, requiring that the decision making process is both transparent and fair. In particular, the public authority (whether a local authority, an adoption agency or the court) must ensure that 'the parents have been involved in the decision-making process, seen as a whole, to a degree sufficient to provide them with the requisite protection of their interests.'[35]

8.4.3 JUSTIFYING A BREACH UNDER ARTICLE 8(2)

If the applicant is able to establish a prima facie breach of Article 8(1), the next question is whether the breach can be justified in accordance with Article 8(2): (i) that the act in question was 'in accordance with the law'; (ii) that it pursued a legitimate aim; and (iii) was 'necessary in a democratic society'.[36] This last requirement gives rise to the most difficult questions, requiring a careful balancing exercise between the various rights and interests at stake. It is at this stage of the decision-making process that we reach the crux of the issue: in carrying out this balancing exercise what weight is to be attributed to the child's interests? In particular, are the child's interests to be regarded as the paramount or determining factor,

---

[29] *Marckx v Belgium* (A/31, ECHR) (1979–80), [45].
[30] *C v X,Y,Z County Council* [2007] EWCA Civ 1206, [31] and [39].
[31] *KA v Finland* (App No 27751/95, ECHR) (2003), [92]. See also *Venema v The Netherlands* (App No 35731/97, ECHR) (2003), [71].
[32] *KA v Finland* (App No 27751/95, ECHR) (2003), [45]. *Hoffman v Austria* (A/255-C, ECHR) (1994).
[33] (A/31, ECHR) (1979–80), [31].
[34] *Haase v Germany* (App No 11057/02, ECHR) (2005), [93]; *Glaser v UK* (App No 32346/96, ECHR) (2000).
[35] *W v United Kingdom* (App No 9749/82, ECHR) (1988), [62]–[64].
[36] These requirements are discussed more generally at pp 6–8.

such that any interference with the adult applicant's rights will be deemed 'necessary in a democratic society' provided the measure in question was taken with the aim of protecting the child? It is the answer to this question which determines whether the welfare-orientated approach of English law can survive implementation of the HRA 1998.

8.4.4   CAN THE PARAMOUNTCY PRINCIPLE BE RECONCILED WITH ARTICLE 8?

Academic commentators were divided on whether the implementation of the HRA 1998 in 2000 would necessitate change to the paramountcy principle. It was certainly arguable that pursuant to s 3 of the HRA 1998 the welfare principle, as traditionally understood under English law, would have to be 're-interpreted' in order to give greater recognition to the independent rights and interests of the child's parents, perhaps along the lines suggested by Herring[37] or by 'downgrading' the interests of the child from the sole to perhaps the primary or principal consideration. It was equally arguable that if such re-interpretation of the word 'paramount' was considered impossible, the paramountcy principle under the CA 1989 and ACA 2002 would find itself subject to a declaration of incompatibility under s 4 of the HRA 1998.

Pre-implementation of the HRA 1998

Immediately preceding implementation, there were clear signs of judicial opposition to any attempt to 're-interpret' or 'downgrade' the welfare principle in light of the ECHR. The family judiciary's approach towards the ECHR, which might be regarded as 'dismissive',[38] was presaged by the House of Lords' decision in *Re KD (a minor) (ward: termination of access)*, a case concerning an application for contact with a child in local authority care. In addressing the possible implications of the ECHR for domestic family law, Lord Oliver held that the difference between the welfare-orientated approach as interpreted and approved by the House of Lords in *J v C* and the rights-based approach of the ECHR was 'semantic only'.

Re KD (a minor) (ward: termination of access) [1988] 1 AC 806, 820 and 824–7

LORD OLIVER:

Such conflict as exists . . . lies only in differing ways of giving expression to the single common concept that the natural bond and relationship between parent and child gives rise to universally recognised norms which ought not to be gratuitously interfered with and which, if interfered with at all, ought to be so only if the welfare of the child dictates it . . .

Parenthood, in most civilised societies, is generally conceived of as conferring on parents the exclusive privilege of ordering, within the family, the upbringing of children of tender age, with all that that entails. That is a privilege which, if interfered with without authority, would be protected by the courts, but it is a privilege circumscribed by many limitations imposed by the general law and, where the circumstances demand, by the courts or by the authorities upon whom the legislature has imposed the duty of supervising the welfare of children and young persons. When the jurisdiction of the court is invoked for the protection of the child the parental privileges do not terminate. They do, however, become immediately subservient to

---

[37] See pp 536–7 above.
[38] Harris-Short (2005), 354.

the paramount consideration which the court has always in mind, that is to say the welfare of the child. That is the basis of the decision of your Lordships House in *J v C*...and I see nothing in [the Strasbourg case law] which contradicts or casts doubt upon that decision or which calls now for any reappraisal of it by your Lordships. In particular, the description of those familial rights and privileges as "fundamental" or "basic" does nothing, in my judgment, to clarify either the nature or the extent of the concept which it is sought to describe...

Whatever the position of the parent may be as a matter of law—and it matters not whether he or she is described as having a "right" in law or a "claim" by the law of nature or as a matter of common sense—it is perfectly clear that any "right" vested in him or her must yield to the dictates of the welfare of the child. If the child's welfare dictates that there be access, it adds nothing to say that the parent has also a right to have it subject to considerations of the child's welfare. If the child's welfare dictates that there should be no access, then it is equally fruitless to ask whether that is because there is no right to access or because the right is overborne by considerations of the child's welfare...As a general proposition a natural parent has a claim to access to his or her child to which the court will pay regard and it would not I think be inappropriate to describe such a claim as a "right". Equally, a normal assumption is...that a child will benefit from continued contact with his natural parent. But both the "right" and the assumption will always be displaced if the interests of the child indicate otherwise and I find nothing in the [Strasbourg case law] which suggests otherwise.

As Jane Fortin has pointed out, Lord Oliver's judgment in *Re KD* provides the courts with an easy answer to the dilemma of whether the welfare principle can be reconciled with the ECHR.

J. Fortin, 'The HRA's impact on litigation involving children and their families', (1999a) 11 *Child and Family Law Quarterly* 237, 252

Lord Oliver's approach has the merit of providing the courts with a simple method of retaining the welfare principle as a means of interpreting Article 8(2). In other words, when dealing with a contact dispute, the court might agree that prima facie the father's right to family life will be infringed by an order refusing him contact. Nevertheless, it might then argue that such an order is in a child's best interests and that any order fulfilling the child's best interests will automatically comply with the terms of Article 8(2)—such an order will be considered *necessary*, to protect the child's health and morals and his or her own rights. In this way the process of applying the welfare principle and considering the requirements of Article 8(2) will become subsumed into each other.

However, Herring questions whether the ECHR arguments can be so easily dismissed as no more than 'semantic'.

J. Herring, 'The Human Rights Act and the welfare principle in family law— conflicting or complementary?', (1999a) 11 *Child and Family Law Quarterly* 223, 231

I respectfully suggest that this statement is not entirely accurate and that there are fundamental differences between the approach of the Children Act and the European Convention on Human Rights. In a case based on the Convention, concerning, say, denying a parent access to a child, the starting point is the parent's right to contact. In order to justify a breach there must be clear and convincing evidence that the contact would infringe the rights and interests of the child to such an extent as to make the infringement necessary and proportionate. However, an approach based on the Children Act's welfare principle might start with a factual presumption that the welfare of the child is promoted by contact with parents, but this could be rebutted by evidence that the welfare is not thus enhanced in the particular case.

The difference is twofold. First, less evidence is required to rebut the factual presumption of welfare than to demonstrate that the breach of a right is *necessary* in a democratic society. Secondly, the nature of the question is different. It is essentially an evidential question in the welfare approach. The law is clear—the order which should be made is that which best promotes the child's welfare. The question is then a factual one—which order will actually promote the child's welfare? Whereas in the European Convention approach, it is a question of judgment—whether the harm to the child is sufficient to make the breach 'necessary' as understood by the law.

A further difference between the approach of the welfare principle and the Convention is that the Convention is in this area essentially restrictive—it tells governments and courts what they may not do. Whereas the welfare principle requires the court to act positively to promote the child's welfare.

Post-implementation case law

Following implementation of the HRA 1998 in 2000, the family bench have continued their fierce defence of the welfare principle against incursion by the rights-based reasoning of the ECHR. In general, the courts have been reluctant to confront the potential incompatibility between the two, preferring either to ignore the HRA altogether or to fall back on a vague, generalized statement that applying the ECHR will lead to the same substantive result as that already arrived at on the basis of welfare. In other words, once the court reaches a decision in accordance with the child's best interests, it is *automatically* deemed to comply with Article 8. The judgment of Wall J in *Re H (Children) (Contact Order) (No 2)* typifies this approach. The case concerned an application by the child's father for direct contact with the child against the mother's wishes. The mother opposed contact because the father was suffering from Huntington's disease and posed a potential risk to the child.

Re H (Children) (Contact Order) (No 2) [2001] 3 FCR 385 (Fam Div)

WALL J:

[59] Finally, it will be apparent that I have made no mention of the European Convention for the Protection of Human Rights and Fundamental Freedoms in this judgment. Inevitably, however, every order made under s 8 of the 1989 Act represents in some measure an interference by a public authority (the court) in the right to respect for family life contained in art 8. The court's interference must, of course, be in accordance with the powers given to the court under the 1989 Act, and proportionate. Every application involves the court balancing the rights of the participants to the application (including the children who are the subjects of it) and arriving at a result which is in the interests of those children (or least detrimental to those interests) and proportionate to the legitimate aims being pursued. However, it seems to me that a proper application of the checklist in s 1(3) of the 1989 Act is equivalent to the balancing exercise required in the application of art 8, which is then a useful cross-check to

ensure that the order proposed is in accordance with the law, necessary for the protection of the rights and freedoms of others and proportionate. In my judgment, and for all the reasons I have given, the order I am making in this case fulfils those criteria.

The same approach was adopted by the Court of Appeal in *Payne v Payne*[39] and confirmed by the House of Lords in *Re B (A Minor) (Adoption: Natural Parent)*. The clear message from these cases was that post-implementation of the HRA it was 'business as usual'. *Re B* was a highly unusual case concerning an application by the father for an adoption order in his favour.[40] The primary purpose of the adoption was to terminate the parental responsibility of the mother who had voluntarily relinquished the child at birth. Having determined that the adoption would be in the child's best interests, Lord Nicholls addressed the ECHR arguments:

Re B (A Minor) (Adoption: Natural Parent) [2001] UKHL 70

LORD NICHOLLS:

Article 8: the right to respect for family life

29.…In considering this point it is important to keep in mind that in the present case the individual whose right has to be respected is the child. The mother has freely and unconditionally agreed to the making of an adoption order, with a full appreciation of the consequences. So there is no question of adoption being a violation of her rights under article 8.

30. As to child A's rights, I agree with the Court of Appeal that the relationship of mother and child is of itself sufficient to establish 'family life'. I agree also that section 15(3) [the statutory provision under the Adoption Act 1976 which governed applications by a sole natural parent] has to be given effect to in such a way as to avoid the result that a court might make an adoption order excluding one natural parent from the life of the child when this would represent an interference disproportionate to the child's needs. Where I part company with the Court of Appeal is that, unlike the Court of Appeal, I think this undesirable and unacceptable result is already precluded by the Adoption Act itself. There is no discordance between the statute and article 8 on this point. There is no need to 'read down' section 15(3)(b) so as to avoid incompatibility which otherwise would exist. There is no need to have recourse to section 3 of the Human Rights Act 1998.

31. My reason for holding this view is as follows. Take a case, such as the instant case, where the natural father alone seeks an adoption order. The court hears evidence and representations from all concerned, including the child's guardian. The mother consents to the application. The court considers the advantages and disadvantages adoption would have for the child. The court decides that an adoption order is best for the child in all the circumstances. I do not see how an adoption order made in this way can infringe the child's rights under article 8. Under article 8 the adoption order must meet a pressing social need and be a proportionate response to that need…Inherent in both these Convention concepts is a balancing exercise, weighing the advantages and the disadvantages. But this balancing exercise, required by article 8, does not differ in substance from the like balancing exercise undertaken by a court when deciding whether, in the conventional phraseology of English law, adoption would be in the best interests of the child. The like considerations fall to be

---

[39] [2001] EWCA Civ 166.
[40] For commentary, see Harris-Short (2002) and below at 13.6.4.

taken into account. Although the phraseology is different, the criteria to be applied in deciding whether an adoption order is justified under article 8(2) lead to the same result as the conventional tests applied by English law. Thus, unless the court misdirected itself in some material respect when balancing the competing factors, its conclusion that an adoption order is in the best interests of the child, even though this would exclude the mother from the child's life, identifies the pressing social need for adoption (the need to safeguard and promote the child's welfare) and represents the court's considered view on proportionality. That is the effect of the judge's decision in the present case. Article 8(2) does not call for more.

The strong and consistent message from the case law is that the HRA 1998 requires no change to the traditional understanding and application of the paramountcy principle.

The Strasbourg jurisprudence

Is the approach of the English judiciary to the paramountcy principle well-founded in the Strasbourg jurisprudence? The answer must be 'no'.[41] At the heart of Article 8(2) and the balancing exercise it requires is the concept of proportionality.[42] 'Proportionality' demands that there exist a 'fair balance' or 'reasonable relationship' between the legitimate aim pursued and the means used to achieve it.[43] Consequently, whilst an act carried out to protect the legitimate rights and interests of the child will have the *potential* to justify a prima facie breach of the rights of the child's parents, it will not *automatically* do so.[44] In some cases, such will be the gravity of the interference with the birth parents' rights that only very weighty welfare considerations will satisfy the ECHR need for proportionality.[45]

The leading European authority on the weight to be accorded to the welfare of the child under Article 8(2) is *Johansen v Norway*, which concerned a mother's challenge to the Norwegian authorities' decision to take her child into care and terminate her parental rights and responsibilities with a view to placing the child for adoption. The Norwegian government expressly argued that in a case of this nature 'rather than attempting to strike a "fair balance" between the interests of the natural parent and the child', the best interests of the child should be paramount. The European Court clearly rejected this interpretation of the required balancing exercise.

Johansen v Norway (App No 17383/90, ECHR) (1997)

78. The Court considers that taking a child into care should normally be regarded as a temporary measure to be discontinued as soon as circumstances permit and that any measures of implementation of temporary care should be consistent with the ultimate aim of reuniting the natural parent and the child... In this regard, a fair balance has to be struck between the interests of the child in remaining in public care and those of the parent in being reunited with the child... In carrying out this balancing exercise, the Court will attach particular importance to the best interests of the child, which, depending on their nature and seriousness, may

---

[41] Bonner, Fenwick, and Harris-Short (2003), 580–1.
[42] Ibid.
[43] Ibid.
[44] Ibid.
[45] Ibid. See also Herring and Taylor (2006), 527–9.

override those of the parent. In particular, as suggested by the Government, the parent cannot be entitled under Article 8 of the Convention...to have such measures taken as would harm the child's health and development.

In the present case the applicant had been deprived of her parental rights and access in the context of a permanent placement of her daughter in a foster home with a view to adoption by the foster parents...These measures were particularly far-reaching in that they totally deprived the applicant of her family life with the child and were inconsistent with the aim of reuniting them. Such measures should only be applied in exceptional circumstances and could only be justified if they were motivated by an overriding requirement pertaining to the child's best interests...

The Court found that the state's reasons for terminating the applicant's parental rights and access to her daughter, whilst relevant, did not correspond to any overriding requirement in the child's best interests and thus were not sufficient to justify the intervention.

Most of the subsequent case law has faithfully followed the *Johansen* approach, often quoting directly from the judgment and emphasizing the need to strike a 'fair balance' between, on the one hand, the rights and interests of the child's parents and, on the other, the rights and interests of the child. This approach has been adopted in both the public and private law context.[46]

It seems difficult to reconcile the *Johansen* approach with the welfare principle as understood in English law.[47] Rather than welfare being the paramount consideration in the sense of a 'trump card' overriding all else, *Johansen* clearly requires a balance to be carried out between the competing rights and interests.[48] Consequently, the child's welfare *may* override the rights and interests of the parents but whether it does will depend on the nature and seriousness of the breach of the parents' rights and the relative strength of the child's interests.[49] There will be some situations, of which adoption may well be a classic example, in which the breach of the parents' rights and interests is so far-reaching and grave that only very weighty and substantial welfare considerations will be sufficient to justify that interference.[50]

The one authority which appears to depart from the balancing exercise required under *Johansen* and provides some scope for defending the paramountcy principle is *Yousef v Netherlands*. The case concerned a guardianship and custody dispute between the child's father and the maternal family, following the death of the child's mother. The father wanted to 'recognize' the child, a procedure under Dutch law by which he would become the child's legal parent. The Netherlands Supreme Court dismissed the father's applications, leaving custody with the maternal grandmother. The father complained to the European Court, alleging a violation of his right to respect for family life under Article 8. Turning to the question of whether this interference could be justified as 'necessary in a democratic society', the European Court held:

Yousef v Netherlands (App No 33711/96, ECHR) (2002)

66. [The government submitted], if there was any clash of Article 8 rights between a child and its father, the interests of the child should always prevail.

---

[46] See, e.g., *Buchberger v Austria* (App No 32899/96, ECHR) (2003), [40]; *Sahin v Germany; Sommerfeld v Germany* (App No 30943/96, ECHR) (2003), [66]; and *Gorgula v Germany* (App No 74969/01, ECHR) (2004), [43].
[47] Bonner, Fenwick, and Harris-Short (2003), 582–3.
[48] Ibid.
[49] Ibid.
[50] Ibid.

> 73. The Court reiterates that in judicial decisions where the rights under Article 8 of parents and those of a child are at stake, the child's rights must be the paramount consideration. If any balancing of interests is necessary, the interests of the child must prevail (see Elsholz v. Germany...and T.P. and K.M. v. the United Kingdom...). This applies also in cases such as the present.
>
> 74. The Court has not found any indication that the domestic courts, in striking the balance they did between the rights of the applicant and those of the child, failed to take the applicant's rights sufficiently into account or decided in an arbitrary manner.
>
> 75. There has therefore not been a violation of Article 8 of the Convention.

However, *Yousef*'s apparent departure from *Johansen* does not signal a change in the European Court's approach to the weight to be attributed to the child's interests under Article 8(2).[51] *Yousef* is an isolated and weak decision.[52] *Johansen* is not referred to but the authorities relied on by the Court (*Elsholz v Germany* and *TP and KM v United Kingdom*) both follow the *Johansen* approach in requiring a balancing exercise between the competing interests.[53] In carrying out the balancing exercise, the welfare of the child is held to be of 'crucial importance'.[54] The Strasbourg jurisprudence does not, however, suggest that 'crucial' equates to 'paramount' as understood in English law.[55] It is, moreover, notable that several decisions since *Yousef* have simply followed the Johansen approach.[56]

It is therefore difficult, despite the *Yousef* decision, to sustain the position that the paramountcy principle is consistent with the Strasbourg case law. It may only be a matter of time before the paramountcy principle as traditionally understood in English law faces a direct challenge before the European Court, forcing the hand of the English judiciary on this fundamentally important issue.

8.4.5 SUMMARY: THE IMPACT OF THE HRA 1998 ON CHILD-RELATED DISPUTES

The judiciary's staunch defence of the welfare principle has prevented the HRA 1998 from having any great influence on private law disputes relating to children. Where the welfare principle does not apply, the ECHR's impact has been greater, with rights-based arguments being more openly received. ECHR arguments have thus been more prominent in cases only indirectly concerned with the 'upbringing' of the child, such as paternity disputes[57] and procedural matters under the CA 1989.[58] The HRA 1998 has also had a more positive impact in the public law context, with the courts drawing on the ECHR to impose increasingly high

---

[51] Harris-Short (2005), 357–8.

[52] Ibid. The European Court makes incidental reference to the child's welfare being paramount in the case of *Zawadka v Poland* (App No 48542/99, ECHR) (2005), at [67]. However, the judgment is clearly directed towards carrying out the required balancing exercise set down in *Johansen*.

[53] Harris-Short (2005), ibid.

[54] Ibid.

[55] Ibid.

[56] See, e.g., *Hoppe v Germany* (App No 28422/95, ECHR) (2003); *Gorgulu v Germany* (App No 74969/01, ECHR) (2004), [43]; *Hansen v Turkey* (App No 36141/97, ECHR) (2004), [98]; and *Suss v Germany* (App No 40324/98, ECHR) (2006).

[57] See, e.g., *Re T (a child) (DNA tests: paternity)* 3 FCR 577, discussed in detail at p 607.

[58] See, e.g., *Re J (Leave to Issue Application for Residence Order)* [2002] EWCA Civ 1364.

standards on local authorities in terms of their decision-making processes.[59] However, the courts' reluctance to engage with the ECHR in the private law context remains a matter of considerable disappointment for commentators hoping that the Convention's rights-based arguments would introduce much greater transparency and intellectual rigour into this area of family law.

8.5 CHILDREN'S RIGHTS

In contrast to the notion of parents' rights, one area of rights-based discourse which has not received a great deal of attention following implementation of the HRA 1998 is children's rights.[60] The explanation for this lies not only in the inadequacies of the ECHR as a vehicle for the protection of children's rights, but deep ambivalence about the concept of children's rights within contemporary legal, political and social thinking. However, despite struggling to gain a secure foothold in mainstream family law, the idea of children's rights provides a potentially important challenge to the centrality of the welfare principle. Many children's rights are based on a very different understanding of childhood from that of a welfare-orientated approach. Whereas the latter tends to emphasize the incapacity and vulnerability of children, much of children's rights discourse tends to emphasize the autonomy of children and their capacity for independent thought and action. The paternalism of the welfare principle and the 'liberationist' tendencies of a children's rights approach are not, however, mutually exclusive: indeed there is considerable overlap between the concept of welfare and rights.[61] Adherents to the welfare approach will readily concede that for children entering their teenage years it is often in their best interests that they should begin to take responsibility for their own futures: to become self-determining beings.[62] Similarly, proponents of children's rights would agree that children, particularly young children, have a right to special protection and care thereby ensuring their future welfare is maximized. As is evident from the case law, difficulties tend to arise when teenagers begin to struggle for independence from those in authority, wanting to determine for themselves how their future welfare will be secured.

We begin this section by looking at the theoretical foundations of children's rights and why the protection of children's rights, as opposed to children's welfare, may be important. We then move on to consider the extent to which children's rights have gained acceptance in English law.

8.5.1 ARE CHILDREN'S RIGHTS IMPORTANT?

Since the implementation of the HRA 1998, a strong 'culture of rights' has developed within the UK. However, children, unlike adults, are still not widely perceived as natural beneficiaries of rights. There remains deep ambivalence about the value of trying to attribute rights

---

[59] See, e.g., *Re M (Care: Challenging Decisions by Local Authority)* [2001] 2 FLR 1300; *Re G (Care: Challenge to Local Authority's Decision)* [2003] EWHC 551; and *Re L (Care Assessment: Fair trial)* [2002] 2 FLR 730. See chapter 12.

[60] For a review of progress in advancing children's rights post-implementation of the HRA 1998, see Fortin (2004) and Fortin (2006).

[61] For more detailed discussion see Fortin (2006), 311–12 and 317–18.

[62] Ibid., 317–18.

to children, with the result that children, as a group, are often excluded from contemporary rights-based discourse.[63] The reasons for such scepticism are varied. For some commentators, such as Onora O'Neill, rights can only ever offer a partial understanding of the obligations and duties owed by society to children.[64] Believing children's situation to be fundamentally different from other oppressed groups, she argues that rights-based discourse is an inappropriate legal and political tool to empower and protect this particularly vulnerable and often disadvantaged group.

O. O'Neill, 'Children's Rights and Children's Lives', (1992) 6 *International Journal of Law and the Family* **24, 36–9**

Appeals to children's rights might have political and rhetorical importance if children's dependence on others is like that of oppressed social groups whom the rhetoric of rights has served well. However, the analogy between children's dependence and that of oppressed groups is suspect. When colonial peoples, or the working classes or religious and racial minorities or women have demanded their rights, they have sought recognition and respect for capacities for rational and independent life and action that are demonstrably there and thwarted by the denial of rights...But the dependence of children is very different from the dependence of oppressed social groups on those who exercise power over them.

Younger children are completely and unavoidably dependent on those who have power over their lives. Theirs is not a dependence which has been artificially produced (although it can be artificially prolonged); nor can it be ended merely by social or political changes, nor are others reciprocally dependent on children...It is not surprising that oppressors often try to suggest that they stand in a paternal relation to those whom they oppress: in that way they suggest that the latter's dependence is natural and irremediable and their own exercise of power a burden which they bear with benevolent fortitude. The vocabulary and trappings of paternalism are often misused to mask the unacceptable faces of power. It is not mere metaphor but highly political rhetoric, when oppressors describe what they do as paternalistic...

The crucial difference between (early) childhood dependence and the dependence of oppressed social groups is that childhood is a stage of life, from which children normally emerge and are helped and urged to emerge by those who have most power over them. Those with power over children's lives usually have some interest in ending childish dependence. Oppressors usually have an interest in maintaining the oppression of social groups...

Children are more fundamentally but less permanently powerless; their main remedy is to grow up.

O'Neill can be criticized for underestimating the similarity of children's oppression at the hands of patriarchal and/or matriarchal authority to that of other oppressed groups. O'Neill portrays the incapacity, dependence, and vulnerability of children as a natural and inevitable state: a state from which a child will 'naturally' emerge upon reaching majority. It is questionable, however, whether the perceived incapacity and dependence of children is any more 'natural' than the 'natural' dependence of slaves and women was once thought to be. It can be argued that rather than a natural state, childhood as currently depicted in western societies is socially constructed, created to serve some wider societal interest.[65] Smith

---

[63] See generally, ibid.
[64] O'Neill (1992), 25–9.
[65] Smith (1997), 109, 133.

suggests that one such interest is that of the state in ensuring that children grow up to be responsible citizens.[66] The interests of individual adults, and in particular parents, are also served by a conception of childhood dominated by ideas of dependency and vulnerability, in which a protective role for the adult is guaranteed.

C. Smith, 'Children's Rights: Judicial Ambivalence and Social Resistance', (1997) 11 *International Journal of Law, Policy and the Family* **103, 134–5**

In contradistinction to the progress and order of modernity, post-modernity heralds a scepticism about the relationship between 'scientific investigation' and universal knowledge. In so doing it introduces a sense of uncertainty about what, if anything, may be construed as truth, and how, in the absence of shared values, understandings and knowledge, order and progress can be maintained...As individuals, we have come to lack an economic identity which was previously determined by secure and progressive employment opportunities, and we have lost a familial identity which was traditionally confirmed by the continuity of stable community and family relationships. Our sense of society has similarly been eroded by increasing 'globalization' externally, and the fragmentation of social structure internally. In these circumstances which characterise post-modernity, Jenks argues that adult-child relationships have come to provide the sense of closeness, affection and stability which it is hard to find elsewhere. He summarises the nature of this bond between adults and children thus:

Oddly enough children are seen as dependable and permanent, in a manner to which no other person or persons can possibly aspire. The vortex created by the quickening of social change and the cultivation of our perceptions of such change means that whereas children used to cling to us, through modernity, for guidance into their/our 'futures', now we, through late modernity, cling to them for nostalgic groundings, because such change is both intolerable and disorientating for us.

If we are prepared to take Jenks' analysis seriously then it may go some way towards explaining why we so stubbornly resist accepting that a child's right to decide should take precedence over an adult's protective interpretation of their best interests. We can talk all we like about respecting children's wishes, listening to their views and responding to them as intentional subjects rather than objects of concern, but we are not prepared to withdraw our protection or to abandon the legal distinction between children and adults. To do so would strike at the very heart of the adult-child relationship which enables adults to locate themselves emotionally, as being affectionate, caring, protective, and socially, as being responsible for moulding the next generation of citizens.

For some, the argument that our current understanding of childhood is fuelled by post-modern angst and uncertainty may seem a little far-fetched. However, Jenks' analysis does serve to highlight O'Neill's somewhat idealistic view of the parent-child relationship. O'Neill perhaps underestimates the extent to which adults, and particularly parents, do have a clear self-interest in maintaining control over their children's lives. Many parents have strong aspirations about the type of people they want their children to be. Very often they have invested heavily, emotionally and financially, in their futures. Recognizing children's capacity for autonomous decision-making, giving them the freedom to determine their own path in life, can jeopardize strongly held parental hopes and dreams.

---

[66] Ibid., 132.

In seeking to convince a sceptical public of the importance of children's rights, children's rights advocates have tried to focus on the realities of children's lives, challenging some of the more idealistic assumptions about childhood, including the parent-child relationship:

M. Freeman, 'Taking Children's Rights More Seriously', (1992) 6 *International Journal of Law and the Family* 52, 55–6

The arguments put [against children's rights] tend to take one or more of three forms.

First, there is the argument that the importance of rights and rights-language themselves can be exaggerated. That there are other morally significant values, love, friendship, compassion, altruism, and that these raise relationships to a higher plain than one based on the observance of duties cannot be gainsaid. This argument may be thought particularly apposite to children's rights, particularly in the context of family relationships. Perhaps in an ideal moral world this is true. Rights may be used to resolve conflicts of interest and in an ideal world there would be harmony and these would not exist. But it is not an ideal world—certainly not for children. Children are particularly vulnerable and need rights to protect their integrity and dignity. 'Solitary, poor, nasty, brutish and short' (Hobbes, 1651) may not be a description of a state of nature . . . but it may come close to describing what a world without rights would look like for many children . . .

The second argument is in one sense related to the first. It assumes that adults already relate to children in terms of love, care and altruism, so that the case for children's rights becomes otiose. This idealizes adult-child relations: it emphasises that adults (and parents in particular) have the best interests of children at heart. There is a tendency for those who postulate such an argument to adopt a *laissez-faire* attitude towards the family. Thus, the only right for children . . . is the child's right to autonomous parents . . .

The third argument equally rests on a myth. It sees childhood as a golden age, as the best years of our life. Childhood is synonymous with innocence. It is the time when, spared the rigours of adult life, we enjoy freedom, experience play and joy. The argument runs: just as we avoid the responsibilities and adversities of adult life in childhood, so there should be no necessity to think in terms of rights, a concept which we must assume is reserved for adults. Whether or not the premise underlying this were correct or not, it would represent an ideal state of affairs, and one which ill-reflects the lives of many of today's children and adolescents . . .

For children's rights advocates, children's rights are important because of their potential to protect children from suffering and exploitation at the hands of others. Rights give children's interests, regardless of age, a status equal to the interests of adults, meaning they cannot be easily disregarded: the child, as person, as individual, has to be respected.

M. Freeman, 'Taking Children's Rights More Seriously', (1992) 6 *International Journal of Law and the Family* 52, 56

Rights are important because those who lack rights are like slaves, means to the ends of others, and never sovereigns in their own right. Those who may claim rights, or for whom rights may be claimed, have a necessary pre-condition to the constitution of humanity, of integrity, of individuality, of personality.

8.5.2 THE THEORETICAL FOUNDATIONS OF CHILDREN'S RIGHTS

There are two main competing approaches to children's rights: (i) the 'will' or 'power' theory; and (ii) the 'interest' theory. These two theories have very different implications for the law's approach to childhood and, in particular, differ in the extent to which they challenge the paternalism of the welfare principle. Tom Campbell provides a detailed explanation of both theories, beginning with the will or power theory of rights.

The will or power theory of rights

T. Campbell, 'The Rights of the Minor: As Person, As Child, As Juvenile, As Future Adult', (1992) 6 *International Journal of Law and the Family* 1, 4–5

On the power theory, a right is a normative capacity that the bearer may choose to use for the furtherance of his or her own interests or projects, a sanctioned exercise of legitimate control over others...In its limited forms, the power theory is that the formal analysis of the structure of rights must be carried out in terms of the mechanisms available for invoking, waiving and enforcing rights, all of which are said to depend on the exercise of will by the right-bearer. Thus a right may give a normative control over others which may be used at the discretion of the right-holder to activate those obligations the performance of which she judges to be advantageous to herself or her projects. It follows that only those capable of claiming, demanding or waiving a right can be the bearers of rights. Hence, for instance, small children, being in no position to exercise this sort of control over the obligations of others, have no rights.

The embarrassment for the power theorists of denying rights to children may seem to be avoided by allowing that a proxy, such as a parent, may exercise, on behalf of a child, the discretionary powers which constitute the rights in question. However, on the power theory, this must be less than a full possession of a right since the bearer's will, the exercise of which is definitive for the existence of the right, is not involved. Indeed, it would appear, on the assumptions of the theory, that the proxy is the right-holder. After all, it is she who possesses the power which is said to constitute the right. In other words, children's rights exercised by proxies are certainly less than full rights as defined by the power theory. Moreover, at least for some theorists, the process of choosing to exercise one's rights is part of what gives importance to rights, for it is the exercise of choice in matters of importance to the individual that enhances the dignity and exhibits the autonomy of the right-holder. On this view, while the natural capacity to make choices of this sort comes to minors in the course of their normal development, it is only in so far as the individual minor has come to possess these capacities, and hence to resemble an adult, that he or she can have rights. For young children there can be no such choices, and hence, no genuine rights.

In the fuller version of the power theory, rights are related substantively to capacities for choice and rational action in that, at least as far as fundamental rights are concerned, all rights relate to the exercise of practical rationality and self-determination, in that rights have the function of protecting and furthering these capacities. In its purest form, the fuller version of the power theory is that all rights are materially based in the presupposition of the value pre-eminence of the distinctively rational elements of human nature. It is because human beings have the power of reasoned self-determination that they can have rights, these rights being for the protection of the exercise of these capacities or related to the prerequisites of rational action, such as life itself. In this way, the whole rights viewpoint is a working out of some ideal of Kantian rationalism as the distinctive value-basis of human existence.

Clearly, on the fuller version of the power theory, minors can have rights only to the extent that they have acquired adult-like capacities for reasoned decision-making and willed conduct under the control of rational moral agency. To some people this is an outrageous denial of the value significance of young children which exposes the intellectual and moral limitations of the power theory. Children are no less precious on account of the immaturity of their characteristically adult capacities.

As Campbell argues, the will or power theory of rights can lead to a complete denial that children, particularly young children, can be sensibly regarded as rights-holders. However, there is scope within this particular theory of rights for a more radical interpretation. The will or power theory does not necessarily exclude children as rights-holders. What it requires from children is the capacity for reasoned, rational thought. Once a child has that capacity, there can no longer be any objection to that child being accorded the same rights as others. The crux of the issue thus becomes at what point it can be said that a child acquires the necessary skills and maturity to hold and exercise rights. In response, the so-called 'child liberationists' argue that children have the capacity for rational, reasoned, decision-making from a much earlier age than western society has generally been willing to acknowledge, a fact attributable to adults' self-interest in retaining control over children.[67] They thus contend that children, even very young children, have the capacity to be self-determining, autonomous beings capable of holding and exercising rights.

However, whilst this theory does not entirely exclude children as rights-holders, it does have important limitations. Attributing rights to children on the basis of their adult-like capacities tends to conceptualize children as 'little adults', making their respective rights and interests virtually indistinguishable. Children's rights to various forms of autonomy and freedom, such as the right to freedom of expression or the right to determine their own health care, are emphasized at the potential expense of other core interests, particularly of young children. This, according to Campbell, is to adopt only a partial view of childhood. It attributes no value to the distinctive interests of children, 'as children'. This leads him to prefer the much broader, interest theory of rights.

The interest theory of rights

T. Campbell, 'The Rights of the Minor: As Person, As Child, As Juvenile, As Future Adult', (1992) 6 *International Journal of Law and the Family* 1, 5–6

According to this—the interest—theory of rights, children have rights if their interests are the basis for having rules which require others to behave in certain ways with respect to these interests. It is enough that there are ways of identifying these interests and arranging and enforcing duties which meet the requirements that they set. There is no presupposition that these interests are expressions of rational capacities, although some of them may be. Nor is there any assumption that the performance of the correlative interest-saving duties must

[67] Ibid., 106. See also Fortin (2009b), 4–5.

be triggered or set aside by the choice of the right-bearer, although this may often be the preferred way to protect the interests concerned. Rights where the exercise of will by the right-holder is a formal requirement or possibility—which I call option rights—are simply one type of right and do not represent the core of the idea of rights...

Taking the offensive, interest theorists claim to be able to explain a wider range of rights than the power theorists who have to resort to subtle reconstructions of those specific rights where there is no evident link to capacities of choice. Thus, the right not to be tortured has to be interpreted by a full power theorist as being grounded in something like the fact that torture interferes with the processes of rational decision-making. The interest theorist may retort that it also hurts. Similarly, the interest theorist can persuasively argue that there is nothing particularly indirect about the ascription of rights to mentally handicapped adults and small children, whereas the power theorist...has difficulty with these classes of persons.

The concept of childhood embraced by the interest theory of rights is much broader and allows for the core interests of even very young children to be elevated to the status of rights. Campbell argues that children's interests change throughout childhood, with different rights being particularly important at different stages of children's development. During the latter stages of childhood, as the child develops the capacity for independent decision-making, the autonomy or freedom interests identified with the will or power theory become of increasing importance. However, during very young childhood, needs-based rights, more closely identified with a traditional welfare approach, predominate.

It can be difficult to identify the core interests of children which are of such fundamental importance that they should be elevated to the status of rights. Identifying those rights that children, as children, would value raises particular difficulties. Eekelaar has developed one possible solution to this dilemma.

J. Eekelaar, 'The Emergence of Children's Rights', (1986) 6 *Oxford Journal of Legal Studies* 161, 169–71

We here meet the problem that children often lack the information or ability to appreciate what will serve them best. It is necessary therefore to make some kind of imaginative leap and guess what a child might retrospectively have wanted once it reaches a position of maturity. In doing this, values of the adult world and of individual adults will inevitably enter. This is not to be deplored, but openly accepted. It encourages debate about these values. There are, however, some broad propositions which might reasonably be advanced as forming the foundation of any child's (retrospective) claims. General physical, emotional and intellectual care within the social capabilities of his or her immediate caregivers would seem a minimal expectation. We may call this the 'basic' interest. What a child should expect from the wider community must be stated more tentatively. I have elsewhere suggested the formulation that, within certain overriding constraints created by the economic and social structure of society (whose extent must be open to debate), all children should have an equal opportunity to maximize the resources available to them during their childhood (including their own inherent abilities) so as to minimize the degree to which they enter adult life affected by avoidable prejudices incurred during childhood. In short, their capacities are to be developed to their best advantage. We may call this the 'developmental' interest...

There is a third type of interest which children may, retrospectively, claim. A child may argue for the freedom to choose his own lifestyle and to enter social relations according to his

own inclinations uncontrolled by the authority of the adult world, whether parents or institutions...We may call them the 'autonomy' interest.

Campbell criticizes this reliance on 'retrospective judgment', arguing that such an approach
is inevitably adult centred.[68] He points out that Eekelaar relies exclusively on an adult perspective and that adults considering childhood with hindsight tend to minimize the sufferings and sacrifices made, dismissing such misery as unimportant in light of the benefits
and advantages they now enjoy.[69] This is a clear problem with any 'substituted judgment'
approach. Giving children a much more direct voice in defining their own interests would
help achieve a better balance.

Children's rights and paternalism

The interest theory of rights is not unproblematic. On the positive side, the strong correlation between interests and rights means that children's rights are more easily reconciled
with the welfare principle, which in turn renders children's rights less challenging for policy
makers and more easily integrated into mainstream family law. Indeed, Fortin argues that
there is no conflict between children's rights and children's welfare.[70] However, on the negative side, tying children's rights so closely to children's interests makes children's rights vulnerable to the paternalism of a welfare-centred approach. As noted above, there is a danger
that children will only be accorded such rights as adults deem to be consistent with welfare.
Thus, whilst children will readily be accorded the right to special protection and care, they
may be denied the right to refuse life-saving medical treatment, such a right being regarded
as inimical to their best interests.

The danger of slipping back into adult paternalism is not just a problem for the interest
theory of rights. In fact, faced with the stark realities of allowing even older children to
determine their own path in life, Campbell emphasizes that both the interest theory and the
power/will theory of rights can be appropriately qualified with paternalistic interventions
where necessary.

**T. Campbell, 'The Rights of the Minor: As Person, As Child, As Juvenile, As
Future Adult'**, (1992) 6 *International Journal of Law and the Family* 1, 15

Similarly flawed is the assumption that rights are incompatible with paternalism. Given the
type of interest theory sketched above, it can readily be appreciated that some things that
people are interested in cannot always be achieved simply by letting them follow their own
immediate beliefs about what will contribute to the achievement of their interests or objectives. In such circumstances it may be right to restrain or require activity simply because this
will better promote that which the individual is interested in. Thus there may be paternalistic
interventions which are justified by reference to the rights of those constrained. To deny
this possibility is to adopt a crude form of the full power theory of rights according to which
it must always be a violation of rights to restrict individual choice. However, any plausible
power theory must allow that not all exercises of choice are to be enshrined in rights, and

[68] Campbell (1992), 20–1.
[69] Ibid.
[70] Fortin (2006), 311–12.

once we acknowledge the limitations of the full power theory, it is easy to see that important interests for which it is reasonable to accord the individual a protective right may be served by compulsory interventions which are properly regarded as paternalistic.

Freeman, a strong proponent of children's rights, agrees that an element of paternalism is often necessary in order to protect children from themselves.[71]

M. Freeman, 'Taking Children's Rights More Seriously', (1992) 6 *International Journal of Law and the Family* 52, 65–6

To respect a child's autonomy is to treat that child as a person and as a rights-holder. It is clear that we can do so to a much greater extent than we have assumed hitherto. But it is also clear that the exercising of autonomy by a child can have a deleterious impact on that child's life chances. It is true that adults make mistakes too (and also make mistakes when interfering with a child's autonomy). Having rights means being allowed to take risks and make choices. There is a reluctance to interfere with an adult's project. This reluctance is tempered when the project pursuer is a child by the sense that choice now may harm choice later...

If we are to make progress we have to recognize the moral integrity of children. We have to treat them as persons entitled to equal concern and respect and entitled to have both their present autonomy recognized and their capacity for future autonomy safeguarded. And this is to recognize that children, particularly younger children, need nurture, care and protection. Children must not, as Hafen (1977) put it, be 'abandoned' to their rights.

The difficult question in seeking to reconcile the competing demands of autonomy and protection is where the line justifying adult intervention should be drawn. Freeman suggests that intervention will be justified to protect children against irrational actions. Which simply begs the question: what will constitute an irrational action? In particular, will any action with which an adult disagrees be labelled irrational?

M. Freeman, 'Taking Children's Rights More Seriously', (1992) 6 *International Journal of Law and the Family* 52, 67–9

[W]hat is to be regarded as 'irrational' must be strictly confined. The subjective values of the would-be protector cannot be allowed to intrude... Nor should we see an action as irrational unless it is manifestly so in the sense that it would undermine future life choices, impair interests in an irreversible way. Furthermore, we must tolerate mistakes... But we also would be failing to recognize a child's integrity if we allowed him to choose an action, such as using heroin or choosing not to attend school, which could seriously and systematically impair the attainment of full personality and development subsequently. The test of 'irrationality' must also be confined so that it justifies intervention only to the extent necessary to obviate the immediate harm, or to develop the capacities of rational choice by which the individual may have a reasonable chance of avoiding such harms.

The question we should ask ourselves is: what sort of action or conduct would we wish, as children, to be shielded against on the assumption that we would want to mature to a

---

[71] See also Fortin (2004), 259–60.

rationally autonomous adulthood and be capable of deciding on our own system of ends as free and rational beings? We would, I believe, choose principles that would enable children to mature to independent adulthood. One definition of irrationality would be such as to preclude action and conduct which would frustrate such a goal. Within the constraints of such a definition we would defend a version of paternalism: not paternalism in its classical sense for, so conceived, there would be no children's rights at all...

To take children's rights more seriously requires us to take seriously nurturance and self-determination. It demands of us that we adopt policies, practices, structures and laws which both protect children and their rights. Hence the *via media* of 'liberal paternalism'.

Whichever theory of rights is preferred, it is difficult to escape the attractions of adult paternalism. And, perhaps not surprisingly, this will emerge as a dominant theme as we explore the current approach to children's rights in English law.

8.5.3 THE DEVELOPMENT OF CHILDREN'S RIGHTS IN ENGLISH LAW

The emancipation of children from the control of their fathers

The twentieth century witnessed a fundamental shift in understanding about the parent-child relationship. At the turn of the nineteenth century, this relationship was governed by the historic concept of 'guardianship', which conferred on the father of his legitimate children complete authority over their person and property.[72] By the early part of the twentieth century, 'paternal authority' had been transformed into 'parental authority', but the nature of the parent-child relationship had not undergone significant change.[73] Parents were understood to possess all the necessary power and authority over a child that would enable them to control every aspect of the child's upbringing. This power and authority was enshrined in the parental right or bundle of rights often simply referred to as the 'right to custody and control'. The primary concern of the law was to protect this right from any outside interference.

During the twentieth century, attitudes towards children began to change with important consequences for the parent-child relationship. Growing concern with the welfare of children initiated the gradual liberation of children from their parents, with the result that children were no longer regarded as their parents' possessions. The control and authority that parents enjoyed over their children was gradually replaced with the embryonic idea that children were also autonomous individuals with enforceable rights of their own. The emerging concept of children's rights had far-reaching significance for the concept of parenthood. If children possess rights then somebody must hold the corresponding duty or responsibility to protect them. That person is the parent. It is these duties and responsibilities that now dominate the concept of parenthood in English law.[74]

Whilst the general concept of parental rights is currently undergoing a certain renaissance, the parental right to custody and control has been fundamentally transformed. This right is now understood as a *conditional* right. It inheres for the benefit of the child and not

---

[72] *In re Agar-Ellis* (1883) 24 Ch D 317.

[73] The process of placing the mother in a position of equality with that of the father began with the Guardianship of Infants Act 1886, s 5.

[74] See chapter 10.

the parent.[75] Thus, the right to custody and control is of only instrumental value: that is, it exists only insofar as necessary for the fulfilment of parental duties. This understanding of the relationship between children's rights and parental rights and duties was usefully summarized by L'Heureux-Dubé J in the Canadian Supreme Court:

Young v Young et al [1993] 4 SCR 3

The power of the custodial parent is not a "right" with independent value which is granted by the courts for the benefit of the parent, but is designed to enable that parent to discharge his or her responsibilities and obligations to the child. It is, in fact, the child's right to a parent who will look after his or her best interests ... It has long been recognized that the custodial parent has a duty to ensure, protect and promote the best interests of the child. That duty includes the sole and primary responsibility to oversee all aspects of day to day life and long-term well-being, as well as major decisions with respect to education, religion, health and well-being.

It is this view of parenthood which underpins the House of Lords' decision in *Gillick v West Norfolk and Wisbech Area Health Authority*,[76] discussed below. As will be seen, it has important implications as to the scope of the parents' decision-making authority within the parent-child relationship.

8.5.4 CHILDREN'S RIGHTS IN THE COURTS

Children's welfare-based rights to care and protection

The courts have had less difficulty embracing children's rights where there is no inconsistency between the child's rights and the child's welfare. To talk of a child's right to be protected from parental abuse or neglect, or to be provided with the basic necessities of life, is uncontentious and raises no challenge to a welfare-orientated approach. Thus, where the issue relates to a young child's health and safety, such as whether a child should be tested for HIV, the judiciary have comfortably employed the language of welfare and rights interchangeably.[77]

Children's autonomy rights

The Gillick *decision*

As expected, the real test of judicial commitment to children's rights came in a case which raised the more challenging issue of a child's right to self-determination.[78] *Gillick* concerned a challenge to a memorandum of guidance issued by central government to local health authorities containing a section on the provision of contraceptive advice and treatment to children under the age of 16. In essence, the guidance suggested that contraceptive advice and treatment could be provided without informing the child's parents or obtaining parental

---

[75] This contrasts with parental rights as enshrined in Article 8 ECHR which are properly conceptualized as autonomous rights which inhere for the benefit of the parent.

[76] [1986] AC 112.

[77] See, e.g., *Re C (HIV Test)* [1999] 2 FLR 1004, 1016 (per Wilson J), and 1021 (per Butler-Sloss LJ) and *R v Secretary of State for Education and Employment and others, ex parte Williamson* [2005] UKHL 15 (per Baroness Hale). Fortin provides a somewhat more pessimistic analysis. See Fortin (2006), 300–3.

[78] See generally, Fortin (2009b), ch 5.

consent. Mrs Gillick, a mother of five girls, wrote to her local health authority requesting assurance that no contraceptive advice or treatment would be given to any of her daughters whilst under the age of 16 without her knowledge and consent. The health authority refused to give such assurance arguing that in accordance with the central guidance, such a decision would be a matter of clinical judgement for the individual doctor. Mrs Gillick consequently sought a declaration that the guidance was unlawful, in particular, that it unlawfully interfered with her parental rights and duties. The House of Lords, by a majority, dismissed her complaint:

Gillick v West Norfolk and Wisbech Area Health Authority [1986] AC 112, 166–75 and 181–90

LORD FRASER:

[P]arental rights to control a child do not exist for the benefit of the parent. They exist for the benefit of the child and they are justified only in so far as they enable the parent to perform his duties towards the child, and towards other children in the family...

From the parents' right and duty of custody flows their right and duty of control of the child, but the fact that custody is its origin throws but little light on the question of the legal extent of control at any particular age...

It is, in my view, contrary to the ordinary experience of mankind, at least in Western Europe in the present century, to say that a child or a young person remains in fact under the complete control of his parents until he attains the definite age of majority, now 18 in the United Kingdom, and that on attaining that age he suddenly acquires independence. In practice most wise parents relax their control gradually as the child develops and encourage him or her to become increasingly independent. Moreover, the degree of parental control actually exercised over a particular child does in practice vary considerably according to his understanding and intelligence and it would, in my opinion, be unrealistic for the courts not to recognise these facts. Social customs change, and the law ought to, and does in fact, have regard to such changes when they are of major importance...

[T]he view that the child's intellectual ability is irrelevant cannot, in my opinion, now be accepted. It is a question of fact for the judge (or jury) to decide whether a particular child can give effective consent to contraceptive treatment.

In times gone by the father had almost absolute authority over his children until they attained majority. A rather remarkable example of such authority being upheld by the court was the case in *In Re Agar-Ellis* (1883) 24 Ch.D. 317...The case has been much criticised in recent years and, in my opinion, with good reason. In *Hewer v Bryant* [1970] 1 Q.B. 357, 369, Lord Denning MR said:

"I would get rid of the rule in *In Re Agar-Ellis* and of the suggested exceptions to it. That case was decided in the year 1883. It reflects the attitude of a Victorian parent towards his children. He expected unquestioning obedience to his commands...I decline to accept a view so much out of date. The common law can, and should, keep pace with the times. It should declare...that the legal right of a parent to the custody of a child ends at the 18th birthday; and even up till then, it is a dwindling right which the courts will hesitate to enforce against the wishes of the child, and the more so the older he is. It starts with a right of control and ends with little more than advice."

I respectfully agree with every word of that and especially with the description of the father's authority as a dwindling right...In my opinion, the view of absolute paternal authority continuing until a child attains majority which was applied in *Agar-Ellis* is so out of line with present day views that it should no longer be treated as having any authority. I regard it as an historical curiosity...

Once the rule of the parents' absolute authority over minor children is abandoned, the solution to the problem in this appeal can no longer be found by referring to rigid parental rights at any particular age. The solution depends upon a judgment of what is best for the welfare of the particular child. Nobody doubts, certainly I do not doubt, that in the overwhelming majority of cases the best judges of a child's welfare are his or her parents. Nor do I doubt that any important medical treatment of a child under 16 would normally only be carried out with the parents' approval. That is why it would and should be "most unusual" for a doctor to advise a child without the knowledge and consent of the parents on contraceptive matters. But, as I have already pointed out, Mrs. Gillick has to go further if she is to obtain the first declaration that she seeks. She has to justify the absolute right of veto in a parent. But there may be circumstances in which a doctor is a better judge of the medical advice and treatment which will conduce to a girl's welfare than her parents...

The only practicable course is to entrust the doctor with a discretion to act in accordance with his view of what is best in the interests of the girl who is his patient. He should, of course, always seek to persuade her to tell her parents that she is seeking contraceptive advice, and the nature of the advice that she receives. At least he should seek to persuade her to agree to the doctor's informing the parents. But there may well be cases, and I think there will be some cases, where the girl refuses either to tell the parents herself or to permit the doctor to do so and in such cases, the doctor will, in my opinion, be justified in proceeding without the parents' consent or even knowledge provided he is satisfied on the following matters: (1) that the girl (although under 16 years of age) will understand his advice; (2) that he cannot persuade her to inform her parents or to allow him to inform the parents that she is seeking contraceptive advice; (3) that she is very likely to begin or to continue having sexual intercourse with or without contraceptive treatment; (4) that unless she receives contraceptive advice or treatment her physical or mental health or both are likely to suffer; (5) that her best interests require him to give her contraceptive advice, treatment or both without the parental consent... For those reasons I do not consider that the guidance interferes with the parents' rights.

LORD SCARMAN:

The question... for the House is—can a doctor in any circumstances lawfully prescribe contraception for a girl under 16 without the knowledge and consent of a parent?...

Parental right and the age of consent...

Parental rights clearly do exist, and they do not wholly disappear until the age of majority. Parental rights relate to both the person and the property of the child... But the common law has never treated such rights as sovereign or beyond review and control. Nor has our law ever treated the child as other than a person with capacities and rights recognised by law. The principle of the law, as I shall endeavour to show, is that parental rights are derived from parental duty and exist only so long as they are needed for the protection of the person and property of the child. The principle has been subjected to certain age limits set by statute for certain purposes: and in some cases the courts have declared an age of discretion at which a child acquires before the age of majority the right to make his (or her) own decision. But these limitations in no way undermine the principle of the law, and should not be allowed to obscure it.

Let me make good, quite shortly, the proposition of principle.

First…when a court has before it a question as to the care and upbringing of a child it must treat the welfare of the child as the paramount consideration in determining the order to be made. There is here a principle which limits and governs the exercise of parental rights of custody, care and control. It is a principle perfectly consistent with the law's recognition of the parent as the natural guardian of the child; but it is also a warning that parental right must be exercised in accordance with the welfare principle and can be challenged, even overridden, if it be not.

Secondly, there is the common law's understanding of the nature of parental right…It is abundantly plain that the law recognizes that there is a right and a duty of parents to determine whether or not to seek medical advice in respect of their child, and, having received advice, to give or withhold consent to medical treatment. The question in the appeal is as to the extent, and duration, of the right and the circumstances in which…it can be overridden by the exercise of medical judgment…

The principle is that parental right or power of control of the person and property of his child exists primarily to enable the parent to discharge his duty of maintenance, protection and education until he reaches such an age as to be able to look after himself and make his own decisions. Blackstone does suggest that there was a further justification for parental right, viz. as a recompense for the faithful discharge of parental duty: but the right of the father to the exclusion of the mother and the reward element as one of the reasons for the existence of the right have been swept away by the guardianship of minors legislation…He also accepts that by statute and by case law varying ages of discretion have been fixed for various purposes. But it is clear that this was done to achieve certainty where it was considered necessary and in no way limits the principle that parental right endures only so long as it is needed for the protection of the child.

Although statute has intervened in respect of a child's capacity to consent to medical treatment from the age of 16 onwards, neither statute nor the case law has ruled on the extent and duration of parental right in respect of children under the age of 16. More specifically, there is no rule yet applied to contraceptive treatment…It is open, therefore, to the House to formulate a rule. The Court of Appeal favoured a fixed age limit of 16…They sought to justify the limit by the public interest in the law being certain. Certainty is always an advantage in the law, and in some branches of the law it is a necessity. But it brings with it an inflexibility and a rigidity which in some branches of the law can obstruct justice, impede the law's development, and stamp upon the law the mark of obsolescence where what is needed is the capacity for development. The law relating to parent and child is concerned with the problems of the growth and maturity of the human personality. If the law should impose upon the process of "growing up" fixed limits where nature knows only a continuous process, the price would be artificiality and a lack of realism in an area where the law must be sensitive to human development and social change. If certainty be thought desirable, it is better that the rigid demarcations necessary to achieve it should be laid down by legislation after a full consideration of all the relevant factors than by the courts confined as they are by the forensic process to the evidence adduced by the parties and to whatever may properly fall within the judicial notice of judges. Unless and until Parliament should think fit to intervene, the courts should establish a principle flexible enough to enable justice to be achieved by its application to the particular circumstances proved by the evidence placed before them.

The underlying principle of the law was exposed by Blackstone and can be seen to have been acknowledged in the case law. It is that parental right yields to the child's right to make his own decisions when he reaches a sufficient understanding and intelligence to be capable of making up his own mind on the matter requiring decision…

In the light of the foregoing I would hold that as a matter of law the parental right to determine whether or not their minor child below the age of 16 will have medical treatment terminates if and when the child achieves a sufficient understanding and intelligence to enable him or her to understand fully what is proposed. It will be a question of fact whether a child seeking advice has sufficient understanding of what is involved to give a consent valid in law. Until the child achieves the capacity to consent, the parental right to make the decision continues save only in exceptional circumstances...

I am, therefore, satisfied that the department's guidance can be followed without involving the doctor in any infringement of parental right.

[On the issue of consent and the purported interference with parental rights and duties, **Lord Bridge** agreed with both **Lord Fraser** and **Lord Scarman**.]

It is difficult to discern the ratio of *Gillick* on the question of the existence and scope of children's rights vis-à-vis the rights of the parents. The issue has sparked considerable academic debate. However, both Lord Fraser and Lord Scarman appear to confirm that the parental right to custody and control is wholly derived from the parents' duties and responsibilities to the child and thus depends on the continuing existence of those duties. Furthermore, they hold that the parental right to custody and control is forever dwindling and diminishing in importance as the child grows older because, as children mature, they become increasingly capable of exercising their own rights and decision-making powers. It follows logically from this that parents' rights cannot be ascertained by reference to any particular fixed age, but depend on the degree of intelligence and understanding of the child in question. Essentially, the question is whether the child has sufficient maturity to make his or her own decisions. Lord Scarman also appears to go one step further than Lord Fraser in holding in unequivocal terms that the child's right and the corresponding parental right cannot coexist. He thus suggests that parents' and children's rights exist on a continuum such that once a child reaches the required level of '*Gillick* competency', the purpose behind the parental right is exhausted and must yield to the right of the child.

For children's rights advocates, Lord Scarman's judgment seemed to hold enormous promise. An interpretation of the *Gillick* decision in line with his judgment would significantly erode parental authority and control over children, particularly as they enter their teenage years. For this reason, many commentators hailed *Gillick* as a landmark decision in securing children's basic autonomy rights. In line with the power or will theory, Lord Scarman's approach suggested that as soon as children were deemed to have the necessary rational will, they would be regarded as autonomous right-holders, able to make decisions free from parental control.

However, to champion children's autonomy when it enables the child to make decisions many would deem in the child's best interests, such as receiving confidential contraceptive advice and treatment before embarking on a sexual relationship, is one thing. To continue to champion that right when the child is refusing life-saving treatment is more difficult, even for the most ardent 'child liberationist'.

It is perhaps for this reason that the more radical interpretation of *Gillick* and its promise of delivering real autonomy for older children has not been realized. In what many regard as a retreat from *Gillick*, children's autonomy rights have been consistently qualified by a return to a more paternalistic approach, swinging the scales heavily back in favour of protecting parental authority.

The retreat from Gillick

The first sign that *Gillick* would be subjected to a conservative application came in *Re E (A minor)*.[79] *Re E* concerned a 15-year-old boy ['A'] with leukaemia who urgently required a blood transfusion. Both the boy and his parents were devout Jehovah's Witnesses and therefore refused to consent to treatment, blood transfusions being contrary to the tenets of their faith. Ward J accepted that a *Gillick* competent child could validly withhold consent to treatment. However, he avoided the difficult consequences of such a conclusion by refusing to find that the child had sufficient understanding and maturity to be regarded as *Gillick* competent, despite his 'obvious intelligence'. The child was thus deemed incapable of refusing treatment.

Re E (A minor) (Wardship: Medical Treatment) [1992] 2 FCR 219, 224–7

Mr. Justice WARD:

...I will deal with the issue as to whether or not the refusal by A is a refusal taken in circumstances such as would, so it is submitted, enable him to override the parental choice. I find that A is a boy of sufficient intelligence to be able to take decisions about his own well-being, but I also find that there is a range of decisions of which some are outside his ability fully to grasp their implications. Impressed though I was by his obvious intelligence, by his calm discussion of the implications, by his assertion even that he would refuse well knowing that he may die as a result, in my judgment A does not have a full understanding of the whole implication of what the refusal of that treatment involves.

Dr. T told me graphically...that A will become increasingly breathless...I did not judge it right to probe [with A] whether or not he knew how frightening it would be. Dr. T did not consider it necessary to spell it out for him, and I did not feel it was appropriate for me to do so.

I am quite satisfied that A does not have any sufficient comprehension of the pain he has yet to suffer, of the fear that he will be undergoing, of the distress not only occasioned by that fear but also—and importantly—the distress he will inevitably suffer as he, a loving son, helplessly watches his parents' and his family's distress. They are a close family, and they are a brave family, but I find that he has no realization of the full implications which lie before him as to the process of dying. He may have some concept of the fact that he will die, but as to the manner of his death and to the extent of his and his family's suffering I find he has not the ability to turn his mind to it nor the will to do so. Who can blame him for that?

If, therefore, this case depended upon my finding of whether or not A is of sufficient understanding and intelligence and maturity to give full and informed consent, I find that he is not.

Ward J later turns to consider the weight which should be accorded to A's wishes in accordance with the welfare principle. Again, there is a clear reluctance to recognize the child's full capacity for autonomous decision-making:

In considering what his welfare dictates, I have to have regard to his wishes. What he wishes is an important factor for me to take into account and, having regard to the closeness of his attaining 16, a very important matter which weighs very heavily in the scales I have to hold in balance.

---

[79] [1992] 2 FCR 219.

He is of an age and understanding at least to appreciate the consequence if not the process of his decision, and by reason of the convictions of his religion, which I find to be deeply held and genuine, says no to a medical intervention which may save his life. What weight do I place upon this refusal? I approach this case telling myself that the freedom of choice in adults is a fundamental human right. He is close to the time when he may be able to take those decisions. I should, therefore, be very slow to interfere. I have also to ask myself to what extent is that assertion of decision, "I will not have a blood transfusion", the product of his full and his free informed thought? Without wishing to introduce into the case notions of undue influence, I find that the influence of the teachings of the Jehovah's Witnesses is strong and powerful . . . I am far from satisfied that at the age of 15 his will is fully free. He may assert it, but his volition has been conditioned by the very powerful expressions of faith to which all members of the creed adhere. When making this decision, which is a decision of life or death, I have to take account of the fact that teenagers often express views with vehemence and conviction—all the vehemence and conviction of youth! Those of us who have passed beyond callow youth can all remember the convictions we have loudly proclaimed which we now find somewhat embarrassing. I respect this boy's profession of faith, but I cannot discount at least the possibility that he may in later years suffer some diminution in his convictions. There is no settled certainty about matters of this kind . . .

When . . . I have to balance the wishes of the father and son against the need for the chance to live a precious life, then I have to conclude that their decision is inimicable to his well-being.

Two important points emerge from *Re E* which have been used in subsequent cases to justify a finding that a child approaching majority lacks the necessary maturity and understanding to qualify as a *Gillick* competent child.[80] The first relates to the child's illness. The courts have readily found that a child's ability to make fully informed decisions is either compromised by the nature of the illness itself, such as in cases of anorexia nervosa,[81] or that the child, whilst comprehending the nature of the illness, does not fully understand the implications of a failure to agree to treatment, in particular, that the child has not faced or does not fully comprehend the realities of death—a somewhat disingenuous conclusion given that information about the painful and inevitably distressing nature of the death is often withheld from the child in the child's best interests.[82] The second point to emerge from *Re E* relates to a child's religious beliefs. Several of these life and death cases concern a child's refusal to consent to treatment on religious grounds. However, Ward J's judgment questions whether a child's sincerely and strongly held religious beliefs should be accepted at face value, suggesting that a child of 15, particularly if raised within a deeply religious family, lacks the necessary life experience to hold a free and fully informed view on religious matters.[83]

Sadly, the boy who was the subject of the application in *Re E (A minor)* refused to give his consent to continuing treatment upon reaching the age of 18 and died shortly thereafter.[84]

---

[80] See, e.g., *Re S (A Minor) (Consent to Medical Treatment)* [1995] 1 FCR 604; *Re L (Medical Treatment: Gillick Competency)* [1998] 2 FLR 810.

[81] See, e.g., *In re W (A Minor) (Medical Treatment: Court's Jurisdiction)* [1993] Fam 64 (anorexia); *Re R (a minor) (wardship: consent to treatment)* [1992] Fam 11 (psychotic mental illness); *A Metropolitan Borough Council v DB* [1997] 1 FLR 767 (drug addiction problems, eclamptic fits); and *Re K, W and H (Minors) (Medical Treatment)* [1993] 1 FLR 854 (mental health problems).

[82] Fortin (2009b), 154.

[83] See also *Re L (Medical Treatment: Gillick Competency)* [1998] 2 FLR 810.

[84] Fortin (2009b), 154.

The next important 'blow' to *Gillick*'s effectiveness as a vehicle for protecting children's autonomy rights came in *Re R (a minor) (wardship: consent to treatment)*. The *Gillick* decision concerned the right of a minor to *consent* to medical treatment and the relationship between the child's right of consent and that of the parents. It did not specifically address two further questions: (i) the right of a minor to *refuse* medical treatment and the relationship between the child's and the parents' right of refusal; and (ii) the child's rights vis-à-vis the power of the court under its inherent jurisdiction. Both of these questions were addressed by Lord Donaldson in the Court of Appeal in *Re R* and on both questions Lord Donaldson, giving the lead judgment, sanctioned strong paternalistic intervention where necessary.[85] *Re R* concerned a disturbed 15-year-old girl who was suffering from a psychotic illness manifesting itself from time to time in periods of violence, paranoia, hallucinations, and suicidal tendencies. When rational and stable she refused to consent to anti-psychotic drugs being administered to her. On the question of whether her refusal to consent to treatment should be treated as determinative of the matter, Lord Donaldson held:

Re R (a minor) (wardship: consent to treatment) [1992] Fam 11, 22–6 (CA)

LORD DONALDSON MR:

It is trite law that in general a doctor is not entitled to treat a patient without the consent of someone who is authorised to give that consent. If he does so, he will be liable in damages for trespass to the person and may be guilty of a criminal assault. This is subject to the necessary exception that in cases of emergency a doctor may treat the patient notwithstanding the absence of consent, if the patient is unconscious or otherwise incapable of giving or refusing consent and there is no one else sufficiently immediately available with authority to consent on behalf of the patient. However consent by itself creates no obligation to treat. It is merely a key which unlocks a door. Furthermore, whilst in the case of an adult of full capacity there will usually only be one keyholder, namely the patient, in the ordinary family unit where a young child is the patient there will be two keyholders, namely the parents, with a several as well as a joint right to turn the key and unlock the door. If the parents disagree, one consenting and the other refusing, the doctor will be presented with a professional and ethical, but not with a legal, problem because, if he has consent of one authorised person, treatment will not without more constitute a trespass or a criminal assault...

In the instant appeal [counsel], appearing for the Official Solicitor, submits that (a) if the child has the right to give consent to medical treatment, the parents' right to give or refuse consent is terminated and (b) the court in the exercise of its wardship jurisdiction is only entitled to step into the shoes of the parents and thus itself has no right to give or refuse consent. Whilst it is true that he seeks to modify the effect of this rather startling submission by suggesting that, if the child's consent or refusal of consent is irrational or misguided, the court will readily infer that in the particular context that individual child is not competent to give or withhold consent, it is necessary to look very carefully at the *Gillick* decision to see whether it supports his argument and, if it does, whether it is binding upon this court.

The key passages upon which counsel relies are to be found in the speech of Lord Scarman...

What [counsel's] argument overlooks is that Lord Scarman was discussing the parent's right "to *determine* whether or not their minor child below the age of 16 will have medical treatment"...A right of determination is wider than a right to consent. The parents can

---

85 For excellent discussion of this decision see ibid., 155–8.

only have a right of determination if *either* the child has no right to consent, that is, is not a keyholder, *or* the parents hold a master key which could nullify the child's consent. I do not understand Lord Scarman to be saying that, if a child was "*Gillick* competent", to adopt the convenient phrase used in argument, the parents ceased to have an independent right of consent as contrasted with ceasing to have a right of determination, that is, a veto. In a case in which the "*Gillick* competent" child refuses treatment, but the parents consent, that consent *enables* treatment to be undertaken lawfully, but in no way determines that the child shall be so treated. In a case in which the positions are reversed, it is the child's consent which is the enabling factor and again the parents' refusal of consent is not determinative. If Lord Scarman intended to go further than this and to say that in the case of a "*Gillick* competent" child, a parent has no right either to consent or to refuse consent, his remarks were obiter, because the only question in issue was Mrs. Gillick's alleged right of veto. Furthermore I consider that they would have been wrong.

One glance at the consequences suffices to show that Lord Scarman cannot have been intending to say that the parental right to consent terminates with the achievement by the child of "*Gillick* competence". It is fundamental to the speeches of the majority that the capacity to consent will vary from child to child and according to the treatment under consideration, depending upon the sufficiency of his or her intelligence and understanding of that treatment. If the position in law is that upon the achievement of "*Gillick* competence" there is a transfer of the right of consent from parents to child and there can never be a concurrent right in both, doctors would be faced with an intolerable dilemma, particularly when the child was nearing the age of 16, if the parents consented, but the child did not. On pain, if they got it wrong, of being sued for trespass to the person or possibly being charged with a criminal assault, they would have to determine as a matter of law in whom the right of consent resided at the particular time in relation to the particular treatment. I do not believe that that is the law...

Both in this case and in *In Re E.* the judges treated *Gillick*... as deciding that a "*Gillick* competent" child has a right to refuse treatment. In this I consider that they were in error. Such a child can consent, but if he or she declines to do so or refuses, consent can be given by someone else who has parental rights or responsibilities. The failure or refusal of the "*Gillick* competent" child is a very important factor in the doctor's decision whether or not to treat, but does not prevent the necessary consent being obtained from another competent source.

The wardship jurisdiction

In considering the wardship jurisdiction of the court, no assistance is to be derived from *Gillick*'s case, where this simply was not in issue... It is, however, clear that the practical jurisdiction of the court is wider than that of parents... It is also clear that this jurisdiction is not derivative from the parents' rights and responsibilities, but derives from, or is, the delegated performance of the duties of the Crown to protect its subjects and particularly children who are the generations of the future.

Whilst it is no doubt true to say, as Lord Upjohn did say in *J v C*... that the function of the court is to 'act as the judicial reasonable parent', all that, in context, he was saying was that the court should exercise its jurisdiction in the interests of the children "reflecting and adopting the changing views, as the years go by, of reasonable men and women, the parents of children, on the proper treatment and methods of bringing up children". This is very far from saying that the wardship jurisdiction is derived from, or in any way limited by, that of the parents. In many cases of wardship the parents or other guardians will be left to make decisions for the child, subject only to standing instructions to refer reserved matters to the court, e.g. the taking of a serious step in the upbringing or medical treatment of a child, and to the court's right and in appropriate cases, duty to override the decision of the parents or other guardians. If it can override such consents, as it undoubtedly can, I see no reason whatsoever why it should not be able, and in an appropriate case willing, to override decisions by "*Gillick* competent" children who are its wards or in respect of whom applications are made for, for example, section 8 orders under the Children Act 1989...

Conclusion

1. No doctor can be required to treat a child, whether by the court in the exercise of its wardship jurisdiction, by the parents, by the child or anyone else. The decision whether to treat is dependent upon an exercise of his own professional judgment, subject only to the threshold requirement that, save in exceptional cases usually of emergency, he has the consent of someone who has authority to give that consent. In forming that judgment the views and wishes of the child are a factor whose importance increases with the increase in the child's intelligence and understanding.

2. There can be concurrent powers to consent. If more than one body or person has a power to consent, only a failure to, or refusal of, consent by all having that power will create a veto.

3. A "*Gillick* competent" child or one over the age of 16 will have a power to consent, but this will be concurrent with that of a parent or guardian.

4. "*Gillick* competence" is a developmental concept and will not be lost or acquired on a day to day or week to week basis. In the case of mental disability, that disability must also be taken into account, particularly where it is fluctuating in its effect.

5. The court in the exercise of its wardship or statutory jurisdiction has power to override the decisions of a "*Gillick* competent" child as much as those of parents or guardians.

6. Waite J. was right to hold that R. was not "*Gillick* competent" and, even if R. had been, was right to consent to her undergoing treatment which might involve compulsory medication.

[**Staughton LJ** expressed no opinion on the question of whether the parent's right to consent to treatment continued to exist alongside that of the competent child but agreed with **Donaldson MR** as to the scope of the court's inherent jurisdiction. **Farquharson LJ** decided the case on the basis that the child lacked *Gillick* competency.]

Lord Donaldson's judgment in *Re R* makes two points clear. First, a *Gillick* competent child has no right to veto treatment: parents do not lose their independent right to consent upon the child becoming *Gillick* competent, the two rights coexist. This means that provided the doctor obtains the consent of either the child or the parent, the treatment can proceed.[86] Second, the court exercising its inherent jurisdiction can override both the child and the parents. Consequently, even if both a *Gillick* competent child and the parents refuse treatment, the court acting in the child's best interests can grant permission for the treatment to proceed.

The strong swing back in favour of paternalism, even in the case of *Gillick* competent children or children over the age of 16, was taken a step further by Lord Donaldson in *Re W (A Minor) (Medical Treatment: Court's Jurisdiction)*. In this case, Lord Donaldson

---

[86] Applied in *Re K, W and H (Minors) (Medical Treatment)* [1993] 1 FLR 854.

held that, despite a 16-year-old having a clear statutory right to consent to treatment under s 8 of the Family Law Reform Act 1969 (FLRA 1969), a 16-year-old's *refusal* to consent could be overridden by anyone holding parental responsibility or the court. It was similarly confirmed in *South Glamorgan County Council v W and B*[87] that the court's inherent jurisdiction was wide enough to override the right of a child of sufficient age and understanding to refuse to submit to a medical and/or psychiatric examination ordered by the court under s 38(6) of the CA 1989. The extent to which *Gillick* autonomy has been undermined by the courts is particularly striking in this case as the child's right to refuse to participate in any such assessment or examination is clearly enshrined in the statute.[88] In a further blow to children's autonomy, it was also suggested in *South Glamorgan County Council v W and B* and confirmed in *A Metropolitan Borough Council v DB*[89] that reasonable force could be used for the purpose of imposing medical and/or psychiatric treatment against the child's wishes where such treatment was deemed to be necessary in the child's best interests.

On the specific issue of consent to medical treatment, there has thus been a dramatic retreat from the 'high point' of children's autonomy rights suggested in Lord Scarman's judgment in *Gillick*. Indeed, *Gillick* has been narrowed to such an extent that whilst *Gillick* competent children can consent to treatment, children have no overriding right to refuse. This means treatment can be forced on children against their wishes provided that their parents or the court gives consent, such consent invariably being given by the court where the treatment is recommended by the doctor as being in the child's best interests. The only real concession to the *Gillick* competent child has been the court's willingness to acknowledge that the older the child, the greater the respect which should be accorded to his or her wishes.

The wider significance of *Gillick*

In many ways, the post-*Gillick* era was disappointing for children's rights advocates, particularly regarding control over medical treatment. However, the conservatism shown in these difficult 'life and death' cases should not obscure the wider significance of *Gillick*. Freed from the acute circumstances of the medical cases, *Gillick* fundamentally transformed the way the law thought about children and parenthood, with the concept of '*Gillick* competency' providing a touchstone for children's rights to self-determination. Two recent decisions exemplify the extent to which the concept of children's autonomy rights have now taken hold in the law.

The first case concerned an application by three teenage children to be separately represented in private law proceedings between their parents. The judge dismissed the application. The Court of Appeal overturned the decision, Thorpe LJ placing significant emphasis on the children's right to freedom of expression and participation, even if such participation was contrary to the court's judgment on welfare.[90]

---

[87] [1993] 1 FLR 574.

[88] It can be assumed that the same approach would be taken to similar provisions contained in the CA 1989 such as s 43(8) dealing with child assessment orders.

[89] [1997] 1 FLR 767.

[90] For a critique of the way in which the Court of Appeal draws a distinction between the children's rights and the children's welfare see Fortin (2006), 310–12.

Mabon v Mabon and others [2005] EWCA Civ 634

THORPE LJ:

[25]...In our system we have traditionally adopted the tandem model for the representation of children who are parties to family proceedings, whether public or private. First the court appoints a guardian ad litem who will almost invariably have a social work qualification and very wide experience of family proceedings. He then instructs a specialist family solicitor who, in turn, usually instructs a specialist family barrister. This is a Rolls Royce model and is the envy of many other jurisdictions. However its overall approach is essentially paternalistic. The guardian's first priority is to advocate the welfare of the child he represents. His second priority is to put before the court the child's wishes and feelings. Those priorities can in some cases conflict. In extreme cases the conflict is unmanageable. That reality is recognised by the terms of rule 9.2A. The direction set by rule 9.2A(6) is a mandatory grant of the application provided that the court considers "that the minor concerned has sufficient understanding to participate as a party in the proceedings concerned." Thus the focus is upon the sufficiency of the child's understanding in the context of the remaining proceedings.

[26] In my judgment the Rule is sufficiently widely framed to meet our obligations to comply with both Article 12 of the United Nations Convention and Article 8 of the ECHR, providing that judges correctly focus on the sufficiency of the child's understanding and, in measuring that sufficiency, reflect the extent to which, in the 21st Century, there is a keener appreciation of the autonomy of the child and the child's consequential right to participate in decision making processes that fundamentally affect his family life...

[28]...Although the tandem model has many strengths and virtues, at its heart lies the conflict between advancing the welfare of the child and upholding the child's freedom of expression and participation. Unless we in this jurisdiction are to fall out of step with similar societies as they safeguard Article 12 rights, we must, in the case of articulate teenagers, accept that the right to freedom of expression and participation outweighs the paternalistic judgment of welfare.

[29] In testing the sufficiency of a child's understanding I would not say that welfare has no place. If direct participation would pose an obvious risk of harm to the child arising out of the nature of the continuing proceedings and, if the child is incapable of comprehending that risk, then the judge is entitled to find that sufficient understanding has not been demonstrated. But judges have to be equally alive to the risk of emotional harm that might arise from denying the child knowledge of and participation in the continuing proceedings...

[32] In conclusion this case provides a timely opportunity to recognise the growing acknowledgement of the autonomy and consequential rights of children, both nationally and internationally. The Rules are sufficiently robustly drawn to accommodate that shift. In individual cases trial judges must equally acknowledge the shift when they make in individual cases a proportionate judgment of the sufficiency of the child's understanding.

The second case posed a direct threat to the *Gillick* decision. The case concerned DOH guidance published in 2004 regarding confidentiality attaching to advice and treatment given to a child under 16 on sexual matters, including contraception, sexually transmitted infections, and abortion. The guidance stated that in certain circumstances a doctor could provide advice and treatment to a child under 16 without first notifying the parents. The applicant challenged the legality of the guidance, arguing that it undermined the right and responsibility of parents to provide guidance, help, and support to their teenage children, as guaranteed by Article 8 ECHR. The applicant did not challenge the child's right to consent to treatment (the issue in *Gillick*). Her challenge was limited to her right as a parent to be notified should her daughter approach a doctor for advice and/or treatment, particularly on matters relating to abortion. Silber J dismissed the application, finding that he was bound by the decision of the House of Lords in *Gillick*. The importance of recognizing the child's autonomy rights was again a prominent theme, with the provisions of the UNCRC given particular weight.

R (Axon) v Secretary of State for Health (Family Planning Association Intervening) [2006] EWHC 37

SILBER J:

64. It is appropriate to bear in mind that the ECHR attaches great value to the rights of children...Furthermore the ratification by the United Kingdom of the United Nations Convention on the Rights of the Child ("UNC") in November 1989 was significant as showing a desire to give children greater rights. The ECHR and the UNC show why the duty of confidence owed by a medical professional to a competent young person is a high one and which therefore should not be overridden except for a very powerful reason. In my view, although family factors are significant and cogent, they should not override the duty of confidentiality owed to the child...

76. ... It is appropriate at this stage to set out some of the relevant provisions of the UNC which was adopted in November 1989 and so post-dated *Gillick*. It has now been ratified by the United Kingdom...

Silber J then set out Articles 5, 12, and 16 of the UNCRC and referred to the decision of Thorpe LJ in *Mabon v Mabon*:

79. Although the facts in *Mabon* were very different from those in the present case, [Thorpe LJ's comments] do illustrate that the right of young people to make decisions about their own lives by themselves at the expense of the views of their parents has now become an increasingly important and accepted feature of family life...

80. In the light of this change in the landscape of family matters, in which rights of children are becoming increasingly important, it would be ironic and indeed not acceptable now to retreat from the approach adopted in *Gillick* and to impose additional new duties on medical professionals to disclose information to parents of their younger patients.

On the question of whether the DOH guidance violated the rights of the parent under Article 8 ECHR, Silber J applied the 'dwindling right' analysis to conclude that the parent's Article 8 rights would yield upon the child acquiring sufficient maturity and understanding to make his or her own decisions on such matters:

127. I am unable to accept [counsel's] contention that by permitting a medical professional to withhold information relating to advice or treatment of a young person on sexual matters, the article 8 rights of the parents of the young person were thereby infringed...

128. In order to decide whether parents have what [counsel] describes as "the right to parental authority over a child" having regard to their having parental duties, the age and maturity of the young person is of critical importance. Lord Lester QC and Mr David Pannick

QC state convincingly and correctly in my view that "as a child matures, the burden of show-ing ongoing family life by reference to substantive links or factors grows" (Human Rights Law and Practice – 2nd Edition (2004)...). This conclusion presupposes correctly that any right to family life on the part of a parent dwindles as their child gets older and is able to understand the consequence of different choices and then to make decisions relating to them.

130. As a matter of principle, it is difficult to see why a parent should still retain an article 8 right to parental authority relating to a medical decision where the young person concerned understands the advice provided by the medical professional and its implications. Indeed, any right under article 8 of a parent to be notified of advice or treatment of a sexual matter as part of the right claimed by [counsel] must depend on a number of factors, such as the age and understanding of their offspring. The parent would not be able to claim such an article 8 right to be notified if their son or daughter was, say, 18 years of age and had sought medical advice on sexual matters because in that case the young person was able to consent without parental knowledge or consent... The reason why the parent could not claim such a right is that their right to participate in decision-making as part of the right claimed by [counsel] would only exist while the child was so immature that his parent had the right of control... Lord Fraser and Lord Scarman in *Gillick*... both adopted the statement of Lord Denning MR *in Hewer v Bryant* [1970]...that the parent's right as against a child is "a dwindling right". As Lord Scarman explained, a parental right yields to the young person's right to make his own decisions when the young person reaches a sufficient understanding and intelligence to be capable of mak-ing up his or her own mind in relation to a matter requiring decision...and this autonomy of a young person must undermine any article 8 rights of a parent to family life. In my view, any article 8 right of the kind advocated by [counsel] must be seen in that light so that once the child is sufficiently mature in this way, the parent only retains such rights to family life and to be notified about medical treatment if but only if the young person so wishes.

131. Indeed whether there is family life and hence a right to family life in a particular family is a question of fact... It is not clear why the parent should have an article 8 right to family life, where first the offspring is almost 16 years of age and does not wish it, second where the parent no longer has a right to control the child for the reasons set out in the last paragraph and third where the young person in Lord Scarman's words... "has sufficient understanding of what is involved to give a consent valid in law".

132. There is nothing in the Strasbourg jurisprudence, which persuades me that any paren-tal right or power of control under article 8 is wider than in domestic law, which is that the right of parents in the words of Lord Scarman "exists primarily to enable the parent to dis-charge his duty of maintenance, protection and education until he reaches such an age as to be able to look after himself and make his own decisions"...The parental right to family life does not continue after that time and so parents do not have article 8 rights to be notified of any advice of a medical professional after the young person is able to look after himself or herself and make his or her own decisions.

Children's rights are thus gradually becoming an accepted part of everyday discourse in the family courts. However, of crucial importance to the development of this discourse is the way in which children's rights are perceived and implemented under the HRA 1998.

8.5.5 CHILDREN'S RIGHTS AND THE ECHR

Children have rights under the ECHR in the same way as adults. Of the greatest potential significance in protecting the welfare and autonomy rights of children are Articles 3 (the right not to be subjected to torture, inhuman, or degrading treatment), 5 (the right to liberty and security of the person), and 8 (the right to respect for private and family life).[91] Despite the judiciary remaining firmly wedded to the paramountcy principle as the best way of protecting children's interests against adult-centred concerns, talking in terms of children's rights rather than welfare is particularly important in an era of growing rights consciousness.[92] As understood under English law, rights are qualitatively different from other legal interests. In the words of Gavin Phillipson, 'rights have a special status'.[93] They have an assumed weight and importance. To talk of children's *rights* thus underlines their significance. This is essential given the current preoccupation with parents' rights under the ECHR. If parents' interests are to be routinely articulated in terms of rights, it is important that children's interests are similarly conceptualized. Otherwise, there is a danger that should the parents' and child's interests conflict (for example, should parents claim the right to discipline their children using physical force in accordance with their religious beliefs), the child's interests (to physical and mental integrity) will be treated as somehow less weighty and important than those of the parents—as simply welfare-based exceptions to the parents' rights as opposed to rights with equal standing.[94] Children's rights, even in areas where the welfare approach would also apply, are thus important. They ensure that children's interests are taken equally seriously in the decision-making process.

One of the potential drawbacks in routinely articulating children's interests as rights is the potential complexity it introduces into the decision-making process. Most child-related disputes involve many potentially conflicting rights, both between the rights of the parents and child and between the child's own rights. Such conflicts should not, however, deter the courts from fully engaging with rights-based reasoning. Building on House of Lords authority in the sphere of media freedom,[95] academics have developed 'a discipline' to resolving such conflicts which seeks to give proper weight and value to all the rights engaged.[96] Termed a 'parallel analysis', Herring and Taylor have applied this discipline to the difficult question of whether one parent should be able to relocate abroad with the child, arguing that in resolving the 'clash of rights' the courts need to focus on the importance of the underlying values which the right protects:

J. Herring and R. Taylor, 'Relocating relocation', (2006) 18 *Child and Family Law Quarterly* 517, 530–1

The difficulty in relocation cases, as in many family law cases, is that each application involves multiple rights, many of which will be incompatible with one another. Although the HRA does not explicitly address the problem of clashing rights in cases between private parties, a jurisprudence on horizontal clashing rights is emerging from the House of Lords...

This approach requires the court to consider the interference with each right individually with an 'intense focus' on the specific right claimed. The discipline that flows from the decisions of the House of Lords builds on the 'parallel analysis' developed in the academic literature and

---

[91] For a detailed discussion of how rights protected under the HRA 1998 could strengthen the claims of autonomous teenagers see Fortin (2006), 314–17, 320–1.

[92] For detailed discussion see Fortin, ibid.

[93] Phillipson (2003), 750.

[94] Fortin (2006), 310.

[95] *Re S (A Child) (Identification: Restrictions on Publication)* [2003] EWCA Civ 963; *Campbell v MGN Ltd* [2004] UKHL 47.

[96] See Choudhry and Fenwick (2005) and Fortin (2006).

requires the following exercise. First, each right should be weighed separately, by considering the values that underlie that right and the extent to which they are engaged in the particular context. Secondly, the justifications for interfering with the right should be considered and the proportionality test applied. Finally, having considered each right separately, the court should carry out the ultimate balancing exercise, by weighing the interference with each right against the other in order to find a solution that minimises the interference with both rights...

Given the range of rights involved in even the simplest case, it is important to consider how a court may assign weight to each right in the 'ultimate balancing exercise': if the rights are simply incommensurable, the rights-based approach will not be capable of producing a principled resolution to the clash of rights. It is our view that a principled balancing of rights can be achieved by focusing on the values that underlie each right. The decisions of the House of Lords...stress the importance of an 'intense focus' on the specific rights claimed in each case and careful consideration of the extent to which the underlying values of the Article in question are engaged by those rights. As Lord Hoffmann considers in *Campbell*, the question in clashing rights cases is how far it is '*necessary* to qualify the one right in order to protect the underlying value which is protected by the other'.

It therefore seems clear that the balancing exercise demands careful attention to the underlying values raised in each particular case.

As Fortin reports, 'the domestic courts have responded to the demands of the HRA in an extraordinarily haphazard manner when dealing with children's cases'.[97] However, it is not in children's interests for the courts to prevaricate on the question of children's rights. A rights-based approach can strengthen rather than weaken the court's focus on the child.[98] A principled, transparent, and fair approach to resolving inevitable conflicts of rights can be utilized. It is thus to be hoped that the limited and 'patchy' progress made by the courts in advancing children's interests through the discourse of rights in certain child-related disputes can be developed and extended into areas of child law that currently remain dominated by adult-centred concerns and perspectives on 'welfare'.[99]

8.6 NON-INTERVENTION IN PRIVATE FAMILY LIFE

The 'non-intervention' or 'no order' principle is central to the legislative scheme set out in the CA 1989.

Children Act 1989, s 1

(5) The Court shall not make an Order under the Act unless it considers that doing so would be better for the child than making no order at all.

Section 1(5) has commonly been interpreted to constitute a *presumption* against making formal orders in matters relating to the upbringing of children unless it can be positively shown that such an order is in the child's best interests. It is strongly questionable, however, whether this interpretation accords with Parliament's original intention.

[97] Fortin (2006), 300.
[98] Ibid., 313–14.
[99] Fortin (2004), 271; Fortin (2006).

A. Bainham, 'Changing families and changing concepts—reforming the language of family law', (1998) 10 *Child and Family Law Quarterly* 1, 2–4

The source of the [no order] principle is beyond doubt. It is three paragraphs of the Law Commission's *Review of Child Law: Guardianship and Custody*. The Commission was concerned primarily with court orders on divorce. It took the view that orders had been made in many cases as 'part of the package' of divorce despite the fact that there was often no dispute between the parents. It thought that orders should be made only where they would be the most effective way of safeguarding or promoting the child's welfare. The Commission also felt that this would accord with 'the fundamental principle that local authority services for families should be provided on a voluntary basis and compulsory intervention confined to cases where compulsion itself is necessary'. The Commission's recommendations are faithfully translated into section 1(5). What the Commission did *not* say and what the statute does *not* say is that court orders are *presumed* to be unnecessary in either the private or public context. Indeed, quite the reverse is true. The Commission recognised that:

'in many, possibly most, uncontested cases an order is needed in the children's own interests, so as to confirm and give stability to the existing arrangements, to clarify the respective roles of the parents, to reassure the parent with whom the children will be living, and even to reassure the public authorities responsible for housing and income support that such arrangements have been made.'

...All the Law Commission proposed, and all the statute did, was to incorporate a piece of common sense—that if a court order is not useful and would not positively advance the welfare of the child there is no point in making it. Viewed in this way it is entirely consistent with the welfare principle, another central principle in section 1.

This is not the interpretation which has been given to the provision by commentators who have repeatedly referred to the 'no order principle' which, they argue, creates a presumption against orders, and there is evidence that this is the way it has been viewed by judges and legal practitioners...A more accurate epithet would have been the 'no *unnecessary* order principle' which would not have implied as a starting-point that an order is, or is not, likely to be unnecessary. This is the neutrality intended by the Law Commission...

It is also commonly suggested that behind this apparently innocuous principle lies a fundamentally important philosophical commitment to a particular relationship between the family and the state. Arguably inspired by the policies of the Thatcher era, in which a minimalist state and the self-sufficiency and autonomy of the family unit were core ideals, it is argued that s 1(5) represents a policy of non-intervention in family life whereby parents are to be left to the task of raising their children free from scrutiny and intervention by the state. However, Andrew Bainham is similarly critical of this interpretation of the provision.

A. Bainham, 'Changing families and changing concepts—reforming the language of family law', (1998) 10 *Child and Family Law Quarterly* 1, 4

The notion of a 'no order principle' had a receptive audience in the late 1980s. More seductive, however, was the notion of 'non-intervention' and it is this latter expression which is, perhaps, more commonly used to describe the principle in section 1(5). Some have even seen in this modest subsection a much wider, non-interventionist *policy* or *philosophy* which would have as its aim to roll back the frontiers of the State and protect, as they would see it, the private realm of family life. Thus the Children Act 1989 is portrayed as a predominantly 'non-interventionist' statute. Leaving aside the rather obvious point that the intervention/non-intervention dichotomy is itself simplistic and unhelpful there is nothing in the Law Commission Report [preceding the Children Act] or in the actual words of the statute to justify so cavalier a view. However, the Act appeared hot on the heels of the Cleveland debacle [child abuse scandal in the late 1980s that attracted widespread publicity] and at the end of the Thatcher era in which it had been fashionable to attack the State and trumpet individualism. So with 'receptive minds' and parrot-like repetition we now have a principle, policy and philosophy of non-intervention in defiance of the facts surrounding the history of the provision.

Whether intended by Parliament or not, a 'non-interventionist' approach to the family has deep foundations in legal and political thought. The principle is grounded in a certain belief about the family and its role in society, in particular, that parents are better placed than the state to know what is best for their children and therefore should be trusted to raise them as they see fit.[100] Allied to this strong faith in the institution of the family, those in favour of a non-interventionist approach (or what Lorraine Fox Harding terms a laissez-faire approach) often harbour a deep mistrust of the state and question the legitimacy of any purported interference into the privacy of family life.

L. Fox Harding, 'The Children Act 1989 in Context: Four Perspectives in Child Care Law and Policy (I)', (1991a) 13 *Journal of Social Welfare and Family Law* 179, 182–6

(1) Laissez-faire and patriarchy

Underlying the *laissez-faire* perspective lies a mistrust of the state and its powers. There is a strong undercurrent of feeling in this view that the state should in general keep out of certain "private" areas of citizens' lives, with restricted exceptions. In particular, domestic and family life are seen as a relatively private arena which should not be invaded by the agents of the state except with due cause, such cause usually being associated with criminality...

The most notable child care authors associated with the *laissez-faire* position are Goldstein *et. al.*, who set out their views in two works, *Beyond the Best Interests of the Child* and *Before the Best Interests of the Child*. In the earlier work, the authors used psychoanalytical theory to develop child placement guidelines which would safeguard the child's psychological needs. Of importance were two "value preferences": that the law must make the child's needs paramount, and a value preference for privacy and minimum state intervention. This stems from the need to safeguard the child's need for continuity, and therefore to safeguard the right of parents to raise their children as they see fit, free of state intrusion, except in cases of neglect and abandonment. The value preference is reinforced by the view that the law is a crude instrument, incapable of effectively managing complex parent-child relationships.

...In their later work, *Before the Best Interests of the Child*, they developed further their theme of parental control undisturbed by state intervention except in extreme cases. The question posed in their book is essentially when the state *is* justified in overriding the autonomy of families. They consider that: "the child's need for safety within the confines of the family must be met by law through its recognition of family privacy as the barrier to state intrusion upon parental autonomy in child rearing". The authors' position is that "A policy

---

[100] *B(R) v Children's Aid Society of Metropolitan Toronto* [1995] 1 SCR 315.

of minimum coercive intervention by the state thus accords not only with our firm belief as citizens in individual freedom and human dignity, but also with our professional understanding of the intricate developmental processes of childhood". In every case the law should ask "whether removal from an unsatisfactory home is the beneficial measure it purports to be"...

The main elements of this perspective therefore appear to be a belief in the benefits for society of a minimum state which engages in only minimal intervention in families; and a complementary belief in the value to all, including children, of undisturbed family life where adults can get on with bringing up their children in their chosen way. It is argued that adults have a right to do this, and it is better for the children too. The bearing and rearing of a child produces a special bond between parents and child and it is damaging to disrupt it, though it is accepted that it may be necessary to do so *in extreme cases* to avert a greater evil...

It may be hypothesised that the thinking of the "new right" on autonomous (and probably patriarchal) families, and on the drawbacks of state intervention in general, had some influence, if only indirectly, on the non-intervention aspect of the [Children] Act. As already noted, it is consonant with other aspects of Conservative policy in the 1980s, and with new right ideology on the issues of family and state.

A non-interventionist approach to family life as enshrined in s 1(5) has important implications in both the public and private law context. A 'hands-off' approach to the family has perhaps the most obvious impact in public law proceedings aimed at protecting the child from parental neglect and abuse. The CA 1989 thus demands a threshold of significant harm is crossed before state intervention can be justified.[101] In private law proceedings, a non-interventionist approach is particularly important in the context of family breakdown. One manifestation of the 'privatizing' trend in family law has been the emphasis on promoting 'privately' negotiated agreements rather than relying on state adjudicated outcomes.[102] However, the question is whether the state should intervene to regulate disputes over essentially 'private' matters where the parties have been able to reach their own agreement. If the state respects the privacy of the family when it is intact, can state intervention on the sole basis of the parent's separation be justified? In attempting to provide such justification, some commentators simply question whether parents can be trusted to promote the child's, as opposed to their own, best interests when the family is in crisis. It is argued that there is a legitimate public interest and even duty to protect the interests of children subject to the risks of family breakdown. Adopting this approach, the non-intervention principle not only compromises commitment to the welfare principle, particularly if the issue has been brought before the court, but is an irresponsible abdication of responsibility. Intervention to protect the child, even in the sphere of private family matters, is thus regarded as legitimate.

G. Douglas et al, 'Safeguarding Children's Welfare in Non-Contentious Divorce: Towards a New Conception of the Legal Process', (2000) 63 *Modern Law Review* **177, 179–80**

...As divorce has become increasingly common and the concept of 'parental responsibility' has come to underpin modern child law, the question of whether it is appropriate for the

---

101 See chapter 12, esp 12.5.3.
102 See, e.g., the contact reforms discussed in detail at 11.5.4.

state, through the court, to scrutinise parents' decisions for their children in the absence of any dispute has been raised. One argument in favour of some sort of 'welfare check' is that given by Gerald Caplan:

By voluntarily approaching the courts to dissolve their marriage, parents explicitly open up their private domain to public scrutiny and intervention. Their request for divorce is a formal statement that their marriage has broken down and constitutes an invitation to the representatives of society to assess the consequences for themselves and their children...

But this view begs several questions. First, it by no means follows that, just because a couple seeks a divorce, they thereby willingly lay themselves open to state scrutiny. After all, there is no alternative to engaging with whatever is required of them by the legal system if they wish to obtain a licence to remarry. Secondly, no 'marker' is flagged up if parents merely separate and do not take divorce proceedings (or if the parents are unmarried), but the needs of the child may be no different. Thirdly, the form and efficacy of intervention must be assessed. 'Intervention' for its own sake may be at best, irrelevant and at worst, iatrogenic. Further, one must query whether, in the age of mass divorce, there are the resources to permit any meaningful and beneficial legal 'intervention' to occur. Indeed, one can trace over the last half century, a progressive withdrawal from any attempt to scrutinise divorces...

Nonetheless, there is very good reason for the state to be concerned about the interests of children when their parents' relationship breaks down and to use the legal system as well as other mechanisms and services, to try to address these. There is a considerable body of research evidence suggesting that children may face detrimental outcomes from parental separation and divorce... Given the level of divorce and separation in this country and the numbers of children affected, there is a strong justification in ensuring that social—and legal—policies and practices are designed to tackle and reduce this risk.

Bainham has expressed similar concern about the trend towards private ordering on divorce. He suggests a normative framework reflecting accepted societal standards should be enshrined within the law to guide the family in post-separation decision-making. In his view, the absence of such normative standards from the CA 1989 is a serious omission:

A. Bainham, 'The Privatisation of the Public Interest in Children', (1990) 53 *Modern Law Review* 206, 207 and 210–14

A basic philosophy enshrined in the 1989 Act is that the state's role in the family is a primarily supportive one and that it should not intervene at all unless it is necessary to do so. There is nothing in the reformed legislation which contradicts (and a great deal which supports) the notion that the family, and specifically child care, is an area which ought to remain unregulated by law unless the need for regulation can be positively demonstrated...

...I have no quarrel with either the intended marginalisation of the judicial role or with the view that child care arrangements brought about by agreement are more likely to work than those which result from attempts at compulsion. But I want to suggest that this scheme, by regarding private agreements as sacrosanct, fails to give adequate recognition to the *public* interest in children. In developing this argument it must be conceded that, on one interpretation, the Act has simply re-defined the public interest and has not diluted it. On this view, the public interest is seen as best served by facilitating parental agreements. In other words, the theory would be that it is in children's best interests (and consequently the public interest) that parents should agree on their future care. But... whichever way the policy shift is described there can be little doubt that an area which hitherto was thought appropriate for legal regulation will in future be substantially de-regulated.

The crucial point is that there has been no attempt in the legislation to influence the nature or content of parental agreements following divorce other than through the somewhat nebulous and indirect notion of continuing parental responsibility. Parental agreement would arguably have been a more acceptable means of meeting the public interest if the legislation had also established some normative standards for child rearing, both in the context of united families and on divorce, to act as a benchmark or basis for private ordering. Yet the legislation tells us nothing about what is involved in the discharge of parental responsibility...

It is disconcerting that the model apparently believed to be representative of what society considers desirable should be one in which private ordering is seen as an end in itself whatever the quality or nature of the agreements reached.

In practice, research carried out by Bailey-Harris, Barron, and Pearce suggests s 1(5) has received a mixed response from the judiciary:

R. Bailey-Harris, J. Barron, and J. Pearce, 'Settlement culture and the use of the "no order" principle under the Children Act 1989', (1999a) 11 *Child and Family Law Quarterly* 53, 59–61

[S]ection 1(5) receives a very mixed response in practice at county court level...[T]he evidence from our study could be interpreted as suggesting two themes. First, the 'no order principle' is invoked by judges to reinforce the concept of parental autonomy and the vigorous promotion of agreement, this results in the court declining or refusing to make an order even when parties have sought one. It is highly questionable whether this use of the principle accords with the original intention of the legislature, and we found that it could be productive of acute dissatisfaction on the part of parents who were expecting an adjudicated outcome. Secondly, and in complete contrast, the principle is very commonly breached or not observed by judges, particularly when legal practitioners press for resolution by consent order...Our file survey showed that, overall, a substantive order was made in 67 per cent of cases, no substantive order in 27 per cent, and an order of 'no order' in 5 per cent. The extent of non observance of the principle by the courts we sampled is thus immediately apparent.

To pursue the first theme: it is possible to argue from the evidence of our study that in practice the courts are using the 'no order principle' in cases to which it was never intended to apply. In many cases where there is originally real conflict between parents who have invoked the court's jurisdiction specifically to resolve their dispute, the principle is invoked by judges to reinforce the promotion of parental autonomy and agreement as the preferred mode of resolution: the court asserts that no order is needed where parents can eventually agree, even though their preferred original intention was to obtain an order.

Our study reveals many examples of judges using the rhetoric of parental autonomy to justify the refusal to make an order, even in proceedings where there is real dispute and where proceedings are protracted...

There is considerable evidence of the dissatisfaction of parents with the outcome of 'no order' when they consider that they have invoked the court's jurisdiction precisely for the exercise of its authority in a matter which they find difficult to resolve themselves. In other words, the use of the 'no order' approach by the court to reinforce its promotion of parental autonomy is often at odds with parental expectations of the process...

8.7 CONCLUSION

The various approaches to child-related disputes are not, of course, mutually exclusive. Finding an acceptable balance or compromise between them is one of the greatest challenges for family lawyers. From the following chapters it will be clear that, despite the recent trend towards a more rights-based culture in family law, the welfare principle predominates. However, despite this, parents' rights, children's rights, and a non-interventionist ethos are all important and will be evident, to varying degrees, in the discussion to follow. So, with these underlying principles in mind, we turn to our first substantive question: who are a child's legal parents?

 ONLINE RESOURCE CENTRE

Questions, suggestions for further reading, and supplementary materials for this chapter (including updates on developments in this area of family law since this book was published) may be found on the Online Resource Centre at www.oxfordtextbooks.co.uk/orc/harrisshort_tcm2e/.

9

BECOMING A LEGAL PARENT AND THE CONSEQUENCES OF LEGAL PARENTHOOD

CENTRAL ISSUES

1. There are many possible answers to the question 'who are a child's parents?' Genetic, gestational, and social parents may all have convincing claims to the status of 'legal parenthood'.

2. Legal parenthood confers a fundamentally important status on both parent and child, making the child a member of the parent's family and bringing with it a core bundle of rights and responsibilities.

3. In the context of natural procreation, the crucial factor in determining a child's legal parents is the genetic tie between parent and child. This is easily established in the case of the mother. Determining the identity of a child's genetic father is more difficult. Disputes focus today on whether scientific tests should be ordered to put the parentage of a child beyond doubt. Adopting both a rights-based and welfare approach, establishing genetic truth is now regarded as the most important consideration.

4. In the context of assisted reproduction, the intended social parents are generally accorded legal parenthood. Freed from biological constraints, this opens up a much more flexible concept of parenthood. For a long time, English law remained faithful to the heterosexual norm that a child should have one legal father and one legal mother. However, the Human Fertilisation and Embryology Act 2008 (HFEA 2008) revolutionized this position by allowing a child, from birth, to have two legal parents of the same sex.

5. Where genetic parentage does not coincide with legal parenthood, the continuing role of the genetic progenitors must be addressed. The right of donor conceived children to information about their genetic background has been a particularly contentious issue.

6. Surrogacy remains a 'grey' area, neither condemned nor approved by law. Although the HFEA 2008 now facilitates surrogacy in a much wider range of circumstances, considerable uncertainty remains where the surrogacy arrangement breaks down.

9.1 INTRODUCTION

One might have thought becoming a parent was a relatively straightforward matter. Man meets woman, they fall in love, embark upon a sexual relationship, woman becomes pregnant and nine months later they become the proud parents of a newborn baby. However, even with the assistance of new fertility treatments, becoming a parent can be anything but straightforward and, whether or not one conceives through natural means, gaining legal recognition of one's status as a parent can prove an even more difficult and complicated process.

Who are a child's parents? If you posed this question to a group of passengers on the Clapham omnibus, you would probably elicit a wide variety of responses. One passenger might respond that it is the man and woman who are linked by blood to the child: the genetic parents. Another passenger might respond that it is the woman who gives birth to the child: the gestational mother, and perhaps her husband or partner.[1] Yet another passenger might respond that it is the people who intend to be the parents: the intentional parents. Another might suggest it is those who actually love, nurture, and care for the child: the social parents. The concept of parenthood and who should be regarded as a child's parents is thus a strongly contested question. Disagreement as to the identity of a child's parents may be further intensified when the question of assisted reproduction is raised. The passengers who confidently asserted that the blood tie should form the basis for determining parenthood may feel less sure of their position when the scenario of a married couple receiving fertility treatment using donated sperm (AID) is put to them. Would our passengers still consider that the sperm donor, the person with the genetic link to the child, and not the husband receiving fertility treatment with his wife, should be regarded as the father? How would they respond to the challenges raised by surrogacy? Would they consider that the man and woman who can claim a genetic link to the child (who may or may not be the commissioning couple)[2] should be regarded as the parents? Would they remain of that view when faced with the possibility that the genetic and gestational mothers may be different? Would they now consider that the gestational, not the genetic, mother should prevail? Alternatively, could they both be recognized as the child's mother? Does the child have to be limited to just two legal parents? And do those legal parents have to be based on the heterosexual norm of one mother and one father?

And what are the legal consequences of all this? Passengers who think that the genetic tie should determine the identity of a child's parents may not agree that any legal rights and responsibilities should flow from that status. They may, for example, baulk at the idea that a man who raped a married woman, whilst correctly described as the father of any resulting child, should have any *legal* status in relation to the child. When pushed further, our passengers may again begin to waiver in their original conviction that it should be the person with the genetic tie, rather than the person who loves, nurtures, and cares for the child, who should be regarded in law as the parent. If, for example, the husband of the raped woman has accepted the child as his own and intends to raise the child, with his wife, as part of their family unit, should he not be accorded the legal rights and responsibilities of parenthood? One response to this dilemma would be to separate the status of being a 'parent' from

---

[1] The genetic and/or gestational parents are often referred to as the 'natural' parents. Cf Baroness Hale's judgment in *Re G* [2006] UKHL 43, [32]–[37] below where she includes social or intentional parents within this term.

[2] The couple for whom the surrogate carries the child.

holding any legal rights and responsibilities with respect to the child. Could the law not recognize that several people may play different but complementary 'parenting' roles in relation to a child, with different legal rights and responsibilities attaching to each?

Our passengers may by now be feeling somewhat bewildered. These are complex and difficult questions. And they are questions that become increasingly difficult to answer as the diversity and fluidity in modern family life intensifies and innovations in assisted reproduction continue to stretch the boundaries of possibility. Asexual reproduction using only one genetic source is now within scientific reach. How long before we are pondering the identity of the parents of a cloned human embryo grown to term outside a woman's uterus? The fluidity of modern family life and the relentless march of 'scientific progress' will require us to find increasingly nuanced answers to the deceivingly simple question, who are a child's parents?

The principal aim of this chapter is to examine how one acquires the status of 'being a parent' under English law, what we shall refer to as 'legal parenthood'. We begin by examining differing concepts of 'parenthood' and possible approaches to determining legal parenthood. We then move on to consider the current legal framework for identifying a child's legal parents where a child is conceived through natural procreation, before examining the problems and challenges raised by use of assisted reproduction techniques, including surrogacy. Finally, we briefly consider adoption, a unique means of acquiring the legal status of parenthood under English law.[3]

9.2 CONCEPTS OF PARENTHOOD AND POSSIBLE APPROACHES TO DETERMINING LEGAL PARENTHOOD

9.2.1 WHAT IS A 'PARENT'?

Martin Johnson has identified four possible components to parenthood:

M. Johnson, 'A Biomedical Perspective on Parenthood', in A. Bainham, S. Day Sclater, and M. Richards (eds), *What is a Parent? A Socio-Legal Analysis* (Oxford: Hart Publishing, 1999), 47–8

First there is a genetic component to parenthood. We now know that biologically the production of a viable human conceptus *requires* two distinctive subsets of chromosomes, one of which *must* be derived from a woman and the other from a man. The mother's egg alone also contributes a much smaller additional and essential chromosome (<1 per cent of total genetic material) in a non-nuclear structure called a mitochondrion, whilst the father's sperm contributes a non-chromosomal structure which is, however, essential for cell survival and proliferation in the embryo. Thus, genetic parents of both sexes are required and make non-equivalent contributions to their off-spring.

Secondly, there is a coital component to parenthood. Since fertilisation occurs inside the body, an act of coitus or mating is required between male and female...

Thirdly, there is a gestational or uterine component to parenthood, which is exclusively the province of the female. The mother provides a uterus and there is accumulating evidence

---

[3] Adoption is considered in detail in chapter 13.

that her behaviour, mental state, diet and health during pregnancy may affect enduringly the health, traits and well-being of the child that is subsequently born. The tendency to overlook this important parental contribution to the child may have over-emphasised the significance of the genetic component to parenthood.

Finally, there is a post-natal component to parenthood. Higher primates such as humans transmit not just their genes, but also their culture from one generation to another. Post-natal parenthood is sometimes called "social parenthood", but since this component of parenthood has evolved it does have an important biological component to it.

These four aspects of parenthood: genetic, coital, gestational, and social may be performed by various people. Leaving aside possible future developments in assisted reproduction, a child must currently have two genetic parents: one male and one female. In most cases, the child's genetic parents will have engaged in an act of coitus to achieve fertilization. However, the development of assisted reproduction techniques means that coitus is no longer an essential element of parenthood and may be absent in a significant minority of cases. In addition to two genetic parents, all children must have a gestational mother. Although the gestational mother will generally also be the genetic mother, the advent of in vitro fertilization (IVF) means that again this will not necessarily be the case. The possibility of using donated eggs (whether in the context of fertility treatment or for the purposes of surrogacy) means that genetic and gestational motherhood can now be located in two different women. Post-natal or social parenthood is the most open component of parenthood. It is often equated with intentional parenthood because it results from an act of will on the part of the parent. Social parents can be identified as those individuals who care for and nurture a child day-to-day. The crucial post-natal or social aspect of parenthood is usually performed by the genetic (and gestational) parents. Social parenthood can, however, be divorced from both genetic and gestational parenthood. Typical situations where this will occur include assisted reproduction using AID, surrogacy, adoption, and cohabitation between a genetic and non-genetic parent, such as step-parents. Once parenthood is freed from its genetic roots, it opens up endless possibilities. Social parenthood can be performed by an infinite number of people, at different times in the child's life, and with no limitation as to gender or status. Thus a child's social parents may range from the child's genetic and gestational mother and her husband to a gay couple who have neither a genetic nor gestational link to the child.

Baroness Hale tried to unpack the complexity and potential significance of these various components of parenthood in *Re G*.[4]

Re G [2006] UKHL 43

BARONESS HALE:

33. There are at least three ways in which a person may be or become a natural parent of a child, each of which may be a very significant factor in the child's welfare, depending upon the circumstances of the particular case. The first is genetic parenthood: the provision of the gametes which produce the child. This can be of deep significance on many levels. For the parent, perhaps particularly for a father, the knowledge that this is "his" child can bring a very special sense of love for and commitment to that child which will be of great benefit

---

[4] [2006] UKHL 43, [32]–[37]. For the facts of this case see below at pp 765–6.

to the child…For the child, he reaps the benefit not only of that love and commitment, but also of knowing his own origins and lineage, which is an important component in finding an individual sense of self as one grows up. The knowledge of that genetic link may also be an important (although certainly not an essential) component in the love and commitment felt by the wider family, perhaps especially grandparents, from which the child has so much to gain.

34. The second is gestational parenthood: the conceiving and bearing of the child. The mother who bears the child is legally the child's mother, whereas the mother who provided the egg is not…While this may be partly for reasons of certainty and convenience, it also recognises a deeper truth: that the process of carrying a child and giving him birth (which may well be followed by breast-feeding for some months) brings with it, in the vast majority of cases, a very special relationship between mother and child, a relationship which is different from any other.

35. The third is social and psychological parenthood: the relationship which develops through the child demanding and the parent providing for the child's needs, initially at the most basic level of feeding, nurturing, comforting and loving, and later at the more sophisticated level of guiding, socialising, educating and protecting…

36. Of course, in the great majority of cases, the natural mother combines all three. She is the genetic, gestational and psychological parent. Her contribution to the welfare of the child is unique. The natural father combines genetic and psychological parenthood. His contribution is also unique…

37. But there are also parents who are neither genetic nor gestational, but who have become the psychological parents of the child and thus have an important contribution to make to their welfare. Adoptive parents are the most obvious example, but there are many others.

Whilst some commentators have welcomed Baroness Hale's apparent inclusion of psychological/social parenthood within her understanding of 'natural' parenthood, her suggestion that genetic parenthood, and genetic/gestational motherhood in particular, should be regarded as of unique importance has proved considerably more contentious.[5]

9.2.2 THE IMPORTANCE OF LEGAL PARENTHOOD

Legal parenthood confers an important legal status on both parent and child. Andrew Bainham argues it represents the most fundamental relationship between parent and child.[6] Unlike parental responsibility (the legal authority to make decisions with respect to a child's upbringing),[7] which can be conferred on a succession of different social carers during the child's minority, legal parenthood can only be held by two individuals at any one time: usually, but no longer necessarily, the child's 'mother' and the child's 'father'. Legal parenthood is also permanent, non-alienable, and has legal consequences for an individual throughout life, not just during childhood.[8] As Bainham argues, legal parenthood makes the child a member of a family. The legal consequences that attach to legal parenthood therefore

[5] For an excellent critique see Diduck (2007). For further discussion see below at pp 765–8.
[6] Bainham (1999), 32–3.
[7] See chapter 10.
[8] Legal parenthood can only be terminated by adoption or the making of a parental order under s 54 of the HFEA 2008.

represent a core body of rights and responsibilities that flow from the fact that X is Y's child and belongs to Y's family. Although for many parents, particularly those deprived of parental responsibility, the authority to make decisions about a child's upbringing may seem more important and meaningful, the rights and responsibilities attaching to legal parenthood are also significant. For example, a child's core familial relationships for the purposes of determining restrictions on marriage and criminal prohibitions relating to incest are determined in accordance with the child's legal parenthood.[9] Entitlements on intestacy are determined by reference to legal parenthood, as are citizenship rights under the British Nationality Act 1981. Perhaps of greatest importance to many, particularly fathers, is that the duty to maintain a child financially rests with the legal parents.[10]

9.2.3 COMPETING APPROACHES TO DETERMINING A CHILD'S LEGAL PARENTS

In determining legal parenthood, the law has to make a choice, as a matter of policy, which of these aspects of parenthood should be given priority: genetic, gestational, or social.[11] The law has not always taken a consistent approach. There is nothing, in principle, to prevent the law according legal parenthood to more than two people, and nothing, in principle, which dictates that a child's parents must consist exclusively of one man and one woman. However, historically, legal parenthood under English law has been strictly gendered, the law insisting on the heterosexual norm that every child at birth should have two legal parents: one legal mother and one legal father.[12] This was made clear in *X, Y and Z v UK*,[13] where the Registrar General refused to register a female-to-male transsexual as the father of a child born to his long-term partner by means of assisted insemination using donated sperm. In refusing his application, the Registrar General took the view that only a biological male could be regarded as the father of a child for the purposes of registration.[14] The applicant challenged that decision in the European Court of Human Rights. The Court, by majority, found in favour of the UK government, holding that there had been no violation of Article 8 or Article 8 in conjunction with Article 14. It was emphasized that the applicant's inability to be recognized as the legal father by being entered as such on the child's birth certificate did not in any way affect his capacity to act as the child's social father, particularly as he could apply for parental responsibility by means of a joint residence order.[15]

---

[9] See Marriage Act 1949, Sch 1 and Sexual Offences Act 2003, ss 64–5.

[10] Child Support Act 1991, s 1(1); Children Act 1989, Sch 1. See chapter 6.

[11] As the coital aspect of parenthood is no longer present in all cases it is excluded as an appropriate basis for determining legal parenthood.

[12] The possibility of adoption by a sole applicant means that a child post-adoption may have only one legal parent.

[13] (App No 21830/93, ECHR) (1997).

[14] Ibid., [17].

[15] Ibid., [50]. It has subsequently been confirmed that the 'fatherhood' provisions in the Family Law Reform Act 1987 and the Human Fertilisation and Embryology Act 1990 (HFEA 1990) are specifically gendered, restricting the acquisition of 'fatherhood' to a man. See: *J v C (Void Marriage: Status of Children)* [2006] EWCA Civ 551. Although the legal parenthood of transsexual parents would now be dealt with in accordance with the terms of the Gender Recognition Act 2004, *J v C* also confirmed that the legal acquisition of male gender by means of a Gender Recognition Certificate has no retrospective effect. If the purported father was thus legally a woman at the time of the child's birth, he cannot acquire the status of 'fatherhood' under English law.

This approach to parenthood is strongly rooted in the heterosexual biological imperative of natural procreation that a child must have one genetic/gestational mother and one genetic father. Day Sclater, Bainham, and Richards argue that in the wake of scientific advances in DNA testing, this genetic model of parenthood has become even more firmly entrenched.[16]

S. Day Sclater, A. Bainham, and M. Richards, 'Introduction', in A. Bainham, S. Day Sclater, and M. Richards (eds), *What is a Parent? A Socio-Legal Analysis* (Oxford: Hart Publishing, 1999), 15

Developments in the technologies and procedures for DNA testing, used to establish paternity, have undoubtedly contributed to the new constructions of fathers in biological rather than social terms. As Neale and Smart argue, the newly emerging model of family life...is one which venerates biological kin ties and has entailed a refashioning of the legal status of biological parenthood; parenthood has begun to supersede marriage as the bedrock of "the family" and as the central mechanism for the legal regulation of domestic life. If marriage is no longer for life, then (biological) parenthood is. Biology now provides the main basis upon which claims to parental status rest. The increasing availability of genetic testing for a range of inherited conditions, as well as for paternity, and the increasing visibility of the microstructures which make up our bodies, have given added impetus to the salience of "biology" and "genetics" in relation to the question of "what is a parent?"

Whilst arguing that the law must afford appropriate recognition to the importance of social parenthood by conferring on social parents the legal rights and duties required to raise a child (parental responsibility), Bainham supports the approach whereby legal parenthood is based exclusively on the genetic tie. His reasons focus on the unique significance of genetic parentage.

A. Bainham, 'Parentage, Parenthood and Parental Responsibility', in A. Bainham, S. Day Sclater, and M. Richards (eds), *What is a Parent? A Socio-Legal Analysis* (Oxford: Hart Publishing, 1999), 27

In allocating parental responsibility to more and more social parents, is it necessary or desirable to go the extra mile and confer on them legal parenthood? It will be my strong contention that this is neither necessary nor desirable and that legal parenthood, with some exceptions, ought to be confined to genetic parents. This is because those legal effects, which are peculiar to parenthood, are fundamental to the genetic link...

What are these fundamental effects of legal parenthood which do not pass with parental responsibility? The first is arguably the most important and is also the most frequently neglected. This is that legal parenthood, but not parental responsibility, makes the child a member of a family, generating for that child a legal relationship with wider kin going well beyond the parental relationship...[T]he social or psychological value of belonging to a particular family is a nebulous subject for lawyers and is more the terrain of the anthropologist or psychologist. What the lawyer *can* point out is that the loss of the legal status of parent will entail the loss, at least in law, of these wider relationships

---

[16] Other commentators have also noted the increasing trend towards the 'geneticization' of parenthood (particularly fatherhood), albeit they are considerably more critical of this approach. See, especially, Sheldon (2009).

Other effects which arise specifically from legal parenthood are financial liability for child support, the right to object or consent to adoption (though this also depends on possessing parental responsibility), and the right to object to a change of the child's surname and to removal of the child from the jurisdiction, the right to appoint a guardian (although...the parent must possess parental responsibility), a presumption of contact where a child is in care and an automatic right to go to court...

Are these distinctive legal effects just anomalies, historical accidents of the piecemeal development of the law?...It is my contention that on the contrary, they continue to serve a vital purpose in that they give expression to the continuing importance of the genetic link. What they all have in common is that they relate to fundamentals which go beyond the everyday decisions involved in upbringing... If we are to move in the direction of giving effect to a child's right to knowledge of genetic origins we are going to need some legal means of preserving the genetic connection and it is the concept of legal parenthood which currently achieves this...

Bainham suggests that three key principles should guide the law's approach to determining legal parenthood: (i) a commitment to truth; (ii) individual autonomy; and (iii) priority for the rights and interests of those primarily affected—the individuals who result from reproduction.[17] In his view, conferring legal parenthood on the basis of biological truth, rather than the 'fiction' of social parenthood, best protects these core values.[18]

Barton and Douglas are more cautious about a genetic approach. They argue that there has been a perceptible swing in the law towards according precedence to intentional or social parenthood, particularly in the wake of the statutory regime introduced by the HFEA 1990 (now further entrenched by the HFEA 2008) for determining legal parenthood in the context of assisted reproduction. Indeed, they suggest 'it is now the primary test of legal parentage'.[19]

A model of legal parenthood which is based on the intention to parent or the 'function' or 'doing' of parenting has always had the potential to revolutionize English law's historical approach to determining a child's legal parents. Freed from the biological imperative, legal parenthood need not be restricted to two people of the opposite sex, or indeed to only two people. The HFEA 1990 and HFEA 2008 have seen this revolutionary potential at least partially realized. The first inroad into the gendered heterosexual model of legal parenthood was made by the Adoption and Children Act 2002 (ACA 2002) which, for the first time, enabled a same-sex couple to adopt. Thus, since 2002, the law has not demanded that a child have one legal mother and one legal father. The HFEA 2008 took this considerably further by permitting the deliberate creation of a child who will be born into a family consisting of two parents of the same sex. A child with two legal mothers but no legal father (strictly, in accordance with the Act, the child will have one 'mother' and a second female 'parent') is thus possible, as is a child with no legal mother but two legal fathers following a successful surrogacy arrangement (strictly two male 'parents'). By removing any continuing discrimination against civil partners and same-sex cohabiting couples in the regulation of access to, and the legal consequences of, assisted reproduction, same-sex couples can, for the first time, become legal parents on the same basis as a heterosexual couple. The legitimacy of same-sex

---

[17] Bainham (2008a), 323–4.

[18] Bainham, ibid. Note that it is not clear from Bainham's argument why genetic truth can only be adequately protected through the attribution of legal parenthood to the genetic parents.

[19] Barton and Douglas (1995), 51.

parenting has been accepted—at least by the legislature. This considerable liberalization of the law on parenthood in the context of assisted reproduction clearly embraces intentional (rather than genetic) parenthood and accepts the equal worth of a diverse range of family relationships. Parenthood has moved a step closer to being a gender neutral activity.

So do these radical changes fundamentally undermine the genetic or biological basis of legal parenthood in English law? As we examine the current legal framework for determining legal parenthood, it will become apparent that there is no clear answer to this question, English law drawing upon both the genetic and social models of parenthood depending on the particular social need. Those searching for a coherent policy underlying the law's approach will be disappointed. Indeed, Jackson describes the current law as 'spectacularly confused and confusing'.[20] The choice as to which model should predominate in any particular context has been driven by pragmatic considerations as much as by matters of policy and principle. In the context of natural procreation and until the recent advances in DNA testing, difficulties in establishing genetic parentage with any certainty influenced legal policy, as did social and legal considerations concerning the vulnerable status of illegitimate children. However, as the accuracy of genetic testing has improved, and the legal category of illegitimacy purged from English law, genetic parentage has become increasingly important in the determination of legal parenthood for children conceived through natural reproduction. In stark contrast, in the context of assisted reproduction different pragmatic considerations, such as the desire to avoid the seemingly nonsensical result of a sperm donor acquiring legal responsibility for financially maintaining his genetic offspring, have driven legal policy, with the result that social or intentional parenthood, with some notable exceptions, has become the central determining principle.

9.3 DETERMINING PARENTHOOD IN THE CONTEXT OF NATURAL REPRODUCTION

9.3.1 ESTABLISHING MATERNITY

In the context of *natural reproduction*, English law has traditionally placed the greatest emphasis on the genetic link between parent and child.[21] Establishing legal parenthood, at least as far as motherhood is concerned, is therefore relatively straightforward. As Lord Simon famously pointed out in the *Ampthill Peerage Case*,[22] in the case of the child's mother this genetic link can be incontrovertibly proved, as a matter of fact, by parturition.[23] The woman who gives birth to the child is the child's genetic mother and thus the legal parent.[24]

9.3.2 ESTABLISHING PATERNITY

Married fathers and the presumption of legitimacy

Determining a child's father is potentially more complicated. Establishing the genetic link between father and child has, in the past, proved difficult. Without the incontrovertible

---

[20] Jackson (2006), 60.

[21] As exemplified by the cases of *B v B and F (No 1)* [1969] P 37 and *Re M (Child Support Act: Parentage)* [1997] 2 FLR 90.

[22] [1977] AC 547.

[23] Ibid., 577.

[24] With the advent of IVF this is no longer necessarily the case outside natural reproduction.

proof of parturition and, in the absence of accurate genetic testing, the law has had to rely on certain presumptions in order to establish paternity. In the case of children born to married parents, the common law has *presumed* that the mother's husband is the child's genetic father and thus the legal parent. This presumption applies if the man was legally married to the mother either at the date of conception or at the date of birth. Where the mother manages to be married to two different men at the date of birth and the date of conception, Bainham argues that she will be able to register her second husband as the father unless challenged by the first.[25]

Where the parents of a child are married, both parents are obliged to register the child within 42 days of the birth.[26] Either the child's mother or her husband can attend at the registrar's office and enter the husband's name as the child's father without producing any further evidence of his paternity. As Bainham points out, despite the operation of the *pater est* presumption, the birth register is supposed to reflect biological truth, it simply being assumed the mother's husband is indeed the biological father.[27] Moreover, the mother and her husband are under a duty to tell the truth, it being a criminal offence to register the husband as the child's father when they know that he is not in fact the biological father.[28] However, it is estimated that in 2–10 per cent of cases the mother's husband is wrongly named as the child's genetic father on the birth certificate.[29]

The common law presumption that the mother's husband is the father has, in the past, been difficult to displace. Until the law was amended by the Family Law Reform Act 1969 (FLRA 1969), s 26, the presumption could only be rebutted by evidence establishing beyond reasonable doubt that the husband could not be the father.[30] Although the civil standard of proof now applies, it was held in *W v K (proof of paternity)* that this would be harder to discharge than is ordinarily the case.[31] In addition to this high standard of proof, severe restrictions were historically imposed on the evidence that could be adduced at trial. For example, out of concern for public decency, the law refused to hear evidence that the parties were not actively engaging in sexual intercourse at the relevant time.[32] This restrictive approach was explained by the fact that the child's legitimate status depended on the presumption that the mother's husband was the legal father. Given the significance of legitimacy, the courts were extremely reluctant to 'bastardize' a child without the strongest possible proof.[33]

In light of recent scientific, social, and legal changes, the courts' reluctance to disturb the common law presumption in favour of the husband has changed. For most of the twentieth century, although priority was *purportedly* accorded to the genetic link between parent and child, the law was more concerned with protecting the *appearance* of legitimacy than with establishing the *truth* about a child's genetic parentage.[34] Thus, as Barton and Douglas point out, legal fatherhood really turned not upon the man's relationship with the child, but on the

---

[25] Bainham (2008b), 454. Cf Lowe and Douglas who argue that the wife should be afforded the presumption of fidelity during marriage and thus her husband at the date of conception should be deemed the legal father. Lowe and Douglas (2007), 322.

[26] Births and Death Registration Act 1953, s 2.

[27] Bainham (2008b), 452–3.

[28] Ibid.

[29] Ibid., fn 108.

[30] Cretney (2003a), 534.

[31] [1988] 1 FLR 86.

[32] Cretney (2003a), 534.

[33] Ibid., 533.

[34] See Bainham (2008b), 451.

status of his relationship with the mother.[35] In recent years this has changed, with the law now firmly committed to upholding the importance of biological truth.

Unmarried fathers and the presumption based on registration of the birth

Increasing numbers of children are now born to parents outside of marriage. For the 45 per cent of children born to unmarried parents in England and Wales, there is no automatic presumption as to their paternity.[36] However, registration on the birth certificate is regarded as good prima facie evidence that the man named is the child's father.[37] In 2008, 86 per cent of children born outside marriage were registered jointly by both parents.[38] In 76 per cent of jointly registered births, the parents were registered as resident at the same address.[39] In most cases, birth registration is therefore an extremely important tool in helping to establish the child's paternity.

There remains, however, a small minority of cases (14 per cent in 2008) in which the birth of a child is solely registered by the child's mother.[40] In these cases there is no presumption as to the child's paternity. In order to try and reduce the number of sole registrations yet further, Parliament passed new legislation in 2009 making joint registration in effect compulsory.[41] Before the 2009 reforms, only the child's mother, where she was unmarried, had a duty to register the child.[42] Registration of the child's father required the active agreement of both parents or the production of an appropriate court order.[43] This meant that where the child's mother did not want the child's father registered on the birth certificate she could simply withhold her consent to joint registration. Tentative proposals for reform were first put forward by the government in its 2006 White Paper on child support.[44] The issue was then detached from the child support reforms and a separate Green Paper published in 2007,[45] followed by a White Paper in June 2008.[46] Although originating from the problems surrounding child support, the proposals were quickly situated within the government's wider policy agenda on securing good, responsible parenting and promoting and supporting active and engaged fathering in particular. A number of potential benefits from joint registration were identified, including improving child outcomes by facilitating active and involved fathering; securing an enhanced legal status for the father;[47] securing improved levels of contact; improving compliance with child support obligations; and changing cultural

---

[35] Barton and Douglas (1995), 53.

[36] ONS (2009a), figure 2.18.

[37] In the absence of an entry in favour of the putative father on the birth register, the making of a parental responsibility order may also constitute good prima facie evidence as to the child's paternity. It was held in *R v Secretary of State for Social Security, ex parte W* [1999] 2 FLR 604, that because the court can only make a parental responsibility order under s 4 of the Children Act 1989 (CA 1989) in favour of the child's father, it must be implicit in making the order that the man is 'found or adjudged' to be the child's father. The same reasoning would presumably apply to the existence of a parental responsibility agreement between the child's parents.

[38] ONS (2009a), p 24.

[39] Ibid.

[40] Ibid., ch. 2, p 24.

[41] Amendments introduced to the Births and Deaths Registration Act 1953 by the Welfare Reform Act 2009. At the time of writing the amendments were not yet in force.

[42] Births and Deaths Registration Act 1953, s 10.

[43] Ibid. See Barton and Douglas (1995), 56–7.

[44] DWP (2006a).

[45] DWP (2007a).

[46] DCSF and DWP (2008).

[47] All fathers registered on the birth certificate acquire parental responsibility. See chapter 10.

expectations about fathers' responsibilities. Although couched in the language of child welfare and children's rights, the importance of securing 'equality' as between the parents was a strong theme running throughout the White Paper.

DCSF and DWP, *Joint birth registration: recording responsibility,* Cm 7293
(London: HMSO, 2008).

> 6. At the heart of our reforms is a desire to promote child welfare and the right of every child to know who his or her parents are. In most cases, a child's right to be acknowledged and cared for by his or her father should not be dependent on the relationship between the parents. To support this right we will ensure that fathers who want to take responsibility for their children do not have to overcome unnecessary obstacles....
>
> 20. The roles of both father and mother are important to a child's development. We want parents to realise that, even when they do not have a close relationship with each other, they should both play an active, supportive role in their children's lives. Joint birth registration alone cannot achieve this, but it gives parents the opportunity to demonstrate their commitment to their children...
>
> 25....The Government considers that it is now time to take steps towards bringing the responsibilities and rights of unmarried fathers more into line with those of unmarried mothers.

Section 2A of the Births and Deaths Registration Act 1953 thus now imposes a duty on the child's mother to provide the registrar with certain prescribed information about the child's father.[48] The registrar will then contact the alleged father requiring him to state whether or not he acknowledges that he is the father.[49] Where he acknowledges paternity he will be registered as the child's father.[50] Where he disputes paternity, scientific tests can be carried out, but only if both the mother and the alleged father consent.[51] In order to protect the interests of potentially vulnerable mothers and children, the mother's duty to identify the child's father is subject to a number of specific exemptions:

Births and Deaths Registration Act 1953, s 2B

> (3) Subsection (1) does not require the mother to provide information relating to the father if she makes in the presence of the registrar a declaration in the prescribed form stating that one or more of the following conditions is met.
>
> (4) Those conditions are—
>
>   (a) that by virtue of section 41 of the Human Fertilisation and Embryology Act 2008 the child has no father,
>
>   (b) that the father has died,

---

[48] The information to be provided to the registrar is to be prescribed in regulations: Births and Deaths Registration Act 1953, s 2B. The mother may also provide information about the father after registration, allowing the child's birth to be re-registered where the alleged father acknowledges paternity: Births and Deaths Registration Act 1953, s 10C.

[49] Births and Deaths Registration Act 1953, s 2C(2).

[50] Ibid., s 2C(2)(c).

[51] Ibid., s 2E.

(c) that the mother does not know the father's identity,

(d) that the mother does not know the father's whereabouts,

(e) that the father lacks capacity (within the meaning of the Mental Capacity Act 2005) in relation to decisions under this Part,

(f) that the mother has reason to fear for her safety or that of the child if the father is contacted in relation to the birth, and

(g) any other conditions prescribed by regulations made by the Minister.

The White Paper did not state who would be responsible for determining whether one of these exemptions was made out. However, the burden will presumably fall, at least in the first instance, on the registrar. That said, it is clear that the registrar will not embark upon an investigation into the truth of the mother's assertions.[52] A more proactive model in which registrars would be required to conduct detailed interviews with mothers and search out absent fathers was explicitly rejected as unduly interventionist and impractical.[53] It will therefore be relatively easy for a mother to avoid joint registration by simply claiming that she does not know the identity or location of the father. In these circumstances, sole registration will be permitted. Sanctions can be imposed against the child's mother and/or the alleged father if one or both of them refuses to cooperate, the penalties available in the case of the mother providing false information being the more severe.[54]

The revised legislation also permits registration of the child's father where he has contacted the registrar declaring his paternity and the child's mother confirms this.[55] Where the putative father has contacted the registrar, the mother will be required either to acknowledge or deny the alleged father's paternity.[56] If the mother disputes paternity, scientific tests can again be used to determine parentage, subject to the parties' consent.[57] If the mother refuses to cooperate, penalties can again be imposed.[58] However, in order to resolve the dispute over paternity the matter will be referred to the court.[59]

Parliament's decision to make joint birth registration mandatory divided academic opinion. Bainham welcomed the reforms as reinforcing the biological/genetic basis of legal fatherhood and helping to address previous inequalities between the parents in the birth registration system. In his view, the rights of the child demand accurate registration of both biological parents on the birth register:

A. Bainham, 'What is the point of birth registration?', (2008b) 20 *Child and Family Law Quarterly* 449, 468–70

Birth registration is manifestly a right of the child...[T]he child's claim to knowledge of the truth is grounded not in welfare, but in the autonomy of the individual, given that at birth we can only be talking about protecting *potential* autonomy. The essential point is that it is for the

[52] DWP (2007a), 19.
[53] Ibid.
[54] Perjury Act 1911, s 4(1A) and Births and Deaths Registration Act 1953, s 36.
[55] Births and Deaths Registration Act 1953, ss 2D(1) and 10B(1).
[56] Ibid., ss 2D(2) and 10B(3).
[57] Ibid., s 2E.
[58] Ibid., s 36
[59] DCSF and DWP (2008), [29].

individual to decide for himself or herself whether or not biological parentage (and the wider kinship links deriving from it) are important or not. But this autonomy is violated where the individual has no means of discovering whether or not these biological connections exist in the first place.

The wider significance of the initial right of birth registration for the child cannot be overstated. From this first right flows the protection of the child's identity, the establishment of wider kinship links and the legal connection of the child to the State, especially through citizenship.

Bainham would therefore have gone further than the 2009 reforms in one important respect. He is particularly critical of the mother's previous 'dominant' and 'controlling' position over whether the father is registered on the birth certificate.[60] In his view, the mother's rights and interests have been unduly prioritized over those of the child (and the father) and she should be under a stricter obligation to reveal the identity of the father where known.[61] He is thus critical of the welfare-based exemptions for joint registration, arguing that such concerns about vulnerable women and children have no place in the birth registration system.

A. Bainham, 'What is the point of birth registration?', (2008b) 20 *Child and Family Law Quarterly* 449, 460

The fundamental point, surely, is that the Registration Service is not a welfare agency or social service and ought not to be cast as such. Given that there is an apparent commitment in the White Paper to ascertaining and recording the child's biological parentage as soon as possible after birth, and that the child is seen as having a right to be aware of his or her biological parentage, there is a gross imbalance in the Paper between its emphasis on the vulnerability of mothers and its total failure to mention their essential duty to tell the truth about paternity. The fact is that the mother is in a uniquely advantaged position in terms of identifying the biological father, except in a small minority of cases in which she will be in genuine doubt about who the father is . . . [I]t is not the function of the birth registration system to concern itself *at all* with the welfare of any of the parties concerned. Its function is to record accurately the central event of the birth and to identify wherever possible, and record as accurately as possible, the details of the child's two birth parents. If this is right, there would need to be a very strong justification for exempting *any* parent, whether mother or father, from the requirement to co-operate in providing this information . . . Given the new requirement to record the name of the father, the mother's existing duty to tell the truth should effectively become a duty to tell the *whole* truth.

Conversely, there have been equally strong criticisms of the government's unquestioning acceptance of the perceived welfare gains from promoting and supporting genetic fatherhood, despite the weak evidential base for suggesting joint birth registration will have any impact on encouraging greater levels of father involvement or ameliorating the socio-economic disadvantages of lone parenthood.

---

[60] Bainham (2008b), 456.
[61] Ibid., 460.

J. Wallbank, ' "Bodies in the Shadows": joint birth registration, parental responsibility and social class', (2009) 21 *Child and Family Law Quarterly* 267, 272–3, 275

In thinking about this issue it is useful to look to the characteristics of the mothers who sole register the birth... They are likely to be 'younger, have lower incomes, have lower levels of educational attainment and have health issues...' [T]hey are among the more socially and economically vulnerable members of society...

[T]he putative fathers are likely to be located within the same vulnerable social group as the mothers... These fathers are the 'bodies in the shadows' casting a long silhouette back to the past incarnation of the 'feckless' father. By encouraging mothers to register the recalcitrant father without his consent, the state is attempting to ensure that they are traceable so that they may be held accountable for child support. It is highly questionable whether any other form of meaningful parental responsibility will necessarily ensue as a result....

By making joint registration the default position, the government attempts to forestall future problems by embedding the values of responsibility at the earliest possible date... Assumptions are, therefore, made about what fathers will provide for children in respect of advancing their welfare. However,... many of the fathers targeted by the reforms are amongst the most vulnerable groups in society and they may lack effective social and economic support systems. As Val Gillies has argued, it is not possible for parenting to transcend socio-economic reality... Joint registration is unlikely to make any practical contribution to improving the lives of vulnerable mothers, fathers and children. However, the government sees joint registration as an early intervention to get fathers to take responsibility for their children. The government's 'almost evangelical faith in the power of parenting to compensate for social disadvantage' is quite staggering.

The reforms have been particularly strongly criticized for the way in which the government's preoccupation with addressing the 'problem' of potentially absent, disengaged fathers has been dogmatically pursued, regardless of the impact such policies might have on socially vulnerable mothers. In a robust response to Bainham, Wallbank argues that it is wrong to valorize such a highly abstract, formal notion of parental equality that renders irrelevant the father's demonstrable commitment to meeting his parental responsibilities and marginalizes the legitimate welfare concerns of mothers.[62]

J. Wallbank, ' "Bodies in the Shadows": joint birth registration, parental responsibility and social class', (2009) 21 *Child and Family Law Quarterly* 267, 277–8, 281–2

The concerns that women have about joint registration have more to do with women's concerns about the level of responsibility that the father will assume in respect of the child... Where social policy and law is increasingly shaped by aspirational views of fatherhood, mothers base their approach to joint registration on concrete practical contributions...

[T]he reforms may do very little, if anything at all, to ensure actual parental responsibility. Neither will they address the socio-economic needs of vulnerable mothers and children. Rather, already vulnerable mothers will find themselves subject to intrusive questioning about their intimate relationships and their reasons for objecting to joint registration. However,

---

[62] See also Fortin (2009a), 353–4.

some would say that mothers should not have the power to veto joint registration and that it is formal legal rights that should be given priority.

Such an approach ignores the responsibility side of the rights and responsibility that mothers flag up, despite the fact that the reform proposals would have us believe that from the child's and the father's right paternal care for the child will seamlessly flow...

Bainham's approach to joint registration relies heavily on a formal rights-based approach and focuses on the unevenness of rights ascription in respect of mothers and fathers. He also sees the right of the child to know her biological origins as a trump card. However, although there have been legal developments which institute the importance of genetic origins they do not and should not outweigh other significant interests which may need taking account of...[A]lthough birth registration may provide evidence of some tie to the child, that is completely meaningless and even perhaps pernicious in respect of a father who us present in paper but remains the body in the shadows, a spectral figure in the child's life, a mere hologram that the child's imagination will need to fill in...

Of course, those who seek formal equality between mothers and fathers will welcome this shift in gendered power relations whereby fathers can insist on being registered against the mother's wishes. Bainham has argued that welfare considerations have no place in birth registration but I would argue that welfare considerations do have a place, especially when we are dealing with the most vulnerable groups in society.

The debate over the joint registration reforms brings into sharp relief some of the most contentious issues currently dominating the law relating to parents and children. At the heart of the strongly opposing views of Bainham and Wallbank are fundamentally competing visions as to the importance of genetic, as opposed to functional or social, parenthood. As mothers typically fulfil the requirements of both genetic and social parenthood, this debate inevitably focuses on the 'problem' of genetic fathers. As Sheldon notes, the reforms are interesting for what they reveal about the previous Labour government's wider policy agenda on fatherhood.

S. Sheldon, 'From "absent objects of blame" to "fathers who want to take responsibility": reforming birth registration law', (2009) 31 *Journal of Social Welfare and Family Law* 373, 374–5

[T]he proposed changes rely on a number of important assumptions about fatherhood and how it should be regulated. Notably, within this reform process, the term 'father' is assumed to mean the genetic father with no seeming awareness that the work is also often used in other ways...Neither is there any evidence of a concern which was highly significant in early family law and policy: the potential adverse impact of recognising the genetic father on the social family unit in which a child may live with his or her new partner. Further...the reform process reflects a commitment to equality between mothers and fathers and a particular vision of what this entails; an emphasis on independent, unmediated relationships between men and their children; a conflation of men's and children's interests, expressed in appeals to child welfare; an understanding of fatherhood as implying active engagement with children rather than a (merely) disciplinary or breadwinner role; and significant 'policy optimism' both about the desire of fathers to be more involved with their offspring and the likely success of initiatives in parenting as a means of addressing broader social problems....

This raises key questions for family lawyers: should the fact of genetic fatherhood itself be sufficient to confer legal rights and responsibilities on the father? Does a children's rights perspective demand legal recognition of the genetic father? Does equality demand that genetic fathers are accorded exactly the same legal rights as genetic (and social) mothers regardless of whether the father intends to meet the responsibilities of social fatherhood—or does 'real equality' demand something more nuanced? Is active and involved fathering by the biological father of such central importance to securing better outcomes for children that it should be promoted and supported by the law even if the welfare of the mother, and possibly the immediate welfare of the child, will be compromised? We will meet these questions repeatedly throughout the following chapters.

Court proceedings to determine the paternity of a child

Where the paternity of a child is disputed, s 55A of the Family Law Act 1986 (FLA 1986) provides that the child, the child's mother, the putative father, the Child Maintenance and Enforcement Commission, or any other sufficiently interested person (including the person with care of the child for the purposes of the Child Support Act 1991 (CSA 1991)) can make a freestanding application to the court for parentage to be determined.

Family Law Act 1986, s 55A

(1) Subject to the following provisions of this section, any person may apply to the High Court, a county court or a magistrate's court for a declaration as to whether or not a person named in the application is or was the parent of another person so named.

(2) ...

(3) Except in a case falling within subsection (4) below, the court shall refuse to hear an application under subsection (1) above unless it considers that the applicant has a sufficient personal interest in the determination of the application (but this is subject to section 27 of the Child Support Act 1991 [which provides that the person with care of the child will be deemed to have sufficient personal interest and exempts the Child Maintenance and Enforcement Commission from this requirement].

(4) The excepted cases are where the declaration sought is as to whether or not—

  (a) the applicant is the parent of a named person;

  (b) a named person is the parent of the applicant; or

  (c) a named person is the other parent of a named child of the applicant.

(5) Where an application under subsection (1) above is made and one of the persons named in it for the purposes of that subsection is a child, the court may refuse to hear the application if it considers that the determination of the application would not be in the best interests of the child.

The court may refuse to hear the application where it considers to do so would not be in the child's best interests. A declaration made pursuant to s 55A is binding on all persons and for all purposes, including the CSA 1991.[63]

---

[63] FLA 1986, s 58(2).

A child may also apply under s 56 of the FLA 1986 for a declaration as to his or her legitimacy. A dispute over parentage may also be determined when raised in existing civil proceedings, such as an application for parental responsibility under s 4 of the CA 1989.

Proving paternity: rebutting the presumptions and the advent of DNA testing

If a child has been born to unmarried parents and the birth register is silent as to paternity, the applicant will simply have to prove their case on the balance of probabilities.[64] Where a presumption applies, the person seeking to challenge the presumption must adduce sufficient evidence to rebut the presumption on the usual civil standard of proof.

Family Law Reform Act 1969, s 26

Any presumption of law as to the legitimacy or illegitimacy of any person may in any civil proceedings be rebutted by evidence which shows that it is more probable than not that that person is illegitimate or legitimate, as the case may be, and it shall not be necessary to prove that fact beyond reasonable doubt in order to rebut the presumption.

The effect of this provision has been explained by Lord Reid.

S v McC & M; W v W [1972] AC 24, 41 (HL)

LORD REID:

That means that the presumption of legitimacy now merely determines the onus of proof. Once evidence has been led it must be weighed without using the presumption as a makeweight in the scale for legitimacy. So even weak evidence against legitimacy must prevail if there is not other evidence to counterbalance it. The presumption will only come in at that stage in the very rare case of the evidence being so evenly balanced that the court is unable to reach a decision on it. I cannot recollect ever having seen or heard of a case of any kind where the court could not reach a decision on the evidence before it.

Presumptions about a child's paternity and the standard of proof required to rebut them remain technically relevant to determining disputes over parentage. However, the advent of widely accessible, accurate DNA testing means that paternity can now be established with virtual certainty. Where the court makes a direction for DNA tests to be taken, legal niceties about the onus and standard of proof required to rebut a presumption are therefore of little, if any, continuing significance: the DNA tests will be determinative. Indeed, the continuing relevance of the presumption of legitimacy has been explicitly questioned by Thorpe LJ.

[64] FLA 1986, s 58(1).

Re H & A (Children) [2002] EWCA Civ 383

THORPE LJ:

30. The judge made it plain that in the absence of scientific evidence then the issue was to be decided on the application of 'a very important, well established principle . . . that is, the presumption of the legitimacy of children born during the currency of the marriage' . . . Twenty years on I question the relevance of the presumption or the justification for its application. In the nineteenth century, when science had nothing to offer and illegitimacy was a social stigma as well as a depriver of rights, the presumption was a necessary tool, the use of which required no justification. That common law presumption, only rebuttable by proof beyond reasonable doubt, was modified by section 26 of the Family Law Reform Act 1969 by enabling the presumption to be rebutted on the balance of probabilities. But as science has hastened on and as more and more children are born out of marriage it seems to me that the paternity of any child is to be established by science and not by legal presumption or inference.

The key question in present-day paternity disputes is thus whether the court should make the direction for tests so that the truth about a child's genetic parentage can be established with the certainty science now offers.

Directing tests under the FLRA 1969, s 20

Possible approaches

The relevant statutory provisions governing the use of scientific tests in disputes over parentage are found in ss 20–25 of the FLRA 1969.

Family Law Reform Act 1969, s 20

(1) In any civil proceedings in which the parentage of any person falls to be determined, the court may, either of its own motion or on an application by any party to the proceedings, give a direction—

  (a) for the use of scientific tests to ascertain whether such tests show that a party to the proceedings is or is not the father or mother of that person; and

  (b) for the taking, within a period specified in the direction, of bodily samples from all or any of the following, namely, that person, any party who is alleged to be the father or mother of that person and any other party to the proceedings;

and the court may at any time revoke or vary a direction previously given by it under this subsection.

Section 20 confers discretion on the court as to whether a direction for tests should be made. In exercising that discretion, several factors could influence the court's decision:

The rights of the child

First, it could be argued that children have a fundamental right to know the truth about their parentage.

United Nations Convention on the Rights of the Child, 1989

> 7. The child shall be registered immediately after birth and shall have the right from birth to a name, the right to acquire a nationality and, as far as possible, the right to know and be cared for by his or her parents . . .
>
> 8. State Parties undertake to respect the right of the child to preserve his or her identity, including nationality, name and family relations as recognised by law without unlawful interference.

Although the word 'parent' in Article 7 is open to differing interpretations, Bainham puts forward a convincing case that it should be taken to refer to genetic, as opposed to social, parentage.

A. Bainham, 'Parentage, Parenthood and Parental Responsibility', in A. Bainham, S. Day Sclater, and M. Richards (eds), *What is a Parent? A Socio-Legal Analysis* (Oxford: Hart Publishing, 1999), 37–8

> [T]he Convention contains no definition of "parents" and its meaning is therefore legitimately a matter of interpretation upon which opinions may differ. It is argued here, for a number of reasons, that the expression should be interpreted in the conventional sense of genetic parents. First, the history of Articles 7 and 8 reveals that the concern of the international community was with the rights of children from the moment of birth and in relation to their birth parents. It was precisely the threat of removal of the child from the birth parents by others which was the *raison d'etre* of Article 8. Secondly, we must remember that the Convention is a *legal* document. In 1989, when it was adopted, there was, for example, no legislation anywhere in the world regulating assisted reproduction which has been the engine for the re-evaluation of traditional definitions of parenthood. Leaving aside adoption, legislation worldwide has traditionally defined parenthood as genetic parenthood. The legal tie has closely followed the genetic connection. Thirdly . . . the jurisprudence generated under another international Convention, the European Convention on Human Rights, again supports the notion of "family life" from birth and has confirmed that this includes the potential relationship of a child with his or her genetic father even where unmarried. Finally . . . the conventional interpretation was adopted by the Court of Appeal in the one reported decision which directly invokes Article 7. For all these reasons it is submitted that "parents" in the Convention was intended to mean genetic parents and thus the onus is very firmly on those who would argue for an unconventional interpretation.

The principle that children have a fundamental right to know the truth about their genetic parentage has found favour amongst some English judges. In *Re R (A Minor) (Contact Biological Father)*, which concerned a contact dispute between the child's mother and her former husband in relation to a child who had been raised to believe, incorrectly, that the man with whom the mother was cohabiting was her father, Butler-Sloss LJ held in unequivocal terms that the child 'has a right in this case to know the truth'.[65]

---

[65] [1993] 2 FLR 762, 768.

Further support for a children's rights approach can be found in Article 8 of the European Convention on Human Rights (ECHR).[66] It has been held that individuals have a 'private life' interest in ascertaining, through paternity proceedings, the identity of their genetic parents.

Mikulić v Croatia (App No 53176/99, ECHR) (2002)

51. As regards paternity proceedings, the Court has held on numerous occasions that such proceedings do fall within the scope of Article 8...

52. The present case differs...in so far as no family tie has been established between the applicant and her alleged father. The Court reiterates, however, that Article 8, for its part, protects not only "family" but also "private" life.

53. Private life, in the Court's view, includes a person's physical and psychological integrity and can sometimes embrace aspects of an individual's physical and social identity. Respect for "private life" must also comprise to a certain degree the right to establish relationships with other human beings...

There appears, furthermore, to be no reason of principle why the notion of "private life" should be taken to exclude the determination of the legal relationship between a child born out of wedlock and her natural father.

54. The Court has held that respect for private life requires that everyone should be able to establish details of their identity as individual human beings and that an individual's entitlement to such information is of importance because of its formative implications for his or her personality...

55. In the instant case the applicant is a child born out of wedlock who is seeking, by means of judicial proceedings, to establish who her natural father is. The paternity proceedings which she has instituted are intended to determine her legal relationship with H.P. [the putative father] through the establishment of the biological truth. Consequently, there is a direct link between the establishment of paternity and the applicant's private life.

The facts of the case accordingly fall within the ambit of Article 8.

The rights of the putative father

A second factor that may incline the court to make a direction for tests is again rights-based but broadens the scope of the enquiry to include other family members. The European Court of Human Rights has held that under Article 8 ECHR the putative father's right to respect for his private and family life includes the right to have his paternal status and any potential relationship with his child recognized and protected under domestic law or, indeed, to have his paternity excluded.[67] This may require the state to have some mechanism in place whereby the putative father can establish or challenge his legal paternity by, for example, DNA testing and registration/de-registration on the birth register. In *Kroon v the Netherlands* it was held that the applicant's inability to obtain recognition of his paternity because the child had been born whilst the mother was still married and was therefore presumed to be the

---

[66] For commentary see: Fortin (2009a), 345–7.

[67] On the 'family life' aspect of Article 8 where de jure or de facto family ties can be established between the child and the putative father see: *Kroon v The Netherlands* (App No 18535/91, ECHR) (1994), [30] and *Rozanski v Poland* (App No 55339/00, ECHR) (2006), [63]–[64]. As to the 'private life' right engaged in issues regarding the determination of a putative father's legal relations with his child, see: *Shofman v Russia* (App No 74826/01, ECHR) (2005), [30] and *Tavli v Turkey* (App No 11449/02, ECHR) (2006), [25].

legitimate child of her former husband, constituted a breach of the genetic father's right to respect for family life under Article 8. Under Dutch law, only the husband could challenge the presumption of paternity in his favour:

Kroon and others v The Netherlands (App No 18535/91, ECHR) (1994)

32. According to the principles set out by the Court in its case-law, where the existence of a family tie with a child has been established, the State must act in a manner calculated to enable that tie to be developed and legal safeguards must be established that render possible as from the moment of birth or as soon as practicable thereafter the child's integration in his family...

40. In the Court's opinion, "respect" for "family life" requires that biological and social reality prevail over a legal presumption which, as in the present case, flies in the face of both established fact and the wishes of those concerned without actually benefiting anyone.... There has accordingly been a violation of Article 8 (art. 8).

The guiding principle to emerge from *Kroon* (that 'biological and social reality' should prevail over legal presumptions) is consistent with the child's right to know the truth of genetic paternity as established in *Mikulić*.[68] It has, however, subsequently been held by the European Court in *Rozanski v Poland* that this principle will be accorded less weight where the parents do not agree about the desirability of establishing the putative father's status.[69] It is, moreover, clear that the right to biological certainty suggested by *Kroon* is not absolute but must be balanced against other competing interests.[70] Thus the interests of the child and, in particular, the importance of preserving stability and certainty in the child's legal relationships have been found by the Court to constitute a *potential* justification for imposing various restraints, such as time-limits, on challenging the child's paternity.[71] The competing Article 8 right of the child's mother not to be subjected to unwanted and potentially destabilizing interference with her existing family life is also a relevant consideration.

The child's best interests

A third approach that may influence the court's determination of the question of DNA tests rejects rights-based arguments in favour of prioritizing the child's welfare. Adopting this approach, it is argued that the question should simply be determined by asking what is in the child's best interests. If making a direction for DNA testing will secure the child's future welfare, tests should be ordered. If the tests may jeopardize the child's future security and happiness, they should be refused.

The problem is that disputes inevitably arise as to whether tests are in the child's best interests. As discussed in chapter 8, the indeterminacy of the welfare principle renders it

---

68 See also: *Tavli v Turkey* (App No 11449/02, ECHR) (2006), [34]–[36].

69 (App No 55339/00, ECHR) (2006), [67].

70 For a short commentary see Bainham (2007), esp. at 280–1.

71 Although violations of Article 8 were found in the cases of *Shofman* (inflexible time-limit for challenging paternity), *Rozanski* (unable to personally bring direct proceedings to establish his paternity), and *Tavli* (unable to re-open paternity proceedings in light of new DNA evidence), in each case the European Court undertook this careful balancing of interests. See: *Shofman v Russia* (App No 74826/01, ECHR) (2005), [43]–[46]; *Rozanski v Poland* (App No 55339/00, ECHR) (2006), [73]–[80]; *Tavli v Turkey* (App No 11449/02, ECHR) (2006), [32]–[38].

subject to differing interpretations depending on prevailing social attitudes and trends, and the individual preferences of the decision-maker. Consequently, whilst at one time protecting the child against the detrimental consequences of illegitimacy may have been the court's overriding consideration, the declining social stigma surrounding illegitimacy and the final abolition of any legal distinction between a legitimate and illegitimate child[72] opened the way for competing discourses concerning the child's welfare to enter the field. Thus today's debates tend to centre on issues such as whether determining the truth about parentage risks destabilizing the child's existing family unit, how likely it is that the mother's partner is the father, the stability of the mother's existing relationship, the likelihood of the child being able to develop a meaningful relationship with the putative father, and whether doubts concerning the child's parentage have already entered the public arena.

The public interest in the smooth administration of justice

Finally, the issue of whether the court should make a direction for DNA tests can be looked at from a completely different perspective. This fourth approach does not focus on the rights and interests of the parties to the dispute but on the wider public interest. It is argued that once court proceedings have been initiated there is a legitimate public interest in establishing the truth. Consequently, in order to ensure the fair and just administration of justice, the best available evidence should be brought before the court, even if it prejudices the particular rights and interests of the individuals concerned.

Case law under the FLRA 1969, s 20

There is evidence of all the arguments considered above being considered in the case law. In seeking to resolve the conflicts created, the courts have not always adopted a consistent approach. In recent years the preferred approach has been to make a direction for tests, the rationale tending to focus on the child's right to know the truth about his or her genetic parentage, an approach which is considered entirely consistent with the child's best interests.

In *S v McC & M; W v W*,[73] the House of Lords attempted to lay down authoritative guidance as to when a direction for tests should be made under s 20(1) of the FLRA 1969. The conjoined cases both concerned an attempt by the wife's husband to rebut the presumption of legitimacy following the wife's adultery. In making a direction for tests, the House of Lords made clear the declining importance being placed on the child's legitimacy and the court's primary concern, not with the child's welfare, but with the wider public interest in establishing the truth. The principles derived from the House of Lords' judgments have been effectively summarized by Balcombe LJ:

In re F (A Minor) (Blood Tests: Parental Rights) [1993] Fam 314, 318 (CA)

BALCOMBE LJ:

From the speeches in the House of Lords the following principles can be derived: (1) The presumption of legitimacy merely determines the onus of proof...(2) Public policy no longer requires that special protection should be given by the law to the status of legitimacy...(3) The interests of justice will normally require that available evidence be not suppressed and

---

[72] FLRA 1987, s 1.
[73] [1972] AC 24.

that the truth be ascertained whenever possible...In many cases the interests of the child are also best served if the truth is ascertained...(4) However, the interests of justice may conflict with the interests of the child. In general the court ought to permit a blood test of a young child to be taken unless satisfied that that would be against the child's interests; it does not need first to be satisfied that the outcome of the test will be for the benefit of the child...(5) "It is not really protecting the child to ban a blood test on some vague and shadowy conjecture that it may turn out to be to its disadvantage: it may equally well turn out to be for its advantage or at least do it no harm".

Given the House of Lords' strong guidance that a direction for blood tests should ordinarily be made, it is somewhat surprising that the Court of Appeal in *In re F* managed to reach the opposite conclusion. *In re F* concerned a typical paternity dispute. The child was conceived whilst the wife was having sexual relations with both her husband and the putative father. The mother's relationship with the putative father ended before the child was born and the child was being raised as the child of the husband within the existing family unit. The putative father applied for parental responsibility and contact under the CA 1989. Paternity was disputed. Although paying lip-service to the requirement that blood tests must be shown to positively harm the child's interests (the approach adopted in *S v McC*),[74] in determining whether a direction for blood tests should be made, the Court of Appeal appeared to apply the different test of whether the tests would promote the child's interests. In determining this question, the Court of Appeal held that the child's interests lay not in ascertaining the 'abstract' truth about her true genetic parentage, but in providing support and protection to the existing family unit.

In re F (A Minor) (Blood Tests: Parental Rights) [1993] Fam 314, 319–22 (CA)

BALCOMBE LJ:

B. [the putative father] criticised the judge's decision on a number of grounds. He submitted that the judge was wrong to base his decision, at least in part, on the probable outcome of B.'s applications for parental responsibility and contact; that in any event the interests of justice and E.'s [the child's] own welfare required that her true paternity be established. In our judgment that submission is fundamentally misconceived. As is apparent from the provisions of section 20(1) of the Family Law Reform Act 1969, the power to direct the use of blood tests to determine parentage only arises "in civil proceedings in which the paternity of any person falls to be determined." If the probable outcome of these proceedings will be the same whoever may be the natural father of E., then there can be no point in exposing E. to the possible disadvantages of a blood test. We agree with the judge that in the circumstances of this case there is no realistic prospect of B. succeeding at the present time in his applications for parental responsibility and contact since we do not see how such orders could benefit E....

On the issue whether it was in E.'s interests to have the identity of her natural father determined with such degree of certainty as scientific tests can provide, B. submitted that it must inevitably be in E.'s interests to know the truth about her parentage; her interests should not be subordinated to those of Mr. and Mrs. F. [the mother and her husband]. This may well be true, but now and for the first few years of her life E.'s physical and emotional welfare are

---

[74] See also *Re L* [2009] EWCA Civ 1239, [11]–[14].

inextricably bound up with the welfare of the family unit of which she forms part: any harm to the welfare of that unit, as might be caused by an order for the taking of blood tests, would inevitably be damaging to E.

The child's right to knowledge of her genetic parentage, as well as the wider public interest in ascertaining the truth, were raised but cursorily dismissed:

B. also referred us to the United Nations Convention on the Rights of the Child…which has been ratified by the United Kingdom, and in particular to article 7 which provides that a child shall have, "as far as possible, the right to know and be cared for by his or her parents." B. submitted that E.'s welfare included her rights under this article. Whether or not B. is included in this definition of a parent within the meaning of this article, it is not in fact possible for E. to be cared for by both her parents (if B. is such). No family unit exists or has ever existed, between B. and Mrs. F., and if B. were able to assert his claims to have a share in E.'s upbringing it would inevitably risk damaging her right to be cared for by her mother, Mrs. F.…

E.'s welfare depends for the foreseeable future primarily upon her relationship with her mother. B. expressly conceded that he did not dispute the right of Mrs F. to have E. living with her. Anything that may disturb that relationship or the stability of the family unit within which E. has lived since her birth is likely to be detrimental to E.'s welfare, and unless that detriment is shown to be counter-balanced by other positive advantages to her which an order for the taking of blood tests could confer, then the judge's refusal to order blood tests was not merely an exercise of his discretion with which we cannot interfere, but one with which in the circumstances of this case we agree.

B. made a number of other points by way of criticism of the judgment below, including the point that the public interest, as well as E.'s own personal interest, requires that the truth about her paternity be ascertained if possible. However, in the last resort it is clear that E.'s interests must be the decisive factor; where, as here, the judge was satisfied that it would be against E.'s interests to order blood tests to be taken—a decision with which we agree— then it was both his duty and his right to refuse the application. It was for these reasons that we dismissed this appeal.

[The first instance judge's refusal to make a direction for blood tests was upheld.]

The Court of Appeal's judgment met with a mixed academic reaction. Barton and Douglas welcomed the court's preference for the presumed legal parenthood of the mother's husband, as evidence of the 'growing importance of the social, as opposed to genetic aspect of parenthood'.[75] Fortin was, however, more critical, arguing, on the basis of evidence from the field of adoption, that the court 'should have given far greater weight to the psychological value to E of knowing the truth about her origins'.[76] She also criticized the court for failing to keep the issue of the child's genetic parentage separate from that of the putative father's prospects of establishing a meaningful social relationship with the child.[77] However, as discussed below, recent case law has prompted Fortin to reconsider these views.[78]

The Court of Appeal's apparent departure from the House of Lords' preference for determining the truth of parentage was, in any event, short lived. The issue returned to the Court

---

[75] Barton and Douglas (1995), 61.
[76] Fortin (1994), 298.
[77] Ibid.
[78] See below at pp 609–10.

of Appeal in *In re H (A Minor) (Blood Tests: Parental Rights)*. The case was very similar on its facts to *In re F* although it was very unlikely the mother's husband could be the child's genetic father as he had had a vasectomy and sexual relations between them were very poor at the time of conception. The mother, nevertheless, disputed the putative father's paternity. In making a direction for scientific tests, Ward LJ reasserted and refined the House of Lords' principles from *S v McC & M*. On the question of welfare, the Court of Appeal confirmed that 'welfare does not dominate this decision', although most of the judgment is devoted to whether blood tests would be in the child's best interests. The decision is also distinctive for the emphasis placed on the child's right to know the truth about his or her genetic parentage, an approach Ward LJ clearly considered entirely consistent with the child's welfare.

In re H (A Minor) (Blood Tests: Parental Rights) [1997] Fam 89 (CA)

WARD LJ:

(5) In my judgment every child has the right to know the truth unless his welfare clearly justifies the cover up. The right to know is acknowledged in the United Nations Convention on the Rights of the Child... there are two separate rights, the one to know, and the other to be cared for by, one's parents...

(9) Given the real risk bordering on inevitability that H. [the child] will at some time question his paternity, then I do not see how this case is not concluded by the unassailable wisdom expressed by Lord Hodson [in *S v McC & M*]...:

"The interests of justice in the abstract are best served by the ascertainment of the truth and there must be few cases where the interests of children can be shown to be best served by the suppression of truth."

If, as she should, this mother is to bring up her children to believe in and to act by the maxim, which is her duty to teach them at her knee, that honesty is the best policy, then she should not sabotage that lesson by living a lie.

(10) If the child has the right to know, then the sooner it is told the better. The issue of biological parentage should be divorced from psychological parentage. Acknowledging the applicant's parental responsibility should not dent the husband's social responsibility for a child whom he is so admirably prepared to care for and love irrespective of whether or not he is the father....

(11) If H. grows up knowing the truth, that will not undermine his attachment to his father figure and he will cope with knowing he has two fathers. Better that than a time-bomb ticking away.

The wider public interest in the smooth administration of justice does not feature in the Court of Appeal's reasoning.

The judgment in *Re H* is also significant for the clear distinction drawn between the child's genetic and social parents. It is thus emphasized that it is perfectly possible for a child to have two 'fathers'—one genetic and one social—and that the two parental roles are not necessarily mutually exclusive. Ward LJ does, however, make it clear that the two parents may serve quite different functions in relation to the child, and whilst the child has a right to know his or her genetic parentage, this does not necessarily involve trying to foster a personal relationship between them. The child's right to know should therefore not be seen as threatening or detracting from the parenting role of the social or psychological parent.

The impact of the Human Rights Act 1998

In re H is now regarded as the leading authority on when it is appropriate to make a direction for DNA tests.[79] Although the child's welfare is not the paramount consideration, the child's rights and interests are very much the focus of concern. However, one argument which was not dealt with by the Court of Appeal in *In re H,* but could not be avoided following the implementation of the Human Rights Act 1998 (HRA 1998), was whether the putative father could rely on any rights under Article 8 to disturb what was now, essentially, an exclusively child-centred approach. Until this point, arguments focusing on the Article 8 rights of the putative father had been absent from the case law. However, the issue was tackled in *Re T (a child) (DNA tests: paternity)*, Bodey J's judgment making it clear that, following implementation of the HRA 1998, it was business as usual. The facts of *Re T* were somewhat unusual. The mother, who was married but unable to conceive a child with her husband, had engaged in sexual intercourse with several men, including the putative father, at around the same time, in the hope of becoming pregnant. It was always intended that the resulting child would be raised within the existing family unit. However, the putative father, who had had some contact with the child, applied for parental responsibility and contact. The husband responded by asserting his paternity. The putative father's application was specifically triggered by the implementation of the HRA 1998. Having confirmed that the child's welfare was not paramount and that the child's interests had to be balanced against the competing interests of the adults, Bodey J went on to address the rights-based arguments:

Re T (a child) (DNA tests: paternity) [2001] 3 FCR 577, 583–6 (Fam Div)

BODEY J:

There is no significant dispute that T [the child] has a right to respect for his private life (in the sense of having knowledge of his identity, which encompasses his true paternity) and a right to respect for his family life with each of his natural parents, all things being equal.

T also has what may (as here) be mutually 'competing' rights to respect for his private and family life, in the *other* sense that the stability of his present de facto family life should not be put at risk, except as may otherwise be held to be in his interests, and pursuant to art 8(2).

It is further common ground that the mother and her husband have a right to respect for their private and family life, comprising a right that the same should not be intruded upon, or interfered with, except as may be necessary to give effect to T's and (if he has them) the applicant's rights.

So far as the applicant is concerned, he may or may not (depending on the facts and on whether he is in truth the biological father) have a right to respect for a family life encompassing—all things being equal—the society of, and a relationship with T, and/or a knowledge of T's progress.

It is accepted between the parties that if and when these various Convention rights pull in opposite directions, then the crucial importance of the rights and best interests of the child fall particularly to be considered…

I am entirely satisfied that in evaluating and balancing the various rights of the adult parties and of T under art 8, the weightiest emerges clearly as being that of T, namely that he should have the possibility of knowing, perhaps with certainty, his true roots and identity.

---

[79] *Re T (a child) (DNA tests: paternity)* [2001] 3 FCR 577, 583.

I find any such interference as would occur to the right to respect for the family/private life of the mother and her husband, to be proportionate to the legitimate aim of providing T with the possibility of certainty as to his real paternity, a knowledge which would accompany him throughout his life.

Applying art 8 in this way (regardless of whether or not the applicant has established what, if he is the father, would constitute family life with T) confirms my previous view that I should grant the applicant's application.

[Bodey J went on to consider, *obiter*, whether the applicant would be able to establish a right to respect for family life for the purposes of Article 8. He concluded that the applicant's relationship with the child and the child's mother lacked sufficient constancy and commitment to create the necessary de facto family ties to establish the family life right under Article 8. The alternative private life limb of Article 8 was not considered.]

Consent requirements for the taking of samples

On the basis of the most recent authorities, it is now tolerably clear that when paternity is disputed the court will make a direction for scientific tests to determine the issue. There is, however, a further hurdle to be negotiated. Regardless of any direction the Court might make, a bodily sample cannot be taken from any party to the litigation for the purpose of carrying out the tests without that person's consent.[80]

The child's consent to the taking of samples

In the case of a minor who is 16 years or over, s 21(2) of the FLRA 1969 provides that the minor can give an effective consent to the taking of bodily samples in the same way as a person of full age and capacity. For minors who are under 16, the consent of the person with 'care and control' is required. If consent is withheld, the court can override the refusal if satisfied that taking the sample would be in the child's best interests:

Family Law Reform Act 1969, s 21

(3) A bodily sample may be taken from a person under the age of sixteen years, not being a person as is referred to in subsection (4) of this section,

　(a) if the person who has the care and control of him consents; or

　(b) where that person does not consent, if the court considers that it would be in his best interests for the sample to be taken.

This appears to set down a straightforward welfare test for determining whether samples should be taken if the person with care and control does not consent. This is different from the qualified welfare test set down in *S v McC* and *In re H* for determining whether a direction for tests should be made under s 20(1). It is not yet clear how the courts will deal with the slightly differing demands of the two provisions. Although the child's welfare is not the only consideration in determining whether a direction for tests should be made, before making a direction under s 20(1) the court will have given detailed consideration to the issue and reached a firm conclusion as to whether or not DNA tests are in the child's best interests or

[80] FLRA 1969, s 21(1)

at least not adverse to them. Section 21 may therefore be rendered a mere formality, the court invariably ordering that samples be taken once the direction for testing is made. Indeed, there is a clear trend in the current case law, at least where consent to the taking of samples is in issue, to conflate the requirements of ss 20 and 21 of the FLRA 1969 and decide the case by means of an unqualified application of the welfare principle.[81] This will invariably lead both to a direction for DNA tests to be carried out and an order for the taking of samples. This was the approach adopted in the case of *Re D (Paternity)* which unusually involved the vehement opposition of an 11-year-old child to the taking of samples.[82] Hedley J's analysis focused exclusively on the child's best interests with no distinction drawn between the requirements of ss 20 and 21 of the FLRA 1969. Despite the child's clear and determined opposition, Hedley J ordered that a sample be taken for the purposes of testing, albeit he stayed the order to remove the immediate pressure on the child.[83]

The decision in *Re D* has generated concern that the emphasis on genetic truth is such that it is being dogmatically pursued even where, on the particular facts, it is strongly arguable that it may be better for the child to preserve stability and security in his or her current relationships. Fortin, who has previously supported the child's right to know, has recently voiced concerns about this trend. She argues that the preoccupation with biological truth has more to do with serving the rights and interests of the adults than those of the child, particularly where paternity disputes are being driven, not by the child's right to information about his or her genetic origins, but by the putative father's desire to establish a social relationship with the child based on nothing more than the genetic tie.

J. Fortin, 'Children's right to know their origins – too far, too fast?', (2009a) 21
Child and Family Law Quarterly 336, 338–54

When writing my critique of *Re F* [see above], I had perhaps overlooked the dangers for children of the assumption that they all have a right to knowledge of their origins . . . The decision in Re D provokes a feeling of unease . . . Surely a child has a right *not* to know the identity of his father if he himself believes, with some grounds, that his entire life would be disrupted by such knowledge? Indeed, the view that *all* children have a right to know their parents' identity may sometimes achieve more harm than good, given the danger of the two issues being confused—the child's need to know about his origins and his possible need for a social relationship with his biological parent . . . When dealing with applications from putative fathers, it is arguable that the domestic courts are extending a child's right to know beyond its appropriate boundaries . . . [T]he disputes being litigated have little to do with children's right to knowledge of their origins. The DNA testing applications brought by putative fathers are not brought to provide the child with information alone, they are the initial stages of attempts to establish a social relationship between father and child based on assumptions about biological connectedness. The putative fathers' assumption that once the biological ties between father and child have been clearly identified, they should be fulfilled by a social relationship produces an elision of the right to know the parent's identity, with the right to know and have a relationship with that parent. Whether or not claims can be justified by reference to the child's own rights, such an elision concentrates the court's attention on the putative father's position and his own interests—countered by those of the mother . . . These are adult-centred

---

81 *Re T (a child) (DNA tests: paternity)* [2001] 3 FCR 577; *Re H and A* [2002] 1 FLR 1145.
82 [2006] EWHC 3545.
83 Ibid., [29]–[30].

arguments which spring from adult-centred disputes over children who are treated as the property of those who can establish biological connectedness. There are dangers that such an approach, unsupported by research will not benefit some children. Indeed, in some cases like *Re D (Paternity)* where the child himself rejects the need to know the identity of his father, it may psychologically damage him. That case reinforces Smart's warning…about the dangers of allowing the law to insist on only one kind of truth—'the truth of science' above those other claims concerned with 'caring, relationality and the preserve of kinship bonds'.

The consent of adult parties and the drawing of adverse inferences

Under s 21(3), the problem of a lack of consent with respect to the child can now usually be avoided. The need for consent is more difficult where one of the adults refuses to cooperate. This is most likely to arise where the putative father is denying paternity to avoid paying child support. There is no statutory equivalent to s 21(3) giving the court the authority to override the putative father's refusal. The courts have, however, made it clear that they will not allow themselves to be dictated to by intransigent parties and the stated intention of one party to withhold consent will not preclude them from making a direction for tests.[84] A refusal to submit to the tests does not amount to contempt of court and cannot be met by the court's punitive powers.[85] To withhold consent is, however, to play a dangerous game. The court can draw whatever inferences it feels appropriate from a party's refusal to cooperate,[86] including an inference as to the actual paternity of the child.[87] As was made clear in *Re A (A Minor) (Paternity: Refusal of Blood Test)*, this is an effective weapon against an intransigent party. The facts of *Re A* are fairly typical of paternity disputes where liability to provide financial support for the child is at stake. At the time of the child's conception, the mother was having sexual relations with three different men. She claimed maintenance against just one, a man the Court of Appeal described as being 'of some substance'.[88] The man refused to comply with a direction for blood tests, arguing that it would be unjust to compel him to submit to a test and risk paternity being conclusively established against him when two other men who were equally likely to be the child's father were not being exposed to the same risk. The argument was dismissed:

Re A (A Minor) (Paternity: Refusal of Blood Test) [1994] 2 FLR 463, 472–3 (CA)

WAITE LJ:

The starting-point must be that the old uncertainties which formerly surrounded issues of disputed paternity when a mother had been sexually involved with two or more men at the time of conception are now banished altogether. Genetic testing, already advanced to a high degree of probability through the negative techniques of exclusion, has now moved on to the point where it has become possible to achieved [sic] positive certainty. That has had a profound effect on cases like the present, where a mother has been having relations with different men at the time of conception. Any man who is unsure of his own paternity and harbours the least doubt as to whether the child he is alleged to have fathered may be that of another man now has it within his power to set all doubt at rest by submitting to a test. It has

---

[84] *In re H (A Minor) (Blood Tests: Parental Rights)* [1997] Fam 89, 101.
[85] *Re G (A minor) (blood test)* [1994] 1 FLR 495, 499–500.
[86] FLRA 1969, s 23.
[87] *Re A (A Minor) (Paternity: Refusal of Blood Test)* [1994] 2 FLR 463, 472.
[88] Ibid., 464.

ceased, therefore, to be possible for any man in such circumstances to be forced against his will to accept paternity of a child whom he does not believe to be his.

Against that background of law and scientific advance, it seems to me to follow, both in justice and in common sense, that if a mother makes a claim against one of the possible fathers, and he chooses to exercise his right not to submit to be tested, the inference that he is the father of the child should be virtually inescapable. He would certainly have to advance very clear and cogent reasons for this refusal to be tested—reasons which it would be just and fair and reasonable for him to be allowed to maintain.

It is open to the party withholding consent to show good cause why his refusal to cooperate is justified. Absent such justification, however, the drawing of an adverse inference against the party disputing paternity seems virtually inevitable, even if, as was made clear in the case of *F v Child Support Agency*,[89] one of the other putative fathers is married to the child's mother and a presumption of legitimacy therefore applies.

Telling the child the truth about paternity

If scientific tests are ordered and the truth about paternity established, the next question is whether, and if so how, the child should be told. Not surprisingly, many mothers who oppose DNA testing are equally resistant to telling the child the result, particularly where it threatens the child's security within the existing family unit. It is, however, clear that the court can compel a parent to tell the child the truth about his or her paternity. *In the Matter of F (children)*,[90] Thorpe LJ held that the question of whether a child should be told the truth is a question relating to the exercise of an aspect of parental responsibility which can be controlled by a specific issue order or under the court's wardship jurisdiction.[91] Moreover, he made it clear that concerns over the enforceability of such orders were unfounded: if the parent refuses to cooperate, the court can put in place alternative mechanisms for ensuring the children are told, possibly involving mental health professionals.[92]

9.4 DETERMINING PARENTHOOD IN THE CONTEXT OF ASSISTED REPRODUCTION

9.4.1 THE BRAVE NEW WORLD OF ASSISTED REPRODUCTION

For family lawyers, post-war developments in assisted reproduction raised a number of challenging new questions. One of the key difficulties for policy-makers is the number of different treatments available and the vast range of circumstances in which people may seek to take advantage of them. Over 30,000 couples now receive fertility treatment each year in the UK, resulting in about 9,000 live births.[93]

---

[89] [1999] 2 FLR 244.
[90] [2007] EWCA Civ 873.
[91] Ibid., [8], [14].
[92] Ibid., [17]–[18].
[93] Speech by Melanie Johnson MP, 12 June 2004: National Infertility Day 2004. Available from: <http://webarchive.nationalarchives.gov.uk/+/www.dh.gov.uk/en/MediaCentre/Speeches/Speecheslist/DH_4071490>.

Whilst scientific advances in reproductive medicine have generally been welcomed for giving much needed hope to infertile couples, there have also been strong voices of dissent. Concern tends to focus on what is perceived as the potential use of these treatments for social, as opposed to medical reasons. Single women and same-sex couples are typically targeted as the most likely 'deviants' to seek to exploit the developments.[94] A married couple unable to conceive for medical reasons are likely to engender considerable sympathy. IVF using their own gametes to assist in conception raises relatively few problems for our traditional concepts of 'family' and 'parenthood'. At the other extreme is the story of same-sex couple, Tony Barlow and Barrie Drewiit. The couple entered into a surrogacy agreement in the United States, as a result of which twins, Aspen and Saffron, were born. The embryos were created using the eggs of one woman, Tracie McCune, making her the twins' genetic mother.[95] The eggs were fertilized in vitro, that is outside the woman's uterus, using the sperm of both Tony and Barrie. It is thus unclear which of the two men is the twins' genetic father.[96] The embryos were then transferred into a second woman, Rosalind Bellamy, the surrogate, who carried the twins to term. Rosalind is thus the twins' gestational mother. This case raises much greater challenges for English law's traditional concepts of 'family' and 'parenthood'.

As the story of Barrie and Tony graphically illustrates, the act of reproduction is no longer tied to the need for heterosexual intercourse. Although artificial insemination using donor sperm has probably been practised on an informal 'DIY' basis for years, the ability to create an embryo in vitro raises the spectre of a previously unknown fragmentation of parenthood. There are now several individuals who can contribute to the creation of a single embryo and who are able to point to equally credible but competing claims to parenthood of the resulting child. Out of the complicated arrangement entered into by Barrie and Tony there is no easy answer to the question of who the law should regard as the twins' legal parents. Should the twins' genetic parentage (the genetic father and Tracie) or social parentage (Barrie and Tony) be accorded legal priority? The decision to use two different women to act as egg donor and surrogate also raises the question of whether the genetic mother (Tracie) or the gestational mother (Rosalind) should be accorded legal priority. A Californian Supreme Court judge seeking to resolve this dilemma decided that Barrie and Tony should be entered as 'parent one' and 'parent two' on the twins' birth certificates.[97] In the eyes of Californian law, Saffron and Aspen thus have no legal mother and two legal fathers. Such an approach fundamentally challenges our traditional concepts of the heterosexual family. The possibilities created by assisted reproduction dramatically expose the extent to which English family law is willing to embrace unconventional family forms.[98]

However, before turning to consider how the law on parenthood has responded to these developments in assisted reproduction, we will briefly consider an increasingly important and closely related question: the right of an individual to access fertility treatment.

---

[94] As to the concerns expressed in the parliamentary debates preceding the HFEA 1990 see: Jackson (2002), 195; Douglas (1993), 57–8; and Roberts (2000), 49.

[95] Hibbs (2001), 736.

[96] Ibid., 737.

[97] Ibid., 736–7.

[98] For an argument concerning the need for English law to embrace postmodern difference and 'otherness' in the context of assisted reproduction, see Langdridge and Blyth (2001).

9.4.2 ACCESS TO TREATMENT: IS PARENTHOOD A RIGHT OR A PRIVILEGE?

Infertility can be devastating for those affected but developments in assisted reproduction mean that there are now several ways in which couples can be helped. However, whilst one may feel considerable sympathy for these couples, it does not necessarily follow that they have a right to demand access to treatment; *a fortiori* individuals and couples who are not infertile but seek access to assisted reproductive techniques for other, perhaps social, reasons. There are several arguments against allowing individuals, to access fertility treatment.

DHSS, *Report of the Committee of Inquiry into Human Fertilisation and Embryology*, Cm 9314 (London: HMSO, 1984)

2.3 Arguments have been put to us both for and against the treatment of infertility. First, we have encountered the view that in an over-populated world it is wrong to take active steps to create more human beings who will consume finite resources. However strongly a couple may wish to have children, such a wish is ultimately selfish. It has been said that if they cannot have children without intervention, they should not be helped to do so. Secondly, there is a body of opinion which holds that it is wrong to interfere with nature, or with what is perceived to be the will of God. Thirdly, it has been argued that the desire to have children is no more than a wish; it cannot be said to constitute a need. Other people have genuine needs which must be satisfied if they are to survive. Thus services designed to meet those needs must have priority for scarce resources.

The Warnock Committee were unpersuaded by these arguments,[99] and following their recommendations, the UK has taken a fairly liberal approach to the provision of fertility treatment. Clinics specializing in assisted reproduction have been established in both the private and the public sector, albeit subject to the strict licensing conditions set down in the HFEA 1990 and closely regulated by the Human Fertilisation and Embryology Authority (HFEA). The wide availability of fertility treatment does not, however, translate into a right to treatment.

The right to access fertility treatment can be conceptualized as a right to found a family or, more broadly, as a right to reproductive freedom. Emily Jackson makes a strong case as to why those who wish to have children should be afforded the freedom to do so, focusing her arguments on the right of individuals to a protected 'zone of privacy' in which decisions concerning reproduction can be made.[100]

E. Jackson, 'Conception and the Irrelevance of the Welfare Principle', (2002) 65 *Modern Law Review* 176, 177–8

Of course for the vast majority of people, deciding whether or not to conceive is not suscep-tible to legal control. People who conceive through heterosexual sexual intercourse do so without any external scrutiny of the merit or otherwise of their decision. Monitoring these exceptionally personal choices in order to identify ill-judged or improper conception decisions

---

[99] DHSS (1984), [2.4].
[100] See also Alghrani and Harris (2006), 192 and 195–6.

would be unreservedly condemned as an unacceptably intrusive abuse of state power...I would suggest that there are broadly two different justifications for the presumption that normally exists in favour of privacy in procreative decision-making. First, interfering with a particular individual's decision to conceive a child would usually involve violating their bodily integrity and sexual privacy...The second and I would argue equally important reason for respecting people's conception choices is that the freedom to decide for oneself whether or not to reproduce is integral to a person's sense of being, in some important sense, the author of their own life plan. For most people, these two justifications for reproductive privacy mesh together in the requirement that we treat both their body and their life plan with respect. We should, however, remember that those individuals whose procreative preferences can be disregarded without simultaneously violating their bodily integrity and sexual privacy nevertheless retain their interest in being able to make exceptionally personal and important decisions according to their own conception of the good.

In considering the right to reproductive freedom, a distinction needs to be made between what Jackson terms 'positive and negative liberty'.[101] There is an important difference between, on the one hand, the state interfering with the decision of an individual to seek fertility treatment in the private sphere and, on the other, the state refusing to provide unfettered access to state funded treatment. The former seeks to impose a negative obligation of non-interference on the state, whilst the latter seeks to impose a positive obligation on the state to guarantee access to treatment for all. The argument in favour of recognizing the former right is considerably stronger than the latter, where other considerations such as the rationing of resources and prioritization of medical treatment within the NHS are legitimate considerations.[102] Where, however, there are no resource issues at stake, the legitimacy of the state seeking to scrutinize and restrict an individual's procreative freedom is harder to sustain.

E. Jackson, 'Conception and the Irrelevance of the Welfare Principle', (2002) 65 *Modern Law Review* 176, 177–8

My claim is that we should refrain from scrutinising the pre-conception decisions of adults who intend to bring about a child's creation just as we would if they had happened to be able to conceive naturally. Notice that this is not the same as saying that people have a *right* to be provided with fertility treatment. On the contrary, my argument here is much more modest. It is simply that we should each have the liberty to shield certain personal decisions from public scrutiny. The decision to conceive a child goes to the heart of an individual's identity and is precisely the sort of choice that we all ought to be able to make within the privacy of our most intimate relationship. I argue that it is therefore unfair to take advantage of the opportunity afforded by their biological incapacity in order to assess the wisdom of an infertile couple's decision to start a family. We may not be able to fund their treatment, or there might be no treatment that is clinically appropriate for them. But evaluating an infertile couple's fitness to parent deprives them of the decisional privacy that the majority of people are rightly able to take for granted.

---

101 Jackson (2002), 184.
102 Ibid., 184–5.

The right to reproductive freedom under Article 8 ECHR

In order to assist an individual seeking access to fertility treatment, the right to reproductive freedom must first be recognized under English law. The prevailing approach, prior to the implementation of the HRA 1998, was that an individual had the right to seek investigation and advice concerning their infertility and a right to be considered for treatment. There was, however, no unfettered right to treatment in either the public or private sector. This general approach, recommended by the Warnock Committee,[103] was endorsed in *R v Ethical Committee of St Mary's Hospital (Manchester), ex parte H*.[104] The implementation of the HRA 1998 has not changed this basic position. The issue of whether there is a Convention right to access fertility treatment arose in *Evans v UK*.[105] *Evans* did not concern a straightforward claim to treatment. Ms Evans was attending a clinic for fertility treatment with her partner, Mr Johnston, when it was discovered she had cancerous tumours in both ovaries. As a result, she underwent the first stage of IVF treatment to remove as many eggs as possible for use in future treatment. The eggs were fertilized using Mr Johnston's sperm and the resulting embryos frozen whilst Ms Evans underwent treatment for cancer. Before she recovered sufficiently for an embryo transfer to be carried out, the couple separated and Mr Johnston withdrew his consent to the further storage and use of the embryos. This meant that under the terms of the HFEA 1990, Sch 3, the embryos had to be removed from storage and destroyed. Ms Evans claimed that Mr Johnston's right to withdraw his consent violated her Article 8 right to respect for private and family life. In line with the approach adopted by the Court of Appeal hearing the case at the domestic level,[106] the Grand Chamber of the European Court held that the right to decide whether to become a genetic parent (and to realize that right by accessing fertility treatment) fell within the ambit of the Article 8 right to respect for private life, this right being broadly interpreted to incorporate any aspect of one's personal liberty and freedom.

Evans v UK (App No 6339/05, ECHR) (2007)

71. It is not disputed between the parties that Article 8 is applicable and that the case concerns the applicant's right to respect for her private life. The Grand Chamber agrees with the Chamber that "private life", which is a broad term encompassing, *inter alia*, aspects of an individual's physical and social identity including the right to personal autonomy, personal development and to establish and develop relationships with other human beings and the outside world...incorporates the right to respect for both the decisions to become and not to become a parent.

72. It must be noted, however, that the applicant does not complain that she is in any way prevented from becoming a mother in a social, legal, or even physical sense, since there is no rule of domestic law or practice to stop her from adopting a child or even giving birth to a child originally created *in vitro* from donated gametes. The applicant's complaint is, more precisely, that the consent provisions of the 1990 Act prevent her from using the embryos she and J [her former partner] created together, and thus, given her particular circumstances, from ever having a child to whom she is genetically related. The Grand Chamber considers

---

103 DHSS (1984), [2.12].
104 [1988] 1 FLR 512.
105 (App No 6339/05, ECHR) (2007).
106 *Evans v Amicus Healthcare Ltd & Others* [2004] EWCA Civ 727, [108].

that this more limited issue, concerning the right to respect for the decision to become a parent in the genetic sense, also falls within the scope of Article 8.

It was subsequently confirmed in *Dickson v UK* that state-imposed restrictions on accessing assisted reproduction engages Article 8 and the right to respect for the decision to become a genetic parent.[107] It is, however, equally clear from *Evans* and *Dickson* that Article 8 is a qualified right; it does not confer an absolute right to become a parent using any technological means possible.

Legitimate restrictions on the right to reproductive freedom: Article 8(2)

Procreative liberty and the need for unequivocal consent

The state can legitimately regulate and restrict the right to fertility treatment in order to safeguard the rights and interests of others. In *Evans*, the Court of Appeal held that the interference with Ms Evans' Article 8 rights was justified to protect the competing Article 8 rights of Mr Johnston, in particular, his *equal* right to procreative liberty including his right to choose not to become a father.

Evans v Amicus Healthcare Ltd & Others [2004] EWCA Civ 727

ARDEN LJ:

109. The next question is whether the interference is justified under article 8(2). In the 1990 Act Parliament has taken the view that each genetic parent should have the right to withdraw their consent for as long as possible. It was not inevitable that Parliament should take that view. Subject to the possible effect of the Convention, Parliament could have taken the view that, as in sexual intercourse, a man's procreative liberty should end with the donation of sperm but that, in the light of the woman's unique role in making the embryo a child, she should have the right to determine the fate of the embryo. But Parliament did not take that view. Nor did Parliament take the view that the court should have any power to dispense with the requirement for consent of both parties, even when circumstances occur which were not envisaged when the original arrangements were made.

110...I consider that the imposition of an invariable and ongoing requirement for consent in the 1990 Act in the present type of situation satisfies article 8(2) of the Convention. The requirement is supported by the arguments set out in the evidence of [the head of the assisted conception and embryology section at the Department of Health], particularly the argument based on the primacy of consent. As this is a sensitive area of ethical judgment, the balance to be struck between the parties must primarily be a matter for Parliament...Parliament has taken the view that no one should have power to override the need for a genetic parent's consent. The wisdom of not having such a power is, in my judgment, illustrated by the facts of this case. The personal circumstances of the parties are different from what they were at the outset of treatment, and it would be difficult for a court to judge whether the effect of Mr Johnston's withdrawal of his consent on Ms Evans is greater than the effect that the invalidation of that withdrawal of consent would have on Mr Johnston. The court has no point of reference by which to make that sort of evaluation. The fact is that each person has

---

107 *Dickson v UK* (App No 44362/04, ECHR) (2007).

a right to be protected against interference with their private life. That is an aspect of the principle of self-determination or personal autonomy. It cannot be said that the interference with Mr Johnston's right is justified on the ground that interference is necessary to protect Ms Evans's right, because her right is likewise qualified in the same way by his right. They must have equivalent rights, even though the exact extent of their rights under article 8 has not been identified.

111. The interference with Ms Evans's private life is also justified under article 8(2) because, if Ms Evans's argument succeeded, it would amount to interference with the genetic father's right to decide not to become a parent. Motherhood could surely not be forced on Ms Evans and likewise fatherhood cannot be forced on Mr Johnston, especially as in the present case it will probably involve financial responsibility in law for the child as well.

The Grand Chamber of the European Court agreed that the HFEA's strict provisions on consent were a proportionate response to the legitimate need to protect the procreative liberty of *both* parties embarking upon fertility treatment.[108]

This strict approach to consent was retained when the legislative framework governing assisted reproduction was reformed in 2008. The HFEA 2008 amends Sch 3 to the HFEA 1990 to introduce a 12-month 'cooling off' period.[109] This allows the embryos to continue to be stored for 12 months following the withdrawal of consent by one party in the hope that an amicable agreement about their future use and storage can be reached. However, if the parties cannot reach agreement the embryos must still be destroyed on the expiration of the 12-month period.

The best interests of the child

The most important way in which the state regulates access to fertility treatment is through the welfare principle, the mechanism by which the rights and interests of any future child can be protected.

Human Fertilisation and Embryology Act 1990, s 13

(5) A woman shall not be provided with treatment services unless account has been taken of the welfare of any child who may be born as a result of the treatment (including the need of that child for supportive parenting), and of any other child who may be affected by the birth.

The child's welfare constitutes a legitimate qualification on the right of the prospective parents to procreative liberty under Article 8(2).[110] However, restricting access to fertility treatment on the basis of the child's welfare has been fiercely criticized. In practice, it is intrinsically difficult to apply the best interests principle to such an abstract question as the welfare of a child who does not yet exist. Indeed, Emily Jackson, one of the strongest critics, argues that to attempt to do so is 'disingenuous and essentially meaningless'.

---

[108] *Evans v UK* (App No 6339/05, ECHR) (2007), [89]–[92].
[109] HFEA 1990, Sch 3, para 4A.
[110] *Dickson v UK* (App No 44362/04, ECHR) (2007), [76].

E. Jackson, 'Conception and the Irrelevance of the Welfare Principle', (2002) 65 *Modern Law Review* 176, 193

Unlike factors that go to the heart of whether infertility treatment is, for example, clinically advisable or publicly affordable, the pre-conception welfare principle represents an invidious and opportunistic invasion of infertile people's privacy. Deciding to try to conceive a child through sexual intercourse is usually assumed to be a *self-regarding* decision that takes place within the privacy of a couple's intimate relationship. Yet biological infertility somehow serves to convert this choice into an *other-regarding* decision that must be judged according to its likely impact upon this 'other', namely the child that might be born... [R]egardless of whether the child's welfare is described as a medical or social outcome, for several interconnected reasons I believe that attempting to ration treatment using section 13(5) is both tautologous and unjust. First if the alternative is non-existence, it will in fact invariably be in the particular future child's best interests to be conceived. It is therefore simply illogical for the HFEA to insist that treatment should... be refused if the centre believes that it would not be in the interests of any resulting child, because, as John Robertson has explained, from the child's perspective, the risk-creating activity is welcome, since there is no alternative way for this child to be born.

The HFEA is responsible for issuing guidance on how fertility clinics are to apply s 13(5). The HFEA has recently taken a much more permissive approach, effectively enshrining a presumption in favour of treatment unless there is evidence that any resulting child would be at risk of significant harm.[111] Indeed, Smith argues that this 'light touch' approach has rendered s 13(5) almost redundant.[112] The European Court added its voice to the debate in *Dickson v UK*.[113] *Dickson* concerned the right of a prisoner serving life imprisonment to access assisted insemination services so that he and his partner, who would be too old to conceive naturally by the time of his anticipated release, could attempt to begin a family. The Home Secretary, applying the policy then in force, refused permission for Mr Dickson to access such services. Although it was accepted by the Court that the child's welfare was, in principle, a legitimate restriction on the applicants' rights to access artificial insemination facilities, it was clear that such is the importance of the procreative right at stake under Article 8 that significant welfare concerns, going beyond those which were evident on the facts of this particular case, would be needed in order for the state to successfully justify its interference.

Dickson v UK (App No 44362/04, ECHR) (2007)

76. [T]he Government argued that the absence of a parent for a long period would have a negative impact on any child conceived and, consequently, on society as a whole.

The Court is prepared to accept as legitimate, for the purposes of the second paragraph of Article 8, that the authorities, when developing and applying the Policy, should concern themselves, as a matter of principle, with the welfare of any child: conception of a child was the very object of the exercise. Moreover, the State has a positive obligation to ensure the effective protection of children... However, that cannot go so far as to prevent parents who

---

111 HFEA (2005), foreword. For detailed discussion see Alghrani and Harris (2006), 196–201.
112 Smith (2010), 51.
113 (App No 44362/04, ECHR) (2007).

so wish from attempting to conceive a child in circumstances like those of the present case, especially as the second applicant was at liberty and could have taken care of any child conceived until such time as her husband was released.

In balancing the private and public interests engaged under Article 8, the Court seemed to place a much more onerous obligation on the state when seeking to justify restrictions imposed on access to reproductive treatment, particularly if the sole ground on which it purported to do so was the welfare of the child.

The question of whether access to treatment should continue to be regulated on the basis of a welfare test was thoroughly reviewed prior to the reforms enshrined in the HFEA 2008. In the preceding White Paper, the government concluded that given recent changes in HFEA guidance, s 13(5) constituted a legitimate and proportionate restriction on an individual's reproductive liberty.[114] Controversially, however, the government decided to amend s 13(5) in one important respect. As originally enacted in the HFEA 1990, s 13(5) required clinics to have particular regard not to the need of the child for *supportive parenting* but to the need of the child for a *father*. Commentators were extremely critical of the way in which this requirement had been applied in practice. Research by Gillian Douglas, for example, suggested that s 13(5) was being used, at least in the early 1990s, to screen out individuals presumed to be socially 'undesirable' parents, such as single mothers and same-sex couples, without any substantive consideration of their actual parenting ability or the likely welfare of any future child.[115] According to her findings, clinics were routinely making ill-informed judgments based on inadequate information and prejudice. In reviewing s 13(5), the government was clearly sensitive to these concerns and expressed some disquiet about the state's role in determining what constitutes an 'acceptable' family form through the imposition of controls on fertility treatment. This concern was reinforced by the government's heightened commitment to the equal treatment of same-sex couples following implementation of the Civil Partnership Act.

DH, *Review of the Human Fertilisation and Embryology Act. Proposals for revised legislation (including establishment of the Regulatory Authority for Tissue and Embryos)*, Cm 6989 (London: HMSO, 2006)

2.25 Responses to the Government's consultation from individual members of the public generally favoured retention of a reference to the child's need for a father, as part of the consideration of the welfare of the child. Many thought that the legislation should be revised to refer to a need for both a mother and a father. The Government has carefully considered this matter, and in particular has taken into account considerations of the proper role of the State, and of clinicians, in seeking to determine family forms via controls on access to medically-assisted conception, particularly in the light of more recent enactments such as the law relating to civil partnerships.

2.26 On balance, the Government has decided to propose that the reference to the need for a father (in consideration of the welfare of the child) should be removed from the Act. The Government is not convinced that the retention of this provision could be

---

114 DH (2006), [2.22]–[2.24].

115 Douglas (1993), 62–9. In more recent years, Smith argues that s 13(5) has posed no real obstacle to single women and lesbians seeking treatment. See Smith (2010), 51.

> justified in terms of evidence of harm, particularly when weighed against the potential harms arising from the consequences of encouraging some women who wish to conceive to make private arrangements for insemination rather than use licensed treatment services.

The Joint Parliamentary Committee charged with scrutinizing the draft legislation were unhappy with this proposal, the majority thinking that it would be detrimental to remove the requirement to take into account the 'need for a father'.[116] They therefore proposed retaining the current provision in s 13(5) but making it clear that it could be interpreted to mean 'second parent' rather than 'father'. The Committee's principal concern appeared to be the spectre of a growth in single parents rather than an increase in the number of same-sex couples accessing treatment. In its response, the government reiterated that the research tends to show that 'the factor of prime importance is quality of parenting rather than parental gender per se',[117] and referred to the view of the House of Commons Science and Technology Committee that s 13(5) could be wrongly interpreted to 'imply that unjustified discrimination against "unconventional families" is acceptable'.[118]

Opposition to the proposed amendment in Parliament was more clearly concerned with the apparent endorsement of fatherless families and the negative message this would send out about the importance of fathers and their role in the upbringing of children. For some, the proposed amendment constituted an unacceptable attack on the normative heterosexual foundations of family life.

L. Smith, 'Clashing Symbols? Reconciling support for fathers and fatherless families after the Human Fertilisation and Embryology Act 2008', (2010) 22 *Child and Family Law Quarterly* 46, 51–2

> [S]ome of the opposition to amendment of s 13(5) represents displaced discomfort with the amendments relating to same-sex parenting, and an attempt legally to fetter same-sex parenting 'through the back door'...[I]t is not the importance of fatherhood per se which concerns opponents. Rather it is fatherhood as an anchor for the traditional, heterosexual parenting paradigm which loses some of its primacy as non-traditional family types become acceptable....
>
> Broadly speaking, the opposition arguments that were presented during the Parliamentary debates can be separated into three strands. First, it was claimed that removal of the reference to the child's need for a father from section 13(5) HFE Act 1990 would send out a powerful and harmful symbolic message that fathers are not needed. Secondly, it was suggested that the move runs counter to recent government backed efforts to promote involved fatherhood and to encourage contact between children and genetic fathers. Finally, it was asserted that it is unacceptable to dismiss the child's need for a father when a weight of evidence indicates that the presence or absence of a father has a vital impact on levels of child well-being...

The government was sympathetic to many of these arguments concerning the importance of 'father presence'. However, at least in this context, its commitment to ensuring the equal treatment of same-sex couples seeking fertility treatment prevailed.

---

[116] Recommendation 22. DH (2007), 15.
[117] For a brief discussion of this research see Smith (2010), 59–62.
[118] DH (2007), [55]–[56].

It is unsurprising that the amendments to s 13(5) proved so contentious. As amended, it not only sanctions the deliberate creation of fatherless children but confers legal approval on non-conventional family forms that present a direct challenge to the normative heterosexual foundations of family life.[119] And whilst this was welcomed by many, s 13(5) did not sit well with the previous Labour government's strong commitment to promoting and supporting genetic fatherhood in other key areas of family law.[120] These contradictions and tensions at the heart of contemporary family policy are carefully drawn out by Smith.

L. Smith, 'Clashing Symbols? Reconciling support for fathers and fatherless families after the Human Fertilisation and Embryology Act 2008', (2010) 22 *Child and Family Law Quarterly* 46, 54–5, 56–7

In recent years the government has placed its support behind same-sex parenting by initiating various pieces of legislation...The provisions contained in the HFE Act represent a further attempt to remove legal obstacles to the recognition of same-sex parenting arrangements. Each of these developments marks a departure from law's historical support for the heterosexual family unit. As such each also implicitly endorses both existing and prospective fatherless families. Moreover, these legislative developments have been bolstered by policy level rhetoric indicating an intention to support diversity rather than conventionality in family life...

In parallel with these developments, however, the government has repeatedly emphasised its commitment to the idea that the traditional married family is the best environment in which to bring up children...These and other, similar, tributes to the hetero-normative family have given opponents of the Act ample opportunity to criticise countervailing efforts to facilitate the establishment of families by same-sex couples. Given that the government has intimated on multiple occasions that being brought up in a traditional heterosexual family unit is inherently advantageous to children, it is no small wonder that its attempts to support same-sex parenting in the present context have been the subject of criticism. Furthermore, the force of the message in support of the marital, necessarily heterosexual family is repeatedly reinforced by more specific and widespread promotion of the importance of fathers in children's lives....

[W]hile lobbyists and judges eulogise the contributions made by fathers to their children's welfare and invoke the powerful language of rights, policy makers have referred to 'the *vital* role played by fathers'. Such statements present the connection between child well-being and father presence as absolute and this gives the government's suggestion that lesbian parents – who by definition will normally form fatherless families – can bring up children satisfactorily a hollow ring. It begins to look as if the government is indeed clashing its own symbols in terms of its various expressions of support for fathers and support for fatherless families.

The right to reproductive freedom under Article 12 ECHR

At least on the face of the ECHR, Article 12 may seem a more promising route to establishing a right to reproductive treatment because, unlike Article 8, Article 12 appears to establish an unqualified right. The 'right to found a family' under Article 12 has, however, been subjected

[119] Smith (2010), 51–2.
[120] See, especially, residence and contact disputes discussed in chapter 11.

to a conservative interpretation by the European Court.[121] There is no clear authority bringing assisted reproduction within the scope of Article 12.[122] However, the argument that the right to utilize assisted reproductive techniques, such as IVF, *should* fall within the right to 'found a family' is convincing, particularly as it has been held that adoption, which is arguably not as close to natural reproduction as IVF, has been found to fall within the scope of the provision.[123] That said, even if the right to artificial reproduction is found, in principle, to fall within the scope of Article 12, the right remains expressly subject to 'national laws governing the exercise of the right'. The state is thus afforded wide discretion as to who should be allowed to take advantage of the right and under what conditions.[124] A state could thus legitimately restrict its treatment to married couples suffering from infertility on medical grounds, particularly as the right to marry and the right to found a family under Article 12 are closely linked in the Strasbourg case law.[125]

Legitimate restrictions on the right to found a family

The right to 'found a family', despite the unqualified nature of the wording of Article 12, has been held to be less than absolute. In *R (Mellor) v Secretary of State for the Home Department*, it was held that the limitations applicable to Article 8 also apply to Article 12. The state can therefore regulate and restrict the 'right to found a family' under Article 12 in order to protect the public interest or the rights and interests of others, including the future child. This was confirmed in *Dickson v UK*, the Chamber holding that, 'an interference with family life which is justified under paragraph 2 of Article 8 of the ECHR cannot at the same time constitute a violation of Article 12'.[126] This qualification on the right to found a family would appear to have survived the House of Lords' judgment in *R (Baiai) v Secretary of State for the Home Department*, in which the House of Lords held that the right to marry could not be qualified by reading into Article 12 the restrictions of Article 8(2).[127] Both Lord Bingham and Baroness Hale appeared to draw a distinction between the two rights protected under Article 12, the right to marry being regarded as particularly 'strong' and 'fundamental' in contrast to the right to found a family which 'the Strasbourg authorities have not in practice upheld . . . with the same firmness'.[128]

9.4.3 DETERMINING PARENTHOOD UNDER THE HFEA 2008

The common law's traditional emphasis on genetic parenthood can look inappropriate when applied in the context of assisted reproduction. For example, when determining the paternity of a child born through the use of AID, it does not seem right for a sperm donor who is unaware of the child's existence to be regarded as the child's legal father,

---

[121] Harris, O'Boyle, and Warbrick (1995), 434.
[122] See Harris (1995), 69.
[123] *X and Y v UK* 12 DR 32, 34 and *X v Netherlands* 24 DR 176, 177–8. For commentary see Harris, O'Boyle, and Warbrick (1995), 441.
[124] Ibid. With respect to adoption see: *Fretté v France* (App No 36515/97, ECHR) (2003).
[125] Harris, O'Boyle, and Warbrick (1995), 442.
[126] *Dickson v UK* (App No 44362/04, ECHR) (2006) [41].
[127] [2008] UKHL 53, [15] (per Lord Bingham), [46] (per Baroness Hale).
[128] Ibid.

particularly if that status involves a duty to maintain the child. It seems equally illogical for the husband of a woman receiving AID treatment to be regarded in law as a stranger to the child he intends to raise as his own. In the case of disputes over maternity, the law has to contend not only with a potential split between genetic and social motherhood but the further complication of a split between genetic and gestational motherhood. As assisted reproduction became more widely available, it became clear that the common law's emphasis on genetic parenthood could not be sustained in this particular context. The HFEA 1990 was intended to provide a comprehensive scheme for determining the legal parenthood of children conceived via assisted reproductive techniques. This scheme was comprehensively revised by the HFEA 2008, which introduced quite radical changes to the way in which legal parenthood is determined in this context. Most notably, Parliament made it much easier for same-sex couples to acquire legal parenthood following fertility treatment by introducing provisions comparable to those in place for heterosexual married and unmarried couples. Respect for a diverse range of family forms and the need for the HFEA to keep pace with other developments in family law underpinned the government's approach.

DH, *Review of the Human Fertilisation and Embryology Act. Proposals for revised legislation (including establishment of the Regulatory Authority for Tissue and Embryos),* **Cm 6989** (London: HMSO, 2006)

2.67 In undertaking its review of the HFE Act, the Government aimed to consider the extent to which changes may be needed to better recognise the wider range of people who seek and receive assisted reproduction treatment in the early 21st Century. The Government has also considered the impact of other legal changes that have occurred since the HFE Act came into force in 1991. For example, the coming into force of the Civil Partnership Act 2004 created a new legal relationship which two people of the same sex can form by registering as civil partners of each other. Important rights and responsibilities flow from forming a civil partnership including for civil partners to be assessed in the same way as spouses for child support.

2.68 Also, whereas it has for many years been possible for a single person to adopt a child, recent changes have enabled unmarried and same-sex couples jointly to adopt children. Other relevant changes include the fact that an unmarried man can acquire parental responsibility for a child through jointly registering the birth together with the child's mother.

2.69 Given other legal changes since the HFE Act was enacted, and in particular, existing policy to create parity between civil partners and married couples, **the Government proposes to revise the status and legal parenthood provisions of the HFE Act to enable a greater range of persons to be recognised as parents following assisted reproduction.** This will involve introducing parenthood provisions for civil partners and other same-sex couples in line with those for married and unmarried couples respectively. Changes will apply both to the recognition of parental status following the use of donor gametes, and the acquisition of parental orders following surrogacy. In the latter case, this means that as well as married couples, civil partners and other couples in a stable relationship will be able to apply for a parental order.

These proposals were given effect in Part 2 of the HFEA 2008.

Mothers—s 33

Genetic, gestational, and social motherhood may now be located in three different women. The Warnock Committee considered that in the interests of certainty the gestational mother should, for all legal purposes, be accorded the legal status of motherhood.[129] This recommendation was enshrined in s 27(1) of the HFEA 1990 and retained without being re-considered in s 33(1) of the HFEA 2008:

Human Fertilisation and Embryology Act 2008, s 33

(1) The woman who is carrying or has carried a child as a result of the placing in her of an embryo or of sperm and eggs, and no other woman, is to be treated as the mother of the child.

Determining maternity is thus straightforward: the woman who gives birth to the child is always regarded as the legal mother. Egg donation, in accordance with the Warnock Committee's recommendations, is regarded as absolute, with the genetic mother/egg donor being treated in exactly the same way as a sperm donor: no legal rights or duties attach by virtue only of her genetic parentage.[130] In most cases of egg/embryo donation, this approach best meets the needs and interests of the child, the intended parents, and the donor. The only context where it may be problematic is surrogacy.[131] In such cases, the genetic/social mother may have an equally compelling case for recognition of her maternal status. The particular problems to which surrogacy arrangements give rise will be discussed below.

Fathers and second female parents—ss 34–40

The following provisions on legal parenthood only apply where the condition set down in s 34 of the HFEA 2008 is satisfied: that the child 'is being or has been carried by a woman as a result of the placing in her of an embryo or of sperm and eggs or her artificial insemination'. In other words, conception by means of natural sexual intercourse is explicitly excluded from the scope of the legislation.

Married fathers—s 35

Determining paternity is considerably more complicated than determining maternity. In making its recommendations, the Warnock Committee were strongly influenced by the importance of maintaining the child's legitimacy and at least the appearance of a traditional family unit. Where the husband's own sperm is used in his wife's treatment, the common law will apply and, as the genetic father, he will be the legal father. Section 38(2) provides that even where donor sperm is used, the husband is still entitled to rely on the common law presumption of legitimacy until that presumption is rebutted by means of DNA tests. Where it is clear that the husband is not the genetic father, s 35(1) provides that he will still be regarded as the child's legal father unless he did not consent to the treatment.

---

[129] DHSS (1984), [6.8].
[130] Ibid.
[131] Douglas (1991), 129.

Human Fertilisation and Embryology Act 2008, s 35

35 Woman married at time of treatment

(1) If—

(a) at the time of the placing in her of the embryo or of the sperm and eggs or of her artificial insemination, W [the woman] was a party to a marriage, and

(b) the creation of the embryo carried by her was not brought about with the sperm of the other party to the marriage,

then, subject to section 38(2) to (4) [the common law presumption of legitimacy], the other party to the marriage is to be treated as the father of the child unless it is shown that he did not consent to the placing in her of the embryo or the sperm and eggs or to her artificial insemination (as the case may be).

The onus to prove the absence of consent is on the husband. It has been suggested, *obiter*, that the fact the husband has not given written consent will not be sufficient by itself to show he did not consent.[132] However, in determining whether the husband has given his consent, the question of what the husband must have consented to in order for legal parenthood to be conferred, has, under the identical provision in the previous legislation, been strictly construed. The issue was dealt with in the difficult case of *Leeds Teaching Hospital NHS Trust v A*. Two couples, Mr and Mrs A (a white couple) and Mr and Mrs B (a black couple), were receiving fertility treatment at the same clinic. Neither couple consented to treatment using donated gametes. By mistake, Mr B's sperm was used to fertilize Mrs A's eggs. The embryos were implanted in Mrs A, resulting in the birth of mixed-race twins. The mistake was immediately apparent and DNA tests confirmed Mr B was the twins' genetic father. Mr B applied for a declaration of parentage under s 55A of the FLA 1986. The legal position was relatively clear. Mrs A was the twins' mother and if Mr A could bring himself within the terms of s 28(2) (the precursor to s 35(1) of the HFEA 2008) he would be deemed the twins' legal father. If, however, he fell outside the scope of the HFEA 1990, the common law position would prevail and Mr B, as the twins' genetic father, would be regarded as the legal father. The application of s 28(2) turned on whether, given the mistake, Mr A could be said to have consented to his wife's treatment. Mr and Mrs A argued that a valid consent had been given.

Leeds Teaching Hospital NHS Trust v A and others [2003] EWHC 259 (QB), [2003] 1 FCR 599

DAME ELIZABETH BUTLER-SLOSS P:

[25] . . . Subsection (2) applies unless it is shown that Mr A 'did not consent to . . . her insemination'. It is obvious that s 28 is not relevant if the sperm given by Mr A was used since he is then the biological father and the twins are the legitimate children of Mr and Mrs A. The question is whether Mr A consented to the insemination of Mrs A by a third person (for the purposes of this argument, 'a donor').

[26] . . . [Counsel] argued that Mr A gave a broad consent to the placing of an embryo sufficient to treat him as the father unless it could be shown that Mr A had not consented. He did not raise the issue nor seek to set aside the presumption.

---

[132] *Re G (Surrogacy: Foreign Domicile)* [2007] EWHC 2814, [39].

[27] The insurmountable problem, in my view, to that approach, is the question—to what did he consent?...The 'course of treatment' to which he consented was that outlined in Mrs A's consent form....Mrs A consented to her eggs being used and mixed with her husband's sperm. She did not consent to her eggs being mixed with named or anonymous donated sperm. She consented to the placing of not more than two resulting embryos in her uterus.

[28] Mr A certainly gave his consent to the placing in his wife of 'an embryo'. The embryo actually placed in Mrs A was a fundamentally different embryo from one that might have been created by the use of Mr A's sperm...The question whether the husband consented is a matter of fact which may be ascertained independently of the views of those involved in the process. On the clear evidence provided in the consent forms Mr A plainly did not consent to the sperm of a named or anonymous donor being mixed with his wife's eggs. This was clearly an embryo created without the consent of Mr and Mrs A.

[**Butler-Sloss P** refused to make a declaration of parentage in favour of Mr A and adjourned the application of Mr B. It was agreed by the parties that the twins should remain living with Mr and Mrs A.]

It is thus clear that in order for a husband's consent under s 28(2) (now s 35(1) of the HFEA 2008) to be valid, he must consent to the actual treatment received. If no such consent was given, he cannot be regarded as the legal father.

Assuming consent, s 35(1) prioritizes the intended social father over the genetic father. This again reflects the intentions of all the parties and will usually best serve the child's interests, the intended parents, and the donor.[133] Section 35(1) is, however, far from revolutionary in negating the importance of the genetic tie. As seen above, attaching children to their fathers through the fact of marriage to the mother, is in many ways nothing more than what the common law has been doing for centuries through the presumption of legitimacy.

Unmarried fathers—ss 36–8

Unmarried fathers are dealt with under ss 36–8. Although overshadowed by the more radical provisions on same-sex parents, s 36 remains in many ways a remarkable provision. It confers the status of legal parenthood on a man who is neither related to the child by blood or by marriage to the child's mother provided the fatherhood conditions set down in s 36 are satisfied.

Human Fertilisation and Embryology Act 2008, ss 36–7

36 Treatment provided to woman where agreed fatherhood conditions apply

If no man is treated by virtue of section 35 [mother's husband] as the father of the child and no woman is treated by virtue of section 42 [mother's civil partner—see below] as a parent of the child but –

  (a) the embryo or the sperm and eggs were placed in W [the woman], or W was artificially inseminated, in the course of treatment services provided in the United Kingdom by a person to whom a licence applies,

---

[133] For a straightforward example of the application of the identical provision on married fathers as contained within the HFEA 1990, see *Re CH (Contact Parentage)* [1996] 1 FLR 569.

(b) at the time when the embryo or the sperm and eggs were placed in W, or W was artificially inseminated, the agreed fatherhood conditions (as set out in section 37) were satisfied in relation to a man, in relation to treatment provided to W under the licence,

(c) the man remained alive at that time, and

(d) the creation of the embryo carried by W was not brought about with the man's sperm,

then, subject to section 38(2) to (4) [presumption of legitimacy], the man is to be treated as the father of the child.

37 The agreed fatherhood conditions

(1) The agreed fatherhood conditions referred to in section 36(b) are met in relation to a man ("M") in relation to treatment provided to W under a licence if, but only if, –

(a) M has given the person responsible a notice stating that he consents to being treated as the father of any child resulting from treatment provided to W under the licence,

(b) W has given the person responsible a notice stating that she consents to M being so treated,

(c) neither M nor W has, since giving notice under paragraph (a) or (b), given the person responsible notice of the withdrawal of M's or W's consent to M being so treated,

(d) W has not, since the giving of the notice under paragraph (b), given the person responsible –

(i) a further notice under that paragraph stating that she consents to another man being treated as the father of any resulting child, or

(ii) a notice under section 44(1)(b) stating that she consents to a woman being treated as a parent of any resulting child, and

(iii) W and M are not within prohibited degrees of relationship in relation to each other.

(2) A notice under subsection 1(a),(b) or (c) must be in writing and must be signed by the person giving it.

Several conditions must be satisfied in order for s 36 to confer legal parenthood on the putative father:

(i) The putative father's sperm must not have been used.

(ii) The mother must have no husband who falls within the terms of s 35 and no civil partner who falls within the terms of s 42. Priority in determining legal parenthood therefore continues to be accorded to these formal legal relationships.

(iii) Treatment must have been provided by a licensed clinic in the UK. This means that unlike married couples falling within the terms of s 35, an unmarried couple making a 'DIY' attempt at AID at home will not be able to rely on the determination of parenthood under s 36. If a couple does embark upon DIY treatment, the common law will apply and the donor, as the genetic father, will be regarded as the child's legal father.[134] This requirement to attend at a licensed clinic allows the state, in the absence of marriage, to exercise greater control over access to treatment.

---

[134] As to the jurisdictional requirement see *U v W (Attorney General Intervening)* [1998] Fam 29, 44–5.

(iv) The agreed fatherhood conditions must be satisfied at the point at which the embryo or the sperm and eggs were placed in the mother or the mother was artificially inseminated.[135] The putative father must also have been alive at this point.

The agreed fatherhood conditions are set down in s 37, which establishes a straightforward process of notification: the mother and the putative father must both have notified the licensed provider in writing that they consent to the man being treated as the legal father of any resulting child. That notification can be withdrawn by either the mother or the putative father at any point up to the point of embryo transfer or insemination of the woman with the eggs and/or sperm. If consent is withdrawn by either party then legal fatherhood cannot be conferred on that man. The putative father is also prevented from being accorded legal fatherhood if, before the point of embryo transfer or insemination, the mother provides a further notice to the clinic, in writing, that she consents to another man or woman being treated as the legal father or second parent of the child. Provided this second man or woman is able to satisfy the agreed fatherhood or agreed female parenthood conditions, then he or she will be deemed the legal parent.

Although s 37(1)(e) prevents legal parenthood from being conferred on a man and woman falling within the prohibited degrees of relationship, legal fatherhood is otherwise conferred on the putative father by a simple process of agreement. There is no requirement for the mother and father to be cohabiting or indeed involved in any kind of intimate relationship. It is perfectly possible for two friends to decide to parent a child together—subject to being able to satisfy the licensed provider that the arrangement gives rise to no welfare concerns under s 13(5).

Where these conditions are satisfied, the man will treated for all legal purposes as the father of the child.[136]

Deceased fathers—ss 39–40

Under the HFEA 1990, Sch 3, para 8(1), it is clear that gametes cannot be preserved and stored, save in tightly defined circumstances, without the gamete provider's written consent.[137] It is, however, possible for a woman to use the frozen sperm or an embryo created using the gametes of her deceased husband/partner provided he specifically consented to their continued storage and use after his death.[138] It is also possible, if the man agreed to being treated as the father of any resulting child,[139] for the mother to enter that man as the child's father in the birth register.[140] Similar provisions apply where an embryo is created using donated sperm but is only transferred to the woman after her husband or partner's death.[141] Again, provided her husband or partner gave written consent to the use of the embryo after his death and to being treated as the child's father, he can be registered posthumously on the birth register. Registration on the birth register does not, however, in these circumstances confer legal fatherhood on the deceased man as the legislation

---

135 HFEA 2008, s 36(b).
136 Ibid., s 48(1).
137 See *R v HFEA, ex parte Blood* [1999] Fam 151 and *L v Human Fertilisation and Embryology Authority & Another* [2008] EWHC 2149.
138 HFEA 1990, Sch 3, para 2(2).
139 HFEA 2008, ss 39(1)(c), 40(1)(e), and 40(2)(c).
140 Ibid., ss 39(1)(d), 39(3), 40(1)(f), 40(2)(g), and 40(4).
141 Ibid., s 40.

specifically provides that he will not be treated in law as the father of the child for any other purposes.[142]

Civil partners and second female parent—ss 42–7

Sections 42–7 of the Act contain the new and clearly more controversial provisions on determining parenthood where a woman receives fertility treatment together with her female partner. The provisions for determining the legal status of the second female parent are identical to those for determining fatherhood but 'marriage' is replaced with 'civil partnership' and 'father' with 'second parent'.

Human Fertilisation and Embryology Act 2008, ss 42–7

42 Woman in civil partnership at time of treatment

(1) If at the time of the placing in her of the embryo or the sperm and eggs or of her artificial insemination, W [the mother] was a party to a civil partnership, then subject to section 45(2) to (4) [presumption of legitimacy], the other party to the civil partnership is to be treated as a parent of the child unless it is shown that she did not consent to the placing in W of the embryo or the sperm and eggs or her artificial insemination (as the case may be)....

43 Treatment provided to woman who agrees that second woman to be parent

(1) If no man is treated by virtue of section 35 [mother's husband] as the father of the child and no woman is treated by virtue of section 42 [mother's civil partner] as a parent of the child, but –

(a) the embryo or the sperm and eggs were placed in W, or W was artificially inseminated, in the course of treatment services provided in the United Kingdom by a person to whom a licence applies,

(b) at the time when the embryo or the sperm and eggs were placed in W, or W was artificially inseminated, the agreed female parenthood conditions (as set out in section 44) were met in relation to another woman, in relation to treatment provided to W under that licence, and

(c) the other woman remained alive at that time,

then, subject to section 45(2) to (4), the other woman is to be treated as a parent of the child.

44 The agreed female parenthood conditions

(1) The agreed female parenthood conditions referred to in section 43(b) are met in relation to another woman ("P") in relation to treatment provided to W under a licence if, but only if, –

(a) P has given the person responsible a notice stating that P consents to P being treated as a parent of any child resulting from treatment provided to W under the licence,

---

[142] Ibid., s 48(3).

(b) W has given the person responsible a notice stating that W agrees to P being so treated,

(c) neither W nor P has, since giving notice under paragraph (a) or (b), given the person responsible notice of the withdrawal of P's or W's consent to P being so treated,

(d) W has not, since the giving of the notice under paragraph (b), given the person responsible –

(i) a further notice under that paragraph stating that W consents to a woman other than P being treated as a parent of any resulting child, or

(ii) a notice under section 37(1)(b) stating that W consents to a man being treated as the father of any resulting child, and

(e) W and P are not within prohibited degrees of relationship in relation to each other.

(2) A notice under subsection (1)(a), (b) or (c) must be in writing and must be signed by the person giving it.

Section 46 reproduces s 40 to permit parenthood to be conferred on a deceased second female parent for the purposes of birth registration where the consent requirements are met.

Where either s 42 or s 43 applies, the woman is treated as the second parent of the child for all legal purposes.[143] The Act further provides that where there is a second female parent, no man is treated as the child's father.[144] Thus, a child can now be born into a family consisting of two female parents and no legal father.

Sperm and egg donors

Where either s 35, 36, 42, or 43 apply, no other person is to be treated as the father of the child.[145] In most cases, this will be sufficient to protect a sperm donor from legal parenthood. However, further protection is provided by s 41 which stipulates that provided a donor has given the requisite consent and his sperm was used in accordance with that consent, the man is not to be treated as the child's father. Where s 41 applies and there is no man who qualifies for legal fatherhood under s 35 or 36, the child will be legally fatherless.[146] For the sake of completeness, s 47 similarly provides that an 'egg donor' is not to be treated as the parent of a child unless parenthood is conferred under s 42, 43, or 46 or the donor has adopted the child. This reiterates the position made clear in s 33 that the genetic mother is to have no claim to 'legal *motherhood*', which exclusively vests in the gestational mother.

Reflections on the parenthood provisions in the HFEA 2008

At first sight, the HFEA 2008 is revolutionary. Having rejected the biological imperative that a child must have one legal father and one legal mother, the Act embraces a strong model of social parenthood unconstrained by genetics, gender, or heterosexuality. Thus an unmarried man or lesbian partner not tied to the child through blood or 'marriage' can acquire legal parenthood by virtue of intention alone. A legally fatherless child with two female

---

[143] Ibid., s 48(1).
[144] Ibid., s 45(1).
[145] Ibid., s 48(1).
[146] See, for example, *Re Q (Parental order)* [1996] 1 FLR 369, decided under the HFEA 1990.

parents is now legally possible. This 'radical' departure from the traditional heterosexual foundations of family life was inevitably strongly opposed. Critics have argued that this attempt to deny the reality that a child must have two biological parents of the opposite sex betrays the needs of the child.

T. Callus, 'First "Designer Babies", Now À La Carte Parents', (2008) 38 *Fam Law* 143, 143, 145, 146–7

[Current legislation] appears to suggest that parental status itself may be dependent upon the mere intention of the would-be (wannabe?) parent. This is not wholly unprecedented. We have recognised the importance of intention in the process of adoption and more recently in the use of donated gametes in assisted conception techniques. However, giving effect to intention has been circumscribed within the heterosexual model, ideally of two parents to reflect the biological reality that a child is created by the fusion of male and female gametes. But the de-sexualisation of procreation through the use of assisted conception has resulted in a diversity of family forms and, in particular, the possibility of same-sex couples to 'parent' children. This has led to confusion between the parental role and parental status...

[The HFEA 2008] is remarkable because [it] grant[s] legal status to wider family forms based on the sole intention of the would-be parents who undergo treatment at a licensed clinic. Moreover, the proposals legally enshrine family models which deny the very basic fact that gametes of complementary sex are required to create the child. According to the Family Education Trust, they represent the 'lego-kit model of family construction'...

By recognising the status of two female parents, the child's identity is thrown into disarray because the recognition of two female parents conceals the necessary heterosexual element of human existence. Admittedly, even the present provisions on the use of donor gametes can lead to deception insofar as the parents may conceal their use of donated gametes, but the proposals double that deception.

[T]he [Act's] provisions are merely one example of a move towards recognising legal parental status on the basis of individual choice. Yet this choice may be transient and exercised in complete ignorance of the interest of the child.

Unquestionably, for many commentators the HFEA 2008 constitutes a step too far from the 'natural' biological imperatives of parenthood. However, others have criticized the Act, not for exploding the heterosexual parenting paradigm, but for its inherent conservatism. It is argued that the HFEA 2008 remains firmly wedded to a gendered, heterosexual model of parenthood that is binary, structured around the central and exclusive role of the legal 'mother', and precludes a more radical re-visioning of parenthood capable of embracing gay fatherhood, the fragmentation of motherhood and fatherhood into multiple biological and social components, and parenting outside the sexual norm.[147]

J. McCandless and S. Sheldon, 'The Human Fertilisation and Embryology Act (2008) and the Tenacity of the Sexual Family Form', (2010) 73 *Modern Law Review* 175, 188, 190–2, 193, 197

[T]he sexual family ideal has retained a significant hold... This can be seen in the ongoing significance of the formally recognised adult couple; law's continued adherence to a two parent

---

[147] See generally Diduck (2007); Lind and Hewitt (2009); McCandless and Sheldon (2010).

model; what we describe as 'parental dimorphism' (which, within the two-parent model, allows only for one mother plus one father or female parent); and the notion that the couple must be (at least potentially) in a sexual relationship...

In the context of widespread political and cultural disagreement regarding on what grounds parents should be recognised, acceptance of the fact that we can have two—and only two—'real' parents has proved a unifying article of faith. The two parent model retains a grip on the law which appears to have outlived any inevitable relationship between legal parenthood and either biological fact or marital convention...[T]his reform process saw no discussion of the question of whether if two parents are better than one, three parents might be better than (or, at least, as good as) two...[L]ack of further attention to this issue signals just how ingrained in our collective imagination is the notion that a child has only two parents, even in the context of assisted reproduction where more than two people may contribute biologically to the reproductive process...

[T]he sexual family model continues to resonate in a steadfast resistance to the possibility that a child can have two 'mothers' (or indeed two 'fathers'). The two parent model thus appears to encompass an assumption of what might be loosely termed 'parental dimorphism', by which we mean that the two parents are seen as occupying complementary yet different legal roles. This was seen...in the fact that a lesbian co-mother is not to be legally recognised as a 'mother'...but as a 'female parent' (a status awarded on grounds which closely parallel those by which men obtain fatherhood)...

It seems not to have been considered that the status provisions might be further adapted to allow two men to be recognised as parents from the moment of birth...[T]o recognise two gay men as parents under the status provisions would be a significant step further again, and one which simply stretches the current legal imagination too far, as it would involve moving beyond the idea that the birth mother is a legal mother (or, alternatively, recognising three parents from the moment of birth)...

Alison Diduck captures the essence of these concerns, concluding:

A. Diduck, ' "If only we can find the appropriate terms to use the issue will be solved": Law, identity and parenthood', (2007) 19 *Child and Family Law Quarterly* 458, 466–7

It thus seems to me that the new legal status 'parent' does not overcome either the biological or 'proper' nuclear family privilege that attaches to the concept of legal parenthood which has underpinned the Human Fertilisation and Embryology Act 1990 since its inception. Like fatherhood under the Human Fertilisation and Embryology Act 1990, lesbian parenthood is acquired on a basis that mimics rather than overcomes traditional norms and biology. It applies a type of presumption of paternity to partnered lesbian women and instantiates rather than challenges hetero normativity and 'nature', It both biologises and heterosexes 'parent' by ascribing that status on the basis of a person forming an exclusive sexual link with the biological parent...[W]e are left with a situation in which legal parenthood remains limited in number and subtly gendered.

9.4.4 THE CHILD'S RIGHT TO KNOW HIS/HER GENETIC PARENTAGE

Assisted reproduction, as regulated under the HFEA 1990, presents a direct challenge to the common law's preference for genetics. A policy choice had to be made and the HFEA favoured social over genetic parenthood. Whilst this may be welcomed as affording greater recognition to the importance of social parenthood, it leaves open the question of what, if any, role genetic parents play in the child's future. The preference for social parenthood in the legislation is arguably at variance with moves elsewhere in English law to recognize the right of children to know the truth about their genetic parentage.[148] In recent years, the government has therefore faced increasing pressure to protect this right of children conceived using donated gametes.

Why is the right to know important?

The importance of knowing the truth about one's genetic background is described in moving terms by Joanna Rose, an AID child:

R (on the application of Rose and another) v Secretary of State for Health and another [2002] EWHC 1593 (Admin), [2002] 3 FCR 731

[7] 'I feel that these genetic connections are very important to me, socially, emotionally, medically, and even spiritually. I believe it to be no exaggeration that non-identifying information [information about the genetic parents that cannot lead to their identity becoming known] will assist me in forming a fuller sense of self identity and answer questions that I have been asking for a long time. I am angry that it has been assumed that this would not be the case, and can see no responsible logic for this (given the usual pre-eminence accorded to the rights and welfare of the child), unless it is believed that if we are created artificially we will not have the natural need to know to whom we are related. I feel intense grief and loss, for the fact that I do not know my genetic father and his family . . .

I need to find out more about my medical, genealogical and social heritage. Other people who come from families, where they have known both of their natural parents are able to discover this through the process of time. This includes information about their background and religion, where certain of their talents and skills may come from (eg parents or relations with musical or artistic skills), why they look the way they do etc. I have a strong need to discover what most people take for granted. While I was conceived to heal the pain of others (ie my parents' inability to conceive children naturally), I do not feel that there are sufficient attempts to heal my pain.'

There is a growing body of research, largely conducted in the field of adoption, providing strong support for the argument that knowledge of one's genetic background is crucial to the development of a secure sense of identity and sense of self. As Michael Freeman explains, 'identity as what we know and what we feel is an organizing framework for holding together our past and our present and it provides some anticipated shape to future life'.[149] Denying children the truth about their genetic parentage can lead to a sense of 'genealogical bewilderment'.[150] O'Donovan highlights just some of the problems that can result.

---

[148] For example, *In re H (A Minor) (Blood Tests: Parental Rights)* [1997] Fam 89, discussed above at p 606.

[149] Freeman (1996), 290.

[150] Van Bueren (1998), 123 and Fortin (2009b), 469.

K. O'Donovan, 'Interpretations of Children's Identity Rights', in D. Fottrell (ed), *Revisiting Children's Rights* (The Hague; Boston: Kluwer Law International, 2000), 75

Effects of identity confusion have been documented as long term. Low self-esteem, loss of trust in others, inability to form intimate relationships, depression, anxiety, lack of parenting skills, have all been noted. Security about identity is the basis for self-confidence.

There is, however, an important distinction between the need for knowledge about one's genetic background and establishing a social relationship with the genetic parents. As Fortin observes, research in the field of adoption suggests that whilst adopted children may experience a strong need for the former, this is not necessarily accompanied by any desire for the latter.[151] Recognition of the right of children to know the truth about their genetic background does not therefore involve any necessary revision of the *legal status* or *social role* of the genetic parent.[152]

There is not however complete consensus surrounding the child's right to know. The analogy often drawn with adoption has been questioned, with commentators suggesting that the secrecy surrounding AID may not be as damaging as that surrounding adoption given the very different circumstances in which they operate. It is argued that the fact that the child is the result of a deliberate procreative act by the would-be parents, is desperately wanted, does not have to face the psychological difficulty of dealing with the fact of relinquishment and, in the majority of cases, has a genetic link with one of the parents, stands AID apart from adoption. In these circumstances, it is suggested that revealing the truth about genetic parentage may not be in the child's best interests, certainly as perceived by the parents:[153]

I. Turkmendag, R. Dingwall, and T. Murphy, 'The removal of donor anonymity in the UK: the silencing of claims by would-be parents', (2008) 22 *International Journal of Law, Policy and the Family* 283, 289

Adoption is a family-building activity that involves pre-existing individuals, whereas donor conception is directed towards creating a child in order to create a family. In other words, adoption is a *substitute* for procreation whereas donor conception is a *form* of procreation: the act has its own integrity and completeness – it is the would-be parent(s)' act and the child is unquestionably their child... In this act, social links are established between the procreator and the child, not with the donor.

Unlike an adopted child, a donor-conceived child usually has a biological connection with one of their social parents as a result of pregnancy and birth. In (traditional) adoption, both parents are biologically unrelated to the child. The donor conceived child usually has access to full genetic information about one of his/her biological parents. In addition, the donor's medical history is available for the resultant child on the HFEA registers. Adopted children are usually deprived of such information unless it is provided on their birth registers.

In gamete donation, it is easy for the parents to hide the method of their child's conception whereas 'adoption can only be the worst-kept "secret" around'... Despite the difference

---

[151] Fortin (2009b), 467.
[152] This is the same point made *In re H (A Minor) (Blood Tests: Parental Rights)* [1997] Fam. 89, per Ward LJ. See discussion above at p 606.
[153] Turkmendag, Dingwall, and Murphy (2008), 302.

between adoption and donor conception, much of the evidence on the harm caused by secrecy and the importance for a child to know her/his origins is drawn from the literature on adoption. If the child knows that he/she was adopted, the feeling of relinquishment and the desire to seek reasons for being 'given up' may well cause emotional distress. By contrast, donor offspring were desired by their parents, parents have often contributed gametes, and their birth stories do not involve relinquishment. It is then questionable whether donor off-spring's interest in knowing their origins is identical to that of adopted children and whether the research findings on the latter can simply be read across.

There has also been some criticism of the importance these arguments place on the role of genetics in determining 'who we are' and 'what we become'. The nature versus nurture argument has long polarized scholars. Bell argues that the current emphasis on genealogical background is simply crude genetic determinism. It is also suggested that the desperate need expressed by some to know the truth about their genetic background is socially constructed. In other words, it is the emphasis placed by society on the importance of genetics that creates the strongly held need to know the truth.[154] Changing social attitudes may therefore be a more effective solution than further entrenching these attitudes by enshrining the right to know in legislation. Melanie Roberts disagrees:

M. Roberts, 'Children by Donation: Do they have a Claim to their Genetic Parentage?', in J. Bridgeman and D. Monk (eds), *Feminist Perspectives on Child Law* (London: Cavendish, 2000), 47, 63

As the importance which society places on the genetic tie is socially constructed, it could be argued that information about the donor's identity should not be provided, as this reinforces the importance of the genetic link. However, denying children information about genitors is not the way in which to diminish the importance placed on the genetic tie and to raise the importance of the social family. Concepts of anonymity and secrecy reinforce the importance of the blood tie. These concepts fuel the notion that the genetic family is the 'norm' and any other family formation is 'unnatural' and must be hidden. Recognition of, and respect for, the different ways in which families can be formed is needed, and the way to achieve this is to be honest and open about the formation and structure of families.

Furthermore, as O'Donovan points out, telling AID or adopted children that their perceived need for knowledge about their genetic origins is socially constructed does nothing to lessen the very real pain and profound sense of loss and bewilderment they are currently suffering.[155]

The right to know in the HFEA 1990

Background to the HFEA

Until recently, the HFEA guaranteed complete secrecy concerning the conception of a child using donated gametes. The complex reasons behind this approach have been strongly

---

[154] Ibid., 291.
[155] Cited in Van Bueren (1998), 123.

criticized by Roberts. She suggests that the medical underpinnings of assisted reproduction have led to the privileging of the prospective parents' interests (the patients being treated) at the expense of the child.

M. Roberts, 'Children by Donation: Do they have a Claim to their Genetic Parentage?', in J. Bridgeman and D. Monk (eds), *Feminist Perspectives on Child Law* (London: Cavendish, 2000), 47, 49, 53–4

Donation is surrounded with secrecy. When artificial insemination by donor was first introduced, it was assumed that secrecy was the best stance to take and was taken for granted. Secrecy stems from fear: fear that the child will reject the social parent in favour of the genitor; fear that the genitor will interfere; and fear of societal disapproval. As use of donor sperm far outweighs the use of donor ova, it is the infertile man in particular who is protected by a policy of secrecy. There is some evidence that there may be particular problems in relation to openness and male infertility. Western culture attaches much significance to the association between fertility and power. Male infertility is thus seen as a source of shame and weakness, with feelings of masculinity being damaged by the discovery of infertility. The myth that fertility and virility are related and the attitudes of others means that couples often wish to keep the problem of infertility and the means of conception secret. A quest for 'normality' can result in secrecy and dishonesty. For men, parenthood means genetic parenthood. Secrecy stems from patriarchal concern to protect male pride in hiding male infertility and what is considered a failure: the inability to pass on one's genetic heritage.

However, the secretive approach that marked the initial years of the HFEA was not inevitable given the somewhat mixed and inconsistent messages from the Warnock Committee. On the one hand, the Committee expressed great concern about the secrecy surrounding AID children:

DHSS, *Report of the Committee of Inquiry into Human Fertilisation and Embryology,* Cm 9314 (London: HMSO, 1984)

4.12...AID has tended, partly because of the legal situation, to be surrounded with secrecy. This secrecy amounts to more than a desire for confidentiality and privacy, for the couple may deceive their family and friends, and often the child as well. Indeed couples who achieve pregnancy may come to look on their AID child as a true child of the marriage. However the sense that a secret exists may undermine the whole network of family relationships. AID children may feel obscurely that they are being deceived by their parents, that they are in some way different from their peers, and that the men whom they regard as their fathers are not their real fathers. We have little evidence on which to judge this. But it would seem probable that the impact on children of learning by accident that they were born as a result of AID would be harmful—just as it would be if they learned by accident that they were adopted or illegitimate. However, while we agree that it is wrong to deceive children about their origins, we regard this as an argument against current attitudes, not against AID in itself.

However, although the Committee were concerned about 'family secrets' they unequivocally endorsed preserving the 'absolute anonymity of the donor'. The rationale was to 'give legal protection to the donor' and protect the integrity of the family unit by 'minimizing the invasion of the third party into the family'.[156]

The legal framework in the HFEA 1990[157]

Donor anonymity was one of the most controversial issues in the parliamentary debates on the HFEA 1990.[158] However, although donor anonymity was initially firmly entrenched in the legislation, that anonymity was removed in 2004 (although not retrospectively) and greater openness further extended by the HFEA 2008. The legal framework governing the collection, storage, and disclosure of information relating to the conception of a child is found in ss 31–5 of the legislation. Sections 31–31ZE are the core provisions on information to be provided to the child and donor. Under s 31(1)–(2), the HFEA is required to keep a register of any identifiable individual who has received treatment services using donated gametes, details of any individual whose gametes have been kept or used in the provision of treatment services, and details of any identifiable individual who was, or may have been, born as a result of treatment services using donated gametes. Under s 31ZA a donor-conceived child has the right, upon reaching the age of 16, to have access to non-identifying information about his or her genetic parentage and/or any genetically related siblings (specifically the number of such siblings, the sex of each, and the year of birth). Upon reaching the age of 18, the child has the right to access identifying information about the donor. Since the new right is not retrospective, children born by AID before 1 April 2005 are restricted to receiving non-identifying information. The exact information to be provided to the child is specified in regulations. Under s 31ZD a donor-conceived child may obtain identifying information about any donor-conceived genetic siblings who have also attained the age of 18 and who have agreed to identifying information being released to a genetically related sibling requesting such information. Finally, the child has the right, upon reaching the age of 16, to know (with the specified person's consent) whether they may be related to a specified person with whom they intend to: (i) enter into a marriage; (ii) enter into a civil partnership; or (iii) engage in an intimate physical relationship.[159] Before any of this information is disclosed, the donor-conceived child and any other affected person (genetic sibling and 'specified person') must have been given the opportunity to receive proper counselling about the implications of the disclosure.[160]

One innovation of the 2008 reforms was the introduction of the right of donors to access non-identifying information about any children (specifically the number of children, the children's sex, and the year of the children's birth) conceived through the use of their donated gametes.[161] The donor may also be notified when a donor-conceived child has made a request for information about the donor. The donor will not, however, be informed about the child's identity.[162] The HFEA is also authorized to establish a voluntary contact register which may assist children, donors, and genetic siblings to make contact with one another where all relevant parties consent but there is no right to identifying information under the legislation.[163]

---

[156] DHSS (1984), [4.22].
[157] As amended by the HFEA 2008.
[158] DH (2001a), [1.15].
[159] HFEA 1990, s 31ZB.
[160] Ibid., ss 31ZA(3)(b), 31ZB(3)(c), 31ZE(3)(c).
[161] Ibid., s 31ZD.
[162] Ibid., s 31ZC.
[163] Ibid., s 31ZF.

Despite the child's right to know now being entrenched in the legislation, children conceived using donated gametes may still face several obstacles in acquiring information about their genetic background. The first and most difficult to overcome through legal change alone is that many parents who conceive using donated gametes may still prefer to conceal the facts about the child's conception.[164] Research carried out into donor insemination families in the UK, Italy, the Netherlands, and Spain, found that only 12 per cent of the mothers interviewed planned to inform the child that they were conceived using donated gametes.[165] Similar studies in the US and Australia found that up to 90 per cent of parents had not disclosed the use of donated gametes to the child.[166] With no legal obligation on the parent (or the state) to tell children about their conception, most will remain ignorant about their genetic background. The Warnock Committee's suggestion that 'by donation' be added to the birth certificate after the non-genetic parent's name in order to alert the child to the truth of their conception (and thereby encourage parents to be open with the child) was considered again in the 2008 reform process but rejected.[167] The Joint Parliamentary Committee in their recommendations on the draft Human Tissue and Embryos Bill expressed deep concern at this omission, commenting that the authorities 'may be colluding in a deception'.[168] In response, whilst acknowledging the importance of donor-conceived children having access to information about their genetic background, the government argued that it is 'preferable that parents are educated about the benefits of telling children that they were donor-conceived rather than forcing the issue through the annotation of birth certificates'.[169] Although the government agreed to keep the issue under review,[170] its failure to act has disappointed some who point out that the government's approach perpetuates a deception and fundamentally undermines the child's right to know:

A. Bainham, 'What is the point of birth registration?', (2008) 20 *Child and Family Law Quarterly* 449, 463–4

Our concern here...is with the process of birth registration in cases where donation has taken place. Here the position stands in stark contrast to the position which we saw in relation to adoption. In the case of donor-conceived children there is only *one* birth certificate. This records as the legal parents the birth mother and her husband or, where the mother is unmarried, her partner who joins in the registration with her...At the point of registration, the registration officer will be completely unaware of the fact that donation has taken place... [T]he baby will be registered as the presumptive biological child of both parties (except in the case of same-sex partners where it will be clear that one cannot be), as is the case with the registration of births which do not involve donation. The birth certificate which is issued will record the legal, and apparently biological, parents of the child. The concern that legal parentage should correspond with biological parentage, which as we have seen is a central feature of birth registration, is absent here except to the extent that the Registration Service has no reason of course to believe or suspect that it is doing anything other than registering two biological parents.

[164] Turkmendag, Dingwall, and Murphy (2008), 298.
[165] DH (2001a), [1.25].
[166] HFEA (2002), [20].
[167] DHSS (1984), [4.25].
[168] DH (2007), 19, Recommendation 28.
[169] Ibid., [69].
[170] Ibid., [70].

In common with adopted children (who have no legal right to be told that they are adopted), donor conceived persons have no legal right to be told that they are donor conceived. But because of the way the registration system works, this is a far more serious matter for the latter than it is for the former. There is no attempt in the context of donation to maintain a clear distinction between genetic and social parents even though many of those registering the birth will be clear that this distinction in fact exists...While it is true that from April 2005 donors have lost their right to anonymity and the child will be able to access identifying information about them at 18, unless there is a revolution in current practice, the great majority will never discover that they are donor-conceived and hence will effectively be unable to exercise these rights to knowledge about biological origins.

A second potential difficulty lies in the consistency of information provided by donors. Since 1991, the HFEA has collected personal information about donors such as name at time of donation, name at time of birth, place of birth, sex, and whether the donor has children. It has also recorded donors' physical characteristics such as height, weight, ethnic group, eye colour, hair colour, and skin colour. Information about donors' religion, occupation, and interests is optional, as is the provision of a pen portrait.[171] Clinics are advised to encourage donors to record as much non-identifying information about themselves as they are happy to provide but studies suggest the information provided is sparse.[172] Many children born before the removal of anonymity will be disappointed by the information they receive. As regards children conceived after 2004, regulations make the provision of information about the donor's religion, occupation, interests, skills, and reasons for donating compulsory but provision of a pen portrait remains optional.[173] The available information is therefore likely to remain limited in scope.[174]

The downside of reform

One of the strongest arguments against removing anonymity was the perceived risk that it would cause a drop in donors. Evidence from Sweden, where donor anonymity was removed in 1985, suggested that such fears may be unfounded: whilst numbers declined immediately following the change in the law, over time they recovered to their former level.[175] Unfortunately, the emerging picture in the UK following the removal of anonymity is not encouraging. Research by the BBC published in September 2006 revealed that almost 70 per cent of fertility clinics either had no access to donor sperm or were finding it extremely difficult to obtain.[176] Many couples are therefore having to wait months for treatment or are even being denied treatment altogether. This has led some commentators to observe that the 'frustration, despair and anxiety' of those seeking treatment has been ignored in a misplaced, and ultimately vain, attempt to promote greater openness.[177]

---

[171] HFEA (2002), [9].

[172] Roberts (2000), 52.

[173] Human Fertilisation and Embryology Authority (Disclosure of Donor Information) Regulations 2004, SI 2004/1511, reg 2(2)(f)–(h).

[174] See Roberts (2000), 52–3.

[175] Ibid., 57; HFEA (2002), [34].

[176] <http://news.bbc.co.uk/1/hi/health/5341982.stm>. See also Turkmendag, Dingwall, and Murphy (2008), 284 and 296–7.

[177] Ibid., 304–5.

9.5 SURROGACY

9.5.1 EARLY ATTITUDES TO SURROGACY

Surrogacy is a controversial topic. The Warnock Committee found the issue particularly difficult and were divided over the correct approach. Having rehearsed the main arguments, the majority of the Committee were swayed by the arguments against surrogacy, particularly in a commercialized form, and strongly opposed introducing any measures that appeared to sanction or encourage the practice.

DHSS, *Report of the Committee of Inquiry into Human Fertilisation and Embryology,* Cm 9314 (London: HMSO, 1984)

8.10 The objections turn essentially on the view that to introduce a third party into the process of procreation which should be confined to the loving partnership between two people, is an attack on the value of the marital relationship... Further, the intrusion is worse than in the case of AID, since the contribution of the carrying mother is greater, more intimate and personal than the contribution of a semen donor. It is also argued that it is inconsistent with human dignity that a woman should use her uterus for financial profit and treat it as an incubator for someone else's child. The objection is not diminished, indeed it is strengthened, where the woman entered an agreement to conceive a child, with the sole purpose of handing the child over to the commissioning couple after birth.

8.11 Again, it is argued that the relationship between mother and child is itself distorted by surrogacy. For in such an arrangement a woman deliberately allows herself to become pregnant with the intention of giving up the child to which she will give birth and this is the wrong way to approach pregnancy. It is also potentially damaging to the child, whose bonds with the carrying mother, regardless of genetic connections, are held to be strong, and whose welfare must be considered to be of paramount importance. Further it is felt that a surrogacy agreement is degrading to the child who is to be the outcome of it, since for all practical purposes, the child will have been bought for money.

8.12 It is also argued that since there are some risks attached to pregnancy, no woman ought to be asked to undertake pregnancy for another, in order to earn money. Nor, it is argued should a woman be forced by legal sanctions to part with a child, to which she has recently given birth, against her will.

8.13 If infertility is a condition which should, where possible, be remedied, it is argued that surrogacy must not be ruled out, since it offers to some couples their only chance of having a child genetically related to one or both of them. In particular, it may well be the only way that the husband of an infertile woman can have a child. Moreover, the bearing of a child for another can be seen, not as an undertaking that trivialises or commercialises pregnancy, but, on the contrary, as a deliberate and thoughtful act of generosity on the part of one woman to another. If there are risks attached to pregnancy, then the generosity is all the greater.

8.14 There is no reason, it is argued, to suppose that carrying mothers will enter into agreements lightly, and they have a perfect right to enter into such agreement if they so wish, just as they have a right to use their own bodies in other ways, according to their own decision. Where agreements are genuinely voluntary, there can be no question of exploitation, nor does the fact that surrogates will be paid for their pregnancy of itself entail exploitation of either party to the agreement.

> 8.17... In the first place we are all agreed that surrogacy for convenience alone, that is, where a woman is physically capable of bearing a child but does not wish to undergo pregnancy, is totally ethically unacceptable. Even in compelling medical circumstances the danger of exploitation of one human being by another appears to the majority of us far to outweigh the potential benefits in almost every case. That people should treat others as a means to their own ends, however desirable the consequences, must always be liable to moral objection. Such treatment of one person by another becomes positively exploitative when financial interests are involved. It is therefore with the commercial exploitation of surrogacy that we have been primarily, but by no means exclusively, concerned.

The majority thus recommended that any agency, profit or non-profit making, creating and supporting surrogacy agreements should be subject to criminal sanctions.[178] They also recommended that professionals knowingly assisting in establishing a surrogacy should be made criminally liable.[179] The Committee held back from recommending that the commissioning parents and the surrogate mother should be liable to criminal prosecution, concerned that children should not be 'born to mothers subject to the taint of criminality'.[180] They did, however, recommend that all surrogacy agreements be designated illegal contracts, unenforceable in the courts.

The minority was less hostile, accepting that there may be rare circumstances where surrogacy could be beneficial to couples as a very last resort.[181] They therefore felt that the door to surrogacy should 'be left slightly ajar'[182] and that medical practitioners should be able to recommend such a course to their patients without acting unlawfully. Whilst agreeing that surrogacy for mere convenience was totally unacceptable and that commercial agencies should be subject to criminal prohibitions, they argued in favour of bringing surrogacy within the remit of the regulatory authority and allowing the licensing of non-profit making agencies to provide proper advice and support to those for whom surrogacy was deemed appropriate.[183] They also recommended that in order to regularize the legal relationship between the child and the commissioning parents some form of adoption procedure should be made available.[184] Given their view that surrogacy should not stand outside the law, they also disagreed with the majority's recommendation that all surrogacy arrangements should be unenforceable, arguing that each case should be dealt with on its own facts.[185]

9.5.2 THE STATUTORY FRAMEWORK FOR SURROGACY

Surrogacy is a difficult area on which to legislate. On one hand, the practice is now so well established (it is estimated that there are currently between 100 and 180 surrogacy agreements made each year and between 50 and 80 births[186]) that it is very difficult to prevent

---

[178] DHSS (1984), [8.18].
[179] Ibid.
[180] Ibid., [8.19].
[181] Ibid., Expression of dissent, [1].
[182] Ibid., [9].
[183] Ibid., [3]–[5].
[184] Ibid., [7].
[185] Ibid., [8].
[186] Brazier, Campbell, and Golombok (1998), 54.

simply by pushing such arrangements beyond the law, particularly as surrogacy can be successfully carried out within the privacy of the home on a DIY basis. There is, moreover, a danger that criminalizing the practice will drive it underground, compromising safety and increasing the dangers of exploitation for all those involved. On the other hand, to bring surrogacy within a regulatory regime would give it the stamp of legitimacy and risk encouraging a practice believed to be of dubious moral and ethical standing. Parliament has therefore taken the middle ground, neither fully endorsing a prohibitive approach, nor facilitating the practice. The current law on surrogacy is found in the Surrogacy Arrangements Act 1985 (SAA 1985) and the HFEA 2008, ss 54–5.

Surrogacy Arrangements Act 1985

The SAA 1985 targets the commercial aspects of surrogacy. Surrogacy agreements are made unenforceable but neither the commissioning parents nor the surrogate commit a criminal offence by entering into such an arrangement. However, those who engage in surrogacy for financial gain are liable to criminal prosecution. The scope of the legislation is broad, covering, for example, the distributor of a newspaper that the distributor knows contains an advertisement relating to the making of surrogacy agreements.

Surrogacy Arrangements Act 1985

1A Surrogacy arrangements unenforceable

No surrogacy arrangement is enforceable by or against any of the persons making it.

2 Negotiating surrogacy arrangements on a commercial basis, etc.

(1) No person shall on a commercial basis do any of the following acts in the United Kingdom, that is—

    (a) initiate any negotiations with a view to the making of a surrogacy arrangement,

    (aa) take part in any negotiations with a view to the making of a surrogacy arrangement,

    (b) offer or agree to negotiate the making of a surrogacy arrangement, or

    (c) compile any information with a view to its use in making, or negotiating the making of, surrogacy arrangements;

and no person shall in the United Kingdom knowingly cause another to do any of those acts on a commercial basis.

(2) A person who contravenes subsection (1) above is guilty of an offence; but it is not a contravention of that subsection—

    (a) for a woman, with a view to becoming a surrogate mother herself, to do any act mentioned in that subsection or to cause such an act to be done, or

    (b) for any person, with a view to a surrogate mother carrying a child for him, to do such an act or to cause such an act to be done.

(2A) A non-profit making body does not contravene subsection 1 merely because –

    (a) the body does an act falling within subsection 1(a) or (c) in respect of which any reasonable payment is at any time received by it or another, or

(b) it does an act falling within subsection (1)(a) or (c) with a view to any reasonable payment being received by it or another in respect of facilitating the making of any surrogacy arrangement.

(2B) A person who knowingly causes a non-profit making body to do an act falling within subsection (1)(a) or (c) does not contravene subsection (1) merely because –

(a) any reasonable payment is at any time received by the body or another in respect of the body doing the act, or

(b) the body does the act with a view to any reasonable payment being received by it or another person in respect of the body facilitating the making of any surrogacy arrangement.

(2C) Any reference in subsection (2A) or (2B) to a reasonable payment in respect of the doing of an act by a non-profit making body is a reference to a payment not exceeding the body's costs reasonably attributable to the doing of the act.

(3) For the purposes of this section, a person does an act on a commercial basis...if –

(a) any payment is at any time received by himself or another in respect of it, or

(b) he does it with a view to any payment being received by himself or another in respect of making, or negotiating or facilitating the making of, any surrogacy arrangement.

In this section 'payment' does not include payment to or for the benefit of a surrogate mother or prospective surrogate mother...

3 Advertisements about surrogacy

(1) This section applies to any advertisement containing an indication (however expressed) –

(a) that any person is or may be willing to enter into a surrogacy arrangement or to negotiate or facilitate the making of a surrogacy arrangement, or

(b) that any person is looking for a woman willing to become a surrogate mother or for persons wanting to carry a child as a surrogate mother.

(1A) This section does not apply to any advertisement placed by, or on behalf of, a non-profit making body if the advertisement relates only to the doing by the body of acts that would not contravene section 2(1) even if done on a commercial basis...

(2) Where a newspaper or periodical containing an advertisement to which this section applies is published in the United Kingdom, any proprietor, editor or publisher of the newspaper or periodical is guilty of an offence.

(3) Where an advertisement to which this section applies is conveyed by means of a telecommunication system so as to be seen or heard (or both) in the United Kingdom, any person who in the United Kingdom causes it to be so conveyed knowing it to contain such an indication as is mentioned in subsection (1) above is guilty of an offence...

(5) A person who distributes or causes to be distributed in the United Kingdom an advertisement to which this section applies (not being an advertisement contained in a newspaper or periodical published outside the United Kingdom or an advertisement conveyed by means of a telecommunication system) knowing it to contain such an indication as is mentioned in subsection (1) above is guilty of an offence.

Contrary to the recommendations of the Warnock Committee, the SAA 1985 excludes not-for-profit agencies from criminal liability for advertising its services and facilitating surrogacy agreements.[187] This has allowed such agencies to facilitate surrogacy arrangements and support and advise infertile couples seeking to enter into such arrangements. COTS (Childlessness Overcome Through Surrogacy) has established itself as the UK's leading surrogacy agency. Agencies, such as COTS, whilst operating within the law, are unregulated as they fall outside the regulatory framework of the HFEA. If, however, the parties to a surrogacy agreement seek treatment from a licensed clinic, the clinic is subject to the HFEA's code of practice which provides that clinics should only consider using assisted conception techniques to produce a surrogate pregnancy where, 'the commissioning mother is unable for physical or other medical reasons to carry a child or where her health may be impaired by doing so'.[188]

The lack of regulation of voluntary agencies assisting commissioning couples and surrogates has given rise to some concern. A review carried out for the government by Professors Brazier, Campbell, and Golombok in 1997, concluded that regulation was desirable but, as surrogacy was more akin to adoption, the HFEA was not the appropriate regulatory body.[189] It thus recommended that all agencies should be registered with the Department of Health on pain of criminal prosecution.[190] It was further suggested surrogacy agencies should be subject to a Code of Practice similar to the HFEA's Code of Practice for fertility clinics and a parental order (see discussion below) should only be made if the commissioning couple had complied with the Code.[191] McFarlane J supported these calls for greater regulation in *Re G (Surrogacy: Foreign Domicile)*.[192] He strongly criticized COTS for its role in facilitating a surrogacy arrangement for a Turkish couple not domiciled in the UK and providing inaccurate legal advice as to the courts' jurisdiction to grant them a parental order under s 30 of the HFEA 1990 and their ability (with the surrogate's permission) to remove the child from the UK for adoption overseas.[193]

Determining parentage in a surrogacy arrangement—the HFEA 1998

The child's mother and father

The SAA 1985, apart from making surrogacy agreements unenforceable, does not deal with the legal consequences of such agreements, in particular as regards the parental status of the commissioning parents and their legal relationship with the child. These aspects of surrogacy are dealt with in the HFEA 2008, which seeks to strike a balance between protecting the surrogate whilst protecting the legal position of the commissioning parents and the child where all parties are happy to honour the original agreement.

The surrogate mother is given the strongest protection. Section 33 provides that having given birth to the child, the surrogate mother and no other woman, even if the commissioning mother is the genetic mother, will be regarded as the child's legal mother. The position of the commissioning father is more complicated. If the surrogate is unmarried and the commissioning father is the genetic father he will be able to rely on the common law

---

[187] The exclusion of not-for-profit agencies from criminal liability was made clear by virtue of amendments introduced to the SAA 1985 by the HFEA 2008, s 59. Surrogacy agencies operating on a voluntary not-for-profit basis therefore now stand on a much more secure legal footing.

[188] HFEA (2003), [3.17].

[189] Ibid., 52–3.

[190] Ibid.

[191] Brazier, Campbell and Golombok (1998), ii.

[192] [2007] EWHC 2814.

[193] Ibid., [23]–[29].

principle that the genetic parent is accorded legal parenthood. If, however, the surrogate is married, the commissioning father will have to rebut the common law presumption that the surrogate's husband is the child's legal father. Similarly, if assisted reproduction techniques are used to bring about the pregnancy, even if the commissioning father's sperm is used in the treatment, the surrogate's husband will be deemed legal father under s 35 unless it can be shown that he did not consent. Finally, if the surrogate is unmarried and donor sperm is used, the commissioning father may fall within the terms of s 36, provided he can satisfy the agreed fatherhood conditions under s 37. The weakest party is the commissioning mother who, under s 33, will be regarded as a complete legal stranger to the child.

Parental orders—s 54 of the HFEA 2008

Section 54 provides the only means by which the commissioning parents can secure their legal status with respect to the child without resorting to complicated and lengthy adoption proceedings. Under s 54, the court can make a 'parental order' in favour of the commissioning parents. A 'parental order' has the same legal effect as an adoption order, conferring legal parenthood on the commissioning parents and extinguishing the legal motherhood of the surrogate.[194] The making of a parental order is subject to a number of conditions:

Human Fertilisation and Embryology Act 2008, s 54

54 Parental orders

(1) On an application made by two people ("the applicants"), the court may make an order providing for a child to be treated in law as the child of the applicants if –

    (a) the child has been carried by a woman who is not one of the applicants, as a result of the placing in her of an embryo or sperm and eggs or her artificial insemination,

    (b) the gametes of at least one of the applicants were used to bring about the creation of the embryo, and

    (c) the conditions in subsections (2) to (8) are satisfied.

(2) The applicants must be –

    (a) husband and wife,

    (b) civil partners of each other, or

    (c) two persons who are living as partners in an enduring family relationship and are not within prohibited degrees of relationship in relation to each other.

(3) Except in a case falling within subsection (11), the applicants must apply for the order during the period of 6 months beginning with the day on which the child is born.

(4) At the time of the application and the making of the order –

    (a) the child's home must be with the applicants, and

    (b) either or both of the applicants must be domiciled in the United Kingdom or in the Channel Islands or the Isle of Man.

(5) At the time of the making of the order both the applicants must have attained the age of 18.

---

[194] HFEA 2008, s 55(1). See also Human Fertilisation and Embryology (Parental Orders) Regulations 2010, SI 2010/985, s 2 and Sched 1.

(6) The court must be satisfied that both –

(a) the woman who carried the child, and

(b) any other person who is a parent of the child but is not one of the applicants (including any man who is the father by virtue of section 35 or 36 or any woman who is a parent by virtue of section 42 or 43), have freely, and with full understanding of what is involved, agreed unconditionally to the making of the order.

(7) Subsection (6) does not require the agreement of a person who cannot be found or is incapable of giving agreement; and the agreement of the woman who carried the child is ineffective for the purpose of that subsection if given by her less than six weeks after the child's birth.

(8) The court must be satisfied that no money or other benefit (other than for expenses reasonably incurred) has been given or received by either of the applicants for or in consideration of –

(a) the making of the order,

(b) any agreement required by subsection (6),

(c) the handing over of the child to the applicants, or

(d) the making of arrangements with a view to the making of the order, unless authorised by the court.

The 2008 reforms saw a significant liberalization of parental orders. Under the 1990 Act, a parental order could only be made in favour of a married couple. The 2008 Act extends this to permit even a male same sex couple who have entered into a surrogacy arrangement to apply to regularize their position in relation to the child. Thus, not only does s 54 of the HFEA remove the necessity for applicants to be married (thereby opening up parental orders to heterosexual cohabiting couples), it also explicitly removes the necessity for the application to be brought by one man and one woman. The crucial qualifying provisions for making an application are now that the applicants are either married, civil partners, or 'two persons who are living as partners in an enduring family relationship'. Interestingly, unlike adoption, single applicants are still barred from applying under s 54, providing another example of the 'two parent paradigm' firmly entrenched in the legislation.[195]

The remaining conditions for making a parental order have been reproduced from the 1990 legislation. The requirement that the surrogate must have been impregnated by artificial means (s 54(1)(a)) is probably aimed at discouraging the 'adultery' involved in basic DIY surrogacy. Section 54(1)(b) serves an important purpose. By insisting that the gametes of one of the commissioning parents were used in creating the embryo, applicants under s 54 are not 'mere' social parents: at least one must have a genetic tie to the child. This distinguishes such cases from pre-natal adoption, preventing surrogacy being used to circumvent the strict regulations concerning eligibility and suitability to adopt.

Sections 54(4)(a) and 54(6) afford strong protection to the surrogate mother. The requirement that the child must be living with the commissioning parents at the time of the application means that the surrogate mother must have voluntarily surrendered the child after birth.[196] Section 54(4)(b) requires one or both of the applicants to be domiciled in the UK.[197] The surrogate is further protected by the requirement that she must freely consent to the

---

[195] See discussion above at pp 630–2.
[196] HFEA 2008, s 54(4)(a).
[197] See *Re G (Surrogacy: Foreign Domicile)* [2007] EWHC 2814.

order being made.[198] Any consent given within six weeks of the birth, when the surrogate is deemed physically and emotionally vulnerable, is invalid.[199] The commissioning parents cannot therefore use s 54 where the surrogate reneges on the agreement and wishes to keep the child. Unlike adoption, the court has no discretion to override the consent requirements: it is 'an absolute veto'.[200] The only alternative would be for the commissioning parents to pursue an adoption order under the ACA 2002 or, less satisfactorily from their perspective, apply for a residence order under s 8 of the CA 1989. There is a further potentially complicating factor in that the other 'parent' of the child, where it is not one of the applicants, must also consent to the order.[201] Where the surrogate is married this may mean her husband's consent is also required.

The prohibition on financial reward set down in s 54(8) was considered in *Re C; Application by Mr and Mrs X under s 30 of the Human Fertilisation and Embryology Act 1990*.[202] The court held, following the approach taken in adoption cases,[203] that payments made to the surrogate in excess of reasonable expenses and which were thus in breach of the HFEA 1990, s 30(7) (the precursor to the HFEA 2008, s 54(8)) could be retrospectively authorized by the court. In deciding whether to make such an order, the court held that it should consider the child's welfare as against the degree to which the transaction has been tainted by wrongdoing.[204] This approach was followed by Hedley J in *X & Y (Foreign Surrogacy)* where he expanded upon the various factors that must be taken into consideration. The case concerned a surrogacy arrangement between a British couple and a Ukrainian woman. A payment had been made to her that covered not only her reasonable expenses but a deposit for a flat in the Ukraine. The tensions inherent in the court's task and Hedley J's disquiet at what the court is being asked to do in giving retrospective authorization to such payments are very clear.

X & Y (Foreign Surrogacy) [2008] EWHC 3030

HEDLEY J:

20. The statute affords no guidance as to the basis, however, of any such approval. It is clearly a policy decision that commercial surrogacy agreements should not be regarded as lawful; equally there is clearly a recognition that sometimes there may be reasons to do so. It is difficult to see what reason Parliament might have in mind other than the welfare of the child under consideration. Given the permanent nature of the order under Section 30 [now s 54], it seems reasonable that the court should adopt the 'lifelong' perspective of welfare in the Adoption and Children Act 2002 rather than the 'minority' perspective of the Children Act 1989. On the other hand, given that there is a wholly valid public policy justification lying behind Section 30(7) [now 54(8)], welfare considerations cannot be paramount but, of course, are important. That approach accords with that adopted in the previous cases and also accords with the approach adopted towards the authorising of breaches of the adoption legislation...

---

[198] HFEA 2008, s 54(6).
[199] Ibid., s 54(7).
[200] *X & Y (Foreign Surrogacy)* [2008] EWHC 3030, [13].
[201] HFEA 2008, s 54(6)(b).
[202] [2002] EWHC 157.
[203] *In re Adoption Application (payment for adoption)* [1987] Fam 81.
[204] [2002] EWHC 157, [30].

21. In relation to the public policy issues, the cases in effect suggest (and I agree) that the court pose itself three questions:

(i) was the sum paid disproportionate to reasonable expenses?

(ii) were the applicants acting in good faith and without 'moral taint' in their dealings with the surrogate mother?

(iii) were the applicants party to any attempt to defraud the authorities?

On the facts of this case I have no doubt that the applicants were acting in good faith and that no advantage was taken (or sought to be taken) of the surrogate mother who was herself a woman of mature discretion. Moreover there was never any suggestion of any attempt to defraud the authorities; quite the opposite: I am satisfied that these applicants sought at all times to comply with the requirements of English and Ukrainian law as they believed them to be.

23. In this case I am satisfied that the welfare of these children require that they be regarded as lifelong members of the applicants' family. Given my findings on the public policy considerations, I am able without great difficulty to conclude that I should in this particular case authorise the payments so made under Section 30(7) of the 1990 Act.

24. I feel bound to observe that I find this process of authorisation most uncomfortable. What the court is required to do is to balance two competing and potentially irreconcilably conflicting concepts. Parliament is clearly entitled to legislate against commercial surrogacy and is clearly entitled to expect that the courts should implement that policy consideration in its decisions. Yet it is also recognised that as the full rigour of that policy consideration will bear on one wholly unequipped to comprehend it let alone deal with its consequences (i.e. the child concerned) that rigour must be mitigated by the application of a consideration of that child's welfare. That approach is both humane and intellectually coherent. The difficulty is that it is almost impossible to imagine a set of circumstances in which by the time the case comes to court, the welfare of any child (particularly a foreign child) would not be gravely compromised (at the very least) by a refusal to make an order... If public policy is truly to be upheld, it would need to be enforced at a much earlier stage than the final hearing of a Section 30 [now s 54] application... It is, of course, not for the court to suggest how (or even whether) action should be taken, I merely feel constrained to point out the problem.

Provided the court is satisfied that all the conditions under s 54 are met, the court has discretion whether to make the order. In exercising that discretion, the Human Fertilisation and Embryology (Parental Orders) Regulations 2010 apply the welfare test as set down in s 1 of the ACA 2002: that the welfare of the child throughout his life must be the court's paramount consideration. The making of parental orders under the HFEA 1990 generated very little case law providing guidance as to how this welfare discretion should be exercised. In fact, only about 40 s 30 orders are made each year,[205] suggesting that the moral uncertainty surrounding surrogacy and the stringent conditions set down under s 30, particularly as to the payment of expenses, may be discouraging commissioning parents from regulating their legal relationship with the child.

Disputes when the surrogacy agreement breaks down

Evidence suggests that in only 4–5 per cent of cases do surrogates refuse to hand over the child.[206] However, where the surrogacy agreement does break down, there is rarely an easy

[205] Brazier et al (1998), 6.
[206] Ibid., 26.

answer as to whether the surrogate should be able to keep the child and, if so, the role if any that should be played by the commissioning parents. The courts have tended to take each case on its facts, applying the welfare principle as best they can. This has led to very different outcomes in individual cases depending on such factors as the circumstances surrounding the surrogacy agreement, the reasons for the surrogate's refusal to proceed with the arrangement, and the court's general attitude towards surrogacy. The following two cases provide extreme examples of the difficult circumstances that can face the court and their reactions in trying to secure, as best they can, the child's interests.

In the early case of *A v C*,[207] the Court of Appeal made no secret of their intense disapproval of the commissioning couple and the circumstances surrounding the surrogacy agreement. The facts of *A v C* were somewhat colourful, and no doubt fuelled the court's hostility. The commissioning father was living with a slightly older woman who was no longer able to conceive. He desperately wanted a child of his own and so it was agreed that he would go down to Bow Street magistrates court to select a suitable prostitute to act as surrogate. A 19-year-old surrogate was found and, in exchange for a substantial fee and the use of a flat during her pregnancy, she agreed to carry the child to be handed over to the commissioning parents after birth. She was artificially inseminated with the commissioning father's sperm. Unfortunately, she subsequently changed her mind and decided to keep the child. Immediately after the birth, the commissioning father applied to make the child a ward of court with care and control being vested in him. On advice, he withdrew this application but pursued an application for contact which both commissioning parents had enjoyed on a regular basis since the child's birth. The Court of Appeal dismissed the application, holding that 'to permit access to continue in the circumstances of this case is to perpetuate the most artificial situation that one can possibly imagine'.[208] In reaching this conclusion, whilst expressing sympathy for the surrogate, the Court showed nothing but extreme distaste for the commissioning father and the 'sordid',[209] 'ugly',[210] 'bizarre and unnatural arrangement'[211] that he had orchestrated. The Court of Appeal made it clear that, in the circumstances, a mere genetic link between father and child was not sufficient to justify an ongoing social relationship.

More recently in *Re N (a child)*[212] the court disapproved just as strongly of the behaviour of the surrogate mother and took the unusual and very surprising step of transferring the child's residence from the surrogate and her husband to the commissioning parents, even though the child had been living with the surrogate and her husband for the 18 months since her birth. The case was unusual given the surrogate mother's deliberate intention to obtain sperm for insemination by deceiving the commissioning parents into entering the surrogacy arrangement when she had no intention to relinquish the child. This deliberate deception led the court to conclude that the child's long term interests would be better served with the commissioning parents, despite the high standards of care the surrogate and her husband had provided and the strong bond they had formed with the child. The Court of Appeal upheld this decision, paying little regard to whether the surrogate and her husband or the commissioning parents were to be regarded as the legal parents. However, whilst Thorpe LJ approached the case as one between two 'natural' parents—the surrogate mother

---

[207] [1985] FLR 445.
[208] Ibid., 457.
[209] Ibid., per Cumming-Bruce LJ.
[210] Ibid., 461, per Stamp LJ.
[211] Ibid., 455, per Ormrod LJ.
[212] [2007] EWCA Civ 1053.

and the commissioning father[213]—Lloyd LJ noted that under the HFEA 1990, the surrogate's husband would be the legal father.[214] Whilst this did not affect his assessment of the child's welfare, it makes the decision all the more remarkable as residence was being granted to two legal strangers to the child.

Whilst this pragmatic approach which seeks to protect each child's welfare has clear advantages, it also has the major disadvantage of uncertainty, particularly for the commissioning couple. The alternative approach of making surrogacy agreements enforceable like any other contractual arrangement would give much better protection to the commissioning parents and much greater certainty to all parties in the vast majority of surrogacy agreements that work. This intentional/contractual model has been adopted elsewhere, most notably California. Douglas, commenting on the decision of the Supreme Court of California in *Johnson v Calvert*,[215] provides an interesting analysis of the pros and cons of such an approach to determining legal parenthood both in surrogacy agreements and beyond.

G. Douglas, 'The Intention to be a Parent and the Making of Mothers', (1994b) 57 *Modern Law Review* 636, 638–41

The California Court's reliance on intention...has potentially interesting consequences for our attitudes to parenthood and family formation in general. For instance, it has been argued that using intention in this way is a means of avoiding gender-based stereotypes and biologically-determined differences when determining issues of parenthood. While men and women cannot physically play the same role in the procreation of children, both can have the intention to become a parent. Giving weight to intention, rather than to biological roles, therefore provides a means to treat claims to parenthood equally, regardless of gender difference. On the other hand, it could be argued that focusing on intention is very much a *male* approach to parenthood because it fits far more closely to men's experience of procreation than to that of most women. Just as the commissioning mother was unable to carry and give birth to her own child, so too was her husband; for men, *all* women who carry children are surrogates. Relying upon their intention to produce and raise a child is a very convenient way for men to assert their parentage over children...

If the intention to have and rear a child were to be the main criterion for legal parenthood, anyone who had this intention could seek out gamete donors and a surrogate and claim the 'product' of these people's labours when the child was born. This would render irrelevant the assumption that to be the parents of a particular child presupposes a relationship (sexual or not) of not more than two persons of different sex. There would be no reason why more than two people could not be recognised as 'parents', nor why they should be of different sex.

But there may be practical difficulties in the emphasis on intent. First how does it relate to the welfare and interests of the child who is produced? The California majority relied upon the argument that 'the interests of children, particularly at the outset of their lives, are unlikely to run contrary to those of adults who choose to bring them into being.'...Secondly, how would proof of intention be established? The easiest way is by written agreement between the parties and there is certainly nothing new about this...Basing parenthood on intention implies a preparedness to recognise the free alienability of parental responsibility and hence

---

[213] Ibid., [13]–[14].
[214] Ibid., [19].
[215] (1993) 5 Cal 4th 84.

the acceptability of surrogacy agreements. It comes closer to characterising children more openly as a form of property which can be transferred to others.

Thirdly, the corollary of recognising intention as the determining factor of parenthood is to accept that *lack* of intention should be a means of avoiding parenthood. Hitherto, the law in the United Kingdom has generally refused to permit someone to avoid liability (if not responsibility) for a child on the ground that he or she had not *intended* the child's conception or birth...

Why, then, not take the more straightforward route of the California court and accept that the intention to act as parent should be the key indicator for parental status? The short answer is because of the disapproval of surrogacy as a form of assisted reproduction... But underlying these restrictions is a deeper assumption. We still require, or at least prefer, some sort of biological link to the child, be it genetic *or* gestational, because we view children as in some way the physical recreations of their parents. We still refuse to face up to the reality of our acceptance of the importance of social parenthood—to an idea of parenthood as departing from the traditional, pseudo-biological model of two people of the opposite sex creating and rearing their offspring. In *Johnson v Calvert*, probably unintentionally, the Supreme Court of California appears to have moved a little closer to such recognition.

9.6 ADOPTION

Adoption is the one method of acquiring legal parenthood in English law that does not require one or other of the parents to have a biological link (genetic or gestational) with the child. It permanently extinguishes the legal parenthood of the child's original parents (usually the genetic/biological parents) and replaces them with the adoptive parents (the social/intended parents) as if the child had been born their legitimate child.[216] Adoption thus provides unique recognition of the value of social parenthood. The absence of a genetic tie between parent and child means, however, that this method of acquiring legal parenthood is subject to the most detailed and rigorous scrutiny by the state. It is covered in detail in chapter 13.

9.7 CONCLUSION

This chapter has been primarily concerned with how one determines the identity of a child's legal parents under English law. As Douglas and Lowe point out, one can situate the various methods of acquiring legal parenthood on a sliding scale, with natural procreation at one end, adoption at the other, and the various methods of assisted reproduction located at various points in the middle.[217] As one progresses along the scale from natural to adoptive parenthood, one moves from a strong emphasis on genetic parenthood to greater acceptance of the value of social parents. However, as the genetic tie weakens, one also moves from no regulation of an individual's attempts to become a parent, to detailed and rigorous scrutiny of one's parenting credentials by the state. Such scrutiny reflects the law's long-standing preference for genetic parenthood and the ambivalence, and even suspicion, in which it holds 'mere' social parents.

---

[216] ACA 2002, ss 46 and 67.
[217] Douglas and Lowe (1992), 416–17.

Legal parenthood is clearly central to defining the child's core family relationships. However, as should be clear from the above discussion, it is not the only 'parent' or 'parent-like' relationship of importance to children. Advances in reproductive technology and the increasing fluidity and diversity in modern family life, have led to 'parenthood' becoming an increasingly fragmented concept. Three distinct concepts of 'parenthood' have thus emerged in English law: genetic parentage, legal parenthood, and social parenthood. This chapter has considered legal parenthood and, where legal parenthood is divorced from genetic parentage, the continuing role, if any, of the genetic parents. In the next chapter, we consider the child's social parents: those individuals who provide care and nurture for a child. Although in most cases the child's social parents will also be the child's legal (and probably genetic) parents, this is no longer necessarily the case: social parenting can be, and often is, located in someone other than the legal parents. The extent to which English law is able to accommodate this additional level of complexity forms the subject matter of the next chapter. It is to the concept of parental responsibility that we now turn.

ONLINE RESOURCE CENTRE

Questions, suggestions for further reading, and supplementary materials for this chapter (including updates on developments in this area of family law since this book was published) may be found on the Online Resource Centre at **www.oxfordtextbooks.co.uk/orc/harrisshort_tcm2e/**.

10

PARENTAL RESPONSIBILITY

CENTRAL ISSUES

1. Understanding of the parent-child relationship has changed dramatically in recent years. From a concept dominated by rights, parenthood is now largely understood in terms of the parents' duties and responsibilities. Parental rights exist only insofar as they are necessary for parents to perform their parental duties.

2. Parenthood and parental responsibility are distinct legal concepts. Although largely undefined in the Children Act 1989 (CA 1989), parental responsibility gives an individual the power and authority to make decisions regarding the child's upbringing. Arguably, it is parental responsibility which confers the real legal status of parenthood.

3. Parental responsibility is conferred *automatically* on all mothers, married fathers, and civil partners accorded legal parenthood under s 42 of the Human Fertilisation and Embryology Act 2008 (HFEA 2008). Unmarried fathers (and second female parents accorded legal parenthood under s 43 of the HFEA 2008) must *acquire* parental responsibility in accordance with the legislative provisions. The difference in treatment between married and unmarried fathers is controversial but, in practice, of diminishing significance. Indeed, commentators are now suggesting that the balance has swung too far in conferring parental rights and responsibilities on disengaged fathers based on nothing more than the genetic tie.

4. A number of individuals can hold parental responsibility at any one time. In addition to the child's legal parents, parental responsibility may be held by social parents, such as step-parents and guardians, and 'corporate parents', such as the state. This raises the important question whether each individual holding parental responsibility can act unilaterally or whether the agreement of all members of the 'parenting team' must be obtained. Despite the clear statutory basis for unilateral action, the courts have imposed a duty to consult and agree on a growing list of important issues.

5. The exercise of parental responsibility can be limited both by the child (upon reaching *Gillick* competence) and by the state. The state's intervention into the private decision-making realm of the parents is controversial,

particularly when those holding parental responsibility are acting reasonably. The courts have been criticized for the limited weight given to parents' views once a dispute reaches court.

6. The parental responsibility of mothers, married fathers, and civil partners accorded legal parenthood under s 42 of the HFEA 2008 cannot be terminated, other than by way of a parental order under the HFEA 2008 or adoption. For these parents, 'parenthood is for life'. The parental responsibility of unmarried fathers, female second parents accorded legal parenthood under s 43 of the HFEA 2008, and 'mere' social parents can be terminated by the court. Arguably, in order to ensure the equal treatment of all parents, it should be possible to terminate the parental responsibility of any irresponsible and disinterested parent.

10.1 INTRODUCTION

Establishing the legal parenthood of a child under English law can be a complex and difficult process. However, establishing legal parenthood is only half the story. Although, as we have seen in chapter 9, a number of important rights and responsibilities attach to the mere fact of the parent–child relationship, in order to hold the full ambit of rights and responsibilities commonly associated with 'being a parent' and raising a child, an individual must also hold 'parental responsibility'. Indeed, it has been emphasized in the case law that it is parental responsibility that really confers the legal 'status of parenthood'.[1] Parental responsibility is thus a distinct legal concept. It is both narrower and wider than parenthood, in that, whilst some enduring rights and responsibilities attach exclusively to the parent–child relationship, other rights and responsibilities relating to the care and upbringing of the child attach exclusively to the concept of parental responsibility. For most parents, this disjunction between parenthood and parental responsibility poses no problems as the law both confers on them the status of legal parenthood and automatically regards them as holding parental responsibility. However, for some unmarried fathers the legal distinction is of enormous significance as they will not *automatically* hold parental responsibility for their children. Conversely, some social parents who have no genetic links with the child and do not hold the status of legal parenthood can acquire parental responsibility in accordance with the legislative provisions. Parental responsibility therefore plays an important role in the legal recognition of social parenthood, leading one commentator to remark that it is a 'potentially radical legal construct'.[2]

In understanding the parent–child relationship in English law, it is important to keep in mind this crucial distinction between the two legal concepts of parenthood and parental responsibility. Whilst chapter 9 dealt with the concept of parenthood, the focus of this chapter will be on parental responsibility. We begin by exploring the concept of parental responsibility and its legal significance in more detail, before considering the various legislative provisions dealing with who automatically holds parental responsibility, and how, and by whom, it may be acquired. We then examine the exercise of parental responsibility and the various restrictions that may be imposed on the decision-making authority of those who

---

[1] *Re S (A Minor) (Parental Responsibility)* [1995] 3 FCR 225, 234.
[2] Diduck (2007), 462.

hold it. The final section briefly considers the rights and responsibilities of those adults who care for a child but do not have parental responsibility.

10.2 WHAT IS PARENTAL RESPONSIBILITY?

10.2.1 FROM RIGHTS TO RESPONSIBILITY

The parent–child relationship

Section 3(1) of the CA 1989[3] defines parental responsibility in the following terms:

Children Act 1989, s 3

(1) In this Act 'parental responsibility' means all the rights, duties, powers, responsibilities and authority which by law a parent of a child has in relation to the child and his property.

'Parental responsibility' as a distinct legal concept was an innovation in the CA 1989. It was intended to mark a fundamental shift in understanding about the parent–child relationship from one dominated by rights to one dominated by duties and responsibilities. This concept of parenthood underpinned the decision of the House of Lords in *Gillick v West Norfolk and Wisbech AHA*:[4]

Gillick v West Norfolk and Wisbech Area Health Authority [1986] AC 112, 170, 183–5 (HL)

LORD FRASER:

[P]arental rights to control a child do not exist for the benefit of the parent. They exist for the benefit of the child and they are justified only in so far as they enable the parent to perform his duties towards the child, and towards other children in the family.

LORD SCARMAN:

Parental rights clearly do exist, and they do not wholly disappear until the age of majority. Parental rights relate to both the person and the property of the child—custody, care, and control of the person and guardianship of the property of the child. But the common law has never treated such rights as sovereign or beyond review and control. Nor has our law ever treated the child as other than a person with capacities and rights recognised by law. The principle of the law, as I shall endeavour to show, is that parental rights are derived from parental duty and exist only so long as they are needed for the protection of the person and property of the child...

The principle is that parental right or power of control of the person and property of his child exists primarily to enable the parent to discharge his duty of maintenance, protection, and education until he reaches such an age as to be able to look after himself and make his own

---

[3] Unless otherwise stated, all references to statutory provisions in this chapter will be to the CA 1989.
[4] For the facts of this case and more detailed extracts from the judgments, see 8.5.4.

decisions...[Blackstone] accepts that by statute and by case law varying ages of discretion have been fixed for various purposes. But it is clear that this was done to achieve certainty where it was considered necessary and in no way limits the principle that parental right endures only so long as it is needed for the protection of the child...

The *Gillick* approach to parenthood was heralded and later unequivocally endorsed by the Law Commission, before being enshrined in s 3.

Law Commission, *Family Law Review of Child Law: Guardianship and Custody,* Law Com No 172 (London: HMSO, 1988c)

2.4 Scattered through the statute book at present are such terms as "parental rights and duties" or the "powers and duties", or the "rights and authority" of a parent. However, in our first Report on Illegitimacy we expressed the view that "to talk of parental 'rights' is not only inaccurate as a matter of juristic analysis but also a misleading use of ordinary language". The House of Lords in *Gillick v West Norfolk and Wisbech Area Health Authority*, has held that the powers which parents have to control or make decisions for their children are simply the necessary concomitant of their parental duties. To refer to the concept of "right" in the relationship between parent and child is therefore likely to produce confusion, as that case itself demonstrated. As against third parties, parents clearly have a prior claim to look after or have contact with their child but...that claim will always be displaced if the interests of the child indicate to the contrary. The parental claim can be recognised in the rules governing the allocation of parental responsibilities, but the content of their status would be more accurately reflected if a new concept of "parental responsibility" were to displace the ambiguous and confusing terms used at present. Such a change would make little difference in substance but it would reflect the everyday reality of being a parent and emphasise the responsibilities of all who are in that position.

The language of parental rights has not, however, been erased entirely from the statute books. Indeed, the 'rights' of parents are expressly included within the statutory definition of parental responsibility. It is, however, clear from the preparatory work of the Law Commission that such parental rights as are enshrined in the CA 1989 are meant in the *Gillick* sense. That is, they are instrumental: they exist only insofar as they are necessary for parents to perform their parental duties and responsibilities. It is therefore parental duties and responsibilities, not parental rights, which *should* be regarded as standing at the heart of parenthood.

Re S (A Minor) (Parental Responsibility) [1995] 3 FCR 225, 234 (CA)

Lord Justice Ward:

It is unfortunate that the notion of "parental responsibility" [in s 3 of the CA 1989]...gives out-moded pre-eminence to the "rights" which are conferred. That it is unfortunate is demonstrated by the very fact that, when pressed in this case to define [the] nature and effect of the order which was so vigorously opposed, counsel, for the mother, was driven to say that her rooted objection was to the rights to which it would entitle the father and power that it would give to him. That is a most unfortunate failure to appreciate the significant change that the Act has brought about where the emphasis is to move away from rights and to concentrate on responsibilities.

The parent–state relationship

The change in emphasis from focusing on parental rights to focusing on parental responsibilities also reflects a wider political agenda concerning the appropriate relationship between the child, the parent, and the state. As expressed by the government in its 1987 review of the public law on children, 'the prime responsibility for the upbringing of children rests with parents'.[5] In other words, in a policy which was typical of the privatizing trend of the Conservative government of the time, caring for and supporting children was seen to be an individual, not a state, responsibility. The government's approach was encapsulated in Margaret Thatcher's now infamous maxim: 'Parenthood is for life'.[6] It served to emphasize the enduring nature of the individual responsibility of *both* parents for their children's upbringing, a responsibility that could not be transferred or surrendered to the state and would not be affected by the parents' changing relationship.[7]

Two distinct ideas therefore underpin the concept of 'parental responsibility' in the CA 1989: one focusing on the parent–child relationship; the other focusing on the parents' relationship with the state.[8] Eekelaar argues that, by the time the CA 1989 was enacted, there had been a decisive shift in emphasis from the Law Commission's initial concern with the duties and obligations owed by parents to their children, to the more politically contentious issue of the appropriate relationship between the parents and the state.[9] This was fuelled by the government's growing anxiety over the breakdown of the traditional family unit and the resulting growth in single motherhood. Traditionally, men were legally tied to their children through the institution of marriage. Changing social trends brought the wisdom of this approach into question. It was widely perceived that the declining popularity of marriage, rising divorce rates, and the ever-increasing number of children born to unmarried mothers was resulting in a gradual transfer of parental responsibility from 'the husband' to the state. The growing 'irresponsibility' of men towards their children, and the wider social consequences of this phenomenon, was a matter of increasing concern.

J. Lewis, 'Family Policy in the Post-War Period', in S. Katz, J. Eekelaar, and M. Maclean (eds), *Cross Currents: Family Law and Policy in the United States and England* (Oxford: OUP, 2000), 81, 91–3

By the early 1990s, the political debate was dominated by those who stressed the irresponsibility and selfishness of men as well as of women. Michael Howard, then Home Secretary, said in a speech to the Conservative Political Centre in 1993: 'If the state will house and pay for their children the duty on [young men] to get involved may seem removed from their

---

[5] DHSS et al (1987), para 5.
[6] Eekelaar (1991c), 43.
[7] See generally Lindley (1999) and Eekelaar (1991c), 42–3.
[8] Eekelaar (1991c), 38–9. See also Freeman (2000), 452.
[9] Ibid., 40.

> shoulders…And since the State is educating, housing and feeding their children the nature of parental responsibility may seem less immediate.'…
>
> The prime concern of political commentators about men's obligation to maintain was often allied with a more generalised concern on the political Right, and the political Left, among politicians and the media, about an increase in male irresponsibility. All argued that the successful socialization of children required the active involvement of two parents. Dennis and Erdos sought to trace the rise of the 'obnoxious Englishman' to family breakdown. Their chief concern was the effect of lone motherhood on the behaviour patterns of young men. Lone parenthood was in their view responsible for at best irresponsible and at worst criminal behaviour in the next male generation.

The state was anxious to find a way of attaching children to their fathers other than through the traditional mechanism of marriage.[10] The most obvious legal status to which parental duties and responsibilities could be attached was parenthood.[11] However, the government has not always been consistent in its attitude towards the parenting role of unmarried fathers. As evidenced by the decision to withhold *automatic* parental responsibility from unmarried fathers,[12] there has persisted deeply entrenched suspicion about the 'value' of this particular group of men as parents. In the debates leading up to the CA 1989, a strong image of the unmarried father as a feckless, irresponsible individual emerged. Whilst successive governments have therefore taken a clear and unequivocal position on the financial responsibilities of men towards their children,[13] they have shown considerably more ambivalence towards unmarried fathers and the *non-financial* responsibilities of parenthood. Indeed, it can be argued that a desire to move the *financial* burden of maintaining children from the state to *both* their parents has been at the heart of the rhetoric on 'parental responsibility'. However, whilst financial considerations clearly remain important, there was in the later years of the previous Labour government a discernable shift in attitude. Ambivalence about unmarried fathers gave way to a strong belief in the value of active engaged fathering to securing the best possible outcomes for children.[14] Suspicion was thus replaced by steadfast optimism, with the government keen to support and encourage fathers to embrace all aspects of their parenting responsibilities. The Labour government's new found faith in the worth of the unmarried father was strongly reflected in its reforms to the birth registration system. No longer feckless and irresponsible, the exercise of parental responsibility, understood in its broadest sense, by unmarried fathers was portrayed as crucial to promoting the child's welfare.

DCFS and DWP, *Joint birth registration: recording responsibility,* **Cm 7293**
(London: HMSO, 2008)

Ministerial foreword:

The role of both father and mother is important to a child's development. By jointly registering a birth an unmarried father gets parental responsibility and can have a say in such important matters as the child's name, medical decisions, schooling and religion. Currently, unmarried

---

[10] Lewis (2000), 96.
[11] See Douglas (2000b), esp. at 223–7.
[12] See detailed discussion below.
[13] As enshrined in the CSA 1991, s 1.
[14] The assumed value of fatherhood is a strong feature of the current debate over contact. See 11.5.1.

fathers do not automatically have these rights, which places unnecessary obstacles in the way of those fathers who want to take responsibility for their children.

Fathers' involvement in their child's life can lead to positive educational achievement, a good, open and trusting parent-child relationship during the teenage years and reduce the risk of mental health issues for children in separated families.

20. Our ambition to increase significantly the number of joint birth registrations is a key part of our aim to develop a culture in which the welfare of children is paramount and which recognises the responsibilities and rights of fatherhood, as well as motherhood.

21. The roles of both father and mother are important to a child's development. We want parents to realise that, even when they do not have a close relationship with each other, they should both play an active, supportive role in their children's lives. Joint birth registration alone cannot achieve this, but it gives parents the opportunity to demonstrate their commitment to their children.

The Labour government's concern with the parental responsibilities of unmarried fathers extended well beyond financial support:

R. Collier and S. Sheldon, *Fragmenting Fatherhood: A Socio-Legal Study* (Oxford and Portland, Oregon: Hart Publishing, 2008), 191–2

Given the broader policy context around the promotion of 'active fathering'...unmarried fathers' failure to obtain PR has been of growing concern to a government keen to foster men's commitment to their families in a more general sense. Granting automatic PR is thus seen as a way of entrenching paternal duty to provide for the child's emotional development, as well as their financial needs. Denying this 'stamp of approval' to unmarried fathers, it was suggested, risked alienating them and refusing the vital encouragement necessary for them to take on board family responsibilities, destabilising the family unit and further contributing to the creation of lone-parent families.

10.2.2 DEFINING PARENTAL RESPONSIBILITY

Parental responsibility has proved difficult to define with any specificity. The definition in s 3(1) raises more questions than it does answers. However, the Law Commission opposed attempts to articulate any kind of definitive list of parental rights and duties, citing impracticality, incompleteness, and a lack of flexibility as potential drawbacks of such an approach.[15]

'Parental responsibility' therefore remains largely undefined in the CA 1989. However, whilst acknowledging that the formulation of a comprehensive list would be difficult, Freeman argues that Parliament's refusal to provide some form of guidance as to what the law expects of those exercising parental rights and duties was to sacrifice 'principle to pragmatism'.[16] Gillian Douglas and Nigel Lowe attempt to identify the most important rights and duties enshrined within the concept:[17]

---

[15] Law Com (1985b), [1.9].

[16] Freeman (2000), 455.

[17] This closely reflects the tentative list put forward by the Law Commission in 1985. Law Com (1985b), [2.25].

N. Lowe and G. Douglas, *Bromley's Family Law* (10th edn, Oxford: OUP, 2007), 377

- Bringing up the child.
- Having contact with the child.
- Protecting and maintaining the child.
- Disciplining the child.
- Determining and providing for the child's education.
- Determining the child's religion.
- Consenting to the child's medical treatment.
- Consenting to the child's marriage.
- Consenting to the child's adoption.
- Vetoing the issue of a child's passport.
- Taking the child outside the United Kingdom and consenting to the child's emigration.
- Administering the child's property.
- Naming the child.
- Representing the child in legal proceedings.
- Disposing of the child's corpse.
- Appointing a guardian for the child.

This list is frequently cited by other commentators. Despite the absence of a clear statutory definition of parental responsibility, there is fairly widespread consensus about what is core to the concept. In short, parental responsibility encapsulates all the decision-making power and authority that parents' need to provide effective long-term care for a child. It is, however, notable that attempts to define parental responsibility tend to result in lists dominated by parents' rights and decision-making power. This probably accurately reflects the public's perception of parental responsibility and how it operates in practice. Despite the efforts of the Law Commission, the government, and the courts to shift the focus away from parental rights, Freeman may thus be justified in his opinion that the changes introduced in the CA 1989 can be exaggerated, and whilst 'the language and symbolism altered...there was not that much substance to the change'.[18]

10.3   WHO HAS PARENTAL RESPONSIBILITY?

Unlike parenthood, where the law can only recognize a maximum of two legal parents, one of the distinguishing features of parental responsibility is that it can be held simultaneously by more than two people.

Children Act 1989, s 2

(5) More than one person may have parental responsibility for the same child at the same time.

---

[18] Freeman (2000), 451.

(6) A person who has parental responsibility for a child at any time shall not cease to have that responsibility solely because some other person subsequently acquires parental responsibility for the child.

There are two routes by which individuals may come to hold parental responsibility: (i) they hold it automatically; or (ii) it has been acquired in accordance with the CA 1989.

10.3.1 MOTHERS

Regardless of marital status, the child's mother will *always* have *automatic* parental responsibility.

Children Act 1989, s 2

(1) Where a child's father and mother were married to each other at the time of his birth, they shall each have parental responsibility for the child.

(2) Where a child's father and mother were not married to each other at the time of his birth—

(a) the mother shall have parental responsibility for the child...

10.3.2 FATHERS

Married fathers

Married fathers also *automatically* acquire parental responsibility for their children provided they were married to the child's mother 'at the time of [the child's] birth'.[19] This phrase is interpreted in accordance with s 1(4) of the Family Law Reform Act 1987 (FLRA 1987) to include any time between conception and birth. It also includes any child whose parents marry after the birth with the effect of 'legitimating' the child.[20] These provisions apply to void marriages, provided one or both of the parties reasonably believed that the marriage was valid.[21]

Unmarried fathers

The position of an unmarried father is considerably more complicated. Fathers who are not married to the child's mother 'at the time of the child's birth' do not automatically have parental responsibility. They must therefore acquire it in accordance with the legislative provisions.[22] Section 4 provides for three ways in which the child's *father* may acquire parental responsibility:

---

[19] CA 1989, s 2(1).

[20] FLRA 1987, s 1(3)(b) and Legitimacy Act 1976, ss 2, 3, and 10.

[21] FLRA 1987, s 1(3)(a) and Legitimacy Act 1976, s 1(1). With respect to the status of a transsexual marriage and its affect on parenthood, see *J v C (Void Marriage: Status of Children)* [2006] EWCA Civ 551.

[22] CA 1989, s 2(2).

Children Act 1989, s 4

(1) Where a child's father and mother were not married to each other at the time of his birth, the father shall acquire parental responsibility for the child if—

(a) he becomes registered as the child's father...;

(b) the father and the child's mother make an agreement (a "parental responsibility agreement") providing for him to have parental responsibility for the child; or

(c) the court, on his application, orders that he shall have parental responsibility for the child.

Registration

Section 4 of the CA 1989 was amended by the Adoption and Children Act 2002 (ACA 2002) to enable unmarried fathers who are entered as the child's father on the birth register to acquire parental responsibility.[23] This is subject to the qualification that parental responsibility will not be acquired by means of registration if the father has previously made an unsuccessful application to the court for a parental responsibility order or, having previously held parental responsibility, the court had ordered that his parental responsibility should cease.[24] In 2008, 86 per cent of children born outside marriage were jointly registered by both parents.[25] As discussed in chapter 9, reforms to the birth registration system in 2009 making joint registration, in effect, compulsory will further increase this number.[26] This means that all but a very small minority of unmarried fathers will now acquire parental responsibility by the simple act of registration. Indeed, the government identified this as one of the major benefits of the birth registration reforms.[27]

Parental responsibility agreements

A parental responsibility agreement is a formal agreement entered into by the child's parents that the father is to share parental responsibility with the mother. The agreement must be made on the prescribed form and registered at the Principal Registry of the Family Division in London.[28] In practice, they are rarely used. In 2004, only 5,831 agreements were registered.[29] It is generally recognized that this low take up does not reflect a lack of interest in or commitment by unmarried fathers to their children, but rather widespread ignorance about parental responsibility. The number of agreements made is likely to fall yet further in light of the 2002 reforms providing for the acquisition of parental responsibility through registration on the birth certificate.

Parental responsibility orders (PRO)

For those small number of men unable to take advantage of the new provisions on birth registration and who have not entered into a parental responsibility agreement, the only

---

[23] ACA 2002, s 111. The new registration provisions came into effect on 1 December 2003 and have no retrospective effect. Fathers whose children were born before this date cannot therefore take advantage of them.

[24] CA 1989, s 4(1C), inserted by the Welfare Reform Act 2009, s 56, Sch 6, Pt 2, para 21(1), (4).

[25] ONS (2009a), p 24.

[26] See detailed discussion above at pp 591–7.

[27] DCSF and DWP (2008), [9].

[28] CA 1989, s 4(2).

[29] Statistics supplied to authors by the Principal Registry of the Family Division.

means by which they may acquire parental responsibility is by applying to the court under s 4 of the CA 1989 for a PRO. For most unmarried men, their lack of parental responsibility only becomes a problem when their relationship with the mother breaks down (if such a relationship ever existed) and a dispute develops over the child. Indeed, it is often at this point that the father learns for the first time that he lacks the necessary legal status to make key decisions with respect to his child's upbringing. Invariably, fathers in this position are faced with an uncooperative mother who objects to his acquisition of parental responsibility. Most applications for parental responsibility orders are therefore opposed.

The Court of Appeal has provided clear guidance on the factors which should be taken into account on an application for parental responsibility.[30] *Re H (Minors) (Local Authority: Parental Rights) (No 3)* concerned an application for a parental rights order under s 4(1) of the FLRA 1987 (the precursor to a parental responsibility order) but the criteria it set down have been approved and applied to applications under s 4 of the CA 1989.

Re H (Minors) (Local Authority: Parental Rights) (No 3) [1991] Fam 151, 158 (CA)

BALCOMBE LJ:

In considering whether to make an order . . . the court will have to take into account a number of factors of which the following will undoubtedly be material (although there may well be others, as the list is not intended to be exhaustive): (1) the degree of commitment which the father has shown towards the child; (2) the degree of attachment which exists between the father and the child, and (3) the reasons of the father for applying for the order.

In subsequent case law, Balcombe LJ emphasized that these three factors provide only a *starting point* for the court.[31] Satisfying the *Re H (No 3)* criteria should not therefore be regarded as giving rise to a *presumption* in favour of making the order.[32] All applications for parental responsibility remain subject to the overriding principle of the child's best interests.

Re RH (a minor) (parental responsibility) [1998] 2 FCR 89, 94 (CA)

BUTLER-SLOSS LJ:

15. The three requirements set out by Balcombe LJ in Re H are, undoubtedly, the starting point for the making of an order but it is clear . . . that he did not intend them to be the only relevant factors in considering a parental responsibility order and that his list was not exhaustive. In any event, such an approach would be contrary to s 1 of the 1989 Act, which applies to parental responsibility orders and the welfare of the child is therefore paramount. The court has the duty in each case to take into account all the relevant circumstances and to decide whether the order proposed is in the best interests of the child. Of course, it is generally in a child's interests to know and have a relationship with his father but the appropriateness of

---

[30] For a more detailed discussion of the case law on applications for parental responsibility orders see Gilmore (2003).

[31] See *Re G (A minor) (Parental Responsibility Order)* [1994] 1 FLR 504.

[32] Ward LJ came close to saying this in *Re P (Parental Responsibility)* [1997] 2 FLR 722, where he held that 'parental responsibility orders were essentially orders which conferred status on the unmarried father, and that the practice had developed where good reason had to be advanced why orders should not be granted in a committed father's favour'.

the order has to be considered on the particular facts of each individual case. If, reviewing all the circumstances, the judge considers that there are factors adverse to the father sufficient to tip the balance against the order proposed, it would not be right to make the order, even though the three requirements can be shown by the father.

When determining the child's best interests in relation to an application for a parental responsibility order, several factors have proved particularly persuasive. The courts have generally taken the position that it is in the child's interests to have a father who is 'sufficiently concerned and interested' that he wishes to acquire the formal legal status of a parent. In support of this approach, the courts have placed great weight on the nature of a parental responsibility order, emphasizing that it confers a status on the unmarried father that a married father would enjoy as of right. Moreover, it is argued that granting parental responsibility and giving the father the court's 'stamp of approval' helps promote a positive image of him, a vital factor in developing the child's own secure sense of identity.[33] It is also stressed that parental responsibility is not about conferring rights on fathers, but imposing duties and responsibilities, something which invariably works to the child's advantage.[34]

Re S (A Minor) (Parental Responsibility) [1995] 3 FCR 225, 234–6 (CA)

Lord Justice Ward:

It would . . . be helpful if the mother could think calmly about the limited circumstances when the exercise of true parental responsibility is likely to be of practical significance. It is wrong to place undue and therefore false emphasis on the rights and duties and the powers comprised in "parental responsibility" and not to concentrate on the fact that what is at issue is conferring upon a committed father the status of parenthood for which nature has already ordained that he must bear responsibility . . .

I have heard, up and down the land, psychiatrists tell me how important it is that children grow up with good self-esteem and how much they need to have a favourable positive image of the absent parent. It seems to me important, therefore, wherever possible, to ensure that the law confers upon a committed father that stamp of approval, lest the child grow up with some belief that he is in some way disqualified from fulfilling his role and that the reason for the disqualification is something inherent which will be inherited by the child, making her struggle to find her own identity all the more fraught.

Lady Justice Butler-Sloss:

It is important for parents . . . to remember the emphasis placed by Parliament on the order which is applied for. It is that of duties and responsibilities as well as rights and powers. Indeed, the order itself is entitled "parental responsibility". A father who has shown real commitment to the child concerned and to whom there is a positive attachment, as well as a genuine *bona fide* reason for the application, ought, in a case such as the present, to assume the weight of those duties and cement that commitment and attachment by sharing the

---

[33] *Re G (A minor) (Parental Responsibility Order)* [1994] 1 FLR 504, 508 and *Re C and V (Contact and Parental Responsibility)* [1998] 1 FLR 392, 397.
[34] *Re C and V (Contact and Parental Responsibility)*, ibid., 397.

responsibilities for the child with the mother. This father is asking to assume that burden as well as that pleasure of looking after his child, a burden not lightly to be undertaken.

In my judgment, this father should be allowed to share the burden of caring for his daughter which does not remove from the mother the day-to-day control of her daughter's welfare. But it gives to the father the status in which he can share in the responsibility for the child's upbringing and demonstrate that he will be as good a parent as he can make himself to this little girl.

Applying these principles, the Court of Appeal granted a parental responsibility order to the father of a seven-year-old girl, despite his recent conviction for the possession of obscene literature including paedophilic photographs of young girls.[35]

The courts' emphasis on the *status* conferred by parental responsibility has been accompanied by a general tendency to down play its *practical* significance. Although it is recognized parental responsibility confers important rights on the father,[36] the courts have made it clear that a parental responsibility order does not give the father a general licence to interfere in the day-to-day upbringing of the child. Fears concerning the father potentially misusing the order to interfere in the mother's day-to-day care have therefore been regarded as insufficient to prevent the order being granted, particularly as such potential misuse can be controlled by the court under s 8.[37]

Re P (A Minor) (Parental Responsibility Order) [1994] 1 FLR 578, 584–6 (Fam Div)

WILSON J:

It is important to be quite clear that an order for parental responsibility to the father does not give him a right to interfere in matters within the day-to-day management of the child's life...

There is, of course, an order for residence in favour of the mother under the Act and that invests the mother with the right to determine all matters which arise in the course of the day-to-day management of this child's life. Thus, as it seems to me, the proposed order for parental responsibility cannot in fact be used in the way in which the magistrates feared that it might be used. Their decision is in effect founded on a misconception...as to the ambit of the rights which would be afforded to the father under the proposed order for parental responsibility. This seems to me...to be a slender basis upon which to decline to make an order which in all respects is overwhelmingly appropriate.

It is to be noted that on any view an order for parental responsibility gives the father no power to override the decision of the mother, who already has such responsibility: in the event of disagreement between them on a specific issue relating to the child, the court will have to resolve it. If the father were to seek to misuse the rights given him under s 4 such misuse could, as a second to last resort, be controlled by the court under a prohibited steps order against him and/or a specific issue order. The very last resort of all would presumably be the discharge of the parental responsibility order. But, on the evidence before the magistrates, and indeed on the basis of their conclusion as to the father's fitness to continue to care

---

[35] See also, ibid.

[36] *Re RH (a minor) (parental responsibility)* [1998] 2 FCR 89. These include the right to be heard in adoption proceedings and proceedings under the Hague Convention, as well as the right to be consulted on important matters regarding the child's upbringing, such as schooling.

[37] See also *Re C and V (contact and parental responsibility)* [1998] 1 FLR 392. See 11.6 on specific issue and prohibited steps orders.

> responsibly for the child during regular and extensive periods of contact in the future, there seems to be no basis for such extremely pessimistic hypotheses...
>
> [The magistrates] placed far too little weight on the role of the father in the life of the child, as it has been in the past and is likely to be in the future, and far too much weight on the spectre of his misuse of the proposed order.
>
> [Wilson J overturned the decision of the magistrates and made a parental responsibility order in favour of the father].

An alternative means by which the father's use of parental responsibility may be restricted is by subjecting the order to express conditions. This device was employed in *Re D (Contact and PR: Lesbian mothers and known father) (No 2)*.[38] The case was unusual as it involved a dispute over the parenting role to be played by a known 'sperm donor' (Mr B) in the life of a child being raised by a lesbian couple (Ms A and Ms C). B had understood that he was to have a continuing role in the child's upbringing, seeing her frequently and participating on an equal basis in important decisions. A and C had envisaged a more limited role: that he would be a 'real father' and enjoy regular contact with her but he would not be a 'parent' involved in decisions regarding her upbringing. A and C feared that granting B parental responsibility would give him 'increased visibility' as 'a third parent', thereby compromising the security of their family unit and exacerbating the problems they faced in gaining social acceptance of their equal parenting roles. In trying to find a solution which recognized and affirmed the child's place within the primary care of A and C, yet also acknowledged the love and commitment of her biological father, Black J took what she describes as a 'creative' approach to parental responsibility.

Re D (Contact and PR: Lesbian mothers and known father) (No 2) [2006] EWHC 2

BLACK J:

33. Ms A and Ms C are anxious because they perceive same sex couples as having great difficulties in forming families which society recognises. Their experience is that most people focus on the biological mother as if she were a single mother of the type to which society has become used, treating the woman who is not the biological mother as redundant or in the background, rather than accepting the two women and their child as a family with two parents... The problem is compounded... by the shortcomings of language which does not yet have the terms to deal with the new ways of living that are evolving.

34. It is in this climate where, it seems to me, the law is advancing at a pace which is probably quicker than the pace of change in the views of society in general, where new ways of living have not yet wholly crystallised, and where language has not yet evolved to accommodate them, that I must adjudicate upon the issue of parental responsibility for Mr B, equipped only with concepts and language which were not designed with this in mind...

89. I confess that I have been anxious about whether making a parental responsibility order would be in D's interests for the sort of reasons that have influenced [the expert child and adolescent psychiatrist], notably the potential threat to the stability of D's immediate family from what I may loosely call "interference" from Mr B as well as the impact on society's perception of the family if he were, in fact, to use it to become more visible in D's life. On the other hand, I am very mindful of the authorities which stress the status aspect of parental responsibility and those which indicate that it is not appropriate to refuse to grant it because of a feared misuse

---

[38] [2006] EWHC 2.

which should more properly be controlled by s 8 orders. I am also mindful of the fact that such matters as those for which I have criticised Mr B in relation to his actions towards D's family fall far short of the sort of activity that has, in the past, been seen as sufficient to found a refusal of parental responsibility. Perhaps most importantly of all, I am considerably influenced by the reality that Mr B is D's father. Whatever new designs human beings have for the structure of their families, that aspect of nature cannot be overcome. It is to be hoped that as society accepts alternative arrangements more readily, as it seems likely will happen over the next few years, the impulse to hide or to marginalise a child's father so as not to call attention to an anomalous family will decline, although accommodating the emotional consequences of untraditional fatherhood and motherhood and of the sort of de facto, non-biological parenthood that is experienced by a step-parent or same sex partner will inevitably remain discomfiting.

90. The dilemma facing me has been greatly eased by Mr B's offer to be bound by conditions which would prevent him from being intrusive in the obvious situations which might be anticipated as problem areas, namely D's schooling and health care. It has rightly been argued on behalf of Ms A and Ms C that it is not possible to anticipate all the situations that may arise and to guard against them but the course that Mr B proposes would cover the obvious ones. The court has power to regulate others, should they arise, through Children Act orders. Given that Mr B will know, following this judgment, the sort of context that the court anticipates there will be for his involvement in D's life, he will be able to forecast the likely consequences of attempts to become involved in areas of her life not covered by the proposed conditions and it is my judgment that that ought to be a brake upon his conduct.

91. Mr B's suggestion has allowed me to take a creative approach to parental responsibility in an attempt to make it serve the novel demands of a case such as this... I propose to grant him parental responsibility for D. The order will be considerably more detailed than normal and will recite that it is granted on the basis

i) that Mr B will not visit or contact D's school for any purpose without the prior written consent of Ms A or Ms C

ii) that Mr B will not contact any health professional involved in D's care without the prior written consent of Ms A or Ms C.

The grant of parental responsibility in this case thus had nothing to do with the actual 'doing' of parenthood; the imposition of conditions on the father's decision-making capacity stripped his parental responsibility of all meaningful practical effect. The order was made for purely symbolic and therapeutic reasons: to reflect the importance Black J attributed to the fact of B's biological fatherhood and to confer a sense of enhanced parental status on a committed and dedicated father unable to play the parenting role he desired.

Re D was an unusual case dealing with a novel situation. However, in restricting the father's exercise of parental responsibility, the decision is consistent with earlier authority holding that the fact that certain parental rights, duties, and responsibilities are currently incapable of being exercised or enforced by the father, whilst relevant, is no bar to the granting of a parental responsibility order.

Re C and another (minors) [1992] 2 All ER 86, 88–9 and 93 (CA)

MUSTILL LJ

This appeal has required us to consider another possible factor, namely enforceability. The question can be posed in this way: is the court, when considering a PRO application, entitled or bound to take into account the fact that under the circumstances at the date of the application one or more or all of the parental rights may be valueless in practice because they are incapable of being exercised by force of circumstances or by order of the court?

Looking at that question as one of first impression without reference to authority, we would think that the answer must be Yes. The enforceability of the rights which he is being invited to confer is something that any judge would be entitled and bound to regard as relevant to the exercise of his discretion...

Given, therefore, that the prospective enforceability of parental rights is a relevant consideration for a judge deciding whether or not to grant them, there is, in our judgment, nothing in the 1987 Act to suggest that it should be an overriding consideration. It would be quite wrong, in our view, to assume that just because few or none of the parental rights happen to be enforceable under conditions prevailing at the date of the application it would necessarily follow as a matter of course that a PRO would be refused. That can be illustrated by looking—as the legislation clearly requires one to look—at the position of a lawful father in analogous circumstances. Conditions may arise (for example in cases of mental illness) where a married father has, regretfully to be ordered, in effect, to step out of his children's lives altogether. In such a case his legal status as a parent remains wholly unaffected, and he retains all his rights in law although none of them may be exercisable in practice. This does not mean that his parental status becomes a dead letter or a mere paper title. It will have real and tangible value, not only as something he can cherish for the sake of his own peace of mind, but also as a status carrying with it rights in waiting, which it may be possible to call into play when circumstances change with the passage of time. It is not difficult to imagine situations in which similar considerations would apply in the case of a natural father. Though existing circumstances may demand that his children see or hear nothing of him, and that he should have no influence upon the course of their lives for the time being, their welfare may require that if circumstances change he should be reintroduced as a presence, or at least as an influence, in their lives. In such a case a PRO, notwithstanding that only a few or even none of the rights under it may currently be exercisable, may be of value to him and also of potential value to the children. Although there may be other factors which weigh against the making of a PRO in such circumstances, it could never be right to refuse such an order out of hand, on the automatic ground that it would be vitiated by the inability to enforce it.

It is, however, important to note that the case law does not all point the same way and a parental responsibility order has been refused in a few cases where parental responsibility would be devoid of any practical meaning or effect. In *M v M (Parental Responsibility)* Wilson J reluctantly refused to make an order where the father had no *capacity* to exercise parental rights and responsibilities. *M v M* was a tragic case in which the child's father was seriously injured in a cycle accident resulting in significant mental impairment.

M v M (Parental Responsibility) [1999] 2 FLR 737, 743–4 (Fam Div)

WILSON J:

[I]t is the third factor, namely the reasons of the father for applying for the order, which, when expanded to serve the demands of this particular inquiry, causes the most difficulty. Balcombe LJ's formulation presupposes that the father is capable of reason. Even more relevantly the statutory provisions themselves, namely ss 4(1) and 3(1) of the Children Act 1989, presuppose that the father is apt to be invested with responsibilities and is capable of exercising rights, of performing duties and of wielding powers in relation to the child. Parental responsibility, including as it does these rights, duties and powers, is not trivial. In *Re S (Parental Responsibility)* [1995] 2 FLR 648, Butler-Sloss LJ...spoke of the 'weight' of the relevant duties.

I ask whether it can be said with any degree of realism that this father's capacities are such that he should be invested with 'responsibility' for [the child]. It seems to me that he was only just across the borderline into being able to instruct lawyers to represent him in these proceedings. The general effect of the evidence is that, far from being able to exercise parental responsibility over another, for example to weigh up the merits of rival schools or to balance the potential benefits and risks of a surgical operation, this father requires something akin to parental responsibility to be exercised by others over himself...

I respect the weight of authority that misuse of a parental responsibility order can be controlled and that its spectre should not generally inhibit the making of an order. But those propositions presuppose the father's understanding of the concept of parental responsibility and of the likely repercussions of misuse...

I confess to having entertained a secret ambition that I would never be constrained to deny parental responsibility to a loving father. In the light of the tragedy which has broken the father's life, I feel a real sense of discomfort at a conclusion which does not at least give him that status. But my duty is to [the child] and, in my judgment, it dictates otherwise.

Hedley J has also refused to grant a severely restricted parental responsibility order in a case similar to *Re D (Contact and PR: Lesbian mothers and known father) (No 2)*. As in *Re D*, *TJ v CV* concerned a known 'sperm donor' (TJ) who had assisted his sister [S] and her civil partner (CV) to conceive a child and who wished to play a continuing parental role. Hedley J considered it would be in the child's best interests to maintain a relationship with his father. However, he was equally clear that TJ should not have the status of a parent or play any kind of 'parental' role. In such circumstances, he held that the grant of a parental responsibility order would be inappropriate.[39]

TJ v CV and others [2007] EWHC 1952

HEDLEY J:

26....It has become a somewhat hallowed process for the court to consider questions of commitment, attachment and motivation. However, as was pointed out in *Re H (Parental Responsibility)* [1998] 1FLR 855 these applications remain subject to the overriding provision of Section 1(1) of the Children Act 1989. That is particularly important where the case is outside the ordinary run of parental dispute on separation. TJ has certainly shown commitment and acceptable motivation and the contact sessions certainly do not preclude developing attachment. Yet this case is different. TJ accepts that CV and S should comprise the nuclear family and that he has no desire to undermine that and I accept the genuineness of that statement. It is, however, wholly inconsistent with the exercise of parental responsibility.

---

[39] See also *R v E and F (Female Parents: Known Father)* [2010] EWHC 417. Bennett J similarly refused a known 'sperm donor' parental responsibility, holding that where it was not intended that the donor would 'parent' the child (meaning not just caring emotionally and physically for the child but taking responsibility for all the day-to-day decisions) conferring the status of parental responsibility would not be appropriate. Bennett J was also strongly influenced by the expert evidence suggesting granting parental responsibility to the 'sperm donor' would be perceived as a direct threat to the autonomy of the nuclear family.

Moreover, it is perceived by CV and S... as a direct threat to their autonomy as a family unit. I am satisfied that it would be wholly contrary to the best interests of [the child] to grant TJ parental responsibility. TJ would undoubtedly seek to exercise it and forcefully to advance his views. CV and S would feel assailed and undermined in their status as parents. The inevitable resulting conflict would bode ill for [the child].

27. What then should the court do? Black J granted parental responsibility hedged about with conditions and undertakings. It is permissible to adjourn the application indefinitely. The court could dismiss it or pursuant to Section 1(5) of the Act make no order upon it. On the facts of this case I see no benefit in a restricted grant of parental responsibility. It will raise false hopes in TJ leading to frustration and will fuel all the fears of CV and S leading to conflict. Furthermore I see no basis for adjournment. As I have indicated I share the guardian's view that the matter should be resolved now. This family will derive no benefit from what will be perceived as a Damoclean sword suspended over them. On the other hand I am reluctant to dismiss the application for the essential conditions are fulfilled by TJ, it is simply that it will only work to BA's detriment in this case. Accordingly I have decided under Section 1(5) to make no order; it would certainly not be better for this child to make the order than not to make it – quite the reverse. That making of no order must be treated as a final order and, absent a radical change of circumstances, I cannot see the court revisiting this issue for many years, if at all.

In *Re G (Parental Responsibility Order)*,[40] Hedley J similarly refused to uphold a 'suspended' parental responsibility order because it could not be exercised in any meaningful way. The child had been conceived following a 'one night stand' and was being raised by his mother and her new partner. The mother and step-father were strongly opposed to contact, leading the judge at first instance to reduce direct contact from twice a month to just twice a year. However, in recognition of the father's commitment to his son and his determination to build a relationship with him, the judge made an order for parental responsibility. He then suspended that order on the mother's undertaking that she would provide certain information to the father about the child's health, education, and whereabouts. Hedley J set aside the order holding that a parental responsibility order could not be suspended under s 4 of the CA 1989 and that it would be most unusual to make a parental responsibility order with one hand and then 'effectively draw all its teeth' with the other.[41] He suggested it would not be in the child's best interests to make an order for parental responsibility in circumstances where it had been determined that the father should not actually exercise that responsibility except in the most limited way.[42]

However, save for these few cases—which tend to be somewhat unusual on their facts— the courts have shown a strong propensity towards granting a parental responsibility order. Despite the initial view of the Law Commission that successful applications would be rare, the vast majority of applications for a parental responsibility order, although low in number, are granted.[43] In 2008, 7,072 parental responsibility orders were made in private law proceedings, only 108 refused and 503 withdrawn.[44] Indeed, the ease with which orders are granted makes the rationale for continuing court scrutiny unclear. That said, there are some grounds

---

[40] [2006] EWCA Civ 745.
[41] Ibid., [23].
[42] Ibid.
[43] Law Com (1982b), [7.27].
[44] MOJ (2009), table 5.4.

on which applications will be refused, albeit they tend to be somewhat exceptional. Amongst the reported cases abusive behaviour towards the child,[45] repeated imprisonment,[46] and 'demonstrably improper and wrong' motives for making the application,[47] have all been held to justify refusing the order.

As an adjunct to a residence order

A final method by which the unmarried father of a child may acquire parental responsibility under the CA 1989, is as an *automatic* adjunct to a residence order being made in his favour.

Children Act 1989, s 12

(1) Where the court makes a residence order in favour of the father of a child it shall, if the father would not otherwise have parental responsibility for the child, also make an order under section 4 giving him that responsibility.

A parental responsibility order acquired by this route operates in the same way as a parental responsibility order obtained from a freestanding application under s 4. This is subject to one caveat that where a parental responsibility order is made under s 12(1), the order cannot be terminated whilst the residence order remains in force.[48]

10.3.3 UNMARRIED FATHERS AND PARENTAL RESPONSIBILITY—A NEED FOR FURTHER REFORM OR A STEP TOO FAR?

Recent reform has considerably improved the legal position of unmarried fathers. However, unmarried fathers do not enjoy complete equality with the child's mother or a married father as regards their legal relationship with the child. There remain a small minority of unmarried fathers who, because they are not registered on the birth register or have not entered into a parental responsibility agreement with the mother, must still go to the expense and inconvenience of 'proving their worth' to the court before being accorded the full legal status of fatherhood. Furthermore, the parental responsibility of all unmarried fathers remains subject to termination by the court.[49] These anomalies are a continuing source of grievance for paternal rights activists who argue that all distinctions between the child's parents, whether based on sex or marital status, should be removed. On the other hand, whilst these technical distinctions remain, the reality following the birth registration reforms is that, save for a very small minority, all unmarried fathers will acquire parental responsibility. Any con-

---

[45] *Re RH (a minor) (parental responsibility)* [1998] 2 FCR 89.

[46] *Re P (Parental Responsibility)* [1997] 2 FLR 722.

[47] *Re P (Parental Responsibility)* [1998] 2 FLR 96. See also *W v Ealing London Borough Council* [1993] 2 FLR 788 (sole purpose of application to prevent adoption of the child) and *Re M (Contact: Parental Responsibility)* [2001] 2 FLR 342 (the father perceived the order as giving him the right to interfere in the child's upbringing which would destabilize and undermine the mother's care of the child—particularly important in this case because of the nature of the child's special needs and disabilities).

[48] CA 1989, s 12(4).

[49] See discussion at pp 709–11.

tinuing 'discrimination' is thus more symbolic than real. Indeed, for some commentators, to confer parental responsibility on virtually all unmarried fathers as a consequence of the mere fact of birth registration is to go too far. It is argued that the assumed value of genetic fatherhood which underpins these reforms affords legal status to fathers who have no interest in playing any active part in the upbringing of their child, will do nothing to encourage men to take their parenting responsibilities more seriously, devalues the concept of parental responsibility as a practical parenting tool, and places vulnerable women and children at risk. The arguments both for and against further reform are particularly revealing about prevailing attitudes towards the value of fatherhood in English law.

The arguments for further reform

The continuing distinction between married and unmarried fathers, even if largely symbolic, raises an important point of principle about the extent to which a diversity of family forms should be accorded equal respect under the law. There are strong public policy arguments in favour of recognizing and supporting a wide range of alternative family relationships, particularly where the rights and interests of children are involved. There is now widespread agreement amongst commentators that children should not be disadvantaged because of their parents' marital status. What is important to children is the quality of the parent–child relationship, not whether their parents are married.

The growing influence of human rights discourse in domestic law and policy provides further impetus for ensuring the children of unmarried parents are treated just the same way as children of married parents. From a children's rights perspective, the UN Convention on the Rights of the Child (UNCRC), appears to promote the importance of the child's relationship with *both* parents, regardless of marital status.[50] With particular reference to parental responsibility, Article 18 emphasizes the importance of *equality* between the child's parents.[51]

United Nations Convention on the Rights of the Child 1989, Article 18

1. States Parties shall use their best efforts to ensure recognition of the principle that both parents have common responsibilities for the upbringing and development of the child. Parents or, as the case may be, legal guardians have the primary responsibility for the upbringing and development of the child. The best interests of the child will be their basic concern.

A particularly strong argument in favour of affording equal legal status to married and unmarried fathers is the importance of eradicating any continuing legal distinction between 'legitimate' and 'illegitimate' children. This was acknowledged by the Law Commission during its review of illegitimacy in the 1980s.

Law Commission, *Family Law: Illegitimacy*, Law Com No 118 (London: HMSO, 1982b)

4.23...In the Working Paper we expressed the view that if the concept of illegitimacy were to be removed from family law it would be a *necessary* corollary that the distinction

---

[50] See, e.g., Articles 7, 8, and 9.
[51] For commentary see Lowe (1997a), 201–2.

which the law now draws in relation to parental rights between, on the one hand, those children now "legitimate" and on the other, those now "illegitimate" would disappear along with all other distinctions based on legitimacy or illegitimacy. Thus our recommendation that fathers of illegitimate children should have parental rights was not intended to be an end in itself; it was merely a necessary incident of the abolition of all legal distinctions between children founded solely on their parents' marital status. We nevertheless thought it necessary to draw attention to the significance of parental rights in this context and to the consequences of such rights being automatically vested in all fathers. Our tentative conclusion was that any adverse consequences did not outweigh the benefits to be derived from abolition of the status of illegitimacy, but many commentators disagreed with this view...

4.44...Some commentators expressed the view (contrary to that which we had taken) that it would be perfectly possible to abolish the status of illegitimacy whilst preserving the existing rules whereby parental rights vest automatically only in married parents. We do not accept this view. The argument for "abolishing illegitimacy" (rather than merely removing such legal consequences of that status as are adverse to the child) is essentially that the abolition of any legal distinction based on the parents' marital status would itself have an influence on opinion. The marital status of the child's parents would cease to be *legally* relevant, and thus the need to refer to the child's distinctive legal status would (in this view) disappear. This consequence could not follow if a distinction—albeit relating only to entitlement to parental rights—were to be preserved between children which would be based solely on their parent's status. There would thus remain two classes of children: first, those whose parents were married and thereby enjoyed parental rights; secondly, those whose parents were unmarried and whose fathers did not enjoy such rights. In effect, therefore, the distinction between "legitimate" and "illegitimate" would be preserved.

4.45 We believe, therefore, that it is impossible to avoid the stark choice between abolition of the status of illegitimacy, and its retention (albeit coupled with a removal of the legal disadvantages of illegitimacy so far as they adversely affect the child).

Despite their initial view, the Law Commission finally recommended that fathers should not be accorded automatic parental rights. By retaining these differences between married and unmarried fathers, all legal distinctions between 'legitimate' and 'illegitimate' children have not therefore been removed from English law. The term 'illegitimate' may no longer be an acceptable part of legal discourse, but that should not disguise the fact that the legal relationship between children and unmarried parents is different from that enjoyed by children and their married parents. The Law Commission rationalized this continuing 'discrimination' on the basis that withholding automatic parental responsibility from unmarried fathers did not disadvantage the child, a conclusion with which not everyone would agree.

Reasons against conferring equal status on unmarried fathers

The issue of whether unmarried fathers should be treated equally with mothers and married fathers highlights a basic tension in successive government policies on family life. Whilst wishing to ensure that responsibility for children, particularly those living outside the traditional married family unit, falls on the parents and not the state, successive governments have remained committed to promoting marriage as the preferred basis of family life.[52] Reform which may undermine the status of marriage is thus treated cautiously. It is clear

---

[52] See, e.g., HO (1998) and the criticisms of that approach: HO (1999), ch 4.

from the various consultation papers on parental responsibility that there has been deep-seated resistance to fully embracing a diversity of family forms, with suspicion about the value of unmarried fathers being particularly strong. Thus, whereas the commitment and worth of the married father has been simply assumed, the unmarried father, having failed to demonstrate his commitment to the mother and child through marriage, has been an uncertain figure, tainted by fears as to his reckless, irresponsible, and possibly even danger-ous behaviour.[53] As the Law Commission's review of illegitimacy reveals, these concerns about the unmarried father were widely held. Although attitudes have undoubtedly moved on since the Law Commission was writing in the early 1980s, negative assumptions about the unmarried father remain a key part of the debate.

Law Commission, *Family Law—Illegitimacy*, Law Com No 118 (London: HMSO, 1982b)

4.24 In the Working Paper we summarised the case against automatically extending paren-tal rights to the father of an illegitimate child in the following words—

"3.9…It may be argued that [it is right that the father of a child born out of wedlock should have neither rights nor duties unless and until the court so orders] because of the very wide range of possible factual relationships between the father on the one hand and the mother and the child on the other. If the father wishes to participate in the child's upbringing and can make a substantial contribution to his welfare, the court can make appropriate orders even if the mother wishes to exclude him. If, on the other hand, he has nothing to offer it would, on this view, be wrong to give him rights (albeit rights of which the court would be able to divest him if the child's welfare so required). One can think of extreme and no doubt unrealistic examples. For instance, should a rap-ist, even in theory, be entitled to rights equal to those of the mother in relation to a child conceived as the result of the rape? If so, the rapist would in theory be entitled to ask whether he agreed to the child being adopted, and would have equal rights to the child's custody unless and until proceed-ings were taken formally to divest him of such rights. If such an issue were brought before a court it would of course be resolved by reference to the child's welfare, but, unless and until this was done, the rapist father would as a matter of law have the right to exercise full parental rights over the child and might in theory do so.

3.10 We have used the case of the rapist because it provides the most dramatic example of the consequences of abolishing discrimination not only against the child but also against his genetic father. There will, however, be other cases in which the father's relationship with the mother and her child is such that it might seem wrong to give him any, even *prima facie*, legal recognition, as where a child has been conceived as the result of a casual encounter.

3.11 It may be questioned whether this problem is of any real importance since in practice such a father would not seek to exercise rights. Even if he did, the court would be bound to override his rights if to do so would be in the child's interests. Looking at the position pragmatically, this may well be the right approach, but there are two reasons why it may be thought not to be an entirely satisfactory answer. First, the necessity to take legal proceedings to divest the father of his rights may in itself be distressing to the mother—so much so that it could, for example, affect her deci-sion about placing the child for adoption if the result were that the father had to be made a party to the proceedings. Secondly, it would be necessary for the mother to take legal proceedings if she wanted to secure herself and the child against the risk of intervention by the father. Unless and until she did so, the father could (on the hypothesis that he had the same rights as the father of a legitimate child) properly exercise any of the parental rights over the child…Hence, to avoid this

---

[53] As to family law's construction of fathers see Collier (2001) and (2003).

risk, mothers would no doubt often be advised to take steps to remove the father's rights, thus increasing not only the amount of litigation but also the mother's distress. These consequences must therefore be weighed in the balance in deciding whether or not the law should cease to discriminate against the genetic father."

Responses to the Law Commission's Working Paper identified a number of particular concerns with respect to conferring *automatic* parental responsibility on unmarried fathers:

4.26 . . . (a) It was said that automatically to confer "parental rights" on fathers could well result in a significant growth in the number of mothers who would refuse to identify the father of their child. Mothers would be tempted to conceal the father's identity in order to ensure that in practice he could not exercise any parental rights. If this were to happen, it would detract from the desirable objective of establishing, recognising and fostering genuine familial links.

(b) It was said that to confer rights on the father might well be productive of particular distress and disturbance where the mother had subsequently married a third party, who had put himself *in loco parentis* to the child. The possibility—however unlikely in reality—of interference by the child's father could well engender a damaging sense of insecurity in the family: matters would be all the worse if the father did intervene. Some commentators argued that the result in such a case might be that the mother and her new partner would seek, for instance by an application for custody or adoption, to forestall any possible intervention by the natural father with the result that the child would be prematurely denied the possibility of establishing a genuine link with him.

(c) It was said that automatically to confer "rights" on the father of a child born outside marriage could put him in a position where he might be tempted to harass or possibly even to blackmail the mother at a time when she might well be exceptionally vulnerable to pressure. In this context a number of commentators made what seems to us to be the valid point that what is in issue is not so much how the law is perceived by the professional lawyer or the experienced social worker but how it might be perceived by a fearful and perhaps ill-informed mother. Sometimes what the law is thought to be may be almost as important as what it in fact is. Thus the parents of a child might well attach more significance to the fact that the law had given the father "rights" than would a lawyer who is accustomed to the forensic process and able dispassionately to consider the likelihood of a court in fact permitting a father to exercise those rights, given its overriding concern to promote the child's welfare.

As these responses to the Law Commission indicate, many commentators at the time were of the view that 'unmeritorious', unmarried fathers should be excluded from holding parental responsibility. Furthermore, as the Law Commission go on to point out, the term 'unmeritorious fathers' was not necessarily restricted to a particularly deviant group of men, such as those convicted of a criminal offence.[54] Even men who had cohabited with the child's mother were still viewed as potentially problematic, as were men who had voluntarily acknowledged their paternity through, for example, registration on the birth register.[55] A similarly negative image of the unmarried father emerges from the writings of Deech, a particularly strong opponent of the focus on father's rights (rather than responsibilities) within these debates,

[54] Law Com (1982b), [4.30].
[55] Ibid., [4.35].

at what she perceives to be the risk of marginalizing concern for the mother's autonomy and the welfare of the child.

R. Deech, 'The unmarried father and human rights', (1992) 4 *Journal of Child Law* 3

Applying a contractual approach, if the father wants all the rights appertaining to a married father, he should marry the mother. If he does not want to make that permanent connection, then he is asking for rights without the *quid pro quo* of responsibilities. If she does not want to marry him, she should not be forced into a quasi-marital situation by being subjected to fathers' rights, such as they are, save where imposed by court in the interests of the child. It is also taken as self-evident here that the law alone cannot make a father assume parental responsibilities that he does not want. It can make him pay support but it cannot make him visit or stay at home or care for his child....

Writers, mostly men, have argued for more fathers' rights, especially unmarried fathers', allegedly for the sake of the child's welfare. This connection can represent a confusion of thought. The basic rights of the child are not furthered by delivering more choice to the unmarried father. Legal rights which he may acquire are choices for him; that is, he may or may not choose to exercise them. Such choice is a limitation on the rights of the child. Moreover, the call for fathers' rights confuses abstract legal rights to have a say in long-term decisions about the child, with the existence of actual family contact with the child...If one sees parental rights as including protective rights, for example, the parent's right to consent to medical treatment, which gradually cedes with age to the child's choice, it is not clear that the absent unmarried father has any part to play. The proper exercise of a right such as consent to medical treatment of a minor depends fundamentally on intimate knowledge of the condition and maturity of the child and cannot sensibly be exercised otherwise...

Discrimination against [the unmarried father] is rooted in the perceived habits of fathers, married or not, who are absent from home, uncommunicative and unable to give guidance even when visiting...Criticism of absent fathers is to recognise, not to decry, the importance of a father's involvement...

The result of the intense consideration of fathers' rights internationally and in domestic policies has been seen in new legislation. Many of the rights claimed by men have been given to them. Has the movement gone too far? Has sufficient consideration been given to the need to plan for a child and the child's welfare?...The pressure for father's rights which has had so much effect is not directed towards making men take responsibility but only to allowing absent fathers to plant their name and the occasional visit on their children, as if they were pieces of property.

The question should not be, does the absent unmarried father have too few rights, but does he have too few responsibilities? Parenthood is defined in the Children Act 1989 as including duties, and 'rights' as a term has in general been replaced by 'responsibilities'. But does the average unmarried father know this new law? Does he now accept an equal responsibility to rear the child and provide a home for her, or if he is totally rejected by the mother, to do all in his power, materially and otherwise, to enable her to do so? Let us be clear about what is involved in parental responsibilities to make up for the law's deficiencies in defining them. They include feeding, washing and clothing the child, putting her to bed, housing her, educating and stimulating her, taking responsibility for arranging babysitting and daycare, keeping the child in touch with the wider family circle, checking her medical condition, arranging schooling and transport to school, holidays and recreation, encouraging social and possibly religious or moral development. Fatherhood that does not encompass a fair share of these tasks is an empty egotistical concept and has the consequence that the man does not know the child sufficiently well to be able sensibly to take decisions about education, religion, discipline, medical treatment, change of abode, adoption, marriage and property. Therefore the absent unmarried father as contrasted with the cohabiting father, should not automatically be entitled to these rights.

If it is the case that the mother is usually left with the sole day to day responsibility for the child born out of wedlock, and remembering that it is impossible to force a father to live with his child and her mother, the mother should not, in a one-sided way, be subjected to the absent father's rights and the legal disadvantages of marriage when she is not married and where the case for the improved welfare of the child stemming from the absent father's legal status has not been made out.

In stark contrast to the negative view of unmarried fathers, the unmarried mother is consistently portrayed as an inherently worthy parent, however the child was conceived. The perceived vulnerability of the unmarried mother is a further striking feature of the debates.

Law Commission, *Family Law: Illegitimacy*, Law Com No 118 (London: HMSO, 1982b)

4.39 It may, however, be argued that the father should be entitled to parental rights in cases where *both* parents of the child agree that he should. After all (it might be argued) the law already accords parental rights to all married parents without any prior scrutiny of what is in the child's best interests. Why should it not equally accord such rights to unmarried parents who are in agreement? We see force in this argument, but have nevertheless rejected it. The most powerful factor influencing our decision was the strong body of evidence from those best acquainted with the problems of the single parent family about the vulnerable position of the unmarried mother in many cases. Such mothers may well be exposed to pressure and even harassment, on the part of the natural father; and it would, in our view, give unscrupulous natural fathers undesirable bargaining power if they were to be placed in a position where they might more easily extort from the mother a joint "voluntary" acknowledgment, having the effect of vesting parental rights in the father, perhaps as the price of an agreement to provide for the mother or her child, or even as the price of a continuing relationship with the mother.

Concern for the mother has remained prominent in the debate over unmarried fathers and their 'right' to parental responsibility. All reforms to extend the rights of unmarried fathers have been qualified by the need to secure effective safeguards both for mother and child against the behaviour of 'irresponsible' fathers. This approach to the issue has found favour in the European Court of Human Rights, which considered whether it was discriminatory to withhold automatic parental rights from unmarried fathers in *McMichael v United Kingdom*.

McMichael v United Kingdom (A/308, ECHR) (1995)

94. Finally, the first applicant claimed that he had been a victim of discriminatory treatment in breach of Article 14 (art. 14) of the Convention...

In his submission, he had been discriminated against as a natural father contrary to Article 14 taken in conjunction with Article 6 para. 1 and/or Article 8...in that prior to his marriage to the second applicant he had no legal right to custody of A. [the child] or to participate in the care proceedings...

96. Under Scots law a child's father automatically acquires the parental rights of tutory, custody and access only if married to the child's mother...Further, only a "parent", that is a

person having parental rights, is entitled to attend at all stages of a children's hearing...The natural father of a child born out of wedlock may obtain parental rights by making an application to a court; such an application will be dealt with speedily if the mother consents...

Mr McMichael was therefore in a less advantageous position under the law than a married father...

97. According to the Court's well established case-law, a difference of treatment is discriminatory if it has no reasonable and objective justification, that is, if it does not pursue a legitimate aim or if there is not a reasonable relationship of proportionality between the means employed and the aim sought to be realized...

98. The first applicant's complaint is essentially directed against his status as a natural father under Scots law.

As the Commission remarked, "it is axiomatic that the nature of the relationships of natural fathers with their children will inevitably vary, from ignorance and indifference at one end of the spectrum to a close stable relationship indistinguishable from the conventional matrimonial-based family unit at the other"...As explained by the Government, the aim of the relevant legislation, which was enacted in 1986, is to provide a mechanism for identifying "meritorious" fathers who might be accorded parental rights, thereby protecting the interests of the child and the mother. In the Court's view, this aim is legitimate and the conditions imposed on natural fathers for obtaining recognition of their parental role respect the principle of proportionality. The Court therefore agrees with the Commission that there was an objective and reasonable justification for the difference of treatment complained of.

99. In conclusion, there has been no violation of Article 14 taken in conjunction with Article 6 para. 1 or Article 8...in respect of the first applicant.

The Court's reasoning in *McMichael* was applied to the specific issue of withholding automatic parental responsibility from unmarried fathers under the CA 1989 in *B v United Kingdom*.[56]

Despite attracting the support of the European Court, the purported justifications for withholding equal status from all unmarried fathers have been criticized on several grounds. It can be argued that unmarried fathers are being denied equal status on the basis of a negative stereotype that is unsupported by any kind of objective evidence.[57] To deny all unmarried fathers full legal responsibility for their children on the basis of unsubstantiated concerns about the behaviour of a small minority of men is arguably manifestly unjust. There are, after all, many irresponsible and disinterested married fathers, and indeed mothers, who are nevertheless 'given the benefit of the doubt' and encouraged to take an active role in their children's upbringing by the automatic grant of parental responsibility. Similarly, if the government is committed to encouraging active and meaningful relationships between children and fathers, there is a good case for saying that it should use parental responsibility positively to support that policy. As Pickford argues, denying unmarried fathers parental responsibility does not support the father–child relationship but rather undermines attempts to promote fathers' involvement with their children.[58]

These arguments feed into the wider debate about the cultural and social value of fatherhood in contemporary society. By making all men financially responsible for their children but denying them the full responsibilities of parenthood, the law not only constructs

---

[56] (App No 39067/97, ECHR) (1999).
[57] Bainham (1989), 227 and 230–1.
[58] Pickford (1999), 158.

a negative image of the unmarried father but perpetuates outdated stereotypes of fathers as 'breadwinners' and 'providers', rather than 'nurturers' and 'carers', in contrast to mothers who are depicted as the *automatic* natural carers for their children.[59] If one is committed to true equality in parenting, perpetuating these outdated, gendered stereotypes is deeply problematic. As Nigel Lowe has argued, the law needs to foster a 'culture of responsibility' whereby 'fathers have a duty to provide for their children's emotional and moral development as well as their financial needs'.[60]

In order to remove all legal distinctions between parents there are two further steps the government could take:

- Place unmarried fathers in exactly the same position as mothers and married fathers: give them automatic parental responsibility which, like that of other parents, cannot be terminated or revoked.

- Confer automatic parental responsibility on all unmarried fathers but retain the provisions on termination as an appropriate safeguard in extreme cases. This option could be pursued without compromising the principle of equality by rendering the parental responsibility of all parents subject to termination.[61]

Both of these options would address continuing concerns about the inequalities faced by unmarried fathers, whilst sending out a strong message to counter the problematic gendered stereotypes which arguably continue to pervade this area of law.

Recent reforms—a step too far?

The 2002 reforms which enabled an unmarried father to acquire parental responsibility by registration clearly took much of the heat out of the debate. Prior to the birth registration reforms in 2009, registration on the birth register provided an effective mechanism for identifying those 'meritorious' fathers who had some form of continuing relationship with the child's mother, whilst requiring the minority of remaining fathers (who could be assumed to be more likely to fall into the category of 'irresponsible' or 'dangerous') either to apply to the court or enter into a parental responsibility agreement. However, the decision to make joint birth registration mandatory and thus, in effect, make the acquisition of parental responsibility automatic for virtually all genetic fathers has led to concern that the current focus on promoting (genetic) fatherhood is being unjustifiably pursued at the expense of other legitimate interests.

Far from dangerous and irresponsible, Sheldon and Collier suggest that the image of the unmarried father which has come to dominate family policy in recent years has changed dramatically.

R. Collier and S. Sheldon, *Fragmenting Fatherhood: A Socio-Legal Study* (Oxford and Portland, Oregon: Hart Publishing, 2008), 175–6

[T]he image of unmarried fathers as unworthy, irresponsible and uninterested in their children has been increasingly supplemented (in many contexts even supplanted) by a very

---

[59] See, e.g., Collier (2001) and (2003) and McGlynn (2000) and (2001).
[60] Lowe (1997a), 207. See also Bainham (1989), 226–7.
[61] See further discussion below at pp 709–12.

different depiction: of men who are often deeply committed to their children, yet find themselves subject to discrimination, denied access to their children and unfairly dependent on the whims of selfish, sometimes hostile mothers.

Against the background of this emerging image of the unmarried father as inherently worthy, it is argued that the tendency to use parental responsibility orders to confer mere parental status (or 'legitimation'[62]) on unmarried fathers is shifting parental responsibility further away from its original purpose of providing legal recognition and support to those carrying out the actual work of parenting and leaving parental responsibility devoid of any substantive meaning or purpose. Helen Reece is particularly critical of the decision in *Re D (Contact and PR: Lesbian mothers and known father) (No 2)*, arguing that it represents the 'nadir' of a line of cases in which parental responsibility has become detached from parental decision-making. In her view, by awarding parental responsibility simply on the basis of biological fatherhood the distinction between parenthood and parental responsibility has become blurred.[63] These concerns are exacerbated by the effect of the birth registration reforms leaving parental responsibility 'meaning nothing whatsoever'.[64] As Reece points out, 'if almost all unmarried fathers are compelled to hold parental responsibility, their parental responsibility will no longer even imply official approval of them, as least as individual fathers'.[65] Harris and George echo these concerns:

P. Harris and R. George, 'Parental Responsibility and Shared Residence Orders: Parliamentary Intentions and Judicial Interpretations', (2010) 21 *Child and Family Law Quarterly* 151, 161, 163

From the high point of compliance with the scheme intended by Parliament there has been a consistent trend in the case law downplaying both the potency and primacy of parental responsibility, with the concept being constructed as a form of status recognition with limited or no practical effect . . . [T]he pattern that can be seen is that parental responsibility is increasingly granted to men who are going to play no real part in their children's upbringing, primarily as a means of placating them . . . [W]e would suggest that the courts have robbed parental responsibility of its substantive content. Granting parental responsibility to fathers who are to have little if any involvement in their children's lives, makes it almost impossible to argue that parental responsibility can be something of substantive significance.

In addition to these concerns over devaluing parental responsibility, it is doubtful that the government's objectives will be achieved: that conferring parental responsibility on all unmarried fathers will encourage them to undertake the responsibility and work of caring for their children. Insofar as the birth registration reforms are intended to effect a change in fathers' parenting behaviour, several commentators suggest they are naively optimistic and thus deeply flawed.[66]

[62] Reece (2009), 85.
[63] Ibid., 94, 101, and 102.
[64] Ibid., 85.
[65] Ibid., 97.
[66] See also Wallbank (2009), extracts below at pp 595–6 and McCandless (2008).

L. Smith, 'Clashing symbols? Reconciling support for fathers and fatherless families after the Human Fertilisation and Embryology Act 2008', (2010) 22 *Child and Family Law Quarterly* 46, 55, 62–4, 69

[Joint birth registration] is motivated by the intention to develop a culture in which the welfare of children is paramount and people are clear that fatherhood as well as motherhood always comes with rights as well as responsibilities'. The White Paper sets out the optimistic view that the act of birth registration will, somehow, in and of itself, result in more fathers exercising their rights and responsibilities towards their children. This policy document too is supported by statements about the various unique advantages that children allegedly derive from the presence of an involved father, thus implicitly linking fathers with child welfare.

The position as a result of the reform is that the rights, duties, powers and responsibilities that comprise parental responsibility now follow upon the simple acknowledgement of genetic paternity. This creates an artificial link between biological and social fatherhood which assumes that the latter acts follows the former fact...

The White Paper in which [the birth registration reform] was proposed closely linked the importance of genetic and social parenthood...Thus it seems that faith is being invested in the possibility that a legislative assumption that genetic and social fatherhood are linked will help to make the aspiration a reality.

These legislative and policy developments echo common law developments which have seen parental responsibility degraded from a mechanism for conferring rights and responsibilities to committed and attached fathers, to a simple recognition of status. Whereas, for the purpose of granting parental responsibility, the importance of unmarried fathers was once measured according to the role they actually played, it is now taken as a given. This once again shows a step backwards towards locating the importance of fatherhood in the genetic connection rather than the social relationship.

Smith concludes by suggesting that if the intention is to encourage more fathers to take an active interest in their children, the law would be better remaining faithful to the original purpose of parental responsibility and acknowledging and supporting the actual care a father provides rather than valorizing the genetic tie:

The irony of these developments is that the importance of genetic and social fatherhood has been fused using a tool which was designed to recognize that the two are not necessarily linked. The very existence of parental responsibility as a tool with which to graft practical aspects of parenting onto, or separate from, the duties and rights inherent in legal parenthood has always implied legal recognition that genetic and social parenthood may not always coincide. Moreover, when the concept of parental responsibility was introduced into English law, it encapsulated a view of parenthood as a care-giving role. More importantly...the *problem* with these developments is that merging the significance of genetic and social fatherhood makes it possible to assert that all fathers are valuable. By blurring the distinction between fathers who make an active and valuable contribution to their children's upbringing and those who do not, the trend makes it difficult to separate the former from the latter and thus to reject the importance of any father in terms of his potential contribution to his child's welfare...

[G]enuinely promoting the value of fatherhood actually depends on distinguishing genetic paternity from social parenting. Failing to distinguish between uninvolved genetic fathers and attentive social fathers devalues the care devoted by the latter. In that sense the confusion which suggests that it is simply a father, rather than the supportive parenting a father can provide, that is intrinsically valuable not only undermines fatherless families, but also undermines efforts to promote fatherhood itself. This means that the drive in family law and policy to promote the idea of responsible (ie involved) parenting to fathers has been undermined because the way in which the message has been presented has been counter-productive. By contrast, an approach to parenthood which emphasized the distinction between the fact of genetic parentage and the act of socially parenting could further the goal of promoting active fatherhood by encouraging more men to focus on the value of parenting their children, rather than just genetically fathering them.

According to this approach, legal parenthood should be left to deal with issues of parental status; parental responsibility should deal with those who actually undertake the job of parenting.[67]

10.3.4 SECOND FEMALE PARENTS UNDER SS 42 AND 43 OF THE HFEA 2008

Parental responsibility is conferred on second female parents who acquire legal parenthood under the provisions of either s 42 or s 43 of the HFEA 2008 in accordance with the same principles governing heterosexual parents. Preference is thus accorded to formal legal relationships with civil partners who fall within s 42 of the HFEA 2008 (or who have subsequently 'legitimated' the child by entering into a civil partnership) automatically acquiring parental responsibility in the same way as married fathers.[68] A second female parent who is not a civil partner of the child's mother and therefore became a legal parent under s 43 of the HFEA 2008 must acquire parental responsibility in the same way as an unmarried father: by means of registration; entering into a parental responsibility agreement with the child's mother; or by applying to the court for a parental responsibility order.[69] Under s 12(1A) of the CA 1989, she will also automatically acquire a parental responsibility order under s 4ZA if a residence order is made in her favour.

10.3.5 STEP-PARENTS

The CA 1989 was amended by the ACA 2002 and the Civil Partnership Act 2004 to allow 'step-parents' (defined to include civil partners) to acquire parental responsibility for the children of their spouse or partner.

Children Act 1989, s 4A

(1) Where a child's parent ("parent A") who has parental responsibility for the child is married to, or a civil partner of, a person who is not the child's parent ("the step-parent")—

---

[67] Lind and Hewitt (2009).
[68] CA 1989, s 2(1A).
[69] Ibid., ss 2(2A), 4ZA.

> (a) parent A or, if the other parent of the child also has parental responsibility for the child, both parents may by agreement with the step-parent provide for the step-parent to have parental responsibility for the child; or
>
> (b) the court may, on the application of the step-parent, order that the step-parent shall have parental responsibility for the child.

This allows a step-parent to acquire parental responsibility through agreement with the child's parents or by order of the court. The agreement of the child's father or second female parent will only be required if he or she holds parental responsibility. If a parent holding parental responsibility withholds consent, an application to the court will be necessary.

Section 4A is an important provision. Before its introduction, step-parents wishing to formalize their legal relationship with their step-children had to resort to the sometimes artificial mechanism of obtaining a residence order or adopting the child. As there was usually no dispute over the child's residence, adoption was often the preferred option. However, step-parent adoption has a drastic effect on the legal position of the child: in addition to conferring parental responsibility on the step-parent, the adoption order terminated the parental responsibility and parental status of the non-adopting parent.[70] Indeed, once the adoption order has been made the child is to be treated for all purposes 'as if born as the child of the adopters or adopter'.[71] This effectively removes 'the very parenthood' of the non-adopting parent—usually the child's father—terminating any legal relationship between him and the child.

Growing awareness of the importance of genetic parentage and, wherever possible, preserving the child's familial links with *both* parents, regardless of whether the parents are divorced, separated, or have never lived together, has rendered step-parent adoption deeply problematic.[72] Section 4A thus provides an effective means of recognizing and supporting the social parenting role played by many step-parents, without undermining the importance of the child's relationship with both legal parents. It is thus a more measured response to the realities and complexities of the somewhat transient nature of modern family life. There remains, however, an apparent anomaly. As s 4A is specifically limited to a person who is married to, or a civil partner of, the child's parent, cohabitants cannot acquire parental responsibility for their partner's children via this route. This sits uneasily with the ACA 2002 which permits the 'partner' of a child's parent to apply for an adoption order.[73] It is perhaps regrettable that cohabitants may be forced into taking the more drastic step of adoption in order to consolidate their legal relationship with the child.

---

[70] Under the Adoption Act 1976 the child's parent (parent A) had to make a joint application with his/her spouse (the step-parent), to adopt his/her own child. The ACA 2002 removes this wholly artificial requirement, providing that the partner of a child's parent can make a sole application to adopt the child and that the adoption will have no effect on parent A's own parental responsibility: ss 46(3)(b) and 51(2). However, the position of the child's other parent (the non-adopting parent) remains unchanged.

[71] ACA 2002, s 67(1).

[72] See 13.6.3.

[73] ACA 2002, s 51(2). 'Partner' is defined in s 144 of the ACA 2002 as: 'a person is the partner of a child's parent if the person and the parent are a couple but the person is not the child's parent.' 'Couple' is defined as: '(a) a married couple, or (b) two people (whether of different sexes or the same sex) living as partners in an enduring family relationship'.

10.3.6 HOLDERS OF A RESIDENCE ORDER

An alternative route by which step-parents or cohabitants may acquire parental responsibility for their partner's children is by applying for a residence order under the CA 1989.[74] Indeed, anyone can acquire parental responsibility via this route as s 10 of the CA 1989 provides that *any person* may apply for a residence order with respect to any child, although those falling outside certain defined categories will require leave.[75] The primary purpose of a residence order is to determine the person with whom a child is to live.[76] However, where a residence order is made in favour of anyone other than a legal parent, it also confers parental responsibility.

Children Act 1989, s 12

(2) Where the court makes a residence order in favour of any person who is not the parent or guardian of the child concerned that person shall have parental responsibility for the child while the residence order remains in force.

Parental responsibility acquired by a non-legal parent under this provision is, however, subject to important limitations. First, the non-legal parent's parental responsibility is contingent on the existence of the residence order. If the residence order terminates, so does parental responsibility.[77] This differs from the parental responsibility of a father or second female parent who acquires a parental responsibility order under s 4 or s 4ZA as an adjunct to the grant of a residence order under s 12(1) or s 12(1A). In this situation, the parental responsibility order has life independent from the residence order. Second, there are two specific limits on the scope of a non-legal parent's powers if parental responsibility is acquired under s 12(2):

Children Act 1989, s 12

(3) Where a person has parental responsibility for a child as a result of subsection (2), he shall not have the right—

(b) to agree, or refuse to agree, to the making of an adoption order, or an order under section 84 of the Adoption and Children Act 2002 with respect to the child; or

(c) to appoint a guardian for the child.

Decisions relating to adoption and guardianship are amongst the most important with respect to a child's future and parliament has therefore chosen to reserve such questions exclusively to legal parents.

Residence orders thus provide one potential means by which non-legal parents can obtain formal recognition of their parenting role. When, however, there is no real dispute over the child's residence the question arises whether the use of a residence order to confer parental

---

[74] Residence orders are discussed in detail in chapter 11.
[75] See 11.3.2.
[76] CA 1989, s 8(1).
[77] Ibid., s 12(2).

responsibility on the non-legal parent is appropriate. The issue has now been considered in a number of cases.

In the earlier case law, the judiciary were clearly reluctant to employ what they regarded as a wholly artificial device to confer parental responsibility on a social parent.[78] However, more recently, the courts have become increasingly open to using residence orders as a means of conferring parental responsibility where it is in the child's interests. This more flexible attitude was evident in *Re AB (A Minor) (Adoption: Parental Consent)*.[79] The case concerned an application for joint residence by a cohabiting couple (Mr E and Miss G), in conjunction with an adoption application by the male partner, Mr E. The applications were made with respect to a child who had initially been placed with the couple in their capacity as local authority foster carers. The joint residence order was necessary in order to confer parental responsibility on Miss G, who was the child's primary carer, as the Adoption Act 1976 (the legislation then in force) precluded joint applications to adopt by unmarried couples.[80] Cazalet J held that making an adoption order in favour of Mr E and a joint residence order in favour of both Mr E and Miss G was in the interests of the child to ensure both parents had parental responsibility, even though there was no dispute over where the child should live.

In *Re AB* it was at least intended that the child would live with the holders of the residence order, even though there was no dispute requiring resolution. This is not, however, a prerequisite for making the order. In *Re H (Shared Residence: Parental Responsibility)*, the court went further by endorsing the use of a shared residence order to confer parental responsibility on the child's 'step-father', who had separated from the child's mother, even though, despite what may appear on the face of the order, there was no intention that the child should live with him outside the ordinary periods of staying contact.

Re H (Shared Residence: Parental Responsibility) [1996] 3 FCR 321, 327–8 (CA)

Lord Justice Ward:

It is submitted that it was quite inappropriate to use a shared residence order for the purpose of conferring parental responsibility on a step-father in circumstances like this. I see nothing in the authorities which compel that conclusion...

It is important not to forget that each case will depend upon its own facts... The essential element of the Judge's decision was to alleviate the confusion that would arise in the children's minds if they did not have the comfort and security of knowing not only that the father wished to treat the boy as if he was his father, but that the law would give some stamp of approval to that *de facto* position.

Given the boy's shock at the discovery of his paternity [he was only told that the 'step-father' was not his natural father following the parents' separation when he was 14 years old], everything must be done for this child to lead him to believe that life has not changed. It is important, in my judgment, that the benefits of the parental responsibility order, which by virtue of s. 12(2) of the Children Act flows from the making of a shared residence order, be impressed upon the boy to give him the confidence that he has not suffered some life-shattering blow to his self- esteem.

---

[78] See, e.g., *Re: WB (residence orders)* [1995] 2 FLR 1023 and *Re W (Arrangements to place for adoption)* [1995] Fam 120.

[79] [1996] 1 FCR 633, esp. at 644–5.

[80] This is no longer the case under the ACA 2002, s 49. See discussion at 13.5.2.

Whilst, Thorpe, J. [in *Re WB (Residence Orders)* [1995] 2 FLR 1023] did therefore properly find that on the facts of the case before him the making of a shared residence order would be quite artificial and quite unreflective of the reality, this is not such a case. This is a case where a shared residence order is not artificial but of important practical therapeutic importance. This is a case where its making does reflect the reality of the father's involvement and reflect the need for him to be given some status with the school to continue to play his part as both parties wish to do.

This approach was applied to same-sex partners in *Re G (Residence: same-sex partner)*. There was again no intention at this point in the proceedings that the children's primary home should be with the appellant, Miss W: the application for joint residence was made to consolidate Miss W's legal relationship with the children and prevent her gradual exclusion from their lives.[81] The children were born as a result of privately arranged artificial insemination by donor. The appellant's partner, Miss G, was the biological mother of both children. Miss W had always played an equal role in the care and upbringing of the children and following the couple's separation enjoyed substantial staying contact. Thorpe LJ was clearly influenced by the fact that, whereas a father without parental responsibility in an opposite-sex relationship would have been able to rely on s 4 of the CA 1989, the only legal mechanism available to a parent in a same-sex relationship was s 12(2).[82]

Re G (Children) [2005] EWCA Civ 462

LORD JUSTICE THORPE:

11....[Her Honour Judge Hughes, the first instance judge] recorded the evidence of Miss W to the effect that she wished to have parental responsibility so that she could have proper legal involvement with the girls' lives. She had set out in her written evidence...what practically she sought to achieve by way of involvement in the girls' lives from the foundation of a parental responsibility order. She said that involvement in those areas would give the children a clear understanding; that she was in their lives to love, support and help them and was involved in important areas of their lives. The judge recorded the contrasting evidence of Miss G to the effect that Miss W should be viewed as an extended family member, not in a parental position. She did not wish Miss W to be a parent and did not accept that she could care for the children properly....

[Having considered the leading authorities on joint residence orders and parental responsibility, **Thorpe LJ** continues]

24. Finally, I come to the authorities that demonstrate the evolution of the judicial acceptance of the diversity of the family in modern society. [Counsel] cites the judgment of Singer J in *Re W* [1997] 3 FLR 650, the decision of the House of Lords in *Fitzpatrick v Sterling Housing Association Ltd* [2001] 1 AC 27 and, more recently, the decision of the House in *Ghaidan v Godin-Mendoza* [2004] 3 WLR 113. He has selected a passage from the speech of Baroness Hale in paragraphs 141 and 143 which neatly demonstrates the present state of the judicial recognition and acceptance of family diversity. Baroness Hale said:

[81] In subsequent litigation, the children's primary place of residence under the terms of the shared residence order did become a matter of protracted dispute. See *In re G (Children) (Residence: same-sex partner)* [2006] UKHL 43. Discussed at pp 765–7.

[82] As the donor insemination did not occur in a licensed clinic, this was not a case that would have benefited from the parenthood reforms contained in s 43 of the HFEA 2008.

> "…the presence of children is a relevant factor in deciding whether a relationship is marriage-like but if the couple are bringing up children together, it is unlikely to matter whether or not they are the biological children of both parties. Both married and unmarried couples, both homosexual and heterosexual, may bring up children together. One or both may have children from another relationship: this is not at all uncommon in lesbian relationships and the court may grant them a shared residence order so that they may share parental responsibility. The lesbian couple may have children by donor insemination who are brought up as the children of them both: it is not uncommon for each of them to bear a child in this way.…
>
> 143. It follows that a homosexual couple whose relationship is marriage-like in the same ways that an unmarried heterosexual couple's relationship is marriage-like are indeed in an analogous situation. Any difference in treatment is based upon their sexual orientation."
>
> 25. Although [Counsel] has not asserted discrimination against his client he has made the general observation that had the case concerned the two children of a heterosexual couple who had cohabited between 1995 and 2003 and the father, being the absent parent, had sought the parental responsibility order on the strength of the same degree of past and proposed future commitment as has been demonstrated by Miss W, the outcome would have been evident.
>
> 26. Thus I have reached the clear conclusion that [counsel] is entitled to succeed on more than one of the grounds that he has advocated…

Thorpe LJ's judgment gives welcome recognition to the equal value and importance of those who parent children within a diverse range of family relationships, and in the context of same-sex relationships in particular, but who are not genetically related to them.[83]

10.3.7 SPECIAL GUARDIANS

As with residence orders, special guardianship orders (SGOs) confer parental responsibility on the applicants for the duration of the order.[84] A unique feature of SGOs is that whilst the parental responsibility of others is not terminated by the order, special guardians are entitled to exercise parental responsibility to the exclusion of any other person with parental responsibility.[85] Special guardianship is discussed in more detail in chapter 13.

10.3.8 GUARDIANS

A child's guardian has parental responsibility for the child for the duration of the appointment.[86] A guardian may be appointed by the court, a parent with parental responsibility, a previous guardian, or a special guardian.[87] Appointment by someone other than the court takes effect upon the death of the appointer, and may be revoked or disclaimed by the appointed person.[88] The appointment of an inter-testamentary guardian by a parent,

---

[83] That recognition has arguably been undermined by the reasoning of the House of Lords in the subsequent litigation regarding the sharing of time between the two parties under the terms of the joint residence order. See *Re G* [2005] EWCA Civ 462.

[84] CA 1989, s 14C(1)(a)

[85] Ibid., s 14C(1)(b)

[86] Ibid., s 5(6).

[87] Ibid., ss 5(3) and 5(4).

[88] Ibid., s 6.

guardian, or special guardian is the only mechanism available for conferring parental responsibility on an individual other than a parent or step-parent that does not require judicial scrutiny and approval.

10.3.9 ADOPTION

An adoption order confers parental responsibility on the adopter(s).[89] However, unlike a s 4 PRO, s 4ZA PRO, residence order, or SGO, an adoption order terminates the parental responsibility of any other person holding parental responsibility.[90] Parental responsibility is thus transferred from the legal parents to the adoptive parent(s) who stand in relation to the child as if the child had been born their natural legitimate child.[91] In accordance with this approach, parental responsibility conferred by an adoption order is permanent and irrevocable save for a further adoption. The acquisition and exercise of parental responsibility by means of adoption is discussed in detail in chapter 13.

10.3.10 LOCAL AUTHORITIES

The state in the guise of the local authority automatically acquires parental responsibility for a child with respect to whom a care or emergency protection order is made.[92] However, to reinforce the lifelong responsibilities of the child's parents, the parents' parental responsibility is not terminated but is shared with the local authority. Whilst parental responsibility is shared, the local authority has the power to determine the extent to which the parents are actually able to exercise their legal responsibility for the child.[93] The acquisition and exercise of parental responsibility by a local authority is discussed in greater detail in chapter 12.

10.4 EXERCISING PARENTAL RESPONSIBILITY

10.4.1 A DUTY TO CONSULT OR A RIGHT OF UNILATERAL ACTION?

The Children Act's approach to the acquisition of parental responsibility means that at any one time there may be several adults who hold parental responsibility for a particular child. While a child's 'parenting team' can co-operate over decisions relating to the child's upbringing, the fact that decision-making is shared poses no particular problems. However, difficulties develop where co-operation breaks down and different members of the 'parenting team' hold different views about what will best serve the child's interests. Disputes may arise over the child's school, medical treatment, surname, and in which religion, if any, the child should be raised.[94] The possibility of disagreement raises the important question of whether individuals holding parental responsibility can act unilaterally without consulting or seeking the agreement of the other members of the 'parenting team'. This is also an important issue where

---

[89] ACA 2002, s 46(1).
[90] Ibid., s 46(2).
[91] Ibid., s 67(1).
[92] CA 1989, s 33(3).
[93] Ibid., s 33(3)(b).
[94] For detailed discussion of these various aspects of parental responsibility see Probert, Gilmore, and Herring (2009).

an individual holding parental responsibility has little or no contact with the child and that person's whereabouts may be unknown. Again, their estrangement from the child, raises the question whether they must nevertheless be consulted and/or their agreement obtained with respect to important decisions concerning the child's upbringing.

These potential difficulties were anticipated by the Law Commission. Their proposed solution was to allow unilateral action by the individual holders of parental responsibility.

Law Commission, Family Law, *Review of Child Law: Guardianship and Custody*, Law Com No 172 (London: HMSO, 1988c)

(b) The power to act independently

2.10...As we explained in our Working Paper on Custody, we believe it important to preserve the equal status of parents and their power to act independently of one another unless and until a court orders otherwise. This should be seen as part of the general aim of encouraging both parents to feel concerned and responsible for the welfare of their children. A few respondents suggested that they should have a legal duty to consult one another on major matters in their children's lives, arguing that this would increase parental cooperation and involvement after separation or divorce. This is an objective which we all share. However, whether or not the parents are living together, a legal duty of consultation seems both unworkable and undesirable. The person looking after the child has to be able to take decisions in the child's best interests as and when they arise. Some may have to be taken very quickly. In reality, as we pointed out in our Working Paper on Custody, it is that person who will have to put those decisions into effect and that person who has the degree of practical control over the child to be able to do so. The child may well suffer if that parent is prevented by the other's disapproval and thus has to go to court to resolve the matter, still more if the parent is inhibited by the fear that the other may disapprove or by the difficulties of contacting him or of deciding whether what is proposed is or is not a major matter requiring consultation. In practice, where the parents disagree about a matter of upbringing the burden should be on the one seeking to prevent a step which the other is proposing, or to impose a course of action which only the other can put into effect, to take the matter to court. Otherwise the courts might be inundated with cases, disputes might escalate well beyond their true importance, and in the meantime the children would suffer. We recommend, therefore, that the equal and independent status of parents be preserved and, indeed, applied to others...who may share parental responsibility in future. This will not, of course, affect any statutory provision which requires the consent of each parent, for example, to the adoption of the child.

This recommendation was enshrined in s 2(7) of the CA 1989.[95]

Children Act 1989, s 2

(7) Where more than one person has parental responsibility for a child, each of them may act alone and without the other (or others) in meeting that responsibility; but nothing in this Part shall be taken to affect the operation of any enactment which requires the consent of more than one person in a matter affecting the child.

---

[95] Specific provision is made for those holding parental responsibility under a special guardianship order. See CA 1989, s 14C(1)(b), (2) and (3).

The only statutory restriction on this right of unilateral action is that a person exercising parental responsibility must not act incompatibly with a court order.[96]

Law Commission, Family Law, *Review of Child Law: Guardianship and Custody*, Law Com No 172 (London: HMSO, 1988c)

2.11 Allied to this is the principle that parents should not lose their parental responsibility even though its exercise may have to be modified or curtailed in certain respects, for example, if it is necessary to determine where a child will live after his parents separate. Obviously, a court order to that effect will put many matters outside the control of the parent who does not have the child with him. However, parents should not be regarded as losing their position, and their ability to take decisions about their children, simply because they are separated or in dispute with one another about a particular matter. Hence they should only be prevented from acting in ways which would be incompatible with an order made about the child's upbringing. If, for example, the child has to live with one parent and go to a school near home, it would be incompatible with that order for the other parent to arrange for him to have his hair done in a way which will exclude him from the school. It would not, however, be incompatible for that parent to take him to a particular sporting occasion over the weekend, no matter how much the parent with whom the child lived might disapprove. These principles form part of our general aim of "lowering the stakes" in cases of parental separation and divorce, and emphasising the continued responsibility of both parents...

Although a right of unilateral action avoids potential difficulties in trying to locate and obtain the agreement of an estranged parent, such an approach creates the possibility of members of the 'parenting team' taking contradictory decisions and undermining one another's care of the child. This is a particular concern for the resident parent who bears the burden of the day-to-day decision-making. As seen above, this issue has been raised in a number of s 4 applications where the mother has argued that parental responsibility may be misused by the father to exercise control over her and undermine her care of the child. In response to these concerns, the case law has stressed that such fears are based on a misunderstanding of the nature of a parental responsibility order: in particular, it does not provide a mandate for the non-resident carer to interfere in the day-to-day decision-making of the resident parent.[97] However, the non-resident parent's limited ability to participate in routine decisions about the child's day-to-day care does not exhaust the purpose and scope of parental responsibility. With respect to more important decisions concerning a child's upbringing, the position as regards consultation between the holders of parental responsibility is very different.

Despite the statutory basis for unilateral decision-making under s 2(7), the courts have imposed a duty to *consult* and, in effect, *agree* on certain important matters regarding the child's upbringing. The first case to suggest such a duty was *Re G (Parental Responsibility: Education)*. The case concerned a dispute between the child's parents over which school the child should attend. On the advice of the child's current headmaster, the child's father, with whom the child had lived since the parents' separation, wished the child to attend a local authority boarding school. The child's mother, who only became aware of the father's intentions at the eleventh hour, was strongly opposed to this course of action. She applied for an

---

[96] CA 1989, s 2(8).
[97] *Re P (A minor) (Parental Responsibility Order)* [1994] 1 FLR 578.

ex parte prohibited steps order[98] preventing the father from sending the child to the school until her own application for a residence order could be determined. The application was dismissed, but, on appeal, the Court of Appeal made it clear that the mother should have been properly consulted over such an important decision.

Re G (Parental Responsibility: Education) [1995] 2 FCR 53, 56 (CA)

Lord Justice Glidewell:

The great difficulty is, of course, on the one hand that the mother was not informed of the decision to send the boy to the boarding school and there is no doubt she should have been. Under s. 2 of the Children Act 1989 she has parental responsibility for both children, even though they are not living with her . . .

So far no order has been made in respect of which the father is acting incompatibly, but equally there is no doubt, to my mind, that the mother, having parental responsibility, was entitled to and indeed ought to have been consulted about the important step of taking her child away from the day school that he had been attending and sending him to a boarding school. It is an important step in any child's life and she ought to have been consulted. Whether the local authority ought to have informed her I am not prepared to say, but that the father should have done I at once accept.

Support for imposing a duty to consult was taken a step further in *Re C (Minors) (Change of Surname)*, which concerned the mother's wish to change the children's surname from that of her former husband to that of her new husband. Following the parents' divorce it was agreed that the children would live with their mother and no residence order was therefore made. The children's contact with their father ceased just before the mother remarried. The fact that there was no residence order in force was significant because under s 13(1) of the CA 1989, had such an order been made, the mother would not have been able to change their surname without the written consent of everyone with parental responsibility or without first obtaining leave of the court. However, following her remarriage, and on the advice of her solicitor, the mother attempted to change the children's surnames by deed poll without consulting her former husband or obtaining his agreement. Steps were then taken for the new surname to be used at official levels such as at school and on medical files. However, whilst the GP was happy to adopt the new surname, the headmaster and the local education authority requested confirmation that everyone with parental responsibility had consented to the change before being prepared to amend their records. In light of the position taken by the local authority, the mother applied for a specific issue order[99] requiring them to acknowledge and adopt the children's new surname. Holman J held that despite the various legislative provisions suggesting a unilateral right of action, on a matter as important as changing the child's surname, all those with parental responsibility should have been *consulted and their agreement* obtained.[100]

---

[98] For further explanation, see 11.6.

[99] For further explanation, see 11.6.

[100] It has subsequently been suggested by the Court of Appeal that where one parent seeks to change the surname by which a child is known (usually the registered surname), the obligation to obtain the consent of all parents will apply regardless of whether a residence order is in force and regardless of which of the parents has parental responsibility. If the parent withholds consent, the leave of the court will be required. See *Dawson v Wearmouth* [1998] Fam 75.

Re C (Minors) (Change of Surname) [1997] 3 FCR 310, 312–19 (Fam Div)

Mr Justice Holman:

Introduction and background

This case...raises [a] question of considerable general importance...whether...one of two or more people who each have parental responsibility for a child can, lawfully, unilaterally cause that child to be known by a new surname without the consent of the other or others...

The argument for the mother

[Counsel's] argument was, in essence, as follows. Section 2(7) provides that where two or more people have parental responsibility each of them may act alone subject to any enactment which requires the consent of more than one person. In relation to a change of name the only relevant enactments are s. 13(1) and s. 33(7) [where the child is in the care of the local authority subject to a care order]. They do not apply to this case since there is no residence or care order in force. Further, in private law cases, s. 13 provides an exhaustive statutory "code" of the circumstances in which the consents of all people having parental responsibility is required. Accordingly the mother had the right and power to change the surname...

In my judgment the conclusion and consequences of this argument are little short of bizarre. Where parents have not agreed about their child or not been able to trust each other so that a residence order has had to be made...the "rights" of both parents in relation to a change of name are carefully preserved; whereas where parents have been able to agree and have not caused or risked harm to their children, the "rights" of either parent can be unilaterally overborne by the other. Further, there would technically, and unless the mother obtained a court order, have been nothing to stop the father in the present case subsequently exercising *his* parental responsibility and executing another deed of name change, which would of course lead to chaos and be potentially very damaging to the children.

Moreover the argument, if correct, would run totally counter to the philosophy of the Children Act, for it would be likely to lead to an insistence on formal residence orders even when the parents were in complete agreement about the issue of with whom the child should live...In my judgment, Parliament neither intended nor enacted the result which the mother contends for...

Holman J went on to hold that the scope of parental responsibility as enshrined in the CA 1989 should be understood in light of any pre-existing limitations on parents' rights and responsibilities contained in the case law and/or legislation. He thus turned to examine the legal position on changing a child's surname as derived from the case law prior to the enactment of the CA 1989:

Analysis

The key is the meaning of "parental responsibility" in s. 3(1), namely "all the rights, duties, powers, responsibilities and authority which by law a parent of a child has in relation to the child and his property". In order to determine what rights, duties, powers, responsibilities and authority a parent actually has, it is necessary to look at the law. Where some provision of the Children Act or some other enactment is exhaustive, then of course that defines "the law". But vast areas of the law of parental responsibility are still derived from, and to be found in, the common law or a mixture of common law and statute...

In cases where there is no residence order, the old law derived from *Y. v Y.* still holds good. "By law" a parent of a child does not have a right, power or authority unilaterally to change its surname without the consent or agreement of the other parent if the child is legitimate. The very right or power itself only exists in law as a bilateral right or power, which is only capable of being exercised jointly with the other parent. So in relation to a change of surname, s. 3(1) has the effect that parental responsibility means a right or power jointly exercisable with all other persons having parental responsibility. The words "but nothing in this Part shall be taken to affect the operation of any enactment which requires the consent of more than one person in a matter affecting the child" in s. 2(7) do not preclude that the consent of more than one person may also be required by some other source of law than an enactment, notwithstanding the first limb of s. 2(7).

Eekelaar strongly criticized this decision, fearing it could be of much wider application.

J. Eekelaar, 'Do parents have a duty to consult?', (1998b) 114 *Law Quarterly Review* 337, 337–40

When two parents have parental responsibility, must one consult the other over important decisions regarding the child?…In 1988 the Law Commission thought it had resolved the question. "Whether or not the parents are living together, a legal duty of consultation seems both unworkable and undesirable" said the Law Commission, and recommended accordingly, but added that "this will not, of course, affect any statutory provision which requires the consent of each parent, for example, to the adoption of the child."…

[In *Re C*] Holman J held that [s 2(7)] did not "preclude that the consent of more than one person may also be required by some other source of law than an enactment, notwithstanding the first limb of s. 2(7)". He found such a source in the law as it existed prior to the implementation of section 2(7) which, in his view, prevented the parent of a legitimate child from changing its surname without the consent of the other parent.

…[I]t is certainly arguable that under a combination of statute and common law prior to the Children Act 1989 there was a legal duty to consult over "important" matters and that, if the second parent disagreed, the parent with the children could not act without permission of the court.

But this can hardly sustain the basis of Holman J.'s conclusion in [*Re C*]. For the Children Act 1975 was repealed by the Children Act 1989 and cannot form the source of rights thereafter and to hold that the common law position (whatever it was immediately before the implementation of the 1989 Act) overrides section 2(7) is to make the statute subject to the prior law it purported to replace and deprives it of all effect. An argument might be attempted that section 2(7) is consistent with the perpetuation of a duty to consult on the ground that all it does is to clarify that, should consultation fail to bring about agreement, either parent may take action "without the other" leaving the aggrieved party to seek eventual resolution of the dispute in court. Such an interpretation would depart from the intentions of the Law Commission…but there must now be some danger that it could be accepted…

It is suggested that the Law Commission was right in thinking that a general duty to consult would be unworkable. Apart from the problem of defining the range of issues upon which consultation would be required (what are "serious" issues? choice of school, probably; choice of curriculum, of extra-curricular activities? perhaps, perhaps not), what amounts to consultation or attempts at consultation? It cannot be sound policy to provide parties with increased opportunities for legal conflict and dispute…In most cases the best safeguard against surprise decisions lies in the hands of the outside parent. If he sees his children regularly, he will normally know about these "important issues", or will discover them quickly. It is striking that in [*Re C*] the attempt to change the children's name occurred only after direct contact between the father and the children had stopped for over a year. It is difficult to justify imposing a general duty to consult on the parent who is looking after the children when the other parent is not under a legally enforceable duty to involve himself with (or even visit) the children (and nor could such a duty be realistically imposed).

Holman J. commented that if the parents retained the right to independent action, there would have been nothing to stop the father from exercising *his* parental authority and executing another deed of name change, causing "chaos" and being potentially very damaging to the children. This argument against independent action could be made with respect to any exercise of parental responsibility, but is a red herring. Parental responsibility can best be understood as the legitimation of *practical actions* in exercising parenthood. A parent who is not actively involved in a child's life cannot effectively bring about a change in the name by which the child is known. Of course, should he attempt to do so and thus come into conflict with the other parent, the matter would need to be resolved by a court. But that would equally be the case if there was a requirement for his consent.

Indeed, Eekelaar's concern that, following *Re C*, a more general duty to consult and obtain agreement on a wide range of 'important' decisions might be imposed, has been borne out by the subsequent case law. Circumcision and immunization[101] have recently been added to the 'small group of important decisions'[102] on which consultation is necessary.

Re J (child's religious upbringing and circumcision) [2000] 1 FCR 307 (CA)

DAME ELIZABETH BUTLER-SLOSS P:

There is, in my view, a small group of important decisions made on behalf of a child which, in the absence of agreement of those with parental responsibility, ought not to be carried out or arranged by a one-parent carer although she has parental responsibility under s 2(7) of the Children Act 1989. Such a decision ought not to be made without the specific approval of the court. Sterilisation is one example. The change of a child's surname is another. Some of the examples, including the change of a child's surname, are based upon statute (see s 13(1) of the 1989 Act).

The issue of circumcision has not, to my knowledge, previously been considered by this court, but in my view it comes within that group. The decision to circumcise a child on grounds, other than medical necessity is a very important one; the operation is irreversible, and should only be carried out where the parents together approve of it or, in the absence of parental agreement, where a court decides that the operation is in the best interests of the child.

The problem with this approach is the considerable uncertainty it causes. Thus, whilst it is now clear that certain specific issues—schooling; change of surname; circumcision; sterilization; and immunization—fall within the class of case where consultation and agreement is necessary, other decisions potentially falling within this group will have to be determined on a case by case basis. The case law provides little guidance as to whether any particular

---

[101] *Re C (Welfare of child: immunisation)* [2003] EWHC 1376.
[102] Ibid., [16]–[17].

decision will be regarded as sufficiently important as to require consultation. In *Re J* Thorpe LJ suggested that such decisions should be regarded as exceptional and both Thorpe LJ and Butler-Sloss P pointed to the irreversible nature of a decision regarding circumcision. However, neither changing a child's surname nor decisions as to which school a child should attend can properly be regarded as irreversible. This alone cannot therefore be the distinguishing feature. Predictably, the growing list of issues on which consultation is required has led to increasing concern that the autonomy of the primary carer are being undermined. In particular, it is feared that the line between the exception and the rule i.e. those day-to-day decisions which should be regarded as more properly lying within the sole decision-making authority of the residential parent, is gradually being eroded. This concern is exacerbated by the approach adopted in *Re C (Welfare of child: immunisation)*.[103] Sumner J was keen to point out that although the particular bond between a child and its primary carer may be a relevant consideration when determining the welfare of the child, once a dispute of this nature reaches the court both parents have equal standing with no particular preference being afforded to the wishes and feelings of the resident parent.

The proper mechanism for resolving disputes between those holding parental responsibility is to apply for a specific issue or prohibited steps order under s 8 of the CA 1989 or, if the CA 1989 cannot provide an appropriate remedy, to invoke the inherent jurisdiction of the court.[104] In determining the dispute the child's welfare is the paramount consideration.

10.4.2 LIMITATIONS ON THE EXERCISE OF PARENTAL RESPONSIBILITY

The need for consultation and agreement between the holders of parental responsibility can serve as an important limitation on the decision-making authority of a parent. However, even where there is agreement their authority may still be subject to challenge by a third party. There are two major sources of external restraint on the decision-making authority of those holding parental responsibility: (i) the child and (ii) the state.

The *Gillick* competent child

Following the decision of the House of Lords in *Gillick v West Norfolk and Wisbech Health Authority*,[105] it is now well established that where children are of sufficient understanding to be deemed capable of making their own decisions, the child's parents lose their *exclusive* decision-making powers with respect to the care and upbringing of the child. As interpreted in the subsequent case law, *Gillick* competent children have the right, alongside their parents, to provide a valid consent on a range of important matters, such as contraception and medical treatment. As decision-making authority is effectively shared between them, neither the parent nor the child has a right of veto. Consequently, if, for example, the child and the parents are in dispute over the child's medical treatment, the doctors can proceed provided they have the consent of *either* the parents or the child.[106]

---

[103] Ibid. For a good critique of this decision see O'Donnell (2004).
[104] *Re T (A Minor) (Child: Representation)* [1994] Fam 49. See also *Re R (A minor) (Blood transfusion)* [1993] 2 FLR 757.
[105] [1986] AC 112.
[106] For detailed discussion see 8.5.4.

The state

A second and potentially more powerful constraint on the decision-making authority of those with parental responsibility is the state. Current policy generally dictates that parents should be left to raise their children as they see fit. Parental autonomy and protecting the privacy of the family unit against unnecessary intervention are seen as serving the child's interests (and thereby those of the state). With respect to the vast majority of decisions regarding the child's upbringing, the autonomy and authority of those holding parental responsibility is therefore respected.[107] However, the state retains the authority to override the unanimous wishes of those with parental responsibility where such intervention is necessary to protect the health and welfare of the child.[108]

It would generally be agreed that whatever rights a child's parents may have, they do not have the right to harm the child. There would probably also be general agreement that it is a legitimate function of the state to intervene into the private decision-making realm of the family to protect a child who is vulnerable to such harm. It is important to remember, however, that not all cases in which the state seeks to intervene concern neglectful or abusive parents whose parenting would otherwise give rise to child protection concerns. Indeed, the parents embroiled in these disputes are most often devoted, committed parents who provide exemplary care. The problem occurs because the state disagrees with the parents' firmly held views as to the child's best interests and the nature of the harm being caused. The state, through the courts, justifies intervening into the private decision-making realm of the family on the basis of its historical obligation to protect the health and welfare of all minors falling within the protective jurisdiction of the Crown. The fundamental question, however, is whether, where the state and the parents disagree as to the child's welfare, the views of the parents or the state should prevail. To put the question another way: is the child's welfare for the individual family or the wider community to determine? For the courts, once their jurisdiction has been invoked, the answer is clear.

In re A (Children) (Conjoined Twins: Surgical Separation) [2001] Fam 147, 178–9 (CA)

WARD LJ:

There is, however, this important safeguard to ensure that a child receives proper treatment. Because the parental rights and powers exist for the performance of their duties and responsibilities to the child and must be exercised in the best interests of the child, "...the common law has never treated such rights as sovereign or beyond review and control": per Lord Scarman in *Gillick* case...

Overriding control is vested in the court. This proposition is well established and has not been the subject of any challenge in this appeal. Because of the comment in the media questioning why the court should be involved, I add this short explanation. Long, long ago the sovereign's prerogative to protect infants passed to the Lord Chancellor and through him to the judges and it forms a part of the inherent jurisdiction of the High Court. The Children Act 1989 now contains a statutory scheme for the resolution of disputes affecting the upbringing of children. If a person having a recognisable interest brings such a dispute to the court, the court must decide it.

---

[107] See O'Donnell (2004), esp. at 223.
[108] Ibid.

The protective jurisdiction of the court is most commonly invoked by a local authority or an NHS Trust seeking to override the unanimous views of those holding parental responsibility where a dispute has arisen over the child's medical treatment. There are two routes by which such a dispute may be brought before the courts: the third party may apply for a specific issue order under s 8 of the CA 1989 which authorizes them to administer or withhold certain treatment against the wishes of those with parental responsibility. Alternatively, the third party can invoke the High Court's inherent jurisdiction. Whichever procedural route is adopted, the welfare of the child is the court's paramount consideration.

The current approach: protecting the child's welfare and the paramountcy principle

The legal principles to be applied in disputes of this nature were set down in one of the most controversial cases to be decided in recent years: *Re T (a minor) (wardship: medical treatment)*. The court was asked to give permission for a liver transplant operation to be performed on a very young child against the wishes of the parents. The unanimous medical view was that without the operation the child would not live beyond two-and-a-half years. The Court of Appeal controversially refused the hospital's application.

Re T (a minor) (wardship: medical treatment) [1997] 1 WLR 242, 253–4 (CA)

WAITE LJ:

The law's insistence that the welfare of a child shall be paramount is easily stated and universally applauded, but the present case illustrates, poignantly and dramatically, the difficulties that are encountered when trying to put it into practice... Loving and devoted parents have taken, after anxious consideration, a decision to withhold consent to operative transplant treatment. Although it is relatively novel treatment, still unavailable in many countries, doctors of the highest expertise have unanimously recommended it for this child on clinical grounds, taking the view that it involves a relatively minor level of risk which they regard as well worth taking in the child's long-term interests (which in this instance include an extension of life itself)...

What is the court to do in such a situation? It is not an occasion—even in an age preoccupied with "rights"—to talk of the rights of a child, or the rights of a parent, or the rights of the court. The cases cited by Butler-Sloss L.J. are uncompromising in their assertion that the sole yardstick must be the need to give effect to the demands of paramountcy for the welfare of the child. They establish that there are bound to be occasions when such paramountcy will compel the court, acting as a judicial parent, to substitute the judge's own views as to the claims of child welfare over those of natural parents—even in a case where the views of the latter are supported by qualities of devotion, commitment, love and reason. The judge, after anxious consideration, reached the conclusion that this case provides such an occasion. Was he right to do so?...

In this instance... I consider that the judge was betrayed into an error of law by his concern with the need to form a judgment about the reasonableness of the mother's approach. An appraisal of parental reasonableness may be appropriate in other areas of family law (in adoption, for example, where it is enjoined by statute) but when it comes to an assessment of the demands of the child patient's welfare, the starting point—and the finishing point too—must always be the judge's own independent assessment of the balance of advantage or disadvantage of the particular medical step under consideration. In striking that balance, the judge will of course take into account as a relevant, often highly relevant, factor the attitude taken by a natural parent, and that may require examination of his or her motives. But the result of such an inquiry must never be allowed to prove determinative. It is a mistake to view the issue as one in which the clinical advice of doctors is placed in one scale and the reasonableness of the parent's view in the other. Had the judge viewed the evidence more broadly from the standpoint of his own perception of the child's welfare when appraised in all its aspects, he would have been bound, in my view, to take significant account of other elements in the case...

All these cases depend on their own facts and render generalisations—tempting though they may be to the legal or social analyst—wholly out of place. It can only be said safely there is a scale, at one end of which lies the clear case where parental opposition to medical intervention is prompted by scruple or dogma of a kind which is patently irreconcilable with principles of child health and welfare widely accepted by the generality of mankind; and that at the other end lie highly problematic cases where there is genuine scope for a difference of view between parent and judge. In both situations it is the duty of the judge to allow the court's own opinion to prevail in the perceived paramount interests of the child concerned, but in cases at the latter end of the scale, there must be a likelihood (though never of course a certainty) that the greater the scope for genuine debate between one view and another the stronger will be the inclination of the court to be influenced by a reflection that in the last analysis the best interests of every child include an expectation that difficult decisions affecting the length and quality of its life will be taken for it by the parent to whom its care has been entrusted by nature.

Several important principles emerge from the Court of Appeal's judgments in *Re T*. All three members of the Court made it clear that it is the paramountcy principle alone which applies. The courts are not therefore engaged in reviewing the parents' decision to determine whether it falls within a band of reasonable responses, with the court only being free to override the views of the parents if their decision is deemed unreasonable. The courts must undertake their own independent assessment of the child's welfare *de novo*. That is not to say that the views of the parents are irrelevant. Indeed, the Court of Appeal recognize that the parents' wishes may be crucial to the child's welfare if their opposition to the proposed course of action will directly impact upon the quality of care the child will receive or necessitate alternative care being sought. Furthermore, Waite LJ suggests that where the welfare arguments are finely balanced, the parents' reasonable views may carry considerable force. In such marginal cases, Waite LJ indicates that it would be appropriate to fall back on the principle that it is generally in the child's best interests for such difficult decisions to be taken by the people who care for and know the child best. In this case, the fact that the parents were well-informed health professionals, experienced in caring for sick children, seemed to add force to the Court of Appeal's view that, when all the relevant factors were taken into account, the parents' decision should be accorded significant weight within the welfare assessment.[109]

Whilst *Re T* was clearly exceptional, the legal principles set down by the Court of Appeal have been consistently applied in the case law. However, in *Re C (HIV Test)*, the court's attitude towards the parents' views was very different. In *Re C* the mother was HIV positive. The parents held unconventional views as to the diagnosis, cause, and appropriate treatment of HIV and therefore opposed the child, aged five months, being tested for the virus, maintaining that even if she tested positive they would not be prepared to consent to conventional treatment, preferring to rely on a healthy, holistic lifestyle. The mother was also determined to continue

---

[109] Downie (2000), 198.

breastfeeding despite the increased risks of transmitting the disease to the child. Wilson J, whose decision was upheld by the Court of Appeal, granted the local authority's application for the child to be temporarily removed from her parents and tested. By the time the case was heard by the Court of Appeal, the parents had left the country, taking the child with them.

Re C (HIV Test) [1999] 2 FLR 1004, 1006–17 (Fam Div)

WILSON J:

The parents contend that the application for an order is an affront to their parental autonomy...[W]elfare shall be the paramount consideration in my determination of this application.

[I]n some, if not all, circumstances [is] it possible, and, if so, helpful, to discern in the law a rebuttable presumption that the united appraisal of both parents will be correct in identifying where the welfare of their child lies. Support for that proposition is arguably derived from s 1(5) of the 1989 Act, which prohibits the court from making any order under the Act unless it considers that to do so would be better for the child than not to do so. Not to do so is to leave the decision in the hands of those with parental responsibility for the child; and so any applicant for an order has, in effect, to persuade the court that there are positive grounds for taking the matter out of those hands. Furthermore, under Art 8...the parents and the baby all have a right to respect for their family life...

I collect from *Re T* the proposition that the views of these parents, looked at widely and generously, are an important factor in the decision, even, to some extent, irrespectively of the validity of the underlying grounds for their views.

But *Re T* also shows that the views of the parents may have another significance. The intervention proposed for the child may be, in effect, unworkable without their consent...A different, yet allied, situation may arise where to override the parents' wishes is to risk causing them such emotional distress as will disable them from caring properly for the child or, at any rate, as will indirectly affect the child's own emotional stability to a significant extent.

For all these reasons a court invited to override the wishes of parents must move extremely cautiously...

The concluding words of the father's eloquent final submissions were these: 'Whatever the outcome of this case, we would have lost if we had not stood up for our rights.' But this case is not at heart about the rights of the parents. And if...the father regards the rights of a tiny baby as subsumed within the rights of the parents, he is wrong. This baby has rights of her own. They can be considered nationally or internationally.

[Wilson J then set down Articles 5, 6, and 24 of the UNCRC 1989 before confirming that under national law the case must be decided on the basis of the child's welfare. He went on to conclude that the arguments in favour of testing the baby were overwhelming.]

This conclusion was strongly endorsed by the Court of Appeal:

Re C (HIV Test) [1999] 2 FLR 1004, 1020–1 (CA)

Butler-Sloss LJ:

[Counsel] says that there has to be a space within which parents can reject the current orthodoxy, even though that may be based upon good medical evidence. There is an alternative view. They should be entitled to parental autonomy to make that choice, and that is something with which the courts should not intervene. He says that this is a continuing and developing area of medicine and that the parents ought to be free to make these decisions without the interference of the court...

The issue before this court is an issue of knowledge. What is the position of this child? In my view, the child is clearly at risk if there is ignorance of the child's medical condition. The degree of intrusion into the child of a medical test is slight. The degree of intrusion into the family of taking the child to the hospital for a medical test would for most people be comparatively slight. The parents have magnified this into a major issue because they do not accept any of the premises upon which the tests will be carried out. But the welfare of the child is paramount. The court has been asked to deal with the case. It cannot shirk its duty. The space sought by [counsel], which is a space in which parental decisions are final, undoubtedly exists, but it exists subject to s 1(1) of the Children Act. It does not matter whether the parents are responsible or irresponsible. It matters whether the welfare of the child demands that such a course should be taken...We are not talking about the rights of parents. We are talking about the rights of the child. Wilson J set out various Articles of the UN Convention on the Rights of the Child 1989. We do not in a sense need that. It is all encapsulated in s 1 of the Children Act, but it does give added strength to this most important of all points, that the parents' views, which are not the views of the majority, cannot stand against the right of the child to be properly cared for in every sense.

In accordance with *Re T*, the parents' views in *Re C (HIV Test)* were again mitigated through the welfare principle with the result that their somewhat unorthodox position was overruled by the court. Although there are undoubtedly some who would support the parents' approach, the weight of evidence before the judge provided no support for the parents' arguments. *Re C* perhaps therefore provides an example of the type of views described by Waite LJ in *Re T* as promoted by nothing more than 'scruple or dogma', totally and patently inconsistent with the child's welfare. Clearly, Waite LJ did not anticipate that such views should be accorded any great respect when carrying out the welfare assessment, and that is borne out by the decision in *Re C*.

Where there is room for genuine debate as to the child's interests and the parents adopt an entirely reasonable position within that debate, *Re T* suggested that their views would be treated with greater respect. This was put to the test in *Re A*, the case of the conjoined twins. The hospital treating the twins wished to undertake separation surgery to save the life of the stronger twin, Jodie, with the inevitable result that the weaker twin, Mary, would die. Without surgery, the prognosis for both twins was very poor, with the doctors predicting both twins would die within a few months. The parents, who were Roman Catholics with strong religious views on the matter, as well as practical concerns about raising a severely disabled child on the remote island where they lived, opposed the operation. As the huge media debate concerning this case indicates, there was scope for genuine disagreement amongst reasonable people as to what course of action would best serve the interests of the children. This was therefore one of those difficult, marginal cases in which deference to the parents' views might have been expected.

In re A (Children) (Conjoined Twins: Surgical Separation) [2001] Fam 147 (CA)

WARD LJ:

9. Giving due weight to the parents' wishes

9.1 The parents and the courts

...Since the parents have the right in the exercise of their parental responsibility to make the decision, it should not be a surprise that their wishes should command very great respect.

Parental right is, however, subordinate to welfare. That was the view of the House of Lords in In Re *KD (A Minor) (Ward: Termination of Access)* [1998] AC 806, 824–825 where Lord Oliver of Aylmerton said:

"...Parenthood, in most civilised societies, is generally conceived of as conferring upon parents the exclusive privilege of ordering, within the family, the upbringing of children of tender age, with all that that entails. That is a privilege which, interfered with without authority, would be protected by the courts, but it is a privilege circumscribed by many limitations imposed both by the general law and, where circumstances demand, by the courts or by the authorities upon whom the legislature has imposed the duty of supervising the welfare of children and young persons. When the jurisdiction of the court is invoked for the protection of the child the parental privileges do not terminate. They do, however, become immediately subservient to the paramount consideration which the court has always in mind, that is to say, the welfare of the child...".

In *J v C* [1970] AC 668, 715 Lord McDermott set out the rule which has served the test of time:

"While there is now no rule of law that the rights and wishes of unimpeachable parents must prevail over other considerations, such rights and wishes, recognised as they are by nature and society, can be capable of ministering to the total welfare of the child in a special way and must therefore preponderate in many cases. The parental rights, however, remain qualified and not absolute for the purposes of the investigation, the broad nature of which is still as described in the fourth of the principles enunciated by FitzGibbon LJ in *In Re O'Hara* [1990] 2 IR 232, 240."

That fourth principle, which itself was derived from *R v Gyngall* [1893] 2 QB 232, is stated thus:

"4. In exercising the jurisdiction to control or to ignore the parental right the court must act cautiously, not as if it were a private person acting with regard to his own child, and acting in opposition to the parent only when judicially satisfied that the welfare of the child requires that the parental right be suspended or superseded."

Finally, it is perhaps useful to repeat the passage in the judgment of Sir Thomas Bingham MR in *In Re Z (A Minor) (Identification: Restrictions on Publication)* [1997] Fam 1, 32–33, in accordance with which Johnson J approached this part of the case. Sir Thomas Bingham MR said:

"I would for my part accept without reservation that the decision of a devoted and responsible parent should be treated with respect. It should certainly not be disregarded or lightly set aside. But the role of the court is to exercise an independent and objective judgment. If that judgment is in accord with that of the devoted and responsible parent, well and good. If it is not, then it is the duty of the court after giving due weight to the view of the devoted and responsible parent, to give effect to its own judgment. That is what it is there for. Its judgment may of course be wrong. So may that of the parent. But once the jurisdiction of the court is invoked its clear duty is to reach and give the best judgment that it can."

That is the law. That is what governs my decision. That is what I am desperately trying to do...

9.2 The role of the court: reviewer or decision-maker?

Is the court reviewing the parental decision as it reviews an administrative decision or does the court look at the matter afresh, in the round, with due weight given to the parental wish? If there was doubt about that, it has been resolved in favour of the latter approach by the decision of this court in In Re *T (A Minor) (Wardship: Medical Treatment)* [1997] 1 WLR 242...

9.3 The weight to be given to these parents' wishes

I would wish to say emphatically that this is not a case where opposition is "prompted by scruple or dogma." The views of the parents will strike a chord of agreement with many who reflect upon their dilemma. I cannot emphasise enough how much I sympathise with them in the cruelty of the agonising choice they had to make. I know because I agonise over the dilemma too. I fear, however, that the parents' wish does not convince me that it is in the children's best interest:

(i) From Jodie's point of view they have taken the worst possible scenario that she would be wheelchair bound, destined for a life of difficulty. They fail to recognise her capacity sufficiently to enjoy the benefits of life that would be available to her were she free and independent.

(ii) She may indeed need special care and attention and that may be very difficult fully to provide in their home country. This is a real and practical problem for the family, the burden of which in ordinary family life should not be underestimated. It may seem unduly harsh on these desperate *parents* to point out that it is the *child's* best interests which are paramount, not the *parents'*. Coping with a disabled child sadly inevitably casts a great burden on parents who have to struggle through these difficulties. There is, I sense, a lack of consistency in their approach to their daughters' welfare. In Mary's case they are overwhelmed by the legitimate, as I have found it to be, need to respect and protect her right to life. They surely cannot so minimise Jodie's rights on the basis that the burden of possible disadvantage for her and the burdens of caring for such a child for them can morally be said to outweigh her claim to the human dignity of independence which only cruel fate has denied her.

(iii) They are fully entitled to recoil at the idea, as they see it, of killing Mary. That is wholly understandable. This lies at the core of their objection. Yet they came to this country for treatment. They were aware of the possibility that Mary might be stillborn and they seemed reconciled to an operation which would separate Jodie from her. They seemed to have been prepared, and presented their case to Johnson J on the basis that they would agree to the operation if Mary predeceased Jodie. The physical problems for Jodie would be the same, perhaps even worse in such an event. The parents appear to have been willing to cope in any event, and the burdens for parents and child cannot have changed. Mary is lost to them anyway.

(iv) In their natural repugnance at the idea of killing Mary they fail to recognise their conflicting duty to save Jodie and they seem to exculpate themselves from, or at least fail fully to face up to, the consequence of the failure to separate the twins, namely, death for Jodie. In my judgment, parents who are placed on the horns of such a terrible dilemma simply have to choose the lesser of their inevitable loss. If a family at the gates of a concentration camp were told they might free one of their children but if no choice were made both would die, compassionate parents with equal love for their twins would elect to save the stronger and see the weak one destined for death pass through the gates.

This is a terribly cruel decision to force upon the parents. It is a choice no loving parent would ever want to make. It gives me no satisfaction to have disagreed with their views of what is right for their family and to have expressed myself in terms they will feel are harshly and unfairly critical of them. I am sorry about that. It may be no great comfort to them to know that in fact my heart bleeds for them. But if, as the law says I must, it is I who must now make the decision, then whatever the parents' grief, I must strike a balance between the twins and do what is best for them.

[The Court of Appeal went on to hold that it would be in the twins' best interests for the operation to separate them to be performed.]

The parents' views were similarly rejected in the case of Charlotte Wyatt. The Wyatt case is significant because whereas *Re T*, *Re C*, and *Re A* all concerned intervention by the medical authorities with a view to prolonging the life of a vulnerable infant, the Wyatt case raised the opposite question: the proceedings were brought by the NHS Trust with a view to with-holding potentially life-prolonging treatment against the parents' wishes. Cases such as this raise important questions about the appropriate distribution of NHS resources and whether the state is under a positive duty to preserve life at all costs, particularly as advances in tech-nology mean that patients can be kept alive for much longer periods, even though suffering from the most severe disabilities and with little or no prospect of recovery. The Wyatt case was not, however, argued on this basis, the court simply focusing on the competing views of the doctors and the parents as to the child's best interests. Charlotte had been born at just 26 weeks gestation and was severely disabled. The issue was whether, should her breath-ing deteriorate, she should be given artificial ventilation to keep her alive, even though the chances of her surviving another 12 months, even with such intervention, were minimal. Again, whilst the court listened carefully to the parents' wishes and expressed great sympa-thy for their views, the court, in discharging its paramount obligation to protect the child's welfare, preferred the unanimous view of the medical professionals that artificial ventilation should not be pursued.

Re Wyatt (a child) (medical treatment: parents' consent) [2004] EWHC 2247 (Fam)

Mr Justice Hedley:

The Law to be Applied

21. This case evokes some of the fundamental principles that undergird our humanity. They are not to be found in Acts of Parliament or decisions of the courts but in the deep recesses of the common psyche of humanity whether they be attributed to humanity being created in the image of God or whether it be simply a self-defining ethic of a generally acknowledged humanism...

22. Charlotte, of course, is a baby. Whilst the sanctity of her life and her right to dignity are to be respected, she can exercise no choice of her own. In those circumstances someone must choose for her. That is usually her parents but here it is the court. That choice must be exercised on the basis of what is in her best interests. It is the understanding and application of that concept that presents the true difficulty in this kind of case.

23. Best interests must be given a generous interpretation...

25. In the course of argument the European Convention on Human Rights was referred to but no separate submissions were developed even though key rights are undoubtedly engaged. That was because although English domestic law has undoubtedly been signifi-cantly affected by the concept of Convention rights, it is recognised that in this case at least the convention now adds nothing to domestic law...

The Views of the Parents

32. Although this forms part of the consideration of best interests, it is a matter of suf-ficient importance to be dealt with in its own right. There is no doubt these parents have not relinquished hope and do not wish to accept Charlotte's death as inevitable. There is no doubt as to the genuineness of their view nor is there any doubt that they believe that they are in Charlotte's best interests. Moreover, there is no doubt that they have thought long and hard

about the issues that confront them. Their views must be entitled to the greatest respect but what weight is to be attached to them?

33. There is no doubt that the law places final responsibility on the judge. This is not because parliament has expressly said so, though of course it could and indeed might, but because the court is discharging its historic duty of overseeing the best interests of those who, for whatever reason, cannot make decisions for themselves. So although I have no doubt about the law, it leaves me a little uncomfortable. Under Part IV of the Children Act 1989 the State is only entitled to intervene in private family life if it can establish a factual basis for doing so by at least showing a risk of significant harm attributable to the care being given to the child. Then, and only then, may a court consider the welfare of the child. Here, of course, no question arises as to the care given to this child; her condition is entirely organic. Nevertheless I am being asked to override the views of these parents as to what is best for their daughter and undoubtedly I have the jurisdiction to do so.

34. I think the only way I can allay my discomfort is to remind myself in my consideration of Charlotte's best interests that Mr and Mrs Wyatt know her best. I should pay proper attention to their intuitive feelings whilst reminding myself that they may project those on to Charlotte. In approaching the case in this way, bearing in mind the breadth of the concept of best interests, I think I come closest to giving proper weight to their views whilst discharging the responsibility placed on the court.

Court's Conclusions on Best Interests

38. I have given this case my most anxious and closest attention. I am only too aware of my own limitations in making so momentous a decision. Yet in the end I have come to a clear view. Subject to two observations that I wish to make at the end of this judgment, I do not believe that any further aggressive treatment, even if necessary to prolong life, is in her best interests. I know that that may mean that she may die earlier than otherwise she might have done but in my judgment the moment of her death will only be slightly advanced. I have asked myself: what can now be done to benefit Charlotte? I can only offer three answers: first, that she can be given as much comfort and as little pain as possible; secondly, that she can be given as much time as possible to spend physically in the presence of and in contact with her parents; thirdly, that she can meet her end whenever that may be in what Mr Wyatt called the TLC of those who love her most. Although I believe and find that further invasive and aggressive treatment would be intolerable to Charlotte, I prefer to determine her best interests on the basis of finding what is the best that can be done for her.

39. In reaching that view I have of course been informed by the medical evidence as to the prospects and cost to her of aggressive treatment. I hope, however, that I have looked much wider than that and seen not just a physical being but a body, mind and spirit expressed in a human personality of unique worth who is profoundly precious to her parents. It is for that personality of unique worth that I have striven to discern her best interests. It is my one regret that my search has led to a different answer than that sought by these parents.

Hedley J made a declaration permitting the hospital to withhold artificial ventilation from Charlotte should her condition deteriorate.[110]

---

[110] This decision was subsequently reviewed and confirmed by Hedley J following receipt of further medical evidence in *Wyatt v Portsmouth Hospitals NHS Trust and Wyatt (by her guardian) (No 3)* [2005] EWHC 693. Both decisions were subsequently upheld by the Court of Appeal in *Re Wyatt* [2005] EWCA Civ 1181. Following improvements in Charlotte's condition, the declaration that the doctors could discontinue treatment by artificial ventilation was lifted in *Re Wyatt* [2005] EWHC 2293. However, a new declaration was

Although the courts clearly strive to reassure parents that considerable weight will be afforded to their views, the great deference which is shown to the medical authorities in these cases has led to concern that in reality it is the health care professionals, and not the parents or the courts, who are determining the future of these children, even if the views of the children's parents are reasonable.[111] As Huxtable and Forbes suggest, when determining the child's welfare, the courts are prone to fall back on the objective, scientific evidence provided by the medical experts. This is a particular concern if the parents' views are, in contrast, treated with caution because of their inherent lack of objectivity, a factor which appears to have influenced Holman J in another difficult case regarding the withdrawal of treatment from a seriously sick child:

NHS Trust v MB [2006] EWHC 507

Mr Justice Holman:

16. x) The views and opinions of both the doctors and the parents must be carefully considered. Where, as in this case, the parents spend a great deal of time with their child, their views may have particular value because they know the patient and how he reacts so well; although the court needs to be mindful that the views of any parents may, very understandably, be coloured by their own emotion or sentiment. It is important to stress that the reference is to the views and opinions of the parents. Their own wishes, however understandable in human terms, are wholly irrelevant to consideration of the objective best interests of the child save to the extent in any given case that they may illuminate the quality and value to the child of the child/parent relationship...

42....I have to caution myself that [the mother] cannot, because of her relationship, be objective; but it is the fact that no other person has spent so much time with M and been as intimate in their contact with him. I do consider that she is, in various respects, very understandably and humanly, deluding herself.

The father's religious beliefs were similarly dismissed as completely irrelevant to an objective assessment of the child's best interests:

49. The father is a practising Muslim. He said in his written statement : "One of my beliefs is that it is not right for people to choose whether another person should live or die." During the course of his oral evidence he said that he believes no one knows what time someone is born to die. No one knows exactly when the God who gives life takes it. We all have a certain time to die and should leave the decision to God.

50. This case concerns a child who must himself be incapable, by reason of his age, of any religious belief. An objective balancing of his own best interests cannot be affected by whether a parent happens to adhere to one particular belief, or another, or none. I have the utmost respect for the father's religious faith and belief, and for the faith of Islam which he

granted in February 2006 when her condition again deteriorated: *Re Wyatt* [2006] EWHC 319. At the time of writing, Charlotte was doing well. The approach taken to the law by Hedley J in the *Wyatt* decision was subsequently approved by Butler-Sloss P in a similar case concerning a nine-month-old baby suffering from Edwards Syndrome and with respect to whom the hospital trust sought a declaration that it would be lawful not to provide further aggressive treatment by artificial ventilation or cardiac massage. See *Re L (Medical Treatment: Benefit)* [2004] EWHC 2713.

[111] Huxtable and Forbes (2004), 352.

practises and professes. But I regard it as irrelevant to the decision which I have to take and I do not take it into account at all.

This preference for the objectivity of science over faith was reiterated by Holman J in *The NHS Hospital Trust v A*, a case concerning Christian parents.

The NHS Hospital Trust v A [2007] EWHC 1696

68. I have already described (and [counsel] has accepted) the legal approach to faith. The presence or absence of religious faith and belief in either the parents or indeed myself are irrelevant. I must decide this case on the basis of medical knowledge and experience, the evidence, and reason. By definition, a miracle defies medical science and all known experience and reason. Whilst I respect the faith of the parents, I must leave entirely out of account any possibility of a miraculous cure.

Concerns about the way in which the views of parents are treated are clearly important. However, it should be remembered that the court's duty is to the child not the parents and, as the views of the parents carry no *independent* weight once the court has embarked upon its own assessment of the child's interests, the views of the parents, including their religious views, cannot be determinative. Whether this is the correct approach to these cases is a more difficult question.

Would a rights-based approach be preferable?

When faced with such difficult decisions, the courts have typically given only limited consideration to the human rights arguments. However, in all of the cases considered above, a rights-based analysis may well have brought an important and valuable new perspective to the issues. *Re T* may be seen as a substantial victory for the right to parental autonomy. Indeed, the views of the parents were upheld to the extent that the Court of Appeal, in effect, sanctioned the inevitable death of a very young child. For this reason, the decision has been subjected to strong criticism, in particular, for the way in which the interests of the child were subsumed within the interests of the child's mother.[112] Of clear importance in the Court of Appeal's decision was the central role to be played by the mother in the child's post-operative care. However, this welfare-orientated approach arguably led to the fundamental rights of the child, including most remarkably the child's right to life, being marginalized in the decision-making process. Waite LJ was unequivocal that a rights-based analysis was wholly misplaced. However, adopting a rights-based analysis may well have helped the court articulate and give more effective consideration to the different and potentially competing interests of the child.

Whilst a rights-based analysis in *Re T* may well have secured better protection of the child's independent interests, *Re C (HIV Test)* exemplifies the type of dispute in which a rights-based approach may have assisted the child's parents. It is in cases such as *Re C*, where the parents' views are inconsistent with mainstream orthodox thinking and thus are likely to be deemed contrary to the child's best interests, that a rights-based approach would ensure independent weight is accorded to their views. Recognition of the parents' right to decision-making

---

[112] Downie (2000), 200.

autonomy gives the parents the space to reject orthodox opinion and raise their children in accordance with their own values and beliefs, free from the 'tyranny of the majority'. Such a right almost certainly falls within the scope of the parents' right to respect for their private and family life under Article 8 ECHR, at least until the child becomes *Gillick* competent.[113] It is of course true that even adopting a rights-based analysis, the rights of the parents are vulnerable to being overridden by the competing rights of the child: it is unlikely that the court would prioritize the parents' right to autonomy over the child's right to life or a form of medical treatment which the evidence suggests is overwhelmingly in his or her best interests.[114] However, by starting from the position that the parents' decision-making authority should be respected, the rights-based approach does at least demand that the state justifies its intervention as being both necessary and proportionate to the legitimate aim of safeguarding the rights and interests of the child. In those cases which do not involve immediate 'life and death' decisions (which arguably would include *Re C*) or marginal cases where there is genuine debate as to the child's welfare, this burden should be much harder for the state to discharge.

The human rights arguments are clearly important where the interests of the parents and the child are potentially in conflict. However, as the *Wyatt* case demonstrates, a rights-based analysis may be of even greater importance in determining the outcome where the rights of the parents and the child are entirely consistent. In cases such as *Re C (HIV Test)* and *Re A (Conjoined Twins)*, the courts' view that the human rights arguments were of little assistance could be rationalized on the basis that the parents' right to decision-making autonomy would almost certainly be overridden by the competing rights of the child. However, in *Wyatt* the balancing exercise had the potential to take on a very different character. An important dimension of the *Wyatt* case was the possible conflict between the child's rights to life, health, and personal integrity, and the views of the medical authorities as to the child's best interests. Indeed, the rights of the child and the rights of the parents may well have stood on the same side of the scales, underpinning and reinforcing, rather than counter-balancing one another. Given this alliance between the parents' and the child's rights, it would thus be much more difficult for the state to justify overriding the decision-making authority of the child's parents on the basis of the child's interests: an important consideration which the court overlooked by examining the issue through the exclusive prism of the welfare principle.

Although the domestic courts have made only limited reference to human rights arguments, the question has been considered by the European Court of Human Rights in *Glass v United Kingdom*. *Glass* concerned a dispute between the family of a severely disabled child and the hospital where he was being treated for respiratory failure. There was a history of problems between the hospital and the child's mother concerning the child's treatment, in particular as regards the administration of morphine. On this occasion, the doctors took the view that the child was dying and should be given diamorphine to relieve his pain and distress. They also placed a 'Do Not Resuscitate' order on the child's notes without consulting his mother. The mother believed her son was being covertly assisted to die by the use of diamorphine and wanted it stopped. Following a fight between the hospital staff and the child's family, the child was discharged into the care of his mother. Remarkably, given the hospital's view that he was dying, the child recovered. The European Court, applying a human rights framework, found against the UK government. However, the decision was firmly based not on the rights of the mother, but on the rights of the child.

---

[113] This would seem to be implicit in the decision of Silber J in *R (on the application of Axon) v Secretary of State for Health* [2006] EWHC 37, [123]–[132].

[114] Ibid., [44]. See also Downie (2000), 201.

Glass and another v United Kingdom (App No 61827/00, ECHR) (2004)

B. The court's assessment

1. As to the existence of an interference with Article 8

70. The court notes that the second applicant, as the mother of the first applicant—a severely handicapped child—acted as the latter's legal proxy. In that capacity, the second applicant had the authority to act on his behalf and to defend his interests, including in the area of medical treatment. The Government have observed that the second applicant had given doctors at St Mary's Hospital on the previous occasions on which he had been admitted authorisation to pursue particular courses of treatment...However, it is clear that, when confronted with the reality of the administration of diamorphine to the first applicant, the second applicant expressed her firm opposition to this form of treatment. These objections were overridden, including in the face of her continuing opposition. The Court considers that the decision to impose treatment on the first applicant in defiance of the second applicant's objections gave rise to an interference with the first applicant's right to respect for his private life, and in particular his right to physical integrity...It is to be noted that the Government have also laid emphasis on their view that the doctors were confronted with an emergency (which is disputed by the applicants) and had to act quickly in the best interests of the first applicant. However, that argument does not detract from the fact of interference. It is, rather, an argument which goes to the necessity of the interference and has to be addressed in that context...

72. [The court] would further observe that, although the applicants have alleged that the impugned treatment also gave rise to an interference with the second applicant's right to respect for her family life, it considers that it is only required to examine the issues raised from the standpoint of the first applicant's right to respect for his personal integrity, having regard, of course, to the second applicant's role as his mother and legal proxy.

The European Court went on to find against the UK on the narrow basis that the hospital's reasons for failing to refer the dispute to the High Court for resolution before the situation deteriorated and the treatment was imposed on the child against the mother's wishes were unconvincing. The state was therefore unable to justify the prima facie breach of the applicant's Article 8 rights. The Court did not address the wider issue of whether the state had struck an appropriate balance, in general terms, between the decision-making authority of the parents, the medical authorities, and the courts. Indeed, it appeared to give broad approval to the existing regulatory framework for resolving disputes over a child's medical treatment: the failure in this case had been a failure to properly invoke those procedures.

Given the limited grounds of the European Court's decision, it is important not to overstate the significance of this case. However, some commentators have suggested that *Glass* signals an important step towards the re-empowerment of parents. The decision imposes a clear obligation on the medical professionals to listen seriously to the concerns of parents and refer any dispute promptly to the High Court.[115] Of greater significance, however, is the underlying conceptual basis for the decision. The European Court adopts a very different approach from that adopted by the domestic courts. The Court starts from the position that the child has a right to self-determination and personal integrity exercised through proxy decision-makers. Any intervention by the medical professionals without the consent of those with parental responsibility therefore constitutes an interference with the child's rights and needs to be justified by the state in accordance with the requirements of Article 8(2). This principle would

---

[115] Huxtable and Forbes (2004), 352.

seem to apply whether or not the dispute is concerned with giving or withholding treatment. Such an approach reinforces the argument that the preferred locus for decision-making with respect to a child is the parents, not the hospital or the courts, and that the burden of justifying any departure from this position must therefore rest with the state.[116] The approach dictated by the European Court may make it increasingly difficult for the domestic courts to determine these disputes on the basis of the paramountcy principle alone.

10.5 TERMINATING PARENTAL RESPONSIBILITY

10.5.1 MOTHERS, MARRIED FATHERS, AND SECOND FEMALE PARENTS UNDER S 42 OF THE HFEA 2008

The restrictive circumstances under which the parental responsibility of mothers, married fathers, and second female parents under s 42 of the HFEA 2008 can be terminated, emphasizes that despite the occurrence of other events affecting the parties, such as, divorce, separation, or the removal of the children into care, parenthood is a lifelong commitment that cannot simply be surrendered to the state. Indeed, the only way in which the parental responsibility of a child's mother, married father, or second legal parent under s 42 of the HFEA 2008 can be terminated, however uninterested or unsuitable they are, is by making a parental order under s 54 of the HFEA 2008 (surrogacy agreements) or, more commonly, an adoption order. Under these orders the 'parenthood' of the child, including parental responsibility, is transferred to the adopters who, like natural parents, can only be divested of their parental responsibility by a second adoption order.

An adoption order in favour of one legal parent can be used to divest the other legal parent of his or her parental responsibility. However, as noted above, adoption has far-reaching effects on the child's core family relationships beyond the termination of parental responsibility. This use of adoption to deprive an absent, irresponsible, or uninterested parent of parental responsibility is therefore an extreme measure. The issue was considered by the House of Lords in *Re B (A Minor) (Adoption: Natural Parent)*.[117] The child's father, who was worried about the security of his position as the child's residential carer, was seeking an adoption order with the sole purpose of permanently excluding the mother from the child's life.[118] Controversially, Lord Nicholls allowed the adoption order to stand, thereby making the child 'legally motherless', even though the father's position could have been consolidated using alternative, less drastic measures under the CA 1989.[119] The controversy surrounding this case highlights the important question of whether specific provision needs to be made for terminating the parental responsibility of mothers, married fathers, and second female parents under s 42 of the HFEA 2008, akin to the measures in place for terminating the parental responsibility of unmarried fathers, second female parents under s 43 of the HFEA 2008, and step-parents. This additional flexibility in the law, whilst inconsistent with the Children Act policy that 'parenthood is for life', would accommodate the somewhat transient nature of parenting in modern family life, recognizing the reality that there are absent, uninterested parents, who do not have a relationship with their children, and should not have to be consulted on important decisions regarding their upbringing. It would also have

---

[116] Ibid., 353.
[117] [2001] UKHL 70.
[118] This decision is discussed in detail at 13.6.3.
[119] For commentary, see Harris-Short (2002).

the additional benefit of formally acknowledging that the problem of the absent parent is not one restricted to the unmarried father: it is a problem of parenthood not fatherhood.

10.5.2 UNMARRIED FATHERS, SECOND FEMALE PARENTS UNDER S 43 OF THE HFEA 2008, AND STEP-PARENTS

Unmarried fathers

The position of unmarried fathers regarding the acquisition of parental responsibility has improved considerably. However, unlike the parental responsibility of married fathers, the parental responsibility of unmarried fathers may still be terminated on application to the court by another holder of parental responsibility or, with leave, by the child.

Children Act 1989, s 4

(2A) A person who has acquired parental responsibility under subsection (1) [methods by which unmarried fathers may acquire parental responsibility] shall cease to have that responsibility only if the court so orders.

(3) The court may make an order under subsection (2A) on the application—

(a) of any person who has parental responsibility for the child; or

(b) with the leave of the court, of the child himself,

subject, in the case of parental responsibility acquired under subsection 1(c), to section 12(4).

(4) The court may only grant leave under subsection (3)(b) if it is satisfied that the child has sufficient understanding to make the proposed application.

In accordance with s 12(4), a parental responsibility order in favour of an unmarried father cannot be terminated whilst a residence order in his favour is in force.

The principles to be applied in determining an application under ss 4(2A) and 4(3) are set down in *Re P (Terminating Parental Responsibility)*. The father was imprisoned for four-and-a-half years for causing serious non-accidental injuries to the child when she was just nine weeks old. The injuries left the child with severe long-term disabilities and she was taken into care. She was successfully placed with long-term foster carers. The father at first denied causing the injuries and the mother, believing him to be telling the truth, entered into a parental responsibility agreement with him. Upon learning the truth, and fearing that the father intended to destabilize the child's care, the mother applied under s 4 to terminate his parental responsibility. Singer J outlined the principles to be applied before granting the mother's application:

Re P (Terminating Parental Responsibility) [1995] 1 FLR 1048, 1050–4 (Fam Div)

SINGER J:

I start from the proposition that parental responsibility—both wanting to have it and its exercise—is a laudable desire which is to be encouraged rather than rebuffed. So that I think one can postulate as a first principle that parental responsibility once obtained should not be terminated in the case of a non-marital father on less than solid grounds, with a presumption for continuance rather than for termination.

The ability of a mother to make such an application therefore should not be allowed to become a weapon in the hands of the dissatisfied mother of the non-marital child: it should be used by the court as an appropriate step in the regulation of the child's life where the circumstances really do warrant it and not otherwise.

I have been referred in outline to four authorities as to the circumstances in which a court will make an order for parental responsibility on application to it under s 4, notwithstanding maternal opposition and, more particularly, as to the criteria and considerations which are relevant...

Such applications for parental responsibility orders are governed by the considerations set out in s 1(1) of the Children Act, namely that the child's welfare is the court's paramount consideration. I can see no reason why that principle should be departed from in considering the termination of a parental responsibility order or agreement.

Key concepts to the consideration of the making an order are evidence of attachment and a degree of commitment, the presumption being that, other things being equal, a parental responsibility order should be made rather than withheld in an appropriate case...

I believe that it is pertinent to consider on this application whether, were there no agreement or order giving rise to the current existence of parental responsibility and were application made for such an order, what would be the court's response? I have to say, notwithstanding the desirability of fostering good relations between parents and children in the interests of children, I find it difficult to imagine why a court should make a parental responsibility order if none already existed in this case...

I therefore conclude that it is appropriate to make an order as sought under s 4(3) bringing to an end the parental responsibility agreement entered into on 4 June 1992.

Although *Re P* emphasizes that the courts will be reluctant to terminate the parental responsibility of an unmarried father without very good grounds, the fact that the parental responsibility of an unmarried father can be terminated at all is, as discussed above, a continuing source of grievance for paternal rights advocates. However, the argument that it constitutes discrimination against unmarried fathers has been dismissed by the European Court of Human Rights in *B v United Kingdom*.[120]

Second female parents under s 43 of the HFEA 2008

The parental responsibility of a second female parent under s 43 of the HFEA 2008 can be terminated on exactly the same basis as that of an unmarried father.[121]

Step-parents

The parental responsibility of step-parents is also subject to termination on the same basis as that of unmarried fathers and second female parents under s 43 of the HFEA 2008.[122] However, the possibility that the parental responsibility of a step-parent may be terminated on application to the court is considerably less controversial. A step-parent's relationship with a child will usually be very different from that of an unmarried father or second female parent under s 43 of the HFEA 2008, the marriage between the step-parent and one of the

---

120 (App No 39067/97, ECHR) (1999).
121 CA 1989, s 4ZA(4)–(5).
122 Ibid., s 4A.

child's parents constituting the principal link between them. It therefore seems sensible to provide for the termination of the step-parent's parental responsibility should the step-parent's relationship with the child change upon his or her separation or divorce from the child's parent.

10.5.3 GUARDIANS, SPECIAL GUARDIANS, AND OTHERS

Guardians, special guardians, and those holding parental responsibility through a residence order do not have a separate parental responsibility order in their favour: the holding of parental responsibility is regarded as an integral part of the appointment or order made. There are therefore no specific provisions for the termination of parental responsibility where parental responsibility is acquired through one of these mechanisms: it automatically terminates when the relevant appointment or order comes to an end.[123] Similarly, the parental responsibility of a local authority is automatically extinguished when the care order terminates.

10.6 CARING FOR CHILDREN WITHOUT PARENTAL RESPONSIBILITY

There will be many occasions when a child will be cared for by someone who does not have parental responsibility, such as, an unmarried father, a step-parent, a grandparent, a teacher, or a family friend. Without parental responsibility, these carers have no legally recognized decision-making authority. As regards the mundane, day-to-day decisions respecting the child, the carer's lack of parental responsibility poses no particular difficulties. Again, however, there may be problems if more important questions arise. For example, if the child is injured whilst in the care of one of these individuals, decisions may have to be made regarding the child's medical treatment. The position of a carer without parental responsibility is governed exclusively by s 3(5) of the CA 1989.

Children Act 1989, s 3

(5) A person who—

(a) does not have parental responsibility for a particular child; but

(b) has care of the child,
may (subject to the provisions of this Act) do what is reasonable in all the circumstances of the case for the purpose of safeguarding or promoting the child's welfare.

This confers sufficient authority on the carer to make any decisions necessary to safeguard or promote the child's welfare. As there is no case law providing authoritative guidance on the correct interpretation of this provision, its exact meaning is unclear. In practice, it most probably means that where the child is being cared for by individuals on a short-term basis, they will only be able to make urgent decisions regarding, for example, whether the child should receive emergency medical treatment. Where, however, the child is in the more

---

[123] Ibid., ss 12(2) and 14C(1)(a).

permanent care of an individual without parental responsibility, it will confer on the child's carer the necessary authority to make longer-term decisions regarding such things as the child's education or religious upbringing.

10.7 CONCLUSION

Parenthood is a very complex issue with different rights and responsibilities attaching to the two core concepts of legal parenthood and parental responsibility. In many ways, the complexity of the law on this issue is a positive factor. It provides scope for the legal recognition of a range of 'parents'—genetic, intentional, and social—who play an important role in the life of the child. In a social context where family life, including parenting, is increasingly transient, this flexibility in the regulation of the parent–child relationship is a great strength. Whilst the child's immediate family environment may be subject to unsettling changes, English law is able to provide positive support for the child's core relationships.

There are, however, some issues of concern. In recent years, the position of unmarried fathers has generated most debate. However, recent reforms to the birth registration system and s 4 of the CA 1989 have considerably improved the overall picture, such that the argument that unmarried fathers face an unjust struggle to achieve recognition of their parenting role is no longer convincing. Indeed, with the vast majority of unmarried fathers now able to acquire parental responsibility by the mere act of registration (or failing that by a relatively straightforward application to the court), the concern is now the other way. There are clear signs that parental responsibility is losing its distinct identity as a legal mechanism for providing legal recognition and support to those actively involved in raising a child and becoming no more than a useful device to confer enhanced parental status on, for the most part, unmarried fathers in the hope that it will encourage them to assume their parenting responsibilities. By routinely conferring parental responsibility on unmarried fathers, some of whom will play only a limited role in the life of the child, genetic fatherhood is being valorized whilst social parenthood and the actual work of parenting is marginalized. This has particularly worrying implications for mothers who still shoulder the bulk of the actual work and responsibility of parenting. From a position in which the law was dominated by overwhelmingly positive images of mothers as natural committed carers alongside negative stereotypes of unmarried fathers as irresponsible and dangerous, we have moved to a position in which the law on parenthood and parental responsibility is now dominated by assumptions as to the value of genetic fatherhood alongside suspicions about obstructive mothers. As we will see in the next chapter, whilst these changing attitudes towards motherhood and fatherhood and the gendered assumptions which underpin them now permeate family law, they are deeply problematic.

ONLINE RESOURCE CENTRE
Questions, suggestions for further reading, and supplementary materials for this chapter (including updates on developments in this area of family law since this book was published) may be found on the Online Resource Centre at **www.oxfordtextbooks.co.uk/orc/harrisshort_tcm2e/.**

11

PRIVATE DISPUTES OVER CHILDREN

CENTRAL ISSUES

1. When determining any private law dispute over a child's upbringing, the child's welfare is the paramount consideration. However, the 'pure' application of that principle has been compromised to varying degrees by the use of 'assumptions' or 'de facto presumptions' when resolving residence and contact disputes.

2. Many more mothers are granted sole residence of their children than fathers. However, when resolving residence disputes, the courts deny that they are applying a presumption in favour of mothers.

3. Claims that the judiciary are discriminating against fathers in their approach to residence disputes must be examined carefully. The existing division of labour within intact families and the difficulties of 'co-parenting' post-separation make such claims difficult to sustain.

4. The courts are making increased use of shared residence orders as a solution to the problems of post-separation parenting. However, there are strong reasons to doubt whether requiring children to split their time equally between the two parents will commonly prove workable

or fair. The use of shared residence orders for symbolic or psychological reasons has also attracted strong academic criticism.

5. When resolving residence disputes between parents and non-parents, the courts have more openly applied a 'de facto presumption' in favour of the natural parent. Views differ as to whether this privileging of 'genetic' over 'social' parenting can be justified.

6. When resolving contact disputes between parents, the courts again apply a strong 'assumption' or 'de facto presumption' in favour of contact with the non-resident parent (usually the father). It is argued that this presumption is sometimes being applied inappropriately, such that abusive men are being granted contact at the expense of the safety and welfare of women and children.

7. Enforcing contact orders is fraught with difficulty. The courts have recently adopted a more 'hard-line' approach to 'intransigent' mothers. Whether imprisoning the mother for disobeying a contact order can ever be in the child's interests, is a fiercely disputed question.

> 8. The Labour Government introduced important reforms in 2006 aimed at moving contact disputes out of the courts. Through 'soft' tools of persuasion, the government hoped to transform the 'culture' of contact such that it becomes 'socially unacceptable' to deny contact with the non-resident parent.

11.1 INTRODUCTION

Private law disputes are typically, although not exclusively, concerned with disagreements between parents over some aspect of their child's upbringing. Disputes over residence and contact following the parents' separation or divorce are extremely common.[1] They are often amongst the most bitter, heart-wrenching and protracted. Perfect solutions which safeguard the welfare of the child whilst satisfying the wishes of both parties are rarely possible. Children cannot be physically split between two parents, and avoiding a win-lose mentality is difficult. Anger, betrayal, bitterness, and suspicion are just some of the emotions which make these disputes so hard to resolve—this is family law at its most raw.

In the last few years, private law disputes over children, prompted by the antics of groups such as Fathers4Justice, have increasingly attracted the media spotlight. It has become popularly portrayed as the modern-day 'battle of the sexes'. The gender dimension of intra-parental disputes has certainly added a heat and ferocity to the debate which has not always been helpful. Fathers' rights groups, supported by high-profile figures such as Bob Geldof, have launched a highly successful media campaign against what they perceive to be the strong bias in favour of women in this area. Anecdotal, 'tug-of-love' stories in which fathers and children are victimized by malevolent, spiteful, selfish mothers, determined to deprive their children of any meaningful relationship with their fathers, are used to maximum impact. Policy-makers, government ministers, even the judiciary, have, to varying degrees, been receptive to these complaints. On the other hand, women's rights groups have responded with their own accusations of violent and abusive men who have no genuine interest in their children simply using residence and contact disputes to exercise power and control over their former partners. Cutting through the highly charged, and increasingly politicized, rhetoric to get a more balanced perspective on the important gender dimensions of this debate is not easy.[2]

This chapter explores the current legal framework for resolving private law disputes over children. We begin by considering procedural issues germane to all private law disputes, including the extent to which children are able to participate in these proceedings. The four main private law orders available under the Children Act 1989 (CA 1989)—residence orders; contact orders; specific issue orders; and prohibited steps orders—will then be considered, as well as recent initiatives to try and improve the way in which residence and contact disputes are handled. Where relevant, the concerns of fathers' rights groups will be addressed. Whether the vocal complaints of these groups are in fact justified will be discussed in light of the wealth of academic literature on these issues, especially from the feminist school.

---

[1] In 2008, nearly 110,000 children in England and Wales experienced parental divorce, amounting to roughly 10 per cent of all children: ONS, Divorces: Couples and children of divorced couples, 1981, 1991, and 2001–2008. See <http://www.statistics.gov.uk/statbase/Product.asp?vlnk=14124>. In 2008, the courts made almost 27,000 residence orders and just over 80,000 contact orders: MOJ (2009), table 5.4.

[2] See Collier (2005).

11.2 PRIVATE LAW ORDERS UNDER THE CHILDREN ACT 1989

The four main private law orders, which are referred to collectively as 's 8 orders', are defined in s 8(1):

Children Act 1989, s 8

(1) In this Act—

"a contact order" means an order requiring the person with whom a child lives, or is to live, to allow the child to visit or stay with the person named in the order, or for that person and the child otherwise to have contact with each other;

"a prohibited steps order" means an order that no step which could be taken by a parent in meeting his parental responsibility for a child, and which is of a kind specified in the order, shall be taken by any person without the consent of the court;

"a residence order" means an order settling the arrangements to be made as to the person with whom a child is to live; and

"a specific issue order" means an order giving directions for the purpose of determining a specific question which has arisen, or which may arise, in connection with any aspect of parental responsibility for a child.

There are three further orders available under Part II of the CA 1989—special guardianship orders,[3] orders for financial relief,[4] and family assistance orders—which are not discussed here in any detail.

11.3 PROCEDURAL MATTERS GERMANE TO ALL S 8 ORDERS

11.3.1 WHEN MAY A S 8 ORDER BE MADE?

A s 8 order may be made in any 'family proceedings' in which a question arises with respect to the child's welfare.[5] The court may act upon its own motion or upon an application being made to the court.[6]

11.3.2 WHO MAY APPLY FOR A S 8 ORDER?

Entitled applicants

Subsections 10(1) and 10(2) identify two categories of applicant who can apply for a s 8 order: 'entitled applicants' and those who have obtained the court's leave. Entitled applicants are further divided into two groups. Under s 10(4), any parent, guardian, or person with a residence order in their favour is entitled to apply for *any s 8 order*.[7] It was established in *M v C*

---

[3] See 13.8.
[4] See 6.5.
[5] CA 1989, s 8(3)–(4). Unless stated otherwise all statutory references in this chapter are to the CA 1989.
[6] S 10(1).
[7] S 10(4).

and Calderdale Metropolitan Borough Council,[8] that 'parent' includes both natural parents (by which is meant the legal parents) regardless of whether they hold parental responsibility. The second group of entitled applicants, specified in s 10(5), are only entitled to apply as of right for a *residence* or *contact* order.

Children Act 1989, s 10

(5) The following persons are entitled to apply for a residence or contact order with respect to a child—

  (a) any party to a marriage (whether or not subsisting) in relation to whom the child is a child of the family;

  (b) any person with whom the child has lived for a period of at least three years;

  (c) any person who—

    (i) in any case where a residence order is in force with respect to the child, has the consent of each of the persons in whose favour the order was made;

    (ii) in any case where the child is in the care of a local authority, has the consent of that authority; or

    (iii) in any other case, has the consent of each of those (if any) who have parental responsibility for the child.

'Child of the family' is defined to include: (i) a child of the parties to a marriage; and (ii) any other child who has been treated by the parties to a marriage as a child of their family.[9]

If an applicant does not fall within one of the categories of entitled applicant, the leave of the court will be required.

Applicants requiring leave

Any person, including a child, who is not entitled under either s 10(4) or (5) may apply, with the court's leave, for *any s 8 order*. This 'open door' policy is subject to specific restrictions imposed on local authority foster parents who may not apply for leave unless they have the consent of the local authority, they are a relative of the child, or the child has been living with them for at least one year preceding the application.[10] The Court of Appeal has held that where foster parents are precluded from applying for a s 8 order by virtue of these restrictions, the court can nevertheless act of its own motion.[11]

Principles to be applied on an application for leave

Applicants under s 10(9)

The principles to be applied on an application for leave, other than by the child forming the subject-matter of the order, are set down in s 10(9).

---

8 [1994] Fam 1.

9 S 105(1). See *Re A (Child of the family)* [1998] 1 FLR 347.

10 S 9(3). Where a child is placed with prospective adopters by a local authority adoption agency, the prospective adopters will be regarded as falling within the restrictions imposed on local authority foster parents by s 9(3). See *Re C (Adoption: Notice)* [1999] 1 FLR 384.

11 *Gloucestershire County Council v P* [2000] Fam 1.

Children Act 1989, s 10

(9) Where the person applying for leave to make an application for a section 8 order is not the child concerned, the court shall, in deciding whether or not to grant leave, have particular regard to—

(a) the nature of the proposed application for the section 8 order;

(b) the applicant's connection with the child;

(c) any risk there might be of that proposed application disrupting the child's life to such an extent that he would be harmed by it; and

(d) where the child is being looked after by a local authority—

(i) the authority's plans for the child's future; and

(ii) the wishes and feelings of the child's parents.

The question of whether considerations beyond those specified in s 10(9) can be taken into account has caused some difficulty. In *Re A and W*, the court held that an application for leave was not a question relating to the child's upbringing and the child's welfare should not therefore be regarded as the paramount consideration.[12] However, a number of authorities have held that the applicant must establish 'a good arguable case' on the merits.[13] To that end, the courts have allowed quite extensive evidence about the applicant's prospects of success on the substantive application.[14] This additional 'gloss' on the s 10(9) criteria was questioned by the Court of Appeal in *Re J (Leave to issue application for residence order)*.[15] Referring to the possibility that applicants under s 10(9), in this case the child's grandparents, would often be able to rely on rights under Articles 6 and 8 of the European Convention on Human Rights (ECHR), Thorpe LJ held that the threshold for leave should not be placed unduly high by the courts going beyond the specified statutory criteria and embarking upon an enquiry into the substantive merits of the case.[16] Wall LJ has subsequently held that *Re J* does not prevent the court from undertaking 'a broad assessment of the merits of the application': what it does is prohibit the court from refusing leave on the basis of the more exacting criteria that the applicant has 'no reasonable prospect of success'.[17]

Obtaining leave does not give rise to any presumptions in favour of the applicant at the substantive hearing.[18]

Where the applicant is 'the child concerned': s 10(8)

Children are able to bring and defend Children Act proceedings in their own name.[19] In order to apply for a s 8 order, the child requires the court's leave under s 10(8).[20] In determining

---

[12] [1992] 2 FLR 154.

[13] See *Re A (A Minor) (Residence Order: Leave to Apply)* [1993] 1 FLR 425; *Re M (minors) (contact: leave to apply)* [1995] 3 FCR 550; *G v F (shared residence: parental responsibility)* [1998] 2 FLR 799; *Re S (Contact: Application by sibling)* [1999] 1 Fam 283.

[14] See, e.g., *Re F and R (Section 8 order: Grandparent's Application)* [1995] 1 FLR 524.

[15] [2002] EWCA Civ 1364.

[16] For a critique of the Court of Appeal's use of the ECHR arguments in this case, see Douglas (2003).

[17] *Re R (Adoption: Contact)* [2005] EWCA Civ 1128.

[18] *Re W (Contact: Application by grandparent)* [1997] 1 FLR 793.

[19] Family Procedure Rules 2010 (FPR 2010), SI 2010/2955, r 12.3(1), r 9.2A.

[20] In order to fall within the terms of this provision, the child must be applying for an order where he or she is 'the child concerned': meaning he or she must be the intended subject-matter of the order. See *Re S*

the application, the court must be satisfied that the child is of sufficient understanding to make the application.[21] Again the child's welfare is not the court's paramount consideration and the court may have regard to the applicant's 'likelihood of success': the child must not be embarking on proceedings 'doomed to failure'.[22] The application must also be sufficiently serious to merit intervention by the court.[23]

In determining a child's application for leave the courts have been reluctant to allow children to make their own applications in the course of proceedings between their parents. Johnson J's disquiet about such applications was clear in *Re H (Residence Order: Child's application for leave)*,[24] in which a 12-year-old boy sought leave to make an application for a residence order in favour of his father in the course of his parent's divorce proceedings. The court refused the application, holding that the child could add nothing by way of argument or cross-examination to that which would be presented to the court on the father's behalf.[25] Johnson J also referred with concern to the 'spectre of a mother being faced across a courtroom by solicitor or counsel acting on behalf of the child she bore'.[26] Changing attitudes towards the participation of children in private family law disputes, including securing separate legal representation for the child where appropriate, may now encourage a more liberal approach to applications of this nature.[27]

Prohibited applicants

Section 9(2) prohibits a local authority from applying for a residence or contact order. This restriction is based on the important principle that a local authority seeking to intervene in the private realm of family life should be required to use its public law powers under Part IV of the CA 1989, rather than invoking private law proceedings. This prevents the local authority from circumventing the strict requirement under Part IV of the Act that the child must be suffering or likely to suffer significant harm before the state can intervene by way of compulsory measures. The local authority is permitted, with leave, to apply for a specific issue or prohibited steps order but the court cannot make a specific issue order or prohibited steps order with a view to achieving a result which could be achieved by making a residence or contact order.[28] This leaves very little room for a local authority to make use of s 8 orders, even if it believes such orders would be a more nuanced response to the problems of a particular family than invoking its more confrontational powers under Part IV.[29]

Restricted applicants under s 91(14)

The requirement that all non-entitled applicants must obtain leave before applying for a s 8 order protects the child and the child's carers from highly stressful, vexatious litigation. Another important tool in the armoury of the judiciary is s 91(14). Section 91(14) empowers

---

(Contact: Application by sibling) [1999] Fam 283. A child applying for a s 8 order with respect to another child will have his or her application for leave determined in accordance with s 10(9).

[21] *Re SC (A Minor) (Leave to seek residence order)* [1994] 1 FLR 96.
[22] Ibid. See also *Re H (Residence order: Child's application for leave)* [1994] 1 FLR 26.
[23] *Re C (A Minor) (Leave to seek section 8 orders)* [1994] 1 FLR 26.
[24] [2000] 1 FLR 780.
[25] Ibid., 783.
[26] Ibid.
[27] See discussion below at 11.3.1.
[28] S 9(5)(a).
[29] See further discussion at 12.5.2.

the court to prohibit a particular individual or individuals from making any further applications to the court without first obtaining the court's leave.

Section 91(14) is controversial. Whilst it seeks to protect the child and the child's carers from endless litigation, to place a bar, albeit not absolute, on any future application interferes with the individual's fundamental right of access to the court. The judiciary have thus been cautious in using this power, particularly where it concerns a parent.[30] In the words of Butler-Sloss LJ, s 91(14) is a 'useful weapon of last resort'.[31] It is not to be used to give the parties a breathing space from litigation or to allow time for new contact arrangements to settle.[32]

A s 91(14) order will most commonly be made where there has been protracted litigation between the parties and it is in the child's best interests to bring proceedings to an end. In such cases, the prohibited applicant will usually have made repeated applications or will have conducted the litigation in an unreasonable manner.[33] A s 91(14) order may be made in the absence of a history of vexatious litigation provided the potential risks to the child of further litigation are sufficiently serious to warrant pre-emptive action.[34] However, in the absence of a history of unreasonable behaviour, the imposition of a s 91(14) order is extremely unlikely unless the circumstances are exceptional.[35] If a s 91(14) order is deemed appropriate, it can be made for a specified term or until further order. The Court of Appeal has, however, indicated that the latter is the better approach.[36]

If an order has been made under s 91(14), the applicant requires leave before making any further applications to the court. The principles to be applied on an application for leave were considered by the Court of Appeal in Re A (Application for leave).[37] The court held that the application was not to be determined in accordance with the principles set down under s 10(9), but on the basis of the simple question: 'does the application demonstrate that there is any need for renewed judicial investigation?'[38] The Court of Appeal has also confirmed that it is impermissible to attach conditions to a s 91(14) order, such as requiring a report from a psychiatrist demonstrating that the applicant has satisfactorily addressed his damaging behaviour, as such conditions would fetter the judge's discretion when hearing any future application and may, in effect, constitute a bar to the applicant seeking leave.[39]

11.3.3 THE PARTICIPATION OF CHILDREN IN PRIVATE LAW DISPUTES

The recognition accorded to the developing decision-making capacity of children and the importance of respecting children's views on issues that affect their lives, now forms a core

---

[30] Useful guidelines on the appropriate use of s 91(14) orders are set down by Butler-Sloss LJ in *Re P (a child) (residence order: child's welfare)* [2000] Fam 15, [41].

[31] Ibid.

[32] *Re G (A Child)* [2008] EWCA Civ 1468, [13]–[14]; *Re A (A Child)* [2009] EWCA Civ 1548, [16]–[17].

[33] *B v B (Residence order: restricting applications)* [1997] 1 FLR 139.

[34] *Re Y (Child orders: restricting applications)* [1994] 2 FLR 699.

[35] See, e.g., *C v W (a minor) (contact: leave to apply)* [1999] 1 FLR 916.

[36] *Re R (Residence: Contact: Restricting Applications)* [1998] 1 FLR 749 and *Re S (children) (restrictions on applications)* [2006] EWCA Civ 1190.

[37] [1998] 1 FLR 1.

[38] Ibid., 4.

[39] *Re S (children) (restrictions on applications)* [2006] EWCA Civ 1190, [72]–[80].

consideration in many areas of family law.[40] This changing attitude towards children is particularly important with respect to their right to participate in court proceedings concerning their future care and upbringing. As noted above, children deemed to be of sufficient maturity and understanding can bring and defend Children Act proceedings in their own name. In the majority of cases, however, children will be mere 'spectators' to their parents' dispute. In such cases, there remain strong differences of opinion as to the extent to which a child should be able to participate in the proceedings. On the one hand, a children's rights approach emphasizes the importance of listening to and respecting the autonomous, decision-making abilities of children in all matters affecting them. Article 12 of the United Nations Convention on the Rights of the Child provides an underpinning of support for this approach, albeit qualified by reference to the 'age and maturity' of the child.[41]

United Nations Convention on the Rights of the Child 1989, Article 12

1. States Parties shall assure to the child who is capable of forming his or her own views the right to express those views freely in all matters affecting the child, the views of the child being given due weight in accordance with the age and maturity of the child.
2. For this purpose, the child shall in particular be provided the opportunity to be heard in any judicial and administrative proceedings affecting the child, either directly, or through a representative or an appropriate body, in a manner consistent with the procedural rules of national law.

On the other hand, there remains deep-seated concern amongst some family practitioners about exposing children to the burdens and responsibilities of the adult-world of decision-making in matters as difficult and sensitive as residence or contact.[42] However, as Fortin notes, there is a crucial difference between allowing the views of children to determine the outcome of court proceedings—in effect 'delegating the decision-making process to them'—and consulting children on matters that affect them.[43] English law is clearly far from adopting the former, more radical approach. However, although consultation is a more ambivalent offering, the family judiciary are taking this requirement more seriously.

English law has traditionally taken a cautious approach to the participation of children in family law proceedings. The child's voice is usually only heard indirectly through the reports and evidence of others. In many cases, the child's voice is not heard at all. In private law proceedings, the main medium through which the child's views will be expressed is a welfare report prepared by a Children and Family Reporter (CFR).[44] However, a welfare report will not be ordered in every case.[45] Furthermore, even if the court does make a direction

---

[40] See, e.g., *Re Roddy (a child) (identification: restriction on publication)*; *Torbay Borough Council v News Group Newspapers* [2003] EWHC 2927, in which a 16-year-old child who had sufficient maturity and understanding was held to have the same rights to personal autonomy under Arts 8 and 10 of the ECHR as an adult.

[41] Support for this rights-based approach is also found in the European Convention on the Exercise of Children's Rights which came into force in 2000. The UK has not yet ratified the Convention.

[42] May and Smart (2004), 315.

[43] Fortin (2009b), 291.

[44] In *Re M (A minor) (Family Proceedings: Affidavits)* [1995] 2 FLR 100, an attempt by the child's father to introduce a sworn affidavit by the child setting down her wishes as to residence was refused by the Court of Appeal and subjected to very strong criticism.

[45] S 7.

for a welfare report to be prepared, there is no clear obligation on the CFR to ascertain the child's wishes and feelings.[46] There are growing concerns that this mechanism for hearing from the child is unsatisfactory. Research carried out by May and Smart revealed that, from their sample of 430 cases, only 47 per cent had a welfare report on file and in only half of those cases had the child been consulted.[47] As the welfare report constitutes the principal means by which the child's wishes can be conveyed to the court, it is particularly worrying that in the wake of the Labour government's 2006 reforms the number of welfare reports ordered in private law proceedings has fallen yet further, with limited Cafcass ('Children And Family Court Advisory and Support Service'—the body charged with representing the child's interests in private law proceedings) resources being diverted away from report writing and into the provision of in-court conciliation services and supporting and monitoring contact arrangements.[48]

In addition to the welfare report, the judge has a wide discretion as to whether to hear directly from the child.[49] The English judiciary have traditionally exercised that discretion cautiously.[50] There are several reasons why judges may be reluctant to speak to children:

P. Parkinson, J. Cashmore, and J. Single, 'Parents' and children's views on talking to judges in parenting disputes in Australia', (2007) 21 *International Journal of Law, Policy and the Family* 84, 85, 102

[T]he accepted view in most common law jurisdictions is that it is better to rely on the work of trained experts to interview children and to interpret their wishes and feelings to the court. Not only are such professionals regarded as better able to interview children, but they are also seen as better qualified to interpret their views in the light of all the circumstances...Writing in 1983, three Canadian judges explained why the practice of judicial interviewing should be regarded as undesirable:

"The interview is conducted in an intimidating environment by a person unskilled in asking questions and interpreting the answers of children. In the relatively short time these interviews take, it is difficult to investigate with sufficient depth and subtlety those perceptions of a child which may explain, justify or represent the child's wishes. Moreover, the interview may be perceived as a violation of the judge's role as an impartial trier of fact who does not enter the adversarial arena. The impartiality may also be compromised by the judge assuming the role of inquisitor in questioning children".

However, attitudes are changing in light of recent research suggesting many children want a greater level of involvement in the court proceedings, including being given the opportunity to speak directly to the judge.[51] Research into the views of Australian children revealed that 85 per cent would have liked the opportunity to speak to the judge; almost all their parents supported this position.[52] The children's and the parents' reasons were broadly similar:

---

46 FPR 2010, r 16.33.
47 May and Smart (2004), 308.
48 Fortin (2009b), 254. See also Fortin, Ritchie, and Buchanan (2006), 226–7.
49 *B v B (Minors) (Residence and care disputes)* [1994] 2 FLR 489.
50 FJC (2008), [4].
51 Ibid. See Fortin, Ritchie, and Buchanan (2006) and Parkinson, Cashmore, and Single (2007), 88–9.
52 Parkinson, Cashmore, and Single (2007), 95.

Both referred to children's right to be heard and the importance of them having a say in the decision-making process. While both parents and children referred to the need for acknowledgment, and the more therapeutic benefits for children in being heard directly, there was a clear focus in many of their responses on the value of this information in the decision-making process. A number of parents and children thought that if children had the opportunity to talk with the judge directly, it was more likely that the truth would come out and that judges could get the 'real picture' without the distortions arising from the parents' conflict. Like the separately represented children in a recent British study...some children in this study also were concerned that their views be conveyed accurately to the court and indicated that speaking directly to the judge would be the best way of ensuring this.

Parents who opposed the child seeing the judge (27 per cent) raised three main concerns: first, that it would be intimidating for the children; second, that judges do not have the time or experience to ensure they are accurately eliciting the children's views; and third, that the children may be being manipulated by one parent.[53] Despite these concerns, the Family Justice Council of England and Wales are now encouraging a more open approach.

Family Justice Council, *Enhancing the Participation of Children and Young People in Family Proceedings: Starting the Debate* (2008)

11. As a broad proposition, we consider that there are good reasons why judges should be less reluctant to see children than has hitherto been the case. These include:

- to enable the child to have a picture of the judge in their mind by actually seeing them; and

- to enable the child to tell the judge directly about specific issues or to express his/ her wishes;

- to reassure the child that they are/have been at the centre of the decision-making process and that the judge has understood and will take into account what they have said, as well as the representations made on behalf of the child;

- following the judgment, to enable the judge to explain their decision to the child, thereby helping the child to understand the process and hopefully assisting them to accept the outcome;

- to promote and implement the child's human rights in terms of their involvement in the process of decision as set out within our domestic legislation and strengthened by the UK Government's ratification of the UN Convention on the Rights of the Child...

It is thus possible that it will become much more common for judges to speak directly to children, although the views of senior family judges appear to remain divided.[54]

Where the child's views are before the court, they are relevant,[55] but they will not be determinative.[56] The weight to be accorded to the child's wishes is highly dependent on the child's

---

[53] Ibid., 99–100.

[54] See *Re W (Children)* [2008] EWCA Civ 538, [33] (per Thorpe LJ); [57] (per Wilson LJ); [59]–[61] (per Charles J).

[55] S 1(3)(a).

[56] *Re M (Family proceedings: Affidavits)* [1995] 2 FLR 100.

age. May and Smart found that whereas younger children were generally regarded as incapable of forming a view, children aged over seven years of age were routinely asked whether they would prefer to live with mum or dad and they appeared to have no difficulty weighing up the various factors and expressing a clearly articulated view.[57] However, although May and Smart felt that the child's views were taken seriously both by the CFR and the court,[58] young adults looking back at their experiences of parental separation expressed less satisfaction with the way in which their views were taken into account both in the welfare report and by the court.[59]

The courts' general reluctance to override the wishes of an older child stems in part from welfare considerations. It has thus been held that having ascertained the child's wishes it is inappropriate to ignore them.[60] However, the courts' reluctance also stems from the futility of ordering contact if it is known that the children will refuse to comply.[61] The courts have recognized that there must come a point, particularly with older children, when it is counter-productive for the court to continue to force the issue. This consideration led Tyrer J in *Re S (Contact: children's views)* to refuse the father's application for contact. His judgment provides strong support for the principle that the autonomous decision-making capacity of children must be respected. The children in this case were aged 16, 14, and 12. The two older children were opposed in varying degrees to direct contact with the father. The father claimed the children were suffering from parental alienation syndrome (where the mother deliberately alienates the child from the father), an allegation the judge dismissed as 'utter nonsense'.

Re S (Contact: children's views) [2002] EWHC 540

TYRER J:

110. These children are not, in the end, children. V [aged 16] and J [aged 14] in particular are young adults. They are ordinary teenagers and this kind of approach to them is invariably counter-productive. They might obey, perhaps they will obey an order of the court, but with what result? What would be the quality of what is being asked of them by me to do if I order them to do it? ...

114. One of the most important elements in this case is to consider the ascertainable wishes and feelings of the particular child. But that is only part of it. The actual words are that I should have regard in particular to the ascertainable wishes of the child concerned, considered in the light of the child's age and understanding.

115. I accept that parental responsibility means that children have to do things that they otherwise might not find congenial ... But, at the same time, children of this age with whom I am dealing are entitled to have respect for their views. They have expressed their views. The children and family reporter is of the opinion that they have thought about their views before expressing them. They are having to choose. They should not have to choose. They should

---

[57] May and Smart (2004), 314–15.

[58] Ibid.

[59] Fortin, Ritchie, and Buchanan (2006), 220–1. Fewer than a third of the young people felt that the court took proper account of their views and less than a third felt that they had been able to say everything they wanted to the CFR. There is clearly scope for improving the way in which CFRs approach their work with children.

[60] *Re F (Minors) (Denial of contact)* [1993] 2 FLR 677.

[61] *Churchard v Churchard* [1984] FLR 635.

be allowed to make decisions without pressure and without the pressure of being asked to effectively select between one parent and another...

117. What is the range of powers that I have? They are pretty formidable. I could use force. I could order them to do things, send them a piece of paper with the court's order upon it and direct them to do things, either directly or through their mother. What would be the effect of such orders, particularly on the elder two? I have no doubt that both V and J would react with sullen resentment. They would feel that this judge, far away, has been told their views and they have not been listened to. It might create some satisfaction, vindication but it would be a pyrrhic victory indeed because, whatever they were ordered to do, if they did it they would do it with bad grace and with a counter-productive result.

118. The alternative is to try persuasion, to give respect to their views, to acknowledge what they are saying, to listen to them and to try and provide opportunities for negotiation. That means, in effect, that they have to be treated as young adults with minds of their own, minds that they are capable of making up for themselves and opinions that are to be taken at face value without being criticised...

120. What do I find finally therefore in terms of what I am going to say and direct about V. I am entirely satisfied that it is not in her interests to make an order. There are four reasons why I have come to that conclusion. Firstly, it is clear that she does not want an order. Secondly, although she would obey it if I made it, she would do it out of duty or duress, depending upon one's point of view. Thirdly, if I made an order and V reacted against it and did not obey it, it would not be enforced by the father if it were broken. He made that plain. I do not consider that the court should make orders in the expectation that they are not going to be respected or obeyed...Last, but by no means least, because there is a statutory provision which expressly deals with this matter, and that statutory provision says that it is plain that the court should not make an order unless it considers that it is better to make an order than not to make an order (subsection 5 of section 1). I do not consider it is better, quite the reverse. I think it would be counterproductive in the extreme if I was to make an order in respect of V.

121. If young people are to be brought up to respect the law, then it seems to me that the law must respect them and their wishes, even to the extent of allowing them, as occasionally they do, to make mistakes.

In particularly complex or difficult cases, the child can be made a party to the proceedings and separately represented by a guardian ad litem.[62] The children's guardian will conduct the proceedings and instruct a solicitor on the child's behalf. Section 41 of the CA 1989 was amended by the Adoption and Children Act 2002 (ACA 2002) to provide explicitly that s 8 proceedings could be designated 'specified proceedings' by rules of court, thereby giving the child an automatic right to separate representation unless the court was satisfied that his or her interests could be adequately protected without it.[63] The desirability of making greater use of guardians in private law proceedings has also been endorsed by the courts.[64] However, no rules of court have been forthcoming and separate representation in private law proceedings remains relatively unusual.[65] In April 2004, the President of the Family Division issued a practice direction clarifying when it would be appropriate for the court to exercise its discretion to make the child a party to the proceedings.

---

[62] FPR 2010, rr 16.2 and 16.4.
[63] S 41, as amended by ACA 2002, s 122.
[64] *Re A (A child) (Separate representation in court proceedings)* [2001] 1 FLR 715.
[65] For excellent commentary see Fortin (2007), 256–64.

Practice Direction: (Family Proceedings: Representation of Children) (2004)
<http://www.hmcourts-service.gov.uk/cms/949.htm>

2. Making the child a party to the proceedings is a step that will be taken only in cases which involve an issue of significant difficulty and consequently will occur in only a minority of cases. Before taking the decision to make the child a party, consideration should be given to whether an alternative route might be preferable, such as asking an officer of the Children and Family Court Advisory and Support Service ("CAFCASS)" to carry out further work or by making a referral to social services or possibly, by obtaining expert evidence.

3. The decision to make the child a party will always be exclusively that of the judge, made in the light of the facts and circumstances of the particular case. The following are offered, solely by way of guidance, as circumstances which may justify the making of an order:

3.1 Where a CAFCASS officer has notified the court that in his opinion the child should be made a party...

3.2 Where the child has a standpoint or interests which are inconsistent with or incapable of being represented by any of the adult parties.

3.3 Where there is an intractable dispute over residence or contact, including where all contact has ceased, or where there is irrational but implacable hostility to contact or where the child may be suffering harm associated with the contact dispute.

3.4 Where the views and wishes of the child cannot be adequately met by a report to the court.

3.5 Where an older child is opposing a proposed course of action.

3.6 Where there are complex medical or mental health issues to be determined or there are other unusually complex issues that necessitate separate representation of the child.

3.7 Where there are international complications outside child abduction, in particular where it may be necessary for there to be discussions with overseas authorities or a foreign court.

3.8 Where there are serious allegations of physical, sexual or other abuse in relation to the child or there are allegations of domestic violence not capable of being resolved with the help of a CAFCASS officer.

3.9 Where the proceedings concern more than one child and the welfare of the children is in conflict or one child is in a particularly disadvantaged position.

3.10 Where there is a contested issue about blood testing.

In the wake of these guidelines, the Labour government issued a consultation paper with a view to formulating new court rules. However, contrary to the general trend towards facilitating the child's separate representation in private law proceedings, it decided not to make private law cases 'specified proceedings' requiring all children to be separately represented under s 41 of the CA 1989.[66] The question of whether the child should be separately represented therefore remains one for the discretion of the judge. However, the consultation paper made it clear that in the government's view it would only be appropriate for the child to be separately represented where there was a 'legal need': 'where the child has evidence to give or a legal submission to make that cannot be given by another party, and where the

[66] DCA (2006b), 17.

court considers there is a need in terms of Article 6 (access to a fair trial) of the European Convention of Human Rights.'[67]

If anything, the consultation paper therefore took a more restrictive approach to separate representation than that set down in the President's guidance. It appeared to be informed by the belief (apparently supported by research) that separate representation could be harmful to children, and that their wishes and feelings, at least in most cases, could be adequately conveyed to the court by Cafcass.[68] The government's caution also reflected its apparent concern that increasing numbers of children (with the associated costs) were being granted party status under the President's Direction.

The consultation paper was the subject of quite adverse comment, not least for its handling of the research evidence.[69] In July 2007, the Ministry of Justice published a summary of the responses received to the paper and its proposals.[70] In light of the lack of support for the government's key proposal that separate representation for children should only be allowed in cases of 'legal need', the government decided to undertake a further period of consultation and discussion to consider alternatives. No further proposals were forthcoming before the 2010 election, leaving future developments on separate representation somewhat uncertain.

Occasionally, where a guardian has been appointed to act on the child's behalf, conflict develops between the guardian's duty to act in the child's best interests and the child's own views. In such circumstances, the child can apply for the guardian to be removed and for the child to conduct his or her own case.[71] In determining such an application, the court must be satisfied that the child has sufficient understanding to participate as a party to the proceedings without the guardian's assistance.[72] Thorpe LJ has recently held that when determining this question the courts must avoid paternalistic judgments and pay much greater respect to the rights and autonomy of the child.

Mabon v Mabon and others [2005] EWCA Civ 634

THORPE LJ:

25. In our system we have traditionally adopted the tandem model for the representation of children who are parties to family proceedings, whether public or private. First the court appoints a guardian ad litem who will almost invariably have a social work qualification and very wide experience of family proceedings. He then instructs a specialist family solicitor who, in turn, usually instructs a specialist family barrister. This is a Rolls Royce model and is the envy of many other jurisdictions. However its overall approach is essentially paternalistic. The guardian's first priority is to advocate the welfare of the child he represents. His second priority is to put before the court the child's wishes and feelings. Those priorities can in some cases conflict. In extreme cases the conflict is unmanageable. That reality is recognised by the terms of rule 9.2A. The direction set by rule 9.2A(6) is a mandatory grant of the application provided that the court considers "that the minor concerned has sufficient understanding to

---

[67] Ibid., 22.
[68] DCA (2006b), [12] and [23].
[69] See, e.g., Wall LJ (2007) and Fortin (2007).
[70] MOJ (2007).
[71] FPR 2010, r 16.6.
[72] Ibid., r 16.6(6).

participate as a party in the proceedings concerned." Thus the focus is upon the sufficiency of the child's understanding in the context of the remaining proceedings.

26. In my judgment the Rule is sufficiently widely framed to meet our obligations to comply with both Article 12 of the United Nations Convention and Article 8 of the ECHR, providing that judges correctly focus on the sufficiency of the child's understanding and, in measuring that sufficiency, reflect the extent to which, in the 21st Century, there is a keener appreciation of the autonomy of the child and the child's consequential right to participate in decision making processes that fundamentally affect his family life...

28. ...Although the tandem model has many strengths and virtues, at its heart lies the conflict between advancing the welfare of the child and upholding the child's freedom of expression and participation. Unless we in this jurisdiction are to fall out of step with similar societies as they safeguard Article 12 rights, we must, in the case of articulate teenagers, accept that the right to freedom of expression and participation outweighs the paternalistic judgment of welfare.

29. In testing the sufficiency of a child's understanding I would not say that welfare has no place. If direct participation would pose an obvious risk of harm to the child arising out of the nature of the continuing proceedings and, if the child is incapable of comprehending that risk, then the judge is entitled to find that sufficient understanding has not been demonstrated. But judges have to be equally alive to the risk of emotional harm that might arise from denying the child knowledge of and participation in the continuing proceedings...

32. In conclusion this case provides a timely opportunity to recognise the growing acknowledgement of the autonomy and consequential rights of children, both nationally and internationally. The Rules are sufficiently robustly drawn to accommodate that shift. In individual cases trial judges must equally acknowledge the shift when they make in individual cases a proportionate judgment of the sufficiency of the child's understanding.

11.4 RESIDENCE ORDERS

11.4.1 THE LEGAL FRAMEWORK

The statutory framework for resolving disputes concerning the residence of a child is deceptively straightforward. As a question relating to the upbringing of a child, s 1(1) of the CA 1989 applies and the child's welfare must be the court's paramount consideration. If the application is opposed the court must have particular regard to the welfare checklist.[73] The difficulty, of course, is in applying the welfare principle to the particular facts of each case. The way the child's best interests have been interpreted by the judiciary in the context of residence disputes has recently proved particularly controversial.

11.4.2 A 'PRESUMPTION' IN FAVOUR OF THE MOTHER?

Over the last few years, fathers' rights groups have been engaged in a high profile media campaign against what they perceive to be the gender bias entrenched within English family law. One of the main targets of their campaign has been the way in which residence disputes are resolved. Groups such as New Fathers 4 Justice[74] and Families Need Fathers[75] argue that

---

[73] S 1(3)–(4). See p 525.
[74] <http://www.newfathers4justice.info>.
[75] <www.fnf.org.uk>.

in granting sole residence to the mother and restricting fathers to unsatisfactory contact, the judiciary are basing their decisions on outdated stereotypes of men and women and their respective parenting roles. Furthermore, it is suggested that deeply engrained within the collective psyche of the judiciary is a privileging of motherhood and a strong ambivalence towards fatherhood. According to this view, the law is guilty of constructing fathers as disinterested, irresponsible, and even dangerous figures: a construction without foundation. In the discussion to follow, we explore whether these criticisms of the law and the judiciary are well-founded.

The statistics

Unfortunately, official statistics on the making of residence orders under the CA 1989 are not broken down into gender. There is therefore no official record of how many sole residence orders are granted to mothers in litigated cases and how many sole residence orders are granted to fathers. However, research carried out on the general population of post-divorce families, which includes those cases where residence and contact is agreed without going to court, strongly suggests that post-divorce parenting is highly gendered. It is estimated that over 80 per cent of children of separated parents live primarily with their mother;[76] 12 per cent of parents operate a shared residence arrangement.[77] The Office for National Statistics (ONS) survey on non-resident parental contact found that from their sample of 649 resident parents and 312 non-resident parents, 93 per cent of the resident parents were female and 89 per cent of the non-resident parents were male.[78]

The case law

The welfare principle and the welfare checklist are completely gender neutral in form. The important question is whether the welfare principle is being interpreted by the judiciary in such a way that it is resulting in substantive gender discrimination against fathers. Sensitive to such accusations, the judiciary have gone to considerable lengths to deny that there is any inherent bias within the law. It is reiterated throughout the case law that when deciding residence disputes the courts do not apply any kind of 'presumption' in favour of the mother: the only relevant factor is the child's best interests. The gender neutral approach of the courts was clearly set down by the Court of Appeal in *Re A (a minor) (residence order)*. The first instance judge, in granting residence to the child's mother, had relied on Principle 6 of the UN Declaration on the Rights of the Child 1959 which provides: 'A child of tender years shall not, save in exceptional circumstances, be separated from his mother'. The Court of Appeal upheld the father's appeal on the basis that the judge's reliance on this outdated, gendered principle was wholly erroneous.

Re A (a minor) (residence order) [1998] 2 FCR 633, 638–9 (CA)

THORPE LJ:

The relevance and value of the declaration is most doubtful. In terms of relevant social policy it could be said to be almost antiquated since it is now nearly 40 years old and in terms of

---

[76] DCA and DfES (2004), 2.
[77] Peacey and Hunt (2008), 19.
[78] Blackwell and Dawe (2003), 1.3.

social development and in terms of understanding of child development and welfare that is an exceedingly long time. Nor is that principle reflected in the United Nations Convention on the Rights of the Child...a convention ratified by this nation, as indeed by most other nations of the developed world. As [opposing counsel] points out, the corresponding article of the convention, art 9, is in strictly neutral terms. It states that the parties shall ensure that a child shall not be separated from his or her parent against their will except when competent authorities, subject to judicial review, determine, or where the parents are living separately and a decision must be made as to the child's place of residence. In modern terminology that is gender neutral...

In brief conclusion, it is, in my judgment, plainly demonstrated that in this case, most unfortunately, the trial judge fell into error in...applying what he erroneously accepted as a principle, that since J was of tender years his interests would best be served by him being cared for by his mother.

The courts have also been keen to recognize the emergence of the so called 'new father', with judges stressing the equal capacity of men in today's society to assume the responsibility of primary carer.[79]

Re S (A Minor) (Custody) [1991] FCR 155, 160 (CA)

Lord Donaldson of Lymington, M.R.:

What is clear is that there is a change in the social order, in the organization of society, whereby it is much more common for fathers to look after young children than it used to be in bygone days. It must follow that more fathers are equipped to undertake these sorts of duties than was formerly the case. From that it must follow that courts could more readily conclude in an individual case that it was in the interests of a young child that it be with its father than they would have done previously. Now, as always, the duty of the court is to consider the welfare of the child, and that is usually the paramount consideration.

At least at the level of rhetoric, gender equality is thus a prominent theme of the case law. However, beneath this rhetoric, there are several important facets of the judiciary's interpretation and application of the welfare principle which arguably work unfairly against fathers.

The 'natural' order of things

In several cases, the courts' denial that they are applying a presumption in favour of mothers is immediately qualified by the suggestion that, despite the absence of any 'presumption in law', it is nevertheless 'natural' for children, particularly young children, to be with their mother. As it was put by Cumming Bruce LJ, it is 'not a principle but a matter of human nature in the case of the upbringing of children of tender years, that given the normal commitment of a father to support the family, the mother, for practical reasons, is usually the right person to bring up her children.'[80]

---

[79] See also *Re K (Residence order: securing contact)* [1999] 1 FLR 583, 591.
[80] *Re H (A Minor: Custody)* [1990] 1 FLR 51, 56 (CA).

These comments reflect a deeply traditional and arguably outdated notion of family life in which the father's role is one of breadwinner and provider and the mother's role that of primary child-care provider. Clare McGlynn is fiercely critical of this approach, arguing that it reflects an 'ideology of motherhood' in which motherhood is portrayed as something instinctive and innate, and thus the natural and appropriate role for all women.[81] As McGlynn points out, this ideology has been underpinned in the law by a welfarist discourse, often termed the 'tender years doctrine', which emphasizes the strong emotional and physical dependence of a young child on the care of his or her mother.[82] The result has been a privileging of the mother–child relationship in law.

R. van Krieken, ' "The Best Interests of the Child" and Parental Separation: on the "Civilizing of Parents" ', (2005) 68 *Modern Law Review* 25, 30

Most commentators will speak of the emergence of a more or less judicially explicit 'maternal preference rule' as the 'dominant doctrine in most Western countries', in conjunction with a 'tender years doctrine', that the younger a child is the more preferable it is for the mother to retain care and control.

In the decades leading up to the 1970s, there were two lines of argument about post-separation childhood which dominated the way in which the best interests standard was interpreted. The first concerning the understanding of the mother-child relationship, and its placement at the centre of children's emotional development, such as in the work of John Bowlby. As Maidment puts it:

For more than the next twenty years psychologists explored the mother-child dyad to the exclusion of all other relationships, fathers were excluded from all aspects of their children's birth, a maternal preference prevailed in custody cases, mothers were discouraged from working and thus leaving their children, and policy-makers discouraged alternative care arrangements for children such as day nurseries.

Bowlby himself was happy to see the biological mother replaced by another carer, what mattered was the continuity of care, but for all practical purposes his position was understood as emphasising the importance of an undisturbed close relationship between mothers and their children: fathers (or secondary carers) were seen as important but not crucial. In a custody dispute between the two it was clear that the mother's claim was the stronger.

The 'ideology of motherhood' remains deeply entrenched within western cultures. In a recent survey conducted by the Equality and Human Rights Commission, over half of mothers with pre-school children expressed a strong sense of moral responsibility to provide day-to-day care for their children and thus a preference for remaining at home rather than working.[83] Whilst McGlynn is principally concerned about the damaging effects of this dominant ideology on achieving wider equality for women, it obviously has equally worrying consequences for men. The privileging of the mother–child relationship devalues the parenting role of men, restricting it to one of the distant, somewhat detached economic provider and questions the capacity of men to fulfil the emotional needs of the child.

---

[81] McGlynn (2000), 31 and (2001), 325–30. See pp 15–16.
[82] Ibid. See also Neale and Smart (1999), 36.
[83] Ellison, Barker, and Kulasuriya (2009), 14.

Despite these concerns, the 'fact of nature' approach has been a strong feature of the residence case law. Indeed, this same appeal to the 'natural order of things' appears in two key judgments of Butler-Sloss LJ:

Re S (A Minor) (Custody) [1991] FCR 155, 158 (CA)

Lord Justice Butler-Sloss:

The welfare of the child is the first and paramount consideration...[T]here is no presumption that one parent should be preferred to another parent at a particular age. It used to be thought many years ago that young children should be with the mother, that girls approaching puberty should be with mother and that boys over a certain age should be with father. Such presumptions, if they ever were such, do not, in my view, exist today. There are *dicta* of this court to the effect that it is likely that a young child, particularly perhaps a little girl, would be expected to be with her mother, but that is subject to the overriding factor that the welfare of the child is the paramount consideration. When there is a dispute between parents as to which parent should take the responsibility of the care of the child on a day to day basis, it is for the justices or for the Judge to decide which of those parents would be the better parent for the child, who cannot have the best situation since they are not together caring for her. I would just add that it is natural for young children to be with mothers, but, where it is in dispute, it is a consideration but not a presumption.

In the second key judgment, Butler-Sloss LJ attempts to clarify what she meant by her comment in *Re S* that 'it is natural for young children to be with mothers'.

Re A (A Minor) (Custody) [1991] FCR 569, 575–6 (CA)

Lord Justice Butler-Sloss:

[The first argument for the mother] was that it was natural for a mother to have the care of a six year old girl. This was, in my judgment, a misunderstanding of the decision of this court in *Re S (A Minor) (Custody)* [1991] FCR 155... where I said at p. 158G that: "it is natural for young children to be with mothers but, where it is in dispute, it is a consideration but not a presumption".

In cases where the child has remained throughout with the mother and is young, particularly when a baby or toddler, the unbroken relationship of the mother and child is one which it would be very difficult to displace, unless the mother was unsuitable to care for the child. But where the mother and child have been separated and the mother seeks the return of the child, other considerations apply and there is no starting-point that the mother should be preferred to the father and only displaced by a preponderance of evidence to the contrary.

In this case the mother and child had been separated at the time of the hearing for nearly 12 months and at the age of six, she is not within the category of very young children. There is no presumption which requires the mother as mother to be considered as the primary caretaker in preference to the father. The welfare of the child is paramount and each parent has to be looked at by the Judge in order to make as best he can the assessment of each and to choose one of them to be the custodial parent. In so far as the Judge appears to have started with the proposition that little girls naturally go to their mothers, the Judge was in error and applied the wrong test. The second point, the conflict of guidance over matters peculiar to her sex, is, in the context of a case like this, and probably generally, unimportant and ought not to be in itself placed in the balance unless there were recognizable difficulties which had already occurred or were likely to occur...

Butler-Sloss LJ thus places two key qualifications on her general statement in *Re S* that it is 'natural for young children to be with their mothers'. The first relates to the age of the child, with Butler-Sloss LJ suggesting that this 'fact of nature' will only be of particular importance in the case of very young children, particularly babies and toddlers. The importance of the 'natural order of things' for this very young group of children is strongly reinforced by the Court of Appeal in *Re W (Residence Order: Baby)*, Lord Donaldson openly suggesting that in the case of a very young baby there is 'a rebuttable presumption of fact' in favour of the mother.

Re W (Residence Order: Baby) [1992] 2 FCR 603, 607 (CA)

Lord Donaldson of Lymington, M.R.:

At the risk of being told by academics hereafter that my views are contrary to well-established authority, I think that there is a rebuttable presumption of fact that the best interests of a baby are served by being with its mother, and I stress the word "baby". When we are moving on to whatever age it may be appropriate to describe the baby as having become a child, different considerations may well apply. But, as far as babies are concerned, the starting point is, I think, that it should be with its mother. That is not to say that it is not a rebuttable presumption. There are many mothers whose circumstances are such that the presumption would be rebutted; but that is not this case...

The second qualification relates to the need for there to exist an unbroken relationship between mother and child. This, in effect, is a variation of the status quo argument: that the unbroken relationship between mother and child establishes a pattern of child-care that will be harmful to the child to disrupt. In the absence of such an unbroken bond, the courts are more willing to displace the 'presumption' that young children should be with their mothers in favour of the alternative carer.[84]

The status quo

The status quo is an important factor in all residence disputes but has again been a particular concern of fathers' rights groups.[85] There is no 'presumption' in favour of maintaining the status quo and the courts have certainly been prepared to move a child from a settled placement.[86] However, in accordance with the welfare checklist, where the child

---

[84] See, e.g., *Re K (residence order: securing contact)* [1999] 1 FLR 583.

[85] Geldof (2003), 189.

[86] See, e.g., *Re N (a child)* [2007] EWCA Civ 1053, a surrogacy case in which the child was removed from the care of the surrogate mother and her husband and placed with the commissioning couple after 18 months of 'high standards of care' living with the former.

is settled and happy, the courts have generally required some good reason for disturbing that position.

Re F (A Child) [2009] EWCA Civ 313

Ward LJ:

9. The mother's case was strongly advanced on an argument that the status quo was with her and that, accordingly, the children should not be moved without good reason. There is obviously a case for an argument about preserving the status quo but I venture to suggest that since the Children Act of 1989 it would be better to address the checklist factors than rely on any presumption of fact which may arise from an argument of that kind. The status quo argument means no more than that, if the children are settled in one place, then the court is to have regard to section 1(3)(b) of the Act and consider the likely effect on them of any change in circumstances...

17. [I]f, as the judge found, the children will be well looked after and be safe and would thrive in either household, a finding he made, then the defect in the judgment is the inadequate explanation of the reasons which justified a change from a settled position, as settled it had become in the 12 months after the final separation of the parties.

In principle the status quo argument can work in favour of either parent.[87] However, the usual pattern following relationship breakdown is for the children to remain in the family home with the mother and for the father to move out into alternative accommodation. This places the mother in much the stronger position in any subsequent dispute, enabling her to quickly establish her position as the sole primary carer. Because of long delays in the court process, the mother is able to entrench that position and, by the time of the final hearing, the courts are reluctant to unsettle the status quo unless there are clear welfare grounds for doing so.[88] There may of course be a very good reason for this trend in parenting patterns in the immediate post-separation period: that it most accurately reflects the division of parenting responsibilities pre-separation and is therefore a 'natural' extension of the parents' established parenting roles. Although some would argue that parenting roles and responsibilities should be re-negotiated upon separation to meet the demands of the new situation, it is perfectly reasonable to look to past patterns of care in evaluating what arrangements will best promote the child's future interests. However, fathers' rights groups see the opportunity afforded to the mother to entrench her position as primary carer as a serious cause of injustice.

Employment obligations and the availability of the primary carer

A further factor tending to advantage the mother is her greater availability, for practical reasons, to take on the role of primary carer post-separation. With many women in the UK choosing not to return to work after the birth of a child or, if returning to work, doing so on a part-time basis,[89] they can more easily assume the burden of child-care without having to rely as heavily on alternative carers, such as members of the extended family or

---

[87] See, e.g., *Re A (A Minor) (Custody)* [1991] FCR 569.

[88] *Re B (Residence order: Status quo)* [1998] 1 FLR 368.

[89] In a survey conducted for the Commission for Equality and Human Rights in 2009, 63% of women were in employment, of which 43% were full time and 57% part time. That compares with 89% of men in employment, of which just 7% were part time, the remaining 93% full time: Ellison, Barker, and Kulasuriya (2009), 33.

child-minders. Of course, as with the status quo argument, the employment and child-care responsibilities of the parties is often established pre-separation and carried through into the immediate post-separation period. The mother's role as the primary carer pre-separation therefore works to her advantage in any post-separation dispute, with the father's more onerous employment obligations working against him. It is clearly arguable that it is in the child's interests to be with a parent wherever possible in preference to some form of alternative care, especially following the distress of parental separation.[90]

11.4.3 VICTIMS OF GENDER DISCRIMINATION—MOTHERS, FATHERS, OR BOTH?

Despite the absence of any legal presumption in favour of mothers, the courts therefore give weight to several factors that tend to favour them as the more suitable primary carer. But does this therefore constitute gender discrimination against fathers? Whilst many scholars within the feminist school would share the concerns of fathers about some of the outdated gender stereotypes underpinning these cases, the contention that the law is thereby discriminating against fathers is more problematic. Indeed, it is important to recognize that the 'maternal preference' rule and the *ideology* of motherhood which underpins it can work against the interests of women as well as men, particularly as competing discourses on 'gender equality' and the 'new father' gain in strength and popularity. Moreover, many feminists are concerned that the highly publicized allegations of bias against fathers are based on erroneous assumptions about the reality of child-care responsibilities in the UK and risk ignoring the huge investment and sacrifices made by women in developing their parenting role—in short, that the success of the fathers' rights movement has led to a worrying devaluation of motherhood.[91]

Problems with the 'maternal preference' approach

The ideology of motherhood and the tender years doctrine have had both positive and negative consequences for women. As Boyd points out, the maternal preference approach can be empowering for women. However, she shares McGlynn's concerns about the wider implications of the 'ideology of motherhood' for women's equality in the public sphere, particularly in the field of employment.

S. Boyd, 'From gender specificity to gender neutrality? Ideologies in Canadian Child Custody Law', in C. Smart and S. Sevenhuijsen (eds), *Child Custody and the Politics of Gender* (London: Routledge, 1989), 126, 133

The ideology attached to the tender years principle had conflicting implications for women. On the positive side, it arguably empowered women by allowing them to leave abusive husbands without forfeiting their children, and to play the role of head of a family unit. In addition, it may have increased women's bargaining power within marriage and during divorce or separation. While usually lacking the economic clout of their husbands, mothers could play upon the emotional incentive which men had to keep their marriage intact, lest they lose their children...On the negative side, the ideological aspects of the tender years doctrine which strengthened

---

[90] See, e.g. *Re W (Residence)* [1999] 2 FLR 390.
[91] For a recent analysis see Collier (2005).

women's position in custody disputes rendered them ill-suited for public life. That is, the ideology underlying the tender years doctrine was one of inequality in that it enhanced the view of women as wives and mothers within the private sphere of the home…[W]omen were considered only as mothers rather than complete human beings. In turn, any deviation from the 'ideal' vision of motherhood such as leaving a child in the care of another person working outside the home, or engaging in an adulterous relationship could defeat the maternal preference…As long as women are allocated primary responsibility for child rearing and housework, even when employed…they tend to take employment which allows them to reconcile paid work with household and child rearing responsibilities. Such work is normally undervalued in terms of prestige and pay, is often part time, and tends to be 'dead-end' leading to few promotions…Pay and prestige differentials between male and female dominated jobs in turn lead to a tendency for mothers to withdraw from the labour force to care for young children, rather than fathers with better salaries and perhaps greater psychological investment in their employment…The 'traditional' sexual division of labour is thus maintained in spite of significant changes to women's pattern of involvement in the labour market.

As more women enter full-time employment and struggle to live up to the 'ideal' of the self-sacrificing, full-time mother, the 'ideology of motherhood' has become less empowering and increasingly problematic for women. Against the background of the 'new father' rhetoric, it has been observed that in other Commonwealth jurisdictions[92] women's parenting has been subjected to intense scrutiny, with women who deviate from the ideal of a 'good mother', including women who work and those who 'abandon' their children upon separation, being viewed particularly harshly. In contrast, the parenting qualities of men face minimal scrutiny.[93] The simple fact that a father applies for residence is enough to make him a good father. As the father often cannot rely on his own positive history as shared or primary carer, this disproportionate and unfair scrutiny of the mother is encouraged by the father's tendency to focus on the mother's defects, often reinforced by the offer of a more suitable feminine influence within his own home.[94]

Boyd argues that there now exists an important tension within the law. The prevailing appeal of the traditional ideology of motherhood has not been displaced but it has been complicated by competing 'gender neutral ideologies' that have devalued the mothering role of many women and 'render[ed] invisible to the legal eye social and economic differences between the sexes'.[95] Judgments are thus increasingly founded on an idealized but essentially illusionary principle of gender equality that leaves women vulnerable both to the decline of 'maternal preference' and the rise of the 'new father' rhetoric.

S. Boyd, 'From gender specificity to gender neutrality? Ideologies in Canadian Child Custody Law', in C. Smart and S. Sevenhuijsen (eds), *Child Custody and the Politics of Gender* (London: Routledge, 1989), 126, 138–42

Increasingly, the starting point for judges in custody cases is a supposedly gender neutral assumption that women and men are equally situated and thus equally able to assume

---

[92] Boyd (1989) (Canada) and Moloney (2001) (Australia).
[93] Moloney ibid., 373.
[94] Brophy (1989), 236.
[95] Boyd (1989), 136.

domestic responsibilities such as child care. The difficulty for judges in the current conjuncture is in applying this gender neutral assumption to an area of social relations which is not yet gender neutral, and where ideologies of male and female behaviour still prevail. The fact that 43 per cent of women with children are not employed…and that women 'continue to bear the primary burden of family and home care' even if employed… may not be appropriately acknowledged when judges apply gender neutral standards…

Recent Canadian cases involving employed mothers illustrate that the gender-neutral principle of equality and its closely related 'individual-based ideology' can be applied in such a way as to undervalue primary caregiving…[M]istaken assumptions of equality encourage judges to jump to the conclusion that mothers and fathers have shared parenting more or less equally if there is evidence that fathers have engaged in child care to any extent more than the standard model of paternal conduct. Especially where mothers have been employed outside the home, it is often erroneously assumed that domestic work and child care are shared equally between parents, an assumption which devalues the double burden of work carried by most employed mothers…Some judges are also too ready to assume that fathers who have engaged in at least minimal child care can easily adopt the role of primary caregiver of children, while minimizing the value of primary caregiving performed by mothers in the past.

These observations provide an important insight into our own residence case law and the way in which the parenting of the mother is evaluated in comparison to that of the alternative carer.[96]

11.4.4 OTHER IMPORTANT CONSIDERATIONS IN PARENT VERSUS PARENT DISPUTES

Gay and lesbian parents

The issue of gay and lesbian parenting has grown in importance in recent years as parents fighting residence disputes have become increasingly confident about openly revealing their sexuality.[97] In many cases one of the parents may well have established a stable home with a new same-sex partner and wants to raise the child within that family environment, raising the question whether living within a same-sex household poses any risks to the child's welfare.[98] The courts have consistently held that homosexuality does not bar a parent from obtaining a residence order. However, the courts have not given unequivocal support to gay and lesbian parenting, making it clear that a parent's sexuality may be relevant to welfare. Indeed, although the leading authority is now quite old, the Court of Appeal have taken a particularly conservative line in evaluating the 'merits' of parenting within a same-sex family when compared with other, more 'conventional', alternatives.

The judgment of Callam J in *B v B (Minors) (Custody, Care and Control)* contains a careful analysis of the available evidence on gay and lesbian parenting. In this case, the mother had

---

[96] See, for example, *Re A (A Minor) (residence order)* [1998] 2 FCR 633; *Re H (A Minor: Custody)* [1990] 1 FLR 51; *Re S (A Minor) (Custody)* [1991] FCR 155; *Re A (A Minor) (Custody)* [1991] FCR 569; *Re K (Residence order: securing contact)* [1996] 1 FLR 583 and *Re W (Residence)* [1999] 2 FLR 390.

[97] We are dealing here with disputes between parents where one parent has left a heterosexual relationship to form a same-sex relationship. Residence disputes between a gay or lesbian couple (where only one parent is the biological and legal parent) are dealt with below.

[98] This issue also arises with respect to adoption and access to IVF treatment for same-sex couples.

left her husband and was living in a lesbian relationship. The dispute concerned a two-year-old boy, the youngest of three siblings. It was agreed between the parties that the two older children would remain with their father. Having considered the available evidence, Callam J granted residence to the mother.

B v B (Minors) (Custody, Care and Control) [1991] 1 FLR 402, 404–11 (Fam Div)

CALLAM J:

I want to deal first with the issue of whether a child should as a matter of principle be brought up in a lesbian household. The particular issue is that I must ask myself whether the proclivities of the mother and the lady with whom she lives are such as to make it undesirable in M's interests that he should be brought up in that home. That in essence is the question to be put. To some extent that question has been watered down, but it is still the one which underlies this case, and I must grasp that particular nettle...

In this case I have had the inestimable advantage of having had an eminent expert...to come forward to give evidence about the precise issue which I have to deal with on the issue of lesbianism...His opinion and advice basically are that one has to assess the problems of lesbianism and children being brought up in such households under two heads: the sexual identity of the child being brought up in such a household and the stigmatisation. It is very much the same thing as talking about corruption on the one hand and reputation on the other.

The professor came to the conclusion that there is no systematic evidence to suggest that homosexual habits in adult life tend to be associated with homosexuality in appearance, and that there is not an increased incidence of homosexuality among the children of homosexual parents. He specifically made the point that gender identity is not only a birth assignment but it is confirmed by upbringing, dressing, toys and behaviour, and that this boy, M, has clear and immediate boyish, unequivocal boyish appearance and conduct, and there is no need for any concern about him on this score.

While he accepts that what children learn during the first 2 years affects crucially how they see themselves in their male or female roles, there is no evidence that lesbian mothers tend to prejudice the differentiation of roles during early childhood, and he specifically says that he has examined this particular mother and that lesbian mothers almost without exception express a wish, as does this mother, that the sexual orientation of their children should be heterosexual...So what this expert has said quite plainly is that he does not take the view that sexual identity would be a problem in M's case, especially as it is clearly evident that the father will continue to play a role in his life whoever has care and control...

The second question which was raised was stigmatisation or reputation. This has always been seen by the courts as difficult to establish because one does not have to be a psychiatrist; there could be embarrassing conduct and comments, especially amongst the child's friends or schoolmates, and that these must be placed against all the other elements in each case or on the evidence in each case. That is really the most difficult part of the case, because stigmatisation or reputation reflect the views of the world as a whole, which consists of tolerant and less tolerant people, and patterns in this type of case do change...

Let me say immediately, on the question of stigmatisation, the [expert] indicated quite plainly that children tend to be teased about matters about which they show sensitivity, and the [expert] indicated that most of his cases in his experience, and he has made a special study of this, of, for example, nicknaming of children and teasing of children, relate to the child personally, and that those stigmatisations that arise do so from features such as large ears, noses, smell or conduct of the child, and that in his experience it is very rare for children to show an interest in the background of the parents of other children and that, in fact, children are far more tolerant of their classmates' background and parents than most people give them credit for...

[The expert] has said that the fears of pyschosexual development being distorted if a child is reared in a lesbian household, or that he will be subjected unduly to taunts and teasing or be ostracised, find no support in the systematic evidence...Such stigmatisation...as there is tends to come from the minority of adults, only exceptionally from peers, and the children are largely unaware of it and unaffected by it. And the professor said quite plainly that the dangers to the child in living in a lesbian household tend to be overestimated and there are, of course, widespread prejudices about lesbianism...

But when all is said and done, I have here a mother of whom the court welfare officer said quite plainly that M is very happy with his mother, and her report shows quite clearly that there is no concern shown at the mother's ability to look after M. The mother has been a blameless, faultless mother so far as care of her children is concerned, except that she has left her husband, she now lives in a lesbian relationship and certain conduct of deception has taken place that should not have taken place. But that does not undermine her qualification as a mother...

However, although residence was granted to the child's mother, Callam J also held, as a point of 'principle', that it is important to distinguish between 'militant lesbians' who seek to convert others to their way of life and 'private lesbians' who keep their sexuality to themselves. It is not clear on what evidence Callam J was asserting the existence of such 'militant lesbianism' or the potential threat posed to the sexual identity of children. However, it is implicit in his comments regarding the mother's desire to keep her sexuality private that lesbianism is essentially undesirable and not something to be positively promoted, especially to children who must continue to be raised on 'a heterosexual basis'. Whilst in many respects a positive judgment for gay and lesbian parents, Callam J can thus be criticized for conveying the much more negative message that homosexuality is not to be regarded as an equally acceptable alternative to heterosexual family life and that gay and lesbian parents seeking residence of their children should demonstrate a certain degree of restraint about their sexual orientation.

The existence of this hierarchy of family relationships from married heterosexual at one end of the scale to militant homosexual (and probably gay) parents at the other, was made more explicit by the Court of Appeal in *C v C (Custody of Child)*, another case in which the mother had formed a lesbian relationship and the father had remarried. The first instance judge granted residence to the mother but the father appealed. Allowing the appeal, both Glidewell LJ and Balcombe LJ held that when determining residence disputes in the post-divorce context the courts should strive to achieve what is as close as possible to the 'ideal' 'normal' family environment for children. In determining that 'ideal', the Court of Appeal refer not to the available expert evidence on gay and lesbian parenting, but to common sense—a kind of majoritarian morality, even if based on prejudice and misunderstanding—to conclude that according to society's normally accepted standards, a lesbian relationship cannot provide the same ideal family environment as a heterosexual married couple.

C v C (Custody of Child) [1991] FCR 254, 260, 262–4 (CA)

Lord Justice Glidewell:

Despite the vast change over the past 30 years or so in the attitude of our society generally to the institution of marriage, to sexual morality, and to homosexual relationships, I regard it as axiomatic that the ideal environment for the upbringing of a child is the home of loving, caring and sensible parents, her father and her mother. When the marriage between father and mother is at an end, that ideal cannot be attained. When the court is called upon to decide which of two possible alternatives is then preferable for the child's welfare, its task is to choose the alternative which comes closest to that ideal.

Even taking account of the changes of attitude to which I have referred, a lesbian relationship between two adult women is an unusual background in which to bring up a child. I think that the mother herself recognizes this, because the Judge recorded her as saying that she was sensitive to the problems that could arise, and did not flaunt the sexual nature of her relationship . . .

I make it clear that I am not saying that the fact that a mother is living in a lesbian relationship is conclusive, or that it disqualifies her from ever having the care and control of her child. A court may well decide that a sensitive, loving lesbian relationship is a more satisfactory environment for a child than a less sensitive or loving alternative. But that the nature of the relationship is an important factor to be put into the balance seems to me to be clear.

For this reason I would allow the appeal and set aside the Judge's order.

Lord Justice Balcombe:

In my judgment, [the judge] should start on the basis that the moral standards which are generally accepted in the society in which the child lives are more likely than not to promote his or her welfare. As society is now less homogeneous than it was 100 or even 50 years ago, those standards may differ between different communities, and the Judge may in appropriate cases be invited to receive evidence as to the standards accepted in a particular community, but in default of such evidence and where, as here, the child does not come from a particular ethnic minority, the Judge is entitled, and indeed bound, to apply his or her own experience in determining what are the accepted standards.

With those preliminary observations, I turn to what should be the judicial approach when faced with the problem with which the judge was faced in this case: to which of two parents should the care and control of a six and a half year old girl be given, where both parents clearly love and are loved by the child, both can give the child good physical care, but the father who has remarried lives with his new wife, while the mother has formed a lesbian relationship with another woman? Of course, the fact that the mother has a lesbian partner is not of itself a reason for denying the mother the care and control of her daughter; the question is: in conducting the balancing exercise what weight should the Judge give to the fact that, if care and control is given to the mother, the child's home will be the mother's home, with all that that involves? I agree with Glidewell L.J. that in those circumstances the Judge can only start with the approach that in our society it is still the norm that children are brought up in a home with a father, mother and siblings (if any) and, other things being equal, such an upbringing is most likely to be conducive to their welfare. If, because the parents are divorced, such an upbringing is no longer possible, then a very material factor in considering where the child's welfare lies is which of the competing parents can offer the nearest approach to that norm. In the present case it is clearly the father . . .

Interestingly, despite the Court of Appeal favouring the 'normal' family environment offered by the father, the first instance judge rehearing the case granted residence to the mother.[99]

[99] *C v C (No 2)* [1992] FCR 206.

There have, of course, been further significant changes in attitude towards gay and lesbian parenting since Balcombe LJ and Glidewell LJ were giving judgment in 1991. Same-sex couples can now become the legal parents of a child if seeking fertility treatment under the Human Fertilisation and Embryology Act 2008 (HFEA 2008) or by means of adoption.[100] It has also been held by the European Court of Human Rights that it is contrary to Articles 8 and 14 ECHR to discriminate between parents on the basis of sexual orientation when determining residence disputes.[101] In *Salgueiro da Silva Mouta v Portugal*, the Portuguese Court of Appeal had denied residence to the child's father on the basis of his 'abnormal' homosexuality:

Salgueiro da Silva Mouta v Portugal (App No 33290/96, ECHR) (1999)

26. . . . It must be determined whether the applicant can complain of . . . a difference in treatment and, if so, whether it was justified.

1. Existence of a difference in treatment . . .

28. The Court does not deny that the Lisbon Court of Appeal had regard above all to the child's interests when it examined a number of points of fact and of law which could have tipped the scales in favour of one parent rather than the other. However, the Court observes that in reversing the decision of the Lisbon Family Affairs Court and, consequently, awarding parental responsibility to the mother rather than the father, the Court of Appeal introduced a new factor, namely that the applicant was a homosexual and was living with another man.

The Court is accordingly forced to conclude that there was a difference of treatment between the applicant and M.'s mother which was based on the applicant's sexual orientation, a concept which is undoubtedly covered by Article 14 of the Convention . . .

2. Justification for the difference in treatment

29. In accordance with the case-law of the Convention institutions, a difference of treatment is discriminatory within the meaning of Article 14 if it has no objective and reasonable justification, that is if it does not pursue a legitimate aim or if there is not a reasonable relationship of proportionality between the means employed and the aim sought to be realised . . .

30. The decision of the Court of Appeal undeniably pursued a legitimate aim, namely the protection of the health and rights of the child; it must now be examined whether the second requirement was also satisfied.

31. In the applicant's submission, the wording of the judgment clearly showed that the decision to award parental responsibility to the mother was based mainly on the father's sexual orientation, which inevitably gave rise to discrimination against him in relation to the other parent.

32. The Government submitted that the decision in question had, on the contrary, merely touched on the applicant's homosexuality. The considerations of the Court of Appeal to which the applicant referred, when viewed in context, were merely sociological, or even statistical, observations. Even if certain passages of the judgment could arguably have been worded differently, clumsy or unfortunate expressions could not in themselves amount to a violation of the Convention.

---

[100] See pp 629–30 and pp 910–16.
[101] As to the change in attitude of the English judiciary see Thorpe LJ's judgment in *Re G (Residence: same-sex partner)* [2005] EWCA Civ 402.

33. The Court reiterates its earlier finding that the Lisbon Court of Appeal, in examining the appeal lodged by M.'s mother, introduced a new factor when making its decision as to the award of parental responsibility, namely the applicant's homosexuality . . . In determining whether the decision which was ultimately made constituted discriminatory treatment lacking any reasonable basis, it needs to be established whether, as the Government submitted, that new factor was merely an *obiter dictum* which had no direct effect on the outcome of the matter in issue or whether, on the contrary, it was decisive.

34. . . . The Court of Appeal . . . weighed the facts differently from the lower court and awarded parental responsibility [equivalent to residence] to the mother. It considered, among other things, that "custody of young children should as a general rule be awarded to the mother unless there are overriding reasons militating against this . . .". The Court of Appeal further considered that there were insufficient reasons for taking away from the mother the parental responsibility awarded her by agreement between the parties.

However, after that observation the Court of Appeal added "Even if that were not the case . . . we think that custody of the child should be awarded to the mother" . . . The Court of Appeal then took account of the fact that the applicant was a homosexual and was living with another man in observing that "The child should live in . . . a traditional Portuguese family" and that "It is not our task here to determine whether homosexuality is or is not an illness or whether it is a sexual orientation towards persons of the same sex. In both cases it is an abnormality and children should not grow up in the shadow of abnormal situations" . . .

35. It is the Court's view that the above passages from the judgment in question, far from being merely clumsy or unfortunate as the Government maintained, or mere *obiter dicta*, suggest, quite to the contrary, that the applicant's homosexuality was a factor which was decisive in the final decision. That conclusion is supported by the fact that the Court of Appeal, when ruling on the applicant's right to contact, warned him not to adopt conduct which might make the child realise that her father was living with another man "in conditions resembling those of man and wife" (ibid.).

36. The Court is therefore forced to find, in the light of the foregoing, that the Court of Appeal made a distinction based on considerations regarding the applicant's sexual orientation, a distinction which is not acceptable under the Convention . . .

The Court cannot therefore find that a reasonable relationship of proportionality existed between the means employed and the aim pursued; there has accordingly been a violation of Article 8 taken in conjunction with Article 14.

The Court's decision therefore seems to prohibit treating sexual orientation, in and of itself, as a relevant consideration in a residence dispute and clearly not as a decisive factor. This throws into question whether the approach endorsed by the Court of Appeal in *C v C* can still be regarded as good law.

Racial, religious, and cultural factors

Race, religion, and culture are often regarded as fundamentally important to a person's sense of identity and belonging. When separating parents are from different racial, cultural, or religious backgrounds, the battle over residence can take on an even greater significance. It is more than just a battle over where the child should live: it is a battle over the child's whole way of life. The courts have recognized the importance of these issues. However, whilst religion, race, and culture are relevant, they are not afforded any special significance in the welfare balance. The European Court of Human Rights has made it clear that a decision concerning residence must not be based 'solely or principally' on the applicant's religion: in and of itself it cannot be a determining factor.[102] The courts must also avoid making abstract judgments about the tenets, beliefs, or practices of particular religions or cultures. The European Court has, however, confirmed that it is legitimate for the domestic authorities to take into account the *effect* of the applicant's religious practices on the child's lifestyle and upbringing.[103] This is the approach adopted by the English courts.

The case of *M v H* concerned a protracted dispute over the child's residence between her mother who lived in Germany and her father who lived in England. In earlier proceedings a shared residence order had been made. The dispute now centred on whether the child should attend school in Germany or in England. The child's mother was a Jehovah's Witness. The child's father was Catholic. In giving judgment for the father, Charles J provides a clear summary of the law as to the relevance of the parent's respective religions.

M v H [2008] EWHC 324

Charles J:

27....I was referred by counsel for the mother to two unreported cases...as support for the proposition, which I accept, that the fact that the mother is a Jehovah's Witness is of itself not a relevant point. The father accepted this and in my view has never been making this point.

28. The point that the father is a Catholic and his beliefs as such is also of itself not a relevant point.

29. So the fact that one parent is a Catholic and the other a Jehovah's Witness is not of itself relevant and a decision should not be based on a preference of one of these religious beliefs and lifestyle based thereon to the other. For example as Scarman LJ says...in Re T [unreported]:

"...it does not follow that, because one parent's way of life is more acceptable to most of us, it is contrary to the welfare of the children that they should adopt the way of life of the other parent that is acceptable only to a minority, and a tiny minority at that. It seems to me that when one has, as in this case such a conflict, all that the court can do is to look at the detail of the whole of the circumstances of the parents and determine where lies the true interest of the children."...

30. [I]t cannot be said that the beliefs and practices of a parent who is a Jehovah's Witness creates a situation that is so inimical to good family life that ordinary considerations have to give way to it in determining what will best promote the welfare of the relevant child. The position is that the two opposing ways of life that are relevant in this case are both socially acceptable and certainly consistent with a decent and respectable life and one in which the welfare of children can be promoted...

31. Rather the relevance of the religious difference relates to the impact in all the circumstances of the case on Sophie's welfare of the respective beliefs of the parents and thus of their respective lifestyles and attitudes based thereon. This is an exercise that can only be carried out in all the circumstances of a given...case and it naturally has many comparative elements....

106. The religious conflict between her parents is not relevant as such in this respect but, as the cases show, the knock on effects of the ways of life of the parents by reference to their

---

[102] *Palau-Martinez v France* (App No 64927/01, ECHR) (2004).
[103] *Ismailova v Russia* (App No 37614/02, ECHR) (2007), [55]–[63].

religious beliefs and practices is relevant and in my view here it is relevant to the question of Sophie's stability and security to assist her development.

107. In my view such stability and security will be assisted by Sophie having a wide group of friends of her own age, and relationships with adults, both from divergent backgrounds rather than a social life centred on the Jehovah's Witnesses. In my view such a peer group, and relationships with adults, would assist her general happiness and thus her security, stability and development. Such adults would include parents of friends, teachers and people running activities.

108. In my view the beliefs and practices of the mother as a Jehovah's Witness to parties and Christmas is likely to limit the width of Sophie's friends of her own age and her contact with adults, who can help and influence her. Further it may well cause her problems at school simply because of the differences it will create between her and her class mates...

110. So, in my view the likely social effects on Sophie of the mother's beliefs and practices as a Jehovah's Witness are factors that favour Sophie going to school in England. Absent such emotional insecurity flowing from the parental conflict those effects would have far less weight. Further, as I have indicated they are not the most important or magnetic considerations in this case. Rather they constitute a factor that supports the conclusion based on those most important and magnetic considerations.

Acutely aware of the sensitivity of the issue, the courts have clearly tried to avoid any suggestion that they are evaluating and choosing between competing religions or cultures. However, as this case demonstrates, this may be virtually impossible to achieve in practice when assessing the *impact* of any relevant cultural and/or religious practices and beliefs on the child's welfare.

In preference to allowing religious or cultural factors to become a dominant factor in residence disputes, the courts have tended to rely on making generous provision for contact to satisfy the child's need for knowledge of both sides of his or her religious and/or cultural heritage.[104]

11.4.5 SHARED RESIDENCE—THE ANSWER?

One of the most important developments to arise from the emphasis on gender neutrality in post-divorce parenting is the argument in favour of shared residence. Fathers' rights groups have been vocal in calling for a presumption in favour of shared residence to address what they perceive to be the current inequalities in the law. A presumption in favour of shared residence, as demanded by fathers' rights groups, would require an equal 50:50 division of the child's time between the two parents, that presumption only to be displaced on positive welfare grounds. Legal reform to entrench a normative model of post-divorce parenting which embraces equality between the parents in the form of shared 50:50 residence also has a strong attraction for some feminist scholars who see equality or 'gender neutral parenting' both pre and post- separation as the key to achieving gender equality in all spheres of life. In many ways, shared residence appears to offer the ideal solution to inequalities in the distribution of child-care responsibilities and the disadvantages suffered by women as a result.[105]

Support for the greater use of shared residence orders is firmly rooted in the discourse on shared parenting. Shared parenting post-divorce is an integral part of the normative model

[104] *Re T (A child)* [2005] EWCA Civ 1397.
[105] Kurki-Suonio (2000), 183.

of the 'civilized divorce'.[106] The hostility promoted by the 'win-lose' mentality of previous models of post-divorce parenting is regarded as particularly damaging to children, with shared parenting perceived as one means by which hostilities can be reduced.[107] The normative model of post-divorce parenting emerging from these debates is explained by Bren Neale and Carol Smart:

B. Neale and C. Smart, 'In Whose Best Interests? Theorising Family Life Following Parental Separation or Divorce', in S. Day Sclater and C. Piper (eds), *Undercurrents of Divorce* (Aldershot: Ashgate, 1999), 33, 37–9

Since the early 1980s the model of lone/reconstituted family has gradually been replaced by that of a co-parenting/biological family. The original family is no longer to be broken under the 'clean break' philosophy, nor is it to be replaced by a reconstituted family...The potential to care for a child without the other parent, even if this is bound up with a new marriage or partnership, has a diminished value under this new ideology and, barring exceptional circumstances, can no longer be legally sanctioned. If the family can't remain intact and under one roof (still, of course the preferred option) then, as Day Sclater and Piper argue...it must re-invent itself as a 'bi-nuclear' family spread across two households. Divorce has thus been recast as a 'stage' (albeit a painful one) in the newly extended life course of the indelible nuclear family...

This new model dovetails with a welfare discourse that has been radically reformulated. Children are no longer said to need one stable home, one primary carer and the restabilising influence of the stepfamily. What they are now said to need is two biological parents and the restabilising influence of the non-residential father. One notable feature of this reformulated welfare discourse is that the child's needs are now defined in terms of what they are lacking: the lack of proper fathering and the limitations of mothering, which has culminated in a link between the 'child of divorce' and the pervasive but largely undefined notion of harm...

The assumption that children are 'damaged' by divorce is accompanied by another assumption—that this damage can be mitigated if particular forms of parenting and therapeutic interventions are put in place. Parents are to ameliorate the worst effects of their actions by prioritising their children's welfare, playing a joint part in their children's day to day care and developing a co-operative and unselfish sharing of parental authority.

As Neale and Smart point out, the shared parenting discourse is underpinned by a significant shift in the welfare discourse. Whereas the interests of children under the 'tender years doctrine' were clearly identified with those of the mother, the rise of the 'new father' rhetoric has seen the interests of children increasingly viewed as dependent on their relationship with their father.[108] As we have seen in other areas of the law, fathers' rights group have thus been able to argue that the imperative for improving the legal position of fathers comes from within the welfare discourse itself:

[T]he new model is underpinned by a fresh articulation of the rights of fathers who argue that, since they are just as capable as mothers of caring for their children they should be granted equal legal rights to them...

[106] Krieken (2005), 34–45.
[107] Brophy (1989), 222 and Krieken (2005), ibid.
[108] Brophy (1989).

It is important to recognise that what is transformed under the new model is how father-hood is constituted within legal and policy discourse. It seems that where mothers, as the day to day carers, were once constructed as vital to their children, it is fathers, as the restabilisers and potential carers, who are now constructed as essential, at least following divorce. That fathers might want a more direct involvement in day to day care is a relatively new phenom-enon, deserving of explanation. According to Beck, it is linked to wider social changes under which the traditional gendering of parental care and financial support is breaking down...

The changed attitude can also be understood in terms of the value that is increasingly placed upon emotional fulfilment within family relationships. If marriage and, perhaps more to the point, remarriage can no longer be relied upon to provide this, then the parent-child relationship may increasingly become the focus of such fulfilment. This, in turn, is linked to the rise in a romanticised vision of children as priceless emotional assets which, in the inter-ests of parental equality, are best divided equally than awarded to one parent alone. Where mothers were once seen to be the holders of onerous responsibilities, requiring sustained emotional commitment, hard physical work and a range of socio-economic sacrifices (and deserving, therefore, of custodial status and state support), they are now seen to be in pos-session of valuable commodities, and any unwillingness to share them seen as discrimina-tory against fathers.

This increasing focus on fatherhood clearly informed the Labour government's approach to post-divorce parenting.

DCA, DfES, and DTI, *Parental Separation: Children's Needs and Parents' Responsibilities*, Cm 6273 (London: HMSO, 2004)

32. If parental separation is handled well, any adverse impact on the child can be mini-mised. If it is handled badly, in particular, if conflict is played out around or through children, it can have very damaging effects. Children need the support of their parents to thrive. They want and need a safe and secure environment, preferably involving both parents. Where this does not happen, the impact on the children can be severe.

33. Research shows that:

- The likelihood of adverse outcomes for children from separated families is roughly twice that for other children...

- Up to half of young offenders come from separated families.

- Young people with a lone parent are twice as likely, and those living with a parent and step-parent are three times as likely to run away as young people living with two birth parents.

- Girls from separated families are at greater risk of teenage pregnancy, and the daughter of a teenage mother is one and a half times more likely to become one herself, than the daughter of an older mother.

- By the time they were 33, those who had experienced parental divorce as children (16 and under) were almost twice as likely to lack formal qualifications as others: 20 percent compared to 11 percent.

- At age 33, men who experienced divorce when aged 0–16 were twice as likely to be unemployed as those who experienced no parental separation: 14 percent compared to

7 percent. Post-separation parental conflict can lead to emotional and behavioural diffi culties for the child and the weight of evidence suggests conflict has a negative impact on the child's development and adjustment.

34. By contrast, effective parenting enables children to fulfil their potential. And children whose fathers have been actively involved in their lives experience better outcomes:

- Higher educational achievements
- More satisfactory relationships in adult life
- Protection from mental health problems
- Less likelihood of being in trouble with the police.

Shared parenting does not necessarily mean 50:50 shared residence as advocated by fathers' rights groups. Although 50:50 shared residence perhaps represents the most 'pure' form of shared parenting, the retention of parental responsibility by both parents (allied with generous contact to the non-resident parent) already ensures that they both have the necessary legal status to remain actively engaged in their children's lives post-separation.

Shared residence under the Children Act—the legal framework

The CA 1989 explicitly provides for shared residence:

Children Act 1989, s 11

(4) Where a residence order is made in favour of two or more persons who do not themselves all live together, the order may specify the periods during which the child is to live in the different households.

There is no requirement when making a shared residence order that the child's time be divided *equally* between the two households. More flexible patterns of shared care are possible.

The early case law was generally hostile to shared residence orders, the prevailing view being that children require one settled home. A shared residence order was therefore regarded as 'wholly exceptional'[109] or at least 'unusual', and it had to be shown that the proposed departure from the conventional orders conferred some positive benefit on the child.[110] Opposition to shared residence was particularly strong where there was continuing hostility between the parents.

However, judicial attitudes towards shared residence have undergone significant change. A more liberal approach was clear from the Court of Appeal judgment in *D v D*. The case was one in which there was 'an exceptionally high level of animosity between the parents'. The children lived with their mother but had substantial levels of contact with their father. The judge found that the mother used the fact she had sole residence as a weapon in the parents'

---

[109] *J v J* [1991] 2 FLR 385; *Re H (A Minor) (Shared Residence)* [1994] 1 FLR 717.
[110] *A v A (Minors) (Shared residence order)* [1994] 1 FLR 669.

'war'. He therefore made an order for shared residence in an attempt to reduce the level of conflict between them.

D v D [2000] EWCA Civ 3009

HALE LJ:

20. [Counsel] who appears for the mother, has argued that the authorities indicate that shared residence orders should only be made either in exceptional circumstances or, at the very least, where it can be demonstrated that they would show a positive benefit for the children. In this particular case there were no exceptional circumstances, no evidence of positive benefit and thus, no reason to change the legal arrangements which had been in place for some time. He also argues that access to information was irrelevant or given too much weight because the father already had parental responsibility and was entitled to that information. Thus that, by itself, could not be regarded as an exceptional circumstance or of positive benefit...

22. The background to the Children Act provision lies in the Law Commission's Working Paper No. 96, published in 1986, on Custody and the Law Commission's Report, Law Com. No. 172, published in 1988, on Guardianship and Custody. If I may summarise the basic principles proposed, the first was that each parent with parental responsibility should retain their equal and independent right, and their responsibility, to have information and make appropriate decisions about their children. If, of course, the parents were not living together it might be necessary for the court to make orders about their future, but those orders should deal with the practical arrangements for where and how the children should be living rather than assigning rights as between the parents...

24....[D]ealing with residence orders the Commission said this at paragraph 4.12 of the Law Com No. 172:

"Apart from the effect on the other parent, which has already been mentioned, the main difference between a residence order and a custody order is that the new order should be flexible enough to accommodate a much wider range of situations. In some cases, the child may live with both parents even though they do not share the same household. It was never our intention to suggest that children should share their time more or less equally between their parents. Such arrangements will rarely be practicable, let alone for the children's benefit. However, the evidence from the United States is that where they are practicable they can work well and we see no reason why they should be actively discouraged. None of our respondents shared the view expressed in a recent case [Riley v Riley] that such an arrangement, which had been working well for some years, should never have been made. More commonly, however, the child will live with both parents but spend more time with one than the other. Examples might be where he spends term time with one and holidays with the other, or two out of three holidays from boarding school with one and the third with the other. It is a far more realistic description of the responsibilities involved in that sort of arrangement to make a residence order covering both parents rather than a residence order for one and a contact order for the other. Hence we recommend that where the child is to live with two (or more) people who do not live together, the order may specify the periods during which the child is to live in each household. The specification may be general rather than detailed and in some cases may not be necessary at all."...

31. It is quite clear that in [A v A (minors) [1994] 1 FLR 669, Butler-Sloss LJ] was moving matters on from any suggestion, which is not in the legislation, that these orders require exceptional circumstances...

32. If...it is either planned or has turned out that the children are spending substantial amounts of their time with each of their parents then, as both the Law Commission and my Lady indicated in the passages that I have quoted it may be an entirely appropriate order to

make. For my part, I would not add any gloss on the legislative provisions, which are always subject to the paramount consideration of what is best for the children concerned.

33. This case is one in which, as the judge said, the arrangements have been settled for some considerable time. The children are, in effect, living with both of their parents. They have homes with each of them...

34. In those circumstances it seems to me that there is indeed a positive benefit to these children in those facts being recognised in the order that the court makes. There is no detriment or disrespect to either parent in that order. It simply reflects the reality of these children's lives. It was entirely appropriate for the judge to make it in this case and neither party should feel that they have won or lost as a result. I would, therefore, dismiss the appeal.

This case is now regarded as marking an important change in approach towards shared residence orders.[111] Hale LJ makes clear that the courts should not feel constrained in making a shared residence order where such an order will reflect the reality of the children's lives. It is, however, often very difficult to determine where the boundary lies between, on the one hand, a reality of shared care justifying a shared residence order and, on the other, a more conventional arrangement best reflected in orders for residence and contact. It is a question of degree. Absolute equality is not required.[112] Nor is geographical proximity between the parents[113] or a pattern of care whereby the child spends alternative weeks in the home of each parent.

It is clear from *D v D* that high levels of hostility between the parents will not prevent the court making a shared residence order where it is otherwise justified; a good relationship between the parties is not a prerequisite.[114] Indeed, subsequent case law has suggested that a shared residence order may actually help to ease the conflict between the parents by sending out the strong message that they have equal *status* in the eyes of the law. This symbolic or psychological benefit of a shared residence order was considered by Wall J in the case of *A v A (Children) (shared residence)*. By the time of the substantive hearing, the children were spending 50 per cent of their time with each parent.

A v A (Children) (shared residence) [2004] EWHC 142

WALL J:

[24]...

7. This is a case where a shared residence order is appropriate. But it also demonstrates clearly that shared residence orders are not a panacea. Shared residence and an equal division of the children's time between their parents' houses is possible in this case because the parents live close to each other, and the children can go to school from either home. The children welcome it because, in C's words...it gives his parents nothing left to fight about. But it is a pragmatic solution, which does nothing to address the underlying hostility between the parents. Whether or not it succeeds; only time will tell...

[119] *Re D* makes it clear that a shared residence order is an order that children live with both parents. It must, therefore, reflect the reality of the children's lives. Where children are living with one parent and are either not seeing the other parent or the amount of time to be spent with the

---

[111] *Re A (Children) (Shared Residence)* [2002] EWCA Civ 1343, [10].
[112] *Re K (A Child)* [2008] EWCA Civ 526, [6]. A division of care approximating to 60:40 is now fairly standard under the terms of a shared residence order.
[113] *Re F (Children)* [2003] EWCA Civ 592; *Re H (Children)* [2009] EWCA Civ 245, [8].
[114] See also *Re R (Children)* [2005] EWCA Civ 542, [11]–[12].

other parent is limited or undecided, there cannot be a shared residence order. However, where children are spending a substantial amount of time with both their parents, a shared residence order reflects the reality of the children's lives. It is not necessarily to be considered an exceptional order and should be made if it is in the best interests of the children concerned...

[122] [I]t is plain that in terms of time spent in each home and the importance of each home to the children, this is a prime case for a shared residence order. Such an order directly reflects the situation on the ground...

[124]...[The] order, in my judgment, requires the court not only to reflect the reality that the children are dividing their lives equally between their parents, but also to reflect the fact that the parents are equal in the eyes of the law, and have equal duties and responsibilities towards their children...

[126]...This case has been about control throughout. Mrs A sought to control the children, with seriously adverse consequences for the family. She failed. Control is not what this family needs. What it needs is co-operation. By making a shared residence order the court is making that point. These parents have joint and equal parental responsibility. The residence of the children is shared between them. These facts need to be recognised by an order for shared residence.[115]

The notion that a shared residence order may be important for symbolic or psychological reasons has been gathering strength. Indeed, it has been suggested in more recent authorities that a shared residence order may be justified for symbolic or psychological reasons (particularly to acknowledge the equal status of the parents) even in the absence of an underlying reality of shared care; in other words, that they constitute separate alternative grounds for the making of an order. This suggestion first emerged in a judgment of Potter P:[116]

Re A (a child) (joint residence: parental responsibility) [2008] EWCA Civ 867

Sir Mark Potter

66. The making of a shared residence order is no longer the unusual order which once it was. Following the implementation of the Act and in the light of s 11(4) of the Act which provides that the court may make residence orders in favour of more than one person, whether living in the same household or not, the making of such an order has become increasingly common. It is now recognised by the court that a shared residence order may be regarded as appropriate where it provides legal confirmation of the factual reality of a child's life or where, in a case where one party has the primary care of a child, it may be psychologically beneficial to the parents in emphasising the equality of their position and responsibilities.

Although *Re A* falls in the sub-category of cases where a shared residence order is necessary to confer parental responsibility on the non-resident parent,[117] Potter P's judgment has been

---

[115] See also *Re P (Shared residence order)* [2005] EWCA Civ 1639, where Wall LJ appears to suggest that where a child's time is split fairly equally between the parents, there needs to be a good reason why an order for shared residence should not be made.

[116] Although see also *Re K (A Child)* [2008] EWCA Civ 528, [6], where Wilson LJ hints at a similar approach.

[117] In this case the child had been raised for two years by his mother's partner who mistakenly believed that he was the legal (genetic) father.

approved by Wilson LJ as summarizing the principles governing shared residence orders and applied to a routine intra-parental residence dispute.

Re W (Shared Residence Order) [2009] EWCA Civ 370

Wilson LJ:

13. With respect to [counsel], I see no subsisting foundation for his submission to us today that, unless the time to be spent by a child in the two households is close to being equal, unusual circumstances are required before a shared residence order should be made. Fifteen years ago his submission would have been valid...But at any rate for the last 8 years the better view has been that, while of course a need remains for the demonstration of circumstances which positively indicate that the child's welfare would thereby be served, there is no such gloss on the appropriateness of an order for shared residence as would be reflected by the words 'unusual' or indeed 'exceptional'...

17....[Counsel] began by presenting to us statistics which he had compiled and which, according to him...indicate that, under the arrangements made by consent between the parties, K [the child] is to spend with the father only 25% of her time...His submission reminded me of comments which, as a temporary member of this court, I made in *Re F (shared residence order)*...to the effect that statistics of that character were usually only of limited value. [Counsel] ultimately described as the main plank of his appeal the fact that a shared residence order did not reflect the situation on the ground...But it was in that same short judgment of mine...that I attempted to explode the *canard* that a shared residence order was appropriate only in circumstances in which the children would be spending their time evenly, or more or less evenly, in the two homes.

The shared residence order was thus upheld even though the 'reality' of the child's care was a long way from 50:50 shared care.[118]

The Court of Appeal is, however, currently somewhat divided as to whether it is appropriate to use shared residence to deal with questions of parental status even where there is no underlying reality of shared care.[119]

Re H (Children) [2009] EWCA Civ 902

Ward LJ:

13. [A] shared residence order must reflect the reality of the children's lives. Where the children are spending a substantial amount of time with both parents, a shared residence order reflects the reality of their lives...[A] residence order is about where a child is to live and it is not about status. I want to emphasise that here the father's status is recognised by the parental responsibility agreement and order which has been made. That gives him equal say in how the children are to be brought up, so that when they are with him he will determine when they brush their teeth and when they go to bed and whether they have cornflakes or porridge for breakfast...So in terms of status he has it, and shared residence is not going to affect status. Shared residence is about the reality of where they live. And the best test I

---

[118] See also, Wilson LJ's judgment in *Re O (A Child)* [2009] EWCA Civ 1266.
[119] This was also the view taken by Hale LJ in *Re A (Children)* [2001] EWCA Civ 1795, [17].

can think of, though my words of wisdom on the subject do not seem, [un]fortunately [sic], as readily to find their way into the law reports, my practical test is to postulate the question, ask the children, where do you live? If the answer is "I live with my mummy but I go and stay with my daddy regularly", then you have the answer to your problem. That answer means a residence order with mummy and contact with daddy, but if the situation truly is such that the children say, "Oh we live with mummy for part of the time and with daddy for the other part of the time", then you have the justification for making a shared residence order.

The House of Lords has recently had reason to address the issue of shared residence orders in *Holmes-Moorhouse v London Borough of Richmond upon Thames*.[120] The case raised the interesting question of the relationship between the court's power to make an order for shared residence and the local authority's obligations to provide public housing to a parent in whose favour such an order has been made and who is claiming to be in priority need as a 'person with whom dependent children reside or might reasonably be expected to reside.'[121] The court had made a shared residence order in favour of the applicant and his former partner by consent, with the children expected to live with each parent on alternate weeks. Despite the order, the local authority refused to accommodate the father even though he claimed to have priority need. The local authority argued that even though the court had made a shared residence order, the local authority had to reach an independent judgment under the Housing Act as to whether the applicant's expectation that a dependent child would live with him was reasonable. The House of Lords agreed, holding that the provision of public housing was a matter for the housing authority exercising its statutory duties and responsibilities and could not be controlled or pre-judged by the court through the making of a shared residence order, whether or not the order was made by consent or following a disputed hearing. As Lord Hoffmann points out, these are two different questions decided by different authorities on a different basis and 'must not be allowed to become entangled with one another'.[122] The fact that an applicant for public housing has a shared residence order in his or her favour (determined on the basis of the child's welfare but which for various reasons may not have been the subject of thorough forensic examination) is just one factor for the housing authority to take into account when determining whether the applicant has a priority need, alongside other material considerations such as the limited availability of suitable family housing in the area.[123] The shared residence order cannot determine the matter.[124]

The judgment of Baroness Hale is particularly interesting for the general guidance it provides on making shared residence orders.

Holmes-Moorhouse v London Borough of Richmond upon Thames [2009] UKHL 7

BARONESS HALE:

30. When any family court decides with whom the children of separated parents are to live, the welfare of those children must be its paramount consideration: Children Act 1989, s 1(1). This means that it must choose from the available options the future which will be best for

---

120 [2009] UKHL 7.
121 Housing Act 1996, ss 193 and 189(1)(b).
122 [2009] UKHL 7, [8], [9], [14], and [17] (per Lord Hoffmann).
123 Ibid., [16] (per Lord Hoffmann).
124 Ibid., [17] (per Lord Hoffmann).

the children, not the future which will be best for the adults. It also means that the court may be creative in devising options which the parents have not put forward. It does not mean that the court can create options where none exist...

37....[I]n my view, this order should not have been made. A residence order is "an order settling the arrangements to be made as to the person with whom a child is to live"...Although, as I have said, the parents are free to depart from it by agreement if they wish, it is an order which can be enforced, by physical removal of the children if need be...It is one thing to make such an order when each parent has a home to offer the children, even if it is not exactly what they have been used to before their parents split up. It is another thing entirely to make such an order when one parent is living in the family home and the other parent has no accommodation at all to offer them and no money with which to feed and clothe them....

38. Family court orders are meant to provide practical solutions to the practical problems faced by separating families. They are not meant to be aspirational statements of what would be for the best in some ideal world which has little prospect of realisation. Ideally there may be many cases where it would be best for the children to have a home with each of their parents. But this is not always or even usually practicable. Family courts have no power to conjure up resources where none exist. Nor can they order local authorities or other public agencies to provide particular services unless there is a specific power to do so...The courts cannot even do this in care proceedings, whose whole aim is to place long term parental responsibility upon the state, to look after and safeguard and promote the welfare of children who are suffering or likely to suffer harm in their own homes...A fortiori they cannot do this in private law proceedings between the parents. No doubt all family courts have from time to time tried to persuade local authorities to act in what we consider to be the best interests of the children whose welfare is for us the paramount consideration. But we have no power to order them to do so. Nor, in my view, should we make orders which will be unworkable unless they do. It is different, of course, if we have good reason to believe that the necessary resources will be forthcoming in the foreseeable future. The court can always ask the local authority for information about this...

39. But the family court should not use a residence order as a means of putting pressure upon a local housing authority to allocate their resources in a particular way despite all the other considerations which...they have to take into account. It is quite clear that this was what the family court was trying to do in this case...

Baroness Hale's approach, emphasizing the importance of s 8 orders being grounded in reality and offering practical solutions to the problems facing post-separation families, has clear echoes of her earlier judgments on shared residence orders. Although it is only possible to speculate, there is nothing in this judgment to suggest Baroness Hale would now depart from the clear principles she established in *D v D* to endorse the approach to shared residence orders that has been favoured in more recent years by some members of the Court of Appeal. Baroness Hale also emphasizes the particular importance of listening to the voice of the child in cases of shared residence, 'because it is the children who will have to divide their time between two homes and it is all too easy for the parents' wishes and feelings to predominate'.[125]

Problems with shared residence orders and the shared parenting ideal

Sharing residence on a 50:50 basis:

In its 2004 Green Paper on contact, the Labour government considered whether the law should entrench a positive presumption in favour of shared residence with the child's time

---

[125] Ibid., [36].

being divided equally on a roughly 50:50 basis. The government's commitment to the shared parenting ethos was clear but despite the political pressure from fathers' rights groups, it rejected amending the CA 1989 in this way, arguing that a 'one size fits all approach' is not appropriate.

DCA, DfES, and DTI, *Parental Separation: Children's Needs and Parents' Responsibilities,* **Cm 6273** (London: HMSO, 2004), 5, 7

4. The government firmly believes that, in the event of parental separation, a child's welfare is best promoted by a continuing relationship with *both* parents, as long as it is safe to do so...

42. Some have proposed that legislative change is needed to introduce "presumptions of contact" to give parents equal rights to equal time with their child after parental separation. Where such arrangements are best for the child, and are agreed between the parents or determined by a court, such arrangements can and should be put in place. The government does not, however, believe that an automatic 50:50 division of the child's time between the two parents would be in the best interests of most children. In many separated families, such arrangements would not work in practical terms, owing to living arrangements or work commitments. Enforcing this type of arrangement through legislation would not be what many children want and could have a damaging impact on some of them. Children are not a commodity to be apportioned equally after separation. The best arrangements for them will depend on a variety of issues particular to their circumstances: a one-size-fits-all formula will not work. The assumption that both parents have equal status and value as parents is enshrined in current law. The actual arrangements made by courts start from that position.

The Labour government's refusal to enshrine a presumption in favour of shared residence in the CA 1989 seems fully justified. Feminist scholars have raised strong concerns about shared residence and the shared parenting paradigm that underpins it. Their concerns have centred on the lack of any empirical foundation for many of the assumptions about contemporary parenting that have fuelled the debate. Furthermore, it is argued that this has led to a devaluing of women's actual physical, emotional, and financial investment in motherhood, and exacerbated rather than ameliorated existing inequalities.[126]

The empirical work of Smart and Neale is instructive in understanding concerns about how the post-divorce parenting debate has developed. Based on a sample of 60 parents, the research reveals the reality of pre- and post-divorce parenting patterns and the differing attitudes of mothers and fathers towards their respective parenting roles. In particular, their findings unveil the 'myth' of the equal, hands-on 'new father' within intact families, one of the driving forces behind the calls for greater equality in post-divorce parenting.

C. Smart and B. Neale, *Family Fragments?* (Cambridge: Polity Press, 1999), 45–66

[I]t is clear that in Western cultures there are significant differences in both the responsibilities associated with mothering and with fathering, and with the meaning(s) associated with being a mother and being a father. Moreover, while motherhood may have imparted a fairly

---

[126] Boyd (1989), 148–52.

stable identity, the meaning of fatherhood has become highly contested and uncertain in Britain in the 1990s...

Almost all of our interviewees became parents while married or cohabiting and so entered into parenthood with the assumption that there would be two parents available to raise the children. Moreover the majority had settled into a form of parenting where responsibilities and duties had been allocated and become established. We found, not surprisingly, that the typical pattern was one where mothers gave up work or worked part-time in order to become primary carers. The fathers therefore tended to develop rather different relationships with their children because they spent less time with them and inevitably took less day-to-day responsibility for them. We found a pattern of relationships which was very similar to that described by Backett in her study of parenting in intact households. Basically fathers were one step removed from their children and their relationship with them was sustained via their relationship with the mother...Of considerable interest in Backett's research was her discovery that fathers did not have to do equal amounts of caring in order to be regarded as good fathers. Thus child-rearing was often described as being equally shared when in fact it was nothing of the sort...

Very few of our fathers were willing to allow their careers or job prospects to suffer in order to take more responsibility for their children while they had a relationship with the mother...[O]nly one father stayed at home in a 'role reversal' arrangement...[F]or most their ability to spend equal amounts of time with their children and to assume a shared responsibility at a day-to-day level was actually compromised by their paid employment.

The accounts of the mothers in our sample focused on two aspects of childcare, the physical work (e.g. feeding, bathing, toilet training) and the emotional care (e.g. monitoring the child's moods, anticipating needs). In some instances mothers were disappointed that fathers did relatively little of the former, or felt angry that after a 'promising start' they lapsed into a more traditional role. In other instances the mothers were not unduly concerned about the physical work, or acknowledged that the fathers had undertaken a reasonable amount of this burden, but they pointed to the fact that fathers rarely seemed to be 'in tune' with the children or that they did not notice or anticipate emotional states, illnesses or preferences. As with the mothers in Backett's study, these mothers tended to assume that they held the 'real' responsibility for the children while the fathers either helped or hindered...

The gendered nature of parenting within the intact family has important implications for the transition to post-separation family life:

The fact that mothers tended to see themselves as responsible and as more experienced in childcare made the transition to post-divorce parenting hard. During their marriage or cohabitation, being a good mother meant taking this responsibility and, to some extent, taking it for granted too. But on divorce they found that they were expected to relinquish this feeling of responsibility to someone who (usually) had not actually shared it during their relationship and who might be viewed as fairly inept at the physical care work, let alone the emotional caring. This division of labour mitigated against sharing responsibility later, especially if children were very young...

How parents view themselves, and how much of their personal identity is bound up with their parenthood, has an important bearing on how parenthood operates in practice. People's biographies as parents assume importance because parental identities are not made instantly or ascribed but, much like other kin relationships, are negotiated and forged over considerable periods of time. From this perspective, parenthood can be seen as part of a nexus of life commitments. It is a matter of conscious choice, which must be weighed against competing life interests such as employment, leisure pursuits, geographical mobility and, following separation, the pursuit of new intimate partnerships. How this balancing is undertaken and to what extent parents make themselves available for their children in preference to other life chances will have a strong influence on how post divorce parenthood is negotiated and established.

Where the activities of parental care are gendered then the parental identities which arise from them are also likely to be gendered. Motherhood and fatherhood are not perceived as identical subject positions. Many of the mothers in our sample had made their parenthood a central part of their lives...

The strong identity as mothers which these parents express arises in part from dominant cultural constructions which idealize motherhood. It also arises, more concretely, from their experience as full-time parents who gave up their jobs when they had children...[E]ven where the mothers in our sample were working full time in the early years of parenthood (nine out of thirty-one cases) they continued to take the main responsibility for the children's day-to-day care, for 'being there' when needed and for organising substitute care. For these women, therefore, their maternal identity was (for a time at least) more significant than identities arising from their engagement in paid work.

The father's identity is less likely to be derived from such an intense focus on parenthood...But this does not mean that men do not have identities as fathers, but this is often linked to their work as financial providers. This work of financial provision is crucially important, yet it means deriving a sense of identity from outside the home and the family. Although some fathers are now more actively involved in their children's lives, they are more likely to spend time sharing leisure pursuits with the children, rather than engaging in the basics of childcare. There is, therefore, a sense in which fathers have more freedom to opt in or out of such interactions and to choose how and when to balance fatherhood with their other commitments or interests. It is now quite acceptable for men to assume either the identity of the 'good provider' father or the 'new man' father...

[S]ome fathers...gradually develop a new identity as fathers as a consequence of having their children living with them part of the time...But relatively few fathers in our sample were either able or willing to do this, and the majority remained 'good provider' fathers (in that they paid child support and saw their children occasionally) or simply fell back on the minimalist paternal identity as mere biological progenitors who had no other investment in fatherhood.

Parenthood therefore still appears to have very different meanings for mothers and fathers, both before and after separation, although the meanings of both are currently subject to change. But it is important to realize that it is how motherhood and fatherhood are perceived and experienced that will have a major impact on how parents negotiate over their children after separation...[127]

To ignore the reality of pre-separation parenting patterns in the debate on post-separation parenting is unhelpful. With women still investing so heavily in motherhood, women will find it extremely difficult to surrender that key part of their identity post-separation and to share the parenting role with someone they regard as having been essentially disengaged from hands-on parenting whilst living together. The empirical evidence reveals the emotional and practical difficulties of establishing a shared or co-parenting regime for both parents, particularly when this was not the pre-separation pattern of parenting.

---

[127] As to the existence of the 'new father' see also Kaganas (2002).

C. Smart and B. Neale, *Family Fragments?* (Cambridge: Polity Press, 1999), 45–66

[T]he challenges of co-parenting are substantial, as are the costs. Developing and sustaining co-parenting involves an enormous amount of time, emotional labour and sacrifice. The needs of new partners, children and the other parent need to be juggled. It is likely to involve constant negotiations over arrangements as well as ongoing debates over children's well-being. We found a perpetual concern over the adjustment of the children to a mobile existence and two different life-styles. Parents also needed to maintain a positive image of the other parent—at least as far as the children were concerned. Painful knowledge of the activities of the other household and of new partners had to be absorbed and sometimes the individual's own needs for independence, a change of residence or career, or a new relationship had to be postponed...

The co-parents are no less likely than other divorced parents to feel negatively about each other or to be in conflict over their children. Those who are co-parenting by consensus make efforts to put aside problems in their interpersonal relationship in the interests of collaboration, although they do not always succeed. But where co-parenting is the product of coercion or hard economic or legal bargaining, the arrangement may be one of conflict...

Co-parenting, then, is not necessarily the product of a shared commitment to its ethos but may represent an uneasy compromise or a deadlock in a context where neither parent has managed to assert authority over the other.

Finally, co-parenting is fragile. Given the sacrifices and difficulties that it can entail, perhaps this is not surprising...The challenges of co-parenting can mean that, over time, the degree of parental collaboration tends to diminish, even where relatively high levels of shared care are maintained.[128]

Shared 50:50 residence can also be difficult for the children, with the inherent tensions and complexities of a shared residence regime often increasing rather than decreasing the hostility between the parents.[129] Moreover, even if the parents find adjusting to shared residence relatively easy, children can find trying to divide their lives between two different homes demanding, particularly in their teenage years as their social and educational commitments grow and they establish their own social network of friends.[130] That is not to say that 50:50 shared residence cannot work well in some cases.[131] However, research on the impact of shared residence on children's welfare suggests caution is required, particularly in litigated cases, before making such orders.

J. Hunt, J. Masson, and L. Trinder, 'Shared Parenting: The Law, the Evidence and Guidance from Families need Fathers', (2009) 39 *Family Law* 831, 834

There is now a small but growing body of research specifically on the outcomes of shared care or 50/50 arrangements. Perhaps not surprisingly, it appears again to be the quality of relationships – between parents and between parents and children – that influences whether

---

[128] Research into shared parenting regimes in Australia paints a similar picture: Rhoades and Boyd (2004), 133.

[129] On the evidence regarding shared residence decreasing hostility between the parents, see Kurki-Suonio (2000), 197.

[130] Smart (2004); Krieken (2005), 38–9.

[131] For a good review of the research evidence see Gilmore (2006), 353–8.

the arrangements work for children or not. Two studies have reported that substantially shared or 50/50 arrangements can work well for children but where relationships are already good. In Australia one major study found that the key ingredients of successful shared care were flexible and child-centred parents who were able to co-operate and, critically, where both parents had opted for shared care rather than having it imposed by a court...A similar message emerges from a study based on interviews with British children...This research found that children were positive about shared care again where arrangements were flexible and child-centred and where children's views were heard.

Shared care, therefore, is one form of arrangement which can work for children. The great challenge, however, is that the parental attributes that help to make it work – flexibility, child-centredness, parental cooperation – are typically absent in litigated or high conflict cases. Indeed, studies of 50/50 shared care report poorer outcomes for children in such cases...In two recent Australian studies, McIntosh found a link between high levels of emotional distress in children, substantially shared care and ongoing parental conflict and acrimony. In a follow up study McIntosh found that sharing care in this population did not help to reduce conflict and acrimony...Instead continuously shared care parents remained locked in conflict 4 years after the initial intervention when conflict had reduced in other arrangements. McIntosh also found that while fathers were satisfied with arrangements nearly half of children wanted to change from shared care. This is similar to the British children in Smart's study...who were unhappy in inflexible arrangements where parents were hostile to each [other] and where children had no influence about how their time was 'parcelled out'...

There are no robust research studies that find that children benefit from 50/50 type arrangements in high conflict or litigating populations. Rather the evidence suggests precisely the opposite, with research finding poorer outcomes for these children. There is also some evidence that shared care arrangements are much less durable than other arrangements in high conflict families.

Making a shared residence order to symbolically affirm equal status:

Making a shared residence order, regardless of the 'reality' of the division of the child's time, in order to affirm the parents' equal status and to try and control the conflict between them seems reasonable and laudable. Any approach which may help 'lessen the stakes' and reduce the problems associated with the 'win-lose' mentality of litigation will ultimately further the child's welfare. However, despite the initial attractions of this approach, it has been criticized for its inconsistency with the original scheme intended by the Law Commission and Parliament, and for undermining the essential purpose of a residence order.

P. Harris and R. George, 'Parental Responsibility and Shared Residence Orders: Parliamentary Intentions and Judicial Interpretations', (2010) 22 *Child and Family Law Quarterly* 151, 155–6, 166–9

The [Law] Commission...recommended that, where both parties had parental responsibility, the court be limited to dealing with concrete and practical issues about with whom the child should live, what contact she would have with others, and any disputed matters relating to the exercise of parental responsibility...[I]t is important to note that the Commission was clear that the orders should reflect the *realities*...In reflecting that overarching policy, while the Commission in their Review favoured shared residence orders where the child shared 'their time more or less equally between their parents', it thought such orders appropriate only in the rare cases where such an order was a 'more realistic description of that [...] sort of arrangement [...] than a residence order for one [parent] and a contact order for the other'. That approach was also echoed in Parliament when Lord Chancellor Mackay explained that 'contact' included 'staying with' the non-residential parent and that 'shared residence [would be] rare'. Thus both the Commission and Parliament appear to have emphasised that shared residence orders were to be contemplated only where they reflected *the reality* of the *concrete* arrangement...

Having reviewed the case law on shared residence orders and the trend to make such orders in order to affirm the equal status of the parents, Harris and George argue that this development is closely linked to the recent degradation of parental responsibility such that the latter is now a meaningless concept:

We suggest that this alternative approach [to shared residence] came about, in part, because of the courts' earlier dilution of the potency of parental responsibility. The problem from the courts' perspective was that, if a man convicted of possessing child pornography and who was to have no direct contact with his child was worthy of parental responsibility, surely a good father who already had parental responsibility and who was to continue to play some active involvement in his child's upbringing ought to have something more.

Using shared residence orders to resolve the difficulty created by the dilution of parental responsibility was not initially obvious, given the courts' historical resistance to such orders. However, we have now reached the point where academics can suggest that 'a[s] parental responsibility has been diluted, shared residence orders have arguably come to represent the new way of giving separated parents equal authority', and practitioners can ask 'whether the rise of the shared residence order is inextricably linked to the perceived ineffectual nature of parental responsibility'...

It is arguable that the courts are starting on the same road with shared residence as was seen with parental responsibility. Whereas parental responsibility was down-graded so as to be given to fathers who had no practical role to play in their children's lives at all, now shared residence is being down-graded to give it to fathers who are involved, but not in day-to-day care. Where parents live in reasonable proximity to one another, and their children spend considerable time living in both households, there is no reason not to call that shared residence. Where the parents live far apart, but their children live, say, with one for the school term and with the other for the holidays, there is equally no difficulty with calling that shared residence. But when the child merely visits one parent, even if those visits involve overnight stays, such arrangements should not be called residence, for they are not.

There has also been a degree of scepticism that in highly conflicted cases the making of a shared residence order will help reduce hostility. Indeed, it has been suggested that by making a shared residence order the expectations of the non-primary carer for 'real equality', i.e. an actual 50:50 sharing of time, will be raised and the dispute will then turn to focus on the minutiae of the division of time under the terms of the order.[132]

132 Harris-Short (2010), 262.

An alternative approach: a 'primary carer' presumption?

One of the key problems emerging from these debates is how to encourage greater equality in post-divorce parenting without undermining women's greater investment in mothering. Boyd suggests an alternative approach. She suggests that residence should be determined on the basis of a primary carer presumption.[133] This approach has the great advantage that it is gender neutral but nevertheless has the capacity to recognize and take account of the actual burden of child-care carried by most women.[134] Equally, whilst valuing the reality of women's investment in motherhood, the work of men who make an equal or greater contribution to parenting is similarly recognized and valued.[135] A presumption in favour of the primary carer also sits well with an approach giving greater weight to the status quo, in which the quality and strength of the child's existing relationships are seen as central in determining the arrangements which will best promote the child's interests during this difficult period of transition. Indeed, as Julie Wallbank points out, it could be argued that rather than 'favouring mothers' and 'discriminating against fathers', this is what the courts are already doing in faithful adherence to the paramountcy of the child's welfare.

J. Wallbank, 'Getting tough on mothers: regulating contact and residence', (2007) 15 *Feminist Legal Studies* 189, 207–8

The question therefore arises about how . . . the roles of mothers and fathers should be treated when the parents' relationship breaks down . . . It is necessary for the courts to consider the pattern of care that existed before the relationship breakdown. The inquiry into future residence should focus on the past relationship of each parent to the child and should do so in a "more precise and individualised way than . . . the best interests standard requires". By looking at the pattern of care that existed during the adults' relationship the traditional objectives of promoting continuity and stability for the child are more effectively accommodated . . . [T]he status quo of the pre-breakdown situation needs to be foregrounded in order to protect the children from undue disruption . . . [D]espite the formal legal position of gender neutrality in relation to residence and contact, it is overwhelmingly the case that women will continue to have primary responsibility for children on separation, with men seeking contact. Very often, courts will do nothing more than make orders to retain the *status quo*. In the vast majority of cases decisions about residence and contact are reached informally. In respect of court decisions, sole residence and contact orders are used to best match the circumstances and the maintenance of the *status quo* is a feature of the welfare checklist. Rather than presenting evidence of a legal bias against the men, the pattern of residence and contact is reflective of the factual situation where women carry out the bulk of childcare.

The major disadvantage of such an approach is that it is essentially reactive rather than proactive: it tends to preserve the status quo in terms of the current patterns of pre- and post-separation parenting with all the wider disadvantages for women that such divisions in child-care create. However, changes in post-separation parenting rely heavily on changes to parenting within intact families, which requires, in turn, a fundamental restructuring of both private and public life, including most importantly the field of employment. This is clearly something beyond the limited reach of the Children Act.[136]

---

[133] Boyd (1989), 148–52.
[134] Ibid.
[135] Ibid.
[136] Brophy (1989), 228, 232, and 234.

11.4.6 A 'PRESUMPTION' IN FAVOUR OF A NATURAL PARENT?

The majority of residence disputes involve competing claims by the child's parents. However, it is not uncommon for residence disputes to involve a non-parent, such as a grandparent or a prospective adopter. Such disputes must be determined in accordance with the welfare principle. However, in interpreting the child's welfare in this context, the key question is whether a 'presumption' in favour of the 'natural' parent can be justified on the basis that it will usually be in the child's best interests to be raised by a natural parent.[137] The issue again raises the important question of the value to be placed on 'biological' as opposed to 'social' or 'psychological' parenthood.[138] It can be argued that increasing weight has been placed on the importance of the 'blood-tie', with the result that social parenthood has been devalued. However, the decision of the Supreme Court in *Re B (A Child)* (see below) may signal a shift away from this approach.

Applying a 'presumption'?

The traditional starting point for determining a residence dispute involving a non-parent is Lord Templeman's judgment in *Re KD (A Minor) (Ward: Termination of Access)*.

In re KD (A Minor) (Ward: Termination of Access) [1988] AC 806, 812 (HL)

LORD TEMPLEMAN:

The best person to bring up a child is the natural parent. It matters not whether the parent is wise or foolish, rich or poor, educated or illiterate, provided the child's moral and physical health are not endangered. Public authorities cannot improve on nature. Public authorities exercise a supervisory role and interfere to rescue a child when the parental tie is broken by abuse or separation. In terms of the English rule the court decides whether and to what extent the welfare of the child requires that the child shall be protected against harm caused by the parent, including harm which could be caused by the resumption of parental care after separation has broken the parental tie.

Whilst it is clear that the only relevant principle to be applied is the welfare principle, this dictum has generally been interpreted and applied in subsequent case law as amounting to a de facto 'presumption' in favour of the natural parents. The test to be applied was expressed by Fox LJ in *Re K (a minor) (ward: care and control)* in the following terms: 'was it demonstrated that the welfare of the child positively demanded the displacement of the parental right?'[139]

---

[137] The term 'natural' parent is generally used throughout the case law to indicate the 'genetic' parent. This essentially ignores the complexity which will arise in a small minority of cases from the fact that the legal parent may not be the genetic parent. However, for the purposes of this discussion we will adopt the use of the term 'natural' parent in accordance with the case law, particularly as the significance of 'natural' parenthood in the welfare balance is clearly linked to the perceived importance of the genetic tie. The term 'non-parent' will be used to denote all non-genetic parents.

[138] See also chapters 9 and 13.

[139] [1990] 1 WLR 431, 434. See also *Re D (Care: natural parent presumption)* [1999] 1 FLR 134 and *Re R (A Child)* [2009] EWCA Civ 358, [116] (per Wall LJ).

Factors justifying the 'presumption'

Jane Fortin identifies several reasons behind the courts' preference for the biological blood tie in residence disputes:

J. Fortin, 'Re D (Care: Natural Parent Presumption) Is blood really thicker than water?', (1999b) 11 *Child and Family Law Quarterly* **435, 437, 442**

In the late 1980s and early 1990s, a series of decisions emerged which gave the biological link a far greater significance than before. An analysis of the decisions suggests that this change in approach was particularly influenced by three concerns. First, in 1988 Lord Templeman had provided a stirring reminder of the 'naturalness' of the child-parent relationship. Secondly, there appeared to be anxieties that comparisons between the homes of relatively well-off foster carers and of disadvantaged birth parents would inevitably favour the former, leading to decisions which might be criticised as amounting to 'social engineering'. Thirdly, ideas about children's rights had also started to have some impact on judicial thinking and the concept of children having a 'right' to be brought up by their birth parents conveniently encapsulated the new approach...

[U]nderpinning such a view is the societal assumption that it is 'natural' for a child to be brought up by at least one of his 'natural' parents. Furthermore, there is also the growing view that children gain a great deal from knowing about their genetic origins and that this knowledge should be enhanced, if possible, by their having a social relationship with their biological parents.

All of these factors have been evident in the developing case law.

Re K (a minor) (ward: care and control) concerned a dispute between the father and the mother's half-sister and her husband ('Mr and Mrs E') with whom the child had lived since the mother's suicide. The Court of Appeal granted residence to the father, stressing that in the case of a residence dispute between a parent and non-parent, the judge was wrong to embark on a straightforward balancing exercise to decide which of the respective parties would be best able to promote the child's welfare. Relying on *Re KD*, the Court of Appeal held that the correct approach was to ask whether the welfare of the child positively demanded that the normal presumption in favour of the natural parent should be displaced. Moreover, any reasons put forward to displace the presumption must, in the words of Waite J, be 'compelling'. The Court of Appeal rationalized their approach on the basis that the natural parent had a 'right' to raise his own child, albeit they identified this parental 'right' with an identical right in the child.

Re K (a minor) (ward: care and control) [1990] 1 WLR 431, 436–7 (CA)

WAITE J:

The judge correctly referred to *Re KD*...for the guidance of principle which it afforded to him in making that choice. The principle is that the court in wardship will not act in opposition to a natural parent unless judicially satisfied that the child's welfare requires that the parental rights should be suspended or superseded. The speeches in the House of Lords make it plain that the term "parental right" is not there used in a proprietary sense, but rather as describing the right of every child, as part of its general welfare, to have the ties of nature maintained, wherever possible, with the parents who gave it life.

Having at the outset correctly stated that guiding principle, the judge proceeded, however, in the remainder of his judgment, as though the question before him had been: "Which claimant will provide the better home?" The question he ought, of course, to have been asking was: "Are there compelling factors which required him to override the prima facie right of this child to an upbringing by its surviving natural parent?" That approach led him to embark on a careful and detailed assessment of the merits of the two competing households with a view to deciding in which of them R would have a better prospect of achieving a sense of security and stability – qualities, certainly, which he will badly need after his sufferings... It was, despite its thoroughness, an exercise misconceived in law.

The parent's *right* to residence is given further weight by Article 8 ECHR.[140] The approach of the European Court is clear from the case of *Görgülü v Germany* where the child ('C') had been living with prospective adopters for two years and was therefore securely settled. The European Court found there had been a violation of the father's Article 8 right, the German courts having failed to do enough to rehabilitate the child with his father.

Görgülü v Germany (App No 74969/01, ECHR) (2004)

44. The Court notes that in the present case, in its decision of 20 June 2001, the Court of Appeal considered that although the applicant was in a position, together with his wife who had already raised two children, to care for C, granting the applicant custody would not be in C's best interest, as a deep social and emotional bond had evolved between the child and his foster family and a separation from the latter would lead to severe and irreparable psychological damage on the part of the child...

45. The Court is aware that the fact that the applicant and C have at no time lived together may be of relevance when striking a balance between the conflicting rights and interests of the applicant and the rights of Mr and Ms B and C. The Court recalls its case-law, which postulates that where the existence of a family tie with a child has been established, the State must act in a manner calculated to enable that tie to be developed... Article 8 of the Convention thus imposes on every State the obligation to aim at reuniting a natural parent with his or her child... In this context, the Court also notes that effective respect for family life requires that future relations between parent and child not be determined by the mere passage of time...

46. The Court concedes that an instant separation from C's foster family might have had negative effects on his physical and mental condition. However, bearing in mind that the applicant is C's biological parent and undisputedly willing and able to care for him, the Court is not convinced that the Naumburg Court of Appeal examined all possible solutions to the problem. In particular, that court does not appear to have examined whether it would be viable to unify C and the applicant under circumstances that would minimise the strain put on C. Instead, the Court of Appeal apparently only focussed on the imminent effects which a separation from his foster parents would have on the child, but failed to consider the long-term effects which a permanent separation from his natural father might have on C. The solution envisaged by the District Court, namely to increase and facilitate contacts between

---

[140] For more detailed discussion, see Fortin (1999b), 444–5.

the applicant and C, who would at an initial stage continue to live with his foster family, was
seemingly not taken into consideration...

The natural parent 'presumption' has also been justified by the need to avoid the dangers
of 'social engineering', particularly when the dispute is between a parent and a 'perfect'
prospective adopter.[141]

Re O (A Minor) (Custody or Adoption) [1992] 1 FCR 378, 380–1, 383 (CA)

Lord Justice Butler-Sloss:

It is not a straightforward choice. If it were a choice of balancing the known defects of every
parent with some added problems that this father has, against idealized perfect adopters, in
a very large number of cases children would immediately move out of the family circle and
towards adopters. That would be social engineering and it is important to bear that in mind in
looking at the problems which arise in this case...

In my judgment, and I entirely agree with the Judge whose approach it was, the first
question is, is the sole remaining parent a fit and suitable person to care for his son? If he is,
adoption does not arise. If he is found to be unfit to care for his own child then clearly this
child has no parent, since the mother has disqualified herself for other reasons, and this child,
therefore, falls to be cared for within the framework either of care proceedings, which do not
arise in this case, or of adoption, which does arise...

It is not a straight balancing matter between father and an unknown adoptive family, it is
a matter of deciding whether the father will do, and, only if he will not do should one look
outside the family circle.

[The mother's appeal against the grant of custody to the child's father was dismissed.]

The need to protect the child's developing sense of identity has also featured strongly in the
residence case law,[142] particularly where there are cultural and religious factors involved.[143] *Re
M (Child's upbringing)* provides what many commentators regard as a quite extreme and worrying example of the natural parent presumption being applied to the exclusion of any proper
consideration of the importance of psychological parenthood. The case concerned a Zulu boy
born in South Africa whose parents worked for a white South African woman (the appellant).
The appellant took the child into her home and when the appellant decided to return to England
it was agreed that the child would return with her to enable him to receive an English education. Once back in England the appellant launched adoption proceedings which were strongly
opposed by the Zulu parents who had understood the arrangement to be a limited one. By the
time the case reached a substantive hearing the child had been in the care of the appellant for
almost 10 years, the last four of which had been spent in England. Thorpe J at first instance held
that, despite the expert evidence that immediately returning the child to South Africa would be
'deeply traumatic' for him, it was in his interests that he should be raised by his natural parents
and his development 'must be, in the last resort and profoundly, Zulu development and not

[141] See also *Re K (Private Placement for Adoption)* [1991] FCR 142.
[142] See generally, *Re N (Residence: Appointment of Solicitor: Placement with Extended Family)* [2001] 1
FLR 1028, [30]–[31] (per Hale LJ).
[143] On the correct approach to be taken to religious and cultural factors when determining a residence
dispute see *Re R (A Minor) (Religious Sect)* [1993] 2 FCR 525; *Re M (Child's upbringing)* [1996] 2 FCR 473; and
Palau-Martinez v France (App No 64927/01, ECHR) (2004).

Afrikaans or English development'.[144] The Court of Appeal agreed, ordering his immediate return to South Africa without further delay.[145] Unfortunately, the child was so unhappy in South Africa that he eventually returned to England to live with the appellant.[146]

Re M is often criticized for its strong adherence to the natural parent presumption despite the child's strong psychological bonds with the appellant.[147] That criticism may well be justified. However, it should also be recognized that the Court of Appeal were faced with a difficult situation where considerable damage had already been caused to the child. Having a positive sense of one's own cultural background is an essential part of developing a secure sense of identity and the Court of Appeal cannot be criticized for trying to mitigate the harm caused to the child by his alienation from the Zulu culture and people—damage for which the appellant was largely responsible by failing to take the necessary steps to maintain the child's relationships with his family in South Africa.[148] That is not to say that these concerns about the child's cultural identity should have been regarded as the overriding consideration. They were, however, important.

A move away from the natural parent 'presumption'?

Not everyone is convinced by these arguments privileging biological parenting. Fortin, for example, suggests that the argument that children have the right to be raised by their natural parents has, at times, been 'distorted' to further the rights and interests of the parents rather than those of the child.[149] The result is that equally important considerations for the child, such as the potential damage caused to the child's psychological health by disrupting the emotional bonds formed with alternative carers, have been accorded insufficient weight. Fortin questions whether it is right to talk of the child's 'right' to be cared for by his or her natural parents when the child has lived apart from them.[150] In those circumstances she questions whether the 'blood-tie' has any real value to the child and whether, indeed, it would make more sense to talk of the child's right to be cared for by his or her *psychological parents*.[151]

The weight to be accorded to the 'blood-tie' in a residence dispute has recently been revisited by the House of Lords in *Re G (Children) (Residence: Same-Sex Partner)* and by the Supreme Court in *Re B (A Child)*. It is clear from both of these decisions that it is wrong to talk of any 'presumption' in favour of the natural parent. It remains somewhat unclear, however, what weight, if any, should be placed on the significance of the 'blood tie' when determining the best interests of the child.

Re G concerned a residence dispute between a same-sex couple, CG and CW. The children were born to CG as a result of donor insemination (prior to the enactment of the HFEA 2008). CW had been fully involved in every aspect of the children's upbringing. In earlier proceedings a shared residence order had been made in favour of both parties to confer parental responsibility on CW; the dispute concerned the sharing of time under that order.[152] The Court of Appeal had held that the children's primary home should be with CW

---

144 *Re M (Child's Upbringing)* [1996] 2 FCR 473, 485 (per Neill LJ citing Thorpe J at first instance).
145 Ibid., 486.
146 Fortin (2009b), 526.
147 Fortin (1999b), 440.
148 The importance of a child's cultural heritage will be discussed in greater detail at 13.6.2.
149 Fortin (2009b), 520.
150 Ibid., 518.
151 Ibid., 518 and 524–5.
152 See earlier discussion of these proceedings at pp 686–7.

because of CG's obstructive attitude towards contact. The House of Lords reversed that decision. Baroness Hale placed great emphasis on the importance of the biological tie, although she denied that this raised a *presumption* in favour of the 'natural mother'.[153]

Re G (Children) (Residence: Same-sex Partner) [2006] UKHL 43

BARONESS HALE:

36. Of course, in the great majority of cases, the natural mother combines all three. She is the genetic, gestational and psychological parent. Her contribution to the welfare of the child is unique. The natural father combines genetic and psychological parenthood. His contribution is also unique. In these days when more parents share the tasks of child rearing and breadwinning, his contribution is often much closer to that of the mother than it used to be; but there are still families which divide their tasks on more traditional lines, in which case his contribution will be different and its importance will often increase with the age of the child.

37. But there are also parents who are neither genetic nor gestational, but who have become the psychological parents of the child and thus have an important contribution to make to their welfare. Adoptive parents are the most obvious example, but there are many others. This is the position of CW in this case...

38....While CW is their psychological parent, CG is...both their biological and their psychological parent. In the overall welfare judgment, that must count for something in the vast majority of cases. Its significance must be considered and assessed. Furthermore, the evidence shows that it clearly did count for something in this case. These children were happy and doing very well in their mother's home. That should not have been changed without a very good reason.

44. My Lords, I am driven to the conclusion that the courts below have allowed the unusual context of this case to distract them from principles which are of universal application. First, the fact that CG is the natural mother of these children in every sense of that term, while raising no presumption in her favour, is undoubtedly an important and significant factor in determining what will be best for them now and in the future. Yet nowhere is that factor explored in the judgment below...

Although denying the existence of a 'presumption' in favour of the natural parent, Baroness Hale's strong preference for biological over psychological parenting is clear. To repeat her words, being both the biological and psychological parent 'must count for something'. It is 'undoubtedly an important and significant factor' in determining the welfare of the child. In his very short judgment, Lord Nicholls appeared to agree:

LORD NICHOLLS:

I wish to emphasise one point. In this case the dispute is not between two biological parents. The present unhappy dispute is between the children's mother and her former partner Ms CW. In this case, as in all cases concerning the upbringing of children, the court seeks to identify the course which is in the best interests of the children. Their welfare is the court's paramount consideration. In reaching its decision the court should always have in mind that in the ordinary way the rearing of a child by his or her biological parent can be expected to be in the child's best interests, both in the short term and also, and importantly, in the longer term.

---

[153] See also the extracts from Baroness Hale's judgment reproduced at pp 584–5.

> I decry any tendency to diminish the significance of this factor. A child should not be removed from the primary care of his or her biological parents without compelling reason. Where such a reason exists the judge should spell this out explicitly.

This decision, whilst explicitly rejecting any notion of a presumption in favour of the natural parent, appeared essentially consistent with existing case law on the importance to be attributed to the genetic or biological tie. However, in the Supreme Court decision of *Re B*, Lord Kerr, giving the judgment of the Court, seemed to retreat from a position in which the blood tie would be accorded particular weight in the welfare balance. *Re B* concerned a dispute between the maternal grandmother and the father over the residence of a four-year-old boy who had lived with the grandmother all his life. The Supreme Court expressed concern at the apparent 'misunderstanding' of the true import of *Re G* and the principles to be derived from that judgment. The Court reasserted the importance of a 'pure' application of the welfare principle, untrammelled by assumptions about the significance of biological parenthood, observing that the argument that a child had a right to be raised by his or her biological parent could obscure or distort a proper analysis of the child's best interests.

Re B (A Child) [2009] UKSC 5

LORD KERR:

19. The theme that it was preferable for children to be raised by their biological parent or parents was developed by the judge... He stated that it was the right of the child to be brought up in the home of his or her natural parent. (It is clear from the context that the judge was using the term 'natural parent' to mean 'biological parent'.) We consider that this statement betrays a failure on the part of the judge to concentrate on the factor of overwhelming – indeed, paramount – importance which is, of course, the welfare of the child. To talk in terms of a child's rights – as opposed to his or her best interests – diverts from the focus that the child's welfare should occupy in the minds of those called on to make decisions as to their residence.

20. The distraction that discussion of rights rather than welfare can occasion is well illustrated in the latter part of [the] judgment. [The judge] suggested that, provided the parenting that Harry's father could provide was "good enough", it was of no consequence that that which the grandmother could provide would be better. We consider that in decisions about residence such as are involved in this case; there is no place for the question whether the proposed placement would be "good enough". The court's quest is to determine what is in the best interests of the child, not what might constitute a second best but supposedly adequate alternative. As the Court of Appeal pointed out... the concept of 'good enough' parenting has always been advanced in the context of public law proceedings and of care within the wider family as opposed to care by strangers...

34. [In reliance on a passage from Lord Nicholls' judgment in *Re G*], the justices stated that a child should not be removed from the primary care of biological parents. A careful reading of what Lord Nicholls actually said reveals, of course, that he did not propound any general rule to that effect. For a proper understanding of the view that he expressed, it is important at the outset to recognise that Lord Nicholls' comment about the rearing of a child by a biological parent is set firmly in the context of the child's welfare. This he identified as "the court's paramount consideration". It must be the dominant and overriding factor that ultimately determines disputes about residence and contact and there can be no dilution of its importance by reference to extraneous matters.

35. When Lord Nicholls said that courts should keep in mind that the interests of a child will normally be best served by being reared by his or her biological parent, he was doing no more than reflecting common experience that, in general, children tend to thrive when brought up by parents to whom they have been born. He was careful to qualify his statement, however, by the words "in the ordinary way the rearing of a child by his or her biological parent can be expected to be in the child's best interests" (emphasis added). In the ordinary way one can expect that children will do best with their biological parents. But many disputes about residence and contact do not follow the ordinary way. Therefore, although one should keep in mind the common experience to which Lord Nicholls was referring, one must not be slow to recognise those cases where that common experience does not provide a reliable guide...

37. ... All consideration of the importance of parenthood in private law disputes about residence must be firmly rooted in an examination of what is in the child's best interests. This is the paramount consideration. It is only as a contributor to the child's welfare that parenthood assumes any significance. In common with all other factors bearing on what is in the best interests of the child, it must be examined for its potential to fulfil that aim.

The Supreme Court thus seems to have 'downgraded' biological parenthood from a factor of undoubted importance and significance (*Re G*), to just one more factor to be taken into account in the welfare balance, its weight to be determined on the individual facts of each case. It is too early to tell how the lower courts will respond.

11.4.7   EFFECT OF A RESIDENCE ORDER

Conferring parental responsibility

The primary effect of a residence order is to determine with whom a child should live.[154] The order does, however, have a number of important subsidiary legal effects, the most important of which is that it confers parental responsibility on the person holding the order.[155]

Restrictions imposed by a residence order

Whilst a residence order is in force certain restrictions are imposed on those holding parental responsibility:

Children Act 1989, s 13

(1) Where a residence order is in force with respect to a child, no person may—
   (a) cause the child to be known by a new surname; or
   (b) remove him from the United Kingdom;

   without either the written consent of every person who has parental responsibility for the child or the leave of the court.

(2) Subsection 1(b) does not prevent the removal of a child, for a period of less than one month, by the person in whose favour the residence order is made.

---

[154] S 8(1).
[155] See 10.3.6.

(3) In making a residence order with respect to a child the court may grant the leave required by subsection 1(b), either generally or for specified purposes.

In many ways, s 13 is redundant as it is clear that a parent cannot remove a child from the jurisdiction[156] or change the child's surname[157] without the consent of everyone with parental responsibility, whether or not a residence order is in force. Where a residence order is in force, the applicant can either apply for leave under s 13(1) or apply for a specific issue order under s 8.[158] In determining the application, the child's welfare will be the paramount consideration. Technically the procedural route chosen will affect the principles to be applied, as the welfare checklist only applies to s 8.[159] However, it has been made clear in the case law that this anomaly will have no substantive effect.[160]

Leave to remove from the jurisdiction

The leading modern authority on the principles to be applied in determining an application for leave to remove a child from the jurisdiction is the Court of Appeal decision in *Payne v Payne*.

Payne v Payne [2001] EWCA Civ 166

THORPE LJ:

26 In summary a review of the decisions of this court over the course of the last 30 years demonstrates that relocation cases have been consistently decided upon the application of the following two propositions: (a) the welfare of the child is the paramount consideration; and (b) refusing the primary carer's reasonable proposals for the relocation of her family life is likely to impact detrimentally on the welfare of her dependent children. Therefore her application to relocate will be granted unless the court concludes that it is incompatible with the welfare of the children...

40 However, there is a danger that if the regard which the court pays to the reasonable proposals of the primary carer were elevated into a legal presumption, then there would be an obvious risk of the breach of the respondent's rights not only under article 8 but also his rights under article 6 to a fair trial. To guard against the risk of too perfunctory an investigation resulting from too ready an assumption that the mother's proposals are necessarily compatible with the child's welfare I would suggest the following discipline as a prelude to conclusion:

(a) Pose the question: is the mother's application genuine in the sense that it is not motivated by some selfish desire to exclude the father from the child's life? Then ask, is the mother's application realistic, by which I mean founded on practical proposals both well researched and investigated? If the application fails either of these tests, refusal will inevitably follow.

---

[156] Child Abduction Act 1984, s 1.

[157] Indeed, it is suggested in *Dawson v Wearmouth* that to change a child's surname the consent of both parents is required whether or not they hold parental responsibility: *Dawson v Wearmouth* [1999] 2 AC 309 (HL).

[158] Note however that the Court of Appeal suggest in *Dawson v Wearmouth* [1998] Fam 75, 80–2, that where a residence order is in force s 13 is the exclusive route for bringing an application. For more detailed discussion of this jurisdictional issue see Gilmore (2004c), 376–8.

[159] S 1(4).

[160] *Dawson v Wearmouth* [1998] Fam 75 (CA), 80–2.

(b) If, however, the application passes these tests then there must be a careful appraisal of the father's opposition: is it motivated by genuine concern for the future of the child's welfare or is it driven by some ulterior motive? What would be the extent of the detriment to him and his future relationship with the child were the application granted? To what extent would that be offset by extension of the child's relationships with the maternal family and homeland?

(c) What would be the impact on the mother, either as the single parent or as a new wife, of a refusal of her realistic proposal?

(d) The outcome of the second and third appraisals must then be brought into an overriding review of the child's welfare as the paramount consideration, directed by the statutory checklist in so far as appropriate.

41 In suggesting such a discipline I would not wish to be thought to have diminished the importance that this court has consistently attached to the emotional and psychological wellbeing of the primary carer. In any evaluation of the welfare of the child as the paramount consideration great weight must be given to this factor.

The Court of Appeal went on to hold that the Human Rights Act 1998 did not require any change in approach.

The decision in Payne has been subjected to considerable criticism, the most common of which is that it is much too heavily weighted in favour of the resident parent, usually the mother, by prioritizing her wishes at the expense of a proper examination of the child's interests (including the child's relationship with his or her father).

M. Hayes, 'Relocation cases: is the Court of Appeal applying the correct principles?', (2006) 18 *Child and Family Law Quarterly* 351, 362, 364

The 'discipline' in *Payne* imposes a gloss on the welfare principle. It tells a judge trying a relocation case to focus on particular matters. On its face the discipline appears relatively even-handed. But a closer analysis reveals that it expects a judge to approach his task in a manner which is weighted towards one party. The judge is expected to give more attention to the proposals of the primary carer, who, in practice, is almost always the mother, than he is to those of the other parent, in practice almost always the father...

The combined effect of paragraphs [40](c) and [41] [see *Payne* above] leads to the outcome that a judge evaluating the impact on a mother of denial of leave does not start his investigation with an open mind. Instead, he is told to approach his task with certain preconceptions in mind. He is instructed to treat the impact of his ruling on the mother as the most significant consideration. He is told that he must have in mind the importance that the court has consistently attached to the emotional and psychological well-being of the primary carer when weighing this matter within his overriding review of the child's welfare. He is told that he must carefully evaluate the impact of refusal of leave on the new family and on the stepfather or prospective stepfather.

By contrast, a judge is not instructed to have any preconceptions in his mind when he carries out his investigation of the detriment to the father under paragraph [40](b)...

The parent/child relationship is a fundamental bond that is central to the deepest emotions experienced by mothers and fathers. It is central to the deepest emotions experienced by children. The discipline values the bond between the child and the primary carer, but gives less value to the bond between the child and the non-residential parent. The weight that a trial judge is required by the discipline in *Payne* and subsequent case-law to give to considerations that favour the mother offends the fundamental principle that justice should be even-handed. The bias has developed because the discipline is built around the assumption that a child's relationship with his mother as the primary caring parent is of most importance to his or her welfare. But, of course, depending on the circumstances of each case, such an assumption may, or may not, be correct.

Hayes' answer to the biases within *Payne* is to insist that the judge undertake a full examination of the welfare principle in every case, with all relevant factors in the welfare checklist given due consideration.[161]

Jonathan Herring and Rachel Taylor have been similarly critical of *Payne* but for very different reasons. They argue that it is not so much the outcomes in the relocation cases which give rise to concern but the process of reasoning that is employed.[162] They criticize the way in which the welfare principle has been used in these cases 'to tilt the scales heavily in favour of the relocating parent'.[163] However, rather than a return to a 'pure' application of the welfare principle, they advocate a rights-based approach which, in their view, would not lead to a greater number of decisions favouring the non-resident parent but would ensure the individual interests of each family member were properly identified and weighed in the decision-making process. Much greater transparency and accountability would thereby be secured. They begin by identifying the competing rights likely to be engaged within the context of a relocation dispute:

J. Herring and R. Taylor, 'Relocating Relocation', (2006) 18 *Child and Family Law Quarterly* 517, 530–2

The rights involved...will depend on the particular facts of the case, but even in simple cases the court is likely to be faced with a range of conflicting rights...[T]he rights of the adults involved will include, at a minimum, the resident parent's Article 8 right to freedom of movement and the non-resident parent's Article 8 right to maintain and develop a relationship with his child. The rights of the child are also complex: in many cases the child herself will have conflicting rights. On the one hand, the child will have a right under Article 8 to stability in her residential family life. On the other hand, it is clear that a child has a right to contact with both parents under Article 8. Even if the overall duration of contact between the father and the child is maintained, changes to the nature of that contact may affect the relationship between the father and child and engage Article 8. Further where the child is old enough to form and express her own views, she may have a right under Article 8 for those views to be considered.

The question of how the inevitable conflict between these competing rights can be resolved is then addressed:

Given the range of rights involved in the simplest case, it is important to consider how a court may assign weight to each right in the 'ultimate balancing exercise': if the rights are incommensurable, the rights-based approach will not be capable of producing a principled

---

[161] Hayes (2006), 371–2.
[162] Herring and Taylor (2006), 518.
[163] Ibid., 518–19.

resolution to the clash of rights. It is our view that a principled balancing of rights can be achieved by focusing on the values that underlie each right....While the answer will vary between cases, it is possible to identify the values that are most commonly raised in relocation cases.

Strasbourg jurisprudence shows that notions of personal autonomy lie at the heart of Article 8 and its interpretation. At the heart of the right to autonomy is the right to develop one's vision of the good life free from improper interference from either the State or other people. This gives us some assistance in considering competing rights under Article 8: the right to autonomy. The closer the desired act is to the individual's vision of their life and their self, the stronger the claim is and the greater the justification required to interfere with it. The more marginal the claim is to the individual's vision of their life the less strong the right and the less that needs to be demonstrated to justify an interference. So, just because two parties can claim competing Article 8 rights does not mean that their claims are equal. Not all interferences with autonomy are equal. Some are major setbacks in plans for life; others are minor interruptions.

[W]hen dealing with a clash between the rights of the mother and father in a relocation case, the court should consider which interference will constitute a greater blight on the vision of the good life that each had. In developing a vision of the good life, it is likely that most parents would place great value both on their freedom of movement and consequent freedom to develop new relationships and opportunities, and on their relationship with their children. In most relocation cases the question will be how far the court's decision will *interfere* with that vision. For example, if refusal prevents a mother from pursuing a new relationship, it is more likely to have a serious impact on her ability to live her chosen vision of the 'good life' than a father having substantial but less frequent contact with his child. When the mother has no particular reason to relocate and the relocation will effectively bring to an end a strong father-child relationship, it would, no doubt, be found that permitting the relocation would be a greater interference with the father's autonomy than denying it would be for the mother...

While the balance of rights will depend on the specific facts of the case, it is clear that the factors that will be considered are very similar to those considered by the courts under the *Payne* approach. Where relocation would not cause detriment to the child and would enable reasonable contact between father and child, it is likely that a mother with carefully considered plans would be permitted to relocate. This is because refusal to allow relocation would negate the mother's freedom to live an autonomous life, whereas permitting relocation would change, but not destroy, the father's enjoyment of a relationship with his child. This is not to deny that the lessening of contact will be a serious interference with the father's rights and that usually his relationship with his child will play an important part in his life, however, denying freedom of movement to the mother is likely to be a greater blight on her vision of the good life.

Payne has also been criticized for being based on outdated gendered assumptions as to the usual pattern of post-separation parenting, in particular that it now incorrectly assumes a pattern of mother as primary carer. The question of whether it needs to be revisited in light of the increase in shared residence was addressed by the Court of Appeal in the case of *Re G*.[164] On the facts, the applicant mother was seeking leave to remove the two children of the marriage to Germany. The trial judge, applying the principles from *Payne*, granted the application alongside a shared residence order to reflect the fact that the children would still spend

---

164 [2007] EWCA Civ 1497.

41 per cent of their time with their father. The father appealed, arguing that the decision in *Payne* assumed a model of child-care in which there was a clear primary carer with sole residence and it was being wrongly applied to relocation cases such as this where residence was shared between the parents. The Court of Appeal strongly rejected the argument:

Re G (Children) [2007] EWCA Civ 1497

Lord Justice Thorpe

13.... The thrust of [counsel's] skeleton is to suggest that the leading authority in this court, the case of *Payne v Payne* [2001] 1 FLR 1052, was now outdated and heavily criticised, both in this jurisdiction and beyond, by judges, practitioners and academics. The decision in *Payne v Payne* was, I think, available in February 2001, and in the skeleton argument it was suggested that it was antiquated, in that it reflected the view of a past age when joint residence orders would only be made in wholly exceptional circumstances. The essential complaint was that in modern times, when joint residence orders have become commonplace, judges were applying the principles in *Payne v Payne*, or some judges were applying the principles in *Payne v Payne*, which were predicated upon a status of sole residence order and sole primary carer. The skeleton, further emphasises two judgments at first instance, where judges of the Family Division have declined to follow the guidelines in *Payne* on the basis that the case before them was a case in which there was no clear primary carer.

14. That, in my judgment, would be an extremely difficult argument to advance in this court. Clearly this court is bound by the decision in *Payne v Payne* so long as there is not a self-evident social shift that requires its reconsideration. I am far from persuaded that there has been any social shift and would only emphasise that the decision in the influential case of *D v D* [2001] 1 FLR 495 was given some months earlier, on 20th November 2000. In *D v D*, both the President and Hale LJ emphasised that joint residence orders were certainly not to be labelled as exceptional. That would be an unwarranted gloss on the statute... That shift from a position that obtained in the 1990s must have been well in the mind of this court, given that both in *Payne* and in *D v D* the presiding judge was the former President, Baroness Butler-Sloss. Furthermore, as [counsel] has pointed out in his skeleton argument, an analysis of the facts in *Payne v Payne* demonstrates that the father there, prior to the judgment in the county court, had been having the children at his home for much the same proportion of the year as the father in this case.

The widespread criticisms of *Payne* were given a more sympathetic hearing in *Re D (Children)*, with Ward LJ noting that there 'is a perfectly respectable argument for the proposition that [*Payne*] places too great an emphasis on the wishes and feelings of the relocating parent, and ignores or relegates the harm done to children by a permanent breach of the relationship which children have with the left behind parent'.[165] He went on to hold that in the right case this would 'constitute a "compelling reason" ' for an appeal to the Supreme Court'—*Re D* was not, however, considered to be the 'right case'.[166]

Neither the restrictions in s 13(1) nor the 'discipline' in *Payne* applies to cases of relocation within the United Kingdom. So called cases of 'internal relocation' usually arise as a result of the non-resident parent attempting to impose conditions as to the other parent's place of

---

165 [2010] EWCA Civ 50, [33].
166 Ibid., [34].

residence in the residence order or by applying for a prohibited steps order to prevent the resident parent from relocating. The Court of Appeal has made it clear that only in exceptional cases will the resident parent's freedom of movement be restricted in this way. The leading authority is *Re E (Residence: Imposition of conditions)*, in which the child's mother wished to relocate from London to Blackpool. The Court of Appeal removed the conditions from her residence order preventing her from doing so.

Re E (Residence: Imposition of Conditions) [1997] EWCA Civ 3084

LADY JUSTICE BUTLER-SLOSS:

18.... The wording of [s 11(7)] is wide enough to give the court the power to make an order restricting the right of residence to a specified place within the United Kingdom. But in my view a restriction upon the right of the carer of the child to chose where to live sits uneasily with the general understanding of what is meant by a residence order. In **Re D (Minors) (Residence: Imposition of Conditions)**..., this Court considered a similar condition placed on a residence order. In that case the mother had originally agreed that she would not bring the children into contact with the man with whom she had been living. On her subsequent application to discharge that condition this Court held that a section 11(7) condition could not exclude another person from the mother's home, thereby interfering with her right to live with whom she liked. Ward LJ said:

"The court was not in a position to overrule her decision to live her life as she chose. What was before the court was the issue of whether she should have the children living with her."

19. That decision in my judgment applies with equal force to the issue in the present appeal.

20. A general imposition of conditions on residence orders was clearly not contemplated by Parliament and where the parent is entirely suitable and the court intends to make a residence order in favour of that parent, a condition of residence is in my view an unwarranted imposition upon the right of the parent to chose where he/she will live within the United Kingdom or with whom. There may be exceptional cases, for instance, where the court, in the private law context, has concerns about the ability of the parent to be granted a residence order to be a satisfactory carer but there is no better solution than to place the child with that parent...

21. The correct approach is to look at the issue of where the children will live as one of the relevant factors in the context of the cross-applications for residence and not as a separate issue divorced from the question of residence. If the case is finely balanced between the respective advantages and disadvantages of the parents, the proposals put forward by each parent will assume considerable importance.

The Court of Appeal has recently confirmed this approach, holding unequivocally that the imposition of a condition on a residence order restricting the primary carer's right to choose where he or she lives 'is a truly exceptional order'.[167] The Court of Appeal has also confirmed that the same principles will apply to cases where a shared residence order is in force and that shared residence will not be a trump card preventing relocation.[168] In all these cases, each parent's proposed place of residence will be an important consideration when deciding or reviewing in whose favour the residence order should be made.

---

167 *Re B* [2007] EWCA Civ 1055, [7].
168 *Re T (A Child)* [2009] EWCA Civ 20, [36].

Changing the child's surname

The principles to be applied in determining a dispute over a child's surname were summarized by Butler-Sloss LJ in *In re W (A Child) (Illegitimate Child: Change of Surname)*.

In re W (A Child) (Illegitimate Child: Change of Surname) [2001] Fam 1

BUTLER-SLOSS LJ:

9 The present position, in summary, would appear to be as follows.

(a) If parents are married they both have the power and the duty to register their child's names. (b) If they are not married the mother has the sole duty and power to do so. (c) After registration of the child's names, the grant of a residence order obliges any person wishing to change the surname to obtain the leave of the court or the written consent of all those who have parental responsibility. (d) In the absence of a residence order, the person wishing to change the surname from the registered name ought to obtain the relevant written consent or the leave of the court by making an application for a specific issue order. (e) On any application, the welfare of the child is paramount, and the judge must have regard to the s 1(3) criteria. (f) Among the factors to which the court should have regard is the registered surname of the child and the reasons for the registration, for instance recognition of the biological link with the child's father. Registration is always a relevant and an important consideration but it is not in itself decisive. The weight to be given to it by the court will depend upon the other relevant factors or valid countervailing reasons which may tip the balance the other way. (g) The relevant considerations should include factors which may arise in the future as well as the present situation. (h) Reasons given for changing or seeking to change a child's name based on the fact that the child's name is or is not the same as the parent making the application do not generally carry much weight. (i) The reasons for an earlier unilateral decision to change a child's name may be relevant. (j) Any changes of circumstances of the child since the original registration may be relevant. (k) In the case of a child whose parents were married to each other, the fact of the marriage is important and I would suggest that there would have to be strong reasons to change the name from the father's surname if the child was so registered. (l) Where the child's parents were not married to each other, the mother has control over registration. Consequently on an application to change the surname of the child, the degree of commitment of the father to the child, the quality of contact, if it occurs, between father and child, the existence or absence of parental responsibility are all relevant factors to take into account.

10 I cannot stress too strongly that these are only guidelines which do not purport to be exhaustive. Each case has to be decided on its own facts with the welfare of the child the paramount consideration and all the relevant factors weighed in the balance by the court at the time of the hearing.

11.4.8 TERMINATING THE ORDER

A residence order can be made for a specified period[169] or until further order but is usually not to have effect beyond the child's 16th birthday unless the circumstances are exceptional.[170] This is subject to s 12(5), which provides that a residence order in favour of any person who is not a parent or guardian of the child can, at that person's request, continue in force

---

[169] S 11(7)(c).
[170] S 9(6).

until the child is 18. Under s 11(5), if a residence order is made in favour of one of two parents both of whom have parental responsibility for the child and the parents live together for a continuous period of more than six months, then the residence order automatically ceases to have effect.

11.5 CONTACT

Contact can take various forms, differing as to both quantity and quality. It may be direct (face-to-face) or indirect (telephone, letters, email) and may take place according to a strictly regulated regime or on a more informal, ad hoc basis. Where there are particular concerns about the child's safety or general welfare, contact may be 'supported' or more closely 'supervised' by a third party, often at designated contact centres.[171] The courts have wide powers under s 11(7) to attach conditions to the contact order or make detailed directions as to how it is to be carried out.[172] Contact disputes are amongst the most bitter, protracted, and difficult in family law. Due in large part to the campaign of fathers' rights groups, contact with the non-resident parent has recently become a matter of pressing legal and political concern. This has resulted in important changes to the law and changes to the way in which such disputes are tackled. However, the polarized and overly simplistic way in which the issue has been portrayed in the media may well have led to many important factors in these disputes being marginalized or ignored.

11.5.1 A 'PRESUMPTION' IN FAVOUR OF CONTACT WITH THE NON-RESIDENT PARENT?

The courts' approach

As a matter pertaining to the 'upbringing' of the child, the paramountcy principle applies. Where an application for contact is opposed, the welfare checklist must be considered.[173] However, whilst the statutory framework for resolving such disputes is clear and there is no *legal* presumption in favour of contact, the courts have, in effect, applied a strong de facto presumption in favour of contact with the non-resident parent.[174] This approach has been articulated in various ways. Some judges have conceptualized it as a *right* of the child to contact with the non-resident parent, albeit that right may have to give way to welfare considerations.

M v M (Child: access) [1973] 2 All ER 81, 85 (Fam Div)

WRANGHAM J:

[T]he companionship of a parent is in any ordinary circumstances of such immense value to the child that there is a basic right in him to such companionship. I for my part would prefer to call it a basic right in the child rather than a basic right in the parent. That only means this,

---

[171] For the difference between 'supported' and 'supervised' contact at contact centres see CASC (2001), 3.18–3.19.

[172] *Re O (A Minor) (Contact: Indirect Contact)* [1996] 1 FCR 317.

[173] S 1(3)–(4).

[174] Bailey-Harris et al (1999b), 114–15. For discussion see Gilmore (2008).

that no court should deprive a child of access to either parent unless it is wholly satisfied that it is in the interests of that child that access should cease, and that is a conclusion at which a court should be extremely slow to arrive.

This rights-based approach is enshrined in the United Nations Convention on the Rights of the Child.

United Nations Convention on the Rights of the Child 1989, Article 9

(3) States Parties shall respect the right of the child who is separated from one or both parents to maintain personal relations and direct contact with both parents on a regular basis, except if it is contrary to the child's best interests.

The non-residential parent may also claim a corresponding right to contact. This right clearly falls within the scope of the right to respect for family life under Article 8 ECHR.[175] However, at least at the level of rhetoric, the English courts have been at pains to make clear that insofar as it makes sense to talk of rights in this context, the right is that of the child and not the parent. The Human Rights Act 1998 has not changed this basic approach.[176]

In preference to the rights-based approach, the courts have tended to conceptualize the 'presumption' in favour of contact as a straightforward application of the welfare principle albeit the courts take as their starting point that the benefits of contact with a non-residential parent can be *assumed*. The courts have emphasized that a long term view should be taken of the child's best interests and that they should not be unduly concerned about any temporary or short-term distress to the child.

M v M (Child: access) [1973] 2 All ER 81, 88 (Fam Div)

LATEY J:

[W]here the parents have separated and one has the care of the child, access by the other often results in some upset in the child. Those upsets are usually minor and superficial. They are heavily outweighed by the long term advantages to the child of keeping in touch with the parent concerned so that they do not become strangers, so that the child later in life does not resent the deprivation and turn against the parent who the child thinks, rightly or wrongly, has deprived him, and so the deprived parent loses interest in the child and therefore does not make the material and emotional contribution to the child's development which that parent by its companionship and otherwise would make.

---

[175] See e.g. *Hokkanen v Finland* (App No 32346/96, ECHR) (1996) and *Glaser v UK* (App No 32346/96, ECHR) (2000). For an illustration of the difference between a rights-based approach and a welfare-based approach see *Sahin v Germany; Sommerfeld v Germany* (App No 30943/96, ECHR) (2003), [79]–[95] where the European Court held that it constituted discrimination under Article 14 to apply a rights-based approach to married fathers but a welfare-based approach to unmarried fathers. See also Herring (1999a), 234–5.

[176] *Re H (Children) (Contact order) (No 2)* [2001] 3 FCR 385.

The absence of any requirement to adduce positive evidence of the benefits of contact means that contact is one issue where, although conceptually very different,[177] *in practice*, the rights-based and welfare-based approaches are unlikely to lead to a substantive difference in approach or outcome.[178] The courts' strong predisposition to order contact was made clear in *Re O (A Minor) (Contact: Indirect Contact)*, now widely regarded as the leading authority.

Re O (A Minor) (Contact: Indirect Contact) [1996] 1 FCR 317, 323–7 (CA)

SIR THOMAS BINGHAM MR:

It may perhaps be worth stating in a reasonably compendious way some very familiar but nonetheless fundamental principles. First of all, and overriding all else as provided in s. 1(1) of the 1989 Act, the welfare of the child is the paramount consideration of any court concerned to make an order relating to the upbringing of a child. It cannot be emphasized too strongly that the court is concerned with the interests of the mother and the father only in so far as they bear on the welfare of the child.

Second, where parents of a child are separated and the child is in the day-to-day care of one of them, it is almost always in the interests of the child that he or she should have contact with the other parent. The reason for this scarcely needs spelling out. It is, of course, that the separation of parents involves a loss to the child, and it is desirable that that loss should so far as possible be made good by contact with the non-custodial parent, that is the parent in whose day-to-day care the child is not...

Fourth, cases do, unhappily and infrequently but occasionally, arise in which a court is compelled to conclude that in existing circumstances an order for immediate direct contact should not be ordered, because so to order would injure the welfare of the child... The courts should not at all readily accept that the child's welfare will be injured by direct contact. Judging that question the court should take a medium-term and long-term view of the child's development and not accord excessive weight to what appear likely to be short-term or transient problems...

Fifth, in cases in which, for whatever reason, direct contact cannot for the time being be ordered, it is ordinarily highly desirable that there should be indirect contact so that the child grows up knowing of the love and interest of the absent parent with whom, in due course, direct contact should be established....

The caring parent also has reciprocal obligations. If the caring parent puts difficulties in the way of indirect contact by withholding presents of [sic] letters or failing to read letters to a child who cannot read, then such parent must understand that the court can compel compliance with its orders; it has sanctions available and no residence order is to be regarded as irrevocable. It is entirely reasonable that the parent with the care of the child should be obliged to report on the progress of the child to the absent parent for the obvious reason that an absent parent cannot correspond in a meaningful way if unaware of the child's concerns...

[T]he truth is that the mother is subject to an enforceable duty to promote contact where the court judges that contact will promote the welfare of the child.

The resident parent's *duty* to promote contact with the non-resident parent has become a central feature of the contact debate.

---

[177] Herring (1999a), 230–2.
[178] *Re L (A Child) (Contact: Domestic Violence)* [2001] Fam 260, 294.

In *Re M (Minors) (Contact)*, Wilson J attempted to re-focus the courts' attention on the welfare test, and the s 1(3) criteria in particular. Rejecting counsel's submission that the circumstances must be 'wholly exceptional' to defeat the presumption in favour of contact, he held:

Re M (Minors) (Contact) [1995] 1 FCR 753, 758 (Fam Div)

WILSON J:

I personally find it helpful to cast the principles into the framework of the check-list of considerations set out in s. 1(3) of the Children Act 1989 and to ask whether the fundamental emotional need of every child to have an enduring relationship with both his parents (s. 1(3)(b)) is outweighed by the depth of harm which, in the light *inter alia* of his wishes and feelings (s. 1(3)(a)), this child would be at risk of suffering (s. 1(3)(e)) by virtue of a contact order.

Although cited with approval by the Court of Appeal in *Re L (A Child) (Contact: Domestic Violence)*,[179] Wilson J's attempt to return to a 'purer' application of the welfare test has not proved persuasive.

Although the presumption in favour of contact is undoubtedly strongest in the post-divorce context,[180] it has been consistently applied to unmarried fathers. In line with the growing importance generally attached to the father–child relationship, the inherent value of maintaining a relationship between children and their fathers through contact has generally been accepted.[181] A distinction has, however, been drawn between cases in which the father has an established, meaningful relationship with the child, so the question is one of *maintaining* an existing relationship, and cases where the applicant is in effect seeking to *establish* a *new* relationship. This distinction was first alluded to in *M v J (Illegitimate child: Access)*.

M v J (Illegitimate Child: Access) (1982) 3 FLR 19, 21 (Fam Div)

SIR GEORGE BAKER P:

There are cases in which the only ground for saying that the welfare of the child, the interests of the child, require that it should be kept in contact with father is that father is the natural father. Or, if objection is taken to the term 'natural'—which indeed is used in the Act of Parliament—then I can say biological or conceiving father. That is particularly true in the cases where the illegitimate child is the result of casual (or almost casual) inter-course. But there are other cases constantly before this and other courts where in addition the father has over a period of time, of a greater or less length, built up contact and association with the child. I think the psychiatrists would call it an 'attachment' to the child ...

It makes it very important for any court to study carefully and to weigh carefully the past behaviour of the father, the behaviour at the time of the hearing and up to the hearing, and

---

[179] [2001] Fam 260, 274. In his judgment Thorpe LJ expressed a preference for an 'assumption' rather than a 'presumption' in favour of contact.

[180] Although now a matter of historical curiosity, it was intended that the presumption in favour of contact, at least in the context of divorce, would be given statutory force in s 11(4) of the Family Law Act 1996 (FLA 1996).

[181] *S v O (Illegitimate child: Access)* (1982) 3 FLR 15.

> the possible foreseeable future. These may weigh in the other side of the scale to cancel out the factors which I have already indicated, and particularly if the second factor—that is the attachment factor—is either missing or is of less strength than in some cases.

However, the validity of adopting different approaches depending upon whether one is seeking to maintain or (re)establish contact, was rejected in *Re H (minors) (access)*.[182] Indeed, so strong is the professional consensus in favour of contact that, in practice, the distinction appears to have carried very little weight.

R. Bailey-Harris, J. Barron, and J. Pearce, 'From Utility to Rights? The Presumption of Contact in Practice', (1999b) 13 *International Journal of Law, Policy and the Family* 111, 117–19

> [S]ome of the case law demonstrates the courts' willingness to *establish* a relationship which was tenuous in the first place or which has been interrupted for a considerable period...Many district judges apparently have an unquestioning belief that contact will always be in the best interests of the children; hence they tend automatically to try to re-establish contact, even after a long break or where the parent has had no opportunity to form any kind of relationship with a very young child, and when there is no certainty that the absent parent will be consistent in maintaining contact in future. This practice holds despite the lack of evidence that this will be for the child's good and even when the child exhibits signs of considerable distress before, during or after contact. It can be interpreted as indicating the court's conception of its duty as one of establishing, rather than simply maintaining, contact.

In a more recent judgment, Thorpe LJ appears to have revived the distinction, suggesting that the strength of the 'assumption' (the term he prefers instead of the more problematic term 'presumption') in favour of contact will vary depending upon the nature of the existing relationship between parent and child.

Re L (A Child) (Contact: Domestic Violence) and others [2001] Fam 260, 294–5

THORPE LJ:

> However the general judicial approach may currently be expressed I doubt that sufficient distinction has been made between cases in which contact is sought in order to maintain an existing relationship, to revive a dormant relationship or to create a non-existent relationship. The judicial assumption that to order contact would be to promote welfare should surely wane across that spectrum. I would not assume the benefit with unquestioning confidence where a child has developed over its early years without any knowledge of its father, particularly if over those crucially formative years a psychological attachment to an alternative father has been achieved.

---

[182] [1992] 1 FLR 148.

Again, however, this attempt to refocus the courts' attention on the actual relationship between non-resident parent and child does not appear to have led to a different approach where the father is seeking to establish rather than maintain an existing relationship.

Is the 'presumption' in favour of contact well-founded?

The non-resident father

The consensus across various disciplines about the importance of contact with the non-resident parent is remarkable. Research by Bailey-Harris et al suggests it is extremely rare for the benefits of contact with the child's *father* to be questioned by any of the professionals involved in a case.[183] The Labour government was equally committed to the 'contact is good' mantra.

DCA, DfES, and DTI, *Parental Separation: Children's Needs and Parents' Responsibilities* (London: HMSO, 2004), 7–8

6. The government believes that both parents have a responsibility to ensure their child has meaningful contact with the other parent. The non-resident parent has a responsibility to sustain their relationship with their child, while the resident parent has a responsibility to enable this to happen. In most families currently—though this is changing—the resident parent will be the mother and the non-resident parent will be the father. Both are equally important to their child.

The evidential base on which this unwavering faith in the value of contact is founded is, however, open to challenge. Bailey-Harris et al suggest that the current consensus on contact is based on nothing more solid than 'self-reinforcing professional received wisdom'.

R. Bailey-Harris, J. Barron, and J. Pearce, 'From Utility to Rights? The Presumption of Contact in Practice', (1999b) 13 *International Journal of Law, Policy and the Family* 111, 117–19

[O]ur overall conclusion was that the various professionals involved supported each other in a somewhat circular and self-confirming fashion. Contact is presumed to be for the good of the child—but no evidence has been produced to demonstrate this. Solicitors nevertheless advise their clients to accede to contact because that is what the courts expect. The judges order contact because no one really opposes it—so if they do they are being 'unreasonable' and not listening to the advice of their solicitors. Court welfare officers (who, of all the professionals are beginning to develop doubts about the 'automatic' pro-contact presumption) nonetheless know that they need to make their arguments all the stronger if they are to persuade the court against ordering contact in any particular case. One district judge told us that the reason for emphasis on 'contact at (almost) any cost' is the belief that the higher courts would overrule a refusal of contact. Thus the rights/rule approach to the determination of contact disputes has become entrenched through the cumulative effect of self-reinforcing professional received wisdom.

---

[183] Bailey-Harris et al (1999b), 118.

Thorpe LJ has recognized the importance of the courts only proceeding on the basis of the best available expert evidence:

Re L (a child) (contact: domestic violence) and others [2001] Fam 260, 295 (CA)

THORPE LJ:

Most judges in our jurisdiction will have had the experience of parenting their own children. But few if any will have had education or training in child health and development. If a judge is challenged to demonstrate his qualification for discerning why one solution rather than another promotes the welfare of the child he may best rely upon the experience gained in his professional life as a specialist in family law, both as practitioner and judge. But, particularly in the most difficult cases, the judge will have the advantage of expert evidence from a mental health professional. The assumption that contact benefits the child cannot be derived from legal precedent or principle. It must find its foundation in the theory and practice of the mental health professions. Perhaps the largest single ingredient of a child's welfare is health, giving that word a broad definition to encompass physical, emotional and psychological development and well-being. So both judicial general assumption and judicial assessment of welfare in the individual case are to be derived from the expertise of mental health professionals whose training and practice has centred on the development needs and vulnerability of children. So for me the proposition that children benefit from contact with the parent with whom they no longer live must be drawn from current opinion shared by the majority of mental health professionals.

Qualified support for the prevailing judicial approach was indeed provided in *Re L* in the form of an expert psychiatric report co-authored by Dr Claire Sturge and Dr Danya Glaser. The report has been widely disseminated and provides some general support for the courts' pro-contact stance.

Re L (a child) (contact: domestic violence) and others [2001] Fam 260, 269 (CA)

BUTLER-SLOSS P:

The benefits of contact to the father were set out in detail including, the importance of the father as one of the two parents, in the child's sense of identity and value, the role model provided by a father and the male contribution to parenting of children and its relevance to the child's perception of family life as an adult.

They set out many different purposes of contact, including: the maintenance or reparation of beneficial relationships, the sharing of information and knowledge and the testing of reality for the child. They set out the more limited advantages of indirect contact which included: experience of continued interest by the absent parent, knowledge and information about the absent parent, keeping open the possibility of development of the relationship and the opportunity for reparation.

However, whilst the report points to a number of factors in favour of contact, it does not provide unqualified support for the current pro-contact culture. The report makes it clear that each case must be considered on its own particular merits with the welfare of the individual child as the core consideration. It therefore provides no support for the sweeping presumption in favour of contact that has been typical of the courts' approach.

Re L (a child) (contact: domestic violence) and others [2001] Fam 260, 269 (CA)

BUTLER-SLOSS P:

[Sturge and Glaser] set out the psychiatric principles of contact between the child and the non-resident parent. They saw the centrality of the child as all-important and the promotion of his or her mental health the central issue amid the tensions surrounding the adults in dispute. The decisions about contact should be child-centred and related to the specific child in its present circumstances but acknowledge that the child's needs will alter over different stages of development. The purpose of the proposed contact must be overt and abundantly clear and have the potential for benefiting the child in some way.

The report also identified a number of specific risks attaching to both direct and indirect contact:

Re L (a child) (contact: domestic violence) and others [2001] Fam 260, 269 (CA)

BUTLER-SLOSS P:

The overall risk was that of failing to meet and actually undermining the child's developmental needs or even causing emotional abuse and damage directly through contact or as a consequence of the contact. Specifically that included: escalating the climate of conflict around the child which would undermine the child's general stability and sense of emotional well being. The result was a tug of loyalty and a sense of responsibility for the conflict in all children except young babies which affected the relationships of the child with both parents. There might be direct abusive experiences, including emotional abuse by denigration of the child or the child's resident carer. There might be continuation of unhealthy relationships such as dominant or bullying relationships, those created by fear, bribes or emotional blackmail, by undermining the child's sense of stability and continuity by deliberately or inadvertently setting different moral standards or standards of behaviour, by little interest in the child himself or by unstimulating or uninteresting contact. They indicated a series of situations where there were risks to contact: where there were unresolved situations, where the contact was unreliable and the child frequently let down, where the child was attending contact against his wishes so he felt undermined, where there was little prospect for change such as wholly implacable situations, where there was the stress on the child and resident carer of ongoing proceedings or frequently re-initiated proceedings.

The Labour government's commitment to contact was driven by wider social and political concerns. As we have seen, the Green Paper preceding the Children and Adoption Act 2006 focused on the social 'dangers' of lone, as opposed to shared, parenting, emphasizing the poor educational and social outcomes for children who experience loss of contact with the non-resident parent post-separation.[184] The government's clear message was that these social ills could be avoided by a 'civilized' divorce in which the importance of 'fathering' was recognized and protected.[185] However, the evidence suggesting children of separated parents are socially and educationally disadvantaged is controversial. In particular, the

---

[184] Discussed at p 746.
[185] DCA, DfES, and DTI (2004), 16–17.

assumption underlying the Green Paper that loss of contact is the principal cause of these problems is highly questionable,[186] with the social and economic difficulties often associated with family breakdown undoubtedly a major factor. Gilmore has undertaken a comprehensive review of the research evidence on whether contact in and of itself can be a 'protective' factor on parental separation and the implications of this research for judicial decision-making:

S. Gilmore, 'Contact/shared residence and child well-being: research evidence and its implications for legal decision-making', (2006) 20 *International Journal of Law, Policy and the Family* 344, 358–9

The research evidence...does not support adoption of a presumption of contact in court decision-making. Overall, the research suggests that it is not contact *per se* but the nature and quality of contact that are important to children's adjustment. The overall picture is of a complex interaction of family dynamics and demographic factors, in varying combinations and degrees of intensity, impacting on children's adjustment following separation. The complexity does not advocate a form of legal decision-making which relies on generalizations. Even Dunn et al (2004) whose findings might, in part, be used to support a presumption of contact caution that the complexity of family situations must be taken into account, and that 'simple rules of thumb such as "contact is to be fostered" are not appropriate. Moreover, while contact with a non-resident parent can be beneficial, it can also be associated with risks to child welfare. Given that interparental conflict is potentially negatively associated with children's adjustment, the adoption of a presumption in disputed contact cases before the courts, with their profile of high conflict...seems particularly contraindicated. In addition, the benefits of contact are generally modest, and other factors (in particular the child's resident parent) play an important role in moderating child well-being. As Hunt and Roberts argue, therefore, 'care needs to be taken not to over-estimate the presumed benefits of contact'.

Contact is clearly not a panacea.[187]

Non-parents

The assumed value of contact between a non-residential parent and the child is not applied to relationships with other family members, no matter how significant. The courts have been fairly consistent in refusing to apply a 'presumption' in favour of contact with members of the extended family, such as siblings, step-parents, or grandparents. In these cases a 'pure' unfettered application of the welfare principle is followed.[188] In *Re H (A Minor) (Contact)*, where the step-father had raised the child as his own, Butler-Sloss LJ was at pains to point out that making provision for ongoing contact in this case was somewhat unusual, even exceptional. Her judgment is particularly telling as to the limited value generally placed on social parenthood, even where an important, meaningful relationship has been established, as contrasted with the *assumed* value of genetic parenting.

---

[186] Rhoades (2002), 81.

[187] See also, Mooney, Oliver, and Smith (2009).

[188] See *Re S (Contact: Application by sibling)* [1999] Fam 283 (siblings); *Re H (A Minor) (Contact)* [1994] 2 FCR 419 (step-father).

11.5.2 DISPLACING THE 'PRESUMPTION'

Even where the courts apply a 'presumption' in favour of contact, individual welfare considerations are not redundant. Whether one approaches the issue from a rights-based or welfare-based perspective, the burden is placed on the resident parent to adduce positive evidence as to why contact should not take place. As it was put by Butler-Sloss LJ in *Re R (a minor) (contact: biological father)*, 'there are cases where serious risk factors are identified which form cogent reasons why there should not be contact between the father or mother and the child and those cogent reasons are sufficient to displace the general proposition of continuing contact.'[189]

Several factors are identified in the case law as *potentially* constituting a 'cogent reason' for displacing the presumption in favour of contact. Thorpe LJ has provided a tentative list:

Re L (A Child) (Contact: Domestic Violence) and others [2001] Fam 260, 300 (CA)

THORPE LJ:

[T]he factors that may offset the assumption in favour of contact are probably too legion to be either listed or categorised. Abuse must form the largest compartment: as well as physical abuse of the other parent and/or a child there is equally sexual and emotional abuse within the family. Then there is the self-abuse of either drugs or alcohol and the failure to maintain sexual boundaries appropriate to the development of the child. Additionally mental illness or personality disorder may be a dominant factor as may malign motives prompting the applicant to pursue a seemingly justifiable application for the covert purpose of threatening or dominating the primary carer.

The more controversial of these factors are considered below.

Implacable hostility of the residential carer

The courts have engaged in a lot of 'hard talking' on the problem of the so-called 'implacably hostile' or 'intransigent' mother. It is clear that the hostility of the residential parent, usually the mother, is not, without more, justification for refusing contact.

Re H (A Minor) (Contact) [1994] 2 FCR 419, 426–7 (CA)

Lady Justice Butler-Sloss:

It would seem to me that this woman is an entirely responsible and respectable member of society. Having done what her own legal advisers advised, I would assume that she would do what the court ordered. If the court ordered, with whatever reservations there might be, that there should be contact between her son and her former husband, that she would obey the order. We ought not to presume problems between parents over contact unless and until they become apparent. It is important that there should not be what the Judge called "a selfish parents' charter"; that if you do not want your child to see the other parent, then

[189] [1993] 2 FLR 762.

> you can make so much fuss that you prevent the court ordering it. That is not the way the courts see these cases. If it is right for the child to see the husband, then that order is there to be obeyed...
>
> The hostility of the mother in itself is a very unattractive argument to place before a court. The mother must appreciate that she must not be a barrier to the child seeing the husband.[190]

Butler-Sloss LJ emphasizes that, despite the mother's hostility, it should not be assumed that she will not obey the court's orders. However, in many cases, the mother's intention to disobey is patently clear. In such circumstances, the courts have held that they will not 'abdicate their responsibility' by capitulating to such 'threats'. The order, if in the child's interests, will still be made[191]—a 'robust' response is to be expected.[192] Mothers who are regarded as 'implacably hostile' may be directed or ordered to attend classes or counselling aimed at persuading them to cooperate.[193]

In some cases the mother's 'hostility' is more accurately described as 'fear' or 'anxiety'. Indeed, this fear or anxiety, even if lacking a rational basis, may be so strong that ordering contact will cause such enormous distress that the mother's ability to care for the child will be compromised. It is accepted that in such extreme cases, provided the mother's fears and anxiety are genuine, an order for contact may well be inimical to the child's interests.[194] Similarly, where the mother's opposition is such that the child, acutely aware of his mother's anxiety and distress, is being placed in an impossibly stressful position, contact should not be ordered. In *Re L (Contact: Genuine fear)*, the father had a history of serious violence (including stabbing his former wife) which the mother claimed had persisted throughout their relationship. She vehemently opposed contact having developed what the judge described as a 'phobic disorder' with respect to the father. Somewhat surprisingly given the facts, the judge found her fears were genuine but had no rational basis. He nevertheless dismissed the father's application for direct contact, making an order for indirect contact instead.

Re L (Contact: Genuine fear) [2002] 1 FLR 621 (Fam Div)

BRUCE BLAIR QC (sitting as a High Court judge):

[42]...[E]ven against the backcloth that I do not regard the mother's phobic disorder as being based on rational thinking, its genuineness and intensity lead me to the judgment that L [the child], in the midst of the conflict, would be likely to suffer marked emotional harm if, at any rate at this stage, an order for direct contact were made and he were exposed to its emotional effect upon the mother, which in my estimation would be profound and possibly destabilising. I think it highly probable that the order would not be obeyed by the mother,

---

[190] See also *Re O (A Minor) (Contact: Indirect Contact)* [1996] 1 FCR 317, 324–5. The same approach has been taken to cases of step-parent hostility, although there are some exceptional cases where the stepfather's stated intention of abandoning the family if contact is ordered has been considered sufficient to rebut the presumption. See *Re H (A minor) (Parental responsibility)* [1993] 1 FLR 484 and *Re B (Contact: Stepfather's opposition)* [1997] 2 FLR 579.

[191] *Re W (A minor) (contact)* [1994] 2 FLR 441.

[192] *Re A (Children)* [2009] EWCA Civ 1141, [21] (per Coleridge J).

[193] CA 1989, ss 11A–11G, as inserted by the Children and Adoption Act 2006 (CAA 2006), s 1.

[194] *B v A (Illegitimate children: access)* (1982) 3 FLR 27.

that she would not co-operate in the process of treatment that would be a prerequisite to its success and that a repetition of the current stalemate would occur with the father, for whom I have a great deal of sympathy, confronted with a dilemma whether to apply for the mother's committal to prison, an alternative which he himself has stated he does not favour.

[43] Accordingly, having conducted the necessary balancing exercise, I feel, with reluctance, unable to grant the father's application for direct contact. Lest the mother perceives this result as some sort of victory, it most certainly is not. To put it another way, if it could ever be regarded by her subjectively as a victory, the victory is a hollow one indeed. She needs to understand that this solution perpetuates a void in L's life which, from his point of view, is serious and creates the strong probability of his harbouring doubts and anxieties about his father which may prejudice his prospect of a well-balanced upbringing.[195]

There will also of course be many cases where the mother's deeply held fears over contact are based on reasonable concerns about the father's behaviour. Wilson J, in a case where the mother's opposition was based on the fact that the father was serving a sentence of life imprisonment for murder, has emphasized that there are three different categories of 'hostility':

Re P (Minors) (Contact: Discretion) [1999] 1 FCR 566, 574–5 (CA)

WILSON J:

It seems to me that a mother's hostility towards contact can arise in three different situations. The first is where there are no rational grounds for it. In such a case the court will be extremely slow to decline to order contact and will do so only if satisfied that an order in the teeth of the mother's hostility would create a serious risk of emotional harm for the child. The second is where the mother advances grounds for her hostility which the court regards as sufficiently potent to displace the presumption that contact is in the child's interests. In that case the mother's hostility as such becomes largely irrelevant: what are relevant are its underlying grounds, which the court adopts. The third is where the mother advances sound arguments for the displacement of the presumption but where there are also sound arguments which run the other way. In such a situation, so it seems to me, the mother's hostility to contact can of itself be of importance, occasionally of determinative importance, provided, as always, that what is measured is its effect upon the child.

The courts have therefore recognized the importance of distinguishing between cases of 'intransigence' or 'implacable hostility' and cases where the hostility arises from legitimate concern. Whether the courts have managed to sustain this distinction in practice is, however, fiercely disputed. Indeed, feminist scholars have criticized the courts for perpetuating the 'myth' of the 'selfish' 'irresponsible' mother, by marginalizing genuine and reasonably held fears over contact. In the current climate, it is argued that *any* opposition to contact is simply dismissed as 'unreasonable'.[196]

---

[195] See also *Re J (A Minor) (Contact)* [1994] 1 FLR 729 and *Re K (Contact: Mother's Anxiety)* [1999] 2 FLR 703.

[196] Kaganas and Day Sclater (2004), 5 and 13 and Rhoades (2002), 73–4.

Domestic violence

The stereotype of the 'selfish' intransigent mother has proved particularly contentious where there is a history of domestic violence between the parties. Rhoades argues that the 'image of the self-interested "no-contact mother" has helped to obscure the extent to which the child's right to contact provides abusive men with litigation-based tools for harassing the child's carer'.[197] In her view, such is the strength of the dominant welfare discourse that 'father absence' is widely regarded as a much greater social problem than domestic violence. The usual contact dispute thus resolves into a 'hostile mother/thwarted father problem and only exceptionally a protective mother/harmful father problem'.[198] Adrienne Barnett agrees, arguing that such is the dominance of the pro-contact culture that women are frightened to raise issues of domestic violence for fear of being labelled a hostile or intransigent mother.[199]

Until recently, judicial attitudes towards the issue of domestic violence have given more than sufficient grounds for concern. *Williams v Williams* provides a striking example of how the courts have minimized the effects of domestic violence on both the mother and child and tended to regard a history of abuse as irrelevant to the issue of contact. It was found on the evidence that there had been violence during the marriage, some witnessed by the children.

Williams v Williams [1985] FLR 509, 512–13

DUNN LJ:

These courts have said over and over again that although you can dissolve marriage you cannot dissolve parenthood and children have a right to maintain contact with both of their parents. This is no more than nature and commonsense require. If these children are denied any contact with their father during their minority, and not only denied access but actively encouraged to be frightened of him, there is a real danger, such as has already begun to happen with the girl, that they may acquire what the psychologist called 'a generalized fear of men'. This mother would not be the first overpossessive mother who would find, when the children are old enough to make up their own minds, that they might turn against her for having deprived them of the opportunity during their childhood of achieving some relationship with their father.

I do not underestimate the traumatic effect upon the mother of the violence that she has suffered at the hands of this man, but it is plain from the evidence that in her dealings with the children she has not sought to forget it, or push the memory into the background, or to help them to come to terms with it; but rather she has fired and stimulated the memories and encouraged them in the minds of the children so that she has made such memories as they have worse and more vivid in the course of conduct that she has taken in the 2 years or so since she has been separated from their father. And in doing that she has placed a very heavy burden of responsibility upon herself...

If the mother stimulates, and continues to stimulate, the children's fears of their father and if the little girl continues to show the signs of emotional instability which, to a large extent at any rate, appears to have been caused by the mother's action, and if the mother refuses to

---

[197] Rhoades (2002), 77.
[198] Ibid., 83.
[199] Barnett (2000), 142–3.

co-operate..., then at some future time the court may have to consider whether this mother is fit to be entrusted with the care of these children and some other arrangement will have to be made in their interests. That is not a threat, it is simply a statement of the situation.

This expectation that, as a 'good mother', a victim of domestic violence should be able to prioritize her child's interests by putting aside her own 'selfish' fears in order to promote a good relationship between father and child was reiterated in subsequent cases.[200]

Research carried out by Bailey-Harris et al suggests that, until recently, these attitudes were deeply entrenched at all levels of the court system. Their study of practice at the county court level revealed that the issue of domestic violence was routinely marginalized, with district judges adopting a 'no fault discourse' in which the accepted mantra was to 'look forward not back'. Past conduct, including domestic violence, was thus rendered irrelevant to the contact application.[201] Interviews with barristers, solicitors, and child welfare professionals, alongside research carried out into the way in which safety concerns were handled at contact centres, suggested these problems were pervasive, with domestic violence being 'minimized' or rendered 'invisible' at every stage of the process.[202] Not surprisingly, these professional attitudes have also been absorbed into the mindset of parents.[203]

The last few years have, however, seen a significant shift in judicial attitudes regarding the relevance of domestic violence to issues of contact. This has been driven by the growing body of evidence as to the harm caused to children who witness incidents of abuse.[204] The potential dangers of promoting contact between a child and a violent parent are dealt with at length in the Sturge and Glaser report.[205]

Re L (A Child) (Contact: Domestic Violence) and others [2001] Fam 260, 270 (CA)

BUTLER-SLOSS P:

The [Sturge and Glaser] report then moved to the central issue of domestic violence. They agreed...that there needs to be greater awareness of the effect of domestic violence on children, both short-term and long-term, as witnesses as well as victims. The research was entirely consistent in showing the deleterious effects on children of exposure to domestic violence and that children were affected as much by exposure to violence as to being involved in it. All children were affected by significant and repeated inter-partner violence even if not directly involved. Research indicates that even when children did not continue in violent situations emotional trauma continued to be experienced. The context of the overall situation was highly relevant to decision making. The contribution of psychiatric disorder to situations of domestic violence and emotional abuse must be considered. In situations of contact there might be a continuing sense of fear of the violent parent by the child. The child might have

[200] See, e.g., *Re P (A Minor) (contact)* [1994] 2 FLR 374.
[201] Bailey-Harris et al (1999b), 123.
[202] Barnett (2000), 143–8 and Humphreys and Harrison (2003), 244 and 252.
[203] Kaganas and Day Sclater (2004), 15 and 19.
[204] Barnett (2000), 139.
[205] See also Humphreys and Harrison (2003), 239–40. Humphreys and Harrison point to similar research suggesting that where children live with domestic violence, the risk that they themselves will be subjected to physical or sexual abuse is markedly increased, with between 30% and 66% of children suffering such direct abuse.

post-traumatic anxieties or symptoms the proximity of the non-resident violent parent might re-arouse or perpetuate. There might be a continuing awareness of the fear the violent parent aroused in the child's main carer. The psychiatric report highlighted the possible effects of such situations on the child's own attitudes to violence, to forming parenting relationships and the role of fathers. Research shows that attitudes in boys were particularly affected.

These concerns are important given the evidence that family breakdown often acts as a catalyst for violence, with the risks of escalation and even homicide being particularly high in the first six months after separation.[206] Worryingly, it has been shown that victims of domestic violence are particularly vulnerable to further abuse when contact is taking place.[207] An analysis of 300 court files carried out by the Department for Constitutional Affairs (DCA) revealed that in 35 per cent of cases there were safety concerns relating to the child or the resident parent.[208]

The marked change in judicial attitude towards domestic violence was led by Wall J, who in three important decisions firmly established that domestic violence and the fear it engenders in the resident parent may constitute a cogent reason to rebut the presumption in favour of contact.[209] Central to Wall J's approach was clear recognition of the effects of domestic violence on women and children, as well as the importance of violent fathers examining their own behaviour and demonstrating their capacity to behave appropriately. These themes were carried through into the Court of Appeal's decision in *Re L (A Child) (Contact: Domestic Violence)*, in which the courts' general approach to contact where there are allegations of past or present domestic violence was comprehensively reviewed. The Court of Appeal had before them Sturge and Glaser's expert report which recommended that in cases of domestic violence there should be a presumption *against* direct contact, with the violent partner having to meet a number of requirements before contact could be deemed beneficial.

Re L (A Child) (Contact: Domestic Violence) and others [2001] Fam 260, 271 (CA)

BUTLER-SLOSS P:

Dr Sturge and Dr Glaser considered the question in what circumstances should the court give consideration to a child having no direct contact with the non-resident parent. In their view there should be no automatic assumption that contact to a previously or currently violent parent was in the child's interests, if anything the assumption should be in the opposite direction and he should prove why he can offer something of benefit to the child and to the child's situation. They said

"Domestic violence involves a very serious and significant failure in parenting – failure to protect the child's carer and failure to protect the child emotionally (and in some cases physically – which meets any definition of child abuse.)

Without the following we would see the balance of advantage and disadvantage as tipping against contact:

  (a) some (preferably full) acknowledgment of the violence;

---

206 Ibid., 241. Barnett (2000), 143.
207 Humphreys and Harrison (2003).
208 DCA, DfES, and DTI (2004), 10. See also Hunt and Macleod (2008), 6 and Trinder et al (2005), iii.
209 *Re K (Contact: Mother's anxiety)* [1999] 2 FLR 703; *Re H (Contact: Domestic Violence)* [1998] 2 FLR 42; and *Re M (minors) (contact: violent parent)* [1999] 2 FLR 231.

(b) some acceptance (preferably full if appropriate i.e. the sole instigator of violence) of responsibility for that violence;

(c) full acceptance of the inappropriateness of the violence particularly in respect of the domestic and parenting context and of the likely ill effects on the child;

(d) a genuine interest in the child's welfare and full commitment to the child i.e. a wish for contact in which he is not making the conditions;

(e) a wish to make reparation to the child and work towards the child recognising the inappropriateness of the violence and the attitude to and treatment of the mother and helping the child to develop appropriate values and attitudes;

(f) an expression of regret and the showing of some understanding of the impact of their behaviour on the ex-partner in the past and currently;

(g) indications that the parent seeking contact can reliably sustain contact in all senses."

They suggested that without (a)–(f) above they could not see how the non-resident parent could fully support the child and play a part in undoing the harm caused to the child and support the child's current situation and need to move on and develop healthily. There would be a significant risk to the child's general well-being and his emotional development.

The Court of Appeal also had before them a report by the Advisory Board on Family Law, Children Act Sub-Committee (chaired by Wall J) on parental contact in cases of domestic violence ('the CASC report').[210] The CASC report did not support a presumption against contact in cases of domestic violence but set down a number of guidelines as to how allegations of domestic violence should be handled in such disputes.[211] Both the expert evidence of Drs Sturge and Glaser and the recommendations of the CASC report informed the Court's approach.

Re L (A Child) (Contact: Domestic Violence) and others [2001] Fam 260, 272–5 (CA)

BUTLER-SLOSS P:

The family judges and justices need to have a heightened awareness of the existence of and consequences (some long-term), on children of exposure to domestic violence between their parents or other partners. There has, perhaps, been a tendency in the past for courts not to tackle allegations of violence and to leave them in the background on the premise that they were matters affecting the adults and not relevant to issues regarding the children. The general principle that contact with the non-resident parent is in the interests of the child may sometimes have discouraged sufficient attention being paid to the adverse effects on children living in the household where violence has occurred. It may not necessarily be widely appreciated that violence to a partner involves a significant failure in parenting – failure to protect the child's carer and failure to protect the child emotionally.

In a contact or other application under section 8 of the Children Act 1989, where allegations of domestic violence are made which might have an effect on the outcome, those allegations must be adjudicated upon and found proved or not proved. It will be necessary to scrutinise such allegations which may not always be true or may be grossly exaggerated. If however there is a firm basis for finding that violence has occurred, the psychiatric advice becomes

210 CASC (2000).
211 Ibid., Sec 5.

very important. There is not, however, nor should there be, any presumption that, on proof of domestic violence, the offending parent has to surmount a prima facie barrier of no contact. As a matter of principle, domestic violence of itself cannot constitute a bar to contact. It is one factor in the difficult and delicate balancing exercise of discretion. The court deals with the facts of a specific case in which the degree of violence and the seriousness of the impact on the child and on the resident parent have to be taken into account. In cases of proved domestic violence, as in cases of other proved harm or risk of harm to the child, the court has the task of weighing in the balance the seriousness of the domestic violence, the risks involved and the impact on the child against the positive factors, if any, of contact between the parent found to have been violent and the child. In this context, the ability of the offending parent to recognise his past conduct, be aware of the need to change and make genuine efforts to do so, will be likely to be an important consideration...

In expressing these views I recognise the danger of the pendulum swinging too far against contact where domestic violence has been proved. It is trite but true to say that no two child cases are exactly the same. The court always has the duty to apply section 1 of the Children Act 1989 that the welfare of the child is paramount and, in considering that welfare, to take into account all the relevant circumstances, including the advice of the medical experts as far as it is relevant and proportionate to the decision in that case...

In conclusion, on the general issues, a court hearing a contact application in which allegations of domestic violence are raised, should consider the conduct of both parties towards each other and towards the children, the effect on the children and on the residential parent and the motivation of the parent seeking contact. Is it a desire to promote the best interests of the child or a means to continue violence and/or intimidation or harassment of the other parent? In cases of serious domestic violence, the ability of the offending parent to recognise his or her past conduct, to be aware of the need for change and to make genuine efforts to do so, will be likely to be an important consideration.

The importance of taking allegations of domestic violence seriously is thus clearly established. However, the Court of Appeal firmly rejected any suggestion that past or present violence by the non-resident parent should constitute a bar to contact. More controversially, they also rejected the recommendation by Drs Sturge and Glaser that where there is a history of violence there should be a presumption against direct contact.[212]

The Court of Appeal's rejection of this more robust approach in favour of a 'pure' application of the welfare principle disappointed many.[213] However, the Court of Appeal set down a number of positive requirements, now enshrined in a Practice Direction, which should ensure that an allegation of domestic violence is taken seriously and dealt with more effectively by the courts.[214] The Practice Direction provides that all applications for residence and contact are to be sent to Cafcass for initial screening[215] and in every case where there are concerns over domestic violence (whether as a result of screening or allegations raised by the parties) which may affect the court's decision over contact, the court must hold a fact-finding hearing to determine the nature and degree of any domestic violence.[216] Where, following this hearing, there has been a positive finding of domestic violence, the court is instructed to

---

[212] Sturge and Glaser (2000), 623.
[213] For a good critique of the decision see Kaganas (2000).
[214] Practice Direction (2008).
[215] Ibid., [6].
[216] Ibid., [8]–[23].

consider the impact of this on the child. Notably, 'harm' in the welfare checklist is defined to include, 'impairment suffered from seeing or hearing the ill-treatment of another'.[217]

Practice Direction, *Residence and Contact Orders: Domestic Violence and Harm* (2008) <http://www.hmcourts-service.gov.uk/cms/files/Revised_PD_Domestic_Violence140109.pdf>

26. When deciding the issue of residence or contact the court should, in the light of any findings of fact, apply the individual matters in the welfare checklist with reference to those findings; in particular, where relevant findings of domestic violence have been made, the court should in every case consider any harm which the child has suffered as a consequence of that violence and any harm which the child is at risk of suffering if an order for residence or contact is made and should only make an order for contact if it can be satisfied that the physical and emotional safety of the child and the parent with whom the child is living can, as far as possible, be secured before during and after contact.

27. In every case where a finding of domestic violence is made, the court should consider the conduct of both parents towards each other and towards the child; in particular, the court should consider;

(a) the effect of the domestic violence which has been established on the child and on the parent with whom the child is living;

(b) the extent to which the parent seeking residence or contact is motivated by a desire to promote the best interests of the child or may be doing so as a means of continuing a process of violence, intimidation or harassment against the other parent;

(c) the likely behaviour during contact of the parent seeking contact and its effect on the child;

(d) the capacity of the parent seeking residence or contact to appreciate the effect of past violence and the potential for future violence on the other parent and the child;

(e) the attitude of the parent seeking residence or contact to past violent conduct by that parent; and in particular whether that parent has the capacity to change and to behave appropriately.

Where the court has made a finding of domestic violence but nevertheless considers that direct contact is in the best interests of the child, the court must also consider whether the contact should be supervised or whether conditions need to be imposed requiring the violent party to seek advice and/or treatment for his behaviour.[218] The CA 1989 also includes provision for an abusive parent to be directed or ordered to attend 'programmes, classes and counselling or guidance sessions of a kind that may, by addressing a person's violent behaviour, enable or facilitate contact with a child'.[219] Where direct contact is considered inappropriate the court must consider whether to make an order for indirect contact.[220]

The Court of Appeal has made it absolutely clear that this Practice Direction must be obeyed.[221] However, in light of the delay and costs involved in holding a split hearing, more

---

[217] Ss 31(9) and 105.
[218] Practice Direction (2008), [28].
[219] S 11A(5).
[220] Practice Direction (2008), [29].
[221] *Re Z (Children)* [2009] EWCA Civ 430, [27].

recent, somewhat worrying, guidance issued by Wall P cautions against holding fact-finding hearings on allegations of domestic violence unless the court is satisfied that the outcome is likely to be affected by any findings of domestic abuse.[222]

The Practice Direction also deals with contact orders made by consent, making it clear that even where the parties are agreed on an order, the court must decide whether an order for residence or contact is in the interests of the child.[223] The application for a contact order must thus still be scrutinized and the order refused unless the court is satisfied that there is no risk of harm to the child.[224] In determining whether the child is at risk, the judge may make a direction for Cafcass to report to the court.[225] The role of the court in scrutinizing consent orders for signs that the child may be at risk from domestic violence is vital given recent evidence that despite the marked change in professional attitudes regarding this issue, Cafcass officers conducting in-court conciliation sessions continue to marginalize, minimize, or ignore allegations of domestic violence, their primary concern being to help the parties reach agreement on restoring or improving contact.[226]

Is there a problem over contact?

Several important considerations may displace the presumption in favour of contact. However, contrary to the impression which the media may have created, the strength of the presumption in favour of contact is such that it is very rare for contact to be refused. The statistics are striking: less than 1 per cent of applications are refused.[227] Moreover, the majority of applicants obtain both the type and amount of contact sought.[228] Which begs the question: why are so many fathers angry and disillusioned over contact? The answer: the problems surrounding enforcement. And it is to this problem we now turn.

11.5.3 ENFORCING CONTACT ORDERS

According to fathers' rights groups, non-compliance with contact orders is a huge problem, with large numbers of women routinely flouting orders out of pure malevolence and spite. The courts have borne the brunt of the criticism, coming under sustained attack for their apparent inability or unwillingness to tackle the problem effectively. In response, it is argued on behalf of mothers that they are simply acting to protect their children, their concerns about the child's welfare having been given inadequate weight when contact was ordered. The problem of non-compliance with contact orders has generated bitter debate in which gender has again emerged as the dominant factor.

---

[222] The President's Guidance in Relation to Split Hearings, May 2010, [8]. Available at: <http://www. familylaw.co.uk/system/uploads/attachments/0000/4506/Practice_Direction_Split_Hearings_May_2010. pdf>. On the question of whether interim contact should be ordered in cases where a split hearing is necessary, see *S v S (Interim Contact)* [2009] EWHC 1575.

[223] Strong concern about this issue arose in 2006 when it was revealed that 29 children in 13 cases had been murdered by their father whilst on contact visits. In three cases the court had made a contact order by consent. The Family Justice Council was asked to report on the issue. For their recommendations, see Craig (2007).

[224] Practice Direction (2008), [4]–[5].

[225] Ibid.

[226] Trinder et al (2010).

[227] DCA, DfES, and DTI (2004), 13.

[228] Hunt and Macleod (2008), 4.

Modes of enforcement

Breach of a contact order constitutes contempt of court punishable by fine or committal to prison for a maximum of two years. Committal proceedings can be initiated by another party to the proceedings or, in exceptional cases, by the court acting of its own motion.[229] Alternatively, under s 11J of the CA 1989, the court can make an enforcement order imposing 'an unpaid work requirement' on the party in breach.[230] Repeated refusals to allow contact with the non-residential parent can also be addressed by changing the child's place of residence.

Whether the courts should seek to secure compliance with a contact order by invoking one of these measures is exceptionally difficult. If the mother disregards the order and the court fails to act, the welfare of the child, as determined by the court, will be undermined. On the other hand, decisive action which sees the mother imprisoned or deprived of residence is unlikely to further the child's interests, particularly if the father cannot provide the child with an alternative home. Matters are further complicated where the child, having become alienated from the father, also opposes contact.[231] The welfare of the child is not, however, the only consideration: there is a wider public interest in ensuring compliance with the courts' terms. In determining the weight to be afforded to these various factors the courts have adopted strongly differing views.

Committal proceedings

The dilemma facing the courts where one party to a contact dispute seeks to enforce the order by committal has been graphically illustrated by Ward LJ:

Re M (A Minor) (Contempt of Court: Committal of Court's own Motion) [1999] Fam 263, 281–2 (CA)

WARD LJ:

The interests of the children.

The judge was, of course, uniquely well placed to assess what the welfare of the children demanded with regard to the maintenance of a link with their father through contact, but here the judge was assuming that coercive powers of the court would achieve that desired result. He did not, however, appear to consider what effect a committal application (carrying with it the possibility of a prison sentence) may have had on the children, especially in the light of his findings about the mother's proven capacity to influence the children against their father. It does not require much imagination to envisage the domestic scene where mother dramatically proclaims to the children that she is about to face a prison sentence because she is doing what they want - saving them from contact with their horrible father. There is an almost inevitable and serious risk that the committal proceedings might themselves exacerbate the poor relationship between children and father and so hinder not help contact. The committal proceedings do not carry such a certain outcome of good for the children as would justify the judge proceeding of his own motion on the basis of their benefit.

---

[229] Re M (A Minor) (Contempt of Court: Committal of Court's own Motion) [1999] Fam 263.
[230] Inserted by s 4 of the CAA 2006.
[231] See, e.g., Re N (A Minor) (Access: Penal Notice) [1992] 1 FLR 134.

The courts have therefore been extremely reluctant to enforce contact orders by imprisoning the child's residential carer. Indeed, in *Churchard v Churchard* it was held that concerns about the impact of committal proceedings on the child and the child's relationship with the non-resident parent rendered such proceedings utterly 'futile'. The children in this case were strongly opposed to contact and had taken to barricading themselves in the loft when the father came to the house. The father applied to commit the mother to prison.

Churchard v Churchard [1984] FLR 635, 638–9 (CA)

ORMROD LJ:

To accede to the father's application for the committal order would not conceivably be in the best interests of the children. It would mean two things: first, if committed, that their mother would be taken away from them for a time and their father would be branded in their eyes as the man who had put their mother in prison. That is a brand from which no parent in my experience can ever hope to recover. It is the most deadly blow a parent can inflict on his children. There is no doubt and it should be clearly understood—I am speaking for myself now—throughout the legal profession that an application to commit for breach of orders relating to access (and I limit my comments to breaches of orders relating to access) are inevitably futile and should not be made. The damage which they cause is appalling. The damage in this case which they have caused is obvious. To apply for a legalistic but futile remedy, because it is the only thing left to do, is, in my judgment, the last hope of the destitute. The court is only concerned with the welfare of the children and ought not to trouble itself too much about its own dignity.

These cases are exceedingly intractable. They can only be dealt with by tact not force. Force is bound to fail. My conclusion, therefore, is that, as far as the application to commit the mother is concerned, the judge was plainly right.

This strong opposition to the use of committal orders in the context of contact disputes led to a line of authorities in which committal was understood to be a weapon of very last resort, if appropriate at all.[232] More recently, there has, however, been a clear hardening of attitudes, Ormrod LJ's strong reluctance to invoke coercive measures against the residential carer being explicitly questioned. This more robust approach has been marked by a shift in the welfare discourse with a much greater focus on the importance of securing the long-term benefits of contact with the non-residential parent than the short-term distress caused by the imprisonment of the residential carer.[233] The courts' greater willingness to invoke committal proceedings has also been marked by a move away from an almost exclusive focus on the child's welfare to place much greater emphasis on the need to uphold the dignity and authority of the court. The leading authority on this more hard-line approach is *A v N (Committal: Refusal of contact)* in which the mother of a four-and-a-half-year-old girl was adamant that she would rather go to prison than allow the girl to have contact with her father. The mother was committed to prison for 42 days for her persistent breach of the court's orders. The Court of Appeal refused her appeal.

---

[232] See, e.g., *Re N (A Minor) (Access: Penal Notice)* [1992] 1 FLR 134 and *Re M (A Minor) (Contempt of Court: Committal of Court's own Motion)* [1999] Fam 263.

[233] See, e.g., *Re L (Minors) (Access Order: Enforcement)* [1989] 2 FLR 359 and *B v S* [2009] EWCA Civ 548. In the latter case the Court of Appeal upheld the mother's committal to prison even though she had a three-month-old baby and the father no longer wished to see her committed.

A v N (Committal: Refusal of contact) [1997] 2 FCR 475, 482–4 (CA)

Lord Justice Ward:

[In an application for committal for breach] the upbringing of the child is not a paramount consideration. It is obviously a material consideration and every Judge who does any family work at all is always alive to the grievous effect the implementation of an order is likely to have on the life of the children whom the mother is unwisely seeking to protect in her own misguided way.... [The judge] was fully mindful of the distressing consequence of imprisonment on the child...but he balanced against that the long-term damage that she will suffer, especially if she grows up under a deliberate false impression as to whom her father really is. He did, therefore, take proper account of welfare factors and his balance is not one with which I would interfere.

The stark reality of this case is that this is a mother who has flagrantly set herself upon a course of collision with the court's order. She has been given endless opportunities to comply with sympathetic attempts made by the Judge to meet her flimsy objections to contact taking place. She has spurned all of those attempts. For it to be submitted that the hardship to the child is the result of the court imposing the committal order is wholly to misunderstand the position. This little child suffers because the mother chooses to make her suffer. This mother had it within her power to save T that suffering, but she did not avail of that opportunity...In my judgment, it is time that it is realized that against the wisdom of the observations of Ormrod, L.J. is to be balanced the consideration that orders of the court are made to be obeyed. They are not made for any other reason...

[I]t is perhaps appropriate that the message goes out in loud and in clear terms that there does come a limit to the tolerance of the court to see its orders flouted by mothers even if they have to care for their young children. If she goes to prison it is her fault, not the fault of the Judge who did no more than his duty to the child which is imposed upon him by Parliament.

The Court of Appeal's condemnation of the mother for selfishly undermining the child's welfare resonates with the discourse of the 'selfish' 'irresponsible' mother that has come to dominate the substantive case law on contact. Unsurprisingly, this more hard-line approach has been met with concern by feminist scholars.[234]

Enforcement measures under the CA 1989

The CAA 2006 introduced a number of new measures into the CA 1989 aimed at improving implementation and enforcement of contact. The CA 1989 provides that the court may ask an officer of Cafcass to monitor and, if necessary, report back to the court as to compliance.[235] The period of monitoring may not exceed 12 months.[236] The intention behind it is to ensure breaches are immediately brought to the judge's attention. Furthermore, additional advice, support, and assistance to help parents adjust to contact in difficult cases may now be more readily available under a family assistance order.[237] Family assistance orders have been little used in private law disputes,[238] although their potential has been recognized in the academic literature.[239] The CAA 2006 thus amended s 16 of the CA 1989 to remove the

[234] Barnett (2000), 141.
[235] S 11H(2).
[236] S 11H(6).
[237] S 16(4A).
[238] For statistics see CASC (2001), 26.
[239] Seden (2001).

requirement that a family assistance order may only be made in exceptional circumstances.[240] It also extends the period for which the order may be made to 12 months.[241]

On the specific issue of enforcement, the CAA 2006 amended the CA 1989 to increase the range of measures available to the courts. As an alternative to imposing a fine or imprisonment, the courts may make an enforcement order imposing an 'unpaid work requirement' unless the person in breach can satisfy the court, on the balance of probabilities, that there was a reasonable excuse for non-compliance.[242] Before making the enforcement order the court must be satisfied that (i) the order is necessary to secure compliance with the contact order, and (ii) the enforcement order is *proportionate* to the seriousness of the offence.[243] The court must also take into account the child's welfare, though not as the paramount consideration. Compliance with an unpaid work requirement is monitored by an officer of Cafcass.[244]

Where breach of a contact order causes financial loss, such as the cost of a cancelled holiday, the court can order the person in breach to pay compensation.[245] To avoid the order, the person in breach must satisfy the court, on the balance of probabilities, that he or she had a reasonable excuse for failing to comply. In determining whether to make the order and, if so, for how much, the court must take into account the individual's financial circumstances and the welfare of the child concerned.

Transferring residence

A similar hardening of attitudes is discernable in the courts' use of their final weapon in intractable contact disputes: removing residence from the 'intransigent' parent.[246] The Court of Appeal has again made it clear that the transfer of residence is a 'judicial weapon of last resort'—such a move should not be taken lightly.[247] Where the child has been denied contact with the non-resident parent there will be obvious risks in transferring residence to a parent who may well be a relative stranger. However, despite the risks, the courts have made it clear that they are increasingly willing to employ this measure against 'unreasonable mothers' to protect the child's long-term interests. The key question for the court is whether there is a greater risk of harm to the child by reason of the disruption and distress caused by a transfer of residence or by denying him/her a relationship with the non-resident parent.

V v V (Contact: Implacable hostility) [2004] EWHC 1215

BRACEWELL J:

45.... If the children move to father they would be uprooted from mother's daily care, where they have lived all their lives. They would have to change schools and settle into a new environment with father and extended family. The mother has more than adequately provided for their needs, except in respect of the relationship with father. The change would

---

240 S 16(3).
241 S 16(5).
242 S 11J(2)–(4).
243 S 11L.
244 S 11M.
245 S 11O.
246 For recent examples see *Re C (a child)* [2007] EWCA Civ 866; *Re A (Suspended Residence Order)* [2010] 1 FLR 1679; *Re S (Transfer of Residence)* [2010] 1 FLR 1785.
247 *Re A (children)* [2009] EWCA Civ 1141, [18].

be traumatic, even though each parent has the capacity to care for the children. If the children stay with mother there is the prospect of ongoing battles about contact to father, continued litigation with mother finding reasons to stop contact until father, exhausted from the proceedings, might well retire. There would be, in my judgment, a real risk that father would become battle-weary and withdraw from the children's lives defeated and demoralised.

46. If the children move to father I am satisfied he would actively support generous contact to mother and encourage the children to have a loving relationship with her; but there is the emotional upheaval for the children to consider as well as the problem of mother not accepting placement with father and perhaps seeking to undermine it.

47. These children need both their parents...I ask the question: how can the best outcome be achieved for these children? Which solution results in the least risk, the least detrimental harm? The starting point is that these children, in my judgment, have already suffered harm by means of the emotional abuse by the mother...[T]he situation cannot be allowed to continue as at present because the children will continue to suffer harm if deprived of their relationship with their father. It is the right of the children to have contact with their father. It is for the mother to establish by credible evidence any basis for denying or restricting contact. She has not done so. Her implacable hostility is not a proper basis for denying or restricting contact.

...48. Any decision to change residence arising from difficulties over contact must be fully justified by affording paramount consideration to the child's welfare. It must not be used to punish a parent.

49. This is a case in which but for the mother's malign influence the children would have benefited by having the regular and substantial contact...I find that, if left with mother, there will be increasing emotional harm to the children and I agree...that mother's conduct is likely to continue. The use of enforcement procedures, such as penal notice, may have the effect of causing the mother to deliver contact but it will not prevent her from continuing to poison the children's minds against their father and family and building up a case against him.

50. Applying the welfare check list in relation to physical, emotional and educational needs, the parents can provide equally for physical and educational needs, but the father is better able to provide for emotional needs. The likely efficient [sic] of a change in circumstances means that the children will undoubtedly be upset initially to leave their mother but in the longer term will benefit from a change of circumstances....

55....Having considered all the factors, weighing all the risks and advantages, I am satisfied that the need for these children to have a relationship with their father can only be met by transferring residence to him. I am confident in his abilities. I, therefore, order a residence order to father.

Although controversial, this more hard-line approach to enforcement finds support in the ECHR. It was held in *Hokkanen v Finland* that the state has a positive obligation under Article 8 to 'facilitate' the parent–child relationship, including taking all reasonable steps to enforce private law orders for contact.[248] However, the European Court recognized that the state's obligation cannot be absolute and that any coercive measures against the parent in breach must be limited by the need to take into account the rights and interests of others, in particular those of the child. These principles were approved and applied in the case of *Glaser v UK*.[249]

---

[248] *Hokkanen v Finland* (Case No 50/1993/445/524, ECHR) (1996).
[249] (App No 32346/96, ECHR) (2000). See also *Damnjonovic v Serbia* (App No 5222/07, ECHR) (2009), [75]–[78] and *Kaleta v Poland* (App No 11375/02, ECHR) (2009), [52].

11.5.4 TAKING CONTACT OUT OF THE COURTS

As the courts struggle to find appropriate and effective solutions to the more difficult and intractable contact disputes, it has been questioned more broadly whether the courts are the most appropriate forum for dealing with disputes of this nature. Long-term, deep-rooted problems, which are incapable of resolution at a discrete point in time often underpin such disputes. The blunt tool of ordering and enforcing contact will not address the underlying cause of the resident parent's hostility. Counselling or therapy may be the only way such problems can be effectively resolved.

Re L (A Child) (Contact: Domestic Violence) and others [2001] Fam 260, 296–8 (CA)

THORPE LJ:

[T]here is in my opinion validity in questioning the future role of the family justice system in relation to contact. I have already expressed how limited is the capacity of the family justice system to produce good outcomes in disputed areas of personal relationship. Yet a great deal of the resources of the system are taken up with contested contact cases. The disputes are particularly prevalent and intractable. They consume a disproportionate quantity of private law judicial time. The disputes are often driven by personality disorders, unresolved adult conflicts or egocentricity. These originating or contributing factors would generally be better treated therapeutically, where at least there would be some prospect of beneficial change, rather than given vent in the family justice system...

I would question whether the investment of public funds in litigation as the conventional mode of resolving contact disputes is comparatively productive. In many cases the same investment in therapeutic services might produce greater benefit. Within the National Health Service, child and mental health services work with warring parents to try and help them separate their parenting role from the breakdown of the partnership. If one parent has a mental illness or personality disorder the service can help the family to manage perhaps by providing sessions with the children to help them understand their situation. Within the voluntary sector there are exceptional facilities... that provide more than neutral space for contact, and perhaps some professional supervision or assessment. Such centres attempt to address the underlying dysfunction in family relationship that expresses itself in the absence or failure of contact. In some cases they may work with the family therapeutically for weeks before attempting any direct contact. It must at least be arguable that that expenditure of effort and cost is likely to achieve more than an equal expenditure on litigation with its tendency to increase alienation through its adversarial emphasis. Of course there will always be many cases that are only fit for referral to litigation. But in my opinion judges with responsibility for case management should be thoroughly informed as to available alternative services in the locality and astute in selecting the service best suited to promote the welfare of the child in each case.[250]

The Labour government shared many of these concerns believing that contact works best when parents are able to negotiate and agree arrangements between themselves without having to rely on outside intervention.[251] It therefore introduced several initiatives aimed

---

[250] See also *Re D (Intractable contact dispute: Publicity)* [2004] EWHC 727.

[251] This was supported by the ONS Omnibus survey which suggested much greater satisfaction with privately negotiated informal arrangements than court-imposed solutions. However, as the government recognizes, this is not at all surprising, and perhaps even significant, given it is only the most intractable cases that reach the courts and in these circumstances an order satisfying both parties is never really a likely outcome. DCA, DfES, and DTI (2004), 9.

at changing the attitudes and behaviour of separating parents through tools of *persuasion*. The hope was to achieve a change in *culture* regarding contact disputes, whereby 'it becomes socially unacceptable for one parent to impede a child's relationship with its other parent wherever it is safe and in the child's best interests'.[252] Parents were thus to be 'educated' to understand that the 'civilized divorce' and 'good parenting' requires them to put their children's interests before their own and that this means facilitating contact. The government hoped that parents who received and understood this 'message' would be able to reach their own agreements for the generous provision of contact.

The government's first step towards this goal was to provide better access to information and advice through existing agencies such as NCH, Sure Start, and Relate. Information targeted at both parents and children[253] includes parenting plans containing examples of various contact arrangements which have been shown to work well.[254] Several measures have been introduced which are aimed at promoting a more conciliatory approach to resolving disputes. A collaborative law programme is being piloted, whereby both parents' lawyers must be committed to achieving settlement: in the absence of which different lawyers must be instructed.[255] Voluntary mediation (currently only used by about 5 per cent of couples) is being promoted alongside this scheme, funded, where the parties are eligible, by legal aid.[256] Finally, where applications are made to the court, it is now mandatory except in cases involving domestic violence for the parties to attend at least one conciliation session with an officer from Cafcass who will try and assist them to reach agreement.[257]

11.6 SPECIFIC ISSUE AND PROHIBITED STEPS ORDERS

In essence, specific issue and prohibited steps orders constitute two sides of the same coin. A SIO is a positive order providing for a particular step to be taken with respect to the child's upbringing. A PSO is a negative order preventing a particular step being taken. As discussed in chapter 10, such orders are commonly used to resolve disputes between the holders of parental responsibility. However, subject to the requirement for leave, anyone may in theory apply to the court for a particular issue to be determined. SIOs and PSOs have been used to resolve a wide range of disputes concerning a child, the one requirement being that it must engage some aspect of parental responsibility.[258] Some of the more common include: changing a child's surname,[259] preventing the removal of a child from the jurisdiction,[260] medical treatment,[261] and the publication of information about the child.[262]

---

[252] DCA, DfES, and DTI (2005), 7.

[253] For comment on engaging children in this process of securing the 'civilized divorce' see Kaganas and Diduck (2004).

[254] DCA, DfES, and DTI (2005), 19–21.

[255] Ibid.

[256] Ibid.

[257] *The Revised Private Law Programme* (April 2010), available at: <www.judiciary.gov.uk/NR/rdonlyres/27290456-8E28-4E79-8C6A-D8B0AB9F286D/0/praticedirectionpfdprivatelawprogramme april2010.pdf>. For an excellent critique of in-court conciliation schemes and their ability to facilitate fair and effective agreements, see Trinder and Kellett (2007).

[258] *Re J (Specific issue order: Leave to apply)* [1995] 1 FLR 669.

[259] *Dawson v Wearmouth* [1999] 2 AC 309; *Re W (A Child) (Illegitimate Child: Change of Surname)* [2001] Fam 1.

[260] *Re K (Application to remove from jurisdiction)* [1998] 2 FLR 1006.

[261] *Re HG (Specific issue order: Sterilisation)* [1993] 1 FLR 587; *Re R (A minor) (Blood Transfusion)* [1993] 2 FLR 757.

[262] *Re Z (a minor) (freedom of publication)* [1997] Fam 1.

Whilst the potential use of SIOs and PSOs is extremely broad, there are some important restrictions on their use. An SIO or PSO cannot be made with a view to achieving a result which could be achieved by making a contact or residence order.[263] Nor may a SIO or PSO be made with a view to placing a child in local authority care.[264] Finally, a SIO or PSO cannot be used to 'oust' someone from the family home, the proper route for such an application being under Part IV of the Family Law Act 1996.[265]

An application for a SIO or PSO is determined on the basis of the child's welfare.

11.7 CONCLUSION

The law on private disputes over children gives rise to a wide range of issues, bringing into sharp relief many of the key themes discussed in the previous three chapters. The courts are routinely called upon to grapple with such fundamental questions as the appropriate parenting roles of mothers and fathers; whether biological or social parenting should be prioritized; whether the 'bi-nuclear' or 'reconstituted' family is the more secure basis for post-separation parenting; whether multiple parenting figures can be sustained; and the extent to which alternative family forms, such as gay and lesbian parenting, should be accepted as equal to conventional heterosexual arrangements. In searching for the answers to these questions, the courts have tried to make the child's welfare their sole consideration. However, nothing demonstrates the vagaries of the welfare principle more effectively than the shifts in the courts' approach to these disputes over the last 40 years. Whilst some evolution of judicial thinking is to be expected, and indeed applauded, in line with the best available evidence on the developmental needs and outcomes for children living in separated families, the case law and legislative reforms considered in this chapter highlight the extent to which these trends are often driven by social and political factors well beyond the control of the courts. Thus whilst orthodox wisdom used to dictate the importance of mothering over fathering, social over biological parenting and the reconstituted over the 'bi-nuclear' family, various social and political factors have converged to transform these trends so that what we now see, at least in the post-divorce or post-separation context, is a dramatic reversal in the fortunes of one figure: the genetic father. Although there may be some disquiet that the highly politicized debate surrounding fathers' rights has distorted many of the underlying issues, the greater value placed on genetic fathering is not necessarily a cause for concern. Indeed, it may be something to be welcomed. However, in such a highly charged political atmosphere as that generated by some fathers' rights groups, the courts must ensure they do not become distracted by this powerful and often superficially persuasive rhetoric. Decision-making in the courts must remain firmly focused on the needs and interests of the individual child.

ONLINE RESOURCE CENTRE

Questions, suggestions for further reading, and supplementary materials for this chapter (including updates on developments in this area of family law since this book was published) may be found on the Online Resource Centre at **www.oxfordtextbooks.co.uk/orc/harrisshort_tcm2e/**.

---

263 CA 1989, s 9(5)(a). See *Re H (Prohibited steps order)* [1995] 1 WLR 667.
264 Ibid., ss 9(5)(b) and 100(2).
265 *Pearson v Franklin* [1994] 1 WLR 370; *Re D (Prohibited steps order)* [1996] 2 FLR 273.

12

CHILD PROTECTION

CENTRAL ISSUES

1. Child protection is a challenging topic. It requires the state to draw a difficult balance between respecting the integrity of the family whilst ensuring vulnerable family members are protected. Tragic cases attracting strong media interest serve as a constant reminder of the dangers of under and over-reacting to suspicions of abuse.

2. Part III of the Children Act 1989 (CA 1989) seeks to support families through the provision of voluntary services to 'children in need'. These aims will be seriously compromised if local authorities are under-resourced.

3. The state cannot remove children from their parents' care on the basis of a simple best interests test: a threshold involving 'significant harm' must first be established. The threshold for state intervention at various stages of the child protection process has been extremely controversial.

4. The state's poor record in caring for children has given rise to considerable concern. The state has responded with more robust monitoring of the implementation of local authority care plans and a strong drive towards securing permanency for looked after children.

5. The Human Rights Act 1998 (HRA 1998) has reinforced the child's and the parents' rights throughout the child protection process, necessitating some changes to both substantive law and procedure.

12.1 INTRODUCTION

The death of a child at the hands of her parents always engenders strong feelings. When that child is known to be at risk and is supposedly under the care and protection of the state, the child's death attracts great public anger and concern. Maria Colwell, Jasmine Beckford, Kimberley Carlile, Victoria Climbié, and Baby Peter are just some of the children who have died in such tragic circumstances.[1] Finding answers to what went wrong and, more

---

[1] For short accounts of the circumstances surrounding the deaths of Maria Colwell, Jasmine Beckford, Kimberley Carlile, and Victoria Climbié see Cretney (2003a), ch 20. As to Baby Peter, see LSCB (2009).

importantly, how such deaths can be prevented is exceptionally difficult. Deception and manipulation by the child's parents, the naïve optimism of social workers, the complacency of heath professionals and teachers, the basic incompetence of over-worked, inexperienced, and poorly trained staff, and a serious lack of local authority resources are all too familiar stories. However, even the best resourced, trained, and supported professionals would not be able to prevent the death of every child at risk of harm from abusive parents. Child protection is an inherently difficult process. Every case requires a delicate balancing exercise to be performed between respecting and supporting the integrity of the family whilst ensuring vulnerable family members are protected. A strong, robust, and highly interventionist approach by social work, health, and legal professionals can be just as harmful as the 'hands-off' complacency which marked the cases of Victoria Climbié and Baby Peter.[2] The unjustified removal of large numbers of children in Cleveland in 1987, Rochdale in 1990, and Orkney in 1991 because of misplaced suspicions of ritualized sexual abuse provides a chilling reminder of the dangers of misguided, 'crusading', albeit well-meaning, professionals.[3] Although state intervention into the family is not necessarily a bad thing—indeed help offered to the family by the local authority on a consensual basis can be both positive and supportive—the wrongful removal of a child can be devastating. The legal framework provided by the CA 1989[4] has to ensure that child protection professionals are able to respond quickly and effectively to children at risk of harm, whilst guarding against unnecessary and potentially harmful intervention into the family unit. It is a difficult balance. However, nowhere more than here is getting that balance right of such vital importance to the child.

This chapter considers the law governing state intervention into family life where a child is considered to be 'in need' or at risk of harm. We begin by outlining the competing approaches to state intervention and the principles underpinning the CA 1989. We then examine the legal framework governing voluntary state intervention for children in need under Part III of the CA 1989 before considering the law and procedure regulating compulsory intervention into family life by means of care proceedings under Part IV. We conclude by considering the various emergency and interim measures available to protect a child thought to be at risk of immediate harm.

12.2 PRINCIPLES OF STATE INTERVENTION INTO FAMILY LIFE

12.2.1 COMPETING APPROACHES AND THE CHILDREN ACT 1989

When determining the basis upon which state intervention into family life is justified, two key questions have to be addressed: (1) the principles which should govern the state's initial intervention; and (2) the long-term goals which should guide decision-making once some form of intervention is deemed necessary. Lorraine Fox-Harding has identified four models of state intervention into family life which suggest differing answers to these two key questions. She terms these approaches: laissez-faire and patriarchy; state paternalism and child protection; the defence of the birth family and parental rights; and children's rights and child liberation.

---

[2] Lord Laming (2003).
[3] Butler-Sloss (1988).
[4] Unless otherwise stated, all references to statutory provisions in this chapter are to the CA 1989.

L. Fox-Harding, 'The Children Act 1989 in Context: Four Perspectives in Child Care Law and Policy (1)', (1991a) 13 *Journal of Social Welfare and Family Law* 179, 181–2

(1) Laissez-faire and patriarchy

The term *laissez-faire* is used here to describe the perspective which sees the role of the state in child care as ideally one of minimal intervention, while the privacy and sanctity of the original family should in most circumstances be respected. However, in *extreme* cases of poor parental care, state intervention is not only acceptable but preferably of a strong and authoritative kind, transferring the child from the original parent(s) to a secure substitute placement with a new set of parent figures. The new family unit should then be accorded the same rights, and respect by the state, as the original one . . .

(2) State paternalism and child protection

The terms "state paternalism and child protection" are taken to indicate a school of thought which favours much more extensive state intervention to protect children from poor parental care. Where parental care is deemed inadequate, then in this perspective finding the child a new permanent home where good quality care will be provided is usually the appropriate response. Therefore the rights and liberties of parents and the integrity of the original birth family are given a low priority in this perspective; while the welfare of the child, as this is construed, is paramount.

(3) The defence of the birth family and parents' rights

A third, pro-birth family perspective encapsulates the idea that birth or biological families are extremely important both for children and parents, and should be maintained wherever possible. Where families have to be separated through children entering substitute care, then parent-child links should usually be kept up. The role of the state is seen as, ideally, neither paternalist nor *lasseiz-faire*, but positively supportive of families, providing various services that they need to function well and remain together. At the same time, class, poverty and deprivation are seen as important elements in child care, explaining much of what appears to be inadequate parenting, while the (usually coercive) response of the state is disproportionately directed to lower class and deprived families.

(4) Children's rights and child liberation

The terms "children's rights and child liberation" are used here for a perspective which emphasises the importance of *the child's* own viewpoint and wishes, seeing the child as a separate entity with rights to autonomy and freedom, rather like an adult. The idea of the control of children, either through the state or by adults individually, is called into question by the emphasis on rights and liberation, as therefore are notions of custody and parental rights. The strength and competence of children, and their similarity to adults, are emphasised, rather than their vulnerability; children are not seen as in need of protection, but empowerment; but it is not clear how far children would be expected to carry the burdens and duties of adult status as well. A less extreme position would emphasise that children should at least have more say in what happens to them.

Fox-Harding contends that elements of all four approaches can be identified in the CA 1989, albeit she argues that paternalism and defence of the birth parent's rights predominate.[5] Indeed, these were strong themes in the government's Review of Child Care Law preceding the legislation. The importance placed on preserving the integrity of the birth family and supporting it wherever possible both before and after intervention is particularly clear.

DHSS, *Review of Child Care Law. Report to ministers of an interdepartmental working party* (London: HMSO, 1985)

2.8 A distinction is often drawn between the interests of children and the interests of their parents. In the great majority of families, including those who are for one reason or another in need of social services, this distinction does not exist. The interests of the children are best served by their remaining with their families and the interests of their parents are best served by allowing them to undertake their natural and legal responsibility to care for their own children. Hence the focus of effort should be to enable and assist parents to discharge those responsibilities. Even where a child has to spend some time away from home, every effort should be made to maintain and foster links between the child and his family to care for the child in partnership with rather than in opposition to his parents, and to work towards his return to them.

2.13 . . . "[T]he child is not the child of the state" and it is important in a free society to maintain the rich diversity of lifestyles which is secured by permitting families a large measure of autonomy in the way in which they bring up their families who through force of circumstances are in need of help from social services or other agencies. Only where their children are put at unacceptable risk should it be possible compulsorily to intervene. Once such a risk of harm to the child has been shown, however, his interests must clearly predominate.

As Fox-Harding notes, the emphasis placed on providing extensive state *support* for the birth family is surprising.[6] Given the CA 1989 was sponsored by a Conservative government whose political ideology traditionally favours protecting the autonomy of the family and affords only a minimal role to the state, a more laissez-faire approach might have been expected. This would also have been more consistent with what some commentators have identified as the 'privatizing' trend underpinning the CA 1989, which, as encapsulated by s 1(5) (the 'no order' principle), seeks to place the primary responsibility for the care and upbringing of children on the child's parents and is generally characterized by a marked withdrawal of the state from family life.[7] None of this is consistent with the imposition of wide-ranging duties on local authorities to provide a comprehensive range of services to help and support families in need. Yet this is what Part III of the CA 1989 purports to do.

Unfortunately, no matter how much help and support is provided, there will always be some families for whom support will have to give way to more coercive forms of intervention. One of the hardest questions in child protection is determining when that point is reached. A balance must be found between striving to preserve the integrity of the birth family whilst ensuring the child is not left in a situation of known risk or deprived of a permanent placement outside the family because of hopelessly optimistic efforts to achieve a

---

[5] Fox-Harding (1991b), 299.
[6] Ibid.
[7] Bainham (2005), 49.

reconciliation with the parents. Since the implementation of the CA 1989, there have been important shifts in attitude regarding whether the birth family's rights or a stronger, more coercive model of state intervention should predominate. When the CA 1989 was implemented there was a perhaps somewhat idealistic hope that the state would focus its efforts and resources on trying to support the birth family under Part III. However, in more recent years the pendulum has swung back towards more decisive intervention with a view to securing permanency for the child. Growing concern about the life-chances of children left to 'drift' in and out of care,[8] has led to a renewed focus on ensuring effective planning for children known to social services and securing long term alternative placements for those children in care.[9] Given the evidence regarding the woeful life-experiences and long-term prospects of 'looked after' children, this recent emphasis on the importance of permanency planning, even at the potential expense of long-term engagement with the birth family, is understandable.[10] However, the swing back towards a greater emphasis on securing permanency is perhaps surprising given the renewed focus on the birth parents' rights in the wake of the HRA 1998.

12.2.2 THE HUMAN RIGHTS DIMENSION

The fundamental rights of the child and the parents must be safeguarded throughout the child protection process. From the child's perspective, two key rights under the European Convention on Human Rights (ECHR) are engaged: Article 3 and Article 8.[11] These provisions impose positive obligations on the state to protect a child from parental abuse. Clearly the state cannot provide absolute guarantees against the abuse of children. Given the secretive nature of child abuse, particularly sexual abuse, many incidences of abuse will go undetected without any degree of fault or responsibility resting with state officials. Even in those cases known to the local authority, the need to prioritize and allocate scare resources means that the protection afforded to individual children cannot ever be absolute. However, the European Court of Human Rights has held that under Articles 3 and 8 the state owes individual children a positive duty as regards the detection, investigation, and management of child abuse. That obligation includes the need to remove children from situations of known risk where appropriate.[12]

However, as the European Court also recognizes, where the local authority is or should be aware that a child is at risk, it is not a straightforward matter of simply removing the child.[13] In all of these cases children have important countervailing rights: whilst ensuring the child is adequately protected against abuse, the state must also respect the integrity of the child's family. In particular, when considering what child protection measures are necessary, Article 8 requires the state to take all necessary steps to ensure that any measures of intervention are proportionate to the harm suffered and that no child is unnecessarily removed from the care of his or her family. It is a difficult line for the local authority to tread. Both over-reacting (removing without good cause) and under-reacting (failing to remove)

---

8 DfES (2004).

9 Parkinson (2003), 147–8.

10 DfES (2004).

11 See also Article 19 of the United Nations Convention on the Rights of the Child 1989 (UNCRC). For an excellent analysis of the impact of human rights law on child protection see Kaganas (2010).

12 *Z and others v United Kingdom* (App No 29392/95, ECHR) (2001).

13 Ibid., [74].

may give rise to liability under s 7 of the HRA 1998 or (at the suit of the child) in common law negligence.[14]

The child's parents enjoy similar rights under the ECHR.[15] The European Court has consistently stressed that under Article 8 the state has both negative and positive obligations towards the child's parents. The various demands of Article 8 are summarized in the case of *Haase v Germany*.

Haase v Germany (App No 11057/02, ECHR) (2005)

90.... While the authorities enjoy a wide margin of appreciation in assessing the necessity of taking a child into care, in particular where an emergency situation arises, the Court must still be satisfied in the particular case that there existed circumstances justifying the removal of the child, and it is for the respondent State to establish that a careful assessment of the impact of the proposed care measure on the parents and the child, as well as of the possible alternatives to taking the child into public care, was carried out prior to implementation of such a measure...

92. Following any removal into care, a stricter scrutiny is called for in respect of any further limitations by the authorities, for example on restrictions on parental rights and access, and on any legal safeguards designed to secure the effective protection of the right of parents and children to respect for their family life. Such further limitations entail the danger that the family relations between the parents and a young child might be effectively curtailed...

93. The taking into care of a child should normally be regarded as a temporary measure to be discontinued as soon as circumstances permit, and any measures of implementation of temporary care should be consistent with the ultimate aim of reuniting the natural parent and child...In this regard a fair balance has to be struck between the interests of the child remaining in care and those of the parent in being reunited with the child...In carrying out this balancing exercise, the Court will attach particular importance to the best interests of the child which, depending on their nature and seriousness, may override those of the parent...In particular, a parent cannot be entitled under Article 8 to have such measures taken as would harm the child's health and development...

94. Whilst Article 8 contains no explicit procedural requirements, the decision-making process involved in measures of interference must be fair and such as to ensure due respect for the interests safeguarded by Article 8. The Court must therefore determine whether, having regard to the circumstances of the case and notably the importance of the decisions to be taken, the applicants have been involved in the decision-making process, seen as a whole, to a degree sufficient to provide them with the requisite protection of their interests...

---

[14] *TP and KM v United Kingdom* (App No 28945/95, ECHR) (2001). See also *D v East Berkshire Community Health NHS Trust; K and another v Dewsbury Healthcare NHS Trust and another; K and another v Oldham NHS Trust and another* [2003] EWCA Civ 1151.

[15] Note, however, that whilst the parents may bring a claim under the HRA 1998, the local authority does not owe them a duty of care under common law negligence, at least if they are the suspected perpetrators of the abuse. See *D v East Berkshire Community Health NHS Trust and others; Mak and another v Dewsbury Healthcare NHS Trust and another; RK and another v Oldham NHS Trust and another* [2005] UKHL 23 and *Lawrence v Pembrokeshire County Council* [2007] EWCA Civ 446. It has been held that a duty of care may be owed to parents in circumstances where, because the parent is not the suspected abuser, there is no potential conflict of interest between parent and child. See *Merthyr Tydfil County Borough Council v C* [2010] EWHC 62.

The judiciary have broadly welcomed the reception of a rights-based discourse into the public law on children.[16] The right to respect for family life reinforces the importance of preserving the integrity of the family unit which has long formed a core principle of child protection policy. The courts have thus issued strong warnings as to the need for fundamental changes in the prevailing 'culture' and 'mindset' of local authorities, demanding far-reaching improvements in both the procedural and substantive aspects of local authority decision-making before, during, and after formal care proceedings.[17] With the Article 8 rights of the child and the parents engaged, ECHR arguments are now a routine feature of public law cases.[18] Indeed, arguments over alleged breaches of Articles 6 and 8 ECHR are so commonly made that concern is now being expressed that human rights arguments are hindering local authority applications and causing unnecessary expense and delay.[19]

12.2.3 THE PROBLEM OF RESOURCES

The strong protection given to the parents' rights under Article 8 makes the recent shift in favour of permanency planning at the potential expense of repeated attempts at rehabilitation with the birth family all the more surprising. However, the recent emphasis on permanency planning is arguably driven more by pragmatic concerns than any major ideological shift in child protection policy. A model of state intervention based on providing a range of effective support services to families in need is resource-intensive, requiring large-scale investment in local authority services. Without such investment, an approach focusing on supporting the birth family is almost certain to fail. This is an issue where idealism meets head on the harsh economic realities of life. The serious problem of poorly resourced local authorities[20] means there is a tendency to divert resources away from voluntary family support services to deal with the more serious and immediate problems of children requiring compulsory care.[21] A local authority culture of crisis intervention and management is thereby perpetuated.[22] Keenan argues that inadequate funding is a key factor behind the adoption of a more hard-line, authoritarian approach to child protection.[23]

12.3 STATE SUPPORT FOR CHILDREN AND FAMILIES UNDER PART III

Part III of the CA 1989 enshrines the then Conservative government's commitment to promoting the upbringing of children within their birth families by the provision of help and support to families in need. In accordance with the principle that 'prevention is better than

---

[16] For further discussion see Harris-Short (2005), 340–50.

[17] *Re G (Care: Challenge to Local Authority's Decision)* [2003] EWHC 551; *Re L (Care: Assessment: Fair Trial)* [2002] EWHC 1379.

[18] *Re V (a child) (care proceedings: human rights claims)* [2004] EWCA Civ 54.

[19] *Re V (Care: Pre-birth actions)* [2004] EWCA Civ 1575; *Re J (a child) (care proceedings: fair trial)* [2006] EWCA Civ 545.

[20] See, e.g., *R (on the application of G) v Barnet London Borough Council; R (on the application of W) v Lambeth London Borough Council; R (on the application of A) v Lambeth London Borough Council* [2003] UKHL 57, [10] (per Lord Nicholls).

[21] Bainham (2005), 419.

[22] See generally, Smith (2002).

[23] Keenan (2006), 48.

cure',[24] this section of the CA 1989 brings together a wide range of services aimed at ensuring that children's needs are met within their families before more coercive intervention becomes necessary. 'Partnership' is the 'buzz' word of these provisions.[25] Intervention under Part III should be non-coercive, based on mutual cooperation, and, most importantly, voluntarily accepted by the parents. The government was keen to remove any stigma attached to receiving help from the local authority, stressing that the provision of services under Part III should be viewed as a positive, supportive measure for the family, not a sign of 'parental shortcomings' or failure.[26] To emphasize the distinction between these services and any compulsory measures taken within the context of care proceedings under Part IV, all coercive measures that the state could formerly take when a child was being voluntarily looked after by the local authority were removed.[27] In practice, this marked a significant erosion of state power and an important correlative strengthening of the parents' rights.[28]

Before the CA 1989, the provision of support and assistance to families in need was contained within a complicated patchwork of legislative provisions.[29] One of the major aims of the CA 1989 was to rationalize and consolidate the legal basis for the provision of services into one comprehensive, coherent piece of legislation.[30] As a result of this consolidation process, the scope of Part III is extremely broad. It covers a wide and disparate range of children's needs, from the provision of respite care for disabled children to the provision of more long-term accommodation for children in need as a result of parental neglect.

12.3.1 THE GENERAL DUTY TO CHILDREN IN NEED: S 17

Section 17(1) sets down the general duty owed by local authorities to children in need.

Children Act 1989, s 17

(1) It shall be the general duty of every local authority (in addition to the other duties imposed on them by this Part)—

   (a) to safeguard and promote the welfare of children within their area who are in need; and

   (b) so far as is consistent with that duty to promote the upbringing of such children by their families,

by providing a range and level of services appropriate to those children's needs.

In order to qualify for the provision of services under s 17 the child must be 'a child in need'. 'Child' is defined in s 105(1) as 'a person under the age of eighteen'. The meaning of a child 'in need' is set down in s 17(10).

---

[24] Bainham (2005), 18.
[25] Ibid., 51.
[26] DHSS et al (1987), [17], [21].
[27] Bainham (2005), 415.
[28] For discussion of the previous powers of the state, see Bainham, ibid., 20.
[29] Ibid., 18.
[30] DHSS et al (1987), [7]–[8].

Children Act 1989, s 17

(10) For the purposes of this Part a child shall be taken to be in need if—

    (a) he is unlikely to achieve or maintain, or to have the opportunity of achieving or maintaining, a reasonable standard of health or development without the provision for him of services by a local authority under this Part;

    (b) his health or development is likely to be significantly impaired, or further impaired without the provision for him of such services; or

    (c) he is disabled...

'Development' is further defined as 'physical, intellectual, emotional, social or behavioural development'.[31] 'Health' is further defined as physical or mental health.[32] It was held by the Supreme Court in *R (on the application of A) v London Borough of Croydon; R (on the application of M) v London Borough of Lambeth*,[33] that a distinction needs to be drawn between the question of whether or not a young person is 'a child' for the purposes of the CA 1989 and the question of whether or not that child is 'in need' for the purposes of Part III.[34] The former is a straightforward objective question of fact (to which there is a right and wrong answer) and, in cases of dispute, is to be determined, on the evidence, by the court.[35] In contrast, the question of whether the child is 'in need' involves 'a number of different value judgments' and is thus to be made by the local authority, 'subject to the control of the courts on the ordinary principles of judicial review.'[36]

The s 17 duty is a general or 'target' duty owed to all children in need within the local authority area. This means there is no specific duty on the local authority to carry out an assessment of a child's needs which can be enforced at the suit of an individual child.

R (on the application of G) v Barnet London Borough Council; R (on the application of W) v Lambeth London Borough Council; R (on the application of A) v Lambeth London Borough Council [2003] UKHL 57

LORD MILLETT:

106. In my opinion [section 17] imposes a general and overriding duty to maintain a level and range of services sufficient to enable the authority to discharge its functions under Part III of the Act.

107. Section 17(1) contains three indications of the nature of the duty which it imposes. The first is that it is described as a general duty. I agree that this is not decisive by itself. It may be contrasted with the specific duties and powers mentioned in Section 17(2). But it does suggest that what is to follow is a general and comprehensive duty owed to all persons within the authority's area rather than a duty which is owed to particular individuals.

108. The second indication is that it is a duty to safeguard and promote the welfare of "children within their area who are in need" and to promote the upbringing of such children by their families. This is couched in terms which suggest that it is a broad and general duty to

---

[31] S 17(11).
[32] Ibid.
[33] [2009] UKSC 8, [26].
[34] Ibid., [26], [32].
[35] Ibid., [27] (per Lady Hale); [51], [53] (per Lord Hope).
[36] Ibid., [26], [28] (per Lady Hale). See also, *Re J (Specific issue order: Leave to apply)* [1995] 1 FLR 669.

cater for the needs of all the children concerned, rather than a duty to meet the needs of any particular child. This feature, too, cannot be decisive, for the words can be read as involving a duty in respect of the welfare and upbringing of each child. But it cannot be assumed that they do involve such a duty, for this is the very question to be decided.

109. In my opinion, however, the third indication is decisive. The duty is not a duty to safeguard and promote the welfare of the children concerned simpliciter, but to do so "by providing a range and level of services appropriate to those children's needs." A social services authority which provides a range and level of services appropriate to meet the various needs of children in its area has discharged its duty under section 17(1). This cannot be read as a duty to meet the needs of any particular child. It is sufficient that the authority maintains services for which his particular needs make him eligible.

The majority went on to dismiss the argument that the general duty under s 17 'crystallizes' into a specific enforceable duty once the child has been assessed and a particular need identified.[37]

To assist the local authority to carry out its s 17(1) duty, Sch 2, Part I sets down a range of more specific duties and powers.[38] These include identifying and assessing children in need within their area,[39] taking reasonable steps to prevent abuse and neglect,[40] taking reasonable steps to prevent the need for care proceedings under Part IV, providing accommodation to a member of the child's household to protect the child from ill-treatment,[41] and providing services for children living at home (including the provision of advice, guidance and counselling, occupational, social, cultural or recreational activities, home help, and assistance with holidays).[42] Section 17(6) further provides that services may include the provision of accommodation (although a child provided with accommodation under s 17 is not a 'looked after' child), giving assistance in kind or, in exceptional circumstances, cash.[43] Services may be provided to the child or a member of the child's family. 'Family' is defined as including any person who has parental responsibility for the child and any other person with whom the child has been living.[44] Before determining what, if any, services to provide under this section the local authority must, so far as is reasonably practicable, ascertain and give due consideration to the child's wishes.[45]

12.3.2 PROVIDING ACCOMMODATION FOR A CHILD

The duty to accommodate: s 20(1)

In stark contrast to the wide discretion conferred on the local authority under s 17, s 20(1) confers a clear duty on the local authority to accommodate a child if certain conditions are met.

---

[37] Lord Nicholls dissented.
[38] S 17(2).
[39] Sch 2, Part I, paras 1 and 3.
[40] Ibid., para 4.
[41] Ibid., para 5.
[42] Ibid., para 8.
[43] S 17(6) was amended by the Adoption and Children Act 2002, s 116 to make clear that accommodation could be provided under s 17 following contrary decisions in *(R)A v Lambeth London Borough Council* [2001] EWCA Civ 1624 and *(R)J v Enfield Borough Council (Secretary of State for Health as Intervener)* [2002] EWHC 432.
[44] S 17(10).
[45] S 17(4A).

Children Act 1989, s 20

(1) Every local authority shall provide accommodation for any child in need within their area who appears to them to require accommodation as a result of—

(a) there being no person who has parental responsibility for him;

(b) his being lost or having been abandoned; or

(c) the person who has been caring for him being prevented (whether or not permanently, and for whatever reason) from providing him with suitable accommodation or care.

In the case of children in need who are over 16 years of age, the duty to provide accommodation will only arise if the local authority considers it likely that the child's welfare will be 'seriously prejudiced' if it does not provide the child with accommodation.[46]

If the local authority is under a duty to accommodate a child pursuant to s 20 of the CA 1989, it cannot avoid the more extensive obligations owed to a 'looked after' child by purporting to accommodate the child under some other statutory duty or power such as the Housing Act 1996 or s 17 of the CA 1989. The issue has become of particular significance for young people approaching the age of 18 whose future entitlement to local authority support services under the leaving care provisions is dependent on whether they have been 'looked after' children under s 20 of the CA 1989. The question of the relationship between a local authority's general powers under s 17 and its more specific duty to accommodate a child under s 20 of the CA 1989 arose in the case *of R (H) v Wandsworth London Borough Council; R(Barhanu) v Hackney London Borough Council; R(B) v Islington London Borough Council*.[47] Holman J held that in determining whether there was a duty under s 20 the local authority may need to exercise judgment over certain matters, such as the impact of the child's wishes on the question of whether it could be said the child 'required' accommodation.[48] However, once it had been determined that the duty did arise there was no room for discretion: the local authority was bound to act pursuant to that duty and could not avoid its more onerous responsibilities by purporting to accommodate the child under some other statutory provision.[49] Holman J's approach has subsequently been endorsed by the House of Lords in *R(M) v Hammersmith and Fulham London Borough Council*[50] and *R (G) v London Borough of Southwark*.[51]

---

[46] S 20(3). See *Re T (Accommodation by local authority)* [1995] 1 FLR 159.

[47] [2007] EWHC 1082.

[48] Baroness Hale similarly suggested in *R(M) v London Borough of Hammersmith and Fulham* [2008] UKHL 14, [43] that not all homeless 16 and 17 year olds would 'require accommodation' (as opposed, for example, to requiring help to secure accommodation) under s 20 and that it would be very unlikely that a competent child would be accommodated as a 'looked after' child against his/her wishes. She reiterated this view in *R(G) v London Borough of Southwark* [2009] UKHL 26, [28](4) and (6). It was emphasized by Dyson LJ in *R (Liverpool City Council) v London Borough of Hillingdon* [2009] EWCA Civ 43, [32]–[34] that whilst the child's wishes regarding his/her accommodation must be given 'due' consideration, they cannot be decisive: they are just one factor in the local authority's overall assessment of the child's needs and welfare. It is not enough for the local authority to simply accede to the child's wishes. See also *Southwark v D* [2007] EWCA Civ 182; *R(A) v Coventry City Council* [2009] EWHC 34.

[49] [2007] EWHC 1082, [53], [55], and [58].

[50] [2008] UKHL 14. For a good critique of this decision, see Driscoll and Hollingsworth (2008).

[51] [2009] UKHL 26, [9].

ONLINE RESOURCE CENTRE
Extended extracts from these authorities can be found on the Online Resource Centre.

It is important to note that the duty imposed on the local authority under s 20(1) is a duty to provide accommodation for the *child*. It does not include providing accommodation for members of the child's family. This was made clear by the House of Lords in *R (on the application of G) v Barnet London Borough Council et al.* Two of the three conjoined cases concerned a child who had been assessed as in need of accommodation because the mother had been rendered homeless and was not entitled to assistance under the homelessness legislation. The local authorities indicated that whilst they were not prepared to accommodate both mother and child under s 17, they would, if necessary, accommodate the child pursuant to their duties under s 20(1). The appellants contended that this policy was unlawful, arguing that as the local authority was under a duty to promote the upbringing of children within their families, s 20(1) should be read as imposing a duty on the local authority to house both mother and child together. In support of this argument, the appellants relied on the CA 1989, s 23(6) which provides that any local authority looking after a child is under a duty to make arrangements to enable the child to live with, amongst others, a parent unless 'that would not be reasonably practicable or consistent with his welfare'. The majority of the House of Lords again rejected this argument:

R (on the application of G) v Barnet London Borough Council; R (on the application of W) v Lambeth London Borough Council; R (on the application of A) v Lambeth London Borough Council [2003] UKHL 57

LORD HOPE:

99. There are...four hurdles that the appellants must cross if they are to succeed in their argument. First, they must show that their children are children in need within the meaning of section 17(10). It was not suggested that there would have been any serious room for doubt on this point. Their mothers were unable to provide them with accommodation, and in both cases the children were at serious risk of having no roof over their heads at all. Leaving them to sleep in doorways was not an option in their case. Children who are reduced to this level of destitution are plainly children in need. Their health or development is likely to be significantly impaired if they are not provided with services by the local social services authority: section 17(10)(b).

100. The appellants must show, in the second place, that the respondents were under a duty to provide their children with accommodation. Local social services authorities are under a duty to provide accommodation for a child in need within their area who appears to them to require accommodation as a result, among other things, of the person who has been caring from [sic] him being prevented (whether or not permanently, and for whatever reason) from providing him with suitable accommodation or care: section 20(1)(c). This provision must be read in the light of the general duties set out in section 17(1). Among these duties there is the duty to safeguard and promote the welfare of the child. At first sight the concept of the carer being prevented from providing the child with suitable accommodation or care does not sit easily with the situation where the carer has chosen to refuse offers of

accommodation or other forms of assistance by the relevant local authority. But the words "for whatever reason" indicate that the widest possible scope must be given to this provision. The guiding principle is the need to safeguard and promote the child's welfare. So it makes no difference whether the reason is one which the carer has brought about by her own act or is one which she was resisting to the best of her ability. On the facts, it is plain that the respondents were under a duty to provide accommodation for the appellants' children under section 20(1).

101. The appellants must then show, in the third place, that section 23(6) applies to their case. That subsection applies where a local social services authority "are looking after a child." This expression is defined in section 22(1), which provides that any reference in the Act to a child "who is looked after by a local authority" is a reference to a child who is either in their care or is provided with accommodation by the authority in the exercise of any functions referred to the social services committee, including the functions under the Act...[I]t is clear that if the stage had been reached where the respondents were fulfilling their duty to provide accommodation for them under section 20(1)(c), the children would have been children who were being looked after by the local authority within the meaning of section 22(1).

102. This brings me to the crucial point in this part of the case, which is whether a local authority looking after a child is under a duty to provide accommodation to any of the persons mentioned in section 23(6)(a) and (b), who include the child's parent, to enable the child to live with that person. The duty, as expressed in the subsection, is to "make arrangements to enable" the child to live with any one of the person mentioned. It is qualified by the words "unless that would not be reasonably practicable and consistent with his welfare". The appellants' argument is that among the arrangements that may be made in the performance of this duty is the provision of accommodation to the person mentioned so that the child will be able to live with that person. They also submit...that neither the cost of doing this nor the availability of resources have any bearing on what is or is not reasonably practicable as to permit this would downgrade the duty into a discretionary power...

104. Section 23(6) appears to have been framed on the...assumption [that the person with whom the child is to be placed or the person with whom the child may be allowed to live already has accommodation which will enable the child to live with that person]. The context in which it appears suggests that this is so. But the wording of the subsection, and its content, reinforce the argument. The arrangements to which it refers are arrangements enabling the child to live with that person. Nothing is said about providing that person with accommodation. Moreover the duty to make the arrangements to which it refers is not restricted to enabling the child to live with his family. If it had been so restricted there might have been some force in the argument that the duty in this subsection was to be read together with the general duty in section 17(1) to promote the upbringing of the child by his family. But the person with whom the child may be enabled to live under this subsection include relatives other than his parents, friends and other person connected with him: section 23(6)(b). The width of this class of persons indicates that what Parliament had in mind when it was enacting this provision was that these were persons who already had accommodation of their own. The fact that the duty is qualified by reference to what is reasonably practicable and consistent with the child's welfare is entirely consistent with this approach. It permits the local authority to have regard to the nature of the accommodation which that person is able to provide before it takes its decision as to whether, and if so with whom, the child is to be accommodated under this subsection. It is not concerned with the resources of the local authority, because the duty does not extend to the provision of accommodation for that person at its own cost or from its own resources.

The power to accommodate: voluntary accommodation under s 20(4)

In addition to its duty to provide accommodation, the local authority has the *power* to provide accommodation to a child if it 'considers that to do so would safeguard or promote the child's welfare'.[52] This power to receive children into voluntary care was intended as a positive, supportive measure for struggling parents. The government hoped that its position within Part III of the legislation would remove the stigma attached to placing children into local authority care and encourage families to seek local authority support when needed.[53] To this end, s 20(7) explicitly provides that a local authority may not provide accommodation for a child if a person with parental responsibility objects and is willing and able to provide or arrange alternative accommodation. To reinforce this point, it is further provided that a person with parental responsibility can remove the child at any time and without notice from local authority care.[54]

The importance of 'partnership' between the local authority and the parents is evident throughout these provisions. However, the Children Act's strong commitment to protecting the voluntary nature of accommodation under Part III and the consequent weakening of the local authority's position relative to that of the parents has been the subject of strong criticism. In particular, commentators have expressed concern that inappropriate use of voluntary care may prevent proper long-term planning for children spending significant periods of time away from their families. It is argued that children in this position can end up drifting in and out of care throughout their childhood, with the local authority being used by parents as nothing more than a convenient dumping ground.[55]

Judith Masson has also expressed concern about the inappropriate use of voluntary care but on rather different grounds. She argues that parents are often pressured into agreeing to voluntary accommodation by the local authority to avoid the threat of care proceedings or because the parents believe they have no choice.[56] In one particularly worrying case, Munby J was strongly critical of the actions of Nottingham County Council in unlawfully removing a new-born baby from its distressed mother in reliance on the fact that she did not 'raise objection'. As Munby J points out, 'helpless acquiescence' or 'submission in the face of asserted State authority' cannot be equated with consent and 'in this context, nothing short of consent will suffice'.[57]

From the perspective of the local authority the use of voluntary care has many advantages. It is more cost effective and avoids the difficulties of making a potentially complicated and expensive application to the court, difficulties likely to be compounded by the new pre-action requirements of the Public Law Outline.[58] However, as Andrew Bainham points out, the use of voluntary accommodation to avoid the necessity of applying for a care order blurs the distinction between voluntary and compulsory care and renders the supposed 'partnership' between the parents and the local authority 'more illusory than

---

[52] S 20(4).

[53] DHSS et al (1987), [21].

[54] S 20(8) and (9). Relying on comments of Munby J in *R(G) v Nottingham City Council* [2008] EWHC 152, Bainham contends that s 3(5) of the CA 1989 provides sufficient authority for anyone with de facto care of the child to refuse to hand the child over to a parent with parental responsibility if the parent appears to pose an imminent risk to the child's health and safety. See Bainham (2008c), 261–2.

[55] Smith (1992), 350.

[56] Masson (1992). Discussed in Bainham (2005), 415.

[57] *R(G) v Nottingham City Council (No 2)* [2008] EWHC 400, [55] and [61].

[58] MOJ (2008), Flowchart: Pre-proceedings Public Law Outline. Superceded by President of the Family Division (2010), Sec. 10. See Kaganas (2010), 53.

real'.[59] Moreover, coercing parents into agreeing to voluntary accommodation is particularly worrying if the local authority would not have been able to make out the grounds for compulsory intervention under Part IV.

These concerns about the use of voluntary care are exacerbated by recent reforms aimed at encouraging voluntary agreements between local authorities and parents as an alternative to court proceedings.[60] As Kaganas points out, whilst proceeding by way of a voluntary agreement may have certain benefits for the parents, this informal mode of 'state regulation' also denies them the protection of the procedural rights and guarantees which characterize court-based proceedings.

F. Kaganas, 'Child protection, gender and rights', in J. Wallbank, S. Choudhry, and J. Herring (eds), *Rights, Gender and Family Law* (Abingdon: Routledge, 2010), 43, 53–5

[W]hile there might be a drop in the number of applications to court, this does not necessarily mean that families are not going to be regulated. What it might mean is that families will be subject to forms of regulation that take even less account of their rights and give them less chance of making their side of the story heard or of resisting the assessments of the professionals. It is true that the safeguards offered by the HRA are triggered at all decision-making stages of the child protection process, but since they relate primarily to information consultation and presence at meetings, they do not necessarily provide a bulwark against pressure to reach agreement...

[T]he partnership between social workers and parents is generally weighted in favour of the professionals. The balance of power between parents and professionals is not equal and professionals are in a position to dictate what is expected of families... This presents risks for parents... The pressure exerted, coupled with parents' lack of understanding, means that they may agree to arrangements they cannot maintain. Failure to abide by the terms of the agreement can be used to demonstrate parents' unfitness or refusal to co-operate...

Clearly then, partnership and co-operative working can involve monitoring and regulation of the family. And that regulation is unimpeded by the kind of scrutiny that court proceedings would entail. The arrangements are not open to challenge by, for example, lawyers or a children's guardian. And any challenge on the part of the parents carries the risk of court proceedings in which they could be branded as uncooperative and unreasonable.

Increased pressure to proceed by way of voluntary agreement rather than under s 31 of the CA 1989 also has worrying implications for the child:

P. Welbourne, 'Safeguarding children on the edge of care: policy for keeping children safe after the *Review of the Child Care Proceedings System, Care Matters* and the *Carter Review of Legal Aid'*, (2008) 20 *Child and Family Law Quarterly* 335, 343–57

The contrast between the situation in the courts, with the children's guardian, lawyers and the welfare principle guiding decision making, and that for a child having arrangements made

---

[59] Bainham (2005), 415–16.
[60] See, in particular, MOJ (2008), Flowchart: Pre-proceedings Public Law Outline. For an excellent discussion of the three key reviews informing the new Public Law Outline see Masson (2007).

in a FGC [Family group conference] or other informal setting is very marked…There is no mechanism for assuring that the best interests of the child will be a primary consideration in local authority gateway meetings, despite the gravity of the decisions being taken, nor in any ADR process used. In these settings the child's interests compete with other, very powerful, interests such as the wishes of family members and financial and audit considerations of the local authority…Alternative dispute resolution places the child in a disadvantaged position as the only non-legally advised 'party' to the process.

Three key aspects of a court hearing are absent: (a) independence of the person making or ratifying the decision about the child's best interests; (b) independent representation of the child and parents; and (c) enforceability of decisions made. Decisions may be reached in 'informal' processes that seriously affect parents' and children's family life, but they are decisions that may be lawfully disregarded by parents, leaving children at continuing risk of serious harm. Agreements need to be carefully monitored for compliance, but there is no right of access to the child following negotiated agreements and no statutory requirement that local authorities carry out regular reviews or systematically follow up the placement. There is no framework for reviewing the progress of children in informal arrangements. There may be reviews under child protection procedures if the child continues to be at risk…but these have a narrower focus on issues of safety and protection…

For the children and families involved in section 31 proceedings, the court's powers are 'draconian' and the parents' (and children's) circumstances 'dire'. For this reason, the right of children to adequate representation is hard to overvalue. Decisions have to be made about their future safety and welfare, and only in court can they be assured of legal representation, a children's guardian and the prioritisation of their interests over those of others.

12.3.3 LOCAL AUTHORITY DUTIES WITH RESPECT TO LOOKED AFTER CHILDREN

Sections 22–3 of the CA 1989 detail the various duties and responsibilities of local authorities with respect to children in their care. Although these provisions are located in Part III of the legislation, the duties are owed to all children 'looked after' by the local authority: this includes not only children who are in voluntary care but children who are in local authority care pursuant to a care order, interim care order, or emergency protection order under Parts IV and V.[61] The core duty of the local authority set down in s 22(3) is to safeguard and promote the child's welfare.[62] This is not the same as making each individual child's welfare the paramount consideration. The justification for not imposing the paramountcy principle on local authorities is clear. Local authorities owe duties and responsibilities to large numbers of children in their care. In such circumstances it would obviously be inappropriate to prioritize the interests of just one child to the detriment of others. This is particularly so given the limited resources with which local authorities typically have to contend. In making decisions with respect to individual children, local authorities therefore have a wide discretion permitting them to take into account a broad range of factors other than the assessed needs and interests of the child in question.[63]

The way in which local authorities discharge their duties and responsibilities under s 22(3) is crucially important. However, the task is not easy. On 31 March 2009, there were

---

[61] S 22(1).
[62] S 22(3)(a).
[63] See, e.g., Re T (Judicial review: local authority decisions concerning child in need) [2003] EWHC 2515.

60,900 looked after children in care, a 2 per cent increase from the previous year.[64] Many of these children have come from abusive homes and have complex and challenging needs. The difficulty of ensuring that all looked after children enjoy the highest possible standards of accommodation and care, particularly where resources are limited, should not be underestimated. However, outcomes for many children are poor. Educational achievement, youth offending rates, and longer term health and employment prospects are all significantly poorer for children who have been in care.

DH, *Adoption—A New Approach. A White Paper*, Cm 5017 (London: HMSO, 2000), 16

- 70% of young people leave care without having gained any GCSE or GNVQ qualifications;

- 25% of looked after children aged 14–16 do not attend school regularly and many have been excluded and have no regular educational placement;

- between 14% and 25% of young women leaving care are either pregnant or have a child, while in the general population only 3% of 20 year old women have a child;

- compared to the general population, those who have been looked after are 60 times more likely to be homeless;

- 39% of male prisoners under 21 have been looked after.

The poor educational achievements of looked after children are particularly worrying. In 2003, only 53 per cent of looked after children obtained at least one GCSE or GNVQ, compared with 95 per cent of all children.[65] Only 9 per cent obtained at least five GCSEs (grades A*–C). In response to this problem, the CA 1989 was amended by the CA 2004 to place a particular duty on the local authority to promote the child's educational achievement.[66] The Children and Young Persons Act 2008 introduced further amendments to place a duty on the local authority to ensure, so far as is reasonably practicable, that the child's placement does not disrupt the child's education and training.[67]

In addition to this general duty to promote the welfare of looked after children, ss 22–3 of the CA 1989 impose a number of more specific duties on the local authority. Before making any decision with respect to a looked after child, the local authority is under a duty, so far as is reasonably practicable, to ascertain and give due respect to the wishes and feelings of the child and the child's parents.[68] This includes an unmarried father without parental responsibility. The local authority must also pay particular regard to the 'child's religious persuasion, racial origin and cultural and linguistic background'.[69]

When a child is in *voluntary care*, the duty to act in partnership with the parents is particularly strong. Indeed, it was held in *R v Tameside Metropolitan BC, ex parte J* that when a child is in care pursuant to Part III of the CA 1989, the local authority must not only consult the child's parents but obtain their consent to any significant changes regarding the child's

---

[64] DCSF (2009), 1.
[65] DfES (2004), 4.
[66] S 22(3A).
[67] S 22C(8)(b). At the time of writing this provision is not yet in force.
[68] S 22(4) and (5). As to the importance of respecting the child's wishes and feelings see *R (CD) v Isle of Anglesey County Council* [2004] EWHC 1635.
[69] S 22(5)(c).

care, including where the child is accommodated.[70] The position with respect to a child 'in care' pursuant to a care order is different because under s 33(3)(a) the local authority acquires parental responsibility for the child and thereby decision-making authority.[71]

In determining where a looked after child should be accommodated, the local authority has a number of options.[72] Although the child is being looked after by the local authority, the local authority remains under a duty to promote the child's upbringing within his or her family. Section 22C(2)–(4) thus provide that unless it is not practicable to do so or contrary to the child's welfare, the local authority should 'make arrangements' for the child to be accommodated with a parent, a person other than a parent who has PR, or a person in whose favour a residence order was in force before the care order was made.[73] The local authority may provide financial support for the placement.[74] If the local authority is unable to make arrangements for the child in accordance with s 22C(2), then it is under a duty to place the child in the most appropriate placement, giving priority to a relative, friend or connected person who is also a local authority foster parent.[75] If there is no relative or friend able to care for the child then the child can be placed with other local authority foster parents or in a secure unit, residential school, residential home, or hostel.[76] So far as is reasonably practicable the child should be placed within the local authority area, as near to his or her home as possible and, where relevant, with his or her siblings.[77] The majority of looked after children are placed with local authority foster parents previously unknown to the child.[78]

Whilst a child is being looked after by the local authority, great emphasis is placed upon maintaining the child's familial links. The local authority is thus under a duty, if reasonably practicable and consistent with the child's welfare, to promote contact between the child and, amongst others, the parents.[79] Where the child has infrequent contact with family members and is not regularly visited by anyone the local authority may appoint an independent visitor to 'visit, advise and befriend the child'.[80] The local authority is also under a duty to ensure that looked after children are visited by a representative of the authority who will provide them with advice, support, and assistance.[81]

---

[70] [2000] 1 FCR 173, 179–81.

[71] Ibid. See discussion below at 12.5.6.

[72] S 22C(2)–(4) and (6) replacing s 23(2) and (6). At the time of writing s 22C(6) was not yet in force. See also Arrangements for Placement of Children (General) Regulations 1991, SI 1991/890.

[73] Replacing s 23(6) of the CA 1989. At the time of writing s 22C(2)–(4) were not yet in force. See also Placement of Children with Parents etc Regulations 1991, SI 1991/893.

[74] S 22C(10)(a).

[75] S 22C(5)–(9) replacing s 23(2). When in force these provisions will effectively address the problems which had arisen as a result of the possibility of care being provided by a relative or friend under either s 23(2) (child 'placed' and looked after) or s 23(6) (arrangements made by local authority but child not 'looked after'). As it is no longer possible for the local authority to 'make arrangements' for a relative or friend to care for a child, there will be no question of the local authority avoiding its responsibilities to the child as a 'looked after' child by claiming that the placement is a private one which the local authority has merely facilitated. Children to whom a duty to accommodate is owed under s 20 must be placed with relatives or friends as local authority foster parents under s 22C(6). As to the problems which had been caused by the alternative routes to discharging the s 20 duty under s 23(2) or s 23(6), see *London Borough of Southwark v D* [2007] EWCA Civ 182; *SA v KCC* [2010] EWHC 848.

[76] S 22C(6). At the time of writing not yet in force. On 31 March 2009, 13 per cent of looked after children were accommodated in a secure unit, residential school, home, or hostel. DCSF (2009), table A3.

[77] S 22C(8)–(9). At the time of writing not yet in force.

[78] On 31 March 2009, 73 per cent of looked after children were living with foster parents, the vast majority of which were unknown to the child. DCSF (2009), table A3.

[79] Part II, Sch II, para 15(1). The obligation extends to friends and any person connected with the child.

[80] S 23ZB; Part II, Sch II, paras 17(1)–(2).

[81] S 23ZA.

The local authority must review the case of a looked after child within four weeks of the date on which the child first entered care. The second review must be carried out no more than three months after the first and thereafter a review must be carried out every six months.[82] An independent reviewing officer is appointed for every child who is responsible for monitoring the local authority's performance, participating in any reviews of the child's case, ensuring the child's wishes and feelings are taken into consideration, and, if appropriate, referring the child's case to an officer of Cafcass (Children and Family Court Advisory Support Service) who will be able to initiate legal proceedings on the child's behalf.[83]

12.3.4 COOPERATION BETWEEN LOCAL AUTHORITY SERVICES

Children in need under Part III often have a range of complex interrelated needs. A child suffering from parental neglect may be in need of health and nutritional care, therapeutic counselling, and educational support. The parents may need assistance with housing, employment, and basic child-care skills. Section 27 therefore provides that where the local authority requires help in meeting its duties and responsibilities under Part III it may request the help of any local authority, any local education authority, any local housing authority, or any relevant health authority. If an authority is requested to help, they are under a duty to comply 'if it is compatible with their own statutory or other duties and obligations and does not unduly prejudice the discharge of any of their functions'.[84] The various authorities are under a duty to cooperate with one another to meet the needs of the family and safeguard and promote the welfare of the child. The local authority requesting help cannot, however, demand that another authority discharge its duties and responsibilities in any particular way.[85]

Despite the duties imposed by s 27, the inquiry into the death of Victoria Climbié in 2003 identified lack of effective cooperation between the key public authorities as one of the major failings of the child protection system.[86] Parliament responded in the Children Act 2004.[87] Section 10 of the legislation places a duty on the local authority (termed 'the children's services authority') to promote cooperation between the health, education, and police authorities with a view to improving the well-being of children within their area.[88] To facilitate the provision of coordinated services, a pooled fund is established to which all of the various authorities must contribute.[89] Controversially, the legislation also provides for the Secretary of State to establish and maintain an information database covering all children in England and Wales.[90] In 2009, the database ContactPoint was established and became operational across England and Wales providing a centralized record of basic information concerning the child including any contact the child has had with the various health, education, and social welfare services and whether any 'cause for concern' has been identified.[91] The

---

[82] Review of Children's Cases Regulations 1991, SI 1991/895, reg 3.

[83] Ss 25A–C.

[84] S 27(2).

[85] *R v Northavon District Council, ex parte Smith* [2004] 2 AC 402.

[86] Lord Laming (2003).

[87] See also HM Treasury (2003).

[88] CA 2004, s 10(1), (2), and (4).

[89] CA 2004, s 10(6)–(7).

[90] CA 2004, s 12.

[91] CA 2004, s 12(4).

database had the laudable aim of stopping children falling through the state's protective net by improving the recording and sharing of information amongst the relevant professionals about children who may be in need of supportive or protective services. However, ContactPoint attracted strong opposition from those alarmed by the perceived 'big brother' ethos driving the initiative and after a short lifespan of just 18 months the newly elected Coalition government confirmed in August 2010 that ContactPoint was to be dismantled with immediate effect.[92]

12.3.5 PART III: A SUCCESS?

The aims behind Part III of the CA 1989 are certainly admirable. It is difficult to argue with the principle that 'prevention is better than cure' and that, wherever possible, children should be helped and supported within their families. However, as noted above, an approach based on prevention and support will only be successful if properly resourced. The absence of much needed investment in local authority services has resulted in local authorities being crisis led and focusing most of their time and resources on 'managing child protection cases'.[93] Local authorities thus become trapped in a vicious circle. The less time, money, and effort invested in prevention and support, the more resources needed to deal with cases requiring immediate, compulsory intervention. Conversely, if more resources were diverted to providing effective services under Part III, the need for intervention under Parts IV and V should decline. It is therefore disappointing that 20 years after implementation of the CA 1989, 'child protection' cases under Parts IV and V remain the main focus of concern.

12.4 THE CHILD PROTECTION SYSTEM: INVESTIGATING ALLEGATIONS OF CHILD ABUSE

12.4.1 SECTION 47 INVESTIGATION

Individuals concerned about the welfare of a child should refer the matter to their local social services department. There is, however, no general duty on the public to report suspected cases of child abuse to the authorities. Upon referral, the local authority must carry out an investigation and assessment in accordance with the guidelines set down in *Working Together to Safeguard Children*.[94] The local authority must first ascertain whether there are grounds for concern and, in particular, whether there is an urgent need to take protective action. If further enquiries are necessary it should carry out an initial assessment to be completed within 10 days.[95] During that period the local authority should speak to the child's family and, depending on the child's age and understanding, the child. If the local authority has *reasonable cause to suspect* that the child is suffering or likely to suffer significant harm, the local authority must carry out a full investigation under s 47, undertaking such enquiries as are necessary to enable it to decide 'whether they should take any action to safeguard or promote the child's welfare'.[96] In carrying out a 'core assessment' for the purposes of the

---

[92] <http://www.bbc.co.uk/news/education-10887082>.
[93] Smith (2002), 254–5.
[94] DCSF (2010), ch 5.
[95] Ibid., 187.
[96] S 47(1).

s 47 investigation, the local authority should take reasonable steps to see the child unless satisfied it already has sufficient information about the child's condition.[97] If the parents refuse to cooperate with the investigation, the local authority must apply for an emergency protection order (EPO), child assessment order (CAO), or care or supervision order unless satisfied that the child's welfare is adequately protected without one.[98] The preferred route for obtaining access to the child is a CAO under s 43. The court can only make the order if certain conditions are met:

Children Act 1989, s 43

(1) On the application of a local authority or authorised person for an order to be made under this section with respect to a child, the court may make the order if, but only if, it is satisfied that—

  (a) the applicant has reasonable cause to suspect that the child is suffering, or is likely to suffer, significant harm;

  (b) an assessment of the state of the child's health or development, or of the way in which he has been treated, is required to enable the applicant to determine whether or not the child is suffering, or is likely to suffer, significant harm; and

  (c) it is unlikely that such an assessment will be made, or be satisfactory, in the absence of an order under this section.

If the order is made, the assessment can be carried out without the parents' consent. The parents are placed under a duty to produce the child to any person named in the order and must comply with any specified directions for carrying out the assessment.[99] A child of sufficient understanding can, however, refuse to submit to a medical, psychiatric, or other assessment.[100] The order can last for a specified period of no more than seven days from the date on which the assessment is to begin.[101]

The purpose of the local authority investigation is to determine whether action is needed to safeguard and promote the child's welfare.[102] On conclusion of the investigation, the local authority therefore needs to decide how best to proceed. If the concerns prompting the investigation prove to be unsubstantiated or were well-founded but there are no grounds for continuing concern (if, for example, an abuser has left the family home) the local authority can decide to take no further action.[103] If there remains concern about the possibility of future harm, but the local authority has been unable to obtain specific evidence of abuse or neglect, it can simply continue to monitor the situation.[104] In these cases it may offer to provide supportive services to the family under Part III. If the concerns are substantiated and the child is believed to be at continuing risk, the local authority should convene a child

---

[97] DCSF (2010), [5.50]. S 47(4).

[98] S 47(6).

[99] S 43(6).

[100] S 43(8). Although it would seem that the court, exercising its inherent jurisdiction, can override the child's refusal. See *South Glamorgan County Council v W & B* [1993] 1 FLR 514, decided within the context of an interim CO.

[101] S 43(5).

[102] S 47(1).

[103] DCSF (2010), [5.75].

[104] Ibid., [5.76].

protection conference (CPC).[105] The aim of the CPC is to bring together all interested parties and plan how best to safeguard and promote the child's welfare.[106] The parents should normally attend and be provided with sufficient information to enable them to participate effectively in the proceedings.[107] If of sufficient age and understanding, the child may also attend.[108] If the child's attendance is deemed inappropriate, the child's social worker should convey the child's wishes and feelings to the meeting.[109] The CPC must decide whether the child should be subject to a formal child protection plan.[110] The local authority should try to involve the parents in formulating the plan, taking into account their views and securing their agreement where possible.[111] The local authority must record that the child is subject to a child protection plan on their IT system, that record being accessible to other relevant agencies and professionals.[112] The child will be recorded as at risk of harm under either the category of physical abuse, emotional abuse, sexual abuse or neglect.

The plan may include applying to the court for a care or supervision order.[113] However, following a s 47 investigation, the local authority is under no legal duty to initiate care proceedings even if satisfied the child is suffering or is likely to suffer significant harm.[114] This creates an unfortunate gap in the statutory framework. Although the local authority's decision can be challenged through the local authority internal complaints procedure or by way of judicial review,[115] as Eekelaar notes, it is 'surprising that the imposition of extensive and elaborate duties to inquire do not lead to a clear and unambiguous duty to take action on the basis of the results of the inquiries where the child is likely to be harmed if no such action is taken'.[116] Similarly, just as the court is unable to direct the local authority to take any specific steps to protect a child, it is equally unable to grant injunctive relief to restrain the local authority from investigating a child's circumstances under s 47, even if the court is already seized of a private law dispute between the parents.[117] If the local authority decides to initiate care proceedings, the local authority's actions should be challenged by way of defending the proceedings. Only in wholly exceptional circumstances will it be appropriate to bring an application for judicial review.[118]

The potentially indeterminate outcome of a local authority investigation under s 47 can be problematic. Essentially, where there are grounds for continuing concern the local authority may simply decide to keep monitoring the situation and respond as and when appropriate. This can leave parents accused of abuse or neglect in a difficult state of limbo. Whilst care

---

[105] Ibid., [5.81].

[106] Ibid.

[107] *Re M (Care: Challenging decisions by local authority)* [2001] 2 FLR 1300 and *Re G (Care: Challenge to local authority's decision)* [2003] EWHC 551.

[108] DCSF (2010), [5.86].

[109] Ibid.

[110] Ibid., [5.99]–[5.101]. For details of what should be included within the plan see DCSF (2010), [5.105]–[5.106].

[111] Ibid., [5.124]–[5.125].

[112] Ibid., [5.150].

[113] S 47(3)(a).

[114] DCSF (2010), [5.103]. See also, *Nottinghamshire County Council v P* [1994] Fam 18.

[115] *R v East Sussex County Council, ex parte W* [1998] 2 FLR 1082.

[116] Eekelaar (1990), 486.

[117] *D v D (County Court Jurisdiction: Injunctions)* [1993] 2 FLR 802. The Court of Appeal solved this problem by making a prohibited steps order to restrain the father from exercising his parental responsibility to consent to such investigations. The local authority were investigating the mother's treatment of her children at the behest of the father, against the background of a residence dispute.

[118] *Re M (Care Proceedings: Judicial Review)* [2003] EWHC 850.

proceedings constitute a high level of intervention into the family, they do at least provide the opportunity for parents to formally challenge the local authority's allegations and for those allegations to be properly scrutinized by the court. Without such proceedings, it is difficult for parents to 'clear their name' in the face of the local authority's continuing suspicion. This problem was considered in *R(S) v Swindon Borough Council and another*, which concerned a consultant gynaecologist suspected of sexually assaulting the teenage daughter of his former partner. Following his acquittal in the criminal proceedings, he wished to set up home with his new partner, Mrs X, but was unable to do so whilst the local authority, believing he may pose a continuing risk, refused to provide the necessary assurance that it would not take steps to protect Mrs X's two daughters should he and Mrs X begin to cohabit. The claimant sought judicial review of the local authority's position, arguing that it needed to reach a final decision as to whether the allegations were substantiated and, on the basis of that decision, either initiate care proceedings to protect Mrs X's daughters or leave him alone to get on with his life. Scott Baker J dismissed the application, stressing that whilst the local authority must respect the claimant's private and family life, it had an overriding duty to monitor the situation in order to protect the two children. The judgment makes clear that at the early stages of an investigation into child abuse, the thresholds for state intervention are necessarily low and there is therefore no requirement for the local authority to substantiate allegations of abuse on the balance of probabilities.

R(S) v Swindon Borough Council and another [2001] EWHC Admin 334, [2001] 3 FCR 702

SCOTT BAKER J:

[30] [In deciding whether or not to take action to safeguard the child following a s 47 investigation, counsel for the claimant submits] that the test is the same as in s 31—the local authority in this instance rather than the court must be satisfied of the likelihood of significant harm. Absent such satisfaction that is the end of the matter. To use her words the local authority must 'put up' or 'shut up'. They cannot leave the claimant forever in a state of uncertainty . . .

[31] It is a cornerstone of the claimant's case that in assessing the future risk the defendants are not permitted to take into account past events that are not established on balance of probabilities . . .

[34] In my judgment the need to establish facts on the balance of probability has no place in the exercise by a local authority of its various protective responsibilities under the 1989 Act. *Re H* [see below] was concerned with the court's power to make care or supervision orders under s 31 of the 1989 Act. It is at this point in the child protection process that evidence has to be weighed and evaluated and decisions made as to what is proved and what is not. Decisions made earlier in the process have to be made in accordance with the power conferred by the section under which the authority is acting, and in the present case the critical question is whether the authority *have reasonable cause to suspect* a child is likely to suffer significant harm.

[35] It should be noted that if *Re H* governed the approach in cases such as the present the result would be to prevent local authorities from carrying out effective and timely risk assessments. They would be forced to take care proceedings to identify whether grounds for intervention were present. This would be completely contrary to the principle of non-intervention in children cases. I do not accept that a local authority has to be satisfied on balance of probability that a person is an abuser before intervention is justified . . .

Scott Baker J then went on to address the significance of the claimant's acquittal at the criminal trial:

> [37]...Acquittal in criminal sexual abuse proceedings does not mean that a local authority is thereby absolved from further responsibility to protect the child who made the allegations or any other children who may in some way be at risk. Far from it, the various statutory duties under the 1989 Act must, if they are in play, be discharged. A local authority will no doubt look carefully at the result of a criminal trial and any matters of significance that emerged in the course of it. But the fact of an acquittal and observations in the summing up do not prevent a local authority from forming a view which is adverse to the acquitted person...

Scott Baker J also dismissed the ECHR arguments, holding that the balance of interests required under Article 8 added nothing to his analysis under domestic law.

Following the initial CPC, a review meeting should be held within three months.[119] Further reviews should then be held at intervals of no more than six months whilst the child remains subject to a child protection plan.[120] If the child is being looked after by the local authority, this review will be held alongside the six-monthly reviews required under the looked after children regulations.[121] The child protection plan may be terminated at any time if a review meeting concludes the child is no longer at risk of significant harm.[122] Again, however, the local authority should consider whether to continue to provide support services to the family under Part III.[123]

If at any point throughout this process the local authority believes the child to be in need of urgent protection, the local authority should request that the police take the child into police protection or apply for an emergency protection order under Part V.[124]

12.4.2 SECTION 37 INVESTIGATION

An alternative route by which a family may find themselves subject to a local authority investigation under s 37 of the CA 1989:

Children Act 1989, s 37

(1) Where, in any family proceedings in which a question arises with respect to the welfare of any child, it appears to the court that it may be appropriate for a care or supervision order to be made with respect to him, the court may direct the appropriate authority to undertake an investigation of the child's circumstances.

---

[119] DCSF (2010), [5.136].
[120] Ibid., [5.136].
[121] Ibid., [5.136] and [5.148].
[122] Ibid., [5.141].
[123] Ibid., [5.143]
[124] See 12.6.

It was held in *Re H (A minor) (section 37 direction)* that the 'child's circumstances' should be widely construed to include 'any situation which may have a bearing on the child being likely to suffer significant harm in the future'—even if the child is currently settled, well cared for, and happy.[125] The purpose of the investigation is for the local authority to decide whether or not they should apply for a care or supervision order. The local authority must report back to the court within eight weeks.[126] If the local authority decides not to apply for a care or supervision order, the reasons for the decision must be explained and the court informed of any alternative action they propose to take.[127] However, regardless of the local authority's findings, the court has no power to direct them to initiate care proceedings.[128]

12.5 CARE AND SUPERVISION PROCEEDINGS UNDER PART IV

Part IV of the CA 1989 provides for two key orders permitting compulsory intervention into family life: care and supervision orders. A care order is defined under s 31(1)(a) as an order 'placing the child with respect to whom the application is made in the care of a designated local authority'. A supervision order is a less interventionist measure and is simply defined as an order putting the child 'under the supervision of a designated local authority'.[129]

12.5.1 WHO MAY APPLY FOR A CARE OR SUPERVISION ORDER?

Under section 31(1), only a 'local authority' or 'authorized person' may apply for a care or supervision order. 'Authorized person' is defined in s 31(9) as the NSPCC and any other person authorized by the Secretary of State to bring proceedings. To date no such other person has been authorized. The child, the mother, and the father if he has parental responsibility, are automatically joined as respondents.[130] The local authority must serve notice of the proceedings on a father without parental responsibility but he has no right to participate in the proceedings: he must apply for leave to be joined as a party.[131] Leave will, however, ordinarily be granted unless there is some clear reason for refusing the application.[132]

---

125 *Re H (A minor) (section 37 direction)* [1993] 2 FLR 541, 549.

126 S 37(4).

127 S 37(3).

128 *Nottinghamshire County Council v P* [1994] Fam 18.

129 S 31(1)(b).

130 Family Procedure Rules 2010 (FPR 2010), r 12.3(1). A father with parental responsibility whose whereabouts are known can be discharged as a party to the proceedings and service dispensed with, but only in the most exceptional circumstances. See *M & M (Children)* [2009] EWHC 3172.

131 FPR 2010, r 12.8 and PD 12c. Only in exceptional circumstances will this requirement to serve notice of the proceedings on a father without parental responsibility be waived. See *Re A B (Care proceedings: Service on husband ignorant of child's existence)* [2003] EWCA Civ 1842.

132 *Re K (care proceedings: joinder of father)* [1999] 2 FLR 408. *Re P (care proceedings: father's application to be joined as party)* [2001] 1 FLR 781.

12.5.2 WHEN MAY A CARE OR SUPERVISION ORDER BE MADE?

A care or supervision order may be made in any 'family proceedings' or in free-standing care proceedings on application by the local authority or the NSPCC.[133] The court cannot act of its own motion. Indeed, s 100(2) of the CA 1989 explicitly removes the power of the court to place a child into local authority care pursuant to its inherent jurisdiction. This means s 31 now provides the *only* route into care. Although this lack of jurisdiction has frustrated some, it ensures no child can be placed into local authority care on the basis of a simple best interests test (as was the case under the inherent jurisdiction): the threshold of harm justifying state intervention into the family as set down in s 31 must always be established. For similar reasons, the local authority is constrained from acting to protect a child by applying for private law orders under s 8. Section 9(2) thus prohibits a local authority from applying for a residence or contact order and whilst the local authority is permitted, with leave, to apply for a specific issue or prohibited steps order, the court cannot, in accordance with s 9(5)(a), make an order with a view to achieving a result that could be achieved under a residence or contact order. This leaves very little room for local authorities to make use of s 8 orders, even if they believe such orders would be a more nuanced response to the problems of a particular family than invoking their more drastic and confrontational powers under Part IV.

The limitations imposed on local authorities and the various problems such limitations can create for the courts are dramatically illustrated in *Nottinghamshire County Council v P.*[134] As regards local authorities and the courts working in partnership to protect children at risk of harm, this case represents a particular low point with Sir Stephen Brown P expressing clear frustration at the local authority. The case concerned two young girls whose older sister had made allegations of sexual abuse against the father. The parents denied the allegations. The court found that the father had sexually abused the eldest daughter and that the two younger girls were now at serious risk. The court also found that the mother had no capacity to protect the children against their father. However, rather than apply for a care order under Part IV, the local authority applied for a prohibited steps order requiring the father not to reside in the same household as his daughters and prohibiting contact. Owing to the restrictions contained in ss 9(2) and 9(5)(a), Ward J, at first instance, held that he was unable to make the order sought and, in the face of the local authority's refusal to apply for a care order, he instead made a residence order in favour of the mother, subject to two conditions: (i) that the father was not to reside in the family home, and (ii) was not to be allowed contact with the children. All parties appealed:

Nottinghamshire County Council v P [1994] Fam 18, 38–43 (CA)

SIR STEPHEN BROWN P:

In the view of this court the application for a prohibited steps order by this local authority was in reality being made with a view to achieving a result which could be achieved by making a residence or contact order...

---

133 For the meaning of 'family proceedings', see s 8(3)–(4).
134 For commentary on this decision, see Brasse (1993).

The court is satisfied that the local authority was indeed seeking to enter by the "back door" as it were. It agrees with Ward J. that he had no power to make a prohibited steps order in this case...

A wider question arises as to policy. We consider that this court should make it clear that the route chosen by the local authority in this case was wholly inappropriate. In cases where children are found to be at risk of suffering significant harm within the meaning of section 31 of the Children Act 1989 a clear duty arises on the part of local authorities to take steps to protect them. In such circumstances a local authority is required to assume responsibility and to intervene in the family arrangements in order to protect the child. Part IV specifically provides them with wide powers and a wide discretion .. .

A prohibited steps order would not afford the local authority any authority as to how it might deal with the children. There may be situations, for example where a child is accommodated by a local authority, where it would be appropriate to seek a prohibited steps order for some particular purpose. However, it could not in any circumstances be regarded as providing a substitute for an order under Part IV of the Act of 1989. Furthermore, it is very doubtful indeed whether a prohibited steps order could in any circumstances be used to "oust" a father from a matrimonial home... It is a most regrettable feature of this case that the local authority having initially intervened under Part V of the Act of 1989 in order to obtain an emergency protection order did not then proceed to seek orders under section 31 in Part IV of the Act...

Having refused the application for a prohibited steps order, the judge was left with what he described as a "dilemma" ...

The judge purported to act in reliance upon the powers contained in section 10(1) of the Act of 1989 and of the power to attach conditions to a residence order under section 11(7). However these are also provisions falling within the private law section of Part II of the Act of 1989. The complaint is made... that the judge was in effect seeking to make an order in favour of the local authority for although it was not stated to be directed to the local authority it expressly sought to place upon it the duty of regulating and supervising contact. Furthermore, the order as drawn up assumed the nature of an injunction directed to the father to which was attached a penal notice. The question immediately arises as to who might seek to enforce the conditions which the judge attached to the order. It was not on the face of it an order made in favour of the local authority, which in any event was prohibited by section 9(2) from making an application for a residence order or contact order. Furthermore, the court was precluded by the same section from making such an order in favour of a local authority. The local authority accordingly acquired no powers or responsibility as a result. The mother was not a willing party to the grant of an injunction against the father, whom she did not wish to exclude from the matrimonial home.

[Counsel] furthermore raised the question as to what might happen if the mother were to apply to discharge the orders with the consent of the children. These considerations demonstrate the artificiality of the course which was adopted by the judge. I have no doubt that the judge would not disagree that it was an artificial course which he adopted. He said in terms that he was driven to take some step in order to protect the children.

In our judgment these orders cannot stand. Even if the judge had a theoretical power to assume authority by reason of section 10 of the Act of 1989, the orders were plainly not appropriate even in the unhappy circumstances of this case. In the result the appeals against these orders must be allowed.

In the result there are now no orders in force which are capable of regulating and safeguarding the position of these children... Since the fact of the risk of significant harm to the children has been established and not contradicted there remains upon the local authority the clear duty to take steps to safeguard the welfare of these children. It should not shrink from taking steps under Part IV of the Act...

> This court is deeply concerned at the absence of any power to direct this authority to take steps to protect the children. In the former wardship jurisdiction it might well have been able to do so. The operation of the Children Act 1989 is entirely dependent upon the full co-operation of all those involved. This includes the courts, local authorities, social workers, and all who have to deal with children. Unfortunately, as appears from this case, if a local authority doggedly resists taking the steps which are appropriate to the case of children at risk of suffering significant harm it appears that the court is powerless. The authority may perhaps lay itself open to an application for judicial review but in a case such as this the question arises, at whose instance? The position is one which it is to be hoped will not recur and that lessons will be learnt from this unhappy catalogue of errors.
>
> [The residence order with attached conditions was set aside].

Once the local authority has made an application under s 31 and the court is satisfied the threshold conditions are satisfied, the court has much greater freedom to shape its orders in accordance with the child's needs.[135]

12.5.3 THE THRESHOLD CRITERIA

In *Humberside County Council v B*, Booth J established a two stage approach to care proceedings.[136] First, before the court acquires the jurisdiction to make a care or supervision order, the threshold criteria set down in s 31(2) must be satisfied. This is a question of fact to which the child's welfare is irrelevant. Once the threshold criteria have been established, the court can move on to the second stage of the enquiry: whether it is in the child's best interests to make the order. This is generally known as the welfare stage.

Section 31(2) performs a crucial 'gate-keeping' function. It ensures the state can only take coercive action against a child's primary carers once a certain threshold of harm has been established. It thus plays a crucial role in balancing the importance of respecting family integrity against the need to protect children from inadequate or abusive parenting.[137]

Children Act 1989, s 31

(2) A court may only make a care order or supervision order if it is satisfied—

(a) that the child concerned is suffering, or is likely to suffer, significant harm; and

(b) that the harm, or likelihood of harm, is attributable to—

(i) the care given to the child, or likely to be given to him if the order were not made, not being what it would be reasonable to expect a parent to give to him; or

(ii) the child's being beyond parental control.

There are thus two basic limbs to the threshold criteria, both of which must be satisfied:

(1) The child must be suffering or be likely to suffer significant harm; and

(2) The harm must be attributable to the care given to the child not being what it would be reasonable to expect a parent to give or to the child being beyond parental control.

We will take these requirements in turn.

---

[135] See below at pp 850–1.
[136] [1993] 1 FLR 257.
[137] *Re G (Care proceedings: threshold conditions)* [2001] EWCA Civ 968 (per Hale LJ).

Is suffering or likely to suffer significant harm

'harm'

Harm is very widely defined in s 31(9) as the 'ill-treatment or the impairment of health or development including, for example, impairment suffered from seeing or hearing the ill-treatment of another'.[138] 'Ill-treatment' includes 'sexual abuse and forms of ill-treatment which are not physical'. Importantly this includes harm caused by emotional abuse. 'Health' includes both physical and mental health. 'Development' means 'physical, intellectual, emotional, social or behavioural development'. In determining whether a child has been subjected to 'harm', the courts are prepared to tolerate diverse standards of parenting taking into account the social, cultural, and religious background of the family.

Re L (Care: Threshold Criteria) [2007] 1 FLR 2050

HEDLEY J:

[50] What about the court's approach, in the light of all that, to the issue of significant harm? In order to understand this concept and the range of harm that it's intended to encompass, it is right to begin with issues of policy. Basically it is the tradition of the UK, recognised in law, that children are best brought up within natural families...It follows inexorably from that, that society must be willing to tolerate very diverse standards of parenting, including the eccentric, the barely adequate and the inconsistent. It follows too that children will inevitably have both very different experiences of parenting and very unequal consequences flowing from it. It means that some children will experience disadvantage and harm, while others flourish in atmospheres of loving security and emotional stability. These are the consequences of our fallible humanity and it is not the provenance of the state to spare children all the consequences of defective parenting. In any event, it simply could not be done.

The importance to be accorded to diversity in family life has been reiterated by Baroness Hale in the House of Lords.

Re B (Children) (Care Proceedings: Standard of Proof) [2008] UKHL 35

BARONESS HALE:

20. Taking a child away from her family is a momentous step, not only for her, but for her whole family, and for the local authority which does so. In a totalitarian society, uniformity and conformity are valued. Hence the totalitarian state tries to separate the child from her family and mould her to its own design. Families in all their subversive variety are the breeding ground of diversity and individuality. In a free and democratic society we value diversity and individuality. Hence the family is given special protection in all the modern human rights instruments including the European Convention on Human Rights (art 8), the International Covenant on Civil and Political Rights (art 23) and throughout the United Nations Convention on the Rights of the Child. As Justice McReynolds famously said in Pierce v Society of Sisters 268 US 510 (1925), at 535, "The child is not the mere creature of the State".

---

[138] As amended by the Adoption and Children Act 2002, s 120.

'significant'

Section 31(10) provides that where the question of whether the harm suffered is significant turns on the child's health or development, then the child's health or development should be compared with that which could be reasonably expected of a similar child.[139] 'Significant' is not otherwise defined by the legislation. It was held by Booth J in *Humberside CC v B* that the term 'significant' denotes harm that is 'considerable', 'noteworthy', or 'important'—'harm that the court should take into account in considering a child's future'.[140] Ward LJ provides further guidance in *MA, SA and HA v MA, HA and City and County of Swansea*.[141] He makes clear that the threshold for establishing the 'significance' of the harm is not low,[142] the CA 1989 requiring that the harm must be significant enough to 'justify the intervention of the State and disturb the autonomy of the parents to bring up their children by themselves in the way they choose.'[143] He also stresses the relevance of Article 8 when assessing the significance of the harm, pointing out that Article 8 requires that there must be a ' "relevant and sufficient" reason for crossing the threshold'.[144]

'is suffering'

This is the most straightforward way of establishing the first limb of the threshold criteria. It raises a simple question of fact: is the child suffering significant harm? The usual civil standard of proof applies, so the burden is on the local authority to prove the alleged facts on the balance of probabilities.[145] Although relatively straightforward, questions have arisen regarding *when* the alleged state of affairs must be shown to exist. In *Re M (a minor) (care orders: threshold conditions)* the child (G) when just four months old witnessed his father brutally murder his mother, for which the father was serving life imprisonment. The local authority applied for a care order. After a short period in foster care, G went to live with Mrs W, his mother's cousin, who was also caring for his three older half-siblings. By the time the local authority's application for a care order was heard, the child was well-settled and well-cared for in Mrs W's home. Mrs W applied for a residence order. This was supported by the local authority who decided not to pursue its application. However, the guardian ad litem ('GAL', now 'children's guardian', who represents the child's interests in the proceedings) and the father supported making a care order, hoping the child could be adopted outside the family. The question arose whether, in this commonplace scenario of a child being 'rescued' from a harmful situation by the local authority, the child had to be suffering significant harm at the time of the hearing, or whether it sufficed for the purposes of the threshold criteria that the child had been suffering significant harm at the point the local authority first intervened to protect the child. The House of Lords, emphasizing the need to 'avoid the tyranny of language', preferred the latter interpretation.

---

[139] See *Re O (A minor) (care order: education: procedure)* [1992] 2 FLR 7, 10.
[140] [1993] 1 FLR 257, 263.
[141] [2009] EWCA Civ 853.
[142] Ibid., [52].
[143] Ibid., [54].
[144] Ibid.
[145] Discussed in detail below at pp 843–6.

Re M (a minor) (care orders: threshold conditions) [1994] 2 AC 424, 433–4 (HL)

LORD MACKAY:

There is nothing in section 31(2) which in my opinion requires that the conditions to be satisfied are disassociated from the time of the making of the application by the local authority. I would conclude that the natural construction of the conditions in section 31(2) is that where, at the time the application is to be disposed of, there are in place arrangements for the protection of the child by the local authority on an interim basis which protection has been continuously in place for some time, the relevant date with respect to which the court must be satisfied is the date at which the local authority initiated the procedure for protection under the Act from which these arrangements followed. If after a local authority had initiated protective arrangements the need for these had terminated, because the child's welfare had been satisfactorily provided for otherwise, in any subsequent proceedings, it would not be possible to found jurisdiction on the situation at the time of initiation of these arrangements. It is permissible only to look back from the date of disposal to the date of initiation of protection as a result of which local authority arrangements had been continuously in place thereafter to the date of disposal.

It has to be borne in mind that this in no way precludes the court from taking account at the date of the hearing of all relevant circumstances. The conditions in subsection (2) are in the nature of conditions conferring jurisdiction upon the court to consider whether or not a care order or supervision order should be made. Conditions of that kind would in my view normally have to be satisfied at the date on which the order was first applied for. It would in my opinion be odd if the jurisdiction of the court to make an order depended on how long the court took before it finally disposed of the case.

It was subsequently suggested in *Southwark London Borough Council v B* that the relevant date at which the 'local authority initiated the procedure for protection' may include voluntary arrangements entered into under Part III provided protective arrangements have been continuously in place since that date.[146]

The issue of timing arose again in *Re G (Care proceedings: threshold conditions).*[147] The question this time was whether the local authority could rely on information acquired *after* they had first intervened to protect the child in order to help establish that the threshold conditions were satisfied at the point of intervention. The Court of Appeal drew a distinction between: (i) information and events which went towards proving the alleged state of affairs at the point of intervention; and (ii) completely unrelated information and events which, whilst in themselves capable of constituting evidence of significant harm, had no bearing on the initial reasons for the local authority intervening. It was held that whilst the former was clearly relevant and should be admitted, evidence falling into the latter category could not be relied upon by the local authority to 'retrospectively valid[ate] a concern which was not in fact justified at the time'.[148] Wall LJ has provided further clarification on this issue, holding in *Re L (children) (care proceedings)*[149] that the local authority is free to advance grounds for establishing the threshold criteria at trial which are different from the grounds relied on when it first intervened provided the alternative grounds actually existed (whether

[146] [1998] 2 FLR 1095, 1109.
[147] [2001] EWCA Civ 968.
[148] Ibid., [15].
[149] [2006] EWCA Civ 1282.

or not known to the local authority) at the date of intervention.[150] This differs from the situation where a new unrelated event giving rise to grounds for concern occurs *after* the date of intervention, which, in accordance with Hale LJ's judgment in *Re G*, would remain excluded from consideration. In such circumstances the local authority would simply have to start proceedings again.

'is likely to suffer'

The alternative basis on which the local authority can satisfy the first limb of the threshold criteria under s 31(2)(a) is the likelihood of future significant harm. It has been suggested that when looking forward the local authority is not restricted to the immediate or even medium-term future, anticipated harm even years in advance will suffice.[151] Nor does the local authority have to identify the precise harm relied on.[152] However, satisfying the prospective limb of s 31(2)(a) is in many ways a difficult task, relying as it does on various hypotheses about the future. The two leading authorities on establishing the likelihood of future significant harm are the House of Lords' decisions in *Re H and others (minors) (sexual abuse: standard of proof)*[153] and *Re B (Children) (Care proceedings: Standard of proof)*.[154]

Re H concerned applications for care orders with respect to three children (D2, D3, and D4). A fourth child (D1, the eldest sister) alleged she had been sexually abused by the stepfather (Mr R) over a number of years. He was charged with rape but acquitted at the criminal trial. The local authority continued with the care proceedings, the sole ground for the care orders being the likelihood of future significant harm given the alleged sexual abuse of the eldest daughter. It did not contend that any of the three children were currently suffering significant harm. The House of Lords were all agreed that 'likely' should be interpreted to mean there was a 'real possibility' of future significant harm: there was no need to show that the harm was 'probable' in the sense of 'more likely than not'. However, the House of Lords were divided as to the evidential base required in order to make a positive finding that the child was likely to suffer significant harm. The majority held that the court must be satisfied on the balance of probabilities that there was a real possibility the child would suffer significant harm, the burden of proof resting on the local authority. Lord Nicholls went on to hold that the court could only proceed on the basis of 'proper material', meaning the court would only be able to find a real possibility of future harm on the basis of established facts not mere doubts or suspicions—which in this case meant the local authority would need to prove on the balance of probabilities that the eldest daughter had been sexually abused. The minority disagreed, arguing that a number of 'unproven' facts, when taken together, could prove equally probative. The point is important, going as it does to the heart of child protection policy. Is the state justified in removing a child from his or her parents on the basis of mere suspicion of past neglect or abuse? The majority say 'no', setting a much higher threshold for state intervention than the minority.

---

[150] Ibid., [42]–[45]
[151] *Re H (A minor) (section 37 direction)* [1993] 2 FLR 541, 548 (per Scott Baker J).
[152] *F v Leeds City Council* [1994] 2 FLR 60.
[153] [1996] AC 563.
[154] [2008] UKHL 35.

Re H and others (minors) (sexual abuse: standard of proof) [1996] AC 563, 588–92, 572–4 (HL)

LORD NICHOLLS [with whom Lord Goff and Lord Mustill agreed]:

Suspicion and the threshold conditions . . .

[The local authority] case for the making of a care order is based exclusively on the second limb. In support of the allegation that D2, D3 and D4 are likely to suffer significant harm, the local authority rely solely upon the allegation that over many years D1 was subject to repeated sexual abuse by Mr. R.

The judge held that the latter allegation was not made out. Mr. R did not establish that abuse did not occur. The outcome on this disputed serious allegation of fact was that the local authority, upon whom the burden of proof rested, failed to establish that abuse did occur. However, the judge remained suspicious and, had it been relevant, he would have held there was a reasonable possibility that D1's allegations were true. The question arising from these conclusions can be expressed thus: when a local authority assert but fail to prove past misconduct, can the judge's suspicions or lingering doubts on that issue form the basis for concluding that the second limb of section 31(2)(a) has been established? . . .

A conclusion based on facts

The starting point here is that courts act on evidence. They reach their decisions on the basis of the evidence before them. When considering whether an applicant for a care order has shown that the child is suffering harm or is likely to do so, a court will have regard to the undisputed evidence. The judge will attach to that evidence such weight or importance as he considers appropriate. Likewise with regard to disputed evidence which the judge accepts as reliable. None of that is controversial. But the rejection of a disputed allegation as not proved on the balance of probability leaves scope for the possibility that the non-proven allegation may be true after all. There remains room for the judge to have doubts and suspicions on this score. This is the area of controversy.

In my view these unresolved judicial doubts and suspicions can no more form the basis of a conclusion that the second threshold condition in section 31(2)(a) has been established than they can form the basis of a conclusion that the first has been established . . .

A decision by a court on the likelihood of a future happening must be founded on a basis of present facts and the inferences fairly to be drawn therefrom. . . .

An alleged but non-proven fact is not a fact for this purpose . . . [T]here must be facts from which the court can properly conclude there is a real possibility that the child will suffer harm in the future . . . [I]f the facts are disputed, the court must resolve the dispute so far as necessary to reach a proper conclusion on the issue it has to decide . . .

The range of facts which may properly be taken into account is infinite . . . And facts, which are minor or even trivial if considered in isolation, when taken together may suffice to satisfy the court of the likelihood of future harm. The court will attach to all the relevant facts the appropriate weight when coming to an overall conclusion on the crucial issue.

I must emphasise a further point. I have indicated that unproved allegations of maltreatment cannot form the basis for a finding by the court that either limb of section 31(2)(a) is established. It is, of course, open to a court to conclude there is a real possibility that the child will suffer harm in the future although harm in the past has not been established. There will be cases where, although the alleged maltreatment itself is not proved, the evidence does establish a combination of profoundly worrying features affecting the care of the child within the family. In such cases it would be open to a court in appropriate circumstances to find that, although not satisfied the child is yet suffering significant harm, on the basis of such facts as are proved there is a likelihood that he will do so in the future.

That is not the present case. The three younger girls are not at risk unless D1 was abused by Mr. R in the past. If she was not abused, there is no reason for thinking the others may be. This is not a case where Mr. R has a history of abuse. Thus the one and only relevant fact is whether D1 was abused by Mr. R as she says. The other surrounding facts, such as the fact that D1 made a complaint and the fact that her mother responded unsatisfactorily, lead nowhere relevant in this case if they do not lead to the conclusion that D1 was abused. To decide that the others are at risk because there is a possibility that D1 was abused would be to base the decision, not on fact, but on suspicion: the suspicion that D1 may have been abused. That would be to lower the threshold prescribed by Parliament...

Conclusion

As I read the Act, Parliament decided that the threshold for a care order should be that the child is suffering significant harm, or there is a real possibility that he will do so. In the latter regard the threshold is comparatively low. Therein lies the protection for children. But, as I read the Act, Parliament also decided that proof of the relevant facts is needed if this threshold is to be surmounted. Before the section 1 welfare test and the welfare 'checklist' can be applied, the threshold has to be crossed. Therein lies the protection for parents. They are not to be at risk of having their child taken from them and removed into the care of the local authority on the basis only of suspicions, whether of the judge or of the local authority or anyone else. A conclusion that the child is suffering or is likely to suffer harm must be based on facts, not just suspicion.

Lord Lloyd and Lord Browne-Wilkinson both dissented, concerned that the majority approach set the threshold for state intervention too high and left children in unacceptable situations of risk.[155]

LORD BROWNE-WILKINSON:

I agree that the judge can only act on evidence and on facts which, so far as relevant, have been proved. He has to be satisfied by the evidence before him that there is a real possibility of serious harm to the child.

Where I part company is in thinking that the facts relevant to an assessment of risk ('is likely to suffer...harm') are not the same as the facts relevant to a decision that harm is in fact being suffered. In order to be satisfied that an event has occurred or is occurring the evidence has to show on balance of probabilities that such event did occur or is occurring. But in order to be satisfied that there is a risk of such an occurrence, the ambit of the relevant facts is in my view wider. The combined effect of a number of factors which suggest that a state of affairs, though not proved to exist, may well exist is the normal basis for the assessment of future risk. To be satisfied of the existence of a risk does not require proof of the occurrence of past historical events but proof of facts which are relevant to the making of a prognosis.

Let me give an example, albeit a dated one. Say that in 1940 those responsible for giving air-raid warnings had received five unconfirmed sightings of approaching aircraft which might

---

[155] See also Keating (1996) and (2009). Cf Cobley and Lowe (2009), 468.

be enemy bombers. They could not, on balance of probabilities, have reached a conclusion that any one of those sightings was of an enemy aircraft: nor could they logically have put together five non-proven sightings so as to be satisfied that enemy aircraft were in fact approaching. But their task was not simply to decide whether enemy aircraft were approaching but whether there was a risk of an air raid. The facts relevant to the assessment of such risk were the reports that unconfirmed sightings had been made, not the truth of such reports. They could well, on the basis of those unconfirmed reports, have been satisfied that there was a real possibility of an air raid and given warning accordingly...

My Lords, I am anxious that the decision of the House in this case may establish the law in an unworkable form to the detriment of many children at risk. Child abuse, particularly sex abuse, is notoriously difficult to prove in a court of law. The relevant facts are extremely sensitive and emotive. They are often known only to the child and to the alleged abuser. If legal proof of actual abuse is a prerequisite to a finding that a child is at risk of abuse, the court will be powerless to intervene to protect children in relation to whom there are the gravest suspicions of actual abuse but the necessary evidence legally to prove such abuse is lacking. Take the present case. Say that the proceedings had related to D1, the complainant, herself. After a long hearing a judge has reached the conclusion on evidence that there is a "real possibility" that her evidence is true, i.e. that she has in fact been gravely abused. Can Parliament really have intended that neither the court nor anyone else should have jurisdiction to intervene so as to protect D1 from any abuse which she may well have been enduring? I venture to think not.

The majority position was affirmed by the House of Lords in *Re B (Children) (Care Proceedings: Standard of Proof)*. Thus the court cannot be satisfied that child A is likely to suffer significant harm on the basis that there is a 'real possibility' or 'suspicion' that child B has suffered similar harm in the past.

Re B (Children) (Care Proceedings: Standard of Proof) [2008] UKHL 35

LORD HOFFMANN:

2. If a legal rule requires a fact to be proved (a "fact in issue"), a judge or jury must decide whether or not it happened. There is no room for a finding that it might have happened. The law operates a binary system in which the only values are 0 and 1. The fact either happened or it did not. If the tribunal is left in doubt, the doubt is resolved by a rule that one party or the other carries the burden of proof. If the party who bears the burden of proof fails to discharge it, a value of 0 is returned and the fact is treated as not having happened. If he does discharge it, a value of 1 is returned and the fact is treated as having happened.

3. The effect of the decision of the House in *Re H (Minors) (Sexual Abuse: Standard of Proof)* [1996] AC 563 is that section 31(2)(a) of the Children Act 1989 requires any facts used as the basis of a prediction that a child is "likely to suffer significant harm" to be proved to have happened. Every such fact is to be treated as a fact in issue. The majority of the House rejected the analogy with facts which merely form part of the material from which a fact in issue may be inferred, which need not each be proved to have happened. There is of course no conceptual reason for rejecting this analogy, which in the context of some predictions (such as Lord Browne-Wilkinson's example of air raid warnings) might be prudent and appropriate. But the House decided that it was inappropriate for the purposes of section 31(2)(a). It is this rule which the House reaffirms today.

BARONESS HALE:

22. This case is about the meaning of the words "is likely to suffer significant harm". How is the court to be satisfied of such a likelihood? This is a prediction from existing facts, often from a multitude of such facts, about what has happened in the past, about the characters and personalities of the people involved, about the things which they have said and done, and so on. But do those facts have to be proved in the usual way, on the balance of probabilities? Or is it sufficient that there is a "real possibility" that they took place, even if the judge is unable to say that it is more likely than not that they did? . . .

32. In our legal system, if a judge finds it more likely than not that something did take place, then it is treated as having taken place. If he finds it more likely than not that it did not take place, then it is treated as not having taken place. He is not allowed to sit on the fence. He has to find for one side or the other. Sometimes the burden of proof will come to his rescue: the party with the burden of showing that something took place will not have satisfied him that it did. But generally speaking a judge is able to make up his mind where the truth lies without needing to rely upon the burden of proof.

33. The judge's findings in this case were expressed in such a way as squarely to raise the issue of principle. Is it possible to be satisfied that a child is likely to suffer a particular kind of harm in the future when the basis for suggesting this is that there is a "real possibility" that another child has suffered the same kind of harm in the past? There are, of course, many degrees of possibility - from a fifty/fifty chance that it happened down to an infinitesimal chance that it did. In this case, the judge seems to have concluded that there was a "real possibility" because he could not conclude that there was none . . .

54. The reasons given by Lord Nicholls for adopting the approach which he did in *Re H* remain thoroughly convincing. The threshold is there to protect both the children and their parents from unjustified intervention in their lives. It would provide no protection at all if it could be established on the basis of unsubstantiated suspicions: that is, where a judge cannot say that there is no real possibility that abuse took place, so concludes that there is a real possibility that it did. In other words, the alleged perpetrator would have to prove that it did not. [Counsel] accepts that it must be proved on the balance of probabilities that a child "is suffering" significant harm. But nevertheless he argues that those same allegations, which could not be proved for that purpose, could be the basis of a finding of likelihood of future harm. If that were so, there would have been no need for the first limb of section 31(2)(a) at all. Parliament must be presumed to have inserted it for a purpose. Furthermore, the Act draws a clear distinction between the threshold to be crossed before the court may make a final care or supervision order and the threshold for making preliminary and interim orders. If Parliament had intended that a mere suspicion that a child had suffered harm could form the basis for making a final order, it would have used the same terminology of "reasonable grounds to suspect" or "reasonable grounds to believe" as it uses elsewhere in the Act. Instead . . . it speaks of what the child is suffering or is likely to suffer . . .

59. To allow the courts to make decisions about the allocation of parental responsibility for children on the basis of unproven allegations and unsubstantiated suspicions would be to deny them their essential role in protecting both children and their families from the intervention of the state, however well intentioned that intervention may be. It is to confuse the role of the local authority, in assessing and managing risk, in planning for the child, and deciding what action to initiate, with the role of the court in deciding where the truth lies and what the legal consequences should be. I do not under-estimate the difficulty of deciding where the truth lies but that is what the courts are for.

'Is attributable to the care given to the child not being what it would be reasonable to expect a parent to give to him'

The second limb of the threshold test raises the difficult question of whether the local authority must be able to prove on the balance of probabilities that the harm is attributable to one or other or both of the parents before the s 31(2) criteria are met. This question again has important implications as to the overall threshold for state intervention into the family. It was confirmed by Lady Hale in *Re S-B (Children)* that the test to be applied when identifying the perpetrator is the balance of probabilities.[156] The problem arises when the local authority is unable to discharge that burden with respect to any one particular individual. The problem of the 'unknown perpetrator' was addressed by the House of Lords in the case of *Lancashire CC v B*.[157] Lord Nicholls again gave judgment for the majority but on this occasion took a much more interventionist approach, arguably sanctioning state intervention in circumstances where, contrary to his judgment in *Re H*, there was only a *suspicion*, as opposed to established fact, that the child had suffered significant harm *at the hands of the parents*. The case concerned the now common scenario where the care of the child had been shared between the parents and a child-minder, although the problem of the 'unknown perpetrator' also frequently arises where the parents have separated and the local authority is unable to establish whether one or other or both of the parents is responsible for the harm. There was no dispute that the child had suffered significant harm. The question was whether in order to satisfy the second limb of the threshold, it had to be established, on the balance of probabilities, which of the three possible perpetrators: the mother, the father, or the child-minder, had been responsible for the harm.

Lancashire CC v B [2000] 2 AC 147, 164–7 (HL)

LORD NICHOLLS:

In a case based on present harm ("is suffering...significant harm") the attributable condition requires the court to be satisfied that the harm is attributable to the care given to the child or, which is not this case, to the child's being beyond parental control. That nexus must be established on the basis of proved facts. But that prompts the question: care by whom? The contention of A's parents is that, having regard to the statutory context and the legislative policy behind Part IV of the Children Act 1989, "the care given to the child" in section 31(2)(b)(i) means the care given to the child by the parents or other primary carers. The contrary contention, advanced by the local authority and A.'s guardian, is that no such limiting words are to be read into the statute: the relevant phrase means the care given by anyone who plays a part in the care arrangements for the child.

Counsel [for the parents] submitted that a strictly literal interpretation of the phrase under consideration would lead to an absurdity. Parliament cannot have intended that a child should be at risk of being removed from his family, and the parents at risk of losing their child, because of an unforeseeable failure of care by a third party to whom the parents, wholly unexceptionably, had temporarily entrusted the child....

This is a forceful argument, up to a point. I accept that the interpretation of the attributable condition urged on behalf of the respondents [the Local Authority]...is too wide and loose. For this one needs to look no further than [counsel for the appellant's] example of the one-off temporary entrustment of the child to a person reasonably believed by the parents

---

[156] [2009] UKSC 17, [34].
[157] [2000] 2 AC 147.

to be suitable. Injury inflicted by the temporary carer would satisfy the threshold conditions. But the appellants' argument goes too far in the other direction. The interpretation urged on behalf of the appellants is too rigid. As with the respondents' submission, so also with the appellants' submission: the conclusion to which it leads cannot be right. As the present case exemplifies, the appellants' argument, if accepted, produces the result that where a child has repeatedly sustained non-accidental injuries the court may nevertheless be unable to intervene to protect the child by making a care order or, even, a supervision order. In the present case the child is proved to have sustained significant harm at the hands of one or both of her parents or at the hands of a daytime carer. But, according to this argument, if the court is unable to identify which of the child's carers was responsible for inflicting the injuries, the child remains outside the threshold prescribed by Parliament as the threshold which must be crossed before the court can proceed to consider whether it is in the best interests of the child to make a care order or supervision order. The child must, for the time being, remain unprotected, since section 31 of the Children Act 1989 and its associated emergency and interim provisions now provide the only court mechanism available to a local authority to protect a child from risk of further harm.

I cannot believe Parliament intended that the attributable condition in section 31(2)(b) should operate in this way. Such an interpretation would mean that the child's future health, or even her life, would have to be hazarded on the chance that, after all, the non-parental carer rather than one of the parents inflicted the injuries. Self-evidently, to proceed in such a way when a child is proved to have suffered serious injury on more than one occasion could be dangerously irresponsible.

There is a further factor which weighs with me. Sadly, the unhappy facts of the present case are far from being exceptional. As the Court of Appeal observed, the task of caring for children is often shared nowadays between parents and others. When questions of non-accidental injury or abuse arise, the court is frequently unable to discover precisely what happened. This is not surprising. And yet, on the appellants' construction of the attributable condition, in this common form situation of shared caring the court is powerless to make even a supervision order if the judge is unable to penetrate the fog of denials, evasions, lies and half-truths which all too often descends in court at fact finding hearings ...

Against this background, I consider that a permissible and preferable interpretation of section 31(2)(b)(i), between the two extremes, is as follows. The phrase "care given to the child" refers primarily to the care given to the child by a parent or parents or other primary carers. That is the norm. The matter stands differently in a case such as the present one, where care is shared and the court is unable to distinguish in a crucial respect between the care given by the parents or primary carers and the care given by other carers. Different considerations from the norm apply in a case of shared caring where the care given by one or other of the carers is proved to have been deficient, with the child suffering harm in consequence, but the court is unable to identify which of the carers provided the deficient care. In such a case, the phrase "care given to the child" is apt to embrace not merely the care given by the parents or other primary carers; it is apt to embrace the care given by any of the carers. Some such meaning has to be given to the phrase if the unacceptable consequences already mentioned are to be avoided. This interpretation achieves that necessary result while, at the same time, encroaching to the minimum extent on the general principles underpinning section 31(2). Parliament seems not to have foreseen this particular problem. The courts must therefore apply the statutory language to the unforeseen situation in the manner which best gives effect to the purposes the legislation was enacted to achieve.

Lord Nicholls recognized the difficulties caused by this approach but held that the known risk of harm to the child outweighed any potential unfairness to the parents:

> I recognise that the effect of this construction is that the attributable condition may be satisfied when there is no more than a possibility that the parents were responsible for inflicting the injuries which the child has undoubtedly suffered. That is a consequence which flows from giving the phrase, in the limited circumstances mentioned above, the wider meaning those circumstances require. I appreciate also that in such circumstances, when the court proceeds to the next stage and considers whether to exercise its discretionary power to make a care order or supervision order, the judge may be faced with a particularly difficult problem. The judge will not know which individual was responsible for inflicting the injuries. The child may suffer harm if left in a situation of risk with his parents. The child may also suffer harm if removed from parental care where, if the truth were known, the parents present no risk. Above all, I recognise that this interpretation of the attributable condition means that parents who may be wholly innocent, and whose care may not have fallen below that of a reasonable parent, will face the possibility of losing their child, with all the pain and distress this involves. That is a possibility, once the threshold conditions are satisfied, although by no means a certainty. It by no means follows that because the threshold conditions are satisfied the court will go on to make a care order. And it goes without saying that when considering how to exercise their discretionary powers in this type of case judges will keep firmly in mind that the parents have not been shown to be responsible for the child's injuries.
>
> I recognise all these difficulties. This is indeed a most unfortunate situation for everyone involved: the child, the parents, the child-minder, the local authority and the court. But, so far as the threshold conditions are concerned, the factor which seems to me to outweigh all others is the prospect that an unidentified, and unidentifiable, carer may inflict further injury on a child he or she has already severely damaged.

It is indicative of the difficulty in finding an acceptable balance between, on the one hand, respecting the integrity of the family and, on the other, protecting the child that whilst Lord Nicholls has been criticized for placing the threshold for intervention too high in *Re H*, he has been criticized in *Lancashire CC v B* for being overly interventionist at the parents' expense.[158]

Following the House of Lords decision in *Lancashire CC v B*, it is clear that in order to satisfy the second limb of the threshold it is not necessary to identify the perpetrator of the harm. However, establishing the identity of the perpetrator where possible remains of considerable importance as the proceedings progress to the welfare stage and the court is required to determine the future arrangements for the child. Thus, whilst unnecessary to meet the threshold criteria, where the perpetrator can be identified on the balance of probabilities, the court has a duty to do so.[159] There is, however, a limit as to what the court can be expected to do.[160] The Court of Appeal has emphasized that where identification is simply not possible on the evidence, it is the 'duty of the judge to state that as his or her conclusion.'[161] The question then arises what more, if anything, the court should do where the perpetrator cannot be identified. The Supreme Court addressed this particular aspect of the problem in the case of *Re S-B (Children)*, holding that it is still important for the court

---

[158] Hall (2000), 426.
[159] *NH v A County Council, NH and RD &SD* [2009] EWCA Civ 472, [12].
[160] Ibid.
[161] Ibid.

to identify the 'pool of possible perpetrators' because 'it will help to identify the real risks to the child and the steps needed to protect him. It will help the professionals working with the family. And it will be of value to the child in the long run.'[162]

The test for identifying the 'pool of possible perpetrators' was addressed in *North Yorkshire CC v SA*.[163] The Court of Appeal held that applying a test of 'no possibility' to *exclude* a possible perpetrator from the pool was 'patently too wide': it may leave in the pool 'anyone who had even a fleeting contact with the child in circumstances in which there was the opportunity to cause injuries'.[164] Butler-Sloss P suggested that the test for *inclusion* in the pool should be 'likelihood or real possibility'.[165] This approach gained the approval of Lady Hale in *Re S-B*.

Re S-B (Children) [2009] UKSC 17

LADY HALE:

43. The cases are littered with references to a "finding of exculpation" or to "ruling out" a particular person as responsible for the harm suffered. This is...to set the bar far too high. It suggests that parents and other carers are expected to prove their innocence beyond reasonable doubt. If the evidence is not such as to establish responsibility on the balance of probabilities it should nevertheless be such as to establish whether there is a real possibility that a particular person was involved. When looking at how best to protect the child and provide for his future, the judge will have to consider the strength of that possibility as part of the overall circumstances of the case.

Two further points regarding the correct interpretation of the 'attributable to' limb of the threshold criteria should be noted. It was established by the House of Lords in *Lancashire CC v B* that the phrase 'attributable to' connotes a causal connection between the harm and the care being given to the child, but the care in question need not be the 'sole or dominant or direct cause'; a contributory cause, such as a parent's failure to protect, is sufficient.[166] Lord Nicholls also addressed the standard of care to be expected of the caregiver, emphasizing that it was not a question of fault but establishing that the care had fallen below an objectively acceptable level.[167] In determining this objective standard of care, it has been held by Munby J that social and cultural differences are relevant. In *Re K* concerned applications for various orders with respect to a 16-year-old Kurdish Iraqi girl whose family had moved to the UK following her father being granted asylum. In accordance with the family's cultural and religious practices, the girl had entered into an arranged (not forced) marriage at the age of 15 in a religious ceremony in the UK. She subsequently alleged that she had been raped and sexually abused by her 'husband' and physically abused by her father. The police and local authority intervened and she became estranged from her family. Although she maintained her allegations of rape, she later returned to the family home and refused to cooperate with social services. The local authority applied for a supervision order and orders under the court's inherent jurisdiction to prevent the parents removing

---

162 [2009] UKSC 17, [40].
163 [2003] EWCA Civ 839.
164 Ibid., [25].
165 Ibid., [26].
166 [2000] 2 AC 147, 162.
167 Ibid.

her from the UK or consenting to a further marriage whilst she was under the age of 18. The applications were dismissed. In considering the question of whether the harm suffered by the girl as a result of the arranged marriage was attributable to the care given by the parents, Munby J held that whilst the care afforded by the parents was to be judged in accordance with an objective standard, the court must be sensitive to the social, cultural, and religious worldview of the family and evaluate the parents' behaviour accordingly.[168] Taking into account the parents' cultural and religious beliefs and the fact that the mother was herself married to the father at the age of 14, Munby J went on to observe that he would be very reluctant to find that parents who had only recently settled in the UK had fallen below an acceptable standard of parenting if when judged against the standards of their own community they would be regarded as having done nothing wrong.[169] Indeed, it was evident in this case that the parents were genuinely upset and bemused as to why an arranged marriage at the age of 15 should have been regarded as abusive and have caused such outrage amongst the relevant professionals.

Establishing the threshold criteria

The standard of proof

In order to satisfy both limbs of the threshold criteria, the local authority will need to establish a number of key facts. It was held by Lord Nicholls in *Re H*, that the usual civil standard of proof applies, placing the burden on the local authority to satisfy the court on the balance of probabilities as to any disputed issues of fact. None of this is particularly contentious. However, more controversially, Lord Nicholls went on to explain how, in his view, this standard of proof would be applied in the case of serious allegations of child abuse.

Re H and others [1996] AC 563, 586

LORD NICHOLLS:

Where the matters in issue are facts the standard of proof required in non-criminal proceedings is the preponderance of probability, usually referred to as the balance of probability. This is the established general principle. There are exceptions such as contempt of court applications, but I can see no reason for thinking that family proceedings are, or should be, an exception...

The balance of probability standard means that a court is satisfied an event occurred if the court considers that, on the evidence, the occurrence of the event was more likely than not. When assessing the probabilities the court will have in mind as a factor, to whatever extent is appropriate in the particular case, that the more serious the allegation the less likely it is that the event occurred and, hence, the stronger should be the evidence before the court concludes that the allegation is established on the balance of probability. Fraud is usually less likely than negligence. Deliberate physical injury is usually less likely than accidental physical injury. A stepfather is usually less likely to have repeatedly raped and had non-consensual oral sex with his under age stepdaughter than on some occasion to have lost his temper and slapped her. Built into the preponderance of probability standard is a generous degree of flexibility in respect of the seriousness of the allegation.

[168] Ibid., [25]–[26].
[169] Ibid.

> Although the result is much the same, this does not mean that where a serious allegation is in issue the standard of proof required is higher. It means only that the inherent probability or improbability of an event is itself a matter to be taken into account when weighing the probabilities and deciding whether, on balance, the event occurred. The more improbable the event, the stronger must be the evidence that it did occur before, on the balance of probability, its occurrence will be established.

Lord Nicholls' judgment was interpreted to mean that the more serious the allegation, the more cogent and convincing the evidence would need to be to tip the balance of probabilities in favour of the local authority.[170] This approach to the standard of proof was subjected to convincing criticism.[171] Dissenting in *Re H*, Lord Lloyd pointed out that it could lead to 'bizarre' consequences:

Re H and others [1996] AC 563, 577

Lord Lloyd:

In my view the standard of proof under that subsection ought to be the simple balance of probability, however serious the allegations involved. I have reached that view for a number of reasons, but mainly because section 31(2) provides only the threshold criteria for making a care order. It by no means follows that an order will be made even if the threshold criteria are satisfied. The court must then go on to consider the statutory checklist in section 1(3) of the Act. But if the threshold criteria are not met, the local authority can do nothing, however grave the anticipated injury to the child, or however serious the apprehended consequences. This seems to me to be a strong argument in favour of making the threshold lower rather than higher. It would be a bizarre result if the more serious the anticipated injury, whether physical or sexual, the more difficult it became for the local authority to satisfy the initial burden of proof, and thereby ultimately, if the welfare test is satisfied, secure protection for the child.

The untested assumptions underlying Lord Nicholls' judgment, as well as its wider implications for protecting children at risk of harm, also attracted strong academic criticism.[172]

H. Keating, 'Shifting standards in the House of Lords—*Re H and others (Minors) (Sexual abuse: standard of proof)',* (1996) 8 *Child and Family Law Quarterly* 157, 160–1

The path of reasoning adopted by Lord Nicholls seems logical but, arguably, he both starts and finishes at strange locations. His argument is premised on the very broad assertion that

---

170 *Re U (a child) (serious injury: standard of proof); Re B (a child) (serious injury: standard of proof)* [2004] EWCA Civ 567, [13]. The Court of Appeal rejected the approach adopted by Bodey J in *Re ET (serious injuries: standard of proof)* [2003] 2 FLR 1205, in which it was held that in practice the difference between the criminal and civil standards of proof had been rendered 'largely illusory'.

171 See, e.g., Keenan (2005), 179–82.

172 See also, Keenan, ibid., 181–2.

serious abuse is less likely than minor abuse by, for example, stating that a stepfather is usually less likely to have repeatedly raped his stepdaughter than to have slapped her. But do we
know this? Even if true, does it follow that we should be more sceptical of serious allegations
when made? One could take the opposite view that the very seriousness of them means
that they are less likely to be made unless true...More fundamentally, the outcome is that
in serious cases of abuse—which are notoriously difficult to prove—we are making the task
harder. Lord Lloyd is right to describe this result as bizarre....Given that the threshold is only
the starting point in the decision-making process, a simple balance of probabilities standard
is both more workable and less dangerous. It does not amount to an unwarranted intervention into family life and does not leave local authorities powerless to protect children.

The House of Lords revisited the issue in *Re B (Children) (Care: Proceedings)*.[173] The suggestion that Lord Nicholls had intended to apply a 'heightened' civil standard of proof to care
proceedings was firmly denied, in the words of Baroness Hale, 'it is time for us to loosen
its grip and give it its quietus.'[174] The House of Lords unanimously held that the usual civil
standard of proof was to be applied without further gloss or elaboration. That said, both
Lord Hoffmann and Baroness Hale went on to state that the inherent improbability of an
event occurring *may* be relevant, an alleged improbable 'fact' being harder to prove on the
balance of probabilities than a probable one. However, whilst noting the potential relevance
of inherent probabilities to discharging the burden of proof, both expressly disagreed with
Lord Nicholls' basic assertion that the seriousness of the allegation bears any relationship to
the inherent improbability of the event occurring.

Re B (Children) [2008] UKHL 35

LORD HOFFMANN:

15....There is only one rule of law, namely that the occurrence of the fact in issue must
be proved to have been more probable than not. Common sense, not law, requires that in
deciding this question, regard should be had, to whatever extent appropriate, to inherent
probabilities. If a child alleges sexual abuse by a parent, it is common sense to start with
the assumption that most parents do not abuse their children. But this assumption may be
swiftly dispelled by other compelling evidence of the relationship between parent and child
or parent and other children. It would be absurd to suggest that the tribunal must in all cases
assume that serious conduct is unlikely to have occurred. In many cases, the other evidence
will show that it was all too likely. If, for example, it is clear that a child was assaulted by
one or other of two people, it would make no sense to start one's reasoning by saying that
assaulting children is a serious matter and therefore neither of them is likely to have done so.
The fact is that one of them did and the question for the tribunal is simply whether it is more
probable that one rather than the other was the perpetrator.

BARONESS HALE:

70....I would go further and announce loud and clear that the standard of proof in finding the
facts necessary to establish the threshold under section 31(2) or the welfare considerations

---

[173] [2008] UKHL 35.
[174] Ibid., [64].

in section 1 of the 1989 Act is the simple balance of probabilities, neither more nor less. Neither the seriousness of the allegation nor the seriousness of the consequences should make any difference to the standard of proof to be applied in determining the facts. The inherent probabilities are simply something to be taken into account, where relevant, in deciding where the truth lies...

72. As to the seriousness of the allegation, there is no logical or necessary connection between seriousness and probability. Some seriously harmful behaviour, such as murder, is sufficiently rare to be inherently improbable in most circumstances. Even then there are circumstances, such as a body with its throat cut and no weapon to hand, where it is not at all improbable. Other seriously harmful behaviour, such as alcohol or drug abuse, is regrettably all too common and not at all improbable. Nor are serious allegations made in a vacuum. Consider the famous example of the animal seen in Regent's Park. If it is seen outside the zoo on a stretch of greensward regularly used for walking dogs, then of course it is more likely to be a dog than a lion. If it is seen in the zoo next to the lions' enclosure when the door is open, then it may well be more likely to be a lion than a dog.

The House of Lords have thus silenced many of the critics of Lord Nicholls' judgment in *Re H*.[175]

12.5.4 THE WELFARE STAGE

Once the court is satisfied the threshold conditions are met, it acquires jurisdiction to make an order. It can thus move on to the second stage of the proceedings. Whether the court should make the order sought is a question relating to the child's upbringing and the child's welfare is thus the paramount consideration.[176] Section 1(4) directs the court to have particular regard to the welfare checklist in s 1(3), of which the following are of particular note.

'Ascertainable wishes and feelings of the child'

In certain specified public law cases,[177] including applications for care or supervision orders, the child is made a party to the proceedings. To this end, s 41 provides that the court shall appoint a children's guardian to safeguard the child's interests unless satisfied that it is not necessary to do so.[178] The core responsibilities of children's guardians include providing the court with their professional assessment as to the child's best interests and advising the court as to the child's wishes and feelings.[179] Children's guardians are also responsible for appointing and instructing a solicitor to represent the child unless the guardian is authorized to conduct litigation.[180] If the child and the guardian disagree over the handling of the case, the child may instruct the solicitor directly provided the solicitor, the children's guardian, or the court considers the child is of sufficient understanding to

---

[175] Keating (2009).
[176] *Humberside County Council v B* [1993] 1 FLR 257, 261.
[177] S 41(6).
[178] See also FPR 2010, r 16.3.
[179] FPR 2010, r 16.20
[180] Criminal Justice and Court Services Act 2000, s 15.

do so.[181] In such circumstances, the guardian will continue to act, subject to the directions of the court, and may, with leave, appoint his or her own legal representation.[182]

Although the child may be a party to public law proceedings, the child is not entitled to attend court if represented by a children's guardian or solicitor.[183] Indeed, the courts have strongly discouraged guardians from allowing children to be present at hearings, requiring such presence to be justified to the judge.[184] The judge may choose to speak to the child directly. Before doing so, the judge will usually make it clear that the decision is one for the judge to make and the court will not follow the child's wishes if they are not in the child's best interests.[185]

'Any harm which he has suffered or is at risk of suffering'

In order to get to this stage of the proceedings it must already have been established that the child is suffering or is likely to suffer significant harm. At this point the court may take into account not only the harm established at the threshold stage but any additional harm the child may suffer as a result of the court making or refusing to make the orders sought. Importantly, this includes any harm the child may suffer as a result of separation from his or her primary carers.[186]

The Court of Appeal has held that when considering harm at the welfare stage, the same principles set down by Lord Nicholls in the House of Lords in *Re H and others* will apply. Only harm which is established on the balance of probabilities can therefore be considered, mere suspicion about existing or likely future harm must be excluded.

Re M and R (minors) (sexual abuse: expert evidence) [1996] 4 All ER 239, 246–8 (CA)

BUTLER-SLOSS LJ:

In the case before us [counsel] submitted that the House of Lords [in *Re H and others*] were concerned only with the threshold stage and that the majority view had no relevance to the welfare stage. So far as the latter stage was concerned, he submitted that since the judge in the present case was also clearly of the view that there was a real possibility that the children had been sexually abused, this was sufficient to establish that the children were at risk of suffering like harm in the future. Since a risk of harm is included in the welfare checklist set out in s 1(3) of the 1989 Act, the judge was wrong to exclude it from consideration. [Counsel] submitted that the justification for approaching s 1 in a way rejected by the House of Lords for s 31 was that under s 1 the welfare of the child was the paramount consideration, which justified and indeed required the court to act on possibilities rather than proof on the preponderance of probability...

---

[181] FPR 2010, r 16.21. For a more detailed explanation see *Re M (Minors) (Care Proceedings: Child's Wishes)* [1994] 1 FLR 749.
[182] FPR 2010, r 16.21.
[183] FPR 2010, r 12.14(3).
[184] *Re C (A Minor) (Care: Child's Wishes)* [1993] 1 FLR 832, 840–1.
[185] *Re M (Minors) (Care proceedings: Child's wishes)* [1994] 1 FLR 749, 755.
[186] *Humberside County Council v B* [1993] 1 FLR 257, 267.

In our judgment these submissions cannot be supported. They amount to the assertion that under s 1 the welfare of the child dictates that the court should act on suspicion or doubts, rather than facts. To our minds the welfare of the child dictates the exact opposite...

The court must reach a conclusion based on facts, not on suspicion or mere doubts. If, as in the present case, the court concludes that the evidence is insufficient to prove sexual abuse in the past, and if the fact of sexual abuse in the past is the only basis for asserting a risk of sexual abuse in the future, then it follows that there is nothing (except suspicion or mere doubts) to show a risk of future sexual abuse...

Section 1(3)(e)...does not deal with what *might* possibly have happened or what future risk there *may* possibly be. It speaks in terms of what *has* happened or what *is* at risk of happening. Thus, what the court must do (when the matter is in issue) is to decide whether the evidence establishes harm or the risk of harm.

We cannot see any justification for the suggestion that the standard of proof in performing this task should be less than the preponderance of probabilities. Were such a suggestion to be adopted, it would mean in effect that instead of acting on what was established as probably the case, the court would have to act on what was only possibly the case, or even on the basis of what was probably not the case. This, as Lord Nicholls pointed out in *Re H*, is the same as saying that the court should act on the basis of suspicion rather than on the basis of fact.

Such a proposition has, to our minds, only to be stated to be rejected. The same applies to the suggestion that the paramountcy of the welfare of the child requires such a method of proceeding, for this equally entails the proposition that the future of the child should be decided on the basis of suspicion rather than fact. We can find nothing in the 1989 Act which begins to suggest that Parliament intended that all-important decisions as to the future of a child should be made on such a basis, which to our minds would be a recipe for making decisions which were not in the best interests of the child...

Finally, we find support for our analysis of the position from the odd results which would follow were [counsel's] submissions to be accepted.

Firstly, it would be extraordinary if Parliament intended that evidence which is insufficient to establish that a child is likely to suffer significant harm for the purposes of s 31, should nevertheless be treated as sufficient to establish that a child is at risk of suffering harm for the purposes of s 1...

Secondly, it is clear from the speech of Lord Nicholls in *Re H*...that s 31 provides, among other things, protection for parents...

That protection would be entirely removed in circumstances similar to those of the present case, if, on reaching the second stage for reasons which might well not justify permanently removing the children, the court could act on the basis of such suspicions to make an order for permanent removal which would not be justified on the matters that had been properly proved.

As at the threshold stage, a different approach is taken to the question of the *identity* of the perpetrator. In line with the House of Lords decision in *Lancashire CC v B*, it was held by Lord Nicholls in *Re O and another (Minors) (Care: Preliminary Hearing)* that when considering the risk of harm to the child at the welfare stage, a possible perpetrator should not be excluded simply because the local authority is unable to establish culpability on the balance of probabilities. Consequently, whilst the question of whether the child has suffered or is at risk of suffering harm must be determined on the basis of facts proved on the balance of probabilities,[187] there is no requirement to establish the identity of the perpetrator on the same basis.

[187] *Re M and R (minors) (sexual abuse: expert evidence)* [1996] 4 All ER 239.

Re O and N (Minors) (Care: Preliminary Hearing) [2003] UKHL 18

LORD NICHOLLS:

THE WELFARE STAGE: 'UNCERTAIN PERPETRATOR' CASES

26. The first area concerns cases of the type involved in the present appeals, where the judge finds a child has suffered significant physical harm at the hands of his parents but is unable to say which. I stress one feature of this type of case. These are cases where it has been proved, to the requisite standard of proof, that the child is suffering significant harm or is likely to do so.

27. Here, as a matter of legal policy, the position seems to me straightforward. Quite simply, it would be grotesque if such a case had to proceed at the welfare stage on the footing that, because neither parent, considered individually, has been proved to be the perpetrator, therefore the child is not at risk from either of them. This would be grotesque because it would mean the court would proceed on the footing that neither parent represents a risk even though one or other of them was the perpetrator of the harm in question.

28. That would be a self-defeating interpretation of the legislation. It would mean that, in 'uncertain perpetrator' cases, the court decides that the threshold criteria are satisfied but then lacks the ability to proceed in a sensible way in the best interests of the child. The preferable interpretation of the legislation is that in such cases the court is able to proceed at the welfare stage on the footing that each of the possible perpetrators is, indeed, just that: a possible perpetrator...This approach accords with the basic principle that in considering the requirements of the child's welfare the court will have regard to all the circumstances of the case...

31. In 'uncertain perpetrator' cases the correct approach must be that the judge conducting the disposal hearing will have regard, to whatever extent is appropriate, to the facts found by the judge at the preliminary hearing...When the facts found at the preliminary hearing leave open the possibility that a parent or other carer was a perpetrator of proved harm, it would not be right for that conclusion to be excluded from consideration at the disposal hearing as one of the matters to be taken into account. The importance to be attached to that possibility, as to every feature of the case, necessarily depends on the circumstances. But to exclude that possibility altogether from the matters the judge may consider would risk distorting the court's assessment of where, having regard to all the circumstances, the best interests of the child lie...

34. I wholly understand that parents are apprehensive that, if each of them is labelled a possible perpetrator, social workers and others may all too readily rule out the prospect of rehabilitation with either of them because the child would be 'at risk' with either of them...

35. I understand this concern. Whether it is well founded, generally or in particular cases, is an altogether different matter. Whether well founded or not, the way ahead cannot be for cases to proceed on an artificial footing.

As Lord Nicholls clearly acknowledges, his approach means that a parent faces losing his or her child without the state ever proving on the balance of probabilities that the parent in question was responsible for the harm caused. In *Re B (Children)*, Baroness Hale dismissed the argument that this was inconsistent with the decisions of the House of Lords in *Re H* and the Court of Appeal in *Re M and R*, holding that 'the court cannot shut its eyes to the undoubted harm which has been suffered simply because it does not know who was responsible'.[188]

---

[188] [2008] UKHL 35, [61].

Whilst now well established that at the welfare stage the court can treat all possible but unproven perpetrators as posing a potential risk to the child, it remains somewhat unclear as to whether the court should attempt to assess the *degree of risk* posed by the individual in question. Lord Nicholls seemed to suggest in *Re O & N* that it was entirely appropriate for the court to attempt to assess the degree of likelihood that a particular individual was the perpetrator of the harm.[189] Lady Hale has been more cautious, suggesting it is unhelpful to try and assign percentage chances to each possible perpetrator. Whilst not precluding the possibility that the court could find that one individual is 'more likely' to be the perpetrator than others within the pool,[190] she has given strong support to Thorpe LJ's comment that the courts 'should be cautious about amplifying a judgment in which they have been unable to identify a perpetrator: "better to leave it thus" '.[191]

'The range of powers available to the court'

Once the threshold criteria have been established, the court has considerable freedom to shape its orders in accordance with the child's needs. It is open to the court on an application for a care order to make a supervision order and on an application for a supervision order to make a care order. As care proceedings constitute family proceedings, the court may also make a s 8 or a special guardianship order. This enables the court, even where the threshold conditions are satisfied, to make a private law order preventing the removal of the child into local authority care.[192] Despite the wide scope of the court's discretion, it is clear that there must be 'cogent and strong reasons to force upon the local authority a more Draconian order than that for which they have asked'.[193] However, even where all the parties are agreed on the most appropriate order, the court is still under a duty to conduct an 'appropriate judicial investigation' and having considered all the circumstances of the case make the order it considers to be in the child's best interests.[194]

When determining the appropriate order the court must consider the need for a proportionate response: that is, it should adopt the least interventionist measure possible to protect the child. It was held by Hale J in *Oxfordshire County Council v B* that, 'one should approach these cases on the basis that the less Draconian order was likely to be better for the child than the more Draconian or interventionist one'.[195] The importance of this principle has been reinforced by the implementation of the HRA 1998: in order to justify any prima facie interference with the rights of the parents under Article 8(1), any measures taken by the state must, under Article 8(2), be shown to have been no more than necessary to protect the competing rights and interests of the child. This was reiterated by Hale LJ in *Re C and B*, a case concerning the removal of two very young children from their parents on the basis of the intellectual and emotional impairment caused to two older siblings by their mother's deteriorating mental health. Hale LJ held that the removal of the two younger children without any evidence that either of them were currently suffering significant harm was a wholly disproportionate response.

---

[189] [2003] UKHL 18.
[190] *Re T (a child)* [2009] EWCA Civ 1208, [60]–[65].
[191] *Re S-B* [2009] UKSC 17, [44].
[192] *Northamptonshire CC v S* [1993] 1 FLR 554.
[193] *Oxfordshire County Council v B* [1998] 3 FCR 521, 525.
[194] *Re T (A Child)* [2009] EWCA Civ 121, [44] and [49].
[195] [1998] 3 FCR 521, 526.

Re C and B (children) (care order: future harm) [2000] 2 FCR 614 (CA)

HALE LJ:

30. I ... accept that there are cases in which the local authority is not bound to wait until the inevitable happens: it can intervene to protect long before that. But there has to be a balance. The cases where it is appropriate to do that are likely to involve long-standing problems which interfere with the capacity to provide even 'good enough' parenting in a serious way, such as serious mental illness, or a serious personality disorder, or intractable substance abuse, or evidence of past chronic neglect, or abuse, or evidence of serious ill-treatment and physical harm. None of those was involved in this case. Nor can it follow that every case where there is any significant risk of harm to a young child should result in a care order in which the care plan is adoption. Again, one quite understands why this may be considered by the local authority to be the appropriate course of action because, if there is early intervention before problems have escalated, the chance of placing the child successfully for adoption are much increased. The prospects are much less favourable if the child remains and damage is in fact sustained.

31. Nevertheless one comes back to the principle of proportionality. The principle has to be that the local authority works to support, and eventually to reunite, the family, unless the risks are so high that the child's welfare requires alternative family care. I cannot accept [counsel's] submission that this was a case for a care order with a care plan of adoption or nothing. There could have been other options ...

34. There is a long line of European Court of Human Rights jurisprudence ... which emphasises that the intervention has to be proportionate to the legitimate aim. Intervention in the family may be appropriate, but the aim should be to reunite the family when the circumstances enable that, and the effort should be devoted towards that end. Cutting off all contact and the relationship between the child or children and their family is only justified by the overriding necessity of the interests of the child.

[The appeal against the care orders with respect to the two younger children were allowed and the case remitted for rehearing by a High Court judge.]

12.5.5 THE CARE PLAN

A crucial consideration at the welfare stage is the local authority care plan.[196] The CA 1989 provides that where the local authority makes an application on which a care order may be made, the local authority must prepare a care plan.[197] The content of the care plan is prescribed by regulations and should include: the child's identified needs, including needs arising from race, culture, religion, special education, or health needs; the aim of the plan; the proposed timescale for implementation; the proposed placement; arrangements for contact and reunification; a contingency plan if the placement breaks down; the parents' and the child's wishes and views; and plans for the parents ongoing participation in the decision-making process.[198] The local authority should produce evidence to support the plan focusing on its feasibility and the likelihood of success.[199] Where the local authority is continuing to work towards rehabilitation with the family but, in the event of failure, it is possible the child

[196] Although always an important consideration, the care plan was only given statutory force in 2002. The care plan is now often the primary focus of the care proceedings.
[197] S 31A(1).
[198] Set down in *Re J (Minors) (Care: Care Plan)* [1994] 1 FLR 253, 258–9.
[199] Ibid., 261–2.

may require an alternative long-term placement, the local authority is encouraged to pre-pare and plan for both eventualities: what is termed concurrent or twin-track planning.[200]

Section 31(3A) provides that the court cannot make a care order until it has considered the care plan which, according to Wall J in *Re J (Minors) (Care: Care Plan)*, will be subjected to 'rigorous scrutiny'. However, although the court must give careful consideration to the plan and must be satisfied that it is in the child's best interests, there is in practice very little the court can do if it disagrees with what the local authority intends: the care plan is for the local authority not the court to determine. As observed by Munby J, if the court seeks to alter the local authority's care plan it must 'achieve its objective by persuasion rather than by compulsion.'[201] Where persuasion fails and the local authority will not reconsider its pos-ition, the only option available to the court is to refuse to make the care order.

Re S and D (Child Case: Powers of Court) [1995] 1 FCR 626, 634–5 (CA)

BALCOMBE LJ:

We were asked to give assistance to Judges who find themselves in the situation in which this Judge found himself, namely: what is the judge to do when faced with such a dilemma? He has only two alternatives; he may make a care order knowing that the local authority will then act in a way which he considers to be undesirable; or he may make no care order, which will often, as here, leave an unsuitable parent with parental responsibility for the children.

The Judge is therefore faced with the dilemma...that, if he makes a care order, the local authority may implement a care plan which he or she may take the view is not in the child or children's best interests. On the other hand, if he makes no order, he may be leaving the child in the care of an irresponsible, and indeed wholly inappropriate parent.

It seems to me that, regrettable though it may seem, the only course he may take is to choose what he considers to be the lesser of two evils. If he has no other route open to him...then that is the unfortunate position he has to face.

It would be a brave judge who refused to make a care order where the threshold condi-tions were satisfied and the child's welfare otherwise demanded it. In practice such cases are rare.[202]

The frustration caused by the limited range of options available to the court where it disagrees with the local authority care plan is exacerbated by the restrictions placed on the court once a care order has been made. Often the problem is not so much that the court disagrees with the plan, but that the plan is incomplete or uncertain. The High Court used to have the power to monitor implementation of care plans and, if necessary, give directions to the local authority regarding a child within its care. The court could also bring a case back before the court for further consideration and review. The CA 1989 removed these powers.[203] Under the current legislative scheme, once the care order has been made respon-sibility for the child, save for on issues relating to contact, passes to the local authority.[204] Decisions regarding the implementation of the care plan, including making major changes such as abandoning attempts to rehabilitate the child to her family, are regarded as falling

---

[200] *Re D and K (Care plan: Twin track planning)* [1999] 2 FLR 872.
[201] *Re K* [2007] EWHC 393, [15].
[202] Ibid., [21].
[203] S 100(2). See *Re J (Minors) (Care: Care Plan)* [1994] 1 FLR 253, 258.
[204] See below at 12.5.7.

within the discretion of the local authority. Consequently, the only way in which the decision of a local authority can be challenged is by bringing an application to discharge the care order under s 39 of the CA 1989, applying for judicial review, or, if there has been a violation of the child's or the parents' rights under Articles 6 or 8 ECHR, by bringing an application under ss 7 and 8 of the HRA 1998.[205]

Attempts to find a mechanism by which the courts could retain greater control over the local authority's implementation of the care plan have ultimately proved unsuccessful. It was held in *Kent County Council v C* that the court could not add a direction to the care order providing for the continued involvement of the GAL so that the guardian could monitor the local authority's progress towards rehabilitation and, if appropriate, apply for contact with the parents to be terminated.[206] Similarly, it has been held to be inappropriate for the court to adjourn questions of contact with a view to keeping an attempt at rehabilitation under review.[207] The same approach has been taken to the use of interim orders when employed as a means of monitoring or supervising the local authority. It was accepted in *Re J (Minors) (Care: Care Plan)* that a court could refuse to make a final care order if it was not satisfied about 'material aspects of the care plan'.[208] However, Wall J emphasized that interim orders should only be used with caution and should not be used 'as a means of exercising the now defunct supervisory role of the court'.[209] He went on to point out that the court should not be unduly concerned if there were continuing elements of doubt and uncertainty about the plan.

Re J (Minors) (Care: Care Plan) [1994] 1 FLR 253, 264–5 (Fam Div)

WALL J:

I derive from the statute and the authorities the proposition that whilst the court plainly retains the power to adjourn the hearing of what is intended as the final hearing of an application of a care order and to make interim care orders on such an adjournment, such a course is only to be adopted…where all the facts are not as clearly known to the court as can be hoped…

[T]here are cases (of which this is one) in which the action which requires to be taken in the interests of children necessarily involves steps into the unknown and that provided the court is satisfied that the local authority is alert to the difficulties which may arise in the execution of the care plan, the function of the court is not to seek to oversee the plan but to entrust its execution to the local authority.

The courts' inability to monitor or review the implementation of the care plan has been a matter of considerable concern amongst the judiciary. This concern is based on more than simple indignation at the court's inability to control matters once a certain point has been reached. In recent years, worrying evidence has emerged as to the number of children said to be 'lost in care'.[210] These are children for whom no clear care plan has ever been in place or for whom the care plan has simply failed or been forgotten. As was acknowledged by Lord

---

[205] *Re M (Care: Challenging Decisions by Local Authority)* [2001] 2 FLR 1300.
[206] [1993] Fam 57, 62.
[207] *Re S (A Minor) (Care: Contact order)* [1994] 2 FLR 222.
[208] Approving *C v Solihull Metropolitan Council* [1993] 1 FLR 290.
[209] See also *Re L (Sexual abuse: Standard of proof)* [1996] 1 FLR 116, 124–6.
[210] See, e g, Waterhouse (2000) and *Re F; F v Lambeth London Borough Council* [2002] 1 FLR 217.

Nicholls in *Re S (Minors) (Care order: Implementation of care plan)*, these children are grossly let down by the system.[211] Concern about the number of children 'lost in care' prompted calls across the legal profession for the introduction of better judicial safeguards for children in care. It was against this background that *Re S (Minors) (Care order: Implementation of care plan)* came before the House of Lords.

It was contended in *Re S* that the current legislative scheme risked infringing the ECHR rights of the parents and their children in two important respects: (i) by the inability of the court to defer making a care order until uncertainties in the care plan had been resolved; and (ii) by the lack of judicial safeguards once a care order had been made to protect against a local authority failing to implement the plan. The Court of Appeal held that two adjustments were necessary. First, *Re J (Minors) (Care: Care Plan)* (above) needed to be reconsidered to give the judge a much wider discretion to make an interim care order 'where the care plan seems inchoate or where the passage of a relatively brief period of time seems bound to see the fulfilment of some event or process vital to planning and deciding the future'.[212] Second, when formulating the care plan, the local authority, in collaboration with the other professionals and the court, would identify the plan's 'essential milestones' which would then be elevated to a 'starred status'. Failure to achieve a starred milestone within a reasonable timeframe would reactivate the involvement of the other professionals: at the minimum, the local authority would have to inform the children's guardian of the failure in the care plan and either the local authority or the guardian would be able to bring the case back before the court for further directions.[213] This second proposal constituted a quite radical revision of the division of power and responsibilities between the local authority and the court once a care order had been made. Not surprisingly, therefore, the case was appealed to the House of Lords. Lord Nicholls' judgment makes clear the rationale behind the current division of responsibility between the local authority and the court.

Re S (Minors) (Care order: Implementation of care plan); Re W (Minors) (Care order: adequacy of care plan) [2002] UKHL 10

LORD NICHOLLS:

25. . . . The [Children] Act delineated the boundary of responsibility with complete clarity. Where a care order is made the responsibility for the child's care is with the authority rather than the court. The court retains no supervisory role, monitoring the authority's discharge of its responsibilities. That was the intention of Parliament . . .

27. . . . The change brought about by the Children Act gave effect to a policy decision on the appropriate division of responsibilities between the courts and local authorities . . . The particular strength of the courts lies in the resolution of disputes: its ability to hear all sides of a case, to decide issues of fact and law, and to make a firm decision on a particular issue at a particular time. But a court cannot have day to day responsibility for a child. The court cannot deliver the services which may best serve a child's needs. Unlike a local authority, a court does not have close, personal and continuing knowledge of the child. The court cannot respond with immediacy and informality to practical problems and changed circumstances as they arise. Supervision by the court would encourage 'drift' in decision making, a perennial problem in children cases.

---

[211] *Re S (Minors) (Care order: Implementation of care plan); Re W (Minors) (Care order: adequacy of care plan)* [2002] UKHL 10, [29]–[30].

[212] *Re W and B; Re W (Care Plan)* [2001] EWCA Civ 757, [29] (per Thorpe LJ).

[213] Ibid., [30].

> Nor does a court have the task of managing the financial and human resources available to a local authority for dealing with all children in need in its area. The authority must manage these resources in the best interests of all the children for whom it is responsible.
>
> 28. The Children Act, embodying what I have described as a cardinal principle, represents the assessment made by Parliament of the division of responsibility which would best promote the interests of children within the overall care system. The court operates as the gateway into care, and makes the necessary care order when the threshold conditions are satisfied and the court considers a care order would be in the best interests of the child. That is the responsibility of the court. Thereafter the court has no continuing role in relation to the care order. Then it is the responsibility of the local authority to decide how the child should be cared for.

Lord Nicholls begins his judgment by considering the Court of Appeal's more radical innovation: the introduction of starred care plans. Assuming the CA 1989 to be inconsistent with Articles 6 and 8 ECHR (see later discussion), the first question addressed is whether in accordance with s 3 of the HRA 1998 it is possible to interpret the legislation in such a way as to introduce this new starring scheme:

> 39....I am unable to agree that the court's introduction of a 'starring system' can be justified as a legitimate exercise in interpretation of the Children Act in accordance with section 3 of the Human Rights Act...
>
> 41....For present purposes it is sufficient to say that a meaning which departs substantially from a fundamental feature of an Act of Parliament is likely to have crossed the boundary between interpretation and amendment. This is especially so where the departure has important practical repercussions which the court is not equipped to evaluate...
>
> 42....Parliament entrusted to local authorities, not the courts, the responsibility for looking after children who are the subject of care orders. To my mind the new starring system would depart substantially from this principle...
>
> 43....[T]he starring system is inconsistent in an important respect with the scheme of the Children Act. It would constitute amendment of the Children Act, not its interpretation. It would have far-reaching practical ramifications for local authorities and their care of children. The starring system would not come free from additional administrative work and expense. It would be likely to have a material effect on authorities' allocation of scarce financial and other resources. This in turn would affect authorities' discharge of their responsibilities to other children. Moreover, the need to produce a formal report whenever a care plan is significantly departed from, and then await the outcome of any subsequent court proceedings, would affect the whole manner in which authorities discharge, and are able to discharge, their parental responsibilities.
>
> 44. These are matters for decision by Parliament, not the courts. It is impossible for a court to attempt to evaluate these ramifications or assess what would be the views of Parliament if changes are needed.

Lord Nicholls went on to consider whether the current legislative scheme violated the ECHR, concluding that the CA 1989 per se was not incompatible with Article 8:

> 54. Clearly, if matters go seriously awry, the manner in which a local authority discharges its parental responsibilities to a child in its care may violate the rights of the child or his parents under this article [8]. The local authority's intervention in the life of the child, justified at the

outset when the care order was made, may cease to be justifiable under article 8(2). Sedley LJ pointed out that a care order from which no good is coming cannot sensibly be said to be pursuing a legitimate aim. A care order which keeps a child away from his family for purposes which, as time goes by, are not being realised will sooner or later become a disproportionate interference with the child's primary article 8 rights…

55. Further, the local authority's decision making process must be conducted fairly and so as to afford due respect to the interests protected by article 8. For instance, the parents should be involved to a degree which is sufficient to provide adequate protection for their interests…

56. However, the possibility that something may go wrong with the local authority's discharge of its parental responsibilities or its decision making processes, and that this would be a violation of article 8 so far as the child or parent is concerned, does not mean that the legislation itself is incompatible, or inconsistent, with article 8…

57. If an authority duly carries out [its] statutory duties, in the ordinary course there should be no question of infringement by the local authority of the article 8 rights of the child or his parents. Questions of infringement are only likely to arise if a local authority fails properly to discharge its statutory responsibilities. Infringement which then occurs is not brought about, in any meaningful sense, by the Children Act. Quite the reverse. Far from the infringement being compelled, or even countenanced, by the provisions of the Children Act, the infringement flows from the local authority's failure to comply with its obligations under the Act. True, it is the Children Act which entrusts responsibility for the child's care to the local authority. But that is not inconsistent with article 8…

58. Where, then, is the inconsistency which is alleged to exist? As I understand it, the principal contention is that the incompatibility lies in the absence from the Children Act of an adequate remedy if a local authority fails to discharge its parental responsibilities properly and, as a direct result, the rights of the child or his parents under article 8 are violated…

59. In my view this line of argument is misconceived. Failure by the state to provide an effective remedy for a violation of article 8 is not itself a violation of article 8. This is self-evident. So, even if the Children Act does fail to provide an adequate remedy, the Act is not for that reason incompatible with article 8. This is the short and conclusive answer to this point.

Lord Nicholls then considered the arguments under Article 6, concluding that as the parents could effectively challenge any decision made by the local authority regarding implementation of the care plan by judicial review or under ss 7 and 8 of the HRA 1998, any potential breach of their Article 6 rights would be more illusory than real.[214] The child's position was more difficult, Lord Nicholls holding that the *child's* inability to bring legal proceedings to challenge any potential breach of Article 8 gave rise to a *possible* incompatibility between the legislative scheme and the child's rights under Article 6:

82. I must note also a difficulty of another type. This concerns the position of young children who have no parent or guardian able and willing to become involved in questioning a care decision made by a local authority. This is an instance of a perennial problem affecting children. A parent may abuse a child. The law may provide a panoply of remedies. But this avails nothing if the problem remains hidden. Depending on the facts, situations of this type

---

[214] *Re S (Minors) (Care order: Implementation of care plan); Re W (Minors) (Care order: adequacy of care plan)* [2002] UKHL 10, [75]–[81]

may give rise to difficulties with Convention rights. The Convention is intended to guarantee rights which are practical and effective. This is particularly so with the right of access to the courts, in view of the prominent place held in a democratic society by the right to a fair trial…The guarantee provided by article 6(1) can hardly be said to be satisfied in the case of a young child who, in practice, has no way of initiating judicial review proceedings to challenge a local authority's decision affecting his civil rights. (In such a case, as already noted, the young child would also lack means of initiating section 7 proceedings to protect his article 8 rights.)

83. My conclusion is that in these respects circumstances might perhaps arise when English law would not satisfy the requirements of article 6(1) regarding some child care decisions made by local authorities. In one or other of the circumstances mentioned above the article 6 rights of a child…are capable of being infringed.

Having found, however, that the failure of the legislative scheme to provide an effective means by which a child could access the court to challenge the local authority's actions gave rise to a *potential* breach of Article 6, Lord Nicholls declined to decide whether this 'lacuna' did in fact render the legislation incompatible with the child's ECHR rights, concluding that it was unnecessary to do so on the particular facts of the case.

Having dealt with the issue of starred care plans, Lord Nicholls moved on to consider whether greater use should be made of interim care orders to bring cases back before the court where the care plan was inchoate or uncertain. Lord Nicholls' judgment clarifies when the use of interim orders is appropriate, arguably slightly extending the circumstances in which they can be made but signalling no major shift in approach from that set down in *Re J (Minors) (care: care plan)*:

90. From a reading of section 38 as a whole it is abundantly clear that the purpose of an interim care order…is to enable the court to safeguard the welfare of a child until such time as the court is in a position to decide whether or not it is in the best interests of the child to make a care order. When that time arrives depends on the circumstances of the case and is a matter for the judgment of the trial judge. That is the general, guiding principle. The corollary to this principle is that an interim care order is not intended to be used as a means by which the court may continue to exercise a supervisory role over the local authority in cases where it is in the best interests of a child that a care order should be made.

91. An interim care order, thus, is a temporary 'holding' measure…

92. When a local authority formulates a care plan in connection with an application for a care order, there are bound to be uncertainties. Even the basic shape of the future life of the child may be far from clear. Over the last ten years problems have arisen about how far courts should go in attempting to resolve these uncertainties before making a care order and passing responsibility to the local authority. Once a final care order is made, the resolution of the uncertainties will be a matter for the authority, not the court.

93. In terms of legal principle one type of uncertainty is straightforward. This is the case where the uncertainty needs to be resolved before the court can decide whether it is in the best interests of the child to make a care order at all…In such a case the court should finally dispose of the matter only when the material facts are as clearly known as can be hoped…

94. More difficult, as a matter of legal principle, are cases where it is obvious that a care order is in the best interests of the child but the immediate way ahead thereafter is unsatisfactorily obscure. These cases exemplify a problem, or a 'tension', inherent in the scheme of the Children Act. What should the judge do when a care order is clearly in the best interests of the child but the judge does not approve of the care plan?…

95. In this context there are sometimes uncertainties whose nature is such that they are suitable for immediate resolution, in whole or in part, by the court in the course of disposing of the care order application. The uncertainty may be of such a character that it can, and should, be resolved so far as possible before the court proceeds to make the care order. Then, a limited period of 'planned and purposeful' delay can readily be justified as the sensible and practical way to deal with an existing problem . . .

97. Frequently the case is on the other side of this somewhat imprecise line. Frequently the uncertainties involved in a care plan will have to be worked out after a care order has been made and while the plan is being implemented . . .

98. . . . Quite apart from known uncertainties, an element of future uncertainty is necessarily inherent in the very nature of a care plan. The best laid plans 'gang aft a-gley'. These are matters for decision by the local authority, if and when they arise. A local authority must always respond appropriately to changes, of varying degrees of predictability, which from time to time are bound to occur after a care order has been made and while the care plan is being implemented. No care plan can ever be regarded as set in stone.

99. Despite all the inevitable uncertainties, when deciding whether to make a care order the court should normally have before it a care plan which is sufficiently firm and particularised for all concerned to have a reasonably clear picture of the likely way ahead for the child for the foreseeable future. The degree of firmness to be expected, as well as the amount of detail in the plan, will vary from case to case depending on how far the local authority can foresee what will be best for the child at that time . . .

100. Cases vary so widely that it is impossible to be more precise about the test to be applied by a court when deciding whether to continue interim relief rather than proceed to make a care order. It would be foolish to attempt to be more precise. One further general point may be noted. When postponing a decision on whether to make a care order a court will need to have in mind the general statutory principle that any delay in determining issues relating to a child's upbringing is likely to prejudice the child's welfare: section 1(2) of the Children Act.

The House of Lords' judgment in *Re S* thus did little to improve the position of children badly let down by the local authority. That is not to say that the House of Lords did not recognize the need for change. Indeed, Lord Nicholls concluded his judgment by urging the legislature to take appropriate steps to address the problem:

106. I must finally make an observation of a general character. In this speech I have sought to explain my reasons for rejecting the Court of Appeal's initiative over starred milestones. I cannot stress too strongly that the rejection of this innovation on legal grounds must not obscure the pressing need for the Government to attend to the serious practical and legal problems identified by the Court of Appeal or mentioned by me. One of the questions needing urgent consideration is whether some degree of court supervision of local authorities' discharge of their parental responsibilities would bring about an overall improvement in the quality of child care provided by local authorities. Answering this question calls for a wider examination than can be undertaken by a court. The judgments of the Court of Appeal in the present case have performed a valuable service in highlighting the need for such an examination to be conducted without delay.

Parliament responded to address the issue of the child's inability to bring proceedings to challenge a local authority's failure to discharge its statutory duties and responsibilities under the care plan by introducing two important amendments.[215] First, the local authority

---

[215] Amendments introduced by the Adoption and Children Act 2002.

is now under a statutory duty to keep the child's care plan under review.[216] Second, in every case the local authority must now appoint an independent reviewing officer (IRO) who will participate in the local authority's six monthly review of the case, monitor the performance of the local authority, and refer the case to Cafcass if it is deemed appropriate to do so.[217] If the child's Article 8 rights are at risk of being infringed by changes to or non-implementation of the care plan, the potential breach should therefore be brought to the attention of a Cafcass officer who will have the responsibility to bring an action in judicial review or under s 7 of the HRA 1998 on the child's behalf. The effectiveness of the IRO system is, however, questionable. Research conducted by Timms and Thoburn for the NSPCC suggests that many young people within the care system have little faith in the IRO to challenge local authority decision-making effectively, lack of power and independence being key concerns.[218] The researchers go on to comment that the fact that 'very few, if any, cases have been referred by IROs to children's guardians since this section was implemented in 2004 does not encourage confidence that the distress and dissatisfaction with contact and placement plans expressed by some…children…will be alleviated by this particular legislative change.'[219]

12.5.6 EFFECT OF A CARE ORDER

The legal effects of a care order are set down in s 33 of the CA 1989. The primary effect of the order is to place a duty on the local authority to receive the child into care and to keep the child in care whilst the order remains in force.[220] A child can be 'in care' but remain living at home.[221] The care order gives the local authority the power to remove the child from the parents without further recourse to the courts, although, except in emergencies, the local authority must provide the parents with proper notice of the decision and involve them fully in the decision-making process.[222] Whilst the care order is in force, the local authority holds parental responsibility. That responsibility is shared with the parents but the local authority has the power to determine the extent to which the parents may exercise it.[223] This means the local authority not only has the right to make day-to-day decisions with respect to the child's upbringing and, where necessary, override the wishes of the parents, but to effectively exclude them from the decision-making process.[224] Any restrictions imposed on the parental responsibility of the parents must be necessary to safeguard and promote the child's welfare.[225] Whilst the child is in care, the local authority must also comply with the substantive and procedural requirements of Article 8.

Re G (Care: Challenge to Local Authority's Decision) [2003] EWHC 551

MUNBY J:

43. The fact that a local authority has parental responsibility for children pursuant to section 33(3)(a) of the Children Act 1989 does not entitle it to take decisions about those children

---

[216] S 26(2)(f).
[217] Ss 26(2)(k) and 26(2A). Review of Children's Cases Regulations 1991, SI 1991/895, reg 2A.
[218] Timms and Thoburn (2006), 168.
[219] Ibid.
[220] S 33(1).
[221] Placement of Children with Parents etc Regulations 1991, SI 1991/893.
[222] Ibid., reg 11. See *G v N County Council* [2009] 1 FLR 774, [20], [29]–[30].
[223] S 33(3)(a).
[224] *Re P (Children Act 1989, ss 22 and 26: local authority compliance)* [2000] 2 FLR 910.
[225] S 33(4).

without reference to, or over the heads of, the children's parents. A local authority, even if clothed with the authority of a care order, is not entitled to make significant changes in the care plan, or to change the arrangements under which the children are living, let alone to remove the children from home if they are living with their parents, without properly involving the parents in the decision-making process and without giving the parents a proper opportunity to make their case before a decision is made. After all, the fact that the local authority also has parental responsibility does not deprive the parents of their parental responsibility.

44. A local authority can lawfully exercise parental responsibility for a child only in a manner consistent with the substantive *and procedural* requirements of article 8. There is nothing in section 33(3)(b) of the Act that entitles a local authority to act in breach of article 8. On the contrary, section 6(1) of the 1998 Act requires a local authority to exercise its powers under both section 33(3)(a) and section 33(3)(b) of the 1989 Act in a manner consistent with both the substantive and the procedural requirements of article 8.

The CA 1989 imposes further limits on the local authority's parental responsibility. The local authority cannot: (i) cause the child to be brought up in a different religion; (ii) refuse or consent to the child's adoption; or (iii) appoint a guardian.[226] More generally, whilst a care order is in force no one can cause the child to be known by a new surname or remove the child from the jurisdiction without either the written consent of everyone holding parental responsibility or the court's leave.[227]

A care order can be made for a specified period or until further order.

12.5.7 CONTACT WITH A CHILD IN CARE

If the local authority plan is to try and rehabilitate the child with the parents, it is obviously important that the child's familial relationships are sustained through generous provision of contact. Where, however, the local authority's plan is to place the child with a permanent alternative family, the benefits of maintaining contact are more questionable. It used to be the dominant professional view that contact in such circumstances was unhelpful, it being believed that the continued presence of the birth family may prevent the child bonding with the new family and destabilize the placement.[228] That view has changed as the importance of the child maintaining positive links with the birth family has been recognized, not just whilst the child is in care, but in the longer term if the child is adopted.

Re E (Children in Care: Contact) [1994] 1 FCR 584, 594 (CA)

Lord Justice Simon Brown:

[Even] when the s. 31 criteria are satisfied, contact may well be of singular importance to the long-term welfare of the child: firstly in giving the child the security of knowing that his parents love him and are interested in his welfare; secondly, by avoiding any damaging sense of loss to the child in seeing himself abandoned by his parents; thirdly, by enabling the child to commit himself to the substitute family with the seal of approval of the natural parents; and,

---

[226] S 33(6).
[227] S 33(7).
[228] This is discussed in greater detail in the context of adoption. See below at pp 922–3 and 948–60.

> fourthly, by giving the child the necessary sense of family and personal identity. Contact, if maintained, is capable of reinforcing and increasing the chances of success of a permanent placement, whether on a long-term fostering basis or by adoption.

This marked change in professional attitudes towards contact has been reinforced by the European Court of Human Rights. The Court has stated repeatedly that terminating contact between parent and child constitutes a grave interference with Article 8 as it effectively ends any meaningful relationship between them. Any 'radical' decision by the national courts to terminate contact will therefore be subjected to the most 'anxious scrutiny', only being justified in exceptional circumstances.[229]

The importance of contact between a child in care and members of the child's family is firmly entrenched within the CA 1989. The local authority is under a general duty to promote contact between a looked after child and the child's parents.[230] This is reinforced by s 34(1) which provides that the local authority shall allow 'reasonable contact' between them. Initially it will be for the local authority to determine what constitutes reasonable contact. However, one of the most important policy changes enshrined in the CA 1989 was to remove the local authority's almost unfettered authority over contact decisions.[231] Consequently, if there is disagreement over the level of contact, an application can be made to the court for a defined contact order.[232] In determining the application the child's welfare is the paramount consideration.[233] The court also has the power to act of its own motion.[234] Before making a care order the court must consider the local authority's proposed arrangements for contact.[235]

The most important change introduced by the CA 1989 was to remove the local authority's power to terminate contact. That power now rests with the court. The local authority can only prohibit contact between the child and a person specified in s 34(1) for a maximum of seven days if it is an emergency and the local authority is satisfied that it is necessary to safeguard and promote the child's welfare.[236] In all other cases, the local authority must apply to the court under s 34(4) for permission to terminate contact. It is clear from the case law that the court must take this jurisdiction seriously and not simply abdicate its responsibility to the local authority. Thus, it is inappropriate for the court to give the local authority general authorization to terminate or suspend contact should it consider it necessary.[237] This principle applies even if the local authority is certain that at some point in the future contact will need to be terminated.[238]

The court's jurisdiction over contact constitutes an important exception to the principle that once the care order has been made, responsibility for the child passes to the local authority. This exception marks the importance now placed on maintaining contact

---

[229] *S and G v Italy* (App No 39221/98 and 41963/98, ECHR) (2000), [170].
[230] Sch 2, para 15.
[231] For a brief account of the approach to contact prior to the CA 1989 see *Re B (Minors) (Termination of contact: paramount consideration)* [1993] Fam 301, 306–8.
[232] For the test to be applied on an application for leave, see *Re W (Care proceedings: Leave to apply)* [2004] EWHC 3342.
[233] *Re P (Minors) (Contact with Children in Care)* [1993] 2 FLR 156, 160.
[234] S 34(5).
[235] S 34(11).
[236] S 34(6).
[237] *Re L (Sexual abuse: Standard of proof)* [1996] 1 FLR 116; *Re S (children) (termination of contact)* [2004] EWCA Civ 1397.
[238] *Re H (children) (termination of contact)* [2005] EWCA Civ 318.

between a child and the birth family. It raises the possibility, however, of conflict between the local authority's care plan and the court's view on contact, which may in turn reflect a more fundamental disagreement between them as to the child's long-term future. The issue arose in *Re B (Minors) (Termination of contact: paramount consideration)*. The local authority applied to terminate contact between two children and their mother in order to place the children for adoption. The GAL opposed the application, concerned that the possibility of rehabilitation with the mother had not been properly assessed. The Court of Appeal upheld the GAL's appeal, making it clear that where the local authority and the court disagree, the court must do what it considers to be in the child's best interests, even if continuing contact is inconsistent with the local authority's care plan.

Re B (Minors) (Termination of contact: paramount consideration) [1993] Fam 301, 310–12 (CA)

BUTLER-SLOSS LJ:

A section 34 application is clearly a substantive application in which the court is determining a question with respect to the upbringing of the child....

At the moment that an application comes before the court, at whichever tier, the court has a duty to apply section 1, which states that when a court determines any question with respect to the upbringing of a child, the child's welfare shall be the court's paramount consideration...

Contact applications generally fall into two main categories: those which ask for contact as such, and those which are attempts to set aside the care order itself. In the first category there is no suggestion that the applicant wishes to take over the care of the child and the issue of contact often depends on whether contact would frustrate long-term plans for the child in a substitute home, such as adoption, where continuing contact may not be for the long-term welfare of the child. The presumption of contact, which has to be for the benefit of the child, has always to be balanced against the long-term welfare of the child and, particularly, where he will live in the future. Contact must not be allowed to destabilise or endanger the arrangements for the child and in many cases the plans for the child will be decisive of the contact application. There may also be cases where the parent is having satisfactory contact with the child and there are no long-term plans or those plans do not appear to the court to preclude some future contact. The proposals of the local authority, based on their appreciation of the best interests of the child, must command the greatest respect and consideration from the court, but Parliament has given to the court, and not to the local authority, the duty to decide on contact between the child and those named in section 34(1). Consequently, the court may have the task of requiring the local authority to justify their long-term plans to the extent only that those plans exclude contact between parent and child. In the second category, contact applications may be made by parents by way of another attempt to obtain the return of the children. In such a case the court is obviously entitled to take into account the failure to apply to discharge the care order, and in the majority of cases the court will have little difficulty in coming to the conclusion that the applicant cannot demonstrate that contact with a view to rehabilitation with the parent is a viable proposition at that stage, particularly if it had already been rejected at the earlier hearing when the child was placed in care. The task for the parents will be too great and the court would be entitled to assume that the plans of the local authority to terminate contact are for the welfare of the child and are not to be frustrated by inappropriate contact with a view to the remote possibility, at some future date, of rehabilitation.

But in all cases the welfare section has to be considered, and the local authority have the task of justifying the cessation of contact. There may also be unusual cases where either the local authority have not made effective plans or there has been considerable delay in implementing them and a parent, who has previously been found by a court unable or unwilling to care for the child so that a care order has been made, comes back upon the scene as a possible future primary carer. If the local authority with a care order decide not to consider that parent on the new facts, [counsel for the parents] argued that it is for the court, with the enhanced jurisdiction of the Act of 1989, to consider whether even at this late stage there should be some investigation of the proposals of the parent, with the possibility of reconsidering the local authority plans. [Counsel for the local authority] argued that the court cannot go behind the long-term plans of the local authority unless they were acting capriciously or were otherwise open to scrutiny by way of judicial review.

I unhesitatingly reject the local authority argument. As I have already said, their plan has to be given the greatest possible consideration by the court and it is only in the unusual case that a parent will be able to convince the court, the onus being firmly on the parent, that there has been such a change of circumstances as to require further investigation and reconsideration of the local authority plan. If, however, a court were unable to intervene, it would make a nonsense of the paramountcy of the welfare of the child which is the bedrock of the Act, and would subordinate it to the administrative decision of the local authority in a situation where the court is seized of the contact issue. That cannot be right.

But I would emphasise that this is not an open door to courts reviewing the plans of local authorities.

This decision thus makes some limited inroads into the local authority's otherwise unfettered control over the content and implementation of the care plan. It is clear that, although unusual, in the second category of case (where the dispute over contact is really a dispute over whether the child should be rehabilitated with the parents), the court has the jurisdiction to order contact with a view to rehabilitation even if the local authority is thereby forced to reconsider its long term plan to place the child permanently outside the family. Similarly, in the first category of case (where the parent is not seeking to have the child returned to his or her care), although Butler-Sloss LJ recognizes that contact should not be allowed to destabilize or jeopardize the local authority's long term plan—an outcome which will rarely be in the child's best interests—the judge may nevertheless test the local authority's position and can refuse to terminate contact where it is not satisfied that the care plan and contact are necessarily inconsistent.[239] This has subsequently been reiterated by the Court of Appeal in *Re E (Children in care: contact)*. The local authority wished to terminate contact with a view to placing the children in a closed adoption, the GAL and the expert psychiatrist both supported continuing contact. The Court of Appeal upheld the appeal against the judge's order which had authorized the local authority to terminate contact:

Re E (Children in care: contact) [1994] 1 FCR 584, 593–4 (CA)

Lord Justice Simon Brown:

[I]f on a s. 34(4) application the Judge concludes that the benefits of contact outweigh the disadvantages of disrupting any of the local authority's long-term plans which are inconsistent with such contact, then, slow and reluctant though no doubt the Judge would be to reach that conclusion, he must give effect to it by refusing the local authority's application to

---

[239] See also *Berkshire County Council v B* [1997] 1 FLR 171 and *Re K* [2007] EWHC 393, [24], [26].

terminate the contact. That is not to arrogate to himself the task of monitoring or scrutinizing the local authority's plan. That would be impermissible. Rather it is simply to discharge the duty which Parliament by s. 34(4) has laid upon the Judge.

Had the Judge fully recognized the true nature of his task, he could not have made the order he did at the time he did. Rather he must inevitably have recognized that it was premature here to authorize a termination of face-to-face contact. The local authority had not sufficiently, if indeed at all, investigated in relation to this individual case, rather than with regard to adoption generally, the possibility of finding suitable prospective adopters who would accept a degree of face-to-face contact with the parents. Given, as the Judge accepted, the desirability in this case of such face-to-face contact, given that it could never truly threaten any future placement, and given the weight of evidence suggesting the children's special need for it, there really should have been such an investigation.

Section 34 ensures that any attempt by the local authority to terminate contact between parent and child is subjected to independent judicial scrutiny. The court is thus very much cast in the role of safeguarding and defending the parents' rights. Indeed, if necessary, the court can attach a penal notice to the order and enforce it against the local authority by way of committal.[240] However, it is not necessarily always the case that it is the court that is supportive of contact in the face of the local authority's opposition, raising the question whether the court has jurisdiction to terminate contact against the local authority's wishes. Early authority suggested the court could make an order for 'no contact', although it was generally inadvisable as the local authority could simply ignore the order and reach a separate agreement with the parents.[241] More recently, the Court of Appeal has held that, given the clear legislative objectives behind s 34, the court has no such jurisdiction to make an order prohibiting contact.[242]

12.5.8 EFFECT OF A SUPERVISION ORDER

A supervision order provides for a much lower level of intervention into the family than a care order. The effect of the supervision order is to place the child, not the parent, under 'supervision'.

Children Act 1989, s 35

(1) While a supervision order is in force it shall be the duty of the supervisor—

  (a) to advise, assist and befriend the supervised child;

  (b) to take such steps as are reasonably necessary to give effect to the order; and

  (c) where—

    (i) the order is not wholly complied with; or

    (ii) the supervisor considers that the order may no longer be necessary,

  to consider whether or not to apply to the court for its variation or discharge.

---

[240] *Local Authority v HP, MB and P-B (Children)* [2009] EWCA Civ 143, [45], [50].
[241] See *Kent County Council v C* [1993] 1 FLR 308, 311 and *Re D and H (Care: Termination of Contact)* [1997] 1 FLR 841.
[242] *Re W (A Child) (Parental Contact: Prohibition)* [2000] Fam 130, 136–7.

Further provisions with respect to supervision orders are found in Sch 3, Parts I and II. Conditions cannot be attached to a supervision order.[243] The supervision order may, however, require the supervised child to comply with certain directions given by the supervisor. This may include directions that the child reside at a particular place for a particular period of time; keep the supervisor informed of any change in address; allow the supervisor to visit him or her; attend certain appointments; or participate in various activities.[244] The supervision order may also require the child to submit to medical or psychiatric examination.[245] If the child is of sufficient understanding, the child must consent to the inclusion of such a provision in the order.[246] The supervision order (not the supervisor) may also require the child to submit to certain specified psychiatric or medical treatment.[247] The consent of a competent child to such treatment is again required.[248] The supervision order may also include a requirement that a 'responsible person' take all reasonable steps to ensure that the supervised child complies with these directions.[249] The 'responsible person' may also be directed to participate in certain activities, to keep the supervisor informed of the responsible person's and the child's address, and to allow the supervisor to have reasonable contact with the child.[250] A 'responsible person' is defined as 'any person who has parental responsibility for the child and any other person with whom the child is living'.[251] As with a child of sufficient understanding, the 'responsible person' must consent to the inclusion of these provisions.[252]

In contrast to the position under a care order, it has been held that the children's guardian may continue to act until the supervision order has ceased to have effect.[253] The guardian's role will differ depending on the circumstances of each case but may include monitoring the implementation of the order in order to ensure its goals are being met.[254] The hope is that the continued engagement of the guardian can give the supervision order 'added teeth'.

A supervision order can only be made initially for a period of up to 12 months.[255] The order can be extended for further specified periods not exceeding three years in total from the date on which it was first made.[256] The problems caused by the limited duration of supervision orders were raised in *T v Wakefield Metropolitan District Council*.[257] In order to avoid the statutory restrictions, the judge made the order for twelve months and then immediately extended it for a further two years to give the maximum protection of three years. Whilst acknowledging the pragmatism and commonsense behind the judge's order, the Court of Appeal held that such an approach was impermissible as it was clearly artificial for the court to make the order and then immediately extend it, thereby circumventing the clear statutory

---

[243] *Re S (Care or supervision order)* [1996] 1 FLR 753 and *Re V (A Minor) (Care or supervision order)* [1996] 2 FCR 555, 564. Similarly, the court has no jurisdiction to accept undertakings on the making of a supervision order: *Re B (Supervision order: parental undertaking)* [1996] 1 FLR 676.
[244] Sch 3, Part I, paras 2 and 8.
[245] Sch 3, Part I, para 4.
[246] Ibid., para 4(4).
[247] Ibid., para 5.
[248] Ibid., para 5(5).
[249] Ibid., para 3(1)(a) and (b).
[250] Ibid., paras 3(1)(c), 3(3) and Part II, para 8(2).
[251] Ibid., Part I, para 1.
[252] Ibid., para 3(1).
[253] *Re MH (A child) and Re SB and MB (children)* [2001] 2 FLR 1334.
[254] Ibid., [35].
[255] CA 1989, Sch 3, Part II, para 6(1).
[256] Ibid., para 6(3).
[257] [2008] EWCA Civ 199.

language.[258] The Court of Appeal did, however, confirm that on an application for the original order to be extended, it could be extended for a full two-year period rather than being limited to the 12-month maximum period of the initial order.[259]

An application to extend a supervision order is determined on the basis of the child's welfare.[260] It is not necessary for the local authority to prove that the threshold conditions still apply.[261] If after the three-year period has expired the local authority is of the view that the supervision order needs to remain in place, it must make a fresh application under s 31 at which the threshold conditions will again need to be proved to the satisfaction of the court.[262]

When is a supervision order appropriate?

From the point of view of the parents, a supervision order obviously has a number of advantages over a care order. The order is time-limited to an absolute maximum of three years, during which time the child remains living at home. The decision-making capacity of the local authority is severely limited because it does not acquire parental responsibility, and although various obligations can be imposed on the parents, their consent and cooperation is required.[263] The entirely voluntary nature of the parents' participation makes enforcement of a supervision order extremely difficult. The only sanction for non-compliance is for the supervisor to return to court to apply to vary or discharge the order or to issue a fresh application for a care order.[264]

Perhaps the most important limitation on the power of the local authority under a supervision order is that it does not have the authority to remove a child from home should the situation deteriorate and the immediate removal of the child be deemed necessary. In such circumstances, the local authority has to face the delay, expense, and inconvenience of returning to court to apply for a care order or emergency protection order. These restrictions can compromise the local authority's ability to protect the child, making a care order, from their perspective, considerably more advantageous.

Re S (J) (A Minor) (Care or Supervision Order) [1993] 2 FCR 193, 228–31 (Fam Div)

His Honour Judge Coningsby, Q.C.:

[T]he power to remove...—and, indeed, the duty to remove—may occur in circumstances which are not precisely the same as those which would apply to an emergency protection order. The local authority could remove the child under a care order simply because a man moved back into the home who it was considered was undesirable to be in the home, or it could remove the child because the child was not thriving...These things might or might not be sufficient to enable the local authority to go to court and get an emergency protection order. It might be difficult to amass the necessary evidence to do it immediately. Some of those areas...might actually be quite difficult to establish in terms of evidence for the

---

258 Ibid., [18].
259 Ibid., [19].
260 *Re A (Supervision order: extension)* [1995] 1 WLR 482, 486.
261 Ibid.
262 Ibid., 485–6.
263 *Leicestershire County Council v G* [1994] 2 FLR 329.
264 *Re V (A Minor) (Care or supervision order)* [1996] 2 FCR 555, 565.

purposes of an emergency protection order. So I do not accept that the existence of the emergency protection order procedure equates with the wide power which is available to a local authority which has parental responsibility, has its duty under s. 22 and has its duty under the Regulations to remove a child when it is no longer considered to be safe. I am satisfied that the power to remove under the care order procedure is significantly better...

A more significant point is that if I make a care order there will be no recourse to the court if and when it is necessary to remove [the child]. I have already indicated the advantages of not having to come back to court in that situation. But, of course, what is suggested is that it may be a disadvantage because it might be that the local authority would step in too quickly and would remove the child in circumstances where it ought not to do so, and that the court could act as a restraining influence in such a situation....I should assume for the purposes of this decision that the local authority will undertake its obligations under the Act correctly. I do not think it would be right for me to assume that the local authority would jump in too quickly or would take into account wrong considerations or not properly consider the position of the parents.

As the care order confers parental responsibility on the local authority, it not only enables the local authority to remove the child from the parents without the cost and delay of returning to court, it is able to control and monitor the child's welfare much more effectively. A care order can also protect the child over a longer period of time. Unlike a supervision order which is time-limited to three years, a care order remains in force until the court orders otherwise,[265] vesting much greater control in the court as to when the protective measures in place for the child can be safely lifted.[266] A care order may therefore be felt to be more appropriate where it is believed the child will continue to be at risk for a number of years or where it is believed the risk of abuse will be particularly high as the child reaches a certain age.[267] It has also been suggested that a care order is advantageous because of the additional *duties* and *responsibilities* imposed on the local authority.[268]

Re S (J) (A Minor) (Care or Supervision Order) [1993] 2 FCR 193, 223–6 (Fam Div)

His Honour Judge Coningsby, Q.C.:

Then there is a very important provision—s 22...[A]s soon as a child is in care it is the duty of the local authority to safeguard the welfare of the child; in other words, to keep the child safe. So, that is a duty which springs into operation when a care order is made but it is not a duty which is present in the supervision order situation...

When one compares with [the duty under s 22] the arrangements for supervision, one looks at s. 35(1) of the Act...[A]s I understand it, there are no Regulations under this section. So, the obligation is to operate the supervision order to make it work and that is all. There is

---

[265] *Re D (A Minor)* [1993] 2 FLR 423, 429.

[266] *Re D (A Minor) (Care or supervision order)* [1993] 2 FLR 423, 429. Note, however, that it was held by the Court of Appeal in *Re T (A Child)* [2009] EWCA Civ 121, [63], that where the judge has decided rehabilitation with the parents is appropriate and there is no suggestion that the child will need to be urgently removed (thus making the case eminently suitable for a supervision order), it is not for the judge to decide how long the protective regime needs to be in place: that is something to be left to the discretion of the local authority when it comes to decide whether or not it should apply for the supervision order to be extended.

[267] *Re T (A Minor) (Care or supervision order)* [1994] 1 FLR 103.

[268] See above at 12.3.3.

not that obligation under s. 22 to safeguard/keep safe the child. That obligation does not pass to the local authority. It remains with the mother in this case: the only person with parental responsibility.

That is a fundamental difference between these two orders. In the one case it is the local authority which has to undertake the safeguarding of the child, in the other case it is the mother.

Looking at this case: should I leave it to the mother with all the pressures that she is under to keep safe this child? Can I be sure that she will do it? . . .

It is quite a different concept to be supervising the mother in her keeping safe of the child on the one hand and, on the other hand, the social worker actually knowing that he or she has got to make that decision literally on a day to day basis to keep safe the child.

We tend to look at supervision orders and care orders under the same umbrella because the threshold criteria for the coming into operation of the two is the same. But when we actually look at the content of the two orders we find that they are wholly and utterly different. This is because of s. 22 and because of the passing of parental responsibility. Supervision should not in any sense be seen as a sort of watered down version of care. It is wholly different. . . .

The perceived inadequacies of a supervision order led to a number of cases in which the appeal court overturned a supervision order in favour of a care order.[269] However, some of these perceived inadequacies have been questioned and the benefits of proceeding under a supervision order emphasized—not least of which is that, as a less interventionist measure, a supervision order will often constitute a more proportionate response to concerns about the child.[270] Lady Hale when sitting in the lower courts challenged many of the arguments raised in favour of making a care order:

Re O (Minors) (Care or Supervision Order) [1997] 2 FCR 17, 22–5 (Fam Div)

Mrs Justice Hale J:

It is accepted by all the parties before this court that the court should begin with a preference for the less interventionist rather than the more interventionist approach. This should be considered to be in the better interests of the children, again unless there are cogent reasons to the contrary.

The justices in this case referred to three benefits of a care order over a supervision order, which appear to be taken from the case of *Re S (J)*. Firstly, they say that a care order is unlimited in time . . . and requires an application to be made to the court for its discharge or alteration to a supervision order. That, of course, is correct, but they go on to say: "This, we feel, gives the court an on-going opportunity to assess the care and welfare of these children. This situation does not arise with a supervision order". In fact, that is the reverse of the case. Under a care order, apart from questions of contact between the children and significant people in their lives, the court cedes all control over what is to happen to the children to the local authority; the court cannot assess the care and welfare of these children; it has to trust the local authority to do so. A supervision order, on the other hand, is one in which the local

---

[269] *Re T (A minor) (Care or supervision order)* [1994] 1 FLR 103; *Re S (care or supervision order)* [1996] 1 FLR 753; *Re V (A Minor) (Care or supervision order)* [1996] 2 FCR 555; and *Re S(J) (A Minor) (Care or Supervision Order)* [1993] 2 FCR 193.

[270] *Re O (a child) (supervision order: future harm)* [2001] EWCA Civ 16, [27]–[28].

authority will have to return to the court for an extension, or indeed for a care order, should things not go well. That in itself is an important feature of a supervision order rather than a care order, because it has to be borne in mind that a care order gives the local authority the power to remove any or all of these children from their home without resort to a court...

[The justices] also failed to address the issue of how best to develop and maintain a working relationship with the parents... There will be cases in which a care order may be the only way of achieving this; there will be other cases in which a supervision order is going to be the better approach, not least because the parents will perceive it as less heavy handed, and this may be helpful rather than the reverse.

Oxfordshire County Council v B [1998] 3 FCR 521, 529–30 (Fam Div)

HALE J:

[There is] a further reason why it might be thought preferable to place parental responsibility on the local authority. It gives the local authority specific duties in relation to the particular child or children involved, duties which may be thought to go beyond the general duties to the community of children in need in their area which are set out in Sch 2 to the 1989 Act.

It would be unfortunate indeed if an order that were not otherwise justified in the interests of the children were justified on the basis that it was necessary in order to oblige a local authority to fulfil their statutory responsibilities towards children in need. This would seem to be imposing an order upon the children which was not in their best interests and imposing an order on the parents that was an unjustified intervention in their relationship with their children for a purpose for which that order was not, on the face of it, designed. If local authorities fall short in the performance of their statutory obligations there are other remedies available which, on the face of it, would be more appropriate than to choose a form of order which is not in the best interests of the individual children with whom the court is concerned. I am, therefore, somewhat concerned that the reasons given for making a care order appear to place some considerable weight upon the encouragement that it would give to the local authority to maintain the level of intervention and support which had been established...

Particularly in light of the clear requirements of the ECHR, the courts may now be more willing to protect a child under the auspices of a supervision order than earlier case law suggests.

12.5.9 LEAVING CARE

The discharge and variation of care and supervision orders is dealt with under s 39. A care or supervision order may be discharged on application by the local authority/supervisor, the child, or any person who has parental responsibility for the child.[271] An individual who is affected by a condition or requirement imposed by a supervision order may also apply for its variation or discharge.[272] In determining the application, the court applies a simple welfare test.[273] Where a care order is in force, the court can substitute a supervision order

---

[271] S 39(1)–(2). It was confirmed in *Re A (Care: Discharge application by child)* [1995] 1 FLR 599 that the child does not require leave to bring an application.

[272] S 39(3), (3A), and (3B).

[273] *Re S (Discharge of care order)* [1995] 2 FLR 639.

without first having to re-establish that the threshold conditions are met.[274] The making of a residence order, special guardianship order, or adoption order will also have the automatic effect of discharging a care order.[275]

Sadly, for many children the route out of local authority care will not be by way of the discharge of the care order because they are returning home or because they have successfully been adopted. For many children, the care order will simply cease to have effect because they have grown up and have left the care of the local authority. As we have seen, young adults leaving care are exceptionally vulnerable.[276] Most have a poor educational background, little prospect of employment, and poor coping skills. Few have a family on whom they can rely for help and support. Adjusting to a life of independence outside the care system is very difficult for these young people. In recognition of this, the CA 1989 was amended by the Children (Leaving Care) Act 2000 to increase substantially the duties and responsibilities on local authorities to provide assistance and support to looked after children or formerly looked after children who have been in local authority care for a specified period of time.[277] The support now provided, depending on the child's particular status, may include the appointment of a personal advisor, the preparation of a pathway plan, advice and assistance (including financial support) for young people undertaking education, training and employment, and the provision of, or assistance with the cost of obtaining, suitable accommodation.[278]

ONLINE RESOURCE CENTRE

A more detailed discussion of the leaving care provisions can be found on the Online Resource Centre.

12.6 EMERGENCY PROTECTION UNDER PART V

As should be evident, it may be many months before care proceedings are finally resolved. Pending the final hearing, the court may need to take interim steps to protect the child. In serious cases of abuse it often becomes necessary for the local authority to intervene as a matter of urgency. Part V of the Children Act provides for two key mechanisms by which the state may intervene in an emergency to protect a child from harm: (i) police protection, and (ii) EPOs.

12.6.1 POLICE PROTECTION POWERS

Children Act 1989, s 46

Where a constable has *reasonable cause to believe* that a child would otherwise be likely to suffer significant harm, he may—

---

[274] S 39(4) and (5).
[275] *Re SC (A minor) (Leave to seek residence order)* [1994] 1 FLR 96.
[276] See above at p 819.
[277] For the various qualifying conditions see ss 23A, 23C, and Sch 2, para 19B.
[278] Ss 23B, 23C, 23CA, 23E, 24, 24A, 24B, and Sch 2, paras 19B and 19C. For more detailed discussion of all these provisions see Bainham (2005), 444–6.

> (a) remove the child to suitable accommodation and keep him there; or
>
> (b) take such steps as are reasonable to ensure that the child's removal from any hospital, or other place, in which he is then being accommodated is prevented.

Thus, the threshold criteria for police intervention in an emergency is 'reasonable cause to believe' that the child is 'likely to suffer significant harm'—much lower than the threshold for state intervention under s 31. As soon as is reasonably practicable after a child is taken into police protection, the police must inform the local authority, the child, and the parents of the steps they have taken and why.[279] The police do not acquire parental responsibility for the child, but must do what is reasonable to safeguard and promote the child's welfare.[280] The child must be placed in local authority accommodation and the parents allowed such contact as the police consider reasonable and in the child's best interests.[281] As soon as the child is taken into police protection a designated officer must begin an inquiry and release the child if no longer satisfied that there is reasonable cause to believe that the child is likely to suffer significant harm.[282] The child cannot be kept under police protection for more than 72 hours.[283] During this period, there is no mechanism by which the parents can challenge the actions of the police. In order to protect the child beyond this period, the police may apply on behalf of the local authority for an emergency protection order.[284]

Police protection powers should only be used as a last resort.

Department for Children, Schools and Families, *Working Together to Safeguard Children* (London: HMSO, 2010)

> The police also have powers to remove a child to suitable accommodation in cases of emergency. If it is necessary to remove a child a local authority should wherever possible – and unless a child's safety is otherwise at immediate risk – apply for an EPO. Police powers should only be used in exceptional circumstances where there is insufficient time to seek an EPO or for reasons relating to the immediate safety of the child.

However, research suggests that police protection is widely used as the first step in child protection proceedings, often out of administrative convenience and particularly when the local authority wish to initiate protective measures outside normal working hours.

J. Masson, 'Fair Trials in Child Protection', (2006) 28 *Journal of Social Welfare and Family Law* 15, 22

> Where the local authority was unable to obtain an EPO, the social worker contacted the police and requested that the child be taken into police protection. There were three situations

[279] Ss 46(3)(a), 46(3)(c), and 46(4).
[280] S 46(9).
[281] S 46(3)(f) and (10).
[282] S 46(3)(e).
[283] S 46(6).
[284] S 46(7).

where such requests were made. First, if the need to protect was immediate; for example where a parent was insisting that their child left hospital immediately. Secondly, where the magistrates' legal adviser took a restrictive approach to without notice hearings, requiring additional information before considering an application, concern about the time taken to persuade the court to agree would encourage the local authority lawyers to suggest that the social worker should approach the police. Magistrates' legal advisers were also said to suggest this course of action, in order to avoid the need to arrange an immediate hearing. Thirdly, if the need to protect the child arose out of normal working hours, social work emergency duty teams usually contacted the police rather than seeking a court order.

Masson's study of emergency protection carried out between 2001 and 2004 revealed that in 45 per cent of EPO applications, the child had already been taken into police protection.[285] In 74 per cent of those cases the police acted at the request of social services.[286]

The widespread use of police protection is concerning given there are some important disadvantages to invoking these powers rather than proceeding by way of an application for an EPO.

J. Masson, 'Emergency intervention to protect children: using and avoiding legal controls', (2005) 17 *Child and Family Law Quarterly* 75, 79, 95

Police protection is a power, not a court order; the individual officer who exercises the power takes responsibility for it, subject only to a review of its continuation by the designated officer. In most forces, police protection is exercised by ordinary officers with very limited training and experience in child protection, not officers from specialist Family Protection Units. In contrast, EPOs are sought by social workers from specialist child protection teams who generally work closely with specialist lawyers. They can be granted only after a hearing before a magistrate; the court provides an external check that it is appropriate to make the order and give the local authority the power to remove or detain the child...Using police protection avoided the system in the Children Act 1989 for securing legal local authority accountability...Using police protection denied the parents any opportunity to challenge the initial decision to remove or detain the child.

Echoing these concerns, it has been held by the Court of Appeal that, save in exceptional cases, removing a child in an emergency should always be carried out under the auspices of an EPO rather than relying on police protection.

Langley and others v Liverpool City Council and another [2005] EWCA Civ 1173

DYSON LJ:

36....The statutory scheme shows that Parliament intended that, if practicable, the removal of a child from where he or she is living should be authorised by a court order and

---

[285] Masson (2005), 78–9.
[286] Ibid.

effected under section 44. Parliament could have provided simply that specified persons could remove children if the statutory criteria are satisfied without any court involvement at all. But the removal of children, usually from their families, is a very serious matter. It is, therefore, not at all surprising that Parliament decided that the court should play an important part in the process. This is a valuable safeguard. The court must be satisfied that the statutory criteria for removal exist.

37. There are a number of important differences between the section 44 and section 46 regimes. They include the following. First, the court can give directions with respect to contact, examinations and assessments. This is a valuable power not available to the police. Secondly, an EPO gives the applicant parental responsibility, whereas while a child is being kept in police protection under section 46 neither the constable nor the designated officer has parental responsibility. Thirdly, no child can be kept in police protection for more than 72 hours, whereas an EPO may have effect for a period not exceeding 8 days (section 45(1)), and this period may be extended by up to 7 days (section 45(5)).

38. In my judgment, the statutory scheme clearly accords primacy to section 44. Removal under section 44 is sanctioned by the court and it involves a more elaborate, sophisticated and complete process than removal under section 46...

39. It is also relevant to point out that children who require emergency protection and have to be removed are often already well known to the Social Services Department within whose area the children are ordinarily resident. It is obviously preferable for the removal of a child to be effected if possible by, or at least with the assistance of, social workers who are known to the child, rather than by uniformed police officers who will almost certainly be strangers to the child. Whether known to the child or not, a social worker has skills in dealing with the removal of children from their homes which the most sensitive police officer cannot be expected to match.

40. I would, therefore, hold that (i) removal of children should usually be effected pursuant to an EPO, and (ii) section 46 should be invoked only where it is not practicable to execute an EPO. In deciding whether it is practicable to execute an EPO, the police must always have regard to the paramount need to protect children from significant harm.

Although there are clear concerns about the widespread use of police protection, Masson notes that where police protection has been used as a prelude to an application for an EPO, the EPO proceedings are likely to be fairer.[287] The window of time created by the fact the child is safe in police protection makes it more likely the EPO application will be heard on full notice, giving the parents the opportunity to obtain representation and give instructions.[288] It also makes it more likely that the child will be represented by a children's guardian.[289]

12.6.2 EMERGENCY PROTECTION ORDERS

The alternative means by which immediate action can be taken to protect a child is by applying to the court for an EPO. The grounds on which an EPO can be made are set down in s 44.

---

[287] Masson (2006), 24.
[288] Ibid.
[289] Ibid.

Children Act 1989, s 44

(1) Where any person ('the applicant') applies to the court for an order to be made under this section with respect to a child, the court may make the order if, but only if, it is satisfied that—

(a) there is reasonable cause to believe that the child is likely to suffer significant harm if

(i) he is not removed to accommodation provided by or on behalf of the applicant; or

(ii) he does not remain in the place in which he is then being accommodated;

(b) in the case of an application made by a local authority—

(i) enquiries are being made with respect to the child under section 47(1)(b); and

(ii) those enquiries are being frustrated by access to the child being unreasonably refused to a person authorised to seek access and that the applicant has reasonable cause to believe that access to the child is required as a matter of urgency; or

(c) in the case of an application made by an authorised person—

(i) the applicant has reasonable cause to suspect that a child is suffering, or is likely to suffer, significant harm;

(ii) the applicant is making enquiries with respect to the child's welfare; and

(iii) those enquiries are being frustrated by access to the child being unreasonably refused to a person authorised to seek access and the applicant has reasonable cause to believe that access to the child is required as a matter of urgency.

There are thus two basic grounds on which an EPO can be made: (i) that the *court* is satisfied there is *reasonable cause to believe* the child is at immediate risk of suffering significant harm; and (ii) enquiries are being conducted by the local authority or the NSPCC, those enquiries are being frustrated by access to the child being unreasonably withheld, and the *local authority or the NSPCC have reasonable cause to believe* that access is required as a matter of urgency. Where necessary, an EPO can be obtained very quickly. The application can be made ex parte and heard by a single justice sitting outside normal business hours.[290] In practice very few applications are contested and it is rare for a local authority application to be refused.[291]

The legal effects of an EPO are set down in s 44(4).

Children Act 1989, s 44

(4) While an order under this section ('an emergency protection order') is in force it—

(a) operates as a direction to any person who is in a position to do so to comply with any request to produce the child to the applicant;

(b) authorises—

(i) the removal of the child at any time to accommodation provided by or on behalf of the applicant and his being kept there; or

(ii) the prevention of the child's removal from any hospital, or other place, in which he was being accommodated immediately before the making of the order; and

(c) gives the applicant parental responsibility for the child.

[290] Ibid., 89–90.
[291] Ibid., 96 and Masson (2004), 475.

An EPO thus authorizes the local authority to remove the child where necessary to safe-guard the child's welfare.[292] The local authority must return the child to the parents as soon as it considers it safe to do so although whilst the order remains in force the local authority has the power to remove the child again should it be deemed necessary.[293]

In order to protect the child without necessitating the child's removal from home, the court has the power to attach to the EPO a provision excluding a specified individual from residing within the same dwelling-house as the child.[294] In order to make the exclusion order the court must have reasonable cause to believe that by so doing the child will be pro-tected from suffering significant harm or the NSPCC's or local authority's enquiries will cease to be frustrated.[295] The court must also be satisfied that there is another person resid-ing within the dwelling house who is willing and able to care for the child and who consents to the exclusion order.[296] A power of arrest may also be attached.[297] The court may accept an undertaking in lieu of the exclusion order but it cannot attach a power of arrest.[298]

Whilst the EPO is in force the local authority obtains parental responsibility for the child, although it may only take such action as is reasonably required to safeguard or promote the child's welfare.[299] The local authority must allow the child reasonable contact with, amongst others, the parents.[300] The court may also make a direction for a medical or psychiatric examination or other assessment of the child, subject to the child's consent if of sufficient understanding.[301]

An EPO has effect initially for a maximum of eight days.[302] Upon application by the local authority it may be extended once for a further seven days (15 days in total) provided there is reasonable cause to believe that the child is likely to suffer significant harm if the exten-sion is not granted.[303] An application to discharge the order may be brought by the child, the parents, any person with parental responsibility, and any person with whom the child was living immediately before the order was made, subject to the important restriction that an application cannot be brought by anyone who was given notice of the proceedings and was present at the hearing.[304] This restriction makes the growing practice of hearing applications on abridged notice to the parents particularly troublesome.

J. Masson, 'Fair Trials in Child Protection', (2006) 28 *Journal of Social Welfare and Family Law* 15, 24–7

Instead of allowing a hearing without notice or insisting that on the full period of one day's notice, the magistrates' legal adviser could shorten the period of notice. In such cases, the local authority might make its application at 10 a.m. and give notice to the parents of a hearing

---

[292] S 44(5)(a).
[293] S 44(10) and (12).
[294] S 44(1) and (3).
[295] S 44A(2)(a).
[296] S 44A(2)(b).
[297] S 44A(5).
[298] S 44B.
[299] S 44(5)(b).
[300] S 44(6)(a) and (13).
[301] S 44(6)(b) and (7). In appropriate cases, the child's refusal to consent can be overridden by the court exercising its inherent jurisdiction. See *South Glamorgan County Council v W and B* [1993] 1 FLR 574.
[302] S 45(1).
[303] S 45(4)–(6).
[304] S 45(8)–(11).

at 2 p.m. Abridged notice appeared to be seen by both legal advisers and local authority solicitors as a compromise solution, securing a speedy decision for the local authority whilst giving the parents the opportunity to participate in the hearing...

Where notice of the application was abridged, parents were less likely to attend the hearing or to be represented. Only half of the parents who were given short notice of the EPO hearing were represented, compared with over 70% of those with full notice...

Parents who attended were doubly disadvantaged. They lost the right to challenge the EPO available in without notice cases...but had little real opportunity to participate in the proceedings...Children were also less likely to be represented. There were no arrangements between local authorities and CAFCASS to provide children's guardians with early notification of applications...

Overall, the compromise of holding EPO hearings on short notice appeared to undermine the rights of parents rather than to protect them. Although the proceedings might give the appearance of fairness, the more limited opportunity for representation and the loss of the right to challenge the order meant that the parents had less opportunity to be involved in the process than if either the hearing had been on full notice or without any notice at all. The same could also be said for the child, whose own involvement was frequently thwarted because no representative was appointed until after the order had been made.

There is no right of appeal against the making of an EPO or against an application to extend or discharge the order.[305]

An EPO is a drastic order, often made in the absence of the parents[306] and with little effective scrutiny by the courts.[307] These shortcomings are compounded by the severe restrictions placed on challenging the order, raising questions as to the compatibility of this statutory regime with Article 8. The principles to be applied are firmly established in the Strasbourg case law.[308]

Haase v Germany (App No 11057/02, ECHR) (2005)

95. The Court accepts that when action has to be taken to protect a child in an emergency, it may not always be possible, because of the urgency of the situation, to associate in the decision-making process those having custody of the child. Nor may it even be desirable, even if possible, to do so if those having custody of the child are seen as the source of an immediate threat to the child, since giving them prior warning would be liable to deprive the measure of its effectiveness. The Court must however be satisfied that the national authorities were entitled to consider that there existed circumstances justifying the abrupt removal of the child from the care of its parents without any prior contact or consultation. In particular, it is for the respondent State to establish that a careful assessment of the impact of the proposed care measure on the parents and the child, as well as of the possible alternatives to the removal of the child from its family, was carried out prior to the implementation of a care

---

[305] S 45(10). See *Essex County Council v F* [1993] 1 FLR 847 and *Re P (Emergency Protection Order)* [1996] 1 FLR 482.

[306] Masson (2004), 475. Masson points out that even if the proceedings are heard on notice, given the limited time available to them the parents are often unable to actively contest the order.

[307] Ibid., 461 and Masson (2005).

[308] See *K and T v Finland* (App No 25702/94, ECHR) (2001) and *P, C and S v United Kingdom* (App No 56547/00, ECHR) (2002).

measure. The fact that a child could be placed in a more beneficial environment for his or her upbringing will not on its own justify a compulsory measure of removal from the care of the biological parents; there must exist other circumstances pointing to the "necessity" for such an interference with the parents' right under Article 8 to enjoy a family life with their child.

In a detailed obiter judgment, Munby J has identified various points of tension between the statutory regime governing EPOs and the demands of the ECHR, outlining what measures are necessary to avoid incompatibility:

X Council v B (Emergency Protection Orders) [2004] EWHC 2015

MUNBY J

57. . . .

i) An EPO, summarily removing a child from his parents, is a "draconian" and "extremely harsh" measure, requiring "exceptional justification" and "extraordinarily compelling reasons". Such an order should not be made unless the FPC is satisfied that it is both necessary and proportionate and that no other less radical form of order will achieve the essential end of promoting the welfare of the child. Separation is only to be contemplated if immediate separation is essential to secure the child's safety; "imminent danger" must be "actually established".

ii) Both the local authority which seeks and the FPC which makes an EPO assume a heavy burden of responsibility. It is important that both the local authority and the FPC approach every application for an EPO with an anxious awareness of the extreme gravity of the relief being sought and a scrupulous regard for the Convention rights of both the child and the parents.

iii) Any order must provide for the least interventionist solution consistent with the preservation of the child's immediate safety.

iv) If the real purpose of the local authority's application is to enable it to have the child assessed then consideration should be given to whether that objective cannot equally effectively, and more proportionately, be achieved by an application for, or by the making of, a CAO under section 43 of the Act.

v) No EPO should be made for any longer than is absolutely necessary to protect the child. Where the EPO is made on an ex parte (without notice) application very careful consideration should be given to the need to ensure that the initial order is made for the shortest possible period commensurate with the preservation of the child's immediate safety.

vi) The evidence in support of the application for an EPO must be full, detailed, precise and compelling . . .

vii) Save in wholly exceptional cases, parents must be given adequate prior notice of the date, time and place of any application by a local authority for an EPO. They must also be given proper notice of the evidence the local authority is relying upon.

viii) Where the application for an EPO is made ex parte the local authority must make out a compelling case for applying without first giving the parents notice. An ex parte application will normally be appropriate only if the case is genuinely one of emergency or other great urgency – and even then it should normally be possible to give some kind of albeit informal notice to the parents – or if there are compelling reasons to believe that the child's welfare will be compromised if the parents are alerted in advance to what is going on.

ix) The evidential burden on the local authority is even heavier if the application is made ex parte . . .

xii) . . . The local authority must apply its mind very carefully to whether removal is essential in order to secure the child's immediate safety. The mere fact that the local authority has obtained an EPO is not of itself enough. The FPC decides whether to make an EPO. But the local authority decides whether to remove. The local authority, even after it has obtained an EPO, is under an obligation to consider less drastic alternatives to emergency removal. Section 44(5) requires a process within the local authority whereby there is a further consideration of the action to be taken after the EPO has been obtained. Though no procedure is specified, it will obviously be prudent for local authorities to have in place procedures to ensure both that the required decision making actually takes place and that it is appropriately documented.

xiii) Consistently with the local authority's positive obligation under Article 8 to take appropriate action to reunite parent and child, sections 44(10)(a) and 44(11)(a) impose on the local authority a mandatory obligation to return a child who it has removed under section 44(4)(b)(i) to the parent from whom the child was removed if "it appears to [the local authority] that it is safe for the child to be returned." This imposes on the local authority a continuing duty to keep the case under review day by day so as to ensure that parent and child are separated for no longer than is necessary to secure the child's safety. In this, as in other respects, the local authority is under a duty to exercise exceptional diligence.

xiv) Section 44(13) requires the local authority, subject only to any direction given by the FPC under section 44(6), to allow a child who is subject to an EPO "reasonable contact" with his parents. Arrangements for contact must be driven by the needs of the family, not stunted by lack of resources.

These guidelines were strongly endorsed by McFarlane J in *Re X (Emergency Protection Orders)*.[309]

12.7 INTERIM CARE AND SUPERVISION ORDERS

If, following the making of the EPO, there are continuing grounds for concern, the next step is for the local authority to initiate care proceedings. Once proceedings have begun, the court has jurisdiction to adjourn the proceedings and make an interim order to protect the child until the parties are ready to proceed to the final hearing.[310] The court can also make an interim order whilst a s 37 investigation is carried out.[311] Interim orders are dealt with under s 38. The threshold for making an order at this interim stage is higher than that for an EPO but lower than that required for the making of a full care order.

[309] [2006] EWHC 510.
[310] S 38(1).
[311] Ibid.

Children Act 1989, s 38

(2) A court shall not make an interim care order or interim supervision order under this section unless it is satisfied that there are *reasonable grounds for believing* that the circumstances with respect to the child are as mentioned in s.31(2) [child is suffering or is likely to suffer significant harm]. (Emphasis added)

In determining whether the grounds for an interim care order are made out, the Court of Appeal has held that the child should only be removed from the parents pending the final hearing if the child's safety demands it.[312] Thorpe LJ has described this as 'a very high standard'.[313]

An interim order has the same legal effects as a final order. Under an interim care order the local authority therefore acquires parental responsibility and ultimate decision-making authority.[314] The main purpose of an interim care order is to maintain the status quo until the final hearing.

Re G (Minors) (Interim Care Order) [1993] 2 FCR 557, 562–3 (CA)

Lord Justice Waite:

[T]he Judge fell into error in regarding an interim care order as being a step which involved any advance judgment on the part of the court...The making of an interim care order is an essentially impartial step, favouring neither one side or the other, and affording to no one, least of all the local authority in whose favour it is made, an opportunity for tactical or adventitious advantage...

Conditions cannot be attached to an interim care order although a suspected abuser may be excluded from the child's home.[315] Contact between the child and the parents is governed by s 34. However, pending the final hearing, terminating contact will only be considered appropriate in exceptional circumstances.[316]

An interim order will initially have effect for no longer than eight weeks. It may then be extended for periods of no more than four weeks.[317] There is no limit to the number of times the order may be extended. On each renewal application, the court must be satisfied that the threshold conditions under s 38(2) are still met. The time limits enshrined in s 38 were intended to reflect the original intention that care proceedings would take on average 12 weeks.[318] The reality is very different. Care proceedings can take anywhere between 37 and 72 weeks to be resolved.[319] With a view to tackling these delays, a *Protocol for Judicial Case Management in Public Law Children Act Cases* was introduced in June 2003, followed

---

[312] *Re H* [2001] 1 FCR 350, [39]. It has been held that the suggestion made by Ryder J in *Re L* [2008] 1 FLR 575 that there must be 'imminent risk of really serious harm' before intervention can be justified does not establish any new principle of law. See *Re L-A (Children)* [2009] EWCA Civ 822, [7].

[313] *Re L-A (Children)*, ibid.

[314] *Re L (Interim care order: Power of court)* [1996] 2 FLR 742.

[315] S 38A.

[316] *A v M and Walsall Metropolitan Borough Council* [1993] 2 FLR 244.

[317] *Gateshead Metropolitan Borough Council v N* [1993] 1 FLR 811.

[318] DCA (2002), [24].

[319] Masson (2008), 428, 439.

in 2008 by the Public Law Outline, and in 2010 by a new Practice Direction. The Practice Direction states that the timetable for completing the proceedings should now be determined by the individual child's needs.[320]

Although ultimate responsibility for the child passes with the interim care order to the local authority, the court retains control of the care proceedings. This gives the court limited authority to direct the local authority to undertake certain assessments involving the child for the purposes of the final hearing.

Children Act 1989, s 38

(6) Where the court makes an interim care order, or interim supervision order, it may give such directions (if any) as it considers appropriate with regard to the medical or psychiatric examination or other assessment of the child; but if the child is of sufficient understanding to make an informed decision he may refuse to submit to the examination or other assessment.

The scope of the power conferred on the court by s 38 has given rise to considerable controversy and has now been considered by the House of Lords on two occasions. Dispute has centred, in particular, on whether the court can order the local authority, against its wishes, to fund a programme of treatment and therapy which is primarily aimed, not at the child, but the parents. If this jurisdiction exists under the guise of an interim order, the court would be able to force the local authority to provide services for the child's family that the local authority, usually for resource reasons, is otherwise unwilling to offer. The issue was first considered by the House of Lords in *Re C (A Minor) (Interim care order: Residential assessment)* which appeared to widen the scope of permissible directions to include assessments other than those of a medical or psychiatric nature and to include assessments involving the parents as well as the child. The case concerned whether the court could order an expensive residential assessment of the family which was primarily aimed at evaluating the parents' parenting ability.

Re C (A Minor) (Interim care order: Residential assessment) [1997] AC 489, 500–4 (HL)

LORD BROWNE-WILKINSON:

[F]or the purpose of making its ultimate decision whether to grant a full care order, the court will need the help of social workers, doctors and others as to the child and his circumstances. Information and assessments from these sources are necessary not only to determine whether the section 31 threshold has been crossed (including the cause of the existing or anticipated harm to the child from its existing circumstances) but also in exercising its discretion whether or not to make a final care order...Section 38(6) deals with the interaction between the powers of the local authority entitled to make decisions as to the child's welfare in the interim and the needs of the court to have access to the relevant information and assessments so as to be able to make the ultimate decision. It must always be borne in mind that in exercising its jurisdiction under the Act, the court's function is investigative and nonadversarial...

[320] Practice Direction (2010), 3.1. See also FPR 2010, r 12.23.

Against that background, I turn to consider the construction of section 38(6)...

There are two possible constructions of subsection (6)..., one narrow, the other purposive and broader. The Court of Appeal in *Re M (Minors) (Interim Care Order: Directions)* [1996] 3 FCR 137 adopted the narrow view. They held that the words "other assessment of the child" had to be construed as ejusdem generis with the words "medical or psychiatric examination". They attached decisive importance to the fact that the subsection only refers to the examination or assessment "of the child" and makes no reference to the examination or assessment of any other person in relation to the child. They further held that for the court to order a residential assessment of the parents and child together at a specified place would involve the court in an unwarranted usurpation by the court of the local authority's power (as the authority having parental responsibility under the interim care order) to regulate where the child is to reside... [Counsel] for the local authority in the present appeal, submitted that Parliament cannot have intended the court to have power to require the local authority against its own judgment to expend scarce resources: he submitted that the local authority is the only body which can properly assess how such resources are to be allocated as between the social services and the other services it has to provide and as between the various calls on its social services budget.

My Lords, I cannot accept this narrow construction of the subsection. The Act should be construed purposively so as to give effect to the underlying intentions of Parliament. As I have sought to demonstrate, the dividing line between the functions of the court on the one hand and the local authority on the other is that a child in interim care is subject to control of the local authority, the court having no power to interfere with the local authority's decisions save in specified cases. The cases where, despite that overall control, the court is to have power to intervene are set out, inter alia, in subsection (6)... The purpose of subsection (6) is to enable the court to obtain the information necessary for its own decision, notwithstanding the control over the child which in all other respects rests with the local authority. I therefore approach the subsection on the basis that the court is to have such powers to override the views of the local authority as are necessary to enable the court to discharge properly its function of deciding whether or not to accede to the local authority's application to take the child away from its parents by obtaining a care order. To allow the local authority to decide what evidence is to go before the court at the final hearing would be in many cases, including the present, to allow the local authority by administrative decision to pre-empt the court's judicial decision...

Next, it is true that subsection (6)... only refer[s] to the assessment "of the child" and not, as is proposed in the present case, a joint assessment of the child and the parents, including the parents' attitude and behaviour towards the child. But it is impossible to assess a young child divorced from his environment. The interaction between the child and his parents or other persons looking after him is an essential element in making any assessment of the child...

Much the most powerful of [counsel's] submissions is that based on the expenditure of scarce resources by the local authority in the carrying out of an expensive assessment. In the overwhelming majority of care cases, the parties are in straitened circumstances and there is no one to pay for any examination or assessment under section 38(6) other than the local authority. In the present case, the proposed residential assessment is going to cost some £24,000 and the local authority, taking as it does a gloomy view of the result of the assessment, considers that expenditure on that scale is not a sensible allocation of its limited resources, a decision which it is far better qualified to take than the court. I accept the force of this submission but it proves too much. [Counsel] was not able to argue that if the court directed a medical examination of the child himself, which examination would be very expensive, the local authority could refuse to carry it out simply on the grounds of the expense involved and the unwise allocation of limited resources. In such a case, it will be for the court to take into account in deciding whether or not to make an order for the medical examination the expense that it involves. If that is so, the issue of resources cannot affect the proper construction of subsection (6). The consideration of the resource consequences of making the order must be the same whether the court is making an order for medical examination of the child or an order for the other assessment of the child. Therefore it is impossible to construe section 38(6) in the narrow sense simply because the court is less suitable than the local authority to assess the financial considerations.

In my judgment, therefore, subsection (6)...of section 38 of the Act [is] to be broadly construed. [It] confer[s] jurisdiction on the court to order or prohibit any assessment which involves the participation of the child and is directed to providing the court with the material which, in the view of the court, is required to enable it to reach a proper decision at the final hearing of the application for a full care order. In exercising its discretion whether to order any particular examination or assessment, the court will take into account the cost of the proposed assessment and the fact that local authorities' resources are notoriously limited.

This judgment was subsequently seized upon as a potential means of directing the local authority to provide expensive treatment and therapy for individuals other than the child. This gave rise to considerable litigation in the face of local authorities' objections to being forced to fund treatment with which they did not agree.[321] The second House of Lords' decision responded to these concerns, attempting to rein back the potentially expansive scope of s 38(6), and imposing firm restrictions on the nature of the directions that may be imposed. The proposed assessment in this case involved intensive psychotherapy for the child's mother to be provided over a period of months.

Re G (A Minor) (Interim Care Order: Residential Assessment) [2005] UKHL 68

BARONNESS HALE:

64. The purpose of [ss 38(6) and 38(7)] is...not only to enable the court to obtain the information it needs, but also to enable the court to control the information-gathering activities of others. But the emphasis is always on obtaining information. This is clear from the use of the words "examination" and "other assessment". If the framers of the Act had meant the court to be in charge, not only of the examination and assessment of the child, but also of the medical or psychiatric treatment to be provided for her, let alone for her parents, it would have said so. Instead, it deliberately left that in the hands of the local authority.

65. A fortiori, the purpose of section 38(6) cannot be to ensure the provision of services either for the child or his family. There is nothing in the 1989 Act which empowers the court hearing care proceedings to order the provision of specific services for anyone. To imply such a power into section 38(6) would be quite contrary to the division of responsibility which was the "cardinal principle" of the 1989 Act...

66. I appreciate, of course, that it is not always possible to draw a hard and fast line between information-gathering and service-providing. Some information can only be gathered through the provision of services. It may be necessary to observe the parents looking after the child at

---

[321] See, e.g., *Re B (Psychiatric therapy for parents)* [1999] 1 FLR 701; *Re D (Jurisdiction: Programme of assessment or therapy)* [1999] 2 FLR 632; *Re B (Interim care order: directions)* [2002] 1 FLR 545.

close quarters for a short period in order to assess the quality of the child's attachment to the parents, the degree to which the parents have bonded with the child, the current parenting skills of the parents, and their capacity to learn and develop...

67. But the court only has power to insist where this is relevant to the questions which the court has to answer. Where the threshold criteria are in issue, it must be recalled that these are phrased (in section 31(2)) in the present tense...Where the threshold is found or conceded but the proper order is in issue, the welfare checklist is likewise focussed on the present...The capacity to change, to learn and to develop may well be part of that. But it is still the present capacity with which the court is concerned. It cannot be a proper use of the court's powers under section 38(6) to seek to bring about change.

68. These conclusions are reinforced by the Act's emphasis on reaching decisions without delay. It cannot have been contemplated that the examination or assessment ordered under section 38(6) would take many months to complete. It would be surprising if it were to last more than two or three months at most. The important decision for the court is whether or not to make a care order, with all that that entails...The court may sometimes have to accept that it is not possible to know all that is to be known before a final choice is made, because that choice will depend upon how the family and the child respond and develop in the future.

Conclusion

69. In short, what is directed under section 38(6) must clearly be an examination or assessment of the child, including where appropriate her relationship with her parents, the risk that her parents may present to her, and the ways in which those risks may be avoided or managed, all with a view to enabling the court to make the decisions which it has to make under the Act with the minimum of delay. Any services which are provided for the child and his family must be ancillary to that end. They must not be an end in themselves.

Within the framework provided by the House of Lords, Munby J has emphasized the continuing wide scope of s 38(6).

Re A (A Child) [2009] EWHC 865

MUNBY J:

32. The remaining question, therefore, is, precisely what is it that the court has power to direct pursuant to section 38(6)?...It is fundamental that, apart from a "medical or psychiatric examination", all the court can authorise or direct under section 38(6) is something that can properly be described as an "assessment" and, moreover, an assessment "of the child". Hence, the need for the primary focus to be on the child, and hence, also, the familiar distinction between an "assessment" of the child (which is permissible) and a programme of therapy or treatment for the parent (which is not).

33. Whether a particular programme involves permissible assessment, or some other thing which is impermissible, depends upon an evaluation of the 'primary purpose' of what is proposed and whether any otherwise impermissible elements are merely 'ancillary' to what is permissible...

59....[T]here are two preliminary points about section 38(6) that need to be made. In the first place, although, perhaps because they are the most protracted and expensive and most likely to cut across a local authority's planning, and thus most likely to be controversial, we tend to think of section 38(6) assessments in terms of residential assessments . . . section 38(6) is much wider and more general in its scope. It applies to any "examination" (medical or psychiatric) or any "assessment", whether short or long, and in whatever setting. Secondly, subject only to the requirement that the assessment be "of the child", section 38(6) is not expressed as imposing any restrictions at all on what can be directed by the court. The court can direct any "assessment of the child." The only further restriction is that suggested by Lord Browne-Wilkinson's reference in *Re C* to the purpose of section 38(6) as being "to enable the court to obtain the information necessary for its own decision . . . to enable it to reach a proper decision at the final hearing of the application for a full care order." But those words, far from narrowing the scope of section 38(6) merely serve, as it seems to me, to bring out and emphasise the potential breadth of its ambit . . .

62. The argument that section 38(6) does not confer any power to order that a child be placed, whether for the purpose of assessment or otherwise, in a particular placement, that being a matter for the discretion of the local authority once the care order (interim or final) has been made, is, with all respect to those propounding it, quite hopeless . . .

63. The argument, on which [counsel] focussed, that where a residential assessment is directed in accordance with section 38(6), the only kind of place which can lawfully be specified is a 'residential family centre' registered and regulated in accordance with the Care Standards Act 2000 and (in Wales) the Residential Family Centres (Wales) Regulations 2003, is also, in my judgment, lacking in substance. It involves reading into section 38(6) words of restriction which are simply not there . . .

65. Where, one asks, is the vice in what the Justices did here, always bearing in mind the purpose of section 38(6) as explained in *Re C* and *Re G*? I can see none. On the contrary, given the scope and purpose of section 38(6), it would, if anything, be most unfortunate if what the Justices did was unlawful, because it would, to repeat, make it legally impossible for any court, without the agreement of the local authority, ever to direct an assessment in a family setting under the umbrella of an interim care order. And what is the vice in that?

12.8 CHALLENGING LOCAL AUTHORITY DECISIONS

The relationship between the local authority and a family struggling to keep their child is often going to be fraught with tension. Disputes between the local authority and the family are perhaps inevitable. For parents or children who feel they have been treated unfairly or unjustly there are a number of ways in which local authority decisions can be challenged. The route taken will depend on whether the complaint relates to voluntary or compulsory intervention and, if the latter, at what stage the care proceedings have reached.

12.8.1 LOCAL AUTHORITY COMPLAINTS PROCEDURE

Children Act 1989, s 26

(3) Every local authority shall establish a procedure for considering any representations (including any complaint) made to them by—

(a) any child who is being looked after by them or who is not being looked after by them but is in need;

> (b) a parent of his;
>
> (c) any person who is not a parent of his but who has parental responsibility for him;
>
> (d) any local authority foster parent;
>
> (e) such other person as the authority consider has a sufficient interest in the child's welfare to warrant his representations being considered by them,
>
> about the discharge by the authority of any of their qualifying functions in relation to the child.

The 'qualifying functions' to which s 26(3) refers were originally restricted to complaints relating to the local authority's discharge of responsibilities under Part III of the CA 1989. Since 2002, the complaints procedure has also covered Parts IV and V.[322] The procedure for making a complaint under s 26 is set down in regulations.[323]

A complainant who is dissatisfied with the outcome of the s 26 procedure can refer the matter to the Local Authority Ombudsman, although any such complaint is limited to matters of local authority 'maladministration'.[324] Alternatively, the matter can be referred to the Secretary of State under s 84 of the CA 1989. Again, however, the complaint is limited to an alleged failure by the local authority to comply with its statutory duties under the Act.[325]

12.8.2 JUDICIAL REVIEW

The decisions of a local authority are subject to judicial review on the usual grounds: illegality, irrationality, and procedural impropriety. Judicial review will more commonly be used to challenge decisions under Part III as decisions under Part IV should be challenged, where possible, within the ongoing care proceedings.[326] This allows a much fuller consideration of the child's best interests than focusing on the bare legality of the decision.[327] If the care proceedings have been concluded, e.g. the complaint relates to the implementation of the care order, a freestanding application for judicial review will be appropriate.[328]

There are a number of drawbacks to proceeding by way of judicial review. First, before an action for judicial review can proceed, any internal administrative remedy must be exhausted. Although the weight of authority suggests a complaint must first be brought under s 26 of the CA 1989, it remains contentious whether s 26, because of its various limitations, provides a suitable alternative remedy.[329] Second, the grounds for judicial review are strictly limited to the legality of the decision. The child's best interests in light of the wider circumstances of the case cannot be considered. Third, whilst the local authority can be directed to reconsider a particular decision, the court cannot substitute its own view for that of the local authority

---

[322] S 26(3A). For a precise list of the functions under Parts IV and V now covered by the complaints procedure, see Children Act 1989 Representations Procedure (England) Regulations 2006, SI 2006/1783, reg 3.

[323] Children Act 1989 Representations Procedure (England) Regulations 2006, SI 2006/1783.

[324] See Murphy (2003), 130–2.

[325] Ibid., 129–30.

[326] *R (CD) v Isle of Anglesey County Council* [2004] EWHC 1635, [12].

[327] *Re C (Adoption: Religious observance)* [2002] 1 FLR 1119, 1134.

[328] *Re S (Minors) (Care order: Implementation of care plan); Re W (Minors) (Care order: Adequacy of care plan)* [2002] 1 FLR 815, [78].

[329] See *R v London Borough of Barnet, ex parte B* [1994] 1 FLR 592 and *R v Royal Borough of Kingston-Upon-Thames, ex parte T* [1994] 1 FLR 798. For discussion of this point see Murphy (2003), 121–3.

and direct it to undertake a particular course of action.[330] Consequently, a complainant may find that whilst the decision is successfully quashed and sent back to the local authority for reconsideration, the eventual outcome remains the same.[331]

12.8.3 CLAIMS UNDER THE HRA 1998

Where the ECHR rights of the parties are engaged, the local authority's actions may be challenged under the HRA 1998. This avenue of redress is available regardless of whether the decision was taken under Part III, IV, or V of the legislation and includes a failure to act to protect the child.[332] Complaints alleging a breach of the ECHR should be litigated, wherever possible, through the ongoing care proceedings. If there are no such proceedings or the proceedings have been concluded, then a freestanding application can be brought under s 7 of the HRA 1998.[333]

Where a claim under s 7 of the HRA 1998 is successful, the court may 'grant such relief or remedy, or make such order, within its powers as it considers just and appropriate'.[334] This includes granting an injunction ordering the child back to the parents' care.[335] The court may also make an award of damages, although such an award is unlikely for a mere procedural breach.[336] Moreover, for parents facing the loss of their child, damages will be of little consequence.

12.9 CONCLUSION

Protecting children from abuse and neglect involves a difficult balancing exercise. Whilst children must not be left in situations of known risk, the decision to remove a child from the child's parents carries a heavy responsibility. It causes deep loss to both parents and child. Parents in this position are often deeply troubled and vulnerable, they have a right to expect help and support from the state. Better resourced support services may help keep more vulnerable families together. The inadequate funding of services under Part III is thus an issue of crucial importance. However, the sad reality is that even if the state had unlimited resources, for some parents it would never be enough. In serious cases of abuse and neglect or for parents battling against multiple long-term problems, there will come a point at which the child's right to a safe and secure childhood must come first. Deciding when that point has been reached is never easy, but children cannot be expected to wait forever. Whilst the rights of the parents must be taken seriously throughout the child protection process, parents do not have the right to cause irreparable harm to their children. That basic principle should not be forgotten.

---

[330] *Re L (Care proceedings: human rights claims)* [2003] EWHC 665, [14] (per Munby J).

[331] *Re T (Judicial review: Local authority decisions concerning child in need)* [2003] EWHC 2515, [144]–[150]. See Murphy (2003), 115–16.

[332] *Z and others v UK* (App No 29392/95, ECHR) (2001). An action may also lie in tort: *D v East Berkshire Community Health NHS Trust; K and another v Dewsbury Healthcare NHS Trust and another; K and another v Oldham NHS Trust and another* [2003] EWCA Civ 1151.

[333] *Re L (care proceedings: human rights claims)* [2003] EWHC 665 and *Re V (a child) (care proceedings: human rights claims)* [2004] EWCA Civ 54.

[334] HRA 1998, s 8(1).

[335] *G v N (County Council)* [2009] 1 FLR 774, [36].

[336] *Re C (a child)* [2007] EWCA Civ 2.

When children are received into local authority care, they look to the state to give them the safe and secure childhood so many other children are able to take for granted. Munby J is right to observe that 'if the State is to justify removing children from their parents it can only be on the basis that the State is going to provide a better quality of care than that from which the child in care has been rescued.'[337] Sadly, for many children, the state fails them too.[338] As we have seen, the state's own parenting record is poor. However, the children for whom the state has assumed this heavy responsibility are often deeply scarred by their early experiences. They arrive in care deeply troubled and vulnerable. The state does not have a magic wand. It cannot make deep-rooted problems just disappear. However, it can try and repair some of the damage by giving these children the best possible care that it can. And where children cannot return home, successive governments have firmly believed that the best possible care is not that of the state, but the love and support of an alternative 'forever family'. And for most children that means adoption.

ONLINE RESOURCE CENTRE

Questions, suggestions for further reading, and supplementary materials for this chapter (including updates on developments in this area of family law since this book was published) may be found on the Online Resource Centre at **www.oxfordtextbooks.co.uk/orc/harrisshort_tcm2e/**.

---

[337] *Re F; F v Lambeth London Borough Council* [2002] 1 FLR 217, 234.
[338] Ibid.

13

ADOPTION

CENTRAL ISSUES

1. An adoption order terminates the legal relationship between the birth parents and the child. It is permanent and irrevocable. The adoptive parents become the child's legal parents as if the child had been born their own legitimate child. As the social purpose of adoption has changed, this concept of adoption has found itself under increasing pressure.

2. Whenever a decision is made in relation to the adoption of a child, the child's welfare is the paramount consideration. Parental consent to the adoption can be dispensed with if the child's welfare requires it. The exclusively child-centred approach of the Adoption and Children Act 2002 (ACA 2002) raises questions as to whether adequate consideration is given to the birth parents' rights and interests throughout the adoption process.

3. Given the effect of an adoption order on the child's legal status, the child's right to be raised by his or her birth parents in accordance with his or her ethnic, cultural, and religious background is a particularly important issue.

4. Step-parent adoptions and adoptions by a sole natural parent are controversial because of their distorting effect on family relationships. Such adoptions are now discouraged.

5. It can be argued that the law should do more to promote open adoption by ensuring children are provided with information about their birth parents and, where appropriate, making orders for post-adoption contact even against the wishes of the adoptive parents.

6. Special guardianship was introduced by the ACA 2002 as an alternative means of securing permanency for the child. Early indications suggest that it is not perceived as an equally valuable alternative to adoption.

13.1 INTRODUCTION

Adoption is an area of family law beset by tensions and contradictions. As one important route to 'becoming a parent', adoption is for many people a 'good news' story. For adoptive parents, it can fulfil a lifetime's dream to become a parent providing vital recognition of the value and importance of social parenthood. For children in care or voluntarily relinquished by their parents it can be a life-line, providing the opportunity to be part of a 'normal', loving, and devoted 'forever family', perhaps for the first time in their short and often troubled lives. For others, however, behind this 'good news' story lies sadness and despair. A price must be paid for the creation of this new adoptive family—and that price is paid by the birth family. For them, adoption represents the termination of their legal relationship with the child. Put simply, in legal terms, the child is lost to them forever. Often young, vulnerable, and marginalized, it is usually the birth mother who pays the greatest price, many facing a lifetime of unresolved grief. For children too, adoption can be a paradox. Whilst the gains for the child can be enormous, so too can the losses, with many adopted children being profoundly affected by the loss of their birth family relationships. That deep sense of loss can remain with children throughout their lives, often intensifying as they grow older. Adoption is thus a complex issue. It marks both the beginning and the end of what for many is the core, defining relationship of their lives—that of parent and child.

The tensions and contradictions inherent in adoption make this a particularly appropriate topic with which to end the book. Contemporary debates surrounding adoption encapsulate many of the key themes explored within the previous chapters. It brings into focus key questions such as the respective value to be placed on biological as opposed to social parenthood, the value to be placed on traditional as opposed to alternative family forms, the importance of a child's cultural and religious heritage, the importance of preserving original family ties as opposed to supporting and prioritizing new and reconstituted families, the responsibilities of the state when it compulsorily removes a child from its family of birth, and the advantages and disadvantages of law over other methods of social governance. Thus, whilst the number of adoptions has declined dramatically, adoption retains great symbolic importance. What the law has to say about adoption tells us a great deal about prevailing social attitudes to marriage, non-marital relationships, biological parenting, social parenting, and the role of the state in family life. As Murray Ryburn puts it, 'the practice of adoption goes to the heart of many issues that are critical in determining the kind of society we live in or wish to live in'.[1]

This chapter explores the legal framework for adoption as enshrined in the ACA 2002. We begin by examining the legal concept of adoption before turning to consider whether this traditional western concept meets the particular needs of children adopted from care. We then move on to consider the statutory provisions in more detail, beginning with two core principles running throughout the legislation: the welfare principle and the requirement for the birth parents' consent. The statutory test for dispensing with parental consent will be considered, particularly its compatibility or otherwise with the European Convention on Human Rights (ECHR). The adoption process as enshrined in the ACA 2002 is then examined in detail, including the application of the welfare principle to three particularly contentious issues: (i) the importance of the birth family in an adoption dispute; (ii) trans-racial adoption; and (iii) step-parent adoptions and adoptions by a sole natural parent. We conclude our discussion of adoption by examining the increasingly important question of 'open adoption', focusing in particular on adopted children's right to information about their birth families and provision for post-adoption contact. Finally, we turn to consider special guardianship, the main alternative to adoption for securing permanence.

---

[1] Ryburn (1998a), 53–4.

13.2 WHAT IS ADOPTION?

The legal effects of an adoption order are enshrined in ss 46 and 67 of the ACA 2002.[2]

Adoption and Children Act 2002, s 46

(1) An adoption order is an order made by the court...giving parental responsibility for a child to the adopters or adopter.

(2) The making of an adoption order operates to extinguish—

(a) the parental responsibility which any person other than the adopters or adopter has for the adopted child immediately before the making of the order...

Adoption and Children Act 2002, s 67

(1) An adopted person is to be treated in law as if born as the child of the adopters or adopter...

(3) An adopted person—

(a) if adopted by one of a couple is to be treated in law as not being the child of any person other than the adopter and the other one of the couple, and

(b) in any other case, is to be treated in law...as not being the child of any person other than the adopters or adopter...

In the case of a 'stranger-adoption',[3] an adoption order completely terminates any legal relationship between the birth parents and the child. Save for the limited exceptions specified in s 74 of the ACA 2002,[4] it is as if the birth parents had never been: there is a total and absolute transplanting of the legal relationship of parent and child. The adoptive parents become the child's legal parents and are vested with parental responsibility. By an act of legal fiction, they stand in relation to the child as if the child had been born their natural legitimate child. For the adoptive parents, adoption thus represents full and unequivocal recognition of their parental status.

A step-parent adoption has similar effects, although the legal status of the birth parent with whom the child is to live remains unchanged.[5] In contrast, the legal relationship between the non-resident birth parent and the child is completely extinguished just as in a stranger adoption. The child is to be treated as if born to the resident birth parent and his or her new partner.[6]

The courts have strongly endorsed this model of adoption, prioritizing the need to support the adoptive family by treating them in every way as if they were a 'normal' family

---

[2] Unless otherwise stated, all references to statutory provisions in this chapter are to the ACA 2002.

[3] This term refers to adoption by anyone other than a parent or step-parent, including members of the extended family.

[4] Marriage within the prohibited degrees; the offence of engaging in sexual intercourse with an adult relative; and acquisition of British nationality.

[5] S 67(3). It is thus no longer necessary for the birth parent with whom the child is living to adopt his or her own child.

[6] S 67(2)(b).

unit. This has been evident in their approach to whether conditions should be imposed on the adoption order. The courts have firmly resisted this, arguing that to impose conditions on the adoptive family undermines the concept of adoption as a total legal transplant and treats the adoptive parents as something less than an ordinary, natural family, as 'second-class' parents. They have thus generally refused to attach any conditions to the order which interfere with the adoptive parents' decision-making authority. This approach was tested in *Re S (A Minor) (Adoption: Blood Transfusion)*. The prospective adopters were Jehovah's Witnesses who, under pressure from the judge, had undertaken that they would not with-hold consent to the child receiving a blood transfusion without first applying to the court. The adoptive parents appealed, wishing to be released from the undertaking. The Court of Appeal allowed the appeal.

Re S (A Minor) (Adoption: Blood Transfusion) [1995] 2 FCR 177, 182 (CA)

Lord Justice Staughton:

If one were to look over the whole field of imposing conditions on adoptive parents against their will, it might become very common indeed. To my mind this should be a very rare course…The best thing for the child in the ordinary way is that he or she should become as near as possible the lawful child of the adopting parents. That is what the child's welfare requires. I would not, in this case, regard it as in any way appropriate to impose a condition which derogated from that, and which made very little difference as to what would in fact happen, in circumstances which were in any event unlikely to arise.

As with natural parenthood, 'adoption is for life'. Subject only to the very limited circumstances in which an adoption order can be revoked,[7] the legal parenthood of the adoptive parents can only be terminated by a further adoption order. The permanent, irrevocable nature of adoption sets it apart from any other form of social parenthood. This was dramatically illustrated in *Re B (adoption: jurisdiction to set aside)*, in which an adopted child sought to set aside the adoption order 36 years after it was made. The applicant's birth mother was Roman Catholic and the birth father was a Muslim Arab from Kuwait. The child was mistakenly placed with an Orthodox Jewish couple who subsequently adopted him. The applicant sought to set the adoption order aside arguing it had been made under a fundamental mistake of fact as to his racial and ethnic origins. As Simon Brown LJ commented, 'it is difficult to imagine a more ill-starred adoption placement'. The Court of Appeal nevertheless refused the application.

Re B (Adoption: Jurisdiction to Set Aside) [1995] Fam 239, 245–9 (CA)

SWINTON THOMAS LJ:

In my judgment such an application faces insuperable hurdles…

There are certain specific statutory provisions for the revocation of an adoption order…There are cases where an adoption order has been set aside by reason of what is known as a procedural irregularity…Those cases concern a failure to effect proper service

---

[7] See ACA 2002, s 55 (child adopted by a sole natural parent who subsequently marries the other natural parent thereby legitimating the child).

of the adoption proceedings on a natural parent or ignorance of the parent of the existence of the adoption proceedings. In each case the application to set aside the order was made reasonably expeditiously. It is fundamental to the making of an adoption order that the natural parent should be informed of the application so that she can give or withhold her consent. If she has no knowledge at all of the application then, obviously, a fundamental injustice is perpetrated. I would prefer myself to regard those cases not as cases where the order has been set aside by reason of a procedural irregularity, although that has certainly occurred, but as cases where natural justice has been denied because the natural parent who may wish to challenge the adoption has never been told that it is going to happen. . . .

There is no case which has been brought to our attention in which it has been held that the court has an inherent power to set aside an adoption order by reason of a misapprehension or mistake. To allow considerations such as those put forward in this case to invalidate an otherwise properly made adoption order would, in my view, undermine the whole basis on which adoption orders are made, namely that they are final and for life as regards the adopters, the natural parents, and the child. In my judgment [counsel], who appeared as amicus curiae, is right when he submits that it would gravely damage the lifelong commitment of adopters to their adoptive children if there is a possibility of the child, or indeed the parents, subsequently challenging the validity of the order. I am satisfied that there is no inherent power in the courts in circumstances such as arise in this case to set aside an adoption order. Nobody could have other than the greatest sympathy with the applicant but, in my judgment, the circumstances of this case do not provide any ground for setting aside an adoption order which was regularly made.

As the Court of Appeal notes, an adoption order can only be challenged, other than by appealing against the order in the usual way,[8] if there has been a fundamental breach of natural justice. An adoption order was set aside on these grounds in *Re K (Adoption: Foreign Child)*.[9] The case concerned the adoption of a Bosnian Muslim child wrongly assumed to have no surviving relatives. The order was set aside for a 'plethora of procedural irregularities' including the failure to appoint a guardian ad litem, the failure to ensure the guardian appointed by the Bosnian government could participate effectively in the proceedings, and the failure to have proper regard to an edict of the Bosnian government prohibiting the adoption of Bosnian children.[10] In the absence of such significant procedural errors giving rise to a fundamental breach of natural justice, the adoption order must stand.

This restrictive approach was firmly upheld by the Court of Appeal in the difficult case of *W v Norfolk County Council*. The case concerned the removal and subsequent adoption of three children because of what was believed to be the infliction of non-accidental injuries on one of the children. It subsequently transpired that the injuries were probably caused not by abuse but by the fact the child was suffering from scurvy (the child had been fed exclusively with normal soya milk for almost 12 months). The family had thus been the victims of a serious miscarriage of justice and the parents sought to have the adoption orders set side by appealing out of time. By the time the application reached the Court of Appeal the children had been living with their respective adoptive parents for over three years. The Court of Appeal dismissed the application.

---

[8] See *Re M (minors) (adoption)* [1991] 1 FLR 458, in which a natural father was allowed to appeal against an adoption order out of time where the father's ignorance of certain material facts—that the natural mother was suffering from terminal cancer—was held to have vitiated his consent to the adoption.

[9] [1997] 2 FCR 389.

[10] Ibid., 395–7.

W and another v Norfolk County Council [2009] EWCA Civ 59

WALL LJ:

[145]...[A]doption is the process whereby a child becomes a permanent and full member of a new family, and is treated for all purposes as if born to the adopters...

[146] Counsel...recognised that this court would be reluctant as a matter of public policy to set aside adoption orders. This, they accepted, was because if prospective adopters thought that natural parents could, even in limited circumstances, secure the return of a child after an adoption order had been made, this could have a dramatic effect on the number of people putting themselves forward as prospective adopters. Adoption orders have been perceived as final, and as putting the adoptive parents fully in control.

[147] So [counsel] are constrained to fall back on the facts. If the true facts had been known [the three children] would not have been freed for adoption and would not have been adopted. The injustice therefore remains.

[148] In my judgment, however, the public policy considerations relating to adoption, and the authorities on the point – which are binding on this court – simply make it impossible for this court to set aside the adoption orders, even if, as Mr and Mrs W argue, they have suffered a serious injustice.

[149] This is a case in which the court has to go back to first principles. Adoption is a statutory process. The law relating to it is very clear. The scope for the exercise of judicial discretion is severely curtailed. Once orders for adoption have been lawfully and properly made, it is only in highly exceptional and very particular circumstances that the court will permit them to be set aside...

[177] In my judgment...Mr and Mrs W were recognising the reality that the adoption orders in relation to [the three children] were made in good faith on the evidence then available, and that, however, heartbreaking it may be for Mr and Mrs W, those orders must stand.

13.3 THE CHANGING FACE OF ADOPTION

13.3.1 FROM CHILDLESS COUPLES AND TROUBLE-FREE BABIES...

The nature and social purpose of adoption has changed dramatically over the course of the twentieth century.

C. Bridge, 'Adoption law: a balance of interests', in J. Herring (ed), *Family law: issues, debates, policy* (Cullompton: Willan, 2001), 198–9

Formal legal adoption is a relatively modern concept. Its roots lie in the changes evident in society after the first world war: numbers of orphaned children needed the permanency and stability that family life supposedly provided and cohabitation, which had become increasingly common, gave rise to the need for secure legal arrangements for both children and birth parents. The first Adoption Act was passed in 1926 with these social purposes in mind. In comparison with the current law that Act was limited. It did not provide for the child's full integration into the adoptive family, it set out only limited grounds for permitting adoption without parental consent, and did not fully address inheritance issues. Adoption was, as Cretney and Masson suggest, a 'private or amateur activity'.

But as the nature of social problems changed so the nature and purpose of adoption also changed. Adoption became a way of dealing with some of the uncomfortable social and human problems that emerged during the 1950s and 60s. Its upsurge during this period was due, primarily, to the increasing numbers of young single mothers unable to care for their illegitimate babies. Social, moral, financial and a variety of practical measures combined to present adoption as the way out for both mother and child. By having the baby adopted straight after birth the mother was perceived as enabled to resume her life untarnished by the product of past immoral conduct. For the baby, adoption was widely perceived as a lucky escape from the shame of illegitimacy. Illegitimacy still carried a social stigma yet the numbers of such births were high. Sexual liberation had arrived but the contraceptive pill had yet to become widely available and abortion was unlawful. As a result, large numbers of white babies were adopted by childless married couples—those whom Lowe and Douglas describe as seeking to avoid the 'oppressive taint of infertility'. In a secretive process designed to facilitate an irrevocable transfer of all legal rights and powers from birth parents to adoptive parents, such babies became the lawful offspring of their new family, born to them as 'a child of the marriage'. The image this conjured up is one of a traditional family more redolent of the 1950s than the twenty-first century, and although it smacks of legislation of earlier times, that is not so.

At its peak in 1968 there were 24,831 adoptions.[11] However, important social changes in the second half of the twentieth century saw a dramatic decline in the number of adoption orders made. Contraception, the ready availability of abortion, and the loss of stigma surrounding single motherhood and illegitimacy drastically reduced the number of babies available for adoption.[12] Increased understanding of the causes of infertility and the availability of new treatments similarly rendered adoption a less attractive option for childless couples. By 1999, the annual number of adoption orders had reached its lowest point at just 4,100.[13] In only a tiny proportion of these cases was the child voluntarily relinquished by the child's mother immediately after birth. Approximately half were adoptions of children out of care, the other half were made up of step-parent and inter-country adoptions.[14] Thus, by the end of the twentieth century the social role played by adoption had changed dramatically.[15] Adoption was no longer about providing childless couples with unwanted, 'trouble-free babies'. The majority of adoptions were either step-parent adoptions or adoptions of children out of care. Although in recent years the number of children adopted out of care has remained relatively stable at about 2,000 per year,[16] the Labour government was keen to

[11] Cretney (2003a), 596.

[12] Bridge (1993), 83. In 1968 approximately half of the 25,000 adoptions were of babies under 12 months old. By 2007, only 3% of the 4,637 adoptions were of babies under 12 months: DH (1993), 4 and ONS (2009b), table 6.2a.

[13] Cabinet Office (2000), 10.

[14] Ibid.

[15] Ibid.

[16] Ibid. Out of the total number of children looked after by the local authority each year, this represents an adoption rate of about 4%. Cabinet Office (2000), 11.

promote adoption as a central plank in its child protection policy. Central to this policy was the principle that 'no child is un-adoptable'.

13.3.2 LOOKED AFTER CHILDREN—DOES ADOPTION OFFER THE BEST SOLUTION?

One of the major factors driving the ACA 2002 was the Labour government's desire to increase the use of adoption as a route to 'permanence' for looked after children unable to return home: put simply, there should be 'more adoptions more quickly'.[17] The new legislation, hailed as the 'most radical overhaul of adoption law in 25 years', was accompanied by National Adoption Standards and performance targets aimed at increasing by 40 per cent the number of children adopted from care by 2004–5.[18] From the outset, the reforms were marked by a strong 'saving children in care' rhetoric.[19] The Prime Minister's foreword to a key policy paper on the issue set the clear tone for the reforms which were to follow.

Cabinet Office, Performance and Innovation Unit, *The Prime Minister's Review of Adoption* (2000), 3

It is hard to overstate the importance of a stable and loving family life for children. That is why I want more children to benefit from adoption.

We know that adoption works for children. Over the years, many thousands of children in the care of Local Authorities have benefited from the generosity and commitment of adoptive families, prepared to offer them the security and well-being that comes from being accepted as members of new families.

But we also know that many children wait in care for far too long.

Some of the reasons are well known. Too often in the past adoption has been seen as a last resort. Too many local authorities have performed poorly in helping children out of care and into adoption. Too many prospective parents have been confused, or put off, by the process of applying to adopt, and the time the whole procedure takes.

The government's arguments were persuasive. Against the backdrop of the Waterhouse Report into child abuse in care homes in North Wales and emerging evidence as to the worryingly poor outcomes for looked after children, adoption appeared by far the better alternative.[20] Continuing problems with children simply left to 'drift in care' and growing disillusionment with the Children Act's strong emphasis on rehabilitation with the birth family further fuelled the Labour government's calls for reform. There was no shortage of evidence to support their arguments. Research on outcomes for adopted children is generally positive, particularly for children *voluntarily relinquished and placed as babies.*

---

[17] Harris-Short (2001), 407.

[18] DH (2000), 5. These targets have met with limited success. The number of adoption orders made in 2004 was 5,360, an increase of 16% from a low of 4,617 in 1998. However, from a high point of 5,486 in 2002, the number of adoptions appears to be declining again, with the number of orders made in 2007 falling to 4,637. ONS (2009b), table 6.2a.

[19] Harris-Short (2001), 406.

[20] Waterhouse (2000). See p 819.

J. Castle, C. Beckett, and C. Groothues, 'Infant adoption in England. A longitudinal account of social and cognitive progress', (2000) 24 *Adoption and Fostering* 26–7

Baby adoptions are viewed as a group for whom successful outcomes are usual. In general, studies of children placed as babies have shown favourable levels of psychosocial functioning, high parental satisfaction and low levels of adoption disruption. Data from the National Child Development Study (NCDS) indicated that adopted children outperformed birth comparisons on maths and reading tests at age seven, and on a measure of general ability at age eleven.

Although children adopted as babies fare extremely well, there have been conflicting findings regarding psychosocial outcome. In their report of adopted adolescents in residential treatment, Grotevant and McRoy mentioned studies from several countries showing increased referral rates for treatment of emotional disturbance in children adopted as infants by childless couples, compared with the normal population. However, where clinical referrals were concerned, it was possible that adoptive parents were more likely to make use of mental health services because of a lower threshold of concern so there are limitations in generalising from clinical cases to the general population of adopted children.

Castle, Beckett, and Groothues' study of 52 adopted children support these findings, with children placed under six months and reviewed at ages four and six, 'showing favourable cognitive and social progress...and high levels of satisfaction with adoption among parents'.[21] However, the outcomes for children *adopted out of care* are less convincing. Disruption rates for children adopted at around the pre-school age (the average age for children placed out of care in England and Wales) are about 5 per cent.[22] A longitudinal study carried out by Dance and Rushton of 99 children placed from care aged between five and eleven years revealed that whilst six years after placement 49 per cent of adoptions were continuing and positive, 28 per cent were continuing but assessed as 'difficult', and 23 per cent had disrupted (child returned to local authority care).[23] Disruption rates for children placed in adolescence are significantly higher, between a third and a half disrupting within a three to five year period. Studies focusing more specifically on the psychosocial and behavioural adjustment of later placed children also reveal a more mixed picture. Howe, Shemmings, and Feast report that older placed children are 'at increased risk of poor mental health, behavioural problems and relationship difficulties'.[24]

Despite these somewhat mixed outcomes it is important not to lose sight of the fact that children adopted out of care still generally fare better than the *most relevant* comparator groups: similarly disadvantaged children who remain in institutional care or who are placed in long-term foster care.[25] Evidence suggests that when compared against these alternative forms of substitute care, adoption is a superior, generally effective form of intervention with the potential to help children make significant strides towards overcoming their earlier damaging experiences. The greater permanence and security offered by adoption appears to be a particularly significant factor in achieving better outcomes.

---

[21] Castle et al (2000), 32. See also IJzendoorn and Juffer (2005); Maugham, Collishaw, and Pickles (1998); and Brand and Brinich (1999).

[22] Triseliotis (2002), 25.

[23] Dance and Rushton (2005), 269.

[24] Howe, Shemmings, and Feast (2001), 337. See also IJzendoorn and Juffer (2005), 327.

[25] Brand and Brinich (1999) and IJzendoorn and Juffer (2005).

J. Triseliotis, 'Long-term foster care or adoption? The evidence examined',
(2002) 7 *Child and Family Social Work* 23, 31

Two broad conclusions can be drawn...First, because of the type of child currently being adopted or fostered, differences in breakdown rates and in adjustment between these two forms of substitute parenting are diminishing and in some age groups evening out. Yet at least one recent study reported that foster care rarely offers permanence. Its placements are too liable to break down. Second, compared with long-term fostering, adoption still provides higher levels of emotional security, a stronger sense of belonging and a more enduring psychosocial base in life for those who cannot live with their birth families.

The main limitation of long-term fostering is its unpredictability and the uncertain and ambiguous position in which the children find themselves. Taken together these conditions appear to generate long-standing feelings of insecurity and anxiety in children. One other possible explanation for this is the different expectations placed on adopters and foster carers and the different commitment that is brought to the task by each of these two groups of 'substitute' parents.

Studies suggesting more mixed outcomes for children adopted out of care do not therefore necessarily undermine the drive to make greater use of adoption as a route to permanence for looked after children. However, caution is needed when considering adoption for older children with difficult, challenging backgrounds, it will not provide a 'happy ending' for every child and children who are already vulnerable should not be unnecessarily exposed to the risk of failure. Clearly adoption is not a panacea and should not be pursued at all costs. It needs to be underpinned by a clear focus on the welfare of the particular child, not government targets, rigid timescales, and budgetary constraints.[26]

13.3.3 ADOPTING CHILDREN OUT OF CARE—NEW CHALLENGES

As the use of adoption has changed, so too has the profile of adopted children. This explains the poorer outcomes for children adopted out of care. These are not the 'trouble-free babies' that once characterized adoption.[27] Children adopted out of care are typically older[28] and acutely vulnerable as a result of 'challenging backgrounds' marked by abuse and neglect. Not surprisingly, these children have a range of 'complex needs'.[29] Problems are compounded by the length of time looked after children typically spend in care before being adopted, many experiencing a number of unsettling moves before they are successfully placed.[30] These difficult pre-placement experiences increase the risk of an adoption disrupting.[31] The changed

---

[26] See generally Sagar and Hitchings (2007). The social workers interviewed as part of their study all expressed concern at the new target-driven approach to adoption, arguing that it was likely to lead to a greater number of unsuitable placements disrupting. Ibid., 207.

[27] Cabinet Office (2000), 14.

[28] In 1999 the average age of a child adopted out of care was four years and four months. Ibid., 12.

[29] Ibid., 14.

[30] Figures from 1999 suggest that the average length of time a child spent in care before being adopted was two years and ten months, with 36% waiting more than three years. 47% of children experienced two or more placements before being successfully placed for adoption. Ibid., 13–14. See Howe, Shemmings, and Feast (2001), 337.

[31] Dance and Rushton (2005), 279; Selwyn, Frazer, and Quinton (2006).

profile of adopted children raises important policy questions about how adoption practice needs to change to meet the demands of its new 'client group'.

Post-adoption support

Children adopted out of care often have a range of physical, social, and educational needs requiring skilled and sensitive parenting. Adoptive parents face a difficult task for which ongoing professional support may be essential. There is a strong argument that having removed these troubled children from their birth parents, the state cannot simply walk away—it has a continuing responsibility to support the child and the adoptive parents as they face the many challenges of adoption. This approach is clearly at odds with the traditional concept of adoption and, from the government's perspective, one of its major advantages: that once the adoption order has been made the adoptive family is legally and socially autonomous, neither expecting nor requiring any additional assistance or support. So strongly is this notion of the new autonomous family embedded within society's understanding of adoption, that many adoptive parents actively resist post-adoption services and support, believing such intervention makes them less than the ideal.[32] However, it has been argued persuasively by Nigel Lowe that if the adoption of children out of care is to work, this 'mindset' has to change.

N. Lowe, 'The changing face of adoption—the gift/donation model versus the contract/services model', (1997b) 9 *Child and Family Law Quarterly* 371, 382–3

[R]eference [has been] made to the 'mind-set' which seems to stem from the practice of baby adoptions, that essentially adoption is a gift and is the final and irrevocable act in which the mother has given away her child...It is the thesis of this article that this 'mind set' is certainly inadequate for the adoption of older children and, even possibly, for all types of adoption, yet, notwithstanding the virtual ending of baby adoption, this type of thinking still permeates the law, and legal and social work practice...

The 'gift/donation' model sits uneasily with the adoption of older children...and it seems clear that a new model is needed. At the very least with regard to older children (if not all children) it needs to be accepted that adoption is not the end of the process but only a stage (albeit an important stage) in an ongoing and often complex process of family development. It is further suggested that adoption of older children out of care is best understood as some kind of informal 'contract' between the birth family, the child and the adoptive family—a 'contract' which brings with it a pattern of reciprocal obligations between the 'parties' and between the adoption agency...

Under this 'contract/services' model the State should expect to provide substantial support both before, during and after the adoption; the adopters should expect to be informed fully of all the circumstances of the child and to be warned properly of the risks of 'failure' both for the child and for themselves. They should also expect that adoption will not necessarily mean the end of contact with members of the birth family and, although this proposition is made much more tentatively, they may also have to expect that the price of ongoing support is that they may not be in complete control of the child's upbringing...

---

[32] Rushton (2003), 46; Sagar and Hitchings (2007).

Consistent with the general thesis that adoption should not be regarded as the end of the process, the State cannot consider that its obligations towards such children as being *ipso facto* discharged by the making of the order.

Fundamental to Lowe's 'contract/service model' of adoption is the state's responsibility to provide a comprehensive post-adoption support service, including, where appropriate, financial support in the form of an adoption allowance.

N. Lowe et al, *Supporting Adoption—Reframing the Approach* (London: BAAF, 1999), 430–1

[I]t is simply not good enough for the legislation [referring to the Adoption Act 1976] to impose an *implicit* obligation upon local authorities to provide post-adoption support as part of the general adoption service. The legislation should be changed so as to make provision of post-adoption support an *express* duty ... With regard to adoption allowances, it is not acceptable that (a) they should be regarded as the exception rather than the norm, (b) they should be lower than fostering allowances, or (c) they should be dependent upon individual agency policy. We maintain that there is a compelling case for society to continue to bear the costs of looking after these especially vulnerable and frequently highly damaged children, particularly those who had previously been removed from their birth families into care on the basis of 'significant harm', and whom the state undertook to look after into adulthood. At the very least these children should be entitled to the same level of financial support as if they continued to be fostered. The adoption process should not financially disadvantage such children (nor their adopters). We recommend that a national standardised system of eligibility and levels of financial support be introduced, possibly by means of a state allowance rather than one paid by the adoption agency. Ideally we would like to see financial considerations removed from the question of adoption so that decisions can be made based entirely on the welfare of the child.

Adoption should not be regarded as 'a cheap option for bringing up children currently languishing in care'.[33]

Open adoption

Children adopted out of care bring with them a very different relationship with their birth family than babies voluntarily relinquished at birth. As Bridge points out, these children know their families and no matter how inadequate or even abusive their parenting may have been, the children will retain 'history, memories and attachments which cannot be erased'.[34] Statutory provisions aimed at eradicating the birth parents from the child's life and 'drawing a veil of secrecy'[35] over the adoption are obviously pointless in the case of older children who have developed and retain close emotional ties to their birth family. Seeking to deny the importance of these ties may well be inimical to the child's interests. The adoption of children out of care has therefore brought with it a demand for greater openness in adoption.

---

[33] Lowe (1997b), 385–6. Changes introduced by the ACA 2002 to the provision of post-adoption support will be discussed below at 13.7.2.
[34] Bridge (1993), 87.
[35] Ibid., 82.

Openness can take a variety of forms, from simply providing the child with information about the birth family, to facilitating regular direct contact with members of the birth family after the adoption. However, protecting, fostering, and encouraging the child's relationship with the birth parents can be difficult to reconcile with the traditional concept of adoption as a total legal transplant of the parent–child relationship.[36]

Widening the pool of potential adopters

People seeking to adopt often still approach adoption agencies with certain preconceptions in mind. Despite the changed profile of adopted children they expect to find 'trouble-free' babies they can raise as 'their own'.[37] That 'ideal' can rarely be realized. Yet many prospective adopters are reluctant to consider older children with difficult backgrounds and a range of challenging needs, including a birth family to accommodate. The sad result is that there are not enough babies and young toddlers to satisfy the number of prospective adopters and not enough prospective adopters to satisfy the number of older children in need of permanent alternative homes. In order to increase the use of adoption for these difficult to place children, people's misconceptions about adoption must be changed and the pool of potential adopters widened beyond the typical white, married, childless couple. By embracing non-traditional family forms, such as single parents, same-sex couples, and heterosexual cohabiting couples, the chances of children in care being successfully placed are substantially improved without necessarily compromising the child's need for stability and security.[38]

A different model of adoption

The changing profile of adopted children has placed the traditional concept of adoption under increasing pressure. Indeed, the needs of looked after children are so different from the children for which adoption was originally conceived that the Labour government's efforts would arguably have been better focused on developing more appropriate forms of alternative care.[39] As Sagar and Hitchings suggest, not enough attention has been paid to the crucial question of whether adoption *should* be the preferred means of securing permanency for looked after children.[40] At the very least, commentators suggest that the legal concept of adoption needs to be fundamentally transformed if it is to successfully fulfil its changing social purpose.

P. Parkinson, 'Child protection, permanency planning and children's right to family life', (2003) 17 *International Journal of Law, Policy and the Family* 147, 161, and 168

It is correct to say that other permanency options are not as final as adoption. They can be revoked. But there is nothing magic about the concept of adoption which makes it the only form of irreversible parenting order. It is possible to devise new forms of order which provide

---

[36] We consider below at 13.7.1 whether the ACA 2002 makes adequate provision for greater openness in adoption.

[37] Sagar and Hitchings (2007), 203.

[38] Changes introduced by the ACA 2002 as to who can adopt, will be discussed below at 13.5.2.

[39] For arguments against adoption in this context see Parkinson (2003), 156–61.

[40] Sagar and Hitchings (2007), 211–12.

for such permanence without severing the legal relationship of a child's extended family. Indeed, adoption itself might become a more widely used option if it were reinvented to remove the legal fiction of rebirthing into a new family in a way which denies the importance of pre-adoption relationships in the family of origin. The Law Commission of New Zealand has recommended that adoption be recharacterized as having the effect of permanently transferring full parental responsibility from the birth parents to the adoptive parents, making the adoptive parents the legal parents of the child but in so doing the law should recognize that the birth family still exists and may have a role in the child's life. The failure to provide certainty and stability to long-term foster carers may be nothing more than a failure of legal imagination...

Despite these calls for finding more imaginative ways of providing permanence for looked after children, the traditional legal concept of adoption has remained entrenched within the ACA 2002. With that in mind, it is questionable whether the current legal framework is really able to meet the needs of today's adopted children.

13.4 ACA 2002: THE CORE PRINCIPLES

13.4.1 THE WELFARE PRINCIPLE

The ACA 2002 provides that whenever 'a court or adoption agency' is 'coming to a decision' relating to the adoption of a child, the child's welfare must be the paramount consideration.[41] The principle is thus of wide application, binding all key decision-makers throughout the adoption process. In recognition of the life-long consequences of adoption, regard must be had to the welfare of the child 'throughout his life'. This allows the decision-maker to take into account a broad range of factors relating to the child's childhood and beyond.[42] To guide the decision-maker, the legislation provides a 'welfare checklist' similar to that within s 1(3) of the Children Act 1989 (CA 1989):

Adoption and Children Act 2002, s 1

(4) The court or adoption agency must have regard to the following matters (among others)—

    (a) the child's ascertainable wishes and feelings regarding the decision (considered in light of the child's age and understanding),

    (b) the child's particular needs,

---

[41] S 1(1)–(2).

[42] See *ASB and KSB v MQS and SSHD* [2009] EWHC 2491, in which an adoption order was made with respect to a 17-year-old boy, Bennett J being satisfied that the applicants genuinely intended to exercise parental responsibility for him (the adoption was not a mere device to gain the child a right of abode in the UK), the child was happy and settled both at school and in the applicant's home, and there was a real and substantial risk to the child's welfare if he had to return to Pakistan. Bennett J was thus satisfied that the adoption order would 'confer real benefits on him' not just for the remainder of his childhood but throughout his life. Ibid., [35] and [42].

(c) the likely effect on the child (throughout his life) of having ceased to be a member of the original family and becoming an adopted person,

(d) the child's age, sex, background and any of the child's characteristics which the court or agency considers relevant,

(e) any harm (within the meaning of the Children Act 1989 (c. 41)) which the child has suffered or is at risk of suffering,

(f) the relationship which the child has with relatives, and with any other person in relation to whom the court or agency considers the relationship to be relevant, including—

(i) the likelihood of any such relationship continuing and the value to the child of its doing so,

(ii) the ability and willingness of any of the child's relatives, or of any such person, to provide the child with a secure environment in which the child can develop, and otherwise to meet the child's needs,

(iii) the wishes and feelings of any of the child's relatives, of any such person, regarding the child.

Many of these factors are familiar, having come directly from s 1(3) of the CA 1989. Of particular note, however, are the provisions relating specifically to the effect of the adoption on the child's legal status (s 1(4)(c)) and the child's existing and future relationship with the birth family (s 1(4)(f)). The term 'relative' expressly includes the child's parents regardless of whether they hold parental responsibility.[43]

The decision to entrench the paramountcy principle throughout the adoption process constitutes an important change from the previous law in which the welfare of the child was the *first* but not the paramount consideration.[44] This brings the law on adoption into line with the CA 1989 and ensures compliance with Article 21 of the United Nations Convention on the Rights of the Child (UNCRC) which provides that any state recognizing or permitting the system of adoption must ensure that the best interests of the child are the paramount consideration. However, the weight to be attributed to the child's welfare in adoption is controversial. Under the previous legislation the decision-maker had the flexibility to take into account factors other than the child's interests, most importantly the rights and interests of the birth parents. This is precluded by a strict application of the paramountcy principle, a potentially problematic development. As adoption entails the irrevocable severance of the parent–child relationship it has profound affects on both the birth parents and the child. Thus, as Bainham notes, 'the total severance of the parent–child relationship ought not to occur without a thorough examination of the *parent's* claims and interests as well as those of the child'.[45] The paramountcy principle does not permit this examination to occur. In interpreting the welfare of the child, ss 1(4)(c) and 1(4)(f) direct the court or the adoption agency to take into account the wishes and feelings of the birth parents and their relationship with the child. However, as these factors must be mitigated through the framework of the welfare principle, this is not the same as giving *separate* consideration to the rights and interests of the birth parents which are strictly only relevant insofar as they bear upon the interests of the child.[46] Given the importance of adoption

---

[43] ACA 2002, s 1(8)(b).
[44] Adoption Act 1976 (AA 1976), s 6.
[45] Bainham (2005), 266–7.
[46] Harris-Short (2001), 419–20.

for the birth family, it is clearly questionable whether focusing exclusively on the child's interests is right in principle. It also raises serious questions about the compatibility of the ACA 2002 with the ECHR.

Unfortunately, emerging trends in the case law do nothing to assuage these concerns. In interpreting the welfare principle enshrined in s 1(4) the courts have adopted a strong and exclusively child-centred approach, resulting in the rights and interests of the birth parents being squeezed out of consideration at every stage of the decision-making process.[47] This is particularly problematic when considered alongside the issue of parental consent.[48]

13.4.2 PARENTAL CONSENT

At key points along the pathway to adoption, the process can only move forward if the court is satisfied that 'each parent or guardian of the child' has consented or that the parent or guardian's consent should be dispensed with.[49] Whenever the legislation requires parental consent, the issue must be dealt with in accordance with s 52. 'Parent' for these purposes is defined as 'a parent having parental responsibility'.[50] The consent of an unmarried father without parental responsibility is therefore not required. Consent must be given 'unconditionally' and with 'full understanding of what is involved'.[51] Consent given by the mother of a child within six weeks of the child's birth is ineffective.[52] In the absence of parental consent, the court is able to dispense with this requirement if certain conditions are satisfied:

Adoption and Children Act 2002, s 52

(1) The court cannot dispense with the consent of any parent or guardian of a child to the child being placed for adoption or to the making of an adoption order in respect of the child unless the court is satisfied that—

(a) the parent or guardian cannot be found or is incapable of giving consent, or

(b) the welfare of the child *requires* the consent to be dispensed with. [Emphasis added]

Except in the limited circumstances provided for in s 52(1)(a), this provision means parental consent can arguably be dispensed with on the basis of a simple welfare test. This would again constitute an important change from the previous law and has thus proved contentious. Under the AA 1976 there were six grounds on which the court could dispense with parental consent.[53] The most widely used was that the parent or guardian was

---

[47] See, especially, *Re P (a child)* [2008] EWCA Civ 535; *C v XYZ County Council* [2007] EWCA Civ 1206.

[48] We discuss the application of the welfare principle to particularly contentious issues at 13.6.

[49] The two key stages are placing the child for adoption and making the adoption order.

[50] S 52(6).

[51] S 52(5).

[52] S 52(3). In order to place a child under six weeks old for adoption the mother must enter into a written agreement with the adoption agency permitting placement. Once the child is six weeks old the mother should be asked to formally give a 's 19 consent' to placement. Failure to obtain the 's 19 consent' once the child is six weeks old will mean that the consent requirements for making an adoption order under s 47(4) will not have been met and the mother's consent will need to be dispensed with. See *A Local Authority v GC* [2009] 1 FCR 127.

[53] AA 1976, s 16.

withholding his or her agreement unreasonably.[54] Although this was subject to differing interpretations, it was tolerably clear from the case law that in determining whether consent was being unreasonably withheld, the birth parent's rights and interests were highly relevant. In other words, it was accepted that a reasonable parent would have regard to his/ her own wishes and feelings when deciding whether to consent to the child's adoption: the child's welfare was not the only or decisive consideration.[55] When the ACA 2002 was passed there was some uncertainty as to whether s 52(1)(b) would be interpreted to allow the courts the same opportunity to consider the birth parents' various rights and interests. Subsequent case law suggests this will not be the case, although the current state of the law is not entirely satisfactory.

The correct interpretation of s 52(1)(b) was first raised by Wall LJ in *Re S (a child) (adoption order or special guardianship order)*.[56] There had been speculation in the academic literature that the use of the term 'requires' in s 52(1)(b) may be interpreted by the courts to demand a higher threshold for dispensing with consent than a straightforward application of the welfare test.[57] Although reaching no final view on the matter, Wall LJ rejected this argument, suggesting a straightforward welfare test would be applied so that once adoption has been found to be in the child's best interests parental consent would automatically be dispensed with.[58]

Wall LJ was given the opportunity to revisit the issue in *Re P (a child)*.[59] It was argued on behalf of the mother that the preliminary view expressed by Wall LJ in *Re S* was 'at odds' with both the ordinary meaning of the word 'requires' and the intention of Parliament when passing the 2002 Act.[60] Rather than a simple application of the welfare test, it was argued that the word 'requires' conveyed 'a sense of the imperative; something which was a necessity; and a demand which was the antithesis of something voluntary or optional'.[61] In other words, it demanded an 'enhanced' welfare test unlikely to be satisfied where an alternative long-term placement such as fostering was an equally viable if not preferable way forward.[62] In support of this position, counsel for the mother relied on parliamentary material suggesting a balance must be struck between the rights of the birth parents and the rights of the child as demanded by the Strasbourg case law and *Johansen v Norway*[63] in particular. Counsel on behalf of the adoption agency took a different approach, arguing against an 'enhanced' welfare test which would require the court to revisit the question of welfare applying a higher or different test when dealing with parental consent. In her submission, the court should simply apply the welfare test as set down in s 1(4) which would mean, as suggested by Wall LJ in *Re S*, that once adoption had been found to be in the child's best interests, it would automatically follow that parental consent should be dispensed with.[64]

---

[54] AA 1976, s 16(2)(b).

[55] *Re W (An infant)* [1971] AC 682; *Re H; Re W (Adoption: Parental Agreement)* (1983) FLR 614; and *Re C (A Minor) (Adoption: Parental Agreement: Contact)* [1993] 2 FLR 260.

[56] [2007] EWCA Civ 54.

[57] See, e.g., Choudhry (2003), 122–4.

[58] [2007] EWCA Civ 54, [71]–[72].

[59] [2008] EWCA Civ 535.

[60] Ibid., [75].

[61] Ibid., [75].

[62] Ibid., [83]–[84].

[63] (App No 17383/90, ECHR) (1997).

[64] [2008] EWCA Civ 535, [99]–[101].

Having identified one of the key objectives of the 2002 Act as being 'to shift the emphasis to a concentration on the welfare of the child',[65] the Court of Appeal appears to confirm this latter approach, firmly rejecting the need to apply an 'enhanced' welfare test to dispensing with consent. However, in the course of its reasoning, the Court also appears to agree, rather curiously, with the submissions made on behalf of the mother that the word 'requires' does indeed convey the essence of the Strasbourg jurisprudence that adoption must be 'imperative' or 'demanded' rather than 'merely optional or reasonable or desirable'. These apparently contradictory positions can be reconciled, according to the Court of Appeal, through the application of the extended welfare test enshrined in s 1(4) and in particular the requirement that the court is to have regard to the child's welfare *throughout his or her life*—to which the loss of the child's existing familial relationships will be particularly significant.

Re P (a child) [2008] EWCA Civ 535

WALL LJ:

116. . . . The guidance is, we think, simple enough. The judge must, of course, be aware of the importance to the child of the decision being taken. There is, perhaps, no more important or far-reaching decision for a child than to be adopted by strangers. However, the word "requires" in section 52(1)(b) is a perfectly ordinary English word. Judges approaching the question of dispensation under the section must, it seems to us, ask themselves the question to which section 52(1)(b) of the 2002 [Act] gives rise, and answer it by reference to section 1 of the same Act, and in particular by a careful consideration of all the matters identified in section 1(4).

117. In summary, therefore, the best guidance which in our judgment this court can give is to advise judges to apply the statutory language with care to the facts of the particular case. The message is, no doubt, prosaic, but the best guidance, we think, is as simple and as straightforward as that . . .

118. Without wishing to qualify in any way the clarity and simplicity of what we have just said, but in deference to [counsel's] careful argument, we think we should add a few words about the Strasbourg jurisprudence to which he referred us.

119. Plainly Article 8 is engaged; and it is elementary that, if Article 8 is not to be breached, any intervention under Part IV or Part V of the 1989 Act, and any placement or adoption order made without parental consent in accordance with section 52(1)(b) of the 2002 Act, must be proportionate to the legitimate aim of protecting the welfare and interests of the child . . .

120. "Necessary" takes its colour from the context but in the Strasbourg jurisprudence has a meaning lying somewhere between "indispensable" on the one hand and "useful", "reasonable" or "desirable" on the other hand. It implies the existence of what the Strasbourg jurisprudence calls a "pressing social need" . . .

124. In assessing what is proportionate, the court has, of course, always to bear in mind that adoption without parental consent is an extreme – indeed the most extreme – interference with family life. Cogent justification must therefore exist if parental consent is to be dispensed with in accordance with section 52(1)(b). Hence the observations of the Strasbourg court in *Johansen v Norway* (1996) . . .

125. This is the context in which the critical word "requires" is used in section 52(1)(b). It is a word which was plainly chosen as best conveying, as in our judgment it does, the essence of the Strasbourg jurisprudence. And viewed from that perspective "requires" does

---

[65] Ibid., [32].

indeed have the connotation of the imperative, what is demanded rather than what is merely optional or reasonable or desirable.

126. What is also important to appreciate is the statutory context in which the word "requires" is here being used, for, like all words, it will take its colour from the particular context. Section 52(1) is concerned with adoption – the making of either a placement order or an adoption order – and what therefore has to be shown is that the child's welfare "requires" *adoption* as opposed to something short of adoption. A child's circumstances may "require" statutory intervention, perhaps may even "require" the indefinite or long-term removal of the child from the family and his or her placement with strangers, but that is not to say that the same circumstances will necessarily "require" that the child be adopted. They may or they may not. The question, at the end of the day, is whether what is "required" is adoption.

127. In our judgment, however, this does not mean that there is some enhanced welfare test to be applied in cases of adoption, in contrast to what [counsel] called a simple welfare test. The difference, and it is an important, indeed vital, difference, is simply that between section 1 of the 1989 Act and section 1 of the 2002 Act.

128. In the first place, section 1(2) of the 2002 Act, in contrast to section 1(1) of the 1989 Act, requires a judge considering dispensing with parental consent in accordance with section 52(1)(b) to focus on the child's welfare "throughout his life." This emphasises that adoption, unlike other forms of order made under the 1989 Act, is something with lifelong implications. In other words, a judge exercising his powers under section 52(1)(b) has to be satisfied that the child's welfare now, throughout the rest of his childhood, into adulthood and indeed throughout his life, requires that he or she be adopted. Secondly, and reinforcing this point, it is important to bear in mind the more extensive 'welfare checklist' to be found in section 1(4) of the 2002 Act as compared with the 'welfare checklist' in section 1(3) of the 1989 Act; in particular, the provisions of section 1(4)(c) – which specifically directs attention to the consequences for the child "throughout his life" – and section 1(4)(f). This all feeds into the ultimate question under section 52(1)(b): does the child's welfare *throughout his life* require adoption as opposed to something short of adoption?

The Court of Appeal's judgment thus amounts to a defence of the position that the welfare test, as set down in s 1(4), is sufficient, without more, to comply with the requirements of the ECHR. In determining whether this position is convincing it is instructive to return to the requirements of the ECHR as established in *Johansen v Norway*.[66] The applicant mother argued that the decision of the Norwegian authorities to terminate her parental rights and responsibilities and place her daughter (S) for adoption shortly after birth breached her Article 8 right to respect for family life. The Court made clear that such a grave interference with the birth parent's rights could not be justified under Article 8(2) on the basis of a simple welfare test.

Johansen v Norway (App No 17383/90, ECHR) (1997)

78. The Court considers that taking a child into care should normally be regarded as a temporary measure to be discontinued as soon as circumstances permit and that any measures of implementation of temporary care should be consistent with the ultimate aim of reuniting the natural parent and the child. In this regard, a fair balance has to be struck between the

---

[66] The issue of step-parent adoption is dealt with in *Söderbäck v Sweden*. Discussed below at 13.6.3.

interests of the child in remaining in public care and those of the parent in being reunited with the child. In carrying out this balancing exercise, the Court will attach particular importance to the best interests of the child, which, *depending on their nature and seriousness*, may override those of the parent. In particular, as suggested by the Government, the parent cannot be entitled under Article 8 of the Convention to have such measures taken as would harm the child's health and development.

In the present case the applicant had been deprived of her parental rights and access in the context of a permanent placement of her daughter in a foster home with a view to adoption by the foster parents. These measures were particularly far-reaching in that they totally deprived the applicant of her family life with the child and were inconsistent with the aim of reuniting them. Such measures should only be applied in exceptional circumstances and could only be justified if they were motivated by an overriding requirement pertaining to the child's best interests…

84.…The Court does not consider that the decision…in so far as it deprived the applicant of her access and parental rights in respect of her daughter, was sufficiently justified for the purposes of Article 8(2), it not having been shown that the measure corresponded *to any overriding requirement* in the child's best interests.

Therefore the Court reaches the conclusion that the national authorities overstepped their margin of appreciation, thereby violating the applicant's rights under Article 8 of the Convention. (Emphasis added).

It is clear from this decision that in a contested adoption the birth parents have *independent* rights which must be carefully weighed against the rights and interests of the child. Thus, whilst 'particular importance' may be attached to the child's welfare, the child's interests are not paramount in the sense of the *only* or *determinative* consideration. The birth parents' rights are on the scales.[67] Moreover, the court makes clear that the need to strike a *fair* balance between these potentially competing rights means the adoption must be *proportionate* to the child's needs. Where the interference with the birth parents' rights and interests is particularly far-reaching, only very weighty and substantial welfare considerations will therefore be sufficient to justify the interference—in marginal cases where the welfare of the child is finely balanced, the adoption will be neither necessary nor proportionate.[68]

The likely practical effect of the Court of Appeal's decision in *Re P* is that once adoption is deemed to be in the child's best interests, parental consent will be dispensed with without further thought or consideration of the birth parents' interests or the demands of the specific wording of s 52(1)(b). Whether this is sufficient to ensure compliance with the Strasbourg jurisprudence is highly doubtful.

13.5 THE ADOPTION PROCESS

13.5.1 MAKING ARRANGEMENTS FOR THE ADOPTION OF A CHILD

Every local authority must provide an adoption service either directly or through a registered adoption society (referred to as an 'adoption agency'). The adoption service must cover two primary functions: (i) making and participating in arrangements for the adoption of

---

[67] The adoptive parents may also have a right to respect for family life under Article 8.

[68] Harris-Short (2001), 423 and Bonner et al (2003), 582–3. See also the comments of Baroness Hale in *Down Lisburn Health and Social Services Trust v H* [2006] UKHL 36, [33]–[34].

children; and (ii) making and participating in arrangements for the provision of adoption support services. If the child's parents wish to voluntarily relinquish the child for adoption they must approach an adoption agency to make the necessary arrangements. It is an offence for anyone other than an adoption agency to make arrangements for the adoption of a child unless: (i) acting pursuant to an order of the High Court; or (ii) the prospective adopters are parents, relatives, or guardians of the child; or (iii) the prospective adopter is the partner of a parent of the child.[69] The extensive statutory restrictions on arranging a 'private adoption' are intended to prevent a black market developing in unwanted babies. They are reinforced by ss 95 and 96 of the ACA 2002 which make it an offence to make or receive any payment for or in consideration of the adoption of a child, other than a payment to a registered adoption society made by a parent or guardian of the child or a prospective adopter in respect of reasonable expenses incurred by the society in connection with the adoption.[70]

In the case of a looked after child, the local authority begins the adoption process once the local authority care plan identifies adoption as the preferred option for permanence. The plan for adoption will only be confirmed following referral of the case to the local authority adoption panel.[71] The adoption panel's role is to advise the local authority on adoption issues. It therefore makes a recommendation in each individual case as to whether adoption is in the child's best interests. Although the final decision remains with the local authority, it was made clear by the Court of Appeal in *Re B (children),* that an application for a placement order cannot be made by an adoption agency until it is satisfied that the child ought to be placed for adoption and it cannot be satisfied that a child ought to be placed for adoption unless it has obtained and carefully considered the recommendation of the adoption panel. The adoption panel's recommendation must have been properly made on the best available evidence.[72] If the decision of the panel is in some way flawed, the adoption agency cannot place the child for adoption and the case will need to be sent back to the panel for reconsideration.[73] Once the decision to place the child for adoption has been properly made, the local authority is under a duty to take the necessary legal steps to obtain authorization to place the child.[74]

13.5.2 FINDING PROSPECTIVE ADOPTERS

English law currently does not recognize a right to adopt. This has also been the clear position under the ECHR although the Strasbourg jurisprudence may now be moving on the issue. In *EB v France*, the European Court reiterated that there is no right to adopt under the family life limb of Article 8. However, it left open whether such a right may now be found to fall within the right to respect for private life.

E.B. v France (App No 43546/02, ECHR) (2008)

41. The Court, noting that the applicant based her application on Article 14 of the Convention, taken in conjunction with Article 8, reiterates at the outset that the provisions of Article 8 do

---

69 ACA 2002, ss 92–93 and 123.
70 Ss 95 and 96.
71 For explanation of this process see Cabinet Office (2000), 24.
72 [2008] EWCA 835, [70].
73 Ibid.
74 S 22.

not guarantee either the right to found a family or the right to adopt...Neither party contests this. The right to respect for "family life" does not safeguard the mere desire to found a family; it presupposes the existence of a family..., or at the very least the potential relationship between, for example, a child born out of wedlock and his or her natural father..., or the relationship that arises from a genuine marriage, even if family life has not yet been fully established..., or the relationship that arises from a lawful and genuine adoption...

42. Nor is a right to adopt provided for by [French] domestic law or by other international instruments, such as the Convention on the Rights of the Child...or the Hague Convention of 29 May 1993 on the Protection of Children and Co-operation in Respect of International Adoption...

43. The Court has, however, previously held that the notion of "private life" within the meaning of Article 8 of the Convention is a broad concept which encompasses, inter alia, the right to establish and develop relationships with other human beings..., the right to "personal development"...or the right to self-determination as such...It encompasses elements such as names..., gender identification, sexual orientation and sexual life, which fall within the personal sphere protected by Article 8..., and the right to respect for both the decisions to have and not to have a child...

45. It should...be noted that the applicant claimed to have been discriminated against on the ground of her avowed homosexuality, resulting in a violation of the provisions of Article 14 of the Convention taken in conjunction with Article 8.

46. The court is not therefore called upon to rule whether the right to adopt, having regard to, inter alia, to developments in legislation in Europe and the fact that the Convention is a living instrument which must be interpreted in the light of present day conditions...should or should not fall within the ambit of Art 8 of the Convention taken alone.

The European Court's failure to grapple directly with the question of whether the right to adopt is protected within the private life limb of Article 8 has been subjected to convincing criticism, particularly in light of the Court's recent jurisprudence on assisted reproduction.[75]

I. Curry-Sumner, *'E.B. v France:* a missed opportunity', (2009) 21 *Child and Family Law Quarterly* 356, 362

[I]f one does not accept that the right to adopt should fall within the ambit of Article 8, an otherwise unjustifiable distinction will arise between couples wishing to adopt and those wishing to use artificial reproduction techniques. If the court now accepts that the decision to have or not to have a child falls within the scope of Article 8, which the court already acknowledged in *Evans v UK*, why does this not also apply to those who have chosen to follow the route of adoption...[T]he court expressly stated that 'the right to respect for both the decisions to become and not to become a parent' falls within the ambit of Article 8. Is this not also true of adoptions? Obviously, the 'decision to adopt' does not and nor should it lead to a 'right to adopt', in the same way that a 'decision to have a child using artificial insemination techniques does not guarantee a 'right to a child'. However, in recognising that adoption is a method through which individuals and couples are able to realise their wish to raise a child and thus provide a child in need with a familial home, is this decision equally deserving of the protection laid down by the Convention as the desire to raise one's own genetic child?

[75] See 9.4.2.

Although the European Court has avoided giving any determinative answer to the question of whether Article 8 per se protects the right to adopt, it is clear that should the state choose to go beyond its ECHR obligations and allow individuals to apply, it cannot do so in a discriminatory manner.[76]

The selection of prospective adopters under English law is a matter for the adoption agency, although it must comply with any statutory restrictions as to who may apply for an adoption order. In this regard, the pool of prospective adopters was widened considerably by the ACA 2002. Section 49(1) now provides that an application for an adoption order may be made by a 'couple' or one person. 'Couple' is defined in s 144(4) as a married couple, two people who are civil partners of each other, or two people (whether of different sexes or the same sex) living as partners in an enduring family relationship. Hedley J has held that in determining whether a couple are 'living as partners in an enduring family relationship' it is not necessary for them to be living together in the same property—'what is required is: first, an unambiguous intention to create and maintain family life, and secondly, a factual matrix consistent with that intention'.[77] The government's decision to allow same-sex and unmarried opposite-sex couples to adopt was one of the most controversial changes introduced by the ACA 2002. Under the previous legislation an adoption order could not be made in favour of more than one person unless the couple were married.[78] This meant opposite-sex cohabiting couples and same-sex couples could not adopt 'as a couple', although one of them could apply as a single applicant and a residence order made to confer parental responsibility on the non-adopting partner.[79] This reflected the belief that family units headed by a married couple provided adopted children with much greater security and stability—a view which still prevails amongst some members of the legislature and the senior judiciary.[80] With the need to widen the pool of prospective adopters, the Labour government decided late in the legislative process to lift the restriction.

The government's decision pre-empted developments in the Strasbourg jurisprudence which has subsequently held that it is not permissible for states to exclude a prospective adopter from consideration on the grounds (whether direct or indirect) of his or her sexuality.

E.B. v France (App No 43546/02, ECHR) (2008)

48. The prohibition of discrimination enshrined in Article 14...extends beyond the enjoyment of the rights and freedoms which the Convention and the Protocols thereto require each State to guarantee. It applies also to those additional rights, falling within the general scope of any Convention Article, for which the State has voluntarily decided to provide. This principle is well entrenched in the Court's case-law...

49. The present case does not concern adoption by a couple or by the same-sex partner of a biological parent, but solely adoption by a single person. Whilst Article 8 of the Convention is silent as to this question, the Court notes that French legislation expressly grants single persons the right to apply for authorisation to adopt and establishes a procedure to that end. Accordingly, the Court considers that the facts of this case undoubtedly fall within the ambit

---

[76] *EB v France* (App No 43546/02, ECHR) (2008), [49].

[77] *T & M v OCC & C* [2010] EWHC 964, [16]–[17].

[78] AA 1976, s 14.

[79] *Re AB (A Minor) (Adoption: Parental Consent)* [1996] 1 FCR 633. See discussion at p 685.

[80] See, e.g., *Re P (Adoption: Unmarried Couple)* [2008] UKHL 38, [12]–[13] (per Lord Hoffmann) and [108]–[112] (per Baroness Hale).

of Article 8 of the Convention. Consequently, the State, which has gone beyond its obligations under Article 8 in creating such a right – a possibility open to it under Article 53 of the Convention – cannot, in the application of that right, take discriminatory measures within the meaning of Article 14...

50. The applicant alleged in the present case that, in the exercise of her right under the domestic law, she had been discriminated against on the ground of her sexual orientation. The latter is a concept covered by Article 14 of the Convention...The Court also points out that in *Fretté v. France*..., to which the parties expressly referred, the applicant complained that the rejection of his application for authorisation to adopt had implicitly been based on his sexual orientation alone. The Chamber found that Article 14 of the Convention, taken in conjunction with Article 8, was applicable...

51. Accordingly, Article 14 of the Convention, taken in conjunction with Article 8, is applicable in the present case...

ALLEGED VIOLATION OF ARTICLE 14 OF THE CONVENTION TAKEN IN CONJUNCTION WITH ARTICLE 8

53. The applicant maintained that the refusal to grant her authorisation to adopt had been based on her "lifestyle", in other words her homosexuality...

The Court's assessment...

84. The Court...notes that the administrative courts went to some lengths to rule that although regard had been had to the applicant's sexual orientation, it had not been the basis for the decision in question and had not been considered from a hostile position of principle.

85. However, in the Court's opinion the fact that the applicant's homosexuality featured to such an extent in the reasoning of the domestic authorities is significant...[The Court] observes that the manner in which certain opinions were expressed was indeed revealing in that the applicant's homosexuality was a determining factor. In particular, the Court notes that...the psychologist from the children's welfare service recommended that authorisation be refused, referring to, among other things, an "unusual attitude [on the part of the applicant] to men in that men are rejected"...

87. Regarding the systematic reference to the lack of a "paternal referent", the Court disputes not the desirability of addressing the issue, but the importance attached to it by the domestic authorities in the context of adoption by a single person. The fact that it is legitimate for this factor to be taken into account should not lead the Court to overlook the excessive reference to it in the circumstances of the present case.

88. Thus, notwithstanding the precautions taken by the Nancy Administrative Court of Appeal, and subsequently by the *Conseil d'Etat*, to justify taking account of the applicant's "lifestyle", the inescapable conclusion is that her sexual orientation was consistently at the centre of deliberations in her regard and omnipresent at every stage of the administrative and judicial proceedings.

89. The Court considers that the reference to the applicant's homosexuality was, if not explicit, at least implicit. The influence of the applicant's avowed homosexuality on the assessment of her application has been established and, having regard to the foregoing, was a decisive factor leading to the decision to refuse her authorisation to adopt...

90. The applicant therefore suffered a difference in treatment. Regard must be had to the aim behind that difference in treatment and, if the aim was legitimate, to whether the different treatment was justified.

91. The Court reiterates that, for the purposes of Article 14, a difference in treatment is discriminatory if it has no objective and reasonable justification, which means that it does not pursue a "legitimate aim" or that there is no "reasonable proportionality between the means employed and the aim sought to be realised"...Where sexual orientation is in issue, there is a need for particularly convincing and weighty reasons to justify a difference in treatment regarding rights falling within Article 8...

92. In that connection the Court observes that the Convention is a living instrument, to be interpreted in the light of present-day conditions...

93. In the Court's opinion, if the reasons advanced for such a difference in treatment were based solely on considerations regarding the applicant's sexual orientation this would amount to discrimination under the Convention...

94. The Court points out that French law allows single persons to adopt a child..., thereby opening up the possibility of adoption by a single homosexual, which is not disputed. Against the background of the domestic legal provisions, it considers that the reasons put forward by the Government cannot be regarded as particularly convincing and weighty such as to justify refusing to grant the applicant authorisation.

95....In this case, moreover, the applicant presented, in the terms of the judgment of the *Conseil d'Etat*, "undoubted personal qualities and an aptitude for bringing up children", which were assuredly in the child's best interests, a key notion in the relevant international instruments...

96. Having regard to the foregoing, the Court cannot but observe that, in rejecting the applicant's application for authorisation to adopt, the domestic authorities made a distinction based on considerations regarding her sexual orientation, a distinction which is not acceptable under the Convention...

98. There has accordingly been a breach of Article 14 of the Convention taken in conjunction with Article 8.

Although the European Court does not explicitly state as such, the decision in *EB v France* effectively overrules the earlier decision of the Court in *Fretté v France* in which it held that the rejection of a single gay man as a prospective adopter on the basis of his sexual orientation was justified to protect the interests of children, particularly in light of the wide margin of appreciation afforded to states on such sensitive matters.[81]

Of crucial importance to the decision in *EB v France* is the fact that the French authorities permit adoption by single 'heterosexual' applicants and cannot therefore discriminate against single 'homosexual' applicants. The issue would be different if the domestic authorities imposed wider restrictions on adoption such as limiting it to married couples. The question would then be whether the state is justified in precluding from consideration all unmarried cohabiting couples and single applicants, regardless of sexual orientation. The European Court has not yet been called upon to deal specifically with this question. However, in dealing with such restrictions on adoption in Northern Ireland, the House of Lords held that such difference in treatment between married and unmarried couples is contrary to Articles 8 and 14 ECHR.[82] Whilst expressing some sympathy for the view that it is better for children to be raised by a couple who have given each other the commitment of marriage, the House of Lords held that a 'bright line' exclusion of all unmarried couples

---

[81] *Fretté v France* (App No 36515/97, ECHR) (2003). For an excellent critique of the decision in *EB v France* see Curry-Sumner (2009).

[82] Lord Walker dissented on a point of constitutional law.

could not be justified on the basis of protecting the child's welfare. Indeed, to the contrary, the House of Lords took the view that it is in the interests of children for the 'door to adoption' to be opened as widely as possible.[83]

Re P (Adoption: Unmarried Couple) [2008] UKHL 38

LORD HOFFMANN:

16. The question therefore is whether in this case there is a rational basis for having any bright line rule. In my opinion, such a rule is quite irrational. In fact, it contradicts one of the fundamental principles...that the court is obliged to consider whether adoption "by particular...persons" will be in the best interest of the child. A bright line rule cannot be justified on the basis of the needs of administrative convenience or legal certainty, because the law requires the interests of each child to be examined on a case-by-case basis. [The judge] said that "the interests of these two individual applicants must be balanced against the interests of the community as a whole." In this formulation the interests of the particular child,...the most important consideration, have disappeared from sight, sacrificed to a vague and distant utilitarian calculation. That seems to me to be wrong. If, as may turn out to be the case, it would be in the interests of the welfare of this child to be adopted by this couple, I can see no basis for denying the child this advantage in "the interests of the community as a whole"...

18. It is one thing to say that, in general terms, married couples are more likely to be suitable adoptive parents than unmarried ones. It is altogether another to say that one may rationally assume that no unmarried couple can be suitable adoptive parents. Such an irrebuttable presumption defies everyday experience. The Crown suggested that, as they could easily marry if they chose, the very fact that they declined to do so showed that they could not be suitable adoptive parents. I would agree that the fact that a couple do not wish to undertake the obligations of marriage is a factor to be considered by the court in assessing the likely stability of their relationship and its impact upon the long term welfare of the child. Once again, however, I do not see how this can be rationally elevated to an irrebuttable presumption of unsuitability.

19. What are the "interests of the community as a whole" of which [the judge] spoke? He was right to say that a proposal a year or two ago to amend the law by removing the requirement of marriage generated a great deal of passion. People were concerned that it would "send a signal" that the institution of marriage was undervalued, or encourage people not to marry on the ground that being unmarried would be no obstacle to adopting children. But the question for the court is whether these concerns have any rational basis, and, even more important, whether it is right to take them into account in a case in which the law gives priority to the interests of the individual child. In my opinion, neither of these questions can be given an affirmative answer.

20. The judge and the Court of Appeal both emphasised that the question of whether unmarried couples should be allowed to adopt raised a question of social policy and that social policy was in principle a matter for the legislature. That is true in the sense that where questions of social policy admit of more than one rational choice, the courts will ordinarily regard that choice as being a matter for Parliament...But that does not mean that Parliament is entitled to discriminate in any case which can be described as social policy. The discrimination must at least have a rational basis. In this case, it seems to me to be based upon a straightforward fallacy, namely, that a reasonable generalisation can be turned into an irrebuttable presumption for individual cases.

---

[83] [2008] UKHL 38, [54] (per Lord Hope).

LORD HOPE:

54. . . . The aim sought to be realised in regulating eligibility for adoption is how best to safe-guard the interests of the child. Eligibility simply opens the door to the careful and exacting process that must follow before a recommendation is made. The interests of the child require that this door be opened as widely as reasonably possible. Otherwise there will be a risk of excluding from assessment couples whose personal qualities and aptitude for child rearing are beyond question. To exclude couples who are in an enduring family relationship from this process at the outset simply on the ground that they are not married to each other would be to allow considerations favouring marriage to prevail over the best interests of the child. I do not think that this can be said to be either objectively justified or proportionate. From this it must follow that the appellants' exclusion from eligibility would be incompatible with their Convention rights as it would be discriminatory.

LORD MANCE:

134. The present case concerns the strengthening and deepening of private and family relationships that can arise on all sides from adoption. Adoption cements a family unit. It gives the child maintenance rights against the adoptor(s). It makes the child a member of the adoptor(s)' wider family, and confers inheritance rights in that connection. It is a process in relation to which the child's well-being ought to be paramount. The fact that proposed adoptors are a married couple is on any view a material factor. Society is entitled to place weight on the existence of such a bond. But that does not mean that every married couple are suitable or every unmarried couple unsuitable as adoptors. A close scrutiny of all the circumstances is required in the particular child's interests before any adoption can be sanc-tioned. A couple's decision to remain unmarried cannot determine what is in the child's best interests. In today's world, failure to tie the knot is not to be equated with lack of actual com-mitment; and one would have thought that a joint wish to adopt was itself, at least to some extent, a counter-balancing factor. The threshold criterion of marriage which exists under the Northern Irish legislation looks at the matter in terms of the couple's decision whether or not to marry, rather than from the viewpoint of the child or the potential benefits of joint adoption for the child. It excludes all possibility of adoption by all unmarried couples, however long-standing and stable their relationship. It precludes any second stage: any scrutiny at all of the circumstances, the needs or the interests of the particular child. The legislation distinguishes between a married and an unmarried couple, both equally suitable as adoptors, purely on the basis of marital status. The line drawn does not avoid the need for a second stage scrutiny where adoption is possible. It simply makes adoption and the security and benefits which it would bring for the child impossible in the case of this child unless the couple marry.

135. The legislation is thus in my view unjustifiably discriminatory on any objective assess-ment in a manner which cannot in a United Kingdom or Northern Irish context be reconciled with the respect for private and family life protected by article 8 read with article 14.

Lords Hoffmann, Hope, and Mance all expressed confidence that if the issue were to go to Strasbourg, the European Court would take the same view.[84]

Parliament's decision to allow same-sex couples and opposite-sex cohabiting couples to adopt provides important recognition of the diverse nature of family life in contemporary

---

[84] Ibid., [27] (per Lord Hoffmann); [53] (per Lord Hope), [125] (per Lord Mance). Baroness Hale was less certain on this point but held that, in any event, it was open to the domestic courts to go beyond the strictures of the Strasbourg jurisprudence. Ibid., [84], [115].

society. However, the way in which this change was secured, and the concerns which under-pinned the change, have been the subject of criticism.

I. Dey, 'Adapting Adoption: A Case of Closet Politics?', (2005) 19 *International Journal of Law, Policy and Family* 289, 303–5

Nowhere did the shift to a more open approach to adoption meet with more political resistance than over the inclusion of same-sex couples amongst prospective adopters. Anticipating resistance, the Government refused to make the extension of adoption rights to same sex couples a point of principle. It acceded only when convinced by pressure from adoption agencies of the need to reduce delays by extending the pool of prospective adopters to include unmarried couples. Finding adoptive parents in short supply, agencies had extended their recruitment nets well beyond the confines of the conventional family. Agencies had become more circumspect about excluding potential adopters on general grounds such as age or sexual orientation. In doing so, they found that adoption could work without the conventional confines... For hard-to-place children the 'traditional preference' for the idealized conventional family became a prejudice that agencies could no longer afford to indulge... Once the decision had been made in favour of unmarried couples the threat of falling foul of human rights legislation persuaded the Government to avoid an invidious distinction between gay and heterosexual cohabiting couples. There was no vigorous assertion of gay rights to adoption; the emphasis was placed almost entirely on the interests of the child...

[T]he case for not discriminating against same-sex couples went by de-fault. This was not for want of ammunition, for there was no evidence to date that children did less well in homosexual or heterosexual families.

The Labour government's failure to tackle the question of same-sex adoption as a matter of principle has potentially wider repercussions. It is clear under the Equality Act 2010 that an adoption agency cannot refuse to provide adoption services to same-sex couples wishing to adopt, even if such adoptions would contravene the agency's religious beliefs.[85] However, as Dey argues, less direct discriminatory practices in the selection of prospective adopters may well continue. Indeed, s 45(2) of the ACA 2002 provides that in determining the suitability of adopters, regulations may provide that 'proper regard is to be had to the need for stability and permanence in their relationship'.[86] This arguably provides a basis on which the greater 'stability and permanence' offered by traditional heterosexual marriage can continue to be privileged over other 'less enduring' family forms—a position given some support by the House of Lords in *Re P*.[87] Commentators have observed how 'adoption for the homosexual parent only seems to occur where the child has special needs or behavioural problems, and the homosexual parent concerned has exceptional caring qualities to offer, perhaps beyond what may be expected of the "normal parent".[88] It thus seems that there are two pools of prospective adopters: the preferred traditional family unit deemed suitable to care for any child

---

[85] See Equality Act 2010, ss 12 and 29, replacing the Equality Act (Sexual Orientation) Regulations 2007, SI 2007/1263. As a result of these provisions Catholic adoption agencies in England and Wales have either had to close or sever their ties with the church. See <www.telegraph.co.uk/news/newstopics/religion/7952526/Last-Catholic-adoption-agency-faces-closure-after-Charity-Commission-ruling.html>.

[86] It does not appear that this has been expressly included within the regulations. See Adoption Agencies Regulations 2005, SI 2005/389.

[87] [2008] UKHL 38, [12]–[13] (per Lord Hoffmann) and [108]–[112] (per Baroness Hale).

[88] Marshall (2003), 843–4.

and a second group who provide a fall-back option for particularly difficult to place children or who can establish some particular reason on the basis of the child's welfare why placing the child in this less than optimal family setting is justified.[89] There is, in other words, no *general* acceptance of the *equal* parenting worth of single, same sex, and possibly also opposite-sex cohabiting couples. Yet, as Tobin and McNair argue, there is nothing within the empirical research on gay and lesbian parenting to justify this continuing caution.[90]

All people wishing to adopt in England and Wales are subjected to rigorous vetting procedures. Applicants who are unhappy with the decision of an adoption agency as to their suitability to adopt, may apply for the decision to be reviewed by an independent review panel established in accordance with s 12.[91]

13.5.3 PLACING THE CHILD FOR ADOPTION

Placing a child with prospective adopters is a vitally important step in the adoption process. An adoption agency can only place a child for adoption in accordance with ss 18–29 of the ACA 2002. Consent is a crucial issue at this stage of the proceedings because in many contested cases the parents will be unable to re-open consent at the final adoption hearing.

Placing the child with the birth parent's consent

Where the birth parents consent, the adoption agency can place the child without the courts' prior authorization.[92] The birth parents have the option of consenting only to a specific placement or of consenting generally to any placement chosen by the agency.[93] At the same time as consenting to the placement of the child, the birth parents may give their advance consent to the making of an adoption order.[94] Consent can again be general or limited to adoption by the specific individuals with whom the child is to be placed.[95] At the same time as giving consent, or any time thereafter, the parents can give notice to the adoption agency that they do not wish to be informed of any subsequent adoption application.[96] The birth parents can withdraw this notice and their advance consent to the adoption at any time up to the point the adoption order is made.[97]

Where the child is voluntarily relinquished by the mother and the mother wishes to keep the fact of the birth and subsequent adoption secret, questions have arisen as to whether she is entitled to have her wish for confidentiality respected or whether the birth father should be notified and the possibility of a placement with him or the extended maternal or paternal family investigated. Under the AA 1976, the courts took the consistent position that birth fathers should be informed about the adoption and their views considered before the child was placed for adoption. This was always subject to the particular facts of the case including practical considerations such as whether it was feasible to identify and locate the father, as

---

[89] For a worrying small-scale study of social work attitudes towards homosexual applicants post-2002 legislation see, Hitchings and Sagar (2007).

[90] Tobin and McNair (2009), 127.

[91] Independent Review of Determinations (Adoption) Regulations 2005, SI 2005/3332, reg 3.

[92] ACA 2002, s 19(1).

[93] Ibid.

[94] S 20(1).

[95] S 20(2).

[96] S 20(4)(a).

[97] S 20(3) and (4)(b).

well as welfare considerations concerning the child.[98] This approach was followed applying the ACA 2002 in *Re L (Adoption: Contacting Natural Father)*,[99] Munby J holding that 'where there exists family life within the meaning of Art 8 of the ECHR as between the mother and the father, one generally requires "strong countervailing factors"...to justify the exclusion from the adoption process of an unmarried father without parental responsibility'.[100] The issue arose again before the Court of Appeal in *C v X, Y, Z County Council*.[101] It was argued on the child's behalf that this approach to notifying unmarried fathers and members of the extended family had been transformed into a legal duty under the 2002 legislation, such that, even where, as on the facts of this case, the mother wished the child's birth to remain a secret from her family, the local authority nevertheless had an obligation to make inquiries about the father and the wider family. It was suggested that imposing such a duty on the local authority would serve two important purposes: first, it would enable inquiries to be made as to the possibility of a long-term placement for the child within the extended family; second, even if such a placement did not materialize, the information gathered about the birth families would be important for the child as he or she grew older. It was thus contended that s 1(4)(c) and (f) created an expectation of disclosure to the birth family and 'compelling reasons' would be needed to prevent it taking place, particularly to the child's father.[102]

The Court of Appeal disagreed. Despite the current emphasis on the value of the child's relationships (both actual and potential) with the birth family, the Court of Appeal dismissed the argument that there should be a general duty on the local authority to make inquiries in the context of adoption. The singularly 'child-centred' perspective of the ACA 2002 again stood at the heart of the Court of Appeal's reasoning, rendering the rights of the birth family, including the father, of little concern.

C v X, Y, Z County Council [2007] EWCA Civ 1206

ARDEN LJ:

3. In my judgment...when a decision requires to be made about the long-term care of a child, whom a mother wishes to be adopted, there is no duty to make enquiries which it is not in the interests of the child to make, and enquiries are not in the interests of the child simply because they will provide more information about the child's background: they must genuinely further the prospect of finding a long-term carer for the child without delay. This interpretation does not violate the right to family life. The objective of finding long-term care must be the focus of making any further enquiries and that means the court has to evaluate evidence about those prospects. That did not happen in this case....

14. This is a question of statutory interpretation. It is necessary to go back to s 1 [of the ACA 2002]. In my judgment, the governing provision is subs (2), because it lays down a 'paramount' or overarching consideration, and not surprisingly that paramount consideration is the child's welfare. Parliament has added that the reference to welfare is to welfare throughout a child's life and not simply in the short term future or the child's childhood. All the other provisions of s 1 about decision-making take effect subject to this provision.

---

[98] *Re H and G (Adoption: Consultation of Unmarried Fathers)* [2001] 1 FLR 646.
[99] [2007] EWHC 1771.
[100] Ibid., [25]. On the facts of the case Munby J was 'sceptical' as to whether the father would have any right under Article 8.
[101] [2007] EWCA Civ 1206.
[102] Ibid., [23].

15. The result is that s1 is child-centred. It is not "mother-centred". The emphasis is on the interests of the child and not those of the mother. As the European Court of Human Rights ("the Strasbourg court") expressed it in one case, adoption means "giving a family to a child and not the child to a family"... The interests of the child will include the child's interest in retaining its identity, and this is likely to be important to the child in adulthood. But identity is only one factor in the balance that has to be struck. S 1 does not privilege the birth family over adoptive parents simply because they are the birth family...

16. S 1 then lists a number of matters that the court or adoption agency must have in mind when it makes any decision about adoption. Importantly, those matters include delay (subs (3))...

17....The legislation is not prescriptive...[Section] 1 does not establish any preference for any particular result or prescribe any particular conclusion. Importantly, as I have said, it does not express a preference for following the wishes of the birth family or placing a child with the child's birth family, though this will often be in the best interests of the child. The one exception is delay. Delay is always to be regarded as in some degree likely to prejudice the child's welfare: see subs (3). Parliament has here made a value judgement about the likely impact of delay and it is not open to the court or the adoption agency to quarrel with that basic value judgement.

18. In this particular case, subs (4) (c) and (f) are particularly important...

20. Subs (4) (f) requires the court to have regard to the wishes and feelings of a child's relatives and their ability and willingness to provide the child with long-term care. However, that assumes that information is reasonably available about these matters. If the information is not readily available, the court or adoption agency may want to obtain it. But in the light of subs (2) there [sic] are only required to do so, if that is required for the purposes of the child's welfare and if they consider it right to take those steps notwithstanding that any delay is likely to prejudice the child's welfare.

21. It can be seen from this analysis that when a decision requires to be made about the long-term care of the child, whom a mother wishes to be adopted, there is no duty to make enquiries of an absolute kind. There is only a duty to make enquiries, if it is in the interests of the child to make those enquiries. In the present case, the judge considered that in adult life the child would benefit from more information about the child's father. But in the context of the decision-making with which the judge was concerned, I do not consider that that fact could of itself animate indeed the exercise of discretion. The immediate question with which the guardian and local authority were concerned was who would look after the child on a long-term basis. The enquiries had to be focused on that result. That meant looking at the evidence about the prospective carers within the mother's family. It was not enough simply to say that it would be in the child's interests to be placed with her birth family...Finding out more about the child's background for E's information in the future was secondary to that objective, and it would inevitably lead to delay...

24. The logical consequence of my interpretation of s 1 is that exceptional situations can arise in which relatives, or even a father, of a child remain in ignorance about the child at the time of its adoption. But this result is consistent with other provisions of the 2002 Act.

The ECHR arguments are considered by Arden LJ but ultimately she holds that there is nothing within them that requires disclosure. As to the right to respect for family life, she holds in accordance with the Strasbourg jurisprudence that an unmarried father ('who is only a one-night stand') has no right to respect to family life that would be infringed by non-disclosure.[103] As regards the mother's extended family, whilst she recognizes that

---

103 Ibid., [39].

grandparents and other close relatives may have a right to respect for family life, she holds that any prima facie violation will be justified by the fact that the decision as to disclosure will have been based on the child's welfare.[104] No final conclusion is reached on the question of whether the child may have a right to respect for family life which requires inquiries to be made as to whether she can be raised by her natural father. As with the extended family, Arden LJ holds that any such right would be capable of being overridden by the competing welfare considerations under Article 8(2).[105] The child's right to information about her family, as protected under the private life limb of Article 8, is also considered. However, Arden LJ concludes that the current provisions of the ACA 2002 fall well within the state's margin of appreciation in determining appropriate measures to meet this particular requirement of Article 8.[106]

The Court of Appeal's judgment in *C v X, Y, Z Council* sends out a clear message as to the courts' perception of the overriding priorities now entrenched within the ACA 2002. The child's welfare is determinative; avoiding delay is of paramount importance; and the purported rights and interests of the birth family must not divert attention away from these two core objectives. In the words of Thorpe LJ, the ACA 2002 does not compel the adoption agency to 'inform and assess all and sundry'—including the child's father.[107] The opportunity to 'fast-track [the child] into adoption in accordance with her mother's wishes' must not be lost.[108]

Placing the child without consent: placement orders

Where the birth parents do not consent, or the local authority has applied for a care order, the adoption agency must apply to the court under s 21 for a placement order authorizing them to place the child for adoption.[109] A placement order confers general authorization on the adoption agency to place the child with any prospective adopters considered appropriate.[110] The welfare principle applies,[111] and the order can only be made if the parent(s) or guardian(s) consent or the court is satisfied consent should be dispensed with. The consent requirements must be dealt with in accordance with s 52. Further conditions on making the order are set down in s 21(2):

Adoption and Children Act 2002, s 21

(2) The court may not make a placement order in respect of a child unless—

    (a) the child is subject to a care order,

    (b) the court is satisfied that the conditions in section 31(2) of the 1989 Act (conditions for making a care order) are met, or

    (c) the child has no parent or guardian.

---

[104] Ibid.
[105] Ibid., [35].
[106] Ibid., [33].
[107] Ibid., [78].
[108] Ibid., [69].
[109] S 19(3).
[110] S 21(1).
[111] S 1(1) and (7).

Before placing a child for adoption, the threshold conditions for state intervention into family life as set down in s 31 of the CA 1989 must therefore be met: the child must be suffering or likely to suffer significant harm attributable to the parents' care. This ensures that no child can be placed for adoption against the birth parents' wishes on the basis of a simple welfare test.

In order to eliminate delays in the adoption process, the ACA 2002 places a duty on the local authority to apply for a placement order if certain conditions are satisfied:

Adoption and Children Act 2002, s 22

(1) A local authority must apply to the court for a placement order in respect of a child if—

  (a) the child is placed for adoption by them or is being provided with accommodation by them,

  (b) no adoption agency is authorized to place the child for adoption,

  (c) the child has no parent or guardian or the authority consider that the conditions in section 31(2) of the 1989 Act are met, and

  (d) the authority are satisfied that the child ought to be placed for adoption.

(2) If

  (a) an application has been made (and has not been disposed of) on which a care order might be made in respect of a child, or

  (b) a child is subject to a care order and the appropriate local authority are not authorized to place the child for adoption,

the appropriate local authority must apply to the court for a placement order if they are satisfied that the child ought to be placed for adoption.

These provisions in effect require the local authority to apply for a placement order as soon as they are satisfied that a looked after child should be placed for adoption. This duty applies whether a care order is in force and whether an application for a care order has been made provided the local authority 'consider' that the threshold conditions are satisfied. This means that a child can be placed for adoption against the birth parents' wishes without a care order ever being made.

The important question of whether the practice of 'dual planning' could be reconciled with the duties of the local authority under s 22 was addressed by the Court of Appeal in *Re P (a child)*.[112] The legal issue was whether the court could be said to be 'satisfied that the child ought to be placed for adoption' in circumstances where the local authority acknowledged that finding a suitable adoptive placement was likely to prove difficult and, in light of this uncertainty, had adopted a 'dual planning' approach. It was argued on behalf of the mother that if both long-term fostering and adoption were regarded as potentially suitable placements, it could not be said that a placement order 'ought' to be made or was required in the children's best interests.

The Court of Appeal rejected this argument in favour of a pragmatic approach, holding that whilst there were important legal, philosophical, and practical differences between adoption and fostering, provided the local authority were satisfied that adoption was in the

---

[112] [2008] EWCA Civ 535, [134]–[140] and [156]–[159].

child's best interests they could, and indeed ought, to apply for a placement order without precluding undertaking a simultaneous search for long-term foster parents. In the Court of Appeal's judgment, this dual approach was entirely sensible for 'compelling pragmatic reasons': the chances of finding a suitable adoptive home were considerably improved by having the placement order firmly in place whilst any further delay for the child would be avoided if an adoptive home could not be found.

The situation in *Re P (a child)* needs to be distinguished from that which was considered by a differently constituted Court of Appeal in *Re T (children: placement order)*.[113] *Re T* was concerned with a case where, because of the very serious nature of the children's problems, it was recommended that they be placed in a therapeutic foster home for at least six months before a final decision was made as to their long-term placement. Although the local authority agreed that adoption would theoretically be in the long-term interests of the children, that plan remained purely hypothetical given not only the uncertainty of finding a placement but, more importantly, the uncertainty as to whether the children would be deemed suitable for adoption—an uncertainty which would only be resolved after the therapeutic placement. Given it could not be said with certainty that adoption would be in the children's best interests, the Court of Appeal held that it was premature to make a placement order under s 22.[114] Thus, whilst a placement order can and should be made despite uncertainty over finding a suitable placement, a placement order cannot be made if it has not yet been determined that adoption is in the child's best interests.

Section 22 is clearly intended to minimize any delay in placing looked after children for adoption. The importance of moving children through the care system with greater speed has been reinforced by the imposition of tighter timescales for decision-making at every stage of the process.[115] Tackling the problem of 'drift in care' and eradicating any *unnecessary* delays between a child coming into care and being found a permanent alternative home are laudable objectives. The concern that delays in the adoption process can prejudice the chance of a successful outcome is borne out by research.[116] However, there is some disquiet that these provisions create a 'fast-track' to adoption which may not necessarily serve the interests of looked after children.[117] In particular, it is argued that focusing too quickly on adoption may deprive children of the opportunity of being successfully rehabilitated with their birth parents. It is of course a difficult balance. The imposition of strict timetables reflects concern that local authorities and the courts were prevaricating for too long over abandoning attempts at rehabilitation. However, the current drive towards achieving permanence through adoption could mean that even birth parents who have placed children in voluntary care under Part III of the CA 1989 might very quickly find themselves fighting an order which will effectively set in motion the irrevocable termination of their parenthood. The imperative to move quickly to adoption even without a care order being in place is of particular concern if it deprives the birth parents of vital help and support under the auspices of a care order. This is a serious problem where local authority resources are focused on providing services to children in care under Part IV of the CA 1989 (care orders) at the expense of providing effective preventative services to children and their families under Part III (voluntary care) and might again bring the legislation into conflict with Article 8,

[113] [2008] EWCA Civ 248.
[114] Ibid., [18].
[115] DH (2001b), Part A, para 2.
[116] Selwyn, Frazer, and Quinton (2006).
[117] Harris Short (2001); Sagar and Hitchings (2007).

particularly the state's obligation to take all reasonable steps when a child is in care to work towards reuniting the birth family.[118]

Consequences of the child being placed or being authorized to be placed for adoption

Whilst a child is placed or authorized to be placed for adoption, parental responsibility is given to the adoption agency.[119] If the child is placed with prospective adopters then the prospective adopters also acquire parental responsibility for the duration of the placement, the adoption agency having the power to determine to what extent the prospective adopters will be able to exercise their responsibility.[120] The birth parents do not lose parental responsibility by virtue of the fact the child is placed or authorized to be placed for adoption but again the adoption agency has the power to determine to what extent they can exercise that responsibility.[121] If a care order was made at the same time as the placement order or the child was subject to a care order when the placement order was made, the care order ceases to have effect whilst the placement order is in force.[122] The child is therefore no longer 'in care' although a child placed or authorized to be placed for adoption by a local authority is still regarded as a looked after child.[123]

Contact with a child who is placed or authorized to be placed for adoption

Contact is a crucially important issue at this stage of the proceedings as the pattern of contact established at this point can determine whether provision is made for post-adoption contact at the final hearing. For members of the birth family, ensuring contact is continued throughout the placement period can thus be of vital importance.

Although during placement the child has the status of a looked after child, local authorities are exempt from the duty under Sch 2, para 15 of the CA 1989 to endeavour to promote contact between looked after children and their parents.[124] Furthermore, any existing orders for contact made under s 8 or 34 of the CA 1989 cease to have effect.[125] The court can, however, order contact under s 26 of the ACA 2002 upon application by the child, the adoption agency, the birth parents, the child's relatives, a guardian, or any person in whose favour a residence order was in force or who had care of the child under the High Court's inherent jurisdiction immediately before the placement order was made.[126] Any other person may apply with leave of the court.[127] The court may also act of its own motion[128] and is under a duty before making a placement order to consider the adoption agency's proposals for contact.[129]

---

[118] Harris-Short (2001), 424.
[119] S 25(1)–(2).
[120] S 25(3)–(4).
[121] Ibid.
[122] S 29(1).
[123] S 18(3).
[124] Adoption Agencies Regulations 2005, SI 2005/389, reg 45(2)(d).
[125] ACA 2002, s 26(1).
[126] S 26(2)–(3). An application for a s 8 contact order can be heard together with an application for a final adoption order: s 26(5).
[127] S 26(3)(f).
[128] S 26(4).
[129] S 27(4).

A s 26 contact order remains in force whilst the child is placed or authorized to be placed for adoption.[130] The adoption agency retains the authority to terminate contact in an emergency for a maximum of seven days if satisfied that it is necessary to do so to safeguard and promote the child's welfare.[131]

Restrictions on removing a child who is placed for adoption

When a child is placed for adoption under s 19 (with parental consent) only the adoption agency can remove the child from the prospective adopters.[132] If the parents withdraw their consent to the placement the child must be returned to their care within 14 days unless an application has been made for a placement order or the prospective adopters have applied for an adoption order, special guardianship order, or residence order, in which case the child can only be removed with the court's leave.[133] If an adoption agency is authorized to place a child under s 19 but the parents withdraw their consent before the child is placed, the child must be returned to the parents within seven days. Where a placement order is in force, nobody, other than the local authority, can remove the child.[134] Where the adoption agency decides that a child should be removed from prospective adopters, the prospective adopters must return the child within seven days unless they have applied for an adoption order, special guardianship order, or residence order, in which case the court's leave to remove the child is required.[135] Where the prospective adopters wish to return the child to the adoption agency, the adoption agency must receive the child back into care within seven days.[136]

Revoking the placement order

Once a placement order has been made, the birth parents will face an uphill struggle to prevent the adoption proceeding. The placement order is of unlimited duration, remaining in force until revoked or an adoption order is made.[137] Moreover, opportunities to challenge the order are limited. A placement order can be revoked on the application of any person, but only the child or the adoption agency can apply as of right.[138] All other applicants require leave under s 24, and leave will only be granted if the child is not already placed and there has been a change in circumstances since the original order was made.[139]

The test to be applied on an application for leave to revoke a placement order was considered by the Court of Appeal in *Re M (children) (placement order)*.[140] It was argued on the mother's behalf that if she was able to establish a change in circumstances the court would be required to grant leave. The local authority disagreed, contending that establishing a change in circumstances was only 'the necessary precursor to the court's exercise of a discretion' and that in exercising its discretion the children's welfare would be a relevant

---

[130] S 27(1).
[131] S 27(2).
[132] S 30(1).
[133] Ss 32(2) and 32(5).
[134] S 34(1).
[135] Ss 35(2) and 35(5).
[136] S 35(1).
[137] S 21(4).
[138] S 24(1)–(2).
[139] S 24(2)–(3).
[140] [2007] EWCA Civ 1084.

consideration.[141] The Court of Appeal, stacking the odds yet further against the birth parents, agreed with the local authority, holding that establishing a change in circumstances was not determinative of the application. Wilson LJ held that the decision whether to grant leave to revoke a placement order was not 'coming to a decision relating to the adoption of a child' within the meaning of s 1(7) of the Act.[142] The paramountcy principle under s 1(2) does not therefore apply. However, Wilson LJ went on to hold that this does not mean that the children's interests are irrelevant.[143] Indeed, in line with the approach taken to leave applications under s 10(9) of the CA 1989, he held that once a change in circumstances has been established,[144] the court has a discretion as to whether or not to grant leave, in the exercise of which the children's welfare and the applicant's prospects of success on the main application are relevant considerations.[145] He concludes that whilst in most cases the children's welfare will be subsumed within the broader enquiry into the applicant's prospects of success, they remain separate considerations.[146]

The Court of Appeal has also had to tackle a number of difficulties caused by related restrictions set down in s 24: (i) that an application to revoke a placement order cannot be made once the child has been placed for adoption, and (ii) a child cannot be placed for adoption without the court's leave when an application to revoke the placement order is pending. In *Re F (a child)*[147] the Court of Appeal confirmed, by a majority, that a child can lawfully be placed for adoption by the adoption agency even though the adoption agency knows that an application for leave to revoke the placement order has been made. The Court of Appeal held that in accordance with the strict wording of s 24(5), the prohibition on placement without the court's leave only applies once the substantive application for revocation has been made.[148] However, the Court of Appeal emphasized that good practice very clearly demanded that if, to the knowledge of the adoption agency, an application for leave has been issued, the child should not be placed (thereby defeating the application) without the permission of the court and, if necessary, an injunction can be sought to prevent them doing so until the application for leave has been determined.[149] The Court of Appeal also made clear that if the local authority decides to go ahead and place the child before the parent is able to

[141] Ibid., [4].

[142] Section 1(7) provides: "In this section, 'coming to a decision relating to the adoption of a child', in relation to a court, includes – (a) coming to a decision in any proceedings where the orders that might be made by the court include an adoption order (or the revocation of such an order), a placement order (or the revocation of such an order) or an order under section 26 (or the revocation or variation of such an order); (b) coming to a decision about granting leave in respect of any action (other than the initiation of proceedings in any court) which may be taken by an adoption agency or individual under this Act, but does not include coming to a decision about granting leave in any other circumstances.' The Court of Appeal held that an application for leave to revoke a placement order was an application to *initiate proceedings* and therefore was specifically excluded from the scope of s 1(7). Cf an application for leave to defend adoption proceedings, discussed below at pp 929–31.

[143] [2007] EWCA Civ 1084, [24].

[144] Although the change in circumstances will usually relate to the parent and the parent's capacity to resume full-time care of the child, this will not always be the case. A change in circumstances which relates to the child and renders the plan for adoption no longer appropriate may constitute a sufficient change in circumstances for the purposes of s 24 and establish the applicant has a 'real prospect of success' in revoking the order—even if it remains impossible for the child to return home. See *NS-H v Kingston-Upon-Hull City Council and another* [2008] EWCA Civ 493.

[145] [2007] EWCA Civ 1084, [26]–[29].

[146] Ibid., [29].

[147] [2008] EWCA Civ 439.

[148] Ibid., [33], [69].

[149] Ibid., [99], [111].

issue the necessary legal proceedings, the actions of the local authority will be susceptible to judicial review.[150] In determining whether a child has 'been placed' for the purposes of s 24, it was held in *R (on the application of W) v London Borough of Brent*[151] that a child is placed when all the relevant legal and procedural formalities giving the adoption agency authorization to place the child for adoption have been completed and the process of introductions has begun.[152] It is not necessary for the child to have moved permanently to the home of the prospective adopters.[153]

13.5.4 THE ADOPTION APPLICATION

If the child is successfully placed with prospective adopters or, in the case of a non-agency adoption, is already living with the prospective adopter(s), the next stage is to issue the application for an adoption order.

Preliminaries to making the application

Residence conditions

Before prospective adopters can apply to adopt a child, the child must have lived with them for a specified period of time, the exact period depending on the circumstances of the adoption. If the child was placed for adoption by an adoption agency, pursuant to an order of the High Court, or the applicant is a parent of the child, the child must have lived with the prospective adopter(s) for ten weeks preceding the application.[154] If the applicant is the partner of a parent of the child (i.e. a step-parent adoption) the child must have lived with the applicant for six months.[155] If the applicants are local authority foster parents, the child must have lived with them for 12 months unless the court gives leave to apply.[156] In all other cases, the child must have lived with the prospective adopters for not less than three of the previous five years unless again the court gives leave to apply.[157] One of the main purposes of these provisions is to ensure that the local authority or adoption agency has had sufficient opportunity to observe the prospective adopters and the child together in their home environment.[158]

Where the prospective adopters require leave to apply for an adoption order, the Court of Appeal has held that the same principles apply as in an application for leave to revoke a placement order.[159] Thus it was held in *TL v Coventry City Council* that the child's welfare is a relevant but not paramount consideration and the court should take into account whether the application has a real prospect of success.[160]

In addition to the restrictions on removing a child from the care of prospective adopters when the child has been placed for adoption by an adoption agency (see above), once an

---

150 Ibid., [36], [94].
151 [2010] EWHC 175 (Admin).
152 Ibid., [29]. See also *Re S (a child)* [2008] EWCA Civ 1333, [8]–[9].
153 [2010] EWHC 175, [27].
154 S 42(2).
155 S 42(3).
156 S 42(4) and (6).
157 S 42(5)–(6).
158 S 42(7).
159 *Re M (children) (placement order)* [2007] EWCA Civ 1084.
160 [2007] EWCA Civ 1383, [10].

application to adopt has been made in non-agency cases (i.e. private arrangements, foster parent, and step-parent adoptions), the child cannot be removed from the care of the prospective adopters without the court's leave.[161] This prohibition also applies where an application for leave to apply has been made in non-agency cases.[162]

The requirement to give notice

Where the child was not placed with the prospective adopters by an adoption agency, the adoption order cannot be made unless the prospective adopters have given notice to the local authority of their intention to apply.[163] Notice must be given no more than two years or less than three months before the date on which the application is made.[164] Applicants requiring leave cannot give notice of their intention to adopt until leave has been granted.[165] On receiving notice, the local authority must investigate and prepare a report for the court.[166] Once notice of an intention to adopt has been given, nobody can remove the child from the prospective adopters' care without the court's leave, save in the following circumstances: (i) if the child has been in the care of the foster parents for more than one year but less than five years and is being looked after by the local authority pursuant to a voluntary agreement under Part III of the CA 1989, a person with parental responsibility may remove the child from the prospective adopters,[167] or (ii) where a notice of an intention to adopt has been given by a step-parent but the child has lived with the step-parent for less than three years, a parent or guardian can remove the child.[168]

13.5.5 THE FINAL HEARING

Conditions on making the adoption order

Age restrictions

In the case of an application by a single person, the applicant must have attained the age of 21 years.[169] Where the prospective adopters are a couple, both must have attained the age of 21 years unless one of them is a parent of the child in which case the parent must be at least 18 years of age.[170] No maximum age limit is specified in the legislation.

Applications by one person

Applications by one person are subject to additional conditions. An order can be made in favour of one person where the applicant is a parent's partner. Otherwise, if the applicant is married or has a civil partner, the application will only be allowed if: the court is satisfied that the person's spouse/civil partner cannot be found, the spouses/civil partners have separated and are living apart and the separation is likely to be permanent, or the person's

---

161 Ss 36–7.
162 Ss 36 and 40.
163 S 44(2).
164 S 44(3).
165 S 44(4).
166 S 44(5).
167 Ss 38(5) and 40.
168 Ss 39(3) and 40.
169 S 51.
170 S 50.

spouse/civil partner is incapable by reason of ill-health from making an application to adopt.[171] Interestingly there is no similar prohibition on someone living within an 'enduring family relationship' applying to adopt as a single person.[172]

Although it may on the face of it seem odd, a parent may apply to adopt his or her own child. Such adoptions are now rare, but they once served the important purpose of legitimating the child. The law on legitimacy having been comprehensively reformed, adoption by a sole natural parent is now contentious because it terminates any familial ties with one half of the child's family without giving the child the opportunity to build new relationships with an alternative family. Applications by a sole natural parent are subject to additional conditions:

Adoption and Children Act 2002, s 51

(4) An adoption order may not be made on an application under this section by the mother or the father of the person to be adopted unless the court is satisfied that—

(a) the other natural parent is dead or cannot be found,

(b) by virtue of the provisions in subsection (5) [s 28 of the HFEA 1990 and ss 34–47 of the HFEA 2008], there is no other parent, or

(c) there is some other reason justifying the child's being adopted by the applicant alone,

and where the court makes an adoption order on such an application, the court must record that it is satisfied as to the fact mentioned in paragraph (a) or (b) or, in the case of paragraph (c), record the reason.

Section 51(4) reproduces, albeit with a slight change in wording, the same conditions on adoption by a sole natural parent as were contained within s 15(3) of the AA 1976. Section 15(3) was the subject of House of Lords authority in which Lord Nicholls rejected a restrictive interpretation of the requirement that there must be 'some other reason' justifying the adoption. Adopting Lord Nicholls' approach, provided it can be shown that adoption by the natural parent is in the child's best interests these additional conditions will present no real obstacle to the adoption proceeding.

Re B (A Minor) (Adoption: Natural Parent) [2001] UKHL 70

LORD NICHOLLS:

11. . . . The Adoption Act permits adoption in the circumstances of child A, but only if there is reason to exclude the mother. The intervention by the court is to protect the interests of the child . . . [T]he interference must meet a pressing social need and be proportionate to that need. Hale LJ [in the Court of Appeal] said . . . :

'. . . it is difficult indeed to argue that there is a pressing social need to deprive A of all legal relationship with one half of her family of birth. . . . she already has a full and secure legal and factual relationship

---

[171] S 51(3)–(3A).
[172] Bainham (2008d), 481.

with her father. If there is any need to give her more, it can be provided for in a package of orders along the lines discussed. In my view, it would be a disproportionate response to her current needs to turn her from the child of two legal parents, with two legal families, into the child of only one parent, with only one legal family. Section 15(3) has to be given effect in such a way as to avoid that result.'…

22. On its face this permanent exclusion of the child's mother from the life of the child is a drastic and detrimental consequence of adoption so far as the child is concerned. How serious this loss is likely to be depends on the circumstances of the case. In deciding whether to make an order having this consequence the court must always be satisfied that this course is in the best interests of the child. There must be some reason justifying the exclusion of the other natural parent. The reason must be sufficient to outweigh the adverse consequences such an order may have by reason of the exclusion of one parent from the child's life. Consent of the excluded parent is not of itself a sufficient reason, but it is a factor to be taken into account. Its weight will depend on the circumstances.

23. In so far as the Court of Appeal construed section 15(3)(b) more restrictively than this, I am unable to agree. Section 15(3) imposes a prerequisite to the making of an adoption order on the application of the mother or father alone. One or other of the exceptions set out in paragraphs (a) and (b) must be satisfied. The three exceptions listed in paragraph (a) are instances where the other natural parent cannot have, or is unlikely to have, any further part in the child's upbringing and life. But these three exceptions are not an exhaustive list of the circumstances in which a natural parent is unlikely in practice to have a further role in a child's life. Further, there may be other situations when the welfare of the child justifies the exclusion of a natural parent. Abandonment, or persistent neglect or ill-treatment of the child, could be instances.

24. It is not surprising, therefore, that the exception stated in paragraph (b) ['some other reason'] is altogether open-ended. No doubt this was a deliberate choice of language. I can see no ground for importing into this exception an unexpressed limitation whereby 'some other reason' must be comparable with the death or disappearance of the other natural parent. What is required by paragraph (b), and all that is required, is that the reason, whatever it be, must be sufficient to justify the exclusion of the other parent. Whether any particular reason satisfies this test depends on the circumstances. This is a matter left to the decision of the court. On this question of interpretation I respectfully consider the Court of Appeal was unduly restrictive in its approach.

Lord Nicholls held that it would be in the child's best interests to make the adoption order thereby permanently excluding the child's mother from playing any further role in the child's life and giving the father the additional security he desired.[173]

Consent

In most cases, the issue of consent is unlikely to constitute a significant obstacle for the applicants as the question will have been determined at the placement stage. The rather complicated provisions bearing on the consent requirement are contained in s 47.

---

[173] For further discussion see below at p 709.

Adoption and Children Act 2002, s 47

(1) An adoption order may not be made if the child has a parent or guardian unless one of the following conditions is met, but this section is subject to section 52.

(2) The first condition is that, in the case of each parent or guardian of the child, the court is satisfied—

(a) that the parent or guardian consents to the making of the adoption order,

(b) that the parent or guardian has consented under section 20 (and has not withdrawn the consent) and does not oppose the making of the adoption order, or

(c) that the parent's or guardian's consent should be dispensed with.

(3) A parent or guardian may not oppose the making of an adoption order under subsection 2(b) without the court's leave.

(4) The second condition is that—

(a) the child has been placed for adoption by an adoption agency with the prospective adopters in whose favour the order is proposed to be made,

(b) either—

(i) the child was placed for adoption with the consent of each parent or guardian and the consent of the mother was given when the child was at least six weeks old, or

(ii) the child was placed for adoption under a placement order, and

(c) no parent or guardian oppose the making of the adoption order.

(5) A parent or guardian may not oppose the making of an adoption order under the second condition without the court's leave.

(6) The third condition is that the child is free for adoption…[under the AA 1976].

(7) The court cannot give leave under subsection (3) or (5) unless satisfied that there has been a change in circumstances since the consent of the parent or guardian was given or, as the case may be, the placement order was made.

Section 47(4) deals with the position where the child was placed by an adoption agency. In such cases, the child will either have been placed with parental consent or pursuant to a placement order. Although s 47(4)(c) states that the order cannot be made if the adoption is opposed, s 47(5) provides that birth parents falling within this category of case will not be able to oppose the adoption without the court's leave.[174] Section 47(7) then goes on to provide that the court can only grant leave if satisfied there has been a change in circumstances since the consent was given or the placement order made. The relevance of the child's welfare to an application for leave under s 47(7) arose in *Re P (a child) (adoption order: leave to oppose making of adoption order)*.[175] The first question addressed by the Court of Appeal was whether the decision to grant leave was 'coming to a decision relating to the adoption of a child' thereby making the child's welfare the paramount consideration. In accordance with s 1(7) which provides that 'coming to a decision about granting leave in respect of any action (other than the initiation of proceedings)' is a decision relating to the adoption of a child, the

---

[174] The parents will be notified of the proceedings and made respondents thereto. Family Procedure Rules 2010, r 14.3(1).

[175] [2007] EWCA Civ 616.

Court of Appeal held that as an application for leave to defend the adoption order was *not* an application for leave to *initiate proceedings*, s 1(7) required the paramountcy principle to be applied.[176] Consequently, the Court of Appeal held that an application for leave to defend adoption proceedings involved a two-stage process.

Re P (a child) (adoption order: leave to oppose making of adoption order) [2007] EWCA Civ 616

WALL LJ:

26. In our judgment, analysis of the statutory language in sections 1 and 47 of the 2002 Act leads to the conclusion that an application for leave to defend adoption proceedings under section 47(5) of the 2002 Act involves a two stage process. First of all, the court has to be satisfied, on the facts of the case, that there has been a change in circumstances within section 47(7). If there has been no change in circumstances, that is the end of the matter, and the application fails. If, however, there has been a change in circumstances within section 47(7) then the door to the exercise of a judicial discretion to permit the parents to defend the adoption proceedings is opened, and the decision whether or not to grant leave is governed by section 1 of the 2002 Act. In other words, "the paramount consideration of the court must be the child's welfare throughout his life".

The Court of Appeal then expanded on what was meant by a 'change in circumstances':

30. . . . We do not think it permissible to put any gloss on the statute, or to read into it words which are not there. The change in circumstances since the placement order was made must, self-evidently and as a matter of statutory construction, relate to the grant of leave. It must equally be of a nature and degree sufficient, on the facts of the particular case, to open the door to the exercise of the judicial discretion to permit the parents to defend the adoption proceedings. In our judgment, however, the phrase "a change in circumstances" is not ambiguous, and resort to Hansard is both unnecessary and inappropriate.

31. Furthermore, in our judgment, the importation of the word "significant" puts the test too high. Self-evidently, a change in circumstances can embrace a wide range of different factual situations. Section 47(7) does not relate the change to the circumstances of the parents. The only limiting factor is that it must be a change in circumstances "since the placement order was made". Against this background, we do not think that any further definition of the change in circumstances involved is either possible or sensible.

32. We do, however, take the view that the test should not be set too high, because, as this case demonstrates, parents in the position of S's parents should not be discouraged either from bettering themselves or from seeking to prevent the adoption of their child by the imposition of a test which is unachievable. We therefore take the view that whether or not there has been a relevant change in circumstances must be a matter of fact to be decided by the good sense and sound judgment of the tribunal hearing the application.

Particularly in light of these words of caution regarding the unfairness of stacking the odds too highly against the birth parents, making the welfare of the child the paramount

---

[176] Ibid., [19]–[21]. Cf where leave is sought to revoke a placement order discussed above at pp 923–4.

consideration on an application by the parents for leave may seem a little odd—this is, after all, a procedural hurdle and not the substantive hearing at which the child's welfare will clearly be determinative. Moreover, the Court of Appeal make clear that in determining the application for leave, there is no need for the court to conduct a full welfare enquiry with oral evidence and cross-examination.[177] Having made the child's welfare paramount, the parents may thus feel, perhaps with some justification, that they are not then afforded a full and fair hearing on the matter. It is perhaps revealing that in discussing the application of the paramountcy principle to the parents' request for leave, the Court of Appeal note, '[t]he object of the 2002 Act was to simplify the adoption process and to reduce delays in children being placed for adoption and adopted'.[178] The Court of Appeal can perhaps be criticized for pursuing this object with vigour, despite the impact on the birth parents' interests. However, it must be remembered that by this stage of the proceedings the parents will almost certainly have had the opportunity to put their case fully in the care proceedings and again at the placement stage.[179] Moreover, the child is very likely to be securely settled in the prospective adopters' home. The prospect of the parents successfully defending the adoption application will therefore be very small.

The same restrictions on defending the adoption application apply under s 47(2)(b) where the birth parents gave advance consent to the adoption under s 20. If the parents wish to defend the proceedings, leave will be required in accordance with ss 47(3) and 47(7), the application to be determined in accordance with the principles set down in *Re P*.

If the parents' application for leave under s 47(3) or s 47(5) is refused, the adoption application will be unopposed, thus satisfying the necessary conditions for making an adoption order.

In all other cases (i.e. step-parent adoptions and private placements), consent will not have been dealt with at an earlier stage of the proceedings and will thus fall to be determined at the final hearing. Section 47 thus provides that the court will only be able to make the adoption order if satisfied that the birth parents consent to the adoption or that their consent should be dispensed with in accordance with the terms of s 52.[180]

Welfare

Making an adoption order is clearly a 'decision relating to the adoption of a child'. The welfare principle in s 1(2) therefore applies and the child's welfare must be the court's paramount consideration. That said, as most applications will now be unopposed it is difficult to envisage many cases in which the adoption order will be refused. Under the previous legislation, almost 97% of contested adoption applications were successful.[181] As Ryburn notes, although adoption is the final decision in a 'cumulative process where there were many other decisions along the way', it is difficult to imagine any other area of the law where the odds are so highly stacked against one party to the dispute.[182]

---

177 Ibid., [53].
178 Ibid., [53].
179 Ibid.
180 See 13.4.2 above.
181 Ryburn (1998a), 56.
182 Ibid.

13.6   IN THE BEST INTERESTS OF THE CHILD? CONTROVERSIAL ISSUES

Although the birth parents face several obstacles in resisting an adoption, the court must still be satisfied both at the placement stage and at the final hearing that the adoption is in the child's best interests. In determining whether a child should be adopted a number of particularly controversial questions have dominated the case law.

13.6.1   BIRTH FAMILY V THE 'PERFECT' ADOPTIVE COUPLE

At the heart of many contested adoptions is the question of whether a child should be raised within the birth family, preferably by the parents, or be given the opportunity to start a new life with the adoptive parents. A contested adoption thus raises in stark form the value to be placed on 'genetic' as opposed to 'social' or 'psychological' parenting. We have seen within the context of residence disputes how the law has tended to favour biological over social parenting.[183] The key factors justifying the 'natural parent presumption' in residence disputes are particularly important in disputes concerning adoption. For example, the need to protect the child's developing sense of identity takes on particular significance when the order being sought will extinguish all legal ties with the birth family. Concerns over the dangers of 'social engineering' also take on a particular resonance when the birth parents, with all their problems and inadequacies, are facing competing claims from a 'perfect' adoptive couple who will have successfully come through a difficult and far-reaching vetting procedure.

The child's right to be brought up by his or her birth family has, in the past, formed the starting point for determining a contested adoption. This was made clear by Butler-Sloss LJ in *Re K (Private Placement for Adoption)*.[184] The case concerned a private arrangement between the birth parents and the prospective adopters which was entered into shortly after the child's birth and at a time when the birth mother was under enormous stress. The birth parents changed their mind and sought to have the child returned to their care. At the time of the hearing the child had been in the prospective adopters' care for seven-and-a-half months. The Court of Appeal returned the child to her parents.

Re K (Private Placement for Adoption) [1991] FCR 142, 147–8 (CA)

Lady Justice Butler-Sloss:

The mother must be shown to be entirely unsuitable before another family can be considered, otherwise we are in grave danger of slipping into social engineering. The question is not: would the child be better off with the plaintiffs? But: is the natural family so unsuitable that... "the welfare of the child positively demanded the displacement of the parental right?" I agree... that it is the right of the child rather than the parent and, borrowing from the philosophy of the Children Act 1989, I would rephrase it as the displacement of the parental responsibility. Once the Judge found that this mother genuinely wanted her child back and was a

---

[183] See 11.4.6.
[184] See also the extract from *Re O (A Minor) (Custody or Adoption)* [1992] 1 FCR 378 at p 764.

mother who cared properly for the other two children, not to give her at least an opportunity to try to rehabilitate the family was to deprive the child of any chance of her own family.

The courts' preference for the birth parents has also extended to the wider kinship network.[185] It was held in *Re L (A minor) (Care proceedings)* that the local authority should look first to the extended family for alternative care before considering stranger adoption. In determining whether members of the birth family are suitable, the court emphasized that adoption should not be regarded as a 'panacea' and that sometimes the known risks of the birth family would be preferable to the unknown risks of adoption.

Re L (A minor) (Care proceedings: wardship) (No 2) [1991] 1 FLR 29, 36–8 (Crown Court)

JUDGE WILLIS:

The whole crux of this case depends on how much weight should be given to the various 'pros' and 'cons' for the two alternative courses for this child, namely, going to the grandparents or being adopted. We received the impression from the guardian, as we did from the local authority witnesses also, that they are far too keen on adoption and consider it the panacea for all problems. They all expressed a number of concerns or problems which might arise in the maternal grandparents' extended family if K [the child] is there. None of them envisaged any real problem in adoption in a child of this age. The impression they tried to give was that, as in every good fairy story, after placement, 'everyone lives happily ever after'...

The local authority's case is that there are far too many problems if K goes back to the family, i.e. to grandparents, and that a fresh start with adoption is a less risky course. K will be 'grafted' into a new family with the absence of access problems. This argument, however, fails to address the considerable problems which are more likely to arise in adoption, namely the psychological worry of who and what her family are, why she is not with them and why she was adopted...The great advantage in staying with the wider family is that the child maintains her roots. We consider this a very important aspect which has been totally ignored by the local authority and also by the guardian ad litem...[A]doption should only be the last resort when no one in the wider family is available and suitable to look after a child. Parentage is not always perfect, but parentage in the family is preferable to the unknown risks of adoption...We consider that every child has a right, whenever it is possible, to be brought up in its own genetic family. That right should not be taken away from it except in the last resort when there are strong, cogent and positive reasons for so doing. All the local authority's arguments are based on concerns which may or may not happen. Even if they did, the risk to K, we feel, would be less than the risks inherent in adoption.

Whether this preference for the birth family can survive the child-centred approach of the ACA 2002 is questionable. Indeed, in the wake of the new legislation the Court of Appeal has signalled its strong resistance to any 'privileging' of the birth family in adoption disputes, particularly where it may be the cause of delay.

---

[185] Ryburn contends that this is contrary to prevailing social work practice where the 'zero-cost' of stranger adoption is preferred. See Ryburn (1998b), 37.

C v X, Y, Z County Council [2007] EWCA Civ 1206

ARDEN LJ:

I do not consider that this court should require a preference to be given as a matter of policy to the natural family of a child. Section 1 does not impose any such policy. Rather, it requires the interests of the child to be considered. That must mean the child as an individual. In some cases, the birth ties will be very important, especially where the child is of an age to understand what is happening or where there are ethnic or cultural or religious reasons for keeping the child in the birth family. Where a child has never lived with her birth family, and is too young to understand what is going on, that argument must be weaker. In my judgment, in a case such as this, it is (absent any application by any member of the family which succeeds) overtaken by the need to find the child a permanent home as soon as that can be done.

Even given the more accommodating approach towards the birth family in the previous case law, there were very few cases in which the birth parents successfully opposed the adoption.[186] The explanation for this lies in the strength of the countervailing considerations in a typical contested adoption where there will usually be a long history of serious and persistent failings in parenting. Even where there are no such failings, such as where the birth father was unaware of the child, the court is often faced with the problem of what amounts, in effect, to a fait accompli: by the time of the adoption hearing the child has been living with the adoptive parents for a substantial period of time and strong emotional bonds have developed between them. Where the child is strongly attached to the adoptive parents the courts are extremely reluctant to disrupt this position. In *Re O (adoption: withholding agreement)* the strong attachment which had developed between the child and the prospective adopters was held to constitute a compelling factor capable of displacing the preference for the birth family, even though the father, who had not been told of the child's existence, was perfectly capable of offering the child a secure and stable home.[187] Empirical research suggests that this reluctance to break the child's bond with the alternative carers is well founded. Dyer, for example, argues that breaking the bond between the child and the child's primary attachment figures, whether those attachments are to the birth or psychological parents, can have serious adverse consequences. He points to various empirical studies which link 'disturbed or disrupted attachment to personality disorders; poor functioning in the parental role as an adult; alcoholism; criminality; and sexual offending'.[188] However, against this the court has to balance equally compelling evidence regarding the problems often suffered by adopted adolescents in developing a secure and positive sense of identity.[189] These are difficult cases to which there are no easy answers.

13.6.2 TRANS-RACIAL ADOPTION

Concerns over the child's developing sense of identity are particularly strong when there are ethnic, cultural, or religious factors involved. Indeed, no issue causes greater division within adoption.[190] Advocates on both sides of the debate can be particularly dogmatic in their approach.

---

186 Ryburn (1998a), 56.
187 [1999] 2 FCR 262.
188 Dyer (2004), 11.
189 See detailed discussion at 9.4.4.
190 We are typically talking here about placing black or Asian children in white households: a problem which is exacerbated by the low number of prospective adopters from black or Asian communities. DH (2000), [6.4].

Opponents of trans-racial adoption have focused on two key problems: (i) the difficulties ethnic minority children face in developing a strong, positive ethnic identity when placed in a white household; and (ii) the inability of the child's carers to help the child cope with the racism still endemic within British society. An interview with John Small, a key opponent of trans-racial adoption and a leading figure in the development of social work policy on this issue during the 1980s, reveals the thinking behind current opposition to trans-racial placements:

B. Goldstein, 'Ethnicity and Placement. Beginning the debate', (2000) 24 *Adoption and Fostering* 9, 9–10

The thing which is important to my mind is the psychological damage that is likely to occur when the identities of children are not recognised. For example, if you have a child from a West Indian, African [or] Indian background and they claim that their colour is another [ie white], that must be some deep psychological scar. They look into the mirror and what they see they don't like, and the reason why they don't like that is a direct result of what's happening to them in the social world that they are in. It is the question of what society is doing to children whose personalities are in the process of being formed and are actually influenced by what they see, bearing in mind that they develop their ideas and attitudes and they are shaped by the people with whom they interact.

The psychological research has shown us about self and what constitutes self and how our self-image is derivative of the messages we obtain from significant others. So if society has this negative view of particular ethnic groups and transmits this through the media, through television, through the radio, through the print media, through the attitudes in society, through the attitudes of other children in the playground, those kinds of images come through. Identity is something you internalise from a range of things as you go through life, not something you search for later. This is why the messages parents and society give are important. You have to be very conscious of this with a black child in a racist society. Some white parents, they don't think that is important. They think love is enough—perhaps in a non-racist society but we certainly haven't reached that stage yet...

I realise that some well-meaning, white middle-class people tend to ignore the effects of racism because they can't understand the implications of racism for the black population generally. That leads them to deny that racism exists and, once they deny that, it is unlikely that they will be able to explain these things to their children or to the child that they have adopted.

Opponents of trans-racial adoption have tried to shift the debate away from arguments that can be attacked as ideologically or politically driven because of their association with 'black identity politics', focusing instead on the individualized interests of the child.

P. Hayes, 'Giving due consideration to ethnicity in adoption placements—A principled approach', (2003) 15 *Child and Family Law Quarterly* 255, 256

The initial objections by black separatists to transracial adoption were not focused on the child as an individual, but with the purported interests, and even the survival, of the black community; it was claimed that transracial adoption was a form of exploitation of the black community by the white community that was aimed at weakening and ultimately destroying it through 'genocide'. These collectivist arguments, however, were soon supplemented by the claim that the children involved suffered from identity confusion and social ostracism as a consequence of transracial placements. In the 1980s the same ideas spread to the UK where a campaign modelled on the US was launched; it quickly succeeded in changing attitudes in BAAF [British Association for Adoption and Fostering] and in local authority adoption agencies. Once the weight of opinion against transracial placements was accepted it was soon extended to other forms of ethnic matching.

As Hayes notes, opponents of trans-racial adoption have emphasized that it is the particular vulnerability of ethnic minority children in a racist society and the 'experience-based skills' of black and other ethnic minority parents in dealing with such issues—not their 'biological essences'—that make them the preferred carers for these children.[191]

It is, however, difficult to escape ideologically based arguments when issues of race and ethnicity are in question. Underlying disagreements about trans-racial adoption are fundamentally different 'world-views' on issues such as: the importance of racial identity in a liberal western society, whether ethnic identity is an innate or chosen characteristic, and whether or not it is accurate to describe contemporary British society as inherently racist. Hayes is a strong advocate of trans-racial adoption based it would seem on a clear philosophical commitment to a 'colour-blind' vision of life.[192]

P. Hayes, 'Giving due consideration to ethnicity in adoption placements—A principled approach', (2003) 15 *Child and Family Law Quarterly* 255, 260–2

[A]ttempts at ethnic matching demonstrate a naïve understanding of ethnicity and culture that is every bit as flawed as the idea that all people who are not white can be simply lumped together as 'black'.

Three mistaken assumptions underlie precise ethnic matching: first, it is assumed that ethnic culture is a natural inheritance rather than a conventional construct; secondly, a minority child's culture is invariably assumed to be exclusive and particular to one ethnic group rather than being universally accessible; and thirdly, ethnic cultures are conceived of in essential, rather than nominal, terms.

Nature and convention

Advocates of ethnic matching assume that the cultural elements of a child's ethnicity are passed down rather like genes so that they form a hereditary and predetermined element of the child's make-up. Religions, for example, are not defined as universally accessible communities that people might either enter and leave through choice or become acculturated to as they grow up. Instead, it is assumed that it is somehow natural for a child to inherit the religion of the birth parents or grandparents, whether or not the child has been raised in that religion. This is referred to, misleadingly, as the 'right' and 'need' of the child to belong to a particular religion. In fact, it is nothing to do with the child's individual rights, but is rather a collectivist argument that religiously defined communities can lay claim to a child as one of their own...

---

[191] Goldstein (2000), 14 and Flynn (2000).

[192] See also Patel (2007), esp. at 33. Patel argues against an 'essentialist view' of racial identity, contending that racial identity is 'flexible' and 'fluid' and that the individual is able 'to construct for themselves multiple racial identities'.

Particularism and universalism

Advocates of ethnic matching ignore cultural attributes that are universally accessible in favour of ones that are particular to a single ethnic culture. Culture is always viewed by such advocates as something that divides people, never as something that brings them together. But often culture unites people of different ethnic origins, for example, the character sketches of children advertised for adoption mention commonplace interests and pursuits such as football or pop music. These universally accessible pastimes are, in fact, part of these children's culture, although, as they are not associated with any one particular ethnic group, they are not conceived of as culture by those who favour ethnic matching.

Essentialism and nominalism

Ethnic cultures are not fixed concepts with discrete boundaries. Making essentialist distinctions between ethnic cultures ignores the way in which cultures can blend and change; ignores cultural synthesis, and fails to see that the components of culture are multifaceted so that people who nominally share the same ethnic culture may engage in diverse patterns of living. Culture is not tied to race. People of different races may share the same culture, while people who are racially similar may adopt different cultures. This cultural nominalism is not recognised by advocates of ethnic matching. The failings of the essentialist understanding of ethnic culture are particularly apparent in its inchoate response to the placement of mixed-race children. The culture of mixed-race children—like all minority children—is never seen as transcending their racial heritage, but is rather reduced to it. For mixed-race children this means breaking down their supposed culture into a set of discrete components derived from their various ancestors. Mixed-race children are then told to take pride in the ethnic mix within themselves, while at the same time any further mixing into a transracial placement is said to be potentially damaging to them.

Ethnic identity versus 'colour-blind' human beings

One difference between trans-racially adopted children and inracially adopted children has been singled out for particular criticism by advocates of ethnic matching. Transracially adopted children have often been found to be somewhat more likely to describe themselves as human beings first and foremost, or as taking a 'colour-blind' approach in their social relationships. This is a reasonable and viable way of defining yourself and others. It is, for example, a perspective by no means uncommon among minority adults who appear to be perfectly well-adjusted...

To be colour-blind is to assess each individual on his or her own merits. People who are colour-blind believe that generalisations about an ethnic group a person belongs to may well tell you little or nothing about what he or she is like as an individual. They also believe that a person's colour is not an intrinsic bar to achievement, and that neither should there be any bar to relationships between people of different colours, including the deepest marital and family relationships.

The idea of being colour-blind is closely associated with the philosophy of individualism. Those who adopt the colour-blind approach to life have neither reason nor tendency to assume that everyone else in society, or indeed their own children, necessarily thinks the same way that they do about ethnicity. Such an assumption of uniform thinking is quite at odds with the individualist insistence that people are able to make up their own minds about such issues. It is, therefore, incorrect to suggest that to be colour-blind is to assume that no one is racist, or that everyone takes the view that colour is irrelevant. However, advocates of ethnic matching appear to think that because they are fixated with issues of ethnicity, then so is everyone else, and it may be that they attribute to colour-blind parents their own faulty logic.

Advocates of trans-racial adoption have further stressed the absence of any empirical evidence to support the perceived problems caused by trans-racial placements.[193] The empirical evidence is, however, limited and the conclusions drawn somewhat tentative. On the basis of a review carried out of studies in the UK and USA, Rushton and Minnis conclude that adoption breakdown rates are determined by age at placement rather than the type of placement and that 'developmental outcomes of transracially placed children appear to be good for the majority in terms of educational attainment, peer relations and behaviour'.[194] They also point out, however, that methodological flaws with the various studies preclude definitive conclusions.[195] The conclusions drawn by Moffat and Thoburn from a review of the existing literature and their own study of 254 ethnic minority children are similarly qualified, although again they find no significant evidence of harm resulting from trans-racial placements.

P.G. Moffatt and J. Thoburn, 'Outcomes of permanent family placement for children of minority ethnic origin', (2001) 6 *Child and Family Social Work* 13, 14, 18, and 20

The majority of placements of children of minority ethnic origin were successful, at least in the sense that the young people remained in placement. This applied irrespective of gender, of whether they were of mixed race parentage or had two parents of the same ethnic background, and of whether they were placed in ethnically matched families or transracially. However, a worrying minority of the children experienced placement breakdown. The explanations for the success or otherwise of the placements appear broadly similar to those for white children. For the sample as a whole, no difference was found in breakdown rates between those placed in 'matched' and in 'transracial' placements...

Our qualitative data indicate that not all placements which last are successful when other outcome measures such as well-being, satisfaction or ethnic pride are the outcome measures used. From a combination of the qualitative and the quantitative data we concluded that some white families can successfully parent children of a different ethnic origin, including helping them to combat the adverse effects of racism and feel pride in their appearance, culture and heritage. However, compared with the parents of minority ethnic origin, they have additional tasks to negotiate, and the job they have to do in parenting a child who has already suffered adversity and at least one separation and rejection is difficult enough without making it more difficult. We thus concur with the preference expressed in the UN Convention on the Rights of the Child, the Hague Convention on Inter-country Adoption and the England and Wales Children Act 1989 for children to be placed whenever possible with families from their own local or wider communities. But our data emphasize that placements in 'matched' families are also vulnerable to disruption and that long-term support must be available if the chances of success are to improve.

A recent study by Patel focusing particularly on racial identity is less cautious. She argues that trans-racially adopted children do not develop a confused, problematic, or negative racial identity but develop a specific type of identity that demonstrates 'fluid, flexible and multiple forms of racial identity which, to various degrees, incorporated both birth and

---

[193] Hayes (2003), 256–7 and 268. Simon and Altstein (1996).
[194] Rushton and Minnis (2000), 53.
[195] Ibid.

adoptive heritages.'[196] Patel's study is, however, based on interviews with just six trans-racially adopted adults and is therefore of limited value.

On the basis of the current available evidence, the majority of researchers remain cautious about trans-racial placements, concluding that, despite the absence of any positive evidence that trans-racial adoption is harmful, 'matched' placements provide better safeguards against feelings of ostracism and identity confusion and should therefore be the preferred option where available.[197]

The Labour government recognized the sensitivity of this contentious issue and essentially sought to take the middle-ground preferred by researchers. Its policy on trans-racial adoption was set down in the 2000 White Paper:

Department of Health, *Adoption: a new approach*, Cm 5017 (London: HMSO, 2000)

6.15 Children's birth heritage and religious, cultural and linguistic background are all important factors to consider in finding them a new family. . . . [T]he best family for a child will be one that best reflects their birth heritage, and all councils should be proactive in monitoring their local population of looked after children to enable them to recruit permanent carers who can meet their needs. However, the child's welfare is paramount, and no child should be denied loving adoptive parents solely on the grounds that the child and the parents do not share the same racial or cultural background.

The need to respect the child's religious, racial, and cultural background is enshrined in the ACA 2002:

Adoption and Children Act 2002, s 1(5)

In placing the child for adoption, the adoption agency must give due consideration to the child's religious persuasion, racial origin and cultural and linguistic background.

However, the implementation of this policy raises difficult practical problems. As the White Paper and National Adoption Standards make clear, no child should be denied the chance of a loving permanent home because of attempts to 'match' the child with a family of the same religious, ethnic, or cultural background.[198] Section 1(5) of the ACA 2002 must thus be reconciled with the Labour government's strong commitment to eradicating delay and ensuring no child is left 'languishing' in care. In practice, due to the small number of approved ethnic minority adopters, it is very difficult for the local authority to find suitable 'matched' placements within the prescribed timescales for decision-making and placement.[199] The commitment to protecting a child's ethnic and cultural background enshrined in s 1(5) may therefore routinely give way to the 'no delay principle' enshrined in s 1(3).

It is difficult to predict how the courts will reconcile the demands of s 1(5) with s 1(3) as their approach to trans-racial adoption pre-implementation of the ACA 2002 was erratic. At

---

[196] Patel (2007), 41.
[197] See also Kirton, Feast, and Howe (2000).
[198] DH (2000), [6.15] and DH (2001b), [8]–[9].
[199] As to the reasons why there are currently so few prospective adopters from ethnic minority communities see Frazer and Selwyn (2005) and Sunmonu (2000).

one extreme, the courts expressed outright condemnation of local authority policies which precluded trans-racial adoption. In *Re N (A Minor) (Transracial Placement)*, Bush J went so far as to describe policies focusing on the colour of the child's skin as 'mischievous and highly dangerous'.[200] In other cases the courts were much more open to the argument that children should, wherever possible, be placed with families of the same ethnic and cultural background. In *Re P (A minor) (adoption)* the court was willing to remove an 18-month-old mixed-race child from the white foster parents she had lived with since birth to place her with a Jamaican family.[201] In *Re B (Adoption: Child's Welfare)* the court reached a similar conclusion.[202] The case concerned a Gambian child aged four-and-a-half years who had lived in England with white foster parents for 18 months pursuant to an informal arrangement with the child's parents. The foster parents sought to adopt the child, resisted by the child's parents who wished to take her back to the Gambia. In refusing the adoption application, Wall J made it clear that the starting point for determining such disputes is the child's right to be raised by the birth parents within their own particular culture. The most extreme example of this approach is *Re M (Child's upbringing)*, with the Court of Appeal ordering the phased return of a Zulu child to his natural parents in South Africa, despite having lived with his white foster mother for almost 10 years.[203] As was noted in chapter 11, this controversial decision had disastrous results for the child who was so unhappy in South Africa that he had to return to his foster mother in England.[204]

It was clearly an important factor in all of these cases that carers of the same or similar ethnic background were able to offer the child an alternative home. In *Re B* and *Re M* this was reinforced by the fact that the alterative carers were the children's natural parents. Where no such alternative exists, the courts have been much more reluctant to attach any great weight to the child's ethnic identity, holding that ethnic and cultural needs can be more than adequately met through regular contact with the birth parents and/or by the adoptive parents' commitment to establishing links with the ethnic community from which the child comes. This was the approach adopted in *Re JK* which concerned the adoption of a three-year-old Sikh girl who had been living with the prospective adopters in their capacity as foster parents since birth. The local authority had become concerned about the close bond between the foster parents and the child and, believing she would be better placed with a Sikh family, sought to remove her from their care. No alternative Sikh family had been identified. The importance of the child being raised within a family sharing her own cultural and religious background therefore had to be argued at the level of principle. Not surprisingly, the court was unconvinced.

Re JK (Transracial Placement) [1990] FCR 891, 893–8 (Fam Div)

Sir Stephen Brown P:

It is the policy of the council to follow well known guidelines relating to children of different racial backgrounds. They would seek to match her with a family of a similar background to her natural parents. The problem in this case is that it has not been possible to find such a family.

---

[200] [1990] FCR 241, 245–7.
[201] [1990] 1 FLR 96.
[202] [1995] 1 FLR 895.
[203] [1996] 2 FCR 473.
[204] See discussion at pp 764–5.

The evidence before me has been quite clear and specific that adoption in the Sikh community is very rare indeed save in cases where a blood relative is concerned. Furthermore, it is even more rare in cases where the child is illegitimate. It has not been possible for the social services department to find a Sikh family which would answer the requirements of an adoptive family...

Inevitably with the passage of time the child has become attached to the foster parents' family...This gave rise to concern on the part of the social services department because they have a policy which is not necessarily entirely rigid, but which is a clear policy, of matching children of particular racial backgrounds with families of a similar racial background...

I note that there is no conflict about the principles which should apply in general in approaching the placement of children of certain racial backgrounds but, as I have already observed, the core of this matter is: what is to be done for this child?...

Whilst [the foster parents] are not of an advanced intellectual standard which can assimilate easily the finer details of different races and religions, they have been making a very praiseworthy attempt to help the little girl in this respect: they take her weekly to a Sikh temple in the area...[T]hey say, and I have every reason to believe them, that if the child remains in their care they will see to it that her contact with her own background is followed up and that they will seek assistance in order to be able to deal with this matter. I am perfectly certain that in this area there is available such assistance. The schools have to deal with children of all racial backgrounds, particularly Asian backgrounds, and I have no doubt that there are other facilities readily available.

I have come to the conclusion that it would be a terrible thing for this little girl to be moved from this home at this stage in her life.

[The court held that the child was to remain with the foster parents with a view to adoption.]

The approach adopted in this case is difficult to fault. Whilst the child's ethnic, racial, and cultural identity is of clear importance in determining the child's future welfare, where the only alternative is for the child to return to local authority care, breaking the child's bonds with her current carers is difficult to justify. Quite clearly, institutionalized care or a series of short term placements cannot provide better support for the child's ethnic identity or protect her from exposure to damaging racist attitudes than adoptive parents with a different racial, ethnic, or cultural background.

13.6.3 STEP-PARENT ADOPTION

With about 1,600 adoption orders made in favour of a step-parent every year, such adoptions constitute a significant proportion of the total number of annual adoptions.[205] The continuing popularity of step-parent adoption is surprising. During the 1970s, step-parent adoptions were seen by many as a natural means of consolidating and supporting a new family unit following divorce or separation. Reinforced by the 'clean-break philosophy' underpinning divorce and a more ambivalent attitude towards the role of the father in the post-divorce context, it was thought by some that the child's interests would be better protected within the security and stability of the new nuclear family. The interests of the new family unit were thus prioritized, with the maintenance of links with the non-resident

[205] DH (2000), [8.3].

parent, invariably the father, viewed as potentially destabilizing, adding to the pressures on the new family and preventing it from firmly establishing itself as a 'normal', autonomous unit. However, even at this time, there were some strong concerns about the widespread use of step-parent adoption to exclude the non-resident parent from the child's life. The courts' concerns were clearly set down in *Re B (A Minor) (Adoption By Parent)*, a fairly typical case in which, following the parents' divorce, the father had enjoyed only sporadic contact. The mother and her new husband wished to adopt the child thereby excluding the father from playing any further role in the child's life. The father opposed the adoption.

Re B (A Minor) (Adoption By Parent) [1975] Fam 127, 143, 146 (Fam Div)

[Sir George Baker P gave the first judgment allowing the appeal]

CUMMING BRUCE J:

I appreciate that in this case, as in many, it is strongly in the child's interest that he should be settled in the family life of the mother and her second husband; that he should form a close relationship with the father figure represented by that husband. I also appreciate that in this case, as in many, the fact that the child continues to have a relationship with his natural father is a source of practical inconvenience and irritation to the mother, who wishes to put her first husband out of her life as completely as possible. And, of course, the second husband may be expected to wish to keep the first husband completely out of their family life. Also, it is common experience that the emotional effect on the child of an attempt to maintain dual and frequently conflicting loyalties to both parents, and to the stepfather, is deeply disturbing and sometimes gravely destructive to the stable development of his personality. But...[i]t is quite wrong to use the adoption law to extinguish the relationship between the protesting father and the child, unless there is some really serious factor which justifies the use of the statutory guillotine. The courts should not encourage the idea that after divorce the children of the family can be reshuffled and dealt out like a pack of cards in a second rubber of bridge. Often a parent who has remarried and has custody of the children from the first family is eager to achieve just that result, but such parents, often faced with very grave practical problems, are frequently blind to the real long-term interests of their children.

BAGNALL J:

...There is a body of opinion that where there is a divorce followed by remarriage and a very young child, the best course for the child is to make a complete break and allow the child to be brought up exclusively as a member of the new family established by a parent and a step-parent. That this view has not found favour in these courts is clear...Nevertheless it may well be that, where all parties are in agreement and the relevant parent consents, it can be established that adoption by a parent and the step-parent is for the welfare of the child. In such a case the other parent agrees, so to say, to disappear wholly from the child's life and to accept a change of the child's legal status. Even there I think that parents should hesitate long and think carefully before taking such an irrevocable step. Cases such as this, where the relevant parent refuses to consent to adoption, are quite different. The advantages which adoption may bring to the child can almost always be secured without a change in legal status. Where the application is made by a parent and a step-parent after divorce and remarriage, I am of the opinion that only in very rare and wholly exceptional cases will it be possible to say that adoption against the wishes of a present and expostulating parent is for the welfare of the child. I am likewise of opinion, where such an application is made, that again only in very rare and wholly exceptional cases should it be said that a father who says, 'I do not wish my son to become in law the son of another man' is acting unreasonably. I think it is inadvisable that adoption applications in cases such as this should in any way be encouraged.

This strong opposition to step-parent adoption is now underpinned by important changes in family policy as enshrined in the CA 1989. The clean-break model of divorce has been supplanted by an ideal of cooperative joint parenting post-separation, supported by the enduring nature of parental responsibility and a strong presumption in favour of continuing contact with the non-resident parent. As Neale and Smart explain, the model of the reconstituted nuclear family has been replaced by that of the bi-nuclear family spread across two households.[206] These key policy changes are reinforced by a fundamental re-orientation of the welfare discourse such that the child's best interests are no longer viewed as resting primarily with the new family unit but in preserving strong healthy relationships with both sides of the birth family. These policy changes are fundamentally inconsistent with using adoption to sever irrevocably the child's relationship with the non-resident parent.

Cases in which step-parent adoption will be sanctioned are thus likely to be exceptional. Section 8 orders can confer the desired security on the new family unit and regulate any problematic behaviour by the non-resident parent. The recent amendment to the CA 1989 allowing a step-parent to acquire free-standing parental responsibility further reduces the need to resort to adoption—although, surprisingly, unlike applications for adoption under the ACA 2002, only married or civil partners of a birth parent can take advantage of these provisions.[207]

Finally, it should be noted that, depending on the particular circumstances of the case, the European Court of Human Rights has held that a step-parent adoption does not necessarily violate the rights of the non-adopting parent under Article 8.[208] However, given the gravity of the interference with the birth parent's rights, it must be doubtful that the European Court would find a step-parent adoption necessary and proportionate where there was any kind of ongoing, meaningful relationship between the non-adopting parent and the child.

13.6.4 ADOPTION BY A SOLE NATURAL PARENT

Many of the concerns regarding step-parent adoption apply with added force in the case of an adoption by a sole natural parent. The only real remaining advantage of adopting one's own child, from the perspective of the adopting parent, is that it confers additional security on the resident parent by permanently terminating the parental responsibility of the non-adopting parent. It is thus an effective means of ensuring the non-resident parent can play no future role in the child's upbringing. The advantages of such an order from the child's perspective are more difficult to discern. However, in *Re B (A Minor) (Adoption: Natural Parent)*, the House of Lords controversially allowed an adoption order in favour of the child's natural father to stand. The facts of the case were relatively unusual in that the mother, having voluntarily relinquished the child at birth, wanted nothing more to do

---

[206] Neale and Smart (1999), 37. See p 745.
[207] CA 1989, s 4A. See 10.3.5.
[208] *Söderbäck v Sweden* (App No 113/1997/897/1109, ECHR) (1998).

with her. The father discovered the child's existence by chance and immediately assumed responsibility for her care. The mother did not oppose his application to adopt.

Re B (A Minor) (Adoption: Natural Parent) [2001] UKHL 70

LORD NICHOLLS:

5. The father is seeking an adoption order primarily because he is anxious to secure A's future in his sole care. He feels insecure, and believes he will feel more secure knowing that the mother's parental responsibility for A has been removed. This can only be achieved by an adoption order. The mother has said repeatedly she does not wish to play any part in A's life. But the father is concerned that, without an adoption order, it will remain possible in future years for the mother to pose a threat to A's continued placement with him. He is concerned that the mother may marry and, with her new husband, ask to have A to live with her. The court might look favourably upon such an application. His vulnerability to an attempt by the mother to reclaim A is something which has caused him great anxiety. He is adamant in his wish for an adoption order, although whatever order is made will not affect the strength of his commitment to A. He does not, in principle, exclude the possibility of future contact by the mother with A, provided the placement with him is secure...

6. In his report to the court the Official Solicitor, acting as A's guardian, opposed the application. The sole consequence of an adoption order would be to end the mother's relationship with A. This was not an order which could be said to safeguard and promote A's welfare. There was nothing in the history of the case to suggest that the mother would be likely to seek to disrupt the security of A's placement with her father. But any attempt by her to do so would not necessarily be to A's disadvantage...

25. An adoption order in favour of a single natural parent alone will...have the effect of permanently extinguishing any parental responsibility of the other natural parent...This will afford the adoptive parent a measure of additional security. But it is important here to keep in mind the wide range of powers the court now has under the Children Act 1989 to restrict the possibility of inappropriate intervention in the child's life by the other natural parent. Adoption is not intended to be used simply as the means by which to protect the child's life with one natural parent against inappropriate intervention by the other natural parent.

26. Another consequence adoption has in this type of case is that after adoption the child will be treated in law as if she had been borne to her adoptive parent in wedlock...The significance of this benefit today should not be overstated. The social and legal status of children born outside marriage has changed greatly in recent years. The social stigma and legal disabilities attendant upon 'illegitimacy' have now largely gone. Two children in every five born in this country are born outside marriage. Unless a contrary intention appears, statutes enacted after 1987 are to be interpreted without regard to whether a person's parents were married at any time...

27. Having regard to all these matters, the circumstances in which it will be in the best interests of a child to make an adoption order in favour of one natural parent alone, thereby, in Hale LJ's words, taking away one half of the child's legal family, are likely to be exceptional. Bracewell J [at first instance] regarded the circumstances of the present case as exceptional. She said so. The father's case was that the mother's continuing status as a parent with parental responsibility for A would perpetuate insecurity for him and that this would potentially affect A's stability. The judge accepted this...Given the mother's attitude to A from the moment of A's birth, and her consent, adoption by the father was in A's best interests. Adoption was in A's best interests even though this would have the consequence of excluding the mother.

28. In my view, on the evidence before her this conclusion was open to Bracewell J...That an adoption order as sought by A's father will safeguard and promote A's welfare is a wholly tenable view. A residence order, together with an appropriate prohibited steps order, may not suffice to allay the father's genuine anxieties.

The decision has met with strong criticism. It is certainly questionable whether rendering the child 'legally motherless', given the strong negative message of rejection this sends out, was in the child's interests, particularly when alternative orders were available under the CA 1989 to address the father's insecurity.[209] On a more general level, the case raises interesting questions as to whether parents (both mothers and fathers) should be able to reject parenthood by irrevocably terminating their 'very parenthood' through adoption or whether there should be a less drastic mechanism for removing parental responsibility from absent or uninterested parents which does not have the same distorting effect on the child's core familial relationships.[210]

13.7 POST-ADOPTION ISSUES

13.7.1 OPEN ADOPTION

In order to protect the new relationship between the adoptive parents and the child, adoption was traditionally shrouded in secrecy with very careful restrictions in place to prevent children discovering the truth about their adopted status or birth parents discovering the whereabouts of the new adoptive family. In order to preserve the confidentiality of the placement approximately 80 per cent of people applying for an adoption order still ask for a serial number (rather than using their names) to be assigned to their case.[211] However, the fact that many adopted children are now older with strong emotional ties to their birth families, alongside emerging evidence as to the strong need felt by adopted adults to seek information about their biological parents, has severely challenged the closed nature of adoption. In the past few years, a more open concept of adoption has become entrenched within social work practice. However, the law has been more reluctant to embrace this change—a change which fundamentally challenges the orthodox 'legal transplant' model of adoption remaining entrenched within the legislation.

Openness can take many forms. At one end of the scale it can simply involve providing children with more detailed information about their birth parents and the circumstances surrounding their adoption. At the other end of the scale, it can involve regular direct contact between the child and members of the birth family. Between these extremes, openness can involve infrequent visits, indirect contact such as telephone calls and letters, and fairly frequent exchange of information between the adoptive parents and the birth family in the form of photographs, reports on the child's progress, and news about the birth family. Contact between the child and the birth mother, maternal grandparents, and siblings is common, but rarely involves the father and the wider paternal family.[212]

---

[209] Harris-Short (2002).
[210] See further discussion at 10.5.1. See also Harris-Short (2002) and Bainham (2005), 279.
[211] DCA (2006a), 19.
[212] Neil (2000), 314.

The right to information

Although much of the debate on open adoption now focuses on post-adoption contact, an important aspect of openness is the provision of information about the child's genealogical background and the circumstances surrounding the adoption. In some cases this will be sufficient to meet concerns about the child's identity and help assuage any feelings of confusion or loss. Under the ACA 2002, an adopted person has the right, upon reaching the age of 18, to apply through an adoption agency for information which will allow him/her to obtain a certified copy of the birth record.[213] For people adopted before the ACA 2002 came into force, this information can be obtained directly from the Registrar General. Disclosure of this information can only be withheld in exceptional circumstances by order of the High Court.[214] An adopted person upon reaching the age of 18 also has the right to a copy of the adoption order and any prescribed information which had to be disclosed to the adopters.[215] The Registrar General must also maintain an adoption contact register. Part 1 of the register enables adopted persons over the age of 18 to record whether they would like to make contact with any of their birth relatives. Part II of the register contains information entered by birth relatives as to whether they wish to make contact with the adopted child. Where there is a 'match' between the two parts of the register, the Registrar General will notify the adopted person.[216]

The statutory requirements dealing with the recording, keeping and disclosure of wider information about a child's adoption are contained within ss 56 to 65 of the ACA 2002. The information which an adoption agency must keep in relation to an adoption is prescribed by regulations and referred to as 'section 56 information'. It includes:

- the child's case record (includes the child's permanence report, a written record of the adoption panel proceedings, a record of the agency's decision on placement, any consents);
- any information that has been supplied by a natural parent or relative or other significant person in the adopted person's life, with the intention that the adopted person may, should he wish to, be given that information;
- any information supplied by the adoptive parents or other persons which is relevant to matters arising after the making of the adoption order;
- any information the adopted person has requested should be kept;
- any information given to the adoption agency in respect of an adopted person by the Registrar General (information that would enable an adopted person to obtain a certified copy of the record of his birth);
- any information disclosed to the adoption agency about an entry relating to the adopted person on the Adoption Contact Register.[217]

The adoption agency has discretion not to keep information supplied by a member of the birth family or the adoptive parents if satisfied that it would be prejudicial to the adopted

---

[213] S 60(2).

[214] S 60(3). This gives statutory recognition to the principle established in *R v Registrar General, ex parte Smith* [1991] 2 QB 393.

[215] S 60(2)(b) and (4).

[216] Adopted Children and Adoption Contact Registers Regulations 2005, 2005/924, reg 8.

[217] Disclosure of Adoption Information (Post-Commencement Adoptions) Regulations 2005, SI 2005/888, reg 4.

person's welfare or it would not be reasonably practicable.[218] Any s 56 information which is 'identifying information', i.e. information which directly identifies a person or, whether taken alone or in conjunction with other information, could lead to an individual being identified, is referred to as 'protected information'.[219] Where an agreement is in place permitting disclosure, protected information may be disclosed.[220] Otherwise, an application must be made to the adoption agency which has a wide discretion as to whether disclosure should take place. The adoption agency does not have to proceed with an application if it does not consider it appropriate to do so.[221] If it does consider it appropriate to proceed, it must take all reasonable steps to obtain the views of any affected person.[222] Where the protected information is about a person who is at the time of the application a child, the agency must take all reasonable steps to ascertain the views of the child's parent or guardian and, having regard to the child's age and understanding, the views of the child.[223] It is then within the discretion of the agency whether or not it considers it appropriate to disclose. In exercising this discretion, the adoption agency (where at the time of the application none of the information is about a child) is directed to consider the welfare of the adopted person and the views of any person the information is about.[224] Where the information is about an adopted child who has not yet attained the age of 18, in exercising its discretion the child's welfare must be the agency's paramount consideration.[225] If the information is about any other child, the agency 'must have particular regard to the child's welfare'.[226] In the case of information which is not protected information, the adoption agency simply has a broad discretion whether or not to disclose.[227] In exercising its discretion under these provisions the adoption agency is entitled to adopt a general policy on disclosure but must consider each individual case on its merits.[228] If an applicant is unhappy with the agency's decision, he or she may apply to an independent review panel under s 12 of the ACA 2002 for the decision to be reviewed.[229] The agency must then take into account any recommendation of the review panel in reconsidering its decision. An action will also lie in judicial review.

The child's right to know?

Whilst the adoption agency has a broad discretion to make disclosure of both identifying and non-identifying information to an adopted person, the legislation does not provide a *right* in the *child* to receive any information about the birth parents or the circumstances surrounding the adoption. It is therefore misleading to talk about the child's *right* to information in this context. This contrasts sharply with other areas of the law where the courts

---

[218] Ibid., reg 4(4).

[219] ACA 2002, s 57.

[220] S 57(5). See also Disclosure of Adoption Information (Post-Commencement Adoptions) Regulations 2005, SI 2005/888, reg 11.

[221] ACA 2002, ss 61(2) and 62(2).

[222] Ss 61(3) and 62(4).

[223] S 62(3).

[224] Ss 61(5) and 62(7).

[225] S 62(6)(a).

[226] S 62(6)(b).

[227] S 58.

[228] See *Gunn-Russo v Nugent Care Society and Secretary of State for Health* [2001] EWHC 566 (decided under the AA 1976).

[229] Disclosure of Adoption Information (Post-Commencement Adoptions) Regulations 2005, SI 2005/888, reg 15. This addresses the point raised in *Gaskin v UK* (App No 10454/83, ECHR) (1990).

have moved towards accepting the child's *right* to know the truth about parentage.[230] Despite Parliament's reticence to enshrine such a right in the legislation, the National Adoption Standards provide clear guidance to the adoption agency and the adoptive parents as to the child's *entitlement* to information. The guidance is clearly premised on the assumption that the adoptive parents will be open about the adoption and willing and able to share information with their children about the birth family and the circumstances surrounding the adoption. The National Standards provide:

> 7. Children will be well prepared before joining a new family. This will include clear appropriate information on their birth family and life before adoption, and information about the adopters and their family. Children are entitled to information provided by their birth families, which will be kept safe both by agencies and adopters. It will be provided to adopted children, or adults, at a time and in a manner that reflects their age and understanding, as well as the nature of the information concerned.
>
> 12...Information from agency records will be made available to the child when they are of an age and level of understanding to comprehend it.[231]

In practice, what information is provided to the child and when will be left to the discretion of the adoptive parents. The child is very unlikely to be able to access information without their cooperation.

Post-adoption contact

The most effective way of informing children about their birth family is through direct or indirect contact.

The empirical evidence on post-adoption contact

Based on the work of the child psychiatrist John Bowlby, many child care professionals working in the 1970s considered that to consolidate the child within the new adoptive family existing attachments to the birth family must be severed.

B. Lindley, 'Open adoption—Is the door ajar?', (1997) 9 *Child and Family Law Quarterly* 115, 117–18

> Attachment theory was cited by some clinicians and social work practitioners as justification for the notion of closed, secretive adoption. Bowlby's work on attachment and the vital importance of the early relationship with one care-giver, normally the mother, was used to affirm the view that as far as adoption was concerned the child needed an exclusive environment free from interference from the birth family. Although he modified his theory later in his life, conceding that the child could have multiple attachment figures, albeit in some form of hierarchy, Bowlby's original thesis still remains very influential. This is partly due to the work of Goldstein, Freud and Solnit who asserted that, from their *clinical* experience in the UK and the USA, when children were apart from a parent, there should be a cessation of contact with that parent, otherwise the child would

---

230 See *Re H (a minor) (blood tests: parental rights)* [1997] Fam 89, 107 and discussion at pp 599–608.
231 DH (2001b).

fail to bond with the new parent/carer and would also experience confusion and divided loyalties. They applied this theory both to children placed with new carers/families and to children whose parents were separated or divorced...Although their 'clean break' view was based on clinical rather than research evidence, it had a very strong influence on child care professionals at the time when the 'permanence' movement was developing during the 1970s and 1980s. Indeed, in spite of the recent practice development of greater openness, particularly for older children adopted from the care system, this view remains very influential today.

A child's ability to form multiple attachments strongly undermines the view that birth families must be totally excluded from the child's life if the child is to bond successfully with the adoptive family. Indeed, research suggests that continuing contact with the birth family has no affect on the child's sense of belonging with the adoptive parents and can even positively promote the child's integration into the new family.

B. Lindley, 'Open adoption—Is the door ajar?', (1997) 9 *Child and Family Law Quarterly* 115, 121

Subsequent studies of children moving to new families suggest that, rather than preventing children from settling, openness can *help* the child settle in the new family, providing the adults are not hostile to each other, or the idea. Fratter's study found that contact helped to provide continuity, a positive identity and an understanding for the child of the circumstances of the adoption. It enabled the child to feel free to attach to the new family whilst retaining a link with their birth family. Indeed, she concludes when commenting on the impact of contact, that 'contact was not thought to have adversely affected the attachment of any of the children placed under seven years of age, and had not given rise to divided loyalties, even where there had been fortnightly face-to-face contact'. However, she adds a qualification to this, namely that the attitude of the parents and parent figures to one another is crucial in freeing children from guilt and divided loyalties.

Other studies have found that the stability of the placements of older children was not threatened by maintaining links with their families of origin. They also show that older children may not be willing to move to a new family if contact with their original families is to be severed, although they do not always feel able to voice their opinion...

Moreover, Hill et al found that when earlier attachments are disregarded, the feelings do not go away but are simply driven underground. Triseliotis at al also report some evidence which suggests that older children who are pressurised to abandon meaningful relationships with members of the birth family may find it difficult to attach themselves to the new family...

Direct knowledge of the birth parents can also help the child develop a secure and positive identity, avoiding what has been termed in the literature 'genealogical bewilderment'.[232] Ryburn identifies a number of further important benefits from post-adoption contact, perhaps most obviously these include benefits for both the birth parents and the child.

---

[232] Smith (2004), 330. See further discussion at 9.4.4.

M. Ryburn, 'In whose best interests?—Post-adoption contact with the birth family', (1998) 10 *Child and Family Law Quarterly* 53, 59–61

Advantages of contact for birth parents

Contact for birth parents with their children can make a significant difference. The studies indicate in particular that contact helps parents to resolve the grief of their loss, and to move on in their lives, and there is a well-established principle here. It is extremely difficult to manage grief when it has no clear focus…This, in reality, is the living death of a child…

The studies also indicate that one of the overwhelming needs of birth parents without contact is for reassurance that their child is well and happy, and contact is able, in general, to offer this reassurance. In some instances just the open exchange of information may be sufficient . . . . Perhaps one of the most striking things to emerge from the studies is how concerned birth parents are that contact should not be a source of distress or disruption in the life of their child.

Advantages of contact for children

The research studies suggest that with indirect contact children's information needs begin to be met, but that with direct contact their questions are more likely to be met at a level that is satisfying. One of the key advantages of any contact is that facts can more readily replace speculation and fantasy. Children are also helped through contact to come to terms with difficult aspects of their past lives—aspects that might otherwise be a source of difficulty for them…

Children also appear to gain a sense of reassurance as a consequence of contact, particularly direct contact, with their birth relatives. In particular, it gives them a clear message that the placement is supported by their original family since otherwise they would not be visiting, and it is a visible symbol that their adoptive parents feel positively about their original family or contact would not be permitted. The largest study of adoption and permanent foster care placements ever undertaken in the UK…also found that birth family contact was the single factor which could be identified as enhancing the stability of placements. Finally, contact, in particular direct contact, appears to strengthen children's sense of attachment to their adoptive parents…

Perhaps more surprisingly, Murray also identifies a number of advantages for the adoptive parents:

Effects of secrecy on adopters

Traditionally, adopters have been seen as those with the least to gain through post-adoption contact and certainly it was agencies claiming to represent the voice of adopters who were instrumental in introducing much greater secrecy…Without adequate information at the time of placement, and a way of accessing additional and up-to-date information as it is needed, adopters may feel hampered in the task of parenting a child born to someone else…

Advantages of contact for adopters

The studies indicate that adopters may gain significantly through contact. Adopters with continuing contact following adoption are generally comfortable with it. It would appear that contact can enhance children's attachments to their adopters, it provides a ready source of

> information and it appears to lead to more positive feelings towards birth relatives. This, in
> turn, is likely to aid children in the acquisition of positive identity.
>
> The greatest gain to be attributed to contact—in this case direct contact—is a sense of
> security and permanence in the parenting role.

Although some researchers are more cautious than Ryburn in their reading of the empirical evidence,[233] most generally agree that the impact of post-adoption contact on adoption outcomes is fairly negligible: post-adoption contact with the birth family is not generally harmful to the child but neither is its absence.[234] There is little evidence that post-adoption contact leads to significantly better outcomes.[235]

Post-adoption contact in the courts

Practice within the social work profession has in many ways moved ahead of the empirical evidence. The importance of being open about adoption and the birth family, including promoting contact where appropriate, is emphasized at every stage of the process. There are consequently very few adoptions where there is no provision for some form of direct or indirect contact between the adopters and the birth family.[236] Indeed, unless prospective adopters are willing to facilitate openness their suitability to adopt is likely to be questioned. This positive attitude contrasts sharply with the attitude of the courts which have, in the past, been extremely reluctant to make any kind of formal provision for post-adoption contact—this reluctance stemming it would seem from their difficulty in reconciling a move towards greater openness with the traditional legal understanding of adoption.[237]

Re V (A Minor) (Adoption: Consent) [1987] Fam 57, 68 (CA)

OLIVER LJ:

[T]he stability and security of the child is of course a very important consideration, but, speaking for myself, I confess to a degree of unease about the desirability of seeking to secure stability by an adoption order in a case where the whole process is being approached on the footing that an opposing natural parent is to be accorded immediate and continuing access, not simply for the purpose of keeping her memory alive and investing the child with a sense of his own identity, but on a regular and frequent basis and where it is found as a fact that, to put it no higher, there exists a serious doubt whether she is capable of concealing her desire to have the child reestablished as a member of her family. An adoption order would no doubt frustrate the realisation of that desire, but it cannot be thought realistically to eliminate it. This is the dilemma . . . Once it is found . . . that regular and frequent access, inevitably maintaining and strengthening the family ties between the child and his mother and her other children, is so conducive to the welfare of the child that provision has to be made for it in the adoption order as the underlying basis on which the order is made at all, I find it difficult to reconcile that with the avowed purpose of the adoption of extinguishing any parental rights or duties in

---

[233] See, e.g., Quinton and Selwyn (1998) and (2006).
[234] Neil (2009). See also, Quinton and Selwyn (2006), 473. For an excellent summary of the current position see Smith (2005), 315–17 and Logan and Smith (2005), 6–11.
[235] Neil (2009).
[236] Masson (2000).
[237] See, e.g., *Re C (A Minor) (Adoption Order: Condition)* [1986] 1 FLR 315 (per Sir John Donaldson).

the natural parent. I entertain considerable reservations about whether, on the basis of continuing regular and frequent access by a natural parent who has not shown himself or herself unfit in any way to care for his or her own child, it can be right to impose an irrevocable change of status with a view simply to discouraging him or her from the hope of persuading a court in the future to alter the status quo as regards care and control.

Against the backdrop of these concerns about the inherently contradictory nature of 'open adoption', the guiding principles to be applied on an application for post-adoption contact prior to the implementation of the ACA 2002 were established by the House of Lords in *Re C (A Minor) (Adoption Order: Conditions)*. The House of Lords held that it would only be in exceptional cases that a contact order would be imposed on the adoptive parents.

Re C (A Minor) (Adoption Order: Conditions) [1989] 1 AC 1, 17–18 (HL)

LORD ACKNER:

The cases rightly stress that in normal circumstances it is desirable that there should be a complete break, but that each case has to be considered on its own particular facts. No doubt the court will not, except in the most exceptional case, impose terms or conditions as to access to members of the child's natural family to which the adopting parents do not agree. To do so would be to create a potentially frictional situation which would be hardly likely to safeguard or promote the welfare of the child. Where no agreement is forthcoming the court will, with very rare exceptions, have to choose between making an adoption order without terms or conditions as to access, or to refuse to make such an order and seek to safeguard access through some other machinery, such as wardship. To do otherwise would be merely inviting future and almost immediate litigation.

Following the House of Lords' decision in *Re C*, the courts consistently refused to make provision for contact where the adoptive parents did not agree. Even where they did agree, the courts were extremely reluctant to formalize that agreement in an order, holding that such matters were best left to the 'good sense' of the adopters. In *Re T (A Minor) (Contact after Adoption)* the adoptive parents agreed to maintain contact between the adopted child and the birth mother once a year. The birth mother wanted contact on a slightly more regular basis. The parties were not therefore in dispute about the principle of whether contact should take place but simply as to frequency.

Re T (A Minor) (Contact After Adoption) [1995] 2 FCR 537, 542–4 (CA)

Lady Justice Butler-Sloss:

In this case the only argument, really, that remains is whether the once a year, which was agreed to by the adopters and was found to be the right amount of contact by the judge, should be imposed upon these adopters, or whether it should be left to their good sense so that they could be trusted to do what they believe to be in the best interest of their daughter.

[Counsel], for the mother, has one point which he has put to us very effectively, that the mother has consented to adoption, but that her consent to adoption, although it was unconditional, nonetheless recognized that she would expect to see the child at least once a year, and had hoped to see the child rather more, and that such consent was in the context of this continuing contact in an open adoption. What the Judge was doing by making an order was to give her some degree of security...

It seems to me that that degree of security that she seeks has to be found in the trust that she must have in these adopters. That is a trust which is undoubtedly held by the local authority and the guardian ad litem, because those experts in this field all believe that at this stage of this child's life it is right for her sake that she should continue to see her mother once a year. They have chosen this family on the basis that they also would recognize it was in the interests of this child that she should continue, certainly for the time being, to see her natural mother. These adopters themselves accept that this is right...

In this particular case, if for some reason the adopters decide that the child should not see her natural mother, that is a flexibility which was implicit in the recommendations of the social workers and the guardian ad litem that there should be no order. As I understand it, for the foreseeable future it is said that there will be contact, but the adopters wish to be in control, responding, as they intend to do, to what the child says, what the child wants, and perhaps, much more importantly what the child needs, in their careful parental estimation.

If there is an order and in due course it looks as though the child does not want to see her mother, or there may be reasons why the child ought not to see her mother...on the basis of the Judge's order it will be the adopters who will have to go back to court and ask for the order to be varied, suspended or for there to be no future contact. That would seem to me to impose upon a family who have chosen to take on the responsibility of this child, with all the burdens as well as all the pleasures that that imposes, an additional burden which is unjust to this adoptive family. I do not see why they should have to go to court.

If they do stop the contact for any reason in the future, it would be reasonable, it would seem to me, that they would give a clear indication to the natural mother as to why they do not think there should be contact either short-term or long-term. They should give their reasons clearly so the mother can study them. If they do not do that, or if the reasons turn out to be inadequate or wrong or unjust, the mother has the right to go to the court and ask for leave to claim the contact that she has had in the past...

[I]n my judgment the prevalence and finality of adoption and the importance of letting the new family find its owns feet ought not to be threatened in any way by an order in this case.

As the court notes, should the adoptive parents renege on their agreement as to contact, the birth parents can apply for a contact order under s 8 of the CA 1989. However, once the adoption order has been made the birth parents become 'former parents' and, as such, legal strangers to the child. They therefore no longer qualify as 'parents' for the purposes of s 10(4) of the CA 1989 and will require leave to make the application.[238] The case law under the AA 1976 made it clear that obtaining leave in these circumstances would constitute a formidable hurdle for the birth parents. In *Re C (A Minor) (Adopted child: Contact)*, Thorpe J reasserted the orthodox position that adoption orders are 'permanent and final' and that they should therefore only be re-opened where there has been some 'fundamental change in circumstances.'[239] This approach to leave has been confirmed post-implementation of the ACA 2002 by McFarlane J in *X and Y v A Local Authority*.[240] The question of whether it constitutes a 'fundamental change in circumstances' for the adoptive parents to renege on an agreement as to contact has been the subject of some dispute. It is clear that the adoptive

238 *In re C (A Minor) (Adopted child: Contact)* [1993] Fam 210.
239 Ibid., 216.
240 [2009] EWHC 47, [41]–[42].

parents must, at the very least, provide an explanation as to why they are reneging on the agreement.[241] However, apart from this obligation to provide an explanation for the change of heart, there is very little to assist the birth family. The difficult hurdle facing the birth family on an application for leave is exemplified by *Re S (contact: application by sibling)*. The case concerned an application for leave by the half-sister (also adopted) of an adopted child, 'B'. The applicant was suffering considerable distress at the lack of contact with B. Nobody envisaged at the time of the children's adoptions that the absence of contact would be a source of difficulty for either child. No provision was therefore made. In any event, the adoptive mother of B had been strongly opposed to contact throughout. This was not therefore a case where an earlier agreement had been reneged upon. Nevertheless it was argued that the applicant's unforeseen distress constituted a 'fundamental change in circumstances'. Charles J dismissed the application, emphasizing the importance of leaving such questions to B's adoptive mother unless her behaviour was verging on the irrational.

Re S (contact: application by sibling) [1999] Fam 283, 296–8 (Fam Div)

CHARLES J:

In my judgment I should not seek to define what might constitute changes in circumstances which would warrant the grant of leave to bring an application for a contact order in respect of an adopted child and thereby remove, or go behind, the finality of an adoption order. But in considering whether there has been a fundamental or sufficient change in circumstances to warrant leave being granted it is necessary to consider on the facts of each case (i) the effect, or potential effect, of the difference in circumstances between those that existed at the time the adoption order was made and at the time of the application for leave, and (ii) how that effect impacts on the finality of the adoption order, the discretion and responsibility conferred on the adopters thereby and the regime, or new family, created by the adoption order to safeguard and promote the welfare of the adopted child during his or her childhood. . . .

[I]n my judgment the applicant for leave must satisfy the court at the leave stage that, having regard to the relevant changes in circumstances, the decision of the adopters is sufficiently contrary to the best interests of the child, or sufficiently unreasonable, to warrant the court overriding the discretion conferred on the adopters by the adoption order to determine whether what is proposed by the applicant for leave (e.g. as here, contact with a sibling) should be permitted, by giving itself the jurisdiction and discretion to determine this in section 8 proceedings. This approach is not one where the court asks what the court making the adoption order would have considered to be in the best interests of the relevant child, or children, at the time the adoption order was made if the present circumstances had then existed, but is one that recognises that the relevant adopters could not have had an adoption order on terms forced upon them and thus that the discretion and freedom of action given to them by the adoption order to safeguard and promote the welfare of the child should be respected.

The particular circumstances of each case will be important. For example: (a) where the adoption order was made on a particular understanding the adopters may well have to show good reasons for departing from that understanding to avoid leave being granted because the understanding places a limit on, or a starting point to their freedom and discretion as adoptive parents . . . whereas (b) in cases where there is no such understanding, or other matter, which limits the freedom and discretion of the adoptive parents to decide what is in the best interests of their child, in my judgment the court would have to be satisfied that it appeared

---

[241] *Re T (Adopted children: contact)* [1995] 2 FLR 792.

that the decision of the adoptive parents was outside the range of decisions that a reasonable adoptive parent in their position could take because, for example it was clearly not in the best interests of the child, or for some other reason...

[Having considered the evidence **Charles J** concluded that the position adopted by the adoptive mother was not outside the range of decisions that a reasonable adoptive parent could take and that the application for leave should accordingly be dismissed.]

Post-adoption contact in the ACA 2002

The ACA 2002 arguably marks a shift away from this very cautious approach towards post-adoption contact, potentially making the use of s 8 orders in the context of adoption much more routine. The duty on the court to consider contact at the placement stage should ensure more birth parents retain contact with the child throughout this crucial period which in turn will strengthen their case for post-adoption contact. It has been held that birth parents are entitled to apply as of right for a contact order to be heard together with the adoption application at the final hearing.[242] Moreover, regardless of whether or not the parent has made an application to the court, the court is under a mandatory duty to consider the proposals as to post-adoption contact when deciding whether or not to make the adoption order. The court should be further prompted towards making some provision for contact by the welfare checklist which directs the court's attention to the child's existing relationships with members of the birth family, the value of those relationships continuing, and the wishes and feelings of the child's relatives.[243] The court must also consider the full range of powers available to it, including those under s 8 of the CA 1989. There remains considerable doubt, however, whether these provisions are strong enough to bring about a fundamental change in the court's approach.

Comments made by Wall LJ immediately prior to the implementation of the ACA 2002 did not auger well, it being clear that, despite the new provisions, it was his view that the courts' approach to post-adoption contact would essentially remain unchanged.

Re R (Adoption: Contact) [2005] EWCA Civ 1128

WALL LJ:

48. We were shown section 1 of the new Act, which is due in force later this year, which demonstrates the clear change of thinking there has been since 1976, when the Act was initially enacted, and which demonstrates that the court now will need to take into account and consider the relationship the child had with members of the natural family, and the likelihood of that relationship continuing and the value of the relationship to the child.

49. So contact is more common, but nonetheless the jurisprudence I think is clear. The imposition on prospective adopters of orders for contact with which they are not in agreement is extremely, and remains extremely, unusual.

However, two years later in the case of *Re P (a child)*, the Court of Appeal, Wall LJ giving judgment, appeared to signal a cautious but important change in its approach, holding that

---

[242] ACA 2002, s 46. See *X and Y v A Local Authority (Adoption: Procedure)* [2009] EWHC 47, [18]–[19]
[243] S 1(4)(f) and (6).

the courts now have a much more central role to play in securing post-adoption contact where appropriate.[244]

Re P (a child) [2008] EWCA Civ 535

WALL LJ:

141. We approach this part of our judgment with caution, as we are conscious that these are early days, and the manner in which adoption agencies apply the terms of the 2002 Act will need to be worked out in practice over time...

142. Historically, post adoption contact between children and their birth parents has been perceived as highly exceptional...

147. All this, in our judgment, now falls to be revisited under section 26 and 27 of the 2002 Act, given in particular the terms of sections 1(4)(f), 1(6) and (7) and 46(6). In our judgment, the judge in the instant case was plainly right to make a contact order under section 26 of the 2002 Act, and in our judgment the question of contact between [the children], and between the children and their parents, should henceforth be a matter for the court, not for the local authority, or the local authority in agreement with prospective adopters...

148. ... The making of the placement orders means, of course, that contact under the 1989 Act is no longer possible, but orders under sections 26 and 27 are not only possible but, in our judgment, necessary.

149. Furthermore, when the time comes for [the children] to be finally placed, it will be the court which will have to make the necessary orders – either for adoption, or for revocation of the placement orders if the children are not to be adopted. At that point, in our judgment, as the facts of this case currently stand, it will be for the court, before making an adoption order, to decide, in accordance with section 46(6) of the 2002 Act, what ongoing contact [the children] should have with each other – not for their prospective adopters to do so. The same principle will apply if the children are to be placed in long-term foster care.

150. The effect of the placement order is substantially to disempower [the children's] parents – see section 25(4) of the 2002 Act. In our judgment, as matters currently stand, the existence of the placement orders should not be an inhibition on the ability of [the mother] in particular to apply to the court to determine questions of contact – and in particular the question of contact between D and S. Indeed, it seems to us highly likely that the placement of the children with adopters or foster carers who are unwilling, in particular, to facilitate contact between [the children] would provide a proper basis for leave to be granted to [the mother] under section 24(2) of the 2002 Act (leave to make an application to apply for an order to revoke the placement order) or for leave to apply to oppose the making of an adoption order under section 47(5) of the 2002 Act.

151. On the facts of this case, there is a universal recognition that the relationship between [the children] needs to be preserved. It is on this basis that the local authority / adoption agency is seeking the placement of the children. In our judgment, this means that the question of contact between the two children is not a matter for agreement between the local authority / adoption agency and the adopters: it is a matter which, ultimately, is for the court. It is the court which will have to make adoption orders or orders revoking the placement orders, and in our judgment it is the court which has the responsibility to make orders for contact if they are required in the interests of the two children...

---

[244] See also the more positive comments of Baroness Hale regarding post-adoption contact in *Down Lisburn Health and Social Services Trust v H* [2006] UKHL 36, [6]–[8].

> 153. . . . [I]t is not, in our judgment, a proper exercise of the judicial powers given to the court under the 2002 Act to leave contact between the children themselves, or between the children and their natural parents to the discretion of the local authority and / or the prospective carers of [the children], be they adoptive parents or foster carers. It is the court which must make the necessary decisions if contact between the siblings is in dispute, or if it is argued that it should cease for any reason.
>
> 154. We do not know if our views on contact on the facts of this particular case presage a more general sea change in post adoption contact overall. It seems to us, however, that the stakes in the present case are sufficiently high to make it appropriate for the court to retain control over the question of the children's welfare throughout their respective lives under sections 1, 26, 27 and 46(6) of the 2002 Act; and, if necessary, to make orders for contact post adoption in accordance with section 26 of the 2002 Act, under section 8 of the 1989 Act. This is what Parliament has enacted. In section 46(6) of the 2002 Act Parliament has specifically directed the court to consider post adoption contact, and in section 26(5) Parliament has specifically envisaged an application for contact being heard at the same time as an adoption order is applied for. All this leads us to the view that the 2002 Act envisages the court exercising its powers to make contact orders post adoption, where such orders are in the interests of the child concerned.

Should there be stronger intervention by the courts?

The Court of Appeal's much more positive comments in *Re P* as to the courts' role in securing post-adoption contact will be welcomed by advocates of open adoption. Commentators have argued that many of the courts' previous objections towards the making of formal orders have been somewhat overstated, particularly where the parties are in agreement. It is recognized that flexibility is crucial in dealing with post-adoption contact and that many adoptive parents are resistant to court orders—as opposed to proceeding by way of voluntary agreement—because of their rigidity and the fact that they take control out of the hands of the adoptive parents.[245] However, Lowe and Murch argue that the inflexibility of such orders can be exaggerated, with the court able to specify with no greater particularity that there should be 'reasonable contact', thereby leaving it to the adoptive parents to determine exactly what constitutes 'reasonable contact' in the particular circumstances of the case.[246] Moreover, it is pointed out that there are certain advantages to any voluntary agreement between the adoptive parents and the birth family being underpinned by the security of a contact order.[247] Without a court order the adopters can simply walk away from any earlier agreement, a significant possibility if their agreement was only given reluctantly in exchange for the birth parents' consent to the adoption.[248]

Other leading commentators have, however, questioned whether stronger legal intervention is the answer. Indeed, commentators have suggested that the courts are ill-equipped to deal effectively with disputes over post-adoption contact and a more robust legal response is therefore likely to be wholly ineffective, even counterproductive. Smith argues that whilst the law can provide an overarching framework for the resolution of such disputes, the actual

[245] Harris-Short (2001), 417–18.
[246] Ibid.
[247] Ibid.
[248] Ibid.

job of facilitating post-adoption contact is best left to social welfare professionals working to promote greater trust and cooperation between the parties.[249]

C. Smith, 'Trust v Law: Promoting and Safeguarding Post-Adoption Contact',
(2005) 27 *Journal of Social Welfare and Family Law* 315, 326, 329

Law can require, regulate and enforce post-adoption contact. However, it cannot influence the qualitative experience of relationships and social interaction that enable adults to co-operate in the best interests of children. Additionally, while law can intervene in contact disputes at particular points in time, it lacks the capacity to continuously negotiate and respond to developing needs as these unfold. Law acts to reduce uncertainty but in so doing it constrains flexibility and the necessary use of discretion. Even while law may limit itself to ordering 'reasonable' contact, it reduces scope for the exercise of personal responsibility and moral competence on which mutually beneficial contact relies. As with post-divorce and post-separation contact disputes, law's intervention is unlikely to resolve conflicts unless underlying issues of trust are addressed. Law may enforce contact, but it cannot ensure beneficial experiences for those involved—particularly for children...

However, there are ways of enhancing the willingness and ability of adopters to support contact without recourse to legal regulation. Preparation of prospective adopters is crucial to helping them to understand the value of contact for children. The use of research which reports on adoptive parents' experience of beneficial contact can ameliorate fears and increase understanding, as can the inclusion of adopters and birth relatives preparation sessions. An important part of this work is to encourage adopters' confidence about making decisions in their child's best interests. Agencies should avoid negative evaluations of prospective adopters who want the sense of control and ownership over their children that adoption conveys. There is evidence that this legal construction of (adoptive) parenthood provides a secure base, which enables adoptive parents to be generous about contact arrangements...

The argument that formal intervention of the courts is unnecessary and unhelpful where the parties are in agreement as to the principle of contact and are able to co-operate in making and, where necessary, changing the arrangements in the interests of the child, is persuasive. However, in the absence of consensus the law's withdrawal is more problematic. Adoptive parents are not always reasonable and cannot always be trusted to act in the child's best interests. Where mediatory techniques fail to achieve cooperation, unless the adoptive parents are to be the final arbiter of the child's welfare, legal intervention may well be necessary to uphold and enforce certain normative standards.

Re-conceptualizing adoption

The courts have clearly struggled with the idea that retaining substantial links with the birth family can be consistent with adoption as traditionally understood. Commentators have thus argued that it may be easier to facilitate greater openness in the post-adoption context if adoption were to be 're-conceptualized'.[250] Adoption is a legal and social construct. There is therefore no inherent inconsistency between adoption and the preservation

[249] See also Masson (2000).
[250] See e.g. Bridge (1993), 101–2 and Parkinson (2003), 161.

of ongoing relationships with the birth family—a permanent irrevocable transfer of parental responsibility can be achieved whilst maintaining the child's essential genealogical ties. In other words, the legal fiction that the child is to be treated as if born to the adoptive parents can be removed without compromising the powerful messages of permanence and stability traditionally offered by adoption and which are still so highly valued by both children and adopters. However, not all commentators agree that transforming the legal concept of adoption will help encourage greater openness. Smith and Logan suggest that re-conceptualizing adoption may, from the perspective of the adoptive parents, fundamentally undermine the advantages of adoption over other permanent forms of alternative care which help them facilitate and support ongoing contact with the birth family. In particular, it is the 'total legal transplant' achieved through adoption that confers on the adoptive parents the 'entitlement' to parent, thereby giving them the sense of confidence, authority, and legitimacy to engage constructively with the birth parents.

C. Smith and J. Logan, 'Adoptive Parenthood As A "Legal Fiction"—Its Consequences for Direct Post-Adoption Contact', (2002) 14 *Child and Family Law Quarterly* 281, 292, 293–4, 295, and 300

[W]e want to suggest an alternative understanding of the relationship between adoption and contact, which indicates that emphatic calls for change in policy and law may be misplaced and points to the significance of adoption's legal and social effects in facilitating contact...

We asked each of the 59 adoptive mothers and 49 adoptive fathers whom we interviewed why they wanted to adopt, rather than to care for children through some other arrangement...Unsurprisingly, the vast majority of adopters wanted the legal security and permanence afforded by adoption...However, it was clear from our interviews that adoption achieves far more than legal security—it constructs parenthood. It was the experience and meaning of parenthood—legally, socially and emotionally—that was of enormous significance to the adopters in our sample. For many adoptive parents the phenomenology of parenthood is intrinsically characterised by a sense of ownership and control—those very features of adoption that some advocates of contact wish to dismantle. In answer to an open-ended question about what features of adoption were important to them, at least one adoptive parent in 49 (83%) families spontaneously identified factors associated with 'ownership' of their children...

Adoption is remarkably powerful, not only in its legal effects, but in the way it operates to construct new phenomenological identities and relationships. For our adopters, the experience of ownership and control expresses a complex 'package' of attributes that characterise parenthood, and which can only be achieved through adoption. The perceived relationship between parenthood and 'family belonging' was also apparent, with at least one adopter in 27 (46%) families emphasising the creation of a family as an important consequence of adoption. What is particularly noteworthy, in the context of this discussion, is the way in which ownership and control serve to facilitate the maintenance of direct contact...

It seems to us that what our adopters are trying to convey is a sense of parenthood that is phenomenologically distinct from its legal definition in adoption. They can willingly accommodate direct contact because they are the child's legal, social and emotional parents. Birth parents and other birth family members become something 'other'—the phenomenological equivalent of the legal concept of a 'former' parent. While critics of this 'legal fiction' fear that it distorts the nature of relationships and may hinder, rather than promote, post-adoption contact, we found no indication that this is the case. Rather, the 'legal fiction' and its phenomenological counterpart can act to facilitate contact and to make it a beneficial experience for the children concerned...[W]e are suggesting, on the basis of empirical research, that the way in which adopters experience the 'legal fiction' can confirm their sense of parenthood and, at the same time, accommodate the ongoing significance of birth family members through continuing contact...

[We] disagree with any assertion that the most effective way to promote contact must be through policy change, more intrusive judicial intervention or a social and legal assault on the phenomenology of adoption and adoptive parenthood. On the contrary, our research, which is supported by other studies, suggests that contact will be facilitated by enhancing adopters' confidence and confirming the phenomenology that they describe.

13.7.2 POST-ADOPTION SUPPORT

The ACA 2002 provides that adoption support services must be designed to meet the needs of 'adopted persons, their parents, natural parents and former guardians'.[251] It is clear that the duty to provide adoption support services to 'adopted children' includes post-adoption support. The Adoption Support Services Regulations 2005 explicitly provide that in addition to 'counselling, advice and information',[252] adoption support services must include the payment of adoption allowances, providing assistance in relation to arrangements for contact between an adopted child and the birth family, assisting the adoptive family where the placement is at risk of disrupting, and meeting the 'therapeutic needs' of an adoptive child.[253] Every local authority must appoint an adoption support services advisor who is responsible for advising those affected by an adoption as to how to access appropriate services.[254]

The need for effective post-adoption support services formed a central plank of the Labour government's reforms. It was recognized that if greater use was to be made of adoption for 'looked after' children, better support would be needed to prevent these often challenging placements from breaking down. Under the previous legislation the provision of post-adoption support services was woefully inadequate.[255] The duties imposed on local authorities under the ACA 2002 should lead to a substantial improvement in services. The National Adoption Standards promise prospective adopters:

[A]ccess to a range of multi-agency support services before, during and after adoption. Support services will include practical help, professional advice, financial assistance where needed and information about local and national support groups and services.[256]

---

[251] S 3(1). The duty to provide certain adoption services (i.e. financial support and therapeutic services) is restricted under the regulations to 'agency adoptions'. Other services (i.e. those concerned with facilitating post-adoption contact) must be available to members of the child's wider family including siblings and other birth relatives: Adoption Support Services Regulations 2005, SI 2005/691, reg 4. The local authority has a discretion but not a duty to extend the provision of services to individuals falling outside these prescribed categories: ACA 2002, s 3(3).

[252] ACA 2002, s 2(6).

[253] Adoption Support Services Regulations 2005, SI 2005/691, reg 3.

[254] Ibid., reg 6.

[255] Lowe et al (1999), 430; Rushton (2003), 46; and Selwyn and Quinton (2004), 12.

[256] DH (2001b), C3.

There are, however, weaknesses in the legislative scheme. Under s 4(1) the local authority must on request carry out an assessment of a person's need for adoption support services.[257] However, the local authority is under no duty to meet those needs. The local authority must simply decide whether to provide the person with appropriate support, although if it decides to provide the person with services other than advice and information on more than one occasion it must prepare a plan and keep the plan under review.[258] This is a departure from the key policy paper preceding the reforms which recommended that the local authority should be under a duty to meet the child's assessed needs.[259] The approach taken to the provision of financial support is even more restricted with regulations imposing additional conditions on the payment of adoption allowances. Financial support will only be payable if:

- necessary to ensure that the adoptive parent can look after the child;
- the child needs special care which requires greater expenditure of resources by reason of illness, disability, emotional, or behavioural difficulties, or the continuing consequences of past abuse or neglect;
- necessary for the local authority to make any special arrangements to facilitate the placement or the adoption by reason of the age or ethnic origin of the child or the desirability of placing the child with a sibling;
- necessary to meet the recurring costs in respect of travel for the purpose of visits between the child and a related person;
- the local authority considers it appropriate to make a contribution to meet expenditure necessary for the purpose of accommodating and maintaining the child, including for example, alterations to and adaptations of the home.[260]

Financial support may include an element of remuneration where the adoptive parents were previously local authority foster parents for the child. Such payments are, however, restricted to a time limit of two years unless the circumstances are exceptional.[261]

The absence of a clear duty to meet an individual's assessed need for post-adoption support clearly lies in the resource implications of imposing such a duty on the local authority. If post-adoption support were available as of right, significant investment would be needed into local authority adoption services.[262] However, it is by no means clear that this would be the most appropriate use of scarce public resources. Indeed, concern has been expressed at the impact post-adoption support will have on other local authority services to families in need.[263] The duties owed by local authorities to adoptive families are more extensive than those owed to 'children in need' under s 17 of the CA 1989: children and families seeking help under the CA 1989 have no right to an assessment of their need for support.[264] Providing greater support to adoptive families than other struggling families is not easy to rationalize, particularly if it detracts from the local authority's ability to provide effective

---

[257] The local authority is only under a duty to assess a person's need for particular adoption support services if the local authority is under a duty to extend the provision of the service in question to that particular category of person: Adoption Support Services Regulations 2005, SI 2005/691, reg 13.

[258] ACA 2002, s 4(4)–(5). Adoption Support Services Regulations 2005, SI 2005/691, reg 16.

[259] Cabinet Office (2000), 60.

[260] Adoption Support Services Regulations 2005/691, reg 8.

[261] Ibid.

[262] Harris-Short (2001), 412.

[263] Masson (2003), 646–7.

[264] See 12.3.1.

support services under Part III of the CA 1989.[265] These concerns are heightened by the fact adoptive parents tend to have high levels of 'family functioning', scoring highly on such things as 'problem-solving, communication skills, cohesiveness and future orientation'.[266] Where resources are limited, it is certainly questionable whether adoptive families, many of whom have the capacity to obtain the necessary professional help from the private sector, should be prioritized over other, perhaps more vulnerable, families.

Differences regarding the priority which should be afforded to post-adoption support reflect continuing ambivalence about the nature of adoptive parenthood.

B. Luckock and A. Hart, 'Adoptive family life and adoption support: policy ambivalence and the development of effective services', (2005) 10 *Child and Family Social Work* 125, 126, and 133–4

Are adoptive parents more like foster carers, high on any priority list for extra support, or more like any other parents in the community who have to take their turn, according to their assessed needs and agency eligibility criteria? . . .

[G]overnment tries to have it both ways. It has reinforced the traditional expectations of the autonomy of the adoptive family and explicitly distinguished adoption from 'corporate parenting' and its instability. But it has also emphasized the importance to the success of adoption of additional support. This leads to mixed messages being received on the ground and some confusion about which way to move services forward. Analysis of the new legislation and guidance reveals an inherent ambivalence in policy. This is both in relation to the appropriate focus of adoption support services and about the nature of eligibility for those services of the different people affected by the adoption. This ambivalence . . . can be traced primarily to the ambiguous expectations of the adoptive family and to a persisting uncertainty about how best to understand adoptive family life and kinship itself.

Luckock and Hart argue that we need to recognize adoption gives rise to a wholly distinctive form of family life that should not be gauged against either biological or 'corporate' parenting. By continuing to measure adoptive parenting against these benchmarks, it is argued we obscure the real reason adoptive families should be prioritized and attract high levels of support from the state:

[W]e propose that the invigoration of a responsive culture of adoption support requires a fresh approach to be taken to understanding adoptive family life and kinship and its distinctive claims for support. Instead of attempts to press these claims by emphasizing the special social expectations of adoptive parenting or to limit them by pointing to the autonomy (and consumer power) of adoptive families, eligibility for adoption support needs to be argued in an alternative way. Adoption is a different way of 'doing' family life, and the nature of that difference must be understood if services are to be effective. So what is it that makes the difference distinctive in adoption? And what implications does this have for the nature of local service collaboration?

We think it is time to move on from discussions of difference in adoption that use either normative procreational families or 'corporate parenting' models as their benchmark or

---

[265] Masson (2003), 646–7.
[266] Rushton (2003), 44; O'Brien and Zamostny (2003), 690.

template. The limitations of current government policy, where both points of reference are drawn on simultaneously, show how difficult it is trying to have it both ways.

When the benchmark for adoptive family life is the procreational family and its life-cycle, difference is defined in terms of the additional 'adoption-related' tasks faced by children and parents in 'adjusting' or 'adapting' to the autonomous family norm...When the template is 'corporate parenting', difference is understood in terms of the capacity of adoptive parents to implement care plans designed to enhance child development and achievement.

Both aspects of adoptive family are recognizable...Nonetheless, although recognizable, they do not convey the real difference that makes adoption distinctive and its service claims exceptional. This difference derives, we think, from the *way* adoptive family life and kinship is established rather than simply from the nature of any social tasks that family is expected to perform...

What makes adoptive family life and kinship distinctive, however, is the fact that its origins lie in an enforced transition and an obligatory collaboration with professionals...

It is this quality of being an autonomous family life, yet formed from the outset through the support and surveillance of the state, that makes adoption distinctive within a community of family differences. It is on this basis that its exceptional claims for support should now be based.

13.8 ALTERNATIVES TO ADOPTION: SPECIAL GUARDIANSHIP

Although the Labour government was strongly committed to adoption as the preferred option for children in care, it recognized that there would remain some children for whom adoption was not appropriate. Given the disappointing outcomes for children placed in long-term foster care,[267] the ACA 2002 amended the CA 1989 to make available a new alternative order for securing permanence termed special guardianship. The rationale behind this new order is explained in the 2000 White Paper:

Department of Health, *Adoption: a new approach*, Cm 5017 (London: HMSO, 2000)

5.8 Adoption is not always appropriate for children who cannot return to their birth parents. Some older children do not wish to be legally separated from their birth families. Adoption may not be best for some children being cared for on a permanent basis by members of their wider birth family. Some minority ethnic communities have religious and cultural difficulties with adoption as it is set out in law. Unaccompanied asylum-seeking children may also need secure, permanent homes, but have strong attachments to their families abroad. All these children deserve the same chance as any other to enjoy the benefits of a legally secure, stable permanent placement that promotes a supportive, lifelong relationship with their carers, where the court decides that it is in their best interests.

5.9 In order to meet the needs of these children where adoption is not appropriate, and to modernise the law so it reflects the religious and cultural diversity of our country today, the Government believes there is a case to develop a new legislative option to provide permanence short of the legal separation involved in adoption.

5.10 The Government will legislate to create this new option, which could be called 'special guardianship'. It will be used only to provide permanence for those children for whom

[267] Selwyn and Quinton (2004).

adoption is not appropriate and where the court decides it is in the best interests of the child or young person. It will:

- give the carer clear responsibility for all aspects of caring for the child or young person, and for taking the decisions to do with their upbringing. The child or young person will no longer be looked after by the council;

- provide a firm foundation on which to build a lifelong permanent relationship between the carer and the child or young person;

- be legally secure;

- preserve the basic link between the child or young person and their birth family;

- be accompanied by proper access to a full range of support services including, where appropriate, financial support.

These proposals are now enshrined in ss 14A–14F of the CA 1989. An application for a special guardianship order may be made by: (i) the child's guardian, (ii) any person in whose favour a residence order is in force with respect to the child, (iii) any person with whom the child has lived for at least three years, (iv) any person who has the consent of any person in whose favour a residence order is in force, (v) the local authority if the child is in care, (vi) any person who has the consent of all persons with parental responsibility for the child, and (vii) a local authority foster parent with whom the child has lived for a period of at least one year immediately preceding the application. Anyone else may apply with leave.[268] The court may also make a special guardianship order of its own motion in any family proceedings.[269]

A useful summary of special guardianship is contained in *A local authority v Y, Z and others*.[270] The main effect of the order is to confer parental responsibility on the special guardian.[271] Special guardianship is, however, intended as a stronger, more permanent measure than a residence order. The special guardian is thus entitled to exercise parental responsibility to the exclusion of any other person.[272] Whilst the order is in force the child's surname cannot be changed and the child cannot be removed from the jurisdiction other than by the special guardian for a period of no more than three months without leave of the court.[273] Unlike an adoption order a special guardianship order does not automatically discharge a s 8 order. A contact order in favour of the child's parents may therefore continue in force, although the court must consider whether the order should be varied or discharged.[274] Where no contact order is in force the court must consider whether it should make provision for contact before granting the special guardianship order.[275]

A key feature of special guardianship is that it is intended to confer a much greater sense of security and permanence on the child's carers than that conferred by a residence order, without having the irrevocable consequences of adoption. Section 14D provides that the order may be varied or discharged on application by: (i) the special guardian, (ii) the child if of sufficient understanding, (iii) any parent or guardian of the child, (iv) any person in

---

[268] CA 1989, s 14A(3) and s 14A(5).
[269] Ibid., s 14A(6).
[270] [2006] 2 FLR 41.
[271] CA 1989, s 14C(1)(a).
[272] S 14C(1)(b).
[273] Ss 14C(3) and 14C(4).
[274] S 14B(1)(a).
[275] S 14B(1)(b).

whose favour a residence order is in force with respect to the child, (v) any other person who immediately before the making of the special guardianship order had parental responsibility for the child, or (vi) the local authority.[276] The court may also vary or discharge the order of its own motion. In order to protect the special guardians from potentially destabilizing and distressing challenges to their parenting role, applicants other than the local authority require leave to apply for a variation or discharge of the order.[277] Leave will not be granted, other than on application by the child, unless the court is satisfied that there has been a 'significant change' in circumstances since the order was made.[278] Wilson LJ has somewhat tentatively held that despite the specific requirement in s 14D(5) that the change in circumstances must be 'significant' (a qualification which does not appear in s 24(3) of the ACA 2002), that difference in statutory language should be disregarded and an identical approach taken to an application for leave to discharge a special guardianship order as that set down in *Re M (Children) (Placement Order)*[279] for an application for leave to revoke a placement order.[280] This decision will not help assuage the concerns of commentators such as Parkinson who has argued that the provisions purporting to confer security on the special guardians are weak and the hurdles for challenging the order set too low.[281] In this regard, it has been noted with concern that parents do not require leave to apply for a s 8 order, other than a residence order, when a special guardianship order is in force, thus leaving the special guardians vulnerable to repeated unsettling applications by the birth family.[282]

Although located with the private law orders in Part II of the CA 1989, it is clear that special guardianship is primarily intended to provide an alternative to adoption for looked after children in care. Like adoption, it therefore constitutes an important part of the state's child protection policy. In keeping with this 'public service function', special guardianship is highly regulated and attracts similar support services as fostering and adoption, including financial support—it is not intended as a cheap alternative to the child remaining in local authority care.[283]

The Court of Appeal has provided helpful guidance on special guardianship in three important cases.[284] The three cases were all concerned with one central issue: whether it was more appropriate for the child to be adopted or made the subject of a special guardianship order. The three appeals were heard by differently constituted courts but Wall LJ, giving judgment in *Re S (a child) (adoption order or special guardianship order)*,[285] provided a general 'commentary' on the new legislative provisions which was adopted in all three appeals.

Wall LJ begins his judgment in *Re S* with some general comments as to when a special guardianship order may be deemed more appropriate than adoption, making it clear that there is no presumption that a special guardianship order is preferable to adoption in any particular category of case.

---

[276] S 14D(1).

[277] S 14D(3).

[278] S 14D(5).

[279] [2007] EWCA Civ 1084. Discussed above at pp 923–4.

[280] *Re G (A Child)* [2010] EWCA Civ 300, [11]–[14].

[281] Parkinson (2003), 161.

[282] *Re S (a child) (adoption order or special guardianship order)* [2007] EWCA Civ 54, [62]–[68].

[283] On the issue of financial support, see *B v London Borough of Lewisham* [2008] EWHC 738 and *R (on the application of Barrett) v Kirklees Metropolitan Council* [2010] EWHC 467.

[284] *Re S (a child) (adoption order or special guardianship order)* [2007] EWCA Civ 54; *Re M-J (a child) (adoption order or special guardianship order)* [2007] EWCA Civ 56; *Re AJ (A Child)* [2007] EWCA Civ 55.

[285] [2007] EWCA Civ 54.

Re S (a child) (adoption order or special guardianship order) [2007] EWCA Civ 54

WALL LJ:

46. . . . [I]n addition to the fundamental difference in status between adopted children and those subject to special guardianship orders, there are equally fundamental differences between the status and powers of adopters and special guardians. These, we think, need to be borne in mind when the court is applying the welfare checklist under both section 1(3) of the 1989 Act and section 1 of the 2002 Act.

47. Certain other points arise from the statutory scheme:–

(i) The carefully constructed statutory regime (notice to the local authority, leave requirements in certain cases, the role of the court, and the report from the local authority—even where the order is made by the court of its own motion) demonstrates the care which is required before making a special guardianship order, and that it is only appropriate if, in the particular circumstances of the particular case, it is best fitted to meet the needs of the child or children concerned.

(ii) There is nothing in the statutory provisions themselves which limits the making of a special guardianship order or an adoption order to any given set of circumstances. The statute itself is silent on the circumstances in which a special guardianship order is likely to be appropriate, and there is no presumption contained within the statute that a special guardianship order is preferable to an adoption order in any particular category of case. Each case must be decided on its particular facts; and each case will involve the careful application of a judicial discretion to those facts.

(iii) The key question which the court will be obliged to ask itself in every case in which the question of adoption as opposed to special guardianship arises will be: which order will better serve the welfare of this particular child? . . .

49. We would add . . . that, although the no order principle as such is unlikely to be relevant, it is a material feature of the special guardianship regime that it is "less intrusive" than adoption. In other words, it involves a less fundamental interference with existing legal relationships. The court will need to bear Article 8 of ECHR in mind, and to be satisfied that its order is a proportionate response to the problem, having regard to the interference with family life which is involved. In choosing between adoption and special guardianship, in most cases Article 8 is unlikely to add anything to the considerations contained in the respective welfare checklists. Under both statutes the welfare of the child is the court's paramount consideration, and the balancing exercise required by the statutes will be no different to that required by Article 8. However, in some cases, the fact that the welfare objective can be achieved with less disruption of existing family relationships can properly be regarded as helping to tip the balance.

It is reiterated in *Re M-J* that although special guardianship may constitute a more proportionate response to the parents' inability to care for the child this does not give rise to a presumption in favour of special guardianship as the least interventionist measure.[286]

Wall LJ then goes on to deal with the particular issue of whether special guardianship is more appropriate than adoption when the child is to live with a member of the extended family:

286 [2007] EWCA Civ 56, [17]–[19].

50. It is clear from the White Paper that special guardianship was introduced at least in part to deal with the potential problems arising from the use of adoption in the case of placements within the wider family...

51. A particular concern is that an adoption order has, as a matter of law, the effect of making the adopted child the child of the adopters for all purposes. Accordingly, where a child is adopted by a member of his wider family, the familial relationships are inevitably changed. This is frequently referred to as the "skewing" or "distorting" effect of adoption, and is a factor which the court must take into account when considering whether or not to make an adoption order in such a case. This is not least because the checklist under section 1 of the 2002 Act requires it to do so: – see section 1(4)(f) ("the relationship which the child has with relatives."). However, the weight to be given to this factor will inevitably depend on the facts of the particular case, and it will be only one factor in the overall welfare equation.

52. As will be seen, the three appeals before this court illustrate the different weight to be placed on this factor in different circumstances, and that in some it may be of only marginal importance. In particular, as the case of Re AJ demonstrates, both children and adults are capable of penetrating legal forms and retaining hold of the reality....

In his judgment in *Re AJ*, Wall LJ added that the distorting effect of adoption on the child's core familial relationships should not be over-played.[287]

Finally, Wall LJ confirms that, as the statute explicitly contemplates the court making a special guardianship order of its own motion, the court has the power to impose a special guardianship order on an unwilling party against his or her wishes.[288] In determining whether it should do so, Wall LJ holds that the court should apply the welfare checklist taking into account the reasons for the opposition and how that impacts on the child's welfare. However, he emphasizes that if the court reaches the view that special guardianship will best serve the child's interests, then that is the order it should make.[289]

Commentators are generally sceptical about whether special guardianship orders will successfully bridge the gap between residence orders and adoption. As Parkinson notes, 'the concept may need "selling" to people as a viable alternative to adoption given the way in which adoption is entrenched in people's thinking as the only form of secure parenthood with respect to a non-biological child.'[290] Early empirical research on the use of special guardianship is mixed. Whilst there would appear to be some enthusiasm for special guardianship, the number of orders made in the first 12 months after implementation was low.[291] The evidence suggests that it has failed to establish itself as a genuine alternative to adoption, the latter remaining very much 'the gold standard' for achieving security and permanence for looked after children.[292] Special guardianship is thus having little impact on the number of children finding permanent homes outside of the care system, particularly as it has failed to prove an attractive alternative for foster carers.[293] In contrast, it has quickly positioned itself as a much more effective alternative to the 'lesser order' of residence where children are to be cared for within the extended family and the greater security and permanence of adoption is unnecessary.[294] It thus seems likely that, in time,

[287] [2007] EWCA Civ 55, [44] and [51].
[288] [2007] EWCA Civ 54, [73].
[289] Ibid., [73]–[77].
[290] Parkinson (2003), 147.
[291] Hall (2008), 369–70.
[292] Ibid., 373.
[293] Ibid., 376.
[294] Ibid.

special guardianship will replace residence orders as the preferred legal basis for providing long-term kinship care.

13.9 CONCLUSION

Adoption is a very different way of 'becoming a parent', bringing great rewards, but also many challenges. The law has supported and protected these sometimes fragile family units by treating them in every way as if they were an 'ordinary' natural family. Any legal measures which may mark them out as different, as second-class parents, have been consistently resisted. In many ways, this approach is to be welcomed, recognizing as it does the equal value and importance of social parenting. Adoption can therefore be a liberating force within the law. Freed from biological constraints, it allows a multitude of ways of 'being a family'. Yet adoption is a paradox. Whilst the ACA 2002 recognizes a diverse range of prospective parents, it continues to construct the family unit in accordance with the married (legitimate), heterosexual norm. The courts perpetuate this myth by assimilating adoptive parenting to the biological 'ideal' and refusing to acknowledge that adoptive family life is different: most importantly, that adoptive parenting cannot always be exclusive of the birth family. This reluctance to embrace the difference of adoption betrays the law's true ambivalence towards alternative ways of 'doing family'. The married, heterosexual, autonomous family unit remains the norm and whilst adoption provides a snapshot of the rich complexity of contemporary family life, English law's response to that complexity remains deeply problematic.

BIBLIOGRAPHY

This bibliography contains citations available as hard copy, hard copy and electronic, and solely electronic. Those available as hard copy and electronic are listed in full, with an Online Resource Centre (ORC) symbol in the margin, to indicate that a link is available on the ORC for this book (www.oxfordtextbooks.co.uk/orc/harrisshort_tcm2e/). Those available only via the internet have URLs listed against them. These links are up to date as of November 2010. If a link becomes broken, please navigate to the ORC, as we will regularly monitor links and provide the most up-to-date iterations there.

ACPO (2008). *Guidance on Investigating Domestic Abuse.* <www.acpo.police.uk/asp/policies/Data/Domestic_Abuse_2008.pdf>.

ADAM, S. AND BREWER, M. (2010). *Couple Penalties and Premiums in the UK Tax and Benefit System.* IFS Briefing Note BN 102. <www.ifs.org.uk/bns/bn102.pdf>.

ALGHRANI, A. AND HARRIS, J. (2006). 'Reproductive liberty: Should the foundation of families be regulated?'. *Child and Family Law Quarterly,* 18: 10.

ALLEN, D.W. AND GALLAGHER, M. (2007). 'Does Divorce Law Affect the Divorce Rate? A Review of Empirical Research, 1995-2006', iMAPP Research Brief, 1(1). <www.marriagedebate.com/pdf/imapp.nofault.divrate.pdf>.

ALTMAN, S. (2003). 'A theory of child support'. *International Journal of Law, Policy and the Family,* 17: 173.

ANCILLARY RELIEF ADVISORY GROUP (1998). *Report to the Lord Chancellor of the Ancillary Relief Advisory Group.* London.

ANDREWS, G. (2007). 'The presumption of advancement: equity, equality and human rights'. *Conveyancer and Property Lawyer,* 340.

ARCHBISHOP OF CANTERBURY'S GROUP (1984). *No Just Cause: the Law of Affinity in England and Wales: Some Suggestions for Change.* London: CIO Press.

ARTHUR, S., LEWIS, J., MACLEAN, M., FINCH, S., AND FITZGERALD, R. (2002). *Settling Up: making financial arrangements after divorce or separation.* London: National Centre for Social Research.

ATKINSON, A. AND MCKAY, S. (2005). *Child support reform: the views and experiences of CSA staff and new clients.* DWP RR 232. <research.dwp.gov.uk/asd/asd5/rports2005-2006/rrep232.pdf>.

AUCHMUTY, R. (2007). 'Unfair shares for women: the rhetoric of equality and the reality of inequality', in H. Lim and A. Bottomley (eds), *Feminist Perspectives on Land Law.* Abingdon: Routledge-Cavendish.

AUCHMUTY, R. (2008). 'What's so special about marriage? The impact of *Wilkinson v Kitzinger*'. *Child and Family Law Quarterly,* 20: 475.

AUCHMUTY, R. (2009). 'Beyond couples'. *Feminist Legal Studies*, 17: 205.

BAILEY-HARRIS, R. (1992). 'Child Support: is the Right the Wrong One?'. *International Journal of Law and the Family*, 6: 169.

BAILEY-HARRIS, R. (1996). 'Law and the unmarried couple—oppression or liberation?'. *Child and Family Law Quarterly*, 8: 137.

BAILEY-HARRIS, R. (2005). 'The Paradoxes of Principle and Pragmatism: Ancillary Relief in England and Wales'. *International Journal of Law, Policy and the Family*, 19: 229.

BAILEY-HARRIS, R., BARRON, J., AND PEARCE, J. (1999a). 'Settlement culture and the use of the 'no order' principle under the Children Act 1989'. *Child and Family Law Quarterly*, 11: 53.

BAILEY-HARRIS, R., BARRON, J., AND PEARCE, J. (1999b). 'From Utility to Rights? The Presumption of Contact in Practice'. *International Journal of Law, Policy and the Family*, 13: 111.

BAINHAM, A. (1989). 'When is a parent not a parent? Reflections on the unmarried father and his child in English law'. *International Journal of Law and the Family*, 3: 208.

BAINHAM, A. (1990). 'The Privatisation of the Public Interest in Children'. *Modern Law Review*, 53: 206.

BAINHAM, A. (1998). 'Changing families and changing concepts—reforming the language of family law'. *Child and Family Law Quarterly*, 10: 1.

BAINHAM, A. (1999). 'Parentage, Parenthood and Parental Responsibility', in A. Bainham, S. Day Sclater, and M. Richards (eds), *What is a Parent? A Socio-Legal Analysis*. Oxford: Hart Publishing.

BAINHAM, A. (2005). *Children—The Modern Law* (3rd edn). Bristol: Jordan Publishing.

BAINHAM, A. (2007). '"Truth Will Out": Paternity in Europe'. *Cambridge Law Journal*, 66: 278.

BAINHAM, A. (2008a). 'Arguments About Parentage'. *Cambridge Law Journal*, 67: 322.

BAINHAM, A. (2008b). 'What is the point of birth registration?'. *Child and Family Law Quarterly*, 20: 449.

BAINHAM, A. (2008c). 'Removing babies at birth: A more than questionable practice'. *Cambridge Law Journal*, 67: 260.

BAINHAM, A. (2008d). 'Homosexual adoption'. *Cambridge Law Journal*, 67: 479.

BAMFORTH, N. (2001). 'Same-Sex Partnerships and Arguments of Justice', in R. Wintemute and M. Andenæs (eds), *Legal Recognition of Same-Sex Partnerships*. Oxford: Hart Publishing.

BAMFORTH, N. (2007a). '"The benefits of marriage in all but name?" Same-sex couples and the Civil Partnership Act 2004'. *Child and Family Law Quarterly*, 19: 133.

BAMFORTH, N. (2007b). 'Same-sex partnerships: some comparative constitutional lessons'. *European Human Rights Law Review*, 12: 47.

BARLOW, A. (2004). 'Regulation of Cohabitation, Changing Family Policies and Social Attitudes: A Discussion of Britain within Europe'. *Law and Policy*, 26: 57.

BARLOW, A. AND DUNCAN, S. (2000). 'New Labour's communitarianism, supporting families and the "rationality mistake": Part II'. *Journal of Social Welfare and Family Law*, 22: 129.

BARLOW, A. AND JAMES, G. (2004). 'Regulating Marriage and Cohabitation in 21st Century Britain'. *Modern Law Review*, 67: 143.

BARLOW, A. AND LIND, C. (1999). 'A matter of trust: the allocation of rights in the family home'. *Legal Studies*, 19: 468.

🔟 BARLOW, A., BURGOYNE, C., AND SMITHSON, J. (2007). *The Living Together Campaign: an investigation of its impact on legally aware cohabitants*. Ministry of Justice Research Series 5/07. <www.justice.gov.uk/docs/living-together-research-report.pdf>.

BARLOW, A., BURGOYNE, C., CLERY, E., AND SMITHSON, J. (2008). 'Cohabitation and the law: myths, money and the media', in A. Park et al (eds), *British Social Attitudes: the 24th Report*. London: Sage.

BARLOW, A., DUNCAN, S., JAMES, G., AND PARK, A. (2001). 'Just a piece of paper? Marriage and cohabitation in Britain', in A. Park, J. Curtice, K. Thomson, L. Jarvis, and C. Bromley (eds), *British Social Attitudes: the 18th Report—Public policy, social ties*. London: Sage.

BARLOW, A., DUNCAN, S., JAMES, G., AND PARK, A. (2005). *Cohabitation, marriage and the law*. Oxford: Hart Publishing.

🔟 BARNARD, C. (2008). 'The "opt-out" for the UK and Poland from the Charter of Fundamental Rights: Triumph of rhetoric over reality?', in S. Griller and J. Ziller (eds), *The Lisbon Treaty: EU Constitutionalism without a Constitutional Treaty*. New York: Springer. <www.law.cam.ac.uk/faculty-resources/summary/barnard-uk-opt-out-and-the-charter-of-fundamental-rights/7309>.

BARNES, H., DAY, P., AND CRONIN, N. (1998). *Trial and error: a review of UK child support policy*, Occasional Paper 24. London: Family Policy Studies Centre.

🔟 BARNES, L. (2007). '*Stack v Dowden*: the principles in practice'. <www.familylawweek.co.uk/site.aspx?i=ed642>.

BARNETT, A. (2000). 'Contact and Domestic Violence: The Ideological Divide', in J. Bridgeman and D. Monk (eds), *Feminist Perspectives on Child Law*. London: Cavendish.

BARNETT, H. (1998). *Introduction to feminist jurisprudence*. London: Cavendish Publishing.

BARRON, J. (2002). *Five Years On: A review of legal protection from domestic violence*. Bristol: Women's Aid Federation of England.

BARTON, C. (1998). 'Third Time Lucky for Child Support?—The 1998 Green Paper'. *Family Law*, 28: 668.

BARTON, C. (1999). 'Child Support—Tony's Turn'. *Family Law*, 29: 704.

BARTON, C. (2002). 'White Paper Weddings—the Beginnings, Muddles and Ends of Wedlock'. *Family Law*, 32: 431.

BARTON, C. AND BISSETT-JOHNSON, A. (2000). 'The Declining Number of Ancillary Relief Financial Orders'. *Family Law*, 30: 94.

BARTON, C. AND DOUGLAS, G. (1995). *Law and Parenthood*. London: Butterworths.

🌐 Bell, A., Kazimirski, A., and La Valle, I. (2006). *An investigation of CSA Maintenance Direct Payments: qualitative study*. DWP RR 327. <research.dwp.gov.uk/asd/asd5/rports2005-2006/rrep327.pdf>.

Beveridge Report (1942). *Social Insurance and Allied Services: a Report by Sir William Beveridge*. Cmd 6404. London: HMSO.

Binner, J. and Dnes, A. (2001). 'Marriage, Divorce, and Legal Change: New Evidence from England and Wales'. *Economic Inquiry*, 39: 298.

Bird, R. and Burrows, D. (2009). *Child Maintenance: the new law*. Bristol: Jordan Publishing.

Black, J., Bridge, J., Bond, T., and Gribbin, L. (2007). *A Practical Approach to Family Law*, 8th edn. Oxford: OUP.

Blackstone, W. (1765). *Commentaries on the Laws of England, Volume I: Of the Rights of Persons*. Facsimile edition (1979) S. Katz (ed). Chicago: University of Chicago Press.

🌐 Blackwell, A. and Dawe, F. (2003). *Non-resident parental contact—Final report*. London: Office for National Statistics.

Boden, R. and Childs, M. (1996). 'Paying for Procreation: Child Support Arrangements in the UK'. *Feminist Legal Studies*, 4: 131.

Boele-Woelki, K., Ferrand, F., González Beilfuss, C., Jänterä-Jareborg, M., Lowe, N., Martiny, D., and Pintens, W. (2004). *Principles of European Family Law Regarding Divorce and Maintenance Between Former Spouses*. Antwerp-Oxford: Intersentia.

Bonner, D., Fenwick, H., and Harris-Short, S. (2003). 'Judicial Approaches to the HRA'. *International and Comparative Law Quarterly*, 52: 549.

Booth Committee (1985). *Report of the Matrimonial Causes Procedure Committee*. London: HMSO.

Bottomley, A. (1984). 'Resolving Family Disputes: A Critical View', in M. Freeman (ed), *State, Law and the Family*. London: Tavistock.

Bottomley, A. (1993). 'Self and Subjectivities: Languages of Claim in Property Law'. *Journal of Law and Society*, 20: 56.

Bottomley, A. (1998). 'Women and Trust(s): Portraying the Family in the Gallery of Law', in S. Bright and J. Dewar (eds), *Land Law: Themes and Perspectives*. Oxford: OUP.

Bottomley, A. and Wong, S. (2006). 'Shared Households: a new paradigm for thinking about the reform of domestic property relations', in A. Diduck and K. O'Donovan (eds), *Feminist Perspecitves on Family Law*. Abingdon: Routledge.

Boyd, S. (1989). 'From gender specificity to gender neutrality? Ideologies in Canadian Child Custody Law', in C. Smart and S. Sevenhuijsen (eds), *Child Custody and the Politics of Gender*. London: Routledge.

Bradney, A. (1984). 'Arranged Marriages and Duress'. *Journal of Social Welfare and Family Law*, 6: 278.

Bradney, A. (1994). 'Duress, Family Law and the Coherent Legal System'. *Modern Law Review*, 57: 963.

BRADSHAW, J. AND MILLAR, J. (1991). *Lone Parent Families in the UK*, Department of Social Security Research Report No 6. London: HMSO.

BRADSHAW, J., STIMSON, C., SKINNER, C., AND WILLIAMS, J. (1999). *Absent Fathers?* London: Routledge.

BRAND, A. AND BRINICH, P. (1999). 'Behavior Problems and Mental Health Contacts in Adopted, Foster, and Nonadopted Children'. *Journal of Child Psychology and Psychiatry*, 40: 1221.

BRASSE, G. (1993). 'The section 31 monopoly—Nottinghamshire CC v P considered'. *Family Law*, 23: 691.

BRASSE, G. (2006). 'It's payback time! *Miller, McFarlane* and the compensation culture'. *Family Law*, 36: 647.

BRAZIER, M., CAMPBELL, A., AND GOLOMBOK, S. (1997). *Surrogacy—Review for the UK Health Ministers of current arrangements for payments and regulation. Consultation Document and Questionnaire.* <www.dh.gov.uk/assetRoot/04/01/44/62/04014462.pdf>.

BRAZIER, M., CAMPBELL, A., AND GOLOMBOK, S. (1998). *Surrogacy—Review for Health Ministers of Current Arrangements for Payments and Regulation. Report of the Review Team*, Cm 4068. <www.dh.gov.uk/assetRoot/04/01/43/73/04014373.pdf>.

BRIDGE, C. (1993). 'Changing the nature of adoption: law reform in England and New Zealand'. *Legal Studies*, 13: 81.

BRIDGE, C. (2001). 'Adoption law: a balance of interests', in J. Herring (ed), *Family Law: Issues, Debates, Policy*. Cullompton: Willan.

BRIDGE, S. (1998). 'Transferring tenancies of the family home'. *Family Law*, 28: 26.

BRIDGE, S. (2001). 'Marriage and divorce: the regulation of intimacy', in J. Herring (ed), *Family Law: Issues, Debates, Policy*. Cullompton: Willan.

BRITISH ACADEMY WORKING GROUP (2009). *Social Science and Family Policies*. London: British Academy.

BROPHY J. (1989). 'Custody Law, Child Care, and Inequality in Britain', in C. Smart and S. Sevenhuijsen (eds), *Child Custody and the Politics of Gender*. London: Routledge.

BROWN, J. AND DAY SCLATER, S. (1999). 'Divorce: A Psychodynamic Perspective', in S. Day Sclater and C. Piper (eds), *Undercurrents of Divorce*. Ashgate: Dartmouth.

BRYAN, M. AND SANZ, A. (2008). *Does Housework Lower Wages and Why? Evidence for Britain*. ISER Working Paper 2008-3. <www.iser.essex.ac.uk/publications/working-papers /iser/2008-03.pdf>.

BURGOYNE, C. AND SONNENBERG, S. (2009). 'Financial Practices in Cohabiting Heterosexual Couples: a perspective from economic psychology', in J. Miles and R. Probert (eds) (2009), below.

BURROWS, D. (2009a). 'Do child support committal applications breach human rights?'. *New Law Journal*, 159: 653.

BURROWS, D. (2009b). 'Enforcement of Child Maintenance: *Kehoe*'. *Family Law*, 39: 1086.

Burrows, D. (2010). 'Delay and Enforcement of Child Support Arrears'. *Family Law*, 40: 269.

Burrows, D., Conway, H., and Eames, J. (2006). *Finance on Family Breakdown for Low Income Families: a practical guide*. Bristol: Jordan Publishing.

Burton, M. (2003a). 'Third party applications for protection orders in England and Wales: service provider's views on implementing section 60 of the Family Law Act 1996'. *Journal of Social Welfare and Family Law*, 25: 137.

Burton, M. (2003b). 'Criminalising Breaches of Civil Orders for Protection from Domestic Violence'. *Criminal Law Review*, 301.

Burton, M. (2004a). '*Lomas v Parle*—Coherent and effective remedies for victims of domestic violence: time for an integrated domestic violence court?'. *Child and Family Law Quarterly*, 16: 17.

Burton, M. (2004b). 'Domestic Violence—From Consultation to Bill: closer integration of the civil and criminal justice systems'. *Family Law*, 34: 128.

Burton, M. (2006). 'Judicial Monitoring of Compliance: Introducing "Problem Solving" Approaches to Domestic Violence Courts in England and Wales'. *International Journal of Law, Policy and the Family*, 20: 366.

Burton, M. (2008a). *Legal Responses to Domestic Violence*. Abingdon: Routledge-Cavendish.

Burton, M. (2008b). *Domestic Abuse Literature Review*. <www.legalservices.gov.uk/docs/fains_and_mediation/DomesticAbuseLiteratureReview.pdf>.

Burton, M. (2009a). 'Failing to Protect: Victims' Rights and Police Liability'. *Modern Law Review*, 72: 283.

Burton, M. (2009b). 'Civil law remedies for domestic violence: why are applications for non-molestation orders declining?'. *Journal of Social Welfare and Family Law*, 31: 109.

Burton, M. (2010). 'The human rights of victims of domestic violence: *Opuz v Turkey*'. *Child and Family Law Quarterly*, 22: 131.

Burton, M., McCrory, A., and Buck, T. (2002). *The civil remedies for domestic violence under the Family Law Act 1996: is section 60 the way forward?* Unpublished report submitted to the LCD, October.

Butler-Sloss, E. (1988). *Report of the Inquiry into Child Abuse in Cleveland 1987*. Cm 412. London: HMSO.

Cabinet Office Performance and Innovation Unit (2000). *Prime Minister's Review of Adoption*. <http://webarchive.nationalarchives.gov.uk/+/http://www.cabinetoffice.gov.uk/strategy/downloads/su/adoption/adoption.pdf>.

Calderwood, L. (2008). 'Family Demographics', in K. Hansen and H. Joshi (eds), *Millennium Cohort Survey: Third Survey—A User's Guide to Initial Findings*. London: Centre for Longitudinal Studies.

Callus, T. (2008). 'First "Designer Babies", Now À La Carte Parents'. *Family Law*, 38: 143.

Cameron, E. (2001). 'Foreword' to R. Wintemute and M. Andenæs (eds), *Legal Recognition of Same-Sex Partnerships*. Oxford: Hart Publishing.

CAMPBELL, T. (1992). 'The Rights of Minor: As Person, As Child, As Juvenile, As Future Adult'. *International Journal of Law and the Family*, 6: 1.

CARACCIOLO DI TORELLA, E., AND REID, E. (2002). 'The Changing Shape of the "European Family" and Fundamental Rights'. *European Law Review*, 27: 80.

CARBONE, J. (1996). 'Feminism, Gender and the Consequences of Divorce', in M. Freeman (ed), *Divorce: Where Next?* Ashgate: Dartmouth.

CASC (2000). *Report on the Question of Parental Contact in cases where there is Domestic Violence*. <www.dca.gov.uk/family/abfla/dvconreport.pdf>.

CASC (2001). *Making Contact Work. The Facilitation of Arrangements for Contact between Children and their Non-residential Parents; and the Enforcement of Court Orders for Contact*. <www.dca.gov.uk/family/abfla/mcwrep.pdf>.

CASTLE, J., BECKETT, C., AND GROOTHUES, C. (2000). 'Infant adoption in England. A longitudinal account of social and cognitive progress'. *Adoption and Fostering*, 24: 26.

CENTRE FOR SOCIAL JUSTICE (2009). *Every Family Matters: an in-depth review of family law in Britain*. London: Centre for Social Justice. <www.centreforsocialjustice.org.uk/client/downloads/WEB%20CSJ%20Every%20Family%20Matters_smallres.pdf>.

CHAU, P.-L. AND HERRING, J. (2004). 'Men, Women, People: The Definition of Sex', in B. Brooks-Gordon, L. Gelsthorpe, M. Johnson, and A. Bainham (eds), *Sexuality Repositioned: Diversity and the Law*. Oxford: Hart Publishing.

CHOUDHRY, S. (2003). 'The Adoption and Children Act 2002, The Welfare Principle and the Human Rights Act 1998—A Missed Opportunity'. *Child and Family Law Quarterly*, 15: 119.

CHOUDHRY, S. AND FENWICK, H. (2005). 'Taking the rights of parents and children seriously: confronting the welfare principle under the Human Rights Act'. *Oxford Journal of Legal Studies*, 25: 453.

CHOUDHRY, S. AND HERRING, J. (2006a). 'Righting Domestic Violence'. *International Journal of Law, Policy and the Family*, 20: 95.

CHOUDHRY, S. AND HERRING, J. (2006b). 'Domestic Violence and the Human Rights Act 1998: a new means of legal intervention?'. *Public Law*, 752.

CHOUDHRY, S. AND HERRING, J. (2010). *European Human Rights and Family Law*. Oxford: Hart Publishing.

CHURCH OF ENGLAND (2003). *Response to Civil Partnership consultation*. <www.churchofengland.org/media/45595/civil.pdf>.

CLARKE, L. AND BERRINGTON, A. (1999). 'Socio-demographic predictors of divorce', in *One plus one Marriage and Partnership Research, High Divorce Rates: the state of the evidence on reasons and remedies*. Lord Chancellor's Department Research Report Series 2/99, 1(1). Summary at <www.dca.gov.uk/research/1999/299-1esfr.htm>.

CLIVE, E. (1980). 'Marriage: an unnecessary legal concept?', in J. Eekelaar and S. Katz (eds), *Marriage and Cohabitation in Contemporary Societies*. London: Butterworths.

COAST, E. (2009). 'Currently cohabiting: relationships, attitudes, expectations and outcomes'. LSE Research Online: <eprints.lse.ac.uk/23986/1/Currently_cohabiting_(LSERO).pdf>.

COBLEY, C. AND LOWE, N. (2009). 'Interpreting the threshold criteria under section 31(2) of the Children Act 1989—the House of Lords decision in *Re B*'. *Modern Law Review*, 72: 463.

COLEMAN, K. AND OSBORNE, S. (2010). 'Homicide', in K. Smith et al (eds), *Homicides, Firearm Offences and Intimate Violence 2008/09: supplementary volume 2 to Crime in England and Wales 2008/09*. Home Office Statistical Bulletin 01/10. <rds.homeoffice.gov.uk/rds/pdfs10/hosb0110.pdf>.

COLEMAN, L. AND GLENN F. (2010). *When couples part: Understanding the consequences for adults and children*. London: One Plus One.

COLEMAN, N., SEEDS, K., AND NORDEN, O. (2007). *Child Maintenance Redesign Survey: indications of future behaviours and choice*. DWP Research Report No 444. <www.dh.gov.uk/assetRoot/04/01/44/62/04014462.pdf>.

COLLIER, R. (1994). 'The Campaign Against the Child Support Act: "Errant Fathers" and "Family Men"'. *Family Law*, 24: 384.

COLLIER, R. (1995). *Masculinity, Law and the Family*. London: Routledge.

COLLIER, R. (1999). 'The dashing of a "liberal dream"?—the information meeting, the "new family" and the limits of law'. *Child and Family Law Quarterly*, 11: 257.

COLLIER, R. (2001). 'A Hard Time to be a Father?: Reassessing the Relationship Between Law, Policy, and Family (Practices)'. *Journal of Law and Society*, 28: 520.

COLLIER, R. (2003). 'In Search of the 'Good Father': Law, Family Practices and the Normative Reconstruction of Parenthood', in J. Dewar and S. Parker (eds), *Family Law Processes, Practices and Pressures—Proceedings of the Tenth World Conference of the International Society of Family Law, July 2000, Brisbane, Australia*. Oregon: Hart Publishing.

COLLIER, R. (2005). 'Fathers 4 Justice, law and the new politics of fatherhood'. *Child and Family Law Quarterly*, 17: 511.

COLLIER, R. AND SHELDON, S. (2008). *Fragmenting Fatherhood. A Socio-Legal Study*. Oxford and Portland, Oregon: Hart Publishing.

COLLINS, L. (ed) (2000). *Dicey and Morris on the Conflict of Laws*, 13th edn. London: Sweet & Maxwell.

CONCILIATION PROJECT UNIT (1989). *Report to the Lord Chancellor on the Costs and Effectiveness of Conciliation in England and Wales*. Newcastle: University of Newcastle.

CONSERVATIVE PARTY (2010). *The Conservative Manifesto*. London: Conservative Party. <www.conservatives.com/Policy/Manifesto.aspx>.

CONWAY, H. (2001). 'Protecting Tenancies on Marriage Breakdown'. *Family Law*, 31: 208.

CONWAY, H. (2002). 'Money and Domestic Violence—escaping the *Nwogbe* trap'. *Family Law*, 32: 61.

COOK, D., BURTON, M., ROBINSON, A., AND VALLELY, C. (2004). *Evaluation of Specialist Domestic* Violence *Courts/Fast Track Systems*. London: Crown Prosecution Service/ Department of Constitutional Affairs.

COOKE, E. (2007). '*Miller/McFarlane*: law in search of discrimination'. *Child and Family Law Quarterly*, 19: 98.

COOKE, E. (2009). 'The Future of Ancillary Relief', in G. Douglas and N. Lowe, *The Continuing Evolution of Family Law*. Bristol: Family Law.

COOKE, E., BARLOW, A., AND CALLUS, T. (2006). *Community of Property: a regime for England and Wales?* London: Policy Press.

CPAG (2006). *CPAG response to Government consultation on Henshaw review of child support*. <www.cpag.org.uk/info/briefings_policy/CPAG_response_to_Government_consultation_on_Henshaw_review_of_child_support.pdf>.

CPAG (2010). *Welfare Benefits and Tax Credits Handbook 2010–11*. London: CPAG.

CPAG (current year). *Child support handbook*. London: CPAG.

CPS (2006). *Domestic Violence Monitoring Snapshot*. <www.cps.gov.uk/publications/prosecution/domestic/snapshot_2005_12.html#06>.

CPS (2008). *Guidance on section 1, Domestic Violence, Crime and Victims Act 2004*. <www.cps.gov.uk/legal/d_to_g/guidance_on_section_1_domestic_violence_crime_and_victims_act_2004/>.

CPS (2009). *CPS Policy for Prosecuting Cases of Domestic Violence*. <www.cps.gov.uk/publications/prosecution/domestic/domv.html#a02>.

CRAIG, J (2007). *'Everybody's Business'—How applications for contact orders by consent should be approached by the court in cases involving domestic violence. The Family Justice Council's Report and Recommendations to the President of the Family Division*. <www.family-justice-council.org.uk/docs/contactsummary.pdf>.

CRAIG, P. (2008). *Administrative Law*, 6th edn. London: Sweet & Maxwell.

CRETNEY, A. AND DAVIS, G. (1997). 'The Significance of Compellability in the Prosecution of Domestic Assault'. *British Journal of Criminology*, 37: 75.

CRETNEY, S. (1992). 'Divorce—A Smooth Transition?'. *Family Law*, 22: 472.

CRETNEY, S. (1996a). 'Divorce Reform: Humbug and Hypocrisy or Smooth Transition?', in M. Freeman (ed), *Divorce: Where Next?* Aldershot: Dartmouth.

CRETNEY, S. (1996b). 'From Status to Contract?', in F. Rose (ed), *Consensus ad Idem: Essays in the Law of Contract in Honour of Guenter Treitel*. London: Sweet & Maxwell.

CRETNEY, S. (1998). *Law, Law Reform and the Family*. Oxford: OUP.

CRETNEY, S. (1999). 'Contract Not Apt in Divorce Deal'. *Law Quarterly Review*, 115: 356.

CRETNEY, S. (2003a). *Family Law in the Twentieth Century. A History*. Oxford: OUP.

CRETNEY, S. (2003b). 'Community of Property Imposed by Judicial Decision'. *Law Quarterly Review*, 119: 349.

CRETNEY, S. (2006a). *Same Sex Relationships*. Oxford: OUP.

CRETNEY, S. (2006b). 'Marriage, Mothers-in-Law and Human Rights'. *Law Quarterly Review*, 122: 8.

CRETNEY, S. AND MASSON, J. (1990). *Principles of Family Law*, 5th edn. London: Sweet & Maxwell.

CRETNEY, S., MASSON J., AND BAILEY-HARRIS, R. (2002). *Principles of Family Law*, 7th edn. London: Sweet & Maxwell.

CROMPTON, L. (2004). 'Civil Partnerships Bill 2004: the Illusion of Equality'. *Family Law*, 34: 888.

CURRY-SUMNER, I. (2006). *All's well that ends registered*. Antwerp-Oxford: Intersentia.

CURRY-SUMNER, I. (2009). '*E.B. v France:* a missed opportunity'. *Child and Family Law Quarterly*, 21: 356.

DANCE, C. AND RUSHTON, A. (2005). 'Predictors of outcome for unrelated adoptive placements made during middle childhood'. *Child and Family Social Work*, 10: 269.

DAVIES, C. (1993). 'Divorce Reform in England and Wales: A Visitor's View'. *Family Law*, 23: 331.

DAVIS, G. (1988). *Partisans and Mediators*. Oxford: OUP.

DAVIS, G. (2000). *Monitoring Publicly Funded Family Mediation—Summary Report to the Legal Services Commission*. London: Legal Services Commission.

DAVIS, G. AND MURCH, M. (1988). *Grounds for Divorce*. Oxford: Clarendon Press.

DAVIS, G. AND ROBERTS, M. (1989). 'Mediation and the Battle of the Sexes'. *Family Law*, 19: 305.

DAVIS, G. AND WIKELEY, N. (2002). 'National Survey of Child Support Agency Clients—the Relationship Dimension'. *Family Law*, 32: 522.

DAVIS, G., CRETNEY, S., AND COLLINS, J. (1994). *Simple Quarrels: Negotiating Money and Property Disputes on Divorce*. Oxford: OUP.

DAVIS, G., PEARCE, J., BIRD, R., WOODWARD, H., AND WALLACE, C. (2000). 'Research: Ancillary Relief Outcomes'. *Child and Family Law Quarterly*, 12: 43.

DAVIS, G., WIKELEY, N., AND YOUNG, R., WITH BARRON, J. AND BEDWARD, J. (1998). *Child Support in Action*. Oxford: Hart Publishing.

DAY SCLATER, S. (1999). 'Experiences of Divorce', in S. Day Sclater and C. Piper (eds), *Undercurrents of Divorce*. Dartmouth: Ashgate.

DAY SCLATER, S., BAINHAM, A., AND RICHARDS, M. (1999). 'Introduction', in A. Bainham, S. Day Sclater, and M. Richards (eds), *What is a Parent? A Socio-Legal Analysis*. Oxford: Hart Publishing.

DCA (2002). *Scoping Study on Delay in Children Act Cases Findings and Action Taken*. <www.dca.gov.uk/family/scopestud.htm>.

DCA (2006a). *Confidence and confidentiality. Improving transparency and privacy in family courts*. CP 11/06, Cm 6886. London: HMSO.

DCA (2006b). *Separate Representation of Children*. London: HMSO.

DCA (2006c). Judicial Statistics (Revised) England and Wales for the year 2005, Cm 6903. London: TSO.

DCA (date unknown). <www.dca.gov.uk/constitution/transsex/policy.htm>.

DCA AND DfES (2004). *The Government's Response to the Children Act Sub-Committee (CASC) Report: 'Making Contact Work'*. <www.dfes.gov.uk/childrenandfamilies/docs/CASC%20Final%20Version.doc>.

DCA, DfES, AND DTI (2004). *Parental Separation: Children's Needs and Parents' Responsibilities*, Cm 6273. London: HMSO.

DCA, DfES, AND DTI (2005). *Parental Separation: Children's Needs and Parents' Responsibilities—Next Steps*, Cm 6452. London: HMSO.

DCLG (2009). *Housing in England 2007-8*. London: DCLG. <www.communities.gov.uk/documents/statistics/pdf/1346249.pdf>.

DCLG (2010). *English Housing Survey: headline report 2008-9*. London: DCLG. <www.communities.gov.uk/documents/statistics/pdf/1479789.pdf>.

DCSF (2009). *Statistical First Release – Children looked after in England (including adoption and care leavers) year ending 31 March 2009*, SFR 25/2009. <www.dcsf.gov.uk/rsgateway/DB/SFR/s000878/SFR25-2009Version2.pdf>.

DCSF (2010). *Working together to safeguard children. A guide to inter-agency working to safeguard and promote the welfare of children*. London: HMSO. <http://publications.education.gov.uk/eOrderingDownload/00305-2010DOM-EN-v3.pdf>.

DCSF AND DWP (2008). *Joint birth registration: recording responsibility*. Cm 7293. London: HMSO. <http://publications.education.gov.uk/eOrderingDownload/birth_registration_wp.pdf>.

DE WAAL, A. (2008). *Second Thoughts on the Family*. London: Civitas.

DEECH, R. (1977). 'The Principles of Maintenance'. *Family Law*, 7: 229.

DEECH, R. (1980a). 'Williams and Glyn's and Family Law'. *New Law Journal*, 130: 896.

DEECH, R. (1980b). 'The Case Against the Legal Recognition of Cohabitation'. *International and Comparative Law Quarterly*, 29: 480.

DEECH, R. (1982). 'Financial Relief: The Retreat from Precedent and Principle'. *Law Quarterly Review*, 98: 621.

DEECH, R. (1984). 'Matrimonial property and divorce: a century of progress?', in M. Freeman (ed), *State, Law, and the Family*. London: Tavistock Publications.

DEECH, R. (1990). 'Divorce Law and Empirical Studies'. *Law Quarterly Review*, 106: 229.

DEECH, R. (1992). 'The unmarried father and human rights'. *Journal of Child Law*, 4: 3.

DEECH, R. (1996). 'Property and Money Matters', in M. Freeman (ed), *Divorce: Where Next?* Aldershot: Dartmouth.

DEECH, R. (2009a). *Divorce Law—a disaster?* Gresham Lectures 2009–10, <www.gresham.ac.uk/event.asp?PageId=45&EventId=946> and *Family Law*, 39: 1048.

DEECH, R. (2009b). *Cohabitation and the Law*. Gresham Lectures 2009–10, <www.gresham.ac.uk/event.asp?PageId=45&EventId=946> and *Family Law*, 40: 39.

🕸 DEECH, R. (2009c). *What's a woman worth? The maintenance law.* Gresham Lectures 2009–10, <www.gresham.ac.uk/event.asp?PageId=45&EventId=946> and *Family Law,* 39: 1140.

🕸 DEPARTMENT OF JUSTICE (2008). *Spousal Support Advisory Guidelines.* <www.justice.gc.ca/eng/pi/fcy-fea/spo-epo/g-ld/spag/index.html>.

DEWAR, J. (1997). 'Reducing Discretion in Family Law'. *Australian Journal of Family Law,* 11: 309.

DEWAR, J. (1998a). 'The Normal Chaos of Family Law'. *Modern Law Review,* 61: 467.

DEWAR, J. (1998b). 'Land, Law and the Family Home', in S. Bright and J. Dewar (eds), *Land Law: Themes and Perspectives.* Oxford: OUP.

DEWAR, J. (2003). 'Families', in P. Cane and M. Tushnet (eds), *The Oxford Handbook of Legal Studies.* Oxford: OUP.

DEY, I. (2005). 'Adapting Adoption: A Case of Closet politics?'. *International Journal of Law, Policy and the Family,* 19: 289.

🕸 DfES (2004). *Statistics of Education: Outcome Indicators for Looked After Children— Twelve months to 30 September 2003 England.* London: TSO.

DH (1993). *Adoption: the future,* Cm 2288. London: HMSO.

DH (2000). *Adoption—A New Approach. A White Paper,* Cm 5017. London: HMSO.

🕸 DH (2001a). *Donor Information Consultation—Providing Information about Gamete or Embryo Donors.* <www.dh.gov.uk/dr_consum_dh/groups/dh_digitalassets/@dh/@en/documents/digitalasset/dh_4018774.pdf>.

🕸 DH (2001b). *National Adoption Standards for England.* <www.dh.gov.uk/assetRoot/04/01/47/01/04014701.pdf>.

🕸 DH (2006). *Review of the Human Fertilisation and Embryology Act. Proposals for revised legislation (including establishment of the Regulatory Authority for Tissue and Embryos).* Cm 6989. London: HMSO. <www.dh.gov.uk/dr_consum_dh/groups/dh_digitalassets/@dh/@en/documents/digitalasset/dh_073065.pdf>.

🕸 DH (2007). Government response to the Report from the Joint Committee on the Human Tissue and Embryos (Draft) Bill. Cm 7209. London: HMSO. <www.dh.gov.uk/dr_consum_dh/groups/dh_digitalassets/@dh/@en/documents/digitalasset/dh_079145.pdf>.

DHSS (1974). *Report of the Committee on One-Parent Families, vol. 1,* Cm 5629. London: HMSO.

DHSS (1984). *Report of the Committee of Inquiry into Human Fertilisation and Embryology,* Cm 9314. London: HMSO.

DHSS (1985). *Review of Child Care Law. Report to ministers of an interdepartmental working party.* London: HMSO.

DHSS, HO, LCD, DES, WO, AND SO (1987). *The Law on Child Care and Family Services.* London: HMSO.

🕸 DIBDIN, K., SEALEY, A., AND AKTAR, S. (eds) (2001). *Judicial Statistics Annual Report.* London: The Court Service.

DIDUCK, A. (1995). 'The Unmodified Family: The Child Support Act and the Construction of Legal Subjects'. *Journal of Law and Society*, 22: 527.

DIDUCK, A. (1999). 'Dividing the Family Assets', in S. Day Sclater and C. Piper (eds), *Undercurrents of Divorce*. Ashgate: Dartmouth.

DIDUCK, A. (2001). 'A Family by any other Name . . . or Starbucks comes to England'. *Journal of Law and Society*, 28: 290.

DIDUCK, A. (2003). *Law's Families*. London: Butterworths.

DIDUCK, A. (2005). 'Shifting Familiarity'. *Current Legal Problems*, 58: 235.

DIDUCK, A. (2007). ' "If only we can find the appropriate terms to use the issue will be solved": Law, identity and parenthood'. *Child and Family Law Quarterly*, 19: 458.

DIDUCK, A. AND KAGANAS, F. (2006). *Family Law, Gender and the State*. Oxford: Hart Publishing.

DIDUCK, A. AND ORTON, H. (1994). 'Equality and Support for Spouses'. *Modern Law Review*, 57: 681.

DINGWALL, R. (1988). 'Empowerment or Enforcement? Some Questions about Power and Control in Divorce Mediation', in R. Dingwall and J. Eekelaar (eds), *Divorce Mediation and the Legal Process*. Oxford: OUP.

DINGWALL, R. AND GREATBATCH, D. (1993). 'Who is in charge? Rhetoric and Evidence in the study of mediation'. *Journal of Social Welfare and Family Law*, 14: 367.

DIXON, M. (2007a). 'Anything to declare? Express declaration of trust on Land Registry form TR1: the doubts raised in *Stack v Dowden*'. *Conveyancer and Property Lawyer*, 364.

DIXON, M. (2007b). 'The never-ending story: co-ownership after *Stack v Dowden*'. *Conveyancer and Property Lawyer*, 456.

DNES, A. (1998). 'The Division of Marital Assets Following Divorce'. *Journal of Law and Society*, 25: 336.

DOBASH, R. AND DOBASH, R. (1992). *Women, Violence and Social Change*. London: Routledge.

DOBASH, R. AND DOBASH, R. (2004). 'Women's Violence to Men in Intimate Relationships'. *British Journal of Criminology*, 44: 324.

DOGGETT, M. (1992). *Marriage, Wife-Beating and the Law in Victorian England*. London: Weidenfeld & Nicolson.

DONOVAN, C., HESTER, M., HOLMES, J., AND MCCARRY, M. (2006). *Comparing Domestic Abuse in Same Sex and Heterosexual Relationships*. <www.broken-rainbow.org.uk/cohsar_report.pdf>.

DOUGLAS, G. (1991). *Law, Fertility and Reproduction*. London: Sweet & Maxwell.

DOUGLAS, G. (1993). 'Assisted Reproduction and the Welfare of the Child'. *Current Legal Problems*, 46: 53.

DOUGLAS, G. (1994a). 'Marriage—Nullity'. *Family Law*, 24: 17.

DOUGLAS, G. (1994b). 'The Intention to be a Parent and the Making of Mothers'. *Modern Law Review*, 57: 636.

DOUGLAS, G. (2000a). 'The Family, Gender and Social Security', in N. Harris (ed), *Social Security Law in Context*. Oxford: OUP.

DOUGLAS, G. (2000b). 'Marriage, Cohabitation and Parenthood—from Contract to Status?', in S. Katz, J. Eekelaar, and M. Maclean (eds), *Cross Currents Family Law and Policy in the United States and England*. Oxford: OUP.

DOUGLAS, G. (2003). 'Re J (Leave to issue application for residence order)'. *Child and Family Law Quarterly*, 15: 103.

DOUGLAS, G. (2004a). *An Introduction to Family Law*, 2nd edn. Oxford: OUP.

DOUGLAS, G. (2004b). 'Case Report: Child Support—Human Rights'. *Family Law*, 34: 399.

DOUGLAS, G. (2009). Case comment on *Kehoe v UK*. *Family Law*, 39: 107.

DOUGLAS, G. AND LOWE, N. (1992). 'Becoming a Parent in English Law'. *Law Quarterly Review*, 108: 414.

DOUGLAS, G. AND PERRY, A. (2001). 'How parents cope financially on separation and divorce—implications for the future of ancillary relief'. *Child and Family Law Quarterly*, 13: 67.

DOUGLAS, G., PEARCE, J., AND WOODWARD, H. (2007a). 'Dealing with Property Issues on Cohabitation Breakdown'. *Family Law*, 37: 36.

DOUGLAS, G., PEARCE, J., AND WOODWARD, H. (2007b). *A Failure of Trust: Resolving Property Disputes on Cohabitation Breakdown*. <www.law.cf.ac.uk/researchpapers/papers/1.pdf>.

DOUGLAS, G., PEARCE, J., AND WOODWARD, H. (2008). 'The Law Commission's cohabitation proposals: applying them in practice'. *Family Law*, 38: 351.

DOUGLAS, G., PEARCE, J., AND WOODWARD, H. (2009). 'Money, Property, Cohabitation and Separation: patterns and intentions', in J. Miles and R. Probert (eds) (2009), below.

DOUGLAS, G., MURCH, M., SCANLAN, L., AND PERRY, A. (2000). 'Safeguarding Children's Welfare in Non-Contentious Divorce: Towards a New Conception of the Legal Process?' *Modern Law Review*, 63: 177.

DOWNIE, A. (2000). 'Re C (HIV Test) The limits of parental autonomy'. *Child and Family Law Quarterly*, 12: 197.

DRISCOLL J. AND HOLLINGSWORTH, K. (2008). 'Accommodating Children in Need: R (M) v Hammersmith and Fulham London Borough Council'. *Child and Family Law Quarterly*, 20: 522.

DSS (1990). *Children Come First*, Cm 1264. London: HMSO.

DSS (1995). *Improving Child Support*, Cm 2745. London: HMSO.

DSS (1999). *A New Contract for Welfare: Children's Rights and Parents' Responsibilities*, Cm 4349. London: DSS.

ⓐ DTI (2004). *Final Regulatory Impact Assessment: Civil Partnership Act 2004*. URN 04/1336. <webarchive.nationalarchives.gov.uk/+/http://www.berr.gov.uk/files/file23829.pdf>.

DUNCAN, S. AND PHILLIPS, M. (2008). 'New families? Tradition and change in modern relationships', in Park, A. et al (eds), *British Social Attitudes: the 24th Report*. London: Sage.

ⓐ DWP (2006a). *A fresh start: child support redesign—the Government's response to Sir David Henshaw*, Cm 6895. London: TSO.

DWP (2006b). *A new system of child maintenance*. Cm 6979. London: TSO.

DWP (2007a). *Joint birth registration: promoting parental responsibility*. Cm 7160. London: HMSO.

ⓐ DWP (2007b). *Report on the child maintenance White Paper: Reply by the Government*, Cm 7062. <www.dwp.gov.uk/childmaintenance/pdfs/cmr-response-to-selectcommittee.pdf>.

ⓐ DWP (2009). *Households Below Average Income: An analysis of the income distribution 1994/95 – 2008/09*. <research.dwp.gov.uk/asd/hbai/hbai_2009/pdf_files/full_hbai10.pdf>.

ⓐ DWP (2010a). *Fraud and Error in the Benefit System, October 2008 to September 2009*. London: DWP. <research.dwp.gov.uk/asd/asd2/fem/fem_oct08_sep09.pdf>.

ⓐ DWP (2010b). *Decision Makers' Guide*. <dwp.gov.uk/publications/specialist-guides/decision-makers-guide/>.

DYER, F. (2004). 'Termination of parental rights in light of attachment theory'. *Psychology, Public Policy and Law*, 10: 5.

EDWARDS, S. (1989). *Policing 'Domestic' Violence: women, the law and the state*. London: Sage.

EDWARDS, S. (2001). 'Domestic Violence and Harassment: An assessment of the civil remedies', in J. Taylor-Browne (ed), *What Works in Reducing Domestic Violence? A comprehensive guide for professionals*. London: Whiting and Birch.

EDWARDS, S. AND HALPERN, A. (1991). 'Protection for the Victim of Domestic Violence: Time for Radical Revision?'. *Journal of Social Welfare and Family Law*, 13: 94.

EEKELAAR, J. (1986). 'The Emergence of Children's Rights'. *Oxford Journal of Legal Studies*, 6: 161.

EEKELAAR, J. (1987). 'A Woman's Place—A Conflict Between Law and Social Values'. *Conveyancer and Property Lawyer*, 51: 93.

EEKELAAR, J. (1990). 'Investigation under the Children Act 1989'. *Family Law*, 20: 486.

EEKELAAR, J. (1991a). 'Are Parents Morally Obliged to Care for Their Children?'. *Oxford Journal of Legal Studies*, 11: 340.

EEKELAAR, J. (1991b). *Regulating Divorce*. Oxford: Clarendon Press.

EEKELAAR, J. (1991c). 'Parental Responsibility: State of Nature or Nature of the State?'. *Journal of Social Welfare and Family Law*, 13: 37.

EEKELAAR, J. (1994). 'A Jurisdiction in Search of a Mission: Family Proceedings in England and Wales'. *Modern Law Review*, 57: 839.

EEKELAAR, J. (1995). 'Family Justice: Ideal or Illusion? Family Law and Communitarian Values'. *Current Legal Problems Part II*, 48: 191.

EEKELAAR, J. (1998a). 'Should Section 25 be reformed?'. *Family Law*, 28: 469.

EEKELAAR, J. (1998b). 'Do parents have a duty to consult?'. *Law Quarterly Review*, 114: 337.

EEKELAAR, J. (1999). 'Family Law: Keeping Us "On Message"'. *Child and Family Law Quarterly*, 11: 387.

EEKELAAR, J. (2000). 'Uncovering Social Obligations: Family Law and the Responsible Citizen', in M. Maclean (ed), *Making Law for Families*. Oxford: Hart Publishing.

EEKELAAR, J. (2002). 'Beyond the Welfare Principle'. *Child and Family Law Quarterly*, 14: 237.

EEKELAAR, J. (2004). 'Children between cultures'. *International Journal of Law, Policy and the Family*, 18: 178.

EEKELAAR, J. (2006a). 'Property and Financial Settlements on Divorce: Sharing and Compensating'. *Family Law*, 36: 754.

EEKELAAR, J. (2006b). *Family Law and Personal Life*. Oxford: OUP.

EEKELAAR, J. (2010). 'Financial and Property Settlement: a standard deal?'. *Family Law*, 40: 359.

EEKELAAR, J. AND MACLEAN, M. (1986). *Maintenance after Divorce*. Oxford: OUP.

EEKELAAR, J. AND MACLEAN, M. (1997). 'Property and Financial Adjustment after Divorce in the 1990s—Unfinished Business', in K. Hawkins (ed), *The Human Face of Law*. Oxford: Clarendon Press.

EEKELAAR, J., MACLEAN, M., AND BEINART, S. (2000). *Family Lawyers: The Divorce Work of Solicitors*. Oxford: Hart Publishing.

EHRC (2009). *Working better: fathers, family and work—contemporary perspectives.* Research summary 41. <www.equalityhumanrights.com/uploaded_files/research/41_wb_fathers_family_and_work.pdf>.

ELLISON, G., BARKER, A. AND KULASURIYA, T. (2009). *Work and care: a study of modern parents. Research report: 15.* London: Equality and Human Rights Commission. <www.equalityhumanrights.com/uploaded_files/research/15._work_and_care_modern_parents_15_report.pdf>.

ELLISON, L. (2003). 'Responding to Victim Withdrawal in Domestic Violence Prosecutions'. *Criminal Law Review*, 760.

ELLMAN, I. (1997). 'The Misguided Movement to Revive Fault Divorce, and Why Reformers Should Look Instead to the American Law Institute'. *International Journal of Law, Policy and the Family*, 11: 216.

ELLMAN, I. (2000). 'Divorce', in S. Katz, J. Eekelaar, and M. Maclean (eds), *Cross Currents: Family Law and Policy in the US and England*. Oxford: OUP, 341.

ELLMAN, I. (2005). 'Do Americans Play Football?'. *International Journal of Law, Policy and the Family*, 19: 257.

ELLMAN, I. (2007). 'Financial Settlements on Divorce: Two Steps Forward, Two to Go'. *Law Quarterly Review*, 123: 2.

ESKRIDGE, W. (2001). 'The Ideological Structure of the Same-Sex Marriage Debate (And Some Postmodern Arguments for Same-Sex Marriage)', in R. Wintemute and M. Andenæs (eds), *Legal Recognition of Same-Sex Partnerships*. Oxford: Hart Publishing.

ETHERTON, T. (2009). 'Constructive Trusts and Proprietory Estoppel: the search for clarity and principle'. *Conveyancer and Property Lawyer*, 73: 104.

⊕ FAMILY AND PARENTING INSTITUTE (2009). *Ending Child Poverty: making it happen—a response from the Family and Parenting Institute*. <www.familyandparenting.org/Filestore//Documents/consultations/Ending_Child_Poverty2009.pdf>.

⊕ FAMILY JUSTICE COUNCIL (2008). *Enhancing the Participation of Children and Young People in Family Proceedings: Starting the Debate*. <www.family-justice-council.org.uk/docs/Participation_of_young_people.pdf>.

⊕ FAMILY LAW WEEK (2007). *Child support reform 'a disaster', says Commons Public Accounts* Committee. <www.familylawweek.co.uk/site.aspx?i=ed724>.

⊕ FAMILIES NEED FATHERS (2007). Written Memorandum to Public Bill Committee, on Child Maintenance and Other Payments Bill 2007. <www.publications.parliament.uk/pa/cm200607/cmpublic/childmain/memos/memocm2.htm>.

FEHLBERG, B. (1997). *Sexually Transmitted Debt: surety experience and English law*. Oxford: Clarendon Press.

FEHLBERG, B. AND MACLEAN, M. (2009). 'Child support policy in Australia and the United Kingdom: changing priorities but a similar tough deal for children?' *International Journal of Law, Policy and the Family*, 23: 1.

FEHLBERG, B. AND SMYTH. B. (2002). 'Binding Pre-Nuptial Agreements in Australia: the First Year'. *International Journal of Law, Policy and the Family*, 16: 127.

FELDBLUM (2001). 'The Limitations of Liberal Neutrality Arguments in Favour of Same-sex Marriage', in R. Wintemute and M. Andenæs (eds), *Legal Recognition of Same-Sex Partnerships*. Oxford: Hart Publishing.

FERGUSON, L. (2008). 'Family, Social Inequalities, and the Persuasive Force of Interpersonal Obligation'. *International Journal of Law, Policy and the Family*, 22: 61.

FINEMAN, M. (2004). *The Autonomy Myth: a theory of dependency*. New York: The New Press.

⊕ FINNEY, A. (2006). *Domestic Violence, sexual assault and stalking: findings from the 2004/05 British Crime Survey*, Home Office Online Report 12/06. <www.homeoffice.gov.uk/rds/pdfs06/rdsolr1206.pdf>.

FINNIS, J. (1993). 'Law, Morality and "Sexual Orientation"'. *Notre Dame Law Review*, 69: 1049.

FISHER, H. AND LOW, H. (2009). 'Who wins, who loses and who recovers from divorce?', in J. Miles and R. Probert (eds) (2009), below.

⊕ FLATLEY, J. ET AL (eds) (2010). *Crime in England and Wales 2009/10*. Home Office Statistical Bulletin 12/10. <rds.homeoffice.gov.uk/rds/pdfs10/hosb1210.pdf>.

FLAHERTY, J., VEIT-WILSON, J., AND DORNAN, P. (2004). *Poverty: the facts*, 5th edn. London: CPAG.

FLYNN, L. AND LAWSON, A. (1995). 'Gender, sexuality and the doctrine of detrimental reliance'. *Feminist Legal Studies*, 3: 105.

FLYNN, R. (2000). 'Black carers for white children. Shifting the 'same-race' placement debate'. *Adoption and Fostering*, 24: 47.

FORTIN, J. (1994). '*Re F*: "The Gooseberry Bush Approach"'. *Modern Law Review*, 57: 296.

FORTIN, J. (1999a). 'The HRA's impact on litigation involving children and their families'. *Child and Family Law Quarterly*, 11: 217.

FORTIN, J. (1999b). '*Re D (Care: Natural Parent Presumption)* Is blood really thicker than water?'. *Child and Family Law Quarterly*, 11: 435.

FORTIN, J. (2004). 'Children's Rights: Are the Courts Now Taking Them More Seriously?'. *Kings College Law Journal*, 15: 253.

FORTIN, J. (2006). 'Accommodating children's rights in a post Human Rights Act era'. *Modern Law Review*, 69: 299.

FORTIN, J. (2007). 'Children's representation through the looking glass'. *Family Law*, 37: 500.

FORTIN, J. (2009a). 'Children's right to know their origins—too far, too fast?'. *Child and Family Law Quarterly*, 21: 336.

FORTIN J. (2009b). *Children's Rights and the Developing Law*, 3rd edn. Cambridge: CUP.

FORTIN, J., RITCHIE, C., AND BUCHANAN, A. (2006). 'Young adults' perceptions of court-ordered contact.' *Child and Family Law Quarterly*, 18: 211.

FOX, L. (2001). 'Co-ownership of Matrimonial Property: Radical Proposals for Reform'. *Northern* Ireland *Legal Quarterly*, 52: 20.

FOX, L. (2003). 'Reforming family property—comparisons, compromises and common dimensions'. *Child and Family Law Quarterly*, 15: 1.

FOX, L. (2005). 'Creditors and the concept of "family home": a functional analysis'. *Legal Studies*, 25: 201.

FOX HARDING, L. (1991a). 'The Children Act 1989 in Context: Four Perspectives in Child Care Law and Policy (I)'. *Journal of Social Welfare and Family Law*, 13: 179.

FOX HARDING, L. (1991b). 'The Children Act 1989 in Context: Four Perspectives in Child Care Law and Policy (II)'. *Journal of Social Welfare and Family Law*, 13: 285.

FRAZER, L. AND SELWYN, J. (2005). 'Why are we waiting? The demography of adoption for children of black, Asian and black mixed parentage in England'. *Child and Family Social Work*, 10: 135.

FREEMAN, M. (1984). 'Legal ideologies, patriarchal precedents, and domestic violence', in M. Freeman (ed), *State, Law, and the Family: critical perspectives*. London: Tavistock.

FREEMAN, M. (1989). 'The Abuse of the Elderly—Legal Responses in England', in J. Eekelaar and D. Pearl (eds), *An Aging World: Dilemmas and Challenges for Law and Social Policy*. Oxford: OUP.

FREEMAN, M. (1992). 'Taking Children's Rights More Seriously'. *International Journal of Law and the Family*, 6: 52.

FREEMAN, M. (1996). 'The new birth right? Identity and the child of the reproductive revolution'. *International Journal of Children's Rights*, 4: 273.

FREEMAN, M. (2000). 'Disputing Children', in S. Katz, J. Eekelaar, and M. Maclean (eds), *Cross Currents Family Law and Policy in the United States and England*. New York: OUP.

GAFFNEY-RHYS, R. (2005). 'The Law Relating to Affinity after *B and L v UK*'. *Family Law*, 35: 955.

GAFFNEY-RHYS, R. (2006). '*Sheffield City Council v E and Another*—capacity to marry and the rights and responsibilities of married couples'. *Child and Family Law Quarterly* 18: 139.

GAFFNEY-RHYS, R. (2009). 'The law relating to marriageable age from a national and international perspective'. *International Family Law*, 228.

GARDNER, S. (1993). 'Rethinking Family Property'. *Law Quarterly Review*, 109: 263.

GARDNER, S. (2008). 'Family property today'. *Law Quarterly Review*, 124: 422.

GELDOF, B. (2003). 'The Real Love that Dare Not Speak its Name', in A. Bainham, B. Lindley, M. Richards, and L. Trinder (eds), *Children and their Families*. Oxford and Portland: Hart Publishing.

GENERAL REGISTER OFFICE (2003). *Civil Registration: Delivering Vital Change*. London: HMSO.

GEORGE, R. (2008). '*Stack v Dowden*—Do as we say, not as we do?'. *Journal of Social Welfare and Family Law*, 30: 49.

GEORGE, R., HARRIS, P., AND HERRING, J. (2009). 'Pre-nuptial agreements: for better or for worse?'. *Family Law*, 39: 934.

GIBB, F. (2008). 'Family justice system is at risk, warns new chief judge'. *The Times*, 24 March 2008.

GIBSON, C. (1991). 'The Future for Maintenance'. *Civil Justice Quarterly*, 10: 330.

GIBSON, C. (1994). *Dissolving Wedlock*. London: Routledge.

GILLESPIE, G. (2002). 'Child Support—When the Bough Breaks'. *Family Law*, 32: 528.

GILLIES, V. (2009). Understandings and Experiences of Involved Fathering in the United Kingdom: Exploring Classed Dimensions. *Annals, AAPSS*, 2009: 624.

GILMORE, S. (2003). 'Parental Responsibility and the Unmarried Father—A New Dimension to the Debate'. *Child and Family Law Quarterly*, 15: 21.

GILMORE, S. (2004a). 'Duration of marriage *and* seamless preceding cohabitation?'. *Family Law*, 34: 205.

GILMORE, S. (2004b). '*Re P(Child)(Financial Provision)*—Shoeboxes and comical shopping trips—child support from the affluent to fabulously rich'. *Child and Family Law Quarterly*, 16: 103.

GILMORE, S. (2004c). 'The nature, scope and use of the specific issue order'. *Child and Family Law Quarterly*, 16: 367.

GILMORE, S. (2006). 'Contact/shared residence and child well-being: research evidence and its implications for legal decision-making'. *International Journal of Law, Policy and the Family*, 20: 344.

GILMORE, S. (2007). '*Re B (Contact: Child Support)*—horses and carts: contact and child support'. *Child and Family Law Quarterly*, 19: 357.

GILMORE, S. (2008). 'Disputing Contact: challenging some assumptions'. *Child and Family Law Quarterly*, 20: 285.

GINGERBREAD (2008). *There's only one of me: single parents, welfare reform and the real world.* <www.gingerbread.org.uk/uploads/media/17/6844.pdf>.

GLENDINNING, C., CLARKE, K., AND CRAIG, G. (1994). 'The impact of the Child Support Act on lone mothers and their children'. *Journal of Child Law*, 7: 18.

GLENDON, M. (1974). 'Is There a Future for Separate Property?'. *Family Law Quarterly*, 8: 315.

GLENNON, L. (2005). 'Displacing the 'Conjugal Family' in Legal Policy—A Progressive Move?'. *Child and Family Law Quarterly*, 17: 141.

GLENNON, L. (2008). 'Obligations between adult partners: moving from form to function?'. *International Journal of Law, Policy and the Family*, 22: 22–60.

GLENNON, L. (2010). 'The limitations of equality discourses on the contours of intimate obligations', in J. Wallbank, S.Choudhry, and J. Herring (eds), *Rights, Gender and Family Law*, Abingdon: Routledge.

GLISTER, J. (2010). 'Section 199 of the Equality Act 2010: How Not to Abolish the Presumption of Advancement'. *Modern Law Review*, 73: 807.

GOLDSTEIN, B. (2000). 'Ethnicity and placement. Beginning the debate'. *Adoption and Fostering*, 24: 9.

GONZÁLEZ, L. AND VIITANEN, T. (2006). *The effect of divorce laws on divorce rates in Europe.* IZA Discussion Paper No 2023. <ssrn.com/abstract=892354>.

GOODMAN, A. AND GREAVES, E. (2010). *Cohabitation, marriage and child outcomes.* London: Institute for Fiscal Studies. <www.ifs.org.uk/comms/comm114.pdf>.

GOVERNMENT ACTUARY'S DEPARTMENT (2005). *Marriages abroad.* <www.gad.gov.uk/Demography%20Data/Marital%20Status%20Projections/2003/marriages_abroad.html>.

GRACE, S. (1995). *Policing domestic violence in the 1990s*, Home Office Research Study 139. London: HMSO.

GRAY, K. (1977). *Reallocation of Property on Divorce*. Abingdon: Professional Books.

GRAY, K. AND GRAY, S. (2009). *Elements of Land Law*, 5th edn. Oxford: OUP.

GRAYCAR, R. AND MORGAN, J. (2002). *The Hidden Gender of Law*, 2nd edn. Leichhardt, New South Wales: The Federation Press.

GREATBATCH, D. AND DINGWALL, R. (1999). 'The Marginalization of Domestic Violence in Divorce Mediation'. *International Journal of Law, Policy and the Family*, 13: 174.

HAFEN, B. AND HAFEN, J. (1995–96). 'Abandoning Children to their Autonomy: The United Nations Convention on the Rights of the Child'. *Harvard International Law Journal*, 37: 449.

HALE, B. (2004). 'Unmarried couples in family law'. *Family Law*, 34: 419.

HALE, B. (2009). 'The Future of Marriage', in G. Douglas and N. Lowe (eds), *The Continuing Evolution of Family Law*. Bristol: Jordans.

HALE, M. (1736). *The history of the pleas of the Crown*. (1971) P. Glazebrook (ed). London: Professional Books.

HALL, A. (2008). 'Special guardianship and permanency planning: unforeseen consequences and missed opportunities'. *Child and Family Law Quarterly*, 20: 359.

HALL, S. (2000). 'What price the logic of evidence?'. *Family Law*, 30: 423.

HALLEY, J. (2001). 'Recognition, Rights, Regulation, Normalisation: Rhetorics of Justification in the Same-Sex Marriage Debate', in R. Wintemute and M. Andenæs (eds), *Legal Recognition of Same-Sex Partnerships*. Oxford: Hart Publishing.

HARDING, M. (2009). 'Defending *Stack v Dowden*'. *Conveyancer and Property Lawyer*, 309.

HARDING, R. (2007). 'Sir Mark Potter and the protection of the traditional family: why same-sex marriages is (still!) a feminist issue'. *Feminist Legal Studies*, 15: 223.

HARPER, M., DOWNS, M., LANDELLS, K., AND WILSON, G. (2005). *Civil Partnership: the new law*. Bristol: Jordan Publishing.

HARRIS, D.J., O'BOYLE, M., AND WARBRICK, C. (1995). *Law of the European Convention on Human Rights*. London: Butterworths.

HARRIS, J. (1995). 'The Right to Found a Family', in R. E. Ladd, *Children's Rights Re-Visioned Philosophical Readings*. Wadsworth Publishing.

HARRIS, J. (2000). *An evaluation of the use and effectiveness of the Protection from Harassment Act 1997*, Home Office Research Study 203. London: Home Office.

HARRIS, N. (1996). 'Unmarried cohabiting couples and Social Security in Great Britain'. *Journal of Social Welfare and Family Law*, 18: 123.

HARRIS, P. AND GEORGE, R. (2010). 'Parental Responsibility and Shared Residence Orders: Parliamentary Intentions and Judicial Interpretations.' *Child and Family Law Quarterly*, 22: 151.

HARRIS-SHORT, S. (2001). 'The Adoption and Children Bill—a fast track to failure?'. *Child and Family Law Quarterly*, 13: 405.

HARRIS-SHORT, S. (2002). '*Re B (Adoption: Natural Parent)* Putting the child at the heart of adoption?'. *Child and Family Law Quarterly*, 14: 325.

HARRIS-SHORT, S. (2003). 'An "identity crisis" in the international law of human rights? The challenge of reproductive cloning'. *International Journal of Children's Rights*, 11: 333.

HARRIS-SHORT, S. (2005). 'Family Law and the Human Rights Act 1998—Restraint or Revolution?'. *Child and Family Law Quarterly*, 17: 329.

HARRIS-SHORT, S. (2010). 'Resisting the march towards 50/50 shared residence. Rights, welfare and equality in post-separation families'. *Journal of Social Welfare and Family Law*, 32: 257.

⬤ HARVIE-CLARK, S. (2005). *Family Law (Scotland) Bill: Grounds for Divorce (updated).* *SPICe briefing 05/22.* <www.scottish.parliament.uk/business/research/briefings-05/sb05-22.pdf>.

HASKEY, J. (2001a). 'Cohabitation in Great Britain: past, present and future trends—and attitudes'. *Population Trends*, 103: 4.

HASKEY, J. (2001b). 'Cohabiting couples in Great Britain: accommodation sharing, tenure and property ownership'. *Population Trends*, 103: 26.

HASKEY, J. (2005). 'Living arrangements in contemporary Britain: Having a partner who usually lives elsewhere and Living Apart Together'. *Population Trends*, 122: 35.

HASKEY, J. AND LEWIS, J. (2006). 'Living-Apart-Together in Britain: Context and Meaning'. *International Journal of Law and Context*, 2: 37.

HASSON, E. (2006). 'Wedded to 'fault': the legal regulation of divorce and relationship breakdown'. *Legal Studies*, 26: 267.

HAYES, M. (1990). 'The Law Commission and the Family Home'. *Modern Law Review*, 53: 222.

HAYES, M. (2006). 'Relocation cases: is the Court of Appeal applying the correct principles?'. *Child and* Family *Law Quarterly*, 18: 351.

HAYES, M. AND WILLIAMS, C. (1999). *Family Law: Principles, Policy and Practice*. London: Butterworths.

HAYES, P. (2003). 'Giving due consideration to ethnicity in adoption placements—a principled approach'. *Child and Family Law Quarterly*, 15: 225.

HENRICSON, C. AND BAINHAM, A. (2005). *The child and family policy divide: tension, convergence and rights*. York: Joseph Rowntree Foundation.

⬤ HENSHAW, D. (2006). *Recovering child support: routes to responsibility*, Cm 6894. London: TSO. <www.dwp.gov.uk/docs/henshaw-complete22-7.pdf>.

HERRING, J. (1999a). 'The Human Rights Act and the welfare principle in family law—conflicting or complementary?'. *Child and Family Law Quarterly*, 11: 223.

HERRING, J. (1999b). 'The Welfare Principle and the Rights of Parents', in A. Bainham, S. Day Sclater, and M. Richards (eds), *What is a Parent? A Socio-Legal Analysis*. Oxford: Hart Publishing.

HERRING, J. (2005a). 'Why Financial Orders on Divorce should be Unfair'. *International Journal of Law, Policy and the Family*, 19: 218.

HERRING, J. (2005b). 'Farewell Welfare?'. *Journal of Social Welfare and Family Law*, 27: 159.

HERRING, J. AND TAYLOR, R. (2006). 'Relocating Relocation'. *Child and Family Law Quarterly*, 18: 517.

HESS, E. AND HAY. F. (2007). 'Pensions and equality'. *Family Law*, 37: 310.

HESTER, M. (2005). 'Making it through the criminal justice system: attrition and domestic violence'. *Social Policy and Society*, 5: 79.

ⓦ HESTER, M. (2009). *Who does what to whom? Gender and domestic violence perpetrators*. Bristol: University of Bristol in association with the Northern Rock Foundation. <www. nr-foundation.org.uk/downloads/Who%20Does%20What%20to%20Whom.pdf>.

ⓦ HESTER, M. ET AL (2006). *Domestic Violence Perpetrators: Identifying Needs to Inform Early Intervention*. <www.bristol.ac.uk/sps/research/projects/completed/2006/rj4157/ rj4157researchreport.pdf>.

ⓦ HESTER, M. AND WESTMARLAND, N. (2005). *Tackling Domestic Violence: effective interventions and approaches*, Home Office Research Study 290. <rds.homeoffice.gov.uk/rds/ pdfs05/hors290.pdf>.

ⓦ HESTER, M., PEARCE, J., AND WESTMARLAND, N. (2008). *Early evaluation of the Integrated Domestic Violence Court, Croydon*. MOJ Research Series 18/08. <www.justice. gov.uk/publications/evaluation-integrated-court-croydon.htm>.

ⓦ HESTER, M., WESTMARLAND, J., PEARCE, J., AND WILLIAMSON, E. (2008). *Early evaluation of the Domestic Violence, Crime and Victims Act 2004*. MOJ Research Series 14/08. <www.justice.gov.uk/publications/domestic-violence-crime-victims-act-2004.htm>.

ⓦ HFEA (2002). *Response to the Department of Health's Consultation on 'Donor Information: Providing Information about Sperm, Egg and Embryo Donors'*. <www.hfea. gov.uk/cps/rde/xbcr/SID-3F57D79B-F8EA46AD/hfea/Donor_Info_response.pdf>.

ⓦ HFEA (2003). *Code of Practice* (6th ed.). <www.hfea.gov.uk/cps/rde/xbcr/SID-3F57D79B-EA722370/hfea/Code_of_Practice_Sixth_Edition_-_final.pdf>.

ⓦ HFEA (2005). *Tomorrow's children. Report of the policy review of welfare of the child assessments in licensed assisted conception clinics*. <www.hfea.gov.uk/docs/ TomorrowsChildren_report.pdf>.

HIBBS, M. (2001). 'Surrogacy—who will be left holding the baby?'. *Family Law*, 31: 736.

HIBBS, M., BARTON, C., AND BESWICK, J. (2001). 'Why Marry? Perceptions of the Affianced'. *Family Law*, 31: 197.

HITCHINGS, E. (2009a). 'Chaos or Consistency? Ancillary Relief in the "Everyday" Case', in J. Miles and R. Probert (eds) (2009), below.

HITCHINGS, E. (2009b). 'From pre-nups to post-nups: dealing with marital property agreements'. *Family Law*, 39: 1056.

HITCHINGS, E. (2010). 'The impact of recent ancillary relief jurisprudence in the "everyday" ancillary relief case'. *Child and Family Law Quarterly*, 22: 93.

HITCHINGS, E. AND SAGAR, S. (2007). 'The Adoption and Children Act 2002: A Level Playing Field for Same-Sex Adopters?'. *Child and Family Law Quarterly*, 19: 60.

ⓦ HM CPS INSPECTORATE AND HM INSPECTORATE OF CONSTABULARY (2004). *Violence at Home: A Joint Thematic Inspection of the Investigation and Prosecution of Cases Involving Domestic Violence*. <www.hmcpsi.gov.uk/documents/services/reports/THM/ DomVio0104Rep.pdf>.

⊛ HMCS, HO, AND CPS (2008). *Justice with Safety: Specialist Domestic Violence Courts Review 2007-08.* <www.cps.gov.uk/publications/equality/sdvc_review.html>.

⊛ HM GOVERNMENT (2009). *Together we can end violence against women and girls: a strategy.* <webarchive.nationalarchives.gov.uk/20100419081706/http://homeoffice.gov.uk/documents/vawg-strategy-2009/end-violence-against-women2835.pdf?view=Binary>.

HM GOVERNMENT (2010). *The Coalition: our programme for government.*

HM TREASURY (2003). *Every child matters*, Cm 5860. London: HMSO.

⊛ HM TREASURY AND INLAND REVENUE (2002). *The Child and Working Tax Credits: The Modernisation of Britain's Tax and Benefits System.* London: HM Treasury.

⊛ HM TREASURY, DFES, DWP, AND DTI (2004). *Choice for parents, the best start for children: A ten year strategy for childcare.* London: TSO.

⊛ HO (1998). *Supporting Families: a consultation document.* London: HMSO.

⊛ HO (1999). *Supporting Families: summary of responses to the consultation document.* London: TSO.

HO (2000). *Domestic Violence: Revised Circular to Police.* Home Office Circular No 19/2000.

⊛ HO (2003). *Safety and Justice: the Government's Proposals on Domestic Violence*, Cm 5847. <www.archive2.official-documents.co.uk/document/cm58/5847/5847.pdf>.

⊛ HO (2005). *Domestic Violence: A National Report.* <www.broken-rainbow.org.uk/research/domesticviolence51.pdf>.

⊛ HO (2006a). *National Domestic Violence Delivery Plan: Progress Report 2005/06.*

⊛ HO (2006b). *The Code of Practice for Victims of Crime.*

⊛ HO (2008). *Government Responsee to the Sixth Report from the Home Affairs Committee 2007-8 HC263: Domestic violence, forced marriage and "honour"-based violence.* Cm 7450. London: TSO. <www.official-documents.gov.uk/document/cm74/7450/7450.pdf>.

⊛ HO (2009). *National Domestic Violence Delivery Plan: Annual Progress Report 2008/9.* <webarchive.nationalarchives.gov.uk/20100418065544/http://www.homeoffice.gov.uk/documents/dom-violence-delivery-plan-08-092835.pdf?view=Binary>.

⊛ HODSON, D. (2007). '*Charman*: Sharing in the face of the Dragon'. <www.familylawweek.co.uk/site.aspx?i=ed672>.

HOFF, L. (1990). *Battered Women as Survivors.* London: Routledge.

HOGGETT, B. (1980). 'Ends and Means: The Utility of Marriage as a Legal Institution', in J. Eekelaar and S. Katz, (eds), *Marriage and Cohabitation in Contemporary Societies.* Toronto: Butterworths.

HOLCOMBE, L. (1983). *Wives and Property.* Toronto: University of Toronto Press.

⊛ HOME AFFAIRS SELECT COMMITTEE (2008). *Domestic violence, forced marriage and "honour"-based violence.* HC 263. London: TSO. <www.publications.parliament.uk/pa/cm200708/cmselect/cmhaff/263/26302.htm#evidence>.

HOPKINS, N. (2009). 'Regulating trusts of the home: private law and social policy'. *Law Quarterly Review*, 125: 310.

HORTON, M. (1995). 'Improving child support—a missed opportunity'. *Child and Family Law Quarterly*, 7: 26.

HOWE, D., SHEMMINGS, D., AND FEAST, J. (2001). 'Age at placement and adult adopted people's experience of being adopted'. *Child and Family Social Work*, 6: 337.

HOYLE, C. (1998). *Negotiating Domestic Violence*. Oxford: Clarendon Press.

HOYLE, C. AND SANDERS, A. (2000). 'Police Response to Domestic Violence: From Victim Choice to Victim Empowerment'. *British Journal of Criminology*, 40: 14.

HUMPHREYS, C. AND HARRISON, C. (2003). 'Focusing on safety—domestic violence and the role of child contact centres'. *Child and Family Law Quarterly*, 15: 237.

HUMPHREYS, C. AND KAYE, M. (1997). 'Third-party applications for protection orders: opportunities, ambiguities and traps'. *Journal of Social Welfare and Family Law*, 19: 403.

HUMPHREYS, C. AND THIARA, R. (2003). 'Neither justice nor protection: women's experiences of post-separation violence'. *Journal of Social Welfare and Family Law*, 25: 195.

ⓦ HUNT, J. AND MACLEOD, A. (2008). *Outcomes of applications to court for contact orders after parental separation or divorce. Briefing Note*. London: Ministry of Justice. <www.justice.gov.uk/publications/docs/outcomes-contact-orders-briefing-note.pdf>.

HUNT, J., MASSON, J., AND TRINDER, L. (2009). 'Shared Parenting: The Law, the Evidence and Guidance from Families need Fathers'. *Family Law*, 39: 831.

ⓦ HUTTON, J. (2006). *Ministerial statement: Child Support Redesign*. <webarchive.nationalarchives.gov.uk/+/http://www.dwp.gov.uk/aboutus/2006/24-07-06.asp>.

HUXTABLE, R. AND FORBES, K. (2004). '*Glass v United Kingdom*: maternal instinct v medical opinion'. *Child and Family Law Quarterly*, 16: 339.

IJZENDOORN, M. H. VAN AND JUFFER, F. (2005). 'Adoption Is a Successful Natural Intervention Enhancing Adopted Children's IQ and School Performance'. *Current Directions in Psychological Science*, 14: 326.

INGLEBY, R. (1989). 'Rhetoric and Reality: Regulation of Out-of-Court Activity in Matrimonial Proceedings'. *Oxford Journal of Legal Studies*, 9: 230.

ⓦ INLAND REVENUE (2004). Tax and civil partners, Rev BN 28. <webarchive.nationalarchives.gov.uk/20091222074811/http://www.hmrc.gov.uk/budget2005/revbn28.pdf>.

ⓦ INSTITUTE OF FISCAL STUDIES (2010). 'Conservatives to recognise one third of marriages in tax system'. <www.ifs.org.uk/pr/marriage_pr.pdf>.

JACKSON, E. (2002). 'Conception and the Irrelevance of the Welfare Principle'. *Modern Law Review*, 65: 176.

JACKSON, E. (2006). 'What is a Parent?', in A. Diduck and K. O'Donovan (eds), *Feminist Perspectives on Family Law*. Abingdon: Routledge-Cavendish.

JACKSON, E. AND WASOFF, F., WITH MACLEAN, M. AND DOBASH, R. (1993). 'Financial Support on Divorce: The Right Mixture of Rules and Discretion?'. *International Journal of Law and the Family*, 7: 230.

⚫ James, B. (2007). 'Domestic violence and ex parte applications: getting the affidavits right'. *Family Law Week*, December 2007. <www.familylawweek.co.uk/site.aspx?i=ed901>.

James, G. (2009). 'Mothers and fathers as parents and workers: family-friendly employment policies in an era of shifting identities'. *Journal of Social Welfare and Family Law*, 31: 271.

Johnson, M. (1999). 'A Biomedical Perspective on Parenthood', in A. Bainham, S. Day Sclater, and M. Richards (eds), *What is a Parent? A Socio-Legal Analysis*. Oxford: Hart Publishing.

⚫ Joint Committee on Human Rights (2003). *Third Report, Scrutiny of Bills: Progress Report*, HL 23/HC252 2003/04. London: HMSO.

⚫ Joint Committee on Human Rights (2004). *Fifteenth Report of Session 2003–04: Civil Partnership Bill*. HL Paper 136, HC 885. London: HMSO.

⚫ Joint Committee on Human Rights (2007). *Legislative Scrutiny: Child Maintenance and Other Payments Bill: Third Report of Session 2007-08*. HL Paper 28, HC 198. <www.publications.parliament.uk/pa/jt200708/jtselect/jtrights/28/28.pdf>.

⚫ Joint Committee on Human Rights (2009). *Legislative Scrutiny: Welfare Reform Bill…Fourteenth Report of Sesssion 2008-09*. HL Paper 78, HC 414. <www.publications.parliament.uk/pa/jt200809/jtselect/jtrights/78/78.pdf>.

Jones, S. (2007). 'Civil Partnerships and Social Security'. *Journal of Social Security Law*, 14: 9.

Kaganas, F. (1999a). '*B v B (Occupation Order)* and *Chalmers v Johns*: Occupation orders under the Family Law Act 1996'. *Child and Family Law Quarterly*, 11: 193.

Kaganas, F. (1999b). 'Contact, Conflict and Risk', in S. Day Sclater and C. Piper (eds), *Undercurrents of Divorce*. Aldershot: Ashgate.

Kaganas, F. (2000). '*Re L (Contact: Domestic Violence)* . . . Contact and domestic violence'. *Child and Family Law Quarterly*, 12: 311.

Kaganas, F. (2002). 'Shared parenting—a 70% solution'. *Child and Family Law Quarterly*, 14: 365.

Kaganas, F. (2007). 'Domestic Violence, Men's Groups and the Equivalence Argument', in A. Diduck and K. O'Donovan (eds), *Feminist Perspectives on Family Law*. Abingdon: Routledge-Cavendish.

Kaganas, F. (2010). 'Child protection, gender and rights', in J. Wallbank, S. Choudhry, and J. Herring (eds), *Rights, gender and family law*. Abingdon: Routledge.

Kaganas, F. and Day Sclater, S. (2004). 'Contact Disputes: Narrative Constructions of "Good" Parents'. *Feminist Legal Studies*, 12: 1.

Kaganas, F. and Diduck, A. (2004). 'Incomplete Citizens: Changing Images of Post-Separation Children'. *Modern Law Review*, 67: 959.

Kahn-Freund, O. (1952). 'Inconsistencies and Injustices in the Law of Husband and Wife'. *Modern Law Review*, 15: 133.

Kahn-Freund, O. (1955). 'Matrimonial Property Law in England', in W. Friedmann (ed), *Matrimonial Property Law*. London: Stevens.

KAHN-FREUND, O. (1959). 'Matrimonial Property—Some Recent Developments'. *Modern Law Review*, 22: 241.

KAHN-FREUND, O. (1967). 'The Law Commission: Reform of the Grounds of Divorce. The Field of Choice'. *Modern Law Review*, 30: 180.

KAHN-FREUND, O. (1971). 'Matrimonial Property and Equality Before the Law: Some Sceptical Reflections'. *Human Rights Journal*, 4: 493.

KAY, R. (2004). 'Whose Divorce is it anyway—the Human Rights Aspect'. *Family Law*, 34: 892.

KEATING, H. (1996). 'Shifting standards in the House of Lords—*Re H and others (Minors) (sexual abuse: standard of proof)*'. *Child and Family Law Quarterly*, 8: 157.

KEATING, H. (2009). 'Suspicions, sitting on the fence and standards of proof'. *Child and Family Law Quarterly*, 21: 230.

KEENAN, C. (2005). 'The Impact of *Cannings* on Civil Child Protection Cases'. *Journal of Social Welfare and Family Law*, 27: 173.

KEENAN, C. (2006). 'Lessons from America? Learning from child protection policy in the USA'. *Child and Family Law Quarterly*, 18: 43.

KELLY, L. (1999). *Domestic Violence Matters: an evaluation of a development project*, Home Office Research Study 193. London: Home Office.

KEWLEY, A. (1996). 'Pragmatism before principle: the limitations of civil law remedies for the victims of domestic violence'. *Journal of Social Welfare and Family Law*, 18: 1.

KIERNAN, K. AND MUELLER, G. (1998). *The Divorced and Who Divorces?* Centre for Analysis of Social Exclusion, CASE paper 7. <http://cprints.lse.ac.uk/6529/1/The_Divorced_and_Who_Divorces.pdf>.

KINGDOM, E. (2000). 'Cohabitation Contracts and the Democratization of Personal Relationships'. *Feminist Legal Studies*, 8: 5.

KIRTON, D., FEAST, J., AND HOWE, D., (2000). 'Searching, reunion and transracial adoption'. *Adoption and Fostering*, 24: 6.

KRIEKEN, R. VAN (2005). 'The "Best Interests" of the Child and Parental Separation: on the "Civilising of Parents" '. *Modern Law Review*, 68: 25.

KURKI-SUONIO, K. (2000). 'Joint Custody as an Interpretation of the best interests of the child in critical and comparative perspective'. *International Journal of Law, Policy and the Family*, 14: 183.

LAND REGISTRY (2008). *Review of the Land Registration Rules 2003: Report on consultation.* <www1.landregistry.gov.uk/assets/library/documents/report_on_consultation.pdf>.

LANGDRIDGE, D. AND BLYTH, E. (2001). 'Regulation of assisted conception services in Europe: Implications of the new reproductive technologies for "the family"'. *Journal of Social Welfare and Family Law*, 23: 45.

LAW COMMISSION (1966). *Reform of the Grounds of Divorce: The Field of Choice*, Law Com No 6. London: HMSO.

LAW COMMISSION (1969). *Report on Financial Provision in Matrimonial Proceedings*, Law Com No 25. London: HMSO.

LAW COMMISSION (1970). *Report on Nullity of Marriage*, Law Com No 33. London: HMSO.

LAW COMMISSION (1971). *Family Property Law*, Published Working Paper 42. London: HMSO.

LAW COMMISSION (1973a). *Report on Solemnisation of Marriage in England and Wales*, Law Com No 53. London: HMSO.

LAW COMMISSION (1973b). *First Report on Family Property: A New Approach*, Law Com No 52. London: HMSO.

LAW COMMISSION (1978). *Family Property: The Matrimonial Home (Co-ownership and Occupation Rights) and Household Goods*, Law Com No 86. London: HMSO.

LAW COMMISSION (1980). *The Financial Consequences of Divorce: The Basic Policy. A Discussion Paper*, Law Com No 103. London: HMSO.

LAW COMMISSION (1981). *The Financial Consequences of Divorce*, Law Com No 112. London: HMSO.

LAW COMMISSION (1982a). *The Implications of Williams & Glyn's Bank Ltd v Boland*, Law Com No 115. London: HMSO.

LAW COMMISSION (1982b). *Family Law: Illegitimacy*, Law Com No 118. London: HMSO.

LAW COMMISSION (1985a). *Polygamous Marriages: Capacity to Contract a Polygamous Marriage and Related Issues*, Law Com No 146. London: HMSO.

LAW COMMISSION (1985b). *Family Law Review of Child Law: Guardianship*, Working Paper 91. London: HMSO.

LAW COMMISSION (1988a). *Facing the Future: A Discussion Paper on the Ground for Divorce*, Law Com No 170. London: HMSO.

LAW COMMISSION (1988b). *Family Property: Matrimonial Property*, Law Com No 175. London: HMSO.

LAW COMMISSION (1988c). *Family Law Review of Child Law: Guardianship and Custody*, Law Com No 172. London: HMSO.

LAW COMMISSION (1990). *The Ground for Divorce*, Law Com No 192. London: HMSO.

LAW COMMISSION (1992). *Family Law: Domestic Violence and Occupation of the Family Home*, Law Com No 207. London: HMSO.

LAW COMMISSION (2002). *Sharing Homes: A Discussion Paper*, Law Com No 278. London: HMSO.

LAW COMMISSION (2006). *Cohabitation: The Financial Consequences of Relationship Breakdown*, Law Com CP 179. London: TSO. <www.lawcom.gov.uk/docs/cp179.pdf>.

LAW COMMISSION (2007). *Cohabitation: The Financial Consequences of Relationship Breakdown*, Law Com 307. London: TSO. <www.lawcom.gov.uk/docs/lc307.pdf>.

LAW COMMISSION (2008). *Tenth Programme of Law Reform*, Law Com No 311. London: TSO. <www.lawcom.gov.uk/docs/lc311.pdf>.

LAW COMMISSION (2009). *Conspiracy and Attempts,* Law Com No 318. London: TSO. <www.lawcom.gov.uk/docs/lc318.pdf>.

Law Reform Advisory Committee for Northern Ireland (2000). *Matrimonial Property*, Report No 10. Belfast: TSO.

⓪ Law Society (2002). *Cohabitation: the case for clear law*. London: Law Society.

⓪ Law Society (2003). *Financial Provision on Divorce: clarity and fairness*. London: The Law Society.

Law Society (2006). *Family Law Protocol*, 2nd edn. London: The Law Society.

Lawson, A. (1996). 'The things we do for love: detrimental reliance in the family home'. *Legal Studies*, 26: 218.

LCD (1990). *Judicial Statistics Annual Report for 1989*, Cm 1154. London: HMSO.

LCD (1992). *Judicial Statistics Annual Report for 1991*, Cm 1990. London: HMSO.

LCD (1993). *Looking to the Future—Mediation and the ground for divorce*, Cm 2424. London: HMSO.

LCD (1995). *Looking to the Future, Mediation and the Ground for Divorce*, Cm 2799. London: HMSO.

LCD (1999). 'Implementation of Family Law Act Part II Delayed Pilots Show Disappointing Response to Information Meetings'. Press Release No 159/99, 17 June.

LCD (2001). 'Divorce Law Reform—Government Proposes to Repeal Part II of the Family Law Act 1996'. Press Release No 20/01.

LCD (2002). *Moving Forward Together: A proposed strategy for marriage and relationship support for 2002 and beyond*.

Lee, N. (2010). *Revenue Law: Principles and Practice*, 28th edn. Croydon: Tolley.

Lee, R. (2008). '*Stack v Dowden*—a sequel'. *Law Quarterly Review*, 124: 209.

⓪ Legal Services Commission, *Funding Code Decision-making Guidance*. <www.legalservices.gov.uk/civil/guidance/funding_code.asp>.

⓪ Legal Services Commission, *Funding Code: Part 1—Criteria*. <www.legalservices.gov.uk/docs/civil_contracting/Funding_code_criteria_Jul07.pdf>.

Lewis, J. (1998). 'The problem of lone-mother families in twentieth-century Britain'. *Journal of Social Welfare and Family Law*, 20: 251.

Lewis, J. (2000). 'Family Policy in the Post-war Period', in S. Katz, J. Eekelaar, and M. Maclean (eds), *Cross Currents: Family Law and Policy in the US and England*. Oxford: OUP.

Lewis, J. (2001a). 'Debates and Issues regarding Marriage and Cohabitation in the British and American Literature'. *International Journal of Law, Policy and the Family*, 15: 159.

Lewis, J. (2001b). *The End of Marriage? Individualism and Intimate Relations*. Cheltenham: Edward Elgar.

Lewis, J. (2004). 'Adoption: the nature of policy shifts in England and Wales 1972–2002'. *International Journal of Law, Policy and the Family*, 18: 235.

LEWIS, J. (2009). 'Balancing "time to work" and "time to care": policy issues and implications for mothers, fathers and children'. *Child and Family Law Quarterly*, 21: 443.

LEWIS, J., WITH DATTA, J. AND SARRE, S. (1999). *Individualism and Commitment in Marriage and Cohabitation*, LCD Research Series No 8/99. London: Lord Chancellor's Department.

LEWIS, R. (2004). 'Making Justice Work: Effective Legal Interventions for Domestic Violence'. *British Journal of Criminology*, 44: 204.

ⓐ LIBERTY (2003). *Liberty's second reading briefing on the Domestic Violence, Crimes and Victims Bill in the House of Lords*. <www.liberty-human-rights.org.uk/pdfs/policy03/dec-03-domestic-violence-2nd-reading.pdf>.

LIM, H. (1996). 'Messages from a Rarely Visited Island: Duress and Lack of Consent in Marriage'. *Feminist Legal Studies*, 4: 195.

LIND, C. (2004). 'Sexuality and Same-Sex Relationships in Law', in B. Brooks-Gordon, L. Gelsthorpe, M. Johnson, and A. Bainham (eds), *Sexuality Repositioned*. Oxford: Hart Publishing.

LIND, C. AND HEWITT, T. (2009). 'Law and the complexities of parenting: parental status and parental function'. *Journal of Social Welfare and Family Law*, 31: 391.

LINDLEY, B. (1997). 'Open adoption—Is the door ajar?'. *Child and Family Law Quarterly*, 9: 115.

LINDLEY, B. (1999). 'State Intervention and Parental Autonomy in Children's Cases: Have We Got the Balance Right?', in A. Bainham, S. Day Sclater, and M. Richards (eds), *What is a Parent? A Socio-Legal Analysis*. Oxford—Portland, Oregon: Hart Publishing.

ⓐ LOCAL SAFEGUARDING CHILDREN BOARD, Haringey ('LSCB') (2009). *Serious Case Review: Baby Peter*. <www.haringeylscb.org/executive_summary_peter_final.pdf>.

LOGAN, J. AND SMITH, C. (2005). 'Face-to-Face Contact Post-Adoption: Views from the Triangles'. *British Journal of Social Work,* 35: 3.

ⓐ LORD LAMING (2003). *The Victoria Climbié Inquiry*, London: HMSO.

ⓐ LORD LESTER's Civil Partnership Bill 2002. <www.odysseustrust.org/civil_partnershipsindex.html>.

LOWE, N. (1997a). 'The Meaning and Allocation of Parental Responsibility—A Common Lawyer's Perspective'. *International Journal of Law, Policy and the Family*, 11: 192.

LOWE, N. (1997b). 'The changing face of adoption—the gift/donation model versus the contract/services model'. *Child and Family Law Quarterly*, 9: 371.

LOWE, N. AND DOUGLAS, G. (2007). *Bromley's Family Law*, 10th edn. Oxford: OUP.

LOWE, N., MURCH, M., BORKOWSKI, M., WEAVER, A., BECKFORD, V., WITH THOMAS, C. (1999). *Supporting Adoption—Reframing the approach*. London: BAAF.

LUCKOCK, B. AND HART, A. (2005). 'Adoptive family life and adoption support: policy ambivalence and the development of effective services'. *Child and Family Social Work*, 10: 125.

LUNDBERG, S., POLLAK, R., AND WALES, T. (1997). 'Do Husbands and Wives Pool Their Resources? Evidence from the United Kingdom Child Benefit'. *Journal of Human Resources*, 32: 463.

LUNNEY, M. AND OLIPHANT, K. (2010). *Tort Law: Text and Materials*, 4th edn. Oxford: OUP.

LYON, N., BARNES, M., AND SWEIRY, D. (2006). *Families with children in Britain: Findings from the 2004 Families and Children Study*, Department for Work and Pensions Research Report No 340. London: Corporate Document Services.

MACLEAN, M. AND EEKELAAR, J. (1993). 'Child Support: The British Solution'. *International Journal of Law and the Family*, 7: 205.

MACLEAN, M. AND EEKELAAR, J. (1997). *The Parental Obligation: A study of parenthood across households*. Oxford: Hart Publishing.

MADDEN DEMPSEY, M. (2006). 'What counts as domestic violence? A conceptual analysis'. *William and Mary Journal of Women and the Law*, 12: 301.

MANSFIELD, P., REYNOLDS, J., AND ARAI, L. (1999). 'What policy developments would be most likely to secure an improvement in marital stability?', in *One plus one Marriage and Partnership Research, High Divorce Rates: the state of the evidence on reasons and remedies*, Lord Chancellor's Department Research Series 2/99, vol. 2, paper 7. Summary at <www.dca.gov.uk/research/1999/299-7esfr.htm>.

MAPLETHORPE, N. ET AL. (2010). *Families with Children in Britain: Findings from the 2008 Families and Children Study (FACS)*. DWP RR 656. <research.dwp.gov.uk/asd/asd5/rports2009-2010/rrep656.pdf>.

MARSH, A. AND VEGERIS, S. (2004). *The British Lone Parent Cohort and their Children 1991–2001*, DWP Research Report No 209. Leeds: Corporate Document Service.

MARSHALL, A. (2003). 'Comedy of Adoption—When is a parent not a parent?'. *Family Law*, 33: 840.

MASSON, J. (1992). 'Managing risk under the Children Act 1989: Diversion in Child Care'. *Child Abuse Review*, 1992: 103.

MASSON, J. (2000). 'Thinking about contact—a social or legal problem?'. *Child and Family Law Quarterly*, 12: 15.

MASSON, J. (2003). 'The impact of the Adoption and Children Act 2002—Part 2—The provision of services for children and families'. *Family Law*, 33: 644.

MASSON, J. (2004). 'Human rights in child protection: emergency action and its impact', in P. Lødrup and E. Modvar (eds), *Family Life and Human Rights*. Oslo: Gyldendal Norsk Forlag AS.

MASSON, J. (2005). 'Emergency intervention to protect children: using and avoiding legal controls'. *Child and Family Law Quarterly*, 17: 75.

MASSON, J. (2006). 'Fair trials in Child Protection'. *Journal of Social Welfare and Family Law*, 28: 15.

MASSON, J. (2007). 'Reforming care proceedings—time for a review'. *Child and Family Law Quarterly,* 19: 411.

MASSON J. (2008). 'Controlling costs and maintaining services—the reform of legal aid fees for care proceedings.' *Child and Family Law Quarterly,* 20: 425.

MASSON, J., BAILEY-HARRIS, R., AND PROBERT, R. (2008). *Cretney: Principles of Family Law,* 8th edn. London: Sweet & Maxwell.

MAUGHAN, B., COLLISHAW, S., AND PICKLES, A. (1998). 'School Achievement and Adult Qualifications among Adoptees: A Longitudinal Study'. *Journal of Child Psychology and Psychiatry,* 39: 669.

MAY, V. AND SMART, C. (2004). 'Silence in court?—hearing children in residence and contact disputes'. *Child and Family Law Quarterly,* 16: 305.

McCAFFERTY, C. (2002). 'Gays, Transsexuals and the Right to Marry'. *Family Law,* 32: 362.

McCANDLESS, J. (2008). 'Status and anomaly: Re D (contact and parental responsibility: lesbian mothers and known father) [2006] EWHC 2 (Fam), [2006] 1 FCR 556'. *Journal of Social Welfare and Family Law,* 30: 63.

McCANDLESS, J. AND SHELDON, S. (2010). 'The Human Fertilisation and Embryology Act (2008) and the Tenacity of the Sexual Family Form'. *Modern Law Review,* 73: 175.

McCANN, K. (1985). 'Battered women and the law: the limits of the legislation', in J. Brophy and C. Smart (eds), *Women in Law: explorations in law, family and sexuality.* London: Routledge.

McCOLGAN, A. (1993). 'In Defence of Battered Women who Kill'. *Oxford Journal of Legal Studies,* 13: 508.

McGLYNN, C. (2000). 'Ideologies of motherhood in European Community sex equality law'. *European Law Journal,* 6: 29.

McGLYNN, C. (2001). 'European Union Family Values: Ideologies of "Family" and "Motherhood" in European Union Law'. *Social Politics,* 8: 325.

McLELLAN, D. (1996). 'Contract Marriage—The Way Forward or Dead End?'. *Journal of Law and Society,* 23: 234.

MEE, J. (1999). *The Property Rights of Cohabitees.* Oxford: Hart Publishing.

MEE, J. (2004). 'Property rights and personal relationships: reflections on reform'. *Legal Studies,* 24: 414.

MEE, J. (2009). 'The Limits of Proprietary Estoppel: *Thorner v Majors*'. *Child and Family Law Quarterly,* 21: 367.

MIDDLETON, S., ASHWORTH, K., AND BRAITHWAITE, I. (1997). *Small fortunes: spending on children, childhood poverty and parental sacrifice.* York: Joseph Rowntree Foundation.

MILES, J. (2001). 'Domestic Violence', in J. Herring (ed), *Family Law: Issues, Debates, Policy.* Cullompton: Willan Publishing.

MILES, J. (2003). 'Property law v family law: resolving the problems of family property'. *Legal Studies,* 23: 624.

MILES, J. (2005). 'Principle or Pragmatism in Ancillary Relief: the Virtues of Flirting with Academic Theories and Other Jurisdictions'. *International Journal of Law, Policy and the Family*, 19: 242.

MILES, J. (2008). '*Charman v Charman (no 4)*: making sense of need, compensation and equal sharing after *Miller/McFarlane*'. *Child and Family Law Quarterly*, 20: 378.

MILES, J. (2009). '*Radmacher v Granatino*: upping the ante-nuptial agreement'. *Child and Family Law Quarterly*, 21: 513.

MILES, J. (2011). 'Responsibility in Family Finance and Property Law', in J. Bridgeman, H. Keating, and C. Lind (eds), *Regulating Family Responsibilities*. Aldershot: Ashgate.

MILES, J. AND PROBERT, R. (eds) (2009). *Sharing Lives, Dividing Assets: an inter-disciplinary study*. Oxford: Hart Publishing.

MILL, J. S. (1869). *Three Essays: On Liberty, Representative Government and the Subjection of Women* (1975) R. Wollheim (ed). Oxford: OUP.

MILLAR, J. (1996). 'Family Obligations and Social Policy: The Case of Child Support'. *Policy Studies*, 17: 181.

MILLER, G. (2003). 'Pre-nuptial Agreements and Financial Provision', in G. Miller (ed), *Frontiers of Family Law*. Dartmouth: Ashgate.

MILLWARD, E. (2008). 'The Domestic Violence, Crime and Victims Act 2004: is it working?'. *Family Law*, 38: 493.

MIRRLEES-BLACK, C. (1999). *Domestic Violence: Findings from a new British Crime Survey self-completion questionnaire,* Home Office Research Study 191. London: HMSO.

MITCHELL, M., DICKENS, S., AND O'CONNNOR, W. (2009). *Same-Sex Couples and the Impact of Legislative Changes*. London: NatCen. <www.natcen.ac.uk/study/same-sex-couples>.

MNOOKIN, R. (1975). 'Child Custody Adjudication: Judicial Functions in the Face of Indeterminacy'. *Law and Contemporary Problems*, 39: 225.

MNOOKIN, R. AND KORNHAUSER, L. (1979). 'Bargaining in the Shadow of the Law: The Case of Divorce'. *Yale Law Journal*, 88: 950.

MOJ (2007). *Separate representation of children. Summary of responses to a consultation paper*. CP(R) 20/06. London: HMSO. <http://www.justice.gov.uk/docs/cp2006-responses. pdf>.

MOJ (2008). *The Public Law Outline. Guide to Case Management in Public Law Proceedings*. London: HMSO. <www.bournemouth-poole-lscb.org.uk/inter-agency_safeguarding_ procedures/part_one/pictures/content34/public_law_outline.pdf>.

MOJ (2009). *Judicial and Court Statistics 2008*. Cm 7697. London: TSO. <www.justice. gov.uk/publications/judicialandcourtstatistics.htm>.

MOJ (2010). *Judicial and Court Statistics 2009*. <www.justice.gov.uk/publications/docs/ judicial-court-statistics-2009.pdf>.

MOFFATT, P. AND THOBURN, J. (2001). 'Outcomes of permanent family placement for children of minority ethnic origin'. *Child and Family Social Work*, 6: 13.

MOLONEY, L. (2001). 'Do Fathers 'win' or do mothers "lose"? A Preliminary analysis of closely contested parenting judgments in the Family Court of Australia'. *International Journal of Law, Policy and the Family*, 15: 363.

MOONEY, A., OLIVER, C., AND SMITH, M. (2009). *Impact of Family Breakdown on Children's Well-Being. Evidence Review. Research Report DCSF-RR113*. London: DfCSF and Thomas Coram Research Unit. <www.education.gov.uk/research/data/uploadfiles/DCSF-RR113.pdf>.

MOOR, P. AND LE GRICE, V. (2006). 'Periodical payments orders following *Miller* and *McFarlane*—a series of unfortunate events'. *Family Law*, 36: 655.

MORGAN, P. (2000). *Marriage-Lite: the Rise of Cohabitation and its Consequences*. London: Institute for the Study of Civil Society.

MORLEY, R. AND MULLENDER, A. (1994). *Preventing Domestic Violence to Women*, Crime Prevention Unit Series Paper No 48. London: Home Office.

MORRIS, A. (2000). 'Couples and benefits claims: a comment on *Relying on the State, Relying on Each Other*'. *Journal of Social Security Law*, 7: 228.

MORRIS, A. AND GELSTHORPE, L. (2000). 'Re-visioning Men's Violence Against Female Partners'. *The Howard Journal*, 39: 412.

MORRIS, A. AND NOTT, S. (2005). 'Marriage Rites and Wrongs: Challenges to Orthodoxy'. *Journal of Social Welfare and Family Law*, 27: 43.

MORRIS, C. (2005). 'Divorce in a multi-faith society'. *Family Law*, 35: 727.

MORTIMER COMMISSION (1966). *Putting Asunder, A Divorce Law for Contemporary Society*. London: SPCK.

MOSTYN, N. (1999). 'The Green Paper on Child Support—Children First: a new approach to child support'. *Family Law*, 29: 95.

MULLENDER, A. AND MORLEY, R. (1994). 'Context and Content of a New Agenda', in A. Mullender and R. Morley (eds), *Children Living with Domestic Violence*. London: Whiting and Birch.

MÜLLER-FREIENFELS, W. (2003). 'The Emergence of *Droit de Famille* and *Familienrecht* in Continental Europe and the Introduction of Family Law in England'. *Journal of Family History*, 28: 31.

MUMFORD, A. (2007). 'Working Towards Credit for Parenting: a consideration of tax credits as a feminist enterprise', in A. Diduck and K. O'Donovan (eds), *Feminist Perspectives on Family Law*. Abingdon: Routledge-Cavendish.

MURPHY, J. (2000). 'Rationality and Cultural Pluralism in the Non-Recognition of Foreign Marriages'. *International and Comparative Law Quarterly*, 49: 643.

MURPHY, J. (2003). 'Children in need: the limits of local authority accountability'. *Legal Studies*, 23: 103.

MURPHY, J. (2004). 'Same-sex marriage in England: a role for human rights?'. *Child and Family Law Quarterly*, 16: 245.

ⓦ NATIONAL AUDIT OFFICE (2007). *Legal aid and mediation for people involved in family breakdown*. HC 256. London: TSO. <www.nao.org.uk/publications/nao_reports/06-07/0607256.pdf>.

NEALE, B. AND SMART, C. (1999). 'In Whose Best Interests? Theorising Family Life Following Parental Separation or Divorce', in S. Day Sclater and C. Piper (eds), *Undercurrents of Divorce*. Aldershot: Ashgate.

NEIL, E. (2000). 'The reasons why young children are placed for adoption: findings from a recently placed sample and a discussion of implications for subsequent identity development'. *Child and Family Social Work*, 5: 303.

NEIL, E. (2009). 'Post-Adoption Contact and Openness in Adoptive Parents' Minds: Consequences for Children's Development'. *British Journal of Social Work*, 39: 5.

ⓦ NEUBERGER, D. (2008). 'The conspirators, the tax man, the Bill of Rights, and a bit about lovers'. Chancery Bar Association Annual Lecture, 10 March. <www.chba.org.uk/__data/assets/pdf_file/0008/58256/Lord_Neuberger_Lecture.pdf>.

NEUBERGER, D. (2009). 'The Stuffing of Minerva's Owl? Taxonomy and Taxidermy in Equity'. *Cambridge Law Journal*, 68: 537.

ⓦ NEWCASTLE CENTRE FOR FAMILY STUDIES (2001a). *Information Meetings and Associated Provisions within the Family Law Act 1996: Key Findings from Research*. <www.dca.gov.uk/family/fla/summary/brpaper.pdf>.

ⓦ NEWCASTLE CENTRE FOR FAMILY STUDIES (2001b). *Information Meetings and Associated Provisions within the Family Law Act 1996: Summary of the Final Evaluation Report*. London: LCD. <www.dca.gov.uk/family/fla/fullrep.pdf>.

ⓦ NEWCASTLE CENTRE FOR FAMILY STUDIES (2004). *Picking up the pieces: marriage and divorce two years after information provision*. <www.dca.gov.uk/pubs/reports/family2004-webpageintro.htm>.

ⓦ NOON, R. (2008). 'Compensation for Domestic Abuse after *Singh v Bhakar*'. *Family Law Week* September 2009. <www.familylawweek.co.uk/site.aspx?i=ed25932>.

NORRIE, A. (2010). 'The Coroners and Justice Act 2009—partial defences to murder (1) loss of control'. *Criminal Law Review*, 2010: 275.

NORRIE, K. (2000). 'Marriage is for heterosexuals—may the rest of us be saved from it'. *Child and Family Law Quarterly*, 12: 363.

O'BRIEN, K. AND ZAMOSTNY, K. (2003). 'Understanding Adoptive Families: An Integrative Review of Empirical Research and Future Directions for Counseling Psychology'. *The Counseling Psychologist*, 31: 679.

O'DONNELL, K. (2004). '*Re C (Welfare of Child: Immunisation)*—Room to refuse? Immunisation, welfare and the role of parental decision-making'. *Child and Family Law Quarterly*, 16: 213.

O'DONOVAN, K. (1982). 'Should All Maintenance of Spouses be Abolished?'. *Modern Law Review*, 45: 424.

O'DONOVAN, K. (1985). *Sexual Divisions in Law*. London: Weidenfeld & Nicolson.

O'Donovan, K. (1993). *Family Law Matters*. London: Pluto Press.

O'Donovan, K. (2000). 'Interpretations of Children's Identity Rights', in D. Fottrell (ed), *Revisiting Children's Rights*. The Hague; Boston: Kluwer Law International.

O'Keeffe, M. et al (2007). *UK Study of Abuse and Neglect of Older People: prevalence survey report*. London: NatCen.

O'Leary, L., Natamba, E., Jefferies, J., and Wilson, B. (2010). 'Fertility and partnership status in the last two decades'. *Population Trends*, 140: 5.

O'Neill, O. (1992). 'Children's Rights and Children's Lives'. *International Journal of Law and the Family*, 6: 24.

O'Neill, R. (2005). *Fiscal Policy and the Family*. London: Civitas.

OECD (2008). *Family Database: marriage and divorce rates*. <www.oecd.org/dataoecd/4/19/40321815.pdf>.

Oldham, M. (2001). 'Financial Obligations Within the Family—Aspects of Intergenerational Maintenance and Succession in England and France'. *Cambridge Law Journal*, 60: 128.

ONS (2003). *Census 2001 National Report for England and Wales*. London: TSO.

ONS (2004). *Living in Britain: General Household Survey 2002*. London: TSO.

ONS (2005a). *Social Trends*, 35. London: HMSO.

ONS (2005b). *Focus on Ethnicity and Identity*. London: HMSO.

ONS (2006a). *Marriage, divorce and adoption statistics*, Series FM2, no 31. London: HMSO.

ONS (2006b). *Social Trends*, 36. London: HMSO.

ONS (2007). *Focus on Families*. London: Palgrave Macmillan. <www.statistics.gov.uk/focuson/families/>.

ONS (2008). 'Report: Divorces in England and Wales during 2007'. *Population Trends*, 133: 71.

ONS (2009a). *Social Trends*, 39. <www.statistics.gov.uk/downloads/theme_social/Social-Trends40/ST40_Ch02.pdf>.

ONS (2009b). Marriage, divorce and adoption statistics, Series FM2 no 34. <www.statistics.gov.uk/downloads/theme_population/FM2no34/FM2_No34.pdf>.

ONS (2009c). *Statistical bulletin: Who is having babies?* <www.statistics.gov.uk/pdfdir/births1209.pdf>.

ONS (2010a). *Divorces: England and Wales rate at 29 year low*. <www.statistics.gov.uk/cci/nugget.asp?id=170>.

ONS (2010b). *Marriages: registrations in England and Wales remain stable*. <www.statistics.gov.uk/cci/nugget_print.asp?ID=322>.

ONS (2010c). *Marriage Statistics 2008, provisional*. <www.statistics.gov.uk/downloads/theme_population/Marriages_2008_provisional.xls>.

ⓦ ONS (2010d). *Marital Status population projections, 2008 based*. <www.statistics.gov.uk/pdfdir/marr0610.pdf>.

ⓦ ONS (2010e). *Social Trends*, 40. London: TSO. <www.statistics.gov.uk/socialtrends/>.

ⓦ ONS (2010f). *Civil Partnerships in the UK*. <www.statistics.gov.uk/pdfdir/cpuk0810.pdf>.

ORMEROD, D. (2008). *Smith and Hogan Criminal Law*, 12th edn. Oxford: OUP.

PAHL, J. (1985). *Private Violence and Public Policy: the needs of battered women and the response of public services*. London: Routledge and Kegan Paul.

PAHL, J. (2005). 'Individualisation in Couple Finances: who pays for the children?'. *Social Policy and Society*, 4: 381.

ⓦ PARADINE, K. AND WILKINSON, J. (2004). *Protection and Accountability: The Reporting, Investigation and Prosecution of Domestic Violence Cases*. London: HMIC.

PARKER, S. (1991). 'Child Support in Australia: Children's Rights or Public Interest?'. *International Journal of Law and the Family*, 5: 24.

PARKER, S. (1992). 'Rights and Utility in Anglo-Australian Family Law'. *Modern Law Review*, 55: 311.

PARKINSON, P. (2003). 'Child Protection, Permanency Planning and Children's Right to Family Life'. *International Journal of Law, Policy and the Family*, 17: 147.

PARKINSON, P. (2007). 'Reengineering the Child Support Scheme: An Australian Perspective on the British Government's Proposals'. *Modern Law Review*, 70: 812.

PARKINSON, P., CASHMORE, J., AND SINGLE, J. (2007). 'Parents' and children's views on talking to judges in parenting disputes in Australia'. *International Journal of Law, Policy and the Family*, 21: 84.

PATEL, T. (2007). 'Theorising the racial identity development of transracial adoptees. A symbolic interactionist perspective'. *Adoption and Fostering*, 31: 32.

PEACEY, V. AND HUNT, J. (2008). *Problematic contact after separation and divorce? A national survey of parents*. London: One Parent Families/Gingerbread.

PERRY, A. (2000). 'Lancashire County Council v B. Section 31—threshold or barrier?'. *Child and Family Law Quarterly*, 12: 301.

PERRY, A., DOUGLAS, G., MURCH, M., BADER, K., AND BORKOWSKI, M. (2000). *How parents cope financially on marriage breakdown*. London: Family Policy Studies Centre/Joseph Rowntree.

PHILLIPS, R. (1991). *Untying the Knot: A Short History of Divorce*. Cambridge: CUP.

PHILLIPSON, G. (2003). 'Transforming Breach of Confidence? Towards a Common Law Right of Privacy under the Human Rights Act'. *Modern Law Review*, 66: 726.

PICKFORD, R. (1999). 'What is a Parent? A Socio-Legal Analysis', in A. Bainham, S. Day Sclater, and M. Richards (eds), *What is a Parent? A Socio-Legal Analysis*. Oxford and Portland Oregon: Hart Publishing.

PIPER, C. (1996). 'Norms and Negotiation in Mediation and Divorce', in M. Freeman (ed), *Divorce: Where Next?* Aldershot: Dartmouth.

PIPER, C. AND KAGANAS, F. (1997). 'Family Law Act 1996, section 1(d)—how will "they" know there is a risk of violence?'. *Child and Family Law Quarterly*, 9: 269.

PIRRIE, J. (2003). 'Report of the Child Support Agency, March 2002'. *Family Law*, 33: 105.

PIRRIE, J. (2006). 'Child support in danger'. *Solicitors Journal*, 150: 1089.

PIRRIE, J. (2007). 'The legal dig'. *New Law Journal*, 16 March, 382.

PISKA, N. (2008). 'Intention, Fairness and the Presumption of Resulting Trust after *Stack v Dowden*'. *Modern Law Review*, 71: 120.

PISKA, N. (2009). 'Constructing Trusts and Constructing Intention', in M. Dixon (ed), *Modern Studies in Property Law, volume 5*. Oxford: Hart Publishing.

PIZZEY, E. (1974). *Scream Quietly or the Neighbours will Hear*. London: IF Books.

PLATT, J. (2008). 'The Domestic Violence, Crime and Victims Act 2004 Part 1: is it working?'. *Family Law*, 38: 642.

PLATT, J., ASOKAN, M., FINDLAY, L., AND TRUMAN, D. (2009). *Injunctions and Orders against Anti-Social or Violent Individuals*. Bristol: Jordans Publishing.

PLAYDON, Z. (2004). 'Intersecting Oppressions: Ending Discrimination Against Lesbians, Gay Men and Trans People in the UK', in B. Brooks-Gordon, L. Gelsthorpe, M. Johnson, and A. Bainham (eds), *Sexuality Repositioned*. Oxford: Hart Publishing.

POULTER, S. (1998). *Ethnicity, Law and Human Rights*. Oxford: OUP.

PRACTICE DIRECTION: Residence and Contact Orders: Domestic Violence and Harm (2008).<www.hmcourts-service.gov.uk/cms/files/pd-residence-contact-orders-domestic-violence-090508.pdf>.

PRACTICE DIRECTION: Public Law Proceedings Guide to Case Management (2010). <www.judiciary.gov.uk/NR/rdonlyres/3FEA2F29-47D5-4BEB-8DB2-19B9EDD1ABC5/0/public_law_outline_PD_April_2010.pdf>.

PRICE, D. (2009). 'Pension Accumulation and Gendered Household Structures: what are the implications of changes in family formation for future financial inequality?', in J. Miles and R. Probert (eds) (2009), above.

PROBERT, R. (1999). 'The controversy of equality and the Matrimonial Causes Act 1923'. *Child and Family Law Quarterly*, 11: 33.

PROBERT, R. (2001). 'Trusts and the modern woman—establishing an interest in the family home'. *Child and Family Law Quarterly*, 13: 275.

PROBERT, R. (2002a). 'When are we married? Void, non-existent and presumed marriages'. *Legal Studies*, 22: 398.

PROBERT, R. (2002b). 'Sharing Homes—a Long-awaited Paper'. *Family Law*, 32: 834.

PROBERT, R. (2004a). 'Family Law—a Modern Concept?'. *Family Law*, 34: 901.

PROBERT, R. (2004b). 'Lord Hardwicke's Marriage Act—Vital Change 250 Years On?'. *Family Law*, 34: 585.

PROBERT, R. (2004c). 'Cohabitation in Twentieth Century England and Wales: Law and Policy'. *Law and Policy*, 26: 13.

PROBERT, R. (2004d). '*Sutton v Mischon de Reya and Gawor & Co*—Cohabitation contracts and Swedish sex slaves'. *Child and Family Law Quarterly*, 16: 453.

PROBERT, R. (2005a). 'How Would *Corbett v Corbett* be Decided Today?'. *Family Law*, 35: 382.

PROBERT, R. (2005b). 'The wedding of the Prince of Wales: royal privileges and human rights'. *Child and Family Law Quarterly*, 17: 363.

PROBERT, R. (2007a). '*Hyde v Hyde*: defining or defending marriage?'. *Child and Family Law Quarterly*, 19: 322.

PROBERT, R. (2007b). 'A Review of Cohabitation: The Financial Consequences of Relationship Breakdown'. *Family Law Quarterly*, 41: 521.

PROBERT (2008a). 'Hanging on the telephone: *City of Westminster v IC*'. *Child and Family Law Quarterly*, 20: 395.

PROBERT, R. (2008b). 'Equality in the family home?'. *Feminist Legal Studies*, 15: 341.

PROBERT, R. (2009a). 'Parental Responsibility and Children's Partnership Choices', in R. Probert, S. Gilmore, and J. Herring (eds), *Responsible Parents and Parental Responsibility*. Oxford: Hart Publishing.

PROBERT, R. (2009b). *Marriage Law and Practice in the Long Eighteenth Century: a reassessment*. Cambridge: CUP.

PROBERT, R. (2009c). 'Cohabitation: Current Legal Solutions'. *Current Legal Problems*, 62: 316.

PROBERT, R. (2009d). 'The Cohabitation Bill'. *Family Law*, 39: 150.

PROBERT, R. AND BARLOW, A. (2000). 'Displacing marriage—diversification and harmonisation within Europe'. *Child and Family Law Quarterly*, 12: 153.

PROBERT, R., GILMORE, S., AND HERRING, J. (eds) (2009). *Responsible Parents and Parental Responsibility*. Oxford: Hart Publishing.

QUAID, S. AND ITZIN, C. (2000). 'The criminal justice response to women who kill: an interview with Helena Kennedy', in J. Hanmer and C. Itzin (eds), *Home Truths About Domestic Violence: feminist influences on policy and practice*. London: Routledge.

QUINTON, D. AND SELWYN, J. (1998). 'Contact with birth parents in adoption—a response to Ryburn'. *Child and Family Law Quarterly*, 10: 349.

QUINTON, D. AND SELWYN, J. (2006). 'Adoption: research, policy and practice'. *Child and Family Law Quarterly*, 18: 459.

RAITT, F. (1996). 'Domestic violence and divorce mediation'. *Journal of Social Welfare and Family Law*, 18: 11.

RAKE, K. (2000). *Women's Incomes over the Lifetime*. London: TSO.

REECE, H. (1996). 'The Paramountcy Principle. Consensus or Construct?'. *Current Legal Problems*, 49: 267.

REECE, H. (2003). *Divorcing Responsibly*. Oxford: Hart Publishing.

REECE, H. (2006). 'The End of Domestic Violence'. *Modern Law Review*, 69: 770.

REECE, H. (2009). 'The Degradation of Parental Responsibility', in R. Probert, S. Gilmore, and J. Herring (eds), *Responsible Parents and Parental Responsibility*. Oxford and Portland, Oregon: Hart Publishing.

RESOLUTION (2000). *Fairness for families: proposals for reform of the law on cohabitation*. London: SFLA.

RESOLUTION (2010). *Family agreements: seeking certainty to reduce disputes*. London: Resolution.

RESPECT (2010). *Respect multi-site research into perpetrator programme outcomes*. <www.respect.uk.net/pages/respect-multi-site-research-into-perpetrator-programme-outcomes.html>.

RHEINSTEIN, M. (1972). *Marriage Stability, Divorce and the Law*. London: University of Chicago Press.

RHOADES, H. AND BOYD, S. (2004). 'Reforming custody laws: A comparative study'. *International Journal of Law, Policy and the Family*, 18: 119.

RHOADES, H. (2002). 'The "No Contact Mother": Reconstructions of Motherhood in the Era of the "New Father"'. *International Journal of Law, Policy and the Family*, 16: 71.

RICHARDS, M. (1995). 'But what about the children? Some reflections on the divorce White Paper'. *Child and Family Law Quarterly*, 7: 223.

RICHARDS, M. (1996). 'Divorce Numbers and Divorce Legislation'. *Family Law*, 26: 151.

ROBERTS, M. (1992). 'Who is in charge? Reflections on recent research and the role of the mediator'. *Journal of Social Welfare and Family Law*, 13: 372.

ROBERTS, M. (1996). 'Family Mediation and the Interests of Women—Facts and Fears'. *Family Law*, 26: 239.

ROBERTS, M. (2000). 'Children by Donation: Do they have a Claim to their Genetic Parentage?', in J. Bridgeman and D. Monk (eds), *Feminist Perspectives on Child Law*. London: Cavendish.

ROBINSON, A. AND COOK, D. (2006). 'Understanding Victim Retraction in Cases of Domestic Violence: Specialist Domestic Violence Courts, Government Policy, and Victim-Centred Justice'. *Contemporary Justice Review*, 9: 189.

ROE, S. (2009). 'Intimate violence: 2007/08 BCS', in D. Povey et al (eds), *Homicides, Firearm Offences and Intimate Violence 2007/08: supplementary volume 2 to Crime in England and Wales 2007/08*. Home Office Statistical Bulletin 02/09. <rds.homeoffice.gov.uk/rds/pdfs09/hosb0209.pdf>.

ROE, S. (2010). 'Intimate violence: 2008/09 BCS', in K. Smith et al (eds), *Homicides, Firearm Offences and Intimate Violence 2008/09: supplementary volume 2 to Crime in*

England and Wales 2008/09. Home Office Statistical Bulletin 01/10. <rds.homeoffice.gov. uk/rds/pdfs10/hosb0110.pdf>.

● ROGERSON, C. (2002). *Developing Spousal Support Guidelines in Canada: Beginning the Discussion—Background Paper*. <www.justice.gc.ca/eng/pi/fcy-fea/spo-epo/g-ld/ss-pae/ pdf/ss-pae.pdf>.

ROSS, A. AND SACKER, A. (2010). 'Understanding the dynamics of attitude change', in A. Park et al (eds), *British Social Attitudes, the 26th Report*. London: Sage.

ROTHERHAM, C. (2004). 'The Property Rights of Unmarried Cohabitees: the Case for Reform'. *Conveyancer and Property Lawyer*, 68: 268.

ROWTHORN, R. (1999). 'Marriage and trust: some lessons from economics'. *Cambridge Journal of Economics*, 23: 661.

ROYAL COMMISSION ON MARRIAGE AND DIVORCE (1956). Cm 9678. London: HMSO.

RUMNEY, P. (1999). 'When Rape isn't Rape: Court of Appeal Sentencing Practice in Cases of Marital and Relationship Rape'. *Oxford Journal of Legal Studies*, 19: 243.

RUSHTON, A. (2003). 'Support for adoptive families. A review of current evidence on problems, needs and effectiveness'. *Adoption and Fostering*, 27: 41.

RUSHTON, A. AND MINNIS, H. (2000). 'Research review: Transracial placements'. *Adoption and Fostering*, 24: 53.

RYBURN, M. (1998a). 'In whose best interests?—post-adoption contact with the birth family'. *Child and Family Law Quarterly*, 10: 53.

RYBURN, M. (1998b). 'A new model of welfare: Re-asserting the value of kinship for children in state care'. *Social Policy and Administration*, 32: 28.

SAGAR, T. AND HITCHINGS, E. (2007). 'More adoptions, More Quickly': A Study of Social Workers' Responses to the Adoption and Children Act 2002. *Journal of Social Welfare and Family Law*, 29: 199.

SALTER, D. (2007). 'Couples, Children and Taxation—The Need for Consistency and Coherence' in R. Probert (ed), *Family Life and the Law: Under One Roof*. Dartmouth: Ashgate.

SANDLAND, R. (2000). 'Not "Social Justice": the Housing Association, the Judges, the Tenant and his Lover'. *Feminist Legal Studies*, 8: 227.

SCHERPE, J. (2007a). 'A comparative view of pre-nuptial agreements'. *International Journal of Family Law*, 2007: 18.

SCHERPE, J. (2007b). 'Family and private life, ambits and pieces'. *Child and Family Law Quarterly*, 19: 390.

SCHERPE, J (ed) (2011). *Marital Agreements and Private Autonomy in Comparative Perspective*. Oxford: Hart Publishing.

SCHNEIDER, C. (1992). 'Discretion and Rules: a lawyer's view', in K. Hawkins (ed), *The Uses of Discretion*. Oxford: OUP.

SCHNEIDER, E. (1994). 'The Violence of Privacy', in M. Fineman and R. Mykitiuk (eds), *The Public Nature of Private Violence*. New York: Routledge.

SCHOFIELD, G. (2010). *Bankruptcy and Divorce: a Practical Guide for the Family Lawyer*. Bristol: Family Law.

SCHUZ, R. (1993). 'Divorce Reform'. *Family Law*, 23: 630.

SCHUZ, R. (1996). 'Divorce and Ethnic Minorities', in M. Freeman (ed), *Divorce: Where Next?* Aldershot: Dartmouth.

SCOTT, E. (2002). 'Marital commitment and the legal regulation of divorce', in A. Dnes and R. Rowthorn (eds), *The Law and Economics of Marriage and Divorce*. Cambridge: CUP.

SCOTT, J. AND DEX. S. (2009). 'Paid and unpaid work: can policy improve gender inequalities?', in J. Miles and R. Probert (eds) (2009), above.

SCOTTISH LAW COMMISSION (1981). *Report on Aliment and Financial Provision*. Scot Law Com No 67. Edinburgh: HMSO.

SCOTTISH LAW COMMISSION (1984). *Report on Matrimonial Property*. Scot Law Com No 86. Edinburgh: HMSO.

SCOTTISH LAW COMMISSION (1992). *Report on Family Law*. Scot Law Com No 135. Edinburgh: HMSO.

SCULLY, A. (2003). 'Case commentary: *Parra v Parra*—Big Money Cases, Judicial Discretion and Equality of Division'. *Child and Family Law Quarterly*, 15: 205.

SEDEN, J. (2001). 'Family Assistance Orders and the Children Act 1989: Ambivalence about intervention or a means of safeguarding and promoting children's welfare?'. *International Journal of Law, Policy and the Family*, 15: 226.

SELECT COMMITTEE (1975). *Report from the Select Committee in Violence in Marriage*. London: HMSO.

SELWYN, J. AND QUINTON, D. (2004). 'Stability, permanence, outcomes and support'. *Adoption and Fostering*, 28: 6.

SELWYN, J., FRAZER, L., AND QUINTON, D. (2006). 'Paved with Good Intentions: The Pathway to Adoption and the Costs of Delay'. *British Journal of Social Work*, 36: 561.

SENTENCING GUIDELINES COUNCIL (2006a). *Overarching Principles: Domestic Violence*. <webarchive.nationalarchives.gov.uk/20100519200657/http://www.sentencing-guidelines.gov.uk/docs/domestic_violence.pdf>.

SENTENCING GUIDELINES COUNCIL (2006b). *Breach of a Protective Order*. <webarchive.nationalarchives.gov.uk/20100519200657/http://www.sentencing-guidelines.gov.uk/docs/breach_of_protective_order.pdf>.

SHAH, P. (2003). 'Attitudes to Polygamy in English Law'. *International and Comparative Law Quarterly*, 52: 369.

SHELDON, S. (2009). 'From "absent objects of blame" to "fathers who want to take responsibility": reforming birth registration law'. *Journal of Social Welfare and Family Law*, 31: 373.

SHEPHERD, N. (2009). 'Ending the blame game: getting no fault divorce back on the agenda'. *Family Law*, 39: 122.

SHULTZ, M. (1982). 'Contractual Ordering of Marriage: A New Model for State Policy'. *California Law Review*, 70: 204.

SIMON, R. AND ALTSTEIN, H. (1996). 'The case for Transracial Adoption'. *Children and Youth Services Review*, 18: 5.

SIMON, J. (1964). *With All My Worldly Goods . . .* Holdsworth Club Presidential Address, University of Birmingham.

SMART, C. (1984). *The Ties that Bind: Law, marriage and the reproduction of patriarchal relations*. London: Routledge.

SMART, C. (1989). *Feminism and the Power of Law*. London: Routledge.

SMART, C. (2000). 'Divorce in England 1950–2000: A Moral Tale?', in S. Katz, J. Eekelaar, and M. Maclean (eds), *Cross Currents: Family Law and Policy in the US and England*. Oxford: OUP.

SMART, C. (2004). 'Equal shares: rights for fathers or recognition for children?'. *Critical Social Policy*, 24: 484.

SMART, C. AND NEALE, B. (1999). *Family Fragments?* Cambridge: Polity Press.

SMART, C. AND STEVENS, P. (2000). *Cohabitation Breakdown*. London: Family Policy Studies Centre.

SMITH, C. (1997). 'Children's Rights: Judicial Ambivalence and Social Resistance'. *International Journal of Law, Policy and the Family*, 11: 103.

SMITH, C. (2004). 'Autopoietic Law and the "Epistemic Trap": A Case Study of Adoption and Contact'. *Journal of Law and Society*, 31: 318.

SMITH, C. (2005). 'Trust v Law: Promoting and Safeguarding Post-Adoption Contact'. *Journal of Social Welfare and Family Law*, 27: 315.

SMITH, C. AND LOGAN, J. (2002). 'Adoptive parenthood as a "legal fiction"—Its consequences for direct post-adoption contact'. *Child and Family Law Quarterly*, 14: 281.

SMITH, I. (2002). 'European divorce laws, divorce rates, and their consequences', in A. Dnes and R. Rowthorn (eds), *The law and economics of marriage and divorce*. Cambridge: CUP.

SMITH, L. (1989). *Domestic Violence: An Overview of the Literature*, Home Office Research Study No 107. London: HMSO.

SMITH, L. (2010). 'Clashing symbols? Reconciling support for fathers and fatherless families after the Human Fertilisation and Embryology Act 2008'. *Child and Family Law Quarterly*, 22: 46.

SMITH, R. (2002). 'The wrong end of the telescope: child protection or child safety?'. *Journal of Social Welfare and Family Law*, 24: 247.

SMITH, V. (1992). 'Children Act 1989 The Accommodation Trap'. *Family Law*, 22: 349.

SMYTH, B. (2005). 'Parent-Child Contact in Australia: Exploring Five Different Post-Separation Patterns of Parenting'. *International Journal of Law, Policy and the Family*, 19: 1.

SNAPE, D. AND MOLLOY, D. (1999). *Relying on the State, Relying on Each Other*, Research Report No 103. London: Department of Social Security.

SOLICITORS JOURNAL (2006). 'Family lawyers fear inclusion of conduct in divorces'. *Sol J* 150: 485.

SONI, B. (2007). 'Domestic Violence and Family Law: a new era'. *Family Law Week*, July 2007. <www.familylawweek.co.uk/site.aspx?i=ed725>.

SPAHT, E. (2002). 'Louisiana's covenant marriage law: recapturing the meaning of marriage for the sake of the children', in A. Dnes and R. Rowthorn (eds), *The Law and Economics of Marriage and Divorce*. Cambridge: CUP.

STAFFORD, B. AND ROBERTS, S. (2009). *The impact of financial incentives in welfare systems on family structure*. DWP Research Report No 569. London: DWP.

STONE, L. (1990). *Road to Divorce: England 1530–1987*. Oxford: OUP.

STURGE, C. AND GLASER, D. (2000). 'Contact and Domestic Violence—The Experts' Court Report'. *Family Law*, 30: 615.

STYCHIN, C. (2006). 'Family friendly? Rights, Responsibilities and Relationship Recognition', in A. Diduck and K. O'Donovan (eds), *Feminist Perspectives on Family Law*. Abingdon: Routledge-Cavendish.

STYLIANOU, C. (1998). 'The Tensions between Family Mediation Principles and the Formal Legal System'. *Family Law*, 28: 211.

SUNMONU, Y. (2000). 'Why black carers are deterred from adoption'. *Adoption and Fostering*, 24: 59.

SWADLING, W. (2007). 'The common intention constructive trust in the House of Lords: an opportunity missed'. *Law Quarterly Review*, 123: 511.

SYMES, P. (1985). 'Indissolubility and the clean break'. *Modern Law Review*, 48: 44.

TADROS, V. (2005). 'The Distinctiveness of Domestic Abuse: A Freedom-Based Account', in R. Duff and S. Green (eds), *Defining Crimes*. Oxford: OUP.

TALWAR, D. (2010). 'Many Muslims not legally wed'. BBC website, 2 February. <news.bbc.co.uk/1/hi/uk/8493660.stm>.

TAUB, N. AND SCHNEIDER, E. (1998). 'Women's Subordination and the Role of Law' in D. Kairys (ed), *The Politics of Law: a progressive critique*, 3rd edn. New York: Basic Books.

TIMMS, J. E. AND THOBURN, J. (2006). 'Your Shout! Looked After Children's Perspectives on the Children Act 1989'. *Journal of Social Welfare and Family Law*, 28: 153.

TOBIN, J. AND McNAIR, R. (2009). 'Public international law and the regulation of private spaces: does the Convention on the Rights of the Child impose an obligation on states to allow gay and lesbian couples to adopt?'. *International Journal of Law, Policy and the Family*, 23: 110.

TRINDER, L. AND KELLETT, J. (2007). 'Fairness, efficiency and effectiveness in court-based dispute resolution schemes in England'. *International Journal of Law, Policy and the Family*, 21: 322.

TRINDER, L., FIRTH, A., AND JENKS, C. (2010). ' "So presumably things have moved on since then?" The management of risk allegations in child contact dispute resolution'. *International Journal of Law, Policy and the Family*, 24: 29.

TRINDER, L., CONNOLLY, J., KELLETT, J., AND NOTLEY, C. (2005). *A Profile of Applicants and Respondents in Contact Cases in Essex*. DCA Research Series 1/05. <www.familieslink. co.uk/download/july07/A%20Profile%20of%20Applicants%20and%20Respondents%20 in%20Essex.pdf>.

TRISELIOTIS, J. (2002). 'Long-term foster care or adoption? The evidence examined'. *Child and Family Social Work*, 7: 23.

TURKMENDAG, I., DINGWALL, R., AND MURPHY, T. (2008). 'The removal of donor anonymity in the UK: the silencing of would-be parents'. *International Journal of Law, Policy and the Family*, 22: 283.

UNICEF (2006). *Behind Closed Doors: the Impact of Domestic Violence on Children*. <www.unicef.org/protection/files/BehindClosedDoors.pdf>.

VAN BUEREN, G. (1998). *International Law on the Rights of the Child*. The Hague: Kluwer Law International.

VALLELY, C., ROBINSON, A., BURTON, M., AND TREGIDGA, J. (2005). *Evaluation of Domestic Violence Pilot Sites at Caerphilly (Gwent) and Croydon 2004/05: Final Report*. <www.cps.gov.uk/publications/docs/eval_dv_pilots_04-05.pdf>.

VERKAIK, R. (2006). 'Divorce laws "are destroying marriage" '. *The Independent*, 26 August, 1.

VOGLER, C. (2005). 'Cohabiting couples: rethinking money in the household at the beginning of the twenty first century'. *Sociological Review*, 53: 1.

VOGLER, C. (2009). 'Managing Money in Intimate Relationships: similarities and differences between cohabiting and married couples' in J. Miles and R. Probert (eds) (2009), above.

VOGLER, C., LYONETTE, C., AND WIGGINS, R. (2008). 'Money, power and spending decisions in intimate relationships'. *The Sociological Review*, 56: 117.

WAALDIJK, K. (2003). 'Taking same-sex partnerships seriously: European experiences as British perspective?'. *International Family Law*, 2003: 84.

WALBY, S. (2004). *The Cost of Domestic Violence*. London: DTI.

WALBY, S. AND ALLEN, J. (2004). *Domestic violence, sexual assault and stalking: Findings from the British Crime Survey*, Home Office Research Study 276. London: HMSO.

WALBY, S. AND MYHILL, A. (2001). 'Assessing and managing risk', in J. Taylor-Browne (ed), *What Works in Reducing Domestic Violence? A comprehensive guide for professionals*. London: Whiting Birch.

WALKER, J. (1991). 'Divorce—Whose Fault?'. *Family Law*, 21: 234.

WALKER, J. (1996). 'Is there a future for lawyers in divorce?'. *International Journal of Law, Policy and the Family*, 10: 52.

⦿ WALKER, J. (2000). 'The Development of Family Mediation', in Newcastle Centre for Family Studies, *Information meetings and associated provisions within the Family Law Act 1996: Final Evaluation of Research Studies Undertaken*. <www.dca.gov.uk/family/fla/flapt2.htm>.

WALKER, J. AND MCCARTHY, P. (2004). 'Picking up the Pieces'. *Family Law*, 34: 580.

WALL LJ (2007). 'Separate representation of children'. *Family Law*, 37: 124.

WALLBANK, J. (1997). 'The Campaign for Change of the Child Support Act 1991: Reconstituting the "Absent" Father'. *Social and Legal Studies*, 6: 191.

WALLBANK, J. (2007). 'Getting tough on mothers: regulating contact and residence'. *Feminist Legal Studies*, 15: 189.

WALLBANK, J. (2009). ' "Bodies in the Shadows": joint birth registration, parental responsibility and social class'. *Child and Family Law Quarterly*, 21: 267.

WALSH, E. (2004). 'The Future of Family Mediation', in J. Westcott (ed), *Family Mediation: Past, Present and Future*. Bristol: Jordan Publishing.

⦿ WASOFF, F., MILES, J., AND MORDAUNT, E. (2010). *Legal Practitioners' Perspectives on the Cohabitation Provisions of the Family Law (Scotland) Act 2006*, and Briefing Paper no 51. <www.crfr.ac.uk/researchprojects/rp_cohabitation.html>.

WATERHOUSE, R. (2000). *Lost in care—report of the tribunal of inquiry into the abuse of children in care in the former county council areas of Gwynedd and Clwyd*. London: HMSO.

WELBOURNE, P. (2008). 'Safeguarding children on the edge of care: policy for keeping children safe after the *Review of the Child Care Proceedings System, Care Matters and the Carter Review of Legal Aid*'. *Child and Family Law Quarterly*, 20: 335.

⦿ WELSH ASSEMBLY GOVERNMENT (2009). *Living in Wales, 2008*. <wales.gov.uk/docs/statistics/2009/091130livingwales2008en.pdf>.

WIKELEY, N. (2000). 'Child Support—the New Formula, Part I'. *Family Law*, 30: 820.

WIKELEY, N. (2006a). *Child Support: Law and Policy*. Oxford: Hart Publishing.

WIKELEY, N. (2006b). 'A duty but not a right: child support after *R (Kehoe) v Secretary of State for Work and Pensions*'. *Child and Family Law Quarterly*, 18: 287.

⦿ WIKELEY, N. (2007a). *Written Memorandum to Public Bill Committee, on Child Maintenance and Other Payments Bill 2007*. <www.publications.parliament.uk/pa/cm200607/cmpublic/childmain/memos/memocm1.htm>.

WIKELEY, N. (2007b). 'Child support reform—throwing the baby out with the bathwater?'. *Child and Family Law Quarterly*, 19: 434.

WIKELEY, N. (2007c). 'Family Law and Social Security', in R. Probert (ed), *Family Life and the Law: Under One Roof*. Dartmouth: Ashgate.

WIKELEY, N. (2008). 'The strange demise of the liable relative rule'. *Family Law*, 38: 52.

WIKELEY, N. ET AL (2008). *Relationship separation and child support study.* DWP RR 503. <research.dwp.gov.uk/asd/asd5/rports2007-2008/rrep503.pdf>.

WIKELEY, N., ET AL (2001). *National Survey of Child Support Agency Clients,* DWP Research Report No 152. Leeds: Corporate Document Service.

WILLIAMS, G. (1947). 'Legal Unity of Husband and Wife'. *Modern Law Review,* 10: 16.

WILLIAMSON, E. AND HESTER, M. (2009). *Evaluation of the South Tyneside Domestic Abuse Perpetrator Programme (STDAPP) 2006-2008.* <www.bristol.ac.uk/sps/research/projects/completed/2009/rl6866/finalreport.pdf>.

WILSON, B. AND SMALLWOOD, S. (2008). 'The proportion of marriages ending in divorce'. *Population Trends,* 131: 28.

WILSON, B. AND STUCHBURY, R. (2010). 'Do partnerships last? Comparing marriage and cohabitation using longitudinal census data'. *Population Trends,* 139: 37.

WILSON, G. (2006). 'The non-resident parental role for separated fathers: a review'. *International Journal of Law, Policy and the Family,* 20: 286.

WILSON, G. (2007). 'Financial provision in civil partnerships'. *Family Law,* 37: 31.

WILSON, N. (1999). 'Response of the Judges of the Family Division to Government Proposals (made by way of submission to the Lord Chancellor's Ancillary Relief Advisory Group'). *Family Law,* 29: 159.

WOMEN AND EQUALITY UNIT (2003a). *Civil Partnership: a framework for the legal recognition of same-sex couples.* London: HMSO.

WOMEN AND EQUALITY UNIT (2003b). *Responses to Civil Partnership: A framework for legal recognition of same-sex couples.* London: DTI.

WOMEN'S AID (2005). *Women's Aid Briefing on Domestic Violence A National Report.* <www.womensaid.org.uk/default.asp>.

WONG, S. (2009). 'Caring and Sharing: Interdependency as a basic for property redistribution?', in A. Bottomley and S. Wong (eds), *Changing Contours of Domestic Life, Family and Law.* Oxford: Hart Publishing.

WOOD, H., LUSH, D., AND BISHOP, D. (2005). *Cohabitation: Law, Practice and Precedents,* 3rd edn. Bristol: Family Law.

WORK AND PENSIONS SELECT COMMITTEE (2007), *Fourth Report: Child Support Reform,* HC 219-I, 219-II. <www.publications.parliament.uk/pa/cm/cmworpen.htm>.

YOUNG, C. (2009). 'Taking Spousal Status into Account for Tax Purposes: the pitfalls and penalties', in A. Bottomley and S. Wong (eds), *Changing Contours of Domestic Life, Family and Law.* Oxford: Hart Publishing.

ZUCKERMAN, A. (1978). 'Ownership of the Matrimonial Home—Common Sense and Reformist Nonsense'. *Law Quarterly Review,* 94: 26.

INDEX